ARISTOTLE'S METAPHYSICS

ΑΡΙΣΤΟΤΕΛΟΥΣ ΤΑ ΜΕΤΑ ΤΑ ΦΥΣΙΚΑ

ARISTOTLE'S METAPHYSICS

A REVISED TEXT
WITH INTRODUCTION AND COMMENTARY

BY

W. D. ROSS

FELLOW OF ORIEL COLLEGE

DEPUTY PROFESSOR OF MORAL PHILOSOPHY IN THE
UNIVERSITY OF OXFORD

Volume I

OXFORD
AT THE CLARENDON PRESS

Oxford University Press, Ely House, London W. 1

GLASGOW NEW YORK TORONTO MELBOURNE WELLINGTON
CAPE TOWN SALISBURY IBADAN NAIROBI DAR ES SALAAM LUSAKA ADDIS ABABA
BOMBAY CALCUTTA MADRAS KARACHI LAHORE DACCA
KUALA LUMPUR SINGAPORE HONG KONG TOKYO

FIRST EDITION 1924
REPRINTED LITHOGRAPHICALLY IN GREAT BRITAIN
AT THE UNIVERSITY PRESS, OXFORD
FROM SHEETS OF THE FIRST EDITION
1948, 1953 (WITH CORRECTIONS)
1958, 1966, 1970

PREFACE

THE main object of this preface is to express my sincere thanks to those who have helped me in preparing this edition of the *Metaphysics*. First I would thank the Trustees of the Jowett Copyright Fund and the Master and Fellows of Balliol College, whose generous financial help has made possible the publication of the book; their assistance is commemorated by the Balliol arms on the cover. Next I wish to express my gratitude to the following friends, who have read parts of the book in manuscript and much assisted me by their comments: Professors J. A. Smith and C. C. J. Webb of this University; Professor E. S. Forster of the University of Sheffield; Professor J. L. Stocks of the Victoria University, Manchester; the late Mr. C. Cannan, Secretary to the Delegates of the Press; Mr. R. G. Collingwood, Fellow of Pembroke College; Mr. H. A. Prichard, late Fellow of Trinity College; and particularly Professor H. H. Joachim of this University, who not only commented exhaustively on my treatment of Books ZHΘ but allowed me to make what use I pleased of his own valuable notes on Book Z. My *apparatus criticus* contains unpublished emendations (some of which I have adopted) by Professors Forster, Joachim, and Smith, and Mr. Cannan, as well as some by the late Professor I. Bywater, by the President of Corpus Christi College (Mr. T. Case), and by Professor A. R. Lord of Rhodes University College, Grahamstown. On some points in the later Platonic theory I have had the advantage of exchanging views with Professor A. E. Taylor of the University of Edinburgh. Mr. R. McKenzie, Fereday Fellow of St. John's College, has helped me with information on various lexicographical questions. I would also thank the Secretary and the Assistant Secretaries to the Delegates of the Press, and the vigilant Readers to the Press, for their assistance; and Messrs. Methuen & Co., for allowing me to use in the Introduction a few pages of a book which they recently published for me.

With regard to the structure of the *Metaphysics* I have learnt much from Professor Jaeger's brilliant works. In the study of Aristotle's account of earlier philosophers I have (it is hardly necessary to say) been greatly assisted by the classic works of Zeller, Diels, and Burnet; the fragments of the pre-Socratics are referred to in accordance with the numbering in Diels's *Vorsokratiker*. My debt to M. Robin's study of the later development of Plato's thought, and to Sir Thomas Heath's works on Greek mathematics and astronomy, is no less great.

As the most concise way of indicating the course of the argument, I have prefixed to each section of the commentary (usually to the commentary on each chapter) a brief analysis which is distinguished typographically from the commentary itself. The general course of Aristotle's thought can be best seen by reading the analysis continuously.

No editor of the *Metaphysics* is likely to suppose that he has solved all the outstanding problems of this desperately difficult work, and I am certainly free from that illusion. All I can hope to have done is to have cleared up *some* points left obscure by my great predecessor Hermann Bonitz. I should have liked to attempt an introduction dealing more exhaustively with Aristotle as a metaphysician, but this book is already so long that I have refrained from imposing further on the patience of my readers.

W. D. ROSS.

Oxford.

CONTENTS

VOLUME I

VOLUME II

BOOKS REFERRED TO

(This list is meant only to facilitate reference, and does not aim at completeness.)

Alexander Aphrodisiensis : *In Arist. Met. Commentaria,* ed. M. Hayduck. Berol., 1891.

Alexander Aphrodisiensis : *Die durch Averroes erhaltenen Fragmente Alexanders zur Met. des Arist.,* ed. J. Freudenthal, in *Abh. d. Preuss. Akad.* Berl., 1885.

Apelt, O. : *Beiträge zur Geschichte der griechischen Philosophie.* Leipz., 1891.

Aquinas, St. Thomas : *Interpretatio in Met. Arist.* Papiae, 1480, &c

Asclepius : *In Arist. Met. Libros* A-Z *Commentaria,* ed. M. Hayduck. Berol., 1888.

Bast, F. J. : *Comm. Palaeographica,* in G. H. Schaefer's ed. of Gregorius Corinthius. Leipz., 1811.

Bekker, I. : *Arist. Opera.* 2 voll. Berol., 1831.

Bessarion, J. : *Arist. Opus Met. Latinitate donatum.* Par., 1515, &c.

Blass, F. : *Aristotelisches,* in *Rh. Mus.,* xxx (1875), 481-505.

Bonitz, H. : *Observationes Criticae in Arist. Libros Met.* Berol., 1842.

Bonitz, H. : *Arist. Met.* 2 voll. Bonn, 1848-9.

Bonitz, H. : *Ueber die Categorien des Arist.* Wien, 1853.

Bonitz, H. : *Arist. Studien,* ii, iii. Wien, 1863.

Bonitz, H. : *Index Aristotelicus.* Berol., 1870.

Bonitz, H. : *Arist. Met. übersetzt.* Berol., 1890.

Brandis, C. A. : *Arist. et Theophrasti Met.* 2 voll. Berol., 1823-37.

Brentano, F. : *Arist. Lehre vom Ursprung d. menschlichen Geistes.* Leipz., 1911.

Bullinger, A. : *Arist. Met.* Münch., 1892.

Burnet, J. : *Early Greek Philosophy.* Ed. 3. Lond., 1920.

Burnet, J. : *Greek Philosophy : Thales to Plato.* Lond., 1914.

Bywater, I. : Aristotelia, iv, v, in *Journ. of Philol.,* xxviii (1901-3), 244-7 and xxxii (1913), 109-11.

Casaubon, I.: *Operum Arist. nova editio.* 2 voll. Lugd., 1590, &c.

Chandler, H. W.: *Miscellaneous Emendations and Suggestions.* Lond., 1866.

Christ, W.: *Studia in Arist. libros met. collata.* Berol., 1853.

Christ, W.: *Kritische Beiträge zur Met. des Arist.,* in *Sitzb. d. Bayer. Akad.* Münch., 1885. 406-23.

Christ, W.: *Arist. Met.* Ed. 2. Lips., 1895.

Colle, G.: *Arist., La Mét., Livre I, trad. et comm.* Louvain et Paris, 1912. *Livres II, III.* Ibid., 1922.

Diels, H.: *Doxographi Graeci.* Berol., 1879.

Diels, H.: *Die Fragmente der Vorsokratiker.* Ed. 3. Berl., 1912.

Essen, E.: *Bemerkungen über einige Stellen der Arist. Met.* Stargard, 1862.

Essen, E.: *Das Buch Z der Arist. Met.* Cöslin, Berl., 1863.

Essen, E.: *Ein Beitrag zur Lösung der arist. Frage.* Berl., 1884.

Eucken, R.: *De Arist. dicendi ratione.* Pars prima. Gotting., 1866.

Eucken, R.: *Ueber den Sprachgebrauch des Arist.* Berlin, 1868.

Fonseca, P.: *Comment. in libros Met. Arist.* 2 voll. Rom., 1577-89, &c.

Gillespie, C. M.: *Notes on Arist., Met.* A. 6, in *Journal of Philology,* xxxiv (1915-18), 151-4.

Goebel, K.: *Bemerkungen zu Arist. Met.* Soest, 1889.

Goebel, K.: *Weitere kritische Bemerkungen über Arist. Met.* Soest, 1891.

Goebel, K.: *Kritische Bemerkungen über Arist. Met.* Soest, 1892.

Goebel, K.: *Uebersetzung von Buch Λ der Met. des Arist.* Soest, 1896.

Gomperz, T.: *Beiträge zur Kritik u. Erklärung griech. Schriftsteller,* in *Sitzb. d. K. Akad. in Wien,* lxxxiii (1876), 564-9.

Hayduck, M.: *Emendationes Arist.,* in *Jahrbücher f. Cl. Phil.,* cxix (1879), 109-12.

Heinze, R.: *Xenokrates.* Leipz., 1892.

Innes, H. M.: *On the Universal and Particular in Aristotle's Theory of Knowledge.* Camb., 1886.

Jackson, H.: *Arist. Met.* I, in *Journal of Philology,* vi (1876), 206 f.

Jackson, H.: *Plato's Later Theory of Ideas. I. The Philebus and Arist. Met.* I. 6, in *J. of P.,* x (1881), 253-98.

Jackson, H.: *Arist. Met.* A. 1. 985 b 25 ff.; A. 9. 992 b 29, in *Proc. of Camb. Phil. Soc.* Camb., 1895.

Jackson, H.: *On some Passages in Arist. Met.* Λ, in *J. of P.,* xxix (1903), 139-44.

Jaeger, W. W.: *Emendationum Aristotelearum Specimen.* Berol., 1911.

Jaeger, W. W.: *Studien z. Entstehungsgeschichte d. Met. d. Arist.* Berl., 1912.

Jaeger, W.: *Emendationen zu Arist. Met.* A-Δ, in *Hermes,* lii (1917), 481-519.

Jaeger, W.: *Aristoteles.* Berl., 1923.

Jaeger, W.: *Emendationen zu Arist. Met.*, in *Sitzb. d. Preuss. Akaa.*, xxxiv (1923).

Karsten, S.: *Empedoclis Carm. Reliq.* Amst., 1838.

Kühner, R.: *Ausführliche Grammatik d. griech. Sprache.* 2 voll. in 4. Hannover, 1890–1904.

Lasson, A.: *Arist. Met. ins Deutsche übertragen.* Jena, 1907.

Lütze, F.: *Ueber das ἄπειρον Anaximanders.* Leipz., 1878.

Luthe, W.: *Zur Kritik u. Erklärung von Arist. Met. u. Alexanders Commentar*, in *Hermes*, xv (1880), 189–210.

Luthe, W.: *Begriff u. Angabe d. Met. (σοφία) d. Arist.* Düsseld., 1884.

Maier, H.: *Die Syllogistik d. Arist.* 2 voll. in 3. Tübing., 1896–1900.

Natorp, P.: *Thema u. Disposition d. Arist. Met.*, in *Philos. Monatsh.*, xxiv (1887), 37–65, 540–74.

Natorp, P.: *Ueber Met. K.* 1-8. 1065 a 25, in *Philos. Monatsh.*, xxiv (1888), 178–93.

Philoponus, I.: *In Arist. Phys. Commentaria*, ed. H. Vitelli. 2 voll. Berol., 1887-8.

Prantl, C.: *Arist. Physica.* Lips., 1879.

Ravaisson, F.: *Speusippi de primis rerum principiis placita qualia fuisse videntur ex Arist.* Paris, 1838.

Ravaisson, F.: *Essai sur la Mét.* Ed. 2. Paris, 1913.

Richards, H.: *Aristotelica*, in *J. of P.*, xxxiv (1915–18), 247–54.

Robin, L.: *La Théorie platonicienne des Idées et des Nombres d'après Arist.* Paris, 1908.

Robin, L.: *Sur la Conception arist. de la Causalité*, in *Archiv f. Gesch. d. Philos.*, xxiii (1910), 1–28, 184–210.

Rolfes, E.: *Arist. Met. übersetzt.* 2 voll. Leipz., 1904.

Roscher, W. H.: *Sieben- u. Neunzahl im Kultus u. Mythus d. Griechen*, in *Abh. d. Sächs. Akad.*, xxi, xxiv (1903, 1906).

Schwegler, A.: *Die Met. d. Arist.* 4 voll. Tübing., 1847-8.

[Shute, R. ;] *Book Z, translated.* [Oxf.], n.d.

Simplicius: *In Phys. libros Commentaria*, ed. H. Diels. 2 voll. Berol., 1882–95.

Stein, H.: *Empedoclis Fragmenta.* Bonn., 1852.

Sturz, F. W.: *Empedoclis vita et philos., carm. reliq.* Lips., 1805.

Susemihl, F.: *Arist. quae feruntur Oeconomica*, Appendix. Lips., 1887.

Sylburg, F.: *Arist. opera quae exstant.* 11 voll. Francof., 1584-7.

Syrianus: *In Met. Commentaria*, ed. G. Kroll. Berol., 1902.

Taylor, A. E.: *Varia Socratica.* Oxford, 1911.

Themistius: *In Arist. Met. Librum Λ Paraphrasis*, ed. S. Landauer. Berol., 1903.

Themistius: *In Arist. Phys. Paraphrasis*, ed. H. Schenkl. Berol., 1900.

Trendelenburg, F. A.: *Geschichte d. Kategorienlehre.* Ed. 3. Berl., 1876.

Usener, H.: *Zu Arist.*, in *Rh. Mus.*, N.F. xvi (1861), 312, 313, 488.

[Walker, W. W. :] *The First Book of the Met. of Arist. translated* . . .
by a Cambridge Graduate. London, 1881.

Wilamowitz-Moellendorff, U. von : *Commentariolum grammaticum*, iv.
Gotting., 1889.

Winckelmann, A. W. : Review of Bonitz's *Observationes*, in *N. Jahrb. f.
Philol.*, xxxix (1843), 283–94.

Wirth, C. : *Die ersten drei Capitel d. Met. d. Arist.* Bayreuth, 1884.

Zeller, E. : *Platonische Studien.* Tübing., 1837.

Zeller, E. : *Philosophie d. Griechen.* Vol. i. Ed. 6. Leipz., 1919-20.
Vol. ii, 1. Ed. 4. Leipz., 1889. Vol. ii, 2. Ed. 4. Leipz., 1921.

Zeller, E. : *Bericht üb. d. deutsche Litt. d. sokrat., platon. u. arist.
Philosophie*, in *Arch. f. Gesch. d. Philos.*, ii (1889), 259-99.

INTRODUCTION

I

THE STRUCTURE OF THE *METAPHYSICS*

THE structure of the *Metaphysics* obviously presents many difficulties. It is evident on the face of it that this is not a single finished work, meant to be read in its present form. Not only are Books α, Δ, and K manifest intrusions, but even the other books lack the continuity of thought that one expects in a single work. If we look more to externals, the same fact is impressed on us in other ways. It is noteworthy that with the exception of H, Θ, M, and N all the books begin without a connecting particle—a phenomenon which is rare in Aristotle's works.[1] Accordingly scholars have regarded the *Metaphysics* as produced by the combining of separate treatises, some of them containing only single books, others small groups of books; and the latest and most thorough investigator of the problem[2] has treated each book (with the exception of the group ZH) as a distinct treatise. We shall see reasons for believing this to be in a sense true, but some care must be bestowed on the determination of that sense.

In considering the relation of the various books, we should be guided by two considerations: (1) the connexion of the thought, and (2) the explicit references which one book makes to another. These references have for the most part every appearance of being genuine; in many cases it would be difficult to remove

---

[1] The only other clear instances are *An. Post.* ii, *Phys.* vii, *Pol.* iii, iv; in *Phys.* ii, *De Caelo* ii, *E. N.* vii, *Pol.* ii, vii, *Rhet.* iii the manuscripts differ. The *Politics*, of course, presents as great a problem as the *Metaphysics*.

[2] Jaeger, *Studien zur Entstehungsgeschichte der Metaphysik des Aristoteles*, and *Aristoteles: Grundlegung einer Geschichte seiner Entwicklung*.

them from the text without removing a good deal with them; and in most cases no plausible reason can be suggested for their insertion by a later hand. They have accordingly been treated as important by scholars; but not enough attention has always been paid to their precise form.

It is important to distinguish two questions which may be asked about the order of the books. There is the question of the order in which they were written, and the question of the order in which they were delivered as lectures.[1] The first is evidently a very difficult question to answer. Probably the safest evidence would be statistical evidence about matters of grammar and style, and very little such evidence has been collected. It is only the other question that the explicit references help us to solve. But there is a presumption that the order of delivery would in a general way correspond with the order of writing. The complexity of the matter is illustrated by the evidence with regard to the date of the *Metaphysics* relatively to Aristotle's other works. The *Metaphysics* refers back to the *Posterior Analytics*, the *Physics*, the *De Caelo*, the *De Generatione et Corruptione*, and the *Ethics*, and it does not refer forward to any of Aristotle's works. The *De Generatione* refers back to Δ (336^b 29). The *Physics* has a backward reference (191^b 29) which is usually taken to be to Θ, but since Θ itself refers back to the *Physics* (1049^b 36) and the *Physics* refers forward at 192^a 35 to the *Metaphysics*, and apparently to that part of it to which Θ belongs (ZHΘ), it is probable that the reference in 191^b 29, like that in the *De Generatione*, is to Δ, which as we shall see is probably earlier than the other books of the *Metaphysics*; the reference is probably to Δ. 1017^h 1. Finally, the *De Motu Animalium* refers back to Λ (700^b 8), but it is doubtful whether this work is by Aristotle. These are all the references to the

---

[1] *Top.* 184^b 6 indicates that the *Topics* were read aloud, and the use of the terms ἀκροατής, ἀκρόασις where we should say 'student' and 'study' suggests that this is probably true of Aristotle's other works as well. *E. N.* 1104^b 18 ὡς καὶ πρῴην εἴπομεν may contain a reference to lecturing or reading aloud. But πρῴην may as easily mean 'some little distance back' as 'the day before yesterday'. Jaeger (*Stud.* 145–147) gives reasons for supposing that the publication of Aristotle's works (the dialogues perhaps excepted) consisted in (1) their being read aloud, and (2) copies being taken by hearers.

Metaphysics in the other works, and they suggest that it is among the latest of all Aristotle's works. On the other hand the evidence from diction, so far as it has been collected,[1] establishes an affinity between the *Metaphysics* and not only what is probably one of the latest works, the *Politics*, but also what is probably one of the earliest, the *Physics*.

The Connected Treatises.

There is every reason to suppose that Book A formed the first part of Aristotle's course of metaphysical lectures. It is quite in his manner to begin with an historical inquiry. A does not presuppose any of the other books; the only one that it refers to is B, and this it refers to (993ª 25) as something still to come, while B refers to A as 'our prefatory remarks' (995ᵇ 5) and 'our first discussions' (997ᵇ 4).[2]

B is also in its nature preliminary to the main treatise on metaphysics. It enumerates and discusses dialectically fourteen (or fifteen) problems. These are not thought of as a complete programme for the metaphysician, but as the problems which he must discuss first (995ª 25). B announces itself as following A (995ᵇ 5, 996ᵇ 8, 997ʰ 4), and it is noteworthy that the word πάλαι which is used in the second of these passages is one which may be used in referring to an earlier part of an identical work (*Phys.* 254ª 16, Z. 1039ª 19, *Pol.* 1262ᵇ 29, 1282ª 15). Further indications of the close connexion between A and B are the use of the phrase ἡ ἐπιστήμη ἡ ζητουμένη in A. 983ª 21 (cf. 982ª 4), B. 995ª 24, 996ᵇ 3, and the use of the first person plural in the sense of 'we Platonists' (A. 990ᵇ 9, 11, 16, 18, 23, 991ʰ 7, B. 997ᵇ 3, 1002ᵇ 14).

The significance of B with reference to the structure of the

---

[1] By Eucken, in *De Aristotelis dicendi ratione*, and *Ueber den Sprachgebrauch des Aristoteles*.

[2] Blass's theory that parts of the περὶ φιλοσοφίας are embedded in ΑΛΜ, and distinguished from the remainder of these books by the carefulness of the style and the avoidance of hiatus (*Rh. Mus.* xxx. 485-497) requires too forcible a treatment of the text to be convincing. But the three books περὶ φιλοσοφίας formed a basis for A, MN, and Λ respectively. Their probable contents are well discussed in Jaeger's *Aristoteles*, 125-170.

Metaphysics is evident. B might be a programme which Aristotle carried through fully in later lectures. It might be a mere sketch which he never followed up. Or it might lie somewhere between these extremes: it might be that he discussed some of the problems of B explicitly in the form in which they are raised in this book, while others he considered in a fresh shape and perhaps in new groupings, and others he laid aside or never felt himself able to solve. We shall find that something like this is, so far as we can judge from what is left us, what actually happened.

The first four problems[1] are concerned with the possibility and the province of metaphysics:

(1) Is it the task of one or of more than one science to investigate all the kinds of cause?

(2) Should the science that investigates the first principles of substance also investigate the first principles of demonstration?

(3) Is there one science that investigates all substances?

(4) Does the science that investigates substances investigate their properties as well?

Then come eleven problems which metaphysics actually has to solve:

(5) Are there non-sensible as well as sensible substances? If so, are they of more than one kind?

(6) Is it classes, or the constituent parts, that are the first principles of things?

(7) Are summa genera, or infimae species, more of the nature of principles and substances?

(8) Is there anything other than individual things?

(9) Are the first principles limited in number, or in kind?

(10) Are the principles of perishable and imperishable things the same?

(11) Are unity and being substances, or attributes?

(12) Are the first principles universal or individual?

(13) Do the first principles exist potentially or actually?

(14) Are the objects of mathematics substances? If so, are they separate from sensible things?

---

[1] I follow here the order of the discussion in chs. 2–6, which is more logical than that of the formulation in ch. 1; ch. 1 places the fifth problem before the fourth.

(14ª)[1] What are the grounds for belief in Forms as distinct from sensibles and from mathematical objects?

Γ contains only one explicit reference to B, the reference in 1004ª 33 to the fourth problem, but besides answering this question explicitly chs. 1 and 2 answer the first and the third question implicitly (cf. the summary of results at 1005ª 13). Similarly ch. 3 gives a plain affirmative answer to the second problem (1005ª 19–ᵇ8, especially the summary in ᵇ 5-8). Not content, however, with deciding that metaphysics ought to study the first principles of demonstration, Aristotle proceeds actually to discuss them, and to this the rest of Γ is devoted. This procedure, by which a somewhat formal problem in B is made the starting-point for a further discussion, will meet us again in other connexions. Meantime, however, the unity of ABΓ is assured. It remains to be seen how many of the other books form parts of the same whole.

E contains no formal reference to the problems of B. In effect, however, it takes up the answer given in Γ to the first problem (cf. the opening words with Γ. 1003ª 31), and proceeds to define the sense in which metaphysics deals with the principles of being as being. It clears this matter up in two directions. (1) It develops, alongside of the view that metaphysics studies being as such, a view not yet touched upon, viz. that it studies a particular kind of being—the kind that both has separate, substantial existence and is free from change, as distinct from the objects, on one side, of mathematics and those, on the other, of physics. These two views it tries to reconcile by saying that this kind of being, if it exists, is prior to the other kinds, and the science of it is primary and therefore universal. (2) It points out that 'being' is used in two senses which are not studied by metaphysics : (*a*) incidental being, where A is B only in virtue of something incidental to A or to B, and (*b*) 'being as truth'. The first cannot be studied at all; the second is presumably studied by logic.

The doubt which has sometimes been expressed[2] on the

---

[1] This question (1002ᵇ 12–32) is plainly an appendix to the previous one ; there is nothing answering to it in ch. 1.

[2] e.g. by Natorp, in *Philosophische Monatshefte*, xxiv. 37-65 and 540-574. He is answered by Zeller in *Archiv für die Geschichte der Philosophie*, ii. 265 ff. Natorp's attempt to show that E contains a view

question whether there is any real connexion between E and ABΓ is set at rest by the fact that the first part of K, which is certainly very old and may well be a pupil's notes of a course of lectures by Aristotle himself, is a continuous parallel treatment of the topics discussed in BΓE.

ZHΘ evidently form a fairly continuous work. Not only are there connecting particles at the beginning of H and Θ, but Z refers forward to H,[1] while H begins with a summary of Z (1042[a] 3–22) and Θ refers back to Z in language which implies a close connexion.[2] It is true that other references to Z in H and Θ[3] imply a relative independence, but this is evidently only the independence which sections of a larger whole may have.

It is evident, again, that the reference of Θ to Z as ' our first discussions '[4] implies that ZHΘ is in a sense a distinct treatise from ABΓE. These two groups have usually, as by Brandis and Bonitz, been treated as going together and forming the backbone of the *Metaphysics*; one of the main features of Jaeger's view is his belief that ZHΘ do not belong to this ' backbone '.[5] His arguments must be reviewed ; they are as follows :

(1) M, which he believes to form part of the main treatise, refers for the treatment of sensible substance not to ZHΘ, which are in the main occupied with this subject, but to the *Physics* (Jaeger, p. 97). Jaeger follows Bonitz in interpreting ὕστερον in

of the subject-matter of metaphysics incompatible with that contained in ΓZ, and must therefore be spurious, is unsuccessful.

[1] 1037[a] 20 can hardly refer to Z. 12, which follows almost immediately. It must refer to H. 6, to which 1039[a] 22 perhaps also refers.

[2] 1045[b] 28 εἴρηται simply, 31 ὥσπερ εἴπομεν ἐν τοῖς πρώτοις λόγοις.

[3] 1043[b] 16 ἐν ἄλλοις, 1049[b] 27 ἐν τοῖς περὶ τῆς οὐσίας λόγοις (cf. Z. 1037[b] 10).

[4] 1045[b] 32 (cf. ἐν ἀρχῇ Z. 1029[b] 1).

[5] The following criticism (up to p. xxi) was in print before the appearance of Jaeger's *Aristoteles*, and refers to his argument in the *Studien*. I find myself in agreement with his later view, that the earliest parts of the *Metaphysics* (apart from Λ, which was originally a separate treatise) are A, K init.—1065[a] 26, M. 1086[a] 21—N fin., and that BΓE is a later version of K init.—1065[a] 26, and M init.—1086[a] 21 a later version of M. 1086[a] 21—N fin. ABΓE, ZHΘ, MN, and 1 seem to have been worked up into a whole before αΔKΛ were added.

1076ᵃ 9 as referring to a treatment later in the *Physics*. This is, however, rendered impossible by the μὲν . . . δέ. Bonitz's only reason for his highly unnatural interpretation lies in the absence of other references in MN to ZHΘ. But a passage in N (1088ᵇ 24) may refer to Θ, and both Z and H refer to the discussion in MN as to something that is coming later (1037ᵃ 12, 1042ᵃ 22). And even if 1076ᵃ 9 stood alone, it would be a plain reference to ZHΘ.[1]

Jaeger thinks that 1086ᵃ 23 still more clearly shows that ZHΘ do not form a part of the main metaphysical treatise. He takes it to show that ZHΘ, since they deal with sensible substance, are physics rather than metaphysics. The meaning of the passage is something quite different. What it says is that the views of thinkers who recognize sensible substance *only* (i.e. the pre-Socratics) have, on the one hand, been treated in the *Physics*, and are, on the other, inappropriate to the present inquiry: i.e. their views are not pertinent to the present inquiry just because the present inquiry is confined to non-sensible substance. In Book A, before he had narrowed down his subject to non-sensible substance, he actually discusses their views. The passage does not imply that a discussion of sensible substance is inappropriate to metaphysics, but only that it is inappropriate to the present stage of the inquiry.

(2) Not only E. 1026ᵃ 16, 19, 27-32, but Z and Θ themselves (1037ᵃ 10-17, 1048ᵃ 25-30) imply that metaphysics is concerned solely with insensible being, while in fact ZHΘ are occupied with sensible being (Jaeger, p. 97).

In answer to this it must be pointed out that E itself combines the view that metaphysics studies unchangeable reality with the view that it studies the nature of being as such, the nature common to all being. Now when we ask what ZHΘ are in the main concerned with, the answer is perhaps most aptly given in M. 1076ᵃ 9: 'the actual or formal element in sensible being.' These books study primarily not the matter of sensible being, but the formal element which is common to both sensible and non-sensible being and is thus a principle of being as such. And they study this first as it is in sensible substances just because these are ὁμολογούμεναι, and as a preliminary to the study of it in its purity (Z. 1037ᵃ 13, 1041ⁿ 7, H. 1042ᵃ 22-25). In describing

---

[1] Jaeger now (*Arist.* 212 ff.) takes it so.

themselves as concerned with sensible being ZH admit themselves to be preliminary to the main object of metaphysics but certainly not to be inappropriate as part of a metaphysical treatise. And in the same breath they point forward to MN as a future part of the same treatise (ὕστερον, 1037ᵃ 13, 1042ᵃ 23).

(3) ZHΘ do not continue the discussion of the problems formulated in B. E has indicated that the subject of metaphysics is insensible being ; the first problem, after the four preliminary problems discussed in ΓΕ, is the question whether there are insensible substances (B. 997ᵃ 34). Thus both B and E lead us to expect next a discussion of insensible substance, not of sensible. Further, ZHΘ never refer to the problems raised in B (Jaeger, pp. 101, 102).

It must be admitted that in ZHΘ there is no explicit reference to B, and that these books do not in so many words discuss any of the problems there raised. ZHΘ form a relatively independent whole. But they present a phenomenon very like that presented by Γ. 3-9. Just as there, having shown that it is the business of metaphysics to study the axioms (and thus answered his second problem), Aristotle proceeds forthwith to study them, so here, having shown that metaphysics studies substance (and thus answered his third problem), he discusses it forthwith, and postpones the discussion of the further questions raised in B. A similar phenomenon will be found in I.

If ZHΘ do not refer to B, the facts remain, (a) that not only M but also I (1053ᵇ 17)—both of them books which Jaeger rightly maintains to belong to the main treatise, so far as there is a main treatise—use language which implies that ZH have come before,[1] and (b) that E refers forward to Θ with the word ' later ' (1027ᵇ 29), while Z and H use the same word with reference to M (1037ᵃ 13, 1042ᵃ 23). Thus the order ΑΒΓΕΖΗΘΜΝ appears to be established. Yet ZHΘ form a section in which the problems of B have sunk somewhat into the background.

(4) Z treats the ideal theory as not yet refuted (ch. 14). But it has been refuted in A. 8, 9 (Jaeger, p. 111).

In answer to this two things must be said :

(a) MN also treat this theory as not yet refuted. Jaeger himself believes that when MN were written A. 8, 9 were dropped out

---

[1] Further, N. 1088ᵇ 24 *may* refer to Θ. 1050ᵇ 7 ff.

of the course as being superseded by the fuller discussion in MN. May not ZHΘ belong to this later form of the course?

(*b*) The refutation of the Ideas in Z is a refutation of them only from one particular point of view; it is an appendix to the discussion in ch. 13 of the claims of the universal to be regarded as substance (cf. H. 1042ᵃ 15). The subject is for Aristotle so important that it is natural to him to discuss it more than once, from different points of view.

The connexion of Z with E might appear to be established most easily by a comparison of the closing words of E with the first words of Z. But though the closing words of E would be pointless unless Z was to follow, if it was to follow they produce an intolerable repetition. They are plainly a later addition similar to what occurs at the end of α in all the manuscripts, and at the end of Γ, H, I in Aᵇ. The substantial continuity of ZHΘ with E is, however, evident from the fact that ZH and Θ respectively discuss the two senses of being which E declares to be the subject of metaphysics, being as classified into the categories and potential-and-actual being.

Jaeger has pointed out [1] that MN contain an earlier and a later discussion of Academic theories (M. 1086ᵃ 21—N fin., M init.—1086ᵃ 18). The earlier form is in close connexion with AB; Jaeger points out that in M. 1086ᵃ 21—fin. there are more references to AB than in all the Bks. Z–Λ (1086ᵃ 34, ᵇ 2, 15). 1086ᵇ 20–32 reminds us of B. 999ᵇ 27—1000ᵃ 4 (problem 9), and 1086ᵇ 32–37, 37—1087ᵃ 4 of 1003ᵃ 13–17, 7–9 (problem 12); the solution comes in 1087ᵃ 7–25. But the later version also refers to B (1076ᵃ 39, ᵇ 39). M. 1–9 is devoted expressly to the solution of problem 5 (cf. 1076ᵃ 19 with 997ᵃ 35).

M presents one very curious phenomenon—the repetition in chs. 4, 5 (1078ᵇ 34—1079ᵇ 3, 1079ᵇ 12—1080ᵃ 8), practically word for word, of the arguments against the ideal theory put forward in Λ. 990ᵇ 2—991ᵇ 8, and the appearance in chs. 6–9 of a polemic against the ideal numbers which entirely ignores the polemic against them in Λ. 991ᵇ 9—993ᵃ 10. There can be no doubt that the repeated passage occurred in both contexts among Aristotle's papers; by far the most reasonable explanation of its double occurrence is that Aristotle, having to deal with the same subject a second time, felt that his old treatment of it fully expressed

[1] *Arist.* 186–199.

his views and therefore used it again (cf. the identity of Δ. 2 with *Phys.* ii. 3). Certain slight differences[1] enable us with some confidence to give the relative date of the two versions. In A, Aristotle several times says 'we' where it is clear that 'we' means 'we Platonists', i.e. A belongs to the time when Aristotle was still a Platonist, though a critical one; Jaeger's conjecture (*Stud.* 34, n. 2) that the book may have been read to the Platonic circle at Assos among whom Aristotle lived from 348 to 345 is highly probable. In M he uses the third person of the Platonists, and in at least one instance[2] the criticism is sharper; the book belongs to the period when he has definitely broken with the Academy and set up as an independent teacher. Presumably when he had written M he omitted A. 9 from his course; otherwise the repetition would have been too flagrant.

I is evidently a more or less self-contained treatise, dealing with the nature of unity and of kindred conceptions. It is not referred to in any other book of the *Metaphysics.* But it contains a reference to B in 1053^b 10, and not only a reference but a recapitulation (^{b} 11-24) of a good part of the discussion of unity in B (1001^a 5-24). Here we evidently have Aristotle's formal answer to the eleventh problem. From settling the question raised about unity in B, he is next led to discuss other questions about it. The book is, however, connected with B in another way as well. Aristotle has in 995^b 20 raised the question, whose business it is to study the same, the other, the like, the unlike, and contrariety, and in Γ. 1004^a 17 he has answered that this is the business of the metaphysician. The actual discussion of them is found in I. 4-10. We have seen also that I refers back to Z (1053^b 17). Clearly, then, it belongs to the main treatise, though somewhat loosely connected with

---

[1] For which see notes on A. 9.

[2] Cf. 990^b 4, 1078^b 36. The tone of A is less sharp also than that of the *Topics* and the *Analytics*; cf. *An. Post.* 83^a 32 τὰ γὰρ εἴδη χαιρέτω· τερετίσματά τε γάρ ἐστι, καὶ εἰ ἔστιν, οὐδὲν πρὸς τὸν λόγον ἐστίν. It is, of course, possible that, as Grant suggests, after a period of strong reaction against Platonism Aristotle settled into a more friendly attitude; but the opposite view seems more probable—that A is earlier than M, the *Topics*, and the *Analytics.* The fact that M is occupied less with the original ideal theory than with the number-theories of Plato, Speusippus, and Xenocrates is itself strong evidence of lateness.

the rest of it. It is evident also that it comes logically after, not before, MN. Otherwise it interrupts the discussion of the nature of substance which is carried on in ZHΘMN.[1] The opening words of M indicate pretty plainly that Aristotle has just concluded his discussion of sensible substance. It may also be noticed that the absence of a reference in N. 1087ᵇ 33 to the fuller treatment of unity in I. 1 suggests that I has not preceded N.

It seems, then, that ΑΒΓΕΖΗΘΜΝΙ form a more or less continuous work. This is doubtless the ten-book *Metaphysics* which occurs in the list of Aristotle's works in *Anonymus Menagii*. It is not, however, a complete work. If we ask how far the problems raised in B are dealt with in later books, the answer may be stated as follows :

Problem 1 is answered in Γ. 1, 2 (though not in the precise form in which it is raised), and further elucidated in E. The nature of being as such, thus shown to be the subject of metaphysics, and defined as excluding incidental being and being as truth, and including 'being in the sense of the categories' and 'being in the sense of potentiality and actuality', is discussed in ZH and in Θ.

Problem 2 is answered in Γ. 3. 1005ᵃ 19–ᵇ 8, and the topic thus claimed for metaphysics is considered in the remainder of Γ.

Problem 3 is answered in Γ. 1, 2 (especially 1004ᵃ 2-9), E. 1, and substance is further considered in ZH.

Problem 4 is dealt with in Γ. 2. 1003ᵇ 32—1005ᵃ 18 (1004ᵃ 32 refers explicitly to this problem). Some of the main attributes of substance are further considered in I. 4-9. Thus all the preliminary problems about the possibility and the scope of metaphysics find an answer in Γ.

Problem 5 is dealt with in MN. But the inquiry here, being an examination of the views of the Pythagoreans and the Platonists, is only preliminary to a statement of Aristotle's views (πρῶτον τὰ παρὰ τῶν ἄλλων λεγόμενα θεωρητέον, M. 1076ᵃ 12). M. 1076ᵇ 1, 1077ᵃ 1 refer explicitly to this problem.

Problems 6, 7 are not dealt with expressly anywhere. But

---

[1] It will be remembered that HΘMN are just the books which have a connecting particle in the first sentence. This is what we should expect if ZHΘMN form a connected group of discussions.

Z. 13 incidentally gives Aristotle's answer to them (cf. for problem 6, Z. 10. 1035ᵃ 24, 30 ; for problem 7, Z. 12. 1038ᵃ 19).

Problem 8 is not answered expressly, but Aristotle's attitude towards it may be gathered from Z. 8, 13, 14, M. 10.

Problem 9 is answered in M. 10.

Problem 10 is not dealt with expressly, but Aristotle's view may be gathered from Z. 7-10.

Problem 11 is answered in Z. 16. 1040ᵇ 16-24, I. 2. I. 2. 1053ᵇ 10 refers explicitly to it.

Problem 12 is answered in Z. 13-15, M. 10. M. 10. 1086ᵇ 15 refers explicitly to it.

Problem 13 is not expressly answered, but Aristotle's answer may be inferred from his doctrine that actuality is prior to potentiality (Θ. 8).

Problem 14 is answered in M. 1-3, 6-9, N. 1-3, 5, 6, though not expressly referred to.

Problem 14ᵃ is not expressly dealt with anywhere, but cf. M. 10.

On the whole, then, the programme of B is fairly well carried out, though several of the problems are not dealt with in the form in which they are originally raised. It is only natural that Aristotle's way of conceiving the problems of metaphysics should have been modified in the course of his study of them. He lets his thought follow 'the wind of the argument'; but he never entirely forgets the problems raised in B, and he reminds us of them from time to time.

The Outlying Books.

Four books remain to be considered: α, Δ, K, Λ. Of these α evidently interrupts the connexion between A and B. It refers to no other book, and is referred to by none. The attempt to connect it with B by interpolating at 995ᵃ 19 a free version of a clause occurring in B. 995ᵇ 5 was exposed by Alexander once for all. The very title of the book betrays that it is a late, probably the latest, addition to the corpus of the *Metaphysics*, inserted after the other books had already been numbered. One of the oldest manuscripts (E) has a scholion saying that most scholars ascribed the book to Pasicles of Rhodes, a pupil of Aristotle and a nephew of Eudemus.[1]   Alexander (137. 2), Asclepius (113. 5), and Syrianus (1. 7, 14. 26, 37. 29, 98. 9) think it is by Aristotle ; Alexander has doubts about its being in its proper place, and thinks it a fragmentary preface to θεωρητικὴ φιλοσοφία in general (137. 3—138. 9).   They are right in thinking both the thought and the language thoroughly Aristotelian.   But the lack of connexion between the three chapters strongly confirms Jaeger's view that we have in it Pasicles' somewhat fragmentary notes of a discourse by Aristotle.   The concluding words make it quite clear that the discourse was introductory to a course not on metaphysics but on physics (cf. Al. 137. 13), so that we have to deal here with an error of judgement on the part of those who put together the *Metaphysics* out of such materials as they found ready to their hand (Asc. 4. 4, cf. Al. 515. 9).

Δ is evidently out of place where it is, and as evidently it is a genuine Aristotelian work.   It is referred to in E, Z, Θ, and I, as well as in the *Physics* and the *De Generatione et Corruptione*— either by the vague phrase ἐν ἄλλοις, or as τὰ περὶ τοῦ ποσαχῶς or by some variant of this title ; and under this title it occurs in Diogenes Laertius' list, in which the *Metaphysics* itself does not occur.   It is a useful preliminary to the *Metaphysics*, but it is not preliminary to it in particular.   Some of the notions discussed in it (κολοβόν, ψεῦδος) are not appropriate to the *Metaphysics*, and it is apparently earlier than the physical works while the rest of the *Metaphysics*, in its present form, is later.

K consists of two quite distinct parts and presents two distinct problems. 1059^a 18—1065^a 26 contains a shorter version of the contents of ΒΓΕ; 1065^a26—1069^a 14 contains a series of extracts from *Physics* ii, iii, v.   The two parts are ingeniously connected by a transition from the accidental, which is the subject of E. 2, 3, to chance, which is defined in terms of the accidental.   K is not referred to in any other book,[2] but the first part presupposes A (1059^a 19) and contains an obscure reference (1064^a 36) to a later book (? Λ).   An examination of the first part shows that it is no

---

[1] Asclepius (4. 20) says that some scholars thought that A was written by Pasicles; this is probably due to a confusion between A and α.

[2] The references in I. 1053^b 10, M. 1076^a 39 and [b] 39, 1086^b 15 refer to B. 1001^a 4-24, 998^a 11-15 and 997^b 12-34, 999^b 24—1000^a 4 and 1003^a 6-17, rather than to the less detailed parallels in K. 1060^a 36-[b]6, 1059^a 38-[b] 14, 1060^b 28-30 and 19-23.

mechanical paraphrase of ΒΓΕ such as a disciple might have made but an independent handling of the same topics, omitting much (e. g. 1002^b 32—1003^a 5, 1007^a 20–^{b} 18, 1008^a 7–^{b} 12), rearranging much, and inserting not a little of its own (e. g. 1059^b 14-21, 30, 38, 1061^a 20–^{b} 3, 1065^a 14-21). Both the thought and with one exception the language are thoroughly Aristotelian. The exception is the use of the combination of particles γε μήν in 1060^a 5, 17, 20, ^{b} 3, 12, 1061^b 8, 1062^b 33.[1] This does not prove that it was not written by Aristotle; a writer may use a phrase at one time of his life and then drop it, and Zeller points out that δέ γε is apparently used only in the *Physics*, *Metaphysics*, and *Politics*, and that τε . . . τε is almost confined to the *Politics* and the *Ethics*. But, so long as the contents of K are recognized as Aristotelian, it does not much matter whether the actual form is due to Aristotle or to a pupil who took down Aristotle's lectures. Its much smaller size, as compared with ΒΓΕ, is rather in favour of the view that K represents a student's notes— not, however, of the identical course of lectures which we have in ΒΓΕ (it is too independent for that), but of a corresponding course given on another occasion.

We may even conjecture that K represents an earlier course than ΒΓΕ. B seems to imply that the doctrine of the Ideas has not yet been refuted;[2] i. e. it belongs to a course in which A. 9 was dropped out, and the Ideas were left to be discussed in M. K on the other hand implies that the Ideas have already been refuted (1059^b 3); i. e. it belongs to the period in which ch. 9 was still retained in A and not replaced by the later form of it in M.[3]

The later part of K stands on quite a different basis. It consists

---

[1] οὐδὲ μήν, which occurs twice in this part of K, is not found elsewhere in Aristotle except in *Phys.* vii, the genuineness of which has been seriously doubted. But the argument against K is weakened by the fact that μήν is used throughout the *Metaphysics* much oftener than in most of Aristotle's works.

[2] Otherwise the fifth problem, stated in 997^a 35, becomes meaningless. 997^b 3 presupposes, as Jaeger points out, the account of the ideal theory in A. 6, but not the criticism of it in A. 9.

[3] Jaeger shows in *Arist.* 216-222 that there are several indications in the first part of K of Aristotle's standing closer to the Platonic tradition than he does in ΒΓΕ.

of excerpts taken almost word for word from the *Physics*; there is no independence of treatment. The selection is made with considerable skill, and gives a fairly clear account of the subjects dealt with. The selector has a special taste for definitions (cf. $1065^a 27, 30, 35,$ $^b 1, 16, 22, 33, 1066^a 35, 1067^b 21, 23, 1068^b 20, 26, 27, 30, 31, 1069^a 1, 5$). It seems impossible to determine whether these extracts were made by Aristotle himself with a view to a brief course on physical topics, or by some pupil. If it was the latter, it is clear that he had the text of the *Physics* before him and was not simply taking notes of Aristotle's lectures; the verbal resemblance, down to the very particles, is too great to admit of the latter supposition. The union of the two parts of K into a single book presents a curious problem; it is natural enough that an editor, finding one set of papers ending with the discussion of accident, and another beginning with the discussion of chance, should have put them together so as to fill a fair-sized roll. In any case we must regard the second part as an intruder in the *Metaphysics*, for it is quite against Aristotle's principles to suppose that a single discussion could be at home both in physics and in metaphysics.

We come finally to Book Λ. Λ refers to no other book of the *Metaphysics*.[1] There are three passages in other books which may refer to Λ. E. 1027^a 19 says that the question whether everything is 'for the most part' or some things are eternal must be discussed later, and this is not done except in Λ. 6–8. K. $1064^a 36$ says more definitely 'if there is a substance of this nature—separate and unmovable—as we shall try to prove that there is'. On the other hand, the reference in Z. 1037^a 12 to a later discussion of the question 'whether there is another substance remote from the matter of sensible substances, and whether we must look for a substance distinct from them such as numbers or something of the kind', seems to refer much more probably to MN. And the other two references may be to a lost (or never written) positive part of the treatise of which MN is the preliminary critical part (cf. the formulation of the problem in M. 1076^a 10, 'whether there is apart from sensible substances an unchangeable

---

[1] εἴρηται δὲ πῶς, 1072^a 4, is rightly regarded by Bonitz as referring not to Θ. 8 but to Λ. 1071^b 22–26; εἴρηται *simpliciter* can hardly refer to anything but a preceding passage of the same or a very closely connected book.

and eternal substance ').[1]   Thus not much can be made of these references in favour of a real connexion between Λ and the rest of the *Metaphysics*.   It presents all the appearances of a separate work.   It announces itself in its first sentence as a discussion of substance, without reference to the fact that ZH have already dealt fairly comprehensively with this subject.

Its first five chapters discuss the fundamental nature of sensible substance, thus covering the same ground as ZH, but treating the subject quite independently and in a way which has more affinity with the *Physics* than with the rest of the *Metaphysics* ; cf. the analysis of sensible substance into form, privation, and matter (1069^b 32, 1070^b 11–29, 1071^a 8, 34) with *Phys.* i. 6.   It is to be noted, too, that while ZH are occupied mainly with the logical analysis of sensible substance into form and matter, Λ is concerned rather with a causal explanation of the existence of sensible things, and therefore brings in at an early stage and constantly insists on the necessity of a motive cause as well (1069^b 36, 1070^a 21, 28, ^{b} 22–35, 1071^a 14, 20–24, 28, 34).   It thus prepares the way for the proof of the necessity of a single motive cause of the universe.

All this first part of Λ is extremely terse.   That it represents rather notes for a treatise than a substantive treatise is indicated plainly by the two sentences (1069^b 35, 1070^a 4) beginning with μετὰ ταῦτα ὅτι, 'after this remember to say that '.

From the fact that Λ makes the existence of metaphysics conditional on the absence of any principle common to unchangeable substance and the objects of physics (1069^b 1), Jaeger infers (*Stud.* 122) that Aristotle has not yet assured himself that there is such a thing as metaphysics, and that therefore Λ must be earlier than ΓΕ, than ZHΘ, and than the *Physics*, in all of which the existence of metaphysics is clearly asserted, and must belong to the period of ΑΒ, in which metaphysics is still being looked for, an ἐπιστήμη ἐπιζητουμένη.   He thinks, further (p. 123), that this is confirmed by the absence of any name for metaphysics, either θεολογική or πρώτη φιλοσοφία, in Λ.   But the first argument is unconvincing ; one might as well argue that E is an early

---

[1] Λ cannot itself be the dogmatic sequel to MN ; the connexion between its two parts (cf. the reference in 6. 1071^b 3 to 1. 1069^a 30) forbids this. Also 1075^a 25 ff. contains a polemic which would be unnecessary if MN had come before.

work because of the conditional expression εἰ δ᾽ ἔστι τις οὐσία
ἀκίνητος, αὕτη προτέρα, καὶ φιλοσοφία πρώτη (1026ᵃ 29). Nor could
anything be inferred from the non-occurrence in these few pages
of a name for philosophy; but in fact the name σοφία does occur
(1075ᵇ 20). The similarity of the mode of thought with that of
the *Physics* suggests an early origin, but this is rendered doubtful
by the reference to the astronomical theories of Callippus, which
can hardly be dated before 330–325.[1]

It remains to consider the view of Krische and Goedeckemeyer
that Λ. 1–5 is continuous with K. 1–8 and supplies a parallel to ZHΘ
as those chapters supply a parallel to ΒΓΕ.[2] It must be pointed
out that there is nothing like the degree of affinity between Λ. 1–5
and ZHΘ that there is between K and ΒΓΕ. Λ. 2, 3 bear a general
resemblance to Z. 7–9, but beyond this there are very few points
of contact. Nor does Λ take up the problems raised in K. 1, 2.
It is also to be noted that the relative size of Λ. 1–5 and that of
K. 1–8 are very different; while K. 1–8 is about a third as long
as ΒΓΕ, Z is five times, ZH seven times, and ZHΘ ten times as
long as Λ. 1–5. Λ must be considered an entirely independent
treatise, with one principal aim, that of establishing the existence
of an eternal unmoved mover of the world.

[1] Cf. Heath, *Aristarchus of Samos*, 197, 198, 212. Jaeger states in
Arist. 229 ff. other and stronger arguments for the early date of Λ. Cf.
Λ init. note. He argues (366–379) that Λ. 8, with the exception of 1074ᵃ
31–38, was added later, when the inquiries of Eudoxus and Callippus had
convinced Aristotle of the necessity of a more elaborate theory of the
cause of the celestial movements than the mere reference to the first
mover.

[2] Krische, *Forschungen auf d. Gebiet der alten Philos.* i. 263 f.,
Goedeckemeyer in *Arch. f. Gesch. d. Phil.* xx. 521–542, xxi. 18–29.
Goedeckemeyer treats the following passages as parallel:
1069ᵃ 18–ᵇ 2 = Z. 1, 2.
   ᵇ 3–34 = H. 1042ᵃ 24—1044ᵇ 20.
35—1070ᵃ 9 = Z. 1032ᵃ 12—1034ᵇ 7.
1070ᵃ 9–13 = Z. 1029ᵃ 2–7 or H. 1042ᵃ 26–31.
   13–30 = H. 1043ᵇ 19–23, Z. 1033ᵇ 19—1034ᵃ 8.
He admits that Λ. 4, 5 have no parallel in the preceding books.

Inserted Fragments.

Certain features of the corpus to which Jaeger has called attention (not always for the first time) remain to be mentioned. One of these is the tendency to insert loose fragments at the end of the various books, where there was presumably room left at the end of the roll or a fresh length could easily be added. He has made out a strong case for the occurrence of this in several instances.

(1) He argues (*Stud.* 14–21) that A. 10 is a later alternative version of A. 7, meant to come after the account of earlier views in chs. 1–6 and before the criticism of them in chs. 8, 9.

(2) K. 1065ᵃ 26–end is probably an insertion of this sort on a larger scale (ib. 38–41).

(3) Θ. 10 (which had already been suspected by Christ and Natorp) is a similar insertion (ib. 49–53). 'Being as truth' has been in E. 4 as definitely excluded from the province of metaphysics as 'accidental being' was in E. 2, 3. Only the being of the categories and the being of potentiality and actuality should be discussed by metaphysics, and these accordingly are discussed in ZH and in Θ. 1–9 respectively. The section of E in which a discussion of being as truth is promised, and in which truth as the apprehension of simple entities (as distinct from the truth of the judgement) is recognized (1027ᵇ 25–29), is a later addition inserted after the doctrine of *De An.* 430ᵃ 26 had been worked out and ch. 10 had been inserted into Θ. (K has nothing corresponding to the section in question, but the version there is so short that nothing can be inferred from this.)

(4) Jaeger argues (ib. 53–62), again with much probability, that the discussion of the unity of definition in Z. 12 is a doublet of that in H. 6, and one that comes in very curiously when the subject has just been postponed for future discussion (σκεπτέον ὕστερον Z. 11. 1037ᵃ 20). It is certainly odd in a closely united whole like ZH to find two chapters discussing the same subject without reference to each other. Z. 12, further, is a mere fragment, since it does not discuss definitions got by induction, as Aristotle meant to do after treating of those got by division (1037ᵇ 27—1038ᵇ 34). Now ch. 11 closes (1037ᵃ 21–ᵇ 7) with a summary of the contents of Z up to this point, and ch. 13 begins

with the announcement of a fresh start. Chs. 1–11, then, constitute a definite section of the argument, and Jaeger argues that probably chs. 1–11 and chs. 13–17 occupied separate rolls (Z, it should be noted, is the longest book of the *Metaphysics*), and that the isolated doublet was simply put in for convenience on the spare pages of the first roll.

No one of these instances is perfectly conclusive in itself, but the cumulative effect of them is to suggest very strongly that we have here a *vera causa* of some of the peculiarities in the arrangement of the *Metaphysics*.

The motives for the insertion of α, Δ, K, Λ in their present positions may have been as follows:

(1) α was inserted between A and B because the final words of A seemed to promise the raising of certain preliminary ἀπορίαι before the main ἀπορίαι of B (Al. 137. 5–12).

(2) Δ was inserted after Γ because Γ. 1004ᵃ 28 was taken to promise an examination of varieties in the meaning of terms (Al. 344. 22); perhaps also because E. 1026ᵃ 34 is the first backward reference to Δ.

(3) Λ was put next to MN because like them it is concerned with eternal, non-sensible being.

(4) K was put before Λ because Λ might superficially seem to be a parallel version of ZHΘ as K is of BΓE (Al. 633. 25).

The earliest editions of the Metaphysics.

With regard to the time at which the various treatises were put together to form the *Metaphysics* we have very little to go upon. Alexander (515. 20) expresses the opinion that two particular passages were 'placed together by Aristotle but separated by Eudemus'. Asclepius (4. 9) has a different story, that Aristotle sent the whole work to Eudemus, who thought it unfitting 'that so great a work should be published'; and that after his death, and the loss of parts of the book, later scholars filled up the gaps by drawing upon Aristotle's other works and piecing the whole together as best they could. Zeller has pointed out[1] that Asclepius' story implies the notion of an esoteric doctrine, which certainly does not go back to Eudemus,

---

[1] *Abh. d. Königl. Akad. d. Wissensch.*, Berlin, 1887, 156.

and that the *Metaphysics* is not in point of fact pieced to-gether with extracts from the other works of Aristotle. The authority of Asclepius does not in any case count for much. Alexander's suggestion is more probable; Eudemus may have done some editorial work on the metaphysical as on the ethical treatises.[1]

The oldest list of Aristotle's works, that of Diogenes Laertius, which is probably based on Hermippus (*c.* 200 B.C.), does not contain the *Metaphysics*, but mentions Δ under the title of περὶ τῶν ποσαχῶς λεγομένων ἢ κατὰ πρόσθεσιν. The list in *Anonymus Menagii* gives μεταφυσικὰ κ̄, and in an appendix τῆς μετὰ φυσικὰ ῑ. Both of these references probably point to a ten-book *Meta-physics* (stigma being excluded in the first reckoning and included in the second). The list of Ptolemaeus Chennus (*c.* A.D. 100) includes the *Metaphysics* in thirteen books (i. e. with-out α, or counting it as an appendix to A). The name *Meta-physics*, which occurs first in Nicolaus of Damascus, in the time of Augustus, has been commonly supposed to have been affixed by Andronicus (*c.* 60 B.C.) when he issued his great edition of Aristotle's works;[2] but Jaeger (*Stud.* 180) points out that additions to the canon of classical writers do not seem to have been made after this date. If this be so, Andronicus' *Metaphysics* must have contained fourteen (or thirteen) books, and the ten-book *Meta-physics*, and therefore, of course, the name *Metaphysics*, must be earlier than Andronicus, though presumably later than Her-mippus. But as we have no other trace of an edition earlier than that of Andronicus, this conclusion must remain very doubtful; it is equally probable that Aristotle is an exception to the rule that the canon of classical authors was fixed by the beginning of the imperial period.

---

[1] A casual allusion like Alexander's is more significant than an elaborate story like that told by Asclepius. The story connecting A or α with Eudemus' nephew (Asc. 4. 21 and *Schol.* 589ᵃ 41 Brandis) agrees well with the view that Eudemus did some editorial work on the *Metaphysics*.

[2] The earliest title is τὰ περὶ τῆς πρώτης φιλοσοφίας (*M. A.* 700ᵇ 9). The title τὰ μετὰ τὰ φυσικά is due to the place of the work in complete editions of Aristotle's works (Asc. 1. 19), which in turn was probably dictated by the view that it is proper to proceed from τὰ γνώριμα ἡμῖν (material things, treated of in the physical works) to τὰ γνώριμα ἁπλῶς (Al. 171. 6, Asc. 1. 7).

Jaeger has detected a curious point in the external history of the *Metaphysics*. Each of its books has a certain amount of independence, and it seems probable that each was originally written on a separate roll (the general absence of connecting particles, among other things, suggests this). These rolls must have been of very unequal size. Now at the end of the alternate books α, Γ, E, H, and I (and of these books only) there occur in one or all of the manuscripts words meant evidently to point to the beginning of the next book, as in old printed books the first word of each page is printed as a catchword at the end of the previous page. Jaeger argues (*Stud.* 181) from this that for commercial purposes the *Metaphysics* was probably arranged in seven rolls each containing two books; and unequal as the single books are, the pairs of books are not unlike in size. Thus

$$Aα = 14\tfrac{1}{2} \text{ pages of Bekker} \qquad ΘI = 13\tfrac{1}{2} \text{ pages}$$
$$BΓ = 17\tfrac{1}{2} \text{ ,, ,, ,,} \qquad\qquad KΛ = 16\tfrac{3}{4} \text{ ,,}$$
$$ΔE = 15^{1} \text{ ,, ,, ,,} \qquad\qquad MN = 17\tfrac{3}{4} \text{ ,,}$$
$$ZH = 17\tfrac{3}{4} \text{ ,, ,, ,,}$$

The catch-phrase at the end of Λ may be supposed to have been lost.

II

SOCRATES, PLATO, AND THE PLATONISTS

Socrates.

In considering Aristotle's account of Socrates it will be well to have before us his actual words:

A. 987ᵃ 29–ᵇ 9.

μετὰ δὲ τὰς εἰρημένας φιλοσοφίας
ἡ Πλάτωνος ἐπεγένετο πραγματεία,
τὰ μὲν πολλὰ τούτοις (the Pythagoreans) ἀκολουθοῦσα, τὰ δὲ καὶ
ἴδια παρὰ τὴν τῶν Ἰταλικῶν ἔχουσα
φιλοσοφίαν.

M. 1078ᵇ 9–32.

περὶ δὲ τῶν ἰδεῶν πρῶτον αὐτὴν
τὴν κατὰ τὴν ἰδέαν δόξαν ἐπισκεπτέον, μηθὲν συνάπτοντας πρὸς τὴν
τῶν ἀριθμῶν φύσιν, ἀλλ' ὡς ὑπέλαβον ἐξ ἀρχῆς οἱ πρῶτοι τὰς ἰδέας
φήσαντες εἶναι.

---

¹ Not 9 as Jaeger says.

A. 987ᵃ 29–ᵇ 9.

ἐκ νέου τε γὰρ συνήθης γενόμενος πρῶτον Κρατύλῳ καὶ ταῖς Ἡρακλειτείοις δόξαις, ὡς ἁπάντων τῶν
αἰσθητῶν ἀεὶ ῥεόντων καὶ ἐπιστήμης
περὶ αὐτῶν οὐκ οὔσης, ταῦτα μὲν καὶ
ὕστερον οὕτως ὑπέλαβεν·

Σωκράτους δὲ περὶ μὲν τὰ ἠθικὰ
πραγματευομένου περὶ δὲ τῆς ὅλης
φύσεως οὐθέν, ἐν μέντοι τούτοις τὸ
καθόλου ζητοῦντος καὶ περὶ ὁρισμῶν
ἐπιστήσαντος πρῶτον τὴν διάνοιαν,

ἐκεῖνον ἀποδεξάμενος διὰ τὸ
τοιοῦτον ὑπέλαβεν ὡς περὶ ἑτέρων
τοῦτο γιγνόμενον καὶ οὐ τῶν αἰσθητῶν . . . οὗτος οὖν τὰ μὲν τοιαῦτα
τῶν ὄντων ἰδέας προσηγόρευσε,
τὰ δ' αἰσθητὰ παρὰ ταῦτα καὶ κατὰ
ταῦτα λέγεσθαι πάντα.

M. 1078ᵇ 9–32.

συνέβη δ' ἡ περὶ τῶν εἰδῶν δόξα
τοῖς εἰποῦσι διὰ τὸ πεισθῆναι περὶ
τῆς ἀληθείας τοῖς Ἡρακλειτείοις
λόγοις ὡς πάντων τῶν αἰσθητῶν ἀεὶ
ῥεόντων, ὥστ' εἴπερ ἐπιστήμη τινὸς
ἔσται καὶ φρόνησις, ἑτέρας δεῖν
τινὰς φύσεις εἶναι παρὰ τὰς αἰσθητὰς
μενούσας· οὐ γὰρ εἶναι τῶν ῥεόντων
ἐπιστήμην.

Σωκράτους δὲ περὶ τὰς ἠθικὰς
ἀρετὰς πραγματευομένου καὶ περὶ
τούτων ὁρίζεσθαι καθόλου ζητοῦντος
πρώτου (τῶν μὲν γὰρ φυσικῶν ἐπὶ
μικρὸν Δημόκριτος ἥψατο μόνον . . .
οἱ δὲ Πυθαγόρειοι πρότερον περί
τινων ὀλίγων . . . ἐκεῖνος δ' εὐλόγως
ἐζήτει τὸ τί ἐστιν· συλλογίζεσθαι
γὰρ ἐζήτει, ἀρχὴ δὲ τῶν συλλογι-
σμῶν τὸ τί ἐστιν . . . δύο γάρ ἐστιν
ἅ τις ἂν ἀποδοίη Σωκράτει δικαίως,
τούς τ' ἐπακτικοὺς λόγους καὶ τὸ
ὁρίζεσθαι καθόλου· ταῦτα γάρ ἐστιν
ἄμφω περὶ ἀρχὴν ἐπιστήμης)· —ἀλλ'
ὁ μὲν Σωκράτης τὰ καθόλου οὐ
χωριστὰ ἐποίει οὐδὲ τοὺς ὁρισμούς·
οἱ δ' ἐχώρισαν, καὶ τὰ τοιαῦτα
τῶν ὄντων ἰδέας προσηγόρευσαν.

The only other reference to Socrates by name in the *Meta-physics* occurs in M. 1086ᵃ 37–ᵇ 5 τὰ μὲν οὖν ἐν τοῖς αἰσθητοῖς καθ' ἕκαστα ῥεῖν ἐνόμιζον καὶ μένειν οὐθὲν αὐτῶν, τὸ δὲ καθόλου παρὰ ταῦτα εἶναί τε καὶ ἕτερόν τι εἶναι. τοῦτο δ' . . . ἐκίνησε μὲν Σωκράτης διὰ τοὺς ὁρισμούς, οὐ μὴν ἐχώρισέ γε τῶν καθ' ἕκαστον· καὶ τοῦτο ὀρθῶς ἐνόησεν οὐ χωρίσας.

The part that Aristotle assigns to Socrates in the history of philosophy is a comparatively modest one. In his review of previous philosophers he passes (987ᵃ 29) direct from the Pythagoreans to Plato, and Socrates is introduced incidentally as one of the influences which affected Plato's development. What is the value of Aristotle's testimony? Prof. Taylor makes three statements, (1) 'that Aristotle neither had, nor could have been expected to have, any particular knowledge of the life and thought of Socrates, except what he learned from Plato, or read in the works of the "Socratic men" ' ; [1] (2) 'that every statement of importance made about Socrates in the Aristotelian corpus can be traced to an existing source in the Platonic dialogues ' ; [2] and (3) 'that Aristotle exercised no kind of higher criticism on his documents, but simply accepted what he read in the Σωκρατικοὶ λόγοι of Plato and others as a dramatically faithful presentation of a real historical figure '.[3] With the first statement I am generally in agreement, but I should prefer to say that Aristotle in all probability derived all his knowledge of Socrates from Plato and other members of the Academy. Aristotle was not born till fifteen years after Socrates' death, and if a few stories about Socrates may have reached him at Stagira, it is pretty certain that he can have learnt nothing of importance about Socrates' philosophical views till he became a student of the School of Plato. But there is a great gulf between the first of Prof. Taylor's propositions and the other two, for these in effect ignore the fact that besides the dialogues Aristotle had Plato's ἄγραφα δόγματα (to which in another context [4] he refers), and the whole verbal tradition current in the Academy, on which to draw for his knowledge of the teaching both of Socrates and of Plato. By his examination of Aristotle's statements else-where about Socrates, Prof. Taylor makes good his case that all of these—all at any rate that have a philosophical importance— were or (as I should prefer to say) might have been derived from Plato's dialogues. But the first of the above-quoted passages from M presents *prima facie* a powerful objection to both of the two latter of Prof. Taylor's propositions. For according to the ordinary interpretation of his words Aristotle says that Socrates did not effect the 'separation' of the Ideas but that Plato did ; and since the separation to which Aristotle objects is commonly supposed to be the sort of separation which is frequently put into the mouth of Socrates by Plato,[5] the inference is commonly drawn that Aristotle distinguishes between the historical Socrates and the Socrates of the dialogues, and regards

---

[1] *Varia Socratica*, 40.   [2] ib.

[3] ib. 41.   [4] *Phys.* 209[b] 15.

[5] e. g. in *Parm.* 130 B. Socrates says that he believes in χωρὶς μὲν εἴδη αὐτὰ ἄττα, χωρὶς δὲ τὰ τούτων αὖ μετέχοντα. Cf. *Phaedo* 74 A, &c.

the latter as expressing the views not of Socrates but of Plato himself. This would imply that Aristotle did not take the dialogues at their face value as historical accounts of Socrates' views but exercised an independent judgement about them.

To avoid this difficulty, Prof. Taylor supposes that 'those who first said that there are Ideas', who are the persons stated in the above passage from M to have differed from Socrates by separating the Ideas, are not Plato and his followers but the 'half-Pythagorean and half-Eleatic'[1] school of Megara (including Euclides and Terpsion)—the εἰδῶν φίλοι of *Soph.* 248 A who assert 'an absolute severance between γένεσις (process, fact) and οὐσία',[2] and with whom Plato in the *Sophistes* disagrees on this ground.

The answer to this suggestion lies in a comparison of the passage in M with that in A. In A Aristotle does not mention the separation and in M he does not mention Plato, but the reference in both passages to the influence of Heracliteanism, the identity of the way in which Socrates is introduced in both passages, and the identity, but for the change in number, of the final statement show that 'those who first said there are Ideas' in M means just Plato and his orthodox disciples. Prof. Taylor asks, 'if Plato is distinguished as "those who first said there are εἴδη" from some one else who added that εἴδη are numbers, why does Aristotle constantly attribute the doctrine of the "numbers" to Plato himself?'[3] But the distinction in 1078[b] 9–12 is not between two persons but between two forms of the ideal theory, the theory of Ideas pure and simple as it was held originally (ἐξ ἀρχῆς, ib. 11) by the first believers in Ideas, and the theory of Idea-numbers. The earlier Plato and his first disciples are contrasted with his later self and his later disciples like Xeno-crates.[4] That Aristotle viewed Plato as the author of the ideal theory seems to be confirmed by *E. N.* 1096[a] 12 καίπερ προσάντους τῆς τοιαύτης ζητήσεως γινομένης διὰ τὸ φίλους ἄνδρας εἰσαγαγεῖν τὰ εἴδη. Is it likely that Aristotle would have spoken thus if the Ideas went back to the time of Socrates, who died long before he himself was born?

It is with Plato, then, and not with the Megarians, that Aristotle is contrasting Socrates. This can only mean one or

---

[1] *V. S.* 87.   [2] ib. 84.   [3] ib. 70.
[4] Cf. Ps.-Al. 740. 18 (N.B. the singular ὑπέλαβεν), 741. 22.

other of two things. (1) He treats the Socrates of the dialogues as the historical Socrates, and contrasts the views put into his mouth with others which Plato expresses through other mouths in the dialogues, or expressed in his verbal teaching. Or (2) he treats the Socrates of the dialogues not as equivalent to the historical Socrates but as the mouthpiece of Plato's own views, and contrasts these with those which he believes to have been held by Socrates himself.

The first alternative is ruled out by what is implied both in the A passage and in the M passage, that it was not Socrates but those with whom he is contrasted that first used the word ἰδέα in its technical sense. It is notorious that the word is constantly used in such a sense by the Socrates of the dialogues. We are driven therefore to the second alternative, that Aristotle distinguished clearly between the historical Socrates and the Socrates of the dialogues. Nor is this in the least incompatible with the supposition that all he knew of Socrates he learnt from the Academy, and perhaps even from Plato himself. It is natural to suppose that it was well understood in the Academy that Plato had in the dialogues sometimes used Socrates as the mouthpiece of Platonic and non-Socratic views, and Plato may very well have made this clear in his oral teaching.

Prof. Taylor argues [1] from the reference to Σωκρατικοὶ λόγοι in *Poet.* 1447[b] 11 that Aristotle meant by these a realistic type of composition in which truth to life was of the first importance and in which therefore Plato could not reasonably have ascribed to Socrates views quite different from those which he really held. But surely the important point is that the Σωκρατικοὶ λόγοι are for Aristotle, just as much as the mimes of Sophron and Xenarchus, forms of poetry or drama and not of history, that it is universal and not particular truth that is required of them. They are poetry, though written in prose, just as Empedocles' works are not poetry, though written in verse.

What Prof. Taylor's view implies, if pushed to its logical conclusion, is that whenever Plato had original views to express, he was careful to put them into the mouth of some purely imaginary character. The views expressed by Parmenides and Timaeus, for instance, in the dialogues that bear their names, must be as historical as those expressed by Socrates, and all that we are

[1] *V. S.* 55.

left with as the philosophy of Plato is what is said by the
'strangers' in the *Sophist*, the *Statesman*, and the *Laws*, and
what we learn (mainly from Aristotle) about the theory of ideal
numbers. Is it likely that Aristotle, his ablest pupil, the 'mind
of the school', can have been so completely mistaken as this
view implies that he was with regard to the fundamental nature
of the dialogues? That he misunderstood some of Plato's
views is very probable, but that he should have thought Plato
to be writing original philosophy when he was really only
expounding other men's views seems improbable.

If it be asked why Aristotle refers thus vaguely in M to 'the
first believers in Ideas' and not to Plato by name, the answer is
to be found partly in the nature of Books M and N, partly in
a delicacy for which Aristotle has not received the credit due to
him. (1) MN is a study of various actual or even merely
possible opinions conducted in as impersonal a manner as
possible. It is throughout a criticism of the various forms of
a general way of thinking which was common to the Pythagoreans, Plato, Speusippus, and Xenocrates. 'The Pythagoreans' is so vague an expression that Aristotle feels free to
use it frequently, but Plato is mentioned only once,[1] and
Speusippus and Xenocrates never; all three are constantly
referred to in the vaguest terms.[2] (2) Aristotle seems to prefer,
when he is criticizing Plato, not to mention him by name. Of
the passages in the *Metaphysics* in which Plato is mentioned
by name, Λ. 987ᵘ 29–988ᵘ 17 is mainly historical, with little
criticism; Λ. 988ᵘ 26, 990ᵃ 30, Z. 1028ᵇ 19 are purely historical;
B. 996ᵃ 6, 1001ᵃ 9 are purely aporematic; in Γ. 1010ᵇ 12, Δ. 1019ᵃ 4
Aristotle adopts a Platonic argument and a Platonic distinction;
E. 1026ᵇ 14, K. 1064ᵇ 29, Λ. 1070ᵃ 18 express a qualified approval
(οὐ κακῶς is less faint praise in Greek than its literal equivalent
in English); Λ. 1071ᵇ 32–1072ᵃ 4 expresses partial agreement,
partial criticism; M. 1083ᵃ 32 states Plato's view on a particular
point to be better than those of his followers; only in
I. 1053ᵇ 13 ff. is Plato's view simply attacked. To this last
passage we must add Δ. 1025ᵃ 6, where a particular argument in
the *Hippias Minor* (not necessarily treated as having been

---

[1] 1083ᵃ 32.

[2] c.g. 1076ᵃ 19–21 οἱ μὲν (Plato) . . . οἱ δὲ (Xenocrates) . . . ἕτεροι δέ
τινες (Speusippus).

believed in by Plato) is described as illusory. On the other hand in the criticisms of the ideal theory which occur in A. 9, Z. 6, 8, 11, 14, 15, M, N there are no explicit references to Plato except (1) A. 991^b 3 = M. 1080^a 2, a disparaging reference to the *Phaedo*, and (2) M. 1083^a 32, the comparatively laudatory reference mentioned above. It certainly seems as if Aristotle tried to avoid the direct mention of Plato when he was attacking the Platonic theory.

There is a minor but interesting question, viz. whether Aristotle refers, as is maintained by ' Fitzgerald's canon ',[1] to the historical Socrates as Σωκράτης and to the Platonic Socrates as ὁ Σωκράτης. Prof. Taylor maintains[2] that this canon is quite unfounded. The general practice in Greek is that the article is omitted with the names of persons except (*a*) in referring to a person already named in the context without the article (here ὁ = ' the said '); (*b*) to a person who is present and is pointed to ; (*c*) to a particularly famous person : so the practice is stated by Kühner.[3] Aristotle's practice agrees with this in general. In *Met.* A there are fifty references to philosophers and poets without the article, and two with it—ὁ γὰρ Παρμενίδης 986^h 22, ὁ μὲν γὰρ Πλάτων 990^a 29 (both explicable by (*a*) above). In the other books of the *Metaphysics* we find Πλάτων eleven times ; in one passage[4] the best MSS. are divided as between Πλάτων and ὁ Πλάτων, and the latter form occurs nowhere else in these books. In the *Rhetoric* historical characters are mentioned at least 234 times without the article, and there are (as far as I know) only twenty-one passages (other than those explicable by Fitzgerald's canon) in which they occur with the article ;[5] some of these[6] are explicable by (*a*) above, and the rest probably by (*c*). On the other hand Σωκράτης occurs in Aristotle's genuine works 19 times without the article and 22 times with it. This at once suggests that there is some special reason for the use of the article with this name, and the reason which naturally presents

---

[1] W. Fitzgerald, *Selections from the Nic. Eth. of Aristotle*, 163.
[2] *V. S.* 41-51.
[3] *Gr. Gramm.* § 462 (a).   [4] Λ. 1070^a 18.
[5] 1357^b 34, 1364^a 19, 1365^a 28, 1367^a 9, ^{b} 17, 19, 1368^a 20, 1377^a 19, 22, 1384^b 15, 1386^a 19, 1392^b 12, 1398^a 17, ^{b} 31, 1399^a 33, 1400^b 17, 1401^b 32, 1402^b 11, 1405^b 24, 30, 1417^a 7.
[6] 1357^b 34, 1398^a 17. Cf. *Pol.* 1274^a 31 f., *Poet.* 1453^a 24-29.

itself is that Socrates is both a historical character and a character in Plato's dialogues. The use of the article when he is referred to in the latter capacity may be explained as a sort of generalized form of such expressions as ὁ ἐν Φαίδωνι Σωκράτης, ὁ ἐν τῇ Πολιτείᾳ Σωκράτης.[1] If this distinction is intended by Aristotle, we should expect to find Σωκράτης used generally with a past tense and ὁ Σωκράτης with the present. Σωκράτης occurs with a past tense in *Soph. El.* 183ᵇ 7, *P. A.* 642ᵃ 28, *Met.* 987ᵇ 1, 1078ᵇ 17, 1086ᵇ 3, *E. N.* 1127ᵸ 25, 1144ᵇ 18, 28, 1145ᵇ 23, 25, 1147ᵇ 15, *Pol.* 1260ᵃ 22, *Rhet.* 1398ᵃ 24, 1419ᵃ 8 ὁ Σωκράτης with the present in *Pol.* 1261ᵃ 6, 12, 16, ᵇ 19, 21, 1262ᵇ 6, 9, 1264ᵃ 29, ᵇ 7, 1291ᵃ 12, 1316ᵃ 2, ᵇ 27. There are other passages in which the verb throws no light on the question whether the real or the Platonic Socrates is meant, but the sense does so. In *An. Post.* 97ᵇ 21, *Met.* 1078ᵇ 28, *Rhet.* 1390ᵇ 31, where there is no article, the sense clearly demands a reference to the historical Socrates. In the *Politics* the passages with the article (including 1263ᵇ 30, 1264ᵃ 12, ᵇ 24, 29, 37 as well as those mentioned above) occur, with one exception, in contexts in which the *Republic* is mentioned by name and its theories are under discussion. (The exception is 1265ᵃ 11 πάντες οἱ τοῦ Σωκράτους λόγοι, where the article is appropriately used, since Aristotle is referring to the Platonic dialogues; but the special reference is to the *Laws.* Aristotle either speaks carelessly as if Socrates had been a character in that dialogue, or deliberately identifies the 'Athenian Stranger' with Socrates; Grote suggests that Plato intended this identification, and did not call the chief speaker Socrates, only because it was well known that Socrates had never been in Crete, where the scene is laid.) Thus Fitzgerald's canon accounts for 35 out of the 41 passages. Further, it is not surprising if the article occasionally occurs with a past tense; 'as Mr. Micawber said' is hardly less natural than 'as Mr. Micawber says'. *E. N.* 1116ᵇ 4 ὁ Σωκράτης ᾠήθη refers to *Laches* 125, *Prot.* 360; *Rhet.* 1367ᵇ 8 ὁ Σωκράτης ἔλεγεν to *Menex.* 235 D. There remain four exceptional passages. In *Pol.* 1342ᵸ 23 we have ἐπιτιμῶσι καὶ τοῦτο Σωκράτει, where the reference is clearly to the *Republic*; but (a) Susemihl and Burnet regard the section in which this occurs as spurious, and (b), if it is genuine, Prof.

---

[1] *De Gen. et Corr.* 335ᵇ 10, *Pol.* 1342ᵃ 32.

Cook Wilson's emendation τῷ Σωκράτει may well be right after τοῦτο. In *Rhet.* 1415ᵇ 30 we have λέγει Σωκράτης ἐν τῷ ἐπιταφίῳ, where the *Menexenus* is referred to ; it is pardonable to suggest that in this one passage ὁ has dropped out before the similar letter σ. In *Met.* 1078ᵇ 30, *Rhet.* 1398ᵇ 31 ὁ Σωκράτης clearly refers to the historical person, but the former passage falls under Kühner's (*a*) and the latter probably under his (*c*). The canon is on the whole confirmed very strongly by Aristotle's usage with other proper names. In *E. N.* vii, for instance, Bywater observes [1] that we have the article where the canon requires it in 1145ᵃ 21, 1146ᵃ 21, 1148ᵃ 33, 1149ᵇ 15, 1151ᵇ 18, and miss it only in 1145ᵃ 20. The rule is observed in twenty passages of the *Politics*,[2] and ignored only in 1342ᵇ 23 (dealt with above) and in 1338ᵃ 28, where it is natural to restore ⟨ὁ⟩ 'Οδυσσεύς. In 1262ᵇ 11 ὁ 'Αριστοφάνης means Aristophanes in the *Symposium*. In the *Rhetoric* there are at least eighteen instances of the observance of the rule. Bywater admits only two exceptions—1415ᵇ 30 (dealt with above) and 1400ᵃ 27, where we may restore ⟨ὁ⟩ 'Οδυσσεύς. Prof. Taylor, however, has pointed out several passages in which, of two literary characters referred to, only one has the article,[3] as though Aristotle considered that he had thus given a sufficient clue to his meaning. The article is exceptionally omitted in 1413ᵇ 26 ('Ραδάμανθυς καὶ Παλαμήδης). The *Rhetoric* also, as we have seen, uses the article occasionally of historical characters, and it would seem that in this, the most highly finished of Aristotle's works, rhythmical grounds have led to a relaxation of the usual principle. In the *Poetics* there are at least 31 cases of the use of the article in accordance with the canon,[4] and only the following exceptions :—ὁ θρῆνος 'Οδυσσέως ἐν τῇ Σκύλλῃ 1454ᵃ 30 (not really an exception, because θρῆνος 'Οδυσσέως was presumably the regular way of referring to this part of the *Scylla*), 'Οδυσσεύς 1454ᵇ 26, 'Ορέστης ib. 31, Οἰδίπους 1460ᵃ 30, Σίσυφος 1456ᵃ 22. The dropping out of ὁ before ο and occasionally before σ is clearly *exceptio probans regulam*.

---

[1] *Cont. to Text. Emend. of Aristotle's Nic. Eth.* 52.
[2] Bywater, *Aristotle on the Art of Poetry*, 228.
[3] 1396ᵇ 15, 1399ᵃ 1, ᵇ 28, 1400ᵃ 27, 1401ᵇ 35.
[4] 1451ᵃ 22, 1452ᵃ 25, 27, ᵇ 5, 6, 7, 1453ᵇ 6, 23, 24 *ter*, 29, 1454ᵃ 1, 2, 5, 29, 31, ᵇ 14, 1455ᵃ 5, 6, 7, 27, ᵇ 18, 1460ᵃ 30, ᵇ 26, 1461ᵃ 12, 29, ᵇ 5, 7, 21 *bis*.

The references to Socrates in the *Metaphysics* show that Aristotle held that Plato 'separated' the Ideas, and that Socrates did not. But we must agree with Prof. Taylor[1] that the meaning of this phrase is by no means clear. Aristotle's meaning seems to be that Socrates' attempt to arrive at definitions of common terms (of which there are many examples both in Plato's dialogues and in the *Memorabilia*) concentrated attention on universals, but that Socrates did not, any more than Aristotle himself, draw the conclusion that the universal exists as something apart from the particulars; that either he had no theory on the subject, or he thought as Aristotle does that the universal exists only as the common element in particulars. Now to distinguish the universal from its particulars is in a sense to 'separate' it. It is to think of it separately, and if the thought is not merely mistaken, this implies that the universal is a different entity from the particulars. What Aristotle means is that the Platonists treated the universal not merely as different from the particulars but as having a separate existence as well, i.e. (1) as not existing as an element in particulars at all, or (2) as existing apart from them as well as in them. Now he refers frequently to the Platonic doctrine of the participation of the particulars in the Ideas, which implies the presence of the Idea as an element in particulars. His view of the Platonic doctrine must therefore be the second of those just mentioned.

Whether he is right in this charge is a difficult matter on which to satisfy oneself. Much of Plato's language lends itself to the charge, but it is hard to say how far he may not be simply putting in an emphatic and picturesque way the doctrine of the distinction of the universal from the particulars and of the importance of the universal, a doctrine in which Aristotle believed no less than Plato. Yet it is difficult to suppose that Aristotle could have so thoroughly misinterpreted a master with whom he was presumably for years in daily contact, as to take for a fundamental difference of view what was really a difference of emphasis and expression. It is more probable that he had real grounds for supposing that Plato and his orthodox followers (1) were, in the application of such words as παράδειγμα and εἰκών to the Idea and its particulars, expressing belief in the existence of universals quite apart from particular instances, and (2)

[1] *V. S.* 69 ff.

in their zeal for the universal were losing sight of the particulars which after all are the facts with which any theory of the universe has to start.[1]

There are certain other points in Prof. Taylor's view of Socrates which call for some attention. Aristotle says that there are two things which may be ascribed to Socrates—inductive arguments and general definition. Prof. Taylor holds that inductive argument was in no special way characteristic of Socrates.[2] It would, of course, be as untrue to say that Socrates invented inductive argument as, in Locke's phrase, to suppose that God has been 'so sparing to men to make them barely two-legged creatures, and left it to Aristotle to make them rational'.[3] Prof. Taylor can without difficulty produce instances of the use of ἐπάγεσθαι for inductive argument from the early Hippocratean writings. But surely any one can recognize in Socrates, whether as depicted in the *Memorabilia* or as depicted in what are generally known as the 'Socratic' dialogues of Plato, a careful testing of general opinions by the examination of particular cases that is foreign to the previous schools of Greek philosophy, with which Aristotle is here contrasting Socrates. In this sense the ascription of inductive argument to him as of something characteristic is thoroughly justified. Similarly in the careful and continual search for general definitions which we find both the Xenophontic and the Platonic Socrates pursuing there is something very different from either the bold uncritical definitions of the pre-Socratics[4] or the acquiescence of common sense in mere descriptions or mere examples instead of definitions.

Aristotle's testimony is not, if our argument be sound, 'in favour of the view that Plato's dramatic portraiture of Socrates is, in all essentials, thoroughly historical'.[5] It is against this view. Whether we think it decisive against this view will depend on our estimate of the force of the other arguments put forward in favour of the view, and on our estimate of Aristotle as a witness to facts in the history of philosophy two generations

---

[1] That Plato himself saw those dangers to be implied in the ideal theory is shown clearly enough by the first part of the *Parmenides*; that he ever succeeded in avoiding them is not so clear.

[2] *V. S.* 72 ff.
[3] *Essay* iv. 17. 4.
[4] M. 1078[b] 21.
[5] *V. S.* 89.

before his own time. As regards the latter point, his member-
ship of the Academy for well-nigh twenty years surely implies
that his testimony about Socrates is of great importance. He
may be an unsympathetic and in some directions a hasty critic
of the ideal theory, but on a question of fact, the question
whether it was Plato's own theory or that of Socrates that Plato
expressed through the mouth of Socrates, he is unlikely to be
mistaken.

It is no part of my purpose to discuss the other arguments in
favour of Prof. Taylor's view. Every one must admire the skill
with which he and Prof. Burnet have developed and supported
by argument their hypothesis that the Socrates of the dialogues
is the historic Socrates, a hypothesis which has brought new
life into the study of Plato's dialogues. It is both justifiable
and important to work this hypothesis for all it is worth.
Prof. Taylor has shown conclusively [1] that the main facts in the
biography of Socrates which is commonly accepted even by
those who do not share his view are found in the dialogues of
Plato, and have probably made their way into the accepted
biography from no other source.

The sketch of Socrates' *life* and *character* which he has pieced
together from the dialogues forms a coherent and lifelike whole.
But on the question whether it was Socrates or Plato who first
formulated the ideal theory Aristotle's authority seems to me
decisive. This is compatible with accepting Socrates' account
in the *Phaedo* [2] of his early mental history as substantially true.
Aristotle does not tell us that Socrates was a mere moralist who
had never had any interest in physical or metaphysical questions.
What he says is that *when* Socrates was interesting himself [3] in
ethical questions and not in nature as a whole, Plato took him
as his master, i.e. that Socrates' influence on Plato belongs to
the later part of his career, when, as Prof. Taylor himself
maintains, the oracle given to Chaerephon had deflected the
current of his life and transformed him from the head of the
φροντιστήριον (which may well have been half-Anaxagorean, half-
Pythagorean in its complexion [4]) into the critic of current ethical
notions and the searcher for definitions of ethical terms. The

---

[1] In *Plato's Biography of Socrates*.

[2] 96 A-100 A.   [3] πραγματευομένου A. 987^{b} 2 = M. 1078^{b} 18.

[4] *Plato's Biog. of Soc.* 24.

chronology in itself makes this probable. Prof. Taylor holds [1]
that the oracle was given before the beginning of the Pelopon-
nesian war (i.e. before 431). Plato was born three years after
this, and this consideration alone, if we follow Prof. Burnet and
Prof. Taylor in holding the oracle to have been the turning-
point in Socrates' career,[2] would make it probable that Socrates
was not the medium through which Plato became acquainted
with the Pythagorean views out of which the ideal theory was,
according to Aristotle, developed, but rather, as Aristotle
implies, an influence on Plato independent of Pythagoreanism.

Origin of Plato's views.

We may now turn to Aristotle's account of the origin of
Plato's views. According to him,[3] Plato's philosophy 'in most
respects followed[4] the Pythagoreans', but was modified by two
other influences :—(1) an early acquaintance with Heraclitean
views, as represented by Cratylus, and a consequent conviction
that as sensible things are always in flux, they cannot be the
objects of knowledge ; (2) the influence exerted by Socrates'
efforts to find general definitions of ethical terms. Three
things here are somewhat surprising :—(1) the recognition of
Plato's doctrine as essentially akin to Pythagoreanism ; (2) the
reference to an early association with Cratylus ; (3) the absence
of any reference to the influence of Eleaticism.

(1) With regard to the first point it must be remembered that
Aristotle has in mind the whole body of Plato's teaching, including the doctrine of ideal numbers, which is not found in the
dialogues and therefore does not enter largely into our usual
conception of his philosophy. This whole side of Platonism is
plainly a development from Pythagoreanism. But even the
ideal theory proper bears much resemblance to the Pythagorean.
Aristotle states the relation between the two schools more definitely[5] by saying that while the Pythagoreans held that sensible
things exist by imitation of numbers, Plato held that they exist
by participation in Forms. The change from 'imitation' to 'participation' he regards as merely verbal but the change from

[1] ib. 26.　　　　　[2] ib. 19.　　　　　[3] 987ᵃ 30.
[4] i.e. resembled. Cf. n. on A. 987ᵃ 30.　　　　　[5] 987ᵇ 9.

'numbers' to 'Forms' as more important. He later [1] amplifies his account by saying that Plato agreed with the Pythagoreans (a) in treating unity as a substance, not an attribute, and (b) in treating numbers as the cause of the substantial nature of sensible things; and differed from them (a) in describing the material principle of the Forms not as a single thing, 'the indefinite', but as a 'dyad', the great and small, (b) in saying that numbers are 'apart from' sensible things and not the things themselves, (c) in positing mathematical objects as entities 'intermediate' between Forms and sensibles. Finally,[2] the second of these divergences from the Pythagorean doctrine, and the introduction of the Forms, are said to be due to ἡ ἐν τοῖς λόγοις σκέψις, while the first of the divergences is said to be due to a cause which need not concern us at present.

The phrase ἡ ἐν τοῖς λόγοις σκέψις points back to the earlier statement that Socrates' fixing of attention on definitions was an important factor in the development of Plato's thought. The outcome of the whole passage, then, is that while the Platonic theory of Ideas was essentially akin to the Pythagorean theory of numbers, two modifications were due to Socrates' insistence on the importance of careful definition, the recognition of unity and numbers as something apart from sensibles, and the introduction of the Forms. What is the meaning of this? We know from other passages that the Pythagoreans identified things with numbers; justice, they said, is the number four, opportunity the number seven, and so on. Even sensible things were identified with numbers, and, as is implied in this, numbers were not grasped in their true nature as something abstract and independent of any particular material in which they may be exemplified, but were thought of as themselves material. In fact the notion of immaterial being had not yet been grasped. Attention to the problem of definition naturally led to a twofold divergence from the Pythagorean theory. (a) Plato was led to realize that a number must be different from the various particulars in which it may be embodied, and (b) he was led to see that it is improper to put forward numbers as the very essence of other things; justice, for example, has a nature of its own and is not to be identified with four or any other number. These are the two ways, according to Aristotle, in which Socrates'

[1] ib. 22.   [2] ib. 29.

search for definitions produced features of Platonism which distinguished it from Pythagoreanism. It is an example of the
influence of logical inquiries on metaphysical views.

(2) The recognition of the flux of all sensible things and the
consequent impossibility of knowledge of them is present throughout the dialogues as the underlying assumption which does not
need to be often emphasized because it is so unquestioningly
taken for granted. What we should not have known from the
dialogues is Plato's early acquaintance with Cratylus. This
cannot, I think, be merely Aristotle's inference from the *Theaetetus* and the *Cratylus*; there is nothing in those dialogues to
suggest it. It seems to be a genuine piece of information
derived in all probability direct from Plato ; and it to some
extent confirms the view that as regards Socrates also Aristotle
was not entirely dependent on the dialogues for his information.
His other piece of information about Cratylus [1] may well come
from the same source.

(3) We might be tempted to suppose the Eleatics to be included among the ' Italians ' whom, according to Aristotle, Plato's
philosophy in most respects followed. But a reference to what
precedes and to other passages in which the word is used [2]
shows that only the Pythagoreans are meant. The reason why
Aristotle does not mention the Eleatics here probably is that
he describes Plato as learning the lesson of Eleaticism from
Cratylus and from Socrates. The Heraclitean insistence on
the flux of all sensible things, Socrates' insistence on the fact
that there is something that can be known and defined, led
Plato to draw the Eleatic inference that there is a non-sensible
reality which is the object of knowledge.[3] Eleaticism was
mediated to him by Cratylus and Socrates. One misses, however, a reference to the Eleatic Euclides of Megara, to whom
Plato betook himself after the death of Socrates, and by whom
he was considerably influenced.[4]

These non-sensible objects of knowledge, Aristotle says,[5]
Plato called Ideas, and it is implied that he was the first to use
the term in this technical sense. Students of Greek philosophy

---

[1] Γ. 1010ᵃ 12.

[2] 987ᵃ 10, 988ᵃ 26, *De Caelo* 293ᵃ 20, *Meteor.* 342ᵇ 30.

[3] 987ᵇ 5, 1078ᵇ 15.

[4] Cf. Burnet, *Greek Philosophy* i, pp. 230-237.   [5] 987ᵇ 7.

are much indebted to Prof. Taylor for the comprehensive study which he has made in *Varia Socratica* of the prose usage of the words εἶδος, ἰδέα down to the death of Alexander the Great. No one supposes that Plato used the words in a brand-new sense quite out of relation to their previous use. But there are certain contentions of Prof. Taylor's as to their previous use which seem to be disproved by Prof. Gillespie's study of his argument.[1] One is that 'the meaning "real essence" is the primary, the meaning "logical class" the secondary or derivative':[2] another is that the words, 'wherever they occur in any but a most primitive sense, have a meaning due to their significance in Pythagorean geometry'.[3] Prof. Gillespie has shown that in the Hippocratic writings εἶδος is frequently used in a sense which stands to the logical meaning of 'class' very much as the words 'form', 'kind', 'type' do in the mouth of an unphilosophical Englishman. And he has shown that there is no evidence for the belief that the sense 'geometrical figure' which εἶδος seems to have borne at an early stage in the history of Pythagoreanism had any influence on the general use of the word. As regards Plato's usage it is important to notice that both words as used by him imply a dependent genitive, and he speaks of 'the Forms' with an implied reference to the things of which they are the Forms. This in itself tells against the suggestion that εἶδος means a 'simple real'; the Forms are for Plato simple entities, but that is not what the word *means*. In fact for the Platonic use Prof. Taylor's other translation 'real essence' seems to be just right.

Aristotle's attitude to the ideal theory and the nature of his criticism of it are matters of common knowledge, and it is not necessary to enter into these matters here. But it is worth while to consider what light Aristotle throws on the nature of any modifications that may have taken place in the ideal theory.

'The earlier and the later theory of Ideas.'

We must first consider Dr. Jackson's view that an earlier and a later theory of Ideas can be traced in the dialogues.[4] He

[1] *Classical Quarterly* vi. 179-203.
[2] *V. S.* 181.   [3] ib. 180.
[4] *Journal of Philology* x. 253-298, xi. 287-331, xiii. 1-40, 242-272, xiv. 173-230, xv. 280-305. Cf. Prof. Taylor's convincing criticism in *Mind* v. (N.S.) 304 n., 307-311.

holds that the later theory was distinguished in two main respects from the earlier. (1) It restricted the world of Ideas within very narrow limits; it recognized Ideas only of animal and vegetable types and of the four elements, rejecting Ideas of relations, of negations, of manufactured objects. (2) It stated the relation between the particulars and the Ideas no longer as one of participation, but as one of copying.

(1) Aristotle seems to imply that Plato recognized Ideas only of ὁπόσα φύσει, only of those things which exist by nature;[1] and he tells us that the current doctrine of Platonists in his time rejected not only Ideas of manufactured objects, but also Ideas of relations and of negations.[2] Whether Plato himself rejected the latter two classes we do not know; but we are definitely told that he rejected the first, and it seems possible that the reasons which led him to reject this might have led him to reject the others also. But Dr. Jackson seems to be wrong in holding that this rejection is to be found in the dialogues. In order to reach this result, he has to treat the *Parmenides*, which so far as it comes to any definite conclusion reaffirms the necessity of believing in an Idea answering to every common name, as if it rejected this necessity. He has to treat the μέγιστα γένη of the *Sophist* as not Ideas at all because they are abstractions like being and not-being and not animals, vegetables, or elements; and he has to treat the absence of any mention of Ideas of justice, beauty, and the like in the *Timaeus* as proving that when he wrote the *Timaeus* Plato did not believe in these Ideas; when the fact is that Plato does not speak of such Ideas there because he is writing on physics and they would be quite out of place.

The statements of Aristotle just referred to have been much discussed. It is notorious that Plato in several passages speaks of Ideas of manufactured objects.[3] The theories that have been propounded in view of this fact are conveniently enumerated and well discussed in Robin's *Théorie Platonicienne des Idées et des Nombres*,[4] a work of great learning and acuteness. (a) It may be said that when Plato speaks of Ideas of *artefacta*, he is

---

[1] Λ. 1070ᵃ 18.
[2] A. 991ᵇ 6, 990ᵇ 16, 13.
[3] *Rep.* 596 B, 597 C, *Crat.* 389 B, C.   [4] 174 ff.

speaking loosely and perhaps half-humorously.[1] In reply it must be pointed out that Ideas of *artefacta* are required by the general doctrine that wherever there is a common name there is an Idea, and that the Ideas of bed and table form an integral part of Plato's argument against art in the tenth book of the *Republic*. (*b*) It may be said that Aristotle has misinterpreted Plato in saying that he recognized only Ideas of natural objects.[2] But Aristotle's statements agree with the definition put forward by Xenocrates as expressing Plato's view : τοῦτον ὡς ἀρεσκόμενον τῷ καθηγεμόνι τὸν ὅρον τῆς ἰδέας ἀνέγραψε· αἰτία παραδειγματικὴ τῶν κατὰ φύσιν ἀεὶ συνεστώτων ... χωριστὴ καὶ θεία αἰτία. (*c*) It may be said, as by Dr. Jackson,[4] that Plato changed his opinion. But Aristotle does not speak of any change in the ideal theory in this respect, nor is any real evidence of a change to be found in the dialogues. (*d*) It may be suggested that it was only Plato's disciples who changed the theory. Beckmann[5] supposes that the name of Plato is a later addition in the one passage where he is definitely named. But we should not have recourse to a violent assault on the text till more peaceable methods have first been tried ; and we must take some account of the testimony of Xenocrates. (*e*) Robin suggests that Plato rejected Ideas only of the products of the imitative arts, the copies which merely reproduce the outward form of their originals, and not the Ideas of the products of the useful arts, which have a form dictated by their end as truly as natural objects have ; and that Aristotle misinterpreted him as having denied Ideas of the latter also. This suggestion agrees with the doctrine of the *Republic*, where the actual bed stands at one remove from the Idea (just as a natural object does), the painted bed at two removes. There is no Idea of the painted bed ; its παράδειγμα is not an Idea but the actual bed. If this very plausible suggestion be right, Xenocrates and the Platonic school generally[6] must have gone beyond Plato by banning Ideas of both types of

[1] So Proclus *In Tim.* 29 C, i. 344. 8, Diehl ; Ravaisson, *Essai* i. 294 ff. ; Bonitz, 118 f.

[2] So Zeller, *Plat. Stud.* 262.

[3] Procl. *In Parm.* i. 888. 18, v. 136, Cousin.

[4] So Susemihl, *Genet. Entwickl.* ii. 540 ; Ueberweg, *Unters.* 206 f., *Grundr.* i[9]. 191 ; Zeller, *Ph. d. Gr.* ii. 1[4]. 703, 947 ; Heinze, *Xenokr.* 53 f.

[5] *Num Plato artefactorum ideas statuerit*, 29–35. Cf. Alberti, *Die Frage über Geist u. Ordn. d. plat. Schrift.* 75 f.   [6] A. 991[b] 6.

artefacta, and Aristotle ascribes to the master what was true only of the disciples.

On the question of Ideas of negations, of perishables, and of relations it may be enough to refer to the notes on A. 990^b 13–16, from which it will be seen that the belief in a clean-cut division between an earlier and a later ideal theory held by Plato himself is not supported by Aristotle's statements.

(2) In his other main thesis, that in the later Platonic theory the Ideas were no longer thought of as immanent in particulars but as transcendent, related to them solely as a pattern to its copies, Dr. Jackson is on still weaker ground. The *Parmenides*, on which he here chiefly relies, riddles the transcendence-theory with objections as completely as it does the immanence-theory, and the upshot of the dialogue is the recognition of the inadequacy of both metaphors alike to express the view which Plato still holds, that there must be Ideas to which particulars are somehow related and to which they owe their being. Further, the Aristotelian evidence on which Dr. Jackson takes his stand with regard to the range of the Ideal world ẽntirely fails him with regard to the nature of the relation between Idea and particulars. Aristotle treats μέθεξις as the characteristic Platonic way of stating the relation, and he treats this as differ-ing only verbally from the Pythagorean way of stating the relation between numbers and sensible things, viz. as μίμησις.[1] So little does Aristotle make[2] of the distinction which seems to Dr. Jackson all-important. There is no suggestion whatever in Aristotle of an earlier and a later Platonic theory on this question.

There is, however, in Aristotle much evidence of Platonic theories of which little or no trace can be found in the dialogues, and which partly belong to Plato's later thought as it was expressed in the ἄγραφα δόγματα, and partly are due to develop-ments carried out by Speusippus and Xenocrates.

The Ideal Numbers and Ideal Spatial Magnitudes.

The first stage is the doctrine of the ἀσύμβλητοι ἀριθμοί which appears in *Met.* M. 6–8. This is no real advance or departure from the ideal theory as we know it from the dialogues; it is

---

[1] A. 987^b 10. [2] Cf. 991^a 20.

merely the making explicit, with regard to Ideas of numbers,[1] of what was involved in their being Ideas. The ideal numbers are simply the natural numbers, i.e. the universals twoness, threeness, &c., of which all groups with two, three, &c., members are the particular instances. From their nature as Ideas it follows that they are specifically distinct and incomparable,[2] i.e. incapable of being stated as fractions one of another. Twoness is not the half of fourness. Nor is a natural number an aggregate of units.[3] If, therefore, the Platonists had been true to their principles, the question which Aristotle presses on them, whether the units in ideal numbers are comparable or not, would have fallen to the ground. Their answer would have been that there are no units in ideal numbers. It is *possible* that Plato held this view, but certainly some of the Platonists did not. Aristotle says (1080[b] 8) that the views (*a*) that all units are comparable, and (*b*) that the units in each number are comparable to each other but not to those in any other number, both found support among the Platonists, but he does not expressly assign either to Plato. In view of the general nature of their doctrines we may perhaps ascribe (*a*) to Speusippus and (*b*), the compromise theory, to Xenocrates. The third view (*c*), that all units are incomparable, had no supporters (1080[b] 8, 1081[a] 35).

It should be added that a belief in ideal spatial magnitudes, no less than in ideal numbers, is implied in the Platonic theory as we know it from the dialogues. These also must be 'incomparable'. The idea of quadrilateral is not larger or smaller than or equal to the idea of triangle, nor can they be added together so as to make the idea of some other figure. The substance of what Aristotle has to say about the ideal μεγέθη is indicated in a later section of this essay.

[1] For which cf. *Phaedo* 101 c 5.
[2] 1080[a] 17, 1083[a] 34.
[3] Syr. 113. 24 τὸ δὲ καὶ ἀριθμὸν ἐν ἐκείνοις (sc. τοῖς εἰδητικοῖς ἀριθμοῖς) τὸν μοναδικὸν εἰσάγειν καὶ διὰ τοῦτο διπλασίαν ποιεῖν τὴν αὐτοδυάδα τῆς αὐτομονάδος, σφόδρα ἐστὶν ἐπιπόλαιον· οὐ γὰρ διὰ ποσότητα μονάδων ἕκαστος τῶν ἐκεῖ ἀριθμῶν ἔχει τὴν ἐπωνυμίαν ἣν εἴληφεν, ἀλλὰ κατά τινα χαρακτῆρα θειοτάτης καὶ ἀπλουστάτης οὐσίας ... ὅμοιον οὖν μοναδικὸν πλῆθος ἐπιζητεῖν ἐν τοῖς εἰδητικοῖς ἀριθμοῖς καὶ ἧπαρ ἢ σπλῆνα σπλάγχνων τε τῶν ἄλλων ἕκαστον ἐν τῷ αὐτοανθρώπῳ.

τὰ μεταξύ.

This is the doctrine that mathematical numbers and the other objects of mathematics form an order ot entities intermediate between Ideas and sensible objects. Aristotle expressly ascribes this doctrine to Plato,[1] and he tells us clearly what was the ground of the doctrine.[2] The objects of mathematics could not be sensible particulars because they were eternal and unchangeable; they could not be Ideas because there were many alike, while each Idea is unique. Take, for instance, the propositions 'two triangles on the same base and between the same parallels are equal in area'. What are these two triangles? They are different from the Idea of triangle. This, from its nature as a universal, is unique. If there were two Ideas of triangle, there would have had to be another, genuine Idea whose form they would have possessed.[3] On the other hand, Plato seems to have argued, the two triangles cannot be sensible triangles, since the proposition would still be true if all the sensible triangles that now exist ceased to exist; they are eternal while the sensibles are transient. Therefore there must be a third class of entities to which these belong. Similarly, when we say 2 and 2 makes 4, we are not speaking of the Idea of two, since to suppose this duplicated and then added to itself is absurd. Nor are we speaking of sensible twos, since the proposition would be true even if all the sensible twos ceased to exist.

The doctrine of 'intermediates' is not a purely fantastic and negligible one. It is an answer to a real question, the question involved in the notion of 'any'. What do we mean when we say that 'man is mortal'? We do not mean that 'manness' is mortal; nor that the human race is mortal; nor that A, B, and C, certain definite men, are mortal. We mean that any man is mortal, and it is not unnatural to suppose that the subject of this proposition is a separate entity. The argument may be extended beyond the sphere of mathematics and applied to the objects of all the sciences. Political economy makes statements about what happens when two economic men enter into certain relations.

---

[1] A. 987ᵇ 14. In the note ad loc. I have tried to show that the doctrine is a natural conclusion from views expressed in the dialogues, though it is not actually expressed in any dialogue except the *Timaeus*.

[2] 987ᵇ 16. Cf. B. 1002ᵇ 14.   [3] *Rep.* 597 C.

Who are these economic men? They are not the Idea of the
economic man, and they are not men of flesh and blood. Plato
does not appear to have extended the doctrine of the intermediates beyond pure mathematics, but Aristotle notes the
logical necessity for its extension beyond that sphere, if it is
maintained within that sphere. Astronomy must have as its
object a third heaven between the ideal heaven and the material
heaven; there must be 'intermediate' objects of optics, harmonics,
and medical science.[1]

Aristotle's own conception of the objects of mathematics, or
rather of geometry, itself assigns to them an intermediate
position, though not as a class of separate entities between two
other classes of separate entities. According to him the objects
of geometry are sensible things considered in abstraction from
their sensible qualities. Consider sensible things simply as
having boundaries of a certain shape, and you are considering
the objects of geometry. But a further act of abstraction is
possible. Not only may you think away the 'sensible matter'
of sensible things, but you may think away the 'intelligible
matter' of geometrical objects, their extension,[2] and you then
come to the essence of the straight line, of the circle, &c., i. e. the
formula of its construction which we express by its equation and
which the Platonists expressed, more crudely, by assigning the
number 1 as the form of the point or 'indivisible line', 2 as the
form of the line, 3 as that of the plane, and 4 as that of the solid.[3]
Aristotle seems to accept the distinction between τὸ εὐθεῖ εἶναι
(= δυάς) and τὸ εὐθύ.[4] Thus the object of geometry is intermediate
between the fully concrete sensible thing and the final result of
abstraction, the pure form.

But, Aristotle would say, it makes all the difference between
his own and the Platonic view that he assigns no separate
existence to either the intermediate or the final result of
abstraction, while the Platonists assign a separate existence to
both. The merits of the controversy between them thus turn on
the same point which arises with regard to his discussion of the
Ideas, viz. whether the Platonists meant by their χωρισμός the
recognition of a factual separateness or only that of a cognizable
difference between the things 'separated'.

---

[1] B. 997ᵇ 15–32, M. 1077ᵃ 1–9.   [2] Z. 1036ᵃ 11.
[3] De An. 404ᵇ 18–25.   [4] ib. 429ᵇ 18–20. Cf. H. 1043ᵃ 33.

There is another respect in which the 'separation' of the objects of mathematics resembles that of the Ideas. Aristotle speaks as if τὰ μαθηματικά differed from τὰ αἰσθητά only as the abstract from the concrete. Abstract from the bronzeness of the bronze ball, he says, and you will find a mathematical sphere. But what you will find in fact is a very imperfect approximation to a sphere. In certain contexts Aristotle notes this fact; he points out that in geometry we may 'suppose a line to be a foot long when it is not', and that our proof is not vitiated by this. Similarly he knows that the 'straight lines' and 'circles' used in geometrical diagrams are not really straight lines and circles.' But he does not take account of the fact in his statement of the mode of existence of τὰ μαθηματικά. With Plato, on the other hand, the perception of this fact must have been one of the motives of his separation of mathematical objects from sensibles. τὰ μαθηματικά are not, as Aristotle maintains that they are, qualities present in sensible things; they are perfect figures such as the regular solids, to which the things of sense are but approximations. In this respect the separation of τὰ μαθηματικά is like the separation of the Ideas. For those too are not, as Aristotle implies that they are, qualities present equally and completely in every particular; they are such things as the ideal beauty and the ideal justice which transcend all objects admired as beautiful and all acts which pass for just. In this respect they are unlike Aristotle's universals.

Is Plato right in assigning separate existence to the objects of mathematics? To Aristotle planes, lines, and points exist only potentially in the sensible bodies which exist actually. The plane is that at which the solid may be divided; the line that at which the plane may be divided; the point that at which the line may be divided. Plato asserts their actual existence, and surely rightly. To cut a ball in two is not to bring into existence the common plane of its halves, it is to drive your knife along a plane that is already there.

Thus, to sum up, the doctrine of the 'intermediates' turns (1) on the existence of propositions of the type 'any X is Y'. So far as this goes the doctrine is unjustified. The many twos, for example, involved in the propositions of arithmetic are the pairs of ordinary life, thought of in abstraction from their special

¹ M. 1078ᵃ 19, B. 997ᵇ 35- 998ᵃ 4, *An. Pr.* 49ᵇ 35.

nature and only with regard to their common nature as pairs. Every pair of things is a two; it may be designated from another point of view by another number as well (just as what is one week is also seven days), but this does not prevent it from being fully and perfectly a pair. It is difficult, no doubt, to state how we can be judging about all pairs without thinking of any in particular; but what is needed is not the recognition of a special entity but a closer reflection on the nature of judgement.

(2) But as regards the objects of geometry another consideration comes into play. The 'spheres' and 'circles' of common life are not spheres and circles at all, and it is not of them that geometrical propositions are true. Such propositions are true of the perfect geometrical figures which thought recognizes as existing in space though their boundaries do not coincide with those of any sensible figure. It is these perfect figures which, with the 'mathematical numbers', are Plato's intermediates.

Aristotle sees that whatever numbers are implied in the truth of arithmetic must be retained, and no others, and he therefore rejects the ideal numbers and retains the 'mathematical', though he regards them as having no *separate* existence. But in truth the mathematical numbers, as described by Plato in contrast to the ideal numbers and to sensible aggregates, are just those which arithmetic does not require. Aristotle would have done better to reject them and to accept the ideal numbers.

Aristotle recognizes three views about τὰ μαθηματικά from which he distinguishes his own. There is (a) Plato's view that they are κεχωρισμένα τῶν αἰσθητῶν.[1] There is (b) the Pythagorean view that they are in sensible things and constitute them, the sensible thing being an aggregate of planes, and ultimately of numbers.[2] And there is (c) an intermediate view, that they are ἐν τοῖς αἰσθητοῖς as separate entities though occupying the same space as the αἰσθητά.[3] Alexander[4] thinks that this also was a Pythagorean view, but it is clearly distinguished[5] from the view which is described as that of the Pythagoreans.[6] And, further, it is opposed by arguments[7] which are appropriate only against

[1] B. 997ᵇ 12—998ᵃ 6, M. 1076ᵃ 34.
[2] A. 987ᵇ 27, M. 1080ᵇ 2, 16, N. 1090ᵃ 20–23.
[3] B. 998ᵃ 7–19, M. 1076ᵃ 33.
[4] 724. 33–38.   [5] M. 1080ᵇ 2.
[6] ib. 16.   [7] B. 998ᵃ 11, M. 1076ᵇ 1.

believers in the Ideas. It is therefore to be regarded as the expression of an eclectic, half-Pythagorean, half-Platonic way of thinking.

The derivation of Ideal Numbers from their first principles.

A further phase in the development of Platonic theory was the derivation of the ideal numbers from a formal principle, the One, and a material principle which is variously named. The description of the material principle as '*the great and the small*' is expressly ascribed to Plato in A. 987^b 20, 25, 988^a 8–14, 26, *Phys.* 187^a 17, 203^a 15, 209^b 33. The last passage is specially interesting. 'Plato ought to tell us why the Forms and the numbers are not in place, since τὸ μεθεκτικόν is place, whether τὸ μεθεκτικόν is the great and the small or, as he writes in the *Timaeus*, is matter.' Simplicius observes that it was in the unwritten lectures on the Good that Plato called the receptive material by the name of the great and the small; and Simplicius is probably right. The 'more-and-less' of *Phil.* 24 A is an earlier form of the phrase.

The description of the material principle as a *dyad* is referred to Plato in A. 987^b 25, 33, 988^a 8–14. This principle is, further, frequently referred to as '*the unequal*' or '*inequality*', and the association of this phrase with 'the great and the small'[1] suggests that it also was used by Plato himself.

The material principle is, once more, frequently referred to as '*the indefinite dyad*'. There has been more controversy than the importance of the matter warrants over the question whether this phrase also was used by Plato. The phrase is often found unconnected with any of those mentioned above, but in M. 1083^b 23–36, N. 1088^a 15, 1090^b 32—1091^a 5 it is connected with 'the great and the small', and therefore presumably assigned to Plato. This is confirmed by Theophrastus,[2] Alexander,[3] Simplicius,[4] Syrianus, Asclepius, and Hermodorus (an immediate disciple of Plato).[5] In spite of this evidence Trendelenburg, Susemihl, and Zeller (in *Platonische Studien*) considered that 'the indefinite

---

[1] N. 1087^b 7, 9-11, 1091^b 31.   [2] Fr. xii. 33, Wimmer.

[3] 56. 16-21, 33-35, 85. 16-18. Alexander refers to Aristotle's notes of Plato's lectures on the good.

[4] *Phys.* 454. 22—455. 11 (quoting Alexander).

[5] Quoted in Simpl. *Phys.* 247. 30 –248. 18 (cf. 256. 31—257. 4).

dyad' was not a Platonic expression, and Heinze maintained that it was peculiar to Xenocrates. But Zeller later abandoned this view, and M. Robin [1] shows the weakness of the arguments on which it rests. There is little doubt that this expression also was used by Plato in his lectures. One passage,[2] however, deserves special notice. Aristotle says that 'there are some who make the principle which co-operates with the One an indefinite dyad, but object, reasonably enough, to the phrase "the unequal", owing to the impossible results that follow from it; but they have escaped only so many of the difficulties as follow necessarily from making the unequal, i. e. a relative term, an element'; i. e. whereas Plato had used the expressions 'the unequal' and 'the indefinite dyad' indifferently for the material principle, some of his followers, for the reason stated, confined themselves to the latter, which probably became a more important technical term for them than it was for Plato.

In several passages the material principle is described as *plurality*, and it is stated or implied that the thinkers who described it so were different from those who used the above-mentioned terms.[3] A comparison of N. 1091^{b} 30–35 with 1091^{a} 29–^{b} 1, Λ. 1072^{b} 30–34 suggests that Speusippus adopted this phraseology, and a passage in Plutarch,[4] if it is to be trusted, shows that Xenocrates also adopted it.

In N. 1087^{b} 16 Aristotle tells us that some Platonists described the material principle of the ideal numbers as '*the many and few*', on the ground that 'the great and small' was more appropriate as the principle of ideal *spatial magnitudes*.[5] We find here, again, evidence of an amendment, within the Platonic school, of Plato's own description of the material principle. A similar change is indicated by N. 1087^{b} 17–21, where we are told that some thinkers substituted the more general expression τὸ ὑπερέχον καὶ τὸ ὑπερεχόμενον for 'the great and the small'. Sextus Empiricus [6] treats this as one of the essential Pythagorean oppositions,[7] and M. Robin suggests [8] with some probability that it was Platonizing Pythagoreans of the school of Hippasus who described the material principle in this way.

---

[1] pp. 649-654.   [2] N. 1088^{b} 28.
[3] M. 1085^{b} 4-10, N. 1087^{b} 5, 6, 8, 30, 1091^{b} 31, 1092^{a} 35-^{b} 1.
[4] *De An. Procr.* ii. 1. 1012 d.   [5] Cf. N. 1088^{a} 18.^{b} 5-13, 1089^{b} 11-14.
[6] *Adv. Math.* x. 263 ff.   [7] Cf. Al. 56. 16.   [8] p. 659.

Finally, others are said to have described the material principle as τὸ ἕτερον or τὸ ἄλλο.[1] θάτερον occurs in Plato as an expression for the material principle,[2] but in the context Aristotle distinguishes those who used these as their official titles for the material principle from Plato. Alexander says that they were Pythagoreans,[3] and he may well be right; much of the terminology of the *Timaeus* is very likely Pythagorean rather than Platonic.

It is difficult to discover the precise way in which the Platonists carried through the bold attempt to generate the number-series. For Aristotle the function of the indefinite dyad is essentially duplicative (δυοποιός).[4] It is a sort of plastic material (ἐκμαγεῖον) which has the property of producing two copies of the pattern imposed on it. It 'took the definite dyad and made two dyads'.[6] And so Aristotle is able to say that the Platonic elements can only produce τὸν ἀφ' ἑνὸς διπλασιαζόμενον (ἀριθμόν).[7] 2, 4, 8, &c. are produced from the One by a series of multiplications by the indefinite dyad. Aristotle describes three modes of the production of number. 'In one way, if the One falls on an even number, an odd number is produced' (sc. by addition); 'in another way, if the dyad falls' (sc. on the One), '2 and its powers are produced' (sc. by multiplication); 'in another way, if the odd numbers fall' (sc. on even numbers), 'the other even numbers are produced' (sc. by multiplication). If this line of thought be followed out, the numbers up to 10 would have been produced as follows :

$$1 \times 2 = 2 \qquad 2 \times 2 = 4 \qquad 4 \times 2 = 8$$
$$2 + 1 = 3 \qquad 4 + 1 = 5 \qquad 8 + 1 = 9$$
$$3 \times 2 = 6 \qquad 5 \times 2 = 10$$
$$6 + 1 = 7$$

But it is practically certain that it was not thus that Plato conceived the numbers as being generated. This presentation takes account of the fact that the material principle was a dyad ; it takes no account of its being indefinite, nor of what was

---

[1] N. 1087[b]26.   [2] *Tim.* 35 A, B.

[3] 798. 23. Cf. Damascius, *De princ.* 306 ; ii. 172. 20 sq., Ruelle. Ἀρι-στοτέλης δὲ ἐν τοῖς Ἀρχυτείοις ἱστορεῖ καὶ Πυθαγόραν ἄλλο τὴν ὕλην καλεῖν.

[4] M. 1082[a] 14, 1083[b] 35.

[5] A. 988[a] 1.   [6] M. 1082[a] 13.   [7] N. 1091[a] 10.

[8] M. 1084[a] 3. The interpretation of Λ. 987[b] 34 is too doubtful for any conclusions to be drawn from it.

apparently for Plato its fundamental character, that ot being
'great and small'; 'dyad' seems to have been simply a convenient way of referring to this twofold character of the material
principle.[1] Again, this way of generating numbers is as regards
the odd numbers simply addition (which according to Aristotle's
own view is the only mode of generation of numbers),[2] and as
regards the even numbers it is simply multiplication, which is
just abbreviated addition; but Plato distinguished the ideal from
the mathematical numbers just in this, that while the latter
were addible the former were not.[3]

There are indications that the Platonists proceeded by quite
a different road. Aristotle explains aptly in *Phys.* 206^b 27 why
Plato called the material principle 'great and small'. 'Plato
made the indefinites two in number for this reason, that the
indefinite is thought to exceed and to proceed to infinity both in
the direction of increase and in that of diminution.' This is just
the picture of ἀπειρία that we get in the *Philebus*. It is vague
quantitativeness, that which ranges from the infinitely great to the
infinitely small, and which, to become any definite quantity, must
be determined by πέρας or as Aristotle says, by the One. It is
not, as Aristotle usually depicts it as being, two things, the great
and the small, but, as he occasionally calls it,[4] the great-and-
small, one thing with opposite potentialities. As Simplicius
expresses it,[5] quoting Alexander, who in turn was drawing upon
Plato's lectures on the good, 'each of the numbers, in so far as
it is a particular number and one and definite, shares in the
One; in so far as it is divided and is a plurality, in the indefinite
dyad'. Further light is thrown on the matter, and especially on
the description of the material principle as the unequal, by
a quotation of Simplicius[6] from Hermodorus. According to him,

---

[1] Al. 56. 8–13 gives a rather different explanation. He says that the
dyad was selected as the material principle because it is the first thing
after 1 in the number-series and contains the much and the little in their
lowest terms, since its factors are in the ratio of 2 : 1. But this amounts
to making the *number* 2 the material principle of all numbers (including
itself). The material principle is not the number 2 (the 'definite dyad'),
but the indefinite dyad; Aristotle is careful to preserve this distinction.

[2] M. 1081^b 14.   [3] M. 1082^b 28–36.

[4] B. 998^b 10, M. 1083^b 23, 31, N. 1087^b 8.

[5] *Phys.* 454. 22—455. 11.   [6] ib. 247. 30—248. 18.

Plato divided existing things into two classes, the καθ' αὐτά (e. g. man, dog), and the πρὸς ἕτερα, which are divided in turn into the πρὸς ἐναντία (e. g. good and evil) and the πρός τι (e. g. right and left, high and low). Among the πρὸς ἕτερα some are definite, others indefinite; 'and those that are spoken of as great relatively to small all have the more and the less, as being borne to infinity by being in a higher degree greater or less. Similarly 'broader' and 'narrower', and 'heavier' and 'lighter', and all such terms will be borne to infinity. But terms like 'equal' and 'at rest' and 'in tune' do not admit of the more and less, while their contraries do, for one unequal is more so than another, one moved more moved than another, one thing out of tune more so than another. All things,[1] again, in both kinds of pairs (sc. the pairs of πρὸς ἐναντία terms and the pairs of πρός τι terms), except the one element (sc. the One), admit of the more and the less, so that what is of this sort is called unresting, infinite, formless, and not-being, by reason of negation of being'. One further extract from Simplicius is important; that in which he says that the movement of the dyad ἐπὶ τὸ τῆς ἀπειρίας ἀόριστον proceeds κατ' ἐπίτασιν καὶ ἄνεσιν.[2]

In accordance with these indications and with Plato's thought as expressed in the *Philebus*, it seems most probable that Plato thought of the ideal numbers not as being reached by addition or by multiplication, but, vaguely enough, as successive resting-places determined by the principle of limit in the indefinite ebb and flow of the ἀπειρία, the great-and-small. But it must be remembered that according to Aristotle *Xenocrates* identified the ideal with the mathematical numbers. In his account of the matter a more mathematical generation of the numbers may have come in, and it is probable that Aristotle's account is based on Xenocrates rather than on Plato. If we are right in our view of Plato's meaning, the material principle for him was the great-and-small, a single thing capable of indefinite expansion and of indefinite restriction. But Aristotle habitually speaks of the great and *the* small. It seems probable, then, that Xenocrates presupposed two material principles, the great and the small, and may have thought of them as being equalized by the One and as thus constituting, each of them, one of the units in the number 2. It is probably also to this way of thinking that the identification

---

[1] The reading and translation here become doubtful.   [2] 455. 1.

of the One with the odd [1] or with the middle unit in odd numbers belongs.[2]

There is one statement which *prima facie* contradicts the account we have suggested. In M. 1081ª 22 Aristotle says 'the units in the first two are generated simultaneously, whether, as the first holder of the theory said, from unequals—for they were produced by the equalization of these—or otherwise'. Here Plato himself is credited with thinking of two unequal parts of the material principle, which are equalized by the formal principle and thus produce the two units in the number 2.[3] Aristotle, how-ever, expresses some doubt as to this method of production ; 'does each unit come from the great and small equalized', he asks, 'or one from the small, the other from the great?'[4] It is probable that he is here working on slight and obscure evidence as to Plato's meaning. It is significant that, though he here implies that there are two 'unequals' in the material principle, it is not called 'the unequals' but 'the unequal' or 'inequality'.[5] The reason why the material principle is so called is given in the above-quoted fragment of Hermodorus. 'Unequal' is a synonym for 'indefinite', because if one thing is merely known to be unequal to another we know nothing definite about its actual size. We can hardly doubt that Plato's meaning would be more truly expressed by saying that the number 2 is produced ἐκ τοῦ ἀνίσου ἰσασθέντος, from the unequal or indefinite when equated or defined by the One, than it is in Aristotle's phrase ἐξ ἀνίσων ἰσασθέντων.

To return to the presumably Xenocratean account, it is note-worthy that Aristotle says [6] that 'the Platonists produce many things out of the matter, but the form generates once only'. This, taken in connexion with Aristotle's comments on it, seems to mean that the formal principle, the One, is operative only in the production of a single number, which must, of course, be the first number, two ; [7] it would follow that the subsequent numbers are produced by the operation not of the One but of some other

---

[1] M. 1084ª 36.   [2] M. 1083ᵇ 29.

[3] Cf. N. 1091ª 23, where Plato is not mentioned by name.

[4] M. 1083ᵇ 23.

[5] B. 1001ᵇ 23, l. 1056ª 10, Λ. 1075ª 32, N. 1087ʰ 5, 7, 9–11, 1088ᵇ 29, 1089ᵇ 6, 10, 1091ᵇ 31, 1092ᵇ 1.

[6] A. 988ª 2.   [7] M. 1081ª 22. 1084ᵇ 37.

formal principle on the indefinite dyad. And in fact 4 is described as produced by the operation of the number 2 on the
indefinite dyad,[1] and 8 by the operation of the number 4 on the
indefinite dyad.[2] Similarly, we may suppose, 3 generated 6
and 5 generated 10. But how were 3, 5, 7, and 9 generated?
In one passage[3] Aristotle tells us that the Platonists say there is
no generation of odd number, but elsewhere he says that the One
is the odd,[4] or, more definitely, the middle unit in odd numbers.[5]
It may be that, asked whence came the odd unit in odd numbers,
Xenocrates answered that it is the One itself. If this be so, the
One discharges a double function. In the production of 2 it is
a principle of form or limit operating on the indefinite dyad; in
the production of 3 from 2 it is an actual element in the product,
and so too in the production of 5 from 4, 7 from 6, and 9 from 8.
Aristotle actually charges the Platonists with using the One in
this double way; 'they make the One a first principle in both
ways—on the one hand it acts as form and essence, on the other,
as a part and as matter '.[6] The cause of this mistake is that
' they were pursuing the question both from the point of view of
mathematics and from that of general definitions ';[7] i.e. they
made the mistake which Aristotle elsewhere charges Xenocrates[8]
with making, that of confusing the mathematical with the philosophical treatment of numbers. Alexander gives a different
account of the odd unit in odd numbers—that it is one of the
portions of the indefinite dyad, after the One has determined
it ;[9] but this does not agree with Aristotle's statements.

M. Robin[10] has a different view of the production of the odd
numbers. Suppose the 'indefinite' to be increasing. Then,
says M. Robin, the Platonists think of the One as checking the
process first when the indefinite has reached twice its original
size. The number 2 is thus produced. But the indefinite dyad
goes on increasing: the One again checks it when it has again
doubled itself, and so 4 is produced, and similarly 8. Again, the
indefinite may be supposed to increase from 2 and at the same

[1] M. 1081ᵇ 21, 1082ᵃ 12, 33.   [2] M. 1082ᵃ 30.
[3] N. 1091ᵃ 23, where see note.   [4] M. 1084ᵃ 36.
[5] M. 1083ᵇ 29.   [6] M. 1084ᵇ 18.   [7] ib. 24.
[8] Not by name, but we can be fairly sure that Xenocrates is meant.
Cf. pp. lxxiv–lxxvi.
[9] 57. 22-28.   [10] pp. 446-450.

time, and at the same rate, to decrease from 4; the One checks both processes at the point where they meet, and 3 is produced. 6 is produced from 3 as 4 was from 2. 5 is produced from 4 and 6 as 3 was from 2 and 4, and 10 from 5 as 4 was from 2. Finally, 7 is produced from 6 and 8, and 9 from 8 and 10, as 3 was from 2 and 4. This account has the great merit of assigning to the indefinite dyad nothing but indefinite increase and decrease, and to the One no task except that of limiting this, and thus keeps closely in touch with the *Philebus*, as well as with *Phys.* 206ᵇ 27. Its defect, to my mind, is that the process it describes is neither such as we can well ascribe to Plato nor such as we can well ascribe to Xenocrates, but a cross between the two. When the numbers are treated, as they were by Plato, not as aggregates, but as specifically different forms or universals, the essence of each number is not that it contains so many units (for it does not contain units at all) but that it is the successor of the previous number; in this respect Plato may fairly be supposed to have anticipated Frege. And in view of this it is most unlikely that Plato generated the numbers in any other than their natural order from 2 to 10. On the other hand, the suggested mode of generation is not likely to have been that of Xenocrates, for it takes no account of Aristotle's statement that the odd unit in odd numbers was explained as being the One itself. Xenocrates is more likely to have generated the odd numbers in the way already suggested, by adding 1 to even numbers.

The derivation of Ideal Spatial Magnitudes and their place in the theory.

In several passages we read of ' the things after the numbers ', ' the things after the Ideas ', 'the classes posterior to number'.[1] These are a further set of entities distinct from those we have so far dealt with—the ideal magnitudes, related to mathematical magnitudes as the ideal numbers are to the mathematical. The same differences of opinion present themselves here as with regard to numbers. Some (sc. Plato) distinguish ideal from mathematical magnitudes ; others (sc. Speusippus) believe only in mathematical magnitudes and speak mathematically; others (sc. Xenocrates) believe in mathematical magnitudes but speak

---

[1] A. 992ᵇ 13, M. 1080ᵇ 25, 1085ᵃ 7.

unmathematically.[1] As in the case of numbers, there were
differences of detail between the Platonists as to the principles
from which the ideal magnitudes were derived. (1) According to
some the material principle was the various species of the great
and small, viz. the long and short for lines, the broad and narrow
for surfaces, the deep and shallow for solids ; while they differed
about the formal principle answering to the One.[2] This view of
the material principle answers to Plato's treatment of the great
and small as the material principle of number, and is probably
Plato's view. (2) Others made the formal principle the point,
and the material principle something ' akin to plurality'.[3] As it
was probably Speusippus who specified plurality as the material
principle of numbers, it is probably he who is referred to here.
The point and ' something akin to plurality' would be for him
the principles of *mathematical* magnitudes, since he did not
believe in ideal magnitudes. The diversity of opinions about
the formal principle ascribed to holders of view (1) is probably
that which is indicated in B. 1001^b 24, where it is suggested that
the formal principle of magnitudes is either the One itself or
' some number' (so Alexander interprets M. 1085^a 13). The latter
view is indicated more definitely in N. 1090^b 20-24, where Aristotle
refers to the Platonists as deriving magnitudes ' from matter and
number—lengths from the number 2, planes from 3, solids from 4,
or from other numbers'.[4] If we turn to Z. 1028^b 25-27 we find
that after referring to the views of Plato and Speusippus (both
mentioned by name) Aristotle continues 'but some say that
Forms and numbers have the same nature, and that all other
things follow after them, lines and planes, right on to the
substance of the heavens and to sensible things'. The first
words of this passage point to the identification of ideal with
mathematical number, which we have good reason for ascribing
to Xenocrates, and the reference to lines and planes as following
after numbers seems to refer to the view at present under discussion, in which ideal numbers are made the formal principle
of ideal magnitudes. This view may therefore be probably
ascribed to Xenocrates; the ascription is confirmed by a passage
of Theophrastus,[5] in which Xenocrates is praised for having
carried through his explanation of the contents of the universe

---

[1] M. 1080^b 24-30. [2] A. 992^a 10, M. 1085^a 9, 1089^b 11, N. 1090^b 37.
[3] M. 1085^a 32. [4] Cf. Z. 1036^b 13. [5] Fr. xii. 11 fin., 12 Wimmer.

from first principles—'alike of sensibles, intelligibles, mathematicals, and even things divine'.

As regards Plato himself, he is expressly stated[1] to have 'opposed' the point, which he regarded as simply a 'geometrical dogma' or convention, and to have spoken of the indivisible line as the first principle of the line. It is impossible to say with certainty what led Plato to adopt the strange view that the line is constructed out of indivisible lines, but it was probably because[2] he could not believe either that it is constructed out of divisible lines, i. e. is infinitely divisible (he was apparently alarmed by the vicious infinite regress which this seemed to involve), or that it is constructed (as the Pythagoreans said it was) out of points. Aristotle has a truer conception of continuity and sees that the line is constructed out of *divisible* lines, i. e. is infinitely divisible.

M. Robin[3] treats the ideal magnitudes as occupying a place in the Platonic hierarchy between the ideal numbers and the Ideas. The hierarchy according to him is :

$$\left\{\begin{array}{l}\text{Ideal numbers.}\\\text{Ideal figures.}\\\text{Ideas.}\end{array}\right.$$

$$\left\{\begin{array}{l}\text{Mathematical numbers.}\\\text{Geometrical figures.}\\\text{Sensibles,}\end{array}\right.$$

numbers being laws, types, or patterns of organization according to which are formed both Ideas and sensibles, and figures whether ideal or geometrical serving as intermediaries between the two classes they stand between. But a separation of the ideal numbers from the Ideas seems incompatible with Aristotle's statements, and the Platonic hierarchy was (I think) more probably as follows :

$$\text{Ideal} \quad \left\{\begin{array}{l}\text{Numbers}\\\text{Magnitudes}\end{array}\right\} = \text{the Ideas.}$$

$$\text{Mathematical}\left\{\begin{array}{l}\text{Numbers}\\\text{Magnitudes}\end{array}\right\} = \text{the Intermediates.}$$

$$\text{Sensibles.}$$

---

[1] A. 992^{a} 20.

[2] For the other reasons which may have helped to lead Plato to this belief cf. A. 992^{a} 20 n.

[3] p. 470.

Aristotle describes the ideal magnitudes as 'the things after the Ideas', 'the things after the numbers', and as distinct from the Ideas as well as from mathematical magnitudes.[1] But it is clear from his whole account that they are related to mathematical magnitudes exactly as the ideal numbers are to mathematical numbers. They are in fact the essences or universal natures of the straight line, the triangle, the tetrahedron, &c. It is because they are not numbers that Aristotle infers that they are not Ideas.[2] But it would be more accurate to say that they form a lower, more complex group of Ideas than the ideal numbers—more complex because (according to one form of the theory, at all events) they include ideal numbers as an element in them ; the number 2 is the formal principle of the line, 3 of the plane, 4 of the solid. Each class of entities in the universe is a union of form and matter, but as we pass from ideal numbers to ideal magnitudes, to mathematicals, and to sensibles, the formal element becomes more and more encumbered with matter.

Identification of the Ideas with numbers.

We come now to what was probably the last phase in Plato's development of the ideal theory, a phase which is a much less legitimate development of the theory known to us from the dialogues. Aristotle implies quite definitely that Plato held all the Ideas to be numbers.[3] M. Robin has discussed the relation between the ideal numbers and the Ideas.[4] He states three possible alternatives : (1) that the two are co-ordinate, (2) that the numbers are subordinate to the Ideas, (3) that the Ideas are subordinate to the numbers. On the strength of a sentence in Theophrastus[5] he adopts the third view. What Aristotle himself says, if accepted literally, would imply that none of these views is true, but that Plato simply identified the Ideas with the ideal numbers.[6] But Theophrastus' account is supported by

---

[1] A. 992[b] 13-18.
[2] ib. This presupposes the Platonic identification of all Ideas with numbers, a matter which we shall deal with presently.
[3] A. 987[b] 18-25.   [4] pp. 454 ff.
[5] Fr. xii. 13 W. Πλάτων μὲν οὖν ἐν τῷ ἀνάγειν εἰς τὰς ἀρχὰς δόξειεν ἂν ἅπτεσθαι τῶν ἄλλων, εἰς τὰς ἰδέας ἀνάπτων, ταύτας δ' εἰς τοὺς ἀριθμούς, ἐκ δὲ τούτων εἰς τὰς ἀρχάς.
[6] A. 991[b] 9, 992[b] 16, Λ. 1073[a] 18, M. 1081[a] 7, 1083[a] 18.

Sextus Empiricus;[1] and even if we accept Aristotle's statement that Plato described the same entities as Ideas and as numbers, it is consistent with this that Plato should have thought he was giving a more ultimate account of their nature when he described them as numbers.   M. Robin discusses the theory of Bonitz,[2] and of Zeller in *Platonische Studien*,[3] that the numbers mediate between the Ideas, which are pure quality, and the μαθηματικά, which are pure quantity.   Zeller seems to have later given up this view, and M. Robin is right in maintaining against it that the numbers are pure quality, and that in them 'the reciprocal play of the principles (the One and the indefinite dyad) is manifested in the most immediate and the most evident way'.[4]   Indeed, even Aristotle's way of putting the matter, that for Plato 'the Ideas are numbers' (not 'the numbers are Ideas'), suggests that, for Plato, the numbers were not (as Zeller thought) mere symbols of the Ideas, but rather the last product of the abstractive process which had originally led him from sensibles to Ideas.[5] In describing the Ideas as numbers, as successive products of the One and the great-and-small, he may have seemed to himself to be stating in the clearest way the fact which is so often expressed in the later dialogues, that in the ideal world there is multiplicity as well as unity.   And the series of the numbers produced successively by the One may well have seemed to him to express most clearly the hierarchy of the Ideas—linked through fewer or more intermediates with the supreme Idea— which was in his thoughts as early as the time of the writing of the *Republic*.   If this be so, as One was the number of the good,[6] the simpler and more comprehensive Ideas would be represented

---

[1] *Math*. 10. 258 ἰδοὺ γὰρ καὶ αἱ ἰδέαι ἀσώματοι οὖσαι κατὰ τὸν Πλάτωνα προυφεστᾶσι τῶν σωμάτων, καὶ ἕκαστον τῶν γινομένων πρὸς αὐτὰς γίνεται· ἀλλ' οὐκ εἰσὶ τῶν ὄντων ἀρχαί, ἐπείπερ ἑκάστη ἰδέα κατ' ἰδίαν μεταλαμβανομένη ἓν εἶναι λέγεται, κατὰ σύλληψιν δὲ ἑτέρας ἢ ἄλλων δύο καὶ τρεῖς καὶ τέσσαρες, ὥστε εἶναί τι ἐπαναβεβηκὸς αὐτῶν τῆς ὑποστάσεως, τὸν ἀριθμόν, οὗ κατὰ μετοχὴν τὸ ἓν ἢ τὰ δύο ἢ τὰ τρία ἢ τὰ τούτων ἔτι πλείονα ἐπικατηγορεῖται αὐτῶν.

[2] *Met*. p. 541.

[3] pp. 263, 298.

[4] p. 458.

[5] Cf. N. 1091[b] 13 τῶν δὲ τὰς ἀκινήτους οὐσίας εἶναι λεγόντων οἱ μέν φασιν αὐτὸ τὸ ἓν τὸ ἀγαθὸν αὐτὸ εἶναι, οὐσίαν μέντοι τὸ ἓν αὐτοῦ ᾤοντο εἶναι μάλιστα.

[6] N. 1091[b] 13, *E.E.* 1218[a] 24, Aristox. *Harm. Elem.* ii, p. 30 Meib.

by lower numbers, the more complex and less comprehensive by higher. M. Robin may therefore be right in believing in a parallelism between the relation of the numbers to the Ideas and that of the mathematicals to sensibles.[1]

There is a passage in the *Philebus* which perhaps shows the dawning of the tendency that ultimately led Plato to identify the Ideas with numbers. In explaining πέρας he says[2] that he means by it 'first the equal and equality, then the double and every ratio of number to number or of measure to measure'. And later[3] he defines 'the family of the limit' as 'the family of the equal and the double, and all that puts an end to the dissension of the contraries, and by introducing number makes them symmetrical and harmonious'. This is a remarkable identification of the principle of definiteness with number. Plato seems to be pursuing a fresh line of inquiry without considering its bearing on the ideal theory. But the trend of his later dialogues leads us to suppose that he recognized πέρας and ἀπειρία in the ideal as well as in the sensible world. The inference that the analysis was applied to both has a more definite basis in Aristotle's statement that the principles of the Idea-numbers were the principles of all things.[4] Later he says[5] that while the material principle of both Idea-numbers and sensible things is the great and small, the formal principle of Idea-numbers is the One, and the formal principle of the sensible things is the Ideas (i. e. the Idea-numbers). Yet the former statement is justified ; the principles of both are the One and the great and small, except that in sensible things the great and small is used twice over, once with the One to produce the Ideas, once with the Ideas to produce the sensible things.

Probably, then, 'limit' was used by Plato to mean the formal element both in Ideas and in sensible things. The Ideas are the limiting principle in sensible things ; now in the *Philebus* Plato has got so far as to say that limit must be numerical, and that it is this that qualifies it to be a formal principle. From this it is no great step to saying that the Ideas are numbers. He already in the *Philebus*[6] calls them henads and monads.

Aristotle ascribes to Plato something even more surprising than the identification of all Ideas with numbers. In the *Meta*

---

[1] p. 466. [2] 25 A. [3] 25 E.
[4] A. 987ᵇ 19. [5] 988ᵃ 10. Cf. ᵇ 4. [6] 15 A 6, B 1.

physics[1] he says that some thinkers limited the series of ideal numbers to 10, while others thought it infinite; and in the *Physics*[2] he says that Plato limited it to 10. This view, surprising as it is, has a parallel in Greek philosophy. The Pythagoreans thought that things were numbers; they were prepared to tell you (though not always unanimously) what number marriage or opportunity or justice was. And they too limited the series of numbers to 10; so much were they influenced by the current notation.[3] Plato may similarly have thought that the numbers higher than 10 could be treated as mere combinations of the numbers up to 10—though this involves treating the higher natural numbers, contrary to his own principles, as συμβλητοί; and he may have thought that there were ten simple Ideas of which all others were compounds. But the ascription to him of this limitation of the Ideas to 10 rests on a single passage of Aristotle, and it is possible that Aristotle is taking seriously some mere *obiter dictum* of his master.

If we ask what numbers Plato assigned to definite Ideas, it is not easy to give an answer. The materials are very scanty. In two different contexts Aristotle takes 3 as the Idea of man,[4] but in one passage 2 appears in this capacity,[5] and Aristotle may be merely making suppositions for argument's sake. In another passage[6] he enumerates certain entities which were generated 'within the decad', i.e. either from numbers lower than 11 or direct from the first principles. The passage is a difficult one, but the most probable supposition, in view of a statement by Theophrastus,[7] is that the things mentioned were connected directly with the first principles, so that the passage gives us no instance of an entity which was identified with a number. The most important passage for the identification of the numbers with things is *De An.* 404[b] 18 ff., where we learn that in Plato's 'lectures on philosophy' αὐτὸ τὸ ζῷον was derived from the Idea of One and the first length and breadth and depth (i.e. was identified with the number 10, which = 1 + 2 + 3 + 4).[8] Again, νοῦς was 1, ἐπιστήμη 2, δόξα 3, αἴσθησις 4. The two identifications are not equally fantastic. Two is in fact

---

[1] Λ. 1073[a] 19, M. 1084[a] 12.   [2] 206[b] 32.   [3] Cf. Philolaus, fr. 11, Diels.
[4] M. 1081[a] 11, 1084[a] 14.   [5] 1084[a] 25.   [6] ib. 32.
[7] Fr. xii. 12.   [8] Cf. Z. 1036[b] 13, M. 1084[b] 1, N. 1090[b] 22.

the smallest number of points that can determine a line, three the smallest number that can determine a plane, four the smallest that can determine a solid. And though lines, planes, and solids are not numbers, the numerical determination of them has in co-ordinate geometry proved a powerful engine for the discovery of truth. It is not so with the identification of mental faculties with numbers. There we are in the realm of pure fancy; we are back at the level of the Pythagorean identification of justice with 4 and of marriage with 5. If, as seems to be the case, Plato's thought ultimately moved in this direction, it is not surprising that Aristotle should treat him as in the main a follower of the Pythagoreans,[1] and complain that philosophy had been turned into mathematics.[2]

Speusippus and Xenocrates.

We may now attempt to trace the allusions in the *Metaphysics* to Plato's main successors. Speusippus is mentioned by name only twice, and Xenocrates not at all, but a good deal can be learnt about them by fairly certain inference.

The passages in which Speusippus is mentioned are: (1) Z. 1028^b 21, where we read that 'Speusippus, beginning with the One, sets up even more substances (sc. than the Ideas, mathematical objects, and sensibles recognized by Plato), and originative sources for each substance, one for numbers, another for magnitudes, yet another for soul; and in this way he spins out the series of substances '.[3] (2) Λ. 1072^b 30, 'Those who suppose, as the Pythagoreans and Speusippus do, that the most beautiful and best is not at the beginning, because, though the originative sources even of plants and of animals are causes, beauty and perfection are in what proceeds from these sources, are mistaken '.

Two features of Speusippus' philosophy appear from these references: (1) that he recognized more distinct classes of entities than the three recognized by Plato, and treated them in detachment from one another, recognizing separate principles for each; and that, like Plato, he started with the One as his first principle; (2) that he regarded 'values' as emerging late in the evolution of the universe, and thought of the first

---

[1] Λ. 987^a 30.   [2] 992^a 32.   [3] Cf. n. ad loc.

principles and their earliest products, numbers, as not possessing goodness.

With these indications as to the nature of his views, there is little difficulty in recognizing other passages as referring to him. The second aspect of his philosophy is briefly referred to in Λ. 1075ᵃ 36. It is referred to again in N. 1092ᵃ 11–17 : 'nor does any one judge correctly who likens the originative sources of the universe to that of animals and plants, because the more perfect things always come from things indefinite and imperfect, for which reason he says this is so in the case of the first things also, so that the One itself is not even a reality'. The section 1092ᵃ 21–ᵇ 8 seems to be mainly concerned with Speusippus, to judge from indications such as the reference to unity and plurality as first principles,[1] the reference to numbers as the first of existing things,[2] and the suggestion that number is produced from its first principle 'as from seed'.[3] Probably therefore also the intervening sentences 1092ᵃ 17–21, in which Aristotle charges an unnamed thinker or thinkers with generating place simultaneously with the mathematical solids, refers to Speusippus.

There are two passages which link up with the first of those mentioned above,[4] and introduce us to a fresh aspect of his theory. These are : (1) Λ. 1075ᵇ 37, 'Those who say that *mathematical number is the first entity* and assert the existence of a series of substances and different principles for each substance, make the substance of the universe a chain of disconnected incidents (for on this view one substance makes no difference to another by its existence or non-existence), and set up many principles'. (2) N. 1090ᵇ 13, 'Further, we might inquire, if we are not too easy-going, with regard to number as a whole and the objects of mathematics, into the fact that the earlier entities make no difference to the later ; for if number does not exist, spatial magnitudes will exist none the less for those who say that *the objects of mathematics alone exist*, and if spatial magnitudes do not exist, soul and sensible bodies will exist none the less. But, to judge from the observed facts, nature is not a chain of

[1] ᵃ 28.

[2] l. 22. Cf. Z. 1028ᵇ 21 above, Λ. 1075ᵇ 37, M. 1080ᵇ 14, 1083ᵃ 21, N. 1090ᵇ 13–20, 23 below.

[3] Cf. Λ. 1072ᵇ 35, N. 1092ᵃ 12 above.   [4] Z. 1028ᵇ 21.

disconnected incidents like a bad tragedy.' If further proof
were wanted that the frequently mentioned view that the Ideas
do not exist and that τὰ μαθηματικά are the primary entities was
that of Speusippus, it is supplied by a comparison of Λ. 1072ᵇ 30
above with N. 1091ᵃ 29 -ᵇ 1, ᵇ 22-25. Aristotle here says, 'There
is a difficulty . . . in the relation of the elements and the first
principles to the good˙ and the beautiful; namely, whether any
of the principles is the sort of thing that we mean by "the good
itself" and "the best", or this is not so but these are later in
their origin. The cosmologists seem to agree with some of the
thinkers of the present day, who say that this is not so, but that
it is only when the nature of things has developed that the
good and the beautiful appear in it. This they do by way of
guarding against a real difficulty which arises for those who say,
as some do, that the One is a principle . . . For a great difficulty
arises, in avoiding which some have denied ⟨that the good is
among the first principles⟩, viz. those who agree that the One is
a first principle and an element, *but only of mathematical number.*'
    It is certain, then, that Speusippus is referred to in the
passages where Aristotle mentions the theory which denies
the existence of Ideas owing to the difficulties it involves,[1] but
asserts the separate existence of τὰ μαθηματικά and speaks
mathematically about them.[2]
    The passage already referred to, N. 1091ᵃ 29-ᵇ 25, on the
difficulties arising from ascribing goodness to the One, is
succeeded in ᵇ 32 by the statement 'wherefore one thinker
avoided ascribing goodness to the One, on the ground that,
since genesis is from contraries, it would necessarily follow
that evil was the nature of plurality'. From this it may with
much probability be inferred that Speusippus was the thinker
who is referred to as describing the One and plurality as the
first principles of number,[3] and probably also the thinker who
treated the point (which was 'akin to the One') and 'something
akin to plurality' as the first principles of spatial magnitudes.[4]
    Two passages not in the *Metaphysics* may be mentioned as

---

[1] M. 1086ᵃ 2.
[2] Λ. 1069ᵃ 36, M. 1076ᵃ 21, 1080ᵇ 14, 1083ᵃ 20-24, 1086ᵃ 2, 29, N. 1090ᵃ 7-13, 25, 35.
[3] Λ. 1075ᵃ 32, M. 1085ᵇ 5, N. 1087ᵇ 6, 8, 27, 30, 1092ᵃ 35.
[4] M. 1085ᵃ 32.

throwing further light on the aspects of Speusippus' philosophy mentioned above :

(1) *E. N.* 1096ᵇ 5, 'The Pythagoreans seem to speak more plausibly about the good when they place the One in the column of goods ; whom Speusippus also is thought to have followed'. Aristotle regarded Speusippus' view as the most akin to Pythagoreanism of the Platonic views in two respects : (*a*) in that he does not place beauty and goodness in the beginnings of thing but regards them as having emerged in the course of development,[1] and (*b*) in holding no doctrine of Ideas but regarding τὰ μαθηματικά as the primary entities.[2] The coupling of Speusippus with the Pythagoreans in the present passage is evidently connected with the first of these points. The significance of the allusion is not clear, but seems to be that, while Plato identified the One with the good, Speusippus regarded the One simply as one among the goods and, since it was a first principle, as not possessing the good in as high a degree as later products of evolution (such as the soul).

(2) Theophr. fr. xii. 11 fin., 12, where Theophrastus reprehends Speusippus, and indeed all the Platonists except Xenocrates, for not having pushed far enough their deduction of things from first principles ; 'they generated numbers, planes, and solids, and showed that from the indefinite dyad spring certain things such as place, the void, the infinite, and that from the numbers and the One spring certain entities such as the soul, ... but they do not explain the generation of the heavens· or of other things'. This is borne out by the almost complete absence of physical treatises in Diogenes Laertius' list of Speusippus' works.[3]

Xenocrates was the most prominent member of the Platonic school after Plato and Speusippus, and it would be surprising if he were not alluded to in the *Metaphysics*. There is strong reason to suppose that he is the thinker who is frequently referred to as identifying the Ideas with the objects of mathe-

---

[1] Λ. 1072ᵇ 31.

[2] M. 1080ᵇ 16. The description of the material principle as plurality is also a Pythagorean touch ; cf. A. 986ᵃ 24. In his preoccupation with the significance of the number 10 (*Theol. Arithm.* pp. 61-3 Ast) Speusippus shows, once more, a recurrence to Pythagoreanism. He is said to have written a work on the Pythagorean numbers (ib. p. 61).   [3] iv. 4 f.

matics, in contrast with Plato, who distinguished them, and
with Speusippus, who believed only in the latter.[1] For it is
impossible not to see the similarity between the reference in
Z. 1028^b 24 to some thinkers who 'say that the Forms and the
numbers have the same nature, and all other things follow after
them, lines and planes, right on to the nature of the heavens
and to sensibles' and the passage of Theophrastus in which
Xenocrates in contrast with the other Platonists is praised for
deducing everything from the same first principles and 'giving
everything its place in the universe, alike sensibles, intelligibles,
mathematicals, and, further, things divine'.[2] We may fairly
confidently suppose, then, that it is he who is so often mentioned
as identifying the Ideas with mathematical objects,[3] and as doing
so by setting up 'private hypotheses of his own' and 'destroying, in effect, mathematical number'.[4] In two respects, in
particular, he is said to 'speak unmathematically of mathematical
things'—in his assertions that all magnitudes cannot be divided
into magnitudes, and that not any two units taken at random
make a two.[5] In connexion with the *first* point it must be
remembered that Xenocrates was the main supporter of the
doctrine of 'indivisible lines', against which the treatise *De
Lineis Insecabilibus* is directed.   The *second* point enables us to
identify Xenocrates as being among those whom Aristotle
charges with believing in 'incomparable units'.[6]

[1] Aristotle regards Xenocrates' view as the most mistaken of the three,
and combining all the possible disadvantages, M. 1083^b 2.

[2] These passages should be compared with Sext.Emp. *Adv. Math.* vii.147,
where Xenocrates is said to have recognized three kinds of substance, the
sensible = that which is ' within the heaven ', the intelligible = that which
is without the heaven, the composite or object of opinion = the heaven
itself (which is composite because it is perceptible by sight and also
intelligible by means of astronomy). Zeller (ii. 1^4. 1012, n. 7) identifies
τὰ μαθηματικά of the Theophrastus passage with the οὐρανός of the passage
in Sextus Empiricus.   But taking these passages along with Z. 1028^b 25
we seem to get the following classification : (1) intelligibles, including (*a*)
idea-numbers, and (*b*) spatial magnitudes (these two are rather loosely
described by Theophrastus as intelligibles and mathematicals respectively),
(2) things semi-intelligible, semi-sensible = the heaven = things divine,
(3) sensibles.

[3] Λ. 1069^a 35, M. 1076^a 20, 1080^b 22.

[4] M. 1083^b 1–8, 1086^a 5–11.   [5] M. 1080^b 28.   [6] M. 6.

In a passage [1] which contains clear indications that the same thinker is being referred to (κινεῖν τὰ μαθηματικὰ καὶ ποιεῖν ἰδίας τινὰς δόξας l. 28, ὁποιασοῦν ὑποθέσεις λαμβάνοντας 30, προσγλιχόμενοι ταῖς ἰδέαις τὰ μαθηματικά 31), we are informed that the thinkers in question 'make magnitudes out of matter and number, lengths from the number 2, planes, presumably, from 3, and solids from 4, or perhaps from other numbers'. Probably, then, Xenocrates was among those who held the particular view about the principles of ideal magnitudes which is referred to again in M. 1084ᵃ 37–ᵇ2.[2]

Finally, there is reason to suppose that it was Xenocrates who abandoned the description of the material principle as 'the unequal' while retaining the description of it as 'the indefinite dyad'.[3]

III

ARISTOTLE'S METAPHYSICAL DOCTRINE

The Method of Metaphysics.

THREE main features of Aristotle's method may be indicated. (1) He begins, as in several of his other works, with a history of previous thought, in which he shows how the four causes were successively recognized. It need not be supposed, however, that it was consciously by reflection on the work of his predecessors that he arrived at the doctrine of the four causes. The doctrine is presented as one already established in the *Physics*; [4] the study of earlier thought is intended merely to confirm the completeness of the doctrine or else to suggest other causes besides the four, and in point of fact it does the former. We may say in general of Aristotle that he believes himself to be looking at the facts direct, but that his thought is coloured far more than he knew by that of his predecessors, and above all of Plato. (2) His method is aporematic. It is essential, he says,[5] to start with a clear view of the difficulties of the subject, and with an impartial considera- tion of the pros and cons on each main question. Accordingly

---

[1] N. 1090ᵇ 20–32.

[2] *De An.* 404ᵇ 16–25 suggests that Plato himself also held this view.

[3] N. 1088ᵇ 28–35. For details as to Xenocrates' views about the formal and the material principle cf. Zeller ii. 1⁴. 1014, n. 3.

[4] A. 983ᵃ 33.   [5] B. 995ᵃ 27–ᵇ4.

a whole book (B) is devoted to such a presentation, without any attempt to reach a dogmatic result. Not only here, however, but in many other parts of the *Metaphysics* (notably in Z), the method is thoroughly aporematic; not infrequently, after discussing a question from one point of view without definite result, Aristotle proceeds to discuss it from another with the remark, 'Let us try a fresh start'. The *Metaphysics* as a whole expresses not a dogmatic system but the adventures of a mind in its search for truth. (3) The method adopted is, for the most part, not that of formal syllogistic argument from known premises to a conclusion which they establish. The truths which it is most important for metaphysics to establish are fundamental truths which cannot be inferred from anything more fundamental. Any direct proof of them would inevitably be a *petitio principii*. The proper procedure, then, is to attempt no proof but to commend them by showing the paradoxical consequences of the denial of them. This procedure is consciously adopted by Aristotle with regard to the 'laws of thought',[1] and is actually followed in many of his other discussions. Generally we may say that his method in the *Metaphysics* is not that of advance from premises to conclusion, but a working back from common-sense views and distinctions to some more precise truth of which they are an inaccurate expression, and the confirmation of such truth by pointing out the consequences of its denial.

The Subject of Metaphysics.

The subject of metaphysics is stated differently by Aristotle in different places. In Book A σοφία is said to be the study of 'the first principles and causes'.[2] This formulation reappears in Γ,[3] and it is added that these causes must be causes of something in respect of its own nature, and that this can be nothing less than τὸ ὄν itself. Metaphysics, then, studies the causes which determine the nature not of this or that department of reality, but of reality as a whole. These are the four causes the progressive recognition of which, by earlier thinkers, forms the subject of Book A— matter, form, efficient cause, and final cause. But it is to be noted that one of these—matter—is not actually, in Aristotle's

---

[1] Γ. 1006ᵃ 5–28. For some further remarks on Aristotle's conception of the method of metaphysics cf. notes on Γ. 1003ᵃ 21, E. 1025ᵇ 7–18.
[2] 982ᵇ 9.   [3] 1003ᵃ 26.

view, present throughout reality; the prime mover and the subordinate movers of the celestial spheres are pure forms.

To the causes of the real Γ adds another subject of metaphysical study—the essential attributes of the real,[1] by which he means such relations as those of sameness, contrariety, otherness, genus and species, whole and part, and such attributes as perfection and unity.[2] Some of these conceptions are discussed incidentally in various parts of the work, but Book I is more particularly devoted to them.

The subject-matter is similarly formulated in E.[3] But a different formulation of it is also found there.[4] The branches of knowledge are first divided into the practical, the productive, and the theoretical or disinterested. The last division is then subdivided into (1) physics, which deals with objects existing separately, but not free from movement; (2) mathematics, which deals with objects free from movement, but not existing separately, but imbedded in matter; while (3), if there are objects which both are free from movement and have separate existence, they are the subject of a third science prior to the two others—prior because its subject-matter, being eternal, is prior to the temporal and changeable, and, having separate existence, is more fundamental than that which has none but is considered apart only by an act of abstraction. This science is 'theology'. So far, then, it is a problem whether there is such a thing as theology; this depends on the question whether there is an entity free from change and yet existing separately, i. e. a pure form. But the inquiry whether there is such a form is doubtless considered to be itself a branch of theology; if the answer were in the negative it would be the whole of it. The name theology is found only here and in the corresponding passage of K.[5] The more usual names for metaphysics are σοφία and πρώτη φιλοσοφία. But θεολογική is a suitable name for it when its subject is described not as being qua being but as one particular kind of being. The two views of the subject-matter may, Aristotle proceeds,[6] both be held; it may be doubted whether first philosophy is universal in its scope or deals with one particular kind of reality. But, he adds, the two views are reconcilable; if there is an unchangeable substance, the study of it will be first philosophy

---

[1] 1003ᵃ 21.   [2] 1004ᵇ 1-8, 1005ᵃ 11-18.
[3] 1025ᵇ 3, 1026ᵃ 31, 1028ᵃ 3.   [4] ch. 2.   [5] 1064ᵇ 3.   [6] 1026ᵃ 23.

and universal just because it is first. In studying the primary kind of being, metaphysics studies being as such. The true nature of being is exhibited not in that which cannot exist apart but only as an element in a concrete whole, nor again in that which is infected by potentiality and change—that which, as Plato says,[1] is between being and not-being, but only in that which is both substantial and unchangeable.

The restriction of metaphysics to the study of one department of being (and of others only as owing their nature to this) recurs in Book Λ. Its subject-matter is there first restricted to substance, as the 'first part' of the universe. Next substance is divided, not as in E into two kinds, the changeable and the unchangeable, but into three—the eternal sensible (the heavenly bodies), the perishable sensible, and the insensible. The two former are said to be the subject of physics,[2] and accordingly chs. 2–5, which deal with sensible substance,[3] must be regarded as preliminary to chs. 6–10, which deal with unmovable or insensible substance. Not only Λ. 2–5, however, but the greater part of Z–Θ deals with the principles involved in sensible substance, and would have to be regarded as merely preliminary to the business of metaphysics, were it not that form, one of the principles involved in sensible things, and the principle mainly discussed in these books, is also that which exists separate and unchangeable in God and the 'Intelligences' that move the spheres. It cannot be said that in practice the distinction between physics and metaphysics is well maintained by Aristotle, and it may be noted that the bulk of the *Physics* is what we should call metaphysics. It is not an inductive inquiry into natural law, but an *a priori* analysis of material things and the events that befall them.

Further determination of the subject of Metaphysics.

Book E, having shown that the study of separate unchangeable being is the study of being as such, proceeds to rule out certain senses of being as irrelevant, viz. (1) accidental or incidental being,[4] and (2) being as truth.[5] (1) Accidental being is not studied by metaphysics because it cannot be studied at all. A house, for example, has an indefinite number of accidental attributes; it may be found agreeable by some tenants, injure the health of some, and benefit others. Science cannot

---

[1] *Rep.* 477 A.   [2] 1069[a] 36.   [3] 1069[b] 3.   [4] chs. 2, 3.   [5] ch.4.

investigate this indefinite series of attributes; the science of
building, for instance, concentrates on the building of a house
which shall be a house, a 'shelter for living things and goods',[1]
and ignores its incidental attributes. Similarly, geometry studies
not any and every attribute of the triangle, but only those which
belong to it *qua* triangle. In particular, any science excludes
the discussion of logical puzzles which do not arise from the
specific nature of its subject-matter but from the general nature
of things. Architecture is not interested in the fact that any
house is 'different from practically everything else'; geometry
does not consider whether a triangle is the same thing as a
triangle with its angles equal to two right angles; the art of
music does not ask whether 'that which is musical' is the same
as 'that which is literary'.

Metaphysics, then, does not study those connexions of subject
and attribute in which the attribute does not flow from the nature
of the subject but is incidental or accidental to it. It does not
study these, because they are not objects of knowledge at all.
Two possibilities seem to be contemplated by Aristotle. (*a*) The
accidental, the exception to law, may have a law of its own. If
A is usually B, there may be a law that under certain conditions
A is always or usually not B.[2] If this law is discovered, however,
the apparent accident is found to be no accident, so that still
there is no knowledge of the accidental. But (*b*) in human action,
and perhaps in other cases as well, Aristotle recognizes a real
contingency which can never become an object of knowledge. If
a man behaves in a certain way he is bound to meet a violent
death, but there is nothing from which it necessarily follows that
he will behave in that way, and until he does so it is not determined whether he will die by violence.[3]

The notion of the 'accidental' in Aristotle is somewhat complex. The primary meaning of συμβεβηκός is that which is
suggested by such words as 'incidental', 'coincidence'. The
object of science, according to Aristotle, is to exhibit, as far
as possible, the attributes of things as flowing necessarily from
their essence as expressed in definition. But science is constantly frustrated in its effort. Callias, for instance, is pale;
but paleness cannot be deduced from the essence of man, the
infima species to which Callias belongs. Paleness is incidental

---

[1] H. 1043[a] 16.   [2] 1027[a] 25.   [3] ib. 32–[b] 14.

to Callias. It is not implied, however, that his paleness is not the necessary result of *some* cause; it flows from something in the matter of which Callias is made.[1]

In the present passage, and in Δ. 30, accident is described rather differently. The accidental is that which happens neither always nor for the most part—the exception to law. That it is exceptional follows from its being merely incidental. This description, again, does not imply any breach in the causal nexus. The exception may obey a narrower law of its own.

There is, however, a third element in Aristotle's notion of accident which seems to imply objective contingency, and not merely contingency relative to the present imperfection of our knowledge. In the history of the world there are actually fresh starts which are not the determinate result of anything that has preceded.[2] This is implied not only in the present passage, but in the other principal passages on the subject. In *De Int.* 9 Aristotle argues that the law of excluded middle is not true of judgements about the future. It is true, of course, that A will either be or not be B, but it is not true either that A will be B or that A will not be B. The reason is that there is an ἀρχή—a genuine fresh starting-point for future events—in human deliberation and action.[3] In *De Gen. et Corr.* ii. 11 the realm of causal necessity is confined to those processes which are cyclic—the revolution of the heavenly bodies, the rhythm of the seasons, the passage of rain into cloud and of cloud into rain, &c. Within this framework of necessity room seems to be left for a contingency not only in respect of human free will, but generally in respect of the details of terrestrial history.

(2) The other sense of being in which it is not studied by metaphysics is 'being as truth'. This is excluded because it belongs not to objects but to states of mind, and is therefore studied not by metaphysics but by logic. Aristotle admits, indeed, the notion of 'false things', and presumably therefore that of 'true things'. But either (*a*) a 'false thing' means a non-existent thing, and a 'true thing' an existent thing, in which case false and true are not being used in their proper sense, and we have to do not with 'being as truth' but with being as existence. Or (*b*) a false thing is one which produces the appearance of something that is not there, as does a scene-

---

[1] I. 1058ᵃ 29–ᵇ 12.   [2] 1027ᵇ 11.   [3] 19ᵃ 7.

painting or a dream.¹ These are presumably subjects not for metaphysics but for psychology.²

Two main senses of being remain—the being of which the categories are a classification, and potential and actual being— a distinction which cuts across the former since it is found within each category.³ Of these the former is studied in Z H, the latter in Θ.

The Categories.

The doctrine of the categories⁴ is a peculiarly puzzling one, partly from the lack of any very definite information as to Aristotle's precise object in formulating it, partly from our ignorance of the relative dates of the works in which various aspects of it are presented. There are, however, independent grounds⁵ on which we may arrive at a provisional chronological arrangement of his works, an arrangement which in its main outlines is accepted by most scholars. Of the works concerned, the *Categories* may be placed first, followed by the *Topics, Sophistici Elenchi, Analytics, Metaphysics* Δ, the physical works, the *Ethics*, and the rest of the *Metaphysics*. The authenticity of the *Categories* has been doubted, but on insufficient grounds, and if it is genuine we may reasonably suppose that this work, in which the doctrine is expounded at length, is earlier than those in which it is alluded to as familiar.⁶

In the *Categories* the doctrine is introduced as a classification of the meanings of τὰ κατὰ μηδεμίαν συμπλοκὴν λεγόμενα, i. e. of such expressions as 'man', 'ox', 'runs', 'wins', in opposition to 'man runs', 'man wins', which are κατὰ συμπλοκὴν λεγόμενα. In other words it is a classification of the meanings of words and phrases⁷

---

¹ Δ. 1024ᵇ 17–26.

² ' Being as truth ' is discussed in Θ. 10, as well as in E. 4.

³ τῶν εἰρημένων τούτων Δ. 1017ᵇ 2, τούτων Θ. 1051ᵇ 1.

⁴ For a discussion of various aspects of the doctrine which I have not dwelt on cf. Joseph, *Introduction to Logic*, ch. 3.

⁵ The chief ground is the system of references in one work to another, which presents a consistent chronological scheme, if we allow for some works having been on the stocks concurrently.

⁶ *An. Pr.* 49ᵃ 7, *De An.* 402ᵃ 25, 410ᵃ 15 *may* be definite references to the *Categories*.

⁷ Of words and phrases rather than of terms, for the latter are essentially the termini of propositions, while Aristotle is here thinking of objects of thought and the names for them, apart from the proposition.

in opposition to sentences or judgements. Aristotle's interest is logical, not grammatical, but he approaches the classification of objects of thought by a consideration of the words by which we symbolize them. Trendelenburg thought that the doctrine was based entirely on grammatical considerations; Bonitz had little difficulty, however, in showing that this is an exaggerated view, that Aristotle draws distinctions where grammar draws none, and ignores some which grammar does draw.

The *Categories* refers to the categories by the very general word γένη.[1] The term κατηγορίαι, or some variant upon it, is also used of them from the *Categories* onwards, and it is important to see what it means. The normal use of κατηγορεῖν in the sense of 'to predicate' suggests that κατηγορία means either 'predication' or 'predicate', and in other connexions it is found in both these senses.[2] But the classification in the *Categories* is not a classification of predicates. This is indicated by two facts. (1) Aristotle's instances quoted above show that τὰ κατὰ μηδεμίαν συμπλοκὴν λεγόμενα include the subjects of propositions no less than the predicates; and (2) the first category, that of substance, is divided into two parts, and substance in the most proper, primary, and complete sense is said to be that which is *neither asserted of a subject* nor present in a subject, e. g. an individual man or horse. And this view, that individual substances form the primary subdivision of the first category, is steadily maintained by Aristotle in other works. It will not do to treat this[3] as an excrescence on the doctrine. Bonitz was therefore led to suppose that κατηγορίαι does not in this connexion mean 'predicates'. He points out[4] that in certain passages in which the doctrine of the categories is not in question[5] κατηγορίαι means 'names' or 'designations' rather than 'predicates', and thinks

---

[1] 11ª 38, ᵇ 15.

[2] = predication *De Int.* 21ª 29, *An. Pr.* 41ª 4, 12, ᵇ 31, 44ª 34, 45ᵇ 34, 57ᵇ 19, *An. Post.* 84ª 1 ; = predicate *An. Post.* 96ᵇ 13 (positive predicate × στέρησις *An. Pr.* 52ª 15, *De Gen. et Corr.* 318ᵇ 16). In *Cat.* 3ª 35, 37, *An. Post.* 82ª 20, *Top.* 109ʰ 5, 141ª 4, Δ. 1007ᵇ 35 either translation will serve. The regular term for predicate is τὸ κατηγορούμενον (κατηγόρημα occurs only five times).

[3] As Apelt, for instance, does, *Beiträge*, 142–145.

[4] In his essay on the *Categories* (1853).

[5] *Soph. El.* 181ᵇ 27, *Phys.* 192ᵇ 17, *P. A.* 639ª 30, *Z.* 1028ª 28. The other passages he cites will not bear this interpretation.

that it was from this sense that its technical meaning developed. The categories would then be a classification of the meanings of names, i. e. a classification of nameable objects of thought, and among these would naturally be included individual substances as well as those entities which can stand as predicates. But it is undesirable to divorce the technical sense of the word from its natural meaning of 'predicates', and it is not necessary to do so. Though the primary members of the category of substance are not predicates but subjects, 'substance' itself is a predicate. 'What is this thing? A man. What is a man? An animal. What is an animal? A substance.' 'Substance' is the last predicate we come to if we pursue such a line of inquiry, and the names of the other categories are reached by parallel lines of inquiry. Thus the names of the categories might properly be called 'predicates', and indeed the predicates *par excellence*, since they are the highest terms in the various 'columns of predication'.[1] A passage in the *Categories*[2] shows how the transition from the ordinary to the technical sense of the word took place. 'If one of two contraries is a quality, the other also will be a quality. This is clear if we try the other predicates (κατη-γορίαι); e. g. if justice is contrary to injustice, and justice is a quality, injustice also is a quality: for none of the other predicates (κατηγορίαι) will apply to injustice; for neither quantity nor relation nor place nor any of the terms of this sort will apply, but only quality.' The categories are simply the predicates *par excellence*. And individual substances are in the category of substance not in the sense of being predicates but in the sense that 'substance' is the highest, widest term that can be predicated of them essentially;[3] i. e. in the same sense in which secondary substances are in the category of substance, and particular qualities or quantities are in the category of quality cr quantity. The expressions τὰ σχήματα (or τὰ γένη) τῶν κατη-γοριῶν (or τῆς κατηγορίας) emphasize the fact that the categories are the highest types or classes under which all predicates fall. So too κατηγορίαι τοῦ ὄντος, σχήματα κατηγορίας τοῦ ὄντος mean 'predicates of being, types of predicate of being', i. e. the

---

[1] I. 1054ᵇ 35, 1058ᵃ 13.

[2] 10ᵇ 17–23.

[3] That the categories are a classification of τὸ καθ' αὑτὸ ὄν, i. e. of what things essentially are, is emphasized in Δ. 1017ᵃ 22–30, where see note.

highest predicates under one or other of which falls everything that is.

There is another mode of reference to the categories which becomes common in the later works, and especially in the *Metaphysics*, viz. by the expressions πολλαχῶς λέγεται τὸ ὄν, ποσαχῶς τὸ ὂν σημαίνει, οἷς ὥρισται τὸ ὄν. The assumption in fact is made that to these various classes of entity there answer as many senses of 'be'. To be means one thing for a substance, another for a quality, a quantity, &c. This appears to be a later phase of the theory; indeed the difference between the senses of 'be' is announced as a conclusion which follows from the difference between the main types of 'what things are'. καθ' αὐτὰ δὲ εἶναι λέγεται ὅσαπερ σημαίνει τὰ σχήματα τῆς κατηγορίας· ὁσαχῶς γὰρ λέγεται τοσαυταχῶς τὸ εἶναι σημαίνει. ἐπεὶ οὖν τῶν κατηγορουμένων τὰ μὲν τί ἐστι σημαίνει, τὰ δὲ ποιόν, τὰ δὲ ποσόν, τὰ δὲ πρός τι, τὰ δὲ ποιεῖν ἢ πάσχειν, τὰ δὲ πού, τὰ δὲ ποτέ, ἑκάστῳ τούτων τὸ εἶναι ταὐτὸ σημαίνει, 'being has a different meaning corresponding to each of these kinds of predicate'.[1]

Bonitz emphasized the former aspect of the categories and regarded them as essentially a classification of realities; recent inquirers have emphasized the latter aspect. Apelt[2] regards the categories as primarily a classification of the meanings of the copulative 'is'; Maier regards them as a classification of all the meanings of 'is', the copulative being only one among these. Bonitz appears to give the truer account of the earlier and simpler form of the theory. And even in the later use of the theory there are features which seem incompatible with Apelt's view. If the being that is being classified were simply the copulative 'is', the doctrine could hardly have been used as the basis of the division of motion into its kinds,[3] or of the definition of soul.[4]

Aristotle has no 'deduction of the categories', no argument to show that the real must fall into just these divisions. He seems to have arrived at the ten categories by simple inspection of reality, aided by a study of verbal distinctions. Attempts have

---

[1] Δ. 1017ᵃ 22. Cf. Z. 1030ᵃ 21 ὥσπερ γὰρ καὶ τὸ ἔστιν ὑπάρχει πᾶσιν (to all the categories) ἀλλ' οὐχ ὁμοίως.

[2] pp. 112, 113.

[3] *Phys.* 201ᵃ 8, 261ᵃ 31-36.

[4] *De An.* 402ᵃ 22-25.

been made at a systematic arrangement of the categories, e. g. that of the Greek commentator David (Scholia in Arist. 48ᵇ 28–41 ; reproduced by Pacius) :

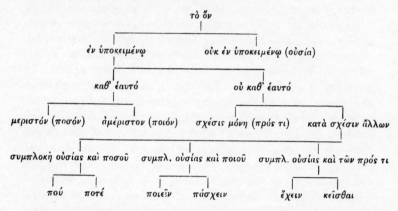

The main difficulties of the doctrine are concerned with the category of substance. It contains two distinct types of thing : (1) individual substances, (2) the species and genera to which they belong. It may seem surprising that these should be grouped together. Why, it might be asked, should one of the universals under which Socrates may be classed, viz. 'man', be picked out as having more affinity with Socrates than other universals under which he may be considered, such as 'white object'?[1] Aristotle's answer would be that Socrates' nature is summed up much more completely in calling him a man than in calling him a white object ; he might be conceived of as changing his colour and yet retaining much that makes him what he is, but take away his manhood and nothing is left that could be called the same individual. 'Man' in fact is the name not of

---

[1] The difficulty is recognized in the *Categories*. 'Every substance seems to mean a "this". . . . But the secondary substances, while they appear to indicate a "this", do not really do so, but rather a quality. Yet they do not indicate simply a quality—they determine quality with reference to a substance ; they indicate a qualified substance' (3ᵇ 10–21). Again, 'the species is more substance than the genus' (2ᵇ 7). The secondary substances are intermediate between primary substances and the other categories ; 'for all the others are predicated of them' as *they* are of the primary substances (3ᵃ 1–4). This line of thought reaches its height in H. 1042ᵃ 21, where genus is said not to be substance at all.

a single quality but of a whole group of interconnected qualities which together make up the most important part, at any rate, of the nature of that which has them.[1] There is therefore good reason for grouping primary and secondary substances together. But if the distinction of individual and species is recognized in the first category, why not in others? Something analogous to such a recognition is found in the *Topics*.[2] ' In indicating the " what it is " we sometimes indicate a substance, sometimes a quality, sometimes one of the other categories. For when, a man being set forth for consideration, we say that what is set forth is a man or an animal, we say what it is and indicate a substance ; when, a white colour being set before us, we say it is white or a colour, we say what it is and indicate a quality. . . . And similarly in the other cases ; for whether any such term is asserted of itself or its genus is asserted of it, we indicate what it is. But when it is asserted of something else, it indicates not what that is, but a quantity or a quality or one of the other categories.' I. e. while from one point of view ' what is it ' may be opposed to ' what qualities has it, of what size is it ', &c., and used as a characteristic name for the category of substance,[3] yet it finds a place in the other categories also, since if *it* is a colour, the proper answer to the question will name not a substance but a quality, colour. Thus the distinction of universal from particular, which was already recognized in the first category, is now found to break out in the other categories also.[4]

Maier seems to go too far in describing this[5] as a thorough and conscious transformation of the doctrine of the categories, the recognition of the distinction between the categories as recurring within the first category. To say this is to lay too much stress on the verbal fact that τί ἐστι, which appears at the beginning of the passage as the name of the first category, is

---

[1] Cf. *Cat.* 2ᵇ 29-37.

[2] 103ᵇ 27-39. The same thought recurs in Z. 1030ᵃ 17-27. Cf. B. 996ᵇ 18-22, Z. 1028ᵇ 1.

[3] It is so used in l. 22.

[4] This is implied in the *Categories* itself, where τὰ ὄντα are divided into (1) τὰ καθ' ὑποκειμένου but not ἐν ὑποκειμένῳ (classes of substances), (2) τὰ ἐν ὑποκειμένῳ but not καθ' ὑποκειμένου (individual qualities, &c.), (3) τὰ καθ' ὑποκειμένου and ἐν ὑποκειμένῳ (types of quality, &c.), (4) τὰ μήτ' ἐν ὑποκειμένῳ μήτε καθ' ὑποκειμένου (individual substances) (1ᵃ 20-ᵇ 9).

[5] *Syllogistik* ii. 2. 321.

later said to indicate now substance, now quality, &c. The truth rather is that Aristotle here recognizes within the other categories something akin to the division of primary and secondary within the first.

From this time onwards both τί ἐστι and τόδε τι or τόδε appear frequently as names for the first category.[1] The latter suggests individual substances; the former, species and genera. Little is gained by showing statistically, as Apelt does,[2] that the former is the more frequent designation. When either occurs alone, it must be understood as a shorthand reference to what was well understood to include both; when greater exactness is aimed at, both are used.[3] In Book Z, which is probably one of the latest, as in the *Categories*, which may be the earliest of Aristotle's extant works, the first category includes both individuals and species.

Though Maier goes too far in describing the categories as primarily a classification of the senses of 'being' rather than of the things that are, he is right in regarding the former as a very important aspect of the theory. The theory enables Aristotle to drag to light various confusions into which his predecessors had fallen through lack of reflection on the meaning of the word 'is'. Maier has distinguished these with great care as being three in number.[4] There is (1) the confusion between the 'is' which implies identity and the 'is' of accidental predication. Instances of the mistake are given in *Soph. El.* 166ᵇ 28–36:

> Coriscus is a man.
>
> Coriscus is different from man.
>
> Therefore Coriscus is different from himself.

Or again,

> Coriscus is other than Socrates.
>
> Socrates is a man.
>
> Therefore Coriscus is other than a man.

If you interpret a merely predicative 'is' as if it expressed

---

[1] τί (ἐστι) in *Soph. El., An. Pr.* and *Post., G. C., E. N., Met.*, τόδε (τι) in *Phys., G. C., De An., Met., Rhet.* Apelt gives a very useful table on pp. 140–141.

[2] p. 139. [3] Z. 1028ᵃ 11, 1030ᵃ 18, 1032ᵃ 14.

[4] pp. 280–287. The fourth confusion Maier points out, that between changeable and eternal being, is solved not by the doctrine of the categories, but by that of potentiality and actuality.

identity,[1] you will land yourself in self-contradiction. To avoid this unpleasant result, Aristotle tells us, 'some thinkers, like Lycophron, took away the 'is' (i. e. insisted on dropping the ἐστί, as Greek grammar allowed them to do, in predicative judgements), 'while others altered the form of speech from ὁ ἄνθρωπος λευκός ἐστιν to ὁ ἄνθρωπος λελεύκωται, *as though " one " or "being" had but one meaning'.*[2] In other words, the cure for the difficulty is neither of their childish expedients but the doctrine of the categories. Antisthenes is charged with having fallen into the same confusion. He 'claimed that nothing should be described save by its own definition, one thing alone being said of one';[3] in other words he did not recognize the predicative as distinct from the identifying judgement.

(2) There is the confusion of existential and copulative being, of 'being simply' and 'being something in particular'. Again the *Sophistici Elenchi*[4] gives instances:

Not-being is thought about.

Therefore not-being is.

Or,

This thing that is, is not man.

Therefore this that is, is not.

(3) There is the confusion of inherent being and subsistent being (to use Maier's terminology), with which Parmenides is charged. 'His reasoning is bad because, if we take merely the white things in the world, and suppose 'white' to have but one meaning, none the less the white things are many and not one; for what is white will not be one either by continuity or in definition. For to be white colour and to be coloured white will be different things—and that without our having to suppose anything *separate* from that which is white; the point is not the separateness but the difference between being white and being that to which white belongs.'[5] Because being is predicable of everything that is, Parmenides concluded that the nature of all that is is just to be being.[6]

---

[1] i. e. if because 'Coriscus is a man' you think yourself justified in substituting 'Coriscus' for 'man' in 'Coriscus is different from man', or because 'Socrates is a man' you think yourself justified in substituting 'man' for 'Socrates' in 'Coriscus is other than Socrates'.

[2] *Phys.* 185^b 25-32.   [3] Δ. 1024^b 32.

[4] 166^b 37—167^a 6. Cf. *Phys.* 187^a 3-6.

[5] *Phys.* 186^a 25-31.   [6] 186^a 32-^{b} 14.

To some extent Plato cleared up these difficulties by his doctrine of the 'intercommunion of Forms'.[1] This was a recognition of the fact that to predicate is not to identify. But Aristotle is not satisfied with Plato's solution. Whereas Aristotle points out the unsoundness of Parmenides' arguments, 'there were some', he says, with evident reference to the *Sophistes*, 'who gave in to both his arguments—to the argument that if being has but one meaning, all things are one, by saying that not-being exists; to the argument from dichotomy, by setting up indivisible spatial magnitudes'.[2] But Plato was reasoning archaically. He thought that to explain the multiplicity in the world he must admit a not-being apart from being. He should instead have taken account of the distinctions expressed in the doctrine of the categories, and asked what sort of unity the world would be if there were no not-being—a unity of substance, of quality, or of what else. And secondly he should have asked what sort of not-being he was invoking. Like being, not-being has a variety of meanings answering to the categories.[3]

Maier argues with much plausibility that in these old difficulties and in Plato's consideration of them we have the original motive of the doctrine of the categories.[4] But something much less elaborate than the categories would have served this purpose; a distinction between substances and attributes, or between substances, qualities, and relations would, it seems, have been enough. The list of ten categories looks much more like an attempt to form an inventory of the elements in the real, and the solution of difficulties about the meaning of 'being' appears to be a by-product, although a very important one.[5]

---

[1] *Soph.* 251, 253 C—259 D.   [2] *Phys.* 187ᵃ 1-3.

[3] N. 1088ᵇ 35—1089ᵃ 19.

[4] The attempt of Rose and of Gercke (*A. G. P.* iv. 424-441) to show that the categories were actually an Academic doctrine is justly rejected by both Apelt and Maier. The isolated references to 'quality', 'quantity', &c., which we find in Plato, form in no sense a doctrine of categories, though they prepared the way for it. Nor have the categories any close connexion with the μέγιστα τῶν γενῶν of the *Sophistes*; the names of the latter—being and not-being, rest and motion, same and other—are enough to show this.

[5] It would be a mistake to infer from the use of forms like πολλαχῶς λέγεται τὸ ὄν that Aristotle's interest is in the meanings of 'being' rather than in the varieties of the existent. Cf. *De An.* 410ᵃ 13 ἔτι δὲ πολλαχῶς λεγομένου

Substance the Main Subject of Metaphysics.

Aristotle does not offer in the *Metaphysics* any treatment of the categories as a whole. The categories other than substance are, as it were, mere 'offshoots and concomitants of being'.[1] Substance is prior to them in three ways:[2] (1) because it can exist apart while they cannot. It would seem natural to take this as an example of the situation described in the *Categories*[3] as that of τὸ μὴ ἀντιστρέφον κατὰ τὴν τοῦ εἶναι ἀκολούθησιν, where A can exist without B but not B without A. But substance is not in fact so related to the other categories. Quality, no doubt, cannot exist without substance. A quality is either the quality of a substance or presupposes substance at a smaller or larger number of removes. But no more can substance exist without quality. A qualityless substance is as impossible as a quality which does not presuppose a substance. The differentia of any substance is a quality.[4] It seems, therefore, that Aristotle must mean not that substance can exist without the other categories, but that it can exist apart while they cannot. The substance is the whole thing, including the qualities, relations, &c., which form its essence, and this can exist apart. It implies qualities but these are not something outside it which it needs in addition to itself. A quality on the other hand needs supplementation by a substance if it is to exist. Obviously, if this is his meaning, Aristotle must be thinking of substance as the individual thing. δεύτεραι οὐσίαι, being universals, cannot according to his own doctrine exist apart, but must be supplemented by the qualities of their individual members.

(2) Substance is prior in definition. In defining a member of any other category you must include the definition of the underlying substance. It is implied that in defining a substance you need not include the definition of anything in any other category; but this is not true, since every differentia of a substance is a quality.

(3) Substance is prior for knowledge. We know a thing better

τοῦ ὄντος (σημαίνει γὰρ τὸ μὲν τόδε τι . . .) πότερον ἐξ ἁπάντων ἔσται ἡ ψυχὴ ἢ οὔ ; The question is whether soul is compounded out of all the kinds of being, not whether it is compounded out of all the senses of ' being '.

[1] This is said of relation in *E. N.* 1096[a] 21.

[2] Z. 1028[a] 32–[b] 2.   [3] 14[a] 30.   [4] Δ. 1020[a] 33, 35–[b] 2, [b] 6.

when we know what it is than when we know what quality, quantity, or place it has. Indeed, if we want to know even something that belongs to a *non*-substantial category, we must ask not what qualities, &c., it has, but what it is, what is its quasi-substance, that which makes it what it is. In this argument it is evident that substance is being thought of not as the concrete thing but as the essential nature. And this ambiguity is present throughout Aristotle's treatment of substance.

The existence of substance, and the distinction between it and the other categories, i.e. between substance and what we may sum up as qualities and relations, is for Aristotle ultimate and self-evident. The primary meaning of substance is ' that which is not asserted of a subject but of which everything else is asserted', or, as he states the matter more fully in the *Categories*,[1] 'that which is neither asserted of a subject nor present in a subject'. There are terms which can figure either as subjects or as predicates; e.g. we can say 'white is a colour', and we can say 'the wood is white'. There are others which can only, according to Aristotle, figure as subjects. Τὸ λευκόν ἐστι ξύλον is not a proper predication but an accidental predication.[2] This doctrine seems to be a mistaken one.[3] But even if the logical doctrine which accompanies it be untrue, Aristotle's distinction between substance and the non-substantial is correct. Reflection on a statement like ' Socrates is white' shows that it is not white or whiteness, nor any of the qualities combined with it in Socrates, nor the sum of these qualities with whiteness, that is said to be white, but that which has all these qualities, the individual thing which is the substratum of them and in which they are united. But Aristotle is not content to leave it at that, to insist on the difference between individual things and their qualities and relations (though this is one of the main moments in his thought, especially in his opposition to Platonism);

---

[1] 2ᵃ 12.   [2] *An. Post.* 83ᵃ 1-17.

[3] Aristotle seems to be misled by the ambiguity of the neuter adjective with τό. τὸ λευκόν may mean ' the white colour' or 'the white thing'. If it means the latter—which it would mean for any one who said τὸ λευκόν ἐστι ξύλον—the statement is as proper a predication as τὸ ξύλον ἐστὶ λευκόν. The one expresses the discovery that what was known to be white is wood, as the other expresses the discovery that what was known to be wood is white.

he strives to find the substantial element in individual substances, and it is to this problem that he now proceeds.

He gives first [1] a *prima facie* account of the denotation of substance. (1) The most obvious substances are bodies, i.e. animals, plants, the four elements, and the parts and compounds of these. (2) The Pythagoreans treat the limits of body—planes, lines, points—as even more substantial than bodies. (3) Plato recognizes Forms and mathematical objects as kinds of substance distinct from bodies. (4) Speusippus recognizes various kinds of substance each with separate originative sources—numbers, magnitudes, soul, &c. (5) Some thinkers (Xenocrates) identify Forms and numbers, and recognize further classes of substance dependent on these—lines, planes, &c., and at the end of the series the physical universe and sensible things ; unlike Speusippus they treat the various grades of substance as dependent each on the simpler kind which goes before. Aristotle's views with regard to bodily substances are to be gathered chiefly from Z H ; his views about the incorporeal substances believed in by the Pythagoreans, Plato, and the Platonists are expressed chiefly in M N. In Λ he unfolds his doctrine with regard to the only incorporeal substances in which he himself believed.

Substratum.

Aristotle next [2] names four main claimants to the title of substance, i.e. not of individual substance but of the substantial element in individual things,—essence (τὸ τί ἦν εἶναι), the universal, genus, substratum. The last has *prima facie*, as we have seen, the strongest claim. By the substratum may be meant (1) matter, (2) the sensible form, or (3) the complex formed by the union of the two. But the identification of substance with substratum tends to lead to the identification of it with matter. In thought we may strip off the attributes one by one, until nothing is left but bare matter, which includes neither positive nor even negative attributes ; [3] for the latter are merely incidental to it. But bare matter is evidently not substance ; it has neither the capacity for separate existence, nor the individuality, the ' thisness ', which are held to be primary characteristics of substance.

[1] Z. 2.   [2] Z. 3.   [3] 1029ᵃ 24.

Matter cannot exist separately; Aristotle has no doubt about that. The bronze, which may be called matter or raw material for the sculptor, since it has not the shape he wishes to impose on it, is not completely raw material; it has a form of its own. (*a*) It has the inner structure peculiar to bronze, which it retains under his hands, and (*b*) it has an outer shape which it loses under his hands, gaining another instead. Bare matter is only a product of the logical analysis in which we divide a given thing into form and that which is not form. And again bare matter is not individual; what is individual must have some character, and bare matter has none.

Essence.

Thus the thought of substance as substratum leads to a wrong result. Instead of abandoning it, however, Aristotle ostensibly retains it, but infers that the substratum must be one of the other two things he had said it might be—form, or the unity of form and matter. The latter is logically posterior to form, and is sufficiently familiar; for these two reasons Aristotle concentrates on form, and proposes to examine it first as it exists in the most generally recognized substances, those perceptible by sense.[1] But, feeling perhaps the difficulty of treating form as a variety of substratum, he here[2] makes a fresh start; he leaves the notion of substratum and passes to another of the four original claimants to substantiality—essence. This, though connected, is not identical with the form which was one variety of substratum. That was τὸ σχῆμα τῆς ἰδέας, the sensible shape; this is the inner nature, what makes a thing what it is, and is unfolded in definition. The essence of a thing, we read, is what that thing is said to be *propter se*. Therefore (1) accidental attributes are excluded from essence. Your essence is not to be musical. You were you before you were musical, and you may cease to be musical and still be you. This exclusion of certain attributes from the essence of an *individual* is somewhat arbitrary. It is obvious that you would not be the same you

[1] This forms the main subject of Z. 4-12. The study of form as it is in sensible things is preliminary to the study of it as it is in itself (1029ᵃ 33, ᵇ 3-12, 1037ᵃ 13, 1041ᵃ 6).

[2] Z. 4.

that you are now if you ceased to be musical. Aristotle is working with a *prima facie* notion of a core of being present throughout the whole existence of an individual and distinguished from the passing attributes. But he is perhaps aware of the possible objection. At all events, for him essence is the object of definition, and the individual is indefinable. After this one reference, therefore, to 'your essence' he refers henceforward to the essence of general types.[1] (2) He excludes, secondly, attributes which *are* in a sense *propter se*, viz. *propria*. To say that A belongs to B *propter se* is ambiguous. A belongs to B *propter se* in one sense if it is included in the essence and definition of B (thus line is *propter se* to triangle, point to line); in another sense, if it is present in B and if B is included in *its* definition (thus straight and curved are *propter se* to line, odd and even to number).[2] What is καθ' αὐτό to B in the second sense—e.g. white to surface—is not the essence of B. For though you cannot define white except by reference to surface, you can define surface without reference to white. (3) Nor is the essence of surface white surface. A definition, which is the statement of the essence of a thing, must not name the thing itself.

(4) Aristotle next asks whether a term which is a complex of a substance + something in another category, e.g. white man, has an essence. It might be objected that any proposed definition of it would have to be condemned, like those considered above under (1), as not *propter se*, since there is no essential connexion between man and white. But '*propter se*' above referred to the relation between the definition and the *definiendum*. A definition is 'not *propter se*' when it errs (*a*) by addition, as when white is defined by the definition appropriate to white man; or (*b*) by omission, as when white man is defined by the definition appropriate to white. It is not necessary to commit either of these mistakes, so that, as far as this goes, white man may have an essence and a definition. But, supposing these errors avoided, would the account of white man arrived at be an essence? No, for an essence is 'just what an individual

---

[1] Probably indeed τὸ σοὶ εἶναι (1029ᵇ 14) is not meant to be taken as the essence of an individual in distinction from the essence of a kind. τὸ σοὶ εἶναι is τὸ ἀνθρώπῳ εἶναι.

[2] *An. Post.* 73ᵃ 34–ᵇ 5.

thing is' (ὅπερ τί or ὅπερ τόδε τι), and white man is not 'just what an individual thing is'; it does not indicate the permanent fundamental nature of anything but the union of a term which does indicate such a nature with an accidental concomitant. Thus lack of necessary connexion within a *definiendum* (and therefore within its definition) is as fatal to any proposed definition of it as would be the lack of necessary connexion between the *definiendum* and the definition.

Of all terms only those which stand for species can be defined. *Summa genera* cannot be defined, since they cannot be analysed into anything simpler than themselves ; and complex terms other than species cannot be defined, since there is no necessary connexion between their elements. In species there is such a necessary connexion ; the genus does not participate in the differentia as in something irrelevant to itself. The genus has no existence apart from the differentiae nor the differentiae apart from the genus.[1] But of other terms an account (λόγος), though not a definition (ὁρισμός), may be given. You can explain any single ὄνομα by stating a combination of words (λόγος) equivalent to it, or any λόγος by giving a more explicit λόγος equivalent to it. And such accounts may be called definitions in a secondary sense of definition. Other things than substantial species may in some sense have a τί ἐστι and a τί ἦν εἶναι, though only in a secondary sense, just as being itself belongs only in a secondary sense to them. Anything in any of the non-substantial categories has, not an essence proper, but an ' essence-of-a-quality ', &c.[2] And in a tertiary sense even a mixed term like white man has an essence,[3] which will be the union of an essence proper and an essence-of-a-quality.

Aristotle proceeds[4] to consider (5) the possibility of defining yet another class of term, the 'coupled term' (συνδεδυασμένον) like 'snub' or 'snub-nose', which stands for τόδε ἐν τῷδε, a particular quality in a particular subject-matter, e. g. concavity in a nose. This is distinguished from terms like 'white man' in that the connexion between the elements is essential. What is white need not be a man, but what is snub must be a nose, what is male must be an animal, what is equal a quantity, what is odd a number. This being so, one might suppose that the

---

[1] H. 6. [2] 1030ª 31.
[3] 1030ᵇ 12. [4] Z. 5.

connexion in these cases is that of genus with differentia, which is similarly described as non-accidental,[1] and that the snub, the male, the equal, the odd are *species* of nose, animal, quantity, and number respectively. This is, however, not Aristotle's view. Sex, for example, is a contrariety not in the λόγος but in τὸ συνειλημμένον τῇ ὕλῃ, in the concrete thing which is a union of matter and form, and it belongs primarily not to form but to matter.[2] In I. 9 Aristotle distinguishes three ways in which attributes may be connected with generic subjects. (a) They may be connected as footed and winged are with animal. These are 'proper attributes of the genus' present in its very form and differentiating species within the genus. (b) They may be connected as male and female are with animal. These are also proper attributes but present not in the form but in the matter, i.e. in the body, and not giving rise to a differentiation of species. (c) They may be connected as white and black are with animal. These are not even *propter se* to the genus and of course give rise to no differentiation of species.[3] It is mentioned as arising from (and confirming) the fact that in case (b) the difference is in the matter, that the same seed, i.e. the same male or formal element in generation, may by different treatment, i.e. by union with this or that female or material element, produce male or female offspring; the difference between male and female comes from matter, not from form. Thus, when some members of a genus have an attribute and others not, (a) the attribute may be peculiar to the genus and be one of its main differentiations. In this case, just as the genus, e. g. animal, is not a single attribute but a mass of interconnected attributes, so the attribute, e. g. footed or winged, carries with it a mass of other attributes, so that land animals and flying animals are real kinds clearly marked off from one another. Then the unity of genus and attribute is a species, a 'secondary substance', and is definable in the strict sense by naming the genus and the differentia. (b) The attribute may be peculiar to the genus but carry with it only a small number of other attributes. In this case the attribute is said to belong to the matter, not to the form. The unity of genus and such an attri-

---

[1] 1030ᵃ 13.   [2] I. 1058ᵇ 1, 21.

[3] In the language of the *Topics*, the attribute may be (a) a *differentia*, (b) a *proprium*, or (c) an *accidens* of the genus.

bute is called a 'coupled term' and is said to be not strictly definable. (c) The attribute may not be peculiar to the genus at all but may belong to certain members of the genus quite externally. In this case the unity of the two is a σύνθετον[1] and is definable in the tertiary sense referred to above.

The distinction of sex might be thought sufficiently important to be recognized as a genuine differentia. But it would cut across the differentiation of animals into the species 'land-animal', 'water-animal', 'air-animal', and Aristotle has therefore to relegate it to a position of less importance.

The reason given for such terms as snub or male not being definable is that any definition would involve 'addition', i.e. the definition of X as 'Y which is X'. This is due to the intimate connexion of the elements in the coupled term. Snub cannot be defined apart from nose nor male apart from animal because what is snub must be a nose and what is male must be an animal. It is inferred that, since *every* term in a category other than substance presupposes a substance, the definition of any such term must involve an 'addition', and therefore be no proper definition. Only substance can be defined. Aristotle does not draw the conclusion that on the same showing no species can be defined, since within a species the elements genus and differentia must have a connexion even more intimate than that between the elements in a coupled term. And on his own principles he is justified in refusing to draw this conclusion. For in the nature of a species the elements genus and differentia are so closely united that one is not ἄλλο to the other at all, and the definition is not therefore ἐκ προσθέσεως.[2]

Pursuing the subject of essence, Aristotle asks in Z. 6 whether a thing is the same as its essence. It is difficult to see the point of this question. Aristotle first points out that terms which are κατὰ συμβεβηκός are not identical with their essence. The meaning seems to be best brought out in a passage later in the chapter, in which it is pointed out that a term like white is in one sense and is not in another identical with its essence. The essence of white is identical with the attribute white, but not with the subject to which the attribute belongs, nor yet with the whole which includes both subject and attribute. This ambiguity in the meaning of the neuter adjective with the definite article

[1] Z. 1029[b] 23.   [2] Z. 12, H. 6.

has to be borne in mind throughout the discussions in Book Z; the extent to which Aristotle is embarrassed by it is rather remarkable.

When Aristotle passes from terms κατὰ συμβεβηκός to terms καθ' αὑτά, i. e. terms which stand neither for mere attributes, like white, nor for unities of subject and accidental attribute, like white man, he does not discuss on its merits the question whether such terms are identical with their essence, but takes as alleged examples of such terms the Platonic Forms, and asks whether, for instance, the Form of good is identical with the essence of goodness; and he draws the conclusion that there is no ground for believing in Platonic Forms if by them is meant anything more than 'what it is to be' so-and-so. It is unfortunate that he has thus improved the occasion by a fling at the Platonic theory, but his own view, that terms καθ' αὑτά are identical with their essence, appears clearly enough. It is supported by three main arguments. It is implied (a) by the nature of knowledge, since to know a thing is obviously to know what it is to be that thing, and (b) by the fact that if it were not so, essence would not exist. If the essence of good is not good, the essence of being will not be. But there is just as much ground for believing in the essence of being as in the essence of anything else, so that on this showing no essence would exist. (c) The identity of a thing with its essence is shown by the infinite regress involved in its denial. If the essence of A is different from A, the essence of the essence of A is different from the essence of A, and so on.

The reasoning of the chapter is weak, and to an unusual degree verbal and dialectical. Its meaning is rendered difficult to seize by the facts (1) that the proof of the non-identity of 'accidental terms' with their essence is not a direct one, but a *reductio ad absurdum*, and (2) that the argument for the identity of 'self-dependent terms' with their essence is conducted with reference to one particular kind of supposed self-dependent terms, the Platonic Forms. But the underlying doctrine has considerable importance. It may perhaps be stated thus. (1) There is a class of πρῶτα καὶ καθ' αὑτὰ λεγόμενα. primary and self-dependent entities, of which 'soul' would be a good example, which stand for certain natures and cannot be distinguished from 'what it is to be' those natures; which are pure form, not complexes of form and matter. (2) There is a class of κατὰ συμβεβηκὸς λεγόμενα, of which 'white man' is an example,—casual conjunctions of mutually independent elements, which, as we have seen from Z. 4, have 'essence' only in a tertiary sense, and are not identical with such essence as they have since they involve an element of matter which can never be stated in definition. Ultimately, as we shall see from Z. 10, 11, even combinations whose elements belong much more directly to one another than those of 'white man' do—entities like 'man', if 'man' means not soul but soul + body—are, though not 'accidental entities', yet distinct from their essence, since definition (which is the unfolding of essence) cannot express the material element in them. (3) There are ambiguous expressions like τὸ λευκόν, which, if they mean the quality in question (e. g. whiteness), are καθ' αὑτά and identical with their essence, but if they mean the thing that has the quality, considered as having it, are κατὰ συμβεβηκός and not identical with their essence.

The discussion is resumed, after a digression, in chs. 10, 11, the main interest of which lies not in Aristotle's answer to the questions he explicitly asks but in the complicated set of entities which emerges in the course of the discussion. There is (1) the pure form, e. g. the circle or the soul, which are identical with their essences;[1] i.e. the pure form of circularity or of vitality. (2) The intelligible individual,[2] the union of form with a particular intelligible matter, i.e. with a particular extension; e. g. the individual geometrical circle. (3) The materiate universal, the union of 'this form' with 'this matter taken as universal'; e.g. 'man', the union of soul with a particular kind of sensible matter.[3] (4) The sensible individual, the union of form with a particular parcel of sensible matter; e. g. Socrates or a particular bronze circle.[4] The recognition of the intelligible individual and that of the materiate universal are important innovations; hitherto the only σύνολον thought of has been, apparently, the sensible individual. But to complete the series a fifth type of entity between the first and the second should be recognized. Circularity is not a pure form but the embodiment in intelligible matter (space) of the equation to the circle, i. e. of a type of arithmetical relation which is capable of other embodiments as well. Aristotle suggests a cruder form of this distinction when he asks whether the line ·is the

[1] 1036ᵃ 1.   [2] ib. 3.
[3] 1035ᵇ 27–30.   [4] 1036ᵃ 3–5, 1035ᵇ 30.

number two or the number two embodied in length.[1]   Thus we
should recognize besides the pure form the σύνολον which includes
'this form' and 'this intelligible matter taken as universal'.
But Aristotle does not draw this conclusion.   He maintains that
geometry and arithmetic deal with entirely different γένη, and
opposes strongly the Pythagorean and Platonic 'reduction of
things to numbers'[2]

Of the four types of entity here recognized by him, only the
first and the last have any real claim to substantiality.   The
intelligible individual is merely one element in the nature of the
sensible individual considered in abstraction from the rest, the
secondary qualities.[3]   The materiate universal, like 'man', which
in the *Categories*[4] is called a secondary substance, is here said not
to be substance at all.[5]   It too exists only in sensible individuals.
Pure form is for Aristotle substance, but few of the things that
prima facie are pure forms turn out to be really pure from matter.
'The circle' in general, which he here identifies with the essence
of circularity, really involves intelligible matter.   'The soul',
which he identifies with the essence of soul, is yet the 'essence
of a particular sort of body',[6] and cannot exist apart from such
a body.   In the long run, God, the intelligences that move the
spheres, and the human reason (or rather the 'active' element in
it) are the only pure forms that Aristotle recognizes.   Finally,
there are difficulties in the view that sensible individuals are
substances.   There is the difficulty—which we shall discuss later—
arising from the facts that the truly real must be knowable, while
the individual is, on the face of it, not completely knowable.[7]
There is the difficulty—perhaps the same difficulty looked at from
another point of view—arising from the presence of matter
or potentiality in the individual, and its resulting subjection to
change and destruction.   The general tendency of Z H Θ is to
carry Aristotle away from his earlier doctrine that the sensible
individual is 'primary substance', to one which identifies primary
substance with pure form and with that alone.

The expression 'intelligible matter' occurs only here and in
1037[a] 4, and in H. 1045[a] 34, 36, where, however, it is used in
a different sense, to express the fact that the genus is to the

---

[1] H. 1043[a] 33. Cf. Z. 1036[b] 12-17.
[2] Z. 1036[b] 12.   [3] 1036[a] 11, M. 2, 3.   [4] 2[a] 17.
[5] 1035[b] 27.   [6] ib. 14-16.   [7] Z. 15.

differentia as matter is to form. On the other hand ἡ τῶν μαθηματικῶν ὕλη in K. 1059^b 15 means the same as ὕλη νοητή here. The
present phrase should probably not be understood in its most obvious sense as meaning matter which is itself intelligible. Matter is
not intelligible;[1] 'intelligible matter' is a shorthand phrase for the
material, pluralizing element in the intelligible, as ὕλη γεννητή is
not generable but is the material element in generable things.

Plato had[2] treated space (χώρα) as the material element or
substratum of sensible things, the stuff out of which they are
moulded by the entrance into it of shapes which are likenesses
of the eternal existents, the Forms.[3] Space in his philosophy
(unless we should rather say, in that of Timaeus) does the work
which matter does in Aristotle's. His analysis of sensible things
is simply into space + τὰ εἰσιόντα καὶ ἐξιόντα. Aristotle recognizes
layer upon layer of matter in sensible things, and only one of these
is identified with space, viz. (1) intelligible matter, the minimum
matter that anything can have ; this exists both in sensible things
and in intelligible individuals.[4] It is this that pluralizes the pure
form of circularity into the many geometrical circles. On this is
superimposed, in sensible things, (2) sensible matter ; but this is
not of one piece. The minimum form of it is (a) ὕλη τοπική, the
matter that makes things capable of local motion ; the heavenly
bodies have this without any of the other kinds of sensible
matter.[5] On this, in sensible things other than the heavenly
bodies, are superimposed (b) the matter or potentiality for
qualitative change, which presupposes (a) ;[6] (c) the matter or
potentiality for growth and diminution, which presupposes (b)[7]
and therefore (a); and (d) ὕλη γεννητὴ καὶ φθαρτή, the matter or
potentiality for generation and destruction, which presupposes
(a), (b), (c).[8] This is ὕλη μάλιστα καὶ κυρίως.[9] (b), (c), and (d),
though they have an order of logical priority, are not given
separately, but are all present in all terrestrial sensible things.

Extension, then, though involved in sensible things, is not for
Aristotle as for Plato the stuff of which they are made. The
stuff of which sensible things are made is something that answers
more to our ordinary notion of matter, something that has solidity

[1] 1036^a 8. [2] *Tim.* 52 A. [3] 50 C.
[4] Z. 1036^a 11. [5] H. 1044^b 7, Θ. 1050^b 21, *Phys.* 260^a 28.
[6] *Phys.* 260^b 4. [7] 260^a 29. [8] H. 1042^b 3.
[9] *De Gen. et Corr.* 320^a 2.

as well as extension. And the matter of the sublunary world is always qualified by one, or by a combination of both, of the members of each of the main ἐναντιότητες, hot and cold, wet and dry, and of the subsidiary ἐναντιότης heavy and light.

But, though space is distinguished from matter, there is no space without matter; there is no actual void.[1] It follows that intelligible individuals do not exist apart from sensible things. Wherever there is a geometrical sphere there is a material sphere—though not necessarily one which is qualitatively distinct from what surrounds it, so as to be sensibly a sphere. Mathematics is not the study of separate entities, but of sensible things considered as possessing size and shape but not as possessing sensible matter and the qualities that go with it.[2] There is, in fact, a series of sciences which abstract progressively more and more from the total nature of sensible things. One science (kinematics) considers them as moving, i. e. as having intelligible matter and local matter but not the other three kinds; another (solid geometry) considers them as having only intelligible matter, but that in three dimensions; another (plane geometry) as having it in two; another (so Aristotle says, but the *obiter dictum* should not be pressed) as having it in one dimension. Another will abstract from all three dimensions and treat them as indivisibles having position, and another (arithmetic) simply as indivisibles.[3]

How do the various types of entity stand with regard to the question of definition? The definition of a *pure form* should take account only of pure form. The *individual*, whether sensible or intelligible, cannot be defined, but is apprehended by the aid of direct perception or intellection.[4] With regard to the *materiate universal*, Aristotle finds it hard to decide whether its definition should include a reference to its matter. 'Finger', he says, 'is defined by reference to man',[5] which implies that man is not defined by reference to finger. Bones, sinew, and flesh are no part of the definition of man.[6] Only the parts of the form are parts of the definition.[7] But a doubt arises in his mind. When a form can be manifested in more than one kind of matter, as a circle can in bronze, stone, or wood, the materials are evidently no part of the definition; even if all circles were of bronze, bronze would be no part of the definition of circle. Are flesh and bones equally

---

[1] *Phys.* iv. 6–9.   [2] M. 2, 3.   [3] M. 1077ᵇ 17–30.
[4] Z. 1036ᵃ 2–6.   [5] 1034ᵇ 28–31.   [6] 1035ᵃ 17–22.   [7] ᵇ 33.

irrelevant to the form of man, lines and continuity to that of circle? Is the circle really a number or a numerical relation, which merely happens to be embodied in extension? No, such terms are essentially τόδε ἐν τῷδε, forms which require a particular kind of matter.[1] Man cannot be defined without reference to bodily parts, i. e. those parts which are κύρια, the dominant parts such as heart or brain in which the essence directly resides, and which are 'simultaneous' with man in the sense that he cannot come into being without them nor survive their destruction.[2] Yet after all Aristotle concludes that the definition of a σύνολον will not refer to matter, for that is indefinite; the definition of man is the definition of the soul.[3]

Aristotle's vacillation on this point led Scotus to postulate for every σύνολον or materiate universal two forms—the *forma partis*, which is an element in the σύνολον (e. g. rationality, which is an element in man), and the *forma totius*, which is the whole of the σύνολόν (e. g. humanity, which is the whole of man, including his body as well as his soul). Zabarella, however, points out that neither rationality nor humanity contains matter as a part, and that both presuppose it as a vehicle and necessary condition, the former implicitly, the latter expressly.

Aristotle admits elsewhere[4] the possibility of three ways of defining a σύνολον, by reference to the matter, to the form, or to both. The first is the way of the so-called physicist, the second that of the dialectician; the truly physical or scientific definition is the third, which recognizes anger, for example, frankly as a λόγος ἔνυλος and defines it as desire for retaliation accompanied by ferment of the blood about the heart.

In Z. 12 Aristotle discusses a question which was often in his mind,[5] though he does not discuss it except here and in H. 6. Definition always mentions a genus and one or more differentiae; wherein, then, consists the unity of the substance defined? Does it not split into two or more externally related elements? His answer consists in pointing out (1) that the genus has no existence apart from its species; it stands to them in a relation analogous to that of matter to form; it is a potentiality which is realized only in them. It therefore offers no obstacle to the unity

---

[1] 1036ᵃ 31–ᵇ 32. Cf. H. 1043ᵇ 2–4.   [2] Z. 1035ᵇ 25.
[3] 1037ᵃ 24–29.   [4] *De An.* 403ᵃ 3–ᵇ 9.
[5] Cf. *De Int.* 17ᵃ 13, *An. Post.* 92ᵃ 29.

of definition. Definition may thus be considered as if it consisted entirely of differentiae. Now (2) each differentia should be a differentiation of the previous one. If we take 'footed' as the first differentia of man, the next to be mentioned should be one which presupposes footedness and is a differentiation of it—not 'wingless' but 'cloven-footed'. Thus the last differentia presupposes all the others and is indeed the essence and definition of man ; all danger of the definition, and the substance, splitting into irrelevant parts is seen to have disappeared. This account of definition looks like a *tour de force* adopted in order to escape a metaphysical difficulty. In the *Posterior Analytics*, where Aristotle has his eye on the actual conditions under which definition has to be effected, his doctrine is different. We must take differentiae *each of which will extend beyond the definiendum* but all together will not.[1] Three is defined as a number which is odd, prime, and not the sum of two numbers—three independent differentiae.[2] Man is defined as an animal which is tame and two-footed.[3] Yet even there it is stated as the *ideal* that each term in the definition should be such as to be presupposed by all the later terms.[4]

Not only in the definition of natural kinds, which has to be by approximation to a general type, but in that of abstract entities like the square, we often have to take account of differentiae logically independent of each other (equality of sides, rightness of one angle). But it is a good counsel of perfection that a single *fundamentum divisionis* should as far as possible be adopted through all the stages of the division implied in definition.

Aristotle now passes from the discussion of essence. He has treated it from many points of view, but he has not answered his original question whether essence is substance. Perhaps the most valuable result is the growing sense of the complexity of the problem. He started with sensible form, matter, and the individual thing which is a complex of the two. He has now recognized in addition (1) essence, the inner nature which makes a thing what it is. He has recognized (2) intelligible matter, present in non-sensible things which might *prima facie* be thought to be pure form. He has recognized (3) the intelligible individual and (4) the materiate universal. And the last of these has revealed an unsuspected implication of matter in essence.

[1] 96ᵃ 32.   [2] ib. 35.   [3] 96ᵇ 31.   [4] 97ᵃ 28–31.

Essence was originally described as substance without matter,[1] and is constantly identified[2] with form and therefore opposed to matter. But the essence of a materiate universal cannot be properly stated without reference to matter—not, of course, prime matter, which has no character and is therefore of no use for purposes of definition, nor yet the particular parcels of matter which are found in individuals, but something intermediate, the kind of matter in which alone the form in question can be embodied. The way is thus prepared for the recognition in H of a relation of the very closest between matter and form.

The question of the unity of definition is resumed in H. 6. It we consider a γενητόν, e. g. a bronze ball, and ask what makes it one, we find it to consist of two elements, matter and form, each of which is adapted to the other.[3] The bronze is potentially round; roundness is a character which can be imposed on bronze. No cause of their unity need be looked for, other than the craftsman who makes the potentially round actually round. But there is intelligible matter as well as sensible. The generic element in the essence of a thing may be regarded as a relatively vague matter or potentiality which is actualized in its different species. And here no efficient cause is needed. The genus does not first exist undifferentiated, as the bronze first exists unrounded. The genus exists only in its species; it is its nature to have one or other of the alternative differentiae. And it is the nature of the differentiae to belong to this particular genus and to no other.[4] The supposed difficulty about the unity of definition arises from looking out for a difference between potentiality and actuality, and a λόγος which unites them. The truth is that the proximate matter and the form are the same thing; the very thing that the one is potentially, the other is actually. If you think of prime matter and of a highly specialized form you may wonder how they are ever to be brought together; but recognize the stages in the preparation or formation of matter,[5] and you will see that matter is at each stage trembling on the verge of its proximate actualization, and needs but the hand of the craftsman, or of the master craftsman nature, to

---

[1] Z. 1032ᵇ 14.
[2] e. g. 1032ᵇ 1, 1035ᵇ 16, 32, H. 1043ᵇ 1, 1044ᵃ 36.
[3] Cf. 1044ᵃ 27–29.   [4] 1045ᵃ 23–35.
[5] Cf. 1044ᵃ 15–20, ᵇ 1–3, Θ. 1048ᵇ 37—1049ᵃ 24.

make it pass over. And similarly between the genus and its first differentia, between the first differentia and the second, and so on, there is no gulf. The genus exists only as characterized by one or other of the alternative first differentiae, each of these only as qualified by one or other of the alternative differentiae at the next stage, and so on right down to the last differentia, which constitutes the *infima species*. To ask how matter and form are one is like asking for the cause of unity in general.[1]

The Universal.

Aristotle proceeds in Z. 13 to the next claimant to the title of substance — the universal,[2] and emphatically denies that this can be the substance of anything. (1) The substance of anything is the substance peculiar to it, but the universal is common. It cannot therefore be the substance either of all its particulars or of any of them, since it is not peculiar to any. (2) Substance is what is not asserted of a subject, but the universal *is* asserted of a subject. Nor can it be an element in the essence. To make it an element in the nature of its particulars is (1) to make it the essence of the class to which the particulars belong; it is (2) to suppose individual substance to consist of elements that are not individual nor substances but qualities, and thus to make quality prior to substance; it is (3) to make the genus substance not only of the species but of each individual in it, and thus not peculiar to that whose substance it is alleged to be. In general, if *infimae species* like man are substance, no mere element in their definition is substance. To say otherwise is to fall into the difficulty of the 'third man' or infinite regress and to make substance consist of actually existing substances, whereas what is actually one cannot be actually two. But a difficulty arises. If a substance cannot consist of universals nor of actual substances, every substance will be incomposite and therefore indefinable. But we have seen that only substance is definable. For the moment, then, we are left with the conclusion that nothing is definable. But we may perhaps find things that are definable in a particular sense.

---

[1] 1045^b 16-23.
[2] The fourth of the original claimants—genus—is not treated separately. The actual treatment of the universal identifies it with the generic element in the nature of a species.

The chapter is clearly dialectical. The result it leads to is one which Aristotle does not accept. He is no doubt in earnest in refusing to find the substance of any separately existing being in a universal character which according to all his principles cannot exist separately. And he is in earnest in refusing to recognize the universal as a *substance* present in the essence of its species or of its individuals. But it is his own doctrine that in some sense the universal is present in the essence of its particulars, and this will emerge later.

Ch. 14 applies to the Platonic Ideas Aristotle's arguments against reducing the substance of individuals to anything universal.

Ch. 15 carries on the thought of ch. 13. In that chapter Aristotle argued that no substance can consist of universals because every universal signifies not a 'this' but a 'such'. He now draws the corollary that since definition is an enunciation of universal marks, it can never adequately express the nature of an individual. The chapter argues that (1) individuals are indefinable, and (2) in particular the Ideas are so since they are thought of by the Platonists as individuals, having separate existence. Individuals are indefinable (*a*) because they contain matter and are therefore perishable. A definition which was at one time true might therefore cease to be true, and therefore could only have been opinion, not knowledge. (*b*) In the discussion of the definability of Ideas the further point, which is applicable to *all* individuals, comes out, that any definition is bound to name only *common* qualities and therefore not to state the unique nature of the individual.

The conclusion that individuals cannot be subjects of definition nor of demonstration creates a serious difficulty for Aristotle, of which much has been made by Zeller. (1) On the one hand, for Aristotle only individuals are really substances. The only forms which have separate substantial existence apart from matter are individuals—God and the intelligences that move the spheres ; the mistake of the Platonists according to Aristotle is not that they believe in immaterial entities but that they identify them with universals.[1] And, at a lower level, the individuals concrete of form and matter are more real, more substantial than the universals in which their common qualities are abstracted

[1] 1040^{b} 27—1041^{a} 3.

from those peculiar to the individuals.[1] (2) On the other hand, definition and demonstration are the very types of knowledge. Science, or knowledge (Aristotle has one word for both), starts with definition and proceeds by demonstration; it demonstrates universal properties as flowing from universal definitions. This is the consistent teaching of the *Posterior Analytics*. Now (3) that which is most real should be for Aristotle most fully knowable, and therefore most strictly the subject of definition and of demonstration. He has said explicitly and more than once that substance alone, or substance primarily, is definable.[2]

In various passages Aristotle hints at a solution of this difficulty. (1) Individuals, though not definable, are known by the aid of intuitive thought (νόησις) or of perception—intelligible individuals like 'this circle' by the former, sensible individuals by the latter.[3] Apart from the abstractive and discursive procedure of science there are other more concrete and direct modes of knowledge (of which one—νόησις—is conceived as actually superior to science) by which the whole individual nature of the individual is grasped in a single act. Aristotle appears to be pointing here to an important fact, the fact that our knowledge of individuals, e. g. of persons or of places, is not held in the form of a set of universal propositions, and could not be completely stated in such a form. But it is to be regretted that he did not work out more fully a theory of νόησις in which this function was correlated with the other functions he assigns to it— the knowledge of the first principles of science, and the knowledge of essences and of incomposite substances.[4]

(2) Aristotle has elsewhere [5] a different solution. It is only knowledge as existing potentially (i. e. as it is in the mind of a man of science when he is not thinking of the object of his science) that is of the universal; actual knowledge is of the individual. Or, as he also puts it, just as sight is directly of 'this' colour, and only incidentally of colour in general because this colour is a colour, so grammatical science is directly 'of this alpha', and only incidentally 'of alpha'. This contention also has truth. To take Aristotle's own example of the science of grammar, the actuality of grammatical knowledge cannot be

---

[1] 1035ᵇ 27, 1038ᵇ 6—1039ᵃ 14, Λ. 1071ᵃ 19-24.
[2] 1030ᵃ 21–ᵇ 7, 1031ᵃ 13, 1039ᵃ 19.   [3] 1036ᵃ 2-8.
[4] Θ. 10.   [5] M. 1087ᵃ 10-25 : cf. *De An.* 417ᵃ 21-29.

confined to the grasping of a set of universal laws. The scholar
who is interpreting a particular passage is in the fullest sense
thinking grammatically or knowing grammar. And what is true
of this is true of all the sciences. To solve a particular problem
by mathematics is to think mathematically. One might go
further and say that actual scientific thought is never concerned with universals cut off from their particulars, but with
universals as the universals of their particulars. There is no
insight into a general law which is not accompanied by some
awareness, perceptual or imaginative, of particulars that fall
under it. When the particulars have been completely lost sight
of, the law is no longer an object of genuine knowledge but a
convenient shorthand or *memoria technica*, which can be re-
vitalized or, as Aristotle says, actualized only by a fresh contact
with particulars.

But this hardly meets the difficulty. For though scientific
work is concerned thus with particulars, it is not concerned with
them in their full particularity. The man of science treats them
as instances of a universal, and is only vaguely aware of their
differing individual natures ; it is his business to abstract, and
his knowledge can therefore never be adequate to the full reality
of individuals. For adequate knowledge of them αἴσθησις and
νόησις seem to be necessary as well as ἐπιστήμη.

Ch. 16 proves two corollaries from the principles laid down in
ch. 13. (1) From the principle that no substance consists of
actual substances it follows that the material parts of substances
—the organs and tissues that make up a living body, and its
more remote constituents the four elements—are not actually
existing substances but mere potentialities. The doctrine is
briefly expressed and difficult, but seems to be as follows :—
A living body may be said to exist actually and to be a substance.
It has a life which is both independent and unified. But when
it exists actually its parts considered as separate entities do not
exist actually, any more than the half lines exist actually in the
undivided line. As the elements are the matter out of which by
the imposition of certain forms or principles of structure tissues
(τὰ ὁμοιομερῆ) are made, and as tissues are the matter out of which
organs (τὰ ἀνομοιομερῆ) are made, so organs are the matter out of
which by the imposition of a certain form, the soul, a living body
is made, ' made ' not in the sense that the elements necessarily

exist before the tissues, the tissues before the organs, or the organs before the living body, but in the sense that logical analysis can draw the distinction between matter and form at these various levels. Now when the hand, e.g., exists in the body it has not the independence characteristic of substance ; its life is merged in the life of the body. And when it is severed from the body, then though it exists it has lost its life, its activity, which was its actuality. It is still but the matter of a living body, only now not of an existing living body but of one which has ceased to be and also perhaps of one that will in time be formed out of its decay and re-formation.

(2) Aristotle has already, in ch. 13, established that no universal can be substance. He there considered particularly the narrowest universals, the genera next above *infimae species*. He now passes to the widest universals, the *transcendentalia*, being and unity, which are not genera but embrace all genera. These too, he shows, because they are 'common' cannot be substance.

Essence is Substance.

Having shown that the substance of things is neither their substratum nor their universal (nor their genus, which is a form of universal), Aristotle next, in ch. 17, essays to show that it is form or essence. The mode of approach is as follows. It is agreed that substance is an originative source and cause, i. e. that it is what makes things what they are. It is the answer to the question Why? Now the question Why? is never of the form Why is A A ?—that is a stupid question. The sort of question that may really be asked is, Why does it thunder ? (i. e. Why is sound produced in the clouds ?) or, By reason of what are bricks and stones a house ? In all these cases we are looking for a cause which is—to speak abstractly—the essence, but is in some cases, as in that of a house (or, generally, of *artefacta*), the end to be subserved, and in some (as in that of thunder) the moving cause. Our question always is, What makes the matter into a particular thing ? The answer is, the presence of the essence of the particular thing, which is not another element in the thing alongside of its material elements, nor anything compounded out of elements. This it is that makes certain elements into flesh and certain others into a syllable, and this is the essence of the thing produced since it is the direct cause of its being.

It is noteworthy that even in naming essence as the answer to the question, What is the explanatory cause of a thing's being, and therefore its substance ? Aristotle indicates that this answer is but an abstract one. If we ask what makes this flesh and these bones into a man, these bricks and stones into a house, these clouds into thundering clouds, it is no doubt a correct answer to say, the presence of the essence of a man, of a house, or of thunder.   But the answer takes us no further.   Aristotle points the way to a more real explanation by saying that what we describe abstractly as the essence is, viewed concretely, sometimes a final, sometimes an efficient, cause.   Normally the real answer to the question is to name the final cause.   No doubt the reason why this flesh and these bones make a man is that they are informed by the form of man, the human soul ; but an answer that cuts deeper is the answer, ' because they are organized in such a way as to subserve the ends for which man exists, intellectual and moral activity '.   In his biological works Aristotle constantly aims at explaining structure by function.   And similarly with *artefacta*.   What makes these bricks and stones into a house ? The fact that they are so arranged as to serve as a shelter for living things and goods.[1]   Normally, then, the formal cause is also a final cause.[2]   But in the production of natural substances and of *artefacta* certain by-products emerge for which no final cause is to be posited,[3] and which are therefore to be explained mechanically, by reference to a moving cause.   Thunder may no doubt be, as the Pythagoreans said, designed to terrorize the inhabitants of Tartarus,[4] but it is safer to explain it as due to the quenching of fire in clouds, or by some similar mechanical explanation.   And, though his language in Z. 17 carelessly suggests that some things are to be explained teleologically and others mechanically,[5] his real view is that the same thing which is due to a final cause is also due to an efficient cause.   The light streams through the lantern to prevent us from stumbling, but also because that which has small parts must pass through that which has larger pores.[6]   And this double action, of final cause and necessity, is normally at work in natural substances as well as in *artefacta*.[7]   Thus Z, while identifying substance, what makes a thing what it is, with essence, points to a less

---

[1] H. 1043[a] 16, 33.   [2] 1044[b] 1.   [3] ib. 12.   [4] *An. Post.* 94[b] 33.
[5] 1041[a] 28-30.   [6] *An. Post.* 94[b] 27-31.   [7] ib. 34-37.

abstract and a more satisfying explanation—the explanation by
final or by mechanical causes or by both. H. 4 emphasizes the
importance of ascertaining *all* the causes of which a given thing
admits—material, efficient, formal, and, where this is applicable,
final cause,[1] as well as that of assigning proximate rather than
remote causes.[2] It further brings out the distinction, somewhat
obliterated in Z.17, between the status of natural substances like
man, and natural phenomena like thunder. In the latter we
have to do not with a simple union of matter and form, but with
a union of substance (itself a union of matter and form) with
a temporary qualification. The substratum of such things is not
matter but substance.[3]

The reduction of essence to efficient or to final causes is,
though mentioned, not stressed in Z. The point which Aristotle
chiefly emphasizes in ch. 17 is that the essence is not to be
thought of either as a component existing alongside of the
material components, or as itself consisting of material components. If we view it in the former way we shall require a
further principle of structure to explain how it is united with the
material components. If we view it in the latter way we shall
want to know how the material components are united to form
the essence, i.e. we shall have to ask about the essence the same
question that we asked originally about the concrete thing—
what makes it what it is? We must pass clean away from any
materialistic understanding of the essence and treat it as the
structure of the concrete thing.

It is chiefly against the materialistic views of the pre-Socratics
that this required to be emphasized. One might have thought
that Plato had in the doctrine of Forms already sufficiently
emphasized the point. But it is proper that Aristotle in rejecting
the Platonic doctrine, which he at least believed to be a doctrine of
transcendent form, should have laid stress on the equally immaterial nature of the immanent form which he himself believed in.

This, then, is Aristotle's answer to the question what is substance. The substance of a thing is the principle of structure,
the presence of which in a collection of materials makes them not
a mere collection but an organized whole. H. 2, 3 carry further

---

[1] 1044ᵃ 33-ᵇ 20.
[2] 1044ᵃ 15-20, ᵇ 1-3. Cf. Θ. 1048ᵇ 37—1049ᵃ 24.
[3] 1044ᵇ 8-11. Cf. Z. 1038ᵇ 5, Θ. 1049ᵃ 27-36.

h

the notion of substance as the cause of being, that which makes a thing what it is.[1] The doctrine is in two ways made more precise. (1) It is pointed out that the differentia or structural principle which makes a thing what it is may be of any one of many types. It may be a question of fusion (as in mead), or of colligation (as in a bundle of sticks), or of position (as in threshold and lintel), or of time (as in breakfast and dinner), or of place (as in the winds), or of sensible quality such as hardness and softness, density and rarity, dryness and wetness. There are again more complex wholes such as hand or foot which involve all, or more than one, of these differentiae. (2) In Z. 17 Aristotle had spoken as if the essence or structural principle of anything—alike of man, of a house, and of thunder—were substance. He now rectifies this impression. None of the differentiae above-named is in the category of substance—they are in the categories of state (if κρᾶσις and δεσμός may be thus classified), position, time, place, or quality. But they present an analogy to substance. They are to the matter in the things named above as the substantial form is to matter in true natural substances. They, like the element of form in true substances, play the part of 'actuality' while matter plays the part of 'potentiality';[2] for these expressions now begin to be used in connexion with form and matter, and tend to take their place.

These differentiae not being substance, the things characterized by them—artefacta, temporary states of substances, and parts of living bodies—are not themselves substances. In fact, of perishable things it is only those that are 'held together by nature', unified by an inherent power of initiating movement, that are substances.[3] The elements, and therefore also the tissues and organs of living bodies, have the power of initiating simple movement upward or downward. But none of these, we have already seen,[4] are in the full sense substance. They are matter at different stages of preparation to play its part in the life of living things. Living things alone have 'nature' in the full sense, the power of purposive and centrally controlled reaction to a variety of stimuli, and these alone of all perishable things are in the full sense substances.

[1] 1043ᵃ 2. [2] ib. 4-7.
[3] 1043ᵇ 21-23. [4] Z. 1040ᵇ 5-14.

The Principle of Individuation.

The question may be asked whether Aristotle thinks of this principle of structure as common to a species or peculiar to an individual. He has argued in Z. 13 that substance must not be κοινόν, but by what is common he seems to mean a genus like 'animal' as opposed to a species like 'man' or 'horse'. Apparently he thinks that 'man' may be the essence, the whole essence, of individual men. The logic of the chapter should have led him to conclude that only the individual, or the immaterial element in the individual, is substance, and it is only the doctrine of *infimae species* that prevents him from drawing this conclusion. That he does not do so seems to be shown by the fact that throughout these chapters it is the essence of universals—surface, white man, snub nose, odd number, man, house—that he is dealing with; the references to 'your essence'[1] and 'the essence of Socrates'[2] are incidental and probably not deliberate. Individuals are indefinable; if they have an essence it is at least inexpressible.[3]

The problem of the principle of individuation was much debated by the schoolmen. The principal views held were the following. (1) St. Thomas assigned the origin of individuality to *materia sensibilis signata*, as opposed to *materia sensibilis in communi*, i.e. to the definite matter present in the individual as opposed to the type of matter present throughout a species, e.g. this flesh and bone as opposed to flesh and bone in general. This view was interpreted in two ways. (a) Some Thomists took *materia signata* to mean a certain amount of matter quantitatively determined. They distinguished indeterminate quantity, which they said was eternally present in matter, and determinate quantity, which 'followed' on form. The former was the original source of division, since it was by virtue of it that matter could be divided into parts and thus constitute separate individuals; the latter made the concrete thing indivisible in itself and divided it from other things, and thus gave it numerical identity and individuality. (b) Those who followed St. Thomas more closely (e.g. Caietanus) held *materia signata* to mean not matter + quantity but matter + the proximate

---

[1] 1029ᵇ 14.   [2] 1032ᵃ 8.   [3] Z. 15.

potentiality for a determinate quantity and for no other. The agent in acting on matter is all the time fitting it to receive the appropriate form and the determinate quantity. (2) Scotus, distinguishing, as we have seen, the *forma totius* from the *forma partis*, made a corresponding distinction between *materia totius* and *materia partis*. The latter was an element in the composite substance ; the former—also called *differentia individualis, entitas individualis*, or *haecceitas*—was what gave existence in individual shape to the form which in itself was universal. (3) Averroes and Zabarella distinguished between the plurality of individuals in the same species, and the numerical unity of each individual and its distinction from others. The former was an imperfection and sprang from the division of matter ; the latter was a per-fection and sprang from form. Form has two functions ; it gives *esse essentiae* and *esse existentiae* ; the generic form gives the first, the specific form the second, and therewith gives in-dividuality since to exist is to exist as an individual. Since matter does not give essence, still less can it give existence, which is to essence as actuality to potentiality. Some forms are by their very nature capable of being shared by more than one individual, and to these forms nature assigns divisible matter, which is the *sine qua non* but not the positive cause of individuality. (4) Others thought that it was the union of matter and form that constituted the individual, and assigned equal importance to the two elements.

When we turn to Aristotle and ask which of these interpreta-tions best expresses his meaning, we find that, on the whole, he tends to describe matter as the source of plurality, if not of individuality. 'Those things are one in number whose matter is one.'[1] 'The whole thing, such and such a form in this flesh and these bones, is Callias or Socrates ; and they are different owing to their matter (for this is different), but the same in species, for the species is indivisible.'[2] 'Man, horse, and terms which are thus applicable to particulars but are universal, are not substance but are complexes of this definition and this matter taken universally ; but it is the *ultimate* matter that is present in Socrates or any other individual.'[3] 'Things are called the same in another sense if they are one both in definition

---

[1] Δ. 1016ᵇ 32.   [2] Z. 1034ᵃ 5-8.   [3] 1035ᵇ 27-31.

and in number, e.g. you are the same with yourself both in form and in matter';[1] here numerical unity is identified with unity in respect of matter. 'That there is but one universe is evident. For if there were many universes as there are many men, their respective moving principles would be one in form but many in number. But all things that are many in number have matter.'[2] 'If we supposed that there were but one circle, none the less to be a circle and to be this circle would be different; the one would be form, the other would be form in matter and would be a particular. This universe, then, and universe simply are different; the latter is of the nature of a form or shape, the former of the nature of something mixed with matter. . . . In the case of all things whose substance is in matter, we see that the things of the same species are many and indeed indefinite in number. . . . But it does not follow that there is more than one universe; nor can there be, if this universe uses up all the matter, as it does. . . . If hookedness is crookedness in a nose or in flesh, and flesh is the matter for hookedness, then if out of all flesh one flesh were made and hookedness belonged to this, nothing else either would be or could become hooked. Similarly if the matter for a man is flesh and bones, then if a man were made out of all the flesh and all the bones and these could not be disintegrated, there could not be another man. Similarly in all other cases; in general, of all the things whose substance involves an underlying matter, none can come into being if there is not matter available.'[3]

The cumulative effect of these passages is very strong. Few passages can be cited in which individuation is ascribed to form. 'Those things whose substance, i.e. whose essence, is one are themselves one.'[4] 'The causes and elements of things in the same species are different, not in species, but in the sense that those of different individuals are different, your matter *and form* and moving cause and mine—though in their universal definition they are the same.'[5] 'We say that one class of existing things is substance, and within this we distinguish matter, which in itself is not a 'this', shape or form, in virtue of which a thing is first called a 'this', and thirdly the complex of the two.'[6] With

---

[1] I. 1054ª 34.   [2] Λ. 1074ª 31-34.
[3] *De Caelo* 278ª 7-ᵇ 3.   [4] Z. 1038ᵇ 14.   [5] Λ. 1071ª 27-29.
[6] *De An.* 412ª 6-9.

this passage must be associated those in which form is described as τόδε τι,[1] but it must be noted that there are others in which it is described as being not τόδε τι but τοιόνδε, and as being universal.[2] In one, and perhaps in both, of two passages in which ἴδιον εἶδος occurs, the form peculiar to a species, not to an individual, is referred to.[3]

The general effect of these passages is that, whereas things in different species differ in form (as well as in matter), things in the same species differ in matter only. The dominating idea is that of the *infima species*, the notion that there are fixed combinations of characteristics which form the core of the individuals in which they are present; these alone nature seeks to secure and to perpetuate. All differences of less importance and permanence than these are deemed unworthy of the name of form and treated as the result of the union of identical form with different matter. The source of mere plurality is bare matter. But the source of the plurality of members of one species is not bare matter but qualified matter—is the fact that there is more of the requisite *kind* of matter than is needed for a single individual realization of the specific form; this seems to be the teaching of the passage quoted from the *De Caelo*. The matter with which the specific form unites is therefore not thought of as qualityless. It is with a certain kind of flesh and bone that the form of man unites. But further, if two parcels of flesh and bone with which the form unites are qualitatively alike, they are no more capable of producing two distinguishable men than if they had been prime matter. They must differ in character, i.e. in form. Socrates and Callias must therefore, while agreeing in their specific form, differ in the quality or form of their matter. Now this difference in the quality of their matter may be reckoned to the side of form or essence, and if this is done we get the notion of an essence of the individual which includes besides the specific form such further permanent characteristics as spring from differences in the matter with which the specific form is in different individuals united.

How far does Aristotle think of the question thus? There are references in Z to 'your essence' and to 'the essence of

---

[1] Δ. 1017[b] 25, H. 1042[a] 28, Θ. 1049[a] 35, Λ. 1070[a] 11.
[2] Z. 1033[b] 19–23, 1036[a] 28.   [3] Λ. 1071[a] 14, *De An.* 407[b] 23.

Socrates ',[1] but these are incidental and must not be stressed. The only clear reference to the individual's having a distinct form as well as a distinct matter is that quoted above from book Λ,[2] and there Aristotle does not seem to realize the importance of his own statement; at all events he passes from it without comment. The passages in which form is described as τόδε τι should probably be interpreted in the light of the more precise passage in which it is described as that in virtue of which, in contrast with matter, a thing can be called τόδε τι. Matter itself is not individual; it is only when form is added that an individual results. An individual must have both being and character; without matter it could not have being, but without form it could not have character. And being and character are inseparable from one another; nothing has either without the other; form and matter exist only in union and are separable only in thought. Of this we might say that Aristotle was well aware, were it not for his doctrine of the existence of certain pure forms, God and the beings that move the spheres; we should perhaps add the human reason,[3] but it would be rash to embark here on that disputed question of interpretation.

With regard to these pure forms we may fairly press Theophrastus' question, how, in view of Aristotle's doctrine that plurality comes from matter, is their plurality to be explained? Later thought treated each such matterless individual as the unique member of a separate species, and this would presumably have been Aristotle's answer if he had put the question to himself.

The Analysis of Becoming.

Things may come into being according to Aristotle in either of three ways—by nature, by art, or spontaneously. The main object of Z. 7–9 is to show that in these three cases similar conditions are involved.

---

[1] 1029^b 14, 1032^a 8.

[2] 1071^a 27–29. Cf. the reference to the (individual) form of the bronze ball which comes into existence simultaneously with the bronze ball, Λ. 1070^a 21–24.

[3] Λ. 1070^a 24–27. Cf. *De An.* iii. 5.

(1) *Natural Generation.*

By nature in this connexion Aristotle means the power, inherent in all living things and in the four elements, of initiating
change.   In natural as in all other generation ' all things that
come to be come to be by some agency and from something and
come to be something '.[1]   The conditions of natural generation
are : (*a*) an individual which already has actually the specific
form which the offspring is to have.   This is the male parent
which has the same nature and specific name as the offspring ;
production is ἐξ (more strictly ὑφ') ὁμωνύμου ; it takes a human
being to beget a human being.[2]   (*b*) A matter capable of being
the vehicle of the specific form.   Such a matter is found in the
surplus blood which is the female parent's contribution to the
act of generation.[3]   (*c*) The specific form which is imposed on
the material.

It is true that the male parent and the offspring may be called
by different names ; a man may beget a woman, a stallion a
mule.   Such offspring are 'mutilations', fallings off from the
perfection of the type.   But even in them if we look deeper we
find a unity of nature and even of name ; it is always a human
being that produces a human being, one bushy-tailed creature
that produces another.   The mule shares the generic though
not the specific nature of his sire, while in a female child
the specific nature of the male parent is reproduced but is
embarrassed by the inferior matter with which it has to cope.[4]

(2) *Artistic Production.*

In artistic production—and this means all production due to
mind—the pre-existence of the form is less obvious.   The
making of a house does not presuppose the existence of an
actual house as generation presupposes an actual man.   Nevertheless in a sense there is a pre-existing house, viz. the form
of house as conceived by the builder.[5]   Such a product is produced ἐξ ὁμωνύμου ἢ ἐκ μέρους ὁμωνύμου,[6] for the house in the

---

[1] Z. 1032ᵃ 13.   [2] 1034ᵃ 21-ᵇ 1, 1032ᵃ 25.   [3] H. 1044ᵃ 35.
[1] 1033ᵇ 33-1034ᵃ 2, 1034ᵇ 1-4, I. 9.
[5] 1032ᵇ 1.   [6] 1034ᵃ 22.

builder's mind is only part of—the formal element in—a house. In all artistic production there are implied two stages, one of νόησις, in which the artist works gradually back from the thought of the object he wishes to produce to that of the means necessary to its production, and one of ποίησις in which, reversing the order, he successively brings these means into existence until at last he has fulfilled his purpose.[1]

(3) *Spontaneous Production.*

The production of results ἀπὸ ταὐτομάτου is of two kinds, one which simulates natural production and one which simulates artistic. To the first the name of ταὐτόματον in a specific sense is applied, to the second that of τύχη.

(*a*) Some types of animal can be produced without seed, i. e. without the action of a male parent, no less than from seed.[2] The possibility of such production is due to the fact that matter, i. e. not prime matter but partially formed matter such as mud, has a certain power of initiating change, and the particular qualitative change that will transform it into a living body.[3] We have no common name by which we designate the mud and the humble creature which springs from it. Such production is neither ἐξ ὁμωνύμου nor ἐκ μέρους ὁμωνύμου. But the production of a living creature at least presupposes the pre-existence of a part of it.

(*b*) Chance production is identical in kind with the second half of the process of artistic production. The first half, the νόησις, is here entirely absent. The process starts with the *unintended* production of the first stage in the making, which in artistic production is intended.[4] This may be produced by external agency, as when an unskilled person happens to rub a patient just in the way in which a doctor would have rubbed him *ex arte*, and thus originates the curative process.[5] Or again, it may depend on the initiative resident in living tissue; the sick body may itself originate the healing process.[6] In either case a part of the result pre-exists. If heat be the first step in the production of health, heat is a part of health or else involves such a part as its necessary result.[7]

[1] 1032[b] 6-21.   [2] 1032[a] 30.   [3] 1034 [b] 4-6.
[4] 1032[b] 23-28.   [5] 1034[a] 20.   [6] ib. 21.   [7] ib. 24-30.

All change presupposes not merely a matter which persists, but a privation which makes way for form. This may, or may not, be designated by a separate name in common speech (disease is so recognized, absence of statue-form is not).[1]

In generation form is not generated any more than matter. If form were itself being produced, it would be being produced out of something else, i. e. by the imposition of form on matter, and if *that* form were being produced, it would be by the imposition of *other* form on other matter, and so *ad infinitum*.[2] The most obvious interpretation of this passage would be that it teaches the eternity of form (though all that it actually *proves* is the existence of form before the process in which it is imposed on matter). But we are met by the fact that Aristotle sometimes speaks of form as coming into and passing out of being instantaneously.[3] In one passage he states both alternatives as possibilities.[4] He does not seem to have thought out the question fully, but the solution may perhaps be found in 1034[b] 18. There Aristotle points out that just as, when a new substance is produced, the form must already exist, so too, when a new quality, quantity, &c., is imposed on a substance, the new quality, &c., must pre-exist; and adds that, while in the former case, the form must pre-exist actually (i. e. as embodied in the male parent), in the latter it need only pre-exist potentially. In the latter case the form is not eternal. But it is not brought into being by a process (which is what γίγνεσθαι always implies), but supervenes instantaneously on a process. It is never coming into being, but *then* it was not (actually) and *now* it is. A white thing may become black, but white does not become black. The white thing becomes black bit by bit, but in each part black supervenes instantaneously on white.[5]

Now artistic production is never the production of a new substance but only of a new shape, &c., in an existing substance. It might seem, therefore, that Aristotle thinks of the pre-existence of the form of the product as only a potential existence. This would, however, be an incorr ct inference. For he does not say that where the production is not production of a new substance the form does not pre-exist, but that in such cases it *need* not pre-exist, actually. The form of house exists actually

---

[1] 1033[a] 5-22.   [2] 1033[a] 24-[b] 19.
[3] 1039[b] 26, H. 1044[b] 21.   [4] H. 1043[b] 15.
[5] 1044[b] 21-26, *Phys.* vi. 4.

before the building of a particular house, for it is already embodied in other houses ; but Aristotle would probably say that when the first house was being built the form existed only potentially.

But if the form of house exists before the building of a particular house, the individual form of the house does not pre-exist ; it comes into being without a process—instantaneously. Contacts, like forms, 'are and are not, without becoming or perishing';[1] and the form of the individual house comes into being timelessly with the last timeless contact of tile with tile, the form of the individual bronze sphere with the last contact of the hammer with the bronze. That which 'becomes' becomes bit by bit, but the form has no parts ; it is the structure of the whole.[2] Similarly, the form of the individual animal comes into being timelessly at the last moment of the vitalizing transformation of the female element by the male.

Even where form pre-exists actually (e. g. where it is natural generation that is in question) it does not pre-exist apart from particular instances. Form is eternal only by virtue of the never-failing succession of its embodiments. If it had substantial existence of its own, a particular thing embodying it could never be produced since one substance cannot contain another. Form indicates a 'such', never a 'this', a characteristic, never the concrete thing that bears it. Thus the Platonic Forms are of no use for explaining the coming into being of substances.[3]

To this account of becoming must be added the account in Λ. 4, 5. The analysis here is more akin to that in the *Physics* in respect of the place assigned to privation. Z works for the most part with the antithesis of form and matter, and privation is, as we have seen, mentioned only incidentally. In Λ it is, along with form and matter, one of the three internal causes (ἐνυπάρ-χοντα αἴτια) which are first mentioned.[4] To these are added the external causes, i. e. (1) the proximate moving cause, e. g. the art of medicine or of building (or to put it otherwise, the form of health or of a house), or, in the case of natural generation, the male parent;[5] (2) in the case of natural generation the remote and common moving cause, the sun as it moves along the ecliptic and produces the sequence of the seasons;[6] (3) the ultimate or first moving

---

[1] *De Caelo* 280ᵇ 27.
[2] *Al.* 486. 13–33. Cf. Λ. 1070ᵃ 21–24.
[3] Z. 1033ᵇ 19–29.
[4] 1069ᵇ 32–34, 1070ᵇ 18, 22.
[5] 1071ᵃ 14 f., 28.
[6] ib. 15.

cause which moves not by mechanical agency, but by being desired and loved.[1] Λ thus takes a wider sweep than Z. The interest of Z in becoming lies in the light it throws on the nature of form; the interest of Λ is in the question how far all things may be said to have the same causes, and how far different causes must be presupposed for different things ?[2] Aristotle points out that, except as regards the first cause, things in different genera have only analogically the same cause ; and he recognizes more clearly than anywhere else the existence of individual as well as specific form, when he says 'your matter and form and moving cause are different from mine, though they are the same in their general description '.[3] And in the same spirit he says that 'universal causes do not exist; the individual is the cause of individuals ; man is the cause of man universally, but there is no universal man ; Peleus is the cause of Achilles, and your father of you '.[4] So, too, the prime cause is not a general principle, but an individual spirit.[5] Book Λ might be described as preaching throughout the importance of the individual.

Potentiality and Actuality.

The expressions potentiality and actuality, almost entirely absent in Z, play a considerable part in H, as Aristotle passes from the static consideration of substance to the dynamic consideration of change. He now, in Θ, undertakes to study these notions, and begins with a distinction of two main senses of δύναμις which may perhaps be rendered by 'power' and 'potentiality'. He will deal first with power, which is defined as 'a source of change in another thing or in the same thing *qua* other'. In proportion as a thing is knit together into one whole it cannot be acted on by itself, for action and passion involve a distinction between agent and patient ; hence, strictly speaking, there is (contrary to Plato's opinion) no such thing as a self-mover. Power is a capacity in A of producing a change in B, or in one part of A of producing change in another part. This may be called transeunt δύναμις, inasmuch as two things are concerned. Potentiality, on the other hand, is a capacity in A of passing into a new state of itself. To the primary kind of power are related

---

[1] 1071ᵃ 36.   [2] 1070ᵘ 31.   [3] 1071ᵃ 27.
[4] ib. 19–23.   [5] 1075ᵃ 11–15.

(1) the complementary half of the same fact, a power in B of being changed by A, and (2) a power in B of not being changed for the worse or destroyed by A. These are akin to the first sense of δύναμις in that they imply an A and a B, but different in that the notion of power proper, i. e. power of initiating change, is absent: (1) implies weakness; (2) a sort of inertial resistance.

Rational and Irrational Powers.

Some powers are present in lifeless things, others in living things, or, to be more precise, in soul, and in that part of the soul which has λόγος, i. e. which can frame an account of an object and of the way to produce it. Some powers, in a word, are irrational, others rational; to the latter class belong the arts or productive forms of knowledge, and, as the *Ethics* informs us, the moral virtues. Both classes are found in living things; to the former belong the innate powers such as the senses, to the latter those which are acquired by practice (which, it is implied, has an element of λόγος in it), or by instruction. Powers of the latter class have this in common, that they are not innate but are developed by exercise. Rational powers are also distinguished from irrational by the fact that they are powers to do either of two contrary things. This follows from the fact that the λόγος of a thing is also the λόγος of its contrary. Because a rational power is a power to do either of two contraries, the conditions of the realization of a rational power are more complex than those of the realization of an irrational power. For the latter it is enough that the agent and the patient should come into that degree of proximity in which their powers become operative. But if proximity were the only necessary condition of the actualization of a rational power, then, since it is a power to do opposites, it would, when the proximity was given, actually do opposites and thus break the law of contradiction. Clearly, therefore, a further condition is needed. This condition is the occurrence of desire or choice of one of the opposites; this given, the power becomes operative, but, of course, only in one of the two ways originally open to it.[1]

[1] Θ. 2, 5.

Vindication of the Conception of Capacity.

In Θ. 3 Aristotle turns to vindicate the conception of capacity against the attack of the Megarian school. The Megarians had said that a thing *can* act only when it is acting. Two reasons for this view may be conjectured. (1) They may have reasoned that the only possible evidence that a thing has a power is that it is actually exercising it, and that to ascribe power to a thing when it is not exercising power must be a mistake. Or (2) they may have been taken in by an easily detected fallacy. Obviously A cannot act-when-it-is-not-acting; they may have inferred that when A is not acting it is not capable of acting. Whatever may have been their grounds, Aristotle answers them as follows: (1) Their view implies that a man is not (e. g.) a builder except when he is building. How, then, account for the fact that after a cessation from building he can quite suddenly begin again, as a man who has never built before cannot do? Is not the condition which makes this possible a disposition left over from previous acts of building, and is not this just what we mean by saying that when he is not building he has the capacity of building? The simple alternatives, he is either building or not building, will not cover the whole facts. (2) Their view implies the denial of the reality of sensible qualities when they are not actually being perceived, and thus involves the doctrine of Protagoras—the most extreme form of sensationalism. (3) It implies that people become blind and deaf many times in a day, i. e. whenever they cease actually to see or hear. (4) If capacity is present only when actuality is present, that which is not happening is incapable of happening, and therefore never will happen; thus the existence of change is denied.

This last argument appears to be fallacious. The real meaning of the Megarian doctrine seems to be that there is no such thing as capacity or possibility. A thing either is happening or it is not happening, and that is all that there is to be said about it. Therefore of that which is not happening they would say, not that it is incapable of happening, but that there is no sense in saying that it is capable of happening; and this does not imply a denial of change—it would be compatible with the assertion that change exists but is always necessary.

It may be noted that though this discussion occurs in the

section devoted to transeunt δύναμις, it really refers to immanent δύναμις, potentiality not power. To this Aristotle professedly proceeds in ch. 6. He expressly says here that it is indefinable, and explains it by citing typical instances. The relation of actuality to potentiality is that of the finished Hermes to the Hermes latent in a block of wood, of the man who is contemplating truth to him who has knowledge 'at the back of his mind', of the man who is actually building to him who knows how to build. The relation is of two main kinds: (1) that of movement to power, (2) that of substance to matter. We recognize in the first of these a reference to the transeunt δύναμις, ἡ κατὰ κίνησιν λεγομένη δύναμις,[1] with which the first half of the book was occupied. A power in A to produce change in B is at the same time an immanent δύναμις in A. In producing change in B, A is itself passing from potentiality to actuality. The second kind is that in which there is no question of A's acting on B, but A merely passes from a relatively unformed to a relatively formed condition, as when the wood which is potentially a statue becomes an actual statue.

Actuality and Movement.

Aristotle has identified one kind of actuality with movement, but he proceeds[2] to specify a narrower sense of both terms in which they are opposed to one another. A movement in the specific sense always points to an end beyond itself, and is therefore not complete or final (τελεία); you learn in order to know, are healed in order to be well. An activity or actuality in the specific sense has its end in itself; seeing, thinking, knowing, living, being happy, aim at nothing beyond themselves. Movement cannot be classed either as δύναμις or as ἐνέργεια proper. It is 'the actuality of that which is potentially, as such'—of bronze, for instance, not qua bronze but qua capable of undergoing change. This is true of all four kinds of movement or change; qualitative change, for example, is the actualization of that which is susceptible to qualitative change, just in so far as it is thus susceptible. Change is thus the actualization of something which is essentially potential, and which in being actualized does not lose this character. That is why it is ἐνέργεια ἀτελής. If the potentiality

[1] 1048ᵃ 25.   [2] 1048ᵇ 18-35.

vanished in actuality there would be no movement, only a new position.[1]

A movement takes time; when you are learning you have not yet learned, when you are being healed you have not yet been healed. An activity is complete in each moment of itself; at the same moment you see and have seen, know and have known. Or, as Aristotle puts it elsewhere, a process must be quick or slow, an activity cannot be either; you may become pleased quickly or slowly, but you cannot enjoy pleasure either quickly or slowly.[2] This distinction has important applications both in theology (in the doctrine of the divine 'activity of immobility') and in ethics (in the doctrine that neither happiness nor pleasure is a process, but an activity or its accompaniment).

Priority of Actuality.

Actuality is, according to Aristotle, prior to potentiality in more than one sense of prior.[3] (1) It is prior in definition. To be capable of being or doing so-and-so is a more complex thing than to be or do so-and-so, and can be defined only by reference to it. (2) It is, in a sense, prior in time. True, in the individual, potentiality comes before actuality, the matter out of which a man is made comes before the man, the musical faculty before its exercise. But the actual comes from the potential by the agency of something actual—and something of the same species as the product. The matter must be quickened by the male parent; the musical faculty must be developed by the instruction of a teacher in whom it has already been developed. Potentiality presupposes actuality because only that is potentially which can come to be actually and only the actual can make the potential to be actual. Aristotle adds an account of the development of faculty different from, though compatible with, that offered above. He has there found it to presuppose actuality in a teacher; he now argues that it presupposes actuality in the learner. It is only by playing a musical instrument that one acquires the faculty of playing it. At first sight this appears paradoxical, but the paradox is removed by reference to a doctrine stated in the *Physics*.[4] Of everything that is coming into being or

---

[1] *Phys.* 201ª 9–ᵇ 15, ᵇ 27—202ª 3 (K. 1065ᵇ 14—1066ª 7, 1066ª 17-26).
[2] *E. N.* 1173ª 34.   [3] Θ. 8.   [4] vi. 6.

is moving some part has already come into being or been moved. Therefore a learner must already know something of what he is learning. All learning, as Aristotle maintains in the *Posterior Analytics*,[1] comes from pre-existing knowledge. A child has not, indeed, scientific knowledge, but he has what is, Aristotle maintains, continuous in character with scientific knowledge,[2] viz. perception, which is never mere passivity, but is from the start something that judges,[3] and has universals for its object, though it be only universals immersed in particularity.[4] Thus, if we take a wide enough view, potentiality does not precede actuality, but 'actuality precedes actuality right back to the actuality of the prime mover'.[5]

(3) Actuality is prior in essence. It is the form or end to which the potentiality points, and which alone gives it its value. Or, if the ἐνέργεια point to an end beyond itself, i. e. if it be not an activity in the specific sense but a movement, it is, at least, nearer to the end than the potentiality. (4) One thing is prior to another in the strictest sense if it can exist without the other, and the other cannot exist without it.[6] Now the eternal can exist without the temporal but not *vice versa*; it is therefore prior to it. But nothing eternal exists potentially. For what has the capacity of being has also the capacity of not being, and therefore might conceivably not be, and is therefore not eternal. The *prius* of the whole universe, the prime mover, is pure actuality without any element of potentiality. And that which comes next to it, sun and stars and the outermost sphere of the heavens, has no potentiality in the fullest sense of potentiality, i.e. potentiality of not-being. It has not matter for generation and destruction but only matter for local movement, the potentiality of moving from here to there. Its eternity and the eternity of its movement is guaranteed by its nature; only the place of its movement changes. This eternity of movement is imitated even by perishable things of the terrestrial world. Here the individuals are

---

[1] 71ᵃ 1.   [2] Cf. Λ. 1, *An. Post.* ii. 19.

[3] *An. Post.* 99ᵇ 35.   [4] ib. 100ᵃ 16–ᵇ 1.

[5] 1050ᵇ 4. To this section of the argument belongs in principle the proof in 1051ᵃ 21–33 that geometrical discovery takes place through constructions latent in the given figure being actualized by an actual exercise of thought.

[6] Cf. Δ. 1019ᵃ 2–4, 11.

not eternal, but by the cyclic transformation of the elements and the succession of the generations eternity of type and eternity of movement are secured.

Further,[1] actuality is better than good potentiality. Potentiality is indifferent as between its opposite actualizations, and therefore inferior to its good actualization. For the same reason it is superior to its bad actualization. Evil therefore has no existence apart from particular evil things. Evil being posterior in nature to potentiality, and potentiality to actuality, and the original and eternal constituents of the universe being, as we have seen, actual not potential, among them neither evil nor defect nor perversion can find a place. Evils (we may perhaps expand the argument by saying) are simply by-products of the effort of terrestrial things to imitate the perfect activity of the first mover—by-products due to the presence in terrestrial things of matter or potentiality. Matter, which *is* one of the eternal constituents of the universe, is not evil but indifferent between evil and good; and form, the other eternal constituent of the universe, is in itself good.

With this suggestive, if rather too easy, argument for optimism, which brings us up to the threshold of the doctrine of Book Λ, our survey of the general metaphysical doctrine may close.[2]

IV

ARISTOTLE'S THEOLOGY

Book Λ is rightly regarded as the coping-stone of the *Metaphysics*. Aristotle has given the name of 'theology' to the highest of the sciences, the science of that kind of being which combines substantial, independent existence with freedom from all change ;[3] and it is in this book that we find his only systematic

---

[1] 1051ᵃ 4–21.

[2] The remainder of Θ. 9 belongs rather to the proof of the temporal priority of actuality, and Θ. 10 does not properly belong to the scheme of the book. Cf. Introduction, p. xxx.

[3] E. 1026ᵃ 10–19, K. 1064ᵃ 33–ᵇ 3.

essay in theology.   There are passages in his other works which throw valuable light on his theological views, and others in which he is clearly accommodating himself to the views of his age.[1] He seems to have put forward in his earlier writings 'proofs of the existence of God' quite different from that which we find in Λ. In the dialogue *De Philosophia* he is reported to have given what may be called an anticipation of the ontological argument ; 'where there is a better', he argued, 'there is a best; now among existing things one is better than another ; therefore there is a best, which must be the divine'.[2]   Nor did he fail to use the teleological argument.   In the same dialogue he pictured a race of men confronted for the first time with the beauty of earth and sea, the majesty of the sun and moon and the starry heavens, and drawing the inevitable conclusion that these mighty works proceed from gods.[3]   Dreams, premonitions,[4] and animal instinct[5] were further used by him as evidence for the belief in gods.   But in his extant works, which express his maturer views, adaptation is usually ascribed to the unconscious teleology of nature rather than to the working out of a divine plan.

In Λ, however, we find him, in the maturity of his powers, arguing for the existence of a God so remote from popular religious ideas that no element of accommodation to the intelligence or the prejudices of his audience is to be suspected ;[6] and arguing, further, from principles that are deep-seated in his

---

[1] These can often be recognized by a reference to ' gods ' in the plural. Cf. *E. N.* 1099[b] 11, 1162[a] 5, 1179[a] 25.

[2] Fr. 1476[b] 22-24.   [3] Fr. 1476[a] 34-[b] 11.   Cf. [a] 11-32.

[4] Fr. 1475[b] 36 — 1476[a] 9.   [5] Cic. *de N. D.* ii. 49. 125.

[6] In Aristotle's conception of God's *modus operandi*, however, there are elements due to popular preconceptions.   Man has always tended to connect the divine with what is distant and what is high above him, and accordingly Aristotle thinks of the stars as 'the most divine of phenomena', and regards the prime mover as acting directly on the outermost sphere of the universe and only very indirectly on the earth.   Again, the description of circular movement as the first movement is due to a prejudice in favour of what is simple and is at the same time free from the 'contrarieties' of up and down which characterize rectilinear movement. In thinking of the world as infinite and of rectilinear motion as the primary kind of motion the Atomists were more truly scientific than Aristotle.

metaphysics. The argument, which is a special form of the 'cosmological' argument for the existence of God, the argument *a contingentia mundi*, pursues a somewhat tortuous course, but may be set out as follows.[1] Substances are the first of existing things.[2] Therefore if all substances are perishable, all things are perishable.[3] But there are two things which are imperishable, as they are ingenerable, change and time. Time must be so, since apart from time there is no before and after.[4] And change must be equally continuous with time; for time is either the same as, or a concomitant of, change.[5] Now the only continuous change is change of place,[6] and the only continuous change of place is circular motion.[7] There must therefore be an eternal circular motion.[8]

Now to produce eternal motion there must be (1) eternal substance. So far the Platonic Forms would suffice. But (2) this eternal substance must have in it a principle capable of causing motion, which the Forms have not.[9] (3) It must not only have this power but exercise it. (4) Its essence must be not power

[1] The first chapter of Alexander's Ἀπορίαι καὶ λύσεις is a proof on Aristotelian lines of the existence of a prime mover. It does not, however, follow Aristotle's proof very closely.

[2] Aristotle's arguments to prove this are found in Z. 1, Λ. 1069ᵃ 19-26. Substance is that which underlies all other entities, which are in the end but attributes of substance.

[3] For suppose something to exist when all substances have perished; this could only be an attribute which was the attribute of nothing—a contradiction in terms.

[4] While if we say time had a beginning or an end, we must say that *before* the beginning or *after* the end time is not. A slightly different proof of the eternity of time is given in *Phys.* 251ᵇ 19-26.

[5] Time is, according to Aristotle, 'the number of change in respect of before and after' (*Phys.* 219ᵇ 1, 220ᵃ 24, ᵇ 8, 223ᵃ 33, *De Caelo* 279ᵃ 14). The eternity of change, which is here inferred from that of time, is proved independently in *Phys.* 250ᵇ 23—251ᵇ 10.

[6] For all other changes are between opposites, and since a thing cannot have opposite movements at the same time, it must rest at the opposites which form the limits of its movement (*Phys.* 261ᵃ 31-ᵇ 26).

[7] For all other changes of place are from opposite to opposite, and therefore subject to the objection indicated in the previous note (*Phys.* 261ᵇ 27—263ᵃ 3, 264ᵃ 7—265ᵃ 12).

[8] 1071ᵇ 4-11.

[9] This is argued in A. 991ᵃ 8-11, ᵇ 3-9, 992ᵃ 29-32, Z. 1033ᵇ 26—1034ᵃ 5.

but activity, for otherwise it would be possible for it sometime not to exercise this power, and change would not be eternal. (5) These substances [1] must be immaterial, since they must be eternal.[2]

Aristotle now turns aside to meet the objection that since what acts must be able to act, while that which is able to act need not necessarily act, power is prior to actuality, and to refer to previous views on this question.[3] He considers that he can meet this objection, and points to experience as showing that there is something that moves with an unceasing circular motion, viz. the starry heavens. He then passes [4] to a further consideration of the prime mover. Since the sphere of the fixed stars moves, there must be something that moves it. Now that which moves and is moved is an intermediate with which we cannot rest content; there must be something that moves without being moved.[5]

This, the last term to which we come in the explanation of change, is the eternal, substantial, purely actual being whose existence he has already proved. The new feature which he has now discovered is its immobility, which might have been inferred directly from its already proved immateriality, since motion involves ὕλη τοπική.

Now, how can anything cause motion without being moved? The physical causation of movement implies the mutual contact of mover and moved, and therefore a reaction of the moved on the mover.[6] The unmoved mover must therefore cause motion

---

[1] Aristotle here for the first time suggests a plurality of moving principles, referring to the 'intelligences' that move the planetary spheres.

[2] 1071^b 12–22. The ground of the last assertion is that matter involves potentiality.

[3] 1071^b 22—1072^a 18.   [4] 1072^a 23.

[5] Aristotle's reason for refusing to be content, as Plato was, with the notion of a self-mover, is that in so far as it moves, it must already have a certain character, while in so far as it is moved, it must have that character only potentially, and actually not have it. E. g. that which warms itself must be warm in order to impart warmth, and cold in order to receive it. The law of contradiction, therefore, forces us to analyse the self-warming into a part which is warm and a part which is cold, i. e. self-imposed change turns out to be change imposed by one thing on another (*Phys.* 257^a 31–^{b} 13).

[6] *Phys.* 202^a 3–7.

in a non-physical way, by being an object of desire. An un-moved mover, according to Aristotle, touches what it moves without being touched by it, but in such a case ' touch ' is being used in a merely metaphorical sense, as is shown by the example which he gives : ' we say sometimes that he who hurts us touches us without our touching him.'[1] Yet the causation of motion by the prime mover is sometimes described as having a quasi-physical character ; for the first mover is said not only to operate directly on the outer sphere of the universe, and only indirectly on the inner spheres, but actually to be at the outside of the universe ;[2] this, however, is an incautious expression which should not be pressed. Aristotle's genuine view undoubtedly is that the prime mover is not in space.[3]

There has been much controversy over the question whether God is for Aristotle only the final cause, or the efficient cause as well, of change. There can be no doubt about the answer. ' Efficient cause ' is simply the translation of Aristotle's ἀρχὴ τῆς κινήσεως, and God is certainly this. The truth is that the opposition of οὗ ἕνεκα to ἀρχὴ κινήσεως is not a well-chosen one. The οὗ ἕνεκα is one kind of ἀρχὴ κινήσεως. The cause of movement may be either (1) an end aimed at, or (2) a force operating a tergo, which may be (a) a physical force, or (b) a mental force, an act of will. What Aristotle does imply is that God's causation is not of either of the two latter types. It cannot be inferred, from the fact that Aristotle describes God as exercising infinite power,[4] that he thinks of Him as an efficient cause of type 2 (b) ; the statement that He causes motion as an object of desire or of love is too explicit for that. Yet He is not an end existing merely in the future ; He exists eternally and thus differs from a merely imagined and anticipated ideal.[5]

The argument is complicated by the fact that the object of knowledge also is described[6] as moving without being moved. It is not, however, meant that the object of knowledge as such causes movement in space. The doctrine is that all existing

---

[1] De Gen. et Corr. 323ᵃ 25-33.

[2] Phys. 267ᵇ 6-9.   [3] De Caelo 279ᵃ 18.

[4] 1073ᵃ 7, Phys. 267ᵇ 22.

[5] Though Prof. Alexander's view of Deity has affinities with Aristotle's, it is in this respect fundamentally different.

[6] 1072ᵃ 26.

things may be arranged in two sets—a column of positives and a column of negatives. Of these the positives are the direct object of knowledge; the negatives are known only as the opposites of the positives. Among the positives, substances come first, and of substances the first is incomposite, fully actual substance, i. e. the kind of being that we have found to be implied as the first cause of movement. But this is not only the primary object of knowledge, the most intelligible of all things ; it is also the most desirable. The knowledge of it inevitably produces desire for it, love of it. And by the desire it inspires it sets the world in motion. What the object of knowledge *as such* 'moves' is simply the mind, and this it moves not to physical action but to thought.[1]

The prime mover moves directly, as we have seen, the 'first heaven'; i.e. it causes the daily rotation of the stars round the earth. Since it moves by inspiring love and desire, it seems to be implied that the 'first heaven' is capable of feeling love and desire, i.e. has soul. And this is confirmed by what Aristotle says elsewhere; the first heaven, the planets, and the sun and moon are all thought of as living beings.[2] The further causal action of the prime mover is somewhat obscure. The motions of the sun, moon, and planets are explained by the hypothesis of a 'nest' of concentric spheres, each with its poles fixed in the shell of the sphere next outside it. Thus each sphere imparts its own motion to the sphere next inside it, and the prime mover, by moving the outermost sphere directly, moves all the other spheres indirectly.[3] It causes the sun to move round the earth once in twenty-four hours, and thus produces the rhythm of day and night, and everything in terrestrial life for which that is responsible. But the rhythm of the seasons, with its consequences of seed-time and harvest and of the breeding-times of animals, is more important in the terrestrial economy, and this is due not,

---

[1] 1072ª 27-ᵇ 1.   [2] *De Caelo* 285ª 29, 292ª 20, ᵇ 1.

[3] The cosmology is confused at this point. If motion is thus transmitted from sphere to sphere, the daily revolution of the sun, moon, and planets is sufficiently explained by the motion transmitted from the outermost sphere (the 'first heaven') to all inside it ; the outermost of the spheres assigned to each of the seven moving bodies (which has this same motion), and the 'intelligences' which move these outermost spheres, become unnecessary.

or not in the same way, to the prime mover, but to the 'intelligences' (as the schoolmen called them) of which Aristotle
recognizes 55 (or 47)[1] as coexisting with the prime mover. In
particular, generation and destruction are due to the sun's motion
in the ecliptic, which is due to one of the 'intelligences'; generation at any particular place tends to occur when the sun is near
that part of the earth, and destruction when it has receded from
it.[2] The 'intelligences', like the first mover, move 'as ends',[3]
i. e. they too move by inspiring desire or love. Their relation
to the prime mover is nowhere specified, but if Aristotle is in
earnest, as he certainly is, in describing the first mover as moving
all things, as that on which the universe and nature depend, and
in insisting on a single ruler of the universe,[4] we must suppose
that the first mover moves the intelligences. And since they
are immaterial this movement will not be physical movement but
the metaphorical 'movement' of desire and love. It will move
them ὡς ἐρώμενον.[5]

If Aristotle's language be taken strictly, then, we have a very
complicated system :

(1) The prime mover.

(2) 55 intelligences actuated by love of the first mover.

(3) The soul of the 'first heaven', actuated by love of the first
mover.

(4) The souls of the 55 spheres, actuated by love of the 55
intelligences respectively.

(5) The 'first heaven', moved by its soul.

(6) The 55 spheres, moved by their souls.

It is unlikely that Aristotle contemplated all this complication.
He nowhere explicitly distinguishes the soul of the first heaven
from God, nor the souls of the spheres from the intelligences.
Averroes and Zabarella identify the form or soul of the first
heaven with the prime mover, and the souls of the spheres with
the intelligences.[6] In so far as God and the intelligences
are the final causes of the spheres which they respectively
move, they are in the normal relation of soul to body, and it

---

[1] 1074ᵃ 11, 13.   [2] *De Gen. et Corr.* 336ᵃ 32, ᵇ 6.   [3] 1074ᵃ 23.

[4] 1070ᵇ 34, 1072ᵇ 13, 1076ᵃ 5.

[5] So Alexander : μεθέξει καὶ τῷ βουλήματι τοῦ πρώτου καὶ μακαριωτάτου
ἐξήρτηται νοός (721. 32).

[6] Zabarella, *De Reb. Nat.*, De Natura Coeli, ch. vi.

might be that in his doctrine of God and the intelligences
Aristotle is bringing into greater distinctness the doctrine of the
De Caelo that the heavenly bodies have life and action.   But if
this be so, the description of God as acting by being the object
of love and desire is simply metaphorical ; it is not the soul of
the first heaven that desires God (for on this view God *is* the
soul of the first heaven), but the first heaven itself.   And
this will be an instance of the desire which matter in general
is, by a bold metaphor, said to have for form.[1]   But in Aristotle's system, taken strictly, matter does not desire form nor
strive towards it ; it has no bias towards form rather than
towards the privation of form ; it is purely passive.   Further,
to regard God as the soul of the first heaven is to regard Him
as controlling it as a soul does its body, by acts of will, and
this would conflict with Aristotle's description of the divine
life as one of pure thought.   It seems preferable to suppose that in Λ 'desire' and 'love' are used in no merely metaphorical sense, and therefore that life and soul are seriously
ascribed to the spheres ;[2] these are living beings which aim at
realizing in their own measure the perfect being enjoyed in full
by God and the intelligences.   The complication of the scheme
of entities set out above should not, then, be diminished by
identifying God with the soul of the 'first heaven' and the intelligences with the souls of the planetary spheres.   The scheme
is simplified in a more satisfactory way if we do not regard the
first heaven and its soul, the planetary spheres and their souls,
as separate entities, but each of the spheres as forming with its
soul a single composite living being.[3]

How, we may ask, does love or desire for the prime mover
produce the physical movements that have to be explained ?
The theory is that each of these unities of soul and body desires
a life as like as possible to that of its moving principle.   The life
of its moving principle is a continuous unchanging activity of

---

[1] *Phys.* 192ᵃ 16-23.

[2] So Aristotle says that motion is a sort of ζωή τοῖς φύσει συνεστῶσι
πᾶσιν, *Phys.* 250ᵇ 14, and that in a sense all things are full of soul, *G. A.*
762ᵃ 21.

[3] Cf. Plut. *Plac.* 881 E, F Ἀριστοτέλης . . . ἑκάστην οἴεται τῶν σφαιρῶν
ζῷον εἶναι σύνθετον ἐκ σώματος καὶ ψυχῆς, ὧν τὸ μὲν σῶμά ἐστιν αἰθέριον κινούμενον κυκλοφορικῶς, ἡ ψυχὴ δὲ λόγος ἀκίνητος αἴτιος τῆς κινήσεως κατ' ἐνέργειαν.

pure thought (with the addition, we must suppose, in the case of
the intelligences, of love of the prime mover). The spheres
cannot reproduce this, but they do the next best by performing
the only perfectly continuous physical movement, viz. movement
in a circle.[1] Circular movement, which in fact involves constant
change of direction, was thought of by Aristotle as involving no
change of direction, and rectilinear movement, the only kind
which really involves no change of direction, was for him ruled
out by the fact that if it is to be continuous it requires infinite
space, in which he disbelieved.[2]

If the spheres are actuated by love of their moving principles
and these by love of the first mover, the questions may be asked,
why should the first heaven move (1) in the direction in which,
and (2) with the speed with which, it actually moves, and, supposing there are reasons for this, (3) why do not all the other spheres
move in the same direction and with the same speed? Aristotle's
answer to the first question is purely anthropomorphic. The
right being the stronger and controlling half of the body, it is
proper that the heavens should move towards the right, i. e.
counter-clockwise.[3] And as they to all appearance move clock-
wise, he has to suppose that not their north but their south pole
is the 'upper' part of the heavens.[4] To the second and the
third question he has no answer. Certain directions and certain
speeds must be assumed if we are to 'save the appearances', to
explain the observed facts; but no teleological explanation of
them is offered. On the other hand, he tries hard to show
how all the changes observed on the earth, changes in position,
quality, and size, flow, as on his theory they must, from the
movements of the spheres,[5] and ultimately from the prime mover.
The heavenly bodies,[6] and particularly the sun,[7] by their approach
to any particular region of the earth produce heat, and by their
withdrawal cold, and thus cause a constant transmutation of the
elements into one another, since heat and cold are two, and the

[1] κινεῖται καὶ ἠρεμεῖ πως ἡ σφαῖρα, *Phys.* 265ᵇ 1.
[2] ib. 265ᵃ 17.
[3] *De Caelo* 288ᵃ 2–12.
[4] ib. 285ᵇ 19.
[5] *Meteor.* 339ᵃ 21–32.
[6] ib. 340ᵇ 10, *De Caelo* 289ᵃ 19–33, *G. A.* 777ᵇ 16—778ᵃ 3.
[7] *Meteor.* 341ᵃ 19, 346ᵇ 20, 354ᵇ 26, *De Gen. et Corr.* 336ᵃ 15–ᵇ 9.

more important two,[1] of the four qualities that characterize
the elements.   If it were not for this constant change of temperature the elements would once for all move to their proper regions
and remain there.[2]

Thus the heavenly bodies produce not only the generation and
destruction, but also the local movements, that are observed
upon the earth ; and the never-ending ebb and flow of movement,
the perpetuation of species as birth repairs the ravages of death,
are the nearest approach which sublunary things, containing as
they do matter for generation and destruction, for qualitative and
quantitative change, as well as for local movement, can make to
the eternal local movement of the heavenly bodies,[3] just as this
in turn is the nearest approach which things that possess ὕλη
τοπική can make to the eternal thought of the pure forms, God
and the intelligences.

Aristotle's recognition of unmoved movers other than the
prime mover involves three difficulties.   (1) In 1074ᵃ 25–31 each
of the celestial movements is said to be ' for the sake of the stars '.
Why then should the intelligences be described as the ends of
these movements ?[4] The answer is that the former are the end
in the sense of the τινί, that for whose good the movements
exist, while the latter are the end in the sense of the τινὸς ἕνεκα,
the ideal at which the movements aim.[5] The movements exist
for the sake of realizing for the stars a mode of activity as like
as possible to that of the intelligences. (2) In 1074ᵃ 31–38
Aristotle argues that the universe must be one since otherwise its
moving principles would be many, and this they cannot be since
they contain no matter to distinguish them from one another.
But the intelligences *are* different from one another and from
God, though they contain no matter, being unchangeable [6] and
without magnitude.[7] It might be suggested that they are pure
forms *specifically* different, each of them being the sole member
of a separate species, as some of the schoolmen maintained that
the angels are.[8] But (*a*) at that rate there might be specifically

---

[1] *Meteor.* 378ᵇ 10-20.   [2] *De Gen. et Corr.* 337ᵃ 7-15.
[3] *De Gen. et Corr.* 336ᵇ 9-19, 26—337ᵃ 7, 338ᵃ 17-ᵇ 19.
[4] 1074ᵃ 23.   [5] 1072ᵇ 2.   [6] 1073ᵃ 33.   [7] ib. 38.
[8] St. Anselm even used language which, by denying that angels constituted a genus like the *genus humanum*, might seem to make each *sui
generis*. But he wrote before the full development of Aristotelian influence made theologians careful in the use of such expressions, and he

different *prime* movers, and Aristotle's argument for the unity of the universe would break down. And (*b*) this way of escape is not open to Aristotle ; for he holds that specific difference implies *a fortiori* numerical difference,[1] which implies matter.[2] The difficulty is an instance of a wider one; if difference implies matter, how does one species differ from another ? The solution, in Aristotelian terms, lies in the doctrine that the genus is the ὕλη νοητή of its species (H. 1045ᵃ 34, Δ. 1024ᵇ 8, Z. 1038ᵃ 6). It is implied that a different portion of this ὕλη νοητή is realized in each species, and that this accounts for the difference of the species. The intelligences, then, will be forms but not pure forms, since they contain an element of matter though not of ' sensible matter '. In this they differ from the first mover.

(3) If, as seems possible, Aristotle regarded the intelligences as actuated by love of the first mover, this itself implies an element of potentiality in them, since they are moved by desire of something which they themselves are not. This implies something quasi-material in them which is not in God.

The intelligences are not mentioned elsewhere in Aristotle. They, and the parallel to them in Plato's somewhat similar theory,[3] reflect (in a form congenial to the philosophy of Plato and Aristotle) the traditional Polytheism in Greek religion, as Plato's ' best soul ' and Aristotle's prime mover reflect the Monarchian element in it and the belief in the supremacy of Zeus. But as in Christian times Monarchianism was the dominant tendency in Greek theology, the tendency which led to the severance between the Eastern and the Western church, so too it is a monistic system which at bottom Aristotle tries to maintain ; and into such a system the intelligences do not really fit.

There can be only one pure form, the first mover or God. The celestial spheres should, to be consistent with Aristotle's fundamental view, have been represented as living beings striving each in its degree to reproduce the unchanging life of the

was concerned not to expound a view of the nature of the angels for its own sake, but only to explain why the fallen angels could not be redeemed, like men, by God taking the nature of them all at once as He did that of all men at once in the incarnation. St. Thomas held the angels to be specifically but not generically different ; Duns Scotus held that not every angel was even specifically different from every other.

[1] Δ. 1016ᵇ 36. [2] 1074ᵃ 33. [3] *Laws* 899.

prime mover, without the intermediary of subordinate moving principles.

It is now time to turn to the way in which the prime mover itself is depicted. We have already seen that it is pure form and pure actuality, the primary object of knowledge and of desire. We must say of it not that it has, but that it is, a life such as the best that we can for brief periods enjoy.[1] This activity is at the same time pleasure ; indeed waking, perceiving, knowing are the pleasantest things in the world just because they are activities. All physical activity being excluded by the immaterial nature of the first mover, Aristotle can only ascribe to it mental activity, and only that kind of mental activity which owes nothing to the body, viz. knowledge ; and only that kind of knowledge which does not grasp conclusions by the aid of premises but is direct, intuitive (νόησις) ; i. e. the prime mover is not only form and actuality, but mind, and hence the term God, which has not so far appeared, begins to be applied to it.[2]

Now knowledge in itself, i. e. when not dependent, as in man, on sense and imagination, is of that which is in itself best, and knowledge in the fullest sense of that which is in the fullest sense best. But that which is in the fullest sense best is, as we have seen, God. The object of God's knowledge is therefore God Himself. 'Now mind does know itself, by participation in the known ; it becomes known by touching and knowing, so that the same thing is mind and object of mind '.[3] No light is thrown here on how this happens, but we may interpret the meaning thus : In νόησις mind is as it were in direct contact with its object (θιγγάνων) ; it is not then knowing one thing by means of another as middle term. Just as in sensation Aristotle supposes the sensible form to be as it were carried over into the mind, leaving the matter behind,[4] so in knowledge he supposes the intelligible form to be carried over. And the character of mind is to have no character of its own but to be characterized entirely by what at the moment it knows ; if it had a character of its own, that would interfere with the perfect reproduction of the object in the knowing mind, as a mirror with a colour of its own reproduces less perfectly the colour of the mirrored object.[5]

---

[1] 1072^{b} 14.   [2] ib. 25.   [3] ib. 20.
[4] *De An.* 424^{a} 18.   [5] ib. 429^{a} 13-22.

Thus in knowledge mind and its object have an identical character, and to know an object is to know one's own mind as it is when it knows the object.

This explanation of self-consciousness, difficult and unsatisfactory as it is, is intended primarily to explain the self-consciousness which accompanies awareness of an object. Consider the language : ἑαυτὸν δὲ νοεῖ ὁ νοῦς κατὰ μετάληψιν τοῦ νοητοῦ· νοητὸς γὰρ γίγνεται θιγγάνων καὶ νοῶν, ὥστε ταὐτὸν νοῦς καὶ νοητόν. It is in and by knowing, sc. something else, that mind *becomes* object of mind. We must not suppose that what it knows primarily is itself, or what is offered as an explanation of its becoming its own object turns into a *petitio principii*. But what Aristotle ascribes to God is knowledge which has *only* itself for its object. νόησις is expressly contrasted with ἐπιστήμη, αἴσθησις, δόξα, διάνοια, each of which is αἰεὶ ἄλλου, and ἑαυτῆς only ἐν παρέργῳ.[1]

An attempt has been made to render Aristotle's conception of the divine knowledge more tolerable by exhibiting it as being, conversely to ordinary knowledge, of itself directly and of the world ἐν παρέργῳ. *Nec tamen sequitur*, says St. Thomas, *quod omnia alia a se ei sunt ignota; nam intellegendo se intellegit omnia alia.*[2] Many others of the schoolmen express the same view, and Brentano tries to support it by reference to a passage[3] in which Aristotle says that the knowledge of correlatives is the same. All things other than God owe their being entirely to God, so that God's self-knowledge must be at the same time a knowledge of all other things. This is a possible and a fruitful line of thought, but it is not that which Aristotle actually adopts. For him, that God should know Himself, and that He should know other things, are alternatives,[4] and in affirming the first alternative he implicitly denies the second. Indeed he denies explicitly much that the second would involve ; he denies to God all knowledge of evil, and all transition from one object of thought to another.[5] The result of this wish to exclude from the divine life any relation to evil and any 'shadow of turning' is the impossible and barren ideal of a knowledge with no object but itself.[6]

---

[1] 1074ᵇ 35.

[2] *In Met.* lib. xii, lect. xi.

[3] *Top.* 105ᵇ 31–34.

[4] 1074ᵇ 22.

[5] ib. 25, 32, 26.

[6] Dr. Caird's view, in his illuminating chapter on Aristotle's theology (*Evolution of Theology in the Greek Philosophers*, ii. 1–30), that Aristotle

This, then, is Aristotle's conception of the life of God ; every activity but knowledge is excluded, and all knowledge except the knowledge of His own knowledge. The relation of God to the world is twofold ; He is the primary object of knowledge and the primary object of desire. We have considered the latter relation ; we now turn to the former. Aristotle's description of God as the πρῶτον νοητόν should be considered in connexion with the doctrine of ' active reason '.

The famous doctrine of the active reason, perhaps the most obscure and certainly the most discussed of all Aristotle's doctrines, is stated in a single chapter of the *De Anima*,[1] and with such brevity that much is left to the intelligence of the reader. 'There must be', says Aristotle, 'within the soul a distinction answering to the general distinction between the matter which underlies each class of things and is potentially each of them, and the efficient cause which makes them—the distinction of which that between an art and its material is an instance.' Two points are here to be noticed. (1) The distinction between the active and the passive reason falls within the soul.[2] This is fatal to any interpretation which identifies the active reason with a divine reason falling entirely outside the individual human being. It is not fatal to the view that the active reason is a divine reason immanent in human souls. The chief difficulty to which such a view is exposed is that the only passage in which Aristotle deals explicitly with the divine nature—Book Λ of the *Metaphysics*—describes God in language which is quite unsuggestive of immanence. (2) The active reason is not a reason which creates out of nothing. It works on a material given to it, which it promotes from potentiality into actuality.[3] What is

ascribes to God a self-consciousness ' which is at the same time a consciousness of the ideal order of the world ' (p. 22), seems to me to take insufficient account of definite statements in Λ.

[1] iii. 5. Good accounts of the various interpretations may be seen in Hicks's ed. of the *De Anima*, lxiv-lxix ; Adamson, *Development of Gk. Phil.* 249-254 ; Webb, *Studies in the Hist. of Nat. Theol.* 264-273.

[2] ἐν τῇ ψυχῇ might conceivably mean only ' in the case of the soul '. But a temporary union of the two reasons within one personality is implied by χωρισθείς l. 22. So, too, Theophrastus says (ap. Them. 108. 23) μεικτὸν γάρ πως ὁ νοῦς ἔκ τε τοῦ ποιητικοῦ καὶ τοῦ δυνάμει.

[3] So Theophrastus describes active νοῦς as ὁ κινῶν, that which sets passive νοῦς to work (ap. Prisc. 29. 14, ap. Them. 108. 24).

meant by this we must try to see from the sequel. 'The one reason', Aristotle proceeds, 'is analogous to matter because it becomes all things ; the other is analogous to the efficient cause because it makes all things.' The first of these statements points to the ordinary activity of apprehension. Just as, according to Aristotle, the sensitive faculty becomes its objects in the sense that their form is, so to say, conveyed over to the sensitive subject and becomes the whole content, the whole nature for the time being, of the sensitive subject, so in knowledge reason becomes identical with its objects. Their whole nature is in some sense in the mind, and there is nothing in the mind except them. The act of apprehension is ascribed, then, to passive reason. What is the rôle that is ascribed to active reason ? In what sense does it make all things ? If we attend to the analogy of art and its material, we notice that art makes its objects by making the material into them. And if the analogy is meant to be exact, we must conclude that the rôle of active reason is to make passive reason *become* its own objects by apprehending them. We shall see here an instance of Aristotle's general principle that ' what is potentially comes to be actually by the agency of something that already is actually '.[1] It is obvious that we come to know things which in the ordinary sense we did not know before. How, Aristotle asks himself, can this happen ? Does not this transition from potential to actual knowledge imply that there is something in us that actually knows already, some element which is cut off from our ordinary consciousness so that we are not aware of this pre-existing knowledge, but which is nevertheless in some sort of communication with the ordinary consciousness or passive reason and leads this on to knowledge ? And when Aristotle refers [2] to the moments in which we can live a life like that of God, he will (on this interpretation) be thinking of moments in which the partition between active and passive reason is broken down and we become aware of our oneness with the principle whose knowledge is always actual and always complete.

According to this line of thought, what the active reason acts on is the passive reason, which is a sort of plastic material on which active reason impresses the forms of knowable objects.

[1] *Met.* 1049ᵇ 24.
[2] *Met.* 1072ᵇ 14, 24, *E. N.* 1177ᵇ 26—1178ᵃ 8, 1178ᵇ 18–32.

But in the same sentence Aristotle introduces another line of thought, which seems to have been suggested by Plato's use of the sun as a symbol for the Idea of Good (*Rep.* 507 B–509 D). The one reason is analogous to matter by becoming all things, the other is analogous to the efficient cause by making all things, in the manner of a positive state like light; for in a sense light makes the potentially existing colours actually existing colours. Some of the conditions of colour are present in the dark, but to make actual seen colours a further condition is necessary, viz. light; and active reason is to the intelligible as light is to the visible. The analogy of light must not be pressed too closely. Light, according to Aristotle, is the functioning-as-transparent of the medium that stretches between the eye and its object;[1] it is by directly producing change in the transparent medium that the object indirectly produces change in the eye and comes to be seen.[2] Active reason is not to be thus thought of as a medium between passive reason and its object; knowledge is a direct not a mediate relation, in Aristotle's view. The analogy is a more general one. Though not a medium, active reason is a third thing, besides passive reason and the object, which has to be taken account of if we would understand the fact of knowledge, as light is a third thing, besides the eye and the object, which we must take account of if we would understand the fact of sight.

Both active reason and light are said to operate as positive states (ὡς ἕξις τις). The expression is not strictly accurate. Both are strictly 'activities' and are described as such.[3] A 'positive state' is properly something intermediate between a potentiality and an activity. But the contrast here thought of is that between positive state and potentiality. Light is the condition of a medium which has already been made actually transparent by the presence of an illuminant,[4] and it is its actuality that makes it possible for the eye which *can* see actually *to* see, and for the visible object actually to be seen. Similarly, the fact that active reason already knows all intelligible objects makes it possible for the passive reason, in itself a potentiality, actually to know, and for the knowable actually to be known.

'The active reason', Aristotle continues, 'is separable and impassive and unmixed, being' (i. e. because it is) 'an actuality.

---

[1] *De An.* 418[b] 9, 419[a] 11.   [2] 419[a] 10.
[3] 430[a] 18, 418[b] 9, 419[a] 11.   [4] 418[b] 12.

For the active is always of higher worth than the passive, and the originative source than the matter.' The meaning of 'separable' here is to be gathered from the occurrence later of the expression 'when it has been separated'. It means that the active reason, united for a certain time with the passive, can be separated from it, and the reference is clearly to the destruction, at death, of the latter and the survival of the former. Else-where [1] Aristotle speaks of 'reason', simply, as surviving death, but that is where the distinction between active and passive reason is not present to his mind; when it is present he evidently thinks of the passive reason as being, like the lower faculties of sense and imagination, an integral part of the soul which is the actuality of a particular body and cannot survive it. The other phrases used, in this sentence, of active reason call for no special comment. They emphasize the facts that it is entirely in-dependent of the body and that it contains no unrealized potentialities but knows always what it ever knows.

'Actual knowledge', Aristotle proceeds, 'is identical with its object; potential knowledge is prior in time in the individual, but in general it is not prior in time, but reason does not at one time function and at another not.' We have seen above that in some sense active reason is 'in the soul', but we certainly are not conscious of it, or are so only in moments of illumination; thus, in some sense, in the individual potential knowledge comes before actual knowledge. But 'on the whole' it does not; active reason knows actually when passive reason as yet knows only potentially. It is clearly implied that active reason, though it is in the soul, goes beyond the individual; we may fairly suppose Aristotle to mean that it is identical in all individuals.

'When it has been separated it is only that which it is essentially, and this alone is immortal and eternal (we do not remember, however, because this is impassive but the passive reason is perishable); and without this nothing thinks.' Though active reason is always impassive and unmixed, it is implied that its true nature is somewhat obscured during its association with the body, but exists in its purity when this association is over. Does this imply that the disembodied reason is conscious, as the embodied reason is not, of the full extent of its knowledge?

The perplexing remark 'we do not remember' receives some

[1] *Met.* 1070^a 26.

light from a passage earlier in the book, in which Aristotle is
speaking of the influence of old age on the mental life.[1] ' Intuitive thought and contemplation, then, die away through the
destruction of something else within ' (i. e. within the body), ' but
are themselves impassive. But reasoning, and loving or hating,
are affections not of reason but of its possessor, in so far as he
possesses it. Hence when he perishes there is neither memory
nor love ; for these belonged not to reason but to the composite being which has perished ; reason is doubtless something
more divine and is impassive.' In the light of that passage it
seems clear [2] that Aristotle here means that memory does not
survive death. The reason is that (1) active reason is impassive ;
it takes no impress from the circumstances of life ; its knowledge has therefore no marks of date or circumstance : while
(2) the passive reason which does take the impress of circumstances has perished at the death of the individual.

The last words of the chapter, καὶ ἄνευ τούτου οὐθὲν νοεῖ, are
capable of a great variety of interpretations, viz. :

(1) ' and without the passive reason the active reason thinks
nothing.'

(2) ' and without the active reason the passive reason thinks
nothing.'

(3) ' and without the passive reason nothing thinks.'

(4) ' and without the active reason nothing thinks.'

It can easily be seen that on none of these interpretations do
these words properly form part of the ground for our 'not re-
membering '. Probably οὐ μνημονεύομεν . . . φθαρτός is parStateti-
cal, and the final words go with what precedes the parenthesis.
They then sum up the teaching of the chapter by saying ' and
without the active reason nothing thinks '.

Alexander identifies the active reason with God, and this view
is adopted by Zabarella, whose argument [3] may be summarized
as follows : ' The active reason is clearly stated to exist entirely
apart from matter.[4] Now in Λ, the only place where Aristotle
discusses *ex professo* what pure immaterial forms there are, the
only such forms that he recognizes are God and the intelligences.
The active reason cannot be any of these inferior beings, for these

---

[1] 408ᵇ 24-30.
[2] Though the point has been much disputed.
[3] *De Reb. Nat.*, De mente agente, capp. 12, 13.   [4] 430ᵃ 17.

have, apparently, the sole function of moving their respective
spheres. The active reason, then, must be God, who as the
πρῶτον νοητόν¹ is the source of intelligibility in all other intelligibles. It is God, then, as active reason, that makes the
potential object of knowledge an actual object of knowledge,
and at the same time enables the passive reason, which in itself
has only the potentiality of knowledge, actually to know, just as
(to use the image which Aristotle borrows from Plato ²) the light
of the sun causes the potentially visible to be actually visible
and the potentially seeing eye actually to see.'

Zabarella's opinion is always worthy of the most serious attention. But it would seem that in his zeal to get a perfect agreement
between the *De Anima* and Λ he has put a somewhat unnatural
interpretation on the former work. The active reason is distinctly presented there as existing in the human soul. And
χωριστός, which he takes to mean 'separate', more probably
means 'separable'; the mode of being of active reason during
the life of the individual seems to be contrasted with its state
when it exists χωρισθείς, presumably after the death of the
individual. Further, it is difficult to suppose with Zabarella
that it is in its character as νοητόν rather than as νοῶν that it
is represented as making the individual's knowledge possible.

A representation of God in the *De Anima* as immanent in the
individual would not necessarily be inconsistent with the representation of Him as also transcendent. But a description of Him
as having all our knowledge before we have it, and imparting it
to us, would be inconsistent with the description of Him in Λ as
knowing only Himself. It is possible that this inconsistency
exists—that the two books represent divergent modes of Aristotle's
thought about the Deity. But it is not necessary to suppose
this. Aristotle makes no actual mention of God in this passage
of the *De Anima*, and though the pure never-ceasing activity of
thought there described is in some respects like that ascribed to
God in the *Metaphysics*, Aristotle probably did not identify the
two. It is more probable that he believed in a hierarchy reaching
continuously from the lowest beings, those most immersed in
matter, up to man, the heavenly bodies, the intelligences, and
God ; the active reason in man being one of the highest members
of this hierarchy but having others as well as God above it.

¹ 1072ᵃ 26-32.   ² *De An.* 430ᵃ 15.

This is the interpretation of the *De Anima* to which the purely deistic doctrine of Λ points.

The conception of God presented in Λ is certainly an unsatisfactory one. God, as conceived by Aristotle, has a knowledge which is not knowledge of the universe, and an influence on the universe which does not flow from His inner life of knowledge as action in man flows from knowledge ; an influence which can hardly be called an activity since it is the sort of influence that one person may unconsciously have on another, or that even a statue or a picture may have on its admirer. Little wonder that generation after generation of commentators has found it hard to believe that this is really Aristotle's view, and has tried to read something different into what he says. Even Alexander tried to find in his master some trace of a recognition of divine providence, and most ancient scholars agreed with him in this. Even Averroes, while denying to God any creative activity and any freedom of will, ascribed to Him — and thought he was following Aristotle in doing so — a knowledge of the general laws of the universe. St. Thomas and Duns Scotus expressed themselves cautiously, but tended to interpret Aristotle's God in a theistic sense. Our own time has witnessed a long controversy between Brentano and Zeller, the former maintaining, the latter denying, the theistic interpretation. Brentano's attempt must be pronounced a failure ;[1] Aristotle has no theory either of divine creation or of divine providence. But there are traces in him of a way of thinking less arid than that which we have seen to be his deliberate theory.

That God's activity is one of knowledge, and of knowledge alone, is not merely the theory of Λ ; it appears to be a part of Aristotle's permanent thought, and is expressed with equal clearness in the *De Caelo*, the *Ethics*, and the *Politics*.[2] On the other hand, in criticizing Empedocles for excluding part of reality from God's knowledge, he, in effect, criticizes his own limitation of God's knowledge to self-knowledge.[3] When Aristotle considers

---

[1] It is examined in detail by K. Elser in *Die Lehre des A. über das Wirken Gottes*, Münster, 1893. I have reviewed the main points of Brentano's argument in *Mind* xxiii. (N.S.) 289-291.

[2] 292ª 22, ᵇ 4, 1158ᵇ 35, 1159ª 4, 1178ᵇ 10, 1325ᵇ 28. πρᾶξις is ascribed to God in *E. N.* 1154ᵇ 25, *Pol.* 1325ᵇ 30, but in a wider sense in which θεωρία is a kind of πρᾶξις (1325ᵇ 20).   [3] *B.* 1000ᵇ 3, *De An.* 410ᵇ 4

the nature of God, he feels that the ascription to Him of any practical interest in the world would detract from His perfection; but when he considers the world he tends to think of God in a way which brings God into closer relation with the world. The comparison of Him to the leader of an army or to the ruler of a people[1] suggests a very different way of thinking from that which is implied in his formal view.

If the question be asked, whether Aristotle thinks of God as creator of the world, the answer must certainly be that he does not. For him matter is ungenerated, eternal; he expressly argues against a creation of the world.[2] This would not necessarily exclude the view that matter is throughout eternity maintained in existence by God, but there is no trace of such a doctrine in Aristotle. Further, the intelligences appear to be independently existing, uncreated beings. And Brentano's attempt to show that the reason of each individual human being is created by God at the birth of the individual breaks down over passages in which the eternal pre-existence of the reason is clearly maintained.[3]

There is one passage of Λ in which Aristotle at first sight seems to suggest that God exists immanently in the world as well as transcendently. 'We should consider in which of two ways the nature of the whole possesses the good and the best— whether as something existing separately and by itself, or as the order of the whole. Perhaps we should say that it possesses the good in both ways, as an army does. For it is true both that its good is in its order, and that its leader is its good, and the latter in a higher degree; for he does not exist by reason of the order, but the order by reason of him.'[4] But, though Aristotle says that the good exists both as a transcendent spirit, and as an immanent order, he does not say that *God* exists in both these ways. God is essentially for him, in Λ, the first cause; and in view of his often-repeated doctrine of the priority of substance, the cause must for him be a substance and not an abstraction such as order is. Yet he treats the order as due to God, so that his God may truly be said to be at work in the world, and in *this* sense immanent.

One of the most conspicuous features of Aristotle's view of the

---

[1] 1075[a] 14, 1076[a] 4. [2] *De Caelo* 279[b] 12 ff., 301[b] 31.
[3] Notably *De An.* 430[a] 23. [4] 1075[a] 11-15.

universe is his thorough-going teleology. Apart from occasional sports and coincidences all that exists and all that happens exists or happens for an end. But it is not so clear what interpretation is to be put on this view. Does he mean (1) that the whole structure and history of the universe is the fulfilment of a divine plan? Or (2) that it is due to the conscious working towards ends of individual beings? Or (3) that there is in nature an unconscious striving towards ends?

(1) The first alternative is out of keeping with the theory of Λ, according to which the sole activity of God is self-knowledge. But there are traces even in Λ of a different way of thought. When God is compared to the captain of an army, to whom the order in the army is due, or to the ruler of a people, or when the universe is compared to a household in which functions more or less definite are assigned to all the members from the highest to the lowest,[1] it is difficult not to suppose that Aristotle is thinking of God as controlling by His will the main lines of development of the world's history. And similar language is not lacking elsewhere. We have seen that Alexander ascribed to Aristotle a belief in providential activity—so far as the maintenance of species is concerned. This interpretation is based on *De Gen. et Corr.* 336^b 31, where Aristotle says that for those beings which, by reason of their distance from the first principle, are incapable of permanent existence (i. e. for men, animals, and plants, in contrast with the stars) God has provided what is next best by arranging for the continuance of generation. Similarly, the praise of Anaxagoras[2] for introducing reason as the cause of order in the world implies the ascription to God of a general ordering of the universe, as also do such phrases as ' God and nature make nothing in vain '.[3] But it is remarkable how little trace there is of this way of thinking, if we discount passages where Aristotle is probably accommodating himself to common opinions; he never uses the word πρόνοια of God, as Socrates and Plato had done;[4] he has no serious belief in divine rewards and punishments; he has no interest as Plato has in justifying the ways of God to man.[5]

---

[1] 1075ª 15, 1076ª 4, 1075ª 19.   [2] Λ. 984^b 15.

[3] *De Caelo* 271ª 33.   [4] Xen. *Mem.* i. 4. 6, &c.; Pl. *Tim.* 30 C, 44 C.

[5] His solution of the problem of evil lies in a reference to τὸ κακοποιόν inherent in matter (*Phys.* 192ª 15). Not that matter has any predisposition towards evil; but, being a potentiality of opposites, it is a potentiality of evil as well as of good.

(2) The second alternative appears to be ruled out by the fact that the teleology in nature is definitely opposed to the working of thought.[1] On the whole, it would seem that view (3) is that which prevails in Aristotle's mind. For the one passage in which he says that God and nature do nothing in vain, there are many in which he says that nature does nothing in vain. The notion of unconscious teleology is, it is true, profoundly unsatisfactory. If we are to view action not merely as producing a result but as being aimed at producing it, we must view the doer of it either as imagining the result and aiming at reaching it, or as merely the agent of some other intelligence which through it is realizing its conscious purposes. Unconscious teleology implies a purpose which is not the purpose of any mind, and hence not a purpose at all. But Aristotle's language suggests that he (like many modern thinkers) did not feel this difficulty, and that, for the most part, he was content to work with the notion of an unconscious purpose in nature itself.

The defects of Aristotle's theology flow, in the main, from its appearance in his system as a sort of appendix to physics, and to his particular physical theory. (1) The latter point may be taken first. Much of his argument for the existence of God rests on premises which have for us no more than antiquarian interest. The notion of the peculiar 'divinity' of the celestial bodies, of their exemption from all change except motion in space; the notion of the universe as a system of concentric spheres; the notion of the priority of circular motion, and of a peculiar analogy between it and the unchanging activity of thought; these and similar features of his thought diminish for us the value of the theology which presupposes them. In particular, they lead him to think of God not as operative with equal directness in all change and being, but as directly operative only at the outermost confines of the universe and as affecting human affairs only through a long series of intermediaries. But (2) the deeper defects of his theology arise not from its being based on a particular physical theory, but from its being based on physics to the exclusion of other possible bases. The primary fact, according to Aristotle, which calls for a supersensual explanation is the fact of movement. He shares with many other thinkers the assumption that movement cannot simply be accepted as an

[1] *Phys.* 199ᵇ 26.

ultimate feature in the nature of the universe, but must be either explained, or asserted to be an illusory appearance. The Eleatics, and less decidedly Plato, had adopted the latter alternative. Aristotle's characteristic philosophical virtue of faithfulness to the given facts made this impossible for him ; he had to allow the reality of motion. But he could not regard it as not needing explanation. He therefore tried to explain it as due to something which was itself exempt from motion. It is exclusively as first mover that a God is necessary to his system. Aristotle does not, indeed, succeed in explaining movement; we are left with the question how a non-physical activity of desire can produce movement in space. But, apart from this difficulty, the God whom he sets up is inadequate to meet the demands of the religious consciousness. These demands are, indeed, not easily satisfied in their entirety. They seem to point in two directions, and the main effort of theology is the effort to reconcile these apparently conflicting demands. On the one hand, there is the demand for a God who shall be all-inclusive and all-explaining, within whom body as well as soul, evil as well as good, shall fall. On the other hand, there is the demand for a God who is pure spirit without any tincture of matter, author of good and not of evil, personal spirit distinct from His worshippers, and entering into personal relations with them. Aristotle's God, to some extent, meets the latter demand. He is spirit, not matter, and one spirit among other spirits; and it is these two features in Aristotle's view that led the Catholic Church to base its theology largely on his. But profound modifications of his view were necessary if his prime mover were to be identified with the God whom Christians worship.[1] The prime mover is not the creator of the universe, for both matter and the subordinate forms are uncreated and eternal; nor is He a providential ruler, since His thought is of Himself alone; nor is He a God of love, since emotion of any sort would mar His life of pure contemplation. Still less does He meet the other set of demands, since His relation to the universe and to human spirits is (in Λ) described as one of transcendence alone.

Aristotle might have been led to a theology which would

---

[1] For an excellent account of St. Thomas's modifications of Aristotle's theology cf. Prof. Webb's *Studies in the History of Natural Theology*, 233–291.

have satisfied at any rate one, and perhaps to some extent both, of these demands, if he had approached the matter by studying the religious consciousness and asking what men really mean by God. He is, it is true, not entirely without regard for the religious consciousness which he finds around him. Many details of the popular religion he treats as worthless,[1] and ascribes to mere anthropomorphism[2] or to utilitarian policy.[3] But in some of its main features—in the universal tendency to believe that there *are* Gods, and in the tendency to think of the heavenly bodies as divine[4]—he is ready to welcome a divination[5] of the truth. He does not, however, carry his analysis of the religious consciousness very far. No doubt religion meant less for the average Greek of his time than it has meant for many other races. But in the mystery-cults, at all events, he would have found something that might have suggested to him that God is required not only by the intellect, to round off our knowledge of the world, but by the heart, to give us strength and courage to live; and such a God, he would have seen, must be something very different from the self-absorbed object of unreciprocated love whom he depicts. At the same time a study of these cults might have suggested to him that God cannot be merely the highest member of a hierarchy, but must somehow be present in His worshippers.

Such a study, however, of the implications of the religious consciousness would have been foreign to his method, which was objective throughout. The facts of the external world, he would have said, require a God of a certain kind; if the religious consciousness demands a God who shall be other than this, so much the worse for the religious consciousness. But it would be justifiable to reply that morality and religion are facts no less than physical change, and may have as direct a bearing on the ultimate nature of the first principle of the universe. In a general sense, Kant was probably right in holding that the practical reason has more to tell us about God than the pure reason.

---

[1] B. 1000ᵃ 18.   [2] 1074ᵇ 5, *Pol.* 1252ᵇ 24.   [3] 1074ᵇ 4.
[4] 1074ᵇ 8-14, *De Caelo* 270ᵇ 5-24, 279ᵃ 30, 284ᵃ 2, *Meteor.* 339ᵇ 19.
[5] μαντεία, *De Caelo* 284ᵇ 3.

V

THE TEXT OF THE *METAPHYSICS*

It was with good reason that W. Christ in his edition of the *Metaphysics* almost entirely ignored the manuscripts used by Bekker other than Laurentianus 87. 12 (A^b) and Parisinus 1853 (E); for the rest of these manuscripts have little independent value. There is, however, one manuscript of great value which was ignored both by Bekker and by Christ, viz. Vindobonensis phil. gr. C. Attention was called to this manuscript by A. Gercke in *Wiener Studien* xiv. 146–148. He referred to it by the symbol W, but as this had been appropriated by Bekker to another codex, I have used the symbol J instead. I made a partial collation of this manuscript in 1904; the collation was later completed for me by Mr. S. Eustratiades. The manuscript has been minutely described by Mr. F. H. Fobes in the *Classical Review* xxvii (1913), 249–250, and its relations to other manuscripts, so far as the *Meteorologica* is concerned, have been discussed by him in *Classical Philology* x (1915), 188–214, and in his edition of the *Meteorologica* (1919). J contains the *Metaphysics* from 994^a 6 to the end, and in addition the *Physics*, the *De Caelo*, the *De Generatione et Corruptione*, the *Meteorologica*, and the *Metaphysics* of Theophrastus. It appears to belong to the beginning of the tenth century and to be the earliest extant manuscript of the *Metaphysics*. It contains not infrequent traces of uncial corruption and of transcription from an archetype in which the words were not divided, e. g. in 1000^b 14, 2^a 21,[1] 27^b 33, 30^b 35, 33^b 17, 41^a 27, 62^n 17, 72^a 6, 74^b 17, 77^b 14, 83^a 12, 88^b 16, 90^b 12. There are 44 places in which EA^b appear to be in error (sometimes only in matters of accent or breathing) and J to preserve the true reading : 994^a 22, 995^a 27, 1002^b 34, 5^b 19, 10^a 31, 12^a 16, ^{b} 19, 30, 16^b 11, 20^a 21, ^{b} 33, 21^a 3, 25^a 6, 29^b 17, 31^b 9, 33^a 21, 35^a 22, 30, 41^b 29, 45^a 4, 46^a 33, ^{b} 4, 47^b 3, 51^b 34, 53^a 20, ^{b} 29, 54^b 34, 58^b 6, 26, 60^n 34, 63^a 9, 67^b 30, 68^b 19, 69^n 22, 71^b 13, 74^b 36, 75^b 23, 78^a 1, 82^a 32, 84^a 21, 89^a 11, 91^b 21, 92^b 18, 93^b 13.[2] E and J being evidently in very close agreement, I have examined all

---

[1] In this section of the Introduction 0^a–93^b = 1000^a–1093^b.

[2] J has been corrected by a second hand, which often follows the text of E ; cf. 1047^b 20–22, 1051^a 11. J occasionally has words omitted by accident in E, e. g. in 994^a 24, 999^a 30, 1020^a 21.

the passages in E in which its reported readings differed from those of J (as well as all those in which Christ's report differs from that of Bekker). In the following passages Bekker's report is right and Christ's wrong: 981^a 21, 982^a 4, 31, 32, 983^a 33, ^{b} 1, 984^b 1, 15, 985^a 19, 986^b 16, 987^a 1, 993^b 13, 996^a 22, 1006^a 21, 7^a 12, ^{b} 31, 10^b 35, 12^b 29, 16^b 19, 19^b 18, 21^a 13, 22^a 26, 27^a 13, 35^a 29, 38^b 13, 39^a 4, 33, 40^b 15, 19, 41^a 25, 45^b 18, 50^b 27, 52^b 13, 53^b 18, 55^a 2, 59^b 37, 61^b 21, 26, 66^a 19, 68^b 15, 69^a 10, 70^b 31, 77^a 20, 80^b 9, 92^b 17, 93^a 11, ^{b} 24. I found unreported readings in 982^a 15, ^{b} 26, 28, 983^b 16, 22, 985^b 17, 26, 991^a 6, ^{b} 18, 999^a 16, 1000^a 29, 6^a 21, ^{b} 3, 9^b 8, 22 *bis*, 17^b 30, 19^a 20, 22, ^{b} 25, 25^a 26, 27^a 29, ^{b} 24, 29^b 26, 33^b 19, 42^b 15, 43^a 28, 46^a 33, 48^b 7, 51^a 30, 52^a 25, 54^b 22, 56^b 4, 57^a 15 *bis*, 58^a 27, 59^b 37, 63^b 2, 67^b 5, 23, 69^b 25, 70^a 8, 71^a 14, 24, 72^b 14, 92^b 14, 21; readings of the second hand [1] in 982^b 31, 1045^b 17, 52^b 13; traces of erasure in 1029^b 3, 31^b 20, 47^b 19, 57^b 14, 80^b 15, 82^a 8, 86^a 7; I have distinguished more accurately between the first and the second hand in 988^b 8, 997^b 26, 1020^a 2, 29^b 17, 18, 22, 34, 41^b 25, 44^b 3, 35, 47^a 3, 48^a 37, ^{b} 35, 49^a 21, ^{b} 7, 51^b 5, 27, 53^b 3, 55^a 7, 58^b 24, 64^b 23, 68^b 12, 70^a 10, 74^b 32, 76^a 4, 80^a 20, 81^a 9, 82^a 32, 88^a 21, ^{b} 8, 89^b 4, 17, 90^b 12.

In A^b Christ had examined only selected passages; I thought it well, therefore, to collate this manuscript throughout. This enables me to confirm Bekker's report against that of Christ in 981^a 21, ^{b} 5, 982^a 4, 31, 32 *bis*, 986^b 16, 989^a 4, 991^a 13, ^{b} 30, 992^b 10, 993^a 8, 994^a 10, 995^b 12, 996^a 14, 997^b 12, 1000^a 10, 1^b 12, 2^a 30, ^{b} 9, 3^b 6, 6^a 8, 7^a 15, ^{b} 31, 9^a 6, 16, 12^b 18, 24, 13^b 6, 15^a 19, ^{b} 18, 16^b 19, 18^b 15, 19^b 33, 20^a 25, ^{b} 8, 28, 21^a 5, 13, 22^b 34, 25^b 25, 30^b 13, 31^a 13, ^{b} 7, 32^b 13, 33^a 33, ^{b} 11, 13, 34^a 28, ^{b} 28, 36^a 11, 38^b 10, 40^a 13, 41^b 6, 44^a 3, 45^b 15, 48^a 31, 49^a 21, 52^b 10, 17, 54^a 31, 32, 34, ^{b} 7, 17, 22, 60^a 17, 31, 61^b 21, 26, 62^a 35, 64^a 12, 65^b 23, 67^b 23, 68^a 35, 70^a 31, 73^b 26, 80^b 9, 82^a 1, 9, ^{b} 21, 89^a 22, 90^b 33. I found new readings in 981^b 2, 3, 6, 982^a 5, 983^a 9, 17,

---

[1] E^2 is a fifteenth-century hand which, besides making minor changes, quotes variant readings, sometimes those of Alexander, e.g. in 982^a 21, 983^a 17 (where Al. is expressly mentioned), 990^a 24, 996^b 24, 998^a 23, 1008^b 11, 14^b 18, 17^b 1, 40^a 22, 56^b 12; sometimes those of J, e.g. in 1008^b 23, 25^a 6, 53^a 20, 58^b 26, 82^a 32; sometimes those of A^b, e.g. in 1004^a 32, 31^a 1, 43^b 9, 44^b 23, 47^b 10; sometimes from other sources, e.g. in 987^b 25, 998^b 27, 1024^a 13, 27^a 34, 35^a 22, 41^b 1, 83^a 13.

^{b} 16, 984^a 20, 985^a 12, 19, 988^a 4, 989^a 26, ^{b} 20, 992^b 33, 993^a 1, 26, ^{b} 27, 994^a 14, 24, 995^a 13, ^{b} 6, 10, 996^a 10, 24, 997^b 10, 999^b 32, 1000^a 14, 25, 29, 32, ^{b} 15, 1^b 28, 2^a 11, 19, 24, ^{b} 8, 19, 20, 3^a 31, ^{b} 26, 4^b 7, 5^b 16, 21, 7^a 25, ^{b} 15, 33, 8^a 23, 33, ^{b} 15, 21, 10^a 17, ^{b} 2, 11^a 28, 31, ^{b} 25, 12^b 16 *bis*, 13^b 19, 14^a 19, ^{b} 28, 15^a 8, 9, 15, ^{b} 20, 16^b 10, 36, 17^b 20, 18^a 9, ^{b} 1, 4, 17, 19, 26, 19^a 7, 9, 25, 35, ^{b} 13, 20^a 15, 34, 21^a 7, 30, ^{b} 6, 21 *bis*, 22, 22^a 18, 30, 35, ^{b} 3, 6, 9, 26, 28, 35, 36, 23^a 2 *bis*, 17, 23, 35, 24^a 7, 8, 27, ^{b} 21, 25^b 22, 23, 26^a 9, 18, 27^b 1, 28^a 19 *bis*, ^{b} 33, 29^b 17, 25, 34, 30^a 18, 23, 24, 34, 31^h 14, 32^a 15, 33^a 5, 7, 8, ^{b} 22, 28, 29, 34^a 11, 15, 17, ^{b} 33, 35^a 23, ^{b} 25, 34, 36^a 17, ^{b} 6, 11, 31, 37^a 4, 8, 14, ^{b} 1, 6, 13, 38^a 3, 14, ^{b} 10, 12, 19, 22, 23, 26, 30, 39^b 18, 24, 32, 40^a 2, ^{b} 20, 41^a 12, 20, 24, ^{b} 13, 15, 43^a 6, 11, 17, 32, ^{b} 30, 44^a 29, ^{b} 2, 3 (? *bis*), 8, 30, 46^a 33, 47^b 25, 48^a 35, ^{b} 7, 49^a 14, 15, 16, 23, 50^a 21, 51^a 28, 52^a 24, ^{b} 33, 53^a 7, ^{b} 18, 54^b 2, 10, 55^a 7, ^{b} 24, 35, 56^a 2, 6, 9 *bis*, ^{b} 23, 57^a 29, 58^a 22, 36, 59^a 9, 35, 61^a 24, 62^a 1, ^{b} 13, 34, 63^b 5, 64^b 3, 20, 65^b 22, 67^a 35, 68^a 2, 69^a 9, 70^b 26, 71^a 8, ^{b} 16, 72^a 35, ^{b} 26, 74^a 27, ^{b} 22, 33, 75^a 10, 78^a 15, 18, 26, 79^a 22, 31, ^{b} 10, 81^b 23, 82^b 8, 84^b 22, 87^a 24, ^{b} 28, 30, 88^a 13, ^{b} 12, 91^b 9. In 982^a 1, 1033^a 3 I discovered readings of the second hand ; I found traces of erasure in 1020^b 18, 54^a 18, 80^a 26, 27, ^{b} 15, 90^b 35; I have distinguished between the first and another hand in 983^a 7, 995^a 5, 1002^a 30, ^{b} 17, 31^a 25, 55^a 26.

From α. 994^a 6 to the end of the *Metaphysics* E and A^b disagree in some 2,366 places ; in 341 of these J agrees with A^b, in the rest with E. The position in detail is as follows :

	J = E	J = A^b
α.	38	1
B.	177	20
Γ.	257	38
Δ.	311	30
E.	43	12
Z.	375	50
H.	79	8
Θ.	149	14
I.	145	24
K.	263	32
Λ. 1069^a 18–1073^a 1	82	12
	1,919	241

	$J = E$	$J = A^b$
Λ. 1073^a 1–1076^a 4	10	16
M.	60	38
N.	36	46
	106	100

It thus appears that the second hand of A^b, apparently of the same period, which begins at 1073^a 1,[1] agrees better than the first hand not only with J but also with E, since the first hand has 2,160 discrepancies in 485 pages, the second only 206 in 118. This is apparently due not to A^b's ceasing to represent an independent tradition (it seems still to represent this), but to the exercise of greater care by the copyist or by his original. For if we take H as typical of the earlier and N of the later books, and consider the disagreements between E and A^b in places in which the true reading can be certainly determined by the sense or the grammar, we find A^b right in H only 12 times out of 38, but in N 25 times out of 39. (J is right in 31 of these passages in H, and in 34 of those in N.) Since EJ obviously belong to one family and A^b to an independent one, it is only to be expected that EJ should sometimes agree in error; there are seven clear cases of this in H and two in N. The error is clearly due to the common archetype. It might be expected, however, that EA^b should be right when they agree against J, and JA^b right when they agree against E. Neither of these expectations is entirely borne out. Cases in which J is right against EA^b have been enumerated above. Of cases in which E is right against JA^b there are none in H but three in N (1087^a 33, 1090^b 3, 1092^a 27). In many of these exceptional cases the divergence is simply a matter of breathing or accent, and it is not surprising that E or J should be right and JA^b or EA^b wrong; in others the error was probably present in the common archetype of all the manuscripts, and the right reading is due to the intelligence of the copyist. For, as Diels has remarked,[2] the writers of our manuscripts were 'not simply writers for hire, but scholastically educated and perhaps even learned copyists, who devoted themselves with more or less skill to the διόρθωσις of their text. They are thus related to the archetype just as many newer recensions are to Bekker's edition.'

[1] Cf. Christ, p. vi. [2] *Zur Textgeschichte der aristotelischen Physik* 19.

The main characteristics of A^b's text as against that of EJ are the following:

(1) Differences of order of words—very frequent.

(2) Differences of inflexion, e. g. of number or of degree.

(3) Use of synonyms, e. g. 998^b 2 συνέστηκε A^b Al., ἐστί EJΓ.

(4) Differences of grammatical structure, e. g. 988^a 9 μόνον κέχρηται A^b, ἐστὶ μόνον κεχρημένος E, 992^b 12 εἰ ... δώσει A^b, ἐὰν ... δῷ E.

(5) Use of ἤ instead of ἤ ...ἤ, and of καί instead of τε ... καί or καί ... καί.

(6) Lacunae. These are in all probability partly due to the omission by a copyist, at some stage or stages of the transmission of the text, of whole lines of the original he was copying; but I have been unable to discover any single standard length of line of which the lacunae are multiples. The omissions must have taken place at more than one stage, and in copying originals with lines of different length. Others may be more fortunate in pursuing this line of inquiry, which has been exemplified by Prof. Clark in *The Descent of Manuscripts*; and for their information I append a list of the longer lacunae in A^b, distinguishing by an asterisk those in which the omission has been facilitated by haplography, and which, therefore, it is not so necessary to trace back to the omission of whole lines of an original:

14 letters	1016^b 11, 29^b 15*, 41^b 3, 66^a 25*.		32 letters	988^a 13, 990^b 33.
			36	988^b 15.
15	1039^b 33*, 52^a 3*.		·37	1030^a 4*, 51^b 7.
16	987^b 12*, 1025^b 26*, 27^b 2*, 30^b 6, 49^a 21, ^{b} 25*.		39	984^a 32.
			41	1032^b 27*, 65^a 18*.
			46	1034^b 29*.
18	1000^b 7, 1020^a 21*.		47	981^a 11.
19	1021^a 11, 34^b 21*, 46^a 23.		48	986^a 9, 1017^a 17*.
20	986^b 3.		49	1015^b 22*, 19^a 7*, 49^a 9*.
21	1003^a 31*, 21^b 20, 56^b 34*.		53	994^a 29*.
23	984^b 1.		57	1015^b 18*.
26	1047^b 25*.		113	1067^b 16*.
28	986^a 20, 1004^b 15*, 15^b 16*.		114	1045^b 19.
			134	981^b 2.
29	985^a 19.		169	989^a 26.
31	1017^b 17.			

It is difficult to make much of this. There is, however, a large consensus of evidence that papyrus rolls were normally written in lines of about 36 letters (Gardthausen ii. 79). Christ (*Sitzungsberichte der k. bayer. Akad. der Wiss.* 1885, 411–417) has pointed out that A^b has indications throughout of divisions answering presumably to 10-line sections in its original. These sections seem to have been of different lengths in different books, but in A the lines were of about $36\frac{1}{2}$ letters on the average. A line of this length, varying down to 32 and up to 39, will account for most of the longer lacunae in A, viz. those of 32, 36, 39, 134, and 169 letters. In Δ the lines averaged about $28\frac{1}{2}$ letters; and a line of 24–31 letters accounts for all the longer lacunae in that book.

The main lacunae in E are the following :

14 letters	1037^n 1.	38 letters	994^a 24.
15	1078^h 8*.	40	999^a 30*.
16	1079^n 20.	42	1020^a 21*.
19	1022^n 5*.	44	1007^n 22*.
26	1044^a 3*.	52	991^b 17.
28	1076^b 30*.	56	1075^a 4*.
29	1037^n 1.	57	1050^n 17*.
31	1051^a 11*.	60	1006^n 26.
35	1000^b 7.	61	1042^a 24.
37	1007^n 31*, 47^b 11*.	c. 750	1048^b 18.

In many of the above passages the sense requires the words which are omitted by one of the manuscript families, but in others this is not so, and the question arises whether these are cases of omission or of later addition. In the bulk of these passages there is no motive for the addition of the words, and the variation is much more likely to have arisen from the carelessness of one copyist than from the excessive zeal of another. There are passages, however, in which a motive for the addition of words can be detected, and others where words have plainly been inserted at a wrong part of the text as well as in their right place ; in such cases I have excised the words in question : cf. 984^b 11, 1009^a 26, 12^b 17, 23^n 21, 73^b 33 (words omitted by E), and 985^n 10, 1028^a 5, 29^b 27, 44^a 18, 59^a 30, 70^b 29 (words omitted by A^b).[1]

---

[1] For the part played by emblemata in the text cf. Index s.v. Emblemata.

It is noteworthy that in the bulk of the above lacunae it is whole clauses or groups of clauses that are omitted, and for the most part clauses not essential to the grammar. The copyists have evidently paid attention to the grammar, and been thereby saved from making more omissions than they have made. The lacunae in 994^a 24, 1007^a 22, 15^b 16, 20^a 21, 25^b 26, 29^b 15, 34^b 21, 29, 45^h 19, 47^b 25, 51^a 11 are exceptions. It is also noteworthy that neither in A^h nor in E are there many considerable lacunae after Θ.

In very many passages A^h on one side, EJ on the other have divergent readings between which there is little or nothing to choose from the point of view of sense, style, or grammar. And, while EJ are older than A^h, A^h presents more traces of uncial corruption and other evidence which points to an original older than that of EJ.[1] In these circumstances it is hard to say which family is more likely to be preserving the original reading. It is natural, then, to turn to the Greek commentators and to the old translations to see which family they support. Alexander (*fl.* 200 A. D.) represents a tradition intermediate between the two. His commentary on Books A–Δ, so far as I have been able to trace his readings, agrees 161 times certainly and 18 times doubtfully with E (or, from 994^a 6 onwards, with EJ), 121 times certainly and 37 times doubtfully with A^h. The pseudo-Alexander's commentary[2] on Books E–N agrees 148 times certainly and 17 times doubtfully with EJ, 184 times certainly and 45 times doubtfully with A^h. Asclepius (*c.* 525) agrees 257 times with EJ, 110 times with A^h; Syrianus (*fl.* 431) 5 times with EJ, twice with A^h; Themistius (born *c.* 315) throws no light on the problem.

Our oldest manuscripts are separated from Aristotle by twelve centuries, Alexander only by five. It is therefore important to see what sort of relations exist in detail between the text of our manuscripts and that presupposed by Alexander's commentary. Where EJA^h Al. do not agree, the normal position is either A^b Al. right, EJ wrong, or EJ Al. right, A^h wrong. These alternatives are about equally common—a not infrequent situation; cf. what the editors of the *Oxyrhynchus Papyri* say of Ox.

---

[1] Christ, p. vii.

[2] Perhaps by Michael of Ephesus (*c.* 1070), to whom it is ascribed i one manuscript.

l

843 (Plato, *Symposium*): 'The text, as so often with papyri, is of an eclectic character, showing a decided affinity with no single manuscript. Compared with the three principal witnesses for the *Symposium* it agrees now with B against TW, now with the two latter as against the former, rarely with T against BW or with W against BT.' Similarly of Ox. 1016 they say that 'as between the two principal manuscripts, B and T, the papyrus shows, as usual, little preference, agreeing first with the one and then with the other'.

In Book B, for instance, the first book for the whole of which J is available, Al. agrees 27 times with A^b and 27 times with EJ. And this is much oftener than any other combination occurs. To show this I note below *all* the cases in Book B of other combinations, together with any other cases in that book which throw light on the relations between the manuscripts and Al. I add in brackets a number of significant cases from other books:

1. J Al. right, EA^b wrong, 995ª 27.
2. EJ right, A^b Al. wrong (1054^b 17 *bis*).
3. JA^b *versus* E Al. : either may be right, 996ª 15.
4. EJA^b right, Al. wrong, 995^b 36, 1000ª 28 (78ª 8).
5. Al. right, EJA^b wrong, 998ª 23, ^{b} 17, 999^b 21.
6 EJA^b *versus* Al. : either may be right, 997ª 5, ^{b} 23, 1000^b 32 (82^b 36).
7. All wrong (in different ways), 1001ª 12.
8. Al.'s transpositions ignored by the MSS. (1005^b 2, 70ª 20, ^{b} 15).
9. Al.'s condemnation ignored (1041ª 28).
10. Al.'s emendations ignored, 996^b 24, 1002^b 24 (7ª 34).
11. ? Al.'s emendations adopted. These cases require close consideration, since it is doubtful whether the manuscript reading is due to Alexander's conjecture or is independent. 1001^b 27 καὶ τὰ ἐπίπεδα EJA^b : om. Al. Alexander notes the absence of these words. But their presence in the manuscripts is probably not due to Alexander's note, for, if it were, the manuscripts would have added καὶ αἱ γραμμαί, which, Alexander notes, must also be understood.

(982ª 21) πάντα E : ἄπαντα A^b : om. Al., who desiderates πάντα.

(995ª 1) λέγεσθαι EJA^b : ἔτι τὸ λέγεσθαι Al., who finds ἔτι superfluous. But if the manuscript reading were due to Alexander's note the MSS. would have read τὸ λέγεσθαι.

(1008ᵃ 25) γάρ Aᵇ : δ’ EJ Al., who says δέ here = γάρ.

(1016ᵇ 11) ἢ ὧν ὁ λόγος μὴ εἶς EJ : om. Aᵇ Al. Alexander notes the absence of a reference to diversity of λόγος but does not suggest its insertion. The reading of EJ seems independent.

(ib.) ἔτι J ci. Al. : ἐπεί EAᵇ.

(1040ᵃ 22) ἔπειτα εἰ Aᵇ : ἔπειτα δὲ εἰ EJ : ἔτι Al., who desiderates ἔπειτα. But the presence of εἰ in the manuscripts seems to show that their reading is not due to Alexander's suggestion.

A consideration of the situations (2), (4), (8), (9), (10), (11) seems to show that in all probability EJAᵇ are independent of Alexander. The facts point to the existence in Alexander's time of three texts of approximately equal correctness, represented now by EJ, Aᵇ, and Alexander's commentary. We shall do well, generally speaking, to treat the consensus of any two of them as taking us as near as we can hope to get to the text of Aristotle. Further, the number of places in which EJ and Aᵇ both disagree with Alexander is relatively so small that where Alexander's reading is not clear the consensus of EJAᵇ is almost as conclusive as the consensus of EJAᵇ Al. is elsewhere. There are, however, a considerable number of cases in which the common archetype of the three texts was in error and in which we must have recourse to manuscripts generally inferior, to Asclepius, or to conjecture.

The lemmata and quotations in the Greek commentators, though much less important than the readings revealed by their actual commentaries, are, as Diels has shown in his work on the *Physics*, not without value. Those in Alexander agree 78 times with E (EJ), and an equal number of times with Aᵇ ; those in pseudo-Alexander 61 times with EJ, 83 times with Aᵇ ; those in Asclepius 357 times with E (EJ), 110 times with Aᵇ ; those in Syrianus 40 times with EJ, 19 times with Aᵇ.

The cases in which Alexander gives the right reading against EAᵇ are numerous and well known. Asclepius occasionally does so : cf. 989ᵃ 28, 29, 995ᵇ 33, 1012ᵇ 9, 25ᵃ 13, 30ᵃ 2, 33ᵃ 1. Even the lemmata and quotations in Asclepius and Syrianus sometimes seem to be right as against the best manuscripts, e. g. in 998ᵃ 29, 999ᵇ 21, 1000ᵇ 7, 4ᵃ 19, 6ᵇ 9, 11ᵃ 1, 32, 24ᵃ 27, 25ᵃ 15, 77ᵇ 18, 79ᵇ 14.

There were three mediaeval translations of the *Metaphysics* : (1) the *Metaphysica vetus*, extending from the beginning to Γ.

1007^a 31, which was apparently executed at Constantinople and was known in Paris shortly before 1210. (2) The *Metaphysica nova*, embracing α, A. 987^a 6-end, B-I, Λ. beginning to 1075^b 11. This translation was probably made either by Gerhard of Cremona or by Michael Scotus. The earliest trace of it is its occurrence in a manuscript dated 1243. The translation was made from the Arabic, diverges very considerably from the Greek text, and is of little use for its establishment. (3) A translation from the Greek, of which the first twelve books were produced between 1260 and 1270, and the last two books not before 1270. This translation may with comparative certainty be ascribed to William of Moerbeke, a Flemish Dominican, who translated much of Aristotle and was for his last nine years (1277–86) Archbishop of Corinth. In Books A–Γ this translation follows the *Metaphysica vetus* very closely, amending it only in the direction of greater literalness, and it remains literal throughout ; as a rule there is no difficulty in inferring the precise Greek which lay before the translator, so that the work has the value of a manuscript of the thirteenth or an earlier century.[1] I collated its readings first in the earliest printed editions to which I had access, that of Andrea de Asula (Ven. 1483) for the first twelve books, and that printed in Johannes Versor's *Quaestiones* (Colon. 1491) for the last two. But to guard against quoting readings which might be peculiar to these editions I subsequently studied the translation in the thirteenth-century MS. Balliol. 277, and the fourteenth-century MSS. Bodl. Canon. 288 and Oriel. 25. The readings quoted represent the consensus of all or the majority of these texts of the translation. The readings agree for the most part with EJ, but not infrequently with A^b, e. g. in Book E 34 times with EJ, 5 times with A^b. Readings ascribed by Bonitz to the Aldine edition or to Bessarion are very often to be found in this earlier source. In the following passages Γ is either alone or almost alone in preserving the true reading : 982^a 27, 998^a 23, 1002^b 34, 6^b 9, 12^a 16, 16^b 11, 20^a 27, 27^b 33, 31^b 8, 9, 38^b 29, 41^b 29, 46^a 33, ^{b} 4, 21, 47^b 21, 53^b 29, 61^b 26, 63^a 9, 68^b 19, 71^b 13, 72^a 5, 75^b 23, 77^a 31, 78^a 28, 81^b 23, 89^a 11, 93^b 13.

It is perfectly clear that neither EJ nor A^b should be followed

---

[1] The three translations have been well discussed by M. Grabmann in *Beitr. zur Gesch. der Phil. des Mittelalters* xvii. 104–169.

exclusively. But the weight of the Greek commentators and of the mediaeval translation is decidedly on the side of EJ, and I have accordingly followed this group of manuscripts, except where the evidence of the Greek commentators, or the sense, or grammar, or Aristotelian usage—what Mr. Bywater was so fond of referring to as the *Sprachgebrauch*—turns the scale in favour of A^b.

Of the other manuscripts quoted by Bekker for the *Metaphysics* D^b, F^b, G^b, H^b, I^b are manuscripts of Alexander, Syrianus, or Asclepius, and I have already indicated the nature of their contribution to the determination of the text. The Laurentian MSS. 81. 1 (S) of the thirteenth century, and 87. 18 (B^b), 87. 26 (C^b) of the fourteenth century form a closely-connected family which has more affinities with EJ than with A^b. S is either alone or almost alone in preserving the true reading in 993^a 16, 1005^b 19, and stands along with more recent manuscripts in preserving it, against EJA^b, in 984^b 26, 986^a 11, 991^b 25, 1004^a 26, 9^b 27, 11^a 1, 14^a 17, 24^a 27, 25^a 9, 13, 27^b 27, 43^a 15, 45^a 8, 46^a 31, ^{b} 21, 22, 47^b 10, 48^b 31, 58^b 30, 62^a 13, 64^b 25, 26, 66 4, 67^b 23, 70^a 8, 71^b 11, 77^b 36, 79^b 19, 82^b 21, 88^1 35, 93^b 4.

Most of the affinities of Vaticanus 256 (T), written in 1321, are with J and S. JT often agree against all the other manuscripts, e.g. in 1014^a 23, 15^b 30, 16^b 11, 19^b 19, 21^a 22, 22^a 27, 23^b 36, 26^a 18, 27^b 8, 46^a 33, 47^b 3, 51^b 34, 53^b 29, 67^b 30. T stands alone or almost alone in preserving the true reading in 1004^a 19, 5^b 19, 11^a 32, 28^b 14, 37^a 26, 51^b 34, 53^b 29, 72^a 5, 84^a 23, 89^a 28 ; it agrees with other late manuscripts in preserving it in 984^b 26, 985^b 33, 986^a 11, 1000^a 29, 4^a 26, 24^a 27, 27^b 24, 45^a 8, 46^a 31, ^{b} 21, 58^b 30, 62^a 13, 70^a 8, 71^b 11, 79^b 19, 82^b 21.

The Marcian MSS. 211 (E^b) of the thirteenth century and 214 (H^a), which Wilamowitz assigns to the fourteenth, are closely connected, and agree more with EJ than with A^b. Marcianus 200 (Q) and Marcianus 206 (f), written in 1447 and 1467 respectively, agree for the most part, the former with E, the latter with E^b, H^a ; Bekker does not cite these manuscripts after Book α, and they seem to be of no importance.

The Latin version of Cardinal Bessarion, made about 1452, agrees for the most part with EJ, but not infrequently he stands alone or almost alone in giving the right reading, e.g. in 1043^b 23, 53^b 29, 66^b 2, 67^b 6, 70^a 11, 72^a 24, 75^b 5, 76^b 32, 78^a 20,

79ᵇ 30, 84ᵃ 21, 23, 90ᵇ 33, 91ᵃ 1 ; he owes something, apparently. to the mediaeval translation, e. g. in 982ᵃ 27, 1002ᵇ 34, 6ᵇ 9, 12ᵃ 16, 16ᵇ 11, 46ᵃ 33, 53ᵃ 20, 61 26, 75ᵇ 23, 77ᵃ 31, 81ᵇ 23, and something to Alexander, e. g. in 1022ᵃ 35, 43ᵇ 23, 70ᵃ 11, 75ᵇ 5, 76ᵇ 32, 78ᵃ 20, 84ᵃ 23, 90ᵇ 33, 91ᵃ 1.

The *editio princeps*, the Aldine of 1498, agrees most closely with T and S ; it has little or nothing of its own that is of value for the determination of the text.

A good deal has been done for the restoration of the text by Sylburg, Brandis, Bekker, Schwegler, and Christ ; but all these together have done less for it than Bonitz, who, partly by careful study of the Greek commentators, partly by attention to what the argument requires, has convincingly amended almost every page of the work.

I have paid special attention to the punctuation, a change in which often makes emendation unnecessary.

With regard to the elision of vowels, the use of *ν paragogicum*, the writing of οὕτως or οὕτω, οὐδείς or οὐθείς, μηδείς or μηθείς, ἐάν or ἄν, ἑαυτοῦ or αὑτοῦ, τοιοῦτον or τοιοῦτο, ταὐτόν or ταὐτό, I have thought it well to follow the oldest MS., J ; but I have written γίγνεσθαι, γιγνώσκειν, not γίνεσθαι, γινώσκειν, irrespective of J.

Christ has argued for the existence, in many passages, of dislocations of the text and the insertion of words in the wrong context. This is a matter on which it is difficult to make up one's mind. There seem to be clear instances in 995ᵃ 19, 1006ᵃ 28, 1029ᵇ 3–12, 1070ᵃ 20, ᵇ 29, and possible instances in 1019ᵃ 20, 1071ᵃ 18. Three of these cases occur in Λ. 1–5, a section which is, more than any other part of the *Metaphysics*, in the form of notes rather than of a finished book ; it is pretty clear that the notes have not always been sorted into the best order.

ΑΡΙΣΤΟΤΕΛΟΥΣ
ΤΑ ΜΕΤΑ ΤΑ ΦΥΣΙΚΑ

SIGLA

E = Parisinus gr. 1853, saec. x
J = Vindobonensis phil. gr. C, saec. x ineuntis
A^b = Laurentianus 87. 12, saec. xii
Γ = Gulielmi de Moerbeka translatio, c. 1260–1275
Al., Asc., Syr., Them. = Alexandri, Asclepii, Syriani, Themistii commentaria
Al.^{l}, etc. = Alexandri, etc., lemmata
Al.^{c}, etc. = Alexandri, etc., citationes

Raro citantur

recc. = codices recentiores
S = Laurentianus 81. 1, saec. xiii
T = Vaticanus 256, anni 1321
i = Bessarionis translatio, c. 1452
a = editio Aldina, anni 1498
M = *Metaphysicorum* liber M
Φ = Aristotelis *Physica*

ΑΡΙΣΤΟΤΕΛΟΥΣ
ΤΩΝ ΜΕΤΑ ΤΑ ΦΥΣΙΚΑ Α

1 Πάντες ἄνθρωποι τοῦ εἰδέναι ὀρέγονται φύσει. σημεῖον δ' 980ᵃ
ἡ τῶν αἰσθήσεων ἀγάπησις· καὶ γὰρ χωρὶς τῆς χρείας
ἀγαπῶνται δι' αὑτάς, καὶ μάλιστα τῶν ἄλλων ἡ διὰ τῶν
ὀμμάτων. οὐ γὰρ μόνον ἵνα πράττωμεν ἀλλὰ καὶ μηθὲν
μέλλοντες πράττειν τὸ ὁρᾶν αἱρούμεθα ἀντὶ πάντων ὡς εἰπεῖν 25
τῶν ἄλλων. αἴτιον δ' ὅτι μάλιστα ποιεῖ γνωρίζειν ἡμᾶς
αὕτη τῶν αἰσθήσεων καὶ πολλὰς δηλοῖ διαφοράς. φύσει
μὲν οὖν αἴσθησιν ἔχοντα γίγνεται τὰ ζῷα, ἐκ δὲ ταύτης
τοῖς μὲν αὐτῶν οὐκ ἐγγίγνεται μνήμη, τοῖς δ' ἐγγίγνεται.
καὶ διὰ τοῦτο ταῦτα φρονιμώτερα καὶ μαθητικώτερα τῶν 980ᵇ
μὴ δυναμένων μνημονεύειν ἐστί, φρόνιμα μὲν ἄνευ τοῦ
μανθάνειν ὅσα μὴ δύναται τῶν ψόφων ἀκούειν (οἷον μέλιττα κἂν εἴ τι τοιοῦτον ἄλλο γένος ζῴων ἔστι), μανθάνει
δ' ὅσα πρὸς τῇ μνήμῃ καὶ ταύτην ἔχει τὴν αἴσθησιν. τὰ 25
μὲν οὖν ἄλλα ταῖς φαντασίαις ζῇ καὶ ταῖς μνήμαις, ἐμπειρίας δὲ μετέχει μικρόν· τὸ δὲ τῶν ἀνθρώπων γένος καὶ
τέχνῃ καὶ λογισμοῖς. γίγνεται δ' ἐκ τῆς μνήμης ἐμπειρία
τοῖς ἀνθρώποις· αἱ γὰρ πολλαὶ μνῆμαι τοῦ αὐτοῦ πράγματος μιᾶς ἐμπειρίας δύναμιν ἀποτελοῦσιν. καὶ δοκεῖ σχεδὸν 981ᵃ
ἐπιστήμη καὶ τέχνη ὅμοιον εἶναι καὶ ἐμπειρία, ἀποβαίνει δ'
ἐπιστήμη καὶ τέχνη διὰ τῆς ἐμπειρίας τοῖς ἀνθρώποις· ἡ
μὲν γὰρ ἐμπειρία τέχνην ἐποίησεν, ὡς φησὶ Πῶλος, ἡ
δ' ἀπειρία τύχην. γίγνεται δὲ τέχνη ὅταν ἐκ πολλῶν 5
τῆς ἐμπειρίας ἐννοημάτων μία καθόλου γένηται περὶ

980ᵃ 26 ἡμᾶς ΕΓ Asc. : τι ἡμᾶς Aᵇ   28 ταύτης] τῆς αἰσθήσεως
ΕΓ Asc.¹   29 δὲ γίγνεται Ε Asc.¹   ᵇ 21 ταῦτα ... καὶ Aᵇ Al. :
τὰ μὲν φρόνιμα τὰ δὲ Ε Asc. : ταῦτα φρονιμώτερα τὰ δὲ καὶ Bywater
23 δυνατὰ ΕΓ   24 καὶ recc.   τι om. Aᵇ   25 ὅσα ΕΓ Asc. :
ὁ Aᵇ   981ᵃ 2 καὶ alt. Aᵇ Asc.¹ : ἡ ΕΓ   3 τοῖς ἀνθρώποις ΕΓ
Asc. : om. Aᵇ   4 Πῶλος Aᵇ et fort. Al. Asc. : Πῶλος ὀρθῶς λέγων
ΕΓ   6 καθόλου μία Ε Asc.¹

B 2

τῶν ὁμοίων ὑπόληψις. τὸ μὲν γὰρ ἔχειν ὑπόληψιν ὅτι
Καλλίᾳ κάμνοντι τηνδὶ τὴν νόσον τοδὶ συνήνεγκε καὶ
Σωκράτει καὶ καθ᾽ ἕκαστον οὕτω πολλοῖς, ἐμπειρίας ἐστίν·

10 τὸ δ᾽ ὅτι πᾶσι τοῖς τοιοῖσδε κατ᾽ εἶδος ἓν ἀφορισθεῖσι,
κάμνουσι τηνδὶ τὴν νόσον, συνήνεγκεν, οἷον τοῖς φλεγματώδεσιν ἢ χολώδεσι [ἢ] πυρέττουσι καύσῳ, τέχνης.——πρὸς μὲν
οὖν τὸ πράττειν ἐμπειρία τέχνης οὐδὲν δοκεῖ διαφέρειν, ἀλλὰ
καὶ μᾶλλον ἐπιτυγχάνουσιν οἱ ἔμπειροι τῶν ἄνευ τῆς ἐμ-

15 πειρίας λόγον ἐχόντων (αἴτιον δ᾽ ὅτι ἡ μὲν ἐμπειρία τῶν
καθ᾽ ἕκαστόν ἐστι γνῶσις ἡ δὲ τέχνη τῶν καθόλου, αἱ δὲ
πράξεις καὶ αἱ γενέσεις πᾶσαι περὶ τὸ καθ᾽ ἕκαστόν εἰσιν·
οὐ γὰρ ἄνθρωπον ὑγιάζει ὁ ἰατρεύων ἀλλ᾽ ἢ κατὰ συμβεβηκός, ἀλλὰ Καλλίαν ἢ Σωκράτην ἢ τῶν ἄλλων τινὰ

20 τῶν οὕτω λεγομένων ᾧ συμβέβηκεν ἀνθρώπῳ εἶναι· ἐὰν
οὖν ἄνευ τῆς ἐμπειρίας ἔχῃ τις τὸν λόγον, καὶ τὸ καθόλου
μὲν γνωρίζῃ τὸ δ᾽ ἐν τούτῳ καθ᾽ ἕκαστον ἀγνοῇ, πολλάκις διαμαρτήσεται τῆς θεραπείας· θεραπευτὸν γὰρ τὸ καθ᾽
ἕκαστον)· ἀλλ᾽ ὅμως τό γε εἰδέναι καὶ τὸ ἐπαίειν τῇ

25 τέχνῃ τῆς ἐμπειρίας ὑπάρχειν οἰόμεθα μᾶλλον, καὶ σοφωτέρους τοὺς τεχνίτας τῶν ἐμπείρων ὑπολαμβάνομεν, ὡς
κατὰ τὸ εἰδέναι μᾶλλον ἀκολουθοῦσαν τὴν σοφίαν πᾶσι·
τοῦτο δ᾽ ὅτι οἱ μὲν τὴν αἰτίαν ἴσασιν οἱ δ᾽ οὔ. οἱ μὲν γὰρ
ἔμπειροι τὸ ὅτι μὲν ἴσασι, διότι δ᾽ οὐκ ἴσασιν· οἱ δὲ τὸ διότι

30 καὶ τὴν αἰτίαν γνωρίζουσιν. διὸ καὶ τοὺς ἀρχιτέκτονας περὶ
ἕκαστον τιμιωτέρους καὶ μᾶλλον εἰδέναι νομίζομεν τῶν χει-

981b ροτεχνῶν καὶ σοφωτέρους, ὅτι τὰς αἰτίας τῶν ποιουμένων
ἴσασιν (τοὺς δ᾽, ὥσπερ καὶ τῶν ἀψύχων ἔνια ποιεῖ μέν, οὐκ
εἰδότα δὲ ποιεῖ ἃ ποιεῖ, οἷον καίει τὸ πῦρ——τὰ μὲν οὖν
ἄψυχα φύσει τινὶ ποιεῖν τούτων ἕκαστον τοὺς δὲ χειροτέχνας

a 8 τοδὶ E Asc.[1] : τόδε A[b]   11 οἷον . . . 12 καύσῳ om. A[b] et fort.
Al. : οἷον τοῖς πυρέττουσι καύσῳ ἢ φλεγματώδεσιν ἢ μελαγχολικοῖς Asc.[1]
12 χολώδεσι Jackson : χολώδεσιν ἢ codd. Γ   13 ἐμπειρία τέχνης
codd. Γ Al.[1] Asc.[1] : ἐμπειρίας τέχνη fort. Al. Asc., Heidel   δοκεῖ
διαφέρειν ΕΓ Asc.[1] : διήνεγκεν A[b] Al.[1]   14 ἐπιτυγχάνουσιν οἱ ἔμπειροι
A[b] Asc. : ἐπιτυγχάνοντας ὁρῶμεν τοὺς ἐμπείρους ΕΓ   18 ἀλλ᾽ A[b]
Asc. : πλὴν ἀλλ᾽ E   19 Σωκράτη E Asc.   20 ἀνθρώπῳ ΕΓ et
fort. Al. Asc. : καὶ ἀνθρώπῳ A[b]   21–22 καὶ τὸ καθόλου recc.   24 ἕκα-
στον] ἕκαστον μᾶλλον ΕΓ   26 ἐμπειρικῶν E   28 αἰτίαν in marg.
E[1]   29 τὸ pr. A[b] Asc. : om. E   b 2 τοὺς . . . 5 ἔθος ΕΑ[b]Γ
Asc. : om. A[b1] et ut vid. Al.   τοὺς] οἱ Γ   ποιεῖν recc.
3 ποιεῖν recc.   ἃ ποιεῖ ΕΓ Asc. : om. A[b2]   4 ποιεῖ E

δι' ἔθος), ὡς οὐ κατὰ τὸ πρακτικοὺς εἶναι σοφωτέρους ὄντας 5
ἀλλὰ κατὰ τὸ λόγον ἔχειν αὐτοὺς καὶ τὰς αἰτίας γνωρίζειν.
ὅλως τε σημεῖον τοῦ εἰδότος καὶ μὴ εἰδότος τὸ δύνασθαι διδάσκειν ἐστίν, καὶ διὰ τοῦτο τὴν τέχνην τῆς ἐμπειρίας ἡγούμεθα
μᾶλλον ἐπιστήμην εἶναι· δύνανται γάρ, οἱ δὲ οὐ δύνανται διδάσκειν. ἔτι δὲ τῶν αἰσθήσεων οὐδεμίαν ἡγούμεθα εἶναι σοφίαν· 10
καίτοι κυριώταταί γ' εἰσὶν αὗται τῶν καθ' ἕκαστα γνώσεις· ἀλλ'
οὐ λέγουσι τὸ διὰ τί περὶ οὐδενός, οἷον διὰ τί θερμὸν τὸ πῦρ,
ἀλλὰ μόνον ὅτι θερμόν. τὸ μὲν οὖν πρῶτον εἰκὸς τὸν
ὁποιανοῦν εὑρόντα τέχνην παρὰ τὰς κοινὰς αἰσθήσεις θαυ-
μάζεσθαι ὑπὸ τῶν ἀνθρώπων μὴ μόνον διὰ τὸ χρήσιμον 15
εἶναί τι τῶν εὑρεθέντων ἀλλ' ὡς σοφὸν καὶ διαφέροντα τῶν
ἄλλων· πλειόνων δ' εὑρισκομένων τεχνῶν καὶ τῶν μὲν
πρὸς τἀναγκαῖα τῶν δὲ πρὸς διαγωγὴν οὐσῶν, ἀεὶ σοφωτέρους τοὺς τοιούτους ἐκείνων ὑπολαμβάνεσθαι διὰ τὸ μὴ πρὸς
χρῆσιν εἶναι τὰς ἐπιστήμας αὐτῶν. ὅθεν ἤδη πάντων τῶν 20
τοιούτων κατεσκευασμένων αἱ μὴ πρὸς ἡδονὴν μηδὲ πρὸς
τἀναγκαῖα τῶν ἐπιστημῶν εὑρέθησαν, καὶ πρῶτον ἐν τούτοις
τοῖς τόποις οὗ πρῶτον ἐσχόλασαν· διὸ περὶ Αἴγυπτον αἱ μαθη-
ματικαὶ πρῶτον τέχναι συνέστησαν, ἐκεῖ γὰρ ἀφείθη σχο-
λάζειν τὸ τῶν ἱερέων ἔθνος. εἴρηται μὲν οὖν ἐν τοῖς ἠθικοῖς 25
τίς διαφορὰ τέχνης καὶ ἐπιστήμης καὶ τῶν ἄλλων τῶν ὁμο-
γενῶν· οὗ δ' ἕνεκα νῦν ποιούμεθα τὸν λόγον τοῦτ' ἐστίν, ὅτι
τὴν ὀνομαζομένην σοφίαν περὶ τὰ πρῶτα αἴτια καὶ τὰς ἀρχὰς ὑπολαμβάνουσι πάντες· ὥστε, καθάπερ εἴρηται πρότερον,
ὁ μὲν ἔμπειρος τῶν ὁποιανοῦν ἐχόντων αἴσθησιν εἶναι δοκεῖ 30
σοφώτερος, ὁ δὲ τεχνίτης τῶν ἐμπείρων, χειροτέχνου δὲ ἀρ-
χιτέκτων, αἱ δὲ θεωρητικαὶ τῶν ποιητικῶν μᾶλλον. ὅτι μὲν 982ᵃ
οὖν ἡ σοφία περί τινας ἀρχὰς καὶ αἰτίας ἐστὶν ἐπιστήμη,
δῆλον.

2   Ἐπεὶ δὲ ταύτην τὴν ἐπιστήμην ζητοῦμεν, τοῦτ' ἂν εἴη

ᵇ6 τὸ τὸν Aᵇ   ἔχειν αὐτοὺς ΕΓ Asc.: αὐτοὺς ἔχειν Aᵇ   7 τε]
δὲ Aᵇ   καὶ μὴ εἰδότος Ε Asc.: om. AᵇΓ   8 ἐστίν, καὶ διὰ τοῦτο Ε
Asc.: νομίζομεν· διὸ AᵇΓ   οἰόμεθα recc.   11 ταύταις Γ
13 θερμόν ΕΓ Asc.¹: θερμὸν τὸ πῦρ Aᵇ   τὸ] τὸν recc.   19 ὑπολαμβάνομεν Aᵇ   21 αἱ] ὅσαι Aᵇ   23 οὗ πρῶτον] οὗπερ Ε Asc.
29 ὥστε Ε Asc.: διὸ AᵇΓ   30 ὁποιανοῦν Aᵇ Asc.ᶜ: ὁποιαντινοῦν Ε
31 δὲ alt. Ε Asc.ᶜ: δ' ὁ Aᵇ: τε γὰρ ὁ Al ᶜ   982ᵃ 1 οἱ δὲ
θεωρητικοὶ Aᵇ²   2 ἀρχὰς καὶ αἰτίας Aᵇ Asc. et fort. Al.: αἰτίας
καὶ ὑρχὰς ΕΓ

5 σκεπτέον, ἡ περὶ ποίας αἰτίας καὶ περὶ ποίας ἀρχὰς ἐπιστήμη σοφία ἐστίν. εἰ δὴ λάβοι τις τὰς ὑπολήψεις ἃς ἔχομεν περὶ τοῦ σοφοῦ, τάχ᾽ ἂν ἐκ τούτου φανερὸν γένοιτο μᾶλλον. ὑπολαμβάνομεν δὴ πρῶτον μὲν ἐπίστασθαι πάντα τὸν
σοφὸν ὡς ἐνδέχεται, μὴ καθ᾽ ἕκαστον ἔχοντα ἐπιστήμην
10 αὐτῶν· εἶτα τὸν τὰ χαλεπὰ γνῶναι δυνάμενον καὶ μὴ
ῥᾴδια ἀνθρώπῳ γιγνώσκειν, τοῦτον σοφόν (τὸ γὰρ αἰσθάνε-
σθαι πάντων κοινόν, διὸ ῥᾴδιον καὶ οὐδὲν σοφόν)· ἔτι τὸν
ἀκριβέστερον καὶ τὸν διδασκαλικώτερον τῶν αἰτιῶν σοφώτερον εἶναι περὶ πᾶσαν ἐπιστήμην· καὶ τῶν ἐπιστημῶν δὲ τὴν
15 αὑτῆς ἕνεκεν καὶ τοῦ εἰδέναι χάριν αἱρετὴν οὖσαν μᾶλλον
εἶναι σοφίαν ἢ τὴν τῶν ἀποβαινόντων ἕνεκεν, καὶ τὴν ἀρ-
χικωτέραν τῆς ὑπηρετούσης μᾶλλον σοφίαν· οὐ γὰρ δεῖν
ἐπιτάττεσθαι τὸν σοφὸν ἀλλ᾽ ἐπιτάττειν, καὶ οὐ τοῦτον
ἑτέρῳ πείθεσθαι, ἀλλὰ τούτῳ τὸν ἧττον σοφόν.——τὰς μὲν οὖν
20 ὑπολήψεις τοιαύτας καὶ τοσαύτας ἔχομεν περὶ τῆς σοφίας
καὶ τῶν σοφῶν· τούτων δὲ τὸ μὲν πάντα ἐπίστασθαι τῷ μάλιστα ἔχοντι τὴν καθόλου ἐπιστήμην ἀναγκαῖον ὑπάρχειν
(οὗτος γὰρ οἶδέ πως πάντα τὰ ὑποκείμενα), σχεδὸν δὲ καὶ
χαλεπώτατα ταῦτα γνωρίζειν τοῖς ἀνθρώποις, τὰ μάλιστα
25 καθόλου (πορρωτάτω γὰρ τῶν αἰσθήσεών ἐστιν), ἀκριβέσταται
δὲ τῶν ἐπιστημῶν αἳ μάλιστα τῶν πρώτων εἰσίν (αἱ γὰρ ἐξ
ἐλαττόνων ἀκριβέστεραι τῶν ἐκ προσθέσεως λεγομένων,
οἷον ἀριθμητικὴ γεωμετρίας)· ἀλλὰ μὴν καὶ διδασκαλικὴ γε
ἡ τῶν αἰτιῶν θεωρητικὴ μᾶλλον (οὗτοι γὰρ διδάσκουσιν, οἱ τὰς
30 αἰτίας λέγοντες περὶ ἑκάστου), τὸ δ᾽ εἰδέναι καὶ τὸ ἐπίστασθαι
αὐτῶν ἕνεκα μάλισθ᾽ ὑπάρχει τῇ τοῦ μάλιστα ἐπιστητοῦ ἐπιστήμῃ (ὁ γὰρ τὸ ἐπίστασθαι δι᾽ αὐτὸ αἱρούμενος τὴν μάλιστα
982ᵇ ἐπιστήμην μάλιστα αἱρήσεται, τοιαύτη δ᾽ ἐστὶν ἡ τοῦ μάλιστα

ᵃ 5 καὶ om. Aᵇ   6 ἐστὶ σοφία Aᵇ   7 τοῦ σοφοῦ ΕΓ Al.¹
Asc.ᶜ: τοὺς σοφούς Aᵇ   τούτων Γ   8 μὲν om. Γ   πάντα Aᵇ et
ut vid. Al.: μάλιστα πάντα ΕΓ   10 τὰ om. Aᵇ   13 τὸν om.
Aᵇ   τῶν αἰτιῶν secl. Baumann   15 αὑτῆς Ε   16 ἢ ... 17
σοφίαν bis scriptum in Ε   17 μᾶλλον Aᵇ Asc.ᶜ: μᾶλλον εἶναι ΕΓ
δεῖ Γ   18 τὸν sup. lin. Ε¹   οὐ τοῦτον ΕΓ Asc.ᶜ: οὐκ αὐτὸν Aᵇ   19
τίθεσθαι Aᵇ¹   20 καὶ τοσαύτας et τῆς ΕΓ Asc.: om. Aᵇ   21 πάντα
Ε¹Γ Asc.ᶜ: ἅπαντα Aᵇ: om. Ε² Al.   23 πως] πῶς ἔχει Aᵇ
πάντα Aᵇ Asc.ᶜ: ἅπαντα Ε   24 ταῦτα om. Γ   26 τε Aᵇ Al.¹
27 προσθέσεως Γi: προθέσεως codd.   λαμβανομένων Aᵇ   30 ἑκάστου Ε Asc.: ἕκαστον Aᵇ   31 αὐτῶν Christ   32 τὸ om. Christ
αὐτὸ scripsi: ἑαυτὸ Ε Asc.: αὐτὸ Aᵇ Al.   μάλιστα om. Γ

ἐπιστητοῦ), μάλιστα δ' ἐπιστητὰ τὰ πρῶτα καὶ τὰ αἴτια (διὰ
γὰρ ταῦτα καὶ ἐκ τούτων τἆλλα γνωρίζεται ἀλλ' οὐ ταῦτα
διὰ τῶν ὑποκειμένων), ἀρχικωτάτη δὲ τῶν ἐπιστημῶν, καὶ
μᾶλλον ἀρχικὴ τῆς ὑπηρετούσης, ἡ γνωρίζουσα τίνος ἕνεκέν 5
ἐστι πρακτέον ἕκαστον· τοῦτο δ' ἐστὶ τἀγαθὸν ἑκάστου, ὅλως
δὲ τὸ ἄριστον ἐν τῇ φύσει πάσῃ. ἐξ ἁπάντων οὖν τῶν εἰρημένων ἐπὶ τὴν αὐτὴν ἐπιστήμην πίπτει τὸ ζητούμενον ὄνομα·
δεῖ γὰρ ταύτην τῶν πρώτων ἀρχῶν καὶ αἰτιῶν εἶναι θεωρητι-
κήν· καὶ γὰρ τἀγαθὸν καὶ τὸ οὗ ἕνεκα ἓν τῶν αἰτίων ἐστίν.   10
   Ὅτι δ' οὐ ποιητική, δῆλον καὶ ἐκ τῶν πρώτων φιλοσοφη-
σάντων· διὰ γὰρ τὸ θαυμάζειν οἱ ἄνθρωποι καὶ νῦν καὶ
τὸ πρῶτον ἤρξαντο φιλοσοφεῖν, ἐξ ἀρχῆς μὲν τὰ πρόχειρα
τῶν ἀτόπων θαυμάσαντες, εἶτα κατὰ μικρὸν οὕτω προϊόντες
καὶ περὶ τῶν μειζόνων διαπορήσαντες, οἷον περί τε τῶν τῆς 15
σελήνης παθημάτων καὶ τῶν περὶ τὸν ἥλιον καὶ ἄστρα
καὶ περὶ τῆς τοῦ παντὸς γενέσεως. ὁ δ' ἀπορῶν καὶ θαυμά-
ζων οἴεται ἀγνοεῖν (διὸ καὶ ὁ φιλόμυθος φιλόσοφός πώς
ἐστιν· ὁ γὰρ μῦθος σύγκειται ἐκ θαυμασίων)· ὥστ' εἴπερ διὰ
τὸ φεύγειν τὴν ἄγνοιαν ἐφιλοσόφησαν, φανερὸν ὅτι διὰ τὸ 20
εἰδέναι τὸ ἐπίστασθαι ἐδίωκον καὶ οὐ χρήσεώς τινος ἕνεκεν.
μαρτυρεῖ δὲ αὐτὸ τὸ συμβεβηκός· σχεδὸν γὰρ πάντων
ὑπαρχόντων τῶν ἀναγκαίων καὶ πρὸς ῥαστώνην καὶ διαγωγὴν ἡ τοιαύτη φρόνησις ἤρξατο ζητεῖσθαι. δῆλον οὖν ὡς δι'
οὐδεμίαν αὐτὴν ζητοῦμεν χρείαν ἑτέραν, ἀλλ' ὥσπερ ἄνθρω- 25
πος, φαμέν, ἐλεύθερος ὁ αὑτοῦ ἕνεκα καὶ μὴ ἄλλου ὤν, οὕτω
καὶ αὐτὴν ὡς μόνην οὖσαν ἐλευθέραν τῶν ἐπιστημῶν· μόνη
γὰρ αὕτη αὑτῆς ἕνεκέν ἐστι. διὸ καὶ δικαίως ἂν οὐκ ἀνθρω-
πίνη νομίζοιτο αὐτῆς ἡ κτῆσις· πολλαχῇ γὰρ ἡ φύσις δούλη τῶν
ἀνθρώπων ἐστίν, ὥστε κατὰ Σιμωνίδην "θεὸς ἂν μόνος τοῦτ' 30
ἔχοι γέρας", ἄνδρα δ' οὐκ ἄξιον μὴ οὐ ζητεῖν τὴν καθ' αὑτὸν

ᵇ 2 καὶ τὰ E Asc. : καὶ Aᵇ : γ' Jaeger   6 ἐστι πρακτέον EΓ Asc.¹ :
πρακτέον ἐστιν Aᵇ ἑκάστου EΓAsc.¹ : ἐν ἑκάστοις Aᵇ   9 αὐτὴν Aᵇ Asc.ᶜ
14 ἀτόπων Aᵇ et ut vid. Al. : ἀπόρων EΓ Asc.ᶜ   16 τὸν] τῶν E
καὶ ἄστρα] καὶ περὶ ἄστρων Aᵇ : omittenda vel καὶ τὰ ἄστρα legenda
ci. Bonitz   18 ὁ φιλόμυθος φιλόσοφός Aᵇ Al. : φιλόμυθος ὁ φιλόσοφός E Asc.   23 καὶ pr.] καὶ τῶν Asc. et fort. Al.   26 φαμέν]
φαίνεται Wirth αὐτοῦ Aᵇ Asc.¹ : αὑτοῦ E   27 αὕτη μόνη ἐλευθέρα
οὖσα E : αὐτὴ ὡς μόνη οὖσα ἐλευθέρα fort. Al.   28 αὕτη EΓ Asc.ᶜ :
αὐτὴ Aᵇ αὑτῆς ἕνεκεν αἰτῆς E ἂν] μὴ E   31 γέρας Aᵇ Plato :
τὸ γέρας E μὴ οὐ] τὸ μὴ οὐ Aᵇ : μὴ E κατ' αὐτὸ E²

ἐπιστήμην. εἰ δὴ λέγουσί τι οἱ ποιηταὶ καὶ πέφυκε φθονεῖν
983ᵃ τὸ θεῖον, ἐπὶ τούτου συμβῆναι μάλιστα εἰκὸς καὶ δυστυχεῖς
εἶναι πάντας τοὺς περιττούς. ἀλλ' οὔτε τὸ θεῖον φθονερὸν ἐνδέχεται εἶναι, ἀλλὰ κατὰ τὴν παροιμίαν πολλὰ ψεύδονται
ἀοιδοί, οὔτε τῆς τοιαύτης ἄλλην χρὴ νομίζειν τιμιω-
5 τέραν. ἡ γὰρ θειοτάτη καὶ τιμιωτάτη· τοιαύτη δὲ διχῶς
ἂν εἴη μόνη· ἥν τε γὰρ μάλιστ' ἂν ὁ θεὸς ἔχοι, θεία τῶν
ἐπιστημῶν ἐστί, κἂν εἴ τις τῶν θείων εἴη. μόνη δ' αὕτη τούτων ἀμφοτέρων τετύχηκεν· ὅ τε γὰρ θεὸς δοκεῖ τῶν αἰτίων
πᾶσιν εἶναι καὶ ἀρχή τις, καὶ τὴν τοιαύτην ἢ μόνος ἢ μά-
10 λιστ' ἂν ἔχοι ὁ θεός. ἀναγκαιότεραι μὲν οὖν πᾶσαι ταύτης,
ἀμείνων δ' οὐδεμία.—δεῖ μέντοι πως καταστῆναι τὴν κτῆσιν
αὐτῆς εἰς τοὐναντίον ἡμῖν τῶν ἐξ ἀρχῆς ζητήσεων. ἄρχονται
μὲν γάρ, ὥσπερ εἴπομεν, ἀπὸ τοῦ θαυμάζειν πάντες εἰ οὕτως
ἔχει, καθάπερ ⟨περὶ⟩ τῶν θαυμάτων ταὐτόματα [τοῖς μήπω τε-
15 θεωρηκόσι τὴν αἰτίαν] ἢ περὶ τὰς τοῦ ἡλίου τροπὰς ἢ τὴν τῆς
διαμέτρου ἀσυμμετρίαν (θαυμαστὸν γὰρ εἶναι δοκεῖ πᾶσι (τοῖς
μήπω τεθεωρηκόσι τὴν αἰτίαν) εἴ τι τῷ ἐλαχίστῳ μὴ μετρεῖται)·
δεῖ δὲ εἰς τοὐναντίον καὶ τὸ ἄμεινον κατὰ τὴν παροιμίαν· ἀπο-
τελευτῆσαι, καθάπερ καὶ ἐν τούτοις ὅταν μάθωσιν· οὐθὲν γὰρ
20 ἂν οὕτως θαυμάσειεν ἀνὴρ γεωμετρικὸς ὡς εἰ γένοιτο ἡ διάμετρος
μετρητή. τίς μὲν οὖν ἡ φύσις τῆς ἐπιστήμης τῆς ζητουμένης,
εἴρηται, καὶ τίς ὁ σκοπὸς οὗ δεῖ τυγχάνειν τὴν ζήτησιν καὶ
τὴν ὅλην μέθοδον.

Ἐπεὶ δὲ φανερὸν ὅτι τῶν ἐξ ἀρχῆς αἰτίων δεῖ λαβεῖν 3
25 ἐπιστήμην (τότε γὰρ εἰδέναι φαμὲν ἕκαστον, ὅταν τὴν πρώτην αἰτίαν οἰώμεθα γνωρίζειν), τὰ δ' αἴτια λέγεται τετρα-
χῶς, ὧν μίαν μὲν αἰτίαν φαμὲν εἶναι τὴν οὐσίαν καὶ τὸ τί
ἦν εἶναι (ἀνάγεται γὰρ τὸ διὰ τί εἰς τὸν λόγον ἔσχατον,

ᵇ 32 δὲ ΕΓ Asc.¹   τι] πη Ε   οἱ sup. lin. Ε¹   καὶ] ὅτι καὶ Γ
983ᵃ 1 συμβαίνειν Αᵇ   3 κατὰ ΕΓ Asc.: καὶ κατὰ Αᵇ   6 μόνον
ΕΓ   ὁ Ε Asc.: om. Αᵇ   7 εἴ τι Αᵇ¹: ἥτις Ε   ἐστί Αᵇ et fort.
Asc.   9 μόνος ΕΓ Asc.ᶜ: μόνον Αᵇ   10 ὁ Ε Asc.ᶜ: om. Αᵇ
ταύτης Αᵇ Asc.: αὐτῆς ΕΓ   11 πως ΕΓ Asc.ˡᶜ: om. Αᵇ   τάξιν
Γ Asc.ˡᶜ   14 περὶ add. Jaeger   τοῖς . . . 15 αἰτίαν post πᾶσι (l. 16)
transp. Jaeger, transponenda ci. Bonitz   15 τὴν alt. ΕΓ Asc.ᶜ: περὶ
τὴν Αᵇ   17 τῷ ἐλαχίστῳ Αᵇ γρ. Ε Al.: τῶν οὐκ ἐλαχίστων Ε Asc.ᶜ
μετρῆται Αᵇ   20 οὕτως θαυμάσειεν ΑᵇΓ Asc.: θαυμάσειεν οὕτως Ε
21 ἐπιστήμης τῆς ζητουμένης Αᵇ Al.ᶜ: ζητουμένης ἐπιστήμης Ε Asc.ᶜ
28 τί Αᵇ Al.ᶜ: τί πρῶτον ΕΓ Asc.ᶜ

αἴτιον δὲ καὶ ἀρχὴ τὸ διὰ τί πρῶτον), ἑτέραν δὲ τὴν ὕλην
καὶ τὸ ὑποκείμενον, τρίτην δὲ ὅθεν ἡ ἀρχὴ τῆς κινήσεως, 30
τετάρτην δὲ τὴν ἀντικειμένην αἰτίαν ταύτῃ, τὸ οὗ ἕνεκα καὶ
τἀγαθόν (τέλος γὰρ γενέσεως καὶ κινήσεως πάσης τοῦτ᾽ ἐστίν),
τεθεώρηται μὲν οὖν ἱκανῶς περὶ αὐτῶν ἡμῖν ἐν τοῖς περὶ φύσεως, ὅμως δὲ παραλάβωμεν καὶ τοὺς πρότερον ἡμῶν εἰς 983ᵇ
ἐπίσκεψιν τῶν ὄντων ἐλθόντας καὶ φιλοσοφήσαντας περὶ
τῆς ἀληθείας. δῆλον γὰρ ὅτι κἀκεῖνοι λέγουσιν ἀρχάς τινας
καὶ αἰτίας· ἐπελθοῦσιν οὖν ἔσται τι προὔργου τῇ μεθόδῳ τῇ νῦν·
ἢ γὰρ ἕτερόν τι γένος εὑρήσομεν αἰτίας ἢ ταῖς νῦν λεγο- 5
μέναις μᾶλλον πιστεύσομεν.—τῶν δὴ πρώτων φιλοσοφησάντων οἱ πλεῖστοι τὰς ἐν ὕλης εἴδει μόνας ᾠήθησαν ἀρχὰς
εἶναι πάντων· ἐξ οὗ γὰρ ἔστιν ἅπαντα τὰ ὄντα καὶ ἐξ οὗ
γίγνεται πρῶτου καὶ εἰς ὃ φθείρεται τελευταῖον, τῆς μὲν
οὐσίας ὑπομενούσης τοῖς δὲ πάθεσι μεταβαλλούσης, τοῦτο στοι- 10
χεῖον καὶ ταύτην ἀρχήν φασιν εἶναι τῶν ὄντων, καὶ διὰ
τοῦτο οὔτε γίγνεσθαι οὐθὲν οἴονται οὔτε ἀπόλλυσθαι, ὡς τῆς
τοιαύτης φύσεως ἀεὶ σωζομένης, ὥσπερ οὐδὲ τὸν Σωκράτην
φαμὲν οὔτε γίγνεσθαι ἁπλῶς ὅταν γίγνηται καλὸς ἢ μουσικὸς οὔτε ἀπόλλυσθαι ὅταν ἀποβάλλῃ ταύτας τὰς ἕξεις, 15
διὰ τὸ ὑπομένειν τὸ ὑποκείμενον τὸν Σωκράτην αὐτόν, οὕτως
οὐδὲ τῶν ἄλλων οὐδέν· ἀεὶ γὰρ εἶναί τινα φύσιν ἢ μίαν ἢ
πλείους μιᾶς ἐξ ὧν γίγνεται τἆλλα σωζομένης ἐκείνης. τὸ
μέντοι πλῆθος καὶ τὸ εἶδος τῆς τοιαύτης ἀρχῆς οὐ τὸ αὐτὸ
πάντες λέγουσιν, ἀλλὰ Θαλῆς μὲν ὁ τῆς τοιαύτης ἀρχηγὸς 20
φιλοσοφίας ὕδωρ φησὶν εἶναι (διὸ καὶ τὴν γῆν ἐφ᾽ ὕδατος
ἀπεφήνατο εἶναι), λαβὼν ἴσως τὴν ὑπόληψιν ταύτην ἐκ τοῦ πάντων ὁρᾶν τὴν τροφὴν ὑγρὰν οὖσαν καὶ αὐτὸ τὸ θερμὸν ἐκ τούτου
γιγνόμενον καὶ τούτῳ ζῶν (τὸ δ᾽ ἐξ οὗ γίγνεται, τοῦτ᾽ ἐστὶν
ἀρχὴ πάντων)—διά τε δὴ τοῦτο τὴν ὑπόληψιν λαβὼν ταύτην 25
καὶ διὰ τὸ πάντων τὰ σπέρματα τὴν φύσιν ὑγρὰν ἔχειν,
τὸ δ᾽ ὕδωρ ἀρχὴν τῆς φύσεως εἶναι τοῖς ὑγροῖς. εἰσὶ δέ

ᵃ 29 ἑτέραν] μίαν ΕΓ   30 δὲ] δὲ τὴν Aᵇ   31 τὸ Aᵇ Al.¹:
καὶ τὸ ΕΓ Asc.ᶜ   33 τεθεώρηται μὲν Aᵇ γρ. Ε: τεθεωρημένων Ε
ἡμῖν om. ΕΓ   ᵇ 1 δὲ om. Ε¹   6 πρώτων Aᵇ Al.¹: πρώτον ΕΓ
13 σωζομένης. ὥσπερ ⟨γὰρ⟩ Jaeger   Σωκράτη Ε   15 ἀποβάλῃ Aᵇ
16 ὑπομένειν Ε Asc.ᶜ: μένειν Aᵇ   17 ἀεὶ Bywater: δεῖ codd. Γ:
δεῖν Wirth   ἢ pr. ΕΓ Asc.ᶜ: om. Aᵇ   21 φησὶν εἶναι ΕΓ Asc.:
εἶναί φησιν Aᵇ   22 ἀπεφαίνετο AᵇΓ   ταύτην om. recc.   24 καὶ
Aᵇ Al.: καὶ τὸ ζῷον ΕΓ Asc.   27 ἀρχὴ τῆς φύσεώς ἐστι Ε Al.

τινες οἱ καὶ τοὺς παμπαλαίους καὶ πολὺ πρὸ τῆς νῦν γενέσεως καὶ πρώτους θεολογήσαντας οὕτως οἴονται περὶ τῆς φύ-
30 σεως ὑπολαβεῖν· Ὠκεανόν τε γὰρ καὶ Τηθὺν ἐποίησαν τῆς
γενέσεως πατέρας, καὶ τὸν ὅρκον τῶν θεῶν ὕδωρ, τὴν καλου-
μένην ὑπ' αὐτῶν Στύγα [τῶν ποιητῶν]· τιμιώτατον μὲν γὰρ
τὸ πρεσβύτατον, ὅρκος δὲ τὸ τιμιώτατόν ἐστιν. εἰ μὲν οὖν
984ª ἀρχαία τις αὕτη καὶ παλαιὰ τετύχηκεν οὖσα περὶ τῆς φύσεως ἡ δόξα, τάχ' ἂν ἄδηλον εἴη, Θαλῆς μέντοι λέγεται
οὕτως ἀποφήνασθαι περὶ τῆς πρώτης αἰτίας (Ἵππωνα γὰρ
οὐκ ἄν τις ἀξιώσειε θεῖναι μετὰ τούτων διὰ τὴν εὐτέλειαν
5 αὐτοῦ τῆς διανοίας)· Ἀναξιμένης δὲ ἀέρα καὶ Διογένης πρότερον ὕδατος καὶ μάλιστ' ἀρχὴν τιθέασι τῶν ἁπλῶν σωμάτων, Ἵππασος δὲ πῦρ ὁ Μεταποντῖνος καὶ Ἡράκλειτος ὁ
Ἐφέσιος, Ἐμπεδοκλῆς δὲ τὰ τέτταρα, πρὸς τοῖς εἰρημένοις
γῆν προστιθεὶς τέταρτον (ταῦτα γὰρ ἀεὶ διαμένειν καὶ οὐ
10 γίγνεσθαι ἀλλ' ἢ πλήθει καὶ ὀλιγότητι, συγκρινόμενα καὶ
διακρινόμενα εἰς ἕν τε καὶ ἐξ ἑνός)· Ἀναξαγόρας δὲ ὁ Κλαζομένιος τῇ μὲν ἡλικίᾳ πρότερος ὢν τούτου τοῖς δ' ἔργοις
ὕστερος ἀπείρους εἶναί φησι τὰς ἀρχάς· σχεδὸν γὰρ ἅπαντα
τὰ ὁμοιομερῆ καθάπερ ὕδωρ ἢ πῦρ οὕτω γίγνεσθαι καὶ
15 ἀπόλλυσθαί φησι, συγκρίσει καὶ διακρίσει μόνον, ἄλλως δ'
οὔτε γίγνεσθαι οὔτ' ἀπόλλυσθαι ἀλλὰ διαμένειν ἀίδια.—ἐκ
μὲν οὖν τούτων μόνην τις αἰτίαν νομίσειεν ἂν τὴν ἐν ὕλης
εἴδει λεγομένην· προϊόντων δ' οὕτως, αὐτὸ τὸ πρᾶγμα ὡδο-
ποίησεν αὐτοῖς καὶ συνηνάγκασε ζητεῖν· εἰ γὰρ ὅτι μάλιστα
20 πᾶσα γένεσις καὶ φθορὰ ἔκ τινος ἑνὸς ἢ καὶ πλειόνων ἐστίν,
διὰ τί τοῦτο συμβαίνει καὶ τί τὸ αἴτιον; οὐ γὰρ δὴ τό γε
ὑποκείμενον αὐτὸ ποιεῖ μεταβάλλειν ἑαυτό· λέγω δ' οἷον
οὔτε τὸ ξύλον οὔτε ὁ χαλκὸς αἴτιος τοῦ μεταβάλλειν ἑκάτερον αὐτῶν, οὐδὲ ποιεῖ τὸ μὲν ξύλον κλίνην ὁ δὲ χαλκὸς ἀν-
25 δριάντα, ἀλλ' ἕτερόν τι τῆς μεταβολῆς αἴτιον. τὸ δὲ τοῦτο
ζητεῖν ἐστὶ τὸ τὴν ἑτέραν ἀρχὴν ζητεῖν, ὡς ἂν ἡμεῖς φαίη-

b 28 παλαιοὺς Aᵇ : πάνυ παλαιοὺς Al.ᶜ   31 καὶ om. Γ   32 τῶν
ποιητῶν om. fort. Al., secl. Christ   984ª 3 οὕτως Aᵇ Al.¹ : τούτου
τὸν τρόπον ΕΓ   γὰρ] μὲν γὰρ ΕΓ Asc.   7 ὁ alt. om. Aᵇ
9 προσθεὶς Ε Al.¹   10 ἢ om. Aᵇ Asc.ᶜ   15 ἁπλῶς Zeller
16 μένειν Aᵇ Asc.   17 ἂν om. Aᵇ   20 γένεσις καὶ φθορὰ Aᵇ Asc. :
φθορὰ καὶ γένεσις ΕΓ   καὶ ΕΓ Asc. : om. Aᵇ   21 γε] τ' Aᵇ¹
24 ὁ δὲ] οὐδ' ὁ Γ

μεν, ὅθεν ἡ ἀρχὴ τῆς κινήσεως. οἱ μὲν οὖν πάμπαν ἐξ ἀρχῆς ἀψάμενοι τῆς μεθόδου τῆς τοιαύτης καὶ ἓν φάσκοντες
εἶναι τὸ ὑποκείμενον οὐθὲν ἐδυσχέραναν ἑαυτοῖς, ἀλλ' ἔνιοί
γε τῶν ἓν λεγόντων, ὥσπερ ἡττηθέντες ὑπὸ ταύτης τῆς ζη- 30
τήσεως, τὸ ἓν ἀκίνητόν φασιν εἶναι καὶ τὴν φύσιν ὅλην οὐ
μόνον κατὰ γένεσιν καὶ φθοράν (τοῦτο μὲν γὰρ ἀρχαῖόν τε
καὶ πάντες ὡμολόγησαν) ἀλλὰ καὶ κατὰ τὴν ἄλλην μετα-
βολὴν πᾶσαν· καὶ τοῦτο αὐτῶν ἴδιόν ἐστιν. τῶν μὲν οὖν ἓν 984^b
φασκόντων εἶναι τὸ πᾶν οὐθενὶ συνέβη τὴν τοιαύτην συνιδεῖν
αἰτίαν πλὴν εἰ ἄρα Παρμενίδῃ, καὶ τούτῳ κατὰ τοσοῦτον
ὅσον οὐ μόνον ἓν ἀλλὰ καὶ δύο πως τίθησιν αἰτίας εἶναι·
τοῖς δὲ δὴ πλείω ποιοῦσι μᾶλλον ἐνδέχεται λέγειν, οἷον τοῖς 5
θερμὸν καὶ ψυχρὸν ἢ πῦρ καὶ γῆν· χρῶνται γὰρ ὡς κινη-
τικὴν ἔχοντι τῷ πυρὶ τὴν φύσιν, ὕδατι δὲ καὶ γῇ καὶ τοῖς
τοιούτοις τοὐναντίον.—μετὰ δὲ τούτους καὶ τὰς τοιαύτας ἀρχάς,
ὡς οὐχ ἱκανῶν οὐσῶν γεννῆσαι τὴν τῶν ὄντων φύσιν, πάλιν
ὑπ' αὐτῆς τῆς ἀληθείας, ὥσπερ εἴπομεν, ἀναγκαζόμενοι τὴν 10
ἐχομένην ἐζήτησαν ἀρχήν. τοῦ γὰρ εὖ καὶ καλῶς τὰ μὲν
ἔχειν τὰ δὲ γίγνεσθαι τῶν ὄντων ἴσως οὔτε πῦρ οὔτε γῆν οὔτ'
ἄλλο τῶν τοιούτων οὐθὲν οὔτ' εἰκὸς αἴτιον εἶναι οὔτ' ἐκείνους
οἰηθῆναι· οὐδ' αὖ τῷ αὐτομάτῳ καὶ τύχῃ τοσοῦτον ἐπιτρέ-
ψαι πρᾶγμα καλῶς εἶχεν. νοῦν δή τις εἰπὼν ἐνεῖναι, κα- 15
θάπερ ἐν τοῖς ζῴοις, καὶ ἐν τῇ φύσει τὸν αἴτιον τοῦ κόσμου
καὶ τῆς τάξεως πάσης οἷον νήφων ἐφάνη παρ' εἰκῇ λέγοντας τοὺς πρότερον. φανερῶς μὲν οὖν 'Αναξαγόραν ἴσμεν
ἁψάμενον τούτων τῶν λόγων, αἰτίαν δ' ἔχει πρότερον Ἑρ-
μότιμος ὁ Κλαζομένιος εἰπεῖν. οἱ μὲν οὖν οὕτως ὑπολαμβά- 20
νοντες ἅμα τοῦ καλῶς τὴν αἰτίαν ἀρχὴν εἶναι τῶν ὄντων
ἔθεσαν, καὶ τὴν τοιαύτην ὅθεν ἡ κίνησις ὑπάρχει τοῖς οὖσιν·

---

^a 28 τῆς τοιαύτης] ταύτης γρ. Ε Asc.¹   29 ἐν ἑαυτοῖς A^b
32 τοῦτο . . . 33 ὡμολόγησαν et ^b 1 καὶ . . . ἐστιν ΕΓ Asc.: om. A^b et
fort. Al.   ^b 1 πᾶσαν Ε Al.: ἅπασαν A^b   ἐν A^b Al.¹ Asc.¹: ἐν μόνον
ΕΓ   2 συνιδεῖν ΕΓ Asc.¹: ἰδεῖν A^b: εἶναι ἰδεῖν Al.¹   3 τοῦτο Γ
5 δὴ A^b Al.¹: om. ΕΓ Asc.^c   11 ἀρχήν] ἀρχὴν τουτέστι τὴν ποιητικὴν τούτων εὖ ἔχειν καὶ καλῶς A^b et fort. Asc.   12 δὲ] δὲ μὴ Γ
13 ἄλλο] ἄλλο τι A^b   13–4 ἐκείνους εἰκὸς οἰηθῆναι ΕΓ   14 καὶ τῇ
τύχῃ A^b   15 ἔχειν ΕΓ   δή] δ' εἰ γρ. Ε: τε Γ   16 τοῖς A^b Asc.:
om. Ε Simpl.^c   τὸν Ε Simpl.^c: τὸ A^b   τοῦ A^b Asc.^c: καὶ τοῦ
ΕΓ Simpl.^c   17 εἰκῇ λέγοντας] μεθύοντας in marg. Ε¹   22 καὶ
ἔθεσαν τὴν τοιαύτην γρ. Ε

ὑποπτεύσειε δ' ἄν τις Ἡσίοδον πρῶτον ζητῆσαι τὸ τοιοῦ- 4
τον, κἂν εἴ τις ἄλλος ἔρωτα ἢ ἐπιθυμίαν ἐν τοῖς οὖσιν ἔθη-
25 κεν ὡς ἀρχήν, οἷον καὶ Παρμενίδης· καὶ γὰρ οὗτος κατα-
σκευάζων τὴν τοῦ παντὸς γένεσιν " πρώτιστον μέν" φησιν
" ἔρωτα θεῶν μητίσατο πάντων", Ἡσίοδος δὲ " πάντων μὲν
πρώτιστα χάος γένετ', αὐτὰρ ἔπειτα | γαῖ' εὐρύστερνος ... | ἠδ'
ἔρος, ὃς πάντεσσι μεταπρέπει ἀθανάτοισιν", ὡς δέον ἐν τοῖς
30 οὖσιν ὑπάρχειν τιν' αἰτίαν ἥτις κινήσει καὶ συνάξει τὰ πράγματα. τούτους μὲν οὖν πῶς χρὴ διανεῖμαι περὶ τοῦ τίς πρώ-
τος, ἐξέστω κρίνειν ὕστερον· ἐπεὶ δὲ καὶ τἀναντία τοῖς ἀγα-
θοῖς ἐνόντα ἐφαίνετο ἐν τῇ φύσει, καὶ οὐ μόνον τάξις καὶ
985ᵃ τὸ καλὸν ἀλλὰ καὶ ἀταξία καὶ τὸ αἰσχρόν, καὶ πλείω τὰ
κακὰ τῶν ἀγαθῶν καὶ τὰ φαῦλα τῶν καλῶν, οὕτως ἄλλος
τις φιλίαν εἰσήνεγκε καὶ νεῖκος, ἑκάτερον ἑκατέρων αἴτιον
τούτων. εἰ γάρ τις ἀκολουθοίη καὶ λαμβάνοι πρὸς τὴν διά-
5 νοιαν καὶ μὴ πρὸς ἃ ψελλίζεται λέγων Ἐμπεδοκλῆς, εὑρή-
σει τὴν μὲν φιλίαν αἰτίαν οὖσαν τῶν ἀγαθῶν τὸ δὲ νεῖκος
τῶν κακῶν· ὥστ' εἴ τις φαίη τρόπον τινὰ καὶ λέγειν καὶ
πρῶτον λέγειν τὸ κακὸν καὶ τὸ ἀγαθὸν ἀρχὰς Ἐμπεδοκλέα,
τάχ' ἂν λέγοι καλῶς, εἴπερ τὸ τῶν ἀγαθῶν ἁπάντων αἴτιον
10 αὐτὸ τἀγαθόν ἐστι [καὶ τῶν κακῶν τὸ κακόν].—οὗτοι μὲν οὖν,
ὥσπερ λέγομεν, καὶ μέχρι τούτου δυοῖν αἰτίαιν ὧν ἡμεῖς διωρί-
σαμεν ἐν τοῖς περὶ φύσεως ἡμμένοι φαίνονται, τῆς τε ὕλης καὶ
τοῦ ὅθεν ἡ κίνησις, ἀμυδρῶς μέντοι καὶ οὐθὲν σαφῶς ἀλλ' οἷον
ἐν ταῖς μάχαις οἱ ἀγύμναστοι ποιοῦσιν· καὶ γὰρ ἐκεῖνοι περι-
15 φερόμενοι τύπτουσι πολλάκις καλὰς πληγάς, ἀλλ' οὔτε
ἐκεῖνοι ἀπὸ ἐπιστήμης οὔτε οὗτοι ἐοίκασιν εἰδέναι ὅ τι
λέγουσιν· σχεδὸν γὰρ οὐθὲν χρώμενοι φαίνονται τούτοις ἀλλ'
ἢ κατὰ μικρόν. Ἀναξαγόρας τε γὰρ μηχανῇ χρῆται τῷ

ᵇ 25 καὶ γὰρ οὗτος ΕΓ Asc.ᶜ : οὗτος γὰρ Αᵇ   26 πρώτιστον recc.
Plato Plut. Simpl.: πρῶτον ΕΑᵇ   28 γέα γαῖα Ε   29 ἔρως Αᵇ
30 τιν' Ε Al. Asc.: τὴν ΑᵇΓ   συνέξει Αᵇ   31 τούτοις ΑᵇΓ
32 ἔξεστι fort. Al. Asc.: ἐξέσται Richards   καὶ om. Γ   985ᵃ 1 καὶ
pr. om. Γ   4 λαμβάνει Αᵇ   7 καὶ λέγειν καὶ om. Γ   9 λέγοιτο
Αᵇⁱ   ἁπάντων Ε Asc.ᶜ : πάντων Αᵇ   10 αὐτὸ om. Γ   καὶ ...
κακόν ΕΓ Asc.ᶜ: om. Αᵇ Al. Asc.   11 ἐλέγομεν Γ   δυεῖν Ε
ὧν] ἐφήψαντο ὧν ΕΓ   12 ἡμμένοι φαίνονται om. ΕΓ   τῆς] περὶ
τῆς Αᵇ   16 εἰδέναι] εἰδόσιν λέγειν ΕΓ: εἰδόσι λέγουσι Gomperz:
εἰδότες λέγειν ci. Christ

νῷ πρὸς τὴν κοσμοποιίαν, καὶ ὅταν ἀπορήσῃ διὰ τίν' αἰτίαν
ἐξ ἀνάγκης ἐστί, τότε παρέλκει αὐτόν, ἐν δὲ τοῖς ἄλλοις 20
πάντα μᾶλλον αἰτιᾶται τῶν γιγνομένων ἢ νοῦν, καὶ Ἐμπεδοκλῆς ἐπὶ πλέον μὲν τούτου χρῆται τοῖς αἰτίοις, οὐ μὴν
οὔθ' ἱκανῶς, οὔτ' ἐν τούτοις εὑρίσκει τὸ ὁμολογούμενον. πολλαχοῦ γοῦν αὐτῷ ἡ μὲν φιλία διακρίνει τὸ δὲ νεῖκος συγ-
κρίνει. ὅταν μὲν γὰρ εἰς τὰ στοιχεῖα διίστηται τὸ πᾶν ὑπὸ 25
τοῦ νείκους, τότε τὸ πῦρ εἰς ἓν συγκρίνεται καὶ τῶν ἄλλων
στοιχείων ἕκαστον· ὅταν δὲ πάλιν ὑπὸ τῆς φιλίας συνίωσιν
εἰς τὸ ἕν, ἀναγκαῖον ἐξ ἑκάστου τὰ μόρια διακρίνεσθαι
πάλιν.—Ἐμπεδοκλῆς μὲν οὖν παρὰ τοὺς πρότερον πρῶτος τὸ τὴν αἰτίαν διελεῖν εἰσήνεγκεν, οὐ μίαν ποιήσας 30
τὴν τῆς κινήσεως ἀρχὴν ἀλλ' ἑτέρας τε καὶ ἐναντίας, ἔτι
δὲ τὰ ὡς ἐν ὕλης εἴδει λεγόμενα στοιχεῖα τέτταρα πρῶτος
εἶπεν (οὐ μὴν χρῆταί γε τέτταρσιν ἀλλ' ὡς δυσὶν οὖσι μό-
νοις, πυρὶ μὲν καθ' αὑτὸ τοῖς δ' ἀντικειμένοις ὡς μιᾷ 985^b
φύσει, γῇ τε καὶ ἀέρι καὶ ὕδατι· λάβοι δ' ἄν τις αὐτὸ
θεωρῶν ἐκ τῶν ἐπῶν)·—οὗτος μὲν οὖν, ὥσπερ λέγομεν, οὕτω τε
καὶ τοσαύτας εἴρηκε τὰς ἀρχάς· Λεύκιππος δὲ καὶ ὁ ἑταῖρος
αὐτοῦ Δημόκριτος στοιχεῖα μὲν τὸ πλῆρες καὶ τὸ κενὸν εἶναί 5
φασι, λέγοντες τὸ μὲν ὂν τὸ δὲ μὴ ὄν, τούτων δὲ τὸ μὲν
πλῆρες καὶ στερεὸν τὸ ὄν, τὸ δὲ κενὸν τὸ μὴ ὄν (διὸ
καὶ οὐθὲν μᾶλλον τὸ ὂν τοῦ μὴ ὄντος εἶναί φασιν, ὅτι
οὐδὲ τοῦ κενοῦ τὸ σῶμα), αἴτια δὲ τῶν ὄντων ταῦτα ὡς
ὕλην. καὶ καθάπερ οἱ ἓν ποιοῦντες τὴν ὑποκειμένην οὐσίαν 10
τἆλλα τοῖς πάθεσιν αὐτῆς γεννῶσι, τὸ μανὸν καὶ τὸ πυκνὸν ἀρχὰς τιθέμενοι τῶν παθημάτων, τὸν αὐτὸν τρόπον
καὶ οὗτοι τὰς διαφορὰς αἰτίας τῶν ἄλλων εἶναί φασιν. ταύτας μέντοι τρεῖς εἶναι λέγουσι, σχῆμά τε καὶ τάξιν καὶ

---

^{a} 19 καὶ om. ΕΓ   ἀπορήσῃ] ἀπορήσῃ γὰρ ΕΓ   διὰ ... 20 τότε
om. Α^b γρ. Ε   20 ἕλκει Ε^1 22 τούτου χρῆται ΕΓ Al.^{1} : χρῆται
τούτου Α^b 23 ἐξευρίσκει Α^b : εὑρίσκεται Γ   24 οὖν Γ   25 πᾶν]
εἶναι Γ   26 τότε τὸ ΕΓ Al. : τό τε Α^b 27 πάλιν πάντα ὑπὸ recc.
30 τὸ ... διελεῖν] ταύτην ... διελὼν ΕΓ Asc.   33 μόνον Γ ^{b} 4 τὰς
om. recc.   6 τὸ pr.] οἷον τὸ ΕΓ   7 κενὸν] κενὸν τε καὶ μανὸν
Ε : κενόν γε καὶ μανὸν recc.   9 τοῦ κενοῦ τὸ σῶμα fort. Al. Asc.,
Schwegler : τὸ κενὸν τοῦ σώματος codd. : τὸ κενὸν ἔλαττον τοῦ σώματος
Zeller   γε ὡς Α^b 12 τῶν παθημάτων ἀρχὰς τιθέμενοι Α^b :
ἀ. τῶν π. τιθ. Γ   ante τὸν γρ. Al. καὶ ὥσπερ τῶν μαθηματικῶν

15 θέσιν· διαφέρειν γάρ φασι τὸ ὂν ῥυσμῷ καὶ διαθιγῇ καὶ
τροπῇ μόνον· τούτων δὲ ὁ μὲν ῥυσμὸς σχῆμά ἐστιν ἡ δὲ
διαθιγὴ τάξις ἡ δὲ τροπὴ θέσις· διαφέρει γὰρ τὸ μὲν Α
τοῦ Ν σχήματι τὸ δὲ ΑΝ τοῦ ΝΑ τάξει τὸ δὲ Ⲍ τοῦ Η
θέσει. περὶ δὲ κινήσεως, ὅθεν ἢ πῶς ὑπάρξει τοῖς οὖσι, καὶ
20 οὗτοι παραπλησίως τοῖς ἄλλοις ῥᾳθύμως ἀφεῖσαν. περὶ μὲν
οὖν τῶν δύο αἰτιῶν, ὥσπερ λέγομεν, ἐπὶ τοσοῦτον ἔοικεν ἐζη-
τῆσθαι παρὰ τῶν πρότερον.

Ἐν δὲ τούτοις καὶ πρὸ τούτων οἱ καλούμενοι Πυθαγόρειοι 5
τῶν μαθημάτων ἁψάμενοι πρῶτοι ταῦτά τε προήγαγον, καὶ
25 ἐντραφέντες ἐν αὐτοῖς τὰς τούτων ἀρχὰς τῶν ὄντων ἀρχὰς
ᾠήθησαν εἶναι πάντων. ἐπεὶ δὲ τούτων οἱ ἀριθμοὶ φύσει
πρῶτοι, ἐν δὲ τούτοις ἐδόκουν θεωρεῖν ὁμοιώματα πολλὰ
τοῖς οὖσι καὶ γιγνομένοις, μᾶλλον ἢ ἐν πυρὶ καὶ γῇ καὶ
ὕδατι, ὅτι τὸ μὲν τοιονδὶ τῶν ἀριθμῶν πάθος δικαιοσύνη
30 τὸ δὲ τοιονδὶ ψυχή τε καὶ νοῦς ἕτερον δὲ καιρὸς καὶ τῶν ἄλλων ὡς εἰπεῖν ἕκαστον ὁμοίως, ἔτι δὲ τῶν ἁρμονιῶν ἐν ἀριθμοῖς ὁρῶντες τὰ πάθη καὶ τοὺς λόγους,—ἐπεὶ δὴ τὰ μὲν ἄλλα
τοῖς ἀριθμοῖς ἐφαίνοντο τὴν φύσιν ἀφωμοιῶσθαι πᾶσαν, οἱ
986ᵃ δ' ἀριθμοὶ πάσης τῆς φύσεως πρῶτοι, τὰ τῶν ἀριθμῶν στοιχεῖα τῶν ὄντων στοιχεῖα πάντων ὑπέλαβον εἶναι, καὶ τὸν
ὅλον οὐρανὸν ἁρμονίαν εἶναι καὶ ἀριθμόν· καὶ ὅσα εἶχον
ὁμολογούμενα ἔν τε τοῖς ἀριθμοῖς καὶ ταῖς ἁρμονίαις πρὸς
5 τὰ τοῦ οὐρανοῦ πάθη καὶ μέρη καὶ πρὸς τὴν ὅλην διακό-
σμησιν, ταῦτα συνάγοντες ἐφήρμοττον. κἂν εἴ τί που
διέλειπε, προσεγλίχοντο τοῦ συνειρομένην πᾶσαν αὐτοῖς εἶναι
τὴν πραγματείαν· λέγω δ' οἷον, ἐπειδὴ τέλειον ἡ δεκὰς
εἶναι δοκεῖ καὶ πᾶσαν περιειληφέναι τὴν τῶν ἀριθμῶν φύσιν,

ᵇ 15 διαφέρειν γάρ φασι ΑᵇΓ Asc.ᶜ : διαφέρει γάρ φησι Ε   ῥοισμῷ
Αᵇ   διαθιγῇ Αᵇ Asc.ᶜ : διαθηγῆι Ε   16 ῥοισμὸς Αᵇ   17 διαθιγὴ
Αᵇ Al. Asc. : διαθηγὴ Ε   18 Ⲍ τοῦ Η Wilamowitz : Ζ τοῦ Ν codd.
19 ὑπάρχει ΕΓ   21 ἐλέγομεν Ε   22 παρὰ τῶν om. ΕΓ Asc.ᶜ
24 πρῶτον recc.   τε om. Ε   προήγον Ε Asc.ᶜ   25 τῶν ὄντων ἀρχὰς
Ε Al. Asc. : om. ΑᵇΓ   26 ἐπὶ Ε   27 τούτοις Αᵇ Al. : τοῖς ἀριθμοῖς
ΕΓ Asc.ᶜ   30 τε om. Ε   31 ἁρμονικῶν recc.   32 ἐπεὶ δὴ Christ :
ἐπειδὴ vulg   τὰ] καὶ τὰ Γ   33 ἐφαίνετο Ε   ἀφωμοιῶσθαι recc. :
ἀφομοιῶσθαι Αᵇ : ἀφομοιωθῆναι Ε   πᾶσιν Ε : πάντα fort. Al., ci. Bonitz
986ᵃ 2 εἶναι ὑπέλαβον ΕΓ   3 εἶχεν Αᵇ : εἴχοντο Γ   4 'ἔν Αᵇ et
ut vid. Al. : δεικνύναι ἕν ΕΓ Asc.ᶜ   6 που ΕΓ et ut vid. Al. : πολὺ Αᵇ
7 προσεπεγλίχοντο Ε   τοῦ] ἕνεκεν add. Αᵇ²   8–9 ἡ δεκὰς τελεία δοκεῖ
in marg. Ε¹   9 εἶναι … φύσιν ΕΓ Asc. : om. Αᵇ et fort. Al.

καὶ τὰ φερόμενα κατὰ τὸν οὐρανὸν δέκα μὲν εἶναί φασιν, 10
ὄντων δὲ ἐννέα μόνον τῶν φανερῶν διὰ τοῦτο δεκάτην τὴν
ἀντίχθονα ποιοῦσιν. διώρισται δὲ περὶ τούτων ἐν ἑτέροις
ἡμῖν ἀκριβέστερον. ἀλλ᾽ οὗ δὴ χάριν ἐπερχόμεθα, τοῦτό ἐστιν
ὅπως λάβωμεν καὶ παρὰ τούτων τίνας εἶναι τιθέασι τὰς
ἀρχὰς καὶ πῶς εἰς τὰς εἰρημένας ἐμπίπτουσιν αἰτίας. φαί- 15
νονται δὴ καὶ οὗτοι τὸν ἀριθμὸν νομίζοντες ἀρχὴν εἶναι καὶ
ὡς ὕλην τοῖς οὖσι καὶ ὡς πάθη τε καὶ ἕξεις, τοῦ δὲ ἀριθμοῦ
στοιχεῖα τό τε ἄρτιον καὶ τὸ περιττόν, τούτων δὲ τὸ μὲν πεπερασμένον τὸ δὲ ἄπειρον, τὸ δ᾽ ἓν ἐξ ἀμφοτέρων εἶναι τούτων (καὶ γὰρ ἄρτιον εἶναι καὶ περιττόν), τὸν δ᾽ ἀριθμὸν ἐκ 20
τοῦ ἑνός, ἀριθμοὺς δέ, καθάπερ εἴρηται, τὸν ὅλον οὐρανόν.—
ἕτεροι δὲ τῶν αὐτῶν τούτων τὰς ἀρχὰς δέκα λέγουσιν εἶναι
τὰς κατὰ συστοιχίαν λεγομένας, πέρας [καὶ] ἄπειρον, περιτ-
τὸν [καὶ] ἄρτιον, ἓν [καὶ] πλῆθος, δεξιὸν [καὶ] ἀριστερόν, ἄρρεν
[καὶ] θῆλυ, ἠρεμοῦν [καὶ] κινούμενον, εὐθὺ [καὶ] καμπύλον, φῶς 25
[καὶ] σκότος, ἀγαθὸν [καὶ] κακόν, τετράγωνον [καὶ] ἑτερόμηκες·
ὅνπερ τρόπον ἔοικε καὶ Ἀλκμαίων ὁ Κροτωνιάτης ὑπολαβεῖν, καὶ ἤτοι οὗτος παρ᾽ ἐκείνων ἢ ἐκεῖνοι παρὰ τούτου παρέλαβον τὸν λόγον τοῦτον· καὶ γὰρ [ἐγένετο τὴν ἡλικίαν] Ἀλκμαίων [ἐπὶ γέροντι Πυθαγόρᾳ,] ἀπεφήνατο [δὲ] παραπλησίως 30
τούτοις· φησὶ γὰρ εἶναι δύο τὰ πολλὰ τῶν ἀνθρωπίνων, λέγων τὰς ἐναντιότητας οὐχ ὥσπερ οὗτοι διωρισμένας ἀλλὰ
τὰς τυχούσας, οἷον λευκὸν μέλαν, γλυκὺ πικρόν, ἀγαθὸν
κακόν, μέγα μικρόν. οὗτος μὲν οὖν ἀδιορίστως ἀπέρριψε περὶ
τῶν λοιπῶν, οἱ δὲ Πυθαγόρειοι καὶ πόσαι καὶ τίνες αἱ ἐναν- 986ᵇ
τιώσεις ἀπεφήναντο. παρὰ μὲν οὖν τούτων ἀμφοῖν τοσοῦτον
ἔστι λαβεῖν, ὅτι τἀναντία ἀρχαὶ τῶν ὄντων· τὸ δ᾽ ὅσαι
παρὰ τῶν ἑτέρων, καὶ τίνες αὗταί εἰσιν. πῶς μέντοι πρὸς
τὰς εἰρημένας αἰτίας ἐνδέχεται συνάγειν, σαφῶς μὲν οὐ 5
διήρθρωται παρ᾽ ἐκείνων, ἐοίκασι δ᾽ ὡς ἐν ὕλης εἴδει τὰ

ᵃ 11 μόνον recc. Γ: μόνων ΕΑᵇ   16 δὴ ΕΓ Al.: δὲ Αᵇ Asc.¹
18 τε om. Ε   πεπερασμένον τὸ δ᾽ ἄπειρον ΕΓ Al. Asc.: ἄπειρον τὸ
δὲ πεπερασμένον Αᵇ   20 καὶ...περιττόν Ε Al.: om. Αᵇ   23 συστο-
χίαν Αᵇ¹   23, 24 καὶ quater om. Ε   24 καὶ alt. et tert. om. Γ
25, 26 καὶ sexies om. ΕΓ et fort. Al.   28 καὶ om. Γ   29, 30 verba
uncinis inclusa ΕΓ Asc.: om. Αᵇ et fort. Al.   30 ἐπὶ] νέος ἐπὶ
Diels   34 μικρὸν μέγα Ε Asc.ᶜ   ἐπέρριψε recc.   ᵇ 2 ἀμφοῖν]
ἀμφοῖν μὲν Αᵇ   3 τὸ...4 ἑτέρων ΕΓ Asc.: om. Αᵇ   5 συναγαγεῖν Αᵇ

στοιχεῖα τάττειν· ἐκ τούτων γὰρ ὡς ἐνυπαρχόντων συνεστά-
ναι καὶ πεπλάσθαι φασὶ τὴν οὐσίαν.—τῶν μὲν οὖν παλαιῶν
καὶ πλείω λεγόντων τὰ στοιχεῖα τῆς φύσεως ἐκ τούτων ἱκα-
10 νόν ἐστι θεωρῆσαι τὴν διάνοιαν· εἰσὶ δέ τινες οἳ περὶ τοῦ
παντὸς ὡς μιᾶς οὔσης φύσεως ἀπεφήναντο, τρόπον δὲ οὐ τὸν
αὐτὸν πάντες οὔτε τοῦ καλῶς οὔτε τοῦ κατὰ τὴν φύσιν. εἰς
μὲν οὖν τὴν νῦν σκέψιν τῶν αἰτίων οὐδαμῶς συναρμόττει περὶ
αὐτῶν ὁ λόγος (οὐ γὰρ ὥσπερ ἔνιοι τῶν φυσιολόγων ἐν ὑπο-
15 θέμενοι τὸ ὂν ὅμως γεννῶσιν ὡς ἐξ ὕλης τοῦ ἑνός, ἀλλ' ἕτερον τρόπον οὗτοι λέγουσιν· ἐκεῖνοι μὲν γὰρ προστιθέασι κίνησιν,
γεννῶντές γε τὸ πᾶν, οὗτοι δὲ ἀκίνητον εἶναί φασιν)· οὐ μὴν
ἀλλὰ τοσοῦτόν γε οἰκεῖόν ἐστι τῇ νῦν σκέψει. Παρμενίδης
μὲν γὰρ ἔοικε τοῦ κατὰ τὸν λόγον ἑνὸς ἅπτεσθαι, Μέλισσος
20 δὲ τοῦ κατὰ τὴν ὕλην (διὸ καὶ ὁ μὲν πεπερασμένον ὁ δ'
ἄπειρόν φησιν εἶναι αὐτό)· Ξενοφάνης δὲ πρῶτος τούτων ἑνίσας (ὁ γὰρ Παρμενίδης τούτου λέγεται γενέσθαι μαθητής) οὐθὲν
διεσαφήνισεν, οὐδὲ τῆς φύσεως τούτων οὐδετέρας ἔοικε θιγεῖν,
ἀλλ' εἰς τὸν ὅλον οὐρανὸν ἀποβλέψας τὸ ἓν εἶναί φησι τὸν
25 θεόν. οὗτοι μὲν οὖν, καθάπερ εἴπομεν, ἀφετέοι πρὸς τὴν
νῦν ζήτησιν, οἱ μὲν δύο καὶ πάμπαν ὡς ὄντες μικρὸν
ἀγροικότεροι, Ξενοφάνης καὶ Μέλισσος· Παρμενίδης δὲ
μᾶλλον βλέπων ἔοικέ που λέγειν· παρὰ γὰρ τὸ ὂν τὸ μὴ
ὂν οὐθὲν ἀξιῶν εἶναι, ἐξ ἀνάγκης ἓν οἴεται εἶναι, τὸ ὄν, καὶ
30 ἄλλο οὐθέν (περὶ οὗ σαφέστερον ἐν τοῖς περὶ φύσεως εἰρήκαμεν), ἀναγκαζόμενος δ' ἀκολουθεῖν τοῖς φαινομένοις, καὶ τὸ
ἓν μὲν κατὰ τὸν λόγον πλείω δὲ κατὰ τὴν αἴσθησιν ὑπολαμβάνων εἶναι, δύο τὰς αἰτίας καὶ δύο τὰς ἀρχὰς πάλιν
τίθησι, θερμὸν καὶ ψυχρόν, οἷον πῦρ καὶ γῆν λέγων· τού-
987ᵃ των δὲ κατὰ μὲν τὸ ὂν τὸ θερμὸν τάττει θάτερον δὲ κατὰ

ᵇ 9 λεγόντων τὰ στοιχεῖα Aᵇ Al.¹: τὰ στοιχεῖα λεγόντων Ε Asc.¹
11 ὡς Aᵇ Al.: ὡς ἂν Ε   12 τὴν om. ut vid. Al. Asc.ᶜ   16 μὲν
om. Γ   γὰρ om. Christ   17 γε om. Aᵇ   19 τὸν om. Aᵇ Asc.ᶜ
21 δὲ] δ' ὁ Richards   22 τούτου Aᵇ Asc.: ὃς τούτου ΕΓ
γενέσθαι Aᵇ et ut vid. Al.: om. ΕΓ   23 οὔτε Aᵇ   οὐδετέρας
ἔοικε τούτων Aᵇ   24 τὸν θεόν ΕΓ Al. Asc.: om. Aᵇ   26 νῦν Ε
Asc.: νῦν παροῦσαν Aᵇ   28 βλέπων om. Ε   που om. Γ
30 σαφεστέρως Ε Asc.ᶜ   31 τὸ ἕν] ἓν Bywater: τὸ ὂν ἓν ex Al. ci.
Christ   32 ὑπολαβὼν Aᵇ   33 τὰς alt. om. Aᵇ   987ᵃ 1 δὲ]
μὲν Aᵇ   κατὰ μὲν] τὸ μὲν κατὰ ΕΓ

τὸ μὴ ὄν.—ἐκ μὲν οὖν τῶν εἰρημένων καὶ παρὰ τῶν συνηδρευκότων ἤδη τῷ λόγῳ σοφῶν ταῦτα παρειλήφαμεν, παρὰ
μὲν τῶν πρώτων σωματικήν τε τὴν ἀρχήν (ὕδωρ γὰρ καὶ
πῦρ καὶ τὰ τοιαῦτα σώματά ἐστιν), καὶ τῶν μὲν μίαν τῶν 5
δὲ πλείους τὰς ἀρχὰς τὰς σωματικάς, ἀμφοτέρων μέντοι
ταύτας ὡς ἐν ὕλης εἴδει τιθέντων, παρὰ δέ τινων ταύτην τε
τὴν αἰτίαν τιθέντων καὶ πρὸς ταύτῃ τὴν ὅθεν ἡ κίνησις, καὶ
ταύτην παρὰ τῶν μὲν μίαν παρὰ τῶν δὲ δύο. μέχρι μὲν
οὖν τῶν Ἰταλικῶν καὶ χωρὶς ἐκείνων μορυχώτερον εἰρήκασιν 10
οἱ ἄλλοι περὶ αὐτῶν, πλὴν ὥσπερ εἴπομεν δυοῖν τε αἰτίαιν
τυγχάνουσι κεχρημένοι, καὶ τούτων τὴν ἑτέραν οἱ μὲν μίαν
οἱ δὲ δύο ποιοῦσι, τὴν ὅθεν ἡ κίνησις· οἱ δὲ Πυθαγόρειοι δύο
μὲν τὰς ἀρχὰς κατὰ τὸν αὐτὸν εἰρήκασι τρόπον, τοσοῦτον
δὲ προσεπέθεσαν ὃ καὶ ἴδιόν ἐστιν αὐτῶν, ὅτι τὸ πεπερα- 15
σμένον καὶ τὸ ἄπειρον [καὶ τὸ ἓν] οὐχ ἑτέρας τινὰς ᾠήθησαν
εἶναι φύσεις, οἷον πῦρ ἢ γῆν ἤ τι τοιοῦτον ἕτερον, ἀλλ᾽ αὐτὸ
τὸ ἄπειρον καὶ αὐτὸ τὸ ἓν οὐσίαν εἶναι τούτων ὧν κατηγο-
ροῦνται, διὸ καὶ ἀριθμὸν εἶναι τὴν οὐσίαν πάντων. περί τε
τούτων οὖν τοῦτον ἀπεφήναντο τὸν τρόπον, καὶ περὶ τοῦ τί ἐστιν 20
ἤρξαντο μὲν λέγειν καὶ ὁρίζεσθαι, λίαν δ᾽ ἁπλῶς ἐπραγμα-
τεύθησαν. ὡρίζοντό τε γὰρ ἐπιπολαίως, καὶ ᾧ πρώτῳ ὑπάρ-
ξειεν ὁ λεχθεὶς ὅρος, τοῦτ᾽ εἶναι τὴν οὐσίαν τοῦ πράγματος ἐνόμιζον, ὥσπερ εἴ τις οἴοιτο ταὐτὸν εἶναι διπλάσιον καὶ τὴν
δυάδα διότι πρῶτον ὑπάρχει τοῖς δυσὶ τὸ διπλάσιον. ἀλλ᾽ 25
οὐ ταὐτὸν ἴσως ἐστὶ τὸ εἶναι διπλασίῳ καὶ δυάδι· εἰ δὲ μή,
πολλὰ τὸ ἓν ἔσται, ὃ κἀκείνοις συνέβαινεν. παρὰ μὲν οὖν
τῶν πρότερον καὶ τῶν ἄλλων τοσαῦτα ἔστι λαβεῖν.

6 Μετὰ δὲ τὰς εἰρημένας φιλοσοφίας ἡ Πλάτωνος ἐπεγένετο πραγματεία, τὰ μὲν πολλὰ τούτοις ἀκολουθοῦσα, τὰ 30
δὲ καὶ ἴδια παρὰ τὴν τῶν Ἰταλικῶν ἔχουσα φιλοσοφίαν.

ᵃ 2 καὶ om. Γ   συνεδρευκότων Aᵇ   3 ταῦτα ΕΓ Asc.ᶜ : τοσαῦτα
Aᵇ   6 τὰς pr. om. E   7 ὡς] οὐδὲν ὡς Γ   8 τιθέντων secl.
Christ   9 παρ᾽ ὧν bis Aᵇ   10 μορυχώτερον γρ. Al., fort. Asc. :
μαλακώτερον Aᵇ γρ. Ε : μετριώτερον ΕΓ Al.¹ : μοναχώτερον Al. : μονι-
μώτερον Asc.ᶜ   11 περὶ τῶν αὐτῶν Ε   15 αὐτῶν ἐστιν ΕΓ
16 καὶ τὸ ἓν Aᵇ et fort. Al. : om. ΕΓ Asc.   19 πάντων Aᵇ Asc. :
ἁπάντων Ε   20 οὖν om. Aᵇ   ἀπεφήναντο τούτον Aᵇ   22 πρώτῳ
ΕΓ Al. : πρώτως Aᵇ Asc.   23 ἐνόμισαν ΕΓ   25 δύο Aᵇ
26 ἴσως ἐστὶ ΕΓ Al.ᶜ : ἐστὶν ἴσως Aᵇ   28 καὶ τῶν ἄλλων secl.
Jaeger   31 ἴδια Aᵇ Asc. : ἰδίᾳ Ε

ἐκ νέου τε γὰρ συνήθης γενόμενος πρῶτον Κρατύλῳ καὶ ταῖς
Ἡρακλειτείοις δόξαις, ὡς ἁπάντων τῶν αἰσθητῶν ἀεὶ ῥεόντων καὶ ἐπιστήμης περὶ αὐτῶν οὐκ οὔσης, ταῦτα μὲν καὶ ὕστε-
987ᵇ ρον οὕτως ὑπέλαβεν· Σωκράτους δὲ περὶ μὲν τὰ ἠθικὰ
πραγματευομένου περὶ δὲ τῆς ὅλης φύσεως οὐθέν, ἐν μέντοι
τούτοις τὸ καθόλου ζητοῦντος καὶ περὶ ὁρισμῶν ἐπιστήσαντος
πρώτου τὴν διάνοιαν, ἐκεῖνον ἀποδεξάμενος διὰ τὸ τοιοῦτον
5 ὑπέλαβεν ὡς περὶ ἑτέρων τοῦτο γιγνόμενον καὶ οὐ τῶν αἰσθη-
τῶν· ἀδύνατον γὰρ εἶναι τὸν κοινὸν ὅρον τῶν αἰσθητῶν
τινός, ἀεί γε μεταβαλλόντων. οὗτος οὖν τὰ μὲν τοιαῦτα τῶν
ὄντων ἰδέας προσηγόρευσε, τὰ δ᾽ αἰσθητὰ παρὰ ταῦτα καὶ
κατὰ ταῦτα λέγεσθαι πάντα· κατὰ μέθεξιν γὰρ εἶναι τὰ
10 πολλὰ ὁμώνυμα τοῖς εἴδεσιν. τὴν δὲ μέθεξιν τοὔνομα
μόνον μετέβαλεν· οἱ μὲν γὰρ Πυθαγόρειοι μιμήσει τὰ ὄντα
φασὶν εἶναι τῶν ἀριθμῶν, Πλάτων δὲ μεθέξει, τοὔνομα μεταβαλών. τὴν μέντοι γε μέθεξιν ἢ τὴν μίμησιν ἥτις ἂν εἴη
τῶν εἰδῶν ἀφεῖσαν ἐν κοινῷ ζητεῖν. ἔτι δὲ παρὰ τὰ αἰσθητὰ
15 καὶ τὰ εἴδη τὰ μαθηματικὰ τῶν πραγμάτων εἶναί φησι
μεταξύ, διαφέροντα τῶν μὲν αἰσθητῶν τῷ ἀΐδια καὶ ἀκίνητα εἶναι, τῶν δ᾽ εἰδῶν τῷ τὰ μὲν πόλλ᾽ ἄττα ὅμοια εἶναι
τὸ δὲ εἶδος αὐτὸ ἓν ἕκαστον μόνον. ἐπεὶ δ᾽ αἴτια τὰ εἴδη
τοῖς ἄλλοις, τἀκείνων στοιχεῖα πάντων ᾠήθη τῶν ὄντων εἶναι
20 στοιχεῖα. ὡς μὲν οὖν ὕλην τὸ μέγα καὶ τὸ μικρὸν εἶναι
ἀρχάς, ὡς δ᾽ οὐσίαν τὸ ἕν· ἐξ ἐκείνων γὰρ κατὰ μέθεξιν τοῦ
ἑνὸς [τὰ εἴδη] εἶναι τοὺς ἀριθμούς. τὸ μέντοι γε ἓν οὐσίαν εἶναι,
καὶ μὴ ἕτερόν γέ τι ὂν λέγεσθαι ἕν, παραπλησίως τοῖς Πυ-
θαγορείοις ἔλεγε, καὶ τὸ τοὺς ἀριθμοὺς αἰτίους εἶναι τοῖς ἄλλοις
25 τῆς οὐσίας ὡσαύτως ἐκείνοις· τὸ δὲ ἀντὶ τοῦ ἀπείρου ὡς ἑνὸς

ᵃ 32 τε om. Aᵇ   συνήθης γενόμενος Aᵇ Al. : συγγενόμενος E Asc.
πρῶτον om. Γ   ᵇ 1 οὗτος E   2 μέντοι] δὲ Aᵇ   5 γιγνομένων
Aᵇ   οὐ E Al. : οὐ περὶ AᵇΓ   αἰσθητῶν] αἰσθητῶν τινός ΕΓ Al.
6 ὅρον Aᵇ Al. : λόγον ΕΓ   7 οὕτως Aᵇ   τὰ μὲν οὖν Aᵇ : μὲν
οὖν τὰ recc.   8 ἰδέας καὶ εἴδη Γ   10 ὁμώνυμα scripsi : τῶν συνωνύμων Aᵇ γρ. ΕΓ Al. Asc. : τῶν συνωνύμων ὁμώνυμα E   11 μόνον
E Al.¹ : om. AᵇΓ Asc.ᶜ   μετέβαλεν E Asc.ᶜ : μετέλαβεν Aᵇ AI.¹
12 τοὔνομα μεταβαλών om. Aᵇ   13 γε om. Aᵇ   14 τῶν εἰδῶν
secl. Gillespie, post μεθέξει l. 12 transposuit Jackson   ἀφῆσαν Aᵇ
17 πολλὰ τὰ Aᵇ   19 πάντων E Al. Asc.ᶜ : ἁπάντων Aᵇ   τῶν ὄντων
ᾠήθη Aᵇ   22 τὰ εἴδη secl. Zeller   τοὺς codd. Γ Al. : καὶ τοὺς
Asc.ᶜ : τὰ ὡς Jackson   23 γέ τι Aᵇ Al.¹ : τι τὸ E Asc.¹   ἕν] εἶναι E
25 τῆς ὅλης οὐσίας γρ. E : τῆς ὕλης οὐσίας Γ

δυάδα ποιῆσαι, τὸ δ' ἄπειρον ἐκ μεγάλου καὶ μικροῦ, τοῦτ'
ἴδιον· καὶ ἔτι ὁ μὲν τοὺς ἀριθμοὺς παρὰ τὰ αἰσθητά, οἱ δ'
ἀριθμοὺς εἶναί φασιν αὐτὰ τὰ πράγματα, καὶ τὰ μαθηματικὰ μεταξὺ τούτων οὐ τιθέασιν. τὸ μὲν οὖν τὸ ἓν καὶ τοὺς
ἀριθμοὺς παρὰ τὰ πράγματα ποιῆσαι, καὶ μὴ ὥσπερ οἱ 30
Πυθαγόρειοι, καὶ ἡ τῶν εἰδῶν εἰσαγωγὴ διὰ τὴν ἐν τοῖς λόγοις ἐγένετο σκέψιν (οἱ γὰρ πρότεροι διαλεκτικῆς οὐ μετεῖχον), τὸ δὲ δυάδα ποιῆσαι τὴν ἑτέραν φύσιν διὰ τὸ τοὺς
ἀριθμοὺς ἔξω τῶν πρώτων εὐφυῶς ἐξ αὐτῆς γεννᾶσθαι ὥσπερ ἔκ τινος ἐκμαγείου. καίτοι συμβαίνει γ' ἐναντίως· οὐ 988ᵃ
γὰρ εὔλογον οὕτως. οἱ μὲν γὰρ ἐκ τῆς ὕλης πολλὰ ποιοῦσιν,
τὸ δ' εἶδος ἅπαξ γεννᾷ μόνον, φαίνεται δ' ἐκ μιᾶς ὕλης
μία τράπεζα, ὁ δὲ τὸ εἶδος ἐπιφέρων εἷς ὢν πολλὰς ποιεῖ.
ὁμοίως δ' ἔχει καὶ τὸ ἄρρεν πρὸς τὸ θῆλυ· τὸ μὲν γὰρ 5
ὑπὸ μιᾶς πληροῦται ὀχείας, τὸ δ' ἄρρεν πολλὰ πληροῖ·
καίτοι ταῦτα μιμήματα τῶν ἀρχῶν ἐκείνων ἐστίν. Πλάτων μὲν οὖν περὶ τῶν ζητουμένων οὕτω διώρισεν· φανερὸν δ'
ἐκ τῶν εἰρημένων ὅτι δυοῖν αἰτίαν μόνον κέχρηται, τῇ τε
τοῦ τί ἐστι καὶ τῇ κατὰ τὴν ὕλην (τὰ γὰρ εἴδη τοῦ τί ἐστιν 10
αἴτια τοῖς ἄλλοις, τοῖς δ' εἴδεσι τὸ ἕν), καὶ τίς ἡ ὕλη ἡ
ὑποκειμένη καθ' ἧς τὰ εἴδη μὲν ἐπὶ τῶν αἰσθητῶν τὸ δ'
ἓν ἐν τοῖς εἴδεσι λέγεται, ὅτι αὕτη δυάς ἐστι, τὸ μέγα καὶ
τὸ μικρόν, ἔτι δὲ τὴν τοῦ εὖ καὶ τοῦ κακῶς αἰτίαν τοῖς στοιχείοις ἀπέδωκεν ἑκατέροις ἑκατέραν, ὥσπερ φαμὲν καὶ τῶν 15
προτέρων ἐπιζητῆσαί τινας φιλοσόφων, οἷον Ἐμπεδοκλέα
καὶ Ἀναξαγόραν.

7   Συντόμως μὲν οὖν καὶ κεφαλαιωδῶς ἐπεληλύθαμεν τίνες
τε καὶ πῶς τυγχάνουσιν εἰρηκότες περί τε τῶν ἀρχῶν
καὶ τῆς ἀληθείας· ὅμως δὲ τοσοῦτόν γ' ἔχομεν ἐξ αὐτῶν, 20

ᵇ 26 τὸ δ' E Al.¹: καὶ τὸ AᵇΓ   27 ἔτι EΓ Al. : ὅτι Aᵇ Asc.
29 τοὺς ἀριθμοὺς EΓ Al. Asc. : τὸν ἀριθμὸν Aᵇ   34 ἔξω τῶν πρώτων
codd. Γ Al. Asc.: ἔξω τῶν περιττῶν Heinze : secl. Zeller   988ᵃ 1–2 οὐκ
ἄρ' Susemihl   2 οἱ Aᵇ Al. : νῦν EΓ Asc.ᶜ   4 ἕν ὂν Walker
πολλὰ Aᵇ   5 μὲν γὰρ] μὲν γὰρ θῆλυ Aᵇ : δὲ Γ   8 διώρισεν E
Al.¹ Asc.ᶜ: διώριζε AᵇΓ   9 μόνον κέχρηται] ἐστὶ μόνον κεχρημένος E
11 ἕν] ἐν καὶ τῇ ὕλῃ γρ. Al.   12 μὲν Aᵇ γρ. Al. : τὰ μὲν EΓ Al.
τὸ δ' ἕν ἐν codd. Γ γρ. Al. : τὰ δ' ἐπὶ Al.   13 ὅτι ... 14 μικρόν EΓ
Al. : om. Aᵇ   14 κακῶς EAᵇΓ Al. Asc. : καλῶς Aᵇ¹   15 ὥσπερ
Aᵇ Al.ᶜ: ὅπερ μᾶλλον EΓ   ἔφαμεν Jackson   16 φιλοσόφων AᵇΓ
Al.ᶜ: φιλοσόφους E

ὅτι τῶν λεγόντων περὶ ἀρχῆς καὶ αἰτίας οὐθεὶς ἔξω τῶν ἐν
τοῖς περὶ φύσεως ἡμῖν διωρισμένων εἴρηκεν, ἀλλὰ πάντες
ἀμυδρῶς μὲν ἐκείνων δέ πως φαίνονται θιγγάνοντες. οἱ μὲν
γὰρ ὡς ὕλην τὴν ἀρχὴν λέγουσιν, ἄν τε μίαν ἄν τε πλείους
25 ὑποθῶσι, καὶ ἐάν τε σῶμα ἐάν τε ἀσώματον τοῦτο τιθῶσιν (οἷον
Πλάτων μὲν τὸ μέγα καὶ τὸ μικρὸν λέγων, οἱ δ' Ἰταλικοὶ
τὸ ἄπειρον, Ἐμπεδοκλῆς δὲ πῦρ καὶ γῆν καὶ ὕδωρ καὶ
ἀέρα, Ἀναξαγόρας δὲ τὴν τῶν ὁμοιομερῶν ἀπειρίαν· οὗτοί
τε δὴ πάντες τῆς τοιαύτης αἰτίας ἡμμένοι εἰσί, καὶ ἔτι ὅσοι
30 ἀέρα ἢ πῦρ ἢ ὕδωρ ἢ πυρὸς μὲν πυκνότερον ἀέρος δὲ λεπτό-
τερον· καὶ γὰρ τοιοῦτόν τινες εἰρήκασιν εἶναι τὸ πρῶτον
στοιχεῖον)·—οὗτοι μὲν οὖν ταύτης τῆς αἰτίας ἥψαντο μόνον,
ἕτεροι δέ τινες ὅθεν ἡ ἀρχὴ τῆς κινήσεως (οἷον ὅσοι φιλίαν
καὶ νεῖκος ἢ νοῦν ἢ ἔρωτα ποιοῦσιν ἀρχήν)· τὸ δὲ τί ἦν εἶναι
35 καὶ τὴν οὐσίαν σαφῶς μὲν οὐθεὶς ἀποδέδωκε, μάλιστα δ' οἱ τὰ
988b εἴδη τιθέντες λέγουσιν (οὔτε γὰρ ὡς ὕλην τοῖς αἰσθητοῖς τὰ
εἴδη καὶ τὸ ἐν τοῖς εἴδεσιν οὔθ' ὡς ἐντεῦθεν τὴν ἀρχὴν τῆς
κινήσεως γιγνομένην ὑπολαμβάνουσιν—ἀκινησίας γὰρ αἴτια
μᾶλλον καὶ τοῦ ἐν ἠρεμίᾳ εἶναι φασιν—ἀλλὰ τὸ τί ἦν εἶναι
5 ἑκάστῳ τῶν ἄλλων τὰ εἴδη παρέχονται, τοῖς δ' εἴδεσι τὸ
ἕν)· τὸ δ' οὗ ἕνεκα αἱ πράξεις καὶ αἱ μεταβολαὶ καὶ αἱ
κινήσεις τρόπον μέν τινα λέγουσιν αἴτιον, οὕτω δὲ οὐ λέγουσιν οὐδ' ὅνπερ πέφυκεν. οἱ μὲν γὰρ νοῦν λέγοντες ἢ φιλίαν
ὡς ἀγαθὸν μὲν ταύτας τὰς αἰτίας τιθέασιν, οὐ μὴν ὡς
10 ἕνεκά γε τούτων ἢ ὂν ἢ γιγνόμενόν τι τῶν ὄντων ἀλλ' ὡς
ἀπὸ τούτων τὰς κινήσεις οὔσας λέγουσιν· ὡς δ' αὕτως καὶ
οἱ τὸ ἐν ἢ τὸ ὂν φάσκοντες εἶναι τὴν τοιαύτην φύσιν τῆς
μὲν οὐσίας αἴτιόν φασιν εἶναι, οὐ μὴν τούτου γε ἕνεκα ἢ εἶναι ἢ
γίγνεσθαι, ὥστε λέγειν τε καὶ μὴ λέγειν πως συμβαίνει αὐ-
15 τοῖς τἀγαθὸν αἴτιον· οὐ γὰρ ἁπλῶς ἀλλὰ κατὰ συμβεβηκὸς
λέγουσιν.—ὅτι μὲν οὖν ὀρθῶς διώρισται περὶ τῶν αἰτίων καὶ
πόσα καὶ ποῖα, μαρτυρεῖν ἐοίκασιν ἡμῖν καὶ οὗτοι πάντες,

ᵃ 25 ἀσώματον τοῦτο Aᵇ Asc.: ἀσωμάτους ΕΓ   34 ἢ pr.] καὶ ΕΓ
35 ἀπέδωκε recc.   ᵇ 1 εἴδη καὶ τὰ ἐν τοῖς εἴδεσι τιθέντες Aᵇ   ὕλη Aᵇ
2 τὸ ἐν Bonitz: τὰ ἐν codd. Al.   οὔθ' Ε Al.: οὐδ' Aᵇ   3 αἴτια
ΕΓ Asc.: αἰτίαν Aᵇ   8 πέφυκε τρόπον Ε²   ἢ ΕΓ Asc.ᶜ: καὶ Aᵇ
9 μὲν Aᵇ Asc.ᶜ: μέν τι ΕΓ   οὐ τὴν Aᵇ   11 οὔσας] εἶναι τούτων
ΕΓ   12 ἐν ἢ τὸ ὂν ΕΓ Al.: ὂν ἢ τὸ ἐν Aᵇ   13 οὐσίας μὲν Ε
ἢ pr. ΕΓ Asc.ᶜ: om. Aᵇ   15 οὐ ... 16 λέγουσιν ΕΓ Al. Asc.ᶜ: om. Aᵇ

οὐ δυνάμενοι θιγεῖν ἄλλης αἰτίας, πρὸς δὲ τούτοις ὅτι ζητη-
τέαι αἱ ἀρχαὶ ἢ οὕτως ἅπασαι ἢ τινὰ τρόπον τοιοῦτον, δῆλον·
πῶς δὲ τούτων ἕκαστος εἴρηκε καὶ πῶς ἔχει περὶ τῶν ἀρχῶν, 20
τὰς ἐνδεχομένας ἀπορίας μετὰ τοῦτο διέλθωμεν περὶ αὐτῶν.

8   Ὅσοι μὲν οὖν ἕν τε τὸ πᾶν καὶ μίαν τινὰ φύσιν ὡς
ὕλην τιθέασι, καὶ ταύτην σωματικὴν καὶ μέγεθος ἔχουσαν,
δῆλον ὅτι πολλαχῶς ἁμαρτάνουσιν. τῶν γὰρ σωμάτων τὰ
στοιχεῖα τιθέασι μόνον, τῶν δ' ἀσωμάτων οὔ, ὄντων καὶ ἀσω- 25
μάτων.   καὶ περὶ γενέσεως καὶ φθορᾶς ἐπιχειροῦντες τὰς
αἰτίας λέγειν, καὶ περὶ πάντων φυσιολογοῦντες, τὸ τῆς κινήσεως αἴτιον ἀναιροῦσιν.   ἔτι δὲ τῷ τὴν οὐσίαν μηθενὸς αἰτίαν
τιθέναι μηδὲ τὸ τί ἐστι, καὶ πρὸς τούτοις τῷ ῥᾳδίως τῶν
ἁπλῶν σωμάτων λέγειν ἀρχὴν ὁτιοῦν πλὴν γῆς, οὐκ ἐπισκε- 30
ψάμενοι τὴν ἐξ ἀλλήλων γένεσιν πῶς ποιοῦνται, λέγω δὲ
πῦρ καὶ ὕδωρ καὶ γῆν καὶ ἀέρα.   τὰ μὲν γὰρ συγκρίσει
τὰ δὲ διακρίσει ἐξ ἀλλήλων γίγνεται, τοῦτο δὲ πρὸς τὸ πρότερον εἶναι καὶ ὕστερον διαφέρει πλεῖστον. τῇ μὲν γὰρ ἂν
δόξειε στοιχειωδέστατον εἶναι πάντων ἐξ οὗ γίγνονται συγκρί- 35
σει πρώτου, τοιοῦτον δὲ τὸ μικρομερέστατον καὶ λεπτότατον ἂν 989ᵃ
εἴη τῶν σωμάτων (διόπερ ὅσοι πῦρ ἀρχὴν τιθέασι, μάλιστα
ὁμολογουμένως ἂν τῷ λόγῳ τούτῳ λέγοιεν· τοιοῦτον δὲ καὶ
τῶν ἄλλων ἕκαστος ὁμολογεῖ τὸ στοιχεῖον εἶναι τὸ τῶν σω-
μάτων· οὐθεὶς γοῦν ἠξίωσε τῶν ἓν λεγόντων γῆν εἶναι 5
στοιχεῖον, δηλονότι διὰ τὴν μεγαλομέρειαν, τῶν δὲ τριῶν
ἕκαστον στοιχείων εἴληφέ τινα κριτήν, οἱ μὲν γὰρ πῦρ οἱ δ'
ὕδωρ οἱ δ' ἀέρα τοῦτ' εἶναί φασιν· καίτοι διὰ τί ποτ' οὐ καὶ
τὴν γῆν λέγουσιν, ὥσπερ οἱ πολλοὶ τῶν ἀνθρώπων; πάντα
γὰρ εἶναί φασι γῆν, φησὶ δὲ καὶ Ἡσίοδος τὴν γῆν πρώ- 10
την γενέσθαι τῶν σωμάτων· οὕτως ἀρχαίαν καὶ δημοτι-
κὴν συμβέβηκεν εἶναι τὴν ὑπόληψιν)·—κατὰ μὲν οὖν τοῦ-

ᵇ 19 τοιοῦτον Bywater : τούτων EAᵇ : τοῦτον recc.   20 δὲ] τε Γ
21 τὰς δὲ Γ   22 τὸ πᾶν καὶ] αὐτὸ Γ   μίαν Aᵇ Asc.ˡᶜ : μίαν εἶναι ΕΓ
25 ὄντων καὶ ἀσωμάτων ΕΓ Al. : om. Aᵇ   26 καὶ φθορᾶς om. Al.
27 πάντων Ε Al.ᶜ : ἀπάντων Aᵇ Asc.ᶜ   28, 29 τῷ i Bywater :
τὸ codd. Al.   30 λέγειν] εἶναι Γ   32 γῆν καὶ ὕδωρ Aᵇ   34 πῇ Ε
989ᵃ 4 ἕκαστος ὁμολογεῖ τὸ ΕΓ Al. : ἕκαστον ὡμολογεῖτο Aᵇ   τὸ
om. Aᵇ : τι Γ   5 γὰρ Γ   ἠξίωσε τῶν Aᵇ et fort. Al. : τῶν ὕστερον
ἠξίωσε καὶ ΕΓ Asc.   7 στοιχείων ἕκαστον recc.   κριτήν τινα ΕΓ
8 οὐ καὶ Ε Al. : οὐδὲ Aᵇ : οὐ Γ   11 γεγενῆσθαι Aᵇ ·   12 συμβέβηκεν εἶναι] εἶχε Aᵇ   μὲν om. Γ

τον τὸν λόγον οὔτ' εἴ τις τούτων τι λέγει πλὴν πυρός,
οὔτ' εἴ τις ἀέρος μὲν πυκνότερον τοῦτο τίθησιν ὕδατος δὲ
15 λεπτότερον, οὐκ ὀρθῶς ἂν λέγοι· εἰ δ' ἔστι τὸ τῇ γενέσει
ὕστερον τῇ φύσει πρότερον, τὸ δὲ πεπεμμένον καὶ συγκεκριμένον ὕστερον τῇ γενέσει, τοὐναντίον ἂν εἴη τούτων, ὕδωρ
μὲν ἀέρος πρότερον γῆ δὲ ὕδατος.——περὶ μὲν οὖν τῶν μίαν
τιθεμένων αἰτίαν οἵαν εἴπομεν, ἔστω ταῦτ' εἰρημένα· τὸ δ'
20 αὐτὸ κἂν εἴ τις ταῦτα πλείω τίθησιν, οἷον Ἐμπεδοκλῆς τέτ-
ταρά φησιν εἶναι σώματα τὴν ὕλην. καὶ γὰρ τούτῳ τὰ μὲν
ταὐτὰ τὰ δ' ἴδια συμβαίνειν ἀνάγκη. γιγνόμενά τε γὰρ ἐξ
ἀλλήλων ὁρῶμεν ὡς οὐκ ἀεὶ διαμένοντος πυρὸς καὶ γῆς τοῦ
αὐτοῦ σώματος (εἴρηται δὲ ἐν τοῖς περὶ φύσεως περὶ αὐτῶν),
25 καὶ περὶ τῆς τῶν κινουμένων αἰτίας, πότερον ἓν ἢ δύο θετέον,
οὔτ' ὀρθῶς οὔτε εὐλόγως οἰητέον εἰρῆσθαι παντελῶς. ὅλως τε
ἀλλοίωσιν ἀναιρεῖσθαι ἀνάγκη τοῖς οὕτω λέγουσιν· οὐ γὰρ ἐκ
θερμοῦ ψυχρὸν οὐδὲ ἐκ ψυχροῦ θερμὸν ἔσται. τί γὰρ αὐτὰ ἂν
πάσχοι τἀναντία, καὶ τίς εἴη ἂν μία φύσις ἡ γιγνομένη
30 πῦρ καὶ ὕδωρ, ὃ ἐκεῖνος οὔ φησιν. Ἀναξαγόραν δ' εἴ τις
ὑπολάβοι δύο λέγειν στοιχεῖα, μάλιστ' ἂν ὑπολάβοι κατὰ
λόγον, ὃν ἐκεῖνος αὐτὸς μὲν οὐ διήρθρωσεν, ἠκολούθησε μέντ'
ἂν ἐξ ἀνάγκης τοῖς ἐπάγουσιν αὐτόν. ἀτόπου γὰρ ὄντος καὶ
ἄλλως τοῦ φάσκειν μεμῖχθαι τὴν ἀρχὴν πάντα, καὶ διὰ
989ᵇ τὸ συμβαίνειν ἄμικτα δεῖν προϋπάρχειν καὶ διὰ τὸ μὴ
πεφυκέναι τῷ τυχόντι μίγνυσθαι τὸ τυχόν, πρὸς δὲ τούτοις
ὅτι τὰ πάθη καὶ τὰ συμβεβηκότα χωρίζοιτ' ἂν τῶν οὐσιῶν
(τῶν γὰρ αὐτῶν μῖξίς ἐστι καὶ χωρισμός), ὅμως εἴ τις ἀκο-
5 λουθήσειε συνδιαρθρῶν ἃ βούλεται λέγειν, ἴσως ἂν φανείη
καινοπρεπεστέρως λέγων. ὅτε γὰρ οὐθὲν ἦν ἀποκεκριμένον,
δῆλον ὡς οὐθὲν ἦν ἀληθὲς εἰπεῖν κατὰ τῆς οὐσίας ἐκείνης,
λέγω δ' οἷον ὅτι οὔτε λευκὸν οὔτε μέλαν ἢ φαιὸν ἢ ἄλλο
χρῶμα, ἀλλ' ἄχρων ἦν ἐξ ἀνάγκης· εἶχε γὰρ ἄν τι τού-

ᵃ 13 λέγει τι Aᵇ   16 ὕστερον ... πρότερον ΕΓ Al. Asc.: πρότερον
... ὕστερον Aᵇ Al.ᶜ Asc.ˡᶜ   25 κινούντων ΕΓ Asc.ˡ   26 εὐλόγως
Aᵇ γρ. Ἐ Al.: ἀλόγως ΕΓ Asc.ᶜ, ci. Al.   ὅλως ... 30 φησιν ΕΓ
Asc.: om. Aᵇ et ut vid. Al.   28 τὶ Asc.: τί codd. Γ   ἂν αὐτὰ
recc.   29 τὶς Asc.: τίς codd.   ἂν εἴη recc.   32 οὐ ΕΓ
Asc.: οὐ σαφῶς Aᵇ   33 ἐπάγουσιν Aᵇ et ut vid. Al.: λέγουσιν ΕΓ
ᵇ 8 οἷον om. ΕΓ   ἢ ἄλλο χρῶμα ΕΓ Asc. et ut vid. Al.: om. Aᵇ
9 ἀχρώματον Aᵇ: ἄχρουν Asc.ᶜ   ἦν om. Aᵇ Asc.ᶜ   τούτων τῶν
χρωμάτων ΕΓ Asc.: τῶν χρωμάτων τούτων Aᵇ

των τῶν χρωμάτων· ὁμοίως δὲ καὶ ἄχυμον τῷ αὐτῷ 10
λόγῳ τούτῳ, οὐδὲ ἄλλο τῶν ὁμοίων οὐθέν· οὔτε γὰρ ποιόν τι
οἷόν τε αὐτὸ εἶναι οὔτε ποσὸν οὔτε τί. τῶν γὰρ ἐν μέρει τι
λεγομένων εἰδῶν ὑπῆρχεν ἂν αὐτῷ, τοῦτο δὲ ἀδύνατον με-
μιγμένων γε πάντων· ἤδη γὰρ ἂν ἀπεκέκριτο, φησὶ δ'
εἶναι μεμιγμένα πάντα πλὴν τοῦ νοῦ, τοῦτον δὲ ἀμιγῆ μόνον 15
καὶ καθαρόν. ἐκ δὴ τούτων συμβαίνει λέγειν αὐτῷ τὰς
ἀρχὰς τό τε ἕν (τοῦτο γὰρ ἁπλοῦν καὶ ἀμιγές) καὶ θάτερον,
οἷον τίθεμεν τὸ ἀόριστον πρὶν ὁρισθῆναι καὶ μετασχεῖν εἴδους
τινός, ὥστε λέγει μὲν οὔτ' ὀρθῶς οὔτε σαφῶς, βούλεται μέντοι
τι παραπλήσιον τοῖς τε ὕστερον λέγουσι καὶ τοῖς νῦν φαινομέ- 20
νοις μᾶλλον.—ἀλλὰ γὰρ οὗτοι μὲν τοῖς περὶ γένεσιν λόγοις
καὶ φθορὰν καὶ κίνησιν οἰκεῖοι τυγχάνουσι μόνον (σχεδὸν
γὰρ περὶ τῆς τοιαύτης οὐσίας καὶ τὰς ἀρχὰς καὶ τὰς αἰτίας
ζητοῦσι μόνης)· ὅσοι δὲ περὶ μὲν ἁπάντων τῶν ὄντων ποιοῦνται
τὴν θεωρίαν, τῶν δ' ὄντων τὰ μὲν αἰσθητὰ τὰ δ' οὐκ αἰσθητὰ 25
τιθέασι, δῆλον ὡς περὶ ἀμφοτέρων τῶν γενῶν ποιοῦνται τὴν
ἐπίσκεψιν· διὸ μᾶλλον ἄν τις ἐνδιατρίψειε περὶ αὐτῶν, τί
καλῶς ἢ μὴ καλῶς λέγουσιν εἰς τὴν τῶν νῦν ἡμῖν προκει-
μένων σκέψιν. οἱ μὲν οὖν καλούμενοι Πυθαγόρειοι ταῖς μὲν
ἀρχαῖς καὶ τοῖς στοιχείοις ἐκτοπωτέροις χρῶνται τῶν φυσιο- 30
λόγων (τὸ δ' αἴτιον ὅτι παρέλαβον αὐτὰς οὐκ ἐξ αἰσθητῶν·
τὰ γὰρ μαθηματικὰ τῶν ὄντων ἄνευ κινήσεώς ἐστιν ἔξω
τῶν περὶ τὴν ἀστρολογίαν), διαλέγονται μέντοι καὶ πραγματεύονται περὶ φύσεως πάντα· γεννῶσί τε γὰρ τὸν οὐρανόν,
καὶ περὶ τὰ τούτου μέρη καὶ τὰ πάθη καὶ τὰ ἔργα διατη- 990ⁿ
ροῦσι τὸ συμβαῖνον, καὶ τὰς ἀρχὰς καὶ τὰ αἴτια εἰς ταῦτα
καταναλίσκουσιν, ὡς ὁμολογοῦντες τοῖς ἄλλοις φυσιολόγοις
ὅτι τό γε ὂν τοῦτ' ἐστὶν ὅσον αἰσθητόν ἐστι καὶ περιείληφεν ὁ
καλούμενος οὐρανός. τὰς δ' αἰτίας καὶ τὰς ἀρχάς, ὥσπερ 5
εἴπομεν, ἱκανὰς λέγουσιν ἐπαναβῆναι καὶ ἐπὶ τὰ ἀνωτέρω
τῶν ὄντων, καὶ μᾶλλον ἢ τοῖς περὶ φύσεως λόγοις ἁρμοτ-
τούσας. ἐκ τίνος μέντοι τρόπου κίνησις ἔσται πέρατος καὶ

ᵇ 10 τῷ] καὶ τῷ Aᵇ   11 ἄλλο τι τῶν Aᵇ   17 θάτερον AᵇΓ Al. :
θάτερον καθάπερ ὃν E   19 λέγει Aᵇ Al.ᶜ: λέγεται ΕΓ   20 τε
E Al.ᶜ Asc.ᶜ: om. Aᵇ   νῦν om. ut vid. Al., Brandis   24 μόνον ΕΓ
30 ἐκτοπωτέροις Al. Bonitz: ἐκτοπωτέρως codd. Γ Asc.   34 περὶ
φύσεως πάντα E Asc.ᶜ: πάντα περὶ φύσεως AᵇΓ   990ª 1 τὰ ult.
om. Aᵇ   6 ἱκανὰς AᵇΓ Al. : ἱκανῶς E

ἀπείρου μόνων ὑποκειμένων καὶ περιττοῦ καὶ ἀρτίου, οὐθὲν
10 λέγουσιν, ἢ πῶς δυνατὸν ἄνευ κινήσεως καὶ μεταβολῆς γένεσιν εἶναι καὶ φθορὰν ἢ τὰ τῶν φερομένων ἔργα κατὰ τὸν
οὐρανόν. ἔτι δὲ εἴτε δοίη τις αὐτοῖς ἐκ τούτων εἶναι μέγεθος
εἴτε δειχθείη τοῦτο, ὅμως τίνα τρόπον ἔσται τὰ μὲν κοῦφα
τὰ δὲ βάρος ἔχοντα τῶν σωμάτων; ἐξ ὧν γὰρ ὑποτίθενται
15 καὶ λέγουσιν, οὐθὲν μᾶλλον περὶ τῶν μαθηματικῶν λέγουσι
σωμάτων ἢ τῶν αἰσθητῶν· διὸ περὶ πυρὸς ἢ γῆς ἢ τῶν
ἄλλων τῶν τοιούτων σωμάτων οὐδ' ὁτιοῦν εἰρήκασιν, ἅτε οὐθὲν
περὶ τῶν αἰσθητῶν οἶμαι λέγοντες ἴδιον. ἔτι δὲ πῶς δεῖ
λαβεῖν αἴτια μὲν εἶναι τὰ τοῦ ἀριθμοῦ πάθη καὶ τὸν ἀριθμὸν
20 τῶν κατὰ τὸν οὐρανὸν ὄντων καὶ γιγνομένων καὶ ἐξ ἀρχῆς
καὶ νῦν, ἀριθμὸν δ' ἄλλον μηθένα εἶναι παρὰ τὸν ἀριθμὸν
τοῦτον ἐξ οὗ συνέστηκεν ὁ κόσμος; ὅταν γὰρ ἐν τῳδὶ μὲν τῷ
μέρει δόξα καὶ καιρὸς αὐτοῖς ᾖ, μικρὸν δὲ ἄνωθεν ἢ κάτωθεν ἀδικία καὶ κρίσις ἢ μῖξις, ἀπόδειξιν δὲ λέγωσιν ὅτι
25 τούτων μὲν ἕκαστον ἀριθμός ἐστι, συμβαίνει δὲ κατὰ τὸν
τόπον τοῦτον ἤδη πλῆθος εἶναι τῶν συνισταμένων μεγεθῶν διὰ
τὸ τὰ πάθη ταῦτα ἀκολουθεῖν τοῖς τόποις ἑκάστοις, πότερον
οὗτος ὁ αὐτός ἐστιν ἀριθμός, ὁ ἐν τῷ οὐρανῷ, ὃν δεῖ λαβεῖν
ὅτι τούτων ἕκαστόν ἐστιν, ἢ παρὰ τοῦτον ἄλλος; ὁ μὲν γὰρ
30 Πλάτων ἕτερον εἶναί φησιν· καίτοι κἀκεῖνος ἀριθμοὺς οἴεται
καὶ ταῦτα εἶναι καὶ τὰς τούτων αἰτίας, ἀλλὰ τοὺς μὲν νοη-
τοὺς αἰτίους τούτους δὲ αἰσθητούς.

Περὶ μὲν οὖν τῶν Πυθαγορείων ἀφείσθω τὰ νῦν (ἱκα- 9
νὸν γὰρ αὐτῶν ἅψασθαι τοσοῦτον)· οἱ δὲ τὰς ἰδέας αἰτίας
990b τιθέμενοι πρῶτον μὲν ζητοῦντες τωνδὶ τῶν ὄντων λαβεῖν τὰς
αἰτίας ἕτερα τούτοις ἴσα τὸν ἀριθμὸν ἐκόμισαν, ὥσπερ εἴ τις

990b 2 — 991a 8 = M. 1078b 34 — 1079b 3

*9 μόνον ΑbΓ   12 δόῃ Ε Asc.¹   εἶναι Ε Asc.¹: εἶναι τὸ Αb
16 ἢ pr.] ἢ περὶ Ε   23 καὶ] ἐκεῖ δὲ ex Al. ci. Luthe: καὶ τόλμα,
ἐν τωιδὶ δὲ Diels   24 γρ. ἀνικία Ε Al.: ἀνεικία ci. Zeller   κρίσις
Αb Al.: διάκρισις Ε   ἀπόδειξις Αb¹   25 μὲν Al.: μὲν ἐν Ε: ἐν ΑbΓ
Bonitz   συμβαίνῃ ci. Bonitz   τὸν τόπον τοῦτον ΕΓ Al.ᶜ: τοῦτον
τὸν τόπον Αb: τοῦτον τὸν τρόπον Asc.ᶜ: τὸν τόπον τοῦτο Luthe: τοῦτον
τὸν τόπον τοῦτο Zeller   26 ἤδη] δὴ τὸ Luthe   διὰ τὸ] διὸ Zeller
28 οὗτος ΕΓ Al.: δὲ Αb: οὕτως Asc.   αἴτιος ex Al. ci. Luthe   ἔστιν
ἀριθμός ΕΓ Asc.ᶜ: ἀριθμός ἐστιν Αb   33 τὰ Αb Al.: τὸ Ε
34 αἰτίας Αb Al.¹: om. ΕΓ Asc.¹

ἀριθμῆσαι βουλόμενος ἐλαττόνων μὲν ὄντων οἴοιτο μὴ δυνή-
σεσθαι, πλείω δὲ ποιήσας ἀριθμοίη (σχεδὸν γὰρ ἴσα—ἢ οὐκ
ἐλάττω—ἐστὶ τὰ εἴδη τούτοις περὶ ὧν ζητοῦντες τὰς αἰτίας ἐκ 5
τούτων ἐπ᾽ ἐκεῖνα προῆλθον· καθ᾽ ἕκαστον γὰρ ὁμώνυμόν τι
ἔστι καὶ παρὰ τὰς οὐσίας, τῶν τε ἄλλων ἔστιν ἐν ἐπὶ πολλῶν, καὶ ἐπὶ τοῖσδε καὶ ἐπὶ τοῖς ἀϊδίοις)· ἔτι δὲ καθ᾽ οὓς τρόπους δείκνυμεν ὅτι ἔστι τὰ εἴδη, κατ᾽ οὐθένα φαίνεται τούτων·
ἐξ ἐνίων μὲν γὰρ οὐκ ἀνάγκη γίγνεσθαι συλλογισμόν, ἐξ ἐνίων 10
δὲ καὶ οὐχ ὧν οἰόμεθα τούτων εἴδη γίγνεται. κατά τε γὰρ
τοὺς λόγους τοὺς ἐκ τῶν ἐπιστημῶν εἴδη ἔσται· πάντων ὅσων
ἐπιστῆμαι εἰσί, καὶ κατὰ τὸ ἐν ἐπὶ πολλῶν καὶ τῶν ἀποφάσεων, κατὰ δὲ τὸ νοεῖν τι φθαρέντος τῶν φθαρτῶν· φάντασμα γάρ τι τούτων ἔστιν. ἔτι δὲ οἱ ἀκριβέστεροι τῶν λόγων 15
οἱ μὲν τῶν πρός τι ποιοῦσιν ἰδέας, ὧν οὔ φαμεν εἶναι καθ᾽
αὑτὸ γένος, οἱ δὲ τὸν τρίτον ἄνθρωπον λέγουσιν. ὅλως τε
ἀναιροῦσιν οἱ περὶ τῶν εἰδῶν λόγοι ἃ μᾶλλον εἶναι βουλόμεθα
[οἱ λέγοντες εἴδη] τοῦ τὰς ἰδέας εἶναι· συμβαίνει γὰρ μὴ
εἶναι τὴν δυάδα πρώτην ἀλλὰ τὸν ἀριθμόν, καὶ τὸ πρός τι 20
τοῦ καθ᾽ αὑτό, καὶ πάνθ᾽ ὅσα τινὲς ἀκολουθήσαντες ταῖς περὶ
τῶν ἰδεῶν δόξαις ἠναντιώθησαν ταῖς ἀρχαῖς.—ἔτι κατὰ
μὲν τὴν ὑπόληψιν καθ᾽ ἣν εἶναί φαμεν τὰς ἰδέας οὐ μόνον
τῶν οὐσιῶν ἔσται εἴδη ἀλλὰ πολλῶν καὶ ἑτέρων (καὶ γὰρ τὸ
νόημα ἐν οὐ μόνον περὶ τὰς οὐσίας ἀλλὰ καὶ κατὰ τῶν ἄλ- 25
λων ἐστί, καὶ ἐπιστῆμαι οὐ μόνον τῆς οὐσίας εἰσὶν ἀλλὰ καὶ
ἑτέρων, καὶ ἄλλα δὲ μυρία συμβαίνει τοιαῦτα)· κατὰ δὲ
τὸ ἀναγκαῖον καὶ τὰς δόξας τὰς περὶ αὐτῶν, εἰ ἔστι με-
θεκτὰ τὰ εἴδη, τῶν οὐσιῶν ἀναγκαῖον ἰδέας εἶναι μόνον. οὐ

ᵇ 5 ἐστὶ τὰ εἴδη AᵇΓ Al. : τὰ εἴδη ἐστὶ E Asc.   τούτοις AᵇΓ Al. :
τούτων E Asc.   6 ἐπ᾽ ἐκεῖνα EΓ Asc. : ἐκεῖ AᵇM   καθ᾽] παρ᾽ Syr.
7 τε E Al. M : om. Aᵇ Asc.   ἄλλων EΓ Asc. M : ἄλλων ὧν Aᵇ Al. :
ἄλλων ἃ γρ. E   ἐν ἐπὶ πολλῶν Aᵇ Al. Asc. : ἐπὶ πολλῶν ἕν EΓ
8 δὲ EΓ Asc.ˡᶜ : om. AᵇM   9 δείκνυμεν EΓ Al. Asc. : δείκνυται
AᵇM   11 τε E Al.ˡ M : γε Aᵇ   12 ἐκ EΓ Al. Asc. M : om. Aᵇ
14 τι EΓ Al.ˡ Asc. M : om. Aᵇ   15 ἀκριβέστεροι Aᵇ et ut
vid. Al. (85. 6) : ἀκριβέστατοι EΓ Al.ˡ Asc.ˡ M   16 φασιν ΓM
18 βουλόμεθα E Asc. : βούλονται AᵇΓ Al. M   19 οἱ λέγοντες
εἴδη secl. Blass   20 προτέραν Richards   τὸ πρός τι] τούτου τὸ
πρός τι καὶ M   21 τοῦ EΓ Al. Asc. : τῶν Aᵇ   22 ἰδεῶν Aᵇ Al.
Asc.ˡ : εἰδῶν EΓM   ἔτι AᵇAl.ˡ M : ἔτι δὲ EΓ Asc.ˡ   24 ἔσονται
AᵇM   26 καὶ pr. E Al. : καὶ αἱ Aᵇ   29 τὰ Aᵇ Al. Asc. M :
om. E   μύνον codd. ΓM : μόνων ut vid. Al. Asc.

30 γὰρ κατὰ συμβεβηκὸς μετέχονται ἀλλὰ δεῖ ταύτῃ ἑκάστου μετέχειν ᾗ μὴ καθ' ὑποκειμένου λέγεται (λέγω δ'
οἷον, εἴ τι αὐτοδιπλασίου μετέχει, τοῦτο καὶ ἀϊδίου μετέχει,
ἀλλὰ κατὰ συμβεβηκός· συμβέβηκε γὰρ τῷ διπλασίῳ
ἀϊδίῳ εἶναι), ὥστ' ἔσται οὐσία τὰ εἴδη· ταῦτα δὲ ἐνταῦθα
991ᵃ οὐσίαν σημαίνει κἀκεῖ· ἢ τί ἔσται τὸ εἶναι φάναι τι παρὰ
ταῦτα, τὸ ἓν ἐπὶ πολλῶν; καὶ εἰ μὲν ταὐτὸ εἶδος τῶν ἰδεῶν
καὶ τῶν μετεχόντων, ἔσται τι κοινόν (τί γὰρ μᾶλλον ἐπὶ
τῶν φθαρτῶν δυάδων, καὶ τῶν πολλῶν μὲν ἀϊδίων δέ, τὸ
5 δυὰς ἓν καὶ ταὐτόν, ἢ ἐπί τ' αὐτῆς καὶ τῆς τινός;)· εἰ δὲ
μὴ τὸ αὐτὸ εἶδος, ὁμώνυμα ἂν εἴη, καὶ ὅμοιον ὥσπερ
ἂν εἴ τις καλοῖ ἄνθρωπον τόν τε Καλλίαν καὶ τὸ ξύλον,
μηδεμίαν κοινωνίαν ἐπιβλέψας αὐτῶν.—πάντων δὲ μάλιστα
διαπορήσειεν ἄν τις τί ποτε συμβάλλεται τὰ εἴδη τοῖς
10 ἀϊδίοις τῶν αἰσθητῶν ἢ τοῖς γιγνομένοις καὶ φθειρομένοις·
οὔτε γὰρ κινήσεως οὔτε μεταβολῆς οὐδεμιᾶς ἐστὶν αἴτια αὐτοῖς.
ἀλλὰ μὴν οὔτε πρὸς τὴν ἐπιστήμην οὐθὲν βοηθεῖ τὴν τῶν ἄλλων (οὐδὲ γὰρ οὐσία ἐκεῖνα τούτων· ἐν τούτοις γὰρ ἂν ἦν), οὔτε
εἰς τὸ εἶναι, μὴ ἐνυπάρχοντά γε τοῖς μετέχουσιν· οὕτω μὲν
15 γὰρ ἂν ἴσως αἴτια δόξειεν εἶναι ὡς τὸ λευκὸν μεμιγμένον
τῷ λευκῷ, ἀλλ' οὗτος μὲν ὁ λόγος λίαν εὐκίνητος, ὃν Ἀναξαγόρας μὲν πρῶτος Εὔδοξος δ' ὕστερον καὶ ἄλλοι τινὲς
ἔλεγον (ῥᾴδιον γὰρ συναγαγεῖν πολλὰ καὶ ἀδύνατα πρὸς
τὴν τοιαύτην δόξαν)· ἀλλὰ μὴν οὐδ' ἐκ τῶν εἰδῶν ἐστὶ τἆλλα
20 κατ' οὐθένα τρόπον τῶν εἰωθότων λέγεσθαι. τὸ δὲ λέγειν
παραδείγματα αὐτὰ εἶναι καὶ μετέχειν αὐτῶν τἆλλα κενο-
λογεῖν ἐστὶ καὶ μεταφορὰς λέγειν ποιητικάς. τί γάρ ἐστι
τὸ ἐργαζόμενον πρὸς τὰς ἰδέας ἀποβλέπον; ἐνδέχεταί τε
991ᵃ 8 — ᵇ 9 = 1079ᵇ 12 — 1080ᵃ 8

ᵇ 30 ἕκαστον Asc.ᶜ   31 μὴ om. γρ. Al.   33 συμβέβηκε ... 34
εἶναι ΕΓ Asc. Μ : om. Aᵇ   34 οὐσία codd. Γ Al.ᶜ Μ : οὐσίᾳ fort.
Al. : οὐσιῶν vel οὐσίας ex Al. coni. Bonitz   ταὐτὰ Al. : ταῦτα codd.
Γ Al.ᶜ   δὲ ἐνταῦθα] γὰρ ἐνταυθί τε Al.ᶜ Bonitz   991ᵃ 4 καὶ] καὶ
δυάδων Aᵇ : καὶ τῶν δυάδων Al.ᶜ Μ   5 ἓν ΕΓ Al. Μ : εἶναι ἓν Aᵇ
Al.ᶜ : σημαίνει ἓν Bywater   τ' αὐτῆς Bonitz : ταύτης codd. Γ : αὐτῆς Μ
6 ὁμονυμία Ε : ὁμωνυμία Γ Asc.ᶜ   7 καλοίη Aᵇ Asc.ᶜ   9 ἂν om.
Aᵇ   10 καὶ Aᵇ Al. : καὶ τοῖς ΕΜ   12 οὔτε Sylburg : οὐδὲ codd.
Asc. Μ   13 οὐδὲ Sylburg : οὔτε codd. Μ   14 γε AᵇΜ : om. Ε
Asc.ᶜ   μὲν om. Γ   15 ὡς Aᵇ Al. : om. ΕΓ Asc.ᶜ Μ   21 αὐτὰ Ε
et ut vid. Al. : ταῦτα Asc.¹ : τε Aᵇ : om. Γ Al.¹ Μ   23 τε AᵇΜ :
δὲ Al.¹ : γὰρ ΕΓ Asc.ᶜ

καὶ εἶναι καὶ γίγνεσθαι ὅμοιον ὁτιοῦν καὶ μὴ εἰκαζόμενον
πρὸς ἐκεῖνο, ὥστε καὶ ὄντος Σωκράτους καὶ μὴ ὄντος γένοιτ' 25
ἂν οἷος Σωκράτης· ὁμοίως δὲ δῆλον ὅτι κἂν εἰ ἦν ὁ
Σωκράτης ἀΐδιος. ἔσται τε πλείω παραδείγματα τοῦ αὐτοῦ,
ὥστε καὶ εἴδη, οἷον τοῦ ἀνθρώπου τὸ ζῷον καὶ τὸ δίπουν,
ἅμα δὲ καὶ τὸ αὐτοάνθρωπος. ἔτι οὐ· μόνον τῶν αἰσθητῶν
παραδείγματα τὰ εἴδη ἀλλὰ καὶ αὐτῶν, οἷον τὸ γένος, 30
ὡς γένος εἰδῶν· ὥστε τὸ αὐτὸ ἔσται παράδειγμα καὶ
εἰκών. ἔτι δόξειεν ἂν ἀδύνατον εἶναι χωρὶς τὴν οὐσίαν καὶ οὗ 991ᵇ
ἡ οὐσία· ὥστε πῶς ἂν αἱ ἰδέαι οὐσίαι τῶν πραγμάτων οὖσαι
χωρὶς εἶεν; ἐν δὲ τῷ Φαίδωνι οὕτω λέγεται, ὡς καὶ τοῦ
εἶναι καὶ τοῦ γίγνεσθαι αἴτια τὰ εἴδη ἐστίν· καίτοι τῶν εἰδῶν
ὄντων ὅμως οὐ γίγνεται τὰ μετέχοντα ἂν μὴ ᾖ τὸ κινῆσον, 5
καὶ πολλὰ γίγνεται ἕτερα, οἷον οἰκία καὶ δακτύλιος, ὧν οὔ
φαμεν εἴδη εἶναι· ὥστε δῆλον ὅτι ἐνδέχεται καὶ τἆλλα καὶ
εἶναι καὶ γίγνεσθαι διὰ τοιαύτας αἰτίας οἵας καὶ τὰ ῥη-
θέντα νῦν.—ἔτι εἴπερ εἰσὶν ἀριθμοὶ τὰ εἴδη, πῶς αἴτιοι ἔσονται; πότερον ὅτι ἕτεροι ἀριθμοί εἰσι τὰ ὄντα, οἷον ὁδὶ μὲν (ὁ) 10
ἀριθμὸς ἄνθρωπος ὁδὶ δὲ Σωκράτης ὁδὶ δὲ Καλλίας; τί
οὖν ἐκεῖνοι τούτοις αἴτιοί εἰσιν; οὐδὲ γὰρ εἰ οἱ μὲν ἀΐδιοι οἱ
δὲ μή, οὐδὲν διαίσει. εἰ δ' ὅτι λόγοι ἀριθμῶν τἀνταῦθα, οἷον ἡ
συμφωνία, δῆλον ὅτι ἐστὶν ἕν γέ τι ὧν εἰσὶ λόγοι. εἰ δὴ
τι τοῦτο, ἡ ὕλη, φανερὸν ὅτι καὶ αὐτοὶ οἱ ἀριθμοὶ λόγοι τινὲς 15
ἔσονται ἑτέρου πρὸς ἕτερον. λέγω δ' οἷον, εἰ ἔστιν ὁ Καλλίας
λόγος ἐν ἀριθμοῖς πυρὸς καὶ γῆς καὶ ὕδατος καὶ ἀέρος,
καὶ ἄλλων τινῶν ὑποκειμένων ἔσται καὶ ἡ ἰδέα ἀριθμός· καὶ
αὐτοάνθρωπος, εἴτ' ἀριθμός τις ὢν εἴτε μή, ὅμως ἔσται λόγος
ἐν ἀριθμοῖς τινῶν καὶ οὐκ ἀριθμός, οὐδ' ἔσται τις διὰ ταῦτα 20

ᵃ 24 ὁτῳοῦν Richards   25 γένοιτ' AᵇM : γίγνοιτ' E   26 οἷος
Aᵇ Al. : οἷος περ E : οἷον M   27 ἔσται ... ᵇ 1 εἰκών om. γρ. Al.
29 τὸ om. M : τοῦ Aᵇ   αὐτοάνθρωπος ΕΓ Asc. M : αὐτοανθρώ-
που Aᵇ   ἔτι δ' οὐ Γ   30 αὐτῶν] αὐτῶν τῶν ἰδεῶν recc.   ὡς γένος τὸ
γένος om. Γ   31 ὡς γένος codd. Γ Asc. : τῶν ὡς γένους M et fort.
Al.   ᵇ 1 ἂν om. Aᵇ   ἀδύνατον bis Aᵇ   3 λέγεται codd. ΓM :
λέγομεν Al. Asc.   8 διὰ] καὶ διὰ Γ   9 εἶεν Γ Al.ˡ   10 ὁ addidi
11 ἄνθρωπος ἀριθμὸς Aᵇ   13 οὐδὲν om. Γ   κἀνταῦθα Γ   14 ὧν] οὗ
Walker 15 τι om. Aᵇ Γ Al.   17 καὶ ἀέρος ... 18 ἀριθμός Aᵇ Al. :
om. E Asc.ᶜ : καὶ ἄλλων ... ἀριθμός om. Γ   18 καὶ pr. om. recc. : ἢ
fort. Al.   καὶ tert.] ὁ Al. et sup. lin. add. E   20 οὐδ' Aᵇ et ut
vid. Al. : καὶ οὐκ ΕΓ   ἰδέα ante διὰ add. Jaeger, post ταῦτα Schwegler

ἀριθμός. ἔτι ἐκ πολλῶν ἀριθμῶν εἷς ἀριθμὸς γίγνεται, ἐξ
εἰδῶν δὲ ἓν εἶδος πῶς; εἰ δὲ μὴ ἐξ αὐτῶν ἀλλ' ἐκ τῶν ἐν
τῷ ἀριθμῷ, οἷον ἐν τῇ μυριάδι, πῶς ἔχουσιν αἱ μονάδες; εἴτε
γὰρ ὁμοειδεῖς, πολλὰ συμβήσεται ἄτοπα, εἴτε μὴ ὁμοει-
25 δεῖς, μήτε αὐταὶ ἀλλήλαις μήτε αἱ ἄλλαι πᾶσαι πά-
σαις· τίνι γὰρ διοίσουσιν ἀπαθεῖς οὖσαι; οὔτε γὰρ εὔλογα
ταῦτα οὔτε ὁμολογούμενα τῇ νοήσει. ἔτι δ' ἀναγκαῖον ἕτερον
γένος ἀριθμοῦ κατασκευάζειν περὶ ὃ ἡ ἀριθμητική, καὶ
πάντα τὰ μεταξὺ λεγόμενα ὑπό τινων, ἃ πῶς ἢ ἐκ τίνων
30 ἐστὶν ἀρχῶν; ἢ διὰ τί μεταξὺ τῶν δεῦρό τ' ἔσται καὶ
αὐτῶν; ἔτι αἱ μονάδες αἱ ἐν τῇ δυάδι ἑκατέρα ἔκ τινος
992ᵃ προτέρας δυάδος· καίτοι ἀδύνατον. ἔτι διὰ τί ἓν ὁ ἀριθμὸς
συλλαμβανόμενος; ἔτι δὲ πρὸς τοῖς εἰρημένοις, εἴπερ εἰσὶν
αἱ μονάδες διάφοροι, ἐχρῆν οὕτω λέγειν ὥσπερ καὶ ὅσοι τὰ
στοιχεῖα τέτταρα ἢ δύο λέγουσιν· καὶ γὰρ τούτων ἕκαστος οὐ
5 τὸ κοινὸν λέγει στοιχεῖον, οἷον τὸ σῶμα, ἀλλὰ πῦρ καὶ γῆν,
εἴτ' ἔστι τι κοινόν, τὸ σῶμα, εἴτε μή. νῦν δὲ λέγεται ὡς ὄντος
τοῦ ἑνὸς ὥσπερ πυρὸς ἢ ὕδατος ὁμοιομεροῦς· εἰ δ' οὕτως, οὐκ
ἔσονται οὐσίαι οἱ ἀριθμοί, ἀλλὰ δῆλον ὅτι, εἴπερ ἐστί τι ἓν
αὐτὸ καὶ τοῦτό ἐστιν ἀρχή, πλεοναχῶς λέγεται τὸ ἕν· ἄλ-
10 λως γὰρ ἀδύνατον.——βουλόμενοι δὲ τὰς οὐσίας ἀνάγειν εἰς τὰς
ἀρχὰς μήκη μὲν τίθεμεν ἐκ βραχέος καὶ μακροῦ, ἔκ τινος
μικροῦ καὶ μεγάλου, καὶ ἐπίπεδον ἐκ πλατέος καὶ στενοῦ,
σῶμα δ' ἐκ βαθέος καὶ ταπεινοῦ. καίτοι πῶς ἕξει ἢ τὸ ἐπίπεδον γραμμὴν ἢ τὸ στερεὸν γραμμὴν καὶ ἐπίπεδον; ἄλλο
15 γὰρ γένος τὸ πλατὺ καὶ στενὸν καὶ βαθὺ καὶ ταπεινόν·
ὥσπερ οὖν οὐδ' ἀριθμὸς ὑπάρχει ἐν αὐτοῖς, ὅτι τὸ πολὺ καὶ
ὀλίγον ἕτερον τούτων, δῆλον ὅτι οὐδ' ἄλλο οὐθὲν τῶν ἄνω

ᵇ 21 ἔτι AᵇΓ Al.¹ Asc.¹ : ἔτι δ' E   22 μηδ' Γ   ἐκ EΓ Asc.¹ᶜ :
om. Aᵇ   ἐν τῷ ἀριθμῷ] ἐναρίθμων E Al.¹ : ἀριθμῶν Γ γρ. E Asc.¹ᶜ
24 συμβήσεται ἄτοπα Aᵇ Al. : ἄτοπα συμβήσεται EΓ Asc.ᶜ   25 μήτε
. . . μήτε] an μηδὲ αἱ αὐταὶ ἀλλήλαις, μηδὲ? Aᵇ Al.¹   αὐταὶ S :
αἱ αὐταὶ EA Al.¹ᶜ : ἑαυταῖς Asc.ᶜ   μήτε δὲ Asc.ᶜ   ἄλλαι] ἄλλαι
αἱ E   27 δ' EJΓ Asc.¹ : τε Aᵇ Al.¹   28 γένος Aᵇ Al.¹ : τι γένος
EJΓ Asc.¹   ὃ EΓ Al. : ὃν Aᵇ   29 τίνων Asc.   ἃ πῶς] ἁπλῶς
EΓ Al.   30 ἔσται fort. Al.   τί Aᵇ Al. Asc. : τί τὰ EΓ   τῶν δεῦρό]
τῶνδέ Aᵇ   31 ἑκατέρα EΓ Al. Asc. : ἑκατέρων Aᵇ   992ᵃ 1 προτέρας EΓ et fort. Al. : ἔτι προτέρας τῆς Aᵇ et ut vid. Asc.   3 ἀδιά-
φοροι γρ. Al.   6 τι E Al. Asc. : om. AᵇΓ   11 βραχέος καὶ
μακροῦ Aᵇ Al.¹ : μακροῦ καὶ βραχέος EΓ Asc.ᶜ   13 ἢ EΓ Al. : om.
Aᵇ Asc.ᶜ   15 καὶ pr.] καὶ τὸ E   16 ἐν EΓ Al. : om. Aᵇ

ὑπάρξει τοῖς κάτω. ἀλλὰ μὴν οὐδὲ γένος τὸ πλατὺ τοῦ βα-
θέος· ἦν γὰρ ἂν ἐπίπεδόν τι τὸ σῶμα. ἔτι αἱ στιγμαὶ ἐκ
τίνος ἐνυπάρξουσιν; τούτῳ μὲν οὖν τῷ γένει καὶ διεμάχετο 20
Πλάτων ὡς ὄντι γεωμετρικῷ δόγματι, ἀλλ᾽ ἐκάλει ἀρχὴν
γραμμῆς—τοῦτο δὲ πολλάκις ἐτίθει—τὰς ἀτόμους γραμμάς.
καίτοι ἀνάγκη τούτων εἶναί τι πέρας· ὥστ᾽ ἐξ οὗ λόγου γραμμὴ
ἔστι, καὶ στιγμὴ ἔστιν.—ὅλως δὲ ζητούσης τῆς σοφίας περὶ
τῶν φανερῶν τὸ αἴτιον, τοῦτο μὲν εἰάκαμεν (οὐθὲν γὰρ λέγομεν 25
περὶ τῆς αἰτίας ὅθεν ἡ ἀρχὴ τῆς μεταβολῆς), τὴν δ᾽ οὐσίαν
οἰόμενοι λέγειν αὐτῶν ἑτέρας μὲν οὐσίας εἶναί φαμεν, ὅπως
δ᾽ ἐκεῖναι τούτων οὐσίαι, διὰ κενῆς λέγομεν· τὸ γὰρ μετέχειν,
ὥσπερ καὶ πρότερον εἴπομεν, οὐθέν ἐστιν. οὐδὲ δὴ ὅπερ ταῖς
ἐπιστήμαις ὁρῶμεν ὂν αἴτιον, δι᾽ ὃ καὶ πᾶς νοῦς καὶ πᾶσα 30
φύσις ποιεῖ, οὐδὲ ταύτης τῆς αἰτίας, ἥν φαμεν εἶναι μίαν
τῶν ἀρχῶν, οὐθὲν ἅπτεται τὰ εἴδη, ἀλλὰ γέγονε τὰ μαθήματα τοῖς νῦν ἡ φιλοσοφία, φασκόντων ἄλλων χάριν
αὐτὰ δεῖν πραγματεύεσθαι. ἔτι δὲ τὴν ὑποκειμένην οὐσίαν 992ᵇ
ὡς ὕλην μαθηματικωτέραν ἄν τις ὑπολάβοι, καὶ μᾶλλον
κατηγορεῖσθαι καὶ διαφορὰν εἶναι τῆς οὐσίας καὶ τῆς ὕλης
ἢ ὕλην, οἷον τὸ μέγα καὶ τὸ μικρόν, ὥσπερ καὶ οἱ φυσιολόγοι φασὶ τὸ μανὸν καὶ τὸ πυκνόν, πρώτας τοῦ ὑποκειμένου 5
φάσκοντες εἶναι διαφορὰς ταύτας· ταῦτα γάρ ἐστιν ὑπεροχή
τις καὶ ἔλλειψις. περί τε κινήσεως, εἰ μὲν ἔσται ταῦτα κίνησις,
δῆλον ὅτι κινήσεται τὰ εἴδη· εἰ δὲ μή, πόθεν ἦλθεν; ὅλη
γὰρ ἡ περὶ φύσεως ἀνήρηται σκέψις. ὅ τε δοκεῖ ῥάδιον
εἶναι, τὸ δεῖξαι ὅτι ἓν ἅπαντα, οὐ γίγνεται· τῇ γὰρ ἐκθέσει 10
οὐ γίγνεται πάντα ἓν ἀλλ᾽ αὐτό τι ἕν, ἂν διδῷ τις πάντα·
καὶ οὐδὲ τοῦτο, εἰ μὴ γένος δώσει τὸ καθόλου εἶναι· τοῦτο δ᾽
ἐν ἐνίοις ἀδύνατον. οὐθένα δ᾽ ἔχει λόγον οὐδὲ τὰ μετὰ τοὺς

ᵃ 20 ἐνυπάρξουσιν Aᵇ Al. : ἐνυπάρχουσι ΕΓ Asc.¹   21 ἐτίθει . . .
22 ἐκάλει Walker   22 ante τοῦτο et τὰς interpunxi   24 σοφίας
ΕΓ Al.¹ Asc. : φιλοσοφίας Ἀᵇ   26 ὅθεν Ε Al. : πόθεν Aᵇ   29 ὃ
περὶ τὰς ἐπιστήμας Aᵇ : ὃ περί τινας ἐπιστήμας Rolfes   30 διὸ Ε
31 οὐδὲ] τόδε Aᵇ   33 ἄλλων Ε Al. : τῶν ἄλλων Aᵇ   ᵇ 4 ἢ ὕλην
AᵇΓ Al. : om. Ε   καὶ alt. om. Γ   6 ταύτας om. Aᵇ   7 καὶ
ἔλλειψις ΕΓ Al. : om. Aᵇ   τε ΕΓ Asc.¹ : δὲ Aᵇ   ἔσται ταῦτα
codd. Γ Al. : ἔστι ταῦτα Asc.¹ : ἔστ᾽ ἐνταῦθα fort. Asc., Jaeger : ἔσται
Heidel   9 σκέψις ἀνήρηται Aᵇ   ὅ τε Aᵇ Al.¹ : καὶ ὃ Ε Asc.¹
10 οὐ . . . ἐκθέσει ΕΓ Al. Asc. : ἐκ τῆς ἐκθέσεως Aᵇ   12 εἰ . . . δώσει
Aᵇ Al.¹ : ἐὰν . . . δῷ ΕΓ   13 ἐν ΕΓ Al. : om. Aᵇ·

ἀριθμοὺς μήκη τε καὶ ἐπίπεδα καὶ στερεά, οὔτε ὅπως ἔστιν ἢ
15 ἔσται οὔτε τίνα ἔχει δύναμιν· ταῦτα γὰρ οὔτε εἴδη οἷόν τε εἶναι
(οὐ γάρ εἰσιν ἀριθμοί) οὔτε τὰ μεταξύ (μαθηματικὰ γὰρ
ἐκεῖνα) οὔτε τὰ φθαρτά, ἀλλὰ πάλιν τέταρτον ἄλλο φαίνεται τοῦτό τι γένος. ὅλως τε τὸ τῶν ὄντων ζητεῖν στοιχεῖα
μὴ διελόντας, πολλαχῶς λεγομένων, ἀδύνατον εὑρεῖν, ἄλλως
20 τε καὶ τοῦτον τὸν τρόπον ζητοῦντας ἐξ οἵων ἐστὶ στοιχείων.
ἐκ τίνων γὰρ τὸ ποιεῖν ἢ πάσχειν ἢ τὸ εὐθύ, οὐκ ἔστι δήπου
λαβεῖν, ἀλλ᾽ εἴπερ, τῶν οὐσιῶν μόνον ἐνδέχεται· ὥστε τὸ τῶν
ὄντων ἁπάντων τὰ στοιχεῖα ἢ ζητεῖν ἢ οἴεσθαι ἔχειν οὐκ ἀληθές. πῶς δ᾽ ἄν τις καὶ μάθοι τὰ τῶν πάντων στοιχεῖα;
25 δῆλον γὰρ ὡς οὐθὲν οἷόν τε προϋπάρχειν γνωρίζοντα πρότερον. ὥσπερ γὰρ τῷ γεωμετρεῖν μανθάνοντι ἄλλα μὲν ἐνδέχεται προειδέναι, ὧν δὲ ἡ ἐπιστήμη καὶ περὶ ὧν μέλλει
μανθάνειν οὐδὲν προγιγνώσκει, οὕτω δὴ καὶ ἐπὶ τῶν ἄλλων,
ὥστ᾽ εἴ τις τῶν πάντων ἔστιν ἐπιστήμη, οἵαν δή τινές φασιν,
30 οὐθὲν ἂν προϋπάρχοι γνωρίζων οὗτος. καίτοι πᾶσα μάθησις διὰ
προγιγνωσκομένων ἢ πάντων ἢ τινῶν ἐστί, καὶ ἡ δι᾽ ἀποδείξεως
⟨καὶ⟩ ἡ δι᾽ ὁρισμῶν (δεῖ γὰρ ἐξ ὧν ὁ ὁρισμὸς προειδέναι καὶ
εἶναι γνώριμα)· ὁμοίως δὲ καὶ ἡ δι᾽ ἐπαγωγῆς. ἀλλὰ μὴν
993ᵃ εἰ καὶ τυγχάνοι σύμφυτος οὖσα, θαυμαστὸν πῶς λανθάνο-
μεν ἔχοντες τὴν κρατίστην τῶν ἐπιστημῶν. ἔτι πῶς τις γνω-
ριεῖ ἐκ τίνων ἐστί, καὶ πῶς ἔσται δῆλον; καὶ γὰρ τοῦτ᾽ ἔχει
ἀπορίαν· ἀμφισβητήσειε γὰρ ἄν τις ὥσπερ καὶ περὶ ἐνίας
5 συλλαβάς· οἱ μὲν γὰρ τὸ ζα ἐκ τοῦ σ καὶ δ καὶ α φασὶν
εἶναι, οἱ δέ τινες ἕτερον φθόγγον φασὶν εἶναι καὶ οὐθένα
τῶν γνωρίμων. ἔτι δὲ ὧν ἐστιν αἴσθησις, ταῦτα πῶς ἄν τις
μὴ ἔχων τὴν αἴσθησιν γνοίη; καίτοι ἔδει, εἴγε πάντων ταῦτα

ᵇ 14 τε om. E Asc.ˡᵒ   οὐδὲ Aᵇ   15 τίνα Aᵇ Al.: εἴ τινα ΕΓ
Asc.   17 τέταρτον om. Γ   φαίνεται τοῦτό τι E et ut vid. Al.:
τοῦτο φαίνεται Aᵇ   19 διελόντα AᵇΓ Al.ˡ   πολλαχῶς λεγομένων
E Al.ˡ: τὰ πολλαχῶς λεγόμενα AᵇΓ   20 οἵων] ὧν AᵇΓ et fort. Al.
21 εὐθύ ΕΓ Al.: εὖ Aᵇ   23 ἢ pr. ΕΓ Al.: om. Aᵇ   26 τῷ ΕΓ
Al. Asc.ᶜ: τῷ γεωμέτρῃ Aᵇ   28 δὲ E Asc.ᶜ   29 πάντων E
Asc.ᶜ: ἁπάντων Aᵇ   οἵαν δή] ὥς ΕΓ Asc.ᶜ   31 ἤ ... 32 καὶ
ἢ Al. Bonitz: ἢ ... ἢ codd. Γ Asc.   33 ἢ Aᵇ   993ᵃ 1 εἰ καὶ
τυγχάνοι Aᵇ Al.ˡ: καὶ εἰ τυγχάνει ΕΓ Asc.ˡ   2 γνωρίσειεν E Asc.ˡ:
γνωρίζει Γ: γνωρίσει Al.   5 ζα Al. Bonitz: σμα codd. Γ Asc.
δ Al. Bonitz: μ codd. Γ Asc.   6 δὲ τὸν ἕτερον τρόπον ἴδιον εἶναι
Aᵇ   8 ἔδει ΕΓ Asc.ᶜ: δεῖ Aᵇ   ταῦτα Asc.ᶜ i et fort. Al.: ταῦτα
codd. Γ

στοιχεῖά ἐστιν ἐξ ὧν, ὥσπερ αἱ σύνθετοι φωναί εἰσιν ἐκ τῶν
οἰκείων στοιχείων.   10

10   Ὅτι μὲν οὖν τὰς εἰρημένας ἐν τοῖς φυσικοῖς αἰτίας
ζητεῖν ἐοίκασι πάντες, καὶ τούτων ἐκτὸς οὐδεμίαν ἔχοιμεν ἂν
εἰπεῖν, δῆλον καὶ ἐκ τῶν πρότερον εἰρημένων· ἀλλ' ἀμυδρῶς
ταύτας, καὶ τρόπον μέν τινα πᾶσαι πρότερον εἴρηνται τρόπον δέ τινα οὐδαμῶς. ψελλιζομένῃ γὰρ ἔοικεν ἡ πρώτη   15
φιλοσοφία περὶ πάντων, ἅτε νέα τε καὶ κατ' ἀρχὰς οὖσα [καὶ
τὸ πρῶτον], ἐπεὶ καὶ Ἐμπεδοκλῆς ὀστοῦν τῷ λόγῳ φησὶν
εἶναι, τοῦτο δ' ἐστὶ τὸ τί ἦν εἶναι καὶ ἡ οὐσία τοῦ πράγματες.
ἀλλὰ μὴν ὁμοίως ἀναγκαῖον καὶ σάρκας καὶ τῶν ἄλλων
ἕκαστον εἶναι τὸν λόγον, ἢ μηδὲ ἕν· διὰ τοῦτο γὰρ καὶ σὰρξ 20
καὶ ὀστοῦν ἔσται καὶ τῶν ἄλλων ἕκαστον καὶ οὐ διὰ τὴν ὕλην,
ἣν ἐκεῖνος λέγει, πῦρ καὶ γῆν καὶ ὕδωρ καὶ ἀέρα. ἀλλὰ
ταῦτα ἄλλου μὲν λέγοντος συνέφησεν ἂν ἐξ ἀνάγκης, σαφῶς δὲ οὐκ εἴρηκεν. περὶ μὲν οὖν τούτων δεδήλωται καὶ
πρότερον· ὅσα δὲ περὶ τῶν αὐτῶν τούτων ἀπορήσειεν ἄν τις, 25
ἐπανέλθωμεν πάλιν· τάχα γὰρ ἂν ἐξ αὐτῶν εὐπορήσαιμέν
τι πρὸς τὰς ὕστερον ἀπορίας.

Α ΕΛΑΤΤΟΝ

1   Ἡ περὶ τῆς ἀληθείας θεωρία τῇ μὲν χαλεπὴ τῇ δὲ 30
ῥᾳδία. σημεῖον δὲ τὸ μήτ' ἀξίως μηδένα δύνασθαι θιγεῖν
αὐτῆς μήτε πάντας ἀποτυγχάνειν, ἀλλ' ἕκαστον λέγειν τι 993ᵇ
περὶ τῆς φύσεως, καὶ καθ' ἕνα μὲν ἢ μηθὲν ἢ μικρὸν ἐπιβάλ-
λειν αὐτῇ, ἐκ πάντων δὲ συναθροιζομένων γίγνεσθαί τι μέγε-
θος· ὥστ' εἴπερ ἔοικεν ἔχειν καθάπερ τυγχάνομεν παροιμια-
ζόμενοι, τίς ἂν θύρας ἁμάρτοι; ταύτῃ μὲν ἂν εἴη ῥᾳδία, 5
τὸ δ' ὅλον τι ἔχειν καὶ μέρος μὴ δύνασθαι δηλοῖ τὸ χαλε-

ᵃ 12 ἔχομεν AᵇΓ Al.ᶜ   15 ψελλιζομένη ΕΓ   16 ἁπάντων Aᵇ
τε καὶ Sa: τε Ε Asc.ᶜ: καὶ Al.ᶜ: om. Aᵇ   καὶ τὸ πρῶτον seclusi,
om. i Al.   19 σαρκὸς ΕΓ Al.ᶜ: σάρκα Τ   20 ἑκάστου Γ   μηδὲ
ἕν] μηδέν Γ: μηδενός Aᵇ Al.   γὰρ ΕΓ Al. Asc.: ἄρα Aᵇ   ἡ σὰρξ
Aᵇ   21 ἐστὶ Γ et fort. Al.   23 ἂν om. Γ   24 τούτων Aᵇ
Al. Asc.: τῶν τοιούτων ΕΓ Al.¹   26 ἀπορήσαιμεν Aᵇ   27 τι
om. Aᵇ   29 ā ἔλαττον] β ex ā fecit Ε   30 ἡ ΕΑᵇΓ Al.¹
γρ. Al. Asc.¹: ὅτι ἡ Al.   31 θιγεῖν] τυχεῖν ΕΓ Asc.¹   ᵇ 1 πάντας
codd. ΓAl.ᶜ: πάντως ex Al. Asc. ci. Brandis   6 ὅλον μὴ δύνασθαι
καὶ μέρος ἔχειν aliquos coniecisse refert Al.   τι Aᵇ Al.: τ' Ε Asc.¹:
om. Γ

πὸν αὐτῆς. ἴσως δὲ καὶ τῆς χαλεπότητος οὔσης κατὰ δύο
τρόπους, οὐκ ἐν τοῖς πράγμασιν ἀλλ᾽ ἐν ἡμῖν τὸ αἴτιον
αὐτῆς· ὥσπερ γὰρ τὰ τῶν νυκτερίδων ὄμματα πρὸς τὸ
10 φέγγος ἔχει τὸ μεθ᾽ ἡμέραν, οὕτω καὶ τῆς ἡμετέρας ψυχῆς
ὁ νοῦς πρὸς τὰ τῇ φύσει φανερώτατα πάντων. οὐ μόνον δὲ
χάριν ἔχειν δίκαιον τούτοις ὧν ἄν τις κοινώσαιτο ταῖς δόξαις, ἀλλὰ καὶ τοῖς ἐπιπολαιότερον ἀποφηναμένοις· καὶ
γὰρ οὗτοι συνεβάλοντό τι· τὴν γὰρ ἕξιν προήσκησαν ἡμῶν·
15 εἰ μὲν γὰρ Τιμόθεος μὴ ἐγένετο, πολλὴν ἂν μελοποιίαν οὐκ
εἴχομεν· εἰ δὲ μὴ Φρῦνις, Τιμόθεος οὐκ ἂν ἐγένετο. τὸν
αὐτὸν δὲ τρόπον καὶ ἐπὶ τῶν περὶ τῆς ἀληθείας ἀποφηναμένων·
παρὰ μὲν γὰρ ἐνίων παρειλήφαμέν τινας δόξας, οἱ δὲ τοῦ
γενέσθαι τούτους αἴτιοι γεγόνασιν. ὀρθῶς δ᾽ ἔχει καὶ τὸ κα-
20 λεῖσθαι τὴν φιλοσοφίαν ἐπιστήμην τῆς ἀληθείας. θεωρητικῆς
μὲν γὰρ τέλος ἀλήθεια πρακτικῆς δ᾽ ἔργον· καὶ γὰρ ἂν
τὸ πῶς ἔχει σκοπῶσιν, οὐ τὸ ἀίδιον ἀλλ᾽ ὃ πρός τι καὶ νῦν
θεωροῦσιν οἱ πρακτικοί. οὐκ ἴσμεν δὲ τὸ ἀληθὲς ἄνευ τῆς
αἰτίας· ἕκαστον δὲ μάλιστα αὐτὸ τῶν ἄλλων καθ᾽ ὃ καὶ
25 τοῖς ἄλλοις ὑπάρχει τὸ συνώνυμον (οἷον τὸ πῦρ θερμότατον·
καὶ γὰρ τοῖς ἄλλοις τὸ αἴτιον τοῦτο τῆς θερμότητος)· ὥστε
καὶ ἀληθέστατον τὸ τοῖς ὑστέροις αἴτιον τοῦ ἀληθέσιν εἶναι.
διὸ τὰς τῶν ἀεὶ ὄντων ἀρχὰς ἀναγκαῖον ἀεὶ εἶναι ἀληθε-
στάτας (οὐ γάρ ποτε ἀληθεῖς, οὐδ᾽ ἐκείναις αἴτιόν τί ἐστι τοῦ
30 εἶναι, ἀλλ᾽ ἐκεῖναι τοῖς ἄλλοις), ὥσθ᾽ ἕκαστον ὡς ἔχει τοῦ
εἶναι, οὕτω καὶ τῆς ἀληθείας.

994ᵃ Ἀλλὰ μὴν ὅτι γ᾽ ἔστιν ἀρχή τις καὶ οὐκ ἄπειρα τὰ 2

ᵇ 8 αἴτιόν ἐστιν αὐτῆς Aᵇ   9 γὰρ καὶ τὰ recc.   12 κοινώσαιτο
Aᵇ Al.¹: κοινωνήσαιτο E sed το eadem ut vid. manu postea additum .
κοινωνῆσαι fort. Al.   τὰς δόξας Richards   13 τοῖς Aᵇ Al. Asc.ᶜ:
τοῖς ἔτι ΕΓ   ἐπιπολαιότερον Aᵇ Al.: ἐπιπολαιοτέρως E Asc.ᶜ
14 συνεβάλοντό Aᵇ Al. Asc.: συμβάλλονταί ΕΓ   προήσκησαν ΕΓ Al
Asc.ᶜ: ἤσκησαν Aᵇ   17 ἐπὶ fort. Al., Jaeger: περὶ AᵇΓ Asc.: om. E
περὶ τῆς E Asc.: om. AᵇΓ   ἀλήθειαν Γ   18 μὲν γὰρ] δὲ Γ γὰρ
incl. Christ   19 δ᾽ AᵇΓ Al.¹ Asc.¹: δὴ E   ἔχει ΕΓ Asc.¹: om. Aᵇ
Al.¹   καλεῖσθαι AᵇΓ Al.¹: καλέσαι E Asc.¹ᶜ   20 τὴν . . . ἀληθείας
ΕΓ Al.¹ Asc.¹: τὴν κατὰ . . . ἀληθείας θεωρητικήν Aᵇ   22 ἐχῆι E
οὐ τὸ ἀίδιον Brandis: οὐκ ἀίδιον Aᵇ Al.: οὐ τὸ ἀίδιον καθ᾽ αὑτὸ recc.
Asc.: οὐ τὸ αἴτιον καθ᾽ αὑτὸ E γρ. Al.: οὐ τὸ καθ᾽ αὑτὸ Γ   ἀλλ δ
scripsi: ἀλλὰ codd.: ἀλλὰ τὸ fort. Al.   27 ὑστέροις ΕΓ Al.ᶜ Asc.:
ὕστερον Aᵇ   29 ἐκείναις ΕΓ Asc.¹: ἐκείνων Aᵇ Al.ᶜ   ἐστι
ΕΓ Asc.¹: om. Aᵇ Al.ᶜ

αἴτια τῶν ὄντων οὔτ᾽ εἰς εὐθυωρίαν οὔτε κατ᾽ εἶδος, δῆλον.
οὔτε γὰρ ὡς ἐξ ὕλης τόδ᾽ ἐκ τοῦδε δυνατὸν ἰέναι εἰς ἄπειρον
(οἷον σάρκα μὲν ἐκ γῆς, γῆν δ᾽ ἐξ ἀέρος, ἀέρα δ᾽ ἐκ πυρός,
καὶ τοῦτο μὴ ἵστασθαι), οὔτε ὅθεν ἡ ἀρχὴ τῆς κινήσεως (οἷον 5
τὸν μὲν ἄνθρωπον ὑπὸ τοῦ ἀέρος κινηθῆναι, τοῦτον δ᾽ ὑπὸ τοῦ
ἡλίου, τὸν δὲ ἥλιον ὑπὸ τοῦ νείκους, καὶ τούτου μηδὲν εἶναι
πέρας)· ὁμοίως δὲ οὐδὲ τὸ οὗ ἕνεκα εἰς ἄπειρον οἷόν τε ἰέναι,
βάδισιν μὲν ὑγιείας ἕνεκα, ταύτην δ᾽ εὐδαιμονίας, τὴν δ᾽ εὐδαιμο-
νίαν ἄλλου, καὶ οὕτως ἀεὶ ἄλλο ἄλλου ἕνεκεν εἶναι· καὶ ἐπὶ 10
τοῦ τί ἦν εἶναι δ᾽ ὡσαύτως. τῶν γὰρ μέσων, ὧν ἐστί
τι ἔσχατον καὶ πρότερον, ἀναγκαῖον εἶναι τὸ πρότερον αἴτιον
τῶν μετ᾽ αὐτό. εἰ γὰρ εἰπεῖν ἡμᾶς δέοι τί τῶν τριῶν αἴτιον,
τὸ πρῶτον ἐροῦμεν· οὐ γὰρ δὴ τό γ᾽ ἔσχατον, οὐδενὸς γὰρ τὸ
τελευταῖον· ἀλλὰ μὴν οὐδὲ τὸ μέσον, ἑνὸς γάρ (οὐθὲν δὲ 15
διαφέρει ἓν ἢ πλείω εἶναι, οὐδ᾽ ἄπειρα ἢ πεπερασμένα). τῶν
δ᾽ ἀπείρων τοῦτον τὸν τρόπον καὶ ὅλως τοῦ ἀπείρου πάντα τὰ
μόρια μέσα ὁμοίως μέχρι τοῦ νῦν· ὥστ᾽ εἴπερ μηδέν ἐστι
πρῶτον, ὅλως αἴτιον οὐδέν ἐστιν.—ἀλλὰ μὴν οὐδ᾽ ἐπὶ τὸ κάτω
οἷόν τε εἰς ἄπειρον ἰέναι, τοῦ ἄνω ἔχοντος ἀρχήν, ὥστ᾽ ἐκ πυ- 20
ρὸς μὲν ὕδωρ, ἐκ δὲ τούτου γῆν, καὶ οὕτως ἀεὶ ἄλλο τι γίγνεσθαι γένος. διχῶς γὰρ γίγνεται τόδε ἐκ τοῦδε—μὴ ὡς τόδε
λέγεται μετὰ τόδε, οἷον ἐξ Ἰσθμίων Ὀλύμπια, ἀλλ᾽ ἢ
ὡς ἐκ παιδὸς ἀνὴρ μεταβάλλοντος ἢ ὡς ἐξ ὕδατος ἀήρ.
ὡς μὲν οὖν ἐκ παιδὸς ἄνδρα γίγνεσθαί φαμεν, ὡς ἐκ τοῦ 25
γιγνομένου τὸ γεγονὸς ἢ ἐκ τοῦ ἐπιτελουμένου τὸ τετελεσμένον
(ἀεὶ γάρ ἐστι μεταξύ, ὥσπερ τοῦ εἶναι καὶ μὴ εἶναι γένεσις,
οὕτω καὶ τὸ γιγνόμενον τοῦ ὄντος καὶ μὴ ὄντος· ἔστι γὰρ ὁ
μανθάνων γιγνόμενος ἐπιστήμων, καὶ τοῦτ᾽ ἐστὶν ὃ λέγεται,

994ᵃ 2 εἰς ΕΓ Al.¹ Asc.ᶜ: ἐπ᾽ Aᵇ   3 εἶναι Ε Asc.ᶜ   εἰς] ἐπ᾽
Ε Al. Asc.ᶜ   6 ὑπὸ pr. ΕΓ Asc.ᶜ: ἐκ Aᵇ   8 οὐδὲ . . . οἷόν]
καὶ . . . οὐχ οἷόν Aᵇ Asc.   εἶναι Aᵇ   10 ἄλλου pr. ΕJΓ Asc.ᶜ:
ἄλλου ἕνεκεν Aᵇ   11 τοῦ] τῶν recc.   δ᾽ om. J   12 τι Al.: om.
Aᵇ Al.¹: ἔξω τι ΕJΓ Asc.¹   13 τῶν ΑᵇΓ Al.: τῶι ΕJ   μετ᾽ αὐτὸ
ΕJ Al.: μεθ᾽ αὐτό ΑᵇΓ   ἡμᾶς εἰπεῖν Aᵇ   τί i Al. Asc.: τι codd.
14 τό γ᾽] γε τ᾽ Aᵇ   15 τὸ] τό γε ΕJ   δέ] γὰρ Γ   18 ἐστι τὸ J
20 τε Aᵇ Al.: τ᾽ ἐστὶν ΕJΓ Asc.¹   εἰς Aᵇ Al.¹: ἐπ᾽ ΕJ Al. Asc.¹
ἰέναι ΕJΓ Al. Asc.¹: ἀπιέναι Aᵇ   22 μὴ . . . 24 ἐκ] ἢ ὡς ἐκ Jaeger
μὴ JΓ γρ. Ε Al. Asc.: ἢ Aᵇ et fecit Ε   23 ἀλλ᾽ ἢ ὡς scripsi: ἀλλ᾽
ὡς ἢ γρ. Ε γρ. J: ἄλλως ἢ J et ut vid. Ε¹: ἢ fecit Ε: ἢ οὐχ οὕτως ἀλλ᾽
ὡς ἢ Aᵇ: ἢ ὡς ex Al. ci. Bonitz   24 ὡς om. ΕJΓ   ἀήρ . . . 25 φαμεν
om. Ε   25 ἀνήρ, γίγνεσθαί φαμεν [ὡς] ἐκ Jaeger   ἀνὴρ J   28 γὰρ
Aᵇ et ut vid. Al.: δὲ ΕJΓ Asc.ᶜ   29 καὶ . . . 30 ἐπιστήμων ΕJΓ Al.
Asc.: om. Aᵇ

D

30 ὅτι γίγνεται ἐκ μανθάνοντος ἐπιστήμων)· τὸ δ᾽ ὡς ἐξ ἀέρος
ὕδωρ, φθειρομένου θατέρου. διὸ ἐκεῖνα μὲν οὐκ ἀνακάμπτει
εἰς ἄλληλα, οὐδὲ γίγνεται ἐξ ἀνδρὸς παῖς (οὐ γὰρ γίγνεται
994b ἐκ τῆς γενέσεως τὸ γιγνόμενον ἀλλ᾽ ⟨ὃ⟩ ἔστι μετὰ τὴν γένεσιν·
οὕτω γὰρ καὶ ἡμέρα ἐκ τοῦ πρωΐ, ὅτι μετὰ τοῦτο· διὸ οὐδὲ τὸ
πρωΐ ἐξ ἡμέρας)· θάτερα δὲ ἀνακάμπτει. ἀμφοτέρως δὲ
ἀδύνατον εἰς ἄπειρον ἰέναι· τῶν μὲν γὰρ ὄντων μεταξὺ
5 ἀνάγκη τέλος εἶναι, τὰ δ᾽ εἰς ἄλληλα ἀνακάμπτει· ἡ γὰρ
θατέρου φθορὰ θατέρου ἐστὶ γένεσις.—ἅμα δὲ καὶ ἀδύνατον τὸ
πρῶτον ἀΐδιον ὂν φθαρῆναι· ἐπεὶ γὰρ οὐκ ἄπειρος ἡ γένεσις
ἐπὶ τὸ ἄνω, ἀνάγκη ἐξ οὗ φθαρέντος πρώτου τι ἐγένετο μὴ
ἀΐδιον εἶναι. ἔτι δὲ τὸ οὗ ἕνεκα τέλος, τοιοῦτον δὲ ὃ μὴ ἄλλου
10 ἕνεκα ἀλλὰ τἆλλα ἐκείνου, ὥστ᾽ εἰ μὲν ἔσται τοιοῦτόν τι
ἔσχατον, οὐκ ἔσται ἄπειρον, εἰ δὲ μηθὲν τοιοῦτον, οὐκ ἔσται τὸ
οὗ ἕνεκα, ἀλλ᾽ οἱ τὸ ἄπειρον ποιοῦντες λανθάνουσιν ἐξαιροῦντες
τὴν τοῦ ἀγαθοῦ φύσιν (καίτοι οὐθεὶς ἂν ἐγχειρήσειεν οὐδὲν
πράττειν μὴ μέλλων ἐπὶ πέρας ἥξειν)· οὐδ᾽ ἂν εἴη νοῦς ἐν
15 τοῖς οὖσιν· ἕνεκα γάρ τινος ἀεὶ πράττει ὅ γε νοῦν ἔχων,
τοῦτο δέ ἐστι πέρας· τὸ γὰρ τέλος πέρας ἐστίν. ἀλλὰ μὴν
οὐδὲ τὸ τί ἦν εἶναι ἐνδέχεται ἀνάγεσθαι εἰς ἄλλον ὁρισμὸν
πλεονάζοντα τῷ λόγῳ· ἀεί τε γὰρ ἔστιν ὁ ἔμπροσθεν μᾶλλον, ὁ δ᾽ ὕστερος οὐκ ἔστιν, οὗ δὲ τὸ πρῶτον μὴ ἔστιν, οὐδὲ
20 τὸ ἐχόμενον· ἔτι τὸ ἐπίστασθαι ἀναιροῦσιν οἱ οὕτως λέγοντες,
οὐ γὰρ οἷόν τε εἰδέναι πρὶν εἰς τὰ ἄτομα ἐλθεῖν· καὶ τὸ
γιγνώσκειν οὐκ ἔστιν, τὰ γὰρ οὕτως ἄπειρα πῶς ἐνδέχεται
νοεῖν; οὐ γὰρ ὅμοιον ἐπὶ τῆς γραμμῆς, ἣ κατὰ τὰς διαιρέσεις μὲν οὐχ ἵσταται, νοῆσαι δ᾽ οὐκ ἔστι μὴ στήσαντα (διόπερ
25 οὐκ ἀριθμήσει τὰς τομὰς ὁ τὴν ἄπειρον διεξιών), ἀλλὰ καὶ
τὴν ὅλην οὐ κινουμένῳ νοεῖν ἀνάγκη. καὶ ἀπείρῳ οὐδενὶ ἔστιν

ᵃ 32 γὰρ EJΓ Al. Asc.ˡᶜ : δὲ Aᵇ   ᵇ 1 ὁ add. Christ : ἃ ci. Christ
ἔστι om. Al. : ἔστι τι Rolfes   2 ἐκ τὸ Aᵇ   τὸ om. Aᵇ Al.   3 θάτερα
EJΓ Al. : θάτερον Aᵇ   5 ἀνακάμπτειν Aᵇ   7 ἢ EJ Al.¹ Asc.ᶜ : om. Aᵇ
9 ἔτι EJΓ Asc.¹ : ἐπεὶ Aᵇ Al.ᶜ   10 τι ex Al. ci. Bonitz : τὸ codd. Γ
15 τοῖς οὖσιν Aᵇ Al. : τοιούτοις EJΓ   16 δέ Christ : γάρ codd. Γ
τέλος πέρας EJΓ Al. : πέρας τέλος Aᵇ   20 ἐχόμενον] ἐχόμενόν ἐστιν
EJΓ   21 πρὶν Aᵇ Al.¹ : πρὶν ἢ EJΓ   ἐλθεῖν EJΓ Al.¹ Asc.ᶜ :
ἔλθῃ Aᵇ   25 ἀριθμήσει EJΓ et ut vid. Al. : ἀριθμεῖ Aᵇ   26 ὅλην
scripsi : ὕλην codd. Γ Al. Asc.   οὐ κινουμένῳ scripsi : ἐν κινουμένῳ
codd. Γ Asc. : κινουμένῳ Al. : κινουμένην Al.¹ γρ. Al.   οὐδενὶ E²J¹²
Aᵇ Al. : οὐδὲν E¹J¹ γρ. EΓ

εἶναι· εἰ δὲ μή, οὐκ ἄπειρόν γ' ἐστὶ τὸ ἀπείρῳ εἶναι.—ἀλλὰ
μὴν καὶ εἰ ἄπειρά γ' ἦσαν πλήθει τὰ εἴδη τῶν αἰτίων, οὐκ
ἂν ἦν οὐδ' οὕτω τὸ γιγνώσκειν· τότε γὰρ εἰδέναι οἰόμεθα
ὅταν τὰ αἴτια γνωρίσωμεν· τὸ δ' ἄπειρον κατὰ τὴν πρόσθε- 30
σιν οὐκ ἔστιν ἐν πεπερασμένῳ διεξελθεῖν.

3   Αἱ δ' ἀκροάσεις κατὰ τὰ ἔθη συμβαίνουσιν· ὡς γὰρ
εἰώθαμεν οὕτως ἀξιοῦμεν λέγεσθαι, καὶ τὰ παρὰ ταῦτα οὐχ 995ᵃ
ὅμοια φαίνεται ἀλλὰ διὰ τὴν ἀσυνήθειαν ἀγνωστότερα καὶ
ξενικώτερα· τὸ γὰρ σύνηθες γνώριμον. ἡλίκην δὲ ἰσχὺν
ἔχει τὸ σύνηθες οἱ νόμοι δηλοῦσιν, ἐν οἷς τὰ μυθώδη καὶ
παιδαριώδη μεῖζον ἰσχύει τοῦ γινώσκειν περὶ αὐτῶν διὰ τὸ 5
ἔθος. οἱ μὲν οὖν ἐὰν μὴ μαθηματικῶς λέγῃ τις οὐκ ἀποδέ-
χονται τῶν λεγόντων, οἱ δ' ἂν μὴ παραδειγματικῶς, οἱ
δὲ μάρτυρα ἀξιοῦσιν ἐπάγεσθαι ποιητήν. καὶ οἱ μὲν πάντα
ἀκριβῶς, τοὺς δὲ λυπεῖ τὸ ἀκριβὲς ἢ διὰ τὸ μὴ δύνασθαι
συνείρειν ἢ διὰ τὴν μικρολογίαν· ἔχει γάρ τι τὸ ἀκριβὲς 10
τοιοῦτον, ὥστε, καθάπερ ἐπὶ τῶν συμβολαίων, καὶ ἐπὶ τῶν
λόγων ἀνελεύθερον εἶναί τισι δοκεῖ. διὸ δεῖ πεπαιδεῦσθαι
πῶς ἕκαστα ἀποδεκτέον, ὡς ἄτοπον ἅμα ζητεῖν ἐπιστήμην
καὶ τρόπον ἐπιστήμης· ἔστι δ' οὐδὲ θάτερον ῥᾴδιον λαβεῖν. τὴν
δ' ἀκριβολογίαν τὴν μαθηματικὴν οὐκ ἐν ἅπασιν ἀπαιτη- 15
τέον, ἀλλ' ἐν τοῖς μὴ ἔχουσιν ὕλην. διόπερ οὐ φυσικὸς ὁ
τρόπος· ἅπασα γὰρ ἴσως ἡ φύσις ἔχει ὕλην. διὸ σκεπτέον
πρῶτον τί ἐστιν ἡ φύσις· οὕτω γὰρ καὶ περὶ τίνων ἡ φυσικὴ
δῆλον ἔσται [καὶ εἰ μιᾶς ἐπιστήμης ἢ πλειόνων τὰ αἴτια καὶ
τὰς ἀρχὰς θεωρῆσαί ἐστιν].   20

ᵇ 27 εἰ om. J¹ : ἢ Γ   γ'] δ' Aᵇ   τῶι J   28 πλήθη J   30 πρόθεσιν
Aᵇ   32 συμβαίνουσιν οὖσιν J   995ᵃ 1 λέγεσθαι codd. Γ Asc.ᶜ :
ἔτι τὸ λέγεσθαι Al.   3 γνώριμον Aᵇ Asc. : γνωριμώτερον EJΓ   4 τὰ
EJΓ Asc.ᶜ : περὶ τὰ Aᵇ   5 τοῦ EJAᵇ²Γ Al. Asc.ᶜ : τὸ Aᵇ¹   διὰ
EΓ Al.ᶜ Asc.ᶜ : om. AᵇJ   6 λέγει J   11 ὥστε] ὥσπερ J
12 τισι δοκεῖ EJΓ Al. : δοκεῖ τισί Aᵇ   πεπαιδεῦσθαι EJ¹   13 ἀποδεκτέον EJΓ Al.ᶜ : ἀποδεικτέον Aᵇ   14 οὐδὲ θάτερον Aᵇ Al. : οὐδέ-
τερον EJΓ Asc.   17 τρόπος codd. Γ γρ. Al. Asc.ᶜ : λόγος Al.
18 ἢ Aᵇ Al. : om. EJ Asc.   τίνων AᵇΓ Al. : τίνος EJ Asc.   19 καὶ
. . . 20 ἐστιν codd. Γ Asc. : om. Al. : a nonnullis ex 995ᵇ 5 falso
hoc loco adiecta esse refert Al.

Β

Ἀνάγκη πρὸς τὴν ἐπιζητουμένην ἐπιστήμην ἐπελθεῖν ἡμᾶς 1
25 πρῶτον περὶ ὧν ἀπορῆσαι δεῖ πρῶτον· ταῦτα δ' ἐστὶν ὅσα
τε περὶ αὐτῶν ἄλλως ὑπειλήφασί τινες, κἂν εἴ τι χωρὶς
τούτων τυγχάνει παρεωραμένον. ἔτι δὲ τοῖς εὐπορῆσαι βου-
λομένοις προὔργου τὸ διαπορῆσαι καλῶς· ἡ γὰρ ὕστερον
εὐπορία λύσις τῶν πρότερον ἀπορουμένων ἐστί, λύειν δ' οὐκ
30 ἔστιν ἀγνοοῦντας τὸν δεσμόν, ἀλλ' ἡ τῆς διανοίας ἀπορία
δηλοῖ τοῦτο περὶ τοῦ πράγματος· ᾗ γὰρ ἀπορεῖ, ταύτῃ παραπλήσιον πέπονθε τοῖς δεδεμένοις· ἀδύνατον γὰρ ἀμφοτέρως προελθεῖν εἰς τὸ πρόσθεν. διὸ δεῖ τὰς δυσχερείας τε-
θεωρηκέναι πάσας πρότερον, τούτων τε χάριν καὶ διὰ τὸ τοὺς
35 ζητοῦντας ἄνευ τοῦ διαπορῆσαι πρῶτον ὁμοίους εἶναι τοῖς ποῖ
δεῖ βαδίζειν ἀγνοοῦσι, καὶ πρὸς τούτοις οὐδ' εἴ ποτε τὸ ζητού-
995b μενον εὕρηκεν ἢ μὴ γιγνώσκειν· τὸ γὰρ τέλος τούτῳ μὲν οὐ
δῆλον τῷ δὲ προηπορηκότι δῆλον. ἔτι δὲ βέλτιον ἀνάγκη
ἔχειν πρὸς τὸ κρῖναι τὸν ὥσπερ ἀντιδίκων καὶ τῶν ἀμφι-
σβητούντων λόγων ἀκηκοότα πάντων.—ἔστι δ' ἀπορία πρώτη
5 μὲν περὶ ὧν ἐν τοῖς πεφροιμιασμένοις διηπορήσαμεν, πότερον μιᾶς ἢ πολλῶν ἐπιστημῶν θεωρῆσαι τὰς αἰτίας· καὶ πότερον τὰς τῆς οὐσίας ἀρχὰς τὰς πρώτας ἐστὶ τῆς ἐπιστήμης
ἰδεῖν μόνον ἢ καὶ περὶ τῶν ἀρχῶν ἐξ ὧν δεικνύουσι πάντες,
οἷον πότερον ἐνδέχεται ταὐτὸ καὶ ἐν ἅμα φάναι καὶ ἀπο-
10 φάναι ἢ οὔ, καὶ περὶ τῶν ἄλλων τῶν τοιούτων· εἴ τ' ἐστι
περὶ τὴν οὐσίαν, πότερον μία περὶ πάσας ἢ πλείονές εἰσι,
κἂν εἰ πλείονες πότερον ἅπασαι συγγενεῖς ἢ τὰς μὲν σοφίας τὰς δὲ ἄλλο τι λεκτέον αὐτῶν. καὶ τοῦτο δ' αὐτὸ τῶν
ἀναγκαίων ἐστὶ ζητῆσαι, πότερον τὰς αἰσθητὰς οὐσίας εἶναι

995b 4–6, cf. 996a 18 — b 26   6–10, cf. 996b 26 — 997a 15
10–13, cf. 997a 15–25   13–18, cf. 997a 34 — 998a 19

---

a 24 ἐπιζητουμένην EJ Al.: ζητουμένην Ab Asc.l   25 πρῶτον
pr. EJΓ Al.: om. Ab   27 τυγχάνει J et ut vid. Al.: τυγχάνῃ EAb.:
τυγχάνοι recc.   30 ἀγνοοῦντας Ab Al. Asc.l: ἀγνοοῦντα EJΓ Asc.
31 ἡ γὰρ ἀπορία JᵃAb   32 ἀμφοτέροις Richards   36 οὐδέποτε
JAbΓ Asc.   b 1 εὕρηκεν] εἰ εὕρηκεν Ab Asc.   2 δὲ alt. om. AbΓ
5 πεπροοιμιασμένοις E   πρότερον J   6 πολλῶν EJΓ Al.c: πολλῶν
ἐστὶν Ab Asc.c   8 πάντες Ab Asc.c Syr.l: ἅπαντες EJ   9 καὶ
ἀποφάναι om. E   10 εἴ τ' AbΓ: εἴτ' vulgo   12 καὶ E

μόνον φατέον ἢ καὶ παρὰ ταύτας ἄλλας, καὶ πότερον μο- 15
ναχῶς ἢ πλείονα γένη τῶν οὐσιῶν, οἷον οἱ ποιοῦντες τά τε
εἴδη καὶ τὰ μαθηματικὰ μεταξὺ τούτων τε καὶ τῶν αἰσθητῶν. περί τε τούτων οὖν, καθάπερ φαμέν, ἐπισκεπτέον, καὶ
πότερον περὶ τὰς οὐσίας ἢ θεωρία μόνον ἐστὶν ἢ καὶ περὶ
τὰ συμβεβηκότα καθ' αὑτὰ ταῖς οὐσίαις, πρὸς δὲ τούτοις 20
περὶ ταὐτοῦ καὶ ἑτέρου καὶ ὁμοίου καὶ ἀνομοίου καὶ ἐναντιό-
τητος, καὶ περὶ προτέρου καὶ ὑστέρου καὶ τῶν ἄλλων
ἁπάντων τῶν τοιούτων περὶ ὅσων οἱ διαλεκτικοὶ πειρῶνται
σκοπεῖν ἐκ τῶν ἐνδόξων μόνων ποιούμενοι τὴν σκέψιν, τίνος
ἐστὶ θεωρῆσαι περὶ πάντων· ἔτι δὲ τούτοις αὐτοῖς ὅσα καθ' 25
αὑτὰ συμβέβηκεν, καὶ μὴ μόνον τί ἐστι τούτων ἕκαστον
ἀλλὰ καὶ ἆρα ἓν ἑνὶ ἐναντίον· καὶ πότερον αἱ ἀρχαὶ καὶ
τὰ στοιχεῖα τὰ γένη ἐστὶν ἢ εἰς ἃ διαιρεῖται ἐνυπάρχοντα
ἕκαστον· καὶ εἰ τὰ γένη, πότερον ὅσα ἐπὶ τοῖς ἀτόμοις λέγεται τελευταῖα ἢ τὰ πρῶτα, οἷον πότερον ζῷον ἢ ἄνθρωπος 30
ἀρχή τε καὶ μᾶλλον ἔστι παρὰ τὸ καθ' ἕκαστον. μάλιστα
δὲ ζητητέον καὶ πραγματευτέον πότερον ἔστι τι παρὰ τὴν
ὕλην αἴτιον καθ' αὑτὸ ἢ οὔ, καὶ τοῦτο χωριστὸν ἢ οὔ, καὶ πότερον ἓν ἢ πλείω τὸν ἀριθμόν, καὶ πότερον ἔστι τι παρὰ τὸ
σύνολον (λέγω δὲ τὸ σύνολον, ὅταν κατηγορηθῇ τι τῆς ὕλης) 35
ἢ οὐθέν, ἢ τῶν μὲν τῶν δ' οὔ, καὶ ποῖα τοιαῦτα τῶν ὄντων.
ἔτι αἱ ἀρχαὶ πότερον ἀριθμῷ ἢ εἴδει ὡρισμέναι, καὶ αἱ ἐν 996ᵃ
τοῖς λόγοις καὶ αἱ ἐν τῷ ὑποκειμένῳ; καὶ πότερον τῶν
φθαρτῶν καὶ ἀφθάρτων αἱ αὐταὶ ἢ ἕτεραι, καὶ πότερον
ἄφθαρτοι πᾶσαι ἢ τῶν φθαρτῶν φθαρταί; ἔτι δὲ τὸ πάντων χαλεπώτατον καὶ πλείστην ἀπορίαν ἔχον, πότερον τὸ 5
ἓν καὶ τὸ ὄν, καθάπερ οἱ Πυθαγόρειοι καὶ Πλάτων ἔλεγεν,

995ᵇ 18-27, cf. 997ᵃ 25-34   27-29, cf. 998ᵃ 20 — ᵇ 14   29-31,
cf. 998ᵇ 14 — 999ᵘ 23   31-36, cf. 999ᵃ 24 — ᵇ 24   996ᵃ 1, 2,
cf. 999ᵇ 24 — 1000ᵃ 4   2-4, cf. 1000ᵃ 5 — 1001ᵃ 3   4-9, cf.
1001ᵃ 4 — ᵇ 25

ᵇ 16 πλείονα EJΓ Asc.ᶜ Syr.ᶜ : πλεοναχῶς τὰ Aᵇ   21 καὶ ult.]
καὶ ταυτότητος καὶ recc.   24 μόνων Aᵇ Asc.ᶜ : μόνον EJΓ   27 ἄρα
JAᵇ : εἰ ἄρα recc.   29 εἰ om. EJ   31 μάλιστα EJΓ Al.¹ Syr.¹ :
μᾶλλον Aᵇ Asc.¹   33 καθ' αὑτὸ ἢ οὔ EJΓ Al. Asc. : om. Aᵇ   καὶ
... οὔ AᵇΓ Al. Asc. : om. EJ   τοῦτο] εἰ τοῦτο Jaeger   36 ποῖα
ταῦτα recc. : ὁπόσα ταῦτα ut vid. Al.   996ᵃ 1 αἱ alt. om. Aᵇ Syr.ᶜ :
εἰ Asc.¹   2 αἱ om. Aᵇ Asc.¹ Syr.ᶜ   6 ἔλεγον E²JΓ Asc.

οὐχ ἕτερόν τί ἐστιν ἀλλ' οὐσία τῶν ὄντων· ἢ οὔ, ἀλλ' ἕτερόν τι
τὸ ὑποκείμενον, ὥσπερ Ἐμπεδοκλῆς φησὶ φιλίαν ἄλλος
δέ τις πῦρ ὁ δὲ ὕδωρ ἢ ἀέρα· καὶ πότερον αἱ ἀρχαὶ
10 καθόλου εἰσὶν ἢ ὡς τὰ καθ' ἕκαστα τῶν πραγμάτων, καὶ
δυνάμει ἢ ἐνεργείᾳ· ἔτι πότερον ἄλλως ἢ κατὰ κίνησιν·
καὶ γὰρ ταῦτα ἀπορίαν ἂν παράσχοι πολλήν. πρὸς δὲ
τούτοις πότερον οἱ ἀριθμοὶ καὶ τὰ μήκη καὶ τὰ σχήματα
καὶ αἱ στιγμαὶ οὐσίαι τινές εἰσιν ἢ οὔ, κἂν εἰ οὐσίαι πότερον
15 κεχωρισμέναι τῶν αἰσθητῶν ἢ ἐνυπάρχουσαι ἐν τούτοις; περὶ
γὰρ τούτων ἁπάντων οὐ μόνον χαλεπὸν τὸ εὐπορῆσαι τῆς
ἀληθείας ἀλλ' οὐδὲ τὸ διαπορῆσαι τῷ λόγῳ ῥᾴδιον καλῶς.

Πρῶτον μὲν οὖν περὶ ὧν πρῶτον εἴπομεν, πότερον μιᾶς **2**
ἢ πλειόνων ἐστὶν ἐπιστημῶν θεωρῆσαι πάντα τὰ γένη τῶν
20 αἰτίων. μιᾶς μὲν γὰρ ἐπιστήμης πῶς ἂν εἴη μὴ ἐναντίας
οὔσας τὰς ἀρχὰς γνωρίζειν; ἔτι δὲ πολλοῖς τῶν ὄντων οὐχ
ὑπάρχουσι πᾶσαι· τίνα γὰρ τρόπον οἷόν τε κινήσεως ἀρχὴν
εἶναι τοῖς ἀκινήτοις ἢ τὴν τἀγαθοῦ φύσιν, εἴπερ ἅπαν ὃ ἂν
ᾖ ἀγαθὸν καθ' αὑτὸ καὶ διὰ τὴν αὑτοῦ φύσιν τέλος ἐστὶν
25 καὶ οὕτως αἴτιον ὅτι ἐκείνου ἕνεκα καὶ γίγνεται καὶ ἔστι
τἆλλα, τὸ δὲ τέλος καὶ τὸ οὗ ἕνεκα πράξεώς τινός ἐστι τέλος,
αἱ δὲ πράξεις πᾶσαι μετὰ κινήσεως; ὥστ' ἐν τοῖς ἀκινήτοις
οὐκ ἂν ἐνδέχοιτο ταύτην εἶναι τὴν ἀρχὴν οὐδ' εἶναί τι αὐτο-
αγαθόν. διὸ καὶ ἐν τοῖς μαθήμασιν οὐθὲν δείκνυται διὰ
30 ταύτης τῆς αἰτίας, οὐδ' ἔστιν ἀπόδειξις οὐδεμία διότι βέλτιον
ἢ χεῖρον, ἀλλ' οὐδὲ τὸ παράπαν μέμνηται οὐθεὶς οὐθενὸς τῶν
τοιούτων, ὥστε διὰ ταῦτα τῶν σοφιστῶν τινὲς οἷον Ἀρίστιππος
προεπηλάκιζεν αὐτάς· ἐν μὲν γὰρ ταῖς ἄλλαις τέχναις,
καὶ ταῖς βαναύσοις, οἷον ἐν τεκτονικῇ καὶ σκυτικῇ, διότι
35 βέλτιον ἢ χεῖρον λέγεσθαι πάντα, τὰς δὲ μαθηματικὰς
996^b οὐθένα ποιεῖσθαι λόγον περὶ ἀγαθῶν καὶ κακῶν.—ἀλλὰ μὴν

996ᵃ 9, 10, cf. 1003ᵃ 5–17   10, 11, cf. 1002ᵇ 32 — 1003ᵃ 5
12–15, cf. 1001ᵇ 26 — 1002ᵇ 11   18 — ᵇ 26, cf. 995ᵇ 4–6, Κ. 1059ᵃ
20–23 (996ᵃ 21 — ᵇ 1, cf. 1059ᵃ 34–38)

ᵃ 9 ἢ EJΓ Syr.¹: ὁ δὲ Aᵇ   11 δυνάμει ἢ ἐνεργείᾳ EJΓ Al. : om.
Aᵇ   14 εἰ οὐσία Aᵇ   15 ἐνυπάρχουσαι om. ΕΓ Syr.¹ et fort. Al.
22 πᾶσι πᾶσαι ΕΓ   23 εἶναι ἐν τοῖς fort. Al. et Asc., Jaeger
τὴν ἀγαθοῦ Aᵇ   24 αὑτοῦ Aᵇ Asc.ᶜ   25 ἔστι] ἔστι καὶ Aᵇ
30 διὸ J   33 αὐτά fort. Asc., Goebel   34 βαναύσοις EJΓ
Asc. : βαναύσοις αὐταῖς Aᵇ   ᵇ 1 κακῶν EJΓ Al. : καλῶν Aᵇ

εἴ γε πλείους ἐπιστῆμαι ·τῶν αἰτίων εἰσὶ καὶ ἑτέρα ἑτέρας
ἀρχῆς, τίνα τούτων φατέον εἶναι τὴν ζητουμένην, ἢ τίνα μάλιστα τοῦ πράγματος τοῦ ζητουμένου ἐπιστήμονα τῶν ἐχόντων
αὐτάς; ἐνδέχεται γὰρ τῷ αὐτῷ πάντας τοὺς τρόπους τοὺς τῶν 5
αἰτίων ὑπάρχειν, οἷον οἰκίας ὅθεν μὲν ἡ κίνησις ἢ τέχνη
καὶ ὁ οἰκοδόμος, οὗ δ' ἕνεκα τὸ ἔργον, ὕλη δὲ γῆ καὶ λίθοι,
τὸ δ' εἶδος ὁ λόγος. ἐκ μὲν οὖν τῶν πάλαι διωρισμένων
τίνα χρὴ καλεῖν τῶν ἐπιστημῶν σοφίαν ἔχει λόγον ἑκάστην
προσαγορεύειν· ἢ μὲν γὰρ ἀρχικωτάτη καὶ ἡγεμονικωτάτη 10
καὶ ᾗ ὥσπερ δούλας οὐδ' ἀντειπεῖν τὰς ἄλλας ἐπιστήμας
δίκαιον, ἡ τοῦ τέλους καὶ τἀγαθοῦ τοιαύτη (τούτου γὰρ ἕνεκα
τἆλλα), ᾗ δὲ τῶν πρώτων αἰτίων καὶ τοῦ μάλιστα ἐπιστητοῦ
διωρίσθη εἶναι, ἡ τῆς οὐσίας ἂν εἴη τοιαύτη· πολλαχῶς γὰρ
ἐπισταμένων τὸ αὐτὸ μᾶλλον μὲν εἰδέναι φαμὲν τὸν τῷ 15
εἶναι γνωρίζοντα τί τὸ πρᾶγμα ἢ τῷ μὴ εἶναι, αὐτῶν δὲ
τούτων ἕτερον ἑτέρου μᾶλλον, καὶ μάλιστα τὸν τί ἐστιν ἀλλ'
οὐ τὸν πόσον ἢ ποῖον ἢ τί ποιεῖν ἢ πάσχειν πέφυκεν. ἔτι δὲ
καὶ ἐν τοῖς ἄλλοις τὸ εἰδέναι ἕκαστον καὶ ὧν ἀποδείξεις
εἰσί, τότ' οἰόμεθα ὑπάρχειν ὅταν εἰδῶμεν τί ἐστιν (οἷον τί 20
ἐστι τὸ τετραγωνίζειν, ὅτι μέσης εὕρεσις· ὁμοίως δὲ καὶ ἐπὶ
τῶν ἄλλων), περὶ δὲ τὰς γενέσεις καὶ τὰς πράξεις καὶ περὶ
πᾶσαν μεταβολὴν ὅταν εἰδῶμεν τὴν ἀρχὴν τῆς κινήσεως·
τοῦτο δ' ἕτερον καὶ ἀντικείμενον τῷ τέλει, ὥστ' ἄλλης ἂν
δόξειεν ἐπιστήμης εἶναι τὸ θεωρῆσαι τῶν αἰτίων τούτων ἕκα- 25
στον.――ἀλλὰ μὴν καὶ περὶ τῶν ἀποδεικτικῶν ἀρχῶν, πότερον
μιᾶς ἐστὶν ἐπιστήμης ἢ πλειόνων, ἀμφισβητήσιμόν ἐστιν (λέγω
δὲ ἀποδεικτικὰς τὰς κοινὰς δόξας ἐξ ὧν ἅπαντες δεικνύουσιν) οἷον ὅτι πᾶν ἀναγκαῖον ἢ φάναι ἢ ἀποφάναι, καὶ
ἀδύνατον ἅμα εἶναι καὶ μὴ εἶναι, καὶ ὅσαι ἄλλαι τοιαῦ- 30
ται προτάσεις, πότερον μία τούτων ἐπιστήμη καὶ τῆς οὐσίας ἢ
ἑτέρα, κἂν εἰ μὴ μία, ποτέραν χρὴ προσαγορεύειν τὴν ζη-

996ᵇ 26 — 997ᵃ 15, cf. 995ᵇ 6-10, 1059ᵃ 23-26

ᵇ 2 ἑτέρα ΕΙΓ Al. Asc. : ἕτεραι Aᵇ   3 τούτων Ι   4 τοῦ
ζητουμένου ΕΙΓ Al.ᶜ et ut vid. Al. : om. Aᵇ   5 τοὺς alt. om. recc.
6 μὲν om. Ι   9 ἐπιστημῶν] ἐπὶ Aᵇ   ἔχει ΕΙΓ Al. Asc.ᶜ : οὐδαμῶς
ἔχει Aᵇ Al.¹   10 ἡγεμονικωτάτη ΕΙΓ Asc.ᶜ: ἢ γενικωτάτη Aᵇ
12 καὶ ἀγαθοῦ Aᵇ   20 οἷον τί ἐστι om. Ι   23 πᾶσαν Aᵇ Asc.ᶜ
Syr.¹: ἅπασαν ΕΙ   24 ὥστ' οὐκ ἄλλης γρ. Ε, ci. Al.   · 32 καὶ
ἂν εἴη μία Aᵇ   προτέραν Ι

τουμένην νῦν. μιᾶς μὲν οὖν οὐκ εὔλογον εἶναι· τί γὰρ μᾶλλον γεωμετρίας ἢ ὁποιασοῦν περὶ τούτων ἐστὶν ἴδιον τὸ ἐπαΐειν;
35 εἴπερ οὖν ὁμοίως μὲν ὁποιασοῦν ἐστίν, ἁπασῶν δὲ μὴ ἐνδέχε-
997ᵃ ται, ὥσπερ οὐδὲ τῶν ἄλλων οὕτως οὐδὲ τῆς γνωριζούσης τὰς
οὐσίας ἴδιόν ἐστι τὸ γιγνώσκειν περὶ αὐτῶν. ἅμα δὲ καὶ τίνα
τρόπον ἔσται αὐτῶν ἐπιστήμη; τί μὲν γὰρ ἕκαστον τούτων
τυγχάνει ὂν καὶ νῦν γνωρίζομεν (χρῶνται γοῦν ὡς γιγνω-
5 σκομένοις αὐτοῖς καὶ ἄλλαι τέχναι)· εἰ δὲ ἀποδεικτικὴ περὶ
αὐτῶν ἐστι, δεήσει τι γένος εἶναι ὑποκείμενον καὶ τὰ μὲν
πάθη τὰ δ' ἀξιώματ' αὐτῶν (περὶ πάντων γὰρ *ἀδύνατον
ἀπόδειξιν εἶναι), ἀνάγκη γὰρ ἔκ τινων εἶναι καὶ περί τι καὶ
τινῶν τὴν ἀπόδειξιν· ὥστε συμβαίνει πάντων εἶναι γένος ἕν
10 τι τῶν δεικνυμένων, πᾶσαι γὰρ αἱ ἀποδεικτικαὶ χρῶνται
τοῖς ἀξιώμασιν.——ἀλλὰ μὴν εἰ ἑτέρα ἡ τῆς οὐσίας καὶ ἡ περὶ
τούτων, ποτέρα κυριωτέρα καὶ προτέρα πέφυκεν αὐτῶν; καθόλου γὰρ μάλιστα καὶ πάντων ἀρχαὶ τὰ ἀξιώματά ἐστιν,
εἴ τ' ἐστὶ μὴ τοῦ φιλοσόφου, τίνος ἔσται περὶ αὐτῶν ἄλλου τὸ
15 θεωρῆσαι τὸ ἀληθὲς καὶ ψεῦδος;——ὅλως τε τῶν οὐσιῶν πότερον μία πασῶν ἐστὶν ἢ πλείους ἐπιστῆμαι; εἰ μὲν οὖν μὴ
μία, ποίας οὐσίας θετέον τὴν ἐπιστήμην ταύτην; τὸ δὲ μίαν
πασῶν οὐκ εὔλογον· καὶ γὰρ ἂν ἀποδεικτικὴ μία περὶ πάντων εἴη τῶν συμβεβηκότων, εἴπερ πᾶσα ἀποδεικτικὴ περὶ
20 τι ὑποκείμενον θεωρεῖ τὰ καθ' αὑτὰ συμβεβηκότα ἐκ τῶν
κοινῶν δοξῶν. περὶ οὖν τὸ αὐτὸ γένος τὰ συμβεβηκότα καθ'
αὑτὰ τῆς αὐτῆς ἐστὶ θεωρῆσαι ἐκ τῶν αὐτῶν δοξῶν. περὶ
τε γὰρ ὃ μιᾶς καὶ ἐξ ὧν μιᾶς, εἴτε τῆς αὐτῆς εἴτε ἄλλης, ὥστε καὶ τὰ συμβεβηκότα, εἴθ' αὗται θεωροῦσιν εἴτ'
25 ἐκ τούτων μία.——ἔτι δὲ πότερον περὶ τὰς οὐσίας μόνον
ἡ θεωρία ἐστὶν ἢ καὶ περὶ τὰ συμβεβηκότα ταύταις; λέγω

997ᵃ 15-25, cf. 995ᵇ 10-13, 1059ᵃ 26-29   25-34, cf. 995ᵇ 18-27,
1059ᵃ 29-34

ᵇ 33 γὰρ] γὰρ οὐ Schwegler   34 περὶ] τῶν περὶ Aᵇ   997ᵃ 4 οὖν
ὡς Γ   5 καὶ] καὶ αἱ Richards, legit fort. Al.   9 ἕν EJΓ Al. :
om. Aᵇ   11 εἴ] ἢ J   14 εἴ τ' Γ: εἴτ' vulgo   15 καὶ] καὶ τὸ Aᵇ
18 εὔλογον EJΓ Asc. Syr. : ἄλογον Aᵇ   19 εἴη] ἂν εἴη Aᵇ   22 ἐστὶ
θεωρῆσαι EJΓ Al. : θεωρῆσαί ἐστι Aᵇ   23 ὃ Aᵇ Al. Asc. : τὸ ὅτι
EJΓ Syr.¹   24 εἴθ' αὗται AᵇΓ Al. Syr.ᶜ : εἴτ' αὗται EJ : εἴθ' αἱ
αὗται Asc. γρ. Al.   θεωροῦσιν Aᵇ Al. : θεωρήσουσιν EJΓ Syr. Asc.ᶜ
ἤ τ' J   25-26 ἡ θεωρία μόνον EJ Al.¹ Asc.¹ Syr.¹

δ' οἷον, εἰ τὸ στερεὸν οὐσία τίς ἐστι καὶ γραμμαὶ καὶ ἐπίπεδα, πότερον τῆς αὐτῆς ταῦτα γνωρίζειν ἐστὶν ἐπιστήμης καὶ
τὰ συμβεβηκότα περὶ ἕκαστον γένος περὶ ὧν αἱ μαθημα-
τικαὶ δεικνύουσιν, ἢ ἄλλης. εἰ μὲν γὰρ τῆς αὐτῆς, ἀπο- 30
δεικτική τις ἂν εἴη καὶ ἡ τῆς οὐσίας, οὐ δοκεῖ δὲ τοῦ τί
ἐστιν ἀπόδειξις εἶναι· εἰ δ' ἑτέρας, τίς ἔσται ἡ θεωροῦσα περὶ
τὴν οὐσίαν τὰ συμβεβηκότα; τοῦτο γὰρ ἀποδοῦναι παγχά-
λεπον.——ἔτι δὲ πότερον τὰς αἰσθητὰς οὐσίας μόνας εἶναι
φατέον ἢ καὶ παρὰ ταύτας ἄλλας, καὶ πότερον μοναχῶς ἢ 35
πλείω γένη τετύχηκεν ὄντα τῶν οὐσιῶν, οἷον οἱ λέγοντες τά 997ᵇ
τε εἴδη καὶ τὰ μεταξύ, περὶ ἃ τὰς μαθηματικὰς εἶναί φασιν ἐπιστήμας; ὡς μὲν οὖν λέγομεν τὰ εἴδη αἴτιά τε καὶ
οὐσίας εἶναι καθ' ἑαυτὰς εἴρηται ἐν τοῖς πρώτοις λόγοις περὶ
αὐτῶν· πολλαχῇ δὲ ἐχόντων δυσκολίαν, οὐθενὸς ἧττον ἄτο- 5
πον τὸ φάναι μὲν εἶναί τινας φύσεις παρὰ τὰς ἐν τῷ
οὐρανῷ, ταύτας δὲ τὰς αὐτὰς φάναι τοῖς αἰσθητοῖς πλὴν ὅτι
τὰ μὲν ἀίδια τὰ δὲ φθαρτά. αὐτὸ γὰρ ἄνθρωπόν φασιν
εἶναι καὶ ἵππον καὶ ὑγίειαν, ἄλλο δ' οὐδέν, παραπλήσιον
ποιοῦντες τοῖς θεοὺς μὲν εἶναι φάσκουσιν ἀνθρωποειδεῖς δέ· 10
οὔτε γὰρ ἐκεῖνοι οὐδὲν ἄλλο ἐποίουν ἢ ἀνθρώπους ἀιδίους, οὔθ'
οὗτοι τὰ εἴδη ἀλλ' ἢ αἰσθητὰ ἀίδια. ἔτι δὲ εἴ τις παρὰ τὰ
εἴδη καὶ τὰ αἰσθητὰ τὰ μεταξὺ θήσεται, πολλὰς ἀπορίας
ἕξει· δῆλον γὰρ ὡς ὁμοίως γραμμαί τε παρά τ' αὐτὰς καὶ
τὰς αἰσθητὰς ἔσονται καὶ ἕκαστον τῶν ἄλλων γενῶν· ὥστ' 15
ἐπείπερ ἡ ἀστρολογία μία τούτων ἐστίν, ἔσται τις καὶ οὐρανὸς
παρὰ τὸν αἰσθητὸν οὐρανὸν καὶ ἥλιός τε καὶ σελήνη καὶ
τἆλλα ὁμοίως τὰ κατὰ τὸν οὐρανόν. καίτοι πῶς δεῖ πιστεῦ-
σαι τούτοις; οὐδὲ γὰρ ἀκίνητον εὔλογον εἶναι, κινούμενον δὲ
καὶ παντελῶς ἀδύνατον· ὁμοίως δὲ καὶ περὶ ὧν ἡ ὀπτικὴ 20
πραγματεύεται καὶ ἡ ἐν τοῖς μαθήμασιν ἁρμονική· καὶ
γὰρ ταῦτα ἀδύνατον εἶναι παρὰ τὰ αἰσθητὰ διὰ τὰς αὐτὰς

997ᵃ 34 — 998ᵃ 19, cf. 995ᵇ 13–18, 1059ᵃ 38 — ᵇ 21

ᵃ 28 ἐστὶν AᵇΓ Asc.ᵒ: om. EJ   ᵇ 2 ἃ om. Aᵇ   5 πολλαχῇ
... δυσκολίαν EJΓ Asc.ᶜ Syr.¹: πολλὰς ... δυσκολίας Aᵇ   7 ὅτι]
τι Aᵇ   10 θεοὺς EJ Al.: τοὺς θεοὺς Aᵇ   δέ EJ Syr.¹: δὲ εἶναι AᵇΓ
12 ἀλλ' Christ: ἀλλ' codd. Γ: ἄλλο Al., ci. Bonitz   14 τ' αὐτὰς
ut vid. Al.: ταύτας Aᵇ: αὐτὰς EJΓ   17 τε om. J

αἰτίας· εἰ γὰρ ἔστιν αἰσθητὰ μεταξὺ καὶ αἰσθήσεις, δῆλον
ὅτι καὶ ζῷα ἔσονται μεταξὺ αὐτῶν τε καὶ τῶν φθαρτῶν.
25 ἀπορήσειε δ' ἄν τις καὶ περὶ ποῖα τῶν ὄντων δεῖ ζητεῖν
ταύτας τὰς ἐπιστήμας. εἰ γὰρ τούτῳ διοίσει τῆς γεωδαισίας
ἡ γεωμετρία μόνον, ὅτι ἡ μὲν τούτων ἐστὶν ὧν αἰσθανόμεθα
ἡ δ' οὐκ αἰσθητῶν, δῆλον ὅτι καὶ παρ' ἰατρικὴν ἔσται τις ἐπιστήμη καὶ παρ' ἑκάστην τῶν ἄλλων μεταξὺ αὐτῆς τε ἰατρι-
30 κῆς καὶ τῆσδε τῆς ἰατρικῆς· καίτοι πῶς τοῦτο δυνατόν; καὶ
γὰρ ἂν ὑγιείν' ἄττα εἴη παρὰ τὰ αἰσθητὰ καὶ αὐτὸ τὸ
ὑγιεινόν. ἅμα δὲ οὐδὲ τοῦτο ἀληθές, ὡς ἡ γεωδαισία τῶν
αἰσθητῶν ἐστὶ μεγεθῶν καὶ φθαρτῶν· ἐφθείρετο γὰρ ἂν
φθειρομένων.—ἀλλὰ μὴν οὐδὲ τῶν αἰσθητῶν ἂν εἴη μεγεθῶν
35 οὐδὲ περὶ τὸν οὐρανὸν ἡ ἀστρολογία τόνδε. οὔτε γὰρ αἱ αἰσθη-
998ᵃ ταὶ γραμμαὶ τοιαῦταί εἰσιν οἵας λέγει ὁ γεωμέτρης (οὐθὲν
γὰρ εὐθὺ τῶν αἰσθητῶν οὕτως οὐδὲ στρογγύλον· ἅπτεται γὰρ
τοῦ κανόνος οὐ κατὰ στιγμὴν ὁ κύκλος ἀλλ' ὥσπερ Πρωταγόρας ἔλεγεν ἐλέγχων τοὺς γεωμέτρας), οὔθ' αἱ κινήσεις καὶ
5 ἕλικες τοῦ οὐρανοῦ ὅμοιαι περὶ ὧν ἡ ἀστρολογία ποιεῖται τοὺς
λόγους, οὔτε τὰ σημεῖα τοῖς ἄστροις τὴν αὐτὴν ἔχει φύσιν.
εἰσὶ δέ τινες οἵ φασιν εἶναι μὲν τὰ μεταξὺ ταῦτα λεγόμενα
τῶν τε εἰδῶν καὶ τῶν αἰσθητῶν, οὐ μὴν χωρίς γε τῶν αἰσθητῶν ἀλλ' ἐν τούτοις· οἷς τὰ συμβαίνοντα ἀδύνατα πάντα
10 μὲν πλείονος λόγου διελθεῖν, ἱκανὸν δὲ καὶ τὰ τοιαῦτα θεωρῆσαι. οὔτε γὰρ ἐπὶ τούτων εὔλογον ἔχειν οὕτω μόνον, ἀλλὰ
δῆλον ὅτι καὶ τὰ εἴδη ἐνδέχοιτ' ἂν ἐν τοῖς αἰσθητοῖς εἶναι
(τοῦ γὰρ αὐτοῦ λόγου ἀμφότερα ταῦτά ἐστιν), ἔτι δὲ δύο στε-
ρεὰ ἐν τῷ αὐτῷ ἀναγκαῖον εἶναι τόπῳ, καὶ μὴ εἶναι ἀκί-
15 νητα ἐν κινουμένοις γε ὄντα τοῖς αἰσθητοῖς. ὅλως δὲ τίνος
ἕνεκ' ἄν τις θείη εἶναι μὲν αὐτά, εἶναι δ' ἐν τοῖς αἰσθητοῖς;
ταὐτὰ γὰρ συμβήσεται ἄτοπα τοῖς προειρημένοις· ἔσται γὰρ
οὐρανός τις παρὰ τὸν οὐρανόν, πλήν γ' οὐ χωρὶς ἀλλ' ἐν τῷ
αὐτῷ τόπῳ· ὅπερ ἐστὶν ἀδυνατώτερον.

ᵇ 23 μεταξύ, καὶ αἰσθήσεις, εἰ δ' αἰσθήσεις, δῆλον ut vid. Al.   25 περὶ
AᵇΓ Al.¹ Syr.¹: παρὰ EJ Asc.¹   26 γεωδεσίας E¹JAᵇ   27 ὧν]
ἃ EJ Syr.¹   31 ὑγιεινά τα Aᵇ   32 γεωδεσία E¹JAᵇ   34 τῶν
EJ Asc.ᶜ: om. Aᵇ   35 περὶ τὸν οὐρανὸν ἢ EJ Al. Asc.: ἢ περὶ
τὸν οὐρανὸν Aᵇ Syr.¹   αἱ EJ Asc.ᶜ: om. Aᵇ   998ᵃ 2 οὔτε J
4 καὶ] καὶ αἱ E Syr.¹   5 ὅμοιαι om. Aᵇ: ὁποῖαι fort. Al.: οἷαι Jaeger
ἢ om. Aᵇ   9 οἱ E¹J²   13 δὲ] τε E   19 ὅ Aᵇ

3 Περί τε τούτων οὖν ἀπορία πολλὴ πῶς δεῖ θέμενον τυ- 20
χεῖν τῆς ἀληθείας, καὶ περὶ τῶν ἀρχῶν πότερον δεῖ τὰ γένη
στοιχεῖα καὶ ἀρχὰς ὑπολαμβάνειν ἢ μᾶλλον ἐξ ὧν ἐνυπαρχόντων ἐστὶν ἕκαστον πρῶτων, οἷον φωνῆς στοιχεῖα καὶ
ἀρχαὶ δοκοῦσιν εἶναι ταῦτ' ἐξ ὧν σύγκεινται αἱ φωναὶ
πρῶτων, ἀλλ' οὐ τὸ κοινὸν ἡ φωνή· καὶ τῶν διαγραμμάτων 25
ταῦτα στοιχεῖα λέγομεν ὧν αἱ ἀποδείξεις ἐνυπάρχουσιν
ἐν ταῖς τῶν ἄλλων ἀποδείξεσιν ἢ πάντων ἢ τῶν πλείστων,
ἔτι δὲ τῶν σωμάτων καὶ οἱ πλείω λέγοντες εἶναι στοιχεῖα
καὶ οἱ ἕν, ἐξ ὧν σύγκειται καὶ ἐξ ὧν συνέστηκεν ἀρχὰς λέγουσιν εἶναι, οἷον Ἐμπεδοκλῆς πῦρ καὶ ὕδωρ καὶ τὰ μετὰ 30
τούτων στοιχεῖά φησιν εἶναι ἐξ ὧν ἐστὶ τὰ ὄντα ἐνυπαρχόντων, ἀλλ' οὐχ ὡς γένη λέγει ταῦτα τῶν ὄντων. πρὸς δὲ
τούτοις καὶ τῶν ἄλλων εἴ τις ἐθέλει τὴν φύσιν ἀθρεῖν, οἷον 998ᵇ
κλίνην ἐξ ὧν μορίων συνέστηκε καὶ πῶς συγκειμένων, τότε
γνωρίζει τὴν φύσιν αὐτῆς.—ἐκ μὲν οὖν τούτων τῶν λόγων οὐκ
ἂν εἴησαν αἱ ἀρχαὶ τὰ γένη τῶν ὄντων· εἰ δ' ἕκαστον μὲν
γνωρίζομεν διὰ τῶν ὁρισμῶν, ἀρχαὶ δὲ τὰ γένη τῶν ὁρισμῶν 5
εἰσίν, ἀνάγκη καὶ τῶν ὁριστῶν ἀρχὰς εἶναι τὰ γένη. κἂν
εἰ ἔστι τὴν τῶν ὄντων λαβεῖν ἐπιστήμην τὸ τῶν εἰδῶν λαβεῖν
καθ' ἃ λέγονται τὰ ὄντα, τῶν γε εἰδῶν ἀρχαὶ τὰ γένη εἰσίν.
φαίνονται δέ τινες καὶ τῶν λεγόντων στοιχεῖα τῶν ὄντων τὸ
ἓν ἢ τὸ ὂν ἢ τὸ μέγα καὶ μικρὸν ὡς γένεσιν αὐτοῖς χρῆ- 10
σθαι.—ἀλλὰ μὴν οὐδὲ ἀμφοτέρως γε οἷόν τε λέγειν τὰς
ἀρχάς. ὁ μὲν γὰρ λόγος τῆς οὐσίας εἷς· ἕτερος δ' ἔσται ὁ
διὰ τῶν γενῶν ὁρισμὸς καὶ ὁ λέγων ἐξ ὧν ἔστιν ἐνυπαρχόν-

998ᵃ 20 — ᵇ 14, ᵇ 14 — 999ᵃ 23, cf. 995ᵇ 27-29, 29-31, 1059ᵇ 21 —
1060ᵃ 1

ᵃ 20 οὖν om. Aᵇ   21 πότερον AᵇΓ Al. Asc.: πότερα EJ Al.[1]
22 ἐνυπαρχόντων EJΓ Asc.ᶜ: ὑπαρχόντων Aᵇ   23 πρῶτων E²Γ Al.:
πρῶτον E¹JAᵇ Al.[1] Asc.ᶜ Syr.[1]   καὶ] ἃ καὶ J   24 φωναὶ Aᵇ et ut
vid. Al.: φωναὶ πᾶσαι EJΓ Asc.ᶜ   25 πρῶτον Aᵇ   26 ἐνυπάρχοντα Aᵇ   27 τῶν ἄλλων EJΓ Asc.ᶜ: τούτων Aᵇ   29 σύγκειται
Asc.ᶜ: σύγκεινται EJAᵇ   30 μετὰ E (sed erasum) JΓ Asc.ᶜ Syr.[1]:
μεταξὺ Aᵇ   ᵇ 1 θέλει Aᵇ   2 κλίνης εἰδῶς ἐξ Susemihl
συνέστηκε Aᵇ Al.: ἐστὶ EJΓ Syr.[1]   τότε] καὶ τότε Aᵇ: ἀθρῶν, τότε
ci. Schwegler, ἀθρεῖ καὶ τότε Christ   4 εἰ Aᵇ Asc. Syr.[1]: ἢ EJΓ
Al.[1]   6 κἂν EJ Asc.[1]: καὶ Aᵇ Syr.[1]   8 καθὸ λέγονται Aᵇ   ἀρχαὶ
τὰ γένη EJΓ Al. Asc.: τὰ γένη ἀρχαί Aᵇ   10 ἢ alt. EJΓ Al.[1] Asc.ᶜ
Syr.: καὶ Aᵇ   καὶ] καὶ τὸ recc.

των.——πρὸς δὲ τούτοις εἰ καὶ ὅτι μάλιστα ἀρχαὶ τὰ γένη εἰσί,
15 πότερον δεῖ νομίζειν τὰ πρῶτα τῶν γενῶν ἀρχὰς ἢ τὰ
ἔσχατα κατηγορούμενα ἐπὶ τῶν ἀτόμων; καὶ γὰρ τοῦτο ἔχει
ἀμφισβήτησιν. εἰ μὲν γὰρ ἀεὶ τὰ καθόλου μᾶλλον ἀρχαί,
φανερὸν ὅτι τὰ ἀνωτάτω τῶν γενῶν· ταῦτα γὰρ λέγεται
κατὰ πάντων. τοσαῦται οὖν ἔσονται ἀρχαὶ τῶν ὄντων ὅσα-
20 περ τὰ πρῶτα γένη, ὥστ' ἔσται τό τε ὂν καὶ τὸ ἓν ἀρχαὶ καὶ
οὐσίαι· ταῦτα γὰρ κατὰ πάντων μάλιστα λέγεται τῶν ὄντων.
οὐχ οἷόν τε δὲ τῶν ὄντων ἓν εἶναι γένος οὔτε τὸ ἓν οὔτε τὸ ὄν·
ἀνάγκη μὲν γὰρ τὰς διαφορὰς ἑκάστου γένους καὶ εἶναι καὶ
μίαν εἶναι ἑκάστην, ἀδύνατον δὲ κατηγορεῖσθαι ἢ τὰ εἴδη τοῦ
25 γένους ἐπὶ τῶν οἰκείων διαφορῶν ἢ τὸ γένος ἄνευ τῶν αὐτοῦ
εἰδῶν, ὥστ' εἴπερ τὸ ἓν γένος ἢ τὸ ὄν, οὐδεμία διαφορὰ οὔτε
ὂν οὔτε ἓν ἔσται. ἀλλὰ μὴν εἰ μὴ γένη, οὐδ' ἀρχαὶ ἔσονται,
εἴπερ ἀρχαὶ τὰ γένη. ἔτι καὶ τὰ μεταξὺ συλλαμβανό-
μενα μετὰ τῶν διαφορῶν ἔσται γένη μέχρι τῶν ἀτόμων
30 (νῦν δὲ τὰ μὲν δοκεῖ τὰ δ' οὐ δοκεῖ)· πρὸς δὲ τούτοις ἔτι μᾶλλον αἱ διαφοραὶ ἀρχαὶ ἢ τὰ γένη· εἰ δὲ καὶ αὗται ἀρχαί,
ἄπειροι ὡς εἰπεῖν ἀρχαὶ γίγνονται, ἄλλως τε κἂν τις τὸ
999ᵃ πρῶτον γένος ἀρχὴν τιθῇ. ἀλλὰ μὴν καὶ εἰ μᾶλλόν γε
ἀρχοειδὲς τὸ ἕν ἐστιν, ἓν δὲ τὸ ἀδιαίρετον, ἀδιαίρετον δὲ
ἅπαν ἢ κατὰ τὸ ποσὸν ἢ κατ' εἶδος, πρότερον δὲ τὸ κατ'
εἶδος, τὰ δὲ γένη διαιρετὰ εἰς εἴδη, μᾶλλον ἂν ἓν τὸ
5 ἔσχατον εἴη κατηγορούμενον· οὐ γάρ ἐστι γένος ἄνθρωπος
τῶν τινῶν ἀνθρώπων. ἔτι ἐν οἷς τὸ πρότερον καὶ ὕστερόν
ἐστιν, οὐχ οἷόν τε τὸ ἐπὶ τούτων εἶναί τι παρὰ ταῦτα (οἷον
εἰ πρώτη τῶν ἀριθμῶν ἡ δυάς, οὐκ ἔσται τις ἀριθμὸς παρὰ
τὰ εἴδη τῶν ἀριθμῶν· ὁμοίως δὲ οὐδὲ σχῆμα παρὰ τὰ εἴδη
10 τῶν σχημάτων· εἰ δὲ μὴ τούτων, σχολῇ τῶν γε ἄλλων
ἔσται τὰ γένη παρὰ τὰ εἴδη· τούτων γὰρ δοκεῖ μάλιστα εἶναι

ᵇ 15 πότερον Aᵇ Al. : πότερα EJΓ Al.¹   17 εἰ] ἢ fecit E   ἀεὶ
Al. : δεῖ Aᵇ : ὅτι EJ Asc. Syr.¹ : om. Γ   ἀρχαί JΓ Al. Asc.¹ et fecit
E : ἀρχάς Aᵇ   18 ταῦτα … 19 πάντων codd. Asc. : om. fort.
Al., secl. Jaeger (cf. l. 21)   22 τῶν ὄντων EJΓ Al. Asc. Syr.¹ : om.
Aᵇ   ἓν pr. … ὄν EJΓ Asc. Syr.¹ : οὔτε τὸ ἓν οὔτε τὸ ὂν εἶναι γένος Aᵇ
24 τοῦ JAᵇΓ Al. : ἄνευ τοῦ E Syr.¹   25 ἐπὶ AᵇΓ Al. : καὶ E Syr.¹ :
om. J   τῶν alt. EJΓ Al. : τοῦ τῶν Syr.¹ : τούτων τῶν Aᵇ   27 ὂν
οὔτε ἓν Aᵇ Asc.ᶜ : ἓν οὔτε ὂν E²Γ : τὸ ἓν οὔτε τὸ ὂν E¹J   28 ἔτι δὲ τὰ
μεταξὺ καὶ Γ   31 αὗταὶ EJ   999ᵃ 3 κατ' pr. Aᵇ Al. Asc.ᶜ : κατὰ τὸ EJ
5 γένος Aᵇ Asc.ᶜ : τὸ γένος EJ   ἄνθρωπος scripsi : ὁ ἄνθρωπος Aᵇ :
ἄνθρωπος EJ Asc.ᶜ   7 ἔστιν] καὶ ἔστιν J   9 τῶν EJΓ Asc.ᶜ :
τὰ τῶν Aᵇ   οὐδὲ om. Aᵇ

γένη)· ἐν δὲ τοῖς ἀτόμοις οὐκ ἔστι τὸ μὲν πρότερον τὸ δ' ὕστερον. ἔτι ὅπου τὸ μὲν βέλτιον τὸ δὲ χεῖρον, ἀεὶ τὸ βέλτιον
πρότερον· ὥστ' οὐδὲ τούτων ἂν εἴη γένος.——ἐκ μὲν οὖν τούτων
μᾶλλον φαίνεται τὰ ἐπὶ τῶν ἀτόμων κατηγορούμενα ἀρχαὶ 15
εἶναι τῶν γενῶν· πάλιν δὲ πῶς αὖ δεῖ ταύτας ἀρχὰς ὑπολαβεῖν οὐ ῥᾴδιον εἰπεῖν. τὴν μὲν γὰρ ἀρχὴν δεῖ καὶ τὴν
αἰτίαν εἶναι παρὰ τὰ πράγματα ὧν ἀρχή, καὶ δύνασθαι
εἶναι χωριζομένην αὐτῶν· τοιοῦτον δέ τι παρὰ τὸ καθ' ἕκαστον
εἶναι διὰ τί ἄν τις ὑπολάβοι, πλὴν ὅτι καθόλου κατηγο- 20
ρεῖται καὶ κατὰ πάντων; ἀλλὰ μὴν εἰ διὰ τοῦτο, τὰ μᾶλλον καθόλου μᾶλλον θετέον ἀρχάς· ὥστε ἀρχαὶ τὰ πρῶτ'
ἂν εἴησαν γένη.

4   Ἔστι δ' ἐχομένη τε τούτων ἀπορία καὶ πασῶν χαλε-
πωτάτη καὶ ἀναγκαιοτάτη θεωρῆσαι, περὶ ἧς ὁ λόγος ἐφέ- 25
στηκε νῦν. εἴτε γὰρ μὴ ἔστι τι παρὰ τὰ καθ' ἕκαστα, τὰ
δὲ καθ' ἕκαστα ἄπειρα, τῶν δ' ἀπείρων πῶς ἐνδέχεται λαβεῖν ἐπιστήμην; ᾗ γὰρ ἕν τι καὶ ταὐτόν, καὶ ᾗ καθόλου τι
ὑπάρχει, ταύτῃ πάντα γνωρίζομεν.——ἀλλὰ μὴν εἰ τοῦτο
ἀναγκαῖόν ἐστι καὶ δεῖ τι εἶναι παρὰ τὰ καθ' ἕκαστα, ἀναγκαῖον 30
ἂν εἴη τὰ γένη εἶναι παρὰ τὰ καθ' ἕκαστα, ἤτοι τὰ ἔσχατα ἢ
τὰ πρῶτα· τοῦτο δ' ὅτι ἀδύνατον ἄρτι διηπορήσαμεν.——ἔτι εἰ
ὅτι μάλιστα ἔστι τι παρὰ τὸ σύνολον ὅταν κατηγορηθῇ τι τῆς
ὕλης, πότερον, εἰ ἔστι, παρὰ πάντα δεῖ εἶναί τι, ἢ παρὰ μὲν ἔνια
εἶναι παρὰ δ' ἔνια μὴ εἶναι, ἢ παρ' οὐδέν; εἰ μὲν οὖν μηδέν ἐστι 999ᵇ
παρὰ τὰ καθ' ἕκαστα, οὐθὲν ἂν εἴη νοητὸν ἀλλὰ πάντα αἰσθητὰ
καὶ ἐπιστήμη οὐδενός, εἰ μή τις εἶναι λέγει τὴν αἴσθησιν ἐπιστήμην. ἔτι δ' οὐδ' ἀΐδιον οὐθὲν οὐδ' ἀκίνητον (τὰ γὰρ αἰσθητὰ
πάντα φθείρεται καὶ ἐν κινήσει ἐστίν)· ἀλλὰ μὴν εἴ γε ἀΐδιον 5
μηθέν ἐστιν, οὐδὲ γένεσιν εἶναι δυνατόν. ἀνάγκη γὰρ εἶναί τι
τὸ γιγνόμενον καὶ ἐξ οὗ γίγνεται καὶ τούτων τὸ ἔσχατον ἀγένη-

ᵃ 14 οὐδὲν recc.   16 ὑπολαβεῖν ἀρχὰς ΕΓ Asc.¹ Syr.¹   17 εἰπεῖν
om. Aᵇ Asc.¹   18 εἶναι ante δεῖ 17 Aᵇ   26 εἰ γὰρ AᵇΓ   27 δ' ΕAᵇ
Asc. Syr.¹: γ' J   30 ἀναγκαῖον ... 31 ἕκαστα JAᵇΓ Asc. : om. Ε
32 εἰ ΕJΓ Al. Asc.: δ' Aᵇ   33 τι pr. ΕJΓ Asc.¹ᶜ: om. Aᵇ   σύνο-
λον] σύνολον, λέγω δὲ σύνολον Jaeger   34 ἔστι] ἔστι τι ΕJΓ: ἔστιν
εἰδός τι recc.   ᵇ 1 ἢ παρ' οὐδέν secl. Essen   4 δ' om. ΕJ
Asc.¹ Syr.¹   6 μηθέν ΕJ Asc. Syr.¹: οὐδέν Aᵇ Al.ᶜ   7 ἀγένη-
τον ΕJ Al.ᶜ Asc.ᶜ: ἀγέννητον Aᵇ

τον, εἴπερ ἵσταταί τε καὶ ἐκ μὴ ὄντος γενέσθαι ἀδύνατον· ἔτι δὲ
γενέσεως οὔσης καὶ κινήσεως ἀνάγκη καὶ πέρας εἶναι (οὔτε
10 γὰρ ἄπειρός ἐστιν οὐδεμία κίνησις ἀλλὰ πάσης ἔστι τέλος,
γίγνεσθαί τε οὐχ οἷόν τε τὸ ἀδύνατον γενέσθαι· τὸ δὲ γεγονὸς ἀνάγκη εἶναι ὅτε πρῶτον γέγονεν)· ἔτι δ᾽ εἴπερ ἡ ὕλη
ἔστι διὰ τὸ ἀγένητος εἶναι, πολὺ ἔτι μᾶλλον εὔλογον εἶναι
τὴν οὐσίαν, ὅ ποτε ἐκείνη γίγνεται· εἰ γὰρ μήτε τοῦτο ἔσται
15 μήτε ἐκείνη, οὐθὲν ἔσται τὸ παράπαν, εἰ δὲ τοῦτο ἀδύνατον,
ἀνάγκη τι εἶναι παρὰ τὸ σύνολον, τὴν μορφὴν καὶ τὸ εἶδος.—
εἰ δ᾽ αὖ τις τοῦτο θήσει, ἀπορία ἐπὶ τίνων τε θήσει τοῦτο
καὶ ἐπὶ τίνων οὔ. ὅτι μὲν γὰρ ἐπὶ πάντων οὐχ οἷόν τε,
φανερόν· οὐ γὰρ ἂν θείημεν εἶναί τινα οἰκίαν παρὰ τὰς τι-
20 νὰς οἰκίας. πρὸς δὲ τούτοις πότερον ἡ οὐσία μία πάντων ἔσται,
οἷον τῶν ἀνθρώπων; ἀλλ᾽ ἄτοπον· ἓν γὰρ πάντα ὧν ἡ
οὐσία μία. ἀλλὰ πολλὰ καὶ διάφορα; ἀλλὰ καὶ τοῦτο
ἄλογον. ἅμα δὲ καὶ πῶς γίγνεται ἡ ὕλη τούτων ἕκαστον
καὶ ἔστι τὸ σύνολον ἄμφω ταῦτα;———ἔτι δὲ περὶ τῶν ἀρχῶν
25 καὶ τόδε ἀπορήσειεν ἄν τις. εἰ μὲν γὰρ εἴδει εἰσὶν ἕν, οὐθὲν
ἔσται ἀριθμῷ ἕν, οὐδ᾽ αὐτὸ τὸ ἓν καὶ τὸ ὄν· καὶ τὸ ἐπίστασθαι πῶς ἔσται, εἰ μή τι ἔσται ἓν ἐπὶ πάντων;—ἀλλὰ μὴν
εἰ ἀριθμῷ ἓν καὶ μία ἑκάστη τῶν ἀρχῶν, καὶ μὴ ὥσπερ
ἐπὶ τῶν αἰσθητῶν ἄλλαι ἄλλων (οἷον τῆσδε τῆς συλλαβῆς
30 τῷ εἴδει τῆς αὐτῆς οὔσης καὶ αἱ ἀρχαὶ εἴδει αἱ αὐταί· καὶ
γὰρ αὗται ὑπάρχουσιν ἀριθμῷ ἕτεραι),—εἰ δὲ μὴ οὕτως ἀλλ᾽
αἱ τῶν ὄντων ἀρχαὶ ἀριθμῷ ἕν εἰσιν, οὐκ ἔσται παρὰ τὰ
στοιχεῖα οὐθὲν ἕτερον· τὸ γὰρ ἀριθμῷ ἓν ἢ τὸ καθ᾽ ἕκαστον
λέγειν διαφέρει οὐθέν· οὕτω γὰρ λέγομεν τὸ καθ᾽ ἕκαστον,
1000ᵃ τὸ ἀριθμῷ ἕν, καθόλου δὲ τὸ ἐπὶ τούτων. ὥσπερ οὖν εἰ τὰ
τῆς φωνῆς ἀριθμῷ ἦν στοιχεῖα ὡρισμένα, ἀναγκαῖον ἦν ἂν το-

ᵇ 8 γίγνεσθαι Al.   9 καὶ alt. om. Γ   13 ἐστὶν ἀΐδιος διὰ ci.
Christ   ἀγένητος recc.   14 ὅ ποτε Ε Al. Asc.: ὁπότε JAᵇΓ Al.ᶜ
γίγνεται εἶναι· εἰ Γ   21 ἕν ... ὧν Syr.ᶜ et ut vid. Al. Asc.: οὐ
γὰρ ἓν ἅπαντα ὧν JAᵇΓ Al.¹ Asc.ᶜ et fecit Ε: οὐ γὰρ πάντων γρ. Syr.
ἢ EJ Asc.ᶜ Syr.ᶜ: om. Aᵇ   22 τοῦτο EJΓ Asc.ᶜ: τούτοις Aᵇ
23 ἢ EJΓ Asc.¹ et ut vid. Al.: om. Aᵇ   24 περὶ ... 25 τόδε
EJΓ Asc.: om. Aᵇ   26 αὐτὸ ἓν καὶ ὂν EJ: αὖ τὸ ἓν καὶ τὸ ὂν Syr.¹
30 αἱ pr. om. EJ   31 εἰ δὴ Susemihl   32 ἀρχαὶ om. EJΓ
ἕν om. E¹J   1000ᵃ 1 τὸ pr.] τῷ J   οὖν] ἂν ci. Fonseca
2 φωνῆς ἐν ἀριθμῷ EJΓ   ὡρισμένῳ Aᵇ   ἂν om. recc.

σαῦτα εἶναι τὰ πάντα γράμματα ὅσαπερ τὰ στοιχεῖα, μὴ
ὄντων γε δύο τῶν αὐτῶν μηδὲ πλειόνων.

Οὐθενὸς δ' ἐλάττων ἀπορία παραλέλειπται καὶ τοῖς 5
νῦν καὶ τοῖς πρότερον, πότερον αἱ αὐταὶ τῶν φθαρτῶν καὶ
τῶν ἀφθάρτων ἀρχαί εἰσιν ἢ ἕτεραι. εἰ μὲν γὰρ αἱ αὐταί,
πῶς τὰ μὲν φθαρτὰ τὰ δὲ ἄφθαρτα, καὶ διὰ τίν' αἰτίαν;
οἱ μὲν οὖν περὶ Ἡσίοδον καὶ πάντες ὅσοι θεολόγοι
μόνον ἐφρόντισαν τοῦ πιθανοῦ τοῦ πρὸς αὑτούς, ἡμῶν δ' ὠλι- 10
γώρησαν (θεοὺς γὰρ ποιοῦντες τὰς ἀρχὰς καὶ ἐκ θεῶν γεγονέναι, τὰ μὴ γευσάμενα τοῦ νέκταρος καὶ τῆς ἀμβρο=
σίας θνητὰ γενέσθαι φασίν, δῆλον ὡς ταῦτα τὰ ὀνόματα
γνώριμα λέγοντες αὑτοῖς· καίτοι περὶ αὐτῆς τῆς προσφο-
ρᾶς τῶν αἰτίων τούτων ὑπὲρ ἡμᾶς εἰρήκασιν· εἰ μὲν γὰρ 15
χάριν ἡδονῆς αὐτῶν θιγγάνουσιν, οὐθὲν αἴτια τοῦ εἶναι τὸ
νέκταρ καὶ ἡ ἀμβροσία, εἰ δὲ τοῦ εἶναι, πῶς ἂν εἶεν ἀΐδιοι δεόμενοι τροφῆς)—ἀλλὰ περὶ μὲν τῶν μυθικῶς σοφι-
ζομένων οὐκ ἄξιον μετὰ σπουδῆς σκοπεῖν· παρὰ δὲ τῶν δι'
ἀποδείξεως λεγόντων δεῖ πυνθάνεσθαι διερωτῶντας τί δή 20
ποτ' ἐκ τῶν αὐτῶν ὄντα τὰ μὲν ἀΐδια τὴν φύσιν ἐστὶ
τὰ δὲ φθείρεται τῶν ὄντων. ἐπεὶ δὲ οὔτε αἰτίαν λέγουσιν
οὔτε εὔλογον οὕτως ἔχειν, δῆλον ὡς οὐχ αἱ αὐταὶ ἀρχαὶ
οὐδὲ αἰτίαι αὐτῶν ἂν εἶεν. καὶ γὰρ ὅνπερ οἰηθείη λέγειν
ἄν τις μάλιστα ὁμολογουμένως αὑτῷ, Ἐμπεδοκλῆς, καὶ 25
οὗτος ταὐτὸν πέπονθεν· τίθησι μὲν γὰρ ἀρχήν τινα αἰτίαν
τῆς φθορᾶς τὸ νεῖκος, δόξειε δ' ἂν οὐθὲν ἧττον καὶ τοῦτο
γεννᾶν ἔξω τοῦ ἑνός· ἅπαντα γὰρ ἐκ τούτου τἆλλά ἐστι
πλὴν ὁ θεός. λέγει γοῦν " ἐξ ὧν πάνθ' ὅσα τ' ἦν ὅσα τ'
ἔσθ' ὅσα τ' ἔσται ὀπίσσω, | δένδρεά τ' ἐβλάστησε καὶ ἀνέ- 30
ρες ἠδὲ γυναῖκες, | θῆρές τ' οἰωνοί τε καὶ ὑδατοθρέμμονες

ᵃ 3 τὰ alt. om. Aᵇ   7 αὐταί Aᵇ Al. : αὐταί εἰσι EJΓ   8 φθαρτὰ
τὰ δὲ ἄφθαρτα Aᵇ Al. : ἀφθαρτὰ τὰ δὲ φθαρτά EJΓ Asc.   10 αὐτούς
Christ: αὑτούς codd.   14 αὑτοῖς Aᵇ   καίτοι καὶ περὶ EJ   προσφο-
ρᾶς] φύσεως γρ. E   16 αὐτοὶ Γ   18 μὲν om. Γ   μυθικῶν Aᵇ
24 ἂν αὑτῶν E : αὐτῶν J   25 αὑτῷ Aᵇ   27 φορᾶς J   δόξειε
δ' EΓ Al.¹ : δόξειεν J : ὡς δόξειεν Aᵇ   οὐθὲν ... 28 γεννᾶν EJΓ Al.¹ :
οὐδὲν δ' ... γεννᾷ Aᵇ   28 ἔξω ... γὰρ] ἐκ γὰρ τοῦ ἑνός ἅπαντα καὶ Al.
29-30 ὅσα τ' ἔσθ' recc. : ὅσα τ' ἐστὶν Aᵇ Al.ᶜ: om. EJΓ   30 ὀπίσσω
om. AᵇΓ Simpl.ᶜ   ἄνδρες J : ἀνέρες τ' Aᵇ   31 τ' om. Aᵇ

ἰχθῦς, | καί τε θεοὶ δολιχαίωνες ". καὶ χωρὶς δὲ τούτων δῆ-
1000ᵇλον· εἰ γὰρ μὴ ἦν ἐν τοῖς πράγμασιν, ἓν ἂν ἦν
ἅπαντα, ὡς φησίν· ὅταν γὰρ συνέλθῃ, τότε δ' " ἔσχατον
ἵστατο νεῖκος ". διὸ καὶ συμβαίνει αὐτῷ τὸν εὐδαιμονέ-
στατον θεὸν ἧττον φρόνιμον εἶναι τῶν ἄλλων· οὐ γὰρ γνω-
5 ρίζει ἅπαντα· τὸ γὰρ νεῖκος οὐκ ἔχει, ἡ δὲ γνῶσις
τοῦ ὁμοίου τῷ ὁμοίῳ. " γαίῃ μὲν γάρ," φησί, " γαῖαν
ὀπώπαμεν, ὕδατι δ' ὕδωρ, | αἰθέρι δ' αἰθέρα δῖον, ἀτὰρ
πυρὶ πῦρ ἀΐδηλον, | στοργὴν δὲ στοργῇ, νεῖκος δέ τε νείκεϊ
λυγρῷ." ἀλλ' ὅθεν δὴ ὁ λόγος, τοῦτό γε φανερόν, ὅτι
10 συμβαίνει αὐτῷ τὸ νεῖκος μηθὲν μᾶλλον φθορᾶς ἢ τοῦ
εἶναι αἴτιον· ὁμοίως δ' οὐδ' ἡ φιλότης τοῦ εἶναι, συνάγουσα
γὰρ εἰς τὸ ἓν φθείρει τὰ ἄλλα. καὶ ἅμα δὲ αὐτῆς τῆς μεταβολῆς αἴτιον οὐθὲν λέγει ἀλλ' ἢ ὅτι οὕτως πέφυκεν·
" ἀλλ' ὅτε δὴ μέγα νεῖκος ἐνὶ μελέεσσιν ἐθρέφθη, | εἰς τιμάς
15 τ' ἀνόρουσε τελειομένοιο χρόνοιο | ὅς σφιν ἀμοιβαῖος πλα-
τέος παρ' ἐλήλαται ὅρκου'" ὡς ἀναγκαῖον μὲν ὂν μεταβάλ-
λειν· αἰτίαν δὲ τῆς ἀνάγκης οὐδεμίαν δηλοῖ. ἀλλ' ὅμως
τοσοῦτόν γε μόνος λέγει ὁμολογουμένως· οὐ γὰρ τὰ μὲν
φθαρτὰ τὰ δὲ ἄφθαρτα ποιεῖ τῶν ὄντων ἀλλὰ πάντα
20 φθαρτὰ πλὴν τῶν στοιχείων. ἡ δὲ νῦν λεγομένη ἀπορία
ἐστὶ διὰ τί τὰ μὲν τὰ δ' οὔ, εἴπερ ἐκ τῶν αὐτῶν ἐστίν.—ὅτι
μὲν οὖν οὐκ ἂν εἴησαν αἱ αὐταὶ ἀρχαί, τοσαῦτα εἰρήσθω·
εἰ δὲ ἕτεραι ἀρχαί, μία μὲν ἀπορία πότερον ἄφθαρτοι καὶ
αὗται ἔσονται ἢ φθαρταί· εἰ μὲν γὰρ φθαρταί, δῆλον ὡς
25 ἀναγκαῖον καὶ ταύτας ἔκ τινων εἶναι (πάντα γὰρ φθείρεται εἰς ταῦτ' ἐξ ὧν ἔστιν), ὥστε συμβαίνει τῶν ἀρχῶν
ἑτέρας ἀρχὰς εἶναι προτέρας, τοῦτο δ' ἀδύνατον, καὶ εἰ
ἵσταται καὶ εἰ βαδίζει εἰς ἄπειρον· ἔτι δὲ πῶς ἔσται τὰ

ᵇ 1 ἦν AᵇΓ Asc.: ἐνῆν EJ   ἐν] τὸ νεῖκος ἐν Aᵇ²   2 συνέλθῃ
EJ et ut vid. Al. Asc.: συνέλθωσιν Aᵇ   δ' om. EJΓ   3 ἱστᾶ
τὸ E²   διὸ] ὃ Aᵇ   4 γνωρίζει τὰ στοιχεῖα πάντα ΕJΓ   7 αἰθέρι
... 8 ἀΐδηλον om. EJΓ   7 δῖον Asc.ᶜ De An.: θεῖον Aᵇ   ἀτὰρ ...
8 ἀΐδηλον recc.: om. Aᵇ   8 στοργῇ δὲ στοργήν De An.: στοργῇ τε
στοργήν EJΓ   δέ τι J   9 λυγμῷ J   11 αἴτιον om. Aᵇ
13 τὸ αἴτιον Aᵇ   14 ἄλλο τε J   15 ὃ Aᵇ   πλατέος om. Γ
16 παρ' ἐλήλαται Sturz: παρελήλαται Aᵇ Simpl.ᶜ: παρελήλατο EJ
Asc.ᶜ: dissoluit Γ   ὥστ' Γ   17 τῆς] ἐξ E: om. J   18 μόνος
Aᵇ et ut vid. Al.: μόνον EJΓ   24 αὐταὶ J Asc.ᶜ: αἱ αὐταὶ Aᵇ
25 πάντα Aᵇ Asc.: ἅπαντα EJ   28 τὰ om. Aᵇ

φθαρτά, εἰ αἱ ἀρχαὶ ἀναιρεθήσονται; εἰ δὲ ἄφθαρτοι, διὰ
τί ἐκ μὲν τούτων ἀφθάρτων οὐσῶν φθαρτὰ ἔσται, ἐκ δὲ τῶν 30
ἑτέρων ἄφθαρτα; τοῦτο γὰρ οὐκ εὔλογον, ἀλλ' ἢ ἀδύνατον ἢ πολλοῦ λόγου δεῖται. ἔτι δὲ οὐδ' ἐγκεχείρηκεν οὐδεὶς
ἑτέρας, ἀλλὰ τὰς αὐτὰς ἁπάντων λέγουσιν ἀρχάς. ἀλλὰ 1001ᵃ
τὸ πρῶτον ἀπορηθὲν ἀποτρώγουσιν ὥσπερ τοῦτο μικρόν τι
λαμβάνοντες.

Πάντων δὲ καὶ θεωρῆσαι χαλεπώτατον καὶ πρὸς τὸ
γνῶναι τἀληθὲς ἀναγκαιότατον πότερόν ποτε τὸ ὂν καὶ τὸ 5
ἓν οὐσίαι τῶν ὄντων εἰσί, καὶ ἑκάτερον αὐτῶν οὐχ ἕτερόν τι
ὂν τὸ μὲν ἓν τὸ δὲ ὄν ἐστιν, ἢ δεῖ ζητεῖν τί ποτ' ἐστὶ τὸ
ὂν καὶ τὸ ἓν ὡς ὑποκειμένης ἄλλης φύσεως. οἱ μὲν γὰρ
ἐκείνως οἱ δ' οὕτως οἴονται τὴν φύσιν ἔχειν. Πλάτων
μὲν γὰρ καὶ οἱ Πυθαγόρειοι οὐχ ἕτερόν τι τὸ ὂν οὐδὲ τὸ 10
ἓν ἀλλὰ τοῦτο αὐτῶν τὴν φύσιν εἶναι, ὡς οὔσης τῆς οὐσίας
αὐτοῦ τοῦ ἑνὶ εἶναι καὶ ὄντι· οἱ δὲ περὶ φύσεως, οἷον Ἐμπεδοκλῆς ὡς εἰς γνωριμώτερον ἀνάγων λέγει ὅ τι τὸ ἕν
ἐστιν· δόξειε γὰρ ἂν λέγειν τοῦτο τὴν φιλίαν εἶναι (αἰτία
γοῦν ἐστὶν αὕτη τοῦ ἓν εἶναι πᾶσιν), ἕτεροι δὲ πῦρ, οἱ δ' 15
ἀέρα φασὶν εἶναι τὸ ἓν τοῦτο καὶ τὸ ὄν, ἐξ οὗ τὰ ὄντα
εἶναί τε καὶ γεγονέναι. ὡς δ' αὕτως καὶ οἱ πλείω τὰ
στοιχεῖα τιθέμενοι· ἀνάγκη γὰρ καὶ τούτοις τοσαῦτα λέγειν
τὸ ἓν καὶ τὸ ὂν ὅσας περ ἀρχὰς εἶναί φασιν. συμβαίνει
δέ, εἰ μέν τις μὴ θήσεται εἶναί τινα οὐσίαν τὸ ἓν καὶ τὸ 20
ὄν, μηδὲ τῶν ἄλλων εἶναι τῶν καθόλου μηθέν (ταῦτα γὰρ
ἐστι καθόλου μάλιστα πάντων, εἰ δὲ μὴ ἔστι τι ἓν αὐτὸ
μηδ' αὐτὸ ὄν, σχολῇ τῶν γε ἄλλων τι ἂν εἴη παρὰ τὰ

1001ᵃ 4 — ᵇ 25, ᵇ 26 — 1002ᵇ 11, cf. 996ᵃ 4-9, 12-15, 1060ᵃ
36 — ᵇ 19

ᵇ 32 εἴρηκεν ex Al. ci. Bonitz   1001ᵃ 1 post ἑτέρας add. λέγειν
Aᵇ, λέγει Jᵛ   λέγουσιν ἁπάντων Aᵇ   10 τὸ pr. om. E   12 αὐτοῦ
. . . ὄντι Christ : αὐτοῦ τοῦ ἑνὶ εἶναι καὶ τοῦ ὄντι ci. Bonitz : αὐτοῦ τὸ ἕν
εἶναι καὶ ὄν τι Aᵇ : ταὐτὸ ἓν εἶναι καὶ ὄντι EJ : αὐτὸ τὸ ἕν εἶναι καὶ ὄν τι
Γ Al.ᶜ : τῆς αὐτῆς, καὶ ταὐτοῦ ἑνὶ εἶναι καὶ ὄντι fort. Al.   13 ὅ τι
Brandis : ὅτι vulgo : ὅ τί ποτε Aᵇ   ἓν Aᵇ et ut vid. Al. : ἓν ὄν EJΓ
14 λέγειν τί τοῦτο Aᵇ   15 γοῦν] γὰρ Γ   19 ἓν καὶ τὸ ὂν Aᵇ Al. :
ὂν καὶ τὸ ἓν EJΓ   20 θήσεται . . . οὐσίαν] τινὸς οὐσίαν λέγει γρ. Al.
τινα οὐσίαν EJΓ Al.ᶜ Asc.¹ : τινας οὐσίας Aᵇ Syr.¹   τὸ ἓν in marg. E
22 δὲ EJΓ Al.ᶜ : γὰρ Aᵇ : δὴ Susemihl

λεγόμενα καθ᾽ ἕκαστα), ἔτι δὲ μὴ ὄντος τοῦ ἑνὸς οὐσίας,
25 δῆλον ὅτι οὐδ᾽ ἂν ἀριθμὸς εἴη ὡς κεχωρισμένη τις φύσις
τῶν ὄντων (ὁ μὲν γὰρ ἀριθμὸς μονάδες, ἡ δὲ μονὰς ὅπερ
ἕν τί ἐστιν)· εἰ δ᾽ ἔστι τι αὐτὸ ἓν καὶ ὄν, ἀναγκαῖον οὐσίαν
αὐτῶν εἶναι τὸ ἓν καὶ τὸ ὄν· οὐ γὰρ ἕτερόν τι καθόλου
κατηγορεῖται ἀλλὰ ταῦτα αὐτά.—ἀλλὰ μὴν εἴ γ᾽ ἔσται
30 τι αὐτὸ ὂν καὶ αὐτὸ ἕν, πολλὴ ἀπορία πῶς ἔσται τι παρὰ
ταῦτα ἕτερον, λέγω δὲ πῶς ἔσται πλείω ἑνὸς τὰ ὄντα. τὸ
γὰρ ἕτερον τοῦ ὄντος οὐκ ἔστιν, ὥστε κατὰ τὸν Παρμενίδου
συμβαίνειν ἀνάγκη λόγον ἓν ἅπαντα εἶναι τὰ ὄντα καὶ
1001ᵇ τοῦτο εἶναι τὸ ὄν. ἀμφοτέρως δὲ δύσκολον· ἄν τε γὰρ μὴ
ᾖ τὸ ἓν οὐσία ἄν τε ᾖ τὸ αὐτὸ ἕν, ἀδύνατον τὸν ἀριθμὸν
οὐσίαν εἶναι. ἐὰν μὲν οὖν μὴ ᾖ, εἴρηται πρότερον δι᾽ ὅ· ἐὰν
δὲ ᾖ, ἡ αὐτὴ ἀπορία καὶ περὶ τοῦ ὄντος. ἐκ τίνος γὰρ
5 παρὰ τὸ ἓν ἔσται αὐτὸ ἄλλο ἕν; ἀνάγκη γὰρ μὴ ἓν εἶ-
ναι· ἅπαντα δὲ τὰ ὄντα ἢ ἓν ἢ πολλὰ ὧν ἓν ἕκαστον.
ἔτι εἰ ἀδιαίρετον αὐτὸ τὸ ἕν, κατὰ μὲν τὸ Ζήνωνος ἀξίωμα
οὐθὲν ἂν εἴη (ὃ γὰρ μήτε προστιθέμενον μήτε ἀφαιρούμενον
ποιεῖ μεῖζον μηδὲ ἔλαττον, οὔ φησιν εἶναι τοῦτο τῶν ὄντων,
10 ὡς δηλονότι ὄντος μεγέθους τοῦ ὄντος· καὶ εἰ μέγεθος,
σωματικόν· τοῦτο γὰρ πάντῃ ὄν· τὰ δὲ ἄλλα πῶς μὲν
προστιθέμενα ποιήσει μεῖζον, πῶς δ᾽ οὐθέν, οἷον ἐπίπεδον
καὶ γραμμή, στιγμὴ δὲ καὶ μονὰς οὐδαμῶς)· ἀλλ᾽ ἐπειδὴ
οὗτος θεωρεῖ φορτικῶς, καὶ ἐνδέχεται εἶναι ἀδιαίρετόν τι
15 ὥστε [καὶ οὕτως] καὶ πρὸς ἐκεῖνον τιν᾽ ἀπολογίαν ἔχειν (μεῖζον μὲν γὰρ οὐ ποιήσει πλεῖον δὲ προστιθέμενον τὸ τοιοῦτον)—
ἀλλὰ πῶς δὴ ἐξ ἑνὸς τοιούτου ἢ πλειόνων τοιούτων ἔσται
μέγεθος; ὅμοιον γὰρ καὶ τὴν γραμμὴν ἐκ στιγμῶν εἶναι
φάσκειν. ἀλλὰ μὴν καὶ εἴ τις οὕτως ὑπολαμβάνει ὥστε

ᵃ 25 φύσις τις EJΓ Syr.¹   28 ἓν καὶ τὸ ὄν Aᵇ Al.: ὃν καὶ τὸ
ἕν EJΓ Asc.ᶜ   καθόλου codd. Γ Al. Asc. Syr.: καθ᾽ οὗ Bonitz
33 ἀνάγκη συμβαίνειν λόγον Aᵇ: λόγον συμβαίνειν ἀνάγκη Γ   ᵇ 1 δύσ-
κολον E   2 τὸ alt. EJΓ Al.¹: τι Aᵇ   4 ἔκ τινος J   γὰρ Aᵇ
Al.ᶜ: γὰρ καὶ EJΓ Syr.¹   5 μὴ ἓν Aᵇ et fort. Al.: μηδὲν EJΓ Asc.
Syr.¹   9 μηδὲ ἔλαττον AᵇΓ Al.: om. EJ   οὗ J   11 σωματικοῦ
ci. Christ   12 προστιθεμένων Aᵇ   13 ἐπειδὴ EJΓ Asc.ᶜ: εἰ δὴ
Aᵇ Al.   14 οὗτος EJΓ Al.: οὕτως Aᵇ Asc.ᶜ   καὶ Aᵇ Al. Asc.ᶜ:
καὶ οὐκ EJΓ   τι Aᵇ Al.: om. EJΓ   15 ὥστε καὶ οὕτως] καὶ οὕτως
ὥστε ci. Christ, καὶ οὕτως Lasson: καὶ οὕτως seclusi   ὄντως ci. Fonseca
καὶ alt. om. Γi et fort. Al.   ἔχει ἀπολογίαν E (sed ν post ἔχει erasum)
JΓ   17 τοιούτων Aᵇ Al.: om. EJΓ Syr.¹

γενέσθαι, καθάπερ λέγουσί τινες, ἐκ τοῦ ἑνὸς αὐτοῦ καὶ 20
ἄλλου μὴ ἑνός τινος τὸν ἀριθμόν, οὐθὲν ἧττον ζητητέον διὰ
τί καὶ πῶς ὁτὲ μὲν ἀριθμὸς ὁτὲ δὲ μέγεθος ἔσται τὸ γε-
νόμενον, εἴπερ τὸ μὴ ἓν ἢ ἀνισότης καὶ ἡ αὐτὴ φύσις
ἦν. οὔτε γὰρ ὅπως ἐξ ἑνὸς καὶ ταύτης οὔτε ὅπως ἐξ ἀριθμοῦ τινὸς καὶ ταύτης γένοιτ' ἂν τὰ μεγέθη, δῆλον.   25

5   Τούτων δ' ἐχομένη ἀπορία πότερον οἱ ἀριθμοὶ καὶ
τὰ σώματα καὶ τὰ ἐπίπεδα καὶ αἱ στιγμαὶ οὐσίαι τινές
εἰσιν ἢ οὔ. εἰ μὲν γὰρ μή εἰσιν, διαφεύγει τί τὸ ὂν καὶ τίνες
αἱ οὐσίαι τῶν ὄντων· τὰ μὲν γὰρ πάθη καὶ αἱ κινήσεις
καὶ τὰ πρός τι καὶ αἱ διαθέσεις καὶ οἱ λόγοι οὐθενὸς δο- 30
κοῦσιν οὐσίαν σημαίνειν (λέγονται γὰρ πάντα καθ' ὑποκειμένου τινός, καὶ οὐθὲν τόδε τι)· ἃ δὲ μάλιστ' ἂν δόξειε
σημαίνειν οὐσίαν, ὕδωρ καὶ γῆ καὶ πῦρ καὶ ἀήρ, ἐξ ὧν
τὰ σύνθετα σώματα συνέστηκε, τούτων θερμότητες μὲν καὶ 1002ᵃ
ψυχρότητες καὶ τὰ τοιαῦτα πάθη, οὐκ οὐσίαι, τὸ δὲ σῶμα
τὸ ταῦτα πεπονθὸς μόνον ὑπομένει ὡς ὄν τι καὶ οὐσία τις
οὖσα. ἀλλὰ μὴν τό γε σῶμα ἧττον οὐσία τῆς ἐπιφανείας,
καὶ αὕτη τῆς γραμμῆς, καὶ αὕτη τῆς μονάδος καὶ τῆς 5
στιγμῆς· τούτοις γὰρ ὥρισται τὸ σῶμα, καὶ τὰ μὲν ἄνευ
σώματος ἐνδέχεσθαι δοκεῖ εἶναι τὸ δὲ σῶμα ἄνευ τούτων
ἀδύνατον. διόπερ οἱ μὲν πολλοὶ καὶ οἱ πρότερον τὴν
οὐσίαν καὶ τὸ ὂν ᾤοντο τὸ σῶμα εἶναι τὰ δὲ ἄλλα
τούτου πάθη, ὥστε καὶ τὰς ἀρχὰς τὰς τῶν σωμάτων 10
τῶν ὄντων εἶναι ἀρχάς· οἱ δ' ὕστεροι καὶ σοφώτεροι τούτων εἶναι δόξαντες ἀριθμούς. καθάπερ οὖν εἴπομεν, εἰ μὴ
ἔστιν οὐσία ταῦτα, ὅλως οὐδὲν ἐστὶν οὐσία οὐδὲ ὂν οὐθέν· οὐ
γὰρ δὴ τά γε συμβεβηκότα τούτοις ἄξιον ὄντα καλεῖν.
—ἀλλὰ μὴν εἰ τοῦτο μὲν ὁμολογεῖται, ὅτι μᾶλλον οὐσία τὰ 15
μήκη τῶν σωμάτων καὶ αἱ στιγμαί, ταῦτα δὲ μὴ ὁρῶμεν
ποίων ἂν εἶεν σωμάτων (ἐν γὰρ τοῖς αἰσθητοῖς ἀδύνατον
εἶναι), οὐκ ἂν εἴη οὐσία οὐδεμία. ἔτι δὲ φαίνεται ταῦτα

ᵇ 27 καὶ τὰ ἐπίπεδα desideravit Al.   28 μὲν om. E   32 ἂν om. J
33 καὶ ἀήρ Aᵇ Asc.: om. EJΓ   1002ᵃ 4 ἥττων E   5 αὕτη alt.]
ἡ γραμμὴ Aᵇ   7-8 τούτων εἶναι ἀδύνατον recc.   9 τὰ δὲ ἄλλα Aᵇ
Asc.: τἆλλα δὲ EJ   11 ὕστεροι Aᵇ Asc.ᶜ: ὕστερον EJΓ   καὶ EJ
Asc.ᶜ: καὶ οἱ Aᵇ   13 οὐδὲν Aᵇ et ut vid. Al.: οὐδεμία EJΓ Asc.ᶜ
ἔσται ci. Bonitz   14 δὴ] ἂν Aᵇ   15 ὡμολόγηται J   18 δὲ
om. EJΓ Asc.ᶦ

πάντα διαιρέσεις ὄντα τοῦ σώματος, τὸ μὲν εἰς πλάτος
20 τὸ δ' εἰς βάθος τὸ δ' εἰς μῆκος. πρὸς δὲ τούτοις ὁμοίως
ἔνεστιν ἐν τῷ στερεῷ ὁποιονοῦν σχῆμα· ὥστ' εἰ μηδ'
ἐν τῷ λίθῳ Ἑρμῆς, οὐδὲ τὸ ἥμισυ τοῦ κύβου ἐν τῷ κύβῳ
οὕτως ὡς ἀφωρισμένον· οὐκ ἄρα οὐδ' ἐπιφάνεια (εἰ γὰρ
ὁποιαοῦν, κἂν αὕτη ἂν ἦν ἡ ἀφορίζουσα τὸ ἥμισυ), ὁ δ'
25 αὐτὸς λόγος καὶ ἐπὶ γραμμῆς καὶ στιγμῆς καὶ μονάδος,
ὥστ' εἰ μάλιστα μὲν οὐσία τὸ σῶμα, τούτου δὲ μᾶλλον
ταῦτα, μὴ ἔστι δὲ ταῦτα μηδὲ οὐσίαι τινές, διαφεύγει τί
τὸ ὂν καὶ τίς ἡ οὐσία τῶν ὄντων. πρὸς γὰρ τοῖς εἰρημένοις
καὶ τὰ περὶ τὴν γένεσιν καὶ τὴν φθορὰν συμβαίνει ἄλογα.
30 δοκεῖ μὲν γὰρ ἡ οὐσία, ἐὰν μὴ οὖσα πρότερον νῦν ᾖ ἢ πρότερον οὖσα ὕστερον μὴ ᾖ, μετὰ τοῦ γίγνεσθαι καὶ φθείρεσθαι
ταῦτα πάσχειν· τὰς δὲ στιγμὰς καὶ τὰς γραμμὰς καὶ τὰς
ἐπιφανείας οὐκ ἐνδέχεται οὔτε γίγνεσθαι οὔτε φθείρεσθαι,
ὁτὲ μὲν οὔσας ὁτὲ δὲ οὐκ οὔσας. ὅταν γὰρ ἅπτηται ἢ δι-
1002b αιρῆται τὰ σώματα, ἅμα ὁτὲ μὲν μία ἁπτομένων ὁτὲ δὲ
δύο διαιρουμένων γίγνονται· ὥστ' οὔτε συγκειμένων ἔστιν ἀλλ'
ἔφθαρται, διῃρημένων τε εἰσὶν αἱ πρότερον οὐκ οὖσαι (οὐ γὰρ
δὴ ἥ γ' ἀδιαίρετος στιγμὴ διῃρέθη εἰς δύο), εἴ τε γίγνονται καὶ
5 φθείρονται, ἐκ τίνος γίγνονται; παραπλησίως δ' ἔχει καὶ
περὶ τὸ νῦν τὸ ἐν τῷ χρόνῳ· οὐδὲ γὰρ τοῦτο ἐνδέχεται
γίγνεσθαι καὶ φθείρεσθαι, ἀλλ' ὅμως ἕτερον ἀεὶ δοκεῖ εἶναι, οὐκ οὐσία τις οὖσα. ὁμοίως δὲ δῆλον ὅτι ἔχει καὶ περὶ
τὰς στιγμὰς καὶ τὰς γραμμὰς καὶ τὰ ἐπίπεδα· ὁ γὰρ
10 αὐτὸς λόγος· ἅπαντα γὰρ ὁμοίως ἢ πέρατα ἢ διαιρέσεις
εἰσίν.

Ὅλως δ' ἀπορήσειεν ἄν τις διὰ τί καὶ δεῖ ζητεῖν 6
ἀλλ' ἄττα παρά τε τὰ αἰσθητὰ καὶ τὰ μεταξύ, οἷον ἃ

ᵃ 19 διαίρεσις Aᵇ   21 ἕν ἐστιν recc.   σχῆμα EJΓ Al. Asc. :
σχῆμα ἢ οὐδέν Aᵇ   21–22 μηδὲν τῷ J   24 αὐτὴ Aᵇ   25 καὶ
alt.] καὶ ἐπὶ EJΓ Al.   30 μὲν EJ Asc.ᶜ : om. AᵇΓ   ἡ οὐσία, ἐὰν
i Brandis : ἐὰν ἡ οὐσία Aᵇ et ut vid. Asc. : ἡ οὐσία EJΓ   πρότερον
EJ γρ. Aᵇ Al. Asc. : τὸ πρότερον Aᵇ   νῦν om. Aᵇ   ᾖ i et ut vid.
Asc., Brandis : εἶναι EJΓ : om. Aᵇ   31 μὴ] δὲ μὴ Γ   ᾖ Aᵇ et
ut vid. Asc. : om. EJΓ   ᵇ 2 γίγνονται E (sed o ex ε facto) Aᵇ
Asc.ᶜ : γίγνοται J   συγκειμένου Aᵇ   3 ἔφθαρτο fecit E   5 τίνος
scripsi : τινος vulgo   7 εἶναι] ἀεὶ εἶναι J : ὡς Aᵇ : an εἶναι, ὡς ?
9 τὰς alt. om. EJ   10 διαίρεσις E Asc.ᶜ   13 ἀλλ' ἄττα EJΓ
Al. Asc. : ἄλλα τοιαῦτα Aᵇ Syr.ˡ   τε Aᵇ Syr.ˡ : om. EJ Al.ˡ Asc.ˡ
τὰ alt. om. E

τίθεμεν εἴδη. εἰ γὰρ διὰ τοῦτο, ὅτι τὰ μὲν μαθηματικὰ
τῶν δεῦρο ἄλλῳ μέν τινι διαφέρει, τῷ δὲ πόλλ᾽ ἄττα 15
ὁμοειδῆ εἶναι οὐθὲν διαφέρει, ὥστ᾽ οὐκ ἔσονται αὐτῶν αἱ
ἀρχαὶ ἀριθμῷ ἀφωρισμέναι (ὥσπερ οὐδὲ τῶν ἐνταῦθα
γραμμάτων· ἀριθμῷ μὲν πάντων οὐκ εἰσὶν αἱ ἀρχαὶ ὡρισμέναι, εἴδει δέ, ἐὰν μὴ λαμβάνῃ τις τησδὶ τῆς συλλαβῆς ἢ τησδὶ τῆς φωνῆς· τούτων δ᾽ ἔσονται καὶ ἀριθμῷ 20
ὡρισμέναι—ὁμοίως δὲ καὶ ἐπὶ τῶν μεταξύ· ἄπειρα γὰρ
κἀκεῖ τὰ ὁμοειδῆ), ὥστ᾽ εἰ μὴ ἔστι παρὰ τὰ αἰσθητὰ καὶ
τὰ μαθηματικὰ ἕτερ᾽ ἄττα οἷα λέγουσι τὰ εἴδη τινές,
οὐκ ἔσται μία ἀριθμῷ ἀλλ᾽ εἴδει οὐσία, οὐδ᾽ αἱ ἀρχαὶ τῶν
ὄντων ἀριθμῷ ἔσονται ποσαί τινες ἀλλὰ εἴδει·—εἰ οὖν τοῦτο 25
ἀναγκαῖον, καὶ τὰ εἴδη ἀναγκαῖον διὰ τοῦτο εἶναι τιθέναι.
καὶ γὰρ εἰ μὴ καλῶς διαρθροῦσιν οἱ λέγοντες, ἀλλ᾽ ἔστι
γε τοῦθ᾽ ὃ βούλονται, καὶ ἀνάγκη ταῦτα λέγειν αὐτοῖς,
ὅτι τῶν εἰδῶν οὐσία τις ἕκαστόν ἐστι καὶ οὐθὲν κατὰ συμβεβηκός.—ἀλλὰ μὴν εἴ γε θήσομεν τά τε εἴδη εἶναι καὶ 30
ἐν ἀριθμῷ τὰς ἀρχὰς ἀλλὰ μὴ εἴδει, εἰρήκαμεν ἃ συμβαίνειν ἀναγκαῖον ἀδύνατα.——σύνεγγυς δὲ τούτων ἐστὶ τὸ
διαπορῆσαι πότερον δυνάμει ἔστι τὰ στοιχεῖα ἤ τιν᾽ ἕτερον
τρόπον. εἰ μὲν γὰρ ἄλλως πως, πρότερόν τι ἔσται τῶν ἀρχῶν ἄλλο (πρότερον γὰρ ἡ δύναμις ἐκείνης τῆς αἰτίας, 1003ᵃ
τὸ δὲ δυνατὸν οὐκ ἀναγκαῖον ἐκείνως πᾶν ἔχειν)· εἰ δ᾽ ἔστι
δυνάμει τὰ στοιχεῖα, ἐνδέχεται μηθὲν εἶναι τῶν ὄντων·
δυνατὸν γὰρ εἶναι καὶ τὸ μήπω ὄν· γίγνεται μὲν γὰρ τὸ
μὴ ὄν, οὐθὲν δὲ γίγνεται τῶν εἶναι ἀδυνάτων.——ταύτας τε 5
οὖν τὰς ἀπορίας ἀναγκαῖον ἀπορῆσαι περὶ τῶν ἀρχῶν, καὶ
πότερον καθόλου εἰσὶν ἢ ὡς λέγομεν τὰ καθ᾽ ἕκαστα. εἰ

1002ᵇ 32 — 1003ᵃ 5, cf. 996ᵃ 10, 11   1003ᵃ 5-17, cf. 996ᵃ 9,
10, 1060ᵇ 19-23

ᵇ 15 πολλὰ τὰ AᵇΓ   17 ἀριθμῶν Aᵇ   ἐνταῦθα EJ γρ. Aᵇ¹ Al.ᶜ
Asc.ᶜ: ἐνταυθὶ Aᵇ¹   19 λανθάνῃ J   τῆσδε . . . 20 τῆσδε Aᵇ
23 οἷα] οἱ J   24 ἀλλ᾽ ci. Al. : καὶ codd. Γ Asc.ᶜ   25 ἀριθμῷ
ἐν ἔσονται Aᵇ   26 τιθέναι om. EJΓ Asc.   28 γε Aᵇ Al.
Asc.ᶜ: om. EJΓ   αὐτοὺς Aᵇ Asc.ᶜ   30 θήσωμεν J   τε om.
EJ   31 ἐν om. EJΓ   32 ἀδύνατα] ἀδύνατα πρότερον Jᵃ Aᵇ
33 τίν᾽ recc.   34 πως JΓⁱ Al. : πῶς EAᵇ

μὲν γὰρ καθόλου, οὐκ ἔσονται οὐσίαι (οὐθὲν γὰρ τῶν κοινῶν
τόδε τι σημαίνει ἀλλὰ τοιόνδε, ἡ δ' οὐσία τόδε τι· εἰ δ'
10 ἔσται τόδε τι καὶ ἐν θέσθαι τὸ κοινῇ κατηγορούμενον, πολλὰ
ἔσται ζῷα ὁ Σωκράτης, αὐτός τε καὶ ὁ ἄνθρωπος καὶ τὸ
ζῷον, εἴπερ σημαίνει ἕκαστον τόδε τι καὶ ἕν)·—εἰ μὲν οὖν
καθόλου αἱ ἀρχαί, ταῦτα συμβαίνει· εἰ δὲ μὴ καθόλου
ἀλλ' ὡς τὰ καθ' ἕκαστα, οὐκ ἔσονται ἐπιστηταί (καθόλου
15 γὰρ ἡ ἐπιστήμη πάντων), ὥστ' ἔσονται ἀρχαὶ ἕτεραι πρό-
τεραι τῶν ἀρχῶν αἱ καθόλου κατηγορούμεναι, ἄνπερ μέλλῃ
ἔσεσθαι αὐτῶν ἐπιστήμη.

Γ

20

Ἔστιν ἐπιστήμη τις ἣ θεωρεῖ τὸ ὂν ᾗ ὂν καὶ τὰ τούτῳ 1
ὑπάρχοντα καθ' αὑτό. αὕτη δ' ἐστὶν οὐδεμιᾷ τῶν ἐν μέρει
λεγομένων ἡ αὐτή· οὐδεμία γὰρ τῶν ἄλλων ἐπισκοπεῖ
καθόλου περὶ τοῦ ὄντος ᾗ ὄν, ἀλλὰ μέρος αὐτοῦ τι ἀποτε-
25 μόμεναι περὶ τούτου θεωροῦσι τὸ συμβεβηκός, οἷον αἱ μαθη-
ματικαὶ τῶν ἐπιστημῶν. ἐπεὶ δὲ τὰς ἀρχὰς καὶ τὰς ἀκρο-
τάτας αἰτίας ζητοῦμεν, δῆλον ὡς φύσεώς τινος αὐτὰς
ἀναγκαῖον εἶναι καθ' αὑτήν. εἰ οὖν καὶ οἱ τὰ στοιχεῖα τῶν
ὄντων ζητοῦντες ταύτας τὰς ἀρχὰς ἐζήτουν, ἀνάγκη καὶ τὰ
30 στοιχεῖα τοῦ ὄντος εἶναι μὴ κατὰ συμβεβηκὸς ἀλλ' ᾗ
ὄν· διὸ καὶ ἡμῖν τοῦ ὄντος ᾗ ὂν τὰς πρώτας αἰτίας
ληπτέον.

Τὸ δὲ ὂν λέγεται μὲν πολλαχῶς, ἀλλὰ πρὸς ἓν καὶ 2
μίαν τινὰ φύσιν καὶ οὐχ ὁμωνύμως ἀλλ' ὥσπερ καὶ τὸ
35 ὑγιεινὸν ἅπαν πρὸς ὑγίειαν, τὸ μὲν τῷ φυλάττειν τὸ δὲ
τῷ ποιεῖν τὸ δὲ τῷ σημεῖον εἶναι τῆς ὑγιείας τὸ δ' ὅτι
1003ᵇ δεκτικὸν αὐτῆς, καὶ τὸ ἰατρικὸν πρὸς ἰατρικήν (τὸ μὲν

Γ. 1, 2, cf. Κ. 3

1003ᵃ 10 ἐν θέσθαι Richards: ἐκθέσθαι codd. et ut vid. Al.: ἐκτί-
θεται Γ: δεῖ ἐκθέσθαι Jaeger   11 ζῷα susp. Christ   14 ἐπιστηταί
EJΓ Al.: ἐπιστήμαι Aᵇ   15 ἡ ἐπιστήμη Aᵇ Al. Asc.: αἱ ἐπιστήμαι
EJΓ   16 αἱ om. EJ   17 ἐπιστήμαι J   22 καθ' αὑτά Al.
25 τοῦτο J   28 αὐτάς Aᵇ Asc.ᶜ et fort. Al.   31 ὄντα EJΓ
διὸ ... ὂν om. Aᵇ   34 ἀλλ' om. Aᵇ

γὰρ τῷ ἔχειν ἰατρικὴν λέγεται ἰατρικὸν τὸ δὲ τῷ εὐφυὲς
εἶναι πρὸς αὐτὴν τὸ δὲ τῷ ἔργον εἶναι τῆς ἰατρικῆς),
ὁμοιοτρόπως δὲ καὶ ἄλλα ληψόμεθα λεγόμενα τούτοις,—
οὕτω δὲ καὶ τὸ ὂν λέγεται πολλαχῶς μὲν ἀλλ' ἅπαν 5
πρὸς μίαν ἀρχήν· τὰ μὲν γὰρ ὅτι οὐσίαι, ὄντα λέγεται,
τὰ δ' ὅτι πάθη οὐσίας, τὰ δ' ὅτι ὁδὸς εἰς οὐσίαν ἢ
φθοραὶ ἢ στερήσεις ἢ ποιότητες ἢ ποιητικὰ ἢ γεννητικὰ
οὐσίας ἢ τῶν πρὸς τὴν οὐσίαν λεγομένων, ἢ τούτων τινὸς
ἀποφάσεις ἢ οὐσίας· διὸ καὶ τὸ μὴ ὂν εἶναι μὴ ὂν φαμεν. 10
καθάπερ οὖν καὶ τῶν ὑγιεινῶν ἁπάντων μία ἐπιστήμη ἔστιν,
ὁμοίως τοῦτο καὶ ἐπὶ τῶν ἄλλων. οὐ γὰρ μόνον τῶν καθ'
ἓν λεγομένων ἐπιστήμης ἐστὶ θεωρῆσαι μιᾶς ἀλλὰ καὶ τῶν
πρὸς μίαν λεγομένων φύσιν· καὶ γὰρ ταῦτα τρόπον τινὰ
λέγονται καθ' ἕν. δῆλον οὖν ὅτι καὶ τὰ ὄντα μιᾶς θεωρῆσαι 15
ᾗ ὄντα. πανταχοῦ δὲ κυρίως τοῦ πρώτου ἡ ἐπιστήμη, καὶ ἐξ
οὗ τὰ ἄλλα ἤρτηται, καὶ δι' ὃ λέγονται. εἰ οὖν τοῦτ' ἐστὶν ἡ
οὐσία, τῶν οὐσιῶν ἂν δέοι τὰς ἀρχὰς καὶ τὰς αἰτίας ἔχειν
τὸν φιλόσοφον.—ἅπαντος δὲ γένους καὶ αἴσθησις μία ἑνὸς
καὶ ἐπιστήμη, οἷον γραμματικὴ μία οὖσα πάσας θεωρεῖ 20
τὰς φωνάς· διὸ καὶ τοῦ ὄντος ᾗ ὂν ὅσα εἴδη θεωρῆσαι μιᾶς
ἐστὶν ἐπιστήμης τῷ γένει, τά τε εἴδη τῶν εἰδῶν. εἰ δὴ τὸ
ὂν καὶ τὸ ἓν ταὐτὸν καὶ μία φύσις τῷ ἀκολουθεῖν ἀλλήλοις ὥσπερ ἀρχὴ καὶ αἴτιον, ἀλλ' οὐχ ὡς ἑνὶ λόγῳ δηλούμενα (διαφέρει δὲ οὐθὲν οὐδ' ἂν ὁμοίως ὑπολάβωμεν, ἀλλὰ 25
καὶ πρὸ ἔργου μᾶλλον)· ταὐτὸ γὰρ εἷς ἄνθρωπος καὶ ἄνθρωπος,
καὶ ὢν ἄνθρωπος καὶ ἄνθρωπος, καὶ οὐχ ἕτερόν τι δηλοῖ κατὰ
τὴν λέξιν ἐπαναδιπλούμενον τὸ εἷς ἄνθρωπος καὶ εἷς ὢν
ἄνθρωπος (δῆλον δ' ὅτι οὐ χωρίζεται οὔτ' ἐπὶ γενέσεως οὔτ'
ἐπὶ φθορᾶς), ὁμοίως δὲ καὶ ἐπὶ τοῦ ἑνός, ὥστε φανερὸν ὅτι 30

ᵇ 2 ἔχειν EJ Asc.ᶜ: ἔχειν τὴν Aᵇ   3 τῷ ἔργον εἶναι] τοῖς ἔργοις Γ
τὴν ἰατρικήν Aᵇ   4 ὁμοίως J   5 δὴ ci. Christ   ἀλλὰ πᾶν E
6 οὐσίαι EJΓ Asc.¹: οὐσία Aᵇ   8 φθοραὶ ἢ στερήσεις EJΓ et ut
vid. Al.: φθορὰ ἢ στέρησις Aᵇ   10 ἀπόφασις Aᵇ   15 λέγεται EJ
20 οἷον EJ Asc.¹: οἷον ἡ Aᵇ   21 ᾗ ὂν J²AᵇΓ et fort. Al.: om. EJ
Al.¹ Asc.ᶜ   22 τε codd. Asc.ᶜ: δὲ ΓAl.¹ᶜ   23 ὂν καὶ τὸ ἓν EJΓ
Al.¹ Asc. Syr.¹: ἐν καὶ τὸ ὂν Aᵇ   26 καὶ ἄνθρωπος AᵇΓ Al.: om. EJ
Asc. Syr. edd.   27 καὶ ἄνθρωπος om. Asc.   28 τὸ] τί E   εἷς ἅ.
καὶ εἷς ὢν scripsi: εἷς ὢν Syr.: ἔστιν εἷς ἅ. καὶ ἅ. καὶ ὢν Asc.ᶜ: εἷς ἐστιν
ἅ. καὶ ἔστιν Aᵇ: ἅ. καὶ ἅ. καὶ εἷς EJ: ἅ. καὶ ὢν ἅ. καὶ εἷς Γ: ἔστιν ἅ. ἅ.
καὶ ἔστιν ut vid. Al.

ἡ πρόσθεσις ἐν τούτοις ταὐτὸ δηλοῖ, καὶ οὐδὲν ἕτερον τὸ ἐν
παρὰ τὸ ὄν, ἔτι δ' ἡ ἑκάστου οὐσία ἕν ἐστιν οὐ κατὰ συμβεβηκός, ὁμοίως δὲ καὶ ὅπερ ὄν τι—ὥσθ' ὅσα περ τοῦ ἑνὸς
εἴδη, τοσαῦτα καὶ τοῦ ὄντος· περὶ ὧν τὸ τί ἐστι τῆς
35 αὐτῆς ἐπιστήμης τῷ γένει θεωρῆσαι, λέγω δ' οἷον περὶ
ταὐτοῦ καὶ ὁμοίου καὶ τῶν ἄλλων τῶν τοιούτων. σχεδὸν δὲ
1004ᵃ πάντα ἀνάγεται τἀναντία εἰς τὴν ἀρχὴν ταύτην· τεθεωρήσθω δ' ἡμῖν ταῦτα ἐν τῇ ἐκλογῇ τῶν ἐναντίων. καὶ
τοσαῦτα μέρη φιλοσοφίας ἔστιν ὅσαι περ αἱ οὐσίαι· ὥστε
ἀναγκαῖον εἶναί τινα πρώτην καὶ ἐχομένην αὐτῶν. ὑπάρ-
5 χει γὰρ εὐθὺς γένη ἔχον τὸ ὄν [καὶ τὸ ἕν]· διὸ καὶ αἱ
ἐπιστῆμαι ἀκολουθήσουσι τούτοις. ἔστι γὰρ ὁ φιλόσοφος
ὥσπερ ὁ μαθηματικὸς λεγόμενος· καὶ γὰρ αὕτη ἔχει
μέρη, καὶ πρώτη τις καὶ δευτέρα ἔστιν ἐπιστήμη καὶ ἄλλαι
ἐφεξῆς ἐν τοῖς μαθήμασιν.—ἐπεὶ δὲ μιᾶς τἀντικείμενα
10 θεωρῆσαι, τῷ δὲ ἑνὶ ἀντίκειται πλῆθος—ἀπόφασιν δὲ καὶ
στέρησιν μιᾶς ἐστὶ θεωρῆσαι διὰ τὸ ἀμφοτέρως θεωρεῖσθαι
τὸ ἓν οὗ ἡ ἀπόφασις ἢ ἡ στέρησις (ἢ ⟨γὰρ⟩ ἁπλῶς λέγομεν
ὅτι οὐχ ὑπάρχει ἐκεῖνο, ἤ τινι γένει· ἔνθα μὲν οὖν †τῷ ἑνὶ
ἡ διαφορὰ πρόσεστι παρὰ τὸ ἐν τῇ ἀποφάσει†, ἀπουσία γὰρ
15 ἡ ἀπόφασις ἐκείνου ἐστίν, ἐν δὲ τῇ στερήσει καὶ ὑποκειμένη τις φύσις γίγνεται καθ' ἧς λέγεται ἡ στέρησις) [τῷ
δ' ἑνὶ πλῆθος ἀντίκειται]—ὥστε καὶ τἀντικείμενα τοῖς εἰρημένοις, τό τε ἕτερον καὶ ἀνόμοιον καὶ ἄνισον καὶ ὅσα
ἄλλα λέγεται ἢ κατὰ ταῦτα ἢ κατὰ πλῆθος καὶ τὸ ἕν,

ᵇ 31 οὐδὲν EJΓ Al.ᶜ Asc.: οὐδὲν ἔτι Aᵇ   34 ὄντος Aᵇ Al.ᶜ Asc.:
ὄντος ἐστίν EJΓ   36 τοιούτων EJAᵇΓ Asc.: τοιούτων καὶ τῶν τούτοις
ἀντικειμένων Sa et fort. Al.   σχεδὸν ... 1004ᵃ 2 ἐναντίων susp. Susemihl, fort. recte (cf. 1004ᵇ 33 — 1005ᵃ 1)   1004ᵃ 1 τεθεωρήσθω Aᵇ
Al.ᶜ (252. 3): τεθεώρηται EJΓ   2 καὶ ... 9 μαθήμασιν ante εἰ 1003ᵇ 22
ponenda ci. Al., ante ἅπαντος 1003ᵇ 19 ponenda vidit Schwegler
4 τινα πρώτην EJΓ Al. Asc.: πρώτην τινὰ Aᵇ   5 ἔχον Aᵇ γρ. Al.:
ἔχοντα EJΓ Al. Asc.   ὂν καὶ τὸ ἕν EJΓ Al.ᶜ Asc.: ἐν καὶ τὸ ὂν Aᵇ: καὶ
τὸ ἐν inclusit Natorp   αἱ Aᵇ Asc.ᶜ: om. EJ   7 ὥσπερ EJΓ Asc.ᶜ:
οὕτως ὥσπερ Aᵇ   9 ἐπεὶ] ἔτι Luthe   10 τῷ ... πλῆθος codd. ΓAl.
Asc.ⁱ: secl. Luthe   12 ἢ ... λέγομεν ex Al. ci. Schwegler: ἡ
ἁπλῶς λεγομένη E¹Aᵇ Asc.: ἡ ἢ ἁπλῶς λεγομένη E²J: ἢ ἁπλῶς λεγομένη Γ   13 ἐκεῖνο E¹Al.: ἐκείνῳ JAᵇΓ et fecit E   τῷ ἑνὶ ἢ an
secludenda?   16 τῷ ... 17 ἀντίκειται seclusi (cf. l. 10): habent
codd. Γ Al.ᶜ Asc.ᶜ   19 ταῦτα Asc.ᶜ T et ut vid. Al.: ταὐτὰ EJ
Aᵇ Γ

τῆς εἰρημένης γνωρίζειν ἐπιστήμης· ὧν ἐστὶ καὶ ἡ ἐναντιό- 20
της· διαφορὰ γάρ τις ἡ ἐναντιότης, ἡ δὲ διαφορὰ ἑτερό-
της. ὥστ' ἐπειδὴ πολλαχῶς τὸ ἓν λέγεται, καὶ ταῦτα πολλαχῶς μὲν λεχθήσεται, ὅμως δὲ μιᾶς ἅπαντά ἐστι γνωρί-
ζειν· οὐ γὰρ εἰ πολλαχῶς, ἑτέρας, ἀλλ' εἰ μήτε καθ' ἓν μήτε
πρὸς ἓν οἱ λόγοι ἀναφέρονται. ἐπεὶ δὲ πάντα πρὸς τὸ πρῶ- 25
τον ἀναφέρεται, οἷον ὅσα ἓν λέγεται πρὸς τὸ πρῶτον ἕν,
ὡσαύτως φατέον καὶ περὶ ταὐτοῦ καὶ ἑτέρου καὶ τῶν ἐναντίων
ἔχειν· ὥστε διελόμενον ποσαχῶς λέγεται ἕκαστον, οὕτως ἀπο-
δοτέον πρὸς τὸ πρῶτον ἐν ἑκάστῃ κατηγορίᾳ πῶς πρὸς ἐκεῖνο
λέγεται· τὰ μὲν γὰρ τῷ ἔχειν ἐκεῖνο τὰ δὲ τῷ ποιεῖν τὰ 30
δὲ κατ' ἄλλους λεχθήσεται τοιούτους τρόπους.—φανερὸν
οὖν [ὅπερ ἐν ταῖς ἀπορίαις ἐλέχθη] ὅτι μιᾶς περὶ τούτων καὶ τῆς οὐσίας ἐστὶ λόγον ἔχειν (τοῦτο δ' ἦν ἐν
τῶν ἐν τοῖς ἀπορήμασιν), καὶ ἔστι τοῦ φιλοσόφου περὶ πάντων δύνασθαι θεωρεῖν. εἰ γὰρ μὴ τοῦ φιλοσόφου, τίς ἔσται 1004^b
ὁ ἐπισκεψόμενος εἰ ταὐτὸ Σωκράτης καὶ Σωκράτης καθή-
μενος, ἢ εἰ ἓν ἑνὶ ἐναντίον, ἢ τί ἐστι τὸ ἐναντίον ἢ ποσαχῶς λέγεται; ὁμοίως δὲ καὶ περὶ τῶν ἄλλων τῶν τοιούτων.
ἐπεὶ οὖν τοῦ ἑνὸς ᾗ ἓν καὶ τοῦ ὄντος ᾗ ὂν ταῦτα καθ' αὑτά 5
ἐστι πάθη, ἀλλ' οὐχ ᾗ ἀριθμοὶ ἢ γραμμαὶ ἢ πῦρ, δῆλον
ὡς ἐκείνης τῆς ἐπιστήμης καὶ τί ἐστι γνωρίσαι καὶ τὰ συμ-
βεβηκότ' αὐτοῖς. καὶ οὐ ταύτῃ ἁμαρτάνουσιν οἱ περὶ αὐτῶν
σκοπούμενοι ὡς οὐ φιλοσοφοῦντες, ἀλλ' ὅτι πρότερον ἡ οὐσία,
περὶ ἧς οὐθὲν ἐπαΐουσιν, ἐπεὶ ὥσπερ ἔστι καὶ ἀριθμοῦ ᾗ ἀρι- 10
θμὸς ἴδια πάθη, οἷον περιττότης ἀρτιότης, συμμετρία ἰσότης, ὑπεροχὴ ἔλλειψις, καὶ ταῦτα καὶ καθ' αὑτοὺς καὶ
πρὸς ἀλλήλους ὑπάρχει τοῖς ἀριθμοῖς (ὁμοίως δὲ καὶ
στερεῷ καὶ ἀκινήτῳ καὶ κινουμένῳ ἀβαρεῖ τε καὶ βάρος
ἔχοντι ἔστιν ἕτερα ἴδια), οὕτω καὶ τῷ ὄντι ᾗ ὂν ἔστι τινὰ 15
ἴδια, καὶ ταῦτ' ἐστὶ περὶ ὧν τοῦ φιλοσόφου ἐπισκέψασθαι

ᵃ 20 τοῖς εἰρημένοις E   ἐστὶ καὶ ἡ ἐναντιότης A^b Al.^{l} Asc.^{c}: ἔν τι
καὶ ἡ ἐναντιότης ἐστί EJΓ   21 διαφορὰ] ἐναντιότης A^b 23 ὅμως
EJΓ Asc. et ut vid. Al.: ὁμοίως A^b γνωρίζειν ἐστί EJΓ   25 ἀναφέρονται τότε ἑτέρας. ἐπεὶ EJΓ   26 ἀναφέρεται recc.: ἀναφέρετε E:
ἀναφέρονται JA^b πρῶτον EJΓ Asc.: πρώτως A^b 30 ἐκεῖνα recc.
32 ὅπερ... ἐλέχθη E^{1}Γ Asc.: om. E^{2}A^b et fort. Al. ^{b} 6 ἀριθμοὶ EJΓ
Asc.^{c}: ἀριθμὸς A^b Al.^{c} γραμμαὶ EJΓ Al.^{c} Asc.^{c}: γραμμὴ A^b
7 ὡς om. A^b 14 ἀβαρεῖ τε EJ Asc.^{c}: καὶ ἀβαρεῖ A^b: καὶ ἀβαρεῖ
τε Eucken   15 οὕτω... 16 ἴδια EJΓ Asc.: om. A^b

τὸ ἀληθές. σημεῖον δέ· οἱ γὰρ διαλεκτικοὶ καὶ σοφισταὶ
τὸ αὐτὸ μὲν ὑποδύονται σχῆμα τῷ φιλοσόφῳ· ἡ γὰρ σοφιστικὴ φαινομένη μόνον σοφία ἐστί, καὶ οἱ διαλεκτικοὶ
20 διαλέγονται περὶ ἁπάντων, κοινὸν δὲ πᾶσι τὸ ὄν ἐστιν,
διαλέγονται δὲ περὶ τούτων δῆλον ὅτι διὰ τὸ τῆς φιλοσοφίας ταῦτα εἶναι οἰκεῖα. περὶ μὲν γὰρ τὸ αὐτὸ γένος στρέ-
φεται ἡ σοφιστικὴ καὶ ἡ διαλεκτικὴ τῇ φιλοσοφίᾳ, ἀλλὰ
διαφέρει τῆς μὲν τῷ τρόπῳ τῆς δυνάμεως, τῆς δὲ τοῦ βίου
25 τῇ προαιρέσει· ἔστι δὲ ἡ διαλεκτικὴ πειραστικὴ περὶ ὧν ἡ
φιλοσοφία γνωριστική, ἡ δὲ σοφιστικὴ φαινομένη, οὖσα δ' οὔ.
    Ἔτι τῶν ἐναντίων ἡ ἑτέρα συστοιχία στέρησις, καὶ πάντα
ἀνάγεται εἰς τὸ ὂν καὶ τὸ μὴ ὄν, καὶ εἰς ἓν καὶ πλῆθος, οἷον
στάσις τοῦ ἑνὸς κίνησις δὲ τοῦ πλήθους· τὰ δ' ὄντα καὶ τὴν
30 οὐσίαν ὁμολογοῦσιν ἐξ ἐναντίων σχεδὸν ἅπαντες συγκεῖσθαι·
πάντες γοῦν τὰς ἀρχὰς ἐναντίας λέγουσιν· οἱ μὲν γὰρ πε-
ριττὸν καὶ ἄρτιον, οἱ δὲ θερμὸν καὶ ψυχρόν, οἱ δὲ πέρας
καὶ ἄπειρον, οἱ δὲ φιλίαν καὶ νεῖκος. πάντα δὲ καὶ τἆλλα
ἀναγόμενα φαίνεται εἰς τὸ ἓν καὶ πλῆθος (εἰλήφθω γὰρ
1005ª ἡ ἀναγωγὴ ἡμῖν), αἱ δ' ἀρχαὶ καὶ παντελῶς αἱ παρὰ τῶν
ἄλλων ὡς εἰς γένη ταῦτα πίπτουσιν. φανερὸν οὖν καὶ ἐκ
τούτων ὅτι μιᾶς ἐπιστήμης τὸ ὂν ᾗ ὂν θεωρῆσαι. πάντα γὰρ
ἢ ἐναντία ἢ ἐξ ἐναντίων, ἀρχαὶ δὲ τῶν ἐναντίων τὸ ἓν
5 καὶ πλῆθος. ταῦτα δὲ μιᾶς ἐπιστήμης, εἴτε καθ' ἓν λέγεται εἴτε μή, ὥσπερ ἴσως ἔχει καὶ τἀληθές. ἀλλ' ὅμως εἰ
καὶ πολλαχῶς λέγεται τὸ ἕν, πρὸς τὸ πρῶτον τἆλλα
λεχθήσεται καὶ τὰ ἐναντία ὁμοίως, [καὶ διὰ τοῦτο] καὶ εἰ
μὴ ἔστι τὸ ὂν ἢ τὸ ἓν καθόλου καὶ ταὐτὸ ἐπὶ πάντων ἢ
10 χωριστόν, ὥσπερ ἴσως οὐκ ἔστιν ἀλλὰ τὰ μὲν πρὸς ἓν τὰ
δὲ τῷ ἐφεξῆς. καὶ διὰ τοῦτο οὐ τοῦ γεωμέτρου θεωρῆσαι τί
τὸ ἐναντίον ἢ τέλειον ἢ ἓν ἢ ὂν ἢ ταὐτὸν ἢ ἕτερον, ἀλλ'

ᵇ 22 ταῦτα εἶναι Aᵇ Asc. : εἶναι αὐτὰ EJΓ   23 ἡ alt. Aᵇ Al.ᶜ
Asc.ᶜ: om. EJ   25 τῇ EJ Al.ᶜ : om. Aᵇ   πείρατι πιστικὴ J
26 ἡ γνωριστικὴ J : γνωστικὴ γρ. J   28 τὸ alt. EJ Asc. : om. Aᵇ
εἰς EJΓ Asc. : om. Aᵇ   30 σχεδὸν E   33 πάντα EJ Asc.ᶜ :
ἅπαντα Aᵇ   34 ἀναγόμενα φαίνεται EJΓ Asc.ᶜ : φαίνεται ἀναγόμενα
Aᵇ   καὶ] καὶ τὸ J   1005ª 2 ταῦτα] εἰς ταῦτα Aᵇ : τὰ αἴτια Asc.
5 καὶ] καὶ τὸ J   δὲ EJΓ Asc.¹ : δὲ καὶ Aᵇ   ἕνα Aᵇ   6 καὶ om.
EJΓ Asc.   7 τὸ ἓν λέγεται Aᵇ   8 καὶ διὰ τοῦτο EJΓ Asc.¹ :
om. Aᵇ   9 ἢ καὶ τὸ Aᵇ   10 τὸ ... τὸ E   12 ἓν ἢ ὂν EJΓ
Asc.ᶜ: ὂν ἢ ἓν Aᵇ

ἢ ἐξ ὑποθέσεως. ὅτι μὲν οὖν μιᾶς ἐπιστήμης τὸ ὂν ᾗ ὂν
θεωρῆσαι καὶ τὰ ὑπάρχοντα αὐτῷ ᾗ ὄν, δῆλον, καὶ ὅτι
οὐ μόνον τῶν οὐσιῶν ἀλλὰ καὶ τῶν ὑπαρχόντων ἡ αὐτὴ 15
θεωρητική, τῶν τε εἰρημένων καὶ περὶ προτέρου καὶ ὑστέρου,
καὶ γένους καὶ εἴδους, καὶ ὅλου καὶ μέρους καὶ τῶν ἄλλων
τῶν τοιούτων.

3 Λεκτέον δὲ πότερον μιᾶς ἢ ἑτέρας ἐπιστήμης περί τε
τῶν ἐν τοῖς μαθήμασι καλουμένων ἀξιωμάτων καὶ περὶ 20
τῆς οὐσίας. φανερὸν δὴ ὅτι μιᾶς τε καὶ τῆς τοῦ φιλοσόφου
καὶ ἡ περὶ τούτων ἐστὶ σκέψις· ἅπασι γὰρ ὑπάρχει τοῖς
οὖσιν ἀλλ' οὐ γένει τινὶ χωρὶς ἰδίᾳ τῶν ἄλλων. καὶ χρῶνται μὲν πάντες, ὅτι τοῦ ὄντος ἐστὶν ᾗ ὄν, ἕκαστον δὲ τὸ γένος
ὄν· ἐπὶ τοσοῦτον δὲ χρῶνται ἐφ' ὅσον αὐτοῖς ἱκανόν, τοῦτο 25
δ' ἔστιν ὅσον ἐπέχει τὸ γένος περὶ οὗ φέρουσι τὰς ἀποδεί-
ξεις· ὥστ' ἐπεὶ δῆλον ὅτι ᾗ ὄντα ὑπάρχει πᾶσι (τοῦτο γὰρ
αὐτοῖς τὸ κοινόν), τοῦ περὶ τὸ ὂν ᾗ ὂν γνωρίζοντος καὶ περὶ
τούτων ἐστὶν ἡ θεωρία. διόπερ οὐδεὶς τῶν κατὰ μέρος ἐπισκο-
πούντων ἐγχειρεῖ λέγειν τι περὶ αὐτῶν, εἰ ἀληθῆ ἢ μή, 30
οὔτε γεωμέτρης οὔτ' ἀριθμητικός, ἀλλὰ τῶν φυσικῶν ἔνιοι,
εἰκότως τοῦτο δρῶντες· μόνοι γὰρ ᾤοντο περί τε τῆς ὅλης
φύσεως σκοπεῖν καὶ περὶ τοῦ ὄντος. ἐπεὶ δ' ἔστιν ἔτι τοῦ
φυσικοῦ τις ἀνωτέρω (ἐν γάρ τι γένος τοῦ ὄντος ἡ φύσις),
τοῦ καθόλου καὶ τοῦ περὶ τὴν πρώτην οὐσίαν θεωρητικοῦ καὶ ἡ 35
περὶ τούτων ἂν εἴη σκέψις· ἔστι δὲ σοφία τις καὶ ἡ φυ- 1005ᵇ
σική, ἀλλ' οὐ πρώτη. ὅσα δ' ἐγχειροῦσι τῶν λεγόντων τινὲς
περὶ τῆς ἀληθείας ὂν τρόπον δεῖ ἀποδέχεσθαι, δι' ἀπαιδευσίαν τῶν ἀναλυτικῶν τοῦτο δρῶσιν· δεῖ γὰρ περὶ τούτων
ἥκειν προεπισταμένους ἀλλὰ μὴ ἀκούοντας ζητεῖν.—ὅτι μὲν 5
οὖν τοῦ φιλοσόφου, καὶ τοῦ περὶ πάσης τῆς οὐσίας θεωροῦντος
ᾗ πέφυκεν, καὶ περὶ τῶν συλλογιστικῶν ἀρχῶν ἐστιν ἐπισκέψασθαι, δῆλον· προσήκει δὲ τὸν μάλιστα γνωρίζοντα
περὶ ἕκαστον γένος ἔχειν λέγειν τὰς βεβαιοτάτας ἀρχὰς

1005ᵃ 19–ᵇ2, cf. K. 4 ᵇ8–34, cf. 1061ᵇ34–1062ᵃ2 (23–26, cf.
1062ᵃ31–35)

ᵃ 21 δὲ Γ   22 τούτων ἐπίσκεψις Aᵇ   24 ὄντως E   25 ὄν]
ἕν Aᵇ¹   30 εἰ] ἤ εἰ E¹: εἰ ἢ E²J   32 τε EJΓ Asc.ᶜ: om. Aᵇ
ᵇ 1 σοφία τις EJΓ Al.ᶜ: τις σοφία Aᵇ   2 ὅσα ... 5 ζητεῖν post
δῆλον l. 8 ponenda censet Al.   8 τὸν om. J

10 τοῦ πράγματος, ὥστε καὶ τὸν περὶ τῶν ὄντων ᾗ ὄντα τὰς
πάντων βεβαιοτάτας. ἔστι δ' οὗτος ὁ φιλόσοφος. βεβαιοτάτη δ' ἀρχὴ πασῶν περὶ ἣν διαψευσθῆναι ἀδύνατον·
γνωριμωτάτην τε γὰρ ἀναγκαῖον εἶναι τὴν τοιαύτην (περὶ
γὰρ ἃ μὴ γνωρίζουσιν ἀπατῶνται πάντες) καὶ ἀνυπόθετον.
15 ἣν γὰρ ἀναγκαῖον ἔχειν τὸν ὁτιοῦν ξυνιέντα τῶν ὄντων, τοῦτο
οὐχ ὑπόθεσις· ὃ δὲ γνωρίζειν ἀναγκαῖον τῷ ὁτιοῦν γνωρί-
ζοντι, καὶ ἥκειν ἔχοντα ἀναγκαῖον. ὅτι μὲν οὖν βεβαιοτάτη
ἡ τοιαύτη πασῶν ἀρχή, δῆλον· τίς δ' ἔστιν αὕτη, μετὰ
ταῦτα λέγωμεν. τὸ γὰρ αὐτὸ ἅμα ὑπάρχειν τε καὶ μὴ
20 ὑπάρχειν ἀδύνατον τῷ αὐτῷ· καὶ κατὰ τὸ αὐτό (καὶ ὅσα
ἄλλα προσδιορισαίμεθ' ἄν, ἔστω προσδιωρισμένα πρὸς τὰς
λογικὰς δυσχερείας)· αὕτη δὴ πασῶν ἐστὶ βεβαιοτάτη τῶν
ἀρχῶν· ἔχει γὰρ τὸν εἰρημένον διορισμόν. ἀδύνατον γὰρ
ὁντινοῦν ταὐτὸν ὑπολαμβάνειν εἶναι καὶ μὴ εἶναι, καθάπερ
25 τινὲς οἴονται λέγειν Ἡράκλειτον. οὐκ ἔστι γὰρ ἀναγκαῖον,
ἅ τις λέγει, ταῦτα καὶ ὑπολαμβάνειν· εἰ δὲ μὴ ἐνδέχεται ἅμα ὑπάρχειν τῷ αὐτῷ τἀναντία (προσδιωρίσθω δ'
ἡμῖν καὶ ταύτῃ τῇ προτάσει τὰ εἰωθότα), ἐναντία δ' ἐστὶ
δόξα δόξῃ ἡ τῆς ἀντιφάσεως, φανερὸν ὅτι ἀδύνατον ἅμα
30 ὑπολαμβάνειν τὸν αὐτὸν εἶναι καὶ μὴ εἶναι τὸ αὐτό· ἅμα
γὰρ ἂν ἔχοι τὰς ἐναντίας δόξας ὁ διεψευσμένος περὶ τούτου. διὸ πάντες οἱ ἀποδεικνύντες εἰς ταύτην ἀνάγουσιν
ἐσχάτην δόξαν· φύσει γὰρ ἀρχὴ καὶ τῶν ἄλλων ἀξιωμάτων αὕτη πάντων.

35 Εἰσὶ δέ τινες οἵ, καθάπερ εἴπομεν, αὐτοί τε ἐνδέχε- 4
1006ᵃ σθαί φασι τὸ αὐτὸ εἶναι καὶ μὴ εἶναι, καὶ ὑπολαμβάνειν οὕτως. χρῶνται δὲ τῷ λόγῳ τούτῳ πολλοὶ καὶ τῶν
περὶ φύσεως. ἡμεῖς δὲ νῦν εἰλήφαμεν ὡς ἀδυνάτου ὄντος
ἅμα εἶναι καὶ μὴ εἶναι, καὶ διὰ τούτου ἐδείξαμεν ὅτι βε-

ᵇ 10 τὰς EJΓ Al.: τὰς περὶ Aᵇ   15 ξυνιόντα Aᵇ   16 ὑποθέσει
Aᵇ   δ] τὸ Aᵇ   17 ἔχοντι E   βεβαιοτάτη ante ἀρχή l. 18 EJΓ
Al.¹   19 λέγωμεν JSTΓ: λέγομεν EAᵇ   τε Aᵇ Al.ᶜ: om. EJ Asc.¹
21 ἔστω τὰ προδίωρισμένα Aᵇ   22 δ' ἁπασῶν EJΓ   27 ὑπάρχειν
τῷ αὐτῷ EJΓ Al.ᶜ: τῷ αὐτῷ ὑπάρχειν Aᵇ   27–28 προδιωρίσθω
ἡμῖν Aᵇ   29 ἀδύνατον ἅμα EJΓ Asc.: ἅμα ἀδύνατον Aᵇ   31 διεψευσμένος Aᵇ Al.: διαψευσάμενος EJ   32 οἱ Aᵇ Al. Asc.ᶜ: om. EJ
35 αὐτοί τε codd. Al.¹: om. Γ   1006ᵃ 2 χρῶνται JAᵇΓ, ex χρῶντο
fecit E

βαιοτάτη αὕτη τῶν ἀρχῶν πασῶν. ἀξιοῦσι δὴ καὶ τοῦτο 5
ἀποδεικνύναι τινὲς δι' ἀπαιδευσίαν· ἔστι γὰρ ἀπαιδευσία
τὸ μὴ γιγνώσκειν τίνων δεῖ ζητεῖν ἀπόδειξιν καὶ τίνων οὐ
δεῖ· ὅλως μὲν γὰρ ἁπάντων ἀδύνατον ἀπόδειξιν εἶναι (εἰς
ἄπειρον γὰρ ἂν βαδίζοι, ὥστε μηδ' οὕτως εἶναι ἀπόδειξιν),
εἰ δέ τινων μὴ δεῖ ζητεῖν ἀπόδειξιν, τίνα ἀξιοῦσιν εἶναι 10
μᾶλλον τοιαύτην ἀρχὴν οὐκ ἂν ἔχοιεν εἰπεῖν. ἔστι δ' ἀποδεῖξαι ἐλεγκτικῶς καὶ περὶ τούτου ὅτι ἀδύνατον, ἂν μόνον
τι λέγῃ ὁ ἀμφισβητῶν· ἂν δὲ μηθέν, γελοῖον τὸ ζητεῖν
λόγον πρὸς τὸν μηθενὸς ἔχοντα λόγον, ᾗ μὴ ἔχει· ὅμοιος
γὰρ φυτῷ ὁ τοιοῦτος ᾗ τοιοῦτος ἤδη. τὸ δ' ἐλεγκτικῶς ἀπο- 15
δεῖξαι λέγω διαφέρειν καὶ τὸ ἀποδεῖξαι, ὅτι ἀποδει-
κνύων μὲν ἂν δόξειεν αἰτεῖσθαι τὸ ἐν ἀρχῇ, ἄλλου δὲ τοῦ
τοιούτου αἰτίου ὄντος ἔλεγχος ἂν εἴη καὶ οὐκ ἀπόδειξις. ἀρχὴ
δὲ πρὸς ἅπαντα τὰ τοιαῦτα οὐ τὸ ἀξιοῦν ἢ εἶναί τι λέγειν
ἢ μὴ εἶναι (τοῦτο μὲν γὰρ τάχ' ἄν τις ὑπολάβοι τὸ ἐξ 20
ἀρχῆς αἰτεῖν), ἀλλὰ σημαίνειν γέ τι καὶ αὑτῷ καὶ ἄλλῳ·
τοῦτο γὰρ ἀνάγκη, εἴπερ λέγοι τι. εἰ γὰρ μή, οὐκ ἂν
εἴη τῷ τοιούτῳ λόγος, οὔτ' αὑτῷ πρὸς αὑτὸν οὔτε πρὸς
ἄλλον. ἂν δέ τις τοῦτο διδῷ, ἔσται ἀπόδειξις· ἤδη γάρ τι
ἔσται ὡρισμένον. ἀλλ' αἴτιος οὐχ ὁ ἀποδεικνὺς ἀλλ' ὁ ὑπο- 25
μένων· ἀναιρῶν γὰρ λόγον ὑπομένει λόγον. ἔτι δὲ ὁ τοῦτο
συγχωρήσας συγκεχώρηκέ τι ἀληθὲς εἶναι χωρὶς ἀποδείξεως [ὥστε οὐκ ἂν πᾶν οὕτως καὶ οὐχ οὕτως ἔχοι].—πρῶτον
μὲν οὖν δῆλον ὡς τοῦτό γ' αὐτὸ ἀληθές, ὅτι σημαίνει τὸ
ὄνομα τὸ εἶναι ἢ μὴ εἶναι τοδί, ὥστ' οὐκ ἂν πᾶν οὕτως καὶ 30
οὐχ οὕτως ἔχοι· ἔτι εἰ τὸ ἄνθρωπος σημαίνει ἕν, ἔστω τοῦτο
τὸ ζῷον δίπουν. λέγω δὲ τὸ ἓν σημαίνειν τοῦτο· εἰ τοῦτ'

1006ᵃ 5-18, cf. K. 1062ᵃ 2-5   18 — 1007ᵃ 20, cf. 1062ᵃ 5-19
(1006ᵇ 28-34, cf. 1062ⁿ 19-23)

ᵃ 5 πασῶν EJ Asc.ᶜ: ἁπασῶν Aᵇ   δὲ Γ   8 ἁπάντων EJ Asc.ᶜ:
πάντων Aᵇ   14 μὴ ἔχει Aᵇ Al.: μηθένα ἔχει λόγον EJΓ   15 ἤδη
Aᵇ Al.: ἤδη ἔστιν JΓ: om. E Asc.   16 ὅτι] ὅτι ὁ EJ   17 ἂν
δόξειεν αἰτεῖσθαι ante διαφέρειν (l. 16) Γ   αἰτῆσθαι Aᵇ   ἀλλ' οὐδὲ
τοῦ Γ   18 αἰτίου om. Aᵇ   19 οὐ EJ γρ. Al.: οὐχὶ Aᵇ: om. Al.
20 γὰρ om. γρ. Al.   21 ἀλλά] ἀλλὰ τὸ recc.   τι om. Aᵇ   αὑτῷ
EJ   23 οὔθ' αὑτῷ EJ   26 ἔτι ... 27 ἀποδείξεως Aᵇ Al.: om. EJΓ
Asc.   28 ὥστε ... ἔχοι Aᵇ Al.¹: om. EJΓ Asc.: cf. l. 30   29 γ']
τ' J   30 πᾶν EJ Asc.ᶜ: ἅπαν Aᵇ   32 τὸ pr. om. J   εἰ] τὸ εἰ Aᵇ

ἔστιν ἄνθρωπος, ἂν ᾖ τι ἄνθρωπος, τοῦτ᾽ ἔσται τὸ ἀνθρώπῳ
εἶναι (διαφέρει δ᾽ οὐθὲν οὐδ᾽ εἰ πλείω τις φαίη σημαίνειν
1006ᵇ μόνον δὲ ὡρισμένα, τεθείη γὰρ ἂν ἐφ᾽ ἑκάστῳ λόγῳ
ἕτερον ὄνομα· λέγω δ᾽ οἷον, εἰ μὴ φαίη τὸ ἄνθρωπος ἓν
σημαίνειν, πολλὰ δέ, ὧν ἑνὸς μὲν εἷς λόγος τὸ ζῷον δίπουν, εἶεν δὲ καὶ ἕτεροι πλείους, ὡρισμένοι δὲ τὸν ἀριθμόν·
5 τεθείη γὰρ ἂν ἴδιον ὄνομα καθ᾽ ἕκαστον τὸν λόγον· εἰ δὲ
μή [τεθείη], ἀλλ᾽ ἄπειρα σημαίνειν φαίη, φανερὸν ὅτι οὐκ ἂν
εἴη λόγος· τὸ γὰρ μὴ ἓν σημαίνειν οὐθὲν σημαίνειν ἐστίν,
μὴ σημαινόντων δὲ τῶν ὀνομάτων ἀνῄρηται τὸ διαλέγεσθαι
πρὸς ἀλλήλους, κατὰ δὲ τὴν ἀλήθειαν καὶ πρὸς αὐτόν·
10 οὐθὲν γὰρ ἐνδέχεται νοεῖν μὴ νοοῦντα ἕν, εἰ δ᾽ ἐνδέχεται,
τεθείη ἂν ὄνομα τούτῳ τῷ πράγματι ἕν).—ἔστω δή, ὥσπερ
ἐλέχθη κατ᾽ ἀρχάς, σημαῖνόν τι τὸ ὄνομα καὶ σημαῖνον
ἕν· οὐ δὴ ἐνδέχεται τὸ ἀνθρώπῳ εἶναι σημαίνειν ὅπερ ἀνθρώπῳ
μὴ εἶναι, εἰ τὸ ἄνθρωπος σημαίνει μὴ μόνον καθ᾽ ἑνὸς
15 ἀλλὰ καὶ ἕν (οὐ γὰρ τοῦτο ἀξιοῦμεν τὸ ἓν σημαίνειν,
τὸ καθ᾽ ἑνός, ἐπεὶ οὕτω γε κἂν τὸ μουσικὸν καὶ τὸ λευκὸν
καὶ τὸ ἄνθρωπος ἓν ἐσήμαινεν, ὥστε ἓν ἅπαντα ἔσται·
συνώνυμα γάρ). καὶ οὐκ ἔσται εἶναι καὶ μὴ εἶναι τὸ αὐτὸ
ἀλλ᾽ ἢ καθ᾽ ὁμωνυμίαν, ὥσπερ ἂν εἰ ὃν ἡμεῖς ἄνθρωπον
20 καλοῦμεν, ἄλλοι μὴ ἄνθρωπον καλοῖεν· τὸ δ᾽ ἀπορούμενον
οὐ τοῦτό ἐστιν, εἰ ἐνδέχεται τὸ αὐτὸ ἅμα εἶναι καὶ μὴ εἶναι
ἄνθρωπον τὸ ὄνομα, ἀλλὰ τὸ πρᾶγμα. εἰ δὲ μὴ σημαίνει ἕτερον τὸ ἄνθρωπος καὶ τὸ μὴ ἄνθρωπος, δῆλον ὅτι καὶ
τὸ μὴ εἶναι ἀνθρώπῳ τοῦ εἶναι ἀνθρώπῳ, ὥστ᾽ ἔσται τὸ ἀν-
25 θρώπῳ εἶναι μὴ ἀνθρώπῳ εἶναι· ἓν γὰρ ἔσται. τοῦτο γὰρ
σημαίνει τὸ εἶναι ἕν, τὸ ὡς λώπιον καὶ ἱμάτιον, εἰ ὁ λόγος

ᵃ 33 ἄνθρωπος EJΓ Asc.ᶜ: om. Aᵇ et ut vid. Al.   ᾖ] εἰ Aᵇ   ἔσται
Aᵇ Al.: ἐστὶ EJΓ Asc.ᶜ   τὸ JAᵇ, ex τῶι fecit E   34 εἰ EJΓ
Asc.: εἰ ἐπὶ Aᵇ: εἰ ἔτι ci. Christ   ᵇ 1 λόγῳ EJ Asc.ᶜ: τῷ λόγῳ
Aᵇ   2 τὸν ἄνθρωπον EJΓ Asc.   3 ἑνὸς μὲν εἷς EJΓ Asc.: εἷς
μὲν εἴη Aᵇ   τὸ ζῷον τὸ δίπουν J   4 εἰσὶ EJΓ Asc.   5 τῶν
λόγων E   6 τεθείη codd. ΓAl. Asc.: secl. Gomperz   7 ἓν]
ἕν τι recc.   ἐστίν om. E¹   9 αὑτόν ΓAsc.ᶜ i et fort. Al.: αὐτόν
codd. Al.ᶜ   10 οὐδὲ Al.   μὴ Aᵇ Al.: μηθὲν EJΓ   12 κατ᾽]
καὶ κατ᾽ E   σημαίνειν τι Aᵇ   13 ὅπερ EJΓ Al.ᶜ: om. Aᵇ
13-14 μὴ εἶναι ἀνθρώπῳ EJΓ   16 τὸ tert. et 17 τὸ Aᵇ Al. Asc.:
om. EJ   21 τὸ αὐτὸ ἅμα Aᵇ Al.ᶜ: ἅμα τὸ αὐτὸ EJ Asc.ᶜ: ἅμα Γ
26 τὸ εἶναι EJΓ Asc.ᶜ: om. Aᵇ   τὸ om. EJ

εἷς· εἰ δὲ ἔσται ἕν, ἐν σημανεῖ τὸ ἀνθρώπῳ εἶναι καὶ μὴ
ἀνθρώπῳ. ἀλλ' ἐδέδεικτο ὅτι ἕτερον σημαίνει. ἀνάγκη τοίνυν, εἴ τί ἐστιν ἀληθὲς εἰπεῖν ὅτι ἄνθρωπος, ζῷον εἶναι δίπουν (τοῦτο γὰρ ἦν ὃ ἐσήμαινε τὸ ἄνθρωπος)· εἰ δ' ἀνάγκη 30
τοῦτο, οὐκ ἐνδέχεται μὴ εἶναι ⟨τότε⟩ τὸ αὐτὸ ζῷον δίπουν (τοῦτο
γὰρ σημαίνει τὸ ἀνάγκη εἶναι, τὸ ἀδύνατον εἶναι μὴ εἶναι
[ἄνθρωπον])· οὐκ ἄρα ἐνδέχεται ἅμα ἀληθὲς εἶναι εἰπεῖν τὸ
αὐτὸ ἄνθρωπον εἶναι καὶ μὴ εἶναι ἄνθρωπον. ὁ δ' αὐτὸς
λόγος καὶ ἐπὶ τοῦ μὴ εἶναι ἄνθρωπον· τὸ γὰρ ἀνθρώπῳ 1007ᵃ
εἶναι καὶ τὸ μὴ ἀνθρώπῳ εἶναι ἕτερον σημαίνει, εἴπερ καὶ
τὸ λευκὸν εἶναι καὶ τὸ ἄνθρωπον εἶναι ἕτερον· πολὺ γὰρ
ἀντίκειται ἐκεῖνο μᾶλλον, ὥστε σημαίνειν ἕτερον. εἰ δὲ καὶ
τὸ λευκὸν φήσει τὸ αὐτὸ καὶ ἓν σημαίνειν, πάλιν τὸ αὐτὸ 5
ἐροῦμεν ὅπερ καὶ πρότερον ἐλέχθη, ὅτι ἓν πάντα ἔσται καὶ οὐ
μόνον τὰ ἀντικείμενα. εἰ δὲ μὴ ἐνδέχεται τοῦτο, συμβαίνει τὸ λεχθέν, ἂν ἀποκρίνηται τὸ ἐρωτώμενον. ἐὰν δὲ
προστιθῇ ἐρωτῶντος ἁπλῶς καὶ τὰς ἀποφάσεις, οὐκ ἀποκρί-
νεται τὸ ἐρωτώμενον. οὐθὲν γὰρ κωλύει εἶναι τὸ αὐτὸ καὶ 10
ἄνθρωπον καὶ λευκὸν καὶ ἄλλα μυρία τὸ πλῆθος· ἀλλ'
ὅμως ἐρομένου εἰ ἀληθὲς εἰπεῖν ἄνθρωπον τοῦτο εἶναι ἢ οὔ,
ἀποκριτέον τὸ ἓν σημαῖνον καὶ οὐ προσθετέον ὅτι καὶ λευκὸν καὶ μέγα. καὶ γὰρ ἀδύνατον ἄπειρά γ' ὄντα τὰ
συμβεβηκότα διελθεῖν· ἢ οὖν ἅπαντα διελθέτω ἢ μηθέν. 15
ὁμοίως τοίνυν εἰ καὶ μυριάκις ἐστὶ τὸ αὐτὸ ἄνθρωπος καὶ
οὐκ ἄνθρωπος, οὐ προσαποκριτέον τῷ ἐρομένῳ εἰ ἔστιν ἄνθρωπος, ὅτι ἐστὶν ἅμα καὶ οὐκ ἄνθρωπος, εἰ μὴ καὶ τἆλλα
ὅσα συμβέβηκε προσαποκριτέον, ὅσα ἐστὶν ἢ μὴ ἔστιν· ἐὰν
δὲ τοῦτο ποιῇ, οὐ διαλέγεται.—ὅλως δ' ἀναιροῦσιν οἱ τοῦτο λέ- 20
γοντες οὐσίαν καὶ τὸ τί ἦν εἶναι. πάντα γὰρ ἀνάγκη συμβεβηκέναι φάσκειν αὐτοῖς, καὶ τὸ ὅπερ ἀνθρώπῳ εἶναι ἢ
ζῴῳ εἶναι μὴ εἶναι. εἰ γὰρ ἔσται τι ὅπερ ἀνθρώπῳ εἶναι,

ᵇ 27 σημανεῖ ex Al. scripsi : σημαίνει codd. Γ 31 τοῦτο E²AᵇΓ Asc.ᶜ:
τότε E¹J   τότε τὸ fort. Al., ci. Bonitz: τὸ Aᵇ: τότε EJ Asc.
33 ἄνθρωπον om. fort. Al., secl. Christ 34 δ' αὐτὸς EJ Asc.ˡᶜ: αὐτὸς
δὲ Aᵇ Al.¹ 1007ᵃ 1 εἶναι ἄνθρωπον] ἄνθρωπον εἶναι Christ 4 σημαίνει
Aᵇ 5 φησι Aᵇ 6 ἔσται Al. Bonitz: ἐστὶ codd. Γ 9 ἀποκρινεῖται fort.
Al. 10 τὸ αὐτὸ εἶναι Aᵇ 12 ἐρωμένου E 15 ἅπαντα EJΓ Asc.:
τὰ ἄπειρα πάντα Aᵇ διελθετέον Aᵇ 17 ἐρωμένωι E 18 ἅμα] ἀλλὰ
Aᵇ 21 εἶναι μὴ εἶναι Aᵇ 22 ἢ . . . 23 εἶναι tert. om. E¹ 23 μὴ
εἶναι E²JΓ Asc.: τί ἦν εἶναι μὴ εἶναι Al. : μὴ εἶναι τί ἦν εἶναι τινος Aᵇ

τοῦτο οὐκ ἔσται μὴ ἀνθρώπῳ εἶναι ἢ μὴ εἶναι ἀνθρώπῳ
25 (καίτοι αὗται ἀποφάσεις τούτου)· ἐν γὰρ ἦν ὃ ἐσήμαινε,
καὶ ἦν τοῦτό τινος οὐσία. τὸ δ' οὐσίαν σημαίνειν ἐστὶν
ὅτι οὐκ ἄλλο τι τὸ εἶναι αὐτῷ. εἰ δ' ἔσται αὐτῷ τὸ
ὅπερ ἀνθρώπῳ εἶναι ἢ ὅπερ μὴ ἀνθρώπῳ εἶναι ἢ ὅπερ
μὴ εἶναι ἀνθρώπῳ, ἄλλο ἔσται, ὥστ' ἀναγκαῖον αὐτοῖς
30 λέγειν ὅτι οὐθενὸς ἔσται τοιοῦτος λόγος, ἀλλὰ πάντα
κατὰ συμβεβηκός· τούτῳ γὰρ διώρισται οὐσία καὶ τὸ συμ-
βεβηκός· τὸ γὰρ λευκὸν τῷ ἀνθρώπῳ συμβέβηκεν ὅτι
ἔστι μὲν λευκὸς ἀλλ' οὐχ ὅπερ λευκόν. εἰ δὲ πάντα κατὰ
συμβεβηκὸς λέγεται, οὐθὲν ἔσται πρῶτον τὸ καθ' οὗ, εἰ ἀεὶ
35 τὸ συμβεβηκὸς καθ' ὑποκειμένου τινὸς σημαίνει τὴν κατη-
1007ᵇ γορίαν. ἀνάγκη ἄρα εἰς ἄπειρον ἰέναι. ἀλλ' ἀδύνατον· οὐδὲ
γὰρ πλείω συμπλέκεται δυοῖν· τὸ γὰρ συμβεβηκὸς οὐ
συμβεβηκότι συμβεβηκός, εἰ μὴ ὅτι ἄμφω συμβέβηκε
ταὐτῷ, λέγω δ' οἷον τὸ λευκὸν μουσικὸν καὶ τοῦτο λευκὸν
5 ὅτι ἄμφω τῷ ἀνθρώπῳ συμβέβηκεν. ἀλλ' οὐχ ὁ Σωκράτης μουσικὸς οὕτως, ὅτι ἄμφω συμβέβηκεν ἑτέρῳ τινί. ἐπεὶ
τοίνυν τὰ μὲν οὕτως τὰ δ' ἐκείνως λέγεται συμβεβηκότα,
ὅσα οὕτως λέγεται ὡς τὸ λευκὸν τῷ Σωκράτει, οὐκ ἐνδέχεται ἄπειρα εἶναι ἐπὶ τὸ ἄνω, οἷον τῷ Σωκράτει τῷ λευκῷ
10 ἕτερόν τι συμβεβηκός· οὐ γὰρ γίγνεταί τι ἐν ἐξ ἁπάντων.
οὐδὲ δὴ τῷ λευκῷ ἕτερόν τι ἔσται συμβεβηκός, οἷον τὸ μου-
σικόν· οὐθέν τε γὰρ μᾶλλον τοῦτο ἐκείνῳ ἢ ἐκεῖνο τούτῳ
συμβέβηκεν, καὶ ἅμα διώρισται ὅτι τὰ μὲν οὕτω συμβέβηκε τὰ δ' ὡς τὸ μουσικὸν Σωκράτει· ὅσα δ' οὕτως, οὐ
15 συμβεβηκότι συμβέβηκε συμβεβηκός, ἀλλ' ὅσα ἐκείνως,
ὥστ' οὐ πάντα κατὰ συμβεβηκὸς λεχθήσεται. ἔσται
ἄρα τι καὶ ὡς οὐσίαν σημαῖνον. εἰ δὲ τοῦτο, δέδεικται ὅτι
ἀδύνατον ἅμα κατηγορεῖσθαι τὰς ἀντιφάσεις.—ἔτι εἰ ἀλη-

1007ᵇ 18 – 1008ᵃ 2, cf. 1062ᵃ 23·30

ᵃ 25 καίτοι αὗται EJΓ Asc. : καὶ τοιαῦται Aᵇ Al.   ἐσήμαινε Aᵇᴳ
Al.ᶜ : εἰσήμηνε EJ   26 ἐστὶν] αὐτῆς ἐστὶν Aᵇ   27 αὐτῷ τὸ EJΓ
Al. : τι Aᵇ   28 ἢ Aᵇ Al. Asc.ᶜ : om. EJΓ   μὴ ἀνθρώπῳ EJΓ Al.
Asc.ᶜ : ἀνθρώπῳ μὴ Aᵇ   29 εἴη J   ἄλλο EJΓ Al. Asc. : ἄλλο τι
Aᵇ Al.ᶜ   31 τούτῳ … συμβεβηκός om. E¹   34 καθ' οὗ ci. Al. :
καθόλου codd. Γ Al. Asc.   εἰ Aᵇ Al. : εἰ δ' EJΓ Asc.ᶜ   ᵇ 2 πλείω
EJΓ Asc. : δύο Aᵇ   6 οὗτος J   13 τούτῳ Aᵇ   15 συμβέβηκε
EJ Asc.ᶜ : συμβέβηκε τὸ recc. : accidit Γ : om. Aᵇ   17 ὡς scripsi :
ὡς codd. Γ

θεὶς αἱ ἀντιφάσεις ἅμα κατὰ τοῦ αὐτοῦ πᾶσαι, δῆλον· ὡς
ἅπαντα ἔσται ἕν. ἔσται γὰρ τὸ αὐτὸ καὶ τριήρης καὶ τοῖ- 20
χος καὶ ἄνθρωπος, εἰ κατὰ παντός τι ἢ καταφῆσαι ἢ
ἀποφῆσαι ἐνδέχεται, καθάπερ ἀνάγκη τοῖς τὸν Πρωταγόρου λέγουσι λόγον. εἰ γάρ τῳ δοκεῖ μὴ εἶναι τριήρης ὁ
ἄνθρωπος, δῆλον ὡς οὐκ ἔστι τριήρης· ὥστε καὶ ἔστιν, εἴπερ
ἡ ἀντίφασις ἀληθής. καὶ γίγνεται δὴ τὸ τοῦ Ἀναξαγόρου, 25
ὁμοῦ πάντα χρήματα· ὥστε μηθὲν ἀληθῶς ὑπάρχειν. τὸ
ἀόριστον οὖν ἐοίκασι λέγειν, καὶ οἰόμενοι τὸ ὂν λέγειν περὶ
τοῦ μὴ ὄντος λέγουσιν· τὸ γὰρ δυνάμει ὂν καὶ μὴ ἐντελεχείᾳ τὸ ἀόριστόν ἐστιν. ἀλλὰ μὴν λεκτέον γ᾽ αὐτοῖς κατὰ
παντὸς ⟨παντὸς⟩ τὴν κατάφασιν ἢ τὴν ἀπόφασιν· ἄτοπον γὰρ 30
εἰ ἑκάστῳ ἡ μὲν αὐτοῦ ἀπόφασις ὑπάρξει, ἡ δ᾽ ἑτέρου ὃ μὴ
ὑπάρχει αὐτῷ οὐχ ὑπάρξει· λέγω δ᾽ οἷον εἰ ἀληθὲς εἰπεῖν τὸν
ἄνθρωπον ὅτι οὐκ ἄνθρωπος, δῆλον ὅτι καὶ ἢ τριήρης ἢ οὐ
τριήρης. εἰ μὲν οὖν ἡ κατάφασις, ἀνάγκη καὶ τὴν ἀπόφασιν·
εἰ δὲ μὴ ὑπάρχει ἡ κατάφασις, ἥ γε ἀπόφασις ὑπάρξει 35
μᾶλλον ἢ ἡ αὐτοῦ. εἰ οὖν κἀκείνη ὑπάρχει, ὑπάρξει καὶ ἡ 1008ᵃ
τῆς τριήρους· εἰ δ᾽ αὕτη, καὶ ἡ κατάφασις.—ταῦτά τε οὖν
συμβαίνει τοῖς λέγουσι τὸν λόγον τοῦτον, καὶ ὅτι οὐκ ἀνάγκη
ἢ φάναι ἢ ἀποφάναι. εἰ γὰρ ἀληθὲς ὅτι ἄνθρωπος καὶ
οὐκ ἄνθρωπος, δῆλον ὅτι καὶ οὔτ᾽ ἄνθρωπος οὔτ᾽ οὐκ ἄν- 5
θρωπος ἔσται· τοῖν γὰρ δυοῖν δύο ἀποφάσεις, εἰ δὲ μία
ἐξ ἀμφοῖν ἐκείνη, καὶ αὕτη μία ἂν εἴη ἀντικειμένη.—ἔτι
ἤτοι περὶ ἅπαντα οὕτως ἔχει, καὶ ἔστι καὶ λευκὸν καὶ οὐ
λευκὸν καὶ ὂν καὶ οὐκ ὄν, καὶ περὶ τὰς ἄλλας φάσεις καὶ
ἀποφάσεις ὁμοιοτρόπως, ἢ οὒ ἀλλὰ περὶ μέν τινας, περί 10
τινας δ᾽ οὔ. καὶ εἰ μὲν μὴ περὶ πάσας, αὗται ἂν εἶεν·

1008ᵃ 4–7, cf. 1062ᵃ 36 — ᵇ 7

ᵇ 21 τι ΕJΓ Asc.¹: om. Aᵇ   23 λέγουσι λόγον ΕJΓ Asc.ᶜ: λόγον
λέγουσι Aᵇ Al.ᶜ   δοκεῖν Aᵇ   24 ὡς Aᵇ Al.ᶜ: ὅτι ΕJ   ἔσται
recc.   ἔσται Al.   25 ἢ] ἦν ἡ Aᵇ   26 ὑπάρχειν JAᵇ Asc.·
ἐνυπάρχειν Ε: ἐν ὑπάρχειν Γ   27 καὶ . . . λέγειν om. J   τὸ ὂν
λέγειν ΕΓ Al.¹ Asc.ᶜ: λέγειν τὸ ὂν Aᵇ   30 παντὸς ex Al. ci. Bonitz:
om. codd. Γ Al.¹ Asc.   31 αὐτοῦ Christ   ὑπάρχει Γ   32 τὸν
ἄνθρωπον ΕJ Asc.ᶜ: τὸ ἄνθρωπος Aᵇ   33 ἢ τριήρης ἢ om. ΕJΓ Al. Asc.
edd.   1008ᵃ 1 ἢ ἢ ΕJΓ Al.: om. Aᵇ   4 ὅτι] ἔστιν ὅτι Aᵇ   7 ἀμφοῖν
Aᵇ Al.: ἀμφοτέρων ΕJ Asc.   ἐκείνη Γ   ἔτι] τι Aᵇ   10 μὲν
περὶ Aᵇ

F

ὁμολογούμεναι· εἰ δὲ περὶ πάσας, πάλιν ἤτοι καθ' ὅσων τὸ
φῆσαι καὶ ἀποφῆσαι καὶ καθ' ὅσων ἀποφῆσαι καὶ φῆσαι,
ἢ κατὰ μὲν ὧν φῆσαι καὶ ἀποφῆσαι, καθ' ὅσων δὲ ἀπο-
15 φῆσαι οὐ πάντων φῆσαι. καὶ εἰ μὲν οὕτως, εἴη ἄν τι πα-
γίως οὐκ ὄν, καὶ αὕτη βεβαία δόξα, καὶ εἰ τὸ μὴ εἶναι
βέβαιόν τι καὶ γνώριμον, γνωριμωτέρα ἂν εἴη ἡ φάσις ἡ ἀντικειμένη· εἰ δὲ ὁμοίως καὶ ὅσα ἀποφῆσαι φάναι, ἀνάγκη ἤτοι ἀληθὲς διαιροῦντα λέγειν, οἷον ὅτι
20 λευκὸν καὶ πάλιν ὅτι οὐ λευκόν, ἢ οὔ. καὶ εἰ μὲν
μὴ ἀληθὲς διαιροῦντα λέγειν, οὐ λέγει τε ταῦτα καὶ
οὐκ ἔστιν οὐθέν (τὰ δὲ μὴ ὄντα πῶς ἂν φθέγξαιτο ἢ
βαδίσειεν;), καὶ πάντα δ' ἂν εἴη ἕν, ὥσπερ καὶ πρότερον
εἴρηται, καὶ ταὐτὸν ἔσται καὶ ἄνθρωπος καὶ θεὸς καὶ τριή-
25 ρης καὶ αἱ ἀντιφάσεις αὐτῶν (εἰ γὰρ ὁμοίως καθ' ἕκαστον,
οὐδὲν διοίσει ἕτερον ἑτέρου· εἰ γὰρ διοίσει, τοῦτ' ἔσται ἀληθὲς
καὶ ἴδιον)· ὁμοίως δὲ καὶ εἰ διαιροῦντα ἐνδέχεται ἀληθεύειν,
συμβαίνει τὸ λεχθέν, πρὸς δὲ τούτῳ ὅτι πάντες ἂν ἀληθεύοιεν καὶ πάντες ἂν ψεύδοιντο, καὶ αὐτὸς αὑτὸν ὁμο-
30 λογεῖ ψεύδεσθαι. ἅμα δὲ φανερὸν ὅτι περὶ οὐθενός ἐστι
πρὸς τοῦτον ἡ σκέψις· οὐθὲν γὰρ λέγει. οὔτε γὰρ οὕτως οὔτ'
οὐχ οὕτως λέγει, ἀλλ' οὕτως τε καὶ οὐχ οὕτως· καὶ πάλιν
γε ταῦτα ἀπόφησιν ἄμφω, ὅτι οὔθ' οὕτως οὔτε οὐχ οὕτως· εἰ
γὰρ μή, ἤδη ἄν τι εἴη ὡρισμένον.—ἔτι εἰ ὅταν ἡ φάσις
35 ἀληθὴς ᾖ, ἡ ἀπόφασις ψευδής, κἂν αὕτη ἀληθὴς ᾖ, ἡ
κατάφασις ψευδής, οὐκ ἂν εἴη τὸ αὐτὸ ἅμα φάναι καὶ
1008ᵇ ἀποφάναι ἀληθῶς. ἀλλ' ἴσως φαῖεν ἂν τοῦτ' εἶναι τὸ ἐξ
ἀρχῆς κείμενον.—ἔτι ἆρα ὁ μὲν ἢ ἔχειν πως ὑπολαμβάνων ἢ μὴ ἔχειν διέψευσται, ὁ δὲ ἄμφω ἀληθεύει; εἰ γὰρ
ἀληθεύει, τί ἂν εἴη τὸ λεγόμενον ὅτι τοιαύτη τῶν ὄντων ἡ

ᵃ 15 πάντως Ε   17 ἂν EJΓ Al. : γὰρ ἂν Aᵇ   18 ἡ ἀντικειμένη
EJ Al. : ἢ ἡ ἀντικειμένη ἀντίφασις AᵇΓ Asc.   δὲ] δὲ τῷ ἀποφάναι Γ
ὅσα EJΓ Al. Asc.¹: ὧν ἔστιν Aᵇ   φάναι EJ Al. Asc.¹: κατὰ τούτων ἔστι φάναι Aᵇ: φάναι κατὰ τούτων Γ   21 λέγει Aᵇ   οὐ λέγει
om. J   23 βαδίσειεν EJΓ Al. Asc. : νοήσειε Aᵇ   πάντα EJ Asc. :
ἅπαντα Aᵇ   25 εἰ δ' EJΓ Al. Asc.   26 οὐδὲν EJ Asc.ᶜ: οὐδενὶ
Aᵇ   28 ἀληθεύοιεν EJ Asc.¹: ἀληθεύσειεν Aᵇ: ἀληθεύσαιεν Al.¹
31 τούτῳ Γ   33 οὔτε] οὔτε οὔτε Aᵇ   34 εἴη] πω Aᵇ   35 ᾖ alt.
om. AᵇΓ   36 τὸ αὐτὸ ἅμα Aᵇ Asc. : ἅμα τὸ αὐτὸ EJΓ   ᵇ 3 γὰρ]
γὰρ μὴ Aᵇ Al. Asc.   4 λεγόμενον ; ἢ ὅτι fort. Al.

φύσις; εἰ δὲ μὴ ἀληθεύει, ἀλλὰ μᾶλλον ἀληθεύει ἢ ὁ ἐκεί- 5
νως ὑπολαμβάνων, ἤδη πως ἔχοι ἂν τὰ ὄντα, καὶ τοῦτ'
ἀληθὲς ἂν εἴη, καὶ οὐχ ἅμα καὶ οὐκ ἀληθές. εἰ δὲ ὁμοίως
ἅπαντες καὶ ψεύδονται καὶ ἀληθῆ λέγουσιν, οὔτε φθέγξα-
σθαι οὔτ' εἰπεῖν τῷ τοιούτῳ ἔσται· ἅμα γὰρ ταῦτά τε καὶ
οὐ ταῦτα λέγει. εἰ δὲ μηθὲν ὑπολαμβάνει ἀλλ' ὁμοίως 10
οἴεται καὶ οὐκ οἴεται, τί ἂν διαφερόντως ἔχοι τῶν γε φυτῶν; ὅθεν καὶ μάλιστα φανερόν ἐστιν ὅτι οὐδεὶς οὕτω διάκειται οὔτε τῶν ἄλλων οὔτε τῶν λεγόντων τὸν λόγον τοῦτον.
διὰ τί γὰρ βαδίζει Μέγαράδε ἀλλ' οὐχ ἡσυχάζει, οἰόμενος βαδίζειν δεῖν; οὐδ' εὐθέως ἕωθεν πορεύεται εἰς φρέαρ ἢ εἰς 15
φάραγγα, ἐὰν τύχῃ, ἀλλὰ φαίνεται εὐλαβούμενος, ὡς οὐχ
ὁμοίως οἰόμενος μὴ ἀγαθὸν εἶναι τὸ ἐμπεσεῖν καὶ ἀγαθόν;
δῆλον ἄρα ὅτι τὸ μὲν βέλτιον ὑπολαμβάνει τὸ δ' οὐ βέλτιον. εἰ δὲ τοῦτο, καὶ τὸ μὲν ἄνθρωπον τὸ δ' οὐκ ἄνθρωπον
καὶ τὸ μὲν γλυκὺ τὸ δ' οὐ γλυκὺ ἀνάγκη ὑπολαμβάνειν. 20
οὐ γὰρ ἐξ ἴσου ἅπαντα ζητεῖ καὶ ὑπολαμβάνει, ὅταν οἰη-
θεὶς βέλτιον εἶναι τὸ πιεῖν ὕδωρ καὶ ἰδεῖν ἄνθρωπον εἶτα
ζητῇ αὐτά· καίτοι ἔδει γε, εἰ ταὐτὸν ἦν ὁμοίως καὶ ἄνθρωπος καὶ οὐκ ἄνθρωπος. ἀλλ' ὅπερ ἐλέχθη, οὐθεὶς ὃς οὐ
φαίνεται τὰ μὲν εὐλαβούμενος τὰ δ' οὔ· ὥστε, ὡς ἔοικε, 25
πάντες ὑπολαμβάνουσιν ἔχειν ἁπλῶς, εἰ μὴ περὶ ἅπαντα,
ἀλλὰ περὶ τὸ ἄμεινον καὶ χεῖρον. εἰ δὲ μὴ ἐπιστάμενοι
ἀλλὰ δοξάζοντες, πολὺ μᾶλλον ἐπιμελητέον ἂν εἴη τῆς
ἀληθείας, ὥσπερ καὶ νοσώδει ὄντι ἢ ὑγιεινῷ τῆς ὑγιείας·
καὶ γὰρ ὁ δοξάζων πρὸς τὸν ἐπιστάμενον οὐχ ὑγιεινῶς διά- 30
κειται πρὸς τὴν ἀλήθειαν.—ἔτι εἰ ὅτι μάλιστα πάντα οὕτως
ἔχει καὶ οὐχ οὕτως, ἀλλὰ τό γε μᾶλλον καὶ ἧττον ἔνεστιν
ἐν τῇ φύσει τῶν ὄντων· οὐ γὰρ ἂν ὁμοίως φήσαιμεν εἶναι
τὰ δύο ἄρτια καὶ τὰ τρία, οὐδ' ὁμοίως διέψευσται ὁ τὰ

1008ᵇ 12–27, cf. 1063ᵃ 28–35

ᵇ 5 ἢ Aᵇ Al.: om. EJΓ Asc.   8 καὶ οὐκ ἀληθῆ E   9 ἔστιν
EJΓ Asc.   ταυτά ... 10 ταυτὰ EJ   11 γε φυτῶν ci. Bonitz : πεφυκότων E¹JAᵇ: φυτῶν E²Γ Al. Asc.   15 δεῖν Aᵇ Al.: om. EJΓ
Asc. edd.   εὐθὺς Aᵇ   ἢ εἰς Aᵇ Al. Asc.: ἢ EJΓ   17 τὸ om. E
20 post ἀνάγκη add. ὡρισμένως E²   23 ζητῇ J et fecit E: ζητεῖ Aᵇ
ἔδει γε EJ Asc.: γ' ἔδει Aᵇ   32 ἔν ἐστιν J   34 δύο] δύο
εἶναι Aᵇ

35 τέτταρα πέντε οἰόμενος καὶ ὁ χίλια. εἰ οὖν μὴ ὁμοίως,
δῆλον ὅτι ἄτερος ἧττον, ὥστε μᾶλλον ἀληθεύει. εἰ οὖν τὸ
1009ᵃ μᾶλλον ἐγγύτερον, εἴη γε ἄν τι ἀληθὲς οὗ ἐγγύτερον τὸ
μᾶλλον ἀληθές. κἂν εἰ μὴ ἔστιν, ἀλλ' ἤδη γέ τι ἔστι βε-
βαιότερον καὶ ἀληθινώτερον, καὶ τοῦ λόγου ἀπηλλαγμέ-
νοι ἂν εἴημεν τοῦ ἀκράτου καὶ κωλύοντός τι τῇ διανοίᾳ
5 ὁρίσαι.

Ἔστι δ' ἀπὸ τῆς αὐτῆς δόξης καὶ ὁ Πρωταγόρου λόγος, 5
καὶ ἀνάγκη ὁμοίως αὐτοὺς ἄμφω ἢ εἶναι ἢ μὴ εἶναι· εἴτε
γὰρ τὰ δοκοῦντα πάντα ἐστὶν ἀληθῆ καὶ τὰ φαινόμενα,
ἀνάγκη εἶναι πάντα ἅμα ἀληθῆ καὶ ψευδῆ (πολλοὶ γὰρ
10 τἀναντία ὑπολαμβάνουσιν ἀλλήλοις, καὶ τοὺς μὴ ταὐτὰ
δοξάζοντας ἑαυτοῖς διεψεῦσθαι νομίζουσιν· ὥστ' ἀνάγκη τὸ
αὐτὸ εἶναί τε καὶ μὴ εἶναι), καὶ εἰ τοῦτ' ἔστιν, ἀνάγκη τὰ
δοκοῦντα εἶναι πάντ' ἀληθῆ (τὰ ἀντικείμενα γὰρ δοξάζουσιν
ἀλλήλοις οἱ διεψευσμένοι καὶ ἀληθεύοντες· εἰ οὖν ἔχει τὰ
15 ὄντα οὕτως, ἀληθεύσουσι πάντες). ὅτι μὲν οὖν ἀπὸ τῆς αὐτῆς
εἰσὶ διανοίας ἀμφότεροι οἱ λόγοι, δῆλον· ἔστι δ' οὐχ ὁ
αὐτὸς τρόπος πρὸς ἅπαντας τῆς ἐντεύξεως· οἱ μὲν γὰρ πει-
θοῦς δέονται οἱ δὲ βίας. ὅσοι μὲν γὰρ ἐκ τοῦ ἀπορῆσαι
ὑπέλαβον οὕτως, τούτων εὔιατος ἡ ἄγνοια (οὐ γὰρ πρὸς τὸν
20 λόγον ἀλλὰ πρὸς τὴν διάνοιαν ἡ ἀπάντησις αὐτῶν)· ὅσοι
δὲ λόγου χάριν λέγουσι, τούτων δ' ἔλεγχος ἴασις τοῦ ἐν τῇ
φωνῇ λόγου καὶ τοῦ ἐν τοῖς ὀνόμασιν. ἐλήλυθε δὲ τοῖς δια-
ποροῦσιν αὕτη ἡ δόξα ἐκ τῶν αἰσθητῶν, ἡ μὲν τοῦ ἅμα
τὰς ἀντιφάσεις καὶ τἀναντία ὑπάρχειν ὁρῶσιν ἐκ ταὐτοῦ
25 γιγνόμενα τἀναντία· εἰ οὖν μὴ ἐνδέχεται γίγνεσθαι τὸ μὴ
ὄν, προϋπῆρχεν ὁμοίως τὸ πρᾶγμα ἄμφω ὄν, ὥσπερ καὶ
Ἀναξαγόρας μεμῖχθαι πᾶν ἐν παντί φησι καὶ Δημόκρι-
τος· καὶ γὰρ οὗτος τὸ κενὸν καὶ τὸ πλῆρες ὁμοίως καθ'

1009ᵃ 6-16, 22-30, cf. 1062ᵇ 12-24   16-22, 1011ᵃ 3-16, cf.
1063ᵇ 7-16

ᵇ 35 πάντα E   1009ᵃ 1 τι om. Aᵇ   6 ἔτι Christ   7 ἄμφω
αὐτοὺς EJ   9 εἶναι πάντα . . . ψευδῆ Aᵇ Al. : πάντα . . . ψευδῆ εἶναι
EJΓ Asc.   15 ἀληθεύουσι EJΓ Asc.   15-16 ἀπὸ τῆς αὐτῆς
εἴη Asc.¹ : εἰσὶν ἀπὸ τῆς αὐτῆς Aᵇ   16 ἀμφότεροι οἱ] οἱ τοιοῦτοι Aᵇ
17 ἅπαντας EJ Asc.ᶜ : πάντας Aᵇ   21 τοῦ Aᵇ et ut vid. Al. : τοῦ
τ EJ   24 ὑπάρξειν EJ   25 γίγνεσθαι Aᵇ Al. : γενέσθαι EJ
Asc.ᶜ   26 ἄμφω ὄν, τουτέστιν ὄν καὶ μὴ ὄν Aᵇ

ότιοῦν ὑπάρχειν μέρος, καίτοι τὸ μὲν ὂν τούτων εἶναι τὸ δὲ
μὴ ὄν. πρὸς μὲν οὖν τοὺς ἐκ τούτων ὑπολαμβάνοντας ἐροῦμεν 30
ὅτι τρόπον μέν τινα ὀρθῶς λέγουσι τρόπον δέ τινα ἀγνοοῦσιν·
τὸ γὰρ ὂν λέγεται διχῶς, ὥστ᾽ ἔστιν ὂν τρόπον ἐνδέχεται
γίγνεσθαί τι ἐκ τοῦ μὴ ὄντος, ἔστι δ᾽ ὂν οὔ, καὶ ἅμα τὸ
αὐτὸ εἶναι καὶ ὂν καὶ μὴ ὄν, ἀλλ᾽ οὐ κατὰ ταὐτὸ [ὄν]· δυνάμει μὲν γὰρ ἐνδέχεται ἅμα ταὐτὸ εἶναι τὰ ἐναντία, 35
ἐντελεχείᾳ δ᾽ οὔ. ἔτι δ᾽ ἀξιώσομεν αὐτοὺς ὑπολαμβάνειν
καὶ ἄλλην τινὰ οὐσίαν εἶναι τῶν ὄντων ᾗ οὔτε κίνησις ὑπάρχει οὔτε φθορὰ οὔτε γένεσις τὸ παράπαν.—ὁμοίως δὲ καὶ
ἡ περὶ τὰ φαινόμενα ἀλήθεια ἐνίοις ἐκ τῶν αἰσθητῶν ἐλή- 1009ᵇ
λυθεν. τὸ μὲν γὰρ ἀληθὲς οὐ πλήθει κρίνεσθαι οἴονται
προσήκειν οὐδὲ ὀλιγότητι, τὸ δ᾽ αὐτὸ τοῖς μὲν γλυκὺ γευο-
μένοις δοκεῖν εἶναι τοῖς δὲ πικρόν, ὥστ᾽ εἰ πάντες ἔκαμνον
ἢ πάντες παρεφρόνουν, δύο δ᾽ ἢ τρεῖς ὑγίαινον ἢ νοῦν εἶχον, 5
δοκεῖν ἂν τούτους κάμνειν καὶ παραφρονεῖν τοὺς δ᾽ ἄλλους οὔ·
ἔτι δὲ καὶ πολλοῖς τῶν ἄλλων ζῴων τἀναντία [περὶ τῶν αὐτῶν]
φαίνεσθαι καὶ ἡμῖν, καὶ αὐτῷ δὲ ἑκάστῳ πρὸς αὑτὸν οὐ
ταὐτὰ κατὰ τὴν αἴσθησιν ἀεὶ δοκεῖν. ποῖα οὖν τούτων ἀληθῆ
ἢ ψευδῆ, ἄδηλον· οὐθὲν γὰρ μᾶλλον τάδε ἢ τάδε ἀληθῆ, 10
ἀλλ᾽ ὁμοίως. διὸ Δημόκριτός γέ φησιν ἤτοι οὐθὲν εἶναι
ἀληθὲς ἢ ἡμῖν γ᾽ ἄδηλον. ὅλως δὲ διὰ τὸ ὑπολαμβάνειν
φρόνησιν μὲν τὴν αἴσθησιν, ταύτην δ᾽ εἶναι ἀλλοίωσιν, τὸ
φαινόμενον κατὰ τὴν αἴσθησιν ἐξ ἀνάγκης ἀληθὲς εἶναί
φασιν· ἐκ τούτων γὰρ καὶ Ἐμπεδοκλῆς καὶ Δημόκριτος 15
καὶ τῶν ἄλλων ὡς ἔπος εἰπεῖν ἕκαστος τοιαύταις δόξαις
γεγένηνται ἔνοχοι. καὶ γὰρ Ἐμπεδοκλῆς μεταβάλλοντας
τὴν ἕξιν μεταβάλλειν φησὶ τὴν φρόνησιν· "πρὸς παρεὸν
γὰρ μῆτις ἐναύξεται ἀνθρώποισιν." καὶ ἐν ἑτέροις δὲ λέγει
ὅτι "ὅσσον ⟨δ᾽⟩ ἀλλοῖοι μετέφυν, τόσον ἄρ σφισιν αἰεὶ | καὶ τὸ 20

1009ᵃ 30–36, cf. 1062ᵇ 24–33   38 — ᵇ 33, cf. 1063ᵃ 35 — ᵇ 7

ᵃ 33 ὄν] ὅπως Aᵇ   34 καὶ pr. Aᵇ Asc.ᶜ: om. EJΓ   κατὰ EJΓ
Al. Asc.ᶜ: om. Aᵇ   ὄν om. ut vid. Asc., secl. Christ   37 τινὰ
om. EJΓ Asc.¹   ᵇ 4 δοκεῖ EJΓ   7 καὶ om. EJΓ Al.¹ Asc.ᶜ
ἄλλων ζῴων EJΓ Asc.: ζῴων ὑγιαίνουσι Aᵇ Al.¹   περὶ τῶν αὐτῶν Aᵇ
Al.¹: om. EJΓ Asc.   8 πρὸς αὑτὸν JAᵇ   12 ὅλως EJΓ Al.¹:
ὁμοίως Aᵇ: ὅμως ut vid. Al.   17 μεταβαλόντας J   19 ἐναύξεται
E²JAᵇ: ἀέξεται E¹   20 ὅσον E²JAᵇ   δ᾽ Boissonnade: γ᾽ Sturz:
τ᾽ Stein: om. codd. Γ   τόσσον E   αἰεὶ] εἰ Aᵇ

φρονεῖν ἀλλοῖα παρίστατο". καὶ Παρμενίδης δὲ ἀποφαίνε-
ται τὸν αὐτὸν τρόπον· "ὡς γὰρ ἑκάστοτ' ἔχει κρᾶσιν με-
λέων πολυκάμπτων, | τὼς νόος ἀνθρώποισι παρίσταται· τὸ
γὰρ αὐτὸ | ἔστιν ὅπερ φρονέει, μελέων φύσις ἀνθρώποισιν |
25 καὶ πᾶσιν καὶ παντί· τὸ γὰρ πλέον ἐστὶ νόημα." Ἀναξαγόρου δὲ καὶ ἀπόφθεγμα μνημονεύεται πρὸς τῶν ἑταί-
ρων τινάς, ὅτι τοιαῦτ' αὐτοῖς ἔσται τὰ ὄντα οἷα ἂν ὑπολά-
βωσιν. φασὶ δὲ καὶ τὸν Ὅμηρον ταύτην ἔχοντα φαίνεσθαι τὴν δόξαν, ὅτι ἐποίησε τὸν Ἕκτορα, ὡς ἐξέστη ὑπὸ
30 τῆς πληγῆς, κεῖσθαι ἀλλοφρονέοντα, ὡς φρονοῦντας μὲν
καὶ τοὺς παραφρονοῦντας ἀλλ' οὐ ταὐτά. δῆλον οὖν ὅτι, εἰ
ἀμφότεραι φρονήσεις, καὶ τὰ ὄντα ἅμα οὕτω τε καὶ οὐχ
οὕτως ἔχει. ᾗ καὶ χαλεπώτατον τὸ συμβαῖνόν ἐστιν· εἰ
γὰρ οἱ μάλιστα τὸ ἐνδεχόμενον ἀληθὲς ἑωρακότες—οὗτοι
35 δ' εἰσὶν οἱ μάλιστα ζητοῦντες αὐτὸ καὶ φιλοῦντες—οὗτοι τοιαύτας ἔχουσι τὰς δόξας καὶ ταῦτα ἀποφαίνονται περὶ
τῆς ἀληθείας, πῶς οὐκ ἄξιον ἀθυμῆσαι τοὺς φιλοσοφεῖν
ἐγχειροῦντας; τὸ γὰρ τὰ πετόμενα διώκειν τὸ ζητεῖν ἂν
1010ª εἴη τὴν ἀλήθειαν.—αἴτιον δὲ τῆς δόξης τούτοις ὅτι περὶ τῶν
ὄντων μὲν τὴν ἀλήθειαν ἐσκόπουν, τὰ δ' ὄντα ὑπέλαβον
εἶναι τὰ αἰσθητὰ μόνον· ἐν δὲ τούτοις πολλὴ ἡ τοῦ ἀορίστου
φύσις ἐνυπάρχει καὶ ἡ τοῦ ὄντος οὕτως ὥσπερ εἴπομεν·
5 διὸ εἰκότως μὲν λέγουσιν, οὐκ ἀληθῆ δὲ λέγουσιν (οὕτω γὰρ
ἁρμόττει μᾶλλον εἰπεῖν ἢ ὥσπερ Ἐπίχαρμος εἰς Ξενοφά-
νην). ἔτι δὲ πᾶσαν ὁρῶντες ταύτην κινουμένην τὴν φύσιν,
κατὰ δὲ τοῦ μεταβάλλοντος οὐθὲν ἀληθευόμενον, περί γε
τὸ πάντῃ πάντως μεταβάλλον οὐκ ἐνδέχεσθαι ἀληθεύειν.
10 ἐκ γὰρ ταύτης τῆς ὑπολήψεως ἐξήνθησεν ἡ ἀκροτάτη δόξα
τῶν εἰρημένων, ἡ τῶν φασκόντων ἡρακλειτίζειν καὶ οἵαν
Κρατύλος εἶχεν, ὃς τὸ τελευταῖον οὐθὲν ᾤετο δεῖν λέγειν
ἀλλὰ τὸν δάκτυλον ἐκίνει μόνον, καὶ Ἡρακλείτῳ ἐπετίμα
εἰπόντι ὅτι δὶς τῷ αὐτῷ ποταμῷ οὐκ ἔστιν ἐμβῆναι· αὐτὸς

ᵇ 22 ἑκάστοτ' E¹J Theophr. : ἑκάστῳ Aᵇ Al. : ἔκαστος E² Al.ᶜ : ἕκαστοι Γ   ἔχη E : εἶχον Γ   23 πολυπλάγκτων Theophr.   τὼς]
τ' ὡς Aᵇ : ὡς ex τῶς fecit E   24 φύσις ἀνθρώποισιν om. Aᵇ : φύσις
Al.   27 τινάς recc. Γ Al. : τινός EJAᵇ Asc.   31 εἰ om. Aᵇ
33 ἔχη E   ᾗ] ἢ Aᵇ   37 ἀθυμῆσαι JAᵇ Asc.ᶜ : ἀθυμεῖν E et
fort. Al.   38 πετώμενα E   1010ª 8 ἀληθεύομεν Γ   δὲ Γ
14 ὅτι Aᵇ Asc. : om. EJΓ

γὰρ ᾤετο οὐδ' ἅπαξ. ἡμεῖς δὲ καὶ πρὸς τοῦτον τὸν λόγον 15
ἐροῦμεν ὅτι τὸ μὲν μεταβάλλον ὅτε μεταβάλλει ἔχει τινὰ
αὐτοῖς λόγον μὴ οἴεσθαι εἶναι, καίτοι ἔστι γε ἀμφισ-
βητήσιμον· τό τε γὰρ ἀποβάλλον ἔχει τι τοῦ ἀποβαλ-
λομένου, καὶ τοῦ γιγνομένου ἤδη ἀνάγκη τι εἶναι, ὅλως
τε εἰ φθείρεται, ὑπάρξει τι ὄν, καὶ εἰ γίγνεται, ἐξ οὗ 20
γίγνεται καὶ ὑφ' οὗ γεννᾶται ἀναγκαῖον εἶναι, καὶ τοῦτο
μὴ ἰέναι εἰς ἄπειρον. ἀλλὰ ταῦτα παρέντες ἐκεῖνα λέγωμεν, ὅτι οὐ ταὐτό ἐστι τὸ μεταβάλλειν κατὰ τὸ ποσὸν
καὶ κατὰ τὸ ποιόν· κατὰ μὲν οὖν τὸ ποσὸν ἔστω μὴ μένον,
ἀλλὰ κατὰ τὸ εἶδος ἅπαντα γιγνώσκομεν. ἔτι δ' ἄξιον 25
ἐπιτιμῆσαι τοῖς οὕτως ὑπολαμβάνουσιν, ὅτι καὶ αὐτῶν τῶν
αἰσθητῶν ἐπὶ τῶν ἐλαττόνων τὸν ἀριθμὸν ἰδόντες οὕτως
ἔχοντα περὶ ὅλου τοῦ οὐρανοῦ ὁμοίως ἀπεφήναντο· ὁ γὰρ
περὶ ἡμᾶς τοῦ αἰσθητοῦ τόπος ἐν φθορᾷ καὶ γενέσει διατε-
λεῖ μόνος ὤν, ἀλλ' οὗτος οὐθὲν ὡς εἰπεῖν μόριον τοῦ παντός 30
ἐστιν, ὥστε δικαιότερον ἂν δι' ἐκεῖνα τούτων ἀπεψηφίσαντο
ἢ διὰ ταῦτα ἐκείνων κατεψηφίσαντο. ἔτι δὲ δῆλον ὅτι
καὶ πρὸς τούτους ταὐτὰ τοῖς πάλαι λεχθεῖσιν ἐροῦμεν· ὅτι
γὰρ ἔστιν ἀκίνητός τις φύσις δεικτέον αὐτοῖς καὶ πειστέον
αὐτούς. καίτοι γε συμβαίνει τοῖς ἅμα φάσκουσιν εἶναι 35
καὶ μὴ εἶναι ἠρεμεῖν μᾶλλον φάναι πάντα ἢ κινεῖσθαι·
οὐ γὰρ ἔστιν εἰς ὅ τι μεταβαλεῖ· ἅπαντα γὰρ ὑπάρχει
πᾶσιν.—περὶ δὲ τῆς ἀληθείας, ὡς οὐ πᾶν τὸ φαινόμενον 1010ᵇ
ἀληθές, πρῶτον μὲν ὅτι οὐδ' ⟨εἰ⟩ ἡ αἴσθησις ⟨μὴ⟩ ψευδὴς τοῦ
γε ἰδίου ἐστίν, ἀλλ' ἡ φαντασία οὐ ταὐτὸν τῇ αἰσθήσει. εἶτ'
ἄξιον θαυμάσαι εἰ τοῦτ' ἀποροῦσι, πότερον τηλικαῦτά ἐστι
τὰ μεγέθη καὶ τὰ χρώματα τοιαῦτα οἷα τοῖς ἄπωθεν φαί- 5

1010ᵃ 22-25, cf. 1063ᵃ 22-28   25-32, cf. 1063ᵃ 10-17   35 — ᵇ 1,
cf. 1063ᵃ 17-21   ᵇ 1-26, 1011ᵃ 31-34, cf. 1062ᵇ 33 — 1063ᵃ 10

ᵃ 15 τοῦτον JAᵇΓ, ex τούτων fecit E   16 ὅτι] ἔτι J   17 λόγον Aᵇ
Asc.: ἀληθῆ λόγον EJΓ   18 τι] τι ἔτι ex Al. ci. Bonitz   22 ἰέναι
Bekker: εἶναι codd. Γ Al.   εἰς om. Γ   27 εἰδότες Γ   29 φορᾷ E
30 μόνον Γ   οὐθὲν ὡς εἰπεῖν EJΓ Asc.ᶜ: ὡς εἰπεῖν οὐδὲν Aᵇ   31 ἂν]
εἰ Aᵇ   τούτων J Asc. et ut vid. Al.: τοῦτον EAᵇΓ   32 ἢ EJΓ
Al.: εἰ Aᵇ   34 πιστέον E   35 γε συμβαίνει EJ Asc.ᶜ: συμβαίνει γε Aᵇ   36 ἢ κινεῖσθαι πάντα Aᵇ   37 μεταβαλεῖ Richards:
μεταβάλλει EJ Al. Asc.ᶜ: μεταβάλλειν Aᵇ   ᵇ 2 μέν γε ὅτι Brandis
εἰ et μὴ addidi, fort. leg. Al. Asc.: om. codd. Γ Al.¹   3 γε om.
EJΓ Al.¹ Asc.   5 ἄπωθεν scripsi: ἄπωθεν codd.

νεται ἢ οἷα τοῖς ἐγγύθεν, καὶ πότερον οἷα τοῖς ὑγιαίνουσιν
ἢ οἷα τοῖς κάμνουσιν, καὶ βαρύτερα πότερον ἃ τοῖς ἀσθε
νοῦσιν ἢ ἃ τοῖς ἰσχύουσιν, καὶ ἀληθῆ πότερον ἃ τοῖς κα
θεύδουσιν ἢ ἃ τοῖς ἐγρηγορόσιν. ὅτι μὲν γὰρ οὐκ οἴονταί
10 γε, φανερόν· οὐθεὶς γοῦν, ἐὰν ὑπολάβῃ νύκτωρ Ἀθήνησιν
εἶναι ὢν ἐν Λιβύῃ, πορεύεται εἰς τὸ ᾠδεῖον. ἔτι δὲ περὶ
τοῦ μέλλοντος, ὥσπερ καὶ Πλάτων λέγει, οὐ δήπου ὁμοίως
κυρία ἡ τοῦ ἰατροῦ δόξα καὶ ἡ τοῦ ἀγνοοῦντος, οἷον περὶ τοῦ
μέλλοντος ἔσεσθαι ὑγιοῦς ἢ μὴ μέλλοντος. ἔτι δὲ ἐπ᾽ αὐ
15 τῶν τῶν αἰσθήσεων οὐχ ὁμοίως κυρία ἡ τοῦ ἀλλοτρίου καὶ
ἰδίου ἢ τοῦ πλησίον καὶ τοῦ αὐτῆς, ἀλλὰ περὶ μὲν χρώ
ματος ὄψις, οὐ γεῦσις, περὶ δὲ χυμοῦ γεῦσις, οὐκ ὄψις·
ὧν ἑκάστη ἐν τῷ αὐτῷ χρόνῳ περὶ τὸ αὐτὸ οὐδέποτε φη
σιν ἅμα οὕτω καὶ οὐχ οὕτως ἔχειν. ἀλλ᾽ οὐδὲ ἐν ἑτέρῳ
20 χρόνῳ περί γε τὸ πάθος ἠμφισβήτησεν, ἀλλὰ περὶ τὸ ᾧ
συμβέβηκε τὸ πάθος. λέγω δ᾽ οἷον ὁ μὲν αὐτὸς οἶνος δό
ξειεν ἂν ἢ μεταβαλὼν ἢ τοῦ σώματος μεταβαλόντος ὁτὲ
μὲν εἶναι γλυκὺς ὁτὲ δὲ οὐ γλυκύς· ἀλλ᾽ οὐ τό γε γλυκύ,
οἷόν ἐστιν ὅταν ᾖ, οὐδεπώποτε μετέβαλεν, ἀλλ᾽ ἀεὶ ἀλη
25 θεύει περὶ αὐτοῦ, καὶ ἔστιν ἐξ ἀνάγκης τὸ ἐσόμενον γλυκὺ
τοιοῦτον. καίτοι τοῦτο ἀναιροῦσιν οὗτοι οἱ λόγοι ἅπαντες,
ὥσπερ καὶ οὐσίαν μὴ εἶναι μηθενός, οὕτω μηδ᾽ ἐξ ἀνάγκης
μηθέν· τὸ γὰρ ἀναγκαῖον οὐκ ἐνδέχεται ἄλλως καὶ ἄλλως
ἔχειν, ὥστ᾽ εἴ τι ἔστιν ἐξ ἀνάγκης, οὐχ ἕξει οὕτω τε καὶ
30 οὐχ οὕτως.—ὅλως τ᾽ εἴπερ ἔστι τὸ αἰσθητὸν μόνον, οὐθὲν ἂν
εἴη μὴ ὄντων τῶν ἐμψύχων· αἴσθησις γὰρ οὐκ ἂν εἴη. τὸ
μὲν οὖν μήτε τὰ αἰσθητὰ εἶναι μήτε τὰ αἰσθήματα ἴσως
ἀληθές (τοῦ γὰρ αἰσθανομένου πάθος τοῦτό ἐστι), τὸ δὲ τὰ
ὑποκείμενα μὴ εἶναι, ἃ ποιεῖ τὴν αἴσθησιν, καὶ ἄνευ αἰ

[b] 6 ὑγιαίνουσιν ... 7 κάμνουσιν codd. ΓAl. Asc.: κάμνουσιν ... ὑγιαί
νουσιν Christ   7, 8, 9 ἃ Aᵇ et fort. Al.: οἷα EJΓAsc.   8 ἰσχύουσιν
EJAl. Asc.: ἰσχυροῖς Aᵇ   9 ἐγρηγόρωσιν E   9–10 οὐχ οἷόν τέ
γε Aᵇ   10 οὖν Γ   ἐὰν ὑπολάβῃ] ὑπολαβὼν Aᵇ   16 αὐτῆς scripsi:
αὐτῆς codd. ΓAl.: ἄποθεν ex Asc. ci. Bonitz   17 οὐκ] ἀλλ᾽ οὐκ EJ
Asc.ᶜ   18 ὤν ... οὐδέποτε EJΓ Al.ᶜ Asc.¹: ὢν καὶ ... οὐδὲ πώποτε
Aᵇ   20 γε] δὲ Aᵇ   22 μεταβάλλων Aᵇ Al. Asc.ᶜ   μεταβαλλόντος
JAᵇ Asc.   23 γε] τε Aᵇ   24 ᾖ om. J   οὐδέπω J   μετέβαλεν EJΓ
Asc.ᶜ: μεταβάλλει Aᵇ   26 ἅπαντες EJ Asc.¹: πάντες Aᵇ   30 ἄλλως
τ᾽ Al.   31 εἴη μόνον μὴ JΓ   32 μήτε pr. ... αἰσθήματα EJΓ et
ut vid. Asc.: μηδὲ τὰ αἰσθητὰ εἶναι Aᵇ: μηδὲ τὰ αἰσθήματα εἶναι fort.
Al., Christ

σθήσεως, ἀδύνατον. οὐ γὰρ δὴ ἥ γ᾽ αἴσθησις αὐτὴ ἑαυτῆς 35
ἐστίν, ἀλλ᾽ ἔστι τι καὶ ἕτερον παρὰ τὴν αἴσθησιν, ὃ ἀνάγκη
πρότερον εἶναι τῆς αἰσθήσεως· τὸ γὰρ κινοῦν τοῦ κινουμένου
φύσει πρότερόν ἐστι, κἂν εἰ λέγεται πρὸς ἄλληλα ταῦτα, 1011ᵃ
οὐθὲν ἧττον.

6 Εἰσὶ δέ τινες οἳ ἀποροῦσι καὶ τῶν ταῦτα πεπεισμένων
καὶ τῶν τοὺς λόγους τούτους μόνον λεγόντων· ζητοῦσι γὰρ
τίς ὁ κρινῶν τὸν ὑγιαίνοντα καὶ ὅλως τὸν περὶ ἕκαστα κρι- 5
νοῦντα ὀρθῶς. τὰ δὲ τοιαῦτα ἀπορήματα ὅμοιά ἐστι τῷ
ἀπορεῖν πότερον καθεύδομεν νῦν ἢ ἐγρηγόραμεν, δύνανται
δ᾽ αἱ ἀπορίαι αἱ τοιαῦται πᾶσαι τὸ αὐτό· πάντων γὰρ
λόγον ἀξιοῦσιν εἶναι οὗτοι· ἀρχὴν γὰρ ζητοῦσι, καὶ ταύτην
δι᾽ ἀποδείξεως λαμβάνειν, ἐπεὶ ὅτι γε πεπεισμένοι οὐκ εἰσί, 10
φανεροί εἰσιν ἐν ταῖς πράξεσιν. ἀλλ᾽ ὅπερ εἴπομεν, τοῦτο
αὐτῶν τὸ πάθος ἐστίν· λόγον γὰρ ζητοῦσιν ὧν οὐκ ἔστι λό-
γος· ἀποδείξεως γὰρ ἀρχὴ οὐκ ἀπόδειξίς ἐστιν. οὗτοι μὲν
οὖν ῥᾳδίως ἂν τοῦτο πεισθεῖεν (ἔστι γὰρ οὐ χαλεπὸν λαβεῖν)·
οἱ δ᾽ ἐν τῷ λόγῳ τὴν βίαν μόνον ζητοῦντες ἀδύνατον ζη- 15
τοῦσιν· ἐναντία γὰρ εἰπεῖν ἀξιοῦσιν, εὐθὺς ἐναντία λέγοντες.
εἰ δὲ μὴ ἔστι πάντα πρός τι, ἀλλ᾽ ἔνιά ἐστι καὶ αὐτὰ
καθ᾽ αὑτά, οὐκ ἂν εἴη πᾶν τὸ φαινόμενον ἀληθές· τὸ γὰρ
φαινόμενον τινί ἐστι φαινόμενον· ὥστε ὁ λέγων ἅπαντα τὰ
φαινόμενα εἶναι ἀληθῆ ἅπαντα ποιεῖ τὰ ὄντα πρός τι. 20
διὸ καὶ φυλακτέον τοῖς τὴν βίαν ἐν τῷ λόγῳ ζητοῦσιν,
ἅμα δὲ καὶ ὑπέχειν λόγον ἀξιοῦσιν, ὅτι οὐ τὸ φαινόμενον
ἔστιν ἀλλὰ τὸ φαινόμενον ᾧ φαίνεται καὶ ὅτε φαίνεται
καὶ ᾗ καὶ ὥς. ἂν δ᾽ ὑπέχωσι μὲν λόγον, μὴ οὕτω δ᾽
ὑπέχωσι, συμβήσεται αὐτοῖς τἀναντία ταχὺ λέγειν. ἐν- 25
δέχεται γὰρ τὸ αὐτὸ κατὰ μὲν τὴν ὄψιν μέλι φαίνεσθαι

1011ᵃ 3-16, cf. 1063ᵇ 7-16

ᵇ 35 δύνατον Aᵇ   αὐτῆ ἑαυτῆς E: αὐτὴ ἑαυτῶν Asc.ᶜ: αὐτῆς Aᵇ
1011ᵃ 1 ἄλληλα EJΓ Al. Asc.ᶜ: ἄλλα Aᵇ   ταῦτα recc. Asc.ᶜ: ταυτὰ
Aᵇ: ταῦτα αὐτὰ EJΓ   5 κρινῶν Richards: κρίνων codd. Γ   κρίνοντα
AᵇΓ   8 αἱ τοιαῦται EJΓ Al. Asc.ᶜ: αὗται Aᵇ   9 οὗτοι εἶναι AᵇΓ
10 ὅτι γε Aᵇ Asc.ᶜ: γε ὅτι EJ   οὐ πεπεισμένοι EJΓ Asc.ᶜ   15 μόνον
EJΓ Al.¹ Asc.ᶜ: μόνην Aᵇ   16 εἰπεῖν οὐκ ἀξιοῦσιν Richards
18 ἄπαν EJ Asc.ᶜ   ἀληθές... 19 φαινόμενον pr. om. J   25 αὐτοῖς
Aᵇ Asc.: αὑτοῖς EJΓ   26 τῷ αὐτῷ EJΓ Asc.ᶜ: τὸ αὐτὸ τῷ αὐτῷ
fort. Al.

τῇ δὲ γεύσει μή, καὶ τῶν ὀφθαλμῶν δυοῖν ὄντοιν μὴ
ταὐτὰ ἑκατέρᾳ τῇ ὄψει, ἂν ὦσιν ἀνόμοιαι· ἐπεὶ πρός γε
τοὺς διὰ τὰς πάλαι εἰρημένας αἰτίας τὸ φαινόμενον φά-
30 σκοντας ἀληθὲς εἶναι, καὶ διὰ τοῦτο πάνθ' ὁμοίως εἶναι
ψευδῆ καὶ ἀληθῆ· οὔτε γὰρ ἅπασι ταὐτὰ φαίνεσθαι οὔτε
ταὐτῷ ἀεὶ ταὐτά, ἀλλὰ πολλάκις τἀναντία κατὰ τὸν αὐτὸν χρόνον (ἡ μὲν γὰρ ἁφὴ δύο λέγει ἐν τῇ ἐπαλλάξει
τῶν δακτύλων ἡ δ' ὄψις ἕν)·—ἀλλ' οὔ τι τῇ αὐτῇ γε καὶ
35 κατὰ τὸ αὐτὸ αἰσθήσει καὶ ὡσαύτως καὶ ἐν τῷ αὐτῷ
1011ᵇ χρόνῳ, ὥστε τοῦτ' ἂν εἴη ἀληθές. ἀλλ' ἴσως διὰ τοῦτ'
ἀνάγκη λέγειν τοῖς μὴ δι' ἀπορίαν ἀλλὰ λόγου χάριν
λέγουσιν, ὅτι οὐκ ἔστιν ἀληθὲς τοῦτο ἀλλὰ τούτῳ ἀληθές.
καὶ ὥσπερ δὴ πρότερον εἴρηται, ἀνάγκη πρός τι ποιεῖν
5 ἅπαντα καὶ πρὸς δόξαν καὶ αἴσθησιν, ὥστ' οὔτε γέγονεν οὔτ'
ἔσται οὐθὲν μηθενὸς προδοξάσαντος. εἰ δὲ γέγονεν ἢ ἔσται,
δῆλον ὅτι οὐκ ἂν εἴη ἅπαντα πρὸς δόξαν. ἔτι εἰ ἕν, πρὸς
ἓν ἢ πρὸς ὡρισμένον· καὶ εἰ τὸ αὐτὸ καὶ ἥμισυ καὶ ἴσον,
ἀλλ' οὐ πρὸς τὸ διπλάσιόν γε τὸ ἴσον. πρὸς δὴ τὸ δοξά-
10 ζον εἰ ταὐτὸ ἄνθρωπος καὶ τὸ δοξαζόμενον, οὐκ ἔσται ἄνθρωπος τὸ δοξάζον ἀλλὰ τὸ δοξαζόμενον. εἰ δ' ἕκαστον
ἔσται πρὸς τὸ δοξάζον, πρὸς ἄπειρα ἔσται τῷ εἴδει τὸ δοξάζον.

Ὅτι μὲν οὖν βεβαιοτάτη δόξα πασῶν τὸ μὴ εἶναι ἀληθεῖς
ἅμα τὰς ἀντικειμένας φάσεις, καὶ τί συμβαίνει τοῖς οὕτω
15 λέγουσι, καὶ διὰ τί οὕτω λέγουσι, τοσαῦτα εἰρήσθω· ἐπεὶ
δ' ἀδύνατον τὴν ἀντίφασιν ἅμα ἀληθεύεσθαι κατὰ τοῦ
αὐτοῦ, φανερὸν ὅτι οὐδὲ τἀναντία ἅμα ὑπάρχειν ἐνδέχεται
τῷ αὐτῷ· τῶν μὲν γὰρ ἐναντίων θάτερον στέρησίς ἐστιν οὐχ
ἧττον, οὐσίας δὲ στέρησις· ἡ δὲ στέρησις ἀπόφασίς ἐστιν ἀπό
20 τινος ὡρισμένου γένους· εἰ οὖν ἀδύνατον ἅμα καταφάναι καὶ

1011ᵃ 31-34, cf. 1062ᵇ 33 — 1063ᵃ 10   ᵇ 17-22, cf. 1063ᵇ 17-19

ᵃ 28 ταὐθ' EJ   ἀνόμοια Aᵇ et fecit E   30 καὶ] ἐροῦμεν ὅτι συμ-
βαίνει αὐτοῖς τὸ πᾶσι φαινόμενον ἀληθὲς εἶναι καὶ Jaeger   31 ταὐτὰ
EJΓ Asc.ᶜ: ταῦτα Aᵇ   32 ταὐτῷ Al. Asc.ᶜ Tia: ἑαυτῷ Aᵇ: αὐτῷ
EJ Γ   34 οὔ τι] οὔτε recc.: οὔ τοι ci. Bonitz   ᵇ 4 πρός
AᵇΓ Asc.: καὶ πρός EJ   5 ὥστ' οὐ AᵇΓ   8 ἢ Aᵇ   10 ἔσται
Aᵇ Al.: ἔστιν EJΓ   11 δ'] δὲ καθ' Aᵇ   12 πρὸς alt. AᵇΓ Al.
Asc. Syr.: om. EJ   15 διὰ τί] ἂν Aᵇ   16 ἅμα ἀληθεύεσθαι
AᵇΓ Al.¹: ἀληθεύεσθαι ἅμα EJ Asc.¹   19 δὲ EJΓ Al.: om. Aᵇ   ἡ δὲ
στέρησις Aᵇ Al. Asc.: om. EJΓ   20 καὶ] ἢ Aᵇ

ἀποφάναι ἀληθῶς, ἀδύνατον καὶ τἀναντία ὑπάρχειν ἅμα, ἀλλ'
ἢ πῇ ἄμφω ἢ θάτερον μὲν πῇ θάτερον δὲ ἁπλῶς.

7 Ἀλλὰ μὴν οὐδὲ μεταξὺ ἀντιφάσεως ἐνδέχεται εἶναι
οὐθέν, ἀλλ' ἀνάγκη ἢ φάναι ἢ ἀποφάναι ἓν καθ' ἑνὸς ὁτιοῦν.
δῆλον δὲ πρῶτον μὲν ὁρισαμένοις τί τὸ ἀληθὲς καὶ ψεῦδος. 25
τὸ μὲν γὰρ λέγειν τὸ ὂν μὴ εἶναι ἢ τὸ μὴ ὂν εἶναι ψεῦδος, τὸ δὲ τὸ ὂν εἶναι καὶ τὸ μὴ ὂν μὴ εἶναι ἀληθές, ὥστε
καὶ ὁ λέγων εἶναι ἢ μὴ ἀληθεύσει ἢ ψεύσεται· ἀλλ'
οὔτε τὸ ὂν λέγεται μὴ εἶναι ἢ εἶναι οὔτε τὸ μὴ ὄν. ἔτι
ἤτοι μεταξὺ ἔσται τῆς ἀντιφάσεως ὥσπερ τὸ φαιὸν 30
μέλανος καὶ λευκοῦ, ἢ ὡς τὸ μηδέτερον ἀνθρώπου καὶ ἵππου.
εἰ μὲν οὖν οὕτως, οὐκ ἂν μεταβάλλοι (ἐκ μὴ ἀγαθοῦ γὰρ
εἰς ἀγαθὸν μεταβάλλει ἢ ἐκ τούτου εἰς μὴ ἀγαθόν), νῦν
δ' ἀεὶ φαίνεται (οὐ γὰρ ἔστι μεταβολὴ ἀλλ' ἢ εἰς τὰ ἀντικείμενα καὶ μεταξύ)· εἰ δ' ἔστι μεταξύ, καὶ οὕτως εἴη ἄν 35
τις εἰς λευκὸν οὐκ ἐκ μὴ λευκοῦ γένεσις, νῦν δ' οὐχ ὁρᾶται. 1012ᵃ
ἔτι πᾶν τὸ διανοητὸν καὶ νοητὸν ἡ διάνοια ἢ κατάφησιν ἢ
ἀπόφησιν—τοῦτο δ' ἐξ ὁρισμοῦ δῆλον—ὅταν ἀληθεύῃ ἢ ψεύδη-
ται· ὅταν μὲν ὡδὶ συνθῇ φᾶσα ἢ ἀποφᾶσα, ἀληθεύει,
ὅταν δὲ ὡδί, ψεύδεται. ἔτι παρὰ πάσας δεῖ εἶναι τὰς 5
ἀντιφάσεις, εἰ μὴ λόγου ἕνεκα λέγεται· ὥστε καὶ οὔτε ἀληθεύσει τις οὔτ' οὐκ ἀληθεύσει, καὶ παρὰ τὸ ὂν καὶ τὸ μὴ ὂν
ἔσται, ὥστε καὶ παρὰ γένεσιν καὶ φθορὰν μεταβολή τις
ἔσται. ἔτι ἐν ὅσοις γένεσιν ἡ ἀπόφασις τὸ ἐναντίον ἐπιφέ-
ρει, καὶ ἐν τούτοις ἔσται, οἷον ἐν ἀριθμοῖς οὔτε περιττὸς οὔτε 10
οὐ περιττὸς ἀριθμός· ἀλλ' ἀδύνατον· ἐκ τοῦ ὁρισμοῦ δὲ δῆλον. ἔτι εἰς ἄπειρον βαδιεῖται, καὶ οὐ μόνον ἡμιόλια τὰ
ὄντα ἔσται ἀλλὰ πλείω. πάλιν γὰρ ἔσται ἀποφῆσαι τοῦτο

1011ᵇ23–1012ᵃ 24, cf. 1063ᵇ 19–24

ᵇ 22 μὲν EJ Asc.ᶜ : om. AᵇΓ   23 ἀποφάσεως J   24 ἐν EJΓ
Al. Asc. : om. Aᵇ   25 τί om. Aᵇ   26 τὸ μὴ ὂν Aᵇ Asc.ᶜ :
τοῦτο EJΓ   27 τὸ ὂν Aᵇ Al. Asc.ᶜ : ὂν EJ   καὶ τὸ] τὸ δὲ EJ
28 καὶ ὁ λέγων EJΓ Asc.ᶜ : ἐκεῖνο λέγων Aᵇ : καὶ ὁ λέγων τοῦτο Al.ᶜ
29 λέγει EJΓ Al. Asc.   30 ἤτοι EJ Asc. : ἤτοι τὸ Aᵇ Al.¹   ἔσται
EJΓ Asc. et ut vid. Al. : ἐστι Aᵇ Al.¹   31 τοῦ μέλανος J   34 ἀεὶ
EJΓ Al. : om. Aᵇ   μεταβολὴ JAᵇΓ, ex μεταβάλλειν ut vid. fecit E
35 εἴη ἄν τις EJΓ et fort. Asc. : ἡ ἀντίφασις Aᵇ : ἡ ἀντίφασις Al.
1012ᵃ 1 ἡ γένεσις fort. Al.   6 λέγεται Aᵇ   12 τὰ ὄντα EJΓ
Al. Asc.ᶜ : ταῦτα Aᵇ   13 γάρ ἐστιν JΓ   τοῦτο EJΓ Al.ᶜ : τοῦ Aᵇ

πρὸς τὴν φάσιν καὶ τὴν ἀπόφασιν, καὶ τοῦτ' ἔσται τι· ἡ
15 γὰρ οὐσία ἐστί τις αὐτοῦ ἄλλη. ἔτι ὅταν ἐρομένου εἰ λευκόν
ἐστιν εἴπῃ ὅτι οὔ, οὐθὲν ἄλλο ἀποπέφηκεν ἢ τὸ εἶναι· ἀπόφασις δὲ τὸ μὴ εἶναι. ἐλήλυθε δ' ἐνίοις αὕτη ἡ δόξα
ὥσπερ καὶ ἄλλαι τῶν παραδόξων· ὅταν γὰρ λύειν μὴ
δύνωνται λόγους ἐριστικούς, ἐνδόντες τῷ λόγῳ σύμφασιν ἀλη-
20 θὲς εἶναι τὸ συλλογισθέν. οἱ μὲν οὖν διὰ τοιαύτην αἰτίαν
λέγουσιν, οἱ δὲ διὰ τὸ πάντων ζητεῖν λόγον. ἀρχὴ δὲ πρὸς
ἅπαντας τούτους ἐξ ὁρισμοῦ. ὁρισμὸς δὲ γίγνεται ἐκ τοῦ σημαίνειν τι ἀναγκαῖον εἶναι αὐτούς· ὁ γὰρ λόγος οὗ τὸ
ὄνομα σημεῖον ὁρισμὸς ἔσται. ἔοικε δ' ὁ μὲν Ἡρακλείτου
25 λόγος, λέγων πάντα εἶναι καὶ μὴ εἶναι, ἅπαντα ἀληθῆ
ποιεῖν, ὁ δ' Ἀναξαγόρου, εἶναί τι μεταξὺ τῆς ἀντιφάσεως,
πάντα ψεύδη· ὅταν γὰρ μιχθῇ, οὔτε ἀγαθὸν οὔτε οὐκ ἀγαθὸν
τὸ μῖγμα, ὥστ' οὐδὲν εἰπεῖν ἀληθές.

Διωρισμένων δὲ τούτων φανερὸν ὅτι καὶ τὰ μοναχῶς 8
30 λεγόμενα καὶ κατὰ πάντων ἀδύνατον ὑπάρχειν ὥσπερ
τινὲς λέγουσιν, οἱ μὲν οὐθὲν φάσκοντες ἀληθὲς εἶναι (οὐθὲν
γὰρ κωλύειν φασὶν οὕτως ἅπαντα εἶναι ὥσπερ τὸ τὴν
διάμετρον σύμμετρον εἶναι), οἱ δὲ πάντ' ἀληθῆ. σχεδὸν
γὰρ οὗτοι οἱ λόγοι οἱ αὐτοὶ τῷ Ἡρακλείτου· ὁ γὰρ λέγων
35 ὅτι πάντ' ἀληθῆ καὶ πάντα ψεύδη, καὶ χωρὶς λέγει τῶν
1012ᵇ λόγων ἑκάτερον τούτων, ὥστ' εἴπερ ἀδύνατα ἐκεῖνα, καὶ
ταῦτα ἀδύνατον εἶναι. ἔτι δὲ φανερῶς ἀντιφάσεις εἰσὶν
ἃς οὐχ οἷόν τε ἅμα ἀληθεῖς εἶναι—οὐδὲ δὴ ψευδεῖς πάσας·
καίτοι δόξειέ γ' ἂν μᾶλλον ἐνδέχεσθαι ἐκ τῶν εἰρημένων.
5 ἀλλὰ πρὸς πάντας τοὺς τοιούτους λόγους αἰτεῖσθαι δεῖ, καθάπερ ἐλέχθη καὶ ἐν τοῖς ἐπάνω λόγοις, οὐχὶ εἶναί τι ἢ μὴ
εἶναι ἀλλὰ σημαίνειν τι, ὥστε ἐξ ὁρισμοῦ διαλεκτέον λα-

1012ᵃ 24–ᵇ 18, cf. 1063ᵇ 24–35 (ᵇ 13–18, cf. 1062ᵇ 7–9)

ᵃ 15 ἐρωμένου E   εἰ om. Aᵇ   16 ἄλλο EJΓ Asc.¹: om. Aᵇ
ἀποπέφηκεν JΓi et fort. Al.: ἀποπέφυκεν EAᵇ: ἀποπέφακεν Christ
18 καὶ αἱ ἄλλαι E Asc.¹   γὰρ om. Aᵇ   21 λόγον ζητεῖν EJΓ
24 ὁρισμὸς γίνεται EJΓ   27 ὥστε πάντα EJΓ Asc.   30 καὶ τὰ
κατὰ recc.   32 κωλύειν EJΓ Al.ᶜ: κωλύει Aᵇ Asc.ᶜ   34 οὗτοι
Aᵇ Asc.ᶜ: αὐτοῖς EJΓ   τῷ τοῦ Ἡρακλείδου Aᵇ   35 τὸν λόγον J
ᵇ 3 δὴ] δεῖ E   4 δόξειεν ἂν Aᵇ Al.ᶜ   5 πάντας Aᵇ Al.¹: ἅπαντας
EJ Asc.ᶜ   6 οὐχὶ EJ Al. Asc.ᶜ: οὐ Aᵇ   7 λαβόντας EJΓ
Asc.: λαβόντα Aᵇ

βόντας τί σημαίνει τὸ ψεῦδος ἢ τὸ ἀληθές. εἰ δὲ μηθὲν
ἄλλο τὸ ἀληθὲς φάναι ἢ ⟨ὃ⟩ ἀποφάναι ψεῦδός ἐστιν, ἀδύνατον πάντα ψευδῆ εἶναι· ἀνάγκη γὰρ τῆς ἀντιφάσεως 10
θάτερον εἶναι μόριον ἀληθές. ἔτι εἰ πᾶν ἢ φάναι ἢ ἀποφάναι ἀναγκαῖον, ἀδύνατον ἀμφότερα ψευδῆ εἶναι· θάτερον γὰρ μόριον τῆς ἀντιφάσεως ψεῦδός ἐστιν. συμβαίνει
δὴ καὶ τὸ θρυλούμενον πᾶσι τοῖς τοιούτοις λόγοις, αὐτοὺς
ἑαυτοὺς ἀναιρεῖν. ὁ μὲν γὰρ πάντα ἀληθῆ λέγων καὶ τὸν 15
ἐναντίον αὑτοῦ λόγον ἀληθῆ ποιεῖ, ὥστε τὸν ἑαυτοῦ οὐκ ἀληθῆ
(ὁ γὰρ ἐναντίος οὔ φησιν αὐτὸν ἀληθῆ), ὁ δὲ πάντα ψευδῆ
καὶ αὐτὸς αὑτόν. ἐὰν δ' ἐξαιρῶνται ὁ μὲν τὸν ἐναντίον ὡς
οὐκ ἀληθὴς μόνος ἐστίν, ὁ δὲ τὸν αὑτοῦ ὡς οὐ ψευδής,
οὐδὲν ἧττον ἀπείρους συμβαίνει αὐτοῖς αἰτεῖσθαι λόγους ἀλη- 20
θεῖς καὶ ψευδεῖς· ὁ γὰρ λέγων τὸν ἀληθῆ λόγον ἀληθῆ
ἀληθής, τοῦτο δ' εἰς ἄπειρον βαδιεῖται.—φανερὸν δ' ὅτι οὐδ'
οἱ πάντα ἠρεμεῖν λέγοντες ἀληθῆ λέγουσιν οὐδ' οἱ πάντα
κινεῖσθαι. εἰ μὲν γὰρ ἠρεμεῖ πάντα, ἀεὶ ταὐτὰ ἀληθῆ καὶ
ψευδῆ ἔσται, φαίνεται δὲ τοῦτο μεταβάλλον (ὁ γὰρ λέγων 25
ποτὲ αὐτὸς οὐκ ἦν καὶ πάλιν οὐκ ἔσται)· εἰ δὲ πάντα κινεῖται, οὐθὲν ἔσται ἀληθές· πάντα ἄρα ψευδῆ· ἀλλὰ δέδεικται ὅτι ἀδύνατον. ἔτι ἀνάγκη τὸ ὂν μεταβάλλειν· ἔκ
τινος γὰρ εἴς τι ἡ μεταβολή. ἀλλὰ μὴν οὐδὲ πάντα ἠρεμεῖ ἢ κινεῖται ποτέ, ἀεὶ δ' οὐθέν· ἔστι γάρ τι ὃ ἀεὶ κινεῖ τὰ 30
κινούμενα, καὶ τὸ πρῶτον κινοῦν ἀκίνητον αὐτό.

ᵇ 8 σημαίνειν EJ   9 τὸ ... ἀποφάναι scripsi, legit ut vid. Asc.:
τὸ ἀληθὲς φάναι ἢ ἀποφάναι AᵇΓ Al.¹: ἢ τὸ ἀληθὲς φάναι ἢ ἀποφάναι
EJ: ἢ φάναι ἢ ἀποφάναι τὸ ἀληθὲς ἢ ex Al. ci. Bonitz: τὸ ἀληθὲς ἢ
φάναι ἢ ἀποφάναι καὶ τὸ γρ. Al.: ἢ τὸ ἀληθὲς ἀποφάναι Christ: ἢ τὸ
ἀληθὲς φάναι ἢ ἀποφάναι τὸ ἀληθὲς ἢ ci. Maier   13 μόριον Aᵇ
Asc.ᶜ: μέρος EJ   14 θρυλούμενον EJ Al.¹: θρυλλούμενον Aᵇ Asc.¹
15 καὶ τὸ Aᵇ   16 αὑτοῦ JAᵇ   αὑτοῦ Aᵇ   17 τὰ γὰρ ἐναντία Γ
οὔ φησιν αὐτὸν ΕΓ Asc.ᶜ: οὔ φησιν εἶναι αὐτὸν J: ὂν φησιν αὐτὸς εἶναι
ἀληθῆ ἐκεῖνός φησι μὴ εἶναι Aᵇ   18 αὐτὸς αὑτόν Aᵇ   19 ἐστίν
om. Aᵇ Al.¹   τὸν] τὸν αὐτὸς EJΓ   αὑτοῦ J: αὐτοῦ ΕAᵇ
20 ἀπείρου Aᵇ   21 ἀληθῆ alt. EJ Al.ᶜAsc.ᶜ: om. AᵇΓ   22 φανερὸν ... 31 αὐτό om. γρ. Al.   24 πάντα καὶ ἀεὶ Aᵇ   ταῦτα JΓ
28 ἀνάγκη τὸ ὂν EJ Asc.ᶜ: τὸ ὂν ἀνάγκη AᵇΓ   29 εἴς τι EJΓ Asc.ᶜ
et ut vid. Al.: ἔστιν Aᵇ   30 ποτέ JΓ Al. Asc.ᶜ: ποτὲ δέ ΕAᵇ
τι ὃ EJΓ Al. Asc.: τιν' ἃ Aᵇ   30–31 κινεῖται κινούμενα Aᵇ   31
πρώτως γρ. E   αὐτό EJΓ Asc.ᶜ: αὐτὸ ἀρχὴ λέγεται Aᵇ

Δ

Ἀρχὴ λέγεται ἡ μὲν ὅθεν ἄν τις τοῦ πράγματος 1
35 κινηθείη πρῶτον, οἷον τοῦ μήκους καὶ ὁδοῦ ἐντεῦθεν μὲν αὕτη
1013ᵃ ἀρχή, ἐξ ἐναντίας δὲ ἑτέρα· ἡ δὲ ὅθεν ἂν κάλλιστα ἕκαστον
γένοιτο, οἷον καὶ μαθήσεως οὐκ ἀπὸ τοῦ πρώτου καὶ τῆς τοῦ
πράγματος ἀρχῆς ἐνίοτε ἀρκτέον ἀλλ' ὅθεν ῥᾷστ' ἂν μά-
θοι· ἡ δὲ ὅθεν πρῶτον γίγνεται ἐνυπάρχοντος, οἷον ὡς πλοίου
5 τρόπις καὶ οἰκίας θεμέλιος, καὶ τῶν ζῴων οἱ μὲν καρδίαν
οἱ δὲ ἐγκέφαλον οἱ δ' ὅ τι ἂν τύχωσι τοιοῦτον ὑπολαμβά-
νουσιν· ἡ δὲ ὅθεν γίγνεται πρῶτον μὴ ἐνυπάρχοντος καὶ
ὅθεν πρῶτον ἡ κίνησις πέφυκεν ἄρχεσθαι καὶ ἡ μεταβολή,
οἷον τὸ τέκνον ἐκ τοῦ πατρὸς καὶ τῆς μητρὸς καὶ ἡ μάχη
10 ἐκ τῆς λοιδορίας· ἡ δὲ οὗ κατὰ προαίρεσιν κινεῖται τὰ
κινούμενα καὶ μεταβάλλει τὰ μεταβάλλοντα, ὥσπερ αἵ
τε κατὰ πόλεις ἀρχαὶ καὶ αἱ δυναστεῖαι καὶ αἱ βασιλεῖαι
καὶ τυραννίδες ἀρχαὶ λέγονται καὶ αἱ τέχναι, καὶ τούτων
αἱ ἀρχιτεκτονικαὶ μάλιστα. ἔτι ὅθεν γνωστὸν τὸ πρᾶγμα
15 πρῶτον, καὶ αὕτη ἀρχὴ λέγεται τοῦ πράγματος, οἷον
τῶν ἀποδείξεων αἱ ὑποθέσεις. ἰσαχῶς δὲ καὶ τὰ αἴτια
λέγεται· πάντα γὰρ τὰ αἴτια ἀρχαί. πασῶν μὲν οὖν κοινὸν τῶν ἀρχῶν τὸ πρῶτον εἶναι ὅθεν ἢ ἔστιν ἢ γίγνεται ἢ
γιγνώσκεται· τούτων δὲ αἱ μὲν ἐνυπάρχουσαί εἰσιν αἱ δὲ
20 ἐκτός. διὸ ἥ τε φύσις ἀρχὴ καὶ τὸ στοιχεῖον καὶ ἡ διάνοια
καὶ ἡ προαίρεσις καὶ οὐσία καὶ τὸ οὗ ἕνεκα· πολλῶν γὰρ
καὶ τοῦ γνῶναι καὶ τῆς κινήσεως ἀρχὴ τἀγαθὸν καὶ τὸ
καλόν.

Αἴτιον λέγεται ἕνα μὲν τρόπον ἐξ οὗ γίγνεταί τι ἐνυ- 2
25 πάρχοντος, οἷον ὁ χαλκὸς τοῦ ἀνδριάντος καὶ ὁ ἄργυρος
τῆς φιάλης καὶ τὰ τούτων γένη· ἄλλον δὲ τὸ εἶδος καὶ
τὸ παράδειγμα, τοῦτο δ' ἐστὶν ὁ λόγος τοῦ τί ἦν εἶναι καὶ

cap. 2 = *Phys.* 194ᵇ 23 — 195ᵇ 21

ᵇ 34 τι Γ   1013ᵃ 1–2 γένοιτο ἕκαστον AᵇΓ   8 ἡ alt. EJ Al.ᶜ:
om. Aᵇ   14 ἔτι] ἀρχὴ λέγεται ἔτι Aᵇ   15 καὶ EJΓ Asc.ᶜ et
fort. Al.: καὶ γὰρ Aᵇ   17 κοινὸν τῶν ἀρχῶν EJΓ Asc.¹: τῶν ἀρχῶν
κοινὸν Aᵇ   20 ἡ om. J   23 καλόν Al.: κακόν EJAᵇΓ γρ. Al.
Asc.   24 αἴτιον Aᵇ Al.¹ Asc.¹: αἴτιον δὲ EJΓ   25 ὁ pr. EJ
Asc.ᶜ Φ: om. Aᵇ   27 ὁ EJΦ: om. Aᵇ

τὰ τούτου γένη (οἷον τοῦ διὰ πασῶν τὸ δύο πρὸς ἓν καὶ
ὅλως ὁ ἀριθμός) καὶ τὰ μέρη τὰ ἐν τῷ λόγῳ. ἔτι ὅθεν ἡ
ἀρχὴ τῆς μεταβολῆς ἡ πρώτη ἢ τῆς ἠρεμήσεως, οἷον ὁ 30
βουλεύσας αἴτιος, καὶ ὁ πατὴρ τοῦ τέκνου καὶ ὅλως τὸ ποιοῦν
τοῦ ποιουμένου καὶ τὸ μεταβλητικὸν τοῦ μεταβάλλοντος. ἔτι
ὡς τὸ τέλος· τοῦτο δ' ἐστὶ τὸ οὗ ἕνεκα, οἷον τοῦ περιπατεῖν
ἡ ὑγίεια. διὰ τί γὰρ περιπατεῖ; φαμέν. ἵνα ὑγιαίνῃ. καὶ
εἰπόντες οὕτως οἰόμεθα ἀποδεδωκέναι τὸ αἴτιον. καὶ ὅσα 35
δὴ κινήσαντος ἄλλου μεταξὺ γίγνεται τοῦ τέλους, οἷον τῆς
ὑγιείας ἡ ἰσχνασία ἢ ἡ κάθαρσις ἢ τὰ φάρμακα ἢ τὰ 1013^b
ὄργανα· πάντα γὰρ ταῦτα τοῦ τέλους ἕνεκά ἐστι, διαφέρει
δὲ ἀλλήλων ὡς ὄντα τὰ μὲν ὄργανα τὰ δ' ἔργα. τὰ μὲν
οὖν αἴτια σχεδὸν τοσαυταχῶς λέγεται, συμβαίνει δὲ πολλαχῶς λεγομένων τῶν αἰτίων καὶ πολλὰ τοῦ αὐτοῦ αἴτια 5
εἶναι οὐ κατὰ συμβεβηκός (οἷον τοῦ ἀνδριάντος καὶ ἡ ἀν-
δριαντοποιητικὴ καὶ ὁ χαλκὸς οὐ καθ' ἕτερόν τι ἀλλ' ᾗ ἀν-
δριάς· ἀλλ' οὐ τὸν αὐτὸν τρόπον ἀλλὰ τὸ μὲν ὡς ὕλη τὸ
δ' ὡς ὅθεν ἡ κίνησις), καὶ ἀλλήλων αἴτια (οἷον τὸ πονεῖν
τῆς εὐεξίας καὶ αὕτη τοῦ πονεῖν· ἀλλ' οὐ τὸν αὐτὸν τρόπον 10
ἀλλὰ τὸ μὲν ὡς τέλος τὸ δ' ὡς ἀρχὴ κινήσεως). ἔτι δὲ
ταὐτὸ τῶν ἐναντίων ἐστίν· ὁ γὰρ παρὸν αἴτιον τουδί,
τοῦτ' ἀπὸν αἰτιώμεθα ἐνίοτε τοῦ ἐναντίου, οἷον τὴν ἀπουσίαν
τοῦ κυβερνήτου τῆς ἀνατροπῆς, οὗ ἦν ἡ παρουσία αἰτία τῆς
σωτηρίας· ἄμφω δέ, καὶ ἡ παρουσία καὶ ἡ στέρησις, αἴτια 15
ὡς κινοῦντα.—ἄπαντα δὲ τὰ νῦν εἰρημένα αἴτια εἰς τέτταρας τρόπους πίπτει τοὺς φανερωτάτους. τὰ μὲν γὰρ στοιχεῖα
τῶν συλλαβῶν καὶ ἡ ὕλη τῶν σκευαστῶν καὶ τὸ πῦρ
καὶ ἡ γῆ καὶ τὰ τοιαῦτα πάντα τῶν σωμάτων καὶ τὰ
μέρη τοῦ ὅλου καὶ αἱ ὑποθέσεις τοῦ συμπεράσματος ὡς τὸ 20
ἐξ οὗ αἴτιά ἐστιν· τούτων δὲ τὰ μὲν ὡς τὸ ὑποκείμενον, οἷον

---

a 28 τούτων recc.   τὸ] τὰ EJ Al. Asc.^c Φ   32 μεταβαλλομένου
Al. Φ   34 ὑγιαίνει E   b 3 ὄργανα τὰ δ' ἔργα A^b Asc. : ὡς ὄργανα
τὰ δ' ὡς ἔργα EJΓ : ἔργα τὰ δ' ὄργανα Φ et fort. Al.   6 ἀνδριαντο-
ποιητικὴ A^b Al.^c Asc.^c : ἀνδριαντοποιικὴ EJ   10 τῆς EJ Asc.^c
Them. : αἴτιον τῆς A^bΓ   12 τῶν A^b Asc. Φ et ut vid. Al. : ἐνίοτε
τῶν EJΓ   13 ἀπὸν EJΓ Al. Asc. Φ : αὐτὸ A^b   αἰτιώμεθα A^b
14 τῆς τοῦ πλοίου ἀνατροπῆς Φ   15 δέ] δὲ τὸ αὐτὸ A^b   16 δὲ EJΓ
Al.^l Asc. Φ : δὲ καὶ A^b   19 καὶ ἡ γῆ EJΓ Asc.^c : om. A^bΦ
πάντα om. A^bΦ : πάντων Asc.^c   20 ὑποθέσεις EJA^bΓΦ : προτάσεις
Asc.^o et ut vid. Al.

τὰ μέρη, τὰ δὲ ὡς τὸ τί ἦν εἶναι, τό τε ὅλον καὶ ἡ σύνθεσις καὶ τὸ εἶδος. τὸ δὲ σπέρμα καὶ ὁ ἰατρὸς καὶ ὁ βουλεύσας καὶ ὅλως τὸ ποιοῦν, πάντα ὅθεν ἡ ἀρχὴ τῆς μετα-
25 βολῆς ἢ στάσεως.   τὰ δ' ὡς τὸ τέλος καὶ τἀγαθὸν
τῶν ἄλλων· τὸ γὰρ οὗ ἕνεκα βέλτιστον καὶ τέλος τῶν
ἄλλων ἐθέλει εἶναι· διαφερέτω δὲ μηδὲν αὐτὸ εἰπεῖν ἀγαθὸν ἢ φαινόμενον ἀγαθόν.—τὰ μὲν οὖν αἴτια ταῦτα καὶ
τοσαῦτά ἐστι τῷ εἴδει, τρόποι δὲ τῶν αἰτίων ἀριθμῷ μέν
30 εἰσι πολλοί, κεφαλαιούμενοι δὲ καὶ οὗτοι ἐλάττους.   λέγονται
γὰρ αἴτια πολλαχῶς, καὶ αὐτῶν τῶν ὁμοειδῶν προτέρως
καὶ ὑστέρως ἄλλο ἄλλου, οἷον ὑγιείας ὁ ἰατρὸς καὶ ὁ τεχνίτης, καὶ τοῦ διὰ πασῶν τὸ διπλάσιον καὶ ἀριθμός, καὶ ἀεὶ
τὰ περιέχοντα ὁτιοῦν τῶν καθ' ἕκαστα.   ἔτι δ' ὡς τὸ συμ-
35 βεβηκὸς καὶ τὰ τούτων γένη, οἷον ἀνδριάντος ἄλλως Πολύκλειτος καὶ ἄλλως ἀνδριαντοποιός, ὅτι συμβέβηκε τῷ ἀν-
1014ᵃ δριαντοποιῷ Πολυκλείτῳ εἶναι· καὶ τὰ περιέχοντα δὲ τὸ
συμβεβηκός, οἷον ἄνθρωπος αἴτιος ἀνδριάντος, ἢ καὶ ὅλως
ζῷον, ὅτι ὁ Πολύκλειτος ἄνθρωπος ὁ δὲ ἄνθρωπος ζῷον.
ἔστι δὲ καὶ τῶν συμβεβηκότων ἄλλα ἄλλων πορρώτερον καὶ
5 ἐγγύτερον, οἷον εἰ ὁ λευκὸς καὶ ὁ μουσικὸς αἴτιος λέγοιτο
τοῦ ἀνδριάντος, ἀλλὰ μὴ μόνον Πολύκλειτος ἢ ἄνθρωπος.
παρὰ πάντα δὲ καὶ τὰ οἰκείως λεγόμενα καὶ τὰ κατὰ
συμβεβηκός, τὰ μὲν ὡς δυνάμενα λέγεται τὰ δ' ὡς ἐνεργοῦντα, οἷον τοῦ οἰκοδομεῖσθαι οἰκοδόμος ἢ οἰκοδομῶν οἰκο-
10 δόμος.   ὁμοίως δὲ λεχθήσεται καὶ ἐφ' ὧν αἴτια τὰ αἴτια
τοῖς εἰρημένοις, οἷον τοῦδε τοῦ ἀνδριάντος ἢ ἀνδριάντος ἢ ὅλως
εἰκόνος, καὶ χαλκοῦ τοῦδε ἢ χαλκοῦ ἢ ὅλως ὕλης· καὶ ἐπὶ
τῶν συμβεβηκότων ὡσαύτως.   ἔτι δὲ συμπλεκόμενα καὶ
ταῦτα κἀκεῖνα λεχθήσεται, οἷον οὐ Πολύκλειτος οὐδὲ ἀν-
15 δριαντοποιὸς ἀλλὰ Πολύκλειτος ἀνδριαντοποιός.   ἀλλ'
ὅμως ἅπαντά γε ταῦτ' ἐστὶ τὸ μὲν πλῆθος ἕξ, λεγόμενα

ᵇ 25 τὰ δ' Aᵇ Al. : τὰ δ' ἄλλα EJΓ Asc. : τὸ δ' Phil.   27 ἐθέλειν Aᵇ
ἀγαθὸν Aᵇ Al.ᶜ Φ : ἢ ἀγαθὸν EJΓ   28 οὖν om. Aᵇ   30 λέγεται
EJ   32 ἄλλο ἄλλου EJΓ Al. : ἄλλου ἄλλο Aᵇ   ὁ alt. om. EJΓ
34 ἕκαστα EJ Simpl. : ἕκαστον Aᵇ Phil.ᶜ   36 ὅτι] καὶ ὅτι Aᵇ
1014ᵃ 2 οἷον . . . ἢ EJΓ Asc. : οἷον εἰ . . . εἴη ἢ AᵇΦ   4 πορρώτερον
EJΓΦ : πορρώτερα Aᵇ : πρότερον recc.   5 ἐγγύτερον EJΓΦ : ἐγγύτερα
Aᵇ   λέγοιτο] οἴοιτο Aᵇ   7 παρὰ codd. Φ (I) Simpl.¹ Phil.¹ :
om. Φ (EF)   9 τοῦ EJΓΦ : τὸ τοῦ Aᵇ   11 ἢ pr. EJΓΦ : ἢ Aᵇ
12 καὶ Aᵇ Al.ᶜ Φ : ἢ EJΓ   ἢ pr. EΓ Al.ᶜ Φ : ἢ JAᵇ

δὲ διχῶς· ἢ γὰρ ὡς τὸ καθ' ἕκαστον ἢ ὡς τὸ γένος, ἢ
ὡς τὸ συμβεβηκὸς ἢ ὡς τὸ γένος τοῦ συμβεβηκότος, ἢ
ὡς συμπλεκόμενα ταῦτα ἢ ὡς ἁπλῶς λεγόμενα, πάντα δὲ ἢ ὡς
ἐνεργοῦντα ἢ κατὰ δύναμιν. διαφέρει δὲ τοσοῦτον, ὅτι τὰ 20
μὲν ἐνεργοῦντα καὶ τὰ καθ' ἕκαστον ἅμα ἔστι καὶ οὐκ ἔστι
καὶ ὧν αἴτια, οἷον ὅδε ὁ ἰατρεύων τῷδε τῷ ὑγιαζομένῳ
καὶ ὅδε ὁ οἰκοδόμος τῷδε τῷ οἰκοδομουμένῳ, τὰ δὲ κατὰ
δύναμιν οὐκ ἀεί· φθείρεται γὰρ οὐχ ἅμα ἡ οἰκία καὶ ὁ
οἰκοδόμος.   25

3 Στοιχεῖον λέγεται ἐξ οὗ σύγκειται πρώτου ἐνυπάρχοντος ἀδιαιρέτου τῷ εἴδει εἰς ἕτερον εἶδος, οἷον φωνῆς
στοιχεῖα ἐξ ὧν σύγκειται ἡ φωνὴ καὶ εἰς ἃ διαιρεῖται
ἔσχατα, ἐκεῖνα δὲ μηκέτ' εἰς ἄλλας φωνὰς ἑτέρας τῷ
εἴδει αὐτῶν, ἀλλὰ κἂν διαιρῆται, τὰ μόρια ὁμοειδῆ, οἷον 30
ὕδατος τὸ μόριον ὕδωρ, ἀλλ' οὐ τῆς συλλαβῆς. ὁμοίως δὲ
καὶ τὰ τῶν σωμάτων στοιχεῖα λέγουσιν οἱ λέγοντες εἰς ἃ
διαιρεῖται τὰ σώματα ἔσχατα, ἐκεῖνα δὲ μηκέτ' εἰς ἄλλα
εἴδει διαφέροντα· καὶ εἴτε ἓν εἴτε πλείω τὰ τοιαῦτα,
ταῦτα στοιχεῖα λέγουσιν. παραπλησίως δὲ καὶ τὰ τῶν 35
διαγραμμάτων στοιχεῖα λέγεται, καὶ ὅλως τὰ τῶν ἀπο-
δείξεων· αἱ γὰρ πρῶται ἀποδείξεις καὶ ἐν πλείοσιν ἀποδείξεσιν ἐνυπάρχουσαι, αὗται στοιχεῖα τῶν ἀποδείξεων λέ- 1014ᵇ
γονται· εἰσὶ δὲ τοιοῦτοι συλλογισμοὶ οἱ πρῶτοι ἐκ τῶν
τριῶν δι' ἑνὸς μέσου. καὶ μεταφέροντες δὲ στοιχεῖον καλοῦ-
σιν ἐντεῦθεν ὃ ἂν ἓν ὂν καὶ μικρὸν ἐπὶ πολλὰ ἦ χρήσιμον, διὸ καὶ τὸ μικρὸν καὶ ἁπλοῦν καὶ ἀδιαίρετον στοι- 5
χεῖον λέγεται. ὅθεν ἐλήλυθε τὰ μάλιστα καθόλου στοιχεῖα
εἶναι, ὅτι ἕκαστον αὐτῶν ἓν ὂν καὶ ἁπλοῦν ἐν πολλοῖς ὑπάρχει ἢ πᾶσιν ἢ ὅτι πλείστοις, καὶ τὸ ἓν καὶ τὴν στιγμὴν
ἀρχάς τισι δοκεῖν εἶναι. ἐπεὶ οὖν τὰ καλούμενα γένη

ᵃ 17 ἢ ὡς τὸ γένος AᵇΓΦ: om. EJ   γένος EJΦ Phil.ᶜ: τοῦ καθ'
αὑτά add. Aᵇ, καὶ τοῦ καθ' αὑτό Γ, αὑτοῦ recc. et fort. Al.   19 ὡς alt.
om. recc.   πάντα δὲ ἢ AᵇΦ et ut vid. Al.: ἔτι EJΓ   22 καὶ Aᵇ Al.ᶜ Φ:
αὑτά τε καὶ EJΓ   ὅ om. Aᵇ   23 ὁ οἰκοδομῶν Φ   τὰ] τὸ J
26 ἐνυπάρχοντας E   27 τῷ . . . ἕτερον] εἰς τὸ αὑτὸ γρ. Al.
28 διαιρεῖ E   30 κἂν EJ Al.ᶜ Asc.: ἂν καὶ Aᵇ   31 συλλαβῆς
συλλαβῇ Richards   34 διαφέροντα σώματα EJΓ   ᵇ 2 ἐκ τῶν
τριῶν] ἐκ τῶν τριῶν μέσων Aᵇ: τῶν τριῶν Al. et ut vid. Asc.: τῶν τριῶν
μέσων γρ. Al.   8 καὶ pr. EJΓ Al.ᶜ: διὸ καὶ Aᵇ   9 ἀρχὰς καὶ
στοιχεῖά τισι Al.   δοκεῖ AᵇΓ Al.ᶜ

10 καθόλου καὶ ἀδιαίρετα (οὐ γὰρ ἔστι λόγος αὐτῶν), στοιχεῖα
τὰ γένη λέγουσί τινες, καὶ μᾶλλον ἢ τὴν διαφορὰν ὅτι
καθόλου μᾶλλον τὸ γένος· ᾧ μὲν γὰρ ἡ διαφορὰ ὑπάρχει, καὶ τὸ γένος ἀκολουθεῖ, ᾧ δὲ τὸ γένος, οὐ παντὶ ἡ
διαφορά. ἁπάντων δὲ κοινὸν τὸ εἶναι στοιχεῖον ἑκάστου τὸ
15 πρῶτον ἐνυπάρχον ἑκάστῳ.

Φύσις λέγεται ἕνα μὲν τρόπον ἡ τῶν φυομένων γέ- 4
νεσις, οἷον εἴ τις ἐπεκτείνας λέγοι τὸ υ, ἕνα δὲ ἐξ οὗ φύεται πρῶτον τὸ φυόμενον ἐνυπάρχοντος· ἔτι ὅθεν ἡ κίνησις
ἡ πρώτη ἐν ἑκάστῳ τῶν φύσει ὄντων ἐν αὐτῷ ᾗ αὐτὸ
20 ὑπάρχει· φύεσθαι δὲ λέγεται ὅσα αὔξησιν ἔχει δι' ἑτέρου
τῷ ἅπτεσθαι καὶ συμπεφυκέναι ἢ προσπεφυκέναι ὥσπερ
τὰ ἔμβρυα· διαφέρει δὲ σύμφυσις ἁφῆς, ἔνθα μὲν γὰρ
οὐδὲν παρὰ τὴν ἁφὴν ἕτερον ἀνάγκη εἶναι, ἐν δὲ τοῖς συμ-
πεφυκόσιν ἔστι τι ἓν τὸ αὐτὸ ἐν ἀμφοῖν ὃ ποιεῖ ἀντὶ τοῦ
25 ἅπτεσθαι συμπεφυκέναι καὶ εἶναι ἓν κατὰ τὸ συνεχὲς καὶ
ποσόν, ἀλλὰ μὴ κατὰ τὸ ποιόν. ἔτι δὲ φύσις λέγεται
ἐξ οὗ πρώτου ἢ ἔστιν ἢ γίγνεταί τι τῶν φύσει ὄντων, ἀρρυθμίστου ὄντος καὶ ἀμεταβλήτου ἐκ τῆς δυνάμεως τῆς αὐτοῦ,
οἷον ἀνδριάντος καὶ τῶν σκευῶν τῶν χαλκῶν ὁ χαλκὸς ἡ
30 φύσις λέγεται, τῶν δὲ ξυλίνων ξύλον· ὁμοίως δὲ καὶ ἐπὶ
τῶν ἄλλων· ἐκ τούτων γάρ ἐστιν ἕκαστον διασωζομένης τῆς
πρώτης ὕλης· τοῦτον γὰρ τὸν τρόπον καὶ τῶν φύσει ὄντων
τὰ στοιχεῖά φασιν εἶναι φύσιν, οἱ μὲν πῦρ οἱ δὲ γῆν οἱ
δ' ἀέρα οἱ δ' ὕδωρ οἱ δ' ἄλλο τι τοιοῦτον λέγοντες, οἱ δ'
35 ἔνια τούτων οἱ δὲ πάντα ταῦτα. ἔτι δ' ἄλλον τρόπον λέγεται ἡ φύσις ἡ τῶν φύσει ὄντων οὐσία, οἷον οἱ λέγοντες
τὴν φύσιν εἶναι τὴν πρώτην σύνθεσιν, ἢ ὥσπερ Ἐμπεδοκλῆς
1015ᵃ λέγει ὅτι " φύσις οὐδενὸς ἔστιν ἐόντος, | ἀλλὰ μόνον μῖξίς τε
διάλλαξίς τε μιγέντων | ἔστι, φύσις δ' ἐπὶ τοῖς ὀνομάζεται
ἀνθρώποισιν ". διὸ καὶ ὅσα φύσει ἔστιν ἢ γίγνεται, ἤδη
ὑπάρχοντος ἐξ οὗ πέφυκε γίγνεσθαι ἢ εἶναι, οὔπω φαμὲν
5 τὴν φύσιν ἔχειν ἐὰν μὴ ἔχῃ τὸ εἶδος καὶ τὴν μορφήν.

ᵇ 10 οὐ Aᵇ Al.¹: εἰς E: εἶς JΓ   11 τινες εἶναι καὶ Aᵇ   16 φύσις
Aᵇ Al.ᶜ: φύσις δὲ EJΓ Asc.¹   18 πρώτου E² Al.: πρῶτον E¹JAᵇΓ
19 αὐτὸ] αὐτῶι E   21 συμπεφυκέναι ἢ EJΓ Al. Asc.: om. Aᵇ
26 δὲ om. AᵇΓ   27 τῶν EJΓ Al. Asc. Φ: τῶν μὴ Aᵇ   ἀρρυθμίστου
Asc.ᶜ Φ: ἀρυθμίστου codd.   28 αὐτοῦ Aᵇ   29 ἡ EJ Asc.ᶜ:
om. Aᵇ   37 ἢ om. Γ   1015ᵃ 2 τε om. Aᵇ   ἐστὶ καὶ φύσις Aᵇ

φύσει μὲν οὖν τὸ ἐξ ἀμφοτέρων τούτων ἐστίν, οἷον τὰ ζῷα
καὶ τὰ μόρια αὐτῶν· φύσις δὲ ἥ τε πρώτη ὕλη (καὶ αὕτη
διχῶς, ἢ ἡ πρὸς αὐτὸ πρώτη ἢ ἡ ὅλως πρώτη, οἷον τῶν
χαλκῶν ἔργων πρὸς αὐτὰ μὲν πρῶτος ὁ χαλκός, ὅλως δ'
ἴσως ὕδωρ, εἰ πάντα τὰ τηκτὰ ὕδωρ) καὶ τὸ εἶδος καὶ ἡ 10
οὐσία· τοῦτο δ' ἐστὶ τὸ τέλος τῆς γενέσεως. μεταφορᾷ δ'
ἤδη καὶ ὅλως πᾶσα οὐσία φύσις λέγεται διὰ ταύτην, ὅτι
καὶ ἡ φύσις οὐσία τίς ἐστιν. ἐκ δὴ τῶν εἰρημένων ἡ πρώτη
φύσις καὶ κυρίως λεγομένη ἐστὶν ἡ οὐσία ἡ τῶν ἐχόντων
ἀρχὴν κινήσεως ἐν αὑτοῖς ᾗ αὐτά· ἡ γὰρ ὕλη τῷ ταύτης 15
δεκτικὴ εἶναι λέγεται φύσις, καὶ αἱ γενέσεις καὶ τὸ φύεσθαι τῷ ἀπὸ ταύτης εἶναι κινήσεις. καὶ ἡ ἀρχὴ τῆς κινήσεως τῶν φύσει ὄντων αὕτη ἐστίν, ἐνυπάρχουσά πως ἢ δυνάμει ἢ ἐντελεχείᾳ.

5   Ἀναγκαῖον λέγεται οὗ ἄνευ οὐκ ἐνδέχεται ζῆν ὡς 20
συναιτίου (οἷον τὸ ἀναπνεῖν καὶ ἡ τροφὴ τῷ ζῴῳ ἀναγκαῖον, ἀδύνατον γὰρ ἄνευ τούτων εἶναι), καὶ ὧν ἄνευ τὸ
ἀγαθὸν μὴ ἐνδέχεται ἢ εἶναι ἢ γενέσθαι, ἢ τὸ κακὸν ἀπο-
βαλεῖν ἢ στερηθῆναι (οἷον τὸ πιεῖν τὸ φάρμακον ἀναγκαῖον
ἵνα μὴ κάμνῃ, καὶ τὸ πλεῦσαι εἰς Αἴγιναν ἵνα ἀπολάβῃ 25
τὰ χρήματα). ἔτι τὸ βίαιον καὶ ἡ βία· τοῦτο δ' ἐστὶ τὸ
παρὰ τὴν ὁρμὴν καὶ τὴν προαίρεσιν ἐμποδίζον καὶ κωλυτικόν,
τὸ γὰρ βίαιον ἀναγκαῖον λέγεται, διὸ καὶ λυπηρόν (ὥσπερ
καὶ Εὔηνός φησι "πᾶν γὰρ ἀναγκαῖον πρᾶγμ' ἀνιαρὸν
ἔφυ"), καὶ ἡ βία ἀνάγκη τις (ὥσπερ καὶ Σοφοκλῆς λέγει 30
"ἀλλ' ἡ βία με ταῦτ' ἀναγκάζει ποιεῖν"), καὶ δοκεῖ ἡ
ἀνάγκη ἀμετάπειστόν τι εἶναι, ὀρθῶς· ἐναντίον γὰρ τῇ
κατὰ τὴν προαίρεσιν κινήσει καὶ κατὰ τὸν λογισμόν. ἔτι
τὸ μὴ ἐνδεχόμενον ἄλλως ἔχειν ἀναγκαῖόν φαμεν οὕτως
ἔχειν· καὶ κατὰ τοῦτο τὸ ἀναγκαῖον καὶ τἆλλα λέγεταί 35
πως ἅπαντα ἀναγκαῖα· τό τε γὰρ βίαιον ἀναγκαῖον λέγεται ἢ ποιεῖν ἢ πάσχειν τότε, ὅταν μὴ ἐνδέχηται κατὰ 1015ᵇ
τὴν ὁρμὴν διὰ τὸ βιαζόμενον, ὡς ταύτην ἀνάγκην οὖσαν
δι' ἣν μὴ ἐνδέχεται ἄλλως, καὶ ἐπὶ τῶν συναιτίων τοῦ

ᵃ 8 ἢ ἤ] ἡ τὰ Aᵇ: ἢ Christ   ἡ om. Aᵇ   9 πρώτων Aᵇ
11 μεταφορᾷ Aᵇ   15 αὐτοῖς Aᵇ   16 αἱ γενέσεις JΓ Al. et fecit
E: γένεσις Aᵇ   τῷ Aᵇ   17 κινήσεις EJΓ Al.: κίνησις Aᵇ
18 αὕτη EJΓ Al.ᶜ: ἡ αὐτή Aᵇ   19 ἐνεργείᾳ Al.ᶜ et ut vid. Al.
23 τὸ Aᵇ Al. Asc.ᶜ: τι EJΓ   27 τὴν alt. EJ Asc.: om. Aᵇ

ζῆν καὶ τοῦ ἀγαθοῦ ὡσαύτως· ὅταν γὰρ μὴ ἐνδέχηται ἔνθα
5 μὲν τὸ ἀγαθὸν ἔνθα δὲ τὸ ζῆν καὶ τὸ εἶναι ἄνευ τινῶν,
ταῦτα ἀναγκαῖα καὶ ἡ αἰτία ἀνάγκη τίς ἐστιν αὕτη. ἔτι
ἡ ἀπόδειξις τῶν ἀναγκαίων, ὅτι οὐκ ἐνδέχεται ἄλλως
ἔχειν, εἰ ἀποδέδεικται ἁπλῶς· τούτου δ' αἴτια τὰ πρῶτα,
εἰ ἀδύνατον ἄλλως ἔχειν ἐξ ὧν ὁ συλλογισμός. τῶν μὲν
10 δὴ ἕτερον αἴτιον τοῦ ἀναγκαῖα εἶναι, τῶν δὲ οὐδέν, ἀλλὰ
διὰ ταῦτα ἕτερά ἐστιν ἐξ ἀνάγκης. ὥστε τὸ πρῶτον καὶ
κυρίως ἀναγκαῖον τὸ ἁπλοῦν ἐστίν· τοῦτο γὰρ οὐκ ἐνδέχεται
πλεοναχῶς ἔχειν, ὥστ' οὐδὲ ἄλλως καὶ ἄλλως· ἤδη γὰρ
πλεοναχῶς ἂν ἔχοι. εἰ ἄρα ἔστιν ἄττα ἀΐδια καὶ ἀκί-
15 νητα, οὐδὲν ἐκείνοις ἐστὶ βίαιον οὐδὲ παρὰ φύσιν.

Ἓν λέγεται τὸ μὲν κατὰ συμβεβηκὸς τὸ δὲ καθ' **6**
αὑτό, κατὰ συμβεβηκὸς μὲν οἷον Κορίσκος καὶ τὸ μουσικόν, καὶ Κορίσκος μουσικός (ταὐτὸ γὰρ εἰπεῖν Κορίσκος καὶ
τὸ μουσικόν, καὶ Κορίσκος μουσικός), καὶ τὸ μουσικὸν καὶ τὸ
20 δίκαιον, καὶ μουσικὸς ⟨Κορίσκος⟩ καὶ δίκαιος Κορίσκος· πάντα
γὰρ ταῦτα ἓν λέγεται κατὰ συμβεβηκός, τὸ μὲν δίκαιον καὶ τὸ
μουσικὸν ὅτι μιᾷ οὐσίᾳ συμβέβηκεν, τὸ δὲ μουσικὸν καὶ Κορίσκος ὅτι θάτερον θατέρῳ συμβέβηκεν· ὁμοίως δὲ τρόπον
τινὰ καὶ ὁ μουσικὸς Κορίσκος τῷ Κορίσκῳ ἓν ὅτι θάτερον
25 τῶν μορίων θατέρῳ συμβέβηκε τῶν ἐν τῷ λόγῳ, οἷον τὸ
μουσικὸν τῷ Κορίσκῳ· καὶ ὁ μουσικὸς Κορίσκος δικαίῳ Κορίσκῳ ὅτι ἑκατέρου μέρος τῷ αὐτῷ ἑνὶ συμβέβηκεν ἕν.
ὡσαύτως δὲ κἂν ἐπὶ γένους κἂν ἐπὶ τῶν καθόλου τινὸς ὀνομάτων λέγηται τὸ συμβεβηκός, οἷον ὅτι ἄνθρωπος τὸ αὐτὸ
30 καὶ μουσικὸς ἄνθρωπος· ἢ γὰρ ὅτι τῷ ἀνθρώπῳ μιᾷ οὔσῃ
οὐσίᾳ συμβέβηκε τὸ μουσικόν, ἢ ὅτι ἄμφω τῶν καθ' ἕκα-

ᵇ 4 ἐνδέχεται Aᵇ   5 καὶ τὸ omittendum ci. Bonitz   6 αὐτῆς Aᵇ
10 δὴ] δι' Aᵇ   ἀναγκαῖον Aᵇ   14 ἄρα EJΓ Al. Asc. : γὰρ Aᵇ
ἄττα] ἄττα καὶ Aᵇ   ἀΐδια] ἁπλᾶ Al.   15 οὐδέν] οὐδ' ἐν E : οὐδεὶν
ἐν fort. Al. et Asc., Jaeger   16 τὸ δὲ ... 17 μὲν EJΓ Al. Asc. :
om. Aᵇ   18 καὶ Κορίσκος μουσικός] καὶ Κορίσκος καὶ μουσικός Aᵇ :
om. J¹   ταὐτὸ ... 19 καὶ alt. EJΓ Al. Asc. : om. Aᵇ   19 καὶ
pr.] ἕν καὶ ex Al. ci. Bonitz   20 καὶ μουσικὸς om. J¹   Κορίσκος
καὶ δίκαιος Al. : καὶ ὁ Aᵇ : δίκαιος EJ²Γ : om. J¹   21 τὸ alt. EJ Al. :
om. Aᵇ Asc.   22 τὸ ... 23 συμβέβηκεν EJΓ Al. Asc. : om. Aᵇ
27 μέρους Aᵇ   ἕν EJ Al. : om. AᵇΓ   post ἕν add. οὐδὲν γὰρ διαφέρει ἢ Κορίσκῳ τὸ μουσικὸν συμβεβηκέναι EJΓ : om. Aᵇ Al. Asc.   29
ὅτι] ὅτι ὁ Aᵇ   30 τῶν ἀνθρώπων J

στόν τινι συμβέβηκεν, οἷον Κορίσκῳ. πλὴν οὐ τὸν αὐτὸν
τρόπον ἄμφω ὑπάρχει, ἀλλὰ τὸ μὲν ἴσως ὡς γένος καὶ
ἐν τῇ οὐσίᾳ τὸ δὲ ὡς ἕξις ἢ πάθος τῆς οὐσίας.—ὅσα μὲν
οὖν κατὰ συμβεβηκὸς λέγεται ἕν, τοῦτον τὸν τρόπον λέγε- 35
ται· τῶν δὲ καθ᾽ ἑαυτὰ ἓν λεγομένων τὰ μὲν λέγεται τῷ
συνεχῆ εἶναι, οἷον φάκελος δεσμῷ καὶ ξύλα κόλλῃ· 1016ᵃ
καὶ γραμμή, κἂν κεκαμμένη ᾖ, συνεχὴς δέ, μία λέγεται,
ὥσπερ καὶ τῶν μερῶν ἕκαστον, οἷον σκέλος καὶ βραχίων.
αὐτῶν δὲ τούτων μᾶλλον ἓν τὰ φύσει συνεχῆ ἢ τέχνῃ.
συνεχὲς δὲ λέγεται οὗ κίνησις μία καθ᾽ αὑτὸ καὶ μὴ οἷόν 5
τε ἄλλως· μία δ᾽ οὗ ἀδιαίρετος, ἀδιαίρετος δὲ κατὰ χρόνον.
καθ᾽ αὑτὰ δὲ συνεχῆ ὅσα μὴ ἀφῇ ἕν· εἰ γὰρ θείης ἁπτό-
μενα ἀλλήλων ξύλα, οὐ φήσεις ταῦτα εἶναι ἓν οὔτε ξύλον
οὔτε σῶμα οὔτ᾽ ἄλλο συνεχὲς οὐδέν. τά τε δὴ ὅλως συνεχῆ
ἓν λέγεται κἂν ἔχῃ κάμψιν, καὶ ἔτι μᾶλλον τὰ μὴ ἔχοντα 10
κάμψιν, οἷον κνήμη ἢ μηρὸς σκέλους, ὅτι ἐνδέχεται μὴ μίαν
εἶναι τὴν κίνησιν τοῦ σκέλους. καὶ ἡ εὐθεῖα τῆς κεκαμμένης
μᾶλλον ἕν· τὴν δὲ κεκαμμένην καὶ ἔχουσαν γωνίαν καὶ
μίαν καὶ οὐ μίαν λέγομεν, ὅτι ἐνδέχεται καὶ μὴ ἅμα τὴν
κίνησιν αὐτῆς εἶναι καὶ ἅμα· τῆς δ᾽ εὐθείας ἀεὶ ἅμα, καὶ 15
οὐδὲν μόριον ἔχον μέγεθος τὸ μὲν ἠρεμεῖ τὸ δὲ κινεῖται,
ὥσπερ τῆς κεκαμμένης. ἔτι ἄλλον τρόπον ἓν λέγεται τῷ
τὸ ὑποκείμενον τῷ εἴδει εἶναι ἀδιάφορον· ἀδιάφορον δ᾽ ὧν
ἀδιαίρετον τὸ εἶδος κατὰ τὴν αἴσθησιν· τὸ δ᾽ ὑποκείμενον
ἢ τὸ πρῶτον ἢ τὸ τελευταῖον πρὸς τὸ τέλος· καὶ γὰρ οἶνος 20
εἷς λέγεται καὶ ὕδωρ ἕν, ᾗ ἀδιαίρετον κατὰ τὸ εἶδος, καὶ
οἱ χυμοὶ πάντες λέγονται ἕν (οἷον ἔλαιον οἶνος) καὶ τὰ τηκτά,
ὅτι πάντων τὸ ἔσχατον ὑποκείμενον τὸ αὐτό· ὕδωρ γὰρ ἢ
ἀὴρ πάντα ταῦτα. λέγεται δ᾽ ἓν καὶ ὧν τὸ γένος ἓν
διαφέρον ταῖς ἀντικειμέναις διαφοραῖς—καὶ ταῦτα λέγεται 25
πάντα ἓν ὅτι τὸ γένος ἓν τὸ ὑποκείμενον ταῖς διαφοραῖς
(οἷον ἵππος ἄνθρωπος κύων ἕν τι ὅτι πάντα ζῷα), καὶ τρόπον δὴ παραπλήσιον ὥσπερ ἡ ὕλη μία. ταῦτα δὲ ὁτὲ

ᵇ 33-34 καὶ οὐσίᾳ Γ   1016ᵃ 1 φάκελος EJ Al.: φάκελλος Aᵇ
Asc.   3 οἷον om. EJ Asc.ᶜ   5 συνεχὲς . . . 6 χρόνον om. J¹
οὗ codd. Al.ᶜ: οὗ ᾖ α et fort. Al.   15 ἀεὶ] δεῖ Aᵇ   17 ὥσπερ
om. E¹   ἓν om. EJΓ   18 ἀδιάφορον alt. EJΓ Asc.ᶜ: om. Aᵇ:
ἀδιάφορα recc.   21 ἕν] ἂν Aᵇ   24 ταῦτ᾽ ἐστὶν EJΓ   26 ἓν
πάντα Aᵇ   27 τι om. Aᵇ   ζῷον Aᵇ

μὲν οὕτως ἓν λέγεται, ὁτὲ δὲ τὸ ἄνω γένος ταὐτὸν λέγε-
30 ται—ἂν ἦ τελευταῖα τοῦ γένους εἴδη—τὸ ἀνωτέρω τούτων, οἷον
τὸ ἰσοσκελὲς καὶ τὸ ἰσόπλευρον ταὐτὸ καὶ ἓν σχῆμα ὅτι
ἄμφω τρίγωνα· τρίγωνα δ᾽ οὐ ταὐτά. ἔτι δὲ ἓν λέγεται
ὅσων ὁ λόγος ὁ τὸ τί ἦν εἶναι λέγων ἀδιαίρετος πρὸς ἄλλον
τὸν δηλοῦντα [τί ἦν εἶναι] τὸ πρᾶγμα (αὐτὸς γὰρ καθ᾽ αὑτὸν
35 πᾶς λόγος διαιρετός). οὕτω γὰρ καὶ τὸ ηὐξημένον καὶ φθῖ-
νον ἕν ἐστιν, ὅτι ὁ λόγος εἷς, ὥσπερ ἐπὶ τῶν ἐπιπέδων ὁ τοῦ
1016ᵇ εἴδους. ὅλως δὲ ὧν ἡ νόησις ἀδιαίρετος ἡ νοοῦσα τὸ τί ἦν
εἶναι, καὶ μὴ δύναται χωρίσαι μήτε χρόνῳ μήτε τόπῳ
μήτε λόγῳ, μάλιστα ταῦτα ἕν, καὶ τούτων ὅσα οὐσίαι· καθόλου γὰρ ὅσα μὴ ἔχει διαίρεσιν, ἡ μὴ ἔχει, ταύτῃ ἓν λέ-
5 γεται, οἷον εἰ ἡ ἄνθρωπος μὴ ἔχει διαίρεσιν, εἷς ἄνθρωπος,
εἰ δ᾽ ἡ ζῷον, ἓν ζῷον, εἰ δὲ ἡ μέγεθος, ἓν μέγεθος. τὰ μὲν
οὖν πλεῖστα ἓν λέγεται τῷ ἕτερόν τι ἢ ποιεῖν ἢ ἔχειν ἢ
πάσχειν ἢ πρός τι εἶναι ἕν, τὰ δὲ πρώτως λεγόμενα ἓν ὧν ἡ
οὐσία μία, μία δὲ ἢ συνεχείᾳ ἢ εἴδει ἢ λόγῳ· καὶ γὰρ
10 ἀριθμοῦμεν ὡς πλείω ἢ τὰ μὴ συνεχῆ ἢ ὧν μὴ ἓν τὸ εἶδος
ἢ ὧν ὁ λόγος μὴ εἷς. ἔτι δ᾽ ἔστι μὲν ὡς ὁτιοῦν ἕν φαμεν
εἶναι ἂν ἦ ποσὸν καὶ συνεχές, ἔστι δ᾽ ὡς οὔ, ἂν μή τι ὅλον
ἦ, τοῦτο δὲ ἂν μὴ τὸ εἶδος ἔχῃ ἕν· οἷον οὐκ ἂν φαῖμεν
ὁμοίως ἓν ἰδόντες ὁπωσοῦν τὰ μέρη συγκείμενα τοῦ ὑποδή-
15 ματος, ἐὰν μὴ διὰ τὴν συνέχειαν, ἀλλ᾽ ἐὰν οὕτως ὥστε ὑπό-
δημα εἶναι καὶ εἶδός τι ἔχειν ἤδη ἕν· διὸ καὶ ἡ τοῦ κύκλου
μάλιστα μία τῶν γραμμῶν, ὅτι ὅλη καὶ τέλειός ἐστιν.—τὸ
δὲ ἑνὶ εἶναι ἀρχῇ τινί ἐστιν ἀριθμοῦ εἶναι· τὸ γὰρ πρῶτον
μέτρον ἀρχή, ᾧ γὰρ πρώτῳ γνωρίζομεν, τοῦτο πρῶτον μέ-
20 τρον ἑκάστου γένους· ἀρχὴ οὖν τοῦ γνωστοῦ περὶ ἕκαστον τὸ

ᵃ 29 δὲ κατὰ τὸ fort. Al. Asc.   γένος Aᵇ Al. Asc. : γένος ὁ EJΓ
30 τὸ . . . τούτων an spuria ?   τὸ Al. : τὰ codd. : τοῦ Γ : τῶν Asc.ᶜ
32 τρίγωνα pr. Aᵇ Asc.ᶜ : τρίγωνον EJΓ   33 ὁ alt. om. Aᵇ
34 τί ἦν εἶναι seclusi   35 διαιρετός EJΓ Al. : ἀδιαίρετος Aᵇ
ᵇ 1 εἴδους Aᵇ Al.ᶜ : εἴδους εἷς EJΓ   4 γὰρ] δὲ E   ἡ μὴ ἔχει om. Aᵇ
7 ἔχειν ἢ πάσχειν EJAᵇ : πάσχειν ἢ ἔχειν Γ   10 ἀριθμῷ μόνως.
ἐπεὶ δ᾽ ἐστὶν ἢ τὰ μὲν γρ. E²   ἢ pr. EJΓ Al.ᶜ Asc.ᶜ : om. Aᵇ
11 ἢ . . . εἷς EJΓ Asc.ᶜ : om. Aᵇ Al.   ἔτι JΓ γρ. E ci. Al. : ἐπεὶ
EAᵇ Al. Asc.   ἕν] ἓν συνεχείᾳ JΓ Asc.ᶜ   13 τὸ EJΓ Al.
Asc.ᶜ : τι Aᵇ   14 ὁπωσοῦν ἰδόντες Aᵇ   16 ἤδη ἔχειν Aᵇ
18 ἑνὶ EJΓ Al. : ἓν Aᵇ Asc.ᶜ   ἀρχὴ EJΓ Asc.ᶜ : ἀρχὴ τοῦ Jaeger
ἀριθμοῦ susp. Christ : ἀριθμῷ EJΓ Jaeger   19 ἀρχή EJΓ Asc.ᶜ :
ἑκάστου γένους ἀρχή Aᵇ : ἀρχή τινι εἶναί ἐστι Γ   γὰρ] δὲ Christ

ἕν. οὐ ταὐτὸ δὲ ἐν πᾶσι τοῖς γένεσι τὸ ἕν. ἔνθα μὲν γὰρ
δίεσις ἔνθα δὲ τὸ φωνῆεν ἢ ἄφωνον· βάρους δὲ ἕτερον καὶ
κινήσεως ἄλλο. πανταχοῦ δὲ τὸ ἓν ἢ τῷ ποσῷ ἢ τῷ εἴδει ἀδιαίρετον. τὸ μὲν οὖν κατὰ τὸ ποσὸν ἀδιαίρετον,
τὸ μὲν πάντῃ καὶ ἄθετον λέγεται μονάς, τὸ δὲ πάντῃ 25
καὶ θέσιν ἔχον στιγμή, τὸ δὲ μοναχῇ γραμμή, τὸ δὲ διχῇ
ἐπίπεδον, τὸ δὲ πάντῃ καὶ τριχῇ διαιρετὸν κατὰ τὸ ποσὸν
σῶμα· καὶ ἀντιστρέψαντι δὴ τὸ μὲν διχῇ διαιρετὸν ἐπίπεδον, τὸ δὲ μοναχῇ γραμμή, τὸ δὲ μηδαμῇ διαιρετὸν κατὰ
τὸ ποσὸν στιγμὴ καὶ μονάς, ἡ μὲν ἄθετος μονὰς ἡ δὲ θετὸς 30
στιγμή. ἔτι δὲ τὰ μὲν κατ' ἀριθμόν ἐστιν ἕν, τὰ δὲ κατ'
εἶδος, τὰ δὲ κατὰ γένος, τὰ δὲ κατ' ἀναλογίαν, ἀριθμῷ
μὲν ὧν ἡ ὕλη μία, εἴδει δ' ὧν ὁ λόγος εἷς, γένει δ' ὧν τὸ
αὐτὸ σχῆμα τῆς κατηγορίας, κατ' ἀναλογίαν δὲ ὅσα ἔχει ὡς
ἄλλο πρὸς ἄλλο. ἀεὶ δὲ τὰ ὕστερα τοῖς ἔμπροσθεν ἀκολουθεῖ, 35
οἷον ὅσα ἀριθμῷ καὶ εἴδει ἕν, ὅσα δ' εἴδει οὐ πάντα ἀριθμῷ·
ἀλλὰ γένει πάντα ἓν ὅσαπερ καὶ εἴδει, ὅσα δὲ γένει οὐ πάν- 1017ᵃ
τα εἴδει ἀλλ' ἀναλογίᾳ· ὅσα δὲ ἀναλογίᾳ οὐ πάντα γένει. φανερὸν δὲ καὶ ὅτι τὰ πολλὰ ἀντικειμένως λεχθήσεται
τῷ ἑνί· τὰ μὲν γὰρ τῷ μὴ συνεχῆ εἶναι, τὰ δὲ τῷ διαιρετὴν ἔχειν τὴν ὕλην κατὰ τὸ εἶδος, ἢ τὴν πρώτην ἢ τὴν τελευ- 5
ταίαν, τὰ δὲ τῷ τοὺς λόγους πλείους τοὺς τί ἦν εἶναι λέγοντας.

7 Τὸ ὂν λέγεται τὸ μὲν κατὰ συμβεβηκὸς τὸ δὲ καθ'
αὑτό, κατὰ συμβεβηκὸς μέν, οἷον τὸν δίκαιον μουσικὸν
εἶναί φαμεν καὶ τὸν ἄνθρωπον μουσικὸν καὶ τὸν μουσικὸν
ἄνθρωπον, παραπλησίως λέγοντες ὡσπερεὶ τὸν μουσικὸν οἰκο- 10
δομεῖν ὅτι συμβέβηκε τῷ οἰκοδόμῳ μουσικῷ εἶναι ἢ τῷ
μουσικῷ οἰκοδόμῳ (τὸ γὰρ τόδε εἶναι τόδε σημαίνει τὸ συμβεβηκέναι τῷδε τόδε),—οὕτω δὲ καὶ ἐπὶ τῶν εἰρημένων· τὸν
γὰρ ἄνθρωπον ὅταν μουσικὸν λέγωμεν καὶ τὸν μουσικὸν ἄνθρωπον, ἢ τὸν λευκὸν μουσικὸν ἢ τοῦτον λευκόν, τὸ μὲν ὅτι 15

ᵇ 24 ποσὸν Aᵇ et fort. Al.: ποσὸν καὶ ἢ ποσὸν ΕΓ Asc. et fecit J
26 στιγμή. τὸ δὲ μοναχῇ ⟨διαιρετὸν⟩ Jaeger 31 δὲ om. Aᵇ ἐστιν
ΕΓΓ Asc.¹: om. Aᵇ 33 μὲν οὖν ὧν Aᵇ εἷς ΕΓΓ Al.ᶜ Asc.ᶜ:
om. Aᵇ 35 δὲ Aᵇ Asc.ᶜ: δὴ ΕΓΓ 36 ὅσα alt.] ὅ Aᵇ 1017ᵃ
2 δὲ] δὲ ἐν ΕJ Asc. 6 λέγονται recc. 8 μουσικὸς Ε 9 τὸν
alt.] τὸ Al. 10 λέγεται Ε ὡσπερεὶ Aᵇ et ut vid. Al.: ὥσπερ
ΕΓΓ Asc.ᶜ 12 τῷδε Ε² τόδε om. Ε¹ 13 τῷδε τόδε ΕJ Asc.:
τόδε τῷδε AᵇΓ 14 γὰρ Aᵇ Al.: om. ΕJΓ Asc.ᶜ λέγομεν J 15
τὸν λευκὸν] λευκὸν τὸν ΕJ

ἄμφω τῷ αὐτῷ συμβεβήκασι, τὸ δ᾽ ὅτι τῷ ὄντι συμβέβηκε,
τὸ δὲ μουσικὸν ἄνθρωπον ὅτι τούτῳ τὸ μουσικὸν συμβέβηκεν (οὕτω δὲ λέγεται καὶ τὸ μὴ λευκὸν εἶναι, ὅτι ᾧ
συμβέβηκεν, ἐκεῖνο ἔστιν)· —τὰ μὲν οὖν κατὰ συμβεβηκὸς
20 εἶναι λεγόμενα οὕτω λέγεται ἢ διότι τῷ αὐτῷ ὄντι ἄμφω
ὑπάρχει, ἢ ὅτι ὄντι ἐκείνῳ ὑπάρχει, ἢ ὅτι αὐτὸ ἔστιν ᾧ
ὑπάρχει οὗ αὐτὸ κατηγορεῖται· καθ᾽ αὑτὰ δὲ εἶναι λέγεται
ὅσαπερ σημαίνει τὰ σχήματα τῆς κατηγορίας· ὁσαχῶς
γὰρ λέγεται, τοσαυταχῶς τὸ εἶναι σημαίνει. ἐπεὶ οὖν τῶν
25 κατηγορουμένων τὰ μὲν τί ἐστι σημαίνει, τὰ δὲ ποιόν, τὰ δὲ
ποσόν, τὰ δὲ πρός τι, τὰ δὲ ποιεῖν ἢ πάσχειν, τὰ δὲ πού,
τὰ δὲ ποτέ, ἑκάστῳ τούτων τὸ εἶναι ταὐτὸ σημαίνει· οὐθὲν
γὰρ διαφέρει τὸ ἄνθρωπος ὑγιαίνων ἐστὶν ἢ τὸ ἄνθρωπος
ὑγιαίνει, οὐδὲ τὸ ἄνθρωπος βαδίζων ἐστὶν ἢ τέμνων τοῦ ἄν-
30 θρωπος βαδίζει ἢ τέμνει, ὁμοίως δὲ καὶ ἐπὶ τῶν ἄλλων.
ἔτι τὸ εἶναι σημαίνει καὶ τὸ ἔστιν ὅτι ἀληθές, τὸ δὲ μὴ εἶναι
ὅτι οὐκ ἀληθὲς ἀλλὰ ψεῦδος, ὁμοίως ἐπὶ καταφάσεως καὶ
ἀποφάσεως, οἷον ὅτι ἔστι Σωκράτης μουσικός, ὅτι ἀληθὲς
τοῦτο, ἢ ὅτι ἔστι Σωκράτης οὐ λευκός, ὅτι ἀληθές· τὸ δ᾽ οὐκ
35 ἔστιν ἡ διάμετρος σύμμετρος, ὅτι ψεῦδος. ἔτι τὸ εἶναι ση-
1017b μαίνει καὶ τὸ ὂν τὸ μὲν δυνάμει ῥητὸν τὸ δ᾽ ἐντελεχείᾳ
τῶν εἰρημένων τούτων· ὁρῶν τε γὰρ εἶναί φαμεν καὶ τὸ δυνάμει ὁρῶν καὶ τὸ ἐντελεχείᾳ, καὶ [τὸ] ἐπίστασθαι
ὡσαύτως καὶ τὸ δυνάμενον χρῆσθαι τῇ ἐπιστήμῃ καὶ τὸ
5 χρώμενον, καὶ ἠρεμοῦν καὶ ᾧ ἤδη ὑπάρχει ἠρεμία καὶ
τὸ δυνάμενον ἠρεμεῖν. ὁμοίως δὲ καὶ ἐπὶ τῶν οὐσιῶν· καὶ
γὰρ Ἑρμῆν ἐν τῷ λίθῳ φαμὲν εἶναι, καὶ τὸ ἥμισυ τῆς
γραμμῆς, καὶ σῖτον τὸν μήπω ἁδρόν. πότε δὲ δυνατὸν καὶ
πότε οὔπω, ἐν ἄλλοις διοριστέον.

ᵃ 16 αὐτῷ EJ Al. Asc.ᶜ: αὐτῷ ὄντι AᵇΓ   τῷ ὄντι συμβέβηκε EJΓ
Asc.ᶜ: συμβέβηκε τῷ ὄντι Aᵇ   17 τὸ δὲ ... συμβέβηκεν EJΓ Al.
Asc.: om. Aᵇ   18 μὴ Aᵇ Al. Asc.: om. EJΓ   19 ἐκεῖνο Aᵇ Al.ᶜ
Asc.ᶜ et fecit E: ἐκεῖνος JΓ   20 ἄμφω ὄντι Aᵇ   21 ἐκείνῳ
EJ Asc.: ἐκεῖνο AᵇΓ   28 ἔστιν Christ   ἢ τὸ EJΓ Asc.ᶜ:
om. Aᵇ   29 οὐδὲ] ἢ EJΓ Asc.   ἔστιν Christ   29–30 ἄνθρωπον βαδίζειν ἢ τέμνειν EJΓ   35 σύμμετρος Al. Bonitz: ἀσύμμετρος codd. Γ   ᵇ 1 ὂν] ὂν καὶ Aᵇ: ὂν· τὸ ὂν J   ῥητὸν δυνάμει
Aᵇ: δυνάμει γρ. E Al. Asc.: γρ. ῥητὸν E Al. Asc.   2 ὁρῶντες γάρ
φαμεν εἶναι Aᵇ   3 ὁρῶν Aᵇ Al. Asc.: ῥητῶς ὁρῶν EJΓ   τὸ om.
ut vid. Al., secl. Bonitz   5 καὶ ρτ.] καὶ τὸ EJ Asc.   ἤδη] δὴ Aᵇ
7 τῆς] τῇ Aᵇ

8 Οὐσία λέγεται τά τε ἁπλᾶ σώματα, οἷον γῆ καὶ πῦρ 10
καὶ ὕδωρ καὶ ὅσα τοιαῦτα, καὶ ὅλως σώματα καὶ τὰ
ἐκ τούτων συνεστῶτα ζῷά τε καὶ δαιμόνια καὶ τὰ μόρια
τούτων· ἅπαντα δὲ ταῦτα λέγεται οὐσία ὅτι οὐ καθ᾽ ὑποκειμένου λέγεται ἀλλὰ κατὰ τούτων τὰ ἄλλα. ἄλλον δὲ
τρόπον ὃ ἂν ᾖ αἴτιον τοῦ εἶναι, ἐνυπάρχον ἐν τοῖς τοιούτοις 15
ὅσα μὴ λέγεται καθ᾽ ὑποκειμένου, οἷον ἡ ψυχὴ τῷ ζῴῳ.
ἔτι ὅσα μόρια ἐνυπάρχοντά ἐστιν ἐν τοῖς τοιούτοις ὁρίζοντά
τε καὶ τόδε τι σημαίνοντα, ὧν ἀναιρουμένων ἀναιρεῖται τὸ
ὅλον, οἷον ἐπιπέδου σῶμα, ὥς φασί τινες, καὶ ἐπίπεδον
γραμμῆς· καὶ ὅλως ὁ ἀριθμὸς δοκεῖ εἶναί τισι τοιοῦτος 20
(ἀναιρουμένου τε γὰρ οὐδὲν εἶναι, καὶ ὁρίζειν πάντα)· ἔτι τὸ τί
ἦν εἶναι, οὗ ὁ λόγος ὁρισμός, καὶ τοῦτο οὐσία λέγεται ἑκάστου.
συμβαίνει δὴ κατὰ δύο τρόπους τὴν οὐσίαν λέγεσθαι, τό θ᾽
ὑποκείμενον ἔσχατον, ὃ μηκέτι κατ᾽ ἄλλου λέγεται, καὶ ὃ
ἂν τόδε τι ὂν καὶ χωριστὸν ᾖ· τοιοῦτον δὲ ἑκάστου ἡ μορφὴ 25
καὶ τὸ εἶδος.

9 Ταὐτὰ λέγεται τὰ μὲν κατὰ συμβεβηκός, οἷον τὸ
λευκὸν καὶ τὸ μουσικὸν τὸ αὐτὸ ὅτι τῷ αὐτῷ συμβέβηκε,
καὶ ἄνθρωπος καὶ μουσικὸν ὅτι θάτερον θατέρῳ συμβέβηκεν,
τὸ δὲ μουσικὸν ἄνθρωπος ὅτι τῷ ἀνθρώπῳ συμβέβηκεν· ἑκα- 30
τέρῳ δὲ τοῦτο καὶ τούτῳ ἑκάτερον ἐκείνων, καὶ γὰρ τῷ ἀνθρώπῳ τῷ μουσικῷ καὶ ὁ ἄνθρωπος καὶ τὸ μουσικὸν ταὐτὸ
λέγεται, καὶ τούτοις ἐκεῖνο (διὸ καὶ πάντα ταῦτα καθόλου
οὐ λέγεται· οὐ γὰρ ἀληθὲς εἰπεῖν ὅτι πᾶς ἄνθρωπος ταὐτὸ
καὶ τὸ μουσικόν· τὰ γὰρ καθόλου καθ᾽ αὑτὰ ὑπάρχει, τὰ 35
δὲ συμβεβηκότα οὐ καθ᾽ αὑτά· ἀλλ᾽ ἐπὶ τῶν καθ᾽ ἕκαστα 1018ᵃ
ἁπλῶς λέγεται· ταὐτὸ γὰρ δοκεῖ Σωκράτης καὶ Σωκράτης
εἶναι μουσικός· τὸ δὲ Σωκράτης οὐκ ἐπὶ πολλῶν, διὸ οὐ πᾶς
Σωκράτης λέγεται ὥσπερ πᾶς ἄνθρωπος)·—καὶ τὰ μὲν οὕτως
λέγεται ταὐτά, τὰ δὲ καθ᾽ αὑτὰ ὁσαχῶσπερ καὶ τὸ ἕν· καὶ 5

ᵇ 16 τῶν ζῴων Aᵇ Asc. et ut vid Al. : τοῦ ζῴου Γ   17 ἐνυπάρχοντά
. . . τοιούτοις EJΓ Al. Asc. : ἔστιν Aᵇ   18 τε EJΓ Al. : om. Aᵇ
22 ὁ λόγος ἐστὶν ὁρισμός EJΓ : λόγος ἐστὶν ὁ ὁρισμός ut vid. Al.
23 κατὰ EJΓ Asc.ᶜ : om. Aᵇ   25 ᾖ EJΓ Al. : τοιοῦτον ᾖ Aᵇ
τοιοῦτον EJΓ Al.ᶜ : τοῦτο Aᵇ   27 ταὐτὰ δὲ λέγεται JΓ Al.¹ Asc.¹
30 τὸ . . . συμβέβηκεν om. E   ὅτι] ὅτι τὸ μουσικὸν JΓ   31 καὶ τούτων
AᵇJΓ   ἐκείνῳ AᵇΓ   32 τῷ] καὶ τῷ Aᵇ   καὶ ὁ] τὸ Aᵇ   35 τὰ Aᵇ
om. EJ   1018ᵃ 3 δὲ] γὰρ EJΓ Al. Asc.   4 καὶ et 5 τὰ om. Aᵇ
5 ὁσαχῶσπερ ex Al. ci. Jaeger: ὅσα ὥσπερ EJ : ὥσπερ Aᵇ Asc.
τὸ EJ Al. : om. Aᵇ Asc.ᶜ

γὰρ ὧν ἡ ὕλη μία ἢ εἴδει ἢ ἀριθμῷ ταὐτὰ λέγεται καὶ
ὧν ἡ οὐσία μία, ὥστε φανερὸν ὅτι ἡ ταυτότης ἑνότης τίς ἐστιν
ἢ πλειόνων τοῦ εἶναι ἢ ὅταν χρῆται ὡς πλείοσιν, οἷον ὅταν
λέγῃ αὐτὸ αὑτῷ ταὐτόν· ὡς δυσὶ γὰρ χρῆται αὐτῷ.—ἕτερα
10 δὲ λέγεται ὧν ἢ τὰ εἴδη πλείω ἢ ἡ ὕλη ἢ ὁ λόγος τῆς
οὐσίας· καὶ ὅλως ἀντικειμένως τῷ ταὐτῷ λέγεται τὸ ἕτερον.

Διάφορα δὲ λέγεται ὅσ᾽ ἕτερά ἐστι τὸ αὐτό τι ὄντα, μὴ
μόνον ἀριθμῷ ἀλλ᾽ ἢ εἴδει ἢ γένει ἢ ἀναλογίᾳ· ἔτι ὧν
ἕτερον τὸ γένος, καὶ τὰ ἐναντία, καὶ ὅσα ἔχει ἐν τῇ οὐσίᾳ
15 τὴν ἑτερότητα. ὅμοια λέγεται τά τε πάντῃ ταὐτὸ πεπονθότα, καὶ τὰ πλείω ταὐτὰ πεπονθότα ἢ ἕτερα, καὶ ὧν ἡ
ποιότης μία· καὶ καθ᾽ ὅσα ἀλλοιοῦσθαι ἐνδέχεται τῶν ἐναντίων, τούτων τὸ πλείω ἔχον ἢ κυριώτερα ὅμοιον τούτῳ. ἀντικειμένως δὲ τοῖς ὁμοίοις τὰ ἀνόμοια.

20 Ἀντικείμενα λέγεται ἀντίφασις καὶ τἀναντία καὶ τὰ 10
πρός τι καὶ στέρησις καὶ ἕξις καὶ ἐξ ὧν καὶ εἰς ἃ ἔσχατα
αἱ γενέσεις καὶ φθοραί· καὶ ὅσα μὴ ἐνδέχεται ἅμα
παρεῖναι τῷ ἀμφοῖν δεκτικῷ, ταῦτα ἀντικεῖσθαι λέγεται
ἢ αὐτὰ ἢ ἐξ ὧν ἐστίν. φαιὸν γὰρ καὶ λευκὸν ἅμα τῷ
25 αὐτῷ οὐχ ὑπάρχει· διὸ ἐξ ὧν ἐστὶν ἀντίκειται. ἐναντία λέγεται τά τε μὴ δυνατὰ ἅμα τῷ αὐτῷ παρεῖναι τῶν διαφερόντων κατὰ γένος, καὶ τὰ πλεῖστον διαφέροντα τῶν ἐν
τῷ αὐτῷ γένει, καὶ τὰ πλεῖστον διαφέροντα τῶν ἐν ταὐτῷ
δεκτικῷ, καὶ τὰ πλεῖστον διαφέροντα τῶν ὑπὸ τὴν αὐτὴν
30 δύναμιν, καὶ ὧν ἡ διαφορὰ μεγίστη ἢ ἁπλῶς ἢ κατὰ
γένος ἢ κατ᾽ εἶδος. τὰ δ᾽ ἄλλα ἐναντία λέγεται τὰ μὲν
τῷ τὰ τοιαῦτα ἔχειν, τὰ δὲ τῷ δεκτικὰ εἶναι τῶν τοιούτων,
τὰ δὲ τῷ ποιητικὰ ἢ παθητικὰ εἶναι τῶν τοιούτων, ἢ ποιοῦν-
τα ἢ πάσχοντα, ἢ ἀποβολαὶ ἢ λήψεις, ἢ ἕξεις ἢ στερή-
35 σεις εἶναι τῶν τοιούτων. ἐπεὶ δὲ τὸ ἓν καὶ τὸ ὂν πολλαχῶς
λέγεται, ἀκολουθεῖν ἀνάγκη καὶ τἆλλα ὅσα κατὰ ταῦτα
λέγεται, ὥστε καὶ τὸ ταὐτὸν καὶ τὸ ἕτερον καὶ τὸ ἐναντίον,
ὥστ᾽ εἶναι ἕτερον καθ᾽ ἑκάστην κατηγορίαν.—ἕτερα δὲ τῷ εἴδει

ᵃ 8.ἢ pr. EJΓ Asc.ᶜ: om. Aᵇ   ὡς πλείοσιν EJΓ Al.ᶜ Asc.ᶜ: om. Aᵇ
9 αὑτῷ] αὐτῷ Aᵇ: αὑτο fecit E   12 δὲ EJΓ Asc.ˡᶜ: om. Aᵇ   μὴ
Aᵇ Asc.ᶜ: καὶ μὴ EJΓ   15 πάντῃ Aᵇ Al.: om. EJΓ Asc.   16 ταὐτὰ
Al. ia: ταὐτὸ codd. Γ   22 αἱ Aᵇ Al.: οἷον αἱ EJΓ Asc.   25 ἀντί-
κειται] ἀντίκειται τούτοις EJΓ   28 τῶν] τῷ EΓ   32 τῷ ταῦτα
ἔχειν Aᵇ   35 τῶν τοιούτων] τούτων Aᵇ

λέγεται ὅσα τε ταὐτοῦ γένους ὄντα μὴ ὑπάλληλά ἐστι, καὶ 1018ᵇ
ὅσα ἐν τῷ αὐτῷ γένει ὄντα διαφορὰν ἔχει, καὶ ὅσα ἐν τῇ
οὐσίᾳ ἐναντίωσιν ἔχει· καὶ τὰ ἐναντία ἕτερα τῷ εἴδει ἀλλήλων ἢ πάντα ἢ τὰ λεγόμενα πρώτως, καὶ ὅσων ἐν τῷ
τελευταίῳ τοῦ γένους εἴδει οἱ λόγοι ἕτεροι (οἷον ἄνθρωπος 5
καὶ ἵππος ἄτομα τῷ γένει οἱ δὲ λόγοι ἕτεροι αὐτῶν), καὶ
ὅσα ἐν τῇ αὐτῇ οὐσίᾳ ὄντα ἔχει διαφοράν. ταὐτὰ δὲ τῷ
εἴδει τὰ ἀντικειμένως λεγόμενα τούτοις.

11   Πρότερα καὶ ὕστερα λέγεται ἔνια μέν, ὡς ὄντος τινὸς
πρώτου καὶ ἀρχῆς ἐν ἑκάστῳ γένει, τῷ ἐγγύτερον ⟨εἶναι⟩ ἀρχῆς 10
τινὸς ὡρισμένης ἢ ἁπλῶς καὶ τῇ φύσει ἢ πρός τι ἢ πού
ἢ ὑπό τινων, οἷον τὰ μὲν κατὰ τόπον τῷ εἶναι ἐγγύτερον ἢ
φύσει τινὸς τόπου ὡρισμένου (οἷον τοῦ μέσου ἢ τοῦ ἐσχάτου)
ἢ πρὸς τὸ τυχόν, τὸ δὲ πορρώτερον ὕστερον· τὰ δὲ κατὰ
χρόνον (τὰ μὲν γὰρ τῷ πορρώτερον τοῦ νῦν, οἷον ἐπὶ τῶν 15
γενομένων, πρότερον γὰρ τὰ Τρωϊκὰ τῶν Μηδικῶν ὅτι πορρώτερον ἀπέχει τοῦ νῦν· τὰ δὲ τῷ ἐγγύτερον τοῦ νῦν, οἷον
ἐπὶ τῶν μελλόντων, πρότερον γὰρ Νέμεα Πυθίων ὅτι ἐγγύτερον τοῦ νῦν τῷ νῦν ὡς ἀρχῇ καὶ πρώτῳ χρησαμένων)· τὰ
δὲ κατὰ κίνησιν (τὸ γὰρ ἐγγύτερον τοῦ πρώτου κινήσαντος 20
πρότερον, οἷον παῖς ἀνδρός· ἀρχὴ δὲ καὶ αὕτη τις ἁπλῶς)·
τὰ δὲ κατὰ δύναμιν (τὸ γὰρ ὑπερέχον τῇ δυνάμει πρότερον,
καὶ τὸ δυνατώτερον· τοιοῦτον δ' ἐστὶν οὗ κατὰ τὴν προαίρεσιν
ἀνάγκη ἀκολουθεῖν θάτερον καὶ τὸ ὕστερον, ὥστε μὴ κινοῦντός
τε ἐκείνου μὴ κινεῖσθαι καὶ κινοῦντος κινεῖσθαι· ἡ δὲ προαί- 25
ρεσις ἀρχή)· τὰ δὲ κατὰ τάξιν (ταῦτα δ' ἐστὶν ὅσα πρός
τι ἓν ὡρισμένον διέστηκε κατά τινα λόγον, οἷον παραστάτης
τριτοστάτου πρότερον καὶ παρανήτη νήτης· ἔνθα μὲν γὰρ ὁ
κορυφαῖος ἔνθα δὲ ἡ μέση ἀρχή)·—ταῦτα μὲν οὖν πρότερα
τούτου λέγεται τὸν τρόπον, ἄλλον δὲ τρόπον τὸ τῇ γνώσει 30
πρότερον ὡς καὶ ἁπλῶς πρότερον. τούτων δὲ ἄλλως τὰ κατὰ

ᵇ 1 ἐστι] τέ ἐστι Aᵇ   4 ἐν τῷ τελευταίῳ ... 5 εἴδει] an ὄντων
τελευταίων ... εἰδῶν ?   7 ταῦτα J   9 πρότερα Aᵇ Asc.¹: τὰ
πρότερα EJ   10 γένει EJΓ Al.ᶜ Asc. Simpl.ᶜ: om. Aᵇ   τῷ Al.
Bonitz: τὸ codd. Γ Asc. Simpl.ᶜ εἶναι addidi: post τῷ add. Jaeger
15 τῷ] τὸ Aᵇ   πορρώτερον Aᵇ Simpl.ᶜ: πορρωτέρω EJ Asc.ᶜ
16 πρότερα recc. Γ Asc.   17 ἐγγυτέρω recc.   19 τῷ νῦν om.
recc. χρησάμενοι Aᵇ   20 τὸ EJΓ Asc.ᶜ Simpl.ᶜ: τὰ Aᵇ Al.   27
τινα ex Al. ci. Jaeger: τὸν codd. Γ Asc.ᶜ   28 καὶ] καὶ ἡ EJ   31
καὶ] ἢ γρ. E²

τὸν λόγον καὶ τὰ κατὰ τὴν αἴσθησιν. κατὰ μὲν γὰρ τὸν
λόγον τὰ καθόλου πρότερα κατὰ δὲ τὴν αἴσθησιν τὰ καθ᾿
ἕκαστα· καὶ κατὰ τὸν λόγον δὲ τὸ συμβεβηκὸς τοῦ ὅλου
35 πρότερον, οἷον τὸ μουσικὸν τοῦ μουσικοῦ ἀνθρώπου· οὐ γὰρ
ἔσται ὁ λόγος ὅλος ἄνευ τοῦ μέρους· καίτοι οὐκ ἐνδέχεται
μουσικὸν εἶναι μὴ ὄντος μουσικοῦ τινός. ἔτι πρότερα λέγεται τὰ τῶν προτέρων πάθη, οἷον εὐθύτης λειότητος· τὸ μὲν
1019ᵃ γὰρ γραμμῆς καθ᾿ αὑτὴν πάθος τὸ δὲ ἐπιφανείας. τὰ
μὲν δὴ οὕτω λέγεται πρότερα καὶ ὕστερα, τὰ δὲ κατὰ φύσιν
καὶ οὐσίαν, ὅσα ἐνδέχεται εἶναι ἄνευ ἄλλων, ἐκεῖνα δὲ ἄνευ
ἐκείνων μή· ᾗ διαιρέσει ἐχρήσατο Πλάτων. (ἐπεὶ δὲ τὸ εἶναι
5 πολλαχῶς, πρῶτον μὲν τὸ ὑποκείμενον πρότερον, διὸ ἡ
οὐσία πρότερον, ἔπειτα ἄλλως τὰ κατὰ δύναμιν καὶ κατ᾿
ἐντελέχειαν· τὰ μὲν γὰρ κατὰ δύναμιν πρότερά ἐστι τὰ
δὲ κατὰ ἐντελέχειαν, οἷον κατὰ δύναμιν μὲν ἡ ἡμίσεια
τῆς ὅλης καὶ τὸ μόριον τοῦ ὅλου καὶ ἡ ὕλη τῆς οὐσίας, κατ᾿
10 ἐντελέχειαν δ᾿ ὕστερον· διαλυθέντος γὰρ κατ᾿ ἐντελέχειαν
ἔσται.) τρόπον δή τινα πάντα τὰ πρότερον καὶ ὕστερον λεγόμενα κατὰ ταῦτα λέγεται· τὰ μὲν γὰρ κατὰ γένεσιν ἐνδέχεται
ἄνευ τῶν ἑτέρων εἶναι, οἷον τὸ ὅλον τῶν μορίων, τὰ δὲ κατὰ
φθοράν, οἷον τὸ μόριον τοῦ ὅλου. ὁμοίως δὲ καὶ τἆλλα.

15 Δύναμις λέγεται ἡ μὲν ἀρχὴ κινήσεως ἢ μεταβολῆς 12
ἢ ἐν ἑτέρῳ ἢ ᾗ ἕτερον, οἷον ἡ οἰκοδομικὴ δύναμίς ἐστιν ἢ οὐχ
ὑπάρχει ἐν τῷ οἰκοδομουμένῳ, ἀλλ᾿ ἡ ἰατρικὴ δύναμις οὖσα
ὑπάρχοι ἂν ἐν τῷ ἰατρευομένῳ, ἀλλ᾿ οὐχ ᾗ ἰατρευόμενος.
ἡ μὲν οὖν ὅλως ἀρχὴ μεταβολῆς ἢ κινήσεως λέγεται δύνα-
20 μις ἐν ἑτέρῳ ἢ ᾗ ἕτερον, ἡ δ᾿ ὑφ᾿ ἑτέρου ἢ ᾗ ἕτερον (καθ᾿ ἣν
γὰρ τὸ πάσχον πάσχει τι, ὁτὲ μὲν ἐὰν ὁτιοῦν, δυνατὸν αὐτό
φαμεν εἶναι παθεῖν, ὁτὲ δ᾿ οὐ κατὰ πᾶν πάθος ἀλλ᾿ ἂν ἐπὶ
τὸ βέλτιον)· ἔτι ἡ τοῦ καλῶς τοῦτ᾿ ἐπιτελεῖν ἢ κατὰ προαί-
ρεσιν· ἐνίοτε γὰρ τοὺς μόνον ἂν πορευθέντας ἢ εἰπόντας, μὴ

ᵇ32 τὰ sup. lin. E   1019ᵃ 4 ἐχρήσατο AᵇΓ Asc. Simpl.ᶜ : ἐχρῆτο
EJ   7 τὰ μέν ... 8 ἐντελέχειαν EJΓ Asc.ᶜ : om. Aᵇ Simpl.ᶜ   9 καὶ
καὶ τὸ Aᵇ   11 ἔσται καὶ τρόπον Aᵇ   12 ταῦτα Bullinger
16 ἢ Aᵇ Asc. : ἢ EJΓ   ἢ EJΓ Al. : om. Aᵇ Asc.   ἢ om. Aᵇ   ἢ Ε
19 ὅλως] οὕτως Jaeger   20 ἢ om. Aᵇ Asc.   ᾗ] ᾗι EJ   ἢ om. Aᵇ Γ
Asc.   καθ᾿ ... 23 βέλτιον post 26 πάσχειν transponenda ci. Christ
21 μὲν οὖν ἐὰν fort. Al.   δυνατόν ... 22 εἶναι] παθεῖν ᾗ δυνατὸν φαμεν
εἶναι αὐτό EJΓ   δυνατόν] τὸ δυνατὸν Aᵇ : δυνατὸν δυνατὸν γρ. Ε   23
ἢ JAᵇ Al. Asc. : ἢ EΓ

καλῶς δὲ ἢ μὴ ὡς προείλοντο, οὔ φαμεν δύνασθαι λέγειν 25
ἢ βαδίζειν· ὁμοίως δὲ καὶ ἐπὶ τοῦ πάσχειν. ἔτι ὅσαι ἕξεις
καθ' ἃς ἀπαθῆ ὅλως ἢ ἀμετάβλητα ἢ μὴ ῥᾳδίως ἐπὶ τὸ
χεῖρον εὐμετακίνητα, δυνάμεις λέγονται· κλᾶται μὲν γὰρ
καὶ συντρίβεται καὶ κάμπτεται καὶ ὅλως φθείρεται οὐ τῷ
δύνασθαι ἀλλὰ τῷ μὴ δύνασθαι καὶ ἐλλείπειν τινός· 30
ἀπαθῆ δὲ τῶν τοιούτων ἃ μόλις καὶ ἠρέμα πάσχει διὰ δύναμιν καὶ τῷ δύνασθαι καὶ τῷ ἔχειν πώς. λεγομένης δὲ
τῆς δυνάμεως τοσαυταχῶς, καὶ τὸ δυνατὸν ἕνα μὲν τρόπον
λεχθήσεται τὸ ἔχον κινήσεως ἀρχὴν ἢ μεταβολῆς (καὶ γὰρ
τὸ στατικὸν δυνατόν τι) ἐν ἑτέρῳ ἢ ᾗ ἕτερον, ἕνα δ' ἐὰν ἔχῃ 35
τι αὐτοῦ ἄλλο δύναμιν τοιαύτην, ἕνα δ' ἐὰν ἔχῃ μεταβάλ- 1019ᵇ
λειν ἐφ' ὁτιοῦν δύναμιν, εἴτ' ἐπὶ τὸ χεῖρον εἴτ' ἐπὶ τὸ βέλτιον (καὶ γὰρ τὸ φθειρόμενον δοκεῖ δυνατὸν εἶναι φθείρεσθαι, ἢ οὐκ ἂν φθαρῆναι εἰ ἦν ἀδύνατον· νῦν δὲ ἔχει τινὰ
διάθεσιν καὶ αἰτίαν καὶ ἀρχὴν τοῦ τοιούτου πάθους· ὁτὲ μὲν 5
δὴ τῷ ἔχειν τι δοκεῖ, ὁτὲ δὲ τῷ ἐστερῆσθαι τοιοῦτον εἶναι· εἰ
δ' ἡ στέρησίς ἐστιν ἕξις πως, πάντα τῷ ἔχειν ἂν εἴη τι,
[εἰ δὲ μὴ] ὥστε τῷ τε ἔχειν ἕξιν τινὰ καὶ ἀρχήν ἐστι
δυνατὸν [ὁμωνύμως] καὶ τῷ ἔχειν τὴν τούτου στέρησιν, εἰ ἐνδέχεται ἔχειν στέρησιν· (εἰ δὲ μή, ὁμωνύμως))· ἕνα δὲ τῷ μὴ 10
ἔχειν αὐτοῦ δύναμιν ἢ ἀρχὴν ἄλλο ἢ ᾗ ἄλλο φθαρτικήν. ἔτι δὲ
ταῦτα πάντα ἢ τῷ μόνον ἂν συμβῆναι γενέσθαι ἢ μὴ γενέσθαι, ἢ τῷ καλῶς. καὶ γὰρ ἐν τοῖς ἀψύχοις ἔνεστιν ἡ τοιαύτη
δύναμις, οἷον ἐν τοῖς ὀργάνοις· τὴν μὲν γὰρ δύνασθαί φασι
φθέγγεσθαι λύραν, τὴν δ' οὐδέν, ἂν ᾖ μὴ εὔφωνος. ἀδυνα- 15
μία δὲ ἐστὶ στέρησις δυνάμεως καὶ τῆς τοιαύτης ἀρχῆς·
οἵα εἴρηται, ἢ ὅλως ἢ τῷ πεφυκότι ἔχειν, ἢ καὶ ὅτε

ᵃ 25 προείλαντο Aᵇ   30 κἂν Aᵇ   31 ἃ Asc. et fecit E : ἂν
Aᵇ : ἢ JΓ   μόγις Aᵇ Asc.ᶜ   πάσχῃ Aᵇ   32 τῷ . . . τῷ Jaeger:
τὸ . . . τὸ codd. Asc.   35 ἢ EJΓ Al. : om. Aᵇ   ᵇ4 εἰ μὴ ἦν
δυνατόν Aᵇ   6 τὸ . . . τὸ recc.   7 ἕξις EJΓ Al. Asc.ᶜ : om. Aᵇ
8 ὥστε . . . 10 ὁμωνύμως ex Al. conieci : idem ci. Christ, nisi quod εἰ
δὲ μή, ὁμωνύμως ante ὥστε, non post στέρησιν scripsit : εἰ δὲ μὴ τῷ
ἔχειν ἕξιν τινὰ καὶ ἀρχήν ἐστι δυνατὸν ὁμωνύμως, ὥστε τῷ τε ἔχειν τὴν
τούτου στέρησιν, εἰ ἐνδέχεται ἔχειν στέρησιν Aᵇ : ὁμωνύμως δὲ λεγόμενον (λέγομεν Γ) τὸ ὄν, ὥστε τῷ (τῷ τε Asc.) ἔχειν ἕξιν τινὰ καὶ ἀρχήν
ἐστι δυνατὸν καὶ τῷ ἔχειν τὴν τούτου στέρησιν, εἰ ἐνδέχεται ἔχειν στέρησιν
EJΓ et ut vid. Asc.   11 ἄλλο ex Al. scr. Bonitz : ἄλλῳ Aᵇᴳ :
ἐν ἄλλῳ EJ   ἢ om. Aᵇ Asc.   13 καλοῖς Aᵇ   ἔνεστιν ex ἐν
ἔστιν fecit E   14 φασι δύνασθαι Aᵇ   16 ἀρχῆς Aᵇ Al. : ἀρχῆς
ἄρσις τις EJΓ : ἀρχῆς ἄρνησις Asc.ᶜ   17 ὅτε EJΓ Asc.ᶜ : ὅτι Aᵇ

πέφυκεν ἤδη ἔχειν· οὐ γὰρ ὁμοίως ἂν φαῖεν ἀδύνατον εἶναι
γεννᾶν παῖδα καὶ ἄνδρα καὶ εὐνοῦχον. ἔτι δὲ καθ' ἑκατέραν
20 δύναμιν ἔστιν ἀδυναμία ἀντικειμένη, τῇ τε μόνον κινητικῇ
καὶ τῇ καλῶς κινητικῇ. καὶ ἀδύνατα δὴ τὰ μὲν κατὰ τὴν
ἀδυναμίαν ταύτην λέγεται, τὰ δὲ ἄλλον τρόπον, οἷον δυνατόν τε καὶ ἀδύνατον, ἀδύνατον μὲν οὗ τὸ ἐναντίον ἐξ
ἀνάγκης ἀληθές (οἷον τὸ τὴν διάμετρον σύμμετρον εἶναι
25 ἀδύνατον ὅτι ψεῦδος τὸ τοιοῦτον οὗ τὸ ἐναντίον οὐ μόνον ἀληθὲς ἀλλὰ καὶ ἀνάγκη [ἀσύμμετρον εἶναι]· τὸ ἄρα σύμμετρον οὐ μόνον ψεῦδος ἀλλὰ καὶ ἐξ ἀνάγκης ψεῦδος)· τὸ δ'
ἐναντίον τούτῳ, τὸ δυνατόν, ὅταν μὴ ἀναγκαῖον ᾖ τὸ ἐναντίον ψεῦδος εἶναι, οἷον τὸ καθῆσθαι ἄνθρωπον δυνατόν· οὐ
30 γὰρ ἐξ ἀνάγκης τὸ μὴ καθῆσθαι ψεῦδος. τὸ μὲν οὖν δυνατὸν ἕνα μὲν τρόπον, ὥσπερ εἴρηται, τὸ μὴ ἐξ ἀνάγκης ψεῦδος σημαίνει, ἕνα δὲ τὸ ἀληθές [εἶναι], ἕνα δὲ τὸ ἐνδεχόμενον ἀληθὲς εἶναι. κατὰ μεταφορὰν δὲ ἡ ἐν γεωμετρίᾳ
λέγεται δύναμις.. ταῦτα μὲν οὖν τὰ δυνατὰ οὐ κατὰ δύνα-
35 μιν· τὰ δὲ λεγόμενα κατὰ δύναμιν πάντα λέγεται πρὸς
1020ᵃ τὴν πρώτην [μίαν]· αὕτη δ' ἐστὶν ἀρχὴ μεταβολῆς ἐν ἄλλῳ
ἢ ᾗ ἄλλο. τὰ γὰρ ἄλλα λέγεται δυνατὰ τῷ τὰ μὲν ἔχειν
αὐτῶν ἄλλο τι τοιαύτην δύναμιν τὰ δὲ μὴ ἔχειν τὰ δὲ
ὡδὶ ἔχειν. ὁμοίως δὲ καὶ τὰ ἀδύνατα. ὥστε ὁ κύριος ὅρος
5 τῆς πρώτης δυνάμεως ἂν εἴη ἀρχὴ μεταβλητικὴ ἐν ἄλλῳ
ἢ ᾗ ἄλλο.

Ποσὸν λέγεται τὸ διαιρετὸν εἰς ἐνυπάρχοντα ὧν ἑκάτερον ἢ ἕκαστον ἕν τι καὶ τόδε τι πέφυκεν εἶναι. πλῆθος
μὲν οὖν ποσόν τι ἐὰν ἀριθμητὸν ᾖ, μέγεθος δὲ ἂν μετρητὸν
10 ᾖ. λέγεται δὲ πλῆθος μὲν τὸ διαιρετὸν δυνάμει εἰς μὴ συνεχῆ, μέγεθος δὲ τὸ εἰς συνεχῆ· μεγέθους δὲ τὸ μὲν ἐφ' ἓν

ᵇ 18 φαμεν Aᵇ : φαῖμεν Bekker   19 καὶ alt. AᵇΓ Al. Asc. : om.
EJ εὐνουχίαν J γρ. E ἑτέραν EJ   20 δύναμιν EJ Asc.ᶜ : τὴν δύναμιν
Aᵇ   21 δὲ EJΓ Asc.ᶜ   22 οἷον om. ut vid. Al., secl. Christ
25 οὗ] καὶ οὐ E   26 ἀσύμμετρον εἶναι seclusi   28 τὸ fort. om.
Al., omittendum ci. Bonitz   ᾖ om. Aᵇ   32 εἶναι seclusi : habent
codd. Γ Al. Asc.ᶜ   33 εἶναι E Al. : ἤδη JAᵇΓ Asc.   ἐν Aᵇ Al. :
ἐν τῇ EJ Asc.ᶜ   34 τὰ EJ Asc.ᶜ : om. Aᵇ   1020ᵃ 1 πρώτην
μίαν] πρώτην Al. Asc. : μίαν γρ. Asc.   2 ἢ om. JAᵇΓ Al. Asc.
ᾗ om. E¹   δυνατῷ τὰ μὲν J : δυνατὰ τὰ μὲν τῷ ΤΓ et fort. Al.
3 ἄλλο] ad aliud Γ   μὴ] τῷ μὴ EJΓ Asc.ᶜ et fort. Al.   4 τῷ ὡδὶ
fort. Al.   6 ἢ om. JAᵇΓ Al.   8 ἕν τε fecit E

συνεχὲς μῆκος τὸ δ' ἐπὶ δύο πλάτος τὸ δ' ἐπὶ τρία βάθος.
τούτων δὲ πλῆθος μὲν τὸ πεπερασμένον ἀριθμὸς μῆκος δὲ
γραμμὴ πλάτος δὲ ἐπιφάνεια βάθος δὲ σῶμα. ἔτι τὰ
μὲν λέγεται καθ' αὑτὰ ποσά, τὰ δὲ κατὰ συμβεβηκός 15
οἷον ἡ μὲν γραμμὴ ποσόν τι καθ' ἑαυτό, τὸ δὲ μουσικὸν κατὰ συμβεβηκός. τῶν δὲ καθ' αὑτὰ τὰ μὲν κατ'
οὐσίαν ἐστίν, οἷον ἡ γραμμὴ ποσόν τι (ἐν γὰρ τῷ λόγῳ τῷ
τί ἐστι λέγοντι τὸ ποσόν τι ὑπάρχει), τὰ δὲ πάθη καὶ ἕξεις
τῆς τοιαύτης ἐστὶν οὐσίας, οἷον τὸ πολὺ καὶ τὸ ὀλίγον, καὶ 20
μακρὸν καὶ βραχύ, καὶ πλατὺ καὶ στενόν, καὶ βαθὺ καὶ
ταπεινόν, καὶ βαρὺ καὶ κοῦφον, καὶ τὰ ἄλλα τὰ τοιαῦτα.
ἔστι δὲ καὶ τὸ μέγα καὶ τὸ μικρὸν καὶ μεῖζον καὶ
ἔλαττον, καὶ καθ' αὑτὰ καὶ πρὸς ἄλληλα λεγόμενα, τοῦ
ποσοῦ πάθη καθ' αὑτά· μεταφέρονται μέντοι καὶ ἐπ' ἄλλα 25
ταῦτα τὰ ὀνόματα. τῶν δὲ κατὰ συμβεβηκὸς λεγομένων
ποσῶν τὰ μὲν οὕτως λέγεται ὥσπερ ἐλέχθη ὅτι τὸ μουσικὸν
ποσὸν καὶ τὸ λευκὸν τῷ εἶναι ποσόν τι ᾧ ὑπάρχουσι, τὰ δὲ
ὡς κίνησις καὶ χρόνος· καὶ γὰρ ταῦτα πόσ' ἄττα λέγεται
καὶ συνεχῆ τῷ ἐκεῖνα διαιρετὰ εἶναι ὧν ἐστὶ ταῦτα πάθη. 30
λέγω δὲ οὐ τὸ κινούμενον ἀλλ' ὃ ἐκινήθη· τῷ γὰρ ποσὸν εἶναι
ἐκεῖνο καὶ ἡ κίνησις ποσή, ὁ δὲ χρόνος τῷ ταύτην.

14   [Τὸ] ποιὸν λέγεται ἕνα μὲν τρόπον ἡ διαφορὰ τῆς οὐσίας,
οἷον ποιόν τι ἄνθρωπος ζῷον ὅτι δίπουν, ἵππος δὲ τετράπουν,
καὶ κύκλος ποιόν τι σχῆμα ὅτι ἀγώνιον, ὡς τῆς διαφορᾶς 35
τῆς κατὰ τὴν οὐσίαν ποιότητος οὔσης·—ἕνα μὲν δὴ τρόπον 1020ᵇ
τοῦτον λέγεται ἡ ποιότης διαφορὰ οὐσίας, ἕνα δὲ ὡς τὰ ἀκίνητα καὶ τὰ μαθηματικά, ὥσπερ οἱ ἀριθμοὶ ποιοί τινες,
οἷον οἱ σύνθετοι καὶ μὴ μόνον ἐφ' ἓν ὄντες ἀλλ' ὧν μίμημα
τὸ ἐπίπεδον καὶ τὸ στερεόν (οὗτοι δ' εἰσὶν οἱ ποσάκις ποσοὶ ἢ 5
ποσάκις ποσάκις ποσοί), καὶ ὅλως ὃ παρὰ τὸ ποσὸν ὑπάρχει ἐν τῇ οὐσίᾳ· οὐσία γὰρ ἑκάστου ὃ ἅπαξ, οἷον τῶν ἓξ οὐχ

ᵃ 15 ποσά AᵇΓ Al. : ποσὰ ἄττα EJ Asc.¹   17 αὐτὸ Aᵇ Asc.ˡᶜ
19 ποσὸν ἐνυπάρχει ex Al. scr. Bonitz   20 τὸ alt. om. Aᵇ   καὶ]
καὶ τὸ Aᵇ   21 καὶ πλατὺ ... 22 βαρὺ JΓ Al. : om. E : καὶ βαθὺ καὶ
ταπεινόν om. Aᵇ   22 τὰ alt. EJ Al.ᶜ : om. Aᵇ   23 καὶ τὸ
μεῖζον recc.   25 μεταφέρονται Aᵇ Asc.ᶜ : μεταφέρεται EJ
27 τὰ Γ Jaeger : τὸ codd. Asc.ᶜ   30 ἀδιαίρετα J   ταῦτα EJΓ Al.ᶜ
Asc. : τὰ Aᵇ   33 τὸ omittendum ci. Bonitz   ἡ διαφορὰ EJΓ Al.
Asc.ˡᶜ : αἱ διαφοραὶ Aᵇ   34 οἷον] ὥσπερ Aᵇ Asc.   ᵇ 6–7 ὑπάρχει
καὶ τὴν οὐσίαν fort. Al.   7 ὃ Bonitz : τὸ codd. Al. Asc.

ὃ δὶς ἢ τρὶς εἰσὶν· ἀλλ' ὃ ἅπαξ· ἐξ γὰρ ἅπαξ ἕξ. ἔτι ὅσα
πάθη τῶν κινουμένων οὐσιῶν, οἷον θερμότης καὶ ψυχρότης,
10 καὶ λευκότης καὶ μελανία, καὶ βαρύτης καὶ κουφότης, καὶ
ὅσα τοιαῦτα, καθ' ἃ λέγονται καὶ ἀλλοιοῦσθαι τὰ σώματα
μεταβαλλόντων. ἔτι κατ' ἀρετὴν καὶ κακίαν καὶ ὅλως τὸ
κακὸν καὶ ἀγαθόν. σχεδὸν δὴ κατὰ δύο τρόπους λέγοιτ' ἂν
τὸ ποιόν, καὶ τούτων ἕνα τὸν κυριώτατον· πρώτη μὲν γὰρ
15 ποιότης ἡ τῆς οὐσίας διαφορά (ταύτης δέ τι καὶ ἡ ἐν τοῖς
ἀριθμοῖς ποιότης μέρος· διαφορὰ γάρ τις οὐσιῶν, ἀλλ' ἢ οὐ
κινουμένων ἢ οὐχ ᾗ κινούμενα), τὰ δὲ πάθη τῶν κινουμένων ᾗ
κινούμενα, καὶ αἱ τῶν κινήσεων διαφοραί. ἀρετὴ δὲ καὶ
κακία τῶν παθημάτων μέρος τι· διαφορὰς γὰρ δηλοῦσι τῆς
20 κινήσεως καὶ τῆς ἐνεργείας, καθ' ἃς ποιοῦσιν ἢ πάσχουσι καλῶς ἢ φαύλως τὰ ἐν κινήσει ὄντα· τὸ μὲν γὰρ ὡδὶ δυνάμενον κινεῖσθαι ἢ ἐνεργεῖν ἀγαθὸν τὸ δ' ὡδὶ καὶ ἐναντίως
μοχθηρόν. μάλιστα δὲ τὸ ἀγαθὸν καὶ τὸ κακὸν σημαίνει τὸ
ποιὸν ἐπὶ τῶν ἐμψύχων, καὶ τούτων μάλιστα ἐπὶ τοῖς ἔχουσι
25 προαίρεσιν.

Πρός τι λέγεται τὰ μὲν ὡς διπλάσιον πρὸς ἥμισυ καὶ 15
τριπλάσιον πρὸς τριτημόριον, καὶ ὅλως πολλαπλάσιον πρὸς
πολλοστημόριον καὶ ὑπερέχον πρὸς ὑπερεχόμενον· τὰ δ' ὡς
τὸ θερμαντικὸν πρὸς τὸ θερμαντὸν καὶ τὸ τμητικὸν πρὸς τὸ
30 τμητόν, καὶ ὅλως τὸ ποιητικὸν πρὸς τὸ παθητικόν· τὰ δ'
ὡς τὸ μετρητὸν πρὸς τὸ μέτρον καὶ ἐπιστητὸν πρὸς ἐπιστήμην
καὶ αἰσθητὸν πρὸς αἴσθησιν. λέγεται δὲ τὰ μὲν πρῶτα κατ'
ἀριθμὸν ἢ ἁπλῶς ἢ ὡρισμένως, πρὸς αὐτοὺς ἢ πρὸς ἕν (οἷον
τὸ μὲν διπλάσιον πρὸς ἓν ἀριθμὸς ὡρισμένος, τὸ δὲ πολλα-
35 πλάσιον κατ' ἀριθμὸν πρὸς ἕν, οὐχ ὡρισμένον δέ, οἷον τόνδε
1021ᵃ ἢ τόνδε· τὸ δὲ ἡμιόλιον πρὸς τὸ ὑφημιόλιον κατ' ἀριθμὸν
πρὸς ἀριθμὸν ὡρισμένον· τὸ δ' ἐπιμόριον πρὸς τὸ ὑπεπιμόριον
κατὰ ἀόριστον, ὥσπερ τὸ πολλαπλάσιον πρὸς τὸ ἕν· τὸ δ'

ᵇ8 ἐξ om. Aᵇſ   11 ἃ] ὅσα Aᵇ   καὶ EJ Al. Asc. : om. Aᵇſ
15 τι ſ et fecit E : τις AᵇJ   18 αἱ EJ Al. Asc.ᶜ: om. Aᵇ post
διαφοραί del. γὰρ Aᵇ   23 τὸ alt. EJ Asc.ᶜ: om. Aᵇ   26 πρὸς
τὸ ἥμισυ Aᵇ   28 ὡς] ὡς πρὸς Aᵇ   29 τὸ pr., alt., tert. om. E
31 καὶ] καὶ τὸ J   33 ὡρισμένως Jſ Al. Asc.ᶜ γρ. E: ὡρισμένον
EAᵇ   αὐτὸν Asc.ᶜ   34 ὡρισμένος] ὡρισμένος πρὸς ἕν Aᵇ
1021ᵃ2 δ' om. Aᵇ   3 ἀόριστον J Al. Asc.ᶜ: ἀορίστου Aᵇ: ἀορίστους
Eſ

ὑπερέχον πρὸς τὸ ὑπερεχόμενον ὅλως ἀόριστον κατ᾽ ἀριθμόν·
ὁ γὰρ ἀριθμὸς σύμμετρος, κατὰ μὴ συμμέτρου δὲ ἀριθμὸς οὐ 5
λέγεται, τὸ δὲ ὑπερέχον πρὸς τὸ ὑπερεχόμενον τοσοῦτόν
τέ ἐστι καὶ ἔτι, τοῦτο δ᾽ ἀόριστον· ὁπότερον γὰρ ἔτυχέν ἐστιν,
ἢ ἴσον ἢ οὐκ ἴσον)· ταῦτά τε οὖν τὰ πρός τι πάντα κατ᾽
ἀριθμὸν λέγεται καὶ ἀριθμοῦ πάθη, καὶ ἔτι τὸ ἴσον καὶ
ὅμοιον καὶ ταὐτὸ κατ᾽ ἄλλον τρόπον (κατὰ γὰρ τὸ ἓν λέ- 10
γεται πάντα, ταὐτὰ μὲν γὰρ ὧν μία ἡ οὐσία, ὅμοια δ᾽
ὧν ἡ ποιότης μία, ἴσα δὲ ὧν τὸ ποσὸν ἕν· τὸ δ᾽ ἓν τοῦ
ἀριθμοῦ ἀρχὴ καὶ μέτρον, ὥστε ταῦτα πάντα πρός τι
λέγεται κατ᾽ ἀριθμὸν μέν, οὐ τὸν αὐτὸν δὲ τρόπον)· τὰ δὲ
ποιητικὰ καὶ παθητικὰ κατὰ δύναμιν ποιητικὴν καὶ παθη- 15
τικὴν καὶ ἐνεργείας τὰς τῶν δυνάμεων, οἷον τὸ θερμαντικὸν
πρὸς τὸ θερμαντὸν ὅτι δύναται, καὶ πάλιν τὸ θερμαῖνον
πρὸς τὸ θερμαινόμενον καὶ τὸ τέμνον πρὸς τὸ τεμνόμενον
ὡς ἐνεργοῦντα. τῶν δὲ κατ᾽ ἀριθμὸν οὐκ εἰσὶν ἐνέργειαι ἀλλ᾽
ἢ ὃν τρόπον ἐν ἑτέροις εἴρηται· αἱ δὲ κατὰ κίνησιν ἐνέργειαι 20
οὐχ ὑπάρχουσιν. τῶν δὲ κατὰ δύναμιν καὶ κατὰ χρόνους ἤδη
λέγονται πρός τι.οἷον τὸ πεποιηκὸς πρὸς τὸ πεποιημένον
καὶ τὸ ποιῆσον πρὸς τὸ ποιησόμενον. οὕτω γὰρ καὶ πατὴρ
υἱοῦ λέγεται πατήρ· τὸ μὲν γὰρ πεποιηκὸς τὸ δὲ πεπονθός
τί ἐστιν. ἔτι ἔνια κατὰ στέρησιν δυνάμεως, ὥσπερ τὸ ἀδύνα- 25
τον καὶ ὅσα οὕτω λέγεται, οἷον τὸ ἀόρατον. τὰ μὲν οὖν κατ᾽
ἀριθμὸν καὶ δύναμιν λεγόμενα πρός τι πάντα ἐστὶ πρός τι
τῷ ὅπερ ἐστὶν ἄλλου λέγεσθαι αὐτὸ ὅ ἐστιν, ἀλλὰ μὴ τῷ
ἄλλο πρὸς ἐκεῖνο· τὸ δὲ μετρητὸν καὶ τὸ ἐπιστητὸν καὶ τὸ
διανοητὸν τῷ ἄλλο πρὸς αὐτὸ λέγεσθαι πρός τι λέγονται. 30
τό τε γὰρ διανοητὸν σημαίνει ὅτι ἔστιν αὐτοῦ διάνοια, οὐκ
ἔστι δ᾽ ἡ διάνοια πρὸς τοῦτο οὗ ἐστι διάνοια (δὶς γὰρ ταὐτὸν

^a 5 σύμμετρος EJΓ Al. Asc.^c : σύμμετρον A^b   συμμέτρου scripsi :
σύμμετρον codd. Γ Al. Asc.^c : συμμέτρων Apelt   ἀριθμὸς οὐ] ἀριθμὸν
EJΓ Al. Asc.^c : ἀριθμοὶ οὐ Apelt : ἀριθμῷ Zeller   6 λέγεται A^b
Al.^c Asc.^c : λέγονται EJΓ Apelt   δὲ] γὰρ EJΓ Al. Asc.^c   8 ἢ pr.
EJΓ Al.^c Asc.^c : om. A^b   πάντα A^b Asc.¹ : ἅπαντα EJ   10 κατ᾽
EJΓ Al. Asc. : om. A^b   11 μὲν γὰρ EJΓ Al.^c : τὸ μὲν γὰρ ταὐτὸ A^b
ἢ om. A^b Al.^c   ὅμοια . . . 12 μία hic EJΓ Al. : post ἕν (l. 12) A^b
13 πάντα πρός τι EJΓ Asc.^c : μὲν τὰ πρός τι πάντα A^b   20 κατὰ
δύναμιν E   22 πρός τι E¹A^bΓ Asc.^c : τὰ πρός E²J   28 αὐτὸ ὅ
ἐστιν om. fort. Al., secl. Jaeger   29 τὸ ult. A^b Asc.^c : om. EJ
30 πρός τι] τι ἃ A^b   32 πρὸς τὸ οὗ E
2573-1   H

εἰρημένον ἂν εἴη), ὁμοίως δὲ καὶ τινός ἐστιν ἡ ὄψις ὄψις, οὐχ
1021ᵇ οὗ ἐστὶν ὄψις (καίτοι γ᾽ ᾽ ἀληθὲς τοῦτο εἰπεῖν) ἀλλὰ πρὸς
χρῶμα ἢ πρὸς ἄλλο τι τοιοῦτον. ἐκείνως δὲ δὶς τὸ αὐτὸ
λεχθήσεται, ὅτι ἐστὶν οὗ ἐστὶν ἡ ὄψις. τὰ μὲν οὖν καθ᾽
ἑαυτὰ λεγόμενα πρός τι τὰ μὲν οὕτω λέγεται, τὰ δὲ ἂν τὰ
5 γένη αὐτῶν ᾖ τοιαῦτα, οἷον ἡ ἰατρικὴ τῶν πρός τι ὅτι τὸ
γένος αὐτῆς ἡ ἐπιστήμη δοκεῖ εἶναι πρός τι· ἔτι καθ᾽
ὅσα τὰ ἔχοντα λέγεται πρός τι, οἷον ἰσότης ὅτι τὸ ἴσον
καὶ ὁμοιότης ὅτι τὸ ὅμοιον· τὰ δὲ κατὰ συμβεβηκός, οἷον
ἄνθρωπος πρός τι ὅτι συμβέβηκεν αὐτῷ διπλασίῳ εἶναι,
10 τοῦτο δ᾽ ἐστὶ τῶν πρός τι· ἢ τὸ λευκόν, εἰ τῷ αὐτῷ συμβέβηκε διπλασίῳ καὶ λευκῷ εἶναι.

Τέλειον λέγεται ἐν μὲν οὗ μὴ ἔστιν ἔξω τι λαβεῖν μηδὲ 16
ἓν μόριον (οἷον χρόνος τέλειος ἑκάστου οὗτος οὗ μὴ ἔστιν ἔξω
λαβεῖν χρόνον τινὰ ὃς τούτου μέρος ἐστὶ τοῦ χρόνου), καὶ τὸ
15 κατ᾽ ἀρετὴν καὶ τὸ εὖ μὴ ἔχον ὑπερβολὴν πρὸς τὸ γένος,
οἷον τέλειος ἰατρὸς καὶ τέλειος αὐλητὴς ὅταν κατὰ τὸ εἶδος
τῆς οἰκείας ἀρετῆς μηθὲν ἐλλείπωσιν (οὕτω δὲ μεταφέροντες
καὶ ἐπὶ τῶν κακῶν λέγομεν συκοφάντην τέλειον καὶ κλέ-
πτην τέλειον, ἐπειδὴ καὶ ἀγαθοὺς λέγομεν αὐτούς, οἷον κλέ-
20 πτην ἀγαθὸν καὶ συκοφάντην ἀγαθόν· καὶ ἡ ἀρετὴ τελείω-
σίς τις· ἕκαστον γὰρ τότε τέλειον καὶ οὐσία πᾶσα τότε τελεία, ὅταν κατὰ τὸ εἶδος τῆς οἰκείας ἀρετῆς μηδὲν ἐλλείπῃ
μόριον τοῦ κατὰ φύσιν μεγέθους)· ἔτι οἷς ὑπάρχει τὸ τέλος,
σπουδαῖον ⟨ὄν⟩, ταῦτα λέγεται τέλεια· κατὰ γὰρ τὸ ἔχειν τὸ
25 τέλος τέλεια, ὥστ᾽ ἐπεὶ τὸ τέλος τῶν ἐσχάτων τί ἐστι, καὶ
ἐπὶ τὰ φαῦλα μεταφέροντες λέγομεν τελείως ἀπολωλέναι
καὶ τελείως ἐφθάρθαι, ὅταν μηδὲν ἐλλείπῃ τῆς φθορᾶς καὶ

ᵇ 1 γ᾽ om. Aᵇ Al.ᵒ Asc.ᶜ   3 ὅτι ἐστὶν ΕJΓ Al.ᵒ Asc.ᵒ : om.
Aᵇ   οὗ] ὄψις οὗ ΕJΓ Al.ᶜ : ἡ ὄψις οὗ Asc.ᶜ, ci. Bonitz   ἢ om.
Al.ᵒ Asc.ᶜ, omittendum ci. Bonitz   5 ἢ om. Aᵇ   6 πρός
AᵇΓ Al.: τῶν πρός ΕJ Asc.   7 οἷον] οἷον ἡ Aᵇ   9 ἄνθρωπος
scripsi: ὁ ἄνθρωπος Aᵇ Asc.ᶜ : ἄνθρωπος ΕJ   10 εἰ ΕJΓ Al. Asc.ᶜ :
ἢ Aᵇ   12 τὸ τέλειον Aᵇ   μηδὲ ἐν] μηθὲν ΕJΓ Al. Asc.
13 χρόνος Aᵇ Al.: ὁ χρόνος ΕJ   14 καὶ τὰ Aᵇ   15 εὖ Aᵇ
Al.: τοῦ, εὖ ΕJΓ   ἔχοντι δ᾽ Aᵇ   17 ἐλλείπωσιν ΕJΓ Al. Asc.:
ἐλλίπωσιν Aᵇ   20 καὶ ἡ ... 21 τις ΕJΓ Al. Asc.: om. Aᵇ   21 τότε
ΕJΓ Asc.ᶜ : om. Aᵇ   καὶ] τι καὶ ἡ Aᵇ   22 ἐλείπῃ ΕJΓ Al.ᶜ :
ἐλλίπῃ Aᵇ   24 ὄν ex Al. addidi   τὸ alt. Aᵇ Asc.ᶜ : om. ΕJ
27 ἐλλείπῃ ΕJΓ Al. Asc.ᶜ : ἐλλίπῃ Aᵇ

τοῦ κακοῦ ἀλλ' ἐπὶ τῷ ἐσχάτῳ ἦν· διὸ καὶ ἡ τελευτὴ κατὰ
μεταφορὰν λέγεται τέλος, ὅτι ἄμφω ἔσχατα· τέλος δὲ
καὶ τὸ οὗ ἕνεκα ἔσχατον. τὰ μὲν οὖν καθ' αὑτὰ λεγόμενα 30
τέλεια τοσαυταχῶς λέγεται, τὰ μὲν τῷ κατὰ τὸ εὖ μηδὲν
ἐλλείπειν μηδ' ἔχειν ὑπερβολὴν μηδὲ ἔξω τι λαβεῖν, τὰ δ'
ὅλως κατὰ τὸ μὴ ἔχειν ὑπερβολὴν ἐν ἑκάστῳ γένει μηδ'
εἶναί τι ἔξω· τὰ δὲ ἄλλα ἤδη κατὰ ταῦτα τῷ ἢ ποιεῖν τι 1022ᵇ
τοιοῦτον ἢ ἔχειν ἢ ἁρμόττειν τούτῳ ἢ ἀμῶς γέ πως λέγεσθαι πρὸς τὰ πρώτως λεγόμενα τέλεια.

17 Πέρας λέγεται τό τε ἔσχατον ἑκάστου καὶ οὗ ἔξω μηδὲν
ἔστι λαβεῖν πρώτου καὶ οὗ ἔσω πάντα πρώτου, καὶ ὃ ἂν ᾖ 5
εἶδος μεγέθους ἢ ἔχοντος μέγεθος, καὶ τὸ τέλος ἑκάστου
(τοιοῦτον δ' ἐφ' ὃ ἡ κίνησις καὶ ἡ πρᾶξις, καὶ οὐκ ἀφ' οὗ—ὁτὲ
δὲ ἄμφω, καὶ ἀφ' οὗ καὶ ἐφ' ὃ καὶ τὸ οὗ ἕνεκα), καὶ ἡ οὐσία
ἡ ἑκάστου καὶ τὸ τί ἦν εἶναι ἑκάστῳ· τῆς γνώσεως γὰρ τοῦτο
πέρας· εἰ δὲ τῆς γνώσεως, καὶ τοῦ πράγματος. ὥστε φανε- 10
ρὸν ὅτι ὁσαχῶς τε ἡ ἀρχὴ λέγεται, τοσαυταχῶς καὶ τὸ
πέρας, καὶ ἔτι πλεοναχῶς· ἡ μὲν γὰρ ἀρχὴ πέρας τι, τὸ
δὲ πέρας οὐ πᾶν ἀρχή.

18 Τὸ καθ' ὃ λέγεται πολλαχῶς, ἕνα μὲν τρόπον τὸ εἶδος
καὶ ἡ οὐσία ἑκάστου πράγματος, οἷον καθ' ὃ ἀγαθός, 15
αὐτὸ ἀγαθόν, ἕνα δὲ ἐν ᾧ πρώτῳ πέφυκε γίγνεσθαι, οἷον
τὸ χρῶμα ἐν τῇ ἐπιφανείᾳ. τὸ μὲν οὖν πρώτως λεγόμενον
καθ' ὃ τὸ εἶδός ἐστι, δευτέρως δὲ ὡς ἡ ὕλη ἑκάστου καὶ τὸ
ὑποκείμενον ἑκάστῳ πρῶτον. ὅλως δὲ τὸ καθ' ὃ ἰσαχῶς καὶ
τὸ αἴτιον ὑπάρξει· κατὰ τί γὰρ ἐλήλυθεν ἢ οὗ ἕνεκα ἐλή- 20
λυθε λέγεται, καὶ κατὰ τί παραλελόγισται ἢ συλλελόγι-
σται, ἢ τί τὸ αἴτιον τοῦ συλλογισμοῦ ἢ παραλογισμοῦ. ἔτι δὲ
τὸ καθ' ὃ τὸ κατὰ θέσιν λέγεται, καθ' ὃ ἔστηκεν ἢ καθ' ὃ βα-
δίζει· πάντα γὰρ ταῦτα τόπον σημαίνει καὶ θέσιν. ὥστε καὶ
τὸ καθ' αὑτὸ πολλαχῶς ἀνάγκη λέγεσθαι. ἐν μὲν γὰρ 25

ᵇ 28 τῷ ἐσχάτῳ Aᵇ Al.: τοῦ ἐσχάτου EJ Asc. ᾖ] δ' ᾖ ᾖ E   33 μὴ]
μηδ' γρ. E   1022ᵃ 1 τὰ] τὰ δὲ μεταξύ ἐστιν, τὰ γρ. E   καθ' αὑτὰ
EJΓ   2 τούτῳ] τοιούτῳ EJΓ   ἀμῶς ut vid. Γ, fort. Al., Bekker:
ἄλλως codd.   3 πρώτως codd. sed ὡς in ras. in E   4 τε om. EJ
Asc.¹   5 καὶ ... πρώτου om. E   7 καὶ alt. EJΓ Asc.: om. Aᵇ
9 ἡ om. recc.   15 ἀγαθός] ἀγαθὸς ὁ ἀγαθός Christ   16 πρώτων Γ
18 δεύτερον Aᵇ   ὡς ἡ E Asc.ᶜ: ἡ ὡς Aᵇ: ὡς J   20 ὑπάρχει
Al.   ἢ om. Aᵇ   22 τί] ὅτι EJΓ   24 τόπον ... θέσιν Aᵇ Asc.:
θέσιν ... τόπον EJΓ

καθ᾽ αὑτὸ τὸ τί ἦν εἶναι ἑκάστῳ, οἷον ὁ Καλλίας καθ᾽ αὑτὸν
Καλλίας καὶ τὸ τί ἦν εἶναι Καλλίᾳ· ἐν δὲ ὅσα ἐν τῷ τί
ἐστιν ὑπάρχει, οἷον ζῷον ὁ Καλλίας καθ᾽ αὑτόν· ἐν γὰρ
τῷ λόγῳ ἐνυπάρχει τὸ ζῷον· ζῷον γάρ τι ὁ Καλλίας. ἔτι
30 δὲ εἰ ἐν αὑτῷ δέδεκται πρώτῳ ἢ τῶν αὑτοῦ τινί, οἷον ἡ ἐπιφάνεια λευκὴ καθ᾽ ἑαυτήν, καὶ ζῇ ὁ ἄνθρωπος καθ᾽ αὑτόν·
ἡ γὰρ ψυχὴ μέρος τι τοῦ ἀνθρώπου, ἐν ᾗ πρώτῃ τὸ ζῆν. ἔτι
οὗ μὴ ἔστιν ἄλλο αἴτιον· τοῦ γὰρ ἀνθρώπου πολλὰ αἴτια, τὸ
ζῷον, τὸ δίπουν, ἀλλ᾽ ὅμως καθ᾽ αὑτὸν ἄνθρωπος ὁ ἄνθρω-
35 πός ἐστιν. ἔτι ὅσα μόνῳ ὑπάρχει καὶ ᾗ μόνον δι᾽ αὑτὸ κεχωρισμένον καθ᾽ αὑτό.

1022ᵇ   Διάθεσις λέγεται τοῦ ἔχοντος μέρη τάξις ἢ κατὰ τόπον 19
ἢ κατὰ δύναμιν ἢ κατ᾽ εἶδος· θέσιν γὰρ δεῖ τινὰ εἶναι,
ὥσπερ καὶ τοὔνομα δηλοῖ ἡ διάθεσις.

Ἕξις δὲ λέγεται ἕνα μὲν τρόπον οἷον ἐνέργειά τις τοῦ 20
5 ἔχοντος καὶ ἐχομένου, ὥσπερ πρᾶξίς τις ἢ κίνησις (ὅταν γὰρ
τὸ μὲν ποιῇ τὸ δὲ ποιῆται, ἔστι ποίησις μεταξύ· οὕτω καὶ
τοῦ ἔχοντος ἐσθῆτα καὶ τῆς ἐχομένης ἐσθῆτος ἔστι μεταξὺ
ἕξις)—ταύτην μὲν οὖν φανερὸν ὅτι οὐκ ἐνδέχεται ἔχειν ἕξιν
(εἰς ἄπειρον γὰρ βαδιεῖται, εἰ τοῦ ἐχομένου ἔσται ἔχειν τὴν
10 ἕξιν), ἄλλον δὲ τρόπον ἕξις λέγεται διάθεσις καθ᾽ ἣν ἢ εὖ
ἢ κακῶς διάκειται τὸ διακείμενον, καὶ ἢ καθ᾽ αὑτὸ ἢ πρὸς
ἄλλο, οἷον ἡ ὑγίεια ἕξις τις· διάθεσις γάρ ἐστι τοιαύτη.
ἔτι ἕξις λέγεται ἂν ᾗ μόριον διαθέσεως τοιαύτης· διὸ καὶ
ἡ τῶν μερῶν ἀρετὴ ἕξις τίς ἐστιν.

15   Πάθος λέγεται ἕνα μὲν τρόπον ποιότης καθ᾽ ἣν ἀλ- 21
λοιοῦσθαι ἐνδέχεται, οἷον τὸ λευκὸν καὶ τὸ μέλαν, καὶ
γλυκὺ καὶ πικρόν, καὶ βαρύτης καὶ κουφότης, καὶ ὅσα
ἄλλα τοιαῦτα· ἕνα δὲ αἱ τούτων ἐνέργειαι καὶ ἀλλοιώσεις

ᵃ 26–27 καθ᾽ αὑτὸ Καλλίας Al. : om. EJΓ Asc.   27 καὶ ... Καλλίαν J : om. ut vid. Al.   29 ἔτι] ἐν Aᵇ   30 αὑτῷ Aᵇ   δέδεικται
Γ   αὑτοῦ Christ : αὐτοῦ codd.   31 ζῇ Aᵇ Al. Asc.ᶜ : ζῷον E :
ζῶν JΓ   33 ἔστιν Aᵇ Al. : ἔστιν τι EJΓ Asc.ᶜ   35 μόνον]
μόνῳ Asc. ia et fort. Al.   δι᾽ αὑτὸ scripsi : διὸ τὸ EAl.ᶜ : διότι JAᵇΓ
γρ. E   κεχωρισμένον EJAᵇΓ Al.ᶜ : ὡρισμένον Al. Asc. γρ. E :
κεχρωσμένον γρ. Al.   ᵇ 1 τόπον EJ Asc.ᶜ : τὸν τόπον Aᵇ   3 καὶ
AᵇΓ Al.ᶜ : om. EJ Asc.ᶜ   6 ποιεῖται Aᵇ   8 ἔχειν τὴν ἕξιν EJ
9 εἰς ... 10 ἕξιν EJΓ Asc. : om. Aᵇ   10 ἢ om. EJΓ Asc.ᶜ   11 καὶ
EJΓ Asc.ᶜ : om. Aᵇ   13 τοιαύτη Aᵇ   16 τὸ alt. EJΓ Asc.ᵃ
Simpl.ᶜ : om. Aᵇ

ἤδη. ἔτι τούτων μᾶλλον αἱ βλαβεραὶ ἀλλοιώσεις καὶ κινήσεις, καὶ μάλιστα αἱ λυπηραὶ βλάβαι. ἔτι τὰ μεγέθη τῶν 20
συμφορῶν καὶ λυπηρῶν πάθη λέγεται.

22 Στέρησις λέγεται ἕνα μὲν τρόπον ἂν μὴ ἔχῃ τι τῶν
πεφυκότων ἔχεσθαι, κἂν μὴ αὐτὸ ᾖ πεφυκὸς ἔχειν, οἷον
φυτὸν ὀμμάτων ἐστερῆσθαι λέγεται· ἕνα δὲ ἂν πεφυκὸς
ἔχειν, ἢ αὐτὸ ἢ τὸ γένος, μὴ ἔχῃ, οἷον ἄλλως ἄνθρωπος ὁ 25
τυφλὸς ὄψεως ἐστέρηται καὶ ἀσπάλαξ, τὸ μὲν κατὰ τὸ
γένος τὸ δὲ καθ᾿ αὐτό. ἔτι ἂν πεφυκὸς καὶ ὅτε πέφυκεν
ἔχειν μὴ ἔχῃ· ἡ γὰρ τυφλότης στέρησίς τις, τυφλὸς δ᾿ οὐ
κατὰ πᾶσαν ἡλικίαν, ἀλλ᾿ ἐν ᾖ πέφυκεν ἔχειν, ἂν μὴ ἔχῃ.
ὁμοίως δὲ καὶ ἐν ᾧ ἂν ᾖ ⟨πεφυκὸς⟩ καὶ καθ᾿ ὃ καὶ πρὸς ὃ καὶ ὥς, 30
ἂν μὴ ἔχῃ [πεφυκός]. ἔτι ἡ βιαία ἑκάστου ἀφαίρεσις στέρησις
λέγεται. καὶ ὁσαχῶς δὲ αἱ ἀπὸ τοῦ ᾱ ἀποφάσεις λέγονται, τοσαυταχῶς καὶ αἱ στερήσεις λέγονται· ἄνισον μὲν
γὰρ τῷ μὴ ἔχειν ἰσότητα πεφυκὸς λέγεται, ἀόρατον δὲ
καὶ τῷ ὅλως μὴ ἔχειν χρῶμα καὶ τῷ φαύλως, καὶ ἄπουν 35
καὶ τῷ μὴ ἔχειν ὅλως πόδας καὶ τῷ φαύλους. ἔτι καὶ τῷ
μικρὸν ἔχειν, οἷον τὸ ἀπύρηνον· τοῦτο δ᾿ ἐστὶ τὸ φαύλως πως 1023ᵃ
ἔχειν. ἔτι τῷ μὴ ῥᾳδίως ἢ τῷ μὴ καλῶς, οἷον τὸ ἄτμητον
οὐ μόνον τῷ μὴ τέμνεσθαι ἀλλὰ καὶ τῷ μὴ ῥᾳδίως ἢ μὴ
καλῶς. ἔτι τῷ πάντῃ μὴ ἔχειν· τυφλὸς γὰρ οὐ λέγεται ὁ
ἑτερόφθαλμος ἀλλ᾿ ὁ ἐν ἀμφοῖν μὴ ἔχων ὄψιν· διὸ οὐ 5
πᾶς ἀγαθὸς ἢ κακός, ἢ δίκαιος ἢ ἄδικος, ἀλλὰ· καὶ τὸ
μεταξύ.

23 Τὸ ἔχειν λέγεται πολλαχῶς, ἕνα μὲν τρόπον τὸ ἄγειν
κατὰ τὴν αὐτοῦ φύσιν ἢ κατὰ τὴν αὐτοῦ ὁρμήν, διὸ
λέγεται πυρετός τε ἔχειν τὸν ἄνθρωπον καὶ οἱ τύραννοι τὰς 10
πόλεις καὶ τὴν ἐσθῆτα οἱ ἀμπεχόμενοι· ἕνα δ᾿ ἐν ᾧ ἂν

ᵇ 19 τούτων JAᵇΓ, ex τοιούτων fecit E   20 βλαβεραί EJΓ   21 συμφορῶν EJΓ Al. Asc.ᶜ Simpl.ᶜ: ἡδέων Aᵇ   23 ἤν E   28 ἔχειν
EJΓ Asc.ᶜ: om. Aᵇ   30 ἐν ᾧ EJΓ Al. Asc.: om. Aᵇ   ἂν ᾖ
EJΓ Al.: ἐὰν Aᵇ: om. Asc. Christ: ἂν ᾖ vel ἂν ci. Bonitz   πεφυκὸς
ex l. 31 transp. Jaeger   καὶ alt. et 31 ἂν om. Aᵇ   34 τὸ JAᵇ
ἰσότητα om. Aᵇ   35 τὸ AᵇΓ   μὴ ὅλως Aᵇ et fort. Asc.   καὶ τῷ
φαύλως om. Aᵇ Al.   36 τὸ teᵉ Aᵇ   ἔτι om. Aᵇ   1023ᵃ 1
τῷ E¹   τὸ E²AᵇΓ Asc.ᶜ: τῷ E¹J   2 τῷ ... τῷ E¹: τὸ .. τὸ
JAᵇ Asc.ᶜ et fecit E   3 ἢ Aᵇ Al.: ἢ τῷ ÉJΓ   4 τὸ JAᵇΓ et
fecit E   6 καὶ τὸ om. Aᵇ   8 λέγεται λέγεται E   τρόπον AᵇΓ
Al.ᶜ Asc.ᶜ: om. EJ   8 ἄγειν EJΓ Al.ᶜ Asc.ᶜ: ἄγον Aᵇ

τι ὑπάρχῃ ὡς δεκτικῷ, οἷον ὁ χαλκὸς ἔχει τὸ εἶδος τοῦ
ἀνδριάντος καὶ τὴν νόσον τὸ σῶμα· ἕνα δὲ ὡς τὸ περιέχον
τὰ περιεχόμενα· ἐν ᾧ γάρ ἐστι περιέχοντι, ἔχεσθαι ὑπὸ
15 τούτου λέγεται, οἷον τὸ ἀγγεῖον ἔχειν τὸ ὑγρόν φαμεν
καὶ τὴν πόλιν ἀνθρώπους καὶ τὴν ναῦν ναύτας, οὕτω δὲ καὶ
τὸ ὅλον ἔχειν τὰ μέρη. ἔτι τὸ κωλῦον κατὰ τὴν αὐτοῦ
ὁρμήν τι κινεῖσθαι ἢ πράττειν ἔχειν λέγεται τοῦτο αὐτό,
οἷον καὶ οἱ κίονες τὰ ἐπικείμενα βάρη, καὶ ὡς οἱ ποιηταὶ
20 τὸν Ἄτλαντα ποιοῦσι τὸν οὐρανὸν ἔχειν ὡς συμπεσόντ' ἂν
ἐπὶ τὴν γῆν, ὥσπερ καὶ τῶν φυσιολόγων τινές φασιν· τοῦτον δὲ τὸν τρόπον καὶ τὸ συνέχον λέγεται ἃ συνέχει ἔχειν,
ὡς διαχωρισθέντα ἂν κατὰ τὴν αὐτοῦ ὁρμὴν ἕκαστον. καὶ
τὸ ἔν τινι δὲ εἶναι ὁμοτρόπως λέγεται καὶ ἑπομένως τῷ
25 ἔχειν.

Τὸ ἔκ τινος εἶναι λέγεται ἕνα μὲν τρόπον ἐξ οὗ ἐστὶν 24
ὡς ὕλης, καὶ τοῦτο διχῶς, ἢ κατὰ τὸ πρῶτον γένος ἢ κατὰ
τὸ ὕστατον εἶδος, οἷον ἔστι μὲν ὡς ἅπαντα τὰ τηκτὰ ἐξ
ὕδατος, ἔστι δ' ὡς ἐκ χαλκοῦ ὁ ἀνδριάς· ἕνα δ' ὡς ἐκ τῆς
30 πρώτης κινησάσης ἀρχῆς (οἷον ἐκ τίνος ἡ μάχη; ἐκ λοιδορίας, ὅτι αὕτη ἀρχὴ τῆς μάχης)· ἕνα δ' ἐκ τοῦ συνθέτου
ἐκ τῆς ὕλης καὶ τῆς μορφῆς, ὥσπερ ἐκ τοῦ ὅλου τὰ μέρη
καὶ ἐκ τῆς Ἰλιάδος τὸ ἔπος καὶ ἐκ τῆς οἰκίας οἱ λίθοι·
τέλος μὲν γάρ ἐστιν ἡ μορφή, τέλειον δὲ τὸ ἔχον τέλος.
35 τὰ δὲ ὡς ἐκ τοῦ μέρους τὸ εἶδος, οἷον ἄνθρωπος ἐκ τοῦ δί-
ποδος καὶ ἡ συλλαβὴ ἐκ τοῦ στοιχείου· ἄλλως γὰρ τοῦτο
1023ᵇ καὶ ὁ ἀνδριὰς ἐκ χαλκοῦ· ἐκ τῆς αἰσθητῆς γὰρ ὕλης ἡ
συνθετὴ οὐσία, ἀλλὰ καὶ τὸ εἶδος ἐκ τῆς τοῦ εἴδους ὕλης.
τὰ μὲν οὖν οὕτω λέγεται, τὰ δ' ἐὰν κατὰ μέρος τι τούτων τις
ὑπάρχῃ τῶν τρόπων, οἷον ἐκ πατρὸς καὶ μητρὸς τὸ τέκνον
5 καὶ ἐκ γῆς τὰ φυτά, ὅτι ἔκ τινος μέρους αὐτῶν. ἕνα δὲ

ᵃ 13 τὸ περιέχον EJΓ Asc.ᶜ : τὰ περιέχοντα Aᵇ Al.   14 τὰ EJΓ
Al. Asc.ᶜ: καὶ Aᵇ   περιέχοντι Aᵇ Asc.ᶜ : περιέχον J : περιεχόμενόν
τι E : περιεχόμενον Γ   17 ἔχει EΓ   αὐτοῦ Aᵇ Asc.ᶜ   18 αὐτό]
ταῦτα Aᵇ   20 ποιοῦσιν Ἄτλαντα Aᵇ   21 καὶ om. EJΓ   post
φασιν add. Aᵇ ἄτλας δ' οὐρανὸν εὐρὺν ἔχει κρατερῆς ὑπ' ἀνάγκης
22 λέγεται . . . ἔχειν] ἔχειν λέγεται Aᵇ et fort. Al.   23 αὐτοῦ Aᵇ
24 ὁμοιοτρόπως recc.   29 ὥστ' Aᵇ   ὡς om. EΓ   τῆς . . . 30
λοιδορίας EJΓ et ut vid. Asc. : τοῦ πρώτου κινήσαντος, οἷον ἐκ λοιδορίας
ἡ μάχη Aᵇ et fort. Al.   35 τὰ] τὸ Γ   ἄνθρωπος scripsi : ὁ ἄνθρωπος
EJ Asc.ᶜ: ἄνθρωπος Aᵇ   ᵇ 1 ἐκ pr. Aᵇ et ut vid. Al. : ἐκ τοῦ EJ

μεθ' ὃ τῷ χρόνῳ, οἷον ἐξ ἡμέρας νὺξ καὶ ἐξ εὐδίας χειμών,
ὅτι τοῦτο μετὰ τοῦτο· τούτων δὲ τὰ μὲν τῷ ἔχειν μεταβολὴν
εἰς ἄλληλα οὕτω λέγεται, ὥσπερ καὶ τὰ νῦν εἰρημένα, τὰ
δὲ τῷ κατὰ τὸν χρόνον ἐφεξῆς μόνον, οἷον ἐξ ἰσημερίας
ἐγένετο ὁ πλοῦς ὅτι μετ' ἰσημερίαν ἐγένετο, καὶ ἐκ Διονυ- 10
σίων Θαργήλια ὅτι μετὰ τὰ Διονύσια.

25 Μέρος λέγεται ἕνα μὲν τρόπον εἰς ὃ διαιρεθείη ἂν τὸ
ποσὸν ὁπωσοῦν (ἀεὶ γὰρ τὸ ἀφαιρούμενον τοῦ ποσοῦ ᾖ ποσὸν
μέρος λέγεται ἐκείνου, οἷον τῶν τριῶν τὰ δύο μέρος λέγεταί
πως), ἄλλον δὲ τρόπον τὰ καταμετροῦντα τῶν τοιούτων 15
μόνον· διὸ τὰ δύο τῶν τριῶν ἔστι μὲν ὡς λέγεται μέρος,
ἔστι δ' ὡς οὔ. ἔτι εἰς ἃ τὸ εἶδος διαιρεθείη ἂν ἄνευ τοῦ ποσοῦ,
καὶ ταῦτα μόρια λέγεται τούτου· διὸ τὰ εἴδη τοῦ γένους φασὶν εἶναι μόρια. ἔτι εἰς ἃ διαιρεῖται ἢ ἐξ ὧν σύγκειται
τὸ ὅλον, ἢ τὸ εἶδος ἢ τὸ ἔχον τὸ εἶδος, οἷον τῆς σφαίρας 20
τῆς χαλκῆς ἢ τοῦ κύβου τοῦ χαλκοῦ καὶ ὁ χαλκὸς μέρος
(τοῦτο δ' ἐστὶν ἡ ὕλη ἐν ᾗ τὸ εἶδος) καὶ ἡ γωνία μέρος. ἔτι
τὰ ἐν τῷ λόγῳ τῷ δηλοῦντι ἕκαστον, καὶ ταῦτα μόρια τοῦ
ὅλου· διὸ τὸ γένος τοῦ εἴδους καὶ μέρος λέγεται, ἄλλως δὲ τὸ
εἶδος τοῦ γένους μέρος.   25

26 Ὅλον λέγεται οὗ τε μηθὲν ἄπεστι μέρος ἐξ ὧν λέγεται
ὅλον φύσει, καὶ τὸ περιέχον τὰ περιεχόμενα ὥστε ἕν τι
εἶναι ἐκεῖνα· τοῦτο δὲ διχῶς· ἢ γὰρ ὡς ἕκαστον ἓν ἢ ὡς
ἐκ τούτων τὸ ἕν. τὸ μὲν γὰρ καθόλου, καὶ τὸ ὅλως λεγόμενον ὡς ὅλον τι ὄν, οὕτως ἐστὶ καθόλου ὡς πολλὰ περιέχον τῷ 30
κατηγορεῖσθαι καθ' ἑκάστου καὶ ἓν ἅπαντα εἶναι ὡς ἕκαστον,
οἷον ἄνθρωπον ἵππον θεόν, διότι ἅπαντα ζῷα· τὸ δὲ συνεχὲς καὶ πεπερασμένον, ὅταν ἕν τι ἐκ πλειόνων ᾖ, ἐνυπαρχόντων μάλιστα μὲν δυνάμει, εἰ δὲ μή, ἐνεργείᾳ. τούτων
δ' αὐτῶν μᾶλλον τὰ φύσει ἢ τέχνῃ τοιαῦτα, ὥσπερ καὶ 35
ἐπὶ τοῦ ἑνὸς ἐλέγομεν, ὡς οὔσης τῆς ὁλότητος ἑνότητός τινος.
ἔτι τοῦ ποσοῦ ἔχοντος δὲ ἀρχὴν καὶ μέσον καὶ ἔσχατον, ὅσων 1024ᵃ

ᵇ 6 εὐδείας Aᵇ   11 τὰ om. Aᵇ   13 ὁπωσοῦν] ᾖ ποσόν ut vid.
Al.: ὁποσοῦν Γ   17 διαιρεθείη EJ Al.: διαιρεθῇ Aᵇ   19 ᾖ
J¹Aᵇ Al.: τι ᾖ EJ²Γ Asc.ᶜ   21 ὁ ὁ τοῦ Aᵇ   27 τὰ] ἓν καὶ
τὰ Aᵇ   29 τὸ ὅλως EJΓ Asc.ᶜ: ὅλον Aᵇ et fort. Al.   32 διότι
Aᵇ et fort. Asc.: ὅτι EJ   34 μή] μὴ καὶ Γ   ἐνεργείᾳ EJΓ Al.
Asc.: ἐντελεχείᾳ Aᵇ   36 ἐλέγομεν Aᵇ et fort. Al.: λέγομεν EJΓ
ἑνότητος ὁλότητός J   1024ᵃ 1 δὲ Aᵇ Asc.ᶜ: om. EJΓ

μὲν μὴ ᵇποιεῖ ἡ θέσις διαφοράν, πᾶν λέγεται, ὅσων δὲ ποιεῖ,
ὅλον. ὅσα δὲ ἄμφω ἐνδέχεται, καὶ ὅλα καὶ πάντα· ἔστι
δὲ ταῦτα ὅσων ἡ μὲν φύσις ἡ αὐτὴ μένει τῇ μεταθέσει, ἡ
5 δὲ μορφὴ οὔ, οἷον κηρὸς καὶ ἱμάτιον· καὶ γὰρ ὅλον καὶ
πᾶν λέγεται· ἔχει γὰρ ἄμφω. ὕδωρ δὲ καὶ ὅσα ὑγρὰ
καὶ ἀριθμὸς πᾶν μὲν λέγεται, ὅλος δ' ἀριθμὸς καὶ ὅλον
ὕδωρ οὐ λέγεται, ἂν μὴ μεταφορᾷ. πάντα δὲ λέγεται ἐφ'
οἷς τὸ πᾶν ὡς ἐφ' ἑνί, ἐπὶ τούτοις τὸ πάντα ὡς ἐπὶ διῃρημένοις·
10 πᾶς οὗτος ὁ ἀριθμός, πᾶσαι αὗται αἱ μονάδες.

Κολοβὸν δὲ λέγεται τῶν ποσῶν οὐ τὸ τυχόν, ἀλλὰ **27**
μεριστόν τε δεῖ αὐτὸ εἶναι καὶ ὅλον. τά τε γὰρ δύο οὐ κολο-
βὰ θατέρου ἀφαιρουμένου ἑνός (οὐ γὰρ ἴσον τὸ κολόβωμα
καὶ τὸ λοιπὸν οὐδέποτ' ἐστίν) οὐδ' ὅλως ἀριθμὸς οὐδείς· καὶ
15 γὰρ τὴν οὐσίαν δεῖ μένειν· εἰ κύλιξ κολοβός, ἔτι εἶναι κύ-
λικα· ὁ δὲ ἀριθμὸς οὐκέτι ὁ αὐτός. πρὸς δὲ τούτοις κἂν ἀνομοιομερῆ ᾖ, οὐδὲ ταῦτα πάντα (ὁ γὰρ ἀριθμὸς ἔστιν ὡς καὶ
ἀνόμοια ἔχει μέρη, οἷον δυάδα τριάδα), ἀλλ' ὅλως ὧν
μὴ ποιεῖ ἡ θέσις διαφορὰν οὐδὲν κολοβόν, οἷον ὕδωρ ἢ πῦρ,
20 ἀλλὰ δεῖ τοιαῦτα εἶναι ἃ κατὰ τὴν οὐσίαν θέσιν ἔχει. ἔτι
συνεχῆ· ἡ γὰρ ἁρμονία ἐξ ἀνομοίων μὲν καὶ θέσιν
ἔχει, κολοβὸς δὲ οὐ γίγνεται. πρὸς δὲ τούτοις οὐδ' ὅσα ὅλα,
οὐδὲ ταῦτα ὁτουοῦν μορίου στερήσει κολοβά. οὐ γὰρ δεῖ οὔτε
τὰ κύρια τῆς οὐσίας οὔτε τὰ ὁπουοῦν ὄντα· οἷον ἂν τρυπηθῇ ἡ
25 κύλιξ, οὐ κολοβός, ἀλλ' ἂν τὸ οὖς ἢ ἀκρωτήριόν τι, καὶ ὁ
ἄνθρωπος οὐκ ἐὰν σάρκα ἢ τὸν σπλῆνα, ἀλλ' ἐὰν ἀκρωτήριόν τι, καὶ τοῦτο οὐ πᾶν ἀλλ' ὃ μὴ ἔχει γένεσιν ἀφαιρεθὲν
ὅλον. διὰ τοῦτο οἱ φαλακροὶ οὐ κολοβοί.

Γένος λέγεται τὸ μὲν ἐὰν ᾖ ἡ γένεσις συνεχὴς τῶν τὸ **28**

ᵃ 2 μὴ ποιῇ E   3 ἄμφω λέγεται καὶ ὅλον Γ   πᾶν EJΓ Asc.ᶜ
7 ὅλος EJΓ Asc.ᶜ: ὁ δὲ πᾶς ὅλος Aᵇ   καὶ EJΓ Asc.ᶜ: ἢ Aᵇ   8 μὴ
κατὰ μεταφορὰν Aᵇ   πάντα EJΓ Asc.ᶜ: πᾶν Aᵇ   9 οἷς EJΓ Al.
Asc.ᶜ: ὅσοις Aᵇ   τὸ alt. ex Al. scr. Christ: τὰ Aᵇ: om. EJ
10 ὁ om. J Asc.ᶜ   12 δεῖ αὐτὸ EJΓ Al. : om. Aᵇ   13 ἀφῃρη-
μένου fecit E   14 λεῖπον fort. Al.   ὅλως EJΓ Al. Asc.ᶜ: ὅλος
Aᵇ   15 ἔτι] ἔστιν E   δεῖ εἶναι EJΓ   16 κἂν ἀνομοιομερῆ ᾖ
EJΓ Al. Asc.: καὶ ἂν ὁμοιομερῇ ᾖ Aᵇ: καὶ ἀνομοιομερῆ ᾖ γρ. E
17 ὡς JAᵇ Γ Al. : ὃς E   18 ὧν EJΓ Asc.: ὅσων Aᵇ   21 ἀνομοιομερῶν EJΓ Al. Asc.   23 δεῖ] δὴ Aᵇ   27 τι om. EJΓ   οὔτ'
ἂν ἄλλο μὴ Aᵇ   ἔχει recc. Al. Asc.ᶜ: ἔχῃ EJAᵇ   29 ἐὰν ᾖ] ἐν
ἐὰν Aᵇ

εἶδος ἐχόντων τὸ αὐτό, οἷον λέγεται ἕως ἂν ἀνθρώπων γέ- 30
νος ᾖ, ὅτι ἕως ἂν ᾖ ἡ γένεσις συνεχὴς αὐτῶν· τὸ δὲ ἀφ᾽
οὗ ἂν ὦσι πρώτου κινήσαντος εἰς τὸ εἶναι· οὕτω γὰρ λέγονται
Ἕλληνες τὸ γένος οἱ δὲ Ἴωνες, τῷ οἱ μὲν ἀπὸ Ἕλληνος οἱ
δὲ ἀπὸ Ἴωνος εἶναι πρώτου γεννήσαντος· καὶ μᾶλλον οἱ ἀπὸ
τοῦ γεννήσαντος ἢ τῆς ὕλης (λέγονται γὰρ καὶ ἀπὸ τοῦ θή- 35
λεος τὸ γένος, οἷον οἱ ἀπὸ Πύρρας). ἔτι δὲ ὡς τὸ ἐπίπεδον
τῶν σχημάτων γένος τῶν ἐπιπέδων καὶ τὸ στερεὸν τῶν στε- 1024ᵇ
ρεῶν· ἕκαστον γὰρ τῶν σχημάτων τὸ μὲν ἐπίπεδον τοιονδὶ
τὸ δὲ στερεόν ἐστι τοιονδί· τοῦτο δ᾽ ἐστὶ τὸ ὑποκείμενον ταῖς
διαφοραῖς. ἔτι ὡς ἐν τοῖς λόγοις τὸ πρῶτον ἐνυπάρχον, ὃ
λέγεται ἐν τῷ τί ἐστι, τοῦτο γένος, οὗ διαφοραὶ λέγονται αἱ 5
ποιότητες. τὸ μὲν οὖν γένος τοσαυταχῶς λέγεται, τὸ μὲν
κατὰ γένεσιν συνεχῆ τοῦ αὐτοῦ εἴδους, τὸ δὲ κατὰ τὸ πρῶτον
κινῆσαν ὁμοειδές, τὸ δ᾽ ὡς ὕλη· οὗ γὰρ ἡ διαφορὰ καὶ ἡ
ποιότης ἐστί, τοῦτ᾽ ἐστι τὸ ὑποκείμενον, ὃ λέγομεν ὕλην. ἕτερα
δὲ τῷ γένει λέγεται ὧν ἕτερον τὸ πρῶτον ὑποκείμενον καὶ 10
μὴ ἀναλύεται θάτερον εἰς θάτερον μηδ᾽ ἄμφω εἰς ταὐτόν,
οἷον τὸ εἶδος καὶ ἡ ὕλη ἕτερον τῷ γένει, καὶ ὅσα καθ᾽ ἕτερον σχῆμα κατηγορίας τοῦ ὄντος λέγεται (τὰ μὲν γὰρ τί
ἐστι σημαίνει τῶν ὄντων τὰ δὲ ποιόν τι τὰ δ᾽ ὡς διῄρηται
πρότερον)· οὐδὲ γὰρ ταῦτα ἀναλύεται οὔτ᾽ εἰς ἄλληλα οὔτ᾽ 15
εἰς ἕν τι.

29 Τὸ ψεῦδος λέγεται ἄλλον μὲν τρόπον ὡς πρᾶγμα
ψεῦδος, καὶ τούτου τὸ μὲν τῷ μὴ συγκεῖσθαι ἢ ἀδύνατον
εἶναι συντεθῆναι (ὥσπερ λέγεται τὸ τὴν διάμετρον εἶναι
σύμμετρον ἢ τὸ σὲ καθῆσθαι· τούτων γὰρ ψεῦδος τὸ μὲν 20
ἀεὶ τὸ δὲ ποτέ· οὕτω γὰρ οὐκ ὄντα ταῦτα), τὰ δὲ ὅσα ἐστὶ
μὲν ὄντα, πέφυκε μέντοι φαίνεσθαι ἢ μὴ οἷά ἐστιν ἢ ἃ μὴ
ἔστιν (οἷον ἡ σκιαγραφία καὶ τὰ ἐνύπνια· ταῦτα γὰρ ἔστι
μέν τι, ἀλλ᾽ οὐχ ὧν ἐμποιεῖ τὴν φαντασίαν)—πράγματα
μὲν οὖν ψευδῆ οὕτω λέγεται, ἢ τῷ μὴ εἶναι αὐτὰ ἢ τῷ 25
τὴν ἀπ᾽ αὐτῶν φαντασίαν μὴ ὄντος εἶναι· λόγος δὲ ψευ-

ᵃ 31 ὁτιοῦν ἕως Aᵇ   ᾖ om. Aᵇ   ἡ om. fort. Al.   αὐτῶν συνεχής
Aᵇ Asc.ᶜ   32-3 λέγονται οἱ μὲν Ἕλληνες Aᵇ   36 οἱ om. EJΓ
Asc.ᶜ   δὲ om. Aᵇ   ᵇ 1 γένος Aᵇ Asc.ᶜ : τὸ γένος EJ   4 ὃ
EJΓ Al. : om. Aᵇ   7 τὸ alt. om. E   8 ὕλη EJ Al. : ἡ ὕλη
Aᵇ Asc.ᶜ   10 ὧν Aᵇ Asc.ᶜ : ὧν τε EJ   21 οὕτω] τῷ Aᵇ

δῆς ὁ τῶν μὴ ὄντων, ᾗ ψευδής, διὸ πᾶς λόγος ψευδὴς ἑτέρου ἢ οὗ ἐστιν ἀληθής, οἷον ὁ τοῦ κύκλου ψευδὴς τριγώνου.
ἑκάστου δὲ λόγος ἔστι μὲν ὡς εἷς, ὁ τοῦ τί ἦν εἶναι, ἔστι δ' ὡς
30 πολλοί, ἐπεὶ ταὐτό πως αὐτὸ καὶ αὐτὸ πεπονθός, οἷον Σωκράτης καὶ Σωκράτης μουσικός (ὁ δὲ ψευδὴς λόγος οὐθενός
ἐστιν ἁπλῶς λόγος)· διὸ Ἀντισθένης ᾤετο εὐήθως μηθὲν ἀξιῶν
λέγεσθαι πλὴν τῷ οἰκείῳ λόγῳ, ἓν ἐφ' ἑνός· ἐξ ὧν συνέβαινε μὴ εἶναι ἀντιλέγειν, σχεδὸν δὲ μηδὲ ψεύδεσθαι. ἔστι
35 δ' ἕκαστον λέγειν οὐ μόνον τῷ αὑτοῦ λόγῳ ἀλλὰ καὶ τῷ
ἑτέρου, ψευδῶς μὲν καὶ παντελῶς, ἔστι δ' ὡς καὶ ἀληθῶς,
1025ᵃ ὥσπερ τὰ ὀκτὼ διπλάσια τῷ τῆς δυάδος λόγῳ. τὰ μὲν οὖν
οὕτω λέγεται ψευδῆ, ἄνθρωπος δὲ ψευδὴς ὁ εὐχερὴς καὶ
προαιρετικὸς τῶν τοιούτων λόγων, μὴ δι' ἕτερόν τι ἀλλὰ
δι' αὐτό, καὶ ὁ ἄλλοις ἐμποιητικὸς τῶν τοιούτων λόγων,
5 ὥσπερ καὶ τὰ πράγματά φαμεν ψευδῆ εἶναι ὅσα ἐμποιεῖ
φαντασίαν ψευδῆ. διὸ ὁ ἐν τῷ Ἱππίᾳ λόγος παρακρούεται
ὡς ὁ αὐτὸς ψευδὴς καὶ ἀληθής. τὸν δυνάμενον γὰρ ψεύ-
σασθαι λαμβάνει ψευδῆ (οὗτος δ' ὁ εἰδὼς καὶ ὁ φρόνιμος)· ἔτι τὸν ἑκόντα φαῦλον βελτίω. τοῦτο δὲ ψεῦδος
10 λαμβάνει διὰ τῆς ἐπαγωγῆς—ὁ γὰρ ἑκὼν χωλαίνων τοῦ
ἄκοντος κρείττων—τὸ χωλαίνειν τὸ μιμεῖσθαι λέγων, ἐπεὶ
εἴ γε χωλὸς ἑκών, χείρων ἴσως, ὥσπερ ἐπὶ τοῦ ἤθους, καὶ
οὗτος.

Συμβεβηκὸς λέγεται ὃ ὑπάρχει μέν τινι καὶ ἀληθὲς 30
15 εἰπεῖν, οὐ μέντοι οὔτ' ἐξ ἀνάγκης οὔτε ⟨ὡς⟩ ἐπὶ τὸ πολύ, οἷον
εἴ τις ὀρύττων φυτῷ βόθρον εὗρε θησαυρόν. τοῦτο τοίνυν συμβεβηκὸς τῷ ὀρύττοντι τὸν βόθρον, τὸ εὑρεῖν θησαυρόν· οὔτε
γὰρ ἐξ ἀνάγκης τοῦτο ἐκ τούτου ἢ μετὰ τοῦτο, οὔθ' ὡς ἐπὶ τὸ
πολὺ ἄν τις φυτεύῃ θησαυρὸν εὑρίσκει. καὶ μουσικός γ'
20 ἄν τις εἴη λευκός· ἀλλ' ἐπεὶ οὔτε ἐξ ἀνάγκης οὔθ' ὡς ἐπὶ τὸ
πολὺ τοῦτο γίγνεται, συμβεβηκὸς αὐτὸ λέγομεν. ὥστ' ἐπεὶ

ᵇ27 ᾗ] ἢ ci. Al.   ψευδῆ, διὸ ci. Christ   31 καὶ Σωκράτης om. Aᵇ
1025ᵃ2 δέ om. E   3 μὴ EJ Asc.ᶜ: οὐ Aᵇ   4 αὐτάAᵇ   5 καὶ
... φαμεν AᵇΓ Al.: φαμὲν καὶ πράγματα EJ Asc.ᶜ   6 φαντασίαν
ψευδῆ EJ Asc.ᶜ: ψευδῆ φαντασίαν AᵇΓ   ὁ E²J: om. E¹Aᵇ
8 οὕτως Aᵇ   9 ἑκόντα EJΓ Al. Asc.: εἰδότα Aᵇ   φαῦλον recc.:
τὰ φαῦλα EJAᵇΓ et ut vid. Asc.: πράττοντα τὰ φαῦλα ex Al. ci.
Jaeger   11 τὸ alt. om. Aᵇ   13 οὗτος recc. Al. Asc.: οὕτως
Aᵇ: τοῦτο EJΓ   15 ὡς Asc.ᶜ, Eucken: δὲ Aᵇ: om. EJΓ   19
γ'] δὲ Aᵇ Al.   20 οὔτε ... οὔθ'] οὐκ ... οὐδ' Aᵇ

ἔστιν ὑπάρχον τι καὶ τινί, καὶ ἔνια τούτων καὶ ποὺ καὶ ποτέ,
ὅ τι ἂν ὑπάρχῃ μέν, ἀλλὰ μὴ διότι τοδὶ ἦν ἢ νῦν ἢ ἐνταῦθα, συμβεβηκὸς ἔσται. οὐδὲ δὴ αἴτιον ὡρισμένον οὐδὲν
τοῦ συμβεβηκότος ἀλλὰ τὸ τυχόν· τοῦτο δ' ἀόριστον. συνέβη 25
τῷ εἰς Αἴγιναν ἐλθεῖν, εἰ μὴ διὰ τοῦτο ἀφίκετο ὅπως ἐκεῖ
ἔλθῃ, ἀλλ' ὑπὸ χειμῶνος ἐξωσθεὶς ἢ ὑπὸ λῃστῶν ληφθείς.
γέγονε μὲν δὴ ἢ ἔστι τὸ συμβεβηκός, ἀλλ' οὐχ ᾗ αὐτὸ
ἀλλ' ᾗ ἕτερον· ὁ γὰρ χειμὼν αἴτιος τοῦ μὴ ὅπου ἔπλει ἐλθεῖν, τοῦτο δ' ἦν Αἴγινα. λέγεται δὲ καὶ ἄλλως συμβεβη- 30
κός, οἷον ὅσα ὑπάρχει ἑκάστῳ καθ' αὑτὸ μὴ ἐν τῇ οὐσίᾳ ὄντα, οἷον τῷ τριγώνῳ τὸ δύο ὀρθὰς ἔχειν. καὶ ταῦτα
μὲν ἐνδέχεται ἀίδια εἶναι, ἐκείνων δὲ οὐδέν. λόγος δὲ τούτου ἐν ἑτέροις.

E   1025ᵇ

Αἱ ἀρχαὶ καὶ τὰ αἴτια ζητεῖται τῶν ὄντων, δῆλον δὲ
ὅτι ᾗ ὄντα. ἔστι γάρ τι αἴτιον ὑγιείας καὶ εὐεξίας, καὶ τῶν
μαθηματικῶν εἰσὶν ἀρχαὶ καὶ στοιχεῖα καὶ αἴτια, καὶ ὅλως 5
δὲ πᾶσα ἐπιστήμη διανοητικὴ ἢ μετέχουσά τι διανοίας περὶ
αἰτίας καὶ ἀρχάς ἐστιν ἢ ἀκριβεστέρας ἢ ἁπλουστέρας. ἀλλὰ
πᾶσαι αὗται περὶ ὄν τι καὶ γένος τι περιγραψάμεναι περὶ
τούτου πραγματεύονται, ἀλλ' οὐχὶ περὶ ὄντος ἁπλῶς οὐδὲ ᾗ
ὄν, οὐδὲ τοῦ τί ἐστιν οὐθένα λόγον ποιοῦνται, ἀλλ' ἐκ τούτου, 10
αἱ μὲν αἰσθήσει ποιήσασαι αὐτὸ δῆλον αἱ δ' ὑπόθεσιν λαβοῦσαι τὸ τί ἐστιν, οὕτω τὰ καθ' αὑτὰ ὑπάρχοντα τῷ γένει
περὶ ὅ εἰσιν ἀποδεικνύουσιν ἢ ἀναγκαιότερον ἢ μαλακώτερον·
διόπερ φανερὸν ὅτι οὐκ ἔστιν ἀπόδειξις οὐσίας οὐδὲ τοῦ τί ἐστιν
ἐκ τῆς τοιαύτης ἐπαγωγῆς, ἀλλά τις ἄλλος τρόπος τῆς 15
δηλώσεως. ὁμοίως δὲ οὐδ' εἰ ἔστιν ἢ μὴ ἔστι τὸ γένος περὶ ὃ

E. 1, cf. K. 7

ᵃ 22 τι EJΓ Al. Asc.ᶜ: om. Aᵇ   25 ἀλλὰ om. E   26 τῷ EΓ:
τῶ J: τὸ Aᵇ Asc.: τῳ τὸ fort. Al.   28 δὴ om. Γ   ἢ cum Al.ᶜ
scripsi: ἢ Aᵇ: καὶ EΓ Asc.: om. J   29 ὅπου EJ Asc.ᶜ: οὗ Aᵇ
Al.   30 ἦν] εἶναι Aᵇ et sup. lin. E   δὲ om. J   32 οἷον EJΓ
Asc.ᶜ: ὥσπερ Aᵇ   33 μὲν . . . εἶναι] ἴδια αἴτια γρ. Al.
ᵇ3 δὴ Aᵇ Al.   4 ὑγιείας EJ   5 καὶ pr. et 6 ἢ om. Γ   8 ὄν Aᵇ
γρ. E Al. Asc.: ἔν EJΓ

πραγματεύονται οὐδὲν λέγουσι, διὰ τὸ τῆς αὐτῆς εἶναι διανοίας τό τε τί ἐστι δῆλον ποιεῖν καὶ εἰ ἔστιν.—ἐπεὶ δὲ καὶ ἡ
φυσικὴ ἐπιστήμη τυγχάνει οὖσα περὶ γένος τι τοῦ ὄντος (περὶ
20 γὰρ τὴν τοιαύτην ἐστὶν οὐσίαν ἐν ᾗ ἡ ἀρχὴ τῆς κινήσεως καὶ
στάσεως ἐν αὐτῇ), δῆλον ὅτι οὔτε πρακτική ἐστιν οὔτε ποιητική
(τῶν μὲν γὰρ ποιητῶν ἐν τῷ ποιοῦντι ἡ ἀρχή, ἢ νοῦς ἢ τέχνη ἢ δύναμίς τις, τῶν δὲ πρακτῶν ἐν τῷ πράττοντι, ἡ
προαίρεσις· τὸ αὐτὸ γὰρ τὸ πρακτὸν καὶ προαιρετόν),
25 ὥστε εἰ πᾶσα διάνοια ἢ πρακτικὴ ἢ ποιητικὴ ἢ θεωρητική,
ἡ φυσικὴ θεωρητική τις ἂν εἴη, ἀλλὰ θεωρητικὴ περὶ τοιοῦτον ὂν ὅ ἐστι δυνατὸν κινεῖσθαι, καὶ περὶ οὐσίαν τὴν κατὰ
τὸν λόγον ὡς ἐπὶ τὸ πολὺ ὡς οὐ χωριστὴν μόνον. δεῖ δὲ τὸ τί
ἦν εἶναι καὶ τὸν λόγον πῶς ἐστὶ μὴ λανθάνειν, ὡς ἄνευ γε
30 τούτου τὸ ζητεῖν μηδέν ἐστι ποιεῖν. ἔστι δὲ τῶν ὁριζομένων
καὶ τῶν τί ἐστι τὰ μὲν ὡς τὸ σιμὸν τὰ δ' ὡς τὸ κοῖ-
λον. διαφέρει δὲ ταῦτα ὅτι τὸ μὲν σιμὸν συνειλημμένον ἐστὶ
μετὰ τῆς ὕλης (ἔστι γὰρ τὸ σιμὸν κοίλη ῥίς), ἡ δὲ κοιλό-
της ἄνευ ὕλης αἰσθητῆς. εἰ δὴ πάντα τὰ φυσικὰ ὁμοίως τῷ
1026ª σιμῷ λέγονται, οἷον ῥὶς ὀφθαλμὸς πρόσωπον σὰρξ ὀστοῦν,
ὅλως ζῷον, φύλλον ῥίζα φλοιός, ὅλως φυτόν (οὐθενὸς
γὰρ ἄνευ κινήσεως ὁ λόγος αὐτῶν, ἀλλ' ἀεὶ ἔχει ὕλην),
δῆλον πῶς δεῖ ἐν τοῖς φυσικοῖς τὸ τί ἐστι ζητεῖν καὶ ὁρίζε-
5 σθαι, καὶ διότι καὶ περὶ ψυχῆς ἐνίας θεωρῆσαι τοῦ φυσικοῦ,
ὅση μὴ ἄνευ τῆς ὕλης ἐστίν. ὅτι μὲν οὖν ἡ φυσικὴ θεωρητική ἐστι, φανερὸν ἐκ τούτων· ἀλλ' ἔστι καὶ ἡ μαθημα-
τικὴ θεωρητική· ἀλλ' εἰ ἀκινήτων καὶ χωριστῶν ἐστι, νῦν
ἄδηλον, ὅτι μέντοι ἔνια μαθήματα ᾗ ἀκίνητα καὶ ᾗ χωρι-
10 στὰ θεωρεῖ, δῆλον. εἰ δέ τί ἐστιν ἀΐδιον καὶ ἀκίνητον καὶ
χωριστόν, φανερὸν ὅτι θεωρητικῆς τὸ γνῶναι, οὐ μέντοι φυ-

ᵇ 18 τε om. Aᵇ   ἐστιν Aᵇ Al. Asc. : ἔστιν τοῦτο ΕJΓ   21 ἐν
αὐτῇ ΕJΓ Asc.ᶜ : ἐν ἑαυτῇ Aᵇ : ᾗ αὐτή Schwegler   22 ποιητικῶν
ΕJΓ Al. Asc.ᶜ (cf. 1064ª 11)   23 πρακτῶν ΕAᵇAl. sed sup. lin.
ικ Ε¹ : πρακτικῶν JΓ Asc.ᶜ (cf. 1064ª 14)   24 καί] καὶ τὸ Ε²J
25 εἰ om. Aᵇ   πᾶσα Aᵇ Asc.ᶜ : ἅπασα ΕJ   26 ἡ φυσικὴ θεωρητική
ΕJΓ Al. Asc. : om. Aᵇ   28 ὡς alt. ΕΤ : om. JAᵇ Γ Al. Asc.
30 ποιεῖν ἐστιν ΕJΓ   ἔστι δὲ τῶν Aᵇ Al.ᶜ : τῶν δ' ΕJΓ : τῶν δὴ γρ. Ε
31 μέν Aᵇ et ut vid. Al. : μὲν οὕτως ὑπάρχει ΕJΓ Asc.   33 τό ΕJΓ
Asc.ᶜ : τὸ μέν Aᵇ   1026ª 3 ἀεὶ om. Aᵇ   7 ἐστι ΕJΓ Al. Asc. :
τίς ἐστι Aᵇ Al.¹   9 μέντοι] μὲν οὖν Ε   ᾗ Aᵇ   ᾗ] μή Schwegler
10 ἀΐδιον καὶ ἀκίνητον καὶ χωριστόν Aᵇ Al. : ἀκ. καὶ ἀΐδ. καὶ χ. ΕJ : ἀκ.
καὶ χ. καὶ ἀΐδ. Γ

σικῆς γε (περὶ κινητῶν γάρ τινων ἡ φυσική) οὐδὲ μαθηματικῆς, ἀλλὰ προτέρας ἀμφοῖν. ἡ μὲν γὰρ φυσικὴ περὶ
χωριστὰ μὲν ἀλλ᾽ οὐκ ἀκίνητα, τῆς δὲ μαθηματικῆς ἔνια
περὶ ἀκίνητα μὲν οὐ χωριστὰ δὲ ἴσως ἀλλ᾽ ὡς ἐν ὕλῃ· ἡ 15
δὲ πρώτη καὶ περὶ χωριστὰ καὶ ἀκίνητα. ἀνάγκη δὲ πάντα
μὲν τὰ αἴτια ἀίδια εἶναι, μάλιστα δὲ ταῦτα· ταῦτα γὰρ
αἴτια τοῖς φανεροῖς τῶν θείων. ὥστε τρεῖς ἂν εἶεν φιλοσο-
φίαι θεωρητικαί, μαθηματική, φυσική, θεολογική (οὐ γὰρ
ἄδηλον ὅτι εἴ που τὸ θεῖον ὑπάρχει, ἐν τῇ τοιαύτῃ φύσει 20
ὑπάρχει), καὶ τὴν τιμιωτάτην δεῖ περὶ τὸ τιμιώτατον γένος
εἶναι. αἱ μὲν οὖν θεωρητικαὶ τῶν ἄλλων ἐπιστημῶν αἱρετώ-
ταται, αὕτη δὲ τῶν θεωρητικῶν. ἀπορήσειε γὰρ ἄν τις πότερόν ποθ᾽ ἡ πρώτη φιλοσοφία καθόλου ἐστὶν ἢ περί τι γένος καὶ φύσιν τινὰ μίαν (οὐ γὰρ ὁ αὐτὸς τρόπος οὐδ᾽ ἐν 25
ταῖς μαθηματικαῖς, ἀλλ᾽ ἡ μὲν γεωμετρία καὶ ἀστρολογία
περί τινα φύσιν εἰσίν, ἡ δὲ καθόλου πασῶν κοινή)· εἰ μὲν
οὖν μὴ ἔστι τις ἑτέρα οὐσία παρὰ τὰς φύσει συνεστηκυίας, ἡ
φυσικὴ ἂν εἴη πρώτη ἐπιστήμη· εἰ δ᾽ ἔστι τις οὐσία ἀκίνητος,
αὕτη προτέρα καὶ φιλοσοφία πρώτη, καὶ καθόλου οὕτως 30
ὅτι πρώτη· καὶ περὶ τοῦ ὄντος ᾗ ὂν ταύτης ἂν εἴη θεωρῆσαι,
καὶ τί ἐστι καὶ τὰ ὑπάρχοντα ᾗ ὄν.

2 Ἀλλ᾽ ἐπεὶ τὸ ὂν τὸ ἁπλῶς λεγόμενον λέγεται πολλαχῶς, ὧν ἓν μὲν ἦν τὸ κατὰ συμβεβηκός, ἕτερον δὲ τὸ
ὡς ἀληθές, καὶ τὸ μὴ ὂν ὡς τὸ ψεῦδος, παρὰ ταῦτα δ᾽ 35
ἐστὶ τὰ σχήματα τῆς κατηγορίας (οἷον τὸ μὲν τί, τὸ δὲ
ποιόν, τὸ δὲ ποσόν, τὸ δὲ πού, τὸ δὲ ποτέ, καὶ εἴ τι ἄλλο
σημαίνει τὸν τρόπον τοῦτον), ἔτι παρὰ ταῦτα πάντα τὸ δυ- **1026ᵇ**
νάμει καὶ ἐνεργείᾳ·—ἐπεὶ δὴ πολλαχῶς λέγεται τὸ ὄν,
πρῶτον περὶ τοῦ κατὰ συμβεβηκὸς λεκτέον, ὅτι οὐδεμία ἐστὶ

E. 2-4, cf. K. 8. 1064ᵇ 15 — 1065ᵃ 26

ᵃ 12 μαθηματικῆς γε ἀλλ᾽ ἑτέρας προτέρας Aᵇ   14 χωριστὰ
Schwegler: ἀχώριστα codd. Γ Al.   17 εἶναι om. EJΓ Al.¹
18 θείων] θείων ἢ Aᵇ: αἰσθητῶν J γρ. E γρ. Al.   19 οὐ . . .
22 εἶναι an post 23 θεωρητικῶν ponenda ? cf. K. 1064ᵇ 3-6   21 ἀεὶ
Aᵇ   22 τῶν EJΓ Al. Asc.: καὶ τῶν Aᵇ   αἱρετώτεραι EJΓ Asc.
25 τινὰ Aᵇ et ut vid. Al.: om. EJΓ Asc.   26 ἀλλ᾽] ὅτι Γ   27 ἡ
AᵇΓ Asc.º: ἐκείνη EJ   καὶ πᾶσι γρ. E   28 φύσεις Γ   30 καὶ
pr.] καὶ ἡ T   32 τις J   35 ὡς τὸ] ὡς E: τὸ ὡς ci. Bonitz
ᵇ 2 καὶ E et ut vid. Al. Asc.: καὶ τὸ Aᵇ: καὶ ἐν J   ἐπεὶ δὲ Aᵇ: ἐπειδὴ
E   3 ἐστὶ περὶ αὐτὸ] περὶ ταὐτό ἐστι E

περὶ αὐτὸ θεωρία. σημεῖον δέ· οὐδεμιᾷ γὰρ ἐπιστήμῃ ἐπι-
5 μελὲς περὶ αὐτοῦ οὔτε πρακτικῇ οὔτε ποιητικῇ οὔτε θεωρητικῇ.
οὔτε γὰρ ὁ ποιῶν οἰκίαν ποιεῖ ὅσα συμβαίνει ἅμα τῇ οἰκίᾳ
γιγνομένῃ (ἄπειρα γάρ ἐστιν· τοῖς μὲν γὰρ ἡδεῖαν τοῖς δὲ
βλαβερὰν τοῖς δ᾽ ὠφέλιμον οὐθὲν εἶναι κωλύει τὴν ποιηθεῖ-
σαν, καὶ ἑτέραν ὡς εἰπεῖν πάντων τῶν ὄντων· ὧν οὐθενός
10 ἐστιν ἡ οἰκοδομικὴ ποιητική), τὸν αὐτὸν δὲ τρόπον οὐδ᾽ ὁ γεωμέτρης θεωρεῖ τὰ οὕτω συμβεβηκότα τοῖς σχήμασιν, οὐδ᾽ εἰ
ἕτερόν ἐστι τρίγωνον καὶ τρίγωνον δύο ὀρθὰς ἔχον. καὶ τοῦτ᾽
εὐλόγως συμπίπτει· ὥσπερ γὰρ ὄνομά τι μόνον τὸ συμβεβηκός ἐστιν. διὸ Πλάτων τρόπον τινὰ οὐ κακῶς τὴν σοφιστι-
15 κὴν περὶ τὸ μὴ ὂν ἔταξεν. εἰσὶ γὰρ οἱ τῶν σοφιστῶν λόγοι
περὶ τὸ συμβεβηκὸς ὡς εἰπεῖν μάλιστα πάντων, πότερον
ἕτερον ἢ ταὐτὸν μουσικὸν καὶ γραμματικόν, καὶ μουσικὸς
Κορίσκος καὶ Κορίσκος, καὶ εἰ πᾶν ὃ ἂν · ᾖ, μὴ ἀεὶ δέ, γέγονεν, ὥστ᾽ εἰ μουσικὸς ὢν γραμματικὸς γέγονε, καὶ γραμ-
20 ματικὸς ὢν μουσικός, καὶ ὅσοι δὴ ἄλλοι τοιοῦτοι τῶν λόγων
εἰσίν· φαίνεται γὰρ τὸ συμβεβηκὸς ἐγγύς τι τοῦ μὴ ὄντος.
δῆλον δὲ καὶ ἐκ τῶν τοιούτων λόγων· τῶν μὲν γὰρ ἄλλον
τρόπον ὄντων ἔστι γένεσις καὶ φθορά, τῶν δὲ κατὰ συμβεβηκὸς οὐκ ἔστιν. ἀλλ᾽ ὅμως λεκτέον ἔτι περὶ τοῦ συμβεβη-
25 κότος ἐφ᾽ ὅσον ἐνδέχεται, τίς ἡ φύσις αὐτοῦ καὶ διὰ τίν᾽
αἰτίαν ἔστιν· ἅμα γὰρ δῆλον ἴσως ἔσται καὶ διὰ τί ἐπιστήμη
οὐκ ἔστιν αὐτοῦ.—ἐπεὶ οὖν ἐστὶν ἐν τοῖς οὖσι τὰ μὲν ἀεὶ ὡσαύτως ἔχοντα καὶ ἐξ ἀνάγκης, οὐ τῆς κατὰ τὸ βίαιον λεγομένης ἀλλ᾽ ἣν λέγομεν τῷ μὴ ἐνδέχεσθαι ἄλλως, τὰ δ᾽
30 ἐξ ἀνάγκης μὲν οὐκ ἔστιν οὐδ᾽ ἀεί, ὡς δ᾽ ἐπὶ τὸ πολύ, αὕτη
ἀρχὴ καὶ αὕτη αἰτία ἐστὶ τοῦ εἶναι τὸ συμβεβηκός· ὃ γὰρ
ἂν ᾖ μήτ᾽ ἀεὶ μήθ᾽ ὡς ἐπὶ τὸ πολύ, τοῦτό φαμεν συμβεβηκὸς εἶναι. οἷον ἐπὶ κυνὶ ἂν χειμὼν γένηται καὶ ψῦχος,
τοῦτο συμβῆναί φαμεν, ἀλλ᾽ οὐκ ἂν πνῖγος καὶ ἀλέα, ὅτι
35 τὸ μὲν ἀεὶ ἢ ὡς ἐπὶ τὸ πολὺ τὸ δ᾽ οὔ. καὶ τὸν ἄνθρωπον
λευκὸν εἶναι συμβέβηκεν (οὔτε γὰρ ἀεὶ οὔθ᾽ ὡς ἐπὶ τὸ πολύ),
ζῷον δ᾽ οὐ κατὰ συμβεβηκός. καὶ τὸ ὑγιάζειν δὲ τὸν οἰκο-

ᵇ 5 πρακτικὴ οὔτε ποιητικὴ οὔτε θεωρητικὴ J   7 γινομένη J
9 ὄντων] τοιούτων Cannan   13 ὄνομά τι Al. Asc. : ὀνόματι codd.
Γ Al.ᶜ   17 καὶ pr. EJΓ Al. Asc. : ἢ Aᵇ   18 καὶ Κορίσκος
om. E   21 γάρ τι τὸ Ε²   30 πολύ] πολύ, τὰ δ᾽ οὔτ᾽ αἰεὶ
οὔθ᾽ ὡς ἐπὶ τὸ πολύ Jaeger   37 τὸ ... οἰκοδόμον Aᵇ Al. : τὸ τὸν
οἰκοδόμον ὑγείαν ποιῆσαι EJΓ Asc.

δόμον συμβεβηκός, ὅτι οὐ πέφυκε τοῦτο ποιεῖν οἰκοδό- 1027ᵃ
μος ἀλλὰ ἰατρός, ἀλλὰ συνέβη ἰατρὸν εἶναι τὸν οἰκοδόμον.
καὶ ὀψοποιὸς ἡδονῆς στοχαζόμενος ποιήσειεν ἄν τι ὑγιεινόν,
ἀλλ' οὐ κατὰ τὴν ὀψοποιητικήν· διὸ συνέβη, φαμέν, καὶ
ἔστιν ὡς ποιεῖ, ἁπλῶς δ' οὔ. τῶν μὲν γὰρ ἄλλων [ἐνίοτε] δυ- 5
νάμεις εἰσὶν αἱ ποιητικαί, τῶν δ' οὐδεμία τέχνη οὐδὲ δύναμις
ὡρισμένη· τῶν γὰρ κατὰ συμβεβηκὸς ὄντων ἢ γιγνομένων
καὶ τὸ αἴτιόν ἐστι κατὰ συμβεβηκός. ὥστ' ἐπεὶ οὐ πάντα
ἐστὶν ἐξ ἀνάγκης καὶ ἀεὶ ἢ ὄντα ἢ γιγνόμενα, ἀλλὰ τὰ
πλεῖστα ὡς ἐπὶ τὸ πολύ, ἀνάγκη εἶναι τὸ κατὰ συμβεβη- 10
κὸς ὄν· οἷον οὔτ' ἀεὶ οὔθ' ὡς ἐπὶ τὸ πολὺ ὁ λευκὸς μουσικός
ἐστιν, ἐπεὶ δὲ γίγνεταί ποτε, κατὰ συμβεβηκὸς ἔσται (εἰ δὲ
μή, πάντ' ἔσται ἐξ ἀνάγκης)· ὥστε ἡ ὕλη ἔσται αἰτία ἡ ἐν-
δεχομένη παρὰ τὸ ὡς ἐπὶ τὸ πολὺ ἄλλως τοῦ συμβεβηκότος. ἀρχὴν δὲ τηνδὶ ληπτέον, πότερον οὐδέν ἐστιν οὔτ' αἰεὶ 15
οὔθ' ὡς ἐπὶ τὸ πολύ. ἢ τοῦτο ἀδύνατον; ἔστιν ἄρα τι παρὰ
ταῦτα τὸ ὁπότερ' ἔτυχε καὶ κατὰ συμβεβηκός. ἀλλὰ πότερον τὸ ὡς ἐπὶ τὸ πολύ, τὸ δ' ἀεὶ οὐθενὶ ὑπάρχει, ἢ ἔστιν
ἄττα ἀΐδια; περὶ μὲν οὖν τούτων ὕστερον σκεπτέον, ὅτι δ'
ἐπιστήμη οὐκ ἔστι τοῦ συμβεβηκότος φανερόν· ἐπιστήμη μὲν 20
γὰρ πᾶσα ἢ τοῦ ἀεὶ ἢ τοῦ ὡς ἐπὶ τὸ πολύ—πῶς γὰρ ἢ
μαθήσεται ἢ διδάξει ἄλλον; δεῖ γὰρ ὡρίσθαι ἢ τῷ ἀεὶ ἢ
τῷ ὡς ἐπὶ τὸ πολύ, οἷον ὅτι ὠφέλιμον τὸ μελίκρατον τῷ
πυρέττοντι ὡς ἐπὶ τὸ πολύ—τὸ δὲ παρὰ τοῦτο οὐχ ἕξει λέγειν, πότε οὔ, οἷον νουμηνίᾳ· ἢ γὰρ ἀεὶ ἢ ὡς ἐπὶ τὸ πολὺ καὶ 25
τὸ τῇ νουμηνίᾳ· τὸ δὲ συμβεβηκός ἐστι παρὰ ταῦτα. τί μὲν
οὖν ἐστι τὸ συμβεβηκὸς καὶ διὰ τίν' αἰτίαν καὶ ὅτι ἐπιστήμη
οὐκ ἔστιν αὐτοῦ, εἴρηται.

8   Ὅτι δ' εἰσὶν ἀρχαὶ καὶ αἴτια γενητὰ καὶ φθαρτὰ

1027ᵃ 1 συμβεβηκός EJ et ut vid. Al.: κατὰ συμβεβηκός AᵇΓ Asc.
3 ἡδονῇ Aᵇ τινι JAᵇΓ Al. Asc.   4 ὀψοποιητικὴν Aᵇ Asc.ᶜ et fecit
E : ὀψοποικὴν J   5 ἄλλων E Al. Asc.: ἄλλαι JAᵇΓ ἐνίοτε seclusi,
om. ut vid Al. Asc.: αἰτίαι τε καὶ ex Al. ci. Bonitz   7 γιγνομένων
EJ Al. Asc.ᶜ: γενομένων Aᵇ   8 ἐπεὶ Aᵇ Al.ᶜ Asc.ᶜ: ἐπειδὴ EJ
13 ὥστε . . . 16 ἀδύνατον hic codd. Γ Al.: ante 8 ὥστ' collocanda
ci. Bonitz   ἔσται ἡ ὕλη Aᵇ   αἰτία post συμβεβηκότος Aᵇ
14 ἄλλως EJΓ Al. Asc.: om. Aᵇ   15 τήνδε Aᵇ Asc.ˡ   16 εἴη
ἄρα Aᵇ   18 τὸ pr.] τὸ μὲν γρ. E: ἔστι μὲν τὸ Christ   οὐδὲν Asc.
21 πῶς γὰρ ἂν ἢ EJ   25 οὔ E et fort. Asc.: om. JAᵇΓ Al.   ἢ
pr.] ἢ γρ. E   26 τὸ pr. om. Aᵇ Asc.   29 γενητὰ EJ Al. Asc.ˡᶜ:
γεννητὰ Aᵇ

30 ἄνευ τοῦ γίγνεσθαι καὶ φθείρεσθαι, φανερόν. εἰ γὰρ μὴ
τοῦτ', ἐξ ἀνάγκης πάντ' ἔσται, εἰ τοῦ γιγνομένου καὶ φθειρομένου μὴ κατὰ συμβεβηκὸς αἴτιόν τι ἀνάγκη εἶναι. πότερον
γὰρ ἔσται τοδὶ ἢ οὔ; ἐάν γε τοδὶ γένηται· εἰ δὲ μή, οὔ.
τοῦτο δὲ ἐὰν ἄλλο. καὶ οὕτω δῆλον ὅτι ἀεὶ χρόνου ἀφαιρουμέ-
1027ᵇ νου ἀπὸ πεπερασμένου χρόνου ἥξει ἐπὶ τὸ νῦν, ὥστε ὁδὶ ἀποθανεῖται [νόσῳ ἢ] βίᾳ, ἐάν γε ἐξέλθῃ· τοῦτο δὲ ἐὰν διψήσῃ·
τοῦτο δὲ ἐὰν ἄλλο· καὶ οὕτως ἥξει εἰς ὃ νῦν ὑπάρχει, ἢ εἰς
τῶν γεγονότων τι. οἷον ἐὰν διψήσῃ· τοῦτο δὲ εἰ ἐσθίει δρι-
5 μέα· τοῦτο δ' ἤτοι ὑπάρχει ἢ οὔ· ὥστ' ἐξ ἀνάγκης ἀποθανεῖται ἢ οὐκ ἀποθανεῖται. ὁμοίως δὲ κἂν ὑπερπηδήσῃ τις εἰς
τὰ γενόμενα, ὁ αὐτὸς λόγος· ἤδη γὰρ ὑπάρχει τοῦτο ἔν
τινι, λέγω δὲ τὸ γεγονός· ἐξ ἀνάγκης ἄρα πάντα ἔσται τὰ
ἐσόμενα, οἷον τὸ ἀποθανεῖν τὸν ζῶντα· ἤδη γάρ τι γέγονεν,
10 οἷον τὰ ἐναντία ἐν τῷ αὐτῷ. ἀλλ' εἰ νόσῳ ἢ βίᾳ,
οὔπω, ἀλλ' ἐὰν τοδὶ γένηται. δῆλον ἄρα ὅτι μέχρι τινὸς
βαδίζει ἀρχῆς, αὕτη δ' οὐκέτι εἰς ἄλλο. ἔσται οὖν ἡ τοῦ
ὁπότερ' ἔτυχεν αὕτη, καὶ αἴτιον τῆς γενέσεως αὐτῆς ἄλλο
οὐθέν. ἀλλ' εἰς ἀρχὴν ποίαν καὶ αἴτιον ποῖον ἡ ἀναγωγὴ ἡ
15 τοιαύτη, πότερον ὡς εἰς ὕλην ἢ ὡς εἰς τὸ οὗ ἕνεκα ἢ ὡς εἰς
τὸ κινῆσαν, μάλιστα σκεπτέον.

Περὶ μὲν οὖν τοῦ κατὰ συμβεβηκὸς ὄντος ἀφείσθω 4
(διώρισται γὰρ ἱκανῶς)· τὸ δὲ ὡς ἀληθὲς ὄν, καὶ μὴ ὂν ὡς
ψεῦδος, ἐπειδὴ παρὰ σύνθεσίν ἐστι καὶ διαίρεσιν, τὸ δὲ σύν-
20 ολον περὶ μερισμὸν ἀντιφάσεως (τὸ μὲν γὰρ ἀληθὲς τὴν
κατάφασιν ἐπὶ τῷ συγκειμένῳ ἔχει τὴν δ' ἀπόφασιν ἐπὶ
τῷ διῃρημένῳ, τὸ δὲ ψεῦδος τούτου τοῦ μερισμοῦ τὴν ἀντίφα-
σιν· πῶς δὲ τὸ ἅμα ἢ τὸ χωρὶς νοεῖν συμβαίνει, ἄλλος
λόγος, λέγω δὲ τὸ ἅμα καὶ τὸ χωρὶς ὥστε μὴ τὸ ἐφεξῆς
25 ἀλλ' ἕν τι γίγνεσθαι)· οὐ γάρ ἐστι τὸ ψεῦδος καὶ τὸ ἀληθὲς
ἐν τοῖς πράγμασιν, οἷον τὸ μὲν ἀγαθὸν ἀληθὲς τὸ δὲ κακὸν εὐθὺς ψεῦδος, ἀλλ' ἐν διανοίᾳ, περὶ δὲ τὰ ἁπλᾶ καὶ

ᵃ 30 ἄνω Apelt   34 τούτου γρ. E   ἂν Aᵇ sup. lin. et Γ: om.
EJ Asc.   ἄλλου J γρ. E Asc.   ᵇ 1 ὅδε EJ Asc.ˡ   2 νόσῳ
ἢ seclusi (cf. l. 10): habent codd. Γ Al.   τοῦτο. . . διψήσῃ om. Aᵇ et
ut vid. Al.   8 γένος J¹   10 αὐτῷ Aᵇ et ut vid. Al.: αὐτῷ
σώματι EJΓ   13 ἄλλο Aᵇ Al.: om. EJΓ Asc.   15 εἰς alt.
om. Aᵇ   18 ἀληθῶς γρ. E   19 παρὰ EJAᵇΓ Al.: περὶ recc.
24 τὸ alt. EJ Asc.ᶜ: om. Aᵇ Al.ᶜ   τὸ recc. Al.ᵉ: τῷ EJAᵇΓ   25
καὶ] τε καὶ E   27 εὐθὺς recc. Al.: εὐθὺ Aᵇ: om. EJΓ

τὰ τί ἐστιν οὐδ' ἐν διανοίᾳ·—ὅσα μὲν οὖν δεῖ θεωρῆσαι περὶ
τὸ οὕτως ὂν καὶ μὴ ὄν, ὕστερον ἐπισκεπτέον· ἐπεὶ δὲ ἡ συμ-
πλοκή ἐστιν καὶ ἡ διαίρεσις ἐν διανοίᾳ ἀλλ' οὐκ ἐν τοῖς 30
πράγμασι, τὸ δ' οὕτως ὂν ἕτερον ὂν τῶν κυρίως (ἢ γὰρ τὸ
τί ἐστιν ἢ ὅτι ποιὸν ἢ ὅτι ποσὸν ἤ τι ἄλλο συνάπτει ἢ
ἀφαιρεῖ ἡ διάνοια), τὸ μὲν ὡς συμβεβηκὸς καὶ τὸ ὡς ἀληθὲς ὂν ἀφετέον—τὸ γὰρ αἴτιον τοῦ μὲν ἀόριστον τοῦ δὲ τῆς
διανοίας τι πάθος, καὶ ἀμφότερα περὶ τὸ λοιπὸν γένος τοῦ 1028ᵃ
ὄντος, καὶ οὐκ ἔξω δηλοῦσιν οὖσάν τινα φύσιν τοῦ ὄντος—διὸ
ταῦτα μὲν ἀφείσθω, σκεπτέον δὲ τοῦ ὄντος αὐτοῦ τὰ αἴτια
καὶ τὰς ἀρχὰς ᾗ ὄν. [φανερὸν δ' ἐν οἷς διωρισάμεθα περὶ
τοῦ ποσαχῶς λέγεται ἕκαστον, ὅτι πολλαχῶς λέγεται 5
τὸ ὄν.]

ᵇ 28 ἐν] ἐν τῇ E   29 ὄντως Asc.   30 καὶ ἡ AᵇΓ Al. Asc.: ἢ
EJ   31 κυρίως Aᵇ Al. Asc.: κυρίων EJΓ   32 τι Aᵇ Al. Asc.:
εἴ τι EJΓ   33 ἀφαιρεῖ codd.: διαιρεῖ Γ et ut vid. Al., Bonitz
ἀληθὲς EJΓ Al.: ἀληθῶς Aᵇ Asc.   1028ᵃ 2 τοῦ om. Aᵇ   4 φανερὸν ... 6 ὄν damnavit Christ (cf. Z. 1028ᵃ 10), habet Al.: φανερὸν
... ἕκαστον om. Asc.   5 ὅτι ... 6 ὄν EJΓ Asc.: om. Aᵇ
6 post ὄν add. σημαίνει γὰρ τὸ μὲν τί ἐστιν E¹J¹Γ

BOOK A

(I) Wisdom is the knowledge of first causes (chs. 1, 2).

(A) *Wisdom is a knowledge of causes* (ch. 1).

980ª 21. All men by nature desire to know, as is indicated by the love we have for our senses, even apart from their practical uses, and especially for that of sight because it tells us much about the differences between things.

27. (1) Sensation is common to all animals. Further,

28. (2) from sensation in some animals arises memory, which makes them intelligent, and, if they have also hearing, makes them capable of being taught.

The other animals live by imagination and memory, with small share in 'experience', but

ᵇ28. (3) in man many memories of the same thing produce experience. Experience may easily be confused with what are really its results, viz.

981ª 2. (4) science and art. Art arises when from many notions of experience there comes a single universal judgement. To judge that *A* was good for *B, C*, &c., when ill of disease *N*, is a matter of experience; to judge that *A* was good for all men of a certain constitution when ill of a certain disease, a matter of art.

12. Experience is often practically more successful than art, because it is of the particular and practice deals with particulars, and with universals only as concomitants of particulars.

24. But knowledge and wisdom belong to art rather than to experience, because artists know causes and men of experience only facts.

30. For this reason too master-artists are thought to have wisdom rather than manual workers, who act by habit very much as lifeless things do by nature.

ᵇ7. In general, we think art more truly knowledge than experience, because it implies the power to teach.

10. Further, though the senses have most to do with knowledge of particulars, we do not think them to be wisdom because they never tell us the 'why'.

13. At first the inventor of any art was admired, not only for the utility of his invention but for his wisdom; later the inventors of arts that aim at giving pleasure were esteemed wiser than the inventors of useful arts;

20. it was only when both these kinds of art had been established that tne arts which aim neither at pleasure nor at the necessities of life were discovered.   They demand leisure ; and this is why mathematics was founded by the Egyptian priests.

25. The difference between art, science, &c., is stated in the *Ethics* ; our present point is that every one takes wisdom to be concerned with first causes ;

29. this is why the experienced man is thought wiser than the man who has only sensation, the artist than the experienced man, the master-artist than the manual worker, the theoretical than the productive arts.

The purpose of this chapter is stated at 981ᵇ 27.   It is to show that σοφία is universally held to be concerned with the primary causes and principles.   Though the chapter begins without any reference to σοφία, and seems to be merely tracing the development of mind from perception to science through memory, experience, and art, the underlying intention throughout (cf. 981ᵃ 25, ᵇ 1, 5, 10, 16, 18) is to bring out the implications of the words σοφός, σοφία, which are finally summed up in 981ᵇ 27.   For the transition from perception to science cf. *An. Post.* ii. 19.

Jaeger has shown (*Aristoteles* 68 ff.) that chs. 1, 2 are based on a fuller treatment of the same topics by Aristotle in the *Protrepticus*. Cf. for instance 980ᵃ 21–28 with Iamblichus, *Protrept.* 43. 20–27, 44. 9–27 (Pistelli), 981ᵇ 13—982ᵃ 2 with Arist. fr. 53 (Rose, 1886).

980ᵃ 23. On the superiority of sight to the other senses cf. *De Sensu* 437ᵃ 3, where, however, though sight is said to be superior πρὸς τὰ ἀναγκαῖα καὶ καθ' αὑτήν, hearing is said to be superior πρὸς νοῦν καὶ κατὰ συμβεβηκός (cf. 980ᵇ 21–25.)   The passage in the *De Sensu* further explains how it is that sight πολλὰς δηλοῖ διαφοράς.   It is because all bodies have colour, so that in seeing colour we see indirectly the common sensibles—figure, size, movement, number.   Alexander assigns a different reason, that in colour itself there are many varieties, while by touch we perceive only pairs of opposites, hot and cold or dry and wet.

29. τοῖς μὲν αὐτῶν οὐκ ἐγγίγνεται μνήμη.   *De An.* 428ᵃ 10 cites ants, bees, and grubs as animals not having φαντασία, which is implied in memory (*De Mem.* 451ᵃ 14).   But in view of 980ᵇ 23 and *De Part. An.* 648ᵃ 5, 650ᵇ 25 difficulties have been felt about this statement, and Torstrik with some ancient authority emends the text so as to make it draw a contrast between ants and bees as having memory, and grubs as not having it.

ᵇ 21. The difficulties which have been felt about the reading of Aᵇ and Alexander are somewhat unreal.   Aristotle first uses φρονιμώτερα and μαθητικώτερα as almost synonymous, and then by an afterthought distinguishes between them.   Of the emendations the best is that of Bywater, who inserts τὰ δέ after φρονιμώτερα.

φρόνιμος is not here used in the strict sense defined in *E. N.*

1140ᵇ 20 ἀνάγκη τὴν φρόνησιν ἕξιν εἶναι μετὰ λόγου ἀληθῆ περὶ τὰ
ἀνθρώπινα ἀγαθὰ πρακτικήν. φρόνησις as it exists in animals involves
no λόγος. But its existence in animals, in this wider sense, is pointed
out even in the *Ethics* (1141ᵃ 26 ; cf. *De Gen. An.* 753ᵃ 11).

23. οἷον μέλιττα. Bees are here said to have memory, and not
to have hearing. In *Hist. An.* 627ᵃ 17 Aristotle says it is doubtful
whether they hear. In *De An.* 428ᵃ 10 it is implied that they do not
remember ; but see 980ᵃ 29 n.

24. κἂν εἴ τι τοιοῦτον ἄλλο γένος ζῴων ἔστι. E. g. the ant (*De
Part. An.* 650ᵇ 26).

μανθάνει, as the reference to hearing shows, means ' can be
taught '. This is the force of the distinction between μαθεῖν and
εὑρεῖν in *De An.* 429ᵇ 9. In *Hist. An.* 608ᵃ 17 we are told explicitly
that animals which hear κοινωνεῖ τινὸς ἅμα καὶ μαθήσεως καὶ διδασκαλίας,
both from one another and from man.

26. The relation between φαντασία and μνήμη is stated in *De Mem.*
451ᵃ 14. μνήμη is φαντάσματος, ὡς εἰκόνος οὗ φάντασμα, ἕξις. I. e.,
in order that we may have memory we must not only retain an image
but also recognize it as standing for an object. Further, memory
involves, while φαντασία does not, a sense of time (449ᵇ 28). The
nature of φαντασία is discussed in *De An.* 427ᵇ 29—429ᵃ 9.

ἐμπειρίας δὲ μετέχει μικρόν. It is not easy to see what Aristotle
wants to say about ἐμπειρία, the connecting link between memory and
art or science. Animals have a little of it ; on the other hand it
involves thought (981ᵃ 6). In principle it seems not to differ from
memory. If you have many memories of the same object you will have
ἐμπειρία; those animals, then, which have good memories will
occasionally have it, and men will constantly have it. After having
described it, however, as produced by many memories of the *same*
object, Aristotle proceeds to describe it as embracing a memory about
Callias and a memory about Socrates. These are not the same
object, but only instances of the same universal ; say, ' phlegmatic
persons suffering from fever '. An animal, or a man possessing only
ἐμπειρία, acts on such memories, and is unconsciously affected by the
identical element in the different objects. But in man a new activity
sometimes occurs, which never occurs in the lower animals. A man
may grasp the universal of which Callias and Socrates are instances,
and may give to a third patient the remedy which helped them,
knowing that he is doing so because the third patient shares their
general character. This is art or science—for here these two are not
distinguished by Aristotle.

What is revived by memory has previously been experienced as
a unit. Experience, on the other hand, is a coagulation of memories ;
what is active in present consciousness in virtue of experience has
not been experienced together. Therefore (*a*) as embodying the
data of unconsciously selected awarenesses it foreshadows a universal ; but (*b*) as not conscious of what in the past is relevant,
and why, it is not aware of it as universal. I. e. experience is a stage

in which there has appeared ability to interpret the present in the
light of the past, but an ability which cannot account for itself; when
it accounts for itself it becomes art.

Alexander suggests (4. 15) that μικρόν is an intentional under-
statement, and that Aristotle really means that animals have *no* ἐμπειρία.
L. 28 γίγνεται δ' ἐκ τῆς μνήμης ἐμπειρία τοῖς ἀνθρώποις also suggests
this, and ἐμπειρία does not seem to be elsewhere ascribed to the brutes.
But the passage, though not very clear, on the whole seems to distinguish
men from other animals by their possession of art, not by their
possession of experience ; and in point of fact the acquired instincts of
animals exhibit the characteristics of experience as described above.

981^a 2. ἀποβαίνει δ' ἐπιστήμη καὶ τέχνη διὰ τῆς ἐμπειρίας τοῖς
ἀνθρώποις. At first art can only be acquired by experience ; but it
may be transmitted by teaching, so that there are people who have art
without experience (l. 14).

4. ὡς φησὶ Πῶλος. Polus was a well-known pupil of Gorgias, and
this jingle is in Gorgias' style. Polus makes the remark in Pl. *Gorg.*
448 c, but it is implied that it also occurred in his work on oratory
(ib. 462 B).

8. Καλλίᾳ. Callias, the well-known patron of Protagoras and
other sophists (cf. Pl. *Apol.* 20 A, *Prot.* 314 D, 315 D, *Crat.* 391 B, Xen.
Symp. 1. 5, 4. 62). Prof. Taylor suggests, however, that Aristotle
is reproducing 'a personal trick employed by Plato in lecturing, . . .
the trick of using members of the audience as the logical subjects of
sample propositions' (*Varia Socratica* 43). He thinks, therefore,
that Καλλίᾳ refers to Callippus, the assassin of Dion, and Σωκράτει to
the younger Socrates (for whom cf. Z. 1036^b 25). Now Coriscus, who
is often used in this way, and sometimes coupled with Socrates (*Top.*
166^b 32, *De Part. An.* 644^a 25, *De Gen. An.* 767^b 25, 768^a 6), was very
likely a member of Aristotle's audience (cf. Δ. 1015^b 17 n.). But the
association of Callias with Cleon in *An. Pr.* 43^a 27, and with Themis-
tocles in *Soph. El.* 176^a 1, and that of Socrates with Hippias in *Rhet.*
1356^b 33 suggest that the famous Callias and the famous Socrates are
meant.

Prof. H. Jackson has conjectured with much probability, from the
references to Callias in Z. 1033^b 24, 1034^a 6, *An. Pr.* 43^a 36, that
Aristotle had in his lecture-room a picture representing the scene in
Pl. *Prot.* 335 c, where Callias prevents Socrates from leaving the
company (*J. of P.* xxxv. 195 f.).

12. Jackson (*J. of P.* vi. 206) points out that τοῖς φλεγματώδεσιν ἢ
χολώδεσιν answers to τοῖς τοιοῖσδε κατ' εἶδος ἐν ἀφορισθεῖσι, and πυρέττουσι καύσῳ to κάμνουσι τηνδὶ τὴν νόσον, so that the second ἢ must
be excised. φλεγματώδης and χολώδης describe not diseases but
natural ἕξεις. Cf. *E. N.* 1181^b 3, *Probl.* i. 9, 11, 12.

πρὸς μὲν οὖν τὸ πράττειν. The answer to μέν comes in l. 24 ἀλλ' ὅμως.

18. πλὴν ἀλλ' ἢ does not seem to be an Aristotelian combination,
and the reading of A^b, which omits πλήν, is probably the
original one.

19. Σωκράτην. This is the usual form of the accusative in Xenophon, while Σωκράτη is the Platonic form. In Aristotle the genitive and dative are Σωκράτους, Σωκράτει. Σωκράτη occurs in *Top.* 160ᵇ 27, 28, *Phys.* 228ᵃ 3, but in *Cat.* 13ᵇ 14, 18, 22, 14ᵃ 10, 11, 14, *An. Pr.* 43ᵃ 35 Σωκράτην is the better attested reading. It appears better to read it here and avoid hiatus.

20. ᾧ συμβέβηκεν ἀνθρώπῳ εἶναι. It is of course not an accident of Callias, as opposed to his essence and his properties, that he is a man; nor (as Bonitz says) a συμβεβηκὸς καθ' αὑτό or property as opposed to his essence. συμβεβηκός is used simply to indicate that it is not directly man that the doctor cures, but directly Callias and indirectly man because Callias is a man. For this use cf. M. 1087ᵃ 19.

ᵇ 2–5. τοὺς . . . ἔθος. These words, omitted by Aᵇ¹ and Alexander, are sufficiently warranted by the other MSS. and by Asc. 10. 6, and need cause no difficulty if they are treated as parenthetical and ὡς οὐ, &c. (l. 5) is taken to refer to the ἀρχιτέκτονες (ᵃ 30).

In ll. 2, 3 ποιεῖν μέν, οὐκ εἰδότα δὲ ποιεῖν ἃ ποιεῖ is commonly read, and taken as going with τοὺς δ', in which case εἰδότα must be supposed to have its gender by attraction. But E and Aᵇ² read ποιεῖ . . . ποιεῖ for ποιεῖν . . . ποιεῖν, and this is clearly right. These words fall within the ὥσπερ clause and go with τῶν ἀψύχων ἔνια. Aristotle begins by *likening* the action of χειροτέχναι to that of lifeless things, but proceeds to point out a *contrast* (that the latter act as they do by nature and the former by habit), which interrupts the construction and produces a not unnatural anacolouthon.

7. ὅλως τε σημεῖον τοῦ εἰδότος . . . τὸ δύνασθαι διδάσκειν ἐστίν. Cf. Pl. *Alcib.* i. 118 D.

18. τῶν δὲ πρὸς διαγωγὴν οὐσῶν. διαγωγή is used of the contemplative life (e. g. Λ. 1072ᵇ 14), and we might suppose that that is here in question. But l. 21 and 982ᵇ 23 show that Aristotle has in mind a threefold division of τέχναι, (1) αἱ πρὸς τἀναγκαῖα (useful arts), (2) αἱ πρὸς διαγωγήν 981ᵇ 18, πρὸς ἡδονήν 21, πρὸς ῥᾳστώνην καὶ διαγωγήν 982ᵇ 23 (almost = fine arts), (3) αἱ μὴ πρὸς ἡδονὴν μηδὲ πρὸς τἀναγκαῖα 981ᵇ 21 (theoretical arts, or sciences). διαγωγή is by no means confined to the theoretical life (*E. N.* 1127ᵇ 34, 1171ᵇ 13, 1176ᵇ 12, 14, *Pol.* 1334ᵃ 17, 1339ᵇ 17, 1341ᵇ 40).

23. For the Egyptian origin of mathematics cf. Pl. *Phaedr.* 274 C. Herodotus (ii. 109) ascribes a more utilitarian origin to Egyptian geometry, viz. the need of remeasuring the land after inundations. Certain geometrical discoveries may have been made by the priests in the course of solving a problem with which they were specially concerned, that of the orientation of temples. But geometry with the Egyptians never advanced beyond the practical art of mensuration (Heath, *Gk. Math.* i. 120–128). Aristotle might also have referred to the debt which Greek astronomy owed to the astronomical observations of the Babylonian priests, for which cf. *De Caelo* 292ᵃ 8. 'So far as the evidence of history extends', Gomperz remarks (*Greek Thinkers,*

i. 43), 'an organized caste of priests and scholars, combining the
necessary leisure with the equally necessary continuity of tradition,
was at all times indispensable to the beginnings of scientific research.
But its beginning and its end in such cases were only too likely to
coincide, for when scientific doctrines are mixed up with religious
tenets the same lifeless dogmatism will commonly benumb them
both. . . . Thus we may account it a double blessing for the free
progress of thought among the Greeks that their predecessors in
civilization possessed an organized priesthood, and that they themselves
lacked it.'

25. ἐν τοῖς ἠθικοῖς. *E. N.* vi. 1139ᵇ 14—1141ᵇ 8. τἆλλα τὰ ὁμογενῆ
are φρόνησις, σοφία, νοῦς. The reference to the *Ethics* is found in all
the MSS. and in Alexander and Asclepius, and the reasons alleged for
treating it as spurious are illusory. True, the difference between art
and science has hitherto been ignored, as it often is in Aristotle ; but
that is because he has been dealing with the difference between both
of them and unreasoning experience. Now, however, the difference
between art and science becomes important ; it is just that which has
already (l. 21) been indicated between systems of knowledge that aim
at utility or pleasure and those whose end is in themselves ; and
nothing is more natural than to refer to the work in which the difference
is most fully treated. It must not, however, be inferred that the *Ethics*
was written before Book A ; the reference may easily have been added
by Aristotle in a later revision. The question whether *Ethics* VI is
the work of Aristotle is here irrelevant ; if it were not, there would still
have been originally an Aristotelian Book VI covering much the same
ground.

Zeller thinks the *Ethics* earlier than the *Metaphysics*. It is certain
at least that no undoubtedly genuine work of Aristotle quotes any part
of the *Metaphysics* except Δ, which clearly must be considered
separately and may have been written considerably earlier than the
other parts.

28. περὶ τὰ πρῶτα αἴτια. What Aristotle has shown with regard
to σοφία is that (1) artists are thought to be wiser than experienced
people because they know better, i. e. because they know the cause as
well as the fact (ᵃ 25), (2) master-artists are thought to be wiser than
artisans for the same reason (ᵃ 30), (3) none of the senses is thought
to be wisdom, for the same reason (ᵇ 10), (4) the inventors of non-
utilitarian arts are thought to be wiser than the inventors of utilitarian
arts (ᵇ 18). The *Metaphysics* being an essay in σοφία, Aristotle says
his object in tracing in this chapter the development of thought has
been to point out what is implied in the ordinary usage (ὑπολαμβάνουσι
πάντες) of the words σοφός, σοφία ; and, as (1), (2), and (3) above
clearly show, the implication is that σοφία is concerned with αἴτια or
ἀρχαί. Aristotle says here that it is concerned with πρῶτα αἴτια. Wirth
objects to πρῶτα, since Aristotle in this chapter only proves that
wisdom is concerned with *certain* causes (982ᵃ 2), and does not prove
till ch. 2 that it deals with *first* causes (982ᵃ 5, ᵇ 9). But here (981ᵇ

27–29) Aristotle is not stating what he has proved, but what he is trying to prove; he proves half of it in ch. 1 and the rest in ch. 2.

(B) *The causes, the knowledge of which is wisdom, are first causes* (ch. 2).

982ᵃ 4. It will become clear with what causes wisdom is concerned, if we consider the common views about the wise man.

(1) He knows everything, as far as possible, without knowing the particulars one by one.

(2) He knows things that are hard to know (which is why sensation does not imply wisdom).

(3) He is more exact and (4) more capable of teaching the causes of things than others.

(5) Knowledge pursued for its own sake is more truly wisdom than knowledge desirable for its results.

(6) A governing science is more truly wisdom than a subordinate one.

21. The more universal a science is, the better it fulfils the first condition; and also the second, since its objects are furthest removed from sensation.

25. The more primary its objects, the better it fulfils the third condition, since it is more abstract.

28. The more it is concerned with causes, the better it fulfils the fourth condition.

30. The knowledge of what is most knowable, i. e. of the first things and of the causes from which other things are known, best fulfils the fifth condition.

ᵇ 4. The knowledge of the final cause of the world best fulfils the sixth condition.

7. All the characteristics of wisdom, then, point to its being the knowledge of first causes, including the final cause.

11. That it is not a science of production is clear also from the first philosophers or lovers of wisdom. Philosophy arose out of wonder, which implies the awareness of one's ignorance (so that the lover of myth is in a sense a philosopher, myth being composed of wonders). If people philosophized to escape from ignorance, they were evidently pursuing knowledge for its own sake.

22. This is indicated also by the fact that philosophy arose only when the necessities and pleasures of life had been provided for. Philosophy, the only science pursued for its own sake, is the only free science.

28. Hence it might seem a privilege which God would grudge to man, if there is anything in what the poets say. But God is not jealous.

983ᵃ 4. This knowledge is the most divine, (1) as being the most worthy of God, and (2) as being knowledge of the divine, since it is of first causes and God is a cause of all things. It is the least necessary but the best of all sciences.

11. We begin by wondering that things are as they are, e. g. that the diagonal of the square is incommensurate with the side ;

18. we must end in a state in which we should wonder if they were otherwise.

982ᵃ 13. καὶ τὸν διδασκαλικώτερον τῶν αἰτιῶν σοφώτερον εἶναι. In l. 28, taking up the point here made, Aristotle says ' the knowledge that contemplates the causes is διδασκαλικὴ μᾶλλον than the others '. The syllogism implied is :

Knowledge that is διδασκαλικωτέρα is σοφία.

Knowledge of causes is διδασκαλικωτέρα.

Therefore knowledge of causes is σοφία.

L. 13 is meant to state the major, l. 28 the minor premise. τῶν αἰτιῶν is therefore out of place in l. 13. Baumann and Gomperz treat it as an interpolation from l. 29 ; but it is testified to by Alexander as well as by all the MSS., and similar carelessness is not uncommon in Aristotle.

16. The description of ' wisdom ' as the ruling or most authoritative science is difficult. It is easy to see how πολιτική can be described by Aristotle as exercising authority over such sciences as strategy (*E. N.* 1094ᵇ 2). It ascertains the end for man, and orders (ἐπιτάττει) strategy to devise means for the attainment of this end in particular circumstances. But σοφία is not a practical but a purely theoretical science ; in what sense then does it issue commands ? To see Aristotle's meaning we must look to ᵇ 4–7, which supplies the minor premise answering to the major stated in ᵃ 16–19. The argument is :

The most authoritative science is σοφία.

The science which knows the final cause is the most authoritative.

Therefore the science which knows the ultimate causes, and among others the ultimate final cause, is σοφία.

But the notion of ' final cause ' here contains an ambiguity. The final cause, the study of which makes the science that studies it authoritative, is the end for the sake of which everything *ought* to be done (τίνος ἕνεκέν ἐστι πρακτέον ἕκαστον, ᵇ 5) ; it is only the science that studies this end, i. e. πολιτική, that can properly be said ἐπιτάττειν, and therefore, if Aristotle's major premise is right, to be σοφία. But the science which Aristotle infers to be σοφία is that which studies τὸ ἄριστον ἐν τῇ φύσει πάσῃ (ᵇ 7), i. e. the end towards which all creation *in fact* moves ; and this is metaphysics. Thus an argument which could only prove ethics or politics to be the highest wisdom is used to prove metaphysics to be so. Aristotle gets into a similar difficulty in the *Ethics* about the comparative claims of ' politics ' and metaphysics to be the supreme science. He describes 'politics' as the architectonic science, and so *seems* to put it on a higher level than metaphysics; but he sets this aside as a misinterpretation, and says that 'politics' does not use σοφία but ensures its coming into being, and issues orders not to it but for its sake (1145ᵃ 8).

It should be remembered that the present passage is a statement of ἔνδοξα, so that some looseness in the thought may be expected.

21. Aristotle now proceeds to show that the characteristics of wisdom enumerated in ll. 8–19 belong to the universal science (l. 22), the science that deals with the most universal objects (24), with the primary objects (26, ᵇ 2), with causes (29, ᵇ 2), with the good or the best (ᵇ 6). Wisdom, then, will be knowledge of the first or most universal causes of things, and among others of the final cause.

23. πως, i. e. potentially. Cf. *An. Post.* 86ᵃ 22.

τὰ ὑποκείμενα, the instances falling under the universal. The best parallel to this use of the word is in *An. Post.* 91ᵃ 11.

23-25. Aristotle usually, as here by implication, describes knowledge as proceeding from the particular, which is nearer to sense, to the universal, which is further from it. But for the complementary aspect of the truth, the advance from abstract to concrete, cf. *Phys.* 184ᵃ 21–ᵇ 14.

25-28. Cf. Pl. *Phil.* 56 c, *An. Post.* 87ᵃ 31.

29. μᾶλλον seems to go both with διδασκαλική and with τῶν αἰτιῶν θεωρητική. ἡ τῶν αἰτιῶν θεωρητικὴ μᾶλλον practically = ἡ τῶν πρώτων αἰτιῶν θεωρητική, and thus Aristotle shows that the science of first causes is worthier of the name of 'wisdom' than the sciences that grasp secondary causes.

ᵇ **2.** There is a difficulty in the statement that the πρῶτα and αἴτια are μάλιστ' ἐπιστητά. If all ἐπιστήμη presupposes these, which is Aristotle's constant doctrine, how can these themselves be objects of ἐπιστήμη? Strictly speaking they cannot, since ἐπιστήμη is demonstrative and demonstration cannot prove its own premises (*An. Post.* 100ᵇ 10, *E. N.* 1140ᵃ 33, &c.). Really that which knows first principles is νοῦς, or σοφία as including νοῦς, but ἐπιστήμη is occasionally used as here in a wider sense in which it is not distinguished from νοῦς. In *An. Post.* 72ᵇ 19 the ἐπιστήμη of ἄμεσα is said to be ἀναπόδεικτος. In *An. Post.* 88ᵇ 36 ἐπιστήμη ἀναπόδεικτος is mentioned alongside of νοῦς; but these may be only alternative expressions for the same thing. Even the constant use of the phrase ἐπιστήμη ἀποδεικτική suggests that ἐπιστήμη ἀναπόδεικτος was not in ordinary usage a contradiction in terms, though Aristotle preferred to use ἐπιστήμη as implying demonstration.

Jaeger argues that the argument requires τὰ πρῶτα αἴτια (cf. l. 9 and B. 996ᵇ 33, which refers to the present passage), and that Alexander read it. He therefore proposes τὰ πρῶτά γ' αἴτια and thinks that Aᵇ's reading arose from this by dittography. But Alexander may well have had καὶ τὰ (or καὶ) αἴτια (13. 24, 28), and Aristotle could quite well treat πρῶτα and αἴτια as synonyms.

4–7. For the argument cf. ᵃ 16 n.

11. As St. Thomas observes, there is a point in the substitution of φιλοσοφησάντων, φιλοσοφεῖν 13, φιλόσοφος 18 for σοφία, σοφός, which have been used before. For Aristotle is now proving that the study is not practical but actuated simply by love of knowledge.

12–13. διὰ γὰρ ... φιλοσοφεῖν. Cf. Pl. *Theaet.* 155 D.

13. τὰ πρόχειρα. Alexander cites the questions 'why amber attracts chaff-like substances ' (a problem which interested Thales), 'the nature of the rainbow' (discussed by Anaximenes and by other early thinkers), and other meteorological problems.

17–19. The argument is :
Myth is full of things that excite wonder.
He who wonders thinks he is ignorant.
He who thinks he is ignorant desires knowledge.
Therefore the lover of myth is a lover of knowledge.

We may compare the interesting personal confession, probably from one of Aristotle's letters to Antipater, ὅσῳ αὐτίτης καὶ μονώτης εἰμί, φιλομυθότερος γέγονα (fr. 1582ᵇ 14).

22. τὸ συμβεβηκός is used here in a non-technical sense ; it means ' the course of events '.

23. πρὸς ῥᾳστώνην καὶ διαγωγήν is co-ordinate with ἀναγκαίων, as is clearly shown by 981ᵇ 17. ῥᾳστώνη means physical comfort, διαγωγή mental enjoyment. The insertion of τῶν would make the meaning clearer, but is not necessary.

24. φρόνησις is used here not in the strict sense defined in *E. N.* vi. 5, but in the wide sense in which it is not distinguished from σοφία or ἐπιστήμη. This is the regular usage in Plato and is not uncommon in Aristotle. Cf. Bonitz's Index, 834ᵇ 4–12.

27. For the notion of a free science cf. Pl. *Rep.* 499 A, 536 E.

28—983ᵃ 5. Cf. *E.N.*1177ᵇ 31–33, Pl. *Epin.* 988 A, B. The opposite view is expressed in Epicharm. fr. 20 (Diels), Eur. *Bacch.* 395 f., 427–432.

30. κατὰ Σιμωνίδην. Fr. 3 Hiller, quoted already by Plato, *Prot.* 341 E, 344 C. Simonides' line continues ἄνδρα δ' οὐκ ἔστι μὴ οὐ κακὸν ἔμμεναι, on which Aristotle models the end of his sentence.

983ᵃ 2. οὔτε τὸ θεῖον φθονερόν. Cf. Pl. *Phaedr.* 247 A, *Tim.* 29 E.

3. πολλὰ ψεύδονται ἀοιδοί is quoted as a proverb already by Solon, fr. 26 Hiller. Cf. Leutsch and Schneidewin, *Paroemiographi,* i. 371, ii. 128, 615.

6. In assigning to God knowledge of the causes of existing things, Aristotle is inconsistent with his account in Bk. Λ, in which God's thought has no object but Himself. He is speaking of God as commonly conceived.

14. τῶν θαυμάτων ταὐτόματα Alexander (18. 17) explains as τὰ ὑπὸ τῶν θαυματοποιῶν δεικνύμενα παίγνια, ἃ ἐξ αὐτῶν δοκεῖ καὶ αὐτομάτως κινεῖσθαι, i. e. the figures in something like a Punch and Judy show. Cf. the reference in the myth of the cave, Pl. *Rep.* 514 B. St. Thomas's (and Schwegler's) view that τῶν θαυμάτων is predicate is sufficiently

refuted by the mode of reference to these puppets in *De Gen. An.* 734ᵇ 10, 741ᵇ 8. The manuscript reading is intolerably harsh; it would require us to understand some such words as θαυμαστά ἐστιν after ταὐτόματα, and this is very difficult. Bonitz saw that τοῖς . . . αἰτίαν would come better after πᾶσι in l. 16, but this would leave καθάπερ τῶν θαυμάτων ταὐτόματα without a satisfactory construction. Jaeger has put this right by supposing περί to have dropped out by haplography after καθάπερ. καθάπερ in the sense of οἷον is not common, but cf. *Top.* 124ᵇ 16. τοῖς . . . αἰτίαν is probably a marginal addition by Aristotle, which has been inserted in the wrong part of the text.

15. τὴν τῆς διαμέτρου ἀσυμμετρίαν. I. 1053ᵃ 17, *Top.* 106ᵃ 38, 163ᵃ 12, *Phys.* 221ᵇ 24, *De Gen. An.* 742ᵇ 27, *E. N.* 1112ᵃ 22 show that the reference is to the incommensurability of the diagonal of a square with the side, not to that of the diameter of a circle with the circumference.

17. εἴ τι τῷ ἐλαχίστῳ μὴ μετρεῖται. I. e. the natural supposition is that everything must be measurable by the smallest thing of its own kind, and accordingly that there must be a unitary line of which all other lines are multiples.

18. κατὰ τὴν παροιμίαν. The proverb is δευτέρων ἀμεινόνων (Leutsch and Schneidewin, i. 62, 234, ii. 357).

21-23. Bonitz raises the question whether the σοφία that Aristotle here claims to have stated the nature of is science in general or metaphysics. σοφία can be used in the wider sense (e. g. in the *Ethics* it includes mathematics and physics, 1141ᵃ 23, ᵇ 1), and some of the marks of σοφία that Aristotle has here collected are characteristic not of one particular science but of excellence in any (982ᵃ 12-14). But from several phrases in the chapter (982ᵃ 4, 14-16, 25-28, ᵇ4, 8, 983ᵃ 6) it is clear that he is establishing the nature of one among the sciences. Starting with the notion of σοφία simply as the most admirable form of knowledge, he has now determined it as knowledge of the primary or most universal causes, i. e. as metaphysics.

(II) THE KINDS OF FIRST CAUSE; CONFIRMATION OF OUR LIST BY A REVIEW OF THE DOCTRINES OF PREVIOUS PHILOSOPHERS (CHS. 3-10).

(A) *Account of previous systems* (chs. 3-7).

Early treatment of material and efficient causes (chs. 3, 4).

983ᵃ 24. To know a thing is to know its first cause; causes are of four kinds—the essence, the matter, the source of movement, the end or good.

33. We have considered these in the *Physics*, but it will be useful to study the views of our predecessors; we shall thus either find some new kind of cause or have our list confirmed.

ᵇ **6.** (1) Most of the earliest thinkers recognized only *material causes*, i. e. that out of which all things are generated and into which they pass when destroyed. Because such a substratum persists, they think nothing is really generated or destroyed.

18. They differ about the number and nature of these causes. (*a*) Thales says the cause is water, presumably because (i) the nutriment of everything, and (ii) the seed of everything, is moist.

27. Some think the ancient cosmologists held this view, since they made Ocean and Tethys the parents of generation, and made the gods swear by water. This speculation is doubtful, but at any rate Thales is said to have held this view (Hippo hardly deserves consideration).

984ᵃ 5. (*b*) Anaximenes and Diogenes make air the first principle, (*c*) Hippasus and Heraclitus fire.

8. (*d*) Empedocles adds earth and recognizes the four elements, which are eternal and merely change in number when combined or dissociated.

11. (*e*) Anaxagoras says the principles are infinite in number; practically all homogeneous substances are 'generated' and 'destroyed' thus, by congregation and disgregation.

18. (2) Since the substratum cannot move itself, the facts forced philosophers to seek a *source of movement*.

27. (*a*) The oldest philosophers, who recognized only one substratum, did not feel this difficulty; (*b*) some of the monists, as though defeated by it, deny not only generation and destruction but all change. (*c*) The only monist who caught a glimpse of the efficient cause was Parmenides, and he did so only in so far as he recognized in a sense two causes.

ᵇ **5.** (*d*) It is easier for the pluralists to recognize it; e. g. they treat fire as a source of movement, and the other elements as passive.

8 (*e*) Such causes being insufficient to generate the world, philosophers had to look again for the efficient cause. Neither a material element, nor chance, could be held responsible for the goodness in things.

15. (i) When Anaxagoras said that reason was present in nature, as in animals, as the cause of order, he seemed like a sober man among drunkards—though he is said to have been anticipated by Hermotimus.

20. These thinkers treated reason as the cause both of the goodness in things and of movement.

23. One might suspect that the first seeker after such a cause was Hesiod or Parmenides or whoever first treated love as a principle.

32. (ii) To account for the badness in the world as well as the good, Empedocles introduced love and strife.

985ᵃ 4. These as the causes of good and evil must be good itself and evil itself, so that he is the first to treat good and evil as principles.

10. These thinkers had a notion of the material and efficient causes, but an inadequate one, for they use them but little. For

18. (i) Anaxagoras drags in reason as an explanation only when he is in a difficulty, and

21. (ii) Empedocles does not use his causes enough, nor consistently. When strife divides the All into its elements, it *unites* the portions of each single element; and similarly love *divides*.

29. Empedocles was the first who introduced (a) contrary efficient principles, (β) four material elements—though he treats them as two, opposing fire to the others.

ᵇ4. Leucippus and Democritus treat the full or existent and the empty or non-existent as material elements ;

10. they generate everything else by three differentiae—shape, order, and position.

19. These thinkers, like the others, neglected to explain the origin of movement. This then is the extent to which the material and efficient causes were recognized by the earlier thinkers.

983ᵃ 25. τὴν πρώτην αἰτίαν, not, as often, the proximate, but the primary, ultimate cause (ἐξ ἀρχῆς l. 24). Colle thinks that while τῶν ἐξ ἀρχῆς αἰτίων must mean absolutely first causes, τὴν πρώτην αἰτίαν must mean the first cause *peculiar* to the particular kind of thing which is the object of the science in question. He therefore regards τότε . . . γνωρίζειν as a gloss. But since the science in question here is metaphysics, the study of what is, simply as being, the distinction he draws is not relevant, and there is no reason to doubt these words.

26. Here, as in the *Physics* (194ᵇ 23), the doctrine of the four causes is introduced quite abruptly. Aristotle nowhere shows us how he reached it, nor offers any logical deduction of it. The best that he does is to show—what it is the main object of Book A to show—that these four causes are those that one after another came to light in the earlier history of philosophy, and that no others had come to light (993ᵃ 11). The doctrine is found in several of his works besides those that are very largely occupied with it (the *Physics* and the *Metaphysics*); but there is an almost complete silence about it in the *Organon*. The one passage which refers to it is *An. Post.* ii. 11. While in all other respects the notion of the four causes remains fundamentally the same in all the works in which it occurs, the place filled, in other references to the four causes, by the material cause is occupied in that passage by what is called τὸ τίνων ὄντων ἀνάγκη τοῦτ' εἶναι, and this is explained as the two premises from which a conclusion follows. Further, this cause is identified with the formal cause (94ᵃ 34), while the material cause is never identified with the formal. The premises of a syllogism occur as an *instance* of the material cause in *Phys.* 195ᵃ 18 (Δ. 1013ᵇ 20).

27. τὴν οὐσίαν καὶ τὸ τί ἦν εἶναι. Though οὐσία is properly a non-committal word, meaning the most real element in a thing, wherever that is to be found—in the essence of the thing, the universal or class under which it falls, or its material substratum (Z. 1028ᵇ 33)—yet Aristotle tends constantly to use it in the sense of that which he himself believes (Z. 1041ᵇ 7–9) to be the most real element in a thing, viz. its form or essence. The use of it here as equivalent to τὸ τί ἦν εἶναι is an anticipation of the result arrived at in Book Z.

τὸ τί ἦν εἶναι, ' the answer to the question, what was it to be so-and-so '. The phrase is a generalization from such phrases as τί ἦν αὐτῷ (*sc.* τῷ αἵματι) τὸ αἵματι εἶναι (*P. A.* 649ᵇ 22). To state the τί ἦν εἶναι of a thing is to state its form in full (genus and differentia) without mentioning its matter. The only difficulty in the phrase, in its general form, is the imperfect tense. Why not τί ἐστιν εἶναι? Three answers have been given to this question. (1) ἦν is said to be a ' philosophical imperfect ', referring to something stated earlier in the argument, and passages like ἐπεὶ ἦσαν τρεῖς οὐσίαι (Λ. 1071ᵇ 3), ' since there are, as we saw, three kinds of substance ', are quoted as parallels. But the ' philosophical imperfect ' is used only when there has been an actual previous discussion of the subject in hand, which is the case in but few of the passages in which τὸ τί ἦν εἶναι is used. (2) The imperfect may be taken to represent duration. Cf. *De Caelo* 278ᵃ 11 τὸ αἰσθητὸν ἅπαν ἐν τῇ ὕλῃ ὑπῆρχεν, *Rhet.* 1363ᵃ 8 οὗ πάντες ἐφίενται, τοῦτ' ἀγαθὸν ἦν, Pl. *Theaet.* 156 A ἀρχὴ ἤδε αὐτῶν, ὡς τὸ πᾶν κίνησις ἦν. (3) The imperfect may be held to be an expression of Aristotle's doctrine of the existence of form before its embodiment in a particular matter, for which cf. Z. 1032ᵇ 11, 1034ᵇ 12. The only difference between the last two explanations is that the third takes more explicit account of Aristotelian doctrine than the second. In this way it may more fully represent Aristotle's meaning. But Antisthenes is said to have anticipated Aristotle in the use of ἦν in this connexion by defining λόγος as ὁ τὸ τί ἦν, ἢ ἔστι, δηλῶν (Diog. Laert. vi. 1. 3). The phrase is discussed fully by Schwegler in Excursus I to his edition of the *Metaphysics*.

27–29. The argument is :
The λόγος, definition, of a thing is the ultimate ' reason why ' of it.
The final reason why is a cause.
Therefore the οὐσία or τί ἦν εἶναι (= λόγος) is a cause.

ἔσχατον is an adjective agreeing with λόγον. ' The definition is the final thing to which the reason why is pushed back.' πρῶτον, again, is an adjective, agreeing with τί (cf. ᵇ 8 ἐξ οὗ πρώτου). ἔσχατον and πρῶτον are used, very awkwardly, with reference to the same thing.

It is what we come to last in the order of explanation, but it is objectively the first or most fundamental element in the thing.

33. ἐν τοῖς περὶ φύσεως. *Phys.* ii. 3, 7.

^b 1. Aristotle's review of his predecessors is made somewhat difficult to follow by the fact that he partly adopts the chronological order, and partly a logical order, taking up the four causes, or at least the material, the efficient, and the formal cause successively. Thus from l. 6 to 984ᵃ 18 he deals with the material cause, and follows the treatment of it down to Anaxagoras. He omits the Pythagoreans, however, presumably as holding a more difficult view and one that demands fuller treatment. The discussion of them is not only postponed, but is divided into two parts, ch. 5, which is in the main an account of their views, and 989ᵇ 29—990ᵃ 32, which is in the main a criticism. The Atomists, Socrates, Plato, and the Platonists are similarly omitted, and this, as far as Socrates, Plato, and the Platonists are concerned, is no doubt due to the fact that the important part of their doctrine is not that which relates to the material cause. But this is not the case with regard to the Atomists. According to Aristotle they recognized only the material cause, and did not deal even with the question of the efficient cause (985ᵇ 19). The omission of them is due to their coming later in time; they are later tacked on to the discussion of the efficient cause, about which, as Aristotle holds, they had nothing to say (985ᵇ 4–20). Again, in discussing Empedocles' views about the efficient cause, Aristotle adds a summary of his distinctive views in which his doctrine of the material cause is rather irrelevantly introduced (985ᵃ 31).

2. περὶ τῆς ἀληθείας. Aristotle does not mean either simply that these thinkers tried to reach the truth, as do inquirers in *any* field, or that they studied the nature of truth, as an 'epistemologist' does, but that they studied the truth in general, the ultimate nature of things. For this use of ἀλήθεια cf. A. 988ᵃ 20, α. 993 ᵃ 30, ᵇ 17, 20.

5–6. ἡ γὰρ ... πιστεύσομεν. This gives us the link that connects all the remaining part of Book A together. Aristotle's object is not to write a history of philosophy but to confirm by reference to earlier philosophers his own account of the primary causes, which, as we have seen, σοφία investigates. This purpose is reaffirmed in 986ᵃ 13, ᵇ 4, 12, 988ᵃ 20, ᵇ 16, 993ᵃ 11.

7. τὰς ἐν ὕλης εἴδει. Aristotle does not say that the earlier thinkers recognized the material cause. The ultimate material cause, according to him, is matter entirely unformed, while they, with the exception of Anaximander, only went back to some simple but yet definitely characterized form of matter such as one of the four elements. The causes they recognized were not matter, but only 'of the nature of matter'. For the phrase cf. ἐν μορίου εἴδει *De Caelo* 268ᵇ 5, ἐν ὀργάνου εἴδει *Pol.* 1253ᵇ 30; the usage is found several times in Plato. ἐν ὕλης εἴδει is especially common in Aristotle.

The word ὕλη occurs in its Aristotelian sense in an Orphic fragment quoted by Damascius—ὕδωρ ἦν ἐξ ἀρχῆς καὶ ὕλη (Diels, *Vorsokr.*³ ii.

172. 9), but apart from this very doubtful evidence there is no evidence
of its use in this sense by any thinker earlier than Aristotle. Frequently,
however, it means wood as the raw material of shipbuilding or some
other art (e. g. Pl. *Phil.* 54 c 1, *Tim.* 69 a 6), and occasionally it is used
of some material other than wood, e. g. Soph. fr. 743 Dindorf οἳ παρ'
ἄκμονι ... ὕλην ἄψυχον δημιουργοῦντες. Uses like these had prepared the way for the technical use of the word by Aristotle. Prof. Burnet
thinks (§ 148 n.) that the Pythagorean comparison of the structure
of the world to the building of a ship may have led in the same
direction.

13. φύσεως = 'primary substance', the meaning recognized in Δ.
1014ᵇ 26; cf. 1014ᵇ 31 διασωζομένης τῆς πρώτης ὕλης with the phrase
here. It is in this sense that many of the pre-Socratics are said to
have written περὶ φύσεως. φύσις has the same meaning in l. 17. In
ll. 26, 27 it is used abstractly in the sense of 'character'.

13–14. τὸν Σωκράτην ... ὅταν γίγνηται καλός is evidently a joke.
Socrates was notoriously ugly.

14. ἡ μουσικός, a reference to Pl. *Prot.* 335 c; cf. Δ. 1018ª 2 n.

16. οὕτως οὐδέ κτλ. The sentence is grammatically complete at
αὐτόν, but the preceding ὥσπερ brings out a clause with οὕτως by a kind
of instinctive response. It is an instance of what Riddell calls the
'binary structure' (*Apology of Plato*, 198). Cf. B. 1002ᵇ 14–22,
Γ. 1003ª 33–ᵇ 5, Δ. 1017ª 10, 1024ª 8, K. 1066ª 31–34, 1068ᵇ 11,
Λ. 1075ª 7.

17. It is necessary to read ἀεί with Bywater, or δεῖν with Wirth,
instead of δεῖ, since the clause is still concerned with what the early
philosophers thought.

20. τῆς τοιαύτης ... φιλοσοφίας, i. e. the search for the material
cause of all things.

21. διὸ καὶ τὴν γῆν ἐφ' ὕδατος ἀπεφήνατο εἶναι. Cf. *De Caelo* 294ª
28. Aet. iii. 15. 1 says that Thales explained earthquakes in this
way, but this may be doubted; cf. Diels, *D. G.* 225.

22. λαβὼν ἴσως τὴν ὑπόληψιν κτλ. Aristotle evidently had not much
evidence about the line of thought which led Thales to his belief in
the primacy of water. He always speaks of Thales' views with
caution (A. 984ª 2, *De Caelo* 294ª 29, *De An.* 405ª 19, 411ª 8, *Pol.*
1259ª 6, 18), and if Thales ever wrote anything it seems that Aristotle
at least had never seen any work or fragment of a work of his. The
two reasons he suggests for Thales' doctrine (ll. 22-27) are both
physiological. At that period, as Burnet (*E. G. P.* § 10) has pointed
out, meteorological considerations are more likely to have prevailed:
Burnet therefore (as also Zeller and Döring) suggests that Aristotle
simply assigned to Thales the reasons which he knew to have influenced
Hippo in treating water as the matter of all things. Both Aristotle
(984ª 3) and Simplicius (*Phys.* 23. 22, *De Caelo* 615. 11) mention
Hippo in connexion with Thales, and Aristotle (*De An.* 405ᵇ 3)
ascribes to Hippo the second of the two reasons he here ascribes to
Thales. Thales was doubtless influenced by the eastern and Egyptian

notion of the world as resting on an immense watery plain. Cf.
Maspero, *Hist. anc. des Temples de l'Orient*, 27–30.

27. εἰσὶ δέ τινες κτλ. Aristotle is probably thinking of Plato, who
jestingly suggests (*Crat.* 402 B, *Theaet.* 152 E, 160 D, 180 C) that
Heraclitus and his predecessors derived their philosophy from Homer,
Hesiod, and Orpheus. Plato refers to Oceanus and Tethys just as
Aristotle does here, and uses the same word παμπαλαίους (*Theaet.* 181 B).
For a similar statement based on humorous suggestions of Plato's cf.
986ᵇ 21 n. The suggestion has no great historical value, as Aristotle
himself admits (984ᵃ 2). He would not regard Hesiod, at any rate, as
an anticipator of Thales, for in 984ᵇ 27, 989ᵃ 10 he refers to him as
making *chaos* the first of all things, and *earth* the first of the elements
in order of origin. Nor, again, would he regard Orpheus in this
light, for though one of the main versions of the Orphic cosmogony
makes water and slime the primitive elements, the version followed by
Aristotle treats *night* as the first principle, followed by earth and heaven
(cf. Λ. 1071ᵇ 27, N. 1091ᵇ 4), and puts Ocean and Tethys only in the
fourth and fifth places. Cf. Zeller, i⁶. 122–125. Plato quotes two
'Orphic' verses which ascribe an important function to Ocean and
Tethys (*Crat.* 402 B), but Aristotle did not believe in the authenticity
of the so-called Orphic verses (fr. 1475ᵃ 40).

29. θεολογήσαντας. This is Aristotle's regular word in speaking
of the early cosmologists as opposed to the physicists (B. 1000ᵃ 9,
Λ. 1071ᵇ 27, 1075ᵇ 26, N. 1091ᵃ 34, *Meteor.* 353ᵃ 35).

30. Ὠκεανόν τε γάρ κτλ. Cf. Hom. *Il.* xiv. 201, 246.

31. τὸν ὅρκον τῶν θεῶν ὕδωρ. Cf. Hom. *Il.* ii. 755, xiv. 271, xv. 37.
For the significance of the oath of the gods as securing their privileges
in the *dasmos* cf. Cornford, *From Religion to Philosophy*, §§ 10, 11.

32. Christ is probably right in bracketing τῶν ποιητῶν, which comes
in very awkwardly after Στύγα.

984ᵃ 3. Hippo, an eclectic of the time of Pericles, is mentioned by
Aristotle only in one other passage (*De An.* 405ᵇ 2), and there also
with contempt. Alexander (26. 21) says he identified the first principle
with the moist, not specifying this either as water or as air. But our
other authorities, Simplicius (*Phys.* 23. 22, 149. 7, *De Caelo* 615. 11),
Hippolytus (i. 16), and Philoponus (*Phys.* 23. 7, *De An.* 92. 3), all
of whom represent Theophrastus' teaching on the subject, say that
Hippo's first principle was water, and this is more in keeping with the
present passage.

5. Diogenes of Apollonia was an eclectic of the fifth century who
borrowed from Empedocles, Anaxagoras, and Leucippus, as well as from
Anaximenes. For his view about the primary element cf. fr. 5 Diels.

7. Hippasus was a Pythagorean who, in all probability, lived somewhat later than Heraclitus, and formed his system by a fusion of
Pythagorean and Heraclitean elements. It may have been the promi-
nence assigned by the Pythagoreans to fire as identical with the
principle of limit (cf. 984ᵇ 4, 5 nn.) that led him confusedly to treat it
as the one material cause.

πῦρ . . . Ἡράκλειτος. For some judicious remarks on the place of
fire in Heraclitus' system cf. Burnet, *E. G. P.* § 69. The primacy of
fire was not the first article of his creed, as that of water or air was in
the creed of Thales or Anaximenes, but he thought that fire was the
prime element just as literally as they thought that water or air was
so. Fire is for him, however, not 'what remains unaltered in the
change of individual things', but 'that which through unceasing transformation brings this change about' (Zeller, i⁶. 822).

10. ἀλλ' ἢ πλήθει καὶ ὀλιγότητι, συγκρινόμενα καὶ διακρινόμενα εἰς ἕν
τε καὶ ἐξ ἑνός. Alexander gives, without choosing between them, three
possible interpretations, which may be paraphrased thus :

(1) 'Except that they become few or many, being aggregated into
one whole by love or segregated out of one whole by strife.'

(2) 'Except that they *seem* to come into being, by virtue of the
number of the parts of the same kind that are aggregated into one
whole, and *seem* to perish when segregation takes place, because then
the small homogeneous aggregates that remain escape our notice.'

(3) 'But only the number or fewness of things comes into being, by
reason of the segregation or aggregation of these elements.'

The third interpretation appears to take πλήθει καὶ ὀλιγότητι in an
impossible way, and need not be further considered. The other two
differ in two respects. (*a*) The first interpretation takes πλήθει to
mean 'in respect of number'. The elements do not come into being
except in respect of number or fewness, i. e. they only come to be
many or few. The second interpretation takes πλήθει to mean 'by
reason of number'. The elements do not come into being, but fire,
for example, seems to do so in virtue of the aggregation of many bits
of fire. (*b*) The first interpretation takes συγκρινόμενα εἰς ἕν to refer to the aggregation of unlikes by friendship ; the second takes it to
refer to the aggregation of likes, owing to the segregation of unlikes,
by strife.

The second interpretation is in some respects attractive, but (*a*) it
requires us to supply in thought οὐδ' ἀπόλλυσθαι after οὐ γίγνεσθαι ;
(*b*) συγκρίνειν in an account of Empedocles' views refers more
naturally to the union of unlikes by love than to the incidental union
of likes by strife ; (*c*) the first interpretation agrees better with fr. 17 of
Empedocles, which Aristotle is evidently paraphrasing :

δίπλ' ἐρέω· τοτὲ μὲν γὰρ ἓν ηὐξήθη μόνον εἶναι
ἐκ πλεόνων, τοτὲ δ' αὖ διέφυ πλέον' ἐξ ἑνὸς εἶναι.
. . . .
καὶ ταῦτ' ἀλλάσσοντα διαμπερὲς οὐδαμὰ λήγει,
ἄλλοτε μὲν Φιλότητι συνερχόμεν' εἰς ἓν ἅπαντα,
ἄλλοτε δ' αὖ δίχ' ἕκαστα φορεύμενα Νείκεος ἔχθει.
⟨οὕτως ᾗ μὲν ἓν ἐκ πλεόνων μεμάθηκε φύεσθαι⟩
ἠδὲ πάλιν διαφύντος ἑνὸς πλέον' ἐκτελέθουσι,
τῇ μὲν γίγνονταί τε καὶ οὔ σφίσιν ἔμπεδος αἰών·
ᾗ δὲ διαλλάσσοντα διαμπερὲς οὐδαμὰ λήγει,
ταύτῃ δ' αἰὲν ἔασιν ἀκίνητοι κατὰ κύκλον.

12. τοῖς δ᾽ ἔργοις ὕστερος. Alexander's interpretation, 'inferior in the merit of his works', is supported by a parallel in Theophr. *ap.* Simpl. *Phys.* 26. 8 (τῇ μὲν δόξῃ καὶ τῇ δυνάμει πρότερος τοῖς δὲ χρόνοις ὕστερος), and is probably correct. Aristotle prefers Empedocles to Anaxagoras because he adopted fewer first principles, *Phys.* 188ª 17, 189ª 15; cf. *De Gen. et Corr.* 314ª 13. Breier's 'more modern in the nature of his works', which is commended by Bonitz and is to some extent supported by a comparison with 989ᵇ 5, 19, *De Caelo* 308ᵇ 30, interprets ὕστερος in a way which is probably without parallel. It is quite possible to take ὕστερος in its literal sense, as meaning that Anaxagoras wrote later than Empedocles though he was an older man. Empedocles was probably born shortly before 490 and Anaxagoras lived about 498–428, so that the statement might easily be correct.

13–16. σχεδὸν γὰρ . . . ἀΐδια. Anaxagoras held that the σπέρματα, flesh and the like, were ingenerable and indestructible; all that happened was that a number of portions of flesh, which were not recognized as such because they were present in wholes in which some other substance predominated, might be segregated out of these wholes and aggregated together and thus come to be recognized as flesh, or again might go through the reverse process (fr. 17). This was true of *all* the 'seeds'; why then does Aristotle qualify his statement by σχεδόν? The answer is that though Aristotle uses the word ὁμοιομερῆ in referring to Anaxagoras' 'seeds', he included among ὁμοιομερῆ things which Anaxagoras did not include among the 'seeds', but treated as compounds, viz. the four elements of Empedocles (*De Caelo* 302ª 28, *De Gen. et Corr.* 314ª 24). These were, according to Anaxagoras, not eternal, but were produced by combinations of 'seeds'.

14. The word ὁμοιομερῆ, though often used in ancient accounts of Anaxagoras, was probably invented by Aristotle; the common ascription of the word to Anaxagoras is due to misunderstanding by the Doxographi. The idea, though not the word, is found in Pl. *Prot.* 329 D. The word means 'things whose parts are similar to one another and to the whole things'. Aristotle uses it (1) of the elements (992ª 7, *Top.* 135ª 24–ᵇ 6), (2) of ores, metals, and stones (*Meteor.* 388ª 14), (3) of animal and vegetable tissues such as flesh, bone, sinew, wood, bark (*Meteor.* 388ª 16). It is used more specially in sense (3), of organic tissues which are compounded out of the ultimate elements, and out of which are compounded the organs or ἀνομοιομερῆ such as the hand or the mouth. Anaxagoras' own word answering to ὁμοιομερῆ is σπέρματα (fr. 4, Diels i. 400. 31, 401. 14). While Empedocles said that if you divide, say, blood, you resolve it into the four elements, Anaxagoras said that however far you divide it you still get blood.

καθάπερ ὕδωρ ἢ πῦρ. In *De Caelo* 302ª 28, *De Gen. et Corr.* 314ª 24 Aristotle tells us that Anaxagoras treated the ὁμοιομερῆ, such as flesh and bone, as elements, and the elements recognized by Empedocles, such as fire and earth, as compounds. This account is confirmed by many other authorities (cf. Zeller, i⁶. 1210, n. 1). On the other hand Aristotle here *seems* to place water and fire among Anaxagoras' ὁμοιομερῆ, and a similar account is given by Simpl. *Phys.* 27. 5, Philop. *De Gen. et Corr.* 13. 26, Lucr. i. 841. There can be no doubt that the former view was really that held by Anaxagoras ; Aristotle's account in the *De Caelo* and the *De Gen. et Corr.* is perfectly explicit. Some other interpretation must therefore be assigned to καθάπερ ὕδωρ ἢ πῦρ. Bonitz points out that καθάπερ means not ' as for example' but 'in the same way as ' (καθάπερ ὕδωρ ἢ πῦρ goes not with what follows but closely with ὁμοιομερῆ, 'the things which are homoeomerous in the manner of water or fire '), and finds an exact parallel in 992ᵃ 6 ὡς ὄντος τοῦ ἑνὸς ὥσπερ πυρὸς ἢ ὕδατος ὁμοιομεροῦς. Aristotle mentions water and fire because they were for him good instances of ὁμοιομερῆ ; the reference to them is confusing because they were *not* instances of Anaxagoras' σπέρματα. The statements of Simplicius, Philoponus, and Lucretius may be due to a mis-understanding of this passage.

οὗτω may refer either back to the description of Empedocles' views (ll. 9–11), or forward—'in this way, viz. by aggregation and segregation only'.

15. ἄλλως, 'in any other sense'. Zeller's emendation ἁπλῶς is unnecessary.

17. τούτων means 'these facts' rather than 'these thinkers', for Empedocles (985ᵃ 2) and Anaxagoras (984ᵇ 15) had some notion of an efficient as well as of a material cause.

ἐν ὕλης εἴδει. Cf. 983ᵇ 7 n.

27. οἱ μὲν οὖν κτλ., i. e., of the thinkers Aristotle has mentioned, Thales, Anaximenes, and Heraclitus.

29. ἔνιοί γε τῶν ἓν λεγόντων, i. e. the Eleatics. But really it was not the difficulty of finding a cause of change, but the difficulty of thinking out the nature of change, that led them to their doctrine of an un-changing universe.

33. τὴν ἄλλην μεταβολήν, i. e. change of place, quantity, or quality.

ᵇ 1. τῶν ... ἐν φασκόντων εἶναι τὸ πᾶν, like τῶν ἐν λεγόντων ᵃ 30, in-cludes the Milesian school and Heraclitus as well as the Eleatics.

4. The reference to two causes occurs (fr. 8, l. 53) in the second part of Parmenides' poem, that in which he professes to leave the truth of things and state the opinions of mortals :

> ἐν τῶι σοι παύω πιστὸν λόγον ἠδὲ νόημα
> ἀμφὶς ἀληθείης· δόξας δ' ἀπὸ τοῦδε βροτείας
> μάνθανε κόσμον ἐμῶν ἐπέων ἀπατηλὸν ἀκούων (fr. 8. 50–2).

At 986ᵇ 28 Aristotle describes the transition from the ' way of truth ' to the ' way of opinion ' by saying that though Parmenides thinks that of necessity only τὸ ὄν exists, he is forced to follow the observed facts and therefore to admit two causes, τὸ ὄν and τὸ μὴ ὄν. I.e. Parmenides is supposed to allow a lower order of reality to the sensible world and to set about the explanation of it, even though this explanation is not in accordance with his account of true reality. Simplicius describes his procedure in the same way (*Phys.* 39. 10). But this is inconsistent with what Parmenides himself says in the verses quoted above, which imply that the second part of the poem merely states the false opinions of mortals—not of the average Greeks of his time, who would not have recognized the 'way of opinion' as their own, but of the popular philosophy of the day, i. e., as Prof. Burnet points out (*E. G. P.* §§ 90, 91), of the Pythagorean philosophy. Aristotle either is simply mistaken, or knows that he is merely stating what occurs in Parmenides' poem but does not belong to Parmenides' own views. πως (ᵇ 4) perhaps gives some colour to the latter alternative.

Aristotle tells us that the two causes recognized by Parmenides were the hot and the cold (986ᵇ 34, *Phys.* 188ᵃ 20). The μορφαί that Parmenides names are φλογὸς αἰθέριον πῦρ and νὺξ ἀδαής (fr. 8. 56, 59). Fire no doubt is hot and night is cold, but we have no evidence that these were the attributes which Parmenides treated as characteristic of them. Rather they are opposed as light and dark (cf. light and darkness in the Pythagorean list of contraries, 986ᵃ 25), and the mention of heat and cold is an accommodation to Aristotle's own views, in which these played so important a part.

Again, Aristotle several times says the two causes assigned by Parmenides were fire and earth (986ᵇ 34, *Phys.* 188ᵃ 20, *De Gen. et Corr.* 318ᵇ 6, 330ᵇ 14, cf. Theophr. *Phys. Op.* fr. 4, Hippol. i. 11. 1). The identification of the second μορφή with earth must be regarded as a mistake. The second principle is night (cf. Simpl. *Phys.* 25. 16), and by this Parmenides means the Pythagorean 'mist', 'air', or 'void' (cf. what Plato makes the Pythagorean Timaeus say, *Tim.* 58 D). Later in the history of Pythagoreanism, fire and earth probably came to be treated as the primary elements (cf. *Tim.* 31 B, and Burnet, § 147), and this may explain Aristotle's words.

Finally, Aristotle says that Parmenides identified fire and earth with being and not-being (986ᵇ 34, *De Gen. et Corr.* 318ᵇ 6). The words of Parmenides are (fr. 8. 53) :

$$\mu o \rho \phi \grave{a} s \ \gamma \grave{v} \rho \ \kappa a \tau \acute{\epsilon} \theta \epsilon \nu \tau o \ \delta \acute{v} o \ \gamma \nu \acute{\omega} \mu a s \ \grave{o} \nu o \mu \acute{a} \zeta \epsilon \iota \nu,$$
$$\tau \hat{\omega} \nu \ \mu \acute{\iota} a \nu \ o \grave{v} \ \chi \rho \epsilon \acute{\omega} \nu \ \grave{\epsilon} \sigma \tau \iota \nu.$$

I. e. one of the two shapes they were right in recognizing, since it was of the nature of being ; the other they were wrong in recognizing, since it was of the nature of not-being. Considering the negative character of night or the void, we can have no hesitation in recognizing this as the μορφή of which Parmenides did not approve. If he had really meant earth, it would be harder to see why he should have condemned it.

Aristotle suggests that Parmenides caught a glimpse of the nature of the efficient cause, and meant one of the two μορφαί to serve this purpose. There is nothing in the fragments to show which of the two he meant, but Hippolytus (i. 11. 1) says fire was the active principle, and this is doubtless Aristotle's meaning—cf. l. 6.

5. τοῖς δὲ δὴ πλείω ποιοῦσι. Alexander and Bonitz think the reference still is to Parmenides; and, as we have seen, Aristotle does ascribe to him the principles ' hot and cold, or fire and earth '. But this interpretation cannot be reconciled with the opposition τῶν μὲν ἐν φασκόντων εἶναι τὸ πᾶν and τοῖς δὲ πλείω ποιοῦσι. Further, μᾶλλον loses its meaning if the same person is being spoken about in the two opposed clauses. What other thinkers could be meant by οἱ πλείω ποιοῦντες? A natural supposition is that the pluralists here referred to are those whom Parmenides attacks for being pluralists, viz. the early Pythagoreans, who identified their active principle, the limit, with light or fire, and their passive principle, the unlimited, with night, mist, or air (cf. 986ᵃ 25, *Phys.* 213ᵇ 22). But a comparison of ll. 6–8 with 985ᵃ 29–ᵇ 2, *De Gen. et Corr.* 330ᵇ 19 (cf. Burnet, § 107) shows that Empedocles is referred to. The opposition of fire to all the other elements is not known to have been a feature of Pythagoreanism, and it is known to have been a feature of Empedocles' doctrine, at least as conceived by Aristotle. Aristotle is doubtless thinking of the fact that fire plays a leading part in Empedocles' account of the origin of the world and in his biology (cf. fr. 62, Burnet, §§ 112–15).

There is one objection to the supposition that Empedocles is referred to. Aristotle includes him (985ᵃ 2) among those who are said in the next sentence to have been μετὰ τούτους. But this is no fatal objection. Up to now Aristotle has been speaking of thinkers who either recognized no efficient cause at all or assigned a sort of efficient causality to one of the material causes. In the next sentence he passes to a later group of thinkers who recognized an efficient cause distinct from the material causes and in some sense taking the place of a final cause. Empedocles assigned efficient activity both to fire and to friendship and strife; he thus belonged to both groups, and yet one group may fairly be called later than the other. He was the last member of the earlier group and the first member of the later.

8–11. It is not easy to see what Aristotle means by τὰς τοιαύτας ἀρχάς and by τὴν ἐχομένην. Our first inclination would be to suppose that the former means the material and efficient causes, and (since Aristotle proceeds to speak of the cause of goodness in things) that the latter means the final cause. But it is not the case that Anaxagoras sought the final cause; he did not ask himself τίνος ἔνεκα; He sought the cause of the order in things, but he explained this not by an end to be fulfilled but by a pre-existent reason which ordered things. He entered on the line of thought which led others to believe in a final cause, but it led him to believe in an efficient cause, more distinctly conceived than it was by the thinkers who assigned to one of the material causes an efficient activity (ll. 5–8). Even those who spoke of love or desire as a cause (ll. 23–985ᵃ 10) did not think of this teleologically. They did not regard it as choosing means with a view to an end, but simply as forming the elements, and the living things composed of them, into certain unions. Thus, while the inquiry 'what set things changing?' did not lead to the notion of a distinct efficient cause, which is the proper answer to that inquiry, the question 'why are things well ordered?' did lead to that notion. These thinkers (Empedocles and Anaxagoras) did not arrive at the notion of a final cause at all, and they did not arrive at the *pure* notion of an efficient or mechanical cause, for they combined with the notion of force that of intelligence or else of desire. Cf. what Aristotle says in l. 20, 988ᵇ 6, Λ. 1075ᵇ 8. That τὴν ἐχομένην does not mean the final cause is shown further by the fact that Aristotle later (985ᵃ 11, ᵇ 21) refers to the material and efficient causes as alone having been discussed. τὰς τοιαύτας ἀρχάς seems then to mean the material and material-efficient causes (the latter being what is referred to in ll. 5–8), and τὴν ἐχομένην the pure efficient cause.

14. For Aristotle's doctrine of τὸ αὐτόματον and τύχη see Z. 7, 9, K. 1065ᵃ 27–ᵇ 4, and notes.

15. τις, i. e. Anaxagoras. Cf. especially fr. 12.

16. τὸν αἴτιον τοῦ κόσμου. πάντα διεκόσμησε νοῦς (Anaxagoras, fr. 14) suggests that κόσμος may mean 'order' rather than 'universe'. Aristotle constantly uses κόσμος in the sense of 'universe', but probably always with the notion of its being an ordered universe. Cf. οὐκ ἔστι κόσμος ὁ κόσμος ἀλλ' ἀκοσμία, fr. 1476ᵇ 45.

17. οἶον νήφων ἐφάνη. Cf. Socrates' account of his high expectations from Anaxagoras, *Phaedo*, 97 B.

19. We have no independent confirmation of this story about Hermotimus. He is a highly legendary personage, whose soul was said to have often left his body and during its absence acquired information of events at a distance ; he was also said to have been one of the previous incarnations of Pythagoras. The connexion between him and Anaxagoras probably is simply that the separation of his soul from his body was thought to furnish an analogy to Anaxagoras' distinction of mind from matter. So Zeller, i⁶. 1267–9. Aristotle makes a suggestion similar to his present one in *De An.* 404ᵃ 25 Ἀναξαγόρας ψυχὴν εἶναι λέγει τὴν κινοῦσαν καὶ εἴ τις ἄλλος εἴρηκεν ὡς τὸ πᾶν ἐκίνησε νοῦς, but Archelaus is just as likely to be there referred to.

20-22. 'Those who thought thus posited the cause of the goodness in things, and at the same time the cause of movement, as a first principle.' The efficient cause (love, or reason) was described as good, but it was used by these thinkers not in the way appropriate to what is good, viz. as the final cause of the universe, but simply as its efficient cause. Cf. 988ᵇ 6–11, where the point is made more distinctly.

23. τὸ τοιοῦτον, i.e. something which was at the same time the cause of the goodness of things and of their movement.

26. πρώτιστον μέν κτλ. Fr. 13. Simplicius (*Phys.* 39. 18) connects this fragment with fr. 12, which describes the working of love, and Plutarch (*Amat.* 13. 756 f.) treats the subject of μητίσατο as being Ἀφροδίτη. Ἀνάγκη, Δίκη, Γένεσις, and Φύσις have also been suggested,

but Simplicius and Plutarch are probably right.   In any case the verse belongs only to the ' way of opinion '.

The best MSS. have πρῶτον, but πρώτιστον is found in the citations by Plato, Plutarch, and Simplicius, and is metrically more probable.

27. πάντων μὲν πρώτιστα κτλ.   *Theog.* 116–20.   After εὐρύστερνος Aristotle omits the words πάντων ἕδος ἀσφαλὲς αἰεί.   Further, the recognized form of the last line is ἠδ' ἔρος, ὃς κάλλιστος ἐν ἀθανάτοισι θεοῖσιν.   Aristotle seems in quoting from memory to have been confused by a reminiscence of such verses as Hom. *Il.* ii. 579, xvi. 194, *Hymn to Apollo,* 315, 327.

32. ἐξέστω κρίνειν ὕστερον.   The promise is nowhere fulfilled.

985ᵃ 3.   In saying that Empedocles made love the cause of good and strife of evil Aristotle is thinking of such phrases as ἠπιόφρων Φιλότητος ἀμεμφέος ἄμβροτος ὁρμή (fr. 35. 13), Ἁρμονία θεμερῶπις (fr. 122. 2), and again of the description of strife as οὐλόμενον, μαινόμενον, λυγρόν (frr. 17. 19, 115. 14, 109. 3) and as Δῆρις αἱματόεσσα (fr. 122. 2).

5.   For ψελλίζομαι in a similar connexion cf. 993ᵃ 15 ; elsewhere Aristotle expresses the same point by saying there is a lack of διάρθρωσις in early thinkers (986ᵇ 5, 989ᵃ 32, B. 1002ᵇ 27).

10. καὶ ... κακόν, omitted by Aᵇ, Alexander, and Asclepius, was probably suggested to some copyist by Alexander's remark that something of the sort must be supplied to complete the sense.

12. ἐν τοῖς περὶ φύσεως, *Phys.* ii. 3, 7.

18. μηχανῇ, as is shown by the word παρέλκει, refers to the stage *deus ex machina.*

20–21. ἐν δὲ τοῖς ἄλλοις ... νοῦν.   Cf. Socrates' disappointment with Anaxagoras (Pl. *Phaed.* 98 B ἀέρας καὶ αἰθέρας καὶ ὕδατα αἰτιώμενον), and *Laws* 967 B, *Met.* A. 988ᵇ 6.   Anaxagoras' bold statement πάντα διεκόσμησε νοῦς (fr. 12) gives promise of a spiritual explanation of the world, which is never carried out in detail.   Mind started the original vortex-movement, but the subsequent changes are explained in a purely mechanical way (frr. 9, 13, 15, 16, 19).   Yet reason, though not conceived as absolutely immaterial (the description of it as λεπτότατον καὶ καθαρώτατον in fr. 12 implies that it is thought of simply as a very tenuous form of matter), is thought of as knowing and foreseeing (ib.).   Anaxagoras, in fact, is on the verge of discovering a genuinely spiritual and teleological principle of explanation.

23.   For τὸ ὁμολογούμενον in the sense of ' consistency ' cf. 989ᵃ 3, 991ᵇ 27, B. 1000ᵃ 25, *An. Pr.* 47ᵃ 8.

23–29. πολλαχοῦ ... πάλιν.   The same point is made in B. 1000ᵃ 26, ᵇ 9.

25, 27. ὅταν implies an indefinite repetition of the cycle of διάκρισις and σύγκρισις ; this is also implied in frr. 17. 6, 26. 1, 12.

25. στοιχεῖα.   στοιχεῖον, properly ' one of a row ' (στοῖχος), appears to be first used of the regularly lengthening shadow on a sun-dial (cf. Aristoph. *Eccl.* 652).   But in Plato it often means an element of spoken language, answering to γράμμα, an element of written language, and in *Theaet.* 201 E it is metaphorically used of the elements of any complex whole. The illustration in 985^b17 shows how a transition might naturally be made from στοιχεῖον as 'letter' to στοιχεῖον as 'element'. In Aristotle's time the word was already in use in the latter sense; cf. l. 32 τὰ . . . λεγόμενα στοιχεῖα, *Phys.* 187^a 26, 204^b 33, *De Gen. et Corr.* 328^b 31, 329^a 26, *Meteor.* 339^b 5, *De Part. An.* 646^a 13, *De Gen. An.* 736^b 31. N. 1087^b 13 seems to imply that the word was regularly used in this sense by the Platonists. On the general history of the word cf. Diels, *Elementum.*— Empedocles' own word for elements was ῥιζώματα (fr. 6).

27. συνίωσιν (*sc.* τὰ στοιχεῖα). For the plural verb with neuter plural subject cf. 988^b 5, M. 1079^a 20, *An. Pr.* 69^b 4, *An. Post.* 87^b 3, *De Gen. et Corr.* 327^b 10, 337^a 10, *De Resp.* 480^b 15, *De Part. An.* 660^a 33, *De Gen. An.* 717^b 11, 762^b 25. The construction is especially common in the *Metaphysics* and in the *Ethics* (cf. Zell on *E. N.* i. 1. 2, vi. 4. 4).

30. τὸ τὴν αἰτίαν διελεῖν. Cf. ll. 2–4.

32. τὰ . . . λεγόμενα στοιχεῖα. Cf. l. 25 n.

τέτταρα πρῶτος εἶπεν. Thales had made water the ultimate principle, Anaximenes air, Heraclitus fire. Anaximander had recognized, at the first remove from his ultimate element, two main sub-principles, the hot and the cold (Diels³, i. 16. 16, Zeller, i.⁶ 295 n.). Anaximenes is said to have given a list of the main forms of matter derived from air—fire, wind, cloud, water, earth, stones (Diels, 22. 24). Xenophanes had thought all things were earth (fr. 27), or earth and water (frr. 29, 33). Heraclitus had said that fire is transformed into sea, and half of the sea is earth (i. e. has just been transformed from earth into water by liquefaction), while half is πρηστήρ or fiery storm-cloud (i. e. has just been transformed from fire into water); in other words, he had recognized two subsidiary elements, water and earth (fr. 31, cf. Burnet, § 71). Epicharmus may have recognized as elements water, earth, breath, and snow (fr. 49). Thus the way had been prepared for Empedocles' theory ; but none the less it was highly original. When an earlier thinker named more than one element, he had not meant to draw up a list of ultimates from which everything else was derived while they were not derived from one another. The earlier thinkers were at bottom monists ; if they recognize a plurality of elements, it is only as variants of an ultimate unity. What Empedocles did was to treat their secondary principles as primary principles. Further, to account for the variety of existing things his predecessors had had to admit qualitative changes in their elements ; Empedocles, starting with a variety of elements, thought no qualitative change in them need be supposed, but aggregation and disgregation of them would produce all the phenomena. The view of Heraclitus is specially likely to have influenced Empedocles, as it was itself influenced by that of Anaximander; and the importance attached to the number 4 by the Pythagoreans may have led to the selection of that number of elements. Empedocles' own theory became in turn the starting-point for that of Philolaus, who added one more element, the 'fifth body' of which the heavens are made.

33. οὐ μὴν χρῆταί γε τέτταρσιν. Cf. 984ᵇ 5 n.

ᵇ 3. ἐκ τῶν ἐπῶν. Aristotle has in mind such passages as fr. 62, and
probably others not now extant which implied more distinctly an
opposition between fire and the other elements.

4. The introduction of the Atomists here is somewhat confusing, since Aristotle has been dealing with the treatment by earlier
thinkers of the *efficient* cause, about which the Atomists have nothing
to say (l. 19). They ought to have been mentioned in the section
dealing with the *material* cause (983ᵇ 6—984ᵃ 18), but Aristotle broke
off that section when he came to Empedocles and Anaxagoras, who
were the first to recognize *efficient* causes distinct from the elements.
Cf. 983ᵇ 1 n.

Little was known to the ancients about the life of Leucippus.
Epicurus is said (Diog. x. 13) to have denied his existence and
Lucretius never mentions him. Rohde tried to show that he never
existed (*Verhandl. der 34. Philologenvers.*, pp. 64–90) but has been refuted by Diels (*Verhandl. d. 35. Philologenvers.*, pp. 96–109). Leucippus is mentioned quite often by Aristotle, and Prof. Burnet suggests
(§ 171 n.) that Epicurus purposely ignored him.

ἑταῖρος Asc. interprets as 'disciple'. Democritus was a disciple
of Leucippus, but the word does not mean more than 'associate';
Aristippus is said to have described Socrates as ὁ ἑταῖρος ἡμῶν (*Rhet.*
1398ᵇ 31).

5. τὸ πλῆρες καὶ τὸ κενόν. Prof. Burnet (§ 175) suggests that
Leucippus borrowed the terms from Melissus. Cf. Melissus, fr. 7,
sub fin. Leucippus seems to have 'flourished' about 450.

6. τὸ μὲν ὂν τὸ δὲ μὴ ὂν suggests a connexion between the Atomists
and the Eleatics, which is well brought out by Burnet, § 173, and indeed by Aristotle himself (*De Gen. et Corr.* 324ᵇ 35—325ᵃ 32).
Leucippus, Aristotle points out, conceded to the Eleatics 'that motion
was impossible without the void, that the void was not real, and that
nothing of what was real was not real'. He thought he could reconcile this with an admission of the reality of change, by holding that the
real is a *plenum* but the *plenum* is not one, and that there is a not-real
(the void). He in fact 'gave the Pythagorean monads the character
of the Parmenidean One' (Burnet³, p. 336).

9. τὸ κενὸν τοῦ σώματος, the reading of all the MSS., does not give
the right sense. We must read either τὸ σῶμα τοῦ κενοῦ (Fonseca), or
τὸ κενὸν ἔλαττον τοῦ σώματος (Zeller), or (which is the least violent
change) τοῦ κενοῦ τὸ σῶμα (Schwegler). W. Jaeger holds (*Hermes*, lii.
486 f.) that in careless writing οὐθὲν μᾶλλον can have the force of οὐθὲν
ἔλαττον, but the passages he cites in support of this (990ᵃ 15, B. 996ᵇ 33,
Meteor. 356ᵃ 16) are to be otherwise explained.

11, 12. πάθεσιν . . . παθημάτων, a good instance of the identity in
meaning of the two words, maintained by Bonitz (*Arist. Stud.* v)
against Bernays.

τὸ μανὸν καὶ τὸ πυκνὸν ἀρχὰς τιθέμενοι. The statement is too wide.
Anaximenes seems to have been the first to ascribe all changes to rare-

faction and condensation (Burnet, § 26), and Diogenes was almost the only later monist who followed his example.

12. Alexander records the variant reading καὶ ὥσπερ τῶν μαθηματι-κῶν τὸν αὐτὸν τρόπον, where μαθηματικῶν is evidently an old corruption of παθημάτων and καὶ ὥσπερ has been put in to make some sort of construction.

13. τὰς διαφοράς. The differentiae by which the Atomists explained τὰ ἄλλα were of course not differentiae of both the 'material' causes, the full and the empty, but only of the full, i. e. of the atoms.

13-19. Of the three 'differences' of the atoms, the only permanent characteristic of a given atom is shape (*Phys.* 184ᵇ 21, *De Caelo* 275ᵇ 31, *De Gen. et Corr.* 325ᵇ 18, 326ᵃ 15). The atoms are hence often called σχήματα or ἰδέαι (cf. Zeller, iⁿ. 1063 n. 3). The shapes were thought to be infinite in number (Zeller, 1064 n. 2). On the other hand two atoms might be at different angles to one another; cf. AH and AꞀ. This is a difference of θέσις. Or two atoms making the same angle with one another may be on different sides of one another; cf. AN with NA. This is a difference of τάξις.

Aristotle overlooks one difference which thé atoms were supposed to have, that of size (Zeller, 1064–6). On the question whether they also differed in weight cf. Zeller, 1066–8, Burnet, § 179.

15. ῥυσμῷ. ῥυσμός is the regular Ionic form of ῥυθμός and is found in Archilochus (62. 7, Hiller), Anacreon (69. 2), and Callimachus (*Ep.* 43. 5). Cf. βασμός, ἀνδροβασμός. ῥυθμός is used in the sense of 'shape' by Herodotus (v. 58), Hippocrates (*De Artic.* 62 (ii. 214. 2, Kühlewein)), Alexis (*Drop.* 1. 4), and Xenophon (*Mem.* iii. 10. 10). Democritus wrote a book περὶ τῶν διαφερόντων ῥυσμῶν (fr. 5).

διαθιγῆ. Both here and in H. 1042ᵇ 14, *De Gen. et Corr.* 315ᵇ 35, 327ᵃ 18, Simpl. *Phys.* 28. 18, 180. 19 the MSS. vary between διαθιγή and διαθηγή, and the latter is the form that is found in Suidas; in Democr. fr. 223 κακοθηγίη occurs as a variant for κακοθιγίη. The word is commonly derived from διαθιγγάνω and supposed to mean 'mutual contact'. But διαθιγγάνω, in the only passage quoted by L. and S., *H. A.* 634ᵃ 9, means something quite different. Accordingly Prof. Beare has suggested (*Greek Theories of Elementary Cognition*, 37, and *Hermathena*, xxxv. 469) that διαθιγή is a dialectal form of διαθήκη. διαθήκη occurs in the sense of διάθεσις in Democr. fr. 9 (cf. προσθήκη = πρόσθεσις), and this is just the sense we want (διάθεσις = τοῦ ἔχοντος μέρη τάξις, Δ. 1022ᵇ 1). Hesychius gives θήγη = θήκη, θέσις, τάξις.

There are two possible words, διαθιγή derived from διαθιγγάνω, and διαθήγη derived from διατίθημι. There does not seem to be, as Prof. Beare thinks, any intrinsic objection to the derivation of διαθιγή from διαθιγγάνω. The difference between AN and NA may naturally be described as one of 'mutual contact'. Again, διαθιγή does not seem to be a possible dialectal form of διαθήκη; Prof. Beare has done nothing to show the possibility of this. The MS. authority is on the whole in favour of retaining the form διαθιγή, and if we retain it we must derive it from διαθιγγάνω. But the facts to which Prof. Beare has called attention make it quite *possible* that διαθιγή is an illusory form due to a mistaken derivation, and that διαθήγη should be restored everywhere.

16. τροπῇ. τροπή in this sense occurs again in H. 1042ᵇ 14, *De Gen. et Corr.* 315ᵇ 35, 316ᵃ 2, 327ᵃ 18.

17. τὸ μὲν A κτλ. Democritus was interested in the letters of the alphabet (cf. frr. 18ᵇ–20, *De Gen. et Corr.* 315ᵇ 14, and Diels in *Verhandl. der 35. Philologenvers.* 109⁴²), and the instances are probably due to him.

18. Wilamowitz (*Comm. Gr.* iv. 27) points out that the only form of Zeta known to Aristotle was Ι, and accordingly reads τὸ δὲ Ι τοῦ H. This is confirmed by Philo, who has H and Z, and tries, though of course ineffectually, to show that these differ θέσει (*de Aet.*, p. 34. 13, Cumont).

19. περὶ δὲ κινήσεως κτλ. Aristotle complains elsewhere that the Atomists ascribed everything to necessity (*De Gen. An.* 789ᵇ 2), and that they did not say what the natural movement of the atoms is (*De Caelo*, 300ᵇ 8). They assumed that the movement of the atoms is eternal, and gave no reason for it (Λ. 1071ᵇ 32). It is true that they do not expressly call it natural, since they have not Aristotle's distinction of natural and compulsory movement in their minds, but they would have had no difficulty in choosing this alternative, nor was their view any less satisfactory than Aristotle's doctrine of the natural motion of bodies up, down, or in a circle. He is right, however, in saying (789ᵇ 2) that they had no notion of a final cause of the movement.

21. τῶν δύο αἰτιῶν, the material and the efficient cause, cf. ᵃ 12.

Pythagoreans and Eleatics (ch. 5).

985ᵇ 23. (1) Contemporary with and even earlier than these thinkers were the Pythagoreans, whose mathematical training led them to think the principles of mathematics were the principles of all things.

26. Numbers were the first of these, and they thought they saw in numbers many resemblances to actual things and events (justice, &c., being identified with certain modifications of number); they saw that music, too, depends on number;

986ᵃ 1. hence they regarded the elements of numbers as elements of all things, and the universe as a number. They collected correspondences between numbers and things,

6. and tried to make the correspondence complete; e.g. they posited the counter-earth to bring the planets up to the perfect number ten.

13. Our object is to see how the principles they recognize compare with our list. Evidently they treat numbers both as the material principle of things and as modifications and states of things. The elements of number are the even, which is unlimited, and the odd, which is limited ; unity is produced out of these two, and number out of unity, and the world is numbers.

22. Other Pythagoreans recognize ten principles, arranged in two columns :

limit	unlimited
odd	even
one	plurality
right	left
male	female
at rest	in motion
straight	crooked
light	darkness
good	evil
square	oblong.

27. Either Alcmaeon borrowed from these thinkers or they from him ; he says most human things go in pairs, but has no definite list of pairs.

b **2.** Both alike (*a*) treat contraries as first principles, and (*b*) treat the first principles as the *matter* of which things are made.

8. The views of the pluralists may be gathered sufficiently from what has been said.

10. (2) The views of the monists differ from one another both in merit and in the degree of their conformity to nature. The discussion of them does not fit into our inquiry into the causes, for they do not, like some of the physicists, mean by saying the world is one that it is generated out of a single matter; they entirely deny change.

17. But it is pertinent to our inquiry to remark that Parmenides is thinking of what is one in definition, Melissus of what is materially one ; Xenophanes, the first of these monists, does not specify or recognize either aspect, but with reference to the universe says the One is the only God.

25. Xenophanes and Melissus may be dismissed as too crude to deserve notice, but Parmenides has a more seeing eye. Claiming that there is no non-existent apart from the existent, he thinks that one thing alone, viz. being, exists ;

31. but being forced to follow the phenomena, and holding that while only the one exists according to definition many things exist according to sensation, he posits two causes, hot and cold, i. e. fire and earth, which he connects with being and non-being.

987ᵃ 2. (3) *Summary of chs. 3–5.* Thus we have found (*a*) the

earliest thinkers recognizing one or more material principles, (*b*) some
thinkers recognizing also one, or two, efficient causes.

9. The thinkers earlier than the Pythagoreans speak rather obscurely about the causes, except for the points just mentioned ;

13. the Pythagoreans similarly recognize the two causes, but have these
peculiarities—(i) they treated the limited (or one) and the unlimited
not as characteristics of something else such as fire, but as themselves
the substance of the things of which they are predicated, and

20. (ii) they began to define things; but (*a*) they did this superficially, and (*β*) they supposed that the first thing to which a definition
was applicable was the essence of the term defined, as if one were
to identify ' double ' and ' two ' because two is the first thing that is
double.   This makes one number the essence of many things.

985^b 23. πρὸ τούτων seems to indicate that by οὗτοι Aristotle
means the Atomists, about whom he has just been speaking, and not
the general body of philosophers whom he has been discussing since
983^b 6.   The Pythagoreans who were ἐν τούτοις will then be those of
the end of the fifth century, such as Philolaus.

οἱ καλούμενοι Πυθαγόρειοι.   Aristotle refers to the Pythagoreans
occasionally as οἱ Ἰταλικοί or οἱ περὶ Ἰταλίαν, usually as οἱ Πυθαγόρειοι,
but not infrequently as οἱ καλούμενοι Πυθαγόρειοι (cf. 989^b 29, *De Caelo*
284^b 7, 293^a 20, *Meteor.* 342^b 30, 345^a 14).   If the shorter reading in
986^a 29, 30 is the correct one, Pythagoras himself is only once mentioned in Aristotle's extant works (*Rhet.* 1398^b 14).   For Aristotle he
seems to be little if anything more than a legendary figure ; there is a
set of people commonly called Pythagoreans, but Aristotle will not
vouch for the origin of any of their doctrines in Pythagoras himself.

On Aristotle's account of the Pythagoreans cf. A. Rothenbücher,
Das System der Pythagoreer nach den Angaben des Aristoteles ; W. A.
Heidel in *Arch. f. Gesch. d. Phil.* xiv. 384–436, O. Gilbert, ib. xxii.
28–48, 145–165, F. M. Cornford in *Class. Quart.* xvi. 137–150,
xvii. 1–12.

25. τὰς τούτων ἀρχάς.   What exactly they meant by these we shall
see at 986^a 17.   On the Pythagorean view that the principles of
numbers are principles of all things cf. Burnet, §§ 52, 142–147, 153,
Milhaud, *Philosophes-Géomètres de la Grèce*, 101–110.

26. φύσει πρῶτοι, i. e. the simplest of mathematical objects.   Relatively numbers were ἐξ ἀφαιρέσεως, spatial magnitudes ἐκ προσθέσεως.
Cf. 982^a 26.

27. ὁμοιώματα πολλά.   For instances cf. N. 6, Sext. Emp. *Adv.
Math.* vii. 94–109.

29. πάθος here must mean πάθος καθ' αὑτό, i. e. συμβεβηκὸς καθ' αὑτό
or property.   Oddness, evenness, &c., are cited as ἴδια πάθη of number
in Γ. 1004^b 10.   Strictly speaking, then, the text should mean that the
Pythagoreans identified justice, &c., with some property of number

such as oddness or squareness. At 990ᵃ 25, however, we learn that
they thought injustice, &c., were actual numbers. But it is just one of
Aristotle's complaints about them that they confused a property like
' double ' with a number like 2 (987ᵃ 22).

δικαιοσύνη. The Pythagorean description of justice as τὸ ἀντιπεπονθὸς ἄλλῳ (E. N. 1132ᵇ 22) implies that it is treated as a square,
a number in which each of two factors treats the other as the other
treats it. In M. M. 1182ᵃ 11–14 we are expressly told that the Pythagoreans treated it as a square number. Alexander tells us that it was
the *first* square number (which agrees with 987ᵃ 22), but that some
identified it with 4, others with 9. *Theol. Arithm.* (p. 30 Ast), Asc.
(34. 17), Syr. (130. 29), ps.-Al. (741. 5), and Philop. (*Phys.* 388. 30)
say that it was 5, while Plutarch (*de Is. et Os.* 75, p. 381 f.) says
it was 3. These writers, however, evidently represent a less trustworthy
tradition.

30. ψυχή τε καὶ νοῦς. Alexander says the Pythagoreans used
ψυχή in the sense of νοῦς and assigned to it the number 1, since
reason is μόνιμον καὶ ὅμοιον πάντῃ καὶ ἀρχικόν. Similarly Hippolytus
says (i. 15. 2) that the Pythagorean Ecphantus identified νοῦς and
ψυχή. Asc. agrees that reason was represented by 1 (cf. Plut. *Epit.* i.
3. 8, 7. 18 Theo Smyrn., p. 98. 1, 100. 5 Hiller, Stob. *Ecl.* i. 1), but
says that soul was 2, since it has τὸ ποθέν ποι, i. e. moves from premises to a conclusion. Elsewhere we read that soul was 4 (Plut.
Epit. i. 3. 8, Sext. Emp. iv. 6), 6 (Syr. 130. 33, Procl. *in Tim.* 223 E),
or 216 (Syr. 130. 33, 188. 4). All that we can say with certainty is
that Aristotle's words imply that soul and reason were represented by
the same number ; this number was in all probability 1.

καιρός, Alexander tells us, was represented by 7, with reference
to certain critical periods in human life (birth at seven months, cutting
of teeth at seven months after birth, puberty at 14, maturity at 21—
cf. N. 1093ᵃ 14, Theo, p. 103. 1—104. 19). The sun, the cause of all
critical periods, was supposed to come seventh of the heavenly bodies,
counting towards the centre. Asc. gives further reasons for the
connexion of καιρός with the number 7.

τῶν ἄλλων ὡς εἰπεῖν ἕκαστον. Thus the point was 1, the line 2, the
plane 3, the solid 4, the physical body, or body endowed with quality
and colour, 5, the body endowed with soul 6, the body endowed with
reason 7 (Procl. *in Tim.* 340 A, 223 E, *Theol. Arithm.*, p. 55 Ast, Asc. 34.
33, Sext. Emp. *adv. Math.* iv. 4, 5). Another tradition assigns the
number 210 to body (Syr. 143. 6, 188. 3, ps.-Al. 767. 11), 1 to fire,
3 to air, 7 to earth, 9 (? 10, since 1 × 3 × 7 × 10 = 210) to water (Syr.
143. 7), while another, with less probability, assigns 9 to water, 11 to
fire, 13 to air (ps.-Al. 767. 12). Again, knowledge was 2 (Aet. i. 3.
8, Theo, p. 98. 2), opinion 3 (Aet. ib., Asc. 34. 30, Theo, p. 98. 3 ;
another tradition makes it 2, cf. Al. 39. 16, 75. 22, Asc. 65. 3), sensation 4 (Aet. i. 3. 8, Theo, p. 98. 4). Daring was 2 (Plut. *De Is. et Os.*
75, p. 381 f., Al. 74. 13), strife 2 (Plut. ib.), marriage 3 (*Theol. Arithm.*,
p. 16), 5 (Al. 39. 8), or 6 (Stob. *Ecl.* i. 1. 10, *Theol. Arithm.*, p. 33) ;

love, friendship, wisdom, and inventiveness were 8 (*Theol. Arithm.*, p. 55).

31. Pythagoras is said to have discovered the elements of the theory of musical harmony (Nicomachus, *Harm.* v, p. 244. 14 Jan, Diog. Laert. viii. 12, Iambl. *Vit. Pyth.* 115–121), and Burnet (§ 51) is inclined to credit this. The octave, the fifth, and the fourth were at any rate known to Philolaus and Archytas. Cf. Zeller, i.^{6} 507 f.

33. Bonitz thinks that since in the next line πᾶσα ἡ φύσις means 'the whole of nature', it can hardly in this line mean 'the whole of *their* nature', and therefore proposes πάντα for πᾶσαν, and this is to some extent confirmed by Alexander (38. 2). The proposal is attractive, but in view of Aristotle's carelessness in using words or phrases in different meanings in close succession it is hardly necessary.

986^a 2. τὸν ὅλον οὐρανὸν ἁρμονίαν εἶναι. Aristotle tells us (*De Caelo* ii. 9) that the sun, moon, and stars (including those now called fixed stars) were supposed by the Pythagoreans to move at speeds proportional to their distances from the centre of the universe, and to give forth accordingly high or low notes which together made an ἐναρμό-νιον φωνήν, a scale. This information is supplemented by Alexander (39. 22), who says the bodies that moved more slowly gave forth a lower, and those that moved faster a higher note. The moon, the sun, Venus, and Mercury were at distances from the earth which were to one another as 1, 2, 3, 4, and so with the other planets. This account does not agree with the later Pythagorean astronomy with which Aristotle has made us familiar. The later Pythagoreans believed that the middle of the universe was occupied not by the earth but by a central fire, which they called the 'hearth' of the universe. Round this revolved ten bodies, in the following order—counter-earth, earth, moon, sun, the five planets, the heaven of the fixed stars. This belief in ten moving bodies could be reconciled with the notion of a celestial harmony only if account was taken of the fact that Venus and Mercury had the same apparent velocity as the sun, and if the number of the notes was thus reduced to eight. But the evidence indicates that, in its earliest form at all events, the celestial harmony comprised only the moon, the sun, and the five planets. This agrees better with Alexander's account, but he must still be wrong in saying that the distances of the sounding bodies were as 1, 2, 3, 4, 5, 6, 7, since these are not the proportional lengths of the strings whose notes make up an octave. Cf. Zeller, i.^{6} 537–542, Burnet, § 152.

7. προσεγλίχοντο. The word is found again in N. 1090^b 31 προσγλιχόμενοι ταῖς ἰδέαις τὰ μαθηματικά, and in Procl. *in Tim.* 25 D, where it is followed by an indirect question and means 'to inquire earnestly'. It seems best to take it, with Alexander and Asclepius, to mean 'they added it eagerly', τοῦ ... εἶναι being a final genitive; cf. Bonitz, *Index*, 149^b 15–19.

8. Various reasons for regarding 10 as the perfect number may be seen in an extract in *Theol. Arithm.*, p. 61 Ast from a work by Speusippus on the Pythagorean theory of numbers. A favourite

Pythagorean way of representing the number 10 was as a τετρακτύς.
i. e. by the following figure :

$$\begin{matrix} & & \bullet & & \\ & \bullet & & \bullet & \\ \bullet & & \bullet & & \bullet \\ \bullet & \bullet & & \bullet & \bullet \end{matrix}$$

The τετρακτύς was that by which they swore their most solemn oaths,
and was called ὑγιείας ἀρχή (Aet. i. 3. 8, Luc. *de lapsu in sal.* 5, Sext.
Emp. *adv. Math.* vii. 94–100, cf. Philolaus fr. 11, Porphyry, *Vit. Pyth.*
20). On the various forms of τετρακτύς cf. Theo, p. 93. 17—99. 23
Hiller, and on its interpretation F. M. Cornford in *Class. Quart.*
xvii. 1–4.

11. Belief in the counter-earth is ascribed definitely to Philolaus
(Aet. ii. 7. 7, iii. 11. 3), but we have no means of knowing whether it
originated with him.   It is part of the late Pythagorean theory which
denied that the earth was the centre of the universe ; the counter-earth
was held to be between the earth and the central fire.   Pythagoras
himself probably held a generative theory.   In the *De Caelo* (293ª 23),
as here, Aristotle charges the Pythagoreans with having introduced the
counter-earth on purely *a priori* grounds.   But according to Aetius
ii. 29. 4, in his work on the Pythagoreans Aristotle said that some of them
explained eclipses of the moon as being caused, sometimes by the earth,
sometimes by the counter-earth; and with this we may compare *De Caelo*
293ᵇ 21, where Aristotle says that some (and they can only have been
Pythagoreans) thought there might be many bodies near the centre
of the universe, hidden from us by the interposition of the earth, and
explained thus the greater frequency of lunar than of solar eclipses.
Thus they had some facts to suggest the theory of a counter-earth.
' The history of the theory seems to be this.   Anaximenes had assumed
the existence of dark planets to account for lunar eclipses, and
Anaxagoras had revived that view.   Certain Pythagoreans had placed
these dark planets between the earth and the central fire in order to
account for their invisibility, and the next stage was to reduce them
to a single body ' (Burnet, § 151).   Cf. Zeller, i.⁶ 532 n. 2.

12. διώρισται . . . ἐν ἑτέροις.   The subject is, as we have seen,
dealt with in *De Caelo* ii. 13.   Alexander refers also to the now lost
work on the Pythagoreans.   Cf. a similar reference to this work,
fr. 1513ᵇ 8–20.

16. The statement that the Pythagoreans made number the material
cause of things may be compared with the statements that they, unlike
the Platonists, thought that the numbers actually are the things
(986ª 2, 21, 987ᵇ 27, 30, M. 1083ᵇ 17, N. 1090ª 22), or are in the
things (M. 1080ᵇ 1, *Phys.* 203ª 6), or are the constituents of the
things (990ª 22, M. 1080ᵇ 2, 17, 1083ᵇ 11, 18, N. 1090ª·23, 32),
or have spatial magnitude (M. 1080ᵇ 19, 32).   Aristotle insists that
the Pythagorean theory of numbers as the substance of things was no
mere symbolism, but a literal account of the nature of the physical

world (989ᵇ 33, N. 1091ᵃ 18). We are not to suppose that they deliberately rejected the notion that numbers are not spatial. Like all the pre-Socratics, they had not reached the notion of non-spatial reality. ·Presumably they thought of the number 10 as *being*, and not merely as being represented by, a set of bits of matter arranged as a τετρακτύς, and this is no more surprising than that Empedocles should think of love and strife, or Anaxagoras of mind, as material things. No doubt the statement that the Pythagoreans made number the matter of things presents their theory in the absurdest possible form, but Aristotle is merely bringing out the fact that they had not drawn certain distinctions which later philosophy made evident. On the whole subject cf. Zeller, i.⁶ 483-495, Burnet, §§ 52, 143-146.

17. καὶ ὡς πάθη τε καὶ ἕξεις. Alexander suggests various interpretations—(1) that the numbers cause the πάθη καὶ ἕξεις of things and thus are an efficient cause, (2) that number is matter, the even is πάθος, and the odd ἕξις (this interpretation he ascribes to Aspasius), (3) that the even number is ὕλη and πάθος, the odd number ἕξις. Clearly none of these interpretations really interprets the text. πάθη and ἕξεις are to be distinguished, if at all, only as temporary and permanent modifications. The words are occasionally elsewhere coupled in a similar way, e.g. Δ. 1015ᵇ 34, 1020ᵃ 19, K. 1061ᵃ 9, *Phys.* 223ᵃ 18. But what can ἀρχὴ ὡς πάθη τε καὶ ἕξεις mean? If we remember what Aristotle's object is throughout his history of earlier thought, and notice that ὡς πάθη τε καὶ ἕξεις is opposed to ὡς ὕλη, we cannot doubt that another of the four causes is meant. At 987ᵃ 13 Aristotle says that the Pythagoreans recognized two causes, and though his words there are difficult it seems likely that he means the material and the formal cause. In 987ᵃ 20 he says that they ' began to speak about the " what " and to define ', i. e. to recognize the formal cause. He adds that this recognition was marred by their supposition that the first thing to which the definition of a given term applied must be the essence of the term, e. g. that 2 must be the essence of ' double '. Is not the supposition that justice is the first square, which he has already alluded to, just of this nature? 4 was the first thing to which the definition of justice (τὸ ἀντιπεπονθὸς ἄλλῳ) applied ; therefore, they said, 4 was the essence of justice. Another point may be mentioned. Speaking of the relation between a thing and its formal cause, Aristotle says (987ᵇ 11) that the Pythagoreans called this relation 'imitation'; we may connect this with the statement we have already had (985ᵇ 32), that according to them all other things 'seemed to have been·made like to the numbers '. It seems clear, then, that Aristotle is hinting that they thought of numbers as in some sense formal as well as material causes. ἕξεις is a natural enough equivalent for εἴδη (cf. H. 1044ᵇ 32, Λ. 1070ᵃ 12). πάθη is more surprising, but it can be used as equivalent to ποιότης (M. 1083ᵃ 10) or διαφορά (*De Gen. et Corr.* 315ᵃ 9) or εἶδος (*Meteor.* 382ᵃ 29) ; a πάθος may be an element in the essence of a thing (*De Part. An.* 678ᵃ 32). Aristotle means, then, that the Pythagoreans thought the number which a thing

' imitated' temporarily or permanently was a πάθος or ἕξις which made the thing what it was, temporarily or permanently. The use of two words which are not quite technical words for 'formal cause' is appropriate when Aristotle is speaking of thinkers who did not clearly distinguish the various kinds of cause.

From the words καὶ οὗτοι Bonitz infers that Aristotle must mean that the Pythagoreans explain the affections of things by the affections of numbers as earlier thinkers had explained them by the affections—condensation and rarefaction—of some material element. But it is impossible to get this out of τὸν ἀριθμὸν νομίζοντες ἀρχὴν εἶναι καὶ ὡς ὕλην τοῖς οὖσι καὶ ὡς πάθη τε καὶ ἕξεις, and καὶ οὗτοι may just as well only mean that the Pythagoreans like the other philosophers recognized no other causes than some of those which Aristotle himself has formulated To prove this is his main point throughout these chapters.

18. τούτων δὲ τὸ μὲν πεπερασμένον κτλ. The subsumption of the even under the indefinite, the odd under the finite, marks, as Heidel (*Archiv für Gesch. der Phil.* xiv. 390) observes, the meeting of 'two streams of interest, the ethico-religious and the mathematico-scientific'. In view of the fact that Pythagoreanism was primarily an ordered way of life, we are probably entitled to consider the opposition of the definite and indefinite the more fundamental of the two. It appears in the forefront in 986ᵃ 23, 987ᵃ 15, 990ᵃ 8, and the opposition of good and bad which runs through the συστοιχίαι (cf. *E. N.* 1096ᵇ 5 οἱ Πυθαγόρειοι . . . τιθέντες ἐν τῇ τῶν ἀγαθῶν συστοιχίᾳ τὸ ἕν) connects itself much more naturally with that of definite and indefinite than with that of odd and even. Definite and indefinite are the wider terms, and odd and even are the exemplification of them in a sphere which was to the Pythagoreans specially important, that of number. In later times (e. g. in the fragments of 'Philolaus', 1–3, 11) odd and even recede into the background, and limit and the indefinite form by far the most important opposition. Zeller's argument (i.⁶ 490–493) for the primariness of the opposition 'odd and even' does not do justice to the ethical element in Pythagoreanism. Cf. Heidel, l. c. 388, 389.

If we ask why the Pythagoreans connected the even with the indefinite, the odd with the definite, we find various reasons suggested by ancient writers. Aristotle gives the reason thus (*Phys.* 203ᵃ 13): περιτιθεμένων γὰρ τῶν γνωμόνων περὶ τὸ ἕν καὶ χωρὶς ὁτὲ μὲν ἄλλο ἀεὶ γίγνεσθαι τὸ εἶδος, ὁτὲ δὲ ἕν. These words present considerable difficulties (for their meaning cf. Zeller, i.⁶ 455 n. 3, Burnet, § 48, Milhaud, *Philosophes-Géomètres de la Grèce*, 115–117, Heath, *Gk. Math.* i. 83), but Stobaeus (i. 1. 10), Alexander (*apud* Simpl. *Phys.* 457. 12), Simplicius, Philoponus, and Themistius agree in an interpretation which may be illustrated by the following figures :

If you start with one dot and place a gnomon round it, and continue this process, you always get a figure of definite shape, the square ; if you start with two dots you get a series of oblongs varying indefinitely in shape. Or, to put it arithmetically, the sum of the odd numbers up to any point is always a square, the sum of the even numbers is always of the form $n(n+1)$, and the ratio of n to $n+1$ increases as n becomes larger. It is to be noted that ' square ' and ' oblong ' occur in the list of opposites (l. 26) ; this confirms the view that the way of thinking we have just illustrated counted for much with the Pythagoreans. If it be remembered that the Pythagoreans described numbers throughout in what we should call geometrical language, as triangular, square, oblong, gnomons, pyramidal, plane, solid (cf. Heath, *Gk. Math.* i. 76–84), it will seem probable that Aristotle's statement of the way in which they connected the odd with the definite, the even with the indefinite, is trustworthy.

But Heidel (l. c. 392–397) has made it appear extremely probable that the terms were connected in another way as well :

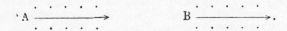

Let us first take ten, an even number (A). The process of halving, represented by the arrow, goes on without let or hindrance, there being no limit set to it by a solid unit. But if we take eleven, an odd number, we find that the unit added sets a limit, preventing the indefinite continuance of the process (B).' Heidel's theory appears to offer the best explanation of several passages in Greek authors (Stob. i. 1. 10, Nicom. *Arithm.* i. 7. 2, Plut. *De Vita et Poesi Homeri* 145, *De E.* 8, p. 388 A, в, *Qu. Rom.* 102, p. 288 D, Simpl. *Phys.* 455. 20), and is quite in the spirit of early Pythagoreanism.

19. According to Alexander and Theo Smyrnaeus the number 1 was regarded by the Pythagoreans as both odd and even and was called ἀρτιοπέριττος, because when added to an even number it makes it odd, and when added to an odd number makes it even (Al. 40. 20, 41. 12, Theo, p. 22. 5 Hiller). Theo says that Archytas took this view. Sir T. Heath suggests alternatively (*Gk. Math.* i. 71) that the unit was called even-odd because it was the principle of even as well as of odd numbers. For this view cf. Theo, p. 99. 24—100. 8. Mr. F. M. Cornford points out (*Class. Quart.* xvii. 3) that in the significance it ascribes to the numbers 1, 2, 3 the Pythagorean scheme falls into line with the early cosmogonies, in which 'there is (1) an undifferentiated unity. (2) From this unity two opposite powers are separated out to form the world order. (3) The two opposites unite again to generate life '.

20. τὸν δ' ἀριθμὸν ἐκ τοῦ ἑνός. The Pythagoreans do not seem to have made 1 the generative principle of the other numbers as the Platonists generated them from 1 and the indefinite dyad. They

started with 2 as the first even and 3 as the first odd number, and generated the later numbers from these, 4 by squaring 2, 5 by adding 2 and 3, &c. (cf. Zeller, i.⁶ 505–507). But since 1 combined oddness and evenness, 2 and 3 may be said to have been produced by a sort of dismemberment of 1.

22. ἕτεροι implies that the ten pairs of opposites were no essential part of the Pythagorean system. Definite and indefinite, odd and even, were the only fundamental antitheses. Zeller refers the longer list, not improbably, to Philolaus. The list is referred to in *E. N.* 1096^b 5 (cf. 1106^b 29, *De Caelo* 285^a 10). In N. 1093^b 11 Aristotle may have a slightly different list in view, since he mentions the powers of certain numbers, which do not occur here ; there, however, he may be referring to a Platonic list. Plut. *de Is. et Os.* 48, p. 370 E gives a slightly different list ; Simpl. *Phys.* 181. 22 gives one with seven, Porph. *Vit. Pyth.* 38 one with six, pairs of opposites ; Al. 694. 19 mentions οὐσία and τρίγωνον among the goods. Aristotle knew that further contrarieties were noted by the Pythagoreans ; e. g. they put ' above ' and ' before ' among the goods (Simpl. *De Caelo* 386. 20). This precise list is of no special importance ; but probably it acquired a certain vogue among the Pythagoreans owing to its recognizing just *ten* pairs of contraries.

23. συστοιχία is a rather puzzling word in Aristotle. Originally it meant a line of soldiers, for instance, or chorus singers, and it came to mean a line or list of cognates. Its application to the Pythagorean doctrine (cf. N. 1093^b 12) must be distinguished from the wider use in Γ. 1004^b 27, K. 1066^a 15, Λ. 1072^a 31, and from a quite different application which it has in I. 1054^b 35, 1058^a 13.

24. ἐν πλῆθος. We have already seen (l. 18 n.) that ' odd ' gnomons added to an odd number always produce one figure, the square, while ' even ' gnomons added to an even number produce a plurality of differently shaped oblongs. Accordingly unity was thought to be connected with oddness and definiteness, plurality with evenness and indefiniteness.

δεξιὸν ἀριστερόν. Milhaud suggests that δεξιόν refers to the regular (πεπερασμένον) movement of the fixed stars ' to the right ', ἀριστερόν to the irregular movement of the planets ' to the left ' (Pl. *Tim.* 36 c). The view that the planets move from west to east, the other stars from east to west is ascribed in Plut. *Epit.* ii. 16. 2 to ' the mathematicians ' and to Alcmaeon, and in Theo. 150. 12 to Pythagoras himself, to whom it may actually go back. Cf. Burnet, § 54. There are obviously other reasons which may have led to the inclusion of ' the right ' in the ' column of goods '. As an instance of this inclusion cf. the Pythagorean rule that the right shoe should be put on first (Iambl. *Vit. Pyth.* 83).

ἄρρεν θῆλυ. Plut. *Qu. Rom.* 102. 288 c–E, *De E.* 8. 388 A–C gives ingenious reasons for the connexion between τὸ ἄρρεν and τὸ περιττόν. The Pythagoreans called the odd numbers male, the even female (Zeller, i.⁶ 461 n. 1). It is to be noted that Plato com-

pares the functions of the limiting form and the indefinite matter
to those of father and mother respectively (*Tim.* 50 D), and that
Aristotle himself uses the same illustration in 988ª 5.   He thinks the
male contains the formative, the female the material principle (*De Gen.
An.* 729ª 9, 28, 730ᵇ 8).   Ordinary Greek thought regarded the father
as supplying the essential principle in generation, and the mother as
furnishing only the nourishment necessary to the seed; cf. Aesch.
Eum. 658–661 :

> οὐκ ἔστι μήτηρ ἡ κεκλημένου τέκνου
> τοκεύς, τροφὸς δὲ κύματος νεοσπόρου, κτλ.

25. ἠρεμοῦν κινούμενον.   Aristotle gives in *Phys.* 201ᵇ 19 ff. the
reason why movement was connected by the Pythagoreans and Plato
(e. g. *Tim.* 57 E) with otherness, inequality, and not-being.   It was
because movement ' was thought to be indefinite '.   The inclusion of
the moving and the resting among the indefinites and the definites
respectively may be connected with the evidently old notion of the
gnomons (cf. l. 18 n.).   The figure produced by putting an odd-
numbered gnomon round an odd number never changes in shape ;
that produced by putting an even-numbered gnomon round an even
number changes shape at each stage.   And, more generally, it was
natural that movement or variation should be connected with the
indefinite, and stability with the definite.

εὐθὺ καμπύλον.   This is a particular application of the opposition
of unity and plurality.   The straight line is that which has one direction
throughout, the crooked line that which changes its direction.

φῶς σκότος.   These are the principles that are criticized in the
' way of opinion ', Parmenides' account of the current (presumably
Pythagorean) beliefs of his time (fr. 8. 53–59, 9. 1–4).   Cf. 984ᵇ 4 n.
There is reason to believe that the Pythagoreans identified darkness,
air, and void.   One of the many ways in which the Pythagoreans
applied the notion of the limit and the unlimited was to think of the
world as formed by the gradual ' drawing and limiting ' (N. 1091ª 17)
of the boundless air (*Phys.* 204ª 31) outside the universe (203ª 7) by
the limit.   ' The Pythagoreans said there was a void, and it entered
into the universe itself from the boundless breath, the universe breathing in even the void ' (213ᵇ 22).   Cf. Burnet, § 53.   The Pythagoreans
probably also connected φῶς with the bounding coloured surface of
things (χροιά in Pythagorean language = ἐπιφάνεια, *De Sensu* 439ª 31),
σκότος with the unexplored, indefinite interior.   Cf. Gilbert in *Archiv
für Gesch. der Phil.* xxii. 150.

26.‑ἀγαθὸν κακόν.   Though good and evil are technically subordinate members of their συστοιχίαι, Aristotle refers to the positive
list as the ' column of goods ' (*E. N.* 1096ᵇ 6), and in this he is
justified.   It must have been because they were thought inferior, rather
than because they were thought to be even or unlimited, that the left
side and the female sex, at least, were put into the second column;
the inference seems to have been that because they were bad and the
bad was unlimited, they must be unlimited.

τετράγωνον ἑτερόμηκες. The connexion between the square, the odd, and the limited has been pointed out in l. 18 n. ἑτερομήκης is used primarily of a rectangle whose adjacent sides are of unequal length. From figures it was transferred to numbers; here it would naturally mean a number having unequal factors. Plato uses both this word and προμήκης more widely (*Theaet.* 148 A) of all numbers other than squares; the later Pythagoreans distinguished them. Nicomachus (*Arithm.* ii. 17) defines the former as having one factor greater than the other by 1, the latter as having one factor greater than the other by more than 1.

27. Alcmaeon is commonly described as a Pythagorean (Diog. Laert. viii. 83, Iambl. *Vit. Pyth.* 104, 267), and he certainly dedicated his book to eminent Pythagoreans (fr. 1). Aristotle does not class him as an ordinary Pythagorean, because in the regions of physiology and medicine he was a decidedly original thinker.

29. ἐγένετο τὴν ἡλικίαν, ἐπὶ γέροντι Πυθαγόρᾳ, and δέ are omitted by A^b, and there is no trace of them in Al.; they are probably a later addition, though the statement is likely enough to be true (cf. Iambl. *Vit. Pyth.* 104). The suspiciousness of the words is increased by the fact that Aristotle only once elsewhere mentions Pythagoras, and nowhere claims any knowledge of his date. Cf. 985^b 23 n.

31. This declaration of the twofoldness of 'most human things' was made by Alcmaeon the basis of a theory according to which ἰσονομία of the δυνάμεις wet and dry, cold and hot, sweet and bitter, &c., was the source of health, and μοναρχία the source of disease (fr. 4)—a view which influenced greatly the later Pythagoreans.

^b **2.** τούτων, the Pythagoreans mentioned in ^a 22-26, and Alcmaeon.

4. τῶν ἑτέρων, the Pythagoreans in question.

6. τὰ στοιχεῖα must be the ἀρχαί referred to in l. 3, i.e. not the numbers but the principles contained in the columns of opposites. Though Aristotle here treats both limit and the unlimited as material causes, in 988^a 26 he treats only the latter as the material cause. I.e., though the Pythagoreans treated things as being made of (πεπλάσθαι ἐκ) limit and the unlimited as if these were both in the same sense elements of things, yet limit from its very nature is not a material element but a regulative principle, a foreshadowing of Aristotle's own 'form' as the unlimited is of 'matter'. In ^a 17 we have already seen that Aristotle ascribes to the Pythagoreans an obscure recognition of the formal principle.

8. τῶν . . . πλείω λεγόντων τὰ στοιχεῖα. Aristotle refers to the thinkers discussed from 984^a 8 onwards, grouping Empedocles, Anaxagoras, the Atomists, and the Pythagoreans together as pluralists.

12. τοῦ κατὰ τὴν φύσιν cannot mean 'in respect of naturalness', which, besides not being in point here, would be τοῦ κατὰ φύσιν. It must mean 'in respect of conformity to the nature of the sensible world'. This was just the point in which the Eleatics, who denied the existence of plurality and change, were lacking; cf. the description of them as ἀφύσικοι which Sextus Empiricus ascribes to Aristotle

(*Adv. Math.* x. 46). Parmenides, however, according to Aristotle, paid more attention to the nature of things than Melissus did (cf. l. 31).

εἰς μὲν οὖν τὴν νῦν σκέψιν κτλ. The inquiry about the Eleatics is foreign to Aristotle's purpose because they denied the existence of plurality, and without plurality the notion of a cause is unmeaning. Cf. *Phys.* 184ᵇ 25—185ᵃ 4.

19. τοῦ κατὰ τὸν λόγον ἑνός. Aristotle's reason for this statement may be seen from the opposition between κατὰ τὸν λόγον and κατὰ τὴν αἴσθησιν in l. 32. He conceives of the first part of Parmenides' poem as stating what we have to think about the world (ἐξ ἀνάγκης ... οἴεται l. 29), the second part as stating what sensation tells us about it. In this he is influenced no doubt by the repeated identification, in the first part, of what can be thought with what is (fr. 5, 6. 1, 8. 34–36). Similarly in *Phys.* 185ᵇ 7, arguing against the Eleatics, he points out that when they say all things are one they may mean by 'one' either 'continuous' or 'indivisible' or 'having the same definition', like μέθυ and οἶνος. Parmenides is presumed to use 'one' in the third sense. His argument is ὅτι πάντα ἕν, εἰ τὸ ὂν ἓν σημαίνει (187ᵃ 1). l. e. all things share the definition of being and therefore are one in definition, κατὰ τὸν λόγον. This seems to describe Parmenides' method of argument correctly; but as regards result he does not mean merely that what is is embraced under one common definition. He means that it is ἓν κατὰ τὴν ὕλην, one solid material whole; the denial of 'that which is not' is, among other things, the denial of a void.

20. τοῦ κατὰ τὴν ὕλην. Simpl. *Phys.* 87. 6, 110. 1 argues that Melissus denied the corporeality of the real, but this is a misinterpretation of the words preserved in fr. 9, which are really part of a refutation of the Pythagorean plurality of reals (Zeller, i.⁶ 770 n. 2, Burnet, § 169). The one, which Melissus declares to be 'infinite in magnitude' (fr. 3), is clearly something material.

ὁ μὲν πεπερασμένον. Cf. Parm. fr. 8. 3², 33, 4², 43.

ὁ δ' ἄπειρόν. Cf. Mel. fr. 3.

21. πρῶτος. Plato's remark (*Soph.* 242 D) that 'the Eleatic school began with Xenophanes *and still earlier*' is not to be taken very literally. He only means that something like Eleatic views might be found occasionally expressed in the old poets; he says the same of the views of Heraclitus (*Theaet.* 179 E). Even his treatment of Xenophanes as a founder of the school is probably not very seriously meant. Xenophanes was a religious teacher rather than a philosopher. Cf. 983ᵇ 27 n.

21-23. ἑνίσας ... διεσαφήνισεν. No other instance of ἑνίζειν is quoted, and no other instance of διασαφηνίζειν in Aristotle. ἑνίζειν is a natural enough coinage on the analogy of μηδίζειν, &c., and means 'to become a partisan of the One'. Cf. Pl. *Theaet.* 181 A 6 τοῦ ὅλου στασιῶται (quoted by Burnet, § 61 n.). διασαφηνίζειν, though not found elsewhere in Aristotle, is found in Xenophon.

22. τούτου λέγεται γενέσθαι μαθητής. The life of Xenophanes may probably be dated approximately at 565–475. Whether we date the birth of Parmenides about 540, or about 514 (Burnet, § 84), it is quite possible that he may have been a pupil of Xenophanes. But Aristotle speaks with hesitation, and there is no independent confirmation of his words, which may be based merely on Pl. *Soph.* 242 D. Xenophanes may have visited Elea, the home of Parmenides, but it is unlikely that he founded a school there (Burnet, § 55). Parmenides' early associations were Pythagorean (Burnet, § 84).

οὐθὲν διεσαφήνισεν. Asclepius, Ueberweg (*Philol.* 26. 709), Zeller (i.⁶ 631 n.), and Burnet (§ 60) take this to mean that Xenophanes did not pronounce in favour either of a finite or of an infinite world. But in *De Caelo* 294ᵃ 23 Aristotle tells us that Xenophanes said the earth was 'rooted to infinity', and quotes a verse of Empedocles in which he attacks those who believed in boundless depths of earth and heights of air. Aristotle's words here probably refer not to the question whether the world is finite, which was mentioned only parenthetically, but to the general question in which Aristotle is mainly interested, the question what sort of cause the Eleatics recognized. οὐθὲν διασαφήνισεν is in fact explained by the words that immediately follow.

23. τῆς φύσεως τούτων οὐδετέρας, 'the nature of either of these causes'. With τούτων we must understand τῶν ἀρχῶν or τῶν αἰτιῶν (ll. 3, 5). The two causes are, of course, the λόγος and ὕλη referred to in ll. 19, 20.

24. οὐρανόν is here used in the last of the three senses distinguished in *De Caelo* 278ᵇ 9–21, i. e. 'the material universe'.

ἀποβλέψας, 'with a view to'. The word has in Aristotle lost its literal meaning.

τὸ ἓν εἶναί φησι τὸν θεόν, 'he says that the One (i. e. the universe) is the God' (i. e. the only God, in opposition to the many gods of the poets). Cf. fr. 23.

27. ἀγροικότεροι. Elsewhere Aristotle calls Melissus' line of argument ἐριστικός, ἀσυλλόγιστος, φορτικός (*Phys.* 185ᵃ 8, 10, 186ᵃ 8, 9). Aristotle thinks meanly of Melissus (1) because he substituted material unity for the conceptual unity recognized by Parmenides (but on this cf. l. 19 n.), (2) because of certain alleged defects in an argument in which Aristotle supposes him to be trying to establish the spatial infinity of the world (*Soph. El.* 167ᵇ 12–20; but on these arguments cf. Burnet, § 166). For a defence of Melissus cf. Offner, in *Archiv für Gesch. der Phil.* iv. 12–33.

28. μᾶλλον βλέπων. Parmenides is similarly ranked higher than Melissus in *Phys.* 185ᵃ 10, 186ᵃ 8, Pl. *Theaet.* 183 E.

30. Cf. *Phys.* i. 3. Parmenides' mistake, Aristotle points out, was that while he only proved that there is one single term which includes everything that is, viz. ὄν, he thought he was proving that there is only one thing, the truth being that the one term ὄν is applicable to many things.

31. Cf. 984ᵇ 4 n.

τὸ ἔν. In view of ll. 14, 29 and Al. 45. 3 there is much to be said for Christ's proposal of τὸ ὃν ἕν. Or perhaps τό should be excised.

34. οἷον . . . λέγων. Cf. 984ᵇ 3–4.

987ᵃ 2. Aristotle now sums up what he has said from 983ᵇ 6 onwards.

4–9. The construction here is somewhat confused. It is not clear whether the accusatives in ll. 4–6 are governed by παρειλήφαμεν or by τιθέντων. The general structure of the sentence leads us to expect accusatives epexegetic of ταῦτα as παρὰ τῶν πρώτων . . . παρά τινων is epexegetic of παρὰ τῶν συνηδρευκότων. Yet to take the accusatives in ll. 4–6 as governed by παρειλήφαμεν involves (1) taking σωματικὴν τὴν ἀρχήν to mean ' we have received the principle bodily ', i. e. we have received it stated as something bodily ; (2) supplying παρά before τῶν μέν and τῶν δέ; and (3) taking ἀμφοτέρων . . . τιθέντων as a genitive absolute—all of which are rather awkward. It seems, then, that the accusatives in ll. 4–6 are governed by τιθέντων, and that this construction has taken the place of an epexegetic object of παρειλήφαμεν such as Aristotle meant to have proceeded to. This originally intended construction appears however in l. 9, where ταύτην can only be the object of παρειλήφαμεν. Christ thinks that this construction prevails in the whole latter part of the sentence (ll. 7–9), and excises τιθέντων in l. 8 as an emblema from l. 7. This would be attractive if it made the sentence a good one, but it leaves the difficulty of the first part untouched ; considering the general confusion of two constructions which the sentence shows, τιθέντων in l. 8 is not surprising.

5. τῶν μέν, i. e. Thales, Hippo, Anaximenes, Diogenes, Hippasus, Heraclitus (984ᵃ 2–8), Melissus (986ᵇ 19).

τῶν δέ, i. e. Leucippus and Democritus (985ᵇ 4–20), though τῶν πρώτων (987ᵃ 4) does not apply very well to these.

9. τῶν μέν, i. e. Parmenides (984ᵇ 3), Anaxagoras (984ᵇ 15–22).

τῶν δέ, i. e. Empedocles (985ᵃ 2–10).

10. τῶν Ἰταλικῶν, the Pythagoreans. Cf. 987ᵃ 31, 988ᵃ 26, *Meteor.* 342ᵇ 29, and οἱ περὶ τὴν Ἰταλίαν *De Caelo* 293ᵃ 20. Pythagoras came from Samos but founded his society at Croton, and soon had disciples in many of the cities of Magna Graecia. The society at Croton was broken up and the members who remained in Italy established themselves at Rhegium. Most of them gradually migrated to Greece, but towards the end of the fifth century many returned, and in the fourth century the school was re-established at Tarentum. There were, however, important settlements of Pythagoreans in Greece, at Thebes and at Phlius.

μορυχώτερον. The MSS. and the Greek commentators give here a large number of variants, which are best explained as attempts to interpret the *hapax legomenon* μορυχώτερον, which is recorded by Alexander as a variant. μαλακώτερον (Aᵇ γρ. E) and μετριώτερον (E) have probably found their way into the MSS. from Alexander's and Asclepius' paraphrases. Alexander gives σκοτεινότερον and μαλακώτερον

as alternative interpretations of μορυχώτερον; the former is probably the
real meaning. Diels (*Hermes*, xl. 301–306) has thrown much light on
the word. It is probably akin to μοριφόν, which Hesychius interprets
as σκοτεινόν, μέλαν, and to ἀμυδρῶς, ἀμαυρῶς, which occur in similar
contexts, 985ᵃ 13, 988ᵃ 23, 993ᵃ 13. μορύσσειν occurs in Hom. *Od.*
xiii. 435, and is explained as = μολύνειν, 'to soil'. Μόρυχος occurs
as a name of Dionysus, and as a personal name both in Athens and
in Syracuse.

13. δύο μὲν τὰς ἀρχὰς κατὰ τὸν αὐτὸν . . . τρόπον looks at first sight
as if it should be interpreted, in the light of δυοῖν αἰτίαιν τυγχάνουσι
κεχρημένοι (l. 11), as the material and the efficient cause. But
recognition of the efficient cause is nowhere else attributed to the
Pythagoreans. It is distinctly implied in one passage (990ᵃ 8–12)
that they did not recognize it. Aristotle might have treated their
'unlimited' as a material, their 'limit' as an efficient cause, but
he does not do so. He treats the numbers, and the elements of
numbers—limit and the unlimited—alike as material causes (986ᵇ 6).
Nor can Aristotle mean, as Alexander suggests (47. 5), that the
Pythagoreans recognised two material causes, the limit and the
unlimited; for he has not referred in this summary to any other
thinkers as recognizing two material causes, so that κατὰ τὸν αὐτὸν
τρόπον would be out of place. We must suppose, then, that κατὰ τὸν
αὐτὸν τρόπον means that like 'the others' (l. 11)—Parmenides, Anaxagoras, and Empedocles—they stated two causes, and like them stated
these obscurely. But while the others had recognized the material
and the efficient causes, the Pythagoreans recognized the material and
the formal. Aristotle then comments first (ll. 15–19) on their treatment of the material cause, and next (ll. 20–27) on their treatment of
the formal. We have already interpreted 986ᵃ 17 as ascribing some
recognition of the formal cause to the Pythagoreans.

18. τὸ ἕν is used here as synonymous with τὸ πεπερασμένον in l. 15.
Cf. N. 1091ᵃ 14–18. καὶ τὸ ἕν in l. 16 seems to have been mistakenly
added by a copyist who looked forward to l. 18.

22. Aristotle has, as τε implies, two complaints against the
Pythagoreans. First, they defined superficially. E. g. they defined
justice as τὸ ἀντιπεπονθὸς ἄλλῳ, a definition which (*E. N.* 1132ᵇ 23)
does not answer to the nature of justice. Secondly, they asked what
is the first thing of which you can predicate ἀντιπεπονθός, and, since
they thought numbers the simplest, most intelligible things in the
world, they answered that it must be a number. The first number that
is ἀντιπεπονθός, i. e. the first product of two factors that treat each other
in the same way, is 4. Therefore, they said, 4 is the ἀντιπεπονθός.
I. e. they reason that because 4 is the first ἀντιπεπονθός therefore it is *the*
ἀντιπεπονθός. Thus they are wrong both in saying that the ἀντιπεπονθός is justice and in saying that 4 is the ἀντιπεπονθός.

26. ἴσως *non dubitantis est, sed cum modestia quadam asseverantis*,
Bz. *Ind.* 347ᵇ 33. Cf. α. 995ᵃ 17, Γ. 1005ᵃ 6, 10, Δ. 1015ᵇ 33,
E. 1026ᵃ 15.

27. πολλὰ τὸ ἓν ἔσται. Alexander gives alternative interpretations,
(1) that friendship, for instance, will be each of several numbers
of which the definition of friendship (e. g. τὸ ἰσάκις ἴσον) is predicable,
(2) that a number will be each of several things whose definition is predicable of it. Bonitz thinks that both of these points are implied. But,
as Aristotle has said only that the *first* number of which a definition
was true was identified with the thing defined, the second must be the
true interpretation.

ὃ κἀκείνοις συνέβαινεν. E. g. 1 was both the point and reason,
4 was justice and the solid, 2 was opinion and daring. Cf. 985ᵇ 29, 30.

28. τῶν πρότερον καὶ τῶν ἄλλων, the earlier and the later of the
thinkers before Plato. Jaeger brackets καὶ τῶν ἄλλων, treating τῶν
ἄλλων as a variant reading for τῶν πρότερον; but this is unnecessary.

Plato (ch. 6).

987ᵃ 29. Plato's system has some features that distinguish it from
that of the Pythagoreans. (1) He was familiar from youth with the
Heraclitean doctrines of Cratylus, that sensible things are in a constant
flux and that there is no knowledge of them. These views he never
abandoned, but

ᵇ**1.** (2) when Socrates, instead of studying the physical universe,
tried to find the universal in morals and fixed attention for the first
time on definitions, Plato accepted his procedure, and thought that
definition must be of non-sensibles because sensibles were always
changing.

7. These non-sensibles he called Forms; sensibles were called after
them, and existed by participation in them. Only the name 'participation' was new; the Pythagoreans had already said that things
exist by 'imitation' of numbers. But they neglected to discuss the
nature of this relation of things to the Forms.

14. Further, he recognizes mathematical objects as existing between
sensibles and Forms, differing from sensibles by being eternal and
unchangeable, from Forms by there being many of the same kind.

18. He thought the elements of Forms were the elements of all
things, 'the great and the small' being the material, 'the one' the
formal cause; the numbers were made out of the great and the small
by participation in the one.

22. He agreed with the Pythagoreans (1) in considering unity a
substance and not an attribute, (2) in making numbers the causes of
the essence of everything else; he differed from them (1) in treating
the indefinite as a dyad, composed of the great and small, (2) in

treating the numbers as existing apart from sensibles, (3) in treating
mathematical objects as an intermediate class.

29. The separation of the one and the numbers from things and
the introduction of the Forms were due to his studies in dialectic, of
which the Pythagoreans were innocent ; the treatment of the material
cause as a dyad was due to the possibility of generating the primary
numbers neatly from a dyad as out of a plastic material.

988ᵃ 1. Yet this is contrary to the facts. These thinkers derive
plurality from matter and make the form generate once only ; but
(*a*) only one table is made out of one piece of matter, and the man who
imposes the form, though he is one, produces the many tables, and
(*b*) the female is impregnated by a single copulation, while the male
impregnates many females ; yet these are analogous to matter and form.

7. Plato, then, has used only the material and the formal cause ;
the Forms are the formal cause of other things, and ' the one ' of the
Forms, while in both cases the matter is the great and the small.

14. Further, he has made his two elements the cause of good and
evil respectively, as Empedocles and Anaxagoras did.

987ᵃ 30. τούτοις, 31 τῶν Ἰταλικῶν, i.e. the Pythagoreans (cf. 987ᵃ 10,
988ᵃ 26).

30. ἀκολουθοῦσα. It is doubtful whether this means that Plato's
system was based on the Pythagorean, or merely that it resembled it.
The word can have the latter meaning (cf. *Poet.* 1449ᵇ 9 ἡ μὲν οὖν
ἐποποιία τῇ τραγῳδίᾳ ... ἠκολούθησεν), but Aristotle evidently wishes
to assert more than a casual resemblance between Pythagoreanism
and Platonism, though he describes Cratylus and Socrates as the
persons who chiefly influenced Plato.

32–ᵇ 8. This passage should be compared with M. 1078ᵇ 12–32,
which gives more detail. The passage in M is immediately followed by
another, 1078ᵇ 34—1080ᵃ 8, which (with the exception of 1079ᵇ 3–11)
reappears almost word for word in A. 990ʰ 2—991ᵇ 9. The main
difference between 987ᵃ 32–ᵇ 8 and the parallel passage in M is the
fact that Plato is not mentioned in the latter. This is in accordance
with the general method of MN ; Plato is only once mentioned in
these books (M. 1083ᵃ 32), and Speusippus and Xenocrates are not
mentioned at all, though all three are under discussion throughout.

The priority of A can be deduced with fair certainty from a comparison of 990ʰ 2—991ᵇ 9 with the parallel passage in M ; and this
conclusion is confirmed by the fact that while B refers back to A
(995ᵇ 5, 996ʰ 8, 14, 997ʰ 4) and M to B (1076ᵃ 39, ʰ 39, 1086ᵃ 34 (?),
ᵇ 15), A never refers back to B nor B to M.

32. ἐκ νέου τε γάρ κτλ. The reference to Cratylus and Socrates is
made in defence of the immediately preceding statement that Plato's
philosophy differed in certain respects from the Pythagorean. I. e.,

Aristotle, at any rate, views Socrates as standing outside of the Pythagorean school and exercising an independent influence on Plato. συνήθης γενόμενος πρῶτον Κρατύλῳ. Aristotle's statement must be accepted in preference to that of Diogenes (iii. 6) and Olympiodorus (*Vit. Plat.* p. 2. 49 Westermann) that Plato became Cratylus' disciple only after the death of Socrates. If Diogenes' statement, that Plato was twenty when he first was taught by Socrates, is to be believed, there was plenty of time before this for him to study under Cratylus. (Prof. Burnet argues that 'the nephew of Charmides must have known Socrates ever since he could remember'; Diogenes' remark, γεγονὼς εἴκοσιν ἔτη διήκουσε Σωκράτους, 'he went through a course of Socrates' conversation', is quite compatible with this.) Diogenes may have been misled by two remarks in the *Cratylus* which imply that Cratylus was considerably younger than Socrates (429 D, 440 D).

Plato studied under Cratylus at Athens, but the vivid and contemptuous picture which he gives (*Theaet.* 179 D—180 D) of the Heraclitean school depicts it as still, in 399 B.C., located at Ephesus. The *Cratylus* indicates no great respect for its efforts in the field of etymology.

For the philosophical views of Cratylus cf. Γ. 1010ᵃ 12, and for Cratylus generally cf. Jackson in *Cambridge Praelections*, 1906, 1–26.

33. ἁπάντων τῶν αἰσθητῶν. The distinction of sensibles and intelligibles was unknown to Heraclitus. If he thought there was no knowledge of sensibles, this does not mean either that he was a complete sceptic or that he thought there was knowledge of intelligibles. What he thought was that appearances were illusory and that the reality of things was the πῦρ ἀείζωον, which was a material thing though it was not perceived by *our* senses.

ᵇ**2.** περὶ δὲ τῆς ὅλης φύσεως οὐθέν. Cf. M. 1078ᵇ 17, *De Part. An.* 642ᵃ 28, Xen. *Mem.* i. 1. 11, iv. 7. 2–8. Socrates says, in Pl. *Apol.* 19 C, 26 D, that he had no more than the ordinary man's knowledge of physical science. Xenophon represents him as interested in nature only in so far as it contributed to human uses, and as valuing the teleological study of it only in so far as it promoted piety (*Mem.* i. 4, iv. 3). The statements of the Platonic Socrates might be regarded as instances of his 'irony', and Xenophon's statements may be to some extent discounted as being in the direct line of his apologetic; but Aristotle is hardly likely to have been mistaken on the point. And Plato's account in the *Phaedo* (96 A) represents Socrates as having abandoned physical science as quite a young man. Cf. Zeller, ii. 1. 132–141.

4. πρώτου. The Pythagoreans had already 'begun to define', but their efforts had been superficial (ᵃ 26–27).

διὰ τὸ τοιοῦτον. Bonitz interprets this as *propter insitas et fixas animo Heracliteas opiniones*. As Apelt points out, a nearer reference may be found for the words in the clause beginning ἀδύνατον γάρ. Similar instances of τοιοῦτον referring forward and being taken up by γάρ are found in B. 998ᵃ 10, E. 1026ᵇ 22, *De An.* 408ᵇ 1.

8. ἰδέας προσηγόρευσε. For the history of the words ἰδέα, εἶδος cf.

Taylor, *Varia Socratica*, 178–267, and for a criticism of his views cf. Gillespie in *Classical Quarterly*, vi. 179–203. It may be noted that Aristotle in speaking of Plato, just like Plato himself, uses both words without distinction.

I find myself in agreement with the conclusions of Prof. Gillespie, viz. ' that in the time of Socrates the words εἶδος and ἰδέα show two trends of meaning in the general vocabulary of science. The first is mainly physical, but without mathematical associations : including many gradations of meaning from the popular to the technical : the *form* of a bodily object—occasionally used for the bodily object itself, like our own words "form" and "shape", but always distinct from σῶμα : sometimes the outer visible form or *shape* : often the inner form, the structure, nature, φύσις, a specially physical conception : often extended to the nature of objects other than bodily : in one treatise of rhetorical character passing, by an easy transition, nearly, if not quite, into the metaphysical notion of essence. The second is semi-logical, classificatory ; used especially in such contexts as "there are four forms, kinds" of anything, whether a substance like the "moist" or a disease or what not ... In this line of development the later meaning of *species* is but a single step further. Prof. Taylor seems to have made out a case for the employment of εἶδος in the Pythagorean mathematics in the sense of geometrical "pattern" or "figure". But there is no evidence whatsoever to show that this highly specialized meaning was a determining factor in the other developments ; it seems to have been a collateral growth.' The meanings of the two words in Plato ' show much greater affinity to the current scientific usage in both its tendencies than to the specialized mathematical meaning'. Thus the linguistic evidence ' bears out the statement of Aristotle (*Metaph.* i. 987ᵃ 31 sqq.) that the Platonic εἴδη were derived from another source than Pythagoreanism'. Prof. Gillespie thinks that the key to Plato's use of the words is to be found in *Crat.* 386 ε sqq. 'In this passage we have two formulae equated with each other. The first, αὐτὸ ὃ ἔστι κερκίς, represents the object of defining thought as opposed to the object of sense ... : it can be easily shown to have arisen from the dialectical question τί ἐστιν ; in this aspect the "idea" is derived from τὴν ἐν τοῖς λόγοις ... σκέψιν, as Aristotle puts it (ibid. 987ᵇ 31). The second formula, τὸ τῆς κερκίδος εἶδος, uses εἶδος in the sense of nature, form, φύσις (a frequent synonym for it in the *Cratylus*), thus bringing it into close connexion with the scientific conception of εἶδος as form. We may perhaps express the difference thus : the "idea" is αὐτὸ ὃ ἔστιν ἕκαστον or οὐσία primarily in its *epistemological* and *ontological* aspects, εἶδος primarily in its *scientific* aspect as cause of the particulars, conceived on the analogy of causation in the arts. Thus the name εἶδος has nothing to do with the doctrine that the ideas are numbers, a doctrine which Aristotle, our only authority for it, always treats as concerned with the relation of the ideas to their elements.'

τὰ δ᾽ αἰσθητὰ παρὰ ταῦτα κτλ. Prof. Burnet, *G. P.* § 233, remarks that Aristotle ' here insists rather on the distinction of sensible things from the forms than on that of the forms from sensible things, and he implies that this is what distinguished Plato from Socrates. We have seen reason already for believing that Socrates recognized no reality in sensible things apart from the forms, and Aristotle's language here confirms this view.' The question whether Socrates had a full-blown theory of Ideas is too large a question to be dealt with here, but Aristotle's evidence is not in favour of that view. It is Plato who is here said to have called the non-sensible objects of definition Ideas, and in the parallel passage in Book M Socrates is represented as having only prepared the way for the ideal theory by attempting to reach universal definitions, and as not having taken the further step of attributing separate existence to universals and calling them Ideas— a step which 'the others' (i. e. Plato) took (1078ᵇ 30). It is clear that in that passage it is the substantial existence of universals, not that of sensibles, that Plato in distinction from Socrates is said to have believed in. The occasions on which Aristotle connects the ideal theory with any name are surprisingly rare, but in them all it is Plato and not Socrates that is mentioned (i. e. apart from this chapter, in Z. 1028ᵇ 19, Λ. 1070ᵃ 18, *Phys.* 203ᵃ 8, 209ᵇ 33).

Apart from the general question it may be doubted whether the current interpretation of παρὰ ταῦτα as 'apart from the Ideas' is the right one. It involves the supplying of εἶναι after παρὰ ταῦτα. This, however, is difficult; it is more natural to take λέγεσθαι with παρὰ ταῦτα as well as with κατὰ ταῦτα, and to translate 'and he said the sensibles were called after these and were called what they were called by virtue of their relation to these'. For this sense of παρά cf. *E. E.* 1228ᵃ 35 ὁ γὰρ θρασὺς παρὰ τὸ θράσος λέγεται παρωνύμως, Pl. *Crat.* 399 A πολλάκις ἐπεμβάλλομεν γράμματα, τὰ δ' ἐξαιροῦμεν, παρ' ὃ βουλό-μεθα ὀνομάζοντες. It is the sense implied in the common Aristotelian word παρώνυμος.

9. πάντα. Λ. 1070ᵃ 18 ὁ Πλάτων ἔφη ὅτι εἴδη ἐστιν ὁπόσα φύσει is commonly interpreted to mean that Plato recognized Ideas only of natural as opposed to artificial objects, and if that interpretation be right the passage conflicts with the present one. Plainly, however, all that that passage tells us is that Plato said there *were* Ideas of all *natural* objects. In any case the statement here is true of the ideal theory as we find it in the *Republic*, where we are told that there is an Idea answering to every group of things (596 A), and where we read of Ideas of bed and table (596B, 597B; cf. the Idea of shuttle, *Crat.* 389B).

κατὰ μέθεξιν γὰρ εἶναι τὰ πολλὰ ὁμώνυμα τοῖς εἴδεσιν. If we keep the reading of Aᵇ and Al., two interpretations may be suggested: (1) 'Most of the things that have the same name and nature as the Forms exist by participation in them' (Al. 50. 24). But on the Platonic view *all* the things that are συνώνυμα with the Forms exist by participation in them. The things of which there were no Forms, if there were any such, were no exception to this rule, and this inter-pretation must therefore be rejected. (2) 'The many particulars, which are συνώνυμα with the Forms, exist by participation in them'

(Al. 51. 6, Bonitz 90. 3). But such a definitive use of the genitive appears impossible. Three other readings suggest themselves. (1) We might with E read τῶν συνωνύμων ὁμώνυμα τοῖς εἴδεσιν, 'most of the things that have the same name and nature have the same name as the Forms by virtue of participation in them',—most, not all, because some συνώνυμα have no Forms answering to them (990ᵇ 10–17). But Aristotle has in the previous clause said that according to Plato *all* sensibles get their names from the Forms; and immediately afterwards he says quite generally that according to Plato all things exist by participation in Forms (l. 12). He is ignoring, then, the later view of some Platonists (and possibly of Plato) that some sensibles had no Forms answering to them. Alternatively, (2) we might excise τοῖς εἴδεσιν, as Prof. Gillespie has proposed (*J. of P.* xxxiv. 151), and translate 'the many (sensibles) exist by participation in their συνώνυμα' the Forms. In 990ᵇ 6, 991ᵃ 6, where Aristotle is *criticizing* the ideal theory, he calls the Form ὁμώνυμον, implying that it has no real common nature with the particulars (for the difference between ὁμώνυμον and συνώνυμον cf. *Cat.* 1ᵃ 1, 6); it might be supposed that here, where he is *stating* the theory, he has no objection to using the word which implies the common nature that Plato thought there was (cf. I. 1059ᵃ 13). Plato has only the word ὁμώνυμον, which he uses without drawing the distinction which Aristotle draws between the two words (*Parm.* 133 D), and the insertion of ὁμώνυμα in some MSS. might be due to a reminiscence of this. But the most satisfactory solution is to adopt the text I have adopted, and to suppose τῶν συνωνύμων, introduced as a gloss by a copyist who took τὰ πολλά to mean 'the majority', to have driven out ὁμώνυμα in the text of Aᵇ.

10. τὴν δὲ μέθεξιν τοὔνομα μόνον μετέβαλεν. It is surprising that Aristotle should describe the change from μίμησις to μέθεξις as only verbal. The former term indicates that the Form and the particular are like one another, i. e. are two instances of the same kind of thing, which involves a profound misunderstanding of the relation between a universal and its particulars; while the latter term describes the relation in a way which if metaphorical is not misleading. It is clear, however, that Plato did not draw any such clear distinction between the two terms, while Aristotle, convinced as he was that Plato illegitimately 'separated' the Form from the particulars, thought that he could not have believed in a relation of genuine immanence between them, and must therefore have meant by 'participation' nothing other than 'imitation'.

Profs. Burnet and Taylor have recently argued that the ideal theory was no discovery of Plato's, but was already familiar to Socrates, and, possibly through Socratic influence, to a whole body of Pythagoreans. In the *Phaedo* (74 A ff.) the theory that equal things are imitations of the 'equal itself' is familiar to the Pythagorean Simmias. Three out of the seven speakers in the dialogue are Pythagoreans. The Ideas are represented as 'something we are always talking about' (76 D). Phrases like αὐτὸ ὃ ἔστι, αὐτὸ καθ' αὑτό are treated as well known (e. g. in 75 D).

Aristotle's evidence is against the view that Socrates held the ideal theory (cf. l. 8 n., M. 1078ᵇ 11 n.), but the extent of the affinity which he recognizes, here and in ᵃ 30, between Pythagoreanism and the ideal theory, has not been sufficiently emphasized by historians of philosophy. Socrates has commonly been regarded as the chief influence on Plato's philosophy; Aristotle evidently regards Plato as having owed more to the Pythagoreans, and may have thought that he owed as much to the Heracliteans (ᵃ 32–ᵇ 1). The dialogues are sufficient evidence that Socrates exercised a great influence on Plato, but the view that Plato took over from Socrates the ideal theory is in conflict with the two oldest authorities other than Plato himself, viz. Xenophon and Aristotle, and rests mainly on the hypothesis that the dialogues must be historically true. Some degree of historical verisimilitude there must no doubt be in a dialogue which introduces historical persons, but the amount of it that is necessary is very much a question of personal taste. It is possible to believe with Aristotle that Socrates had no 'ideal theory', and yet find nothing outrageous in Plato's dramatic presentation of him.

It is easy to see how the elaborate theory of ideal numbers, which plays so large a part in the Platonic system as described by Aristotle, should have led him to describe Plato's system as 'for the most part following the Pythagoreans' (ᵃ 30); it is more surprising that the ideal theory itself should be described as differing only verbally from the Pythagorean doctrine. Aristotle sees that in principle Plato and the Pythagoreans alike broke with the earlier tradition and were trying to discover a non-sensible reality behind sensible things, the universal which is manifested in particulars but is different in kind from them. And he holds that the interest of both was metaphysical, while the main interest of Socrates was ethical.

11. For the description of the Pythagoreans as holding that things 'imitate' the numbers cf. 985ᵇ 33, Aristoxenus ap. Stob. *Ecl.* i. pr. 6 (p. 20. 5 Wachsmuth), and the letter attributed to the wife of Pythagoras in which she declares him to have said that things were made not of but according to number (ib. i. 10. 13). Cf. the description of number ascribed to the followers of Hippasus (Iambl. *in Nicom.*, p. 10. 20 Pistelli)—παράδειγμα πρῶτον κοσμοποιίας. Yet Aristotle elsewhere repeatedly ascribes the other view to the Pythagoreans (cf. 986ᵃ 17 n.). He does not mean that the Pythagoreans thought that things 'imitated' numbers which existed separately from the things (this, he thinks, is one of the differences between them and Plato, l. 27), but that they thought the external, sensible nature of things to be modelled on their inner, numerical nature. Cf. Burnet, *E. G. P.*, § 153. It is probable, however, that the sixth-century Pythagoreans treated things as 'imitating' number, i.e. as exhibiting numerical relations, while those of the fifth century treated number as the very stuff of which things are made. So F. M. Cornford in *Class. Quart.* xvi. 143.

12. Πλάτων δὲ μεθέξει. Prof. Jackson (*J. of P.* x. 294), holding that not numbers but Ideas play in the Platonic system the part that

numbers play in the Pythagorean, and that τῶν εἰδῶν must be connected with the Platonic term μέθεξις and not with the Pythagorean term μίμησις, omits τῶν εἰδῶν in l. 14 and inserts it after μεθέξει here.   He argues that though here Aristotle represents the relation of the particular to the number in the Pythagorean system as identical with the relation of the particular to the Idea in the Platonic, it does not follow that the Platonic number is identical with the Platonic Idea.   The remark is true, but the following considerations prove that in this chapter the Platonic Ideas and numbers are treated as identical :

(1) Mathematical objects are in l. 15 said to be intermediate between sensibles and Ideas, and in l. 28 to be intermediate between sensibles and numbers.

(2) In l. 18 the Forms, in l. 24 the numbers, are said to be the cause of all other things.

(3) *If* the MS. reading is right in l. 22, the Forms and the numbers are expressly identified there.   But, though on different grounds from his, I think Prof. Jackson right in rejecting the MS. reading.

(4) Prof. Jackson thinks that the numbers are the formal causes of the particulars, while the Ideas are the types of the particulars ; but in 988ᵃ 10 the Ideas are expressly said to be the formal causes of all other things, and his attempt (p. 291) to explain this away is not successful.   It is true that in 987ᵇ 29–31 Aristotle distinguishes τὸ τὸ ἓν καὶ τοὺς ἀριθμοὺς παρὰ τὰ πράγματα ποιῆσαι from ἡ τῶν εἰδῶν εἰσαγωγή.   But this does not mean that the numbers and the Ideas were different things.   The assigning of causal significance to numbers was common to the Pythagoreans and to Plato ; the conception of them as existing apart from things, and the introduction of Ideas (i. e. the treatment of them as Ideas, as universals and objects of definition, cf. l. 7) were the result of Plato's dialectical studies.   The Ideas were the same as the numbers, but ἡ τῶν εἰδῶν εἰσαγωγή lays stress on a fresh feature of Plato's originality.

Prof. Jackson's view is that the One is the formal element of the Ideas, the numbers the formal element of particulars, and he claims that the doctrine can be found not only here but in the *Philebus*.   But to this view the following considerations seem fatal :

(1) The view rests largely on the emphasis Prof. Jackson lays on the phrase (*Phil.* 24 C) αὐτό (τὸ ποσόν) τε καὶ τὸ μέτριον.   Emphasizing the τε, he insists that τὸ ποσόν and τὸ μέτριον must be two different things. τὸ ποσόν is what Aristotle calls the numbers ; it is any sort of determinateness the imposition of which on the indefinite produces definite particular entities, e.g. particular illnesses. τὸ μέτριον is what Aristotle calls the One ; it is that unique determinateness the imposition of which on the indefinite produces an Idea, e. g. the Idea of health. Both Ideas and particulars belong to the μικτόν (25 B), but while the components of the Idea are the indefinite and the μέτριον (the One), the components of the particulars are the indefinite and the ποσόν (the numbers).

This is not the place to embark on a detailed discussion of the metaphysics of the *Philebus*, but the following remarks may be made :

It is true that earlier (15 A–C) Plato has propounded the relation of the Idea to its particulars as a problem requiring discussion, and that a definite answer would be given to this problem if we viewed the Idea not as an element in the particulars but as standing outside them, being composed of elements analogous to those of which they are composed, and being a type which they more or less closely resemble. But it cannot be said that the passage 23 C–27 C in any degree works out this suggestion, or that the functions of τὸ ποσόν and of τὸ μέτριον are really distinguished. On Prof. Jackson's theory, for example, particular diseases or instances of bad weather should be composites more or less closely resembling those other composites, the Idea of health and the Idea of good weather; but in point of fact they are treated as indefinites out of which by the imposition of limit health and good weather are produced (25 E, 26 A). It is in fact impossible to find any clear relation between the metaphysics of the *Philebus* and the ideal theory. Plato is working out a new analysis of reality without troubling himself about its relation to his old analysis. Further, the implications which Prof. Jackson finds in the new analysis, (*a*) that the relation of particulars to Ideas must henceforth be described by Plato as imitation and not as participation, and (*b*) that all Ideas save those that are natural types must be abandoned, are not accepted by Plato in the later dialogues. On (*a*) cf. Prof. Taylor in *Mind*, v. 307–311, 320–322, and on (*b*) ib. 304, 305, 313–315, and my notes on 990ᵇ 13, 14, 16, 991ᵇ 6. It is worth noting that 987ᵇ 9–13 indicate that Aristotle at least was not aware of an earlier period in which Plato spoke of participation and a later in which he spoke of imitation.

(2) Nor does Aristotle's positive account of the theory agree with Prof. Jackson's. In this chapter, as we have seen, the Ideas are identified with the numbers, i. e. with the ideal as distinguished from the mathematical numbers; and for this cf. 991ᵇ 9, M. 1080ᵇ 12, 1081ᵃ 21, 1086ᵃ 12, N. 1090ᵃ 16, ᵇ 33, 1091ᵇ 26. The numbers are said to be outside the particulars (ll. 27, 30), while Prof. Jackson holds that they are the formal element in them.—For a criticism of Prof. Jackson's theory cf. Zeller in *Sitzb. der Berl. Akad.* 1887, 197–220.

It is clear, then, that τῶν εἰδῶν is not needed with μεθέξει. On the other hand it would be better away from l. 14. The statement there, as the plural ἀφεῖσαν shows, is meant to apply to the Pythagoreans as well as to Plato, and τῶν εἰδῶν is therefore out of place, though in view of Aristotle's frequent carelessness in such matters we cannot be sure that he did not write it. It seems more likely to be, as Prof. Gillespie suggests (*J. of P.* xxxiv. 152), a gloss like τοῖς εἴδεσιν in l. 10 and τὰ εἴδη in l. 22 than to have been transferred, as Prof. Jackson thinks, from l. 12.

14. ἀφεῖσαν ἐν κοινῷ ζητεῖν. Plato devotes a considerable part of the *Parmenides* to this problem, but no positive solution is left in possession and the question may fairly be said to be left open.

Aristotle's remark to some extent confirms the view that the *Philebus* does not bear directly on the relation of particulars to Ideas (cf. previous note).

According to the usage of ἀφιέναι, the phrase seems to mean 'they left before the world for discussion', rather than 'they omitted to discuss before the world'.

ἔτι δὲ παρὰ τὰ αἰσθητά κτλ. The doctrine of the 'intermediates' is again referred to in l. 28, 991ᵃ 4, ᵇ 29, 992ᵇ 16, B. 995ᵇ 17, 997ᵇ 2, 12, 998ᵃ 7, 1002ᵇ 13, 21, K. 1059ᵇ 6, Λ. 1069ᵃ 34, M. 1076ᵃ 19, 1077ᵃ 11, 1086ᵃ 12, N. 1090ᵇ 35, and is again ascribed to Plato by name in Z. 1028ᵇ 19. It is discussed by Zeller, ii. 1. 780–784, Robin, *Théorie Platonicienne des Idées et des Nombres*, §§ 100–106, 126–129, Cook Wilson in *C. R.* xviii. 248, 249, 251–253, 257–259, Adam, *Republic*, ii. 159–163.

Plato's theory must be distinguished from a Platonist theory, referred to in B. 998ᵃ 7, M. 1076ᵃ 33, which treats mathematical objects as entities intermediate between Ideas and sensibles but as existing in and not apart from the latter.

Among the intermediates were included not only numbers but also geometrical figures (991ᵇ 29, B. 997ᵇ 2). The ground of Plato's belief in mathematical objects as a distinct class of entities is indicated clearly enough in the present passage. An arithmetical statement such as that 2 and 2 makes 4 is not about the number 2 simply, for the number 2 evidently exists only in the singular, whereas the statement is about two 2's and cannot be stated without reference to them. On the other hand we are not thinking of any particular sensible pairs of things when we say that 2 and 2 makes 4. Hence, Plato thought, there must be 2's which are the objects of arithmetic, and are different from the number 2 and from sensible 2's. Similarly geometrical propositions imply the existence of triangles, &c., which are neither the universal of triangle, &c., nor sensible things having an approximately triangular shape.

The doctrine appears to be right with regard to the objects of geometry, and wrong with regard to those of arithmetic. The truths of arithmetic are true, without any qualification or hypothesis, of ordinary pairs of things ; if two X's are added to two X's, then, whatever X may be, four X's, neither more or less, are the sum. And there is no reason to suppose any special class of 2's, other than ordinary pairs of things, for the proposition to be true of. It may seem difficult to suppose that all the pairs of things in the world are what the statement is about, since it is clear that we do not think in detail of all the actual pairs. But it is equally clear that we do not think in detail of all the *mathematical* 2's, if such a class of things be supposed to exist, so that there is nothing to be gained by supposing them to exist. The statement ' 2 and 2 makes 4 ' is no more difficult in this respect than 'all men are mortal'; in the one we are judging about all the particular men in the world, without thinking of them in detail, and in the other we are judging similarly about all the particular pairs in the world. The propositions of geometry, on the

other hand, are not true directly of the approximately triangular
sensible objects in the world, for instance. They are statements
about triangles, and *these* are not triangles. Nor are they statements
about triangularity, though they imply truths about triangularity.
They are statements about pure spatial figures.

Aristotle rejects the 'intermediates' outright. He believes in
mathematical objects, but not as existing 'apart' from sensibles, but
as elements in their nature (M. 2, 3). The merits of his controversy
with Plato, like the merits of his attack on the ideal theory, depend on
the sense in which Plato ascribed 'separate' existence to the entities in
question. If Plato meant that the objects of mathematics are something different from universals and different from material things, then,
as far as geometry is concerned, he was right. If he meant that they
exist, or could exist, where there are no material objects, this amounts
to thinking that there is, or could be, empty space, and our view of his
doctrine will depend on our attitude towards this question. We have no
evidence sufficient to indicate which of the two things he meant ; only
it is clear that if he meant the former, he was badly misunderstood
or misrepresented by Aristotle. Neither of these is an impossible
hypothesis.

There has been much discussion of the question whether the doctrine
is to be found in any of Plato's dialogues. Syrianus (4. 16) connects
it with the Divided Line in the *Republic* (509 D—511 E); Alexander
and Asclepius do not refer to any dialogue. Aristotle refers this theory
distinctly to Plato and not, as he does many other doctrines, vaguely
to 'those who believe in the Forms'. But he is, of course, as likely
to be thinking of Plato's lectures or conversations as of his dialogues.
There are passages in more than one dialogue which, if taken strictly,
imply the existence of 'intermediates' of the sort here described.
Thus in *Phaedo* 74 c Plato speaks of αὐτὰ τὰ ἴσα, which he distinguishes
from sensible equals ; these, since they exist in the plural, cannot be
the Idea of equal. But he does not point out this latter difference ; he
is interested simply in distinguishing the Idea of equal from sensible
equals, and does not notice the third kind of entity which he has
incidentally mentioned. Again in *Rep.* 526 A he speaks of the ἕν
which is ἴσον ἕκαστον πᾶν παντί: he distinguishes it from sensible
single things and ought to, but does not, distinguish it from the Idea
of one. And in *Phil.* 56 E he speaks of μονάδα μονάδος ἑκάστης ... μηδεμίαν ἄλλην ἄλλης διαφέρουσαν, but distinguishes these true arithmetical
units only from sensible units and not from unity. Again, the
description of mathematical studies as leading the soul towards being
(*Rep.* 523 A, 525 A, C, 526 B, 527 B) seems to imply that mathematical
objects are not themselves in the full sense being. Yet the only
entities mentioned are the knowable Idea and the sensible particular.

In all these passages we seem to see Plato on the verge of
recognizing the intermediates as a separate class, but never doing so.
And probably the same must be said of the Divided Line. The logic
of the simile requires that the objects of διάνοια should be a distinct

class of entities, and not distinguished from those of νόησις as Ideas known in one way from the same Ideas known in another way ; and the doctrine of the intermediates would have enabled him to remedy this defect. Yet it seems impossible to say that the doctrine is actually stated in the passage. The *Republic* up to this point, like all the dialogues which probably belong to the same period, has divided the contents of the universe into Ideas, the objects of knowledge, and particulars, the objects of sense ; the natural thing is to suppose that Plato is here subdividing each of these into two parts. If, instead, he were setting up in the objects of διάνοια a class of intermediates, it would not be in his manner to introduce the new doctrine with so little indication of its novelty and so little attempt to indicate his meaning. Should we not have expected a reference to 'units' or 'triangles' in the plural, such as we find in the other passages quoted above, and a statement of the reason for believing in intermediates, such as Aristotle here gives? We find no such reference or statement, and we find the objects of διάνοια illustrated by τετράγωνον αὐτό, διάμετρος αὐτή (510 D). These phrases might stand for perfect particulars *as well as* for Ideas (though αὐτός is, of course, one of the commonest ways of referring to an Idea) ; they could not well be used of the former if it were essential to the argument to *distinguish* them from the latter. Further, the objects of διάνοια (including τὰ μαθηματικά) are said to be νοητά when studied in connexion with the first principle, the Idea of good (καίτοι νοητῶν ὄντων μετ᾽ ἀρχῆς, 511 D). It seems, then, that Plato does not state, as he had undertaken (509 D) to do, a difference between the objects of διάνοια and of νόησις ; his whole stress is on the difference between their methods. (Sir Thomas Heath has pointed out that in *Ep.* vii. 342 A–C, where Plato says that with regard to every ὄν (and the circle is taken as the chief example) five things are involved—the ὄνομα, the λόγος, the εἴδωλον (the three conditions of knowledge), the ἐπιστήμη, and the thing itself, there is no objective entity intermediate between the εἴδωλον (the painted or carved circle) and the circle itself.) But it is quite likely that reflection on the logical requirements of the simile led Plato very soon to formulate the doctrine of the intermediates. It may have been connected with the remoulding of the doctrine of the Divided Line into a classification of entities as either νοητά, ἐπιστητά, δοξαστά, or αἰσθητά (Simpl. on *De An.* 404ᵇ 18–21). There is one passage in which τὰ μαθηματικά (or rather τὰ γεωμετρικά) are recognized as a distinct class of entities, viz. *Tim.* 50 c, where τὰ εἰσιόντα καὶ ἐξιόντα are geometrical figures distinguished both from τὰ ἀεὶ ὄντα, the Ideas, of which they are μιμήματα, and from the sensible things produced by their entrance into the ἐκμαγεῖον, space.

19. τἀκείνων στοιχεῖα πάντων ᾠήθη τῶν ὄντων εἶναι στοιχεῖα. Aristotle states the doctrine more exactly in 988ᵃ 11. The elements of the Ideas were the One and the great and small ; the elements of sensible things were the Ideas and the great and small. Thus the elements of the Ideas together formed the formal element in sensibles, but these had also a material element akin to the material element in Ideas.

20. τὸ μέγα καὶ τὸ μικρόν. This way of describing the material principle is ascribed to Plato by name again in 988ᵃ 13, 26, *Phys.* 187ᵃ 17, 203ᵃ 15, 209ᵇ 35. Various synonymous expressions are found—τὸ ἄνισον, M. 1075ᵃ 33, N. 1087ᵇ 5, 10, 1088ᵇ 29, 1089ᵇ 6, 11, 1091ᵇ 31, 1092ᵇ 1, ἡ ἀνισότης, B. 1001ᵇ 23, τὸ ἄπειρον, 987ᵇ 26, *Phys.* 203ᵃ 5, τὰ ἄπειρα, *Phys.* 203ᵃ 15, 206ᵇ 28, τὸ μὴ ὄν, *Phys.* 192ᵃ 7. It is referred to as a δυάς in 987ᵇ 26, 33, 988ᵃ 13, M. 1083ᵃ 12, *Phys.* 192ᵃ 11, as ἡ τοῦ ἀνίσου δυὰς τοῦ μεγάλου καὶ μικροῦ in M. 1087ᵇ 7. In all these expressions Aristotle appears to be referring to the doctrine of Plato himself; there are certain other expressions about which it is harder to make out whether it is Plato or some of his followers that used them. Thus the expression ἀόριστος δυάς (M. 1081ᵃ 14, 22, ᵇ 21, 25, 32, 1082ᵃ 13, ᵇ 30, 1083ᵇ 36, 1085ᵇ 7, N. 1088ᵃ 15, ᵇ 28, 1089ᵃ 35, 1091ᵃ 5) requires special treatment. There is reason to suppose that the use of the word πλῆθος as a substitute for τὸ μέγα καὶ τὸ μικρόν (N. 1087ᵇ 6, 27, 1091ᵇ 31, 1092ᵃ 28, 35, cf. Λ. 1075ᵃ 33, M. 1085ᵃ 33, ᵇ 5) was peculiar to Speusippus. We learn that some Platonists treated various forms of μέγα καὶ μικρόν as the material principle of spatial magnitudes, and the πολὺ καὶ ὀλίγον as the material of number (N. 1087ᵇ 16, 1089ᵇ 11, cf. A. 992ᵃ 16, N. 1088ᵃ 18, ᵇ 5); and that some preferred to use the more general antithesis of ὑπερέχον καὶ ὑπερεχόμενον (N. 1087ᵇ 18). Others again preferred to call this principle the ἕτερον or ἄλλο (N. 1087ᵇ 26).

The meaning of the doctrine is best brought out in *Phys.* 206ᵇ 27 :—Πλάτων διὰ τοῦτο δύο τὰ ἄπειρα ἐποίησεν, ὅτι καὶ ἐπὶ τὴν αὔξην δοκεῖ ὑπερβάλλειν καὶ εἰς ἄπειρον ἰέναι καὶ ἐπὶ τὴν καθαίρεσιν. I.e. the indefinite or material principle is represented as 'the great and the small' because it is entirely indeterminate in quantity and may be drawn upon to an infinitely great or an infinitely small extent. Aristotle complains (206ᵇ 30) that Plato does not proceed to use the principle for what it is worth; there is no infinitely small number, since 1 is the smallest, and Plato does not recognize infinitely great number but makes 10 the greatest.

Further light is thrown on the conception, or on Aristotle's interpretation of it, by *Phys.* 209ᵇ 33 : Πλάτωνι μέντοι λεκτέον . . . διὰ τί οὐκ ἐν τόπῳ τὰ εἴδη καὶ οἱ ἀριθμοί, εἴπερ τὸ μεθεκτικὸν ὁ τόπος, εἴτε τοῦ μεγάλου καὶ τοῦ μικροῦ ὄντος τοῦ μεθεκτικοῦ εἴτε τῆς ὕλης, ὥσπερ ἐν τῷ Τιμαίῳ γέγραφεν. I.e. Plato has in the *Timaeus* described the receptive element as χώρα, which he identifies with matter (209ᵇ 11), while in the ἄγραφα δόγματα (209ᵇ 14) he has described it as 'the great and the small'. In either case Aristotle holds that Plato means nothing other than 'place', and, since the material principle is an element in the Forms or ideal numbers as well as in material things (987ᵇ 19, 988ᵃ 13, *Phys.* 203ᵃ 9, 207ᵃ 29), Aristotle concludes that Plato ought to have represented the Forms as having spatial position. For the same reason he thinks Plato should, in consistency with his principles, have represented the Forms as subject to movement (992ᵇ 7). Again, if mathematical numbers are to have the same principles as ideal numbers, they must be the same thing (N. 1090ᵇ 36). But there can be little doubt that, as Zeller points out (ii. 1.⁴ 751–762), Aristotle is here misunderstanding or misrepresenting Plato. The great and small which is the material principle of ideal numbers can only be plurality not yet determined as any particular number (not that that is an easy or satisfactory conception); 'the many and few' is indeed a better expression for it (N. 1087ᵇ 16). On the other hand the great and small which is the material principle of sensibles is, as the *Timaeus* clearly enough says, space not yet determined as any particular figure. Such distinctions, whether made by Plato or not, were, as we have seen, part of the Academic doctrine. Lengths were derived from the long and short, planes from the broad and narrow, solids from the deep and shallow—all of them forms of the great and small. Some Platonists, just because the great and small was specially appropriate to spatial magnitudes, the many and few to numbers, preferred to call the material principle in general by the wider name of the exceeding and exceeded. 'The great and small', if thus interpreted, is an apt enough expression for the element of indefiniteness which there is in all things, without implying that it is the same kind of indefiniteness that is present in sensibles and in Ideas. Aristotle's objection might be turned against himself; it might as well be said that because he assigns ὕλη to mathematical objects (Z. 1036ᵃ 9), he is making them the same kind of thing as bronze and wood.

Aristotle, as we have seen, refers the doctrine to Plato's ἄγραφα δόγματα (*Phys.* 209ᵇ 14, 35). Simplicius (*Phys.* 545. 23) identifies these with Plato's lectures *On the Good*, of which notes were taken by Aristotle as well as by other pupils (Simpl. 151. 8, 453. 28).

Though neither Aristotle himself nor Alexander, Asclepius, Syrianus, nor Simplicius connects the doctrine with any of Plato's dialogues, Porphyry (ap. Simpl. *Phys.* 453. 30) connected it with the *Philebus*, and this seems to be in fact the only dialogue in which the doctrine is foreshadowed. *Phil.* 23 c–26 ʙ divides the whole contents of the universe into the following elements: (1) τὸ ἄπειρον, (2) τὸ πέρας, (3) the unity formed by the commixture of these, (4) the cause of the commixture. The first class is said to consist of all the things which admit of τὸ μᾶλλόν τε καὶ ἧττον or of τὸ σφόδρα καὶ ἠρέμα, and this is illustrated by the things which may be hotter or colder, drier or wetter, more or less, faster or slower, greater or smaller. The second class is said to consist of the things which do not admit of differences of degree but do admit of equality, doubleness, or any numerical ratio. This, it is fairly clear, is a description of the limited rather than of limit, and there is a certain amount of confusion between the two; the second class, which is first (23 c) called πέρας, is later (24 ʌ) called τὸ πέρας ἔχον. Similarly, after the above account of it, which is an

account of the limited, we get a second account, which is rather
an account of limit; it is described as ' that which makes the contraries
cease to be at variance with each other, and makes them symmetrical
and harmonious by inserting number '.   The third class is illustrated
by health, music, good weather, beauty, strength, and all good qualities
of soul; all of these are produced by the introduction of limit into
what would otherwise admit of unlimited differences of degree,
e.g. high and low notes or cold and hot weather.   This class in
general is called μικτὴ καὶ γεγενημένη οὐσία.   Finally, reason is said
to belong to, or to be akin to, the fourth class (30 D, 31 A).

Without attempting a detailed exposition of this passage, we may
point out certain things in it which seem to be clear. By the unlimited Plato means that which is quantitatively indeterminate, though
qualitatively it is determined, e.g. as temperature or sound; and by
limit he means quantitative determination.   Heat and cold, or the
height and lowness of notes, are apparently not thought of as different
degrees of the same thing, but as distinct and opposite qualities, for
quantitative determination is described as a ratio (of equality, doubleness, &c.) between heat and cold, or between height and lowness.   It
is by no means clear what, precisely, the third class is meant to
include.   Evidently in *any* actual state of the body the temperature,
and the dryness or humidity, of its parts, will have some definite
determination, so that *any* bodily state should be viewed as belonging
to the third class, the class of things in which determinateness has been
imposed on the indeterminate; but only the healthy state is mentioned
as belonging to this class.   It looks as if Plato recognized only quite
simple ratios between small integers as conferring determinateness
(cf. N. 1092^{b} 27 ἐν εὐλογίστῳ ἀριθμῷ).   Again, there is no hint in the
Philebus of the elaborate doctrine of which Aristotle tells us, according
to which the great and small played a double part, that of uniting with
the One to form the Ideas, and that of uniting with the Ideas to form
particular things (988^{a} 11); Prof. Jackson's gallant effort to trace this
in the dialogue is not successful (cf. 987^{b} 12 n.).   Plato appears
to be putting forward a fresh analysis whose relation to the ideal
theory he has not thought out.   But in the description of the unlimited as τὸ μᾶλλόν τε καὶ ἧττον we cannot fail to see an anticipation
of the description of it as τὸ μέγα καὶ μικρόν, and we must suppose
that the doctrine of the *Philebus* was the starting-point from which
Plato worked in developing the later doctrine.

21. οὐσίαν.   οὐσία is strictly a non-committal word meaning
the true reality of things, whatever that may be (Z. 1028^{b} 33)—whether
matter or form or the compound of both.   But since Plato thought
the reality of things lay in their form, the word here, as often, means
form in opposition to matter.

ἐξ ἐκείνων γὰρ κατὰ μέθεξιν τοῦ ἑνὸς [τὰ εἴδη] εἶναι τοὺς ἀριθμούς.
Alexander and Bonitz think that τοὺς ἀριθμούς is added in apposition
to τὰ εἴδη to indicate that it is the Platonic idea-numbers and not εἴδη
in some other sense, i. e. species such as Aristotle himself believed in,

that are meant. But the apposition is extremely awkward, and the meaning of τὰ εἴδη would have been perfectly clear in this context without any addition. This interpretation must therefore be rejected. Nor is Zeller's interpretation, ' out of the great and the small the Forms become numbers by participation in the One ', a tenable one ; it mistranslates εἶναι, ignores τούς, and attributes to Plato a doctrine of which we have absolutely no evidence. It seems clear that either τὰ εἴδη or τοὺς ἀριθμούς must go. Prof. Jackson's τὰ εἴδη εἶναι τὰ ὡς ἀριθμούς presupposes a distinction of εἴδη ὡς ἀριθμοί and εἴδη in some other sense, which does not agree with Aristotle's general account of the Platonic doctrine.

As far as the sense goes, it does not matter whether we cut out τὰ εἴδη or τοὺς ἀριθμούς, but Prof. Gillespie has pointed out three reasons for preferring the former course (*J. of P.* xxxiv. 153). (1) There is in l. 10 a reference to the εἴδη which is pretty certainly spurious, and in l. 14 one which is not improbably so. It looks as if at some point quite early in the history of the text these three glosses may have been inserted by a single hand. (2) τοὺς ἀριθμούς is the more expressive of the two phrases, ' because it shows that the εἴδη are ἀριθμοί in respect of their origin . . . The Forms are spoken of again lower down as numbers, and the most appropriate place for the substitution of the new term is in this sentence '. (3) Aristotle does not often end a sentence with the unemphatic word εἶναι. For these reasons it seems better to omit τὰ εἴδη, as Zeller latterly preferred to do.

26. δυάδα. Aristotle uses this word freely in speaking of Plato's material principle, and we may safely suppose that Plato used it himself. It is not so clear that he used the phrase ἀόριστος δυάς, for a discussion of which see M. 1081ᵃ 14 n.

31. διὰ τὴν ἐν τοῖς λόγοις ἐγένετο σκέψιν. The best commentary on this, apart from 987ᵇ 1–8 above, is to be found in two other passages dealing with the Platonists—Λ. 1069ᵃ 26, where Aristotle says that they treat universals as substances διὰ τὸ λογικῶς ζητεῖν, and contrasts them with the older thinkers, who treated particular things as substances ; and M. 1084ᵇ 23, where he says that they adopted an erroneous theory of units because they at the same time considered them from the point of view of mathematics and therefore treated them as the constituents of numbers, and ἐκ τῶν λόγων τῶν καθόλου ἐθήρευον and therefore dwelt on the unity that is predicable of any number. Similarly the Platonists are called οἱ ἐν τοῖς λόγοις in Θ. 1050ᵇ 35. The phrase used here is pretty clearly a reminiscence of *Phaedo* 100 A, where τὸν ἐν τοῖς λόγοις σκοπούμενον τὰ ὄντα, ' one who studies things by the method of definitions ', is Socrates' description of his own method. The point seems to be this. The Pythagoreans were doing what the other pre-Socratics did, trying to find the ultimate constituents of things, and they (so Aristotle thinks, at least) thought of numbers as being constituents of things very much as other thinkers had thought of water or air as being their constituents, i.e. as the very stuff of which they are made. Plato, on the other hand,

following in the footsteps of Socrates, was interested in the universal
character of a set of things, and this led to two differences between his
doctrine and the Pythagorean. (1) He did not view the One and the
numbers as the stuff of which things are made, but as their formal
principle, and hence placed them ' apart from ' sensibles, and (2) he
did not confine himself to the Pythagorean language about ' numbers ',
but spoke of ' Forms ' or Ideas and thought of them as essentially the
eternal objects of definition (cf. ll. 1–8).

Prof. Jackson suggests a connexion between this passage and
Pl. *Pol.* 285 A, where ' the Pythagorean misinterpretation of their own
principle ' of measurement is ascribed ' to their want of familiarity with
the dialectic process '. But when Plato ascribes their mistake to τὸ μὴ
κατ᾽ εἴδη συνειθίσθαι σκοπεῖν διαιρουμένους, he means merely that they
did not distinguish two kinds of measurement; and Aristotle can
hardly be referring to anything so little obvious from the context.

32. οἱ γὰρ πρότεροι διαλεκτικῆς οὐ μετεῖχον. Diogenes (viii. 57,
ix. 25) and Sextus Empiricus (*Adv. Math.* vii. 7) tell us that Aristotle
called Zeno the inventor of dialectic. The Pythagoreans, at any rate,
were dogmatic and not dialectical in their procedure (cf. ᵃ 20–25),
In M. 1078ᵇ 25 Aristotle says even of the time of Socrates that
διαλεκτικὴ ἰσχὺς οὔπω ἦν, but there he seems to be speaking with some
irony, and using διαλεκτική in its less favourable sense.

33. Aristotle here represents the reason for Plato's description of the
material element as a ' dyad ' as having lain in the facility of deducing
the numbers from a dyad. The actual reason, as we can see from the
Philebus and from *Phys.* 206ᵇ 27 (quoted in note on l. 20), is that the
quantitatively indeterminate can vary indefinitely in *both* directions.

34. τῶν πρώτων. Alexander (57. 12) explains this as the odd
numbers, i.e. those that are prime (πρῶτοι) to 2, and further on
(57. 28) as the prime numbers generally. The first seems an impossible interpretation. ' Prime number ' is a proper enough sense for
πρῶτος ἀριθμός (cf. I. 1052ᵃ 8, *An. Post.* 73ᵃ 40), but we can hardly
read ' prime to 2 ' into it here, especially as it is not the number 2 but
the indefinite dyad that is being spoken of. The other interpretation
(which appears not to belong to the genuine text of Alexander) is as
difficult. If the function of the indefinite dyad is to double (M. 1081ᵇ
21, 1082ᵃ 13, 1083ᵇ 35), it cannot with the aid of the One produce
anything but the powers of two, i.e. it cannot produce multiples of odd
numbers any more than it can produce prime numbers, so that ' except
the prime numbers ' does not state the exceptions adequately. Asclepius
thinks that the dyad meant is the two factors by whose multiplication
the composite numbers are produced; but this does not in the least
agree with what we learn in books M and N about the Platonic
generation of numbers. Trendelenburg and Schwegler thought that
πρώτων meant ' ideal ', as in M. 1080ᵇ 22, 1081ᵃ 4 (cf. πρώτη δύας in
1081ᵃ 23, &c.), while Brandis combined the two views and thought
ideal odd numbers were meant. But Aristotle is telling us why Plato
made the One and the indefinite dyad the principles of *ideal* numbers

(cf. ll. 18–22), and there would be no sense in saying that he did so because the numbers *except* the ideal numbers could be easily generated from these principles.   If we turn to what might appear the most relevant passage in Plato, *Parm.* 143 c—144 a, we find that 2 is generated by the addition of two units, 3 by the addition of 1 to 2, and other numbers by the multiplication of 2 and 3 or of their powers. (Clearly the prime numbers higher than 3, and all their multiples, are incapable of being produced in this way ; but Plato probably does not mean the account to be exhaustive.)   The *Parmenides* does not help us, for there is no question there of the indefinite dyad ; the numbers, including 2, are produced by the ordinary processes of addition and multiplication from 1 (cf. M. 1084ª 4).   Further, being so produced, they cannot be the ideal numbers, which are inaddible (cf. M. 1083ª 34) ; they are simply mathematical numbers.   But ideal numbers must be referred to here.

Prof. Jackson suggests that, since in *Phys.* 219ᵇ 6 number is said to mean the thing numbered as well as that by which we number it, τοὺς ἀριθμοὺς ἔξω τῶν πρώτων means the ἀριθμητά arising from the union of a great and small with *numbers*, viz. the multitude of particulars, while οἱ πρῶτοι would be those arising from the union of a great and small with the *One*, viz. the Ideas.   Besides involving a theory about the teaching of the *Philebus* which seems untenable (cf. ll. 12, 20, 21 nn.), this involves the necessity of getting out of the one word πρῶτοι a highly technical sense which the word bears nowhere else.   Besides, it is hardly reasonable to explain the fact that Plato made the material principle of the Ideas (cf. ll. 18–22) a dyad by the fact that the numbers could be easily generated from a dyad *with the exception of* the ideal numbers.

We have had to reject the view that τῶν πρώτων = τῶν περιττῶν, but we might, with Heinze, *read* τῶν περιττῶν.   This would be confirmed by N. 1091ª 23 τοῦ μὲν οὖν περιττοῦ γένεσιν οὔ φασιν, ὡς δηλονότι τοῦ ἀρτίου οὔσης γενέσεως, where Aristotle says that the Platonists denied that odd number is generated.   But it is inconceivable that after putting forward the One and the indefinite dyad as the generating principles of numbers they should have said that half the numbers are not generated at all.   The true explanation of the statement in N. 1091ª 23 is probably that given by Syrianus, that Aristotle is reasoning from Platonic language which was not meant to be taken literally.   Cf. n. *ad loc.*   The Platonists did generate odd numbers, but they did not do so εὐφυῶς, for the production of them by inserting the One itself into the middle of an even number (M. 1083ᵇ 29, 1084ª 36) involved a departure from their general principle with regard to the generation of the numbers.   The general principle is that the One is the formative agent, and the great and small is a material which has the property (a strange one, as Aristotle proceeds to point out in 988ª 1–7) of duplicating the Form that is imprinted on it ; ἡ γὰρ ἀόριστος δυὰς δυοποιὸς ἦν, M. 1083ᵇ 35, cf. 1082ª 13.   What the indefinite dyad, on this assumption, can most obviously do is to produce the series 2, 4, 8 (N. 1091ª 10). But secondly, if 3 and 5 were imprinted on it, it would turn out 6 and 10. What it can *not* do is to produce the odd numbers. To produce these, the One has illegitimately to be used not, or not merely, as a formative agent, but as an actual part of the number generated.

Thus ἔξω τῶν περιττῶν gives an excellent sense, if we take it as representing not a part of the Platonic view but a criticism of it. Neither the MSS., however, nor the Greek commentators know any reading but ἔξω τῶν πρώτων, and the corruption is not a likely one. It seems possible to keep the MS. reading in the sense of 'except the prime numbers', if we suppose Aristotle to have forgotten for the moment the number 9. Some of the Platonists, at any rate, treated 10 as the limit of the numerical series (M. 1084ª 12, cf. Λ. 1073ª 20). Within this limit they could quite neatly generate, as we have seen, all the numbers except the prime numbers (3, 5, 7) and the composite number 9. Or, even without supposing the limitation to 10, we may suppose Aristotle to have forgotten the whole class of composite odd numbers.

Another interpretation of ἔξω τῶν πρώτων has been suggested tentatively by Prof. Taylor. According to this Aristotle means that given the One and the indefinite dyad Plato can generate all the numbers except one and two. He supposes that Aristotle identifies the One and the indefinite dyad with the numbers one and two, and in effect charges Plato with assuming these numbers instead of generating them. This view is an attractive one ; the main difficulty is that elsewhere one is not treated as a number, but is opposed to the numbers (cf. N. 1088ª 6–8 n.); according to the Pythagorean definition ἀριθμός is πλῆθος μονάδων. But Aristotle's familiar phrase εἷς ἀριθμῷ implies that in some sense one is a number.

It is difficult to trace the lineaments of Plato's theory through the medium of Aristotle's external and unsympathetic account. In certain respects we may be sure that his account is misleading. That a principle which can only double should be put forward as one of the principles active in the production of all the ideal numbers, odd and even alike, is incredible. Aristotle ascribes to the indefinite dyad the function in the generation of ideal numbers which might be assigned to 2 in an ordinary theory of mathematical number such as is expressed in the *Parmenides*—the function of multiplying some other number by 2 (for other instances of misinterpretation of the indefinite dyad by Aristotle cf. 990^b 19 n., 991^b 31 n.); and this forces him to assign to the One also a function (viz. that of accounting for the odd unit in odd numbers) which can hardly be that which Plato assigned to it. We may take the *Philebus* as our starting-point, but it seems that Plato must have advanced in two respects beyond the analysis there offered. (1) Number is there presupposed and not generated ; one of the two ultimate elements, the limited, consists of the various ratios 1 : 1, 2 : 1, &c., and no attempt is made to get behind these to anything more ultimate. (2) The indefinite has determinate quality although not determinate quantity; its instances are already qualified as temperatures, sounds, &c. Thus both number and quality are presupposed. In the theory of ideal numbers Plato seems to have left quality out of account, and to have tried to generate number. The great and small is thought of as pure indeterminate quantity, not qualified and not determined as any *particular* quantity, but capable of indefinite increase and indefinite diminution. The function of the One was to act as a limit to these movements, to check them at certain points, and at each such check a number was produced.

988ᵃ 1. ἐκμαγείου. The word is Platonic. In Plato it means sometimes a plastic material, sometimes a copy taken in such a material, sometimes a pattern or archetype. Here it is evidently used in the first sense, as in *Theaet.* 191 C, 196 A, *Tim.* 50 C, and Aristotle doubtless had in mind the last-named passage, where Plato uses the word to describe the material principle.

2. ἐκ τῆς ὕλης πολλὰ ποιοῦσιν. The point is not simply that in Plato's doctrine multiplicity proceeds from matter. It does so in Aristotle's own system just as certainly (cf. Λ. 1069ᵇ 30, 1074ᵃ 33). What Aristotle is criticizing is a special feature which he thinks he detects in Plato's theory of matter. He thinks Plato means that from a single union of form and matter a plurality of products results. Cf. M. 1082ᵃ 13, ' the indefinite dyad took the definite dyad and made two dyads'. As against this he points out that from a single portion of matter only one product can be got by a single application of form; the form must be applied to many portions of matter if a plurality of objects is to be produced. We can hardly doubt (cf. previous note) that Aristotle is here misrepresenting Plato's view. Each number must have been produced by a separate union of form with matter; though Plato would have been hard put to it to explain how different numbers are produced if the One is always the same and the great and small contains in itself no reason why it should be checked at one point rather than another on each occasion.

3. The use of ὕλη here illustrates well how the word passed from its ordinary to its technical meaning.

4. τράπεζα. The instance was probably suggested by Pl. *Rep.* 596 A.

εἷς ὤν, ' though one '.

5. τὸ ἄρρεν πρὸς τὸ θῆλυ. Plato actually (*Tim.* 50 D) compares the material cause to a mother and the active cause to a father, and Aristotle himself thinks of the male and female as contributing respectively form and matter to the offspring. Cf. 986ᵃ 24 n.

9. δυοῖν αἰτίαιν μόνον κέχρηται. Aristotle ignores various suggestions of an efficient cause in Plato—the self-moving soul of *Phaedrus* 245 C, D, *Laws* 891–899, the demiurge of *Soph.* 265 B–D and of *Tim.* 28 C ff., the αἰτία τῆς μίξεως of *Phil.* 23 D, 26 E—27 B, and various suggestions of a final cause—the ultimate good or οὗ χάριν of *Phil.* 20 D, 53 E, the object of the creator's purpose in *Tim.* 29 D ff., and in *Laws* 903 C. He doubtless thinks Plato's treatment of these causes

inadequate, but that does not justify him in speaking as if Plato had ignored them entirely. Cf. ᵇ11–14 n.

14. ἔτι δὲ τὴν τοῦ εὖ κτλ. The origin of good is distinctly ascribed to limit in Pl. *Phil.* 25 E—26 B. Cf. Λ. 1075ᵃ 35, N. 1091ᵇ 13, *E. E.* 1218ᵃ 24.

15. ὥσπερ φαμέν κτλ. Cf. 984ᵇ 15, 985ᵃ 2.

Summary account of the treatment of the four causes by earlier thinkers
(ch. 7).

988ᵃ 18. Our account has shown that our predecessors have recognized no causes other than our four, and that they have recognized these, though obscurely.

23. (1) Some describe the first principle as *matter,* making it one or more than one, corporeal or incorporeal ; e. g. Plato, the Pythagoreans, Empedocles, Anaxagoras, and all who describe it as air, fire, water, or something intermediate between fire and air.

33. (2) Some have recognized a *source of movement* in friendship and strife, reason, or love.

34. (3) No one has described the *essential cause* clearly, but the Platonists come nearest to it ; they treat the Forms and the One not as the matter of sensibles and of the Forms respectively, nor as the cause of movement (they describe them rather as causes of rest), but as imparting to them their essence.

ᵇ**6.** (4) The *final cause* they mention in a way, but not as such. (*a*) Those who speak of reason or love treat these as a good, but as the source of movement, not its object ; and (*b*) those who say the One or Being is the good treat it as the essential, not the final cause. Thus they treat the good as a cause only incidentally.

16. Thus our predecessors confirm our account of the number and nature of the causes. Let us next discuss the problems arising out of the earlier treatment of them.

In chs. 3–6 Aristotle has given us his account of previous thinkers ; in this chapter he summarizes this history with reference to the early treatment of the four causes ; in chs. 8 and 9 he will proceed to criticize this treatment.

988ᵃ 20. τῆς ἀληθείας. Cf. 983ᵇ 2 n.

21. ἐν τοῖς περὶ φύσεως, i. e. *Phys.* ii. 3, 7.

26. οἱ δ᾿ Ἰταλικοὶ τὸ ἄπειρον. Cf. 986ᵇ 6 n.

30. πυρὸς μὲν πυκνότερον ἀέρος δὲ λεπτότερον. Such a substance is referred to again in *Phys.* 187ᵃ 14, *De Gen. et Corr.* 328ᵇ 35, 332ᵃ 21. A substance intermediate between *water* and air is referred to in

989ª 14, *Phys.* 203ª 18, 205ª 27, *De Caelo* 303ᵇ 12, *De Gen. et Corr.*
332ª 21 ; a substance intermediate between water and fire in *Phys.*
189ᵇ 3.   The ancient commentators for the most part (e.g. Al.
60. 8) explain these passages as referring to Anaximander ; but such
vagueness in referring to so well-known a thinker would be surprising,
and in spite of the occurrence in some of these passages, especially
De Caelo 303ᵇ 12, *De Gen. et Corr.* 332ª 25, of language which reminds
us of Anaximander, *Phys.* 187ª 20 shows clearly that he is not meant.
He is there mentioned by name, and his view, ἐκ τοῦ ἑνὸς ἐνούσας τὰς
ἐναντιότητας ἐκκρίνεσθαι, is expressly distinguished from the belief in
an intermediate substance out of which all other things are produced
by densification and rarefaction. (*Phys.* 204ᵇ 22–29 seems to draw
the same distinction.)   I. e. Anaximander believed in a primary
substance which had no such definite character as would be implied
in being intermediate between two of the four commonly recognized
elements, but which contained the potency of them all.   Its absolute
indefiniteness distinguishes it from the principles believed in by the
other early physicists, and perhaps explains the omission of his view
in Aristotle's survey.   Cf. Zeller, i.⁶ 283–291, Diels, *Vors.* i. 18.
10–21.

The view in question probably belongs to a somewhat later period
of speculation, since it mediates between the views of Heraclitus and
Anaximenes, between those of Thales and Anaximenes, or between
those of Thales and Heraclitus.   It takes its origin from the thought
of Anaximenes, since he was the first thinker who treated density and
rarity as the characteristic mark of the different kinds of matter.
Simplicius (*Phys.* 25. 8, 149. 13, 151. 21) says that Nicolaus and
Porphyry referred the belief to Diogenes of Apollonia, but claims to
have seen Diogenes' treatise, *De Natura*, and says it treats *air* as the
principle.   This is also Aristotle's account of Diogenes' view (984ª 5,
De An. 405ª 22).   Zeller and Diels conjecture that it was Idaeus of
Himera that believed in the intermediate substance, but of this there
is no evidence, and the only author who mentions Idaeus (Sext. ix.
360) says definitely that he believed in air as the primitive substance.
We must be content to refer the belief in an intermediate substance
to some member or members of the school of Anaximenes, which
evidently lasted for a considerable time and had much influence (cf.
Burnet, §§ 31, 122).

32. By οὗτοι Aristotle evidently means thinkers who did not
recognize an efficient cause ; i. e. the reference is solely to the Ionian
thinkers indicated in ll. 29–32.

34. ἔρωτα.   Aristotle is thinking of Parmenides and perhaps of
Hesiod.   Cf. 984ᵇ 24.

ᵇ2. Bonitz's conjecture of τὸ ἕν for τὰ ἕν is, in view of ª 11, ᵇ 5,
certainly right.

οὔθ' ὡς ἐντεῦθεν κτλ.   The uselessness of the ideas as efficient
causes is a favourite point with Aristotle, cf. 991ª 11, ᵇ 4, 992ª 25, Λ.
1071ᵇ 14, 1075ᵇ 28.

6–11. Cf. 984ᵇ 20–22 n.

11–14. The Platonists, who say the One or the existent is the good, are making goodness an accident of the formal cause as Anaxagoras and Empedocles make it an accident of the efficient cause ; in neither case is the good made a cause in its own right, as the end of being and becoming. Aristotle ignores the distinctly teleological view which Plato expresses in some dialogues. Cf. ᵃ 9 n.

19. τινὰ τρόπον τούτων is peculiar, and Bywater's proposal to read τινὰ τρόπον τοιοῦτον is probably right.

(B) *Criticism of previous systems* (chs. 8–10).
(a) *The pre-Platonic systems* (ch. 8).

988ᵇ 22. (1) Those who recognize one material principle, and that a bodily one, make several mistakes. (*a*) They ignore the existence of incorporeal entities. (*b*) Though they are trying to explain generation and destruction, they do away with the cause of movement. (*c*) They do not recognize the essential cause.

29. (*d*) They recklessly make any of the simple bodies (except earth) the first principle, without considering how the simple bodies are generated from one another. It makes a great difference to their relative priority whether they are produced by congregation or segregation.

34. (i) In one way the body out of which the others are produced by congregation, i. e. the finest, would seem the most elementary. Those who make fire the principle conform best to this argument, and it is confirmed by the fact that none of the later monists made earth the principle, while each of the other elements has got a vote.

989ᵃ 8. Yet most people make earth primary—cf. Hesiod.

15. (ii) But if what is later in generation is prior in nature, and the product of concoction is later in generation, water will be prior to air and earth to water.

19. (2) Equal difficulties beset those who recognize more than one material principle. (*a*) As for *Empedocles*, (i) we see things generated from one another in a way which implies that fire and earth do *not* remain themselves eternally. (ii) He treats the question whether the cause of movement is single or double neither rightly nor plausibly. (iii) Such thinkers do away with alteration, for in order that cold should come from hot or *vice versa* there would have to be one substance which becomes fire and water, which he denies.

.30. (*b*) If we ascribe two elements to *Anaxagoras*, we shall be bringing out fairly the implication of what he says. His saying that all things were originally mixed is absurd, because (i) this implies a previous unmixed state, (ii) it is not everything that can be mixed with everything, (iii) if attributes were mixed with substances they could exist apart from them.

^b **4.** Yet if we make his views articulate there is something modern in them. When nothing had been separated out, nothing true could be said of the then existing substance ;

12. for it to have any particular character, something would have had to be already separated out, but all things were mixed save reason.

16. Thus he recognizes the One, which is simple and unmixed, and the Other, which is like our 'indefinite' before it participates in a form; though his language is neither right nor clear, his views approximate to later views and to the facts.

21. (3) While these thinkers are at home only in discussions about generation, destruction, and movement, those who recognize non-sensibles as well as sensibles evidently study both kinds, and deserve more consideration with a view to the study that lies before us.

29. (*a*) The *Pythagoreans* use stranger principles than the physicists, because they take them from the non-sensible, unchangeable world of mathematics.

33. Yet all their discussions are about nature; they observe the facts about the material universe and use up their principles on it, as if they agreed with the physicists that what is is just what is sensible, though their principles are more suited to act as steps up to the higher kinds of reality.

990^a 8. But (i) how can there be movement if only limit and unlimited, odd and even are presupposed, or how without movement can there be generation, destruction, and the movements of the stars ?

12. (ii) Even if we grant, or they can prove, that spatial magnitude is composed of these principles, how can differences of weight be explained ? They must be speaking about sensibles as much as about mathematicals ; they say nothing expressly about sensibles presumably because they have nothing *special* to say about them.

18. (iii) How can number and its modifications be the causes of physical things and events, if there is no number other than that of which the physical universe is composed?

22. They place opinion, opportunity, &c., in various parts of the universe, and state, as their proof, that each of these is a number and that a plurality of the spatial objects composed of numbers is already

present in each region just because these modifications of number are
appropriate to the several regions. Is the number, which e. g. opinion
is, the same as the corresponding number in the physical universe ?

29. Plato says not ; he makes the one set of numbers intelligible,
the other sensible.

Christ thinks that chs. 8–10 (of which part of ch. 9 agrees almost
verbally with M. 5 and part of 4) were not originally included in this
book, but were added later, when Aristotle determined to omit M and
N and to finish the *Metaphysics* with Λ. The relation between
A. 9 and M. 4 and 5 must be considered later, but it may be said at
once that the grounds for Christ's suggestion are insufficient.

988ᵇ 22. ὅσοι κτλ., 'those who posit the unity of the universe, and
some one kind of thing as its matter '. The first point in the
description would apply to the Eleatics as well as to the school of
Miletus ; the second applies to the latter only.

28–32. Bekker prints ἔτι δὲ τὸ ... ἐστι, καὶ πρὸς τούτοις τὸ κτλ.,
presumably understanding some such words as ἁμαρτήματά ἐστιν
as predicate of the whole sentence. But in this construction the
nominative ἐπισκεψάμενοι is difficult if not impossible. Bonitz, however, supposes Bekker to take τὸ τιθέναι and τὸ λέγειν as objects of
ποιοῦνται and to understand πῶς as meaning πῶς ἔστι. Bonitz himself
takes τὸ λέγειν and πῶς so, but points out that there is no connexion
in sense between τὸ τὴν οὐσίαν ... τὸ τί ἐστι and οὐκ ἐπισκεψάμενοι.
He therefore places a colon after τὸ τί ἐστι and would understand
ἁμάρτημά ἐστι as the predicate of this first clause, while he takes
τὸ ... λέγειν to be governed by ποιοῦνται. But τὸ λέγειν ποιοῦνται is
very difficult, and it is much better to take πῶς ποιοῦνται together and
to read with Bywater τῷ ... τιθέναι, τῷ ... λέγειν, taking these, in
spite of the intervening sentences, as depending in thought on
ἁμαρτάνουσιν in l. 24.

31. For τὴν ... γένεσιν ποιοῦνται = γίγνονται cf. *De Part. An.*
646ª 31.

34. τῇ μὲν γάρ. The response to this comes in 989ª 15 εἰ δ' ἔστι,
the μέν clause being meanwhile summed up in 989ª 12 κατὰ μὲν
οὖν κτλ.

989ª 5–6. οὐθεὶς ... στοιχεῖον. Prof. Burnet has remarked (*G. P.*,
§ 10) on the marked divergence of the Milesian philosophy from the
earlier cosmology, implied in the fact that none of the physicists treated
earth as a primary form of body, though it was very prominent in the
cosmologists, as late as Pherecydes. Theophrastus agreed with
Aristotle in making no exception of Xenophanes, though later writers
did so (Diels, i. 52. 20).

10. Cf. Hes. *Theog.* 116, already quoted in 984ᵇ 28.

14. ἀέρος μὲν πυκνότερον κτλ. Cf. 988ª 30 n.

15. τὸ τῇ γενέσει ὕστερον τῇ φύσει πρότερον. Aristotle derives this
principle from the facts of growth. The seed or the child is not

intelligible except in the light of what it becomes; it is a potency
which we can understand only when we know what it is the potency of.
Cf. Θ. 1050ᵃ 4, *Phys.* 261ᵃ 13.

16. πεπεμμένον καὶ συγκεκριμένον, cf. *Meteor.* 380ᵃ 4.

17. Aristotle allows some value both to the argument in 988ᵇ 34—
989ᵃ 2 and to that in 989ᵃ 15–18. There is thus something to be
said for making either of the extremes, fire or earth, the ultimate
element, but nothing for assigning this position to air or water.

21. τὰ μὲν ταῦτά. Of the four objections raised against the school
of Miletus, the first (988ᵇ 24) and the third (ᵇ 28) apply equally to
Empedocles.

23. ὡς οὐκ ἀεὶ διαμένοντος κτλ. According to Empedocles each of
the four elements did remain unchanged into any of the others. The
apparent generation of one from another was really the ἔκκρισις of it
out of the other. But in *De Caelo* iii. 7 Aristotle tries to show that
this account is unsatisfactory, that the 'elements' really are produced
out of one another and therefore are not elements at all.

24. ἐν τοῖς περὶ φύσεως, *De Caelo* iii. 7. This phrase and ἐν τοῖς
φυσικοῖς may refer to works other than the *Physics*, such as the *De
Caelo* or the *De Gen. et Corr.*; cf. H. 1042ᵇ 8, K. 1062ᵇ 31, Λ. 1073ᵃ
32, M. 1086ᵃ 23.

25. πότερον ἓν ἢ δύο θετέον. Cf. 985ᵃ 23–29. 'Since according to
Empedocles love can do the work of strife and strife that of love,
should he not recognize only one motive principle?' The criticism,
however, is beside the mark, for according to Empedocles love can
separate only likes. To account for the separation of unlikes as well,
two principles must be supposed.

26–30. ὅλως . . . φησιν. These words, omitted by Aᵇ and Alexander,
are found in the other MSS. and in Asclepius. This points to a very
early divergence of the tradition, but there is no reason to regard the
words as not genuine. They are quite suitable in the context, and the
objection which they raise—that Empedocles does not provide a
permanent substratum for change—is a truly Aristotelian one. Empedocles meant to provide four such substrata, but Aristotle has already
in ll. 22–24 argued that the four 'elements' do not really persist
unchanged.

31. δύο λέγειν στοιχεῖα, i. e. mind and the mixture of all other
things. In calling the 'mind' of Anaxagoras an element, Aristotle is
treating it as a material, not, as in 984ᵇ 15, as an efficient principle;
and this is justified by Anaxagoras' own language, since he describes
it as λεπτότατον (fr. 12). He was aiming at the notion of an immaterial
substance, but did not reach it.

32. The subject of ἠκολούθησε is ἐκεῖνος. So Al. 68. 12, and
cf. 993ᵃ 23.

33. τοῖς ἐπάγουσιν αὐτόν, 'to those who led him on to it'. It is
phrases like this (cf. *An. Post.* 71ᵃ 21, 24, 81ᵇ 5, *De Caelo* 268ᵃ 20)
that best show the origin of the technical meaning of ἐπαγωγή.

ἀτόπου γὰρ ὄντος κτλ. Aristotle takes the statement which we may suppose Anaxagoras to have made (cf. fr. 12), that all things 'were mixed', and argues that this implies a previous process of mixing and a still earlier unmixed condition. The argument appears to be purely verbal.

ᵇ1. τὸ μὴ πεφυκέναι κτλ. This is true only of thorough chemical combination, which is what Aristotle meant by μῖξις (cf. *De Gen. et Corr.* 1. 10), but not what Anaxagoras meant; he thought of a mechanical mixture.

3. τὰ πάθη . . . χωρίζοιτ' ἂν τῶν οὐσιῶν. Aristotle is thinking of such passages as fr. 4, where wet and dry, hot and cold, bright and dark, are mentioned alongside of the substance earth, or fr. 10, where black and white, heavy and light, are mentioned alongside of hair and flesh. But Anaxagoras means wet substance and dry substance, &c. The neuter of the adjective (τοῦ διεροῦ, κτλ.) is always open to this misunderstanding. Again Aristotle's argument is somewhat captious.

7. εἰπεῖν is an epexegetic infinitive; 'true to say'. Cf. Γ. 1006ᵇ 29, &c.

15. τοῦτον δὲ ἀμιγῆ. Cf. fr. 12.

20. It seems better to read τοῖς νῦν φαινομένοις with the MSS., even though νῦν does not appear in Alexander's commentary. If νῦν be omitted, μᾶλλον has to be taken with παραπλήσιον, which is awkward in view of the distance between the words. τοῖς νῦν φαινομένοις μᾶλλον means 'what is now more clearly seen to be the case'—now, when the distinction of form and matter has been clearly recognized.

29. οἱ . . . καλούμενοι Πυθαγόρειοι, cf. 985ᵇ 23 n.

34. For the Pythagorean 'generation of the heavens' cf. N. 1091ᵃ 13 ; for their interest in astronomy and physics cf. 986ᵃ 10, N. 6.

990ᵃ 5. ὥσπερ εἴπομεν refers to 989ᵇ 31.

12-14. Aristotle's point is : 'Even if geometrical magnitudes could be generated from the odd and even, how could the physical properties of bodies be explained from these principles ?'

15-16. Casaubon's proposal to interchange μαθηματικῶν and αἰσθητῶν derives some support from Al. 73. 2, but the manuscript reading is probably right. The Pythagoreans mean to be giving an account of sensible objects as well as of mathematical; this is why they have said nothing about any of the elements, viz. because they have nothing *special* to say of them but mean their account of mathematical bodies to apply to these also. Aristotle is not ignoring the Pythagorean derivation of the four elements from various geometrical figures (for which cf. Burnet, § 147). His point is that they have given a purely mathematical account of the elements, *identifying* them with geometrical figures and having nothing to say of their distinctive sensible qualities.

W. Jaeger holds (*Hermes*, lii. 487) that οὐθὲν μᾶλλον has the force of οὐθὲν ἔλαττον, but this can hardly be right. Cf. 985ᵇ 9 n.

18-22. 'How can number be the cause of what exists and happens in the material world, and at the same time that of which the world is composed?' This would make number the cause of number.

19. τὰ τοῦ ἀριθμοῦ πάθη. Cf. 985ᵇ 29 n.

20. οὐρανόν, 22 κόσμος. Philolaus used οὐρανός in the sense of ' the sublunary region', κόσμος in the sense of ' the region of the sun, moon, and planets' (Stob. i. 22. 1, cf. *Epinomis* 997 B) ; and W. R. Newbold in *Archiv für Gesch. der Phil.* xix. 214, thinks that Aristotle is using the words in this sense. But Aristotle nowhere else recognizes the distinction. Elsewhere in his remarks about the Pythagoreans he uses the words as equivalent, and for the most part the Pythagoreans seem to have used them so (Zeller, i.⁶ 548 n. 3). Nor does the distinction in any way help the interpretation of this passage ; it would rather divert attention from the difficulty which Aristotle wishes to emphasize, i. e. how can numbers be the causes of things and at the same time the things themselves ?

23. δόξα was identified with the number 3 (or 2), καιρός with 7 ; for the evidence cf. 985ᵇ 30 n. They are not identified with the same number ; it is difficult therefore to suppose that they were assigned to the same region of the universe. Accordingly Luthe has proposed ἐκεῖ δέ, and Zeller ἤ, for καί in l. 23, while Diels reads δόξα καὶ ⟨τόλμα, ἐν τῳδὶ δὲ⟩ καιρός. τόλμα is stated by Alexander (74. 13) to have been identified with 2, but there is no reason to suppose that Alexander had it in his text. His paraphrase (74. 7) rather confirms the reading ἐκεῖ δέ.

ἄνωθεν ἢ κάτωθεν, further from or nearer to the centre of the universe.

24. ἀδικία. We do not know with what number this was identified. Alexander knows another reading ἀνικία (cf. Asc. 65. 18, 20), which he identifies with 5, and explains by reference to the triangle whose sides are in the ratio 3 : 4 : 5, so that the square on the hypotenuse is not ' conquered by ' the squares on the other two sides. The word is apparently not found elsewhere, and the object which it would indicate is not of the same type as the others mentioned here, so that we should probably prefer the reading of the MSS. of Aristotle, viz. ἀδικία.

κρίσις is probably ' decision '. This use of the word is as old as Parmenides (fr. 8. 15). Asclepius says (65. 13) that 6 was called κρίσις because it is the first number that can be divided into two odd numbers, 1 not being a number. On the other hand Stobaeus (i. 1 pr. 6, p. 20. 13 Wachsmuth) remarks that the Pythagoreans thought the κρίσεις of diseases were at odd numbers of days, and this would point to their having identified κρίσις with an odd number.

μῖξις. Asc. 65. 15 tells us that 12 was called ' mixture ', because it can be divided both into the even numbers 6 and 6 and into the odd numbers 3 and 3. But it seems unlikely that the Pythagoreans went beyond 10 in their identification of things with numbers (986ᵃ 9). Mixture is more likely to have been identified with 5, the first ' mixture ' of odd and even.

25. It is somewhat surprising that the existence of certain συνιστά-μενα μεγέθη in a certain place should be given as the reason for placing certain abstractions, such as opinion, there. Accordingly Bonitz proposes to read τούτων ἓν ἕκαστον . . . συμβαίνῃ δέ. He

takes the first of these two clauses to give the whole of the ἀπόδειξις, and the second to state an awkward result with which the Pythagoreans are confronted, viz. that the place where they put one of the abstractions is already occupied by συνιστάμενα μεγέθη; how then are they to state the relation between the two? The proposal is an attractive one, but is open to two objections, (1) that ἀπόδειξιν λέγωσιν prepares us for something more elaborate than the single clause ὅτι τούτων ἐν ἕκαστον ἀριθμός ἐστιν; (2) that there is no reason for the unusual and very emphatic combination ἐν ἕκαστον. For these reasons it seems better to read with Alexander μὲν ἕκαστον and to retain συμβαίνει with the MSS. and Alexander. The proof is not very well stated; συμβαίνει . . . μεγεθῶν is really irrelevant and the point comes in διὰ . . . ἑκάστοις. 'They allege, as proof, that each of these is a number, and that in this place there is already a plurality of the magnitudes composed of numbers *just because* the qualities of number that constitute these are connected with these groups of places.' Since opinion and the like are also constituted by qualities of number, this does afford a proof, good enough for the Pythagoreans, that opinion and the like are localized in these same places.

26. ἤδη πλῆθος εἶναι τῶν συνισταμένων μεγεθῶν. Alexander (74. 12) takes this to mean that while at the centre of the universe there is τὸ ἕν, in the next region there are τὰ δύο, i. e. opinion and daring, in the next region to that presumably three corresponding things, and so on. This interpretation is unsatisfactory because (1) ἤδη implies that there are already things *other* than opinion, &c., assigned to the various regions, and (2) μεγεθῶν, spatial magnitudes, is inapplicable to opinion and the like. The μεγέθη must be spatial objects of some kind. One naturally thinks of the Pythagorean cosmology with its ten bodies ranged in order from the centre of the universe outwards— counter-earth, earth, moon, sun, Venus, Mercury, Mars, Jupiter, Saturn, heaven of the fixed stars. One of the versions of Alexander (alt. rec. gr. in Hayduck) connects opinion, which was identified with 2 (unless the tradition connecting it with 3, for which cf. 985ᵇ 30 n., is the more correct), with the region of the earth, and opportunity, which was identified with 7, with the region of the sun and moon. In 38. 20, also, Alexander connects opportunity with the sun. But these suggestions are misleading, for (1) the earth can be reckoned as the second body only if we count from the centre, and the sun as the seventh only if we count from the outside; but we cannot be meant to combine the two modes of counting. (2) πλῆθος is not explained by this interpretation. In the cosmology only one star is assigned to each region (except that of the outer heaven), but Aristotle speaks of a plurality of μεγέθη in each region. πλῆθος cannot mean, as Zeller takes it to mean, the *ordinal* number of each heavenly body. Aristotle must mean that in each of the regions of the universe there is a multitude of extended bodies composed of numbers. Now Pythagoras is said to have regarded earth as built up out of cubes, fire of tetrahedra, air of octahedra, water of eicosahedra, the outer sphere of dodecahedra

(Aet. ii. 6. 5). We read in the scholia to Euclid (Heiberg's Euclid, vol. v, p. 654, quoted by Burnet) that the Pythagoreans knew only the cube, the tetrahedron, and the dodecahedron, while the other two regular solids were discovered by Theaetetus; but later Pythagoreans probably used Theaetetus' discovery to complete the correspondence of the elements with the regular solids. They further reduced the regular solids to numbers, in accordance with their general principle (Speusippus, *ap. Theol. Arithm.* pp. 61–63 Ast). Thus each of the elements is a μέγεθος συνιστάμενον, composed of a particular number. συνισταμένων = συνισταμένων ἐκ τῶν ἀριθμῶν, cf. l. 21 τὸν ἀριθμὸν τοῦτον ἐξ οὗ συνέστηκεν ὁ κόσμος. Proclus similarly speaks of the Pythagorean construction of the elements out of the regular solids as τὴν τῶν κοσμικῶν σχημάτων σύστασιν (Diels, i. 346. 2). On the history of this doctrine cf. Heath. *Gk. Math.* i. 158–162. The various regions, then, of which Aristotle is speaking are probably those of the elements. In one region there is already a plurality of portions of fire, because the number of fire is proper to that region; in another a plurality of portions of air, and so on.

The emendations proposed by Zeller and Luthe in this line do nothing to aid the interpretation.

27. τὰ πάθη ταῦτα, the properties of number, or the numbers exhibiting certain properties (for the confusion between these cf. 985^b 29 n.), which constitute the συνιστάμενα μεγέθη.

τοῖς τόποις ἑκάστοις, as the plural ἑκάστοις shows, means 'the several groups of places'. Each portion of fire, for instance, occupies one place: fire altogether occupies a group of places.

πότερον οὗτος κτλ. is to be interpreted in the light of ll. 21, 22. 'Is this number, which we must suppose each of these abstractions (opinion, &c.) to be, the same number that is exhibited in the material universe?' The question raised in ll. 18–22 was, 'How can numbers be the causes of the things and events in the universe, and at the same time the universe itself?'; in ll. 22–29 Aristotle puts a different question, 'How can numbers be opinion, &c., and at the same time be the substance of the material universe?' He wants a distinction to be drawn between abstract number as the cause of the nature of things and concrete number as the substance of the things themselves, and he assumes that the only number with which opinion, for instance, can possibly be identified is abstract number. Thus the question how the number which is the cause of things can also be the substance of things is substantially the same as the question how the number which is, e.g., opinion can be the number which is the substance of a material thing.

29–32. Aristotle says nothing here of the distinction which he elsewhere (e. g. 987^b 14) attributes to Plato between the Idea of a number and the many mathematical or 'intermediate' instances of that number. He is thinking of passages in which this distinction is blurred, and intelligible number in general is opposed to concrete or denominate numbers, ὁρατὰ ἢ ἁπτὰ σώματα ἔχοντες ἀριθμοί (*Rep.* 525 D), such as στρατόπεδα δύο καὶ βοῦς δύο (*Phil.* 56 D).

31. ταῦτα means not, like τούτων in l. 29, opinion and the like, but material things, the συνιστάμενα μεγέθη.

(b) *The theory of Ideas (or Forms)* (ch. 9).

990ª 33. Objections: (i) It supposes Ideas to exist in order to explain sensibles, but in doing this it merely doubles the number of things to be explained.

ᵇ 8. (ii) Of the 'proofs' of the theory, some prove nothing, others would prove the existence of Ideas of things of which we Platonists think there are none. (α) The arguments from the existence of the sciences would prove that there are Forms of all things of which there are sciences. (β) The argument of 'one over many' would prove that there are Forms of negations. (γ) The argument from the possibility of thinking when the object has perished would prove that there are Forms of perishable objects. (δ) Of the more accurate arguments some lead to Ideas of relative terms, others posit the 'third man'.

17. (iii) In general the arguments about the Forms destroy what the school of Ideas thinks more important than the Ideas; number becomes prior to the dyad, the relative to the absolute. In various ways the opinions about the Ideas conflict with the first principles of the theory.

22. (iv) According to the view on which the theory is based there will be Forms of many things besides substances (for there can be a single concept, or a science, of other things); but according to the logical requirements of the theory and the opinions actually held, if the Forms are shared in there are Forms only of substances.

29. For (α) each is shared in not as an accident of something else but as something not predicated of a subject (i. e. not as anything that shares in doubleness shares in eternity because doubleness is eternal), so that the Forms must be substances. But (β) the same names must indicate substance in the sensible world as in the ideal (else what is meant by calling the Idea 'one over many'? If the Ideas and the things that share in them *have* the same form, there is something common, for instance, to the Idea of two and the particular two, as there is to the perishable two and the particular mathematical two; and if they *have not* the same form, they have only their name in common, as Callias and a statue may both be called 'a man').

991ª 8. (v) The main question is, what do the Forms contribute

either to eternal or to transient sensibles? (a) They cause no change
in them, (β) they contribute nothing to the knowledge of them (for,
not being in them, they are not their substance), nor (γ) to their being
(if they were in them they might perhaps be their causes as white is of
the whiteness of that in which it is mixed; but this view of Anaxagoras and Eudoxus is easily refuted).

19. (vi) Other things are not composed of Forms in any
ordinary sense; and to call the Forms patterns and say other things
share in them is empty metaphor. For (a) what is it that works with
its eye on the Ideas? (β) A thing can be or become like another
without being copied from it. (γ) There will be many patterns, and
therefore Forms, of the same thing; to a man there will answer
the Forms of animal, biped, and man. (δ) Not only will the species
be the pattern of the individuals, but the genus will be the pattern of
its species, so that the same thing will be pattern and copy.

b **1.** (vii) How can the Ideas, being the substances of things, exist
apart from the things? In the *Phaedo* they are said to be causes
both of being and of becoming. Yet (a) even if the Forms exist, the
things that share in them do not come into being unless there is a
moving cause, and (β) many things, e. g. houses, come into existence
though we say there are no Forms of them, and therefore other things
also may be or come into being owing to similar causes.

9. (viii) If the Forms are numbers, how will they be causes?
(a) If it is because things are other numbers, how will the one set of
numbers act as causes for the other set? The fact that the former are
eternal, the latter not, makes no difference. (β) If it is because things
in this world are numerical ratios, like a harmony, evidently they are
ratios *of something*, and the numbers themselves will be so too, and not
really numbers.

21. (ix) From many numbers one number is produced, but how can
one Form be produced from more than one? If it is produced not
from numbers but from the units in them, what of the units? If they are
specifically alike, many paradoxes ensue, and so too if they are unlike
(both the units in one number and those in different numbers); for
how will they differ, if they are subject to no affections?

27. (x) They must set up another kind of number, with which
arithmetic deals, and all the so-called intermediates; then (a) from
what principles are these produced, and (β) why are they intermediate?

31. (xi) Each unit in the indefinite dyad must come from a prior
dyad, which is impossible.

992ᵃ 1. (xii) What constitutes the unity of the number when grasped collectively?

2. (xiii) If the units are dissimilar, then (just as people name not the general term body but fire and earth as the elements) the different kinds of unit should have been named; but they speak as if the One were always alike in kind, in which case the numbers it gave rise to would not be substances. If there is a ' one itself' and this is a principle, ' one ' must have more than one meaning.

10. (xiv) We derive lengths from the long and short, planes from the broad and narrow, bodies from the deep and shallow. But (*a*) these principles being generically different, how can the plane contain a line or the solid a plane? The broad is not the genus of the deep, for then a body would be a kind of plane.

19. (*β*) From what will the points contained in lines be derived? Plato opposed the point as a geometrical dogma, and applied the name of ' principle of the line ', a thing he often posited, to the ' indivisible lines '. Yet they must have a limit, so that the argument that establishes the line establishes the point.

24. (xv) In general, though philosophy seeks the cause of sensible phenomena, we have abandoned this search (for we say nothing of the efficient cause), and name other substances without showing how they can be the substances of these ; participation is nothing.

29. (xvi) The Forms have nothing to do with the final cause at which both reason and nature aim ; mathematics has taken the place of philosophy, though it is said that we ought to study it for the sake of other things.

ᵇ 1. (xvii) The underlying substance is stated too mathematically ; (*a*) the great and the small are predicates of matter rather than matter; they answer to the rare and the dense of the physicists.

(*β*) If these are movements, the Forms will be moved ; if they are not, whence did movement come? The theory is fatal to physics.

9. (xviii) They do not prove that all things are one ; even if we grant that the universal is a genus (which it sometimes cannot be), they only establish the existence of a separate One-itself.

13. (xix) It cannot be stated how the ' things after the numbers '— lines, planes, solids—exist or can exist, or what function they have ; they cannot be either Forms or ' intermediates ' or perishables, but must form a fourth class.

18. (xx) To seek the elements of all things that are, without distinguishing the various senses of ' be ', is absurd ; only the elements of *substances* can be discovered.

24. (xxi) If we are to discover the elements of all things we cannot know anything before, as the man who is learning geometry knows no *geometry* before; but all learning, whether by deduction, definition, or induction, implies previous knowledge. Nor can we have this supreme knowledge all along without knowing it.

993ᵃ 2. (xxii) As it may be disputed whether ζ is a compound of σ and δ or a distinct sound, so there may be dispute about the elements of being.

7. (xxiii) If the elements of all things are the same, we ought to know even those sensible things which we do not perceive, which is impossible.

A considerable part of this chapter, 990ᵇ 2—991ᵇ 9, is almost verbally identical with M. 1078 ᵇ 34—1079ᵇ 3, 1079ᵇ 12—1080ᵃ 8. The following differences may be noted:

(1) Book A says (990ᵇ 4) σχεδὸν γὰρ ἴσα—ἢ οὐκ ἐλάττω—ἐστὶ τὰ εἴδη τούτοις. M puts the case more strongly (1078ᵇ 36)—πλείω γάρ ἐστι τῶν καθ' ἕκαστα αἰσθητῶν ὡς εἰπεῖν τὰ εἴδη.

(2) Where A says δείκνυμεν, οἰόμεθα, φαμεν, βουλόμεθα (990ᵇ 9, 11, 16, 19, 23, 991ᵇ 7), M says δείκνυται, οἴονται, φασιν, βούλονται (1079ᵃ 5, 7, 12, 14, 20, 1080ᵃ 6).

(3) M has a section (1079ᵇ 3–11) which does not appear in A.

(4) There are many slight divergences; sometimes A and sometimes M adds an explanatory word or phrase. Cf. M. 1078ᵇ 34—1080ᵃ 8 n.

Of these points the first two are the most significant. The use of the first person implies that Aristotle speaks of himself as a Platonist. Jaeger argues with much force (*Entst.* 33–35) that Book A must have been read before a Platonic circle, and that this was probably the circle that gathered round Hermias at Assos. If this conjecture be right, the book may be dated 348–345 B.C., when Aristotle is known to have been living at the court of Hermias. In M Aristotle no longer speaks of himself as a Platonist, and permits himself at one point (1078ᵇ 36), as we have seen, to exaggerate an objection which was stated more moderately in A. M, then, belongs to a later period, at which Aristotle was no longer in touch with Platonists. This inference about the comparative date of the two versions agrees with that suggested by the references in B to A and by those in M to B, for which see 987ᵃ 32—ᵇ 8 n.

The occurrence of these two versions of the same passage may have been the reason why the authenticity of A was doubted in antiquity (Al. 196, 20, Syr. 23. 9). Really it is an indication of the genuineness of both books. That Aristotle should have used in one context what he had written in another is much more likely than that a forgery should have found its way into the text when there was already a genuine passage covering the same ground.

It is to be noticed that the use of the first person in the sense of 'we

Platonists' is not confined to this passage. It is common to A and B, and confirms the other indications of a close connexion between these books; cf. 992ᵃ 11, 25, 27, 28, B. 997ᵇ 3, 1002ᵇ 14. The same tone may be detected in *E. N.* 1096ᵃ 13.

990ᵇ 2. That τούτοις means individual things, not, as Alexander and Bonitz suppose, classes of things, is shown by τωνδὶ τῶν ὄντων, l. 1. ἴσα is not to be taken very strictly. One Idea was common to many particulars; but, on the other hand, one particular shared in many Ideas, so that, speaking very roughly, Aristotle says their numbers are equal.

6. καθ' ἕκαστον κτλ. The evidence about the text is somewhat puzzling. In l. 7 E and Al., as well as the corresponding passage in M, have τε, which is omitted by Aᵇ and by Asc. Again E, Γ, Asc., and M have ἄλλων, while Aᵇ and Al. have ἄλλων ὧν. Bonitz argues that τῶν ἄλλων forms no proper contrast to καθ' ἕκαστον, and therefore punctuates (as Bekker does) after ἐστι (*sic*) and not after οὐσίας, and would omit τε, and interpret (reading ἄλλων ὧν) 'for each class of things there is something (an Idea) of the same name, even for those things other than substances which have a unity over the plurality of particulars'.

τε, however, is very strongly attested, and the objection to it is removed if we interpret τῶν ἄλλων in the light of the whole phrase καθ' ἕκαστον γὰρ ὁμώνυμόν τι ἔστι καὶ παρὰ τὰς οὐσίας, and not of καθ' ἕκαστον merely. The question remains whether ὧν should be read. The balance of evidence is against it, and the construction without it is at any rate not more difficult than that which we get by reading it. The whole sentence, with τε and without ὧν, will mean : 'for to each thing there answers an entity having the same name as it and existing apart from the substances, and in the case of non-substantial things there is a one-over-many.'

ὁμώνυμον. Aristotle uses this word rather than συνώνυμον, partly because it is Plato's own word, partly perhaps to suggest that there is no common nature shared by the Idea and the particular and that therefore the one can do nothing to explain the other—the point which he has been making in ll. 1–4. Cf. 987ᵇ 9 n.

8. τοῖς ἀϊδίοις is in 991ᵃ 9 expanded into τοῖς ἀϊδίοις τῶν αἰσθητῶν, i. e. the heavenly bodies. Similarly τοῖσδε is expanded into τοῖς γιγνομένοις καὶ φθειρομένοις.

9. δείκνυμεν, 'we Platonists prove'. For the use of the first person cf. note at beginning of chapter.

11. οὐχ ὧν οἰόμεθα = ὧν οὐκ οἰόμεθα, cf. Bonitz, *Index,* 539ᵃ 14–47. The things of which according to Aristotle the Platonists did not think there were Ideas are :

(1) the objects of some 'sciences' (l. 12), i. e., probably, *artefacta* (cf. 991ᵇ 6, Λ. 1070ᵃ 18).

(2) negations (l. 13).

(3) perishable things (l. 14).

(4) relative terms (l. 16).

It is quite clear that Platonism soon departed from the doctrine of the

Republic (596 A) that there is an Idea answering to every group of things. Xenocrates defined the Idea as αἰτία παραδειγματικὴ τῶν κατὰ φύσιν ἀεὶ διεστώτων (Procl. *in Parm.* i. 888. 18 Cousin), and Diogenes Laertius represents Plato himself as making the Ideas αἰτίας τινὰς καὶ ἀρχὰς τοῦ τοιαῦτα εἶναι τὰ φύσει διεστῶτα οἷάπερ ἐστὶν αὐτά (iii. 77). The doctrine of the school is well stated by Syrianus, who says there are not Ideas of bad things (107. 8), of negations (107. 10), of things changeable (107. 12), of 'parts which are not also wholes', like the hand or the head (107. 14), of the accidental attributes of bodies, like sweetness (107. 18), of 'composites, like wise man' (107. 21), of hybrids (107. 26), of the products of the imitative arts (107. 31), or of things that depend on choice or chance (107. 34), but only of universal and perfect substances and of what contributes to their natural state, e. g. of man and of wisdom (107. 38). Again he says there are not Ideas of inessential relations such as higher and lower, right and left, neighbouring, and so on (111. 12), nor of attributes that belong to bodies only, but that there are Ideas of attributes that belong ' both to souls and to bodies and to natures', such as likeness, equality, greatness (114. 5). Cf. similar statements by Plotinus (v. 9. 10 init.), Proclus (*in Rempubl.* i. 32. 17 Kroll, *in Parm.* v. p. 815. 15— 833. 23 Cousin).

It is hard to say to what extent Plato himself limited the class of things of which there are Ideas. The only relevant passage in which Aristotle mentions Plato by name is Λ. 1070ᵃ 18, and here he only says that Plato ἔφη ὅτι εἴδη ἔστιν ὁπόσα φύσει, that there are Ideas of all natural objects, though Aristotle there seems to infer that Plato thought there were *not* Ideas of artificial objects. In the period represented by such dialogues as the *Phaedo* and the *Republic* we find Ideas of types which Aristotle says the Platonists repudiated, e. g. (1) of bed and table (*Rep.* 596 B, 597 C), of shuttle and auger and of every kind of tool (*Crat.* 389 B, C), (2) of the negations of self-control, courage, &c. (*Rep.* 402 C), of ugly, bad, and unjust (ib. 475 E, 476 A), (4) of equal, greater, and less (*Phaedo* 74 A, 75 C, 100 E). Prof. Jackson has tried to show (*J. of P.* x. 253–298, xi. 287–331, xiii. 1– 40, 242–272, xiv. 173–230, xv. 280–305) that there is a 'later theory of Ideas', represented by the *Parmenides*, *Theaetetus*, *Sophistes*, *Politicus*, *Philebus*, and *Timaeus*, in which Plato excludes all Ideas save those which are natural types of the species of animals and of the four elements. This is a theory of Ideas, it will be observed, which outdoes even Syrianus in exclusiveness. For a trenchant criticism of Prof. Jackson's view cf. Prof. Taylor in *Mind*, v. 304, 305, 313–315. Apart from other objections to this view, which it would take too long to enter upon, it may be enough to point to the Ideas of unlike, other, ugly, bad in *Theaet.* 186 A, and of other and not-being in *Soph.* 254 E, 256 D. If not many instances of Ideas of the kinds in question are to be found in the late dialogues, this is because the ideal theory has in general receded considerably into the background and Plato has become interested in other speculations. It would seem that this development of the ideal theory, like so many other developments of it about which Aristotle tells us, either belongs to a very late period of Plato's life and is not expressed at all in the dialogues, or does not belong to Plato but only to his followers. We have really no means of deciding between these two possibilities.

11–15. The very concise mode of reference to the arguments for the Ideas seems to imply that the arguments had been carefully named and tabulated ; τὸ ἓν ἐπὶ πολλῶν and τὸ νοεῖν τι φθαρέντος are evidently technical names current in the school. The 'arguments from the sciences' must have been arguments on the lines of *Rep.* 479 A—480 A, *Tim.* 51 D—52 A. Such arguments have already, in 987^a 32–^{b} 10, been described as the main reason for the belief in Ideas. The general form of the argument is :

If knowledge exists, there must exist an unchangeable object of knowledge.

Knowledge does exist.

Therefore there exists an unchangeable object.

Sensible objects are changeable.

Therefore there exist non-sensible realities.

Alexander (who seems to rely on the first book of Aristotle's *De Ideis*) gives three arguments ἐκ τῶν ἐπιστημῶν. (1) If every science does its work with reference to one identical object and not to any of its individual instances, there must be in the case of each science something apart from sensible things which is eternal and is the pattern of the objects of each science ; and of this nature is the Idea. (2) The objects of sciences must exist ; now the objects of the sciences are things other than the particulars, for these are infinite and indefinite, but the objects of the sciences are definite ; there are, therefore, things other than the particulars, and these are the Ideas. (3) If medicine is the science not of this health but of health simply, there must be a health-itself ; and if geometry is not the science of this equal and this proportionate but of the equal simply and of the proportionate simply, there must be an equal-itself and a proportionate-itself, and these are Ideas.

If we ask what the objects of science were, of which the Platonists of Aristotle's time did not recognize Ideas, the answer probably is, 'the objects of the *productive* sciences, or arts'. It will be noticed that there is no *express* reference in this passage to the Platonists' denial of Ideas of manufactured objects (for which cf. 991^b 6). This is most easily explained if we suppose that they are referred to in the words πάντων ὅσων ἐπιστῆμαί εἰσι, and Alexander interprets the words so.

13. τὸ ἓν ἐπὶ πολλῶν is the argument for the existence of Ideas from the existence of groups of particulars (*Rep.* 596 A, cf. *Phaedo* 74).

καὶ τῶν ἀποφάσεων. It is not absolutely necessary to suppose any change in the Platonic theory in this respect. It is true that Ideas of the vices, of the ugly, the bad, the other. the unlike, and not-being, are referred to in Plato's dialogues, but these are privations with a positive meaning of their own, not bare negations. There was no need to suppose bare negative Ideas; anything that could be explained by participation in a negative Idea could be explained more simply by non-participation in the positive Idea.

14. κατὰ δὲ τὸ νοεῖν τι φθαρέντος τῶν φθαρτῶν. This objection stands on a different footing from the two that precede and the one that follows. In these others Aristotle is arguing that certain arguments for the Ideas involve the existence of Ideas which the Platonists repudiated, though the Platonism of the *Phaedo* and the *Republic* admits them. Here he is arguing that one of the arguments for the Ideas involves the existence of Ideas which neither Plato nor any Platonist ever admitted. In a sense they did admit Ideas of perishables, e. g. an Idea of horse. But Aristotle means that they ought in consistency to have admitted Ideas of the particular perishable horses. There must be an Idea of horse, they say, since we could think of the horse even if all horses had died. Then, Aristotle argues, there must be an Idea of each perishable horse, since we can have an image of it when it has died. I. e., if thought implies the existence of its object, so does memory.

15. οἱ ἀκριβέστεροι τῶν λόγων. There is no reason to suppose, with Alexander (83. 29), that Aristotle means the arguments which prove the existence of the Idea as a παράδειγμα, in contrast to the preceding arguments which merely prove the existence of κοινόν τι παρὰ τὰ καθ' ἕκαστα. The distinction would be a difficult one to maintain, and is not suggested by Aristotle's words. The point rather is this (it has been well brought out by Prof. Jackson in *J. of P.* x. 255): Aristotle has previously pointed out certain *consequences* of Platonic arguments; he now points out certain *implications actually stated* (λέγουσι can mean nothing else) in Plato's more accurate arguments, though unwelcome to his successors. Plato's argument in the *Phaedo* (74 A—77 A) and in the *Republic* (479 A—480 A) states the existence of Ideas of relative terms (cf. 990^b 11 n.), and his argument in the *Parmenides* (132 A, B, D—133 A) states the difficulty of the 'third man'.

16. ὧν οὔ φαμεν εἶναι καθ' αὑτὸ γένος. A change in Aristotle's mode of expression is to be noted here. He does not say that Platonic arguments lead to a belief in Ideas of relations, and that yet the Platonists deny the existence of such Ideas. He says that Platonic arguments lead to Ideas of τὰ πρός τι, 'which, we maintain, do not form an independent class'. Arguments like those in the *Phaedo* lead to belief in an Idea, e. g., of the equal. Yet we do not suppose that all things which happen to be equal to other things form a separate class *in rerum natura*; such a class would include things which in essentials differ from each other; such a classification would cut across any natural classification of the contents of the universe. This points not to a change in the Platonic theory but to a difficulty which the Platonic theory, in the form familiar to us from the dialogues, must have presented to Aristotle and to orthodox Platonists alike.

17. τὸν τρίτον ἄνθρωπον. The argument which 'mentions the third man ', Alexander tells us, is the argument that since a particular man is like the ideal man in being a man, there must be a ' third man ' in which both share. But he mentions various other forms of ' third man ' argument. (1) There is an argument which was ' used by the sophists '. When we say ' man walks ', we mean neither the Idea of man (which is motionless) nor any particular man; we must, then, mean a man of some third kind. (2) Phanias (a pupil of Aristotle) in his book against Diodorus Cronus says that Polyxenus the sophist (a contemporary of Plato) used the following argument : If man exists by participation in the Idea of man, there must be some man who ' will have his being in relation to the Idea'. But this can neither be the ideal man, who *is* an Idea, nor a particular man. Therefore it must be a third man. (3) Alexander gives in the third place an argument which appears to be the same as that which he says is used here, except that it points out that the same regress may be repeated *ad indefinitum.*

Thus ' the third man ' was a phrase that was applied to various forms of argument; but that which Aristotle means here is doubtless that which Alexander supposes him to mean, and which occurs in *Parm.* 132 A, B, D—133 A. But the instance of man is not there used by Plato, and Aristotle probably has in view not the argument in the *Parmenides* itself, but an argument of the Academic school based on it. Alexander, followed by Bonitz, interprets (83. 34) λέγουσιν as meaning εἰσάγουσιν, 'involve', as if the ' third man ' were merely a consequence implied in some Platonic argument; but the word cannot well mean this. What Aristotle says is that the Platonic argument, not his own inference from it, ' mentions the third man '.

The ' third man ' argument depends on the positing of the Idea as an individual substance outside the particulars and imitated by them (this is stated expressly in *Soph. El.* 179ᵃ 3). Aristotle himself would escape it by saying that there is no such Idea but only a universal *in* the particulars. There is not an ideal man but only man-ness, and as man-ness is not a man there is no reason to suppose a ' third man ' predicable of man-ness as well as of man. The question whether the argument is valid as against Plato depends on the further question whether Plato really did describe the Idea as if it were just a sort of fresh particular, an αἰσθητὸν ἀίδιον as Aristotle calls it ; and on this we can hardly enter here. It is clear from the *Parmenides* that Plato saw the difficulty ; that, as Prof. Jackson says, ' he had in reserve a reformed doctrine which was, or seemed to be, safe from attack on this side ' (*J. of P.* x. 256) is more doubtful. What the *Parmenides* itself suggests is rather that he saw the need for a restatement of the ideal theory but did not see his way to such a restatement (τι ἄλλο δεῖ ζητεῖν ᾧ μεταλαμβάνει, 133 A).

Before writing the *Parmenides*, Plato had pointed out that the supposition of *two* Ideas, say of bed, would lead to yet another Idea (*Rep.* 597 c); and *Tim.* 31 A gives another argument analogous to the ' third man '. Aristotle refers to the ' third man ' argument in

Z. 1039ᵃ 2, *Soph. El.* 178ᵇ 36; in K. 1059ᵇ 8 the phrase is used, with a play upon words, in a different connexion.

On the assumption that λέγουσιν means 'involve' and not 'mention', surprise has been felt at Aristotle's failing to say that Plato has actually anticipated his objection in the *Parmenides*, and Ueberweg, among others, used this as an argument against the authenticity of the *Parmenides*. Bäumker has tried (*Rhein. Mus.* xxxiv. 82) to explain the absence of a reference to the *Parmenides* here by the supposition that the argument was invented not by Plato but by Polyxenus the sophist, and that thus Plato is in the *Parmenides* merely quoting a Megarian attack on the ideal theory. But Bäumker's interpretation of the 'third man' argument ascribed to Polyxenus by Alexander is untenable; whatever the argument means, it is not identical with the argument in the *Parmenides*; and it is the latter that Aristotle has in view in *Soph. El.* 178ᵇ 36—179ᵃ 10, and, we may be sure, here too. On this side also, then, our interpretation of λέγουσιν is confirmed. On the difficulties in the supposition that in the first part of the *Parmenides* Plato is merely quoting Megarian attacks on the Ideas, cf. Prof. Taylor in *Mind*, v. 316–318.

18. βουλόμεθα, the reading of E and Asclepius, is pretty certainly right. βούλονται οἱ λέγοντες εἴδη is doubtless a gloss introduced from Book M, and E has illogically combined οἱ λέγοντες εἴδη with βουλόμεθα.

19. συμβαίνει γάρ κτλ., i. e. number, being the Idea under which the dyad falls, must be prior to it; thus the Platonic arguments depose the very first principles of the Platonic theory from their place of dignity. ἡ δυάς probably means the indefinite dyad, as it does in M. 1081ᵇ 18, 1083ᵃ 12. It can be referred to simply as 'the dyad' because it has been already referred to more explicitly in 987ᵇ 20, 25, 33.

It is to be noted tnat Aristotle is not quite fair in assuming that the indefinite dyad is an ordinary member of the class of 2's. We have already (987ᵇ 34) found him misinterpreting the indefinite dyad somewhat similarly. Cf. 991ᵇ 31 n.

20. καὶ τὸ πρός τι τοῦ καθ' αὐτό, sc. πρότερον, to be understood from πρώτην. It is natural to take this, with Alexander (86. 5), as repeating in a different form what has just been said. 'I. e. the relative term number will be prior to the supposed self-subsistent dyad.' Bonitz thinks that number is not a relative term, and therefore interprets 'and the relative term great-and-small will be prior to the supposed self-subsistent Ideas'. But it is harder to get this out of the Greek. Number no doubt is in the category of quantity (*Cat.* 4ᵇ 23), but that is no reason why it should not be also in the category of relation (*Cat.* 11ᵃ 37). Certainly it is the number *of* something, as Alexander points out (86. 5), and πρός τι τὰ τοιαῦτα λέγεται ὅσα αὐτὰ ἅπερ ἐστὶν ἑτέρων εἶναι λέγεται (*Cat.* 6ⁿ 36). This interpretation is confirmed by the fuller form of the argument in M. 1079ⁿ 17.

29–991ᵃ 2. We may best attack the interpretation of this difficult

argument by bringing out the implications of the parenthesis in
990ᵇ 31–34 εἶναι. If anything 'shares in the double itself', it shares
in eternalness, since the double itself is eternal. But for A to share
thus (incidentally) in B does not give it the character B, according to
the Platonists, for no Platonist would say that a sensible thing which is
double of something else is therefore eternal. Therefore the Ideas,
sharing in which gives particulars the character expressed by the name
common to them and the Ideas, cannot be shared in *qua* predicates of
a subject, as 'eternal' is a predicate of the double itself. Therefore
they must be substances. But the same words must indicate substance
in this sensible world as in the ideal world. Therefore the things of
which there are Ideas must be substances. This conclusion, stated in
l. 29, is established by the premises (1) οὐσία τὰ εἴδη ἐστίν (which
is itself proved in ll. 29–34) and (2) ταὐτὰ ἐνταῦθα οὐσίαν σημαίνει
κἀκεῖ. Bonitz argues that the substantiality of the Ideas must be
assumed, not proved, and would therefore read οὐσίας or οὐσιῶν
in l. 34, and, since then ταὐτὰ ... κἀκεῖ must give a reason for this
conclusion, he reads ταὐτὰ γάρ for ταὐτὰ δέ. The argument according
to him is: 'The particulars must share in the Ideas-*qua*-substances,
not *qua*-predicates, and must therefore themselves be substances,
for the same names indicate substance in the sensible as in the ideal
world'. This agrees with Alexander's interpretation, but (1) if
Aristotle were *assuming* that the Ideas are substances, ταὐτὰ ἐνταῦθα
οὐσίαν σημαίνει κἀκεῖ would in itself prove that there are Ideas only of
substances, and the rest of the argument would be otiose. (2) Alexander probably read οὐσία in l. 34 (see Al. 91. 11, 12), though he ignores
it as long as possible and interprets it loosely when he comes to it ;
and we cannot safely infer from 91. 2 that he read ταὐτὰ γάρ. Since
Aristotle has *already* in l. 29 said τῶν οὐσιῶν ἀναγκαῖον ἰδέας εἶναι
μόνον, it is hard to see how οὐσιῶν or οὐσίας, if it had been the original
reading in l. 34, could have been corrupted into οὐσία.

Schwegler's conjectures, ὥστ' εἰ ἔστιν οὐσία τὰ εἴδη, ταὐτὰ ἐνταῦθα,
and ὥστ', εἰ ἔσται, οὐσία τὰ εἴδη· ταὐτὰ δὲ ἐνταῦθα, are no more likely to
be right than those of Bonitz.

29. οὐ γὰρ ... μετέχονται, 'they are not shared in as accidents of a subject that is directly shared in '.

991ᵃ 1. ἢ τί ἔσται κτλ. 'If the same words are not to indicate
substance in the sensible as in the ideal world, what is the relation
between the two worlds, and why should an Idea be posited for each
group of particulars ; what community of nature would there be between
the one and the many if it were a substance and they were not ? '

2. καὶ εἰ μέν κτλ. This is not introduced as if it were a fresh argument against the Ideas, and if it were, it would merely repeat the 'third
man' argument which Aristotle has already referred to in 990ᵇ 17.
Rather it seems to confirm the close relation between particulars
and Ideas which he has asserted in the words ταὐτὰ ἐνταῦθα οὐσίαν
σημαίνει κἀκεῖ. If there is not this close relation, there is a mere
ὁμωνυμία.

4. τῶν πολλῶν μὲν ἀϊδίων δέ, the mathematical 2's. Cf. 987ᵇ 15.

τὸ δυάς. The common reading is τὸ δυὰς εἶναι, but this is an impossible form, and we must either omit εἶναι with ΕΓ Al. and M. 1079ᵃ 36 or read τὸ δυὰς σημαίνει with Bywater (*J. of P.* xxviii. 246).

5. τ' αὐτῆς, Bonitz's emendation of ταύτης, is clearly right. Cf. Z. 1040ᵇ 33, M. 1079ᵃ 36.

9. διαπορεῖν here seems merely to mean 'to raise a difficulty', as in Γ. 1009ᵃ 22, M. 1079ᵇ 21, 1085ᵃ 25. More often it means 'to work through the difficulties', as in B. 995ᵃ 28, 35, ᵇ 5, 996ᵃ 17, K. 1059ᵃ 19, ᵇ 15, M. 1086ᵃ 19, or 'to establish by discussion of the difficulties', as in B. 999ᵃ 31, M. 1086ᵃ 34.

τοῖς ἀϊδίοις τῶν αἰσθητῶν, the heavenly bodies.

12, 13. This argument is met by Plato in *Parm.* 134 D; this is one of the points relied on by Siebeck for the proof of his theory that the *Parmenides* (with the *Sophist* and the *Philebus*) was directed against criticisms urged by Aristotle in discussion. The theory has but little evidence in favour of it.

15. ὡς τὸ λευκὸν μεμιγμένον τῷ λευκῷ, 'as white is the cause of whiteness to the white thing by being mixed in it'.

16. Anaxagoras held (cf. fr. 12 *ad fin.*) that each thing owes its apparent character to the preponderance of one of the infinitely numerous 'seeds' in it. For Aristotle's criticisms of the theory cf. 989ᵃ 33, *Phys.* i. 4.

17. Eudoxus is the famous astronomer mentioned in Λ. 1073ᵇ 17. He seems to have 'flourished' about 365 B.C. We have no further information about his views on the question referred to here. But he is commonly said to have been a friend of Plato, or a Platonist (Al. 97. 17, Asc. 86. 11, Cic. *Divin.* ii. 42. 87, *Rep.* i. 14. 22, Strabo, xiv, p. 656 Casaubon, Procl. *in Eucl.* p. 67. 3 Friedl., Plut. *Adv. Colot.* 32, p. 1126 D, Philostr. *V. Soph.* i. 1), and his theory seems to have been an ideal theory which rejected the transcendence ascribed to the Ideas by Plato and described them as immanent in particulars; which is perhaps the reason why he is sometimes described as a Pythagorean (Diog. Laert. viii. 91, Iambl. *in Nicom. Arithm.* p. 10. 17 Pistelli). This would seem to be not so very different from Aristotle's own theory of the universal immanent in particulars; the difference would be that Eudoxus thought of the Ideas still as substances in the fullest sense, while Aristotle holds that one substance cannot inhere in another, and therefore treats universals as not substances in the proper sense of the word. For his criticism of a theory similar to that of Eudoxus cf. B. 998ᵃ 7 n.

20. κατ' οὐθένα τρόπον κτλ. Alexander hesitates between two interpretations, 'in any of the usual senses of ἐκ' (for which cf. α. 994ᵃ 22, Δ. 24) and 'in any of the ways in which the Platonists are wont to derive them'. As Aristotle has said (987ᵇ 13) that they did not specify the nature of the relation between particulars and Ideas, the former interpretation is the more likely.

22. τί γάρ ἐστι κτλ. Aristotle ignores the account (*Tim.* 28 c, 29 A)

of the Demiurgus as making the world with 'the eternal' for his
pattern. Even if he were entitled to regard this as 'poetical metaphor', there is still the Reason which is the αἰτία τῆς μίξεως (*Phil.*
23 D)—though there indeed there is no distinct reference to the Ideas
and no use of the notion of a 'pattern'.

23. τε gives the connexion better than the other reading γάρ : the
sentence introduces a fresh objection. Alexander is said by Bonitz to
have read γάρ, but this is not clear from 102. 6. In this part of Bk.
A, Aristotle somewhat affects the stringing together of sentences by
τε, a usage which specially characterizes Bks. viii–x of the *Ethics.*
Cf. 989ᵃ 26, 990ᵇ 17, 991ᵃ 27, 992ᵇ 7, 9, 18, and Eucken, *De
Aristotelis dicendi ratione*, i. 14.

31. ὡς γένος εἰδῶν. τῶν ὡς γένους εἰδῶν ('the species as species of
a genus') seems to have been Alexander's reading (105. 25) and is
found in all the MSS. in M. 1079ᵇ 34. εἴδη is often thus qualified
when Aristotle is speaking of species of a genus in distinction from
Platonic Forms (cf. Z. 1038ᵃ 5, I. 1057ᵇ 7, 1058ᵃ 22, M. 1085ᵃ 24).
The reading of the MSS. here, ὡς γένος εἰδῶν, puts the same relation
from the other end, 'the genus as genus of species'.

ᵇ **3.** Cf. *Phaedo* 100 D.

6. ὧν οὔ φαμεν εἴδη εἶναι. In Λ. 1070ᵃ 18 Aristotle says expressly
that Plato ἔφη ὅτι εἴδη ἐστὶν ὁπόσα φύσει, and it is apparently implied
that he did *not* recognize Ideas of objects other than natural objects. Now
in *Rep.* 596 B, 597 C, *Crat.* 389 B, C we find Ideas of bed, table, shuttle,
auger ; cf. the story about Plato and Diogenes (Diog. Laert. vi. 53) in
which Plato is represented as speaking of tableness and cupness. It
does not seem possible with Bonitz to treat these references as not
seriously meant, for they agree with the principle of *Rep.* 596 A that there
is an Idea answering to every group of things with a common name.
We find, however, in *Soph.* 265 B a distinction sharply drawn between
natural objects which are the products of God's demiurgic activity,
and the products of human art, and in the *Timaeus* the Ideas appear
not in a logical character, as universals in general, but as patterns according to which God exercises his demiurgic activity. The argument from their non-appearance in the *Timaeus* in any other capacity
is not conclusive, but it is *possible* that when he wrote the *Timaeus*
Plato had altered his conception of the Ideas in the way indicated. It
is also possible that Plato merely denied that there were Ideas answering to the products of the *imitative* arts—their original being not an
Idea but an actual material object ; and that his followers extended this
ban to Ideas answering to the products of the *useful* arts. Cf. 990ᵇ
11 n., Introduction, pp. xlix–li.

8. For the construction διὰ τοιαύτας αἰτίας οἵας = διὰ τοιαύτας αἰτίας
δι᾽ οἵας cf. M. 1086ᵇ 29, *Ath. Pol.* iv. 2 ἐκ τοῦ αὐτοῦ τέλους . . . οὗπερ.

13–21. The argument is: If numbers are said to be the causes of
things because particular things are numerical ratios between certain
subject-matters (cf. the description of the animal body as due to the
mixture, in a certain ratio, of the four elements, *Tim.* 73 B, C), then the

numbers also should be ratios between certain (no doubt different) subject-matters. Thus for ἀριθμός in l. 18 we should expect λόγος ἐν ἀριθμοῖς. But the stress is on ἄλλων τινῶν ὑποκειμένων. Aristotle is willing for the moment to adopt the Platonic description of the Ideas as numbers, so long as it is clear that they must have a substratum. For the use of ἀριθμός where λόγος would be stricter cf. *De An.* 431ᵃ 23. The distinction is pointed out, though rather awkwardly, in the next sentence. 'Man-himself, whether he is in a sense (τις) a number or not, yet will be a numerical ratio and not a number', i.e. not a number in the proper sense. ἁπλῶς, which Bonitz would insert after ἀριθμός in l. 20, would make the meaning clearer, but is not absolutely necessary.

14. ἐστὶν ἔν γέ τι ὧν εἰσὶ λόγοι. The meaning must be 'the things between which they are ratios are some one class of things'. οὖ has been proposed for ὧν, but Alexander read ὧν (108. 20), and the plural is wanted, since a ratio involves two terms.

20. 'Nor can it be inferred on these grounds that it will be a particular number'. Jaeger may, however, be right in inserting ἰδέα, so as to make the statement general, 'nor can it be inferred on these grounds that any idea is a number'. Alexander interprets so, but did not read ἰδέα (109. 20, 30, 110. 1).

22. ἐν τῷ ἀριθμῷ (Aᵇ) is preferable to ἐναρίθμων, which does not seem to occur in this sense.

23. εἴτε γὰρ ὁμοειδεῖς κτλ. The same dilemma is stated in M. 1080ᵃ 18, where ὁμοειδεῖς and μὴ ὁμοειδεῖς are represented by συμβληταί and ἀσύμβλητοι.

25. The commonly accepted reading, μήτε αἱ αὐταὶ ἀλλήλαις μήτε αἱ ἄλλαι πᾶσαι πάσαις, is taken to mean '(if) neither the units in the same number are homogeneous with each other, nor those in one number with those in another', and that this must be the general meaning is clear from M. 1080ᵃ 18-29, 1081ᵇ 35-37. In M Aristotle recognizes the possibility that units in the same number might be thought to be addible while those in different numbers were not. But αἱ αὐταί cannot mean 'the units in the same number', and Bywater accordingly proposed to read with S αὐταί, so as to give the sense 'if they are not homogeneous, neither the units in the number themselves with one another, nor the other units—i.e. those in other numbers—all with all'. It is to be noticed, however, that Aᵇ Al.¹ read μηδὲ αἱ αὐταί, and that Alexander's paraphrase (112. 5) εἰ γὰρ μήτε ἐκεῖναι ἀλλήλαις ὁμοειδεῖς, μήτε πᾶσαι πάσαις ὁμοειδεῖς μηδὲ αἱ αὐταὶ κατὰ τὸ εἶδος takes αἱ αὐταί as = αἱ αὐταὶ κατὰ τὸ εἶδος and as explanatory of ὁμοειδεῖς. Alexander probably read μηδὲ αἱ αὐταὶ ἀλλήλαις, μηδέ κτλ., with the meaning 'while if they (the units in a number, cf. l. 22) are not similar in kind and (in that sense) the same, and if the other units (i.e. the units in other numbers) are not similar in kind all with all'.

27. ὁμολογούμενα τῇ νοήσει, 'consistently with the way in which we think about units'.

28. A comma, as Prof. Cook Wilson has pointed out, is necessary

after ἀριθμητική. πάντα τὰ μεταξὺ λεγόμενα is co-ordinate not with
ἡ ἀριθμητική but with ἕτερον γένος ἀριθμοῦ. For τὰ μεταξύ cf. 987ᵇ
14.

31. τῇ δυάδι may mean (1) the indefinite dyad, or (2) the number 2.
Alexander and Bonitz take it in the former sense, and the argument
then is: The indefinite dyad must have units in it, like any other 2,
and these must be derived from the principles which the Platonists
treat as the principles of all number, viz. the One and the indefinite
dyad. Thus there will be an indefinite dyad before the indefinite
dyad, which is impossible. ἡ δυάς *simpliciter* can be used thus in the
sense of ' the indefinite dyad ' (cf. 990ᵇ 19 n.) ; this interpretation is,
however, open to the objection that Aristotle does not say ' the units
ought on Platonic principles to be derived from a prior dyad '; he
says that they *are* so derived. This suggests that the other interpretation is probably the true one, viz. ' the units in the number 2 each of
them, according to the Platonists, come from a previous 2 (the indefinite dyad), which is impossible '—doubly impossible, because it
makes 2 prior both to 1 and to itself. For ἡ δυάς *simpliciter* used of
the number 2 cf. M. 1081ᵇ 19, N. 1090ᵇ 22.

Whichever be the true interpretation, Aristotle does injustice to the
notion of the indefinite dyad by supposing it to be a number like other
numbers. The Platonists meant by it simply that of which indefinitely much or indefinitely little can be taken, or plurality in the
abstract. For other instances of Aristotle's misinterpretation of it
cf. 987ᵇ 34 n., 990ᵇ 19 n.

992ª 1. ἔτι διὰ τί ἕν κτλ. Aristotle puts the same point in a slightly
more expanded form in H. 1044ª 2-5. ' If a number contains several
units (and particularly, we may suppose Aristotle to have meant,
if these units are different in kind, as some Platonists held), what is
it that makes the number a unity and not a mere aggregate—of this
the Platonists have given no account.' Aristotle here does not do
justice to Plato's conception of number. Plato's point in distinguishing
the Idea of 2, for instance, from the mathematical or intermediate 2's,
was just that the number 2 is not itself a plurality composed of units,
though no doubt it presupposes them. Cf. 987ᵇ 14 n.

6. εἴτ' ἔστι τι κοινόν, τὸ σῶμα, εἴτε μή. In *De Gen. et Corr.*
320ᵇ 23 Aristotle says there is no κοινὸν σῶμα ; i.e. matter, wherever
it exists, is already qualified by some combination of the πρῶται
ἐναντιώσεις, hot and cold, wet and dry, and is thus already fire, air,
water, or earth, or some compound of them ; unqualified matter is an
abstraction which never exists apart.

νῦν δὲ λέγεται κτλ., i.e. in making the One and the indefinite dyad
the principles, the Platonists speak as if the One were the same in kind
wherever it is found, just as portions of fire small or large are the same
in kind. But the numbers that can be built up out of precisely similar
1's are not substances but ordinary mathematical numbers differing
from one another merely in the number of their units (cf. M. 1081ª 5).
If there are ideal numbers, which is what the Platonists are thinking of

when they make the One-itself a first principle, the units are different in kind, and 'one' or 'unit' has a variety of meanings; they ought to distinguish these. For them to make unity in the abstract their first principle is as wrong as it would have been for Empedocles to make body in the abstract his first principle when he believed there were four ultimately irreducible kinds of body.

Aristotle treats the One, which the Platonists made one of the first principles of number, as meaning the unit out of which the numbers are built up. Since they believe in a qualitative difference between the numbers, they should believe, he argues, in a qualitative difference between the units, and they should specify this and not make the One in the abstract their first principle. But he seems to be misunderstanding the One as we have before (987^b 33, 991^b 31) found him misunderstanding the indefinite dyad. The One is different from the units involved in a number, just as the indefinite dyad is different from the number 2 whose function is to double that which is multiplied by it. The indefinite dyad is plurality not yet determined as any particular number, and the One is the formal principle the application of which to the indefinite dyad forms definite numbers. There is here a difficulty for the Platonists; if the material principle and the formal principle are both always the same, how is it that now one number and now another is produced? It would seem that different formal principles are needed. But Aristotle's view that qualitatively different *material* principles—μονάδες διάφοροι—are needed seems to be mistaken; and so is his treatment of the One here as if it were a material principle like Empedocles' elements.

10-19. We know from 988^a 11-14 that the Platonists treated the great and small as the material principle both of the Forms and of sensible things. Now it is the *ideal* numbers that Aristotle has been discussing since 991^b 9; presumably therefore it is *ideal* lines, planes, and solids that he now proceeds to discuss. These were, however, not thought of as being, strictly speaking, Ideas; they are distinguished from the ideal numbers (of which Aristotle has been speaking up to now), but in the phase of Platonism which he is considering all the Ideas were regarded as ideal numbers (991^b 9). We are dealing in this passage, in fact, with a class of entities which some of the Platonists interposed between the Ideas and the mathematicals—entities which Aristotle refers to as 'the things after the numbers' (992^b 13), 'the classes later than number' (M. 1085^a 7), or 'the things after the Ideas' (M. 1080^b 25). These are the universals of the different kinds of line, plane figure, and solid; they have the property which distinguishes Ideas from mathematicals, that of existing only in the singular number (987^b 17), and they would have been called Ideas were it not that the Platonists had identified all Ideas with numbers. Their status is most clearly indicated in 992^b 13-18.

Being quasi-Ideas, they were naturally supposed by the Platonists to have a great and small as their material principle, or rather various forms of the great and small; the material principle of lines was the long and short, that of planes the broad and narrow, that of solids the deep and shallow. With regard to the formal principle Aristotle in one passage speaks vaguely of this as the One or some number (B. 1001ᵇ 24). But from other passages we learn that the prevailing tendency was to treat the numbers 2, 3, and 4 as the formal principles of the lines, planes, and solids respectively (Z. 1036ᵇ 13, M. 1084ª 37–ᵇ 2, N. 1090ᵇ 20–24). Thus, of the various ideal entities, numbers were derived from 1 and the many-and-few (N. 1089ᵇ 12), lines from 2 and the long-and-short, planes from 3 and the broad-and-narrow, solids from 4 and the deep-and-shallow. The notion must have been somewhat as follows: Consider the long-and-short, i.e. indefinite extension in one dimension; two limiting points in this are necessary and sufficient to determine a line. Now suppose the extension to be broad-and-narrow as well, i.e. to be indefinite extension in two dimensions; three points in this are necessary and sufficient to determine the simplest plane figure, the triangle. Now suppose the extension to be deep and shallow as well, i.e. to be indefinite extension in three dimensions; four points in this are necessary and sufficient to determine the simplest solid, the tetrahedron. It is this same mode of derivation that is referred to in *De An.* 404ᵇ 18–21, where τὸ πρῶτον μῆκος καὶ πλάτος καὶ βάθος means the numbers 2, 3, and 4. (In M. 1085ª 32 we read of another Platonic mode of derivation of spatial magnitudes, in which the point is the formal principle and something 'akin to plurality' is the material principle. This answers to the derivation of numbers from the One and plurality, and there is reason for assigning both these doctrines to Speusippus; cf. 1085ª 32 n.)

It will be seen that the mode of derivation of the ideal magnitudes does in fact treat them as 'after' the Idea-numbers, for the numbers 2, 3, and 4 are the formal principles involved in the formation of lines, planes, and solids respectively.

Aristotle's argument in ll. 10–19 might be turned against himself. He is as far removed as Plato from making the solid a *kind* of plane, the plane a kind of line. How, then, if they are three definite kinds of thing, can there be a plane in a solid or a line in a plane? His answer no doubt would be that though he treats them as different kinds he does not derive them from independent principles. He makes the plane the ἀρχή of the solid and the line the ἀρχή of the plane, and thus gets a connexion between them which he thinks the Platonists cannot on their principles get.

19. ἔτι αἱ στιγμαί κτλ.: i.e., since points cannot be deduced from *any* kind of great and small, how can they be present in lines?

20. τούτῳ μὲν οὖν τῷ γένει κτλ. We have no further direct information about Plato's rejection of the point and assertion that there are indivisible lines. The doctrine is frequently ascribed to Xenocrates (Proclus, *in Tim.* 36 B, ii. 246 Diehl, *in Eucl.* 279. 5 Friedlein, Al. 120. 6, 766. 33, Them. *Phys.* 12. 6, Simpl. *Phys.* 138. 14, 140. 12, 142.

16 *De Caelo* 563. 22, 665. 7, Philop. *Phys.* 83. 20, 84. 20, Syr. 124. 2). The treatise *De Lineis Insecabilibus* is apparently directed against Xenocrates' view, and begins by stating the reasons which had led to the view. These are as follows:

1. Since that which admits an infinite number of divisions is big, what is little will admit only a finite number of divisions (968ᵃ 2–9).

2. Since the Idea of line is the first of all lines, it cannot have parts ; for if it had, they would be prior to it (9–14).

3. Since elements are the things to which there is nothing prior, and parts *are* prior to the whole, the elements can have no parts (14–18).

4. Zeno's argument : (1) Since a body moving along a line must reach the half-way point before it reaches the end, a moving body would have to touch an infinite number of points in a finite time unless there are indivisible lines (18–23). (2) Even if it does so, there is the difficulty that thought, the quickest of movements, will come into contact with an infinity of objects, i.e. will count them, in a finite time ; which is impossible (23–ᵇ 4).

5. If we suppose that all commensurate lines are actually measured, there will be a length by which all of them are measured, and this must be indivisible, since otherwise the unit would be multiple (ᵇ 4–14).

This is probably a full list of the reasons for which various thinkers had believed in indivisible lines, and Plato's reason or reasons are probably to be found among them. In the absence of any very definite evidence the ascription to him of any one of the reasons must be conjectural, but a conjecture may be attempted. (1) In the first place the suggestion naturally presents itself that it was really the *ideal* line that Plato held to be indivisible. The ideal line of course would be so, as every Idea must be so. 'Lineness' is clearly not divisible into lines (cf. 991ᵇ 21). The author of the *De Lineis Insecabilibus* seems to think that reflection about the Idea of line was one of the reasons for the belief in indivisible lines (986ᵃ 9–14), and in *De Gen. et Corr.* 316ᵃ 12 the reason given for the belief of ' some ' in indivisible lines is that if there are none the ideal triangle will be many. Porphyry has some such notion in mind when he says (*ap.* Simpl. *Phys.* 140. 10) that Xenocrates believed in entities divisible in quantity but τῷ εἴδει ἄτομα καὶ πρῶτα. Syrianus (l. c.) and Proclus (*in Tim.* l. c.) similarly hold that Xenocrates was maintaining the indivisibility only of the ideal line. Asclepius explains the belief away still more completely (102. 17) We might suppose that Plato was thinking only of the ideal line, and that Xenocrates, who identified the Ideas with the objects of mathematics and therefore ' spoke un-mathematically about the mathematical ' (M. 1080ᵇ 22, 28), spoke of indivisible mathematical lines where Plato had spoken only of the Idea of line as indivisible. But this suggestion is open to serious objections. (*a*) It does not account for the statement that Plato ' opposed the point '. The existence of points is evidently not affected by a belief in an indivisible Idea or universal of line. (*b*) It does not account for the plural τὰς ἀτόμους γραμμάς. This might no doubt be a careless expression on Aristotle's part, but the presumption is that it is not.

(2) In the second place an attempt has been made to connect Aristotle's statement with the doctrine of minimal triangles in the *Timaeus*. The minimal triangles, it is argued, must have been thought of as having minimal sides (cf. *De Lin. Insec.* 968ᵃ 14–18). A similar notion is involved in the attempt of Antiphon to square the circle. There is, however, no evidence that Plato believed his triangles to be mathematical minima. We are only told that the solids composed out of them were so small as to be invisible (56 B). Yet this suggestion seems to be on the right lines in so far as it ascribes to Plato a belief in genuine mathematical lines which were indivisible; only it is not clear that this belief is to be found in the *Timaeus*.

Plutarch (*Quaest. Plat.* v. 2, 3) ascribes to Plato the view that the circle is composed of very small straight lines. It is quite possible that Plato tried thus to reduce the circle to straight lines, and if he did, he would probably have thought of these lines as indivisible. But, as Apelt observes (*Beiträge* 268), Plutarch seems to be reading between the lines of the *Timaeus* rather than recording an independent tradition, and his view is made somewhat improbable by the 'high and almost holy significance' which Plato ascribes to the circle.

(3) Another interpretation of the passage has been given by Milhaud (*Philosophes-Géomètres de la Grèce* 340–343 and *Archiv für Gesch. der Phil.* xvi. 386–390). He takes Aristotle to be saying that Plato attacked the notion that the point was the element of which the line was made up, and called it rather the generative principle of the line; and that this—viz. that the line cannot be divided into *points*—was what he meant when he posited his 'indivisible lines'. No doubt ἐνυπάρχειν, which is here used, is a word which is used in expressing the relation of a στοιχεῖον or constituent part, in distinction from other ἀρχαί, to that of which it is a part (Δ. 1013ᵃ 4, 7, 24, 1014ᵃ 26). This interpretation also avoids the difficulty involved in taking ἐκάλει to mean 'he spoke of', and gives it a more natural meaning—'he called the point the first principle of the line'. But (*a*) the more natural meaning of τούτῳ τῷ γένει is 'the class of points', not 'the class of points considered as constituent parts of the line'. (*b*) 'Indivisible lines' would be a strange name for lines which can be divided into shorter lines though not into points. Milhaud's argument from the use of ἄτομον in Pl. *Soph.* 229 D is unconvincing. (*c*) Aristotle evidently implies that points *do* ἐνυπάρχειν in the line; the only question is, how on Platonic principles they can do so (ἐκ τίνος ἐνυπάρξουσιν, l. 19). But Aristotle does not believe, any more than Plato, that a line can be put together out of points (B. 1001ᵇ 18, *Phys.* 215ᵇ 18, 231ᵃ 24, 241ᵃ 3); the point is not the constituent element but the limit of the line (l. 23). There is, then, no opposition meant between the point as 'present in the line' and as 'principle of the line'. If Plato's doctrine had been merely what Milhaud holds it to have been, Aristotle could have agreed with every word of it; but

in fact he regards it as absurd (*Phys.* 206ᵃ 17, *De Caelo* 299ᵃ 12). (*d*) The treatise *De Lin. Insec.*, which at least reflects Aristotle's teaching accurately, contains no reference to any such theory of indivisible lines as Milhaud suggests. (*e*) In M. 1084ᵃ 37 we have, in an account of Platonic views, the words ἔτι τὰ μεγέθη καὶ ὅσα τοιαῦτα μέχρι ποσοῦ, οἷον ἡ πρώτη γραμμὴ ⟨ἡ⟩ ἄτομος, εἶτα δυάς. Here there is no doubt that δυάς stands for the line (cf. Z. 1036ᵇ 13, H. 1043ᵃ 33), so that γραμμὴ ἄτομος must stand for the point or for what took its place in Plato's theory. There is, however, this much truth in Milhaud's view, that the doctrine of indivisible lines may have been adopted as if it were the only alternative to the Pythagorean construction of the line out of points. The truth lies in a third view, which is Aristotle's own, that the line is constructed out of *divisible* lines, i.e. is infinitely divisible.

(4) Again, a doctrine which denied the existence of the point and substituted for it indivisible lines can hardly be identical, as Prof. Burnet suggests (*G. P.* § 239), with the doctrine which described the line expressly as 'the fluxion (ῥύσις) of the point' (Simpl. *Phys.* 722. 28, Procl. *in Eucl.* i. p. 97. 6 Friedlein). Simplicius uses this phrase in explaining *Aristotle's* view, of which it is a not unfair paraphrase.

(5) Once more, Simplicius' interpretation of Xenocrates' doctrine (142. 16–27) is not satisfactory. He cannot believe that so good a mathematician could have denied the infinite divisibility of the line, and therefore thinks the doctrine was that there are lines which are indivisible by reason of their smallness but are divisible by nature, and can therefore be divided when they are added to 'other bodies' and these bodies are then divided. A straightforward belief in absolutely indivisible lines is at least no more unreasonable than this, and it is possible to show with much probability from Aristotle's references to the doctrine that such a straightforward belief was what Plato actually held. This is certainly the belief which Aristotle means elsewhere when he refers to 'the indivisible lines' (*Phys.* 206ᵃ 17, *De Caelo* 299ᵃ 12). And in one passage he practically tells us Plato's reason for the belief. In *Phys.* 187ᵃ 1, after stating two arguments used by the Eleatics, he says 'some yielded to both the arguments; to the argument that all things must be one if 'being' always has one meaning they yielded in holding that not-being is, and to the argument from bisection they yielded in positing indivisible magnitudes'. Now from the similarity of this passage to N. 1089ᵃ 2–6 it seems clear that Aristotle is referring to the 'not-being' of the *Sophistes* in the *Physics* as he is in the *Metaphysics*, and the Greek commentators interpret the passage of the *Physics* so. But they think that the second half of the sentence in the *Physics* refers not to Plato but to Xenocrates. It seems clear, however, that the 'some' who 'gave in' to the one argument are the same persons who gave in to the other, and that Plato in particular is meant; otherwise Aristotle would have said 'some gave in to the one argument and some to the other'. Thus Plato's doctrine of indivisible lines is in effect said to be

due to his accepting ' the argument from bisection ', i. e. the argument propounded by Zeno which in the *De Lineis Insecabilibus* also (968ᵃ 18–23) is stated to have been one of the reasons for the belief in indivisible lines. This is the argument which is called Zeno's ' first argument' in *Phys.* 239ᵇ 11 (cf. 233ᵃ 21, *Top.* 160ᵇ 8). I. e. Plato was influenced by the really serious difficulty which meets any one who tries to think out the nature of the infinitely divisible, i. e. by the vicious infinite regress which it seems (but only seems) to involve. At the same time it is possible that there was some confusion in his mind between the mathematical line and the ideal line, which of course must be indivisible. Aristotle, as we have seen, says that one of the reasons for the belief in indivisible lines was the reflection that otherwise the *ideal* triangle would be many (*De Gen. et Corr.* 316ᵃ 12). But this sounds more like Xenocrates, who, as Aristotle tells us, confused the ideal with the mathematical.

The present passage suggests yet another reason which may have led Plato to deny the existence of points. The point, if it was to be real, should have been a combination of form and matter. Now a matter could be assigned to the line, the plane, and the solid (the long and short, &c.), but no such matter could be assigned to the point, since it had no dimensions at all. We have, however, no evidence to show that this difficulty was in Plato's mind.

The imperfects διεμάχετο, ἐκάλει, ἐτίθει indicate that Aristotle is thinking of frequently repeated oral teaching of Plato. Heiberg makes the interesting suggestion that it was the influence of Plato that led to the supersession of στιγμή by σημεῖον as the ordinary word for a point in Greek geometry (*Abh. zur Gesch. der Math.* xviii. 8). στιγμή claims reality for that which has position but no magnitude, while σημεῖον means simply a conventional mark. Aristotle uses στιγμή more often than σημεῖον, but only the latter word is found in Euclid and later.

The imperfects probably also indicate that Book A was written after Plato's death in 348–347. The most probable date is 348–345; cf. p. xxii.

With the expression ἀρχὴ γραμμῆς cf. Pl. *Laws* 894 Λ δῆλον ὡς ὁπόταν ἀρχὴ λαβοῦσα αὔξην εἰς τὴν δευτέραν ἔλθῃ μετάβασιν καὶ ἀπὸ ταύτης εἰς τὴν πλησίον, καὶ μέχρι τριῶν ἐλθοῦσα αἴσθησιν σχῇ τοῖς αἰσθανομένοις, which according to the most probable interpretation refers to the successive generation of the three dimensions, culminating in a solid body.

On the whole subject cf. Zeller, ii. 1.⁴ 1017, 1018, Apelt, *Beitr.* 263–268, Robin, *Théorie Platonicienne*, §§ 112, 215.

διεμάχετο Πλάτων ὡς ὄντι γεωμετρικῷ δόγματι. This is interesting as an instance of the procedure of dialectic τὰς ὑποθέσεις ἀναιροῦσα (*Rep.* 533 c).

21, 22. If the ordinary punctuation be retained, to give its due value to ἐκάλει we must translate ' but what most people call the point he called the principle of the line, and this is what he meant in his frequent assumption of indivisible lines'. But the single accusative after ἐκάλει and the two accusatives after ἐτίθει are both somewhat awkward, and it seems better to get rid of both awkwardnesses by treating τοῦτο δὲ πολλάκις ἐτίθει as parenthetical.

25. εἰάκαμεν, λέγομεν, **27** φαμεν, **28** λέγομεν. For the first person cf. n. on ch. 9 *ad init.*

οὐθὲν γὰρ λέγομεν κτλ. Cf. 988ᵃ 9 n.

29. πρότερον εἴπομεν, cf. 991ᵃ 20.

ὅπερ ταῖς ἐπιστήμαις κτλ. Difficulty has been felt about this, since science is concerned even more essentially with the formal than with the final cause (Z. 1031ᵇ 6, 20). But the clause is not meant to define the nature of the cause in question (that comes in the second clause), but only to emphasize its importance. It says no more than the opening words of the *Ethics*, πᾶσα τέχνη καὶ πᾶσα μέθοδος . . . ἀγαθοῦ τινὸς ἐφίεσθαι δοκεῖ, and the proposed alterations of the text are unnecessary. If any were to be made, that of Rolfes, ὃ περί τινας ἐπιστήμας (ὃ περὶ τὰς ἐπιστήμας Aᵇ), would seem the best.

33. τοῖς νῦν. The reference is primarily to Speusippus. Cf. Λ. 1069ᵃ 26 n.

φασκόντων ἄλλων χάριν κτλ. Cf. Pl. *Rep.* 531 D. 533 B–F.

ᵇ **4.** οἱ φυσιολόγοι, cf. 985ᵇ 11, 12 n.

7. περί τε κινήσεως κτλ. 'If the great and small is movement, the Ideas will be in movement; and if it is not, how can sensible things, which have no elements other than the Ideas and the great and small, be in movement?'

Jaeger's ἔστ' ἐνταῦθα (for ἔσται ταῦτα), though attractive and to some extent confirmed by Asclepius, is not necessary. The above interpretation makes good sense of the MS. reading. For this identification of movement with the indefinite or material principle cf. *Phys.* 201ᵇ 20, Eudemus *ap.* Simpl. *Phys.* 431. 8, 13. We are reminded of the restless movement ascribed to the material principle in *Tim.* 52 D—53 A (cf. 57 E).

10. τῇ γὰρ ἐκθέσει. ἔκθεσις, ἐκτίθεσθαι have two main senses in Aristotle. They mean (1) the 'setting out' of particular instances by which the truth of a conclusion (in the third figure) is confirmed. Thus the syllogism 'All S is P, All S is R. Therefore some R is P' is confirmed by 'setting out' a particular S, e.g. N; we shall then see clearly that some R is P, since N is R and N is P. This usage occurs in *An. Pr.* 28ᵃ 23, ᵇ 14, 30ᵃ 9, 11, 12, ᵇ 31, 57ᵃ 35. (2) They mean the 'setting out' in the appropriate syllogistic form of the terms occurring in an argument previously stated in unsyllogistic form. This usage occurs in *An. Pr.* 48ᵃ 1, 25, 29, 49ᵇ 6, 33, 50ᵃ 1.

There are occasional less technical uses. In *Soph. El.* 179ᵃ 3–5 ἐκτίθεσθαι means 'to isolate in thought' (universals from their particular instances). In *Phys.* 235ᵃ 28–30 it means 'to pick out for separate treatment'; in *Poet.* 1455ᵇ 1 it means 'to set out in general form'. In the *Metaphysics* we have in addition to the present passage Z. 1031ᵇ 21 ὥστε καὶ κατὰ τὴν ἔκθεσιν ἀνάγκη ἕν τι εἶναι ἄμφω,

M. 1086ᵇ 9 ταύτας δὲ τὰς. καθόλου λεγομένας (οὐσίας) ἐξέθεσαν,
N. 1090ᵃ 17 κατὰ τὴν ἔκθεσιν ἑκάστου παρὰ τὰ πολλά. B. 1003ᵃ 10,
commonly quoted as an instance of ἐκτίθεσθαι, seems to require
emendation. In 1086ᵇ 10, where alone in Aristotle the verb is in
the active, it clearly means 'they (the Platonists) assigned separate
existence to' (the universals). In the other three passages of the
Metaphysics ἔκθεσις is generally described as referring similarly to
the hypostatization of universals; but in the Z passage there seems
to be no special reference to Platonic views, and in all three passages
ἔκθεσις seems to refer to a method or procedure rather than to a doctrine.
Alexander describes the procedure in a passage which seems to rest on
knowledge of Academic method (124. 9—125. 4). The Platonists, he
says, took particular men by way of example and observed the likeness
between them and reduced them all to 'this unit' (man). They then
noted the likeness between horses, between dogs, &c. They then
observed what was common to men, horses, dogs, &c., and so rose
to higher and higher units till they reached that of αὐτοουσία, which
embraced everything. This exhibition of terms in a 'tree of Porphyry'
has some affinity to the second of the technical senses of ἔκθεσις, and
there can be little doubt that it is what Aristotle here means. Cf.
ps.-Alexander's account of ἔκθεσις in N. 1090ᵃ 17 (see n. *ad loc.*).
     The senses of ἔκθεσις are discussed fully in Maier, *Syll. des Ar.* ii. 1.
310–320, 2. 141–9.

II. ἂν διδῷ τις πάντα, 'if we grant all their assumptions', i.e. that
there is an Idea answering to every common name. In point of fact,
Aristotle thinks, not every universal is a genuine class, or can
be supposed to have an Idea answering to it. A genus is a common
term which indicates an element in the *essence* of that of which it is
predicated (*Top.* 108ᵇ 22). The universals that are not genera,
of which Aristotle is thinking, may be negative or relative terms
(cf. 990ᵇ 13, 16), or the widest universals like ὄν and ἕν (B. 998ᵇ 22,
H. 1045ᵇ 6).

13. τὰ μετὰ τοὺς ἀριθμούς, the entities which are to geometrical objects as the ideal numbers are to arithmetical numbers. Cf. ᵃ 10–19 n.

18–19. τὸ τῶν ὄντων ζητεῖν στοιχεῖα . . . ἀδύνατον εὑρεῖν. One or
other infinitive is superfluous. Richards proposes to read τά for τό
and to omit ζητεῖν or read ζητοῦντας. But the two infinitives are not
out of keeping with Aristotle's style.

21. ἐκ τίνων γάρ κτλ. Cf. H. 1044ᵇ 8. Actions, affections
like eclipse or sleep, and properties like straightness have not the
elements form and matter as substances have. The substances
which do the actions and have the affections or properties may
be called their substrata as the matter of a substance is called its substratum, but the relation is not the same in both cases. The substratum
of a substance is something contained in it; the substratum of a
property is something implied by it.

22. τῶν οὐσιῶν, sc. τὰ στοιχεῖα εὑρεῖν.

24—993ᵃ 2. Aristotle here attacks the notion of an all-embracing science like Plato's dialectic. He first (24–33) shows that there cannot be a science which *proves* the whole nature of reality; a science cannot be demonstrative throughout but must start with immediately known premises. The only alternative that he considers is that the science of reality should be present in us from birth, and this suggestion he disposes of without difficulty (33–993ᵃ 2). Aristotle himself would adopt a third view, that knowledge of the first principles is not fully present in us at birth, but can be attained by reflection (which is *not* proof) on what is implied in certain particular propositions which any one can see the truth of as soon as he reaches years of intelligence (cf. *An. Post.* ii. 19). E. g. the law of contradiction can be recognized if we will only reflect on what is implied in our knowledge that some particular thing cannot be not-itself. It might seem that this third alternative was open to the Platonists as well as to Aristotle, but there is a further point to be noticed. Aristotle is not speaking of metaphysics, the knowledge of the *general* nature of being, and showing that this cannot be either demonstrative throughout or innate. He is attacking the possibility of a science which should deduce the whole concrete nature of reality from certain principles common to all realities—a science such as Plato sketches under the name of dialectic. Besides the principles common to all reality, Aristotle holds that there are principles peculiar to the various departments of reality (*An. Post.* 76ᵃ 16), and that without the knowledge of these, which is gained by reflection on particular perceptions (993ⁿ 7, *De An.* 432ᵃ 7), the concrete nature of reality cannot be known.

992ᵇ 31. ἢ πάντων ἢ τινῶν. πάντων, as Alexander says (131. 10), applies to definition and induction, τινῶν to demonstration. In demonstration it sometimes happens that the minor premise is not known before the conclusion but simultaneously with it (*An. Post.* 71ᵃ 17); in definition and induction the data must be known beforehand.

31. ἤ, 32 καὶ ἤ, Bonitz's emendation of 31 ἤ, 32 ἤ, is shown to be right by καὶ ἤ in l. 33 and is confirmed by Al. 130. 18, 20.

993ⁿ 1. εἰ καὶ τυγχάνοι σύμφυτος οὖσα an allusion to the Platonic doctrine of ἀνάμνησις (*Meno* 81 c, *Phaedo* 72 E).

2–7. How, asks Aristotle, are we to know when we have got to the ultimate elements in our analysis? There can always be difference of opinion about this, as there can be about the question whether the letter ζ is further analysable or not.

5. τὸ ζα κτλ. The ancient grammarians similarly derive ζ from σ and δ (Dion. Thrax, p. 14 Ullig, Dion. Hal. *De Comp. Verb.* 14. 78, Kühner, § 3. 14). Thus in Aeolic Ζεύς, κωμάζω, &c., are represented by Σδεύς, κωμάσδω, and in Attic Ἀθήνασδε becomes Ἀθήναζε. In N. 1093ᵃ 20, on the other hand, ζ is grouped with ξ and ψ as if it stood for δσ; but cf. 1093ᵃ 24 n. Curtius thought that ζ had the sound of *ds* in ancient Greek. Blass (*Pronunciation of Ancient Greek*, 115–125) holds that in Attica and in central Greece it had the sound of *sd* until Hellenistic times, when it acquired in popular speech the sound of soft *s*, and that it had the value of *ts* or *ds* only in the old Cretan and Italian dialects.   The change of ζ to a voiced sibilant (English *z*) seems, however, to have begun earlier than Blass allows.   Attic inscriptions begin to confuse σ and ζ as early as 340 B. C. (ἐπεψήφισεν = -ζεν *I. G.* ii. 117ᵃ 3, Σεύς 707. 10, cf. Meisterhans-Schwyzer, pp. 88, 92).   Lagercrantz, *Zur Griechischen Laut-geschichte*, 125–149, and Lambert, *de Dialecto Aeolica Quaest. Select.* 9–60, argue that ζ had the sound of a double soft *s*.   Thus the discussion to which Aristotle refers has not yet been settled.

8–10. If all things were produced from the same elements, colours would have the same elements as tones, and a man who has hearing would necessarily know colours.

ταὐτά, Schwegler's emendation of ταῦτα, is confirmed by Al. 133. 22, 134. 5, and by Bessarion's translation.

9–10. ὥσπερ . . . στοιχείων.   There is no sufficient reason for re-garding these words, with Christ, as a gloss on l. 5 οἱ μὲν . . . 6 εἶναι. οἰκείων means ' proper to sound ', not to *each* sound.

Epilogue (ch. 10).

993ᵃ 11. Thus all earlier thinkers are seeking our four causes and no others, but they conceive them vaguely, as is natural in the infancy of philosophy.

17. E. g. Empedocles says bone exists by virtue of the ratio of its elements, i. e. by its essence.   But then flesh, and everything else, will *be* the ratio of its elements, for it exists by reason of this and not of its matter, fire, earth, &c.   This is a consequence implicit in what he says.

24. We must next review the difficulties that may be raised about the four causes ; we shall then be better able to deal with other difficulties.

Jaeger in his discussion of this chapter (*Stud.* 14–21) argues that the opening words refer back more naturally to chs. 3–6 than to chs. 8, 9, and in effect duplicate the opening words of ch. 7 ; and that the closing words (ll. 25–27) refer not to Book α as Alexander supposes, nor to B as Bonitz supposes (for the questions which Aristotle promises to discuss are distinguished from the ὕστερον ἀπορίαι, which must be those of B), but to chs. 8, 9, and duplicate the closing words of ch. 7. In spite of the difference between the contents of the middle parts of chs. 7, 10 the chapters are really alternative versions, of which ch. 10 is shown to be the later by the reference to B in 993ⁿ 27 ; ch. 7 was written before Aristotle had any thought of linking A with B. The editor who reduced Aristotle's manuscripts to order failed to notice the distinction between two sets of problems which is drawn in 993ᵃ 25–27 and therefore thought the end of the chapter referred simply to B and accordingly put the chapter at the end of A. Jaeger points out that there is a tendency for 'erratic passages', which were difficult to place elsewhere, to be placed at the end of books. Cf. E. 1027ᵇ 25—1028ᵃ 3, H. 6, Θ. 10, K. 1065ᵃ 26—1069ᵃ 14, M. 1086ᵃ 21—1087ᵃ 25.

This reasoning is not convincing. Jaeger himself points out that ch. 7 tries to show that earlier thinkers did somehow recognize the four causes, while ch. 10 emphasizes rather the fact that they did so very inadequately. This is surely more natural if ch. 10 was meant to come where it does, *after* the detailed criticism contained in chs. 8, 9. Again, it is hardly likely that this very slight chapter was meant to take the place of the much fuller treatment in ch. 7. The reference to B in 993ᵃ 27 is no indication of late date; there are many indications that A and B belong to about the same period of Aristotle's thought; cf. note on ch. 9 *ad init.* Finally, there is no difficulty in supposing that ὅσα περὶ τῶν αὐτῶν τούτων ἀπορήσειεν ἄν τις (l. 25) refers to the problems raised in B. Those problems are similarly said to arise out of the topics discussed in A (995ᵇ 5). Jaeger asks, what then are the 'later problems' referred to in 993ᵃ 27? But the problems of B are similarly described as only the first of the problems which the philosopher must discuss (995ᵃ 25); we are not to suppose that Aristotle had a definite second set of problems in mind. It seems fair to conclude that this chapter is in its proper place, and that its concluding sentence refers forward to B.

993ᵃ 11. ἐν τοῖς φυσικοῖς, *Phys.* ii. 3, 7.

16. The vulgate reading νέα τε κατ᾽ ἀρχὰς οὖσα καὶ τὸ πρῶτον, 'being young at the beginning and at first', is an extraordinarily pleonastic phrase, and with this reading there seems to be no explanation of τε. The best reading appears to be that proposed by Diels (*Hermes*, xl. 303), νέα τε καὶ κατ᾽ ἀρχάς. τε καί occurs in S and in the Aldine edition. καὶ τὸ πρῶτον, which is omitted by Al. (63. 31) and Bessarion, is probably a gloss on καὶ κατ᾽ ἀρχάς.

17. The reference is to Empedocles fr. 96:

> ἡ δὲ χθὼν ἐπίηρος ἐν εὐστέρνοις χοάνοισι
> τὼ δύο τῶν ὀκτὼ μερέων λάχε Νήστιδος αἴγλης,
> τέσσαρα δ᾽ Ἡφαίστοιο· τὰ δ᾽ ὀστέα λευκὰ γένοντο
> Ἁρμονίης κόλλῃσιν ἀρηρότα θεσπεσίηθεν.

This means that bone contains two parts of earth, two of water, and four of fire (so Aet. v. 22; the statements of Theophr. *De Sensu* 23 and Simplicius *De An.* 68. 10 appear to be mistaken). Empedocles has previously been described as recognizing a material cause (984ᵃ 8) and an efficient cause, and the latter in two ways (984ᵇ 6, 985ᵃ 33, 985ᵃ 5). Here for the first time he is said to have had an inkling of the formal cause; the first recognition of this is elsewhere ascribed to the Pythagoreans (987ᵃ 20) or to Socrates (987ᵇ 3).

19. Bekker's reading, σαρκὸς (E) καὶ τῶν ἄλλων ἑκάστου (Moerbeka, ἕκαστον MSS.) εἶναι τὸν λόγον, ἢ μηθενός (Aᵇ) leaves τὸν λόγον εἶναι without any predicate, and it is difficult to 'understand' a predicate such as οὐσίαν or φύσιν, 'is the substance of flesh,' &c. Bonitz therefore rightly proposed to read σάρκας (Aᵇ) or σάρκα (T) καὶ τῶν ἄλλων ἕκαστον εἶναι τὸν λόγον, ἢ μηδὲ ἕν (E). In *De Part. An.* 642ª 21 Empedocles is similarly described as *identifying* the bodily parts with their 'ratio of mixture'. σάρκας is preferable to σάρκα, as accounting better for the corruption. Once σάρκας had been corrupted to σαρκός, μηθενός naturally followed. The plural σάρκες is common in Aristotle. The readings proposed by Schwegler (σάρκας ... ἕκαστον εἶναι κατὰ (or κατὰ τὸν) λόγον, ἢ μηθέν), Karsten (τινα λόγον for τὸν λόγον, Bekker's reading being otherwise retained), and Christ (εἶναι αἴτιον for εἶναι, Bekker's reading being otherwise retained) are less probable than that of Bonitz.

24. δεδήλωται καὶ πρότερον. Alexander refers this to 989ª 30, where Aristotle has similarly pointed out the implications of *Anaxagoras'* theory (985ª 4–10 might also be mentioned). But ὅσα δὲ περὶ τῶν αὐτῶν τούτων ἀπορήσειεν ἄν τις shows that the reference is more general ; it is to Aristotle's whole account of earlier thought about the first principles.

26. ἐπανέλθωμεν πάλιν. Alexander and Asclepius think this refers to α, but the topics there discussed can hardly be described as arising out of Book A ; the reference seems pretty clearly to be to B. Cf. note at beginning of chapter.

BOOK α

The numbering of this book as Book α implies that those responsible for the arrangement of the *Metaphysics* in books felt it to be something of an excrescence on the general structure of the work. Doubts were early felt about its authorship. A scholion at the beginning of the book in one of the oldest manuscripts (E) says that it was commonly regarded as the work of Pasicles of Rhodes, a pupil of Aristotle and a nephew of Eudemus ; and it is probably a confused reminiscence of this tradition that leads Asclepius (4. 20) to say that Book A was supposed to be the work of Pasicles. Alexander thinks that α is the work of Aristotle, and the contents and style are quite in keeping with this view. The tradition about Pasicles is likely to have some basis, and the truth may be that the fragment was recovered from his notes of Aristotle's lectures.

It appears from 995ª 14–19 that the book, or fragment of a book, is an introduction not to metaphysics but to physics or to theoretical philosophy in general.

Book α.

General considerations about the study of philosophy (ch. 1).

993^a 30. The study of the truth is difficult in that no one can hit with precision the part he wants to hit, easy in that the target is too big to be entirely missed. The small results attained by each thinker make together a considerable total.

^b 7. Further, the difficulty lies not in the facts but in our reason, which is dazzled by the very brightness of the object.

11. We must be grateful not only to those whose opinions we take over, but to the earlier thinkers whose superficial views gave the mind the necessary practice in thinking.

19. Philosophy is rightly called the knowledge of the truth (cf. ^a30, ^b17). For the end of theoretical knowledge is truth, that of practical knowledge being action ; if the latter studies the truth, it is not eternal truth but that which is of the moment and relative to an object.

23. Now we cannot know the truth without the cause ; that which gives other things a certain character itself has that character in the highest degree, so that what makes other things true is itself most true. Hence the first principles of eternal things are most true, being always true and the source of all truth ; thus what has most being has most truth.

993^a 30. On the precise meaning of ἀληθείας cf. Α. 983^b 2 n.

^b 1. Brandis's conjecture πάντως derives some support from Al. 138. 12, 139. 11, 20, 140. 3, but the sense required for πάντως is not that which it generally has in Aristotle, viz. ' in all circumstances ', ' in any and every case '. The opposition required is that between μηδένα and πάντας, as is shown by the following words, καθ' ἕνα μὲν . . . ἐκ πάντων δέ.

2. If φύσεως means nature in the narrower sense in which it is the subject of physics and not of metaphysics (ἡ οὐσία ἡ τῶν ἐχόντων ἀρχὴν κινήσεως ἐν αὐτοῖς ᾗ αὐτά, Δ. 1015^a 14), this confirms the suggestion already made, that the book is an introduction to physics rather than to metaphysics. But the word may mean more widely ' the nature of things ' and be practically equivalent to ἀλήθεια ^a 30.

5. τίς ἂν θύρας ἁμάρτοι ; cf. Leutsch and Schneidewin, *Paroemiographi*, ii. 678.

6. τὸ δ' ὅλον τι ἔχειν κτλ. Aristotle has already implied (in τίς ἂν θύρας ἁμάρτοι ;) that no one entirely misses the nature of things ; the difficulty of the study, he now adds, is shown by the fact that while this is the case, we cannot often hit the precise part of the nature of things that we are aiming at. Cf. *Phys.* 184^a 23, *An. Pr.* 67^a 29.

12. Richards points out that the only dative that properly goes with κοινοῦσθαι is that of the person with whom something is shared, not of the thing shared, and therefore suggests τὰς δόξας. The dative is, however, possible, by a quasi-personification of the δόξαι.

14. τὴν γὰρ ἕξιν κτλ. The construction, as Bonitz observes, is proleptic. ' They formed our ἕξις by practice', i. e. by practice they transformed a natural δύναμις into a trained ἕξις.

15. Timotheus, the famous poet and musician, was a Milesian, but worked chiefly in Athens. He died in 357, and is said to have been born in 446.

16. Not very much is known about Phrynis. The main references in ancient literature are Ar. *Nub.* 971, Plut. *de Mus.* 6. 1133 B. He and Timotheus were ridiculed in Pherecrates' *Chiron*.

17. The best reading appears to be ἐπὶ τῶν περὶ τῆς ἀληθείας, which seems to have been read by Alexander (144. 11 f.). For the construction cf. B. 996ᵇ 21, 1002ᵇ 21, &c. περὶ τῶν περὶ τῆς ἀληθείας ἀποφηναμένων is possible but less natural.

24. ἕκαστον δὲ μάλιστα κτλ. 'Each thing, in virtue of which a common nature belongs to the other things that have that nature, itself is (i. e. has that nature) in a higher degree than the other things.'

Impossibility of (1) *an infinite chain of causes,* (2) *an infinite variety of kinds of cause* (ch. 2).

994ᵃ 1. The causes of things do not (1) form an infinite chain, nor (2) present an infinite number of kinds. (1) (*a*) Neither of material, efficient, final, nor formal causes is there a series which is infinite in the upward direction.

11. For in a chain of terms the first is the cause of the rest, but in an infinite series all the terms except the given result are middle terms, so that since there is no first there is no cause.

19. Nor (*b*) is the chain infinite in the downward direction. ' A comes from B ' (if we exclude the case of mere temporal succession) either (i) as the man from the boy or (ii) as air from water.

25. (i) is the emergence of the developed from the developing ; the developing is a middle term between not-being and being ; to say that the savant comes from the learner means that he who is learning is becoming a savant. (ii) on the other hand implies the destruction of the B out of which A comes.

31. Hence process (i) is not reversible, but (ii) is. In neither case can the series be infinite ; the middle terms involved in (i) imply a last term, and the terms in (ii) revert into each other ; the destruction of either is the genesis of the other.

ᵇ6. (Return to upward direction.) The prime *material* cause, being eternal, cannot be thus destroyed. Since generation is not infinite in the upward direction, ⟨it presupposes an eternal cause, but⟩ a cause which produces effects only by being itself destroyed is not eternal.

9. Since the *final* cause is something which is not for the sake of anything else, those who posit an infinite series are destroying the very nature of the good, and abolishing reason; for reason always acts for an end which is a limit.

16. The *formal* cause cannot be reduced *ad infinitum* to another definition fuller in expression, for (i) the earlier definition in such a series is more of a definition than the later;

20. (ii) to say that it can is to abolish knowledge; it is implied that we cannot know until we reach the unanalysable terms involved in the definition. We cannot know an infinite series; the case is not like that of a line, which is infinitely divisible but can be apprehended by stopping the process of division; the whole line must be apprehended by something in us that does not move from part to part. Nothing infinite can be, and at any rate the notion of infinity is not analysable *ad infinitum*.

27. (2) If the *kinds* of cause were infinite, knowledge would be equally impossible; for to know a thing is to know its causes, but what is additively infinite cannot be traversed by thought in a finite time.

Aristotle has in the first chapter shown that the philosopher must above all know τὰς τῶν ἀεὶ ὄντων ἀρχάς, since these are the cause of the truth of all that depends on them. He now sets himself to show that there *are* ἀρχαί, that the series of causes is not an infinite one, and also that there is not an infinite number of kinds of cause; i.e. that causes are not infinite in number vertically (εἰς εὐθυωρίαν) nor in kind horizontally. Bonitz's doubts as to there being any real connexion between the two chapters are not justified.

Aristotle first (994ᵃ 3–19) shows that the series of causes cannot be infinite in the upper direction, i.e. that if we are seeking the cause of a given effect, we are not led on without limit from *causa* to *causa causae*.

994ᵃ 6–7. τοῦτον . . . νείκους. The reference to Strife shows that Aristotle is taking an illustration from the cosmology of Empedocles. According to this, the sun was πυρὸς ἄθροισμα μέγα (Diog. Laert. viii. 77). I.e. it was formed by Strife, which leads to the segregation of the elements from each other and the aggregation of each together. The same impulse which formed it was doubtless thought to give it its motion. And the sun in turn, being fire, acts on the other elements (cf. A. 984ᵇ6, 985ᵇ 1), and in particular on air (Aet. ii. 8. 2).

17. τοῦτον τὸν τρόπον Alexander interprets as κατ᾽ ἐνέργειαν (151. 26). The actually infinite would be the same as the infinite κατὰ τὴν πρόσθεσιν (ᵇ 30), as opposed to the infinitely divisible (ἄπειρον κατὰ διαίρεσιν *Phys.* 204ᵃ 7, or δυνάμει τε καὶ ἐπὶ καθαιρέσει 206ᵇ 13). But if τοῦτον τὸν τρόπον meant this, καὶ ὅλως τοῦ ἀπείρου would extend the statement to the potentially infinite or infinitely divisible, of which it is not true that all its parts are μέσα ὁμοίως μέχρι τοῦ νῦν.

This is true only of the actually infinite, and τοῦτον τὸν τρόπον must refer to some *species* of the actual infinite. Presumably τὰ ἄπειρα τοῦτον τὸν τρόπον means infinite discrete series such as are here in question, and ὅλως τὸ ἄπειρον includes also infinite continua, e. g. infinite time.

18. μέχρι τοῦ νῦν. Christ's suspicion of these words is unjustified. Aristotle is assuming throughout this section a present effect whose cause is being sought for. μέχρι excludes τὸ νῦν from the general statement, cf. B. 998ᵇ 29.

19. That the series of causes is finite in the downward direction, i. e. that if we start from a given cause, we are not led on without limit from effect to more distant effect, Aristotle proves only for material causes (19 -ᵇ 6).

22. μή is not infrequently used thus, setting aside an irrelevant suggestion, cf. *Phys.* 186ᵃ 14, 15, Hdt. iii. 127. The use of ἐκ in the sense of 'after' is irrelevant, since that after which something else comes is in no sense its ὑποκείμενον or material cause. But there are two cases in which A comes strictly from or out of B, that in which B retains its substantial nature but develops, and that in which B disappears and its substratum takes on a new and opposite substantial nature. The second case is γένεσις proper; the first may be either change of quantity (αὔξησις), as when a boy becomes a man, or of quality (ἀλλοίωσις), as when an ignorant person becomes learned. But it is not coextensive with αὔξησις and ἀλλοίωσις: Aristotle is thinking only of those cases in which the change is development towards an end (τελείωσις) and cannot be reversed (l. 32).

The manuscript variations in ll. 22-24 point to early corruption, and Jaeger supposes μὴ . . . Ὀλύμπια to be a gloss by a copyist familiar with Δ. 1023ᵇ 10 f. These words were, however, read by Alexander (154. 7-15), and the reading ἀλλ' ἢ ὡς in ll. 23 f. makes the sentence a good one without involving any great departure from the manuscripts. Jaeger's punctuation and excision of ὡς in l. 25 make that sentence grammatically more correct, but the sentence as it stands in the manuscripts is not un-Aristotelian.

ᵇ1. The manuscripts read ἀλλ' ἔστι μετά κτλ. Bonitz has tried to emend the passage by omitting, with Alexander, ἔστι. He takes Aristotle to mean 'that which is generated is not generated from the generation but after it, i. e. from that which has already been generated'. But this can only mean 'a man is not generated by the generation of a boy but only from a boy who has already been generated'. On this view τῆς γενέσεως and τὴν γένεσιν do not refer to the γένεσις which is implied in γίγνεται and in τὸ γιγνόμενον : they refer to the generation of the boy, not to that of the man. But the generation of the boy is not referred to anywhere in the context ; and γίγνεται, γενέσεως, γιγνόμενον, γένεσιν must surely all refer to the only generation which is in question, that of the man from the boy. We might try to save the text by inter-

preting ' for that which comes to be does not come to be merely *from*
the coming to be, but is necessarily *after* the coming to be '. Between
man and boy there is not merely such a relation that out of a boy a
man can be produced ; it is part of the very nature of the man that he
should be the later stage, should come after the generation. But it
is illegitimate to insert a ' merely ' which is not in the Greek, and it
seems likely that the true solution is that of Christ, who reads ἀλλ' ὃ
ἔστι. The sense then is ' it is not that which is coming to be something
that comes to be as a result of the coming to be, but that which is
after the coming to be '. τὸ γιγνόμενον then retains the sense it has in
ᵃ 25, 28.

This sense of ἐκ then includes the notion of ' after ', which constitutes the sense rejected in ᵃ 22 (cf. *De Gen. An.* 724ᵃ 21); but it
includes also the notion that B is in some sense the substratum of A.

4. τῶν μὲν γὰρ ὄντων μεταξύ, i. e. the intermediates in the first kind
of change (ὡς ἐκ παιδὸς ἀνήρ), cf. ᵃ 27–28. There must be some
limit to such a process of development.

5. τὰ δ' εἰς ἄλληλα ἀνακάμπτει. The second kind of change (ὡς ἐξ
ὕδατος ἀήρ) is not a development up to a perfect state of maturity, but
may go on indefinitely. But there is not an indefinite series of new
effects. The process returns on itself; the air which came from
water turns again into water.

6-9. This sentence is very obscure. Aristotle has in ᵃ 11–19
given a general argument which applies to all the four causes, to show
that there must always be a first cause. This, he apparently assumes,
must be eternal. In ᵃ 19–ᵇ 6 he has been showing that there must be
a limit to the series of material causes in the downward direction.
Now he returns to the upward direction, and shows that the prime
material cause must be indestructible. There are two difficulties :

(1) It seems pointless to say that the first cause must be indestructible because it is eternal; eternalness so obviously implies indestructi-
bility. But the remark is explained by what immediately precedes.
Aristotle has just been speaking of one kind of material cause which
is destroyed when that of which it is the cause is produced. This
leads him to remark that the prime material cause cannot be of this
nature; rather it is to its effect as boy to man, as the undeveloped to
the developed. (2) ἐπεὶ . . . εἶναι can be understood only if taken as
elliptical : ' since becoming is not infinite in the upward direction,
(there must be an eternal first cause, but) that which is the first thing
by whose destruction something came to be cannot be eternal '.

9-27. Having at l. 6 returned from the downward to the upward
direction, and shown that there is an eternal ultimate material cause,
Aristotle now shows that there is an ultimate final cause (9–16) and an
ultimate formal cause or definition (16–27).

9. It is not clear that Alexander read ἐπεί, so that there is no need
to question the reading of most manuscripts, ἔτι. If ἐπεί were read,
we should have to take the apodosis as beginning with ὥστε, and this
would be difficult with so short a protasis.

16. ἀλλὰ μήν κτλ. 'But neither can the essence be reduced (*sc.*
ad infinitum) to another definition fuller in expression. For the earlier
definition is always more of a definition, and the later less of one ;
but where the first term of a series has not the required character, the
next has not it either.' The definition of 'man' as 'rational animal'
may be reduced to the fuller definition 'rational sensitive living substance', but this process cannot be carried on indefinitely. For this
Aristotle gives two reasons, the first in ll. 18–20, the second in ll. 20–
23 ; ἔτι, not, as Bonitz says, δέ, is what answers to τε l. 18 (cf. Bonitz,
Index, 749ᵇ 39, 40). Of the first of these reasons Alexander's second
interpretation (162. 6–10) *may* be the right one. 'Rational sensitive
living substance' is more of a definition than 'rational animal', since
it leaves less unexplained ; but if it in turn could be reduced to a prior
definition and so *ad infinitum*, there would be no first in the series (no
completely full definition), and therefore no second either. There
would in fact be no definition at all, and 'man' (and all other terms)
would be indefinable. The argument is, on this view, an application
to the formal cause of the general argument in ᵃ 11–19. It is difficult,
however, to take ὁ ἔμπροσθεν to refer to the definition which is arrived
at later, and Alexander's first interpretation (161. 10—162. 6) is
probably right. 'Rational animal', on this interpretation, is more of
a definition of man than 'rational sensitive living substance', which is
rather a definition of the definition of man ; and if 'rational animal' is
not a correct definition of man, neither will any definition such as
'rational sensitive living substance' be a proper definition of it.

20. τὸ ἐπίστασθαι, scientific knowledge ; **21. τὸ γιγνώσκειν,** everyday knowledge.

21. τὰ ἄτομα must mean the most universal terms, those not
analysable into genus and differentia. This use of ἄτομα seems to
be without parallel in Aristotle (cf. B. 995ᵇ 29 n.), but may be compared with the use of ἀμερῆ in *An. Post.* 100ᵇ 2, and of ἀδιαίρετον in
Δ. 1014ᵇ 10, H. 1043ᵇ 35, M. 1084ᵇ 14, *De An.* 430ᵃ 26.

22. οὕτως, i. e. actually. The line is only potentially infinite, i. e.
infinitely divisible, and one can apprehend it by checking the process
of division (στήσαντα) and taking it κατ' ἀθρόα μόρια (Al. 164. 9). But
an actually infinite series cannot be apprehended.

25. τὴν ἄπειρον, the infinitely divisible line.

25–26. ἀλλὰ . . . ἀνάγκη is very difficult. Bonitz says 'quid signi-
ficent, non possum nisi obscura quadam divinatione assequi. Sicuti
linea infinita est propterea, quod potest dividi in infinitum, similis in
materia cernitur infinitas, quae potest infinitas in se recipere qualitates.
Sed cogitari eam semper oportet tamquam quae insit uni cuidam
ex iis rebus, quae motu ac mutatione ex ea procreantur, τὴν ὕλην ἐν
κινουμένῳ νοεῖν ἀνάγκη'. This is perhaps as much as can be made of
the received text. But it is obviously unsatisfactory. The variety of
readings in Alexander points to early corruption. I read, with hesitation, τὴν ὅλην οὐ κινουμένῳ, which at least connects better with what
precedes (διόπερ . . . διεξιών being parenthetical). 'It is not possible

to apprehend the line without calling a halt to the process of dividing, but the whole line also must be apprehended by something in us which does not move (in thought) from part to part.' For the use of οὐ κινουμένῳ cf. τῷ ἠρεμῆσαι καὶ στῆναι τὴν διάνοιαν ἐπίστασθαι καὶ φρονεῖν λέγομεν *Phys*. 247ᵇ 10, ἵστησι γὰρ ὁ λέγων τὴν διάνοιαν καὶ ὁ ἀκούσας ἠρέμησεν *De Int*. 16ᵇ 20, ἔτι δ' ἡ νόησις ἔοικεν ἠρεμήσει τινὶ καὶ ἐπιστάσει μᾶλλον ἢ κινήσει *De An*. 407ᵃ 32.

26. καὶ ἀπείρῳ κτλ. 'And nothing infinite can exist; and if it did, at least the notion of infinity is not infinite', i. e. it is analysable into a finite number of marks. The remark is irrelevant to Aristotle's main point, the finitude of the causal series ; but the reflection is not unnatural in view of the context.

30. τὸ ἄπειρον κατὰ τὴν πρόσθεσιν, in opposition to τὸ ἄπειρον κατὰ τὴν διαίρεσιν, is the actually as opposed to the potentially infinite ; i.e. to the infinitely divisible. Cf. ᵃ 17 n.

Different methods appropriate to different studies (ch. 3).

994ᵇ 32. Our attitude towards lectures is determined by our habits ; the unfamiliar seems unintelligible. The strength of habit is shown by the laws, in which the mythical element prevails by force of habit over our knowledge of its childishness.

995ᵃ 6. Some demand mathematical proof, others examples, others the authority of the poets; some demand accurate treatment everywhere, others are pained by it either because they cannot follow it or because they think it ungentlemanly. We ought to be educated with regard to the method to be expected before we begin the actual study ; we cannot study two such difficult things at once.

14. Mathematical accuracy is to be expected only in the study of immaterial objects, and hence is not suited to natural philosophy. If we ask first what nature is, we shall see what natural philosophy is about.

With the whole chapter cf. *E. N*. i. 3.

995 ᵃ 4. On the connexion between law and myth cf. Λ. 1074ᵇ 3.

7. παραδειγματικῶς. Asclepius cites Plato's dialogues as an instance of paradeigmatic discussion, discussion by means of examples taken from everyday life.

10. συνείρειν = ἐπακολουθεῖν (Al. 168. 5), 'to follow the connexion of thought'. For similar uses cf. Bonitz, *Index*, 726ᵃ 36–38.

12. ἀνελεύθερον εἶναί τισι δοκεῖ is no doubt suggested by Pl. *Theaet*. 184 c.

13. ὡς ἄτοπον (without ὄν) may be compared with *Pol*. 1255ᵃ 9 ὡς δεινόν, Pl. *Gorg*. 495 c ὡς ἕτερον τὴν ἀνδρείαν τῆς ἐπιστήμης δύο ταῦτα ἔλεγες ;

17. ἴσως Alexander explains as being used because the heavenly

bodies though part of φύσις have not matter. But they have ὕλη
τοπική (H. 1042^b 6), and form no exception to the general statement.
ἴσως is simply an instance of the modest form of statement characteristic of Aristotle. Cf. A. 987^a 26 n.

σκεπτέον πρῶτον, as Alexander says (169. 19—170. 4) may mean
either 'we must consider first, in the present treatise, what nature is ',
or ' a man must consider what nature is before turning to metaphysics'.
If the first meaning be assigned to the phrase, book α must be treated
as a preface to a general work on theoretical philosophy, and therefore
as no part of the *Metaphysics*; if the latter be adopted, the sentence
simply says that physics should be studied before metaphysics, and on
this view α might stand as a genuine part of the *Metaphysics*. But
διὸ ... δῆλον ἔσται seems clearly to promise an immediate inquiry
into the meaning of ' nature '; and neither B nor any subsequent
book fits on to these closing words of α.

19. καὶ ... ἐστιν. These words are irrelevant, and are omitted
by Alexander, who, however, states (174. 25) that the words
were inserted here in order that there might be something in α for
B. 995^b 5 to refer to. But in fact B does not in any sense take
its start from these words.

BOOK B

Sketch of the main problems of Metaphysics (ch. 1).

995^n 24. We must first enumerate the questions that should be first
discussed.

A preliminary discussion of problems is useful. (1) A problem is
like a bond which we cannot unloose until we understand its nature.
(2) A student who has not discussed the difficulties does not know the
direction in which he should move, nor even whether he has found
what he is looking for. (3) The man who has heard the contending
arguments is best able to judge between them.

^{b} 4. The problems are : (1) Is it the business of one science to know
the causes?

6. (2) Should the science that studies the first principles of substance also study the first principles of demonstration ?

10. (3) Does one science study all substances ? If more than one,
are they all akin, or are only some of them to be called forms of
Wisdom ?

13. (4) Are there non-sensible substances ; if so, are they of more
than one kind, e. g. Forms and mathematical objects ?

18. (5) Is the study a study of substances only or also of their
essential attributes ? Whose business is it to study same and other,

like and unlike, and the other topics of dialectical discussion, and their essential attributes?

27. (6) Are classes, or constituent parts, the first principles of things?

29. (7) If classes, are *infimae species* or *summa genera* more of the nature of principles and separately existing entities?

31 (8) Above all, is there a cause apart from matter? Has it separate existence? Is it one or more than one? ' Is there anything apart from the concrete thing? Do some concrete wholes have separately existent forms and others not, and if so, which have them?

996ᵃ 1. (9) Are the principles, whether formal or material, limited in number or in kind?

2. (10) Are the principles of perishable and imperishable things the same? Are they all imperishable or are the former perishable?

4. (11) The hardest question : Are unity and being substances or attributes?

9. (12) Are the principles universal or individual?

10. (13) Do they exist potentially or actually? Does their potentiality or actuality imply movement?

12. (14) Are mathematical objects substances, and if so are they separate from sensible things?

995ᵃ 26. αὐτῶν. Bk. B being continuous with Bk. A, αὐτῶν (like τούτων 993ᵃ 24) refers to the first principles which formed the subject of that book.

28. διαπορῆσαι, cf. A. 991ᵃ 9 n.

31. τοῦτο, i.e. the existence of a 'knot'.

ᵇ 4—996ᵃ 15. The ἀπορίαι of Bk. B, with the passages of the *Metaphysics* in which they are discussed, may be set out as follows:

(1) Does one science investigate all kinds of cause? 995ᵇ 5, 6 = 996ᵃ 18–ᵇ 26, cf. Γ. 1, 2.

(2) If it does, should it also discuss the axioms? 995ᵇ 6–10 = 996ᵇ 26—997ᵃ 15, cf. Γ. 3.

(3) Does one science, or more than one, deal with all substances? If more than one, are they all forms of Wisdom? 995ᵇ 10–13 = 997ᵃ 15–25, cf. Γ: 2. 1004ᵃ 2–9, E. 1.

(4) Are there non-sensible substances? If so, are there more than one kind of them? 995ᵇ 13–18 = 997ᵃ 34—998ᵃ 19, cf. Λ. 6–10, M. 1–9, N.

(5) Does one science discuss the essential attributes of substances as well as substances themselves? What science inquires into the same and the other, like and unlike, contrariety, prior and posterior, &c., and their attributes? 995ᵇ18–27 = 997ᵃ25–34, cf. Γ. 2. 1003ᵇ22—1005ᵃ 18.

(6) Are classes, or constituent parts, the principles of things? 995ᵇ 27–29 = 998ᵃ 20–ᵇ 14, cf. Z. 10, 13.

(7) Are *summa genera* or *infimae species* more of the nature of principles and substances? $995^b\,29-31 = 998^h\,14-999^a\,23$, cf. Z. 12. $1038^a\,19$, and Z. 13.

(8) Is there any cause apart from matter? Has such a cause separate existence? Is there one such cause, or more? Is there anything apart from concrete wholes? Do some concrete wholes have separately existent forms and others not, and if so, which have them? $995^b\,31-36 = 999^n\,24-^b\,24$, cf. Z. 8, 13, 14, Λ. 6–10, M. 10.

(9) Are the principles limited in number or in kind? $996^a\,1,2 = 999^h\,24-1000^a\,4$, cf. Λ. 4, 5, M. 10.

(10) Are the principles of perishable and of imperishable things the same? Are the former perishable? $996^a\,2-4 = 1000^a\,5-1001^a\,3$, cf. Z. 7–10.

(11) Are unity and being attributes or substances? $996^a\,4-9 = 1001^a\,4-^b\,25$, cf. Z. 16. $1040^b\,16-24$, I. 2.

(12) Are the principles universal or individual? $996^a\,9, 10 = 1003^a\,5-17$, cf. Z. 13, 15, M. 10.

(13) Do they exist potentially or actually? Does their potentiality or actuality refer to movement? $996^a\,10, 11 = 1002^b\,32-1003^a\,5$, cf. Θ. 8, Λ. 6, 7.

(14) Are mathematical objects substances, and if so are they separate from sensible things? $996^a\,12-15 = 1001^b\,26-1002^b\,11$, cf. M. 1–3, 6–9, N. 1–3, 5, 6.

The whole of B. 2–6 is thus accounted for, except $1002^b\,12-32$, which forms a sort of appendix to $1001^b\,26-1002^b\,11$. Further, Γ. 1–3, E. 1, Z. 7–10, 13–16, Θ. 1–9, I. 2, Λ–N are more or less directly occupied with answering the questions raised in B (though as regards Λ it must be noted that this book does not refer to B and seems to have been an independent treatise). Γ. 4–8 forms a natural appendix to the discussion of the second ἀπορία, and I a natural appendix to the discussion of the fifth. E. 2–4 and Θ. 10 deal with subjects not touched on in the ἀπορίαι, but naturally arising out of them. Z. 1–6, 11, 12, 17, and H are very closely bound up with the chapters of Z which discuss the ἀπορίαι. Only Δ and K stand outside the programme here laid down for study. Aristotle makes no attempt to preserve the order of the problems or to discuss them in exactly the form in which they are raised, but references in Γ. $1004^a\,33$, I. $1053^b\,10$, M. $1076^a\,39$, $^b\,39$, $1086^a\,34$ (?), $^b\,15$ show that he has them more or less in view.

The ἀπορίαι 1–3, 5 form a group of questions regarding the scope of metaphysics. They are restated continuously in B. 2, and they are all discussed in Γ. 1–3. The fourth question is of a different type; it comes after the first group in B. 2, and is discussed not in Γ but in Λ–N. It is similar in character to the eighth, eleventh, twelfth, and fourteenth questions. Questions 6–11 are taken in the same order in B. 3, 4. The remaining three are taken in the reverse order in B. 5, 6. Thus the order in B. 2–6 follows that of B. 1 in the main, but not closely, and at one point distinctly improves on it.

In K. 1, 2 the problems reappear in an order more akin to that of B. 2-6 but not entirely agreeing with it.

Problem	(1)	is restated in	1059^a 20-23 (34-38).
	(2)	,,	,, 23-26
	(3)	,,	,, 26-29
	(4)	.,	,, 38-^{b} 21
	(5)	..	., 29-34
	(6, 7)	,,	1059^b 21—1060^a 1
	(8)	,,	1060^a 3-27, ^{b} 23-28
	(9)	,,	1060^b 28-30
	(10)	,,	1060^a 27-36
	(11, 14)	,,	,, 36-^{b} 19
	(12)	,,	1060^b 19-23
	(13)	does not appear in K.	

5. Aristotle does not say that he has raised this difficulty ἐν τοῖς πεφροιμιασμένοις, i. e. in Bk. A (which he has not done), but that the difficulty concerns the subject discussed there, viz. the first principles. The wrong interpretation of this passage led to the interpolation in a. 995^a 19.

10. τῶν ἄλλων τῶν τοιούτων. It is not very clear what other universal starting-points of knowledge or axioms Aristotle recognizes. The law of excluded middle is the only one, besides the law of contradiction, that is mentioned in B. 2 or discussed in Γ. In *An. Post.* 76^a 41, 77^a 30 he gives as a κοινὴ ἀρχή the law that if equals be taken from equals the remainders are equal. Clearly certain others of Euclid's κοιναὶ ἔννοιαι have an equal right to be included, but Aristotle makes no attempt at a complete list.

12-13. The problem here stated is nowhere restated separately, and may be treated as an appendix to that in ll. 10, 11.

16. οἱ ποιοῦντες κτλ. Plato and his school, cf. A. 987^b 14.

20-27. This problem is not restated in B and may be treated as an appendix to that in ll. 18-20. The two are treated together in Γ. Same, other, like, unlike, contrary, prior, posterior, &c., are here distinguished from the συμβεβηκότα καθ' αὐτά of substances. In Γ. 1003^b 33-36 they are described not as συμβεβηκότα but as εἴδη τοῦ ἑνός and τοῦ ὄντος. In Γ. 1004^b 1-6, 1005^a 11-18 on the other hand, they are described as πάθη or ὑπάρχοντα of being as such. They are further described as ἐναντιώσεις τοῦ ὄντος (K. 1061^b 5). The concepts regarding which Aristotle here asks whose business it is to discuss them, he himself discusses in Bk. I.

29. τοῖς ἀτόμοις, 'the individuals'. So in 998^b 16, 999^a 12, 15, I. 1058^a 18, 19, 20. In Δ. 1018^b 6, Z, 1034^a 8, I. 1058^b 10, K. 1059^b 36 the word is applied to the 'indivisible species'. In B. 998^b 29 either meaning seems possible. Cf. a. 994^b 21 n.

31-34. These problems are not restated in this form in the later chapters, but are really involved in the next group (34-36). The whole group (31-36) is the most important of all (995^b 31, 999^a 24).

996ᵃ 1-2. αἱ ἐν τοῖς λόγοις must mean the elements of, i. e. the characteristics named in, definitions ; and αἱ ἐν τῷ ὑποκειμένῳ must mean the constituent material elements of things. It is the same distinction that is drawn in Z. 11.

6. ἔλεγεν (E¹ Aᵇ) may be retained, the singular being due to the nearer subject Πλάτων. Cf. 996ᵃ 33, 1001ᵃ 13, and Kühner, ii. 1. § 370. 2 (β).

8-9. Love was, of course, on Empedocles' view, not *the* ὑποκείμενον but one of six elements all of which are ὑποκείμενα. Aristotle presumably mentions it here because of its unifying power, the notion being that the other elements are merged in love. Strictly speaking, on Empedocles' view they are not merged in love but merged in one another owing to the operation of love. Aristotle identifies the substratum with φιλία more doubtfully in 1001ᵃ 14.

ὅλλος δέ τις = Hippasus and Heraclitus, ὁ δὲ ὕδωρ—Thales—ἢ ἀέρα —Anaximenes and Diogenes. Cf. A. 984ᵃ 7, 983ᵇ 20, 984ᵃ 5.

11. ἔτι πότερον κτλ. This problem is not restated in B, and must be treated as an appendix to the question δυνάμει ἢ ἐνεργείᾳ. The potency which does not refer to movement is explained in Θ. 6.

PROBLEMS 1-5 (ch. 2.).

First problem.

996ᵃ 18. Is it the business of one science to study all the kinds of causes? 1. (*a*) How can it be so if they are not contrary? (*b*) Many things have not all the kinds of cause; e. g. unchangeable things have no efficient or final cause.

29. Hence mathematics never uses final causes in explaining things, and was therefore regarded by some of the sophists as inferior even to the mechanical arts.

ᵇ 1. 2. On the other hand, if there are several sciences of causes, which is the science we are looking for? Which cause must we know if we are most truly to know the thing caused? A thing, e. g. a house, may have all four causes.

10. (*a*) *Qua* most authoritative, knowledge of the final cause might seem to be what we want; but (*b*) *qua* dealing with what is most intelligible, knowledge of substance or the formal cause. For it is better to know what a thing is than what it is not, and *what* it is rather than its quantity, quality, &c. In other cases, where the term to be defined is not a substance but an attribute that can be demonstrated, we know it when we know its formal cause. But (*c*) with regard to change, we understand this best when we know the efficient cause, which is the opposite of the final cause; thus the study of each of these causes would seem to be the work of a different science.

Second problem.

26. Is it the business of one science to study the first principles of demonstration as well, e. g. the law of excluded middle or of contradiction? Does the same science study these and study substance? If different sciences do so, which of them is the science that we are looking for?

33. *Thesis.* (*a*) It cannot well be the business of one science, for why of one more than another? Nor can it be the business of all. Therefore it is not the task of the science of substance (any more than of any other).

997ª 2. (*b*) How can there be knowledge of these first principles? *What they are* is evidently familiar enough; if *their truth* is to be proved, they will have to be shown to be attributes of an underlying genus, and so, since all demonstrative science uses the axioms, all attributes that can be proved will be attributes of a common genus.

11. *Antithesis.* If the science of substance and the science of the axioms are distinct, which is the more authoritative? The axioms are the principles of all things, and who can study them if not the philosopher?

Third problem.

15. Is there one science of all substances? *Thesis.* If not one, which kind of substance does the supreme science study? *Antithesis.* One science cannot well study them all. For if one science studies all substances, and one science studies all the axioms, these two sciences or one compounded out of them will study *all* attributes.

Fifth problem.

25. Does the science of substances study their attributes also?

30. *Thesis.* If it does, the science of substance will be demonstrative, which it is not thought to be. *Antithesis.* If not, which science studies the attributes of substance?

Fourth problem.

34. Are there non-sensible substances, and if so, are there more than one kind of them, e. g. Forms, and 'intermediates' which are the objects of mathematics?

ᵇ **3.** (A.) We have already stated how the *Forms* are said to be causes and substances. Not least of the many difficulties of the theory is that involved in making the non-sensible realities the same as the sensible except that they are eternal; to make them eternal sensibles is like making the gods eternal men.

12. (B.) *Thesis.* The belief in the *intermediates* involves many difficulties. (*a*) On the same showing there will be heavens and heavenly bodies apart from the ideal and the sensible; but how can they be either immovable or movable?

20. (*b*) There will be intermediate objects of optics and harmonics, i.e. intermediate sensibles, and therefore intermediate senses, and therefore intermediate animals.

25. (*c*) If geometry differs from mensuration only by being of non-sensibles, there will be a medical science intermediate between the ideal medical science and that which we know, and therefore intermediate healthy objects.

32. (*d*) It is not the case that mensuration is of sensible objects; if it were, it would have perished when they perish.

34. *Antithesis.* Astronomy is not concerned with sensible things. The movements of the heaven are not like those of which astronomy speaks any more than sensible lines are like those of geometry.

998ᵃ 7. Some say that intermediates exist, but *in* sensible things. The difficulties of this view may be briefly indicated.

11. (*a*) At this rate the Forms might be in sensibles. (*b*) There would be two solids in the same place. (*c*) The intermediates, being in moving sensibles, could not be unmovable. (*d*) The view is open to all the difficulties of the former view, in an exaggerated form.

996ᵃ 18–ᵇ 26.   *First* ἀπορία.

Aristotle answers the question in Γ. 1, by saying that metaphysics studies all the causes or principles of being *qua* being. The precise difficulties raised here, however, are not solved.

20. Aristotle assumes (1) that of different γένη there are in general different sciences, but (2) that of contraries there is one science. The γένη τῶν αἰτίων being different and not contrary, how can there be one science of them?

21. ἔτι δὲ πολλοῖς κτλ. This, as Colle has pointed out, becomes intelligible as an objection to there being one science of all the kinds of cause, only if that be taken to mean that a science which apprehends one kind of cause necessarily apprehends them all. If the objects of certain sciences are unaffected by some kinds of cause, those sciences will know some kinds of cause without knowing all.

23. τοῖς ἀκινήτοις. Jaeger argues that Aristotle would not have asked 'how can unmoved things have a cause of movement?', and that the meaning must be 'how can there be among unmoved things one which causes movement in other things?'. He therefore reads

ἐν τοῖς ἀκινήτοις, which may have been read by Alexander (181. 34 f.,
37, 182. 3) and Asclepius (152. 18), and is found in l. 27 and in the
parallel passage K. 1059ᵃ 18, as well as in Λ. 1072ᵇ 1. But the argument in ll. 23–27 implies the question 'how can unmoved things *have*
a final cause?', and ἐν τοῖς ἀκινήτοις in l. 27 only puts this in another
way, 'how can there be a final cause in the case of unmoved things?'
At l. 23 ἐν τοῖς ἀκινήτοις may be only Alexander's and Asclepius' paraphrase of τοῖς ἀκινήτοις.

29. In M. 1078ᵃ 31–ᵇ 5 Aristotle shows that τὸ καλόν, if not τὸ
ἀγαθόν, has a place in mathematics.

32. Aristippus is called a sophist because of his subjectivistic or
Protagorean theory of knowledge, for which see Zeller, ii. 1. 347–352.
The Cyrenaics are said to have eschewed physics and logic as well as
mathematics because of their ' uselessness ' (Diog. Laert. ii. 92, Sext.
Math. vii. 11, ps.–Plut. in Eus. *Pr. Ev.* i. 8, 9, cf. Diog. ii. 71, 79).
In this both the Cynics and the Epicureans agreed with them.

33. προεπηλάκιζεν. For the singular cf. l. 6 n.

ᵇ 1. The thesis that *one* science cannot study all the causes has been
stated in ᵃ 20–ᵇ 1 ; Aristotle does not now, as in most of the other
ἀπορίαι, proceed to state the antithesis. He only points out that if
different sciences study the different causes it is hard to say which of
tl.em is Wisdom or first philosophy. Alexander's conjecture in l. 24
would give us the antithesis.

It is to be noticed that in this book ἀλλὰ μήν is used both in passing
from thesis to antithesis (997ᵃ 11, ᵇ 34, 999ᵃ 29, ᵇ 27, 1002ᵃ 15,
ᵇ 30), in passing to a new problem (996ᵇ 26), in passing to a new
argument (999ᵃ 1, 1001ᵇ 19), in pointing out that thesis and antithesis
cannot be combined (998ᵇ 11), and in adding a fresh step to an
argument (998ᵇ 27, 999ᵃ 21, ᵇ 5, 1001ᵃ 29, 1002ᵃ 4).

8. τῶν πάλαι διωρισμένων. Aristotle is referring to the characteristics
of Wisdom or first philosophy stated in A. 982ᵃ 8–19.

10–24. Aristotle gives reasons for regarding knowledge of the final
(ll. 10–13), of the formal (13–22), and of the efficient cause (22–24) as
being Wisdom. He does not suggest that knowledge of the material
cause could be Wisdom, doubtless because knowledge of the matter of
a thing is not positive knowledge of the thing but only knowledge of its
οὗ οὐκ ἄνευ (Al. 187. 12).

14. διωρίσθη. A. 982ᵃ 32–ᵇ 2.
οὐσίας, as often, means essence or formal cause.

15. μᾶλλον μὲν εἰδέναι κτλ. ' The man who recognizes the nature of
a thing by its being so-and-so knows it better than the man who
recognizes it by its not being so-and-so.'

19. καὶ ἐν τοῖς ἄλλοις. Aristotle has first (l. 15) spoken of the case
in which we directly know what a thing is. Now he refers to the case
in which the knowledge is reached by demonstration (καὶ ὧν ἀποδείξεις
εἰσί is epexegetic of ἐν τοῖς ἄλλοις). Substances are defined in the first
way (λόγος τοῦ τί ἐστιν ἀναπόδεικτος, *An. Post.* 94ⁿ 11), attributes or
operations in the second (συλλογισμὸς τοῦ τί ἐστι, πτώσει διαφέρων τῆς

ἀποδείξεως, ib. 94ᵃ 12). The definition, 'the squaring of a rectangle is
the finding of a (geometrical) mean between the sides', is an abbreviated form of the syllogism 'a rectangle can be squared because a
mean can be found between its sides'. (The problem is solved by the
finding of a mean proportional in Eucl. vi. 13, but otherwise in ii. 14.)
Cf. Aristotle's account of the definition of eclipse (*An. Post.* 90ᵃ 15–
18, 93ᵃ 30–ᵇ 7) and of thunder (ib. 93ᵇ 7–12, 94ᵃ 3–7).

24. ὥστ᾽ ἄλλης κτλ. This follows strictly not from what has been
said in ᵇ 1–24, but from what was said in ᵃ 20–ᵇ 1. In view of this
difficulty Alexander conjectured ὥστ᾽ οὐκ ἄλλης. The argument then
would be : 'the knowledge of each of three causes has a claim to be
regarded as Wisdom; therefore each of the three causes must be
studied by a science none other than Wisdom'. Cf. l. 1 n. It is possible, however, to take ὥστ᾽ ἄλλης not as summing up the whole
section ᵇ 1–24, but as suggested by the opposition Aristotle has just
(ᵇ 24) pointed out between the final and the efficient cause.

996ᵇ 26—997ᵃ 15.   *Second ἀπορία.*

26-27. καὶ περὶ . . . πλειόνων. In view of 995ᵇ 6–10, 996ᵇ 31—
997ᵃ 2, 997ᵃ 11–15, Γ. 1005ᵃ 19 we must take this to mean 'whether
it is the task of one science to study the axioms *as well as the four
causes*'. But in K. 1059ᵃ 23 the question is put in the form 'is it the
task of one science or of more than one to study the axioms?'.
It looks as if the writer of K had read the present passage hastily and
ignored the significance of καί.

Aristotle answers the question in Γ. 3 by saying that metaphysics
studies the axioms as well as the ἀρχαί of being.

28. τὰς κοινὰς δόξας. This phrase is the ancestor of κοιναὶ ἔννοιαι,
Euclid's term for the axioms. P. Tannery held that the phrase κοιναὶ
ἔννοιαι is a late interpolation due to Apollonius (*c.* 50 B.C.), but there is
no sufficient basis for this view. Cf. Heath's *Euclid,* i. 221–222.

30. ὅσαι ἄλλαι τοιαῦται, cf. 995ᵇ 10 n.

33-997ᵃ 2. Aristotle here argues dialectically that it cannot be the
special business of the science of substance any more than of any of
the other sciences to study principles common to all reasoning. The
fallacy of the argument is pointed out in Γ. 3 ; the science of substance
is not a special science like geometry, but the science of being as such.

34. The proposals to amend γεωμετρίας (σοφίας Schwegler, ταύτης
ἢ γεωμετρίας Christ) are obviously unnecessary.

35. ἁπασῶν δὲ μὴ ἐνδέχεται, *sc.* because all the sciences would then
overlap.

997ᵃ 2-11. Aristotle assumes that if there is a science of the axioms, it
must either define or demonstrate them ; cf. the two kinds of things
that have to be 'foreknown', ὅτι ἔστι and τί τὸ λεγόμενόν ἐστι, *An.
Post.* 71ᵃ 11. We do not need a science to enable us to *define* the
meaning of the axioms (ll. 3–5) ; and if they could be *demonstrated*
then all demonstrated facts would belong to one genus. The latter

proposition is proved thus (ll. 5–11). If the axioms are supposed to be demonstrable, then (1) there must be some underlying genus (περί τι), (2) some of the axioms must be πάθη proved about this genus (τινῶν), (3) since every proof must start with something unproved, some of them must be unproved ἀξιώματα (ἔκ τινων). (Thus the supposition that the axioms are demonstrable must be corrected into the supposition that some of them can be demonstrated from others which are indemonstrable.) For these three implications of proof cf. *An. Post.* 75ᵃ 39, 76ᵇ 11, 21. Now all demonstrative sciences use the axioms as their premises, and the conclusions of proof must be about the same genus as the premises (this is not stated but is clearly assumed ; cf. ib. 75ᵃ 38, 76ᵃ 5). Therefore if axioms are demonstrable, all δεικνύμενα belong to one genus and all the sciences become one—which for Aristotle is a *reductio ad absurdum.*

The argument is designed only to raise difficulties, and overlooks two points. (1) There is a third way in which there may be a science of axioms. Metaphysics, as Bk. Γ shows, neither defines nor demonstrates them, but commends them to common sense by showing the absurd consequences of their denial. This is not strictly science since it is not demonstrative, but in face of scepticism it is a real service which philosophy may perform. (2) Aristotle ignores the difference between κοιναί and ἴδιαι ἀρχαί (*An. Post.* 72ᵃ 14–18, 76ⁿ 37–41). Each science must have principles dealing with the same genus with which its conclusions deal, but it also uses principles common to all the sciences, i.e. the axioms.

5. τέχναι, not distinguished from ἐπιστῆμαι, cf. A. 981ᵇ 25 n.

997ᵃ 15-25. *Third ἀπορία.*

Aristotle answers this question in Γ. 2. 1004ᵃ 2–9, E. 1 by pointing out that the three main kinds of entity are studied by three sciences, those that exist independently but are mutable by physics, those that are immutable but do not exist independently by mathematics, those that are immutable and exist independently by theology. But the last of the three really studies the general nature of all substances ; it is 'universal because it is first ' (E. 1026ᵃ 30).

22-25. If the περὶ ὅ, the subject genus, viz. all substances, be the object of one science, and if the ἐξ ὧν, the axioms, be the object of one science, no matter whether these two sciences be identical or not (this, the question just discussed in the previous ἀπορία, is still undecided), then the συμβεβηκότα (= πάθη, l. 7) will be the object of one science, i.e. of these two sciences if they are identical, or of one compounded out of them if they are not. The plural αὗται can still be used, for even if the sciences are one in fact they are described differently ; one is the science of substance, the other the science of the axioms. It seems best to take ἐκ τούτων μία as ' one compounded out of these ' (Al. 193. 6). It might mean simply ' one of them ', but if one science knows the substances, another the axioms, it would not be natural to

suggest that one of them alone could know the attributes inferred from
the axioms to belong to the substances. It is hard to get Bonitz's
' one dependent on these ' out of the Greek.

997ᵃ 25-34.   *Fifth ἀπορία.*

Aristotle answers this question in Γ. 2. 1003ᵇ 32—1005ᵃ 18 by
saying that the science which studies substances must study also their
general attributes.

30-32. The argument is : if Wisdom is the science of substance
and is demonstrative, it must be demonstrative of substance ; but substance or essence cannot be demonstrated (*An. Post.* ii. 3–8). The
fallacy is obvious ; really Wisdom defines substances and demonstrates
their attributes.

997ᵃ 34—998ᵃ 19.   *Fourth ἀπορία.*

Aristotle answers the problem by asserting in Λ. 6–10 the existence of
certain non sensible substances, viz. God and the pure forms that move
the planetary spheres, and by denying in M and N the substantiality of
Ideas and mathematical objects.

ᵇ 3. λέγομεν, cf. A. 990ᵇ 9 n.

4. ἐν τοῖς πρώτοις λόγοις, A. 6.

7. οὐρανῷ, the sensible universe, cf. A. 986ᵇ 24 n.

12. It is of course a mistake to describe the Forms as ' eternal
sensibles'. They were certainly not thought of as sensibles at all.
Aristotle's point, however, is that, in his view, the Platonists treated the
Forms too much as akin to sensibles. They did not grasp the nature
of the universal as something essentially *in* particulars, but placed it
outside the particulars and thus made it a particular itself. If not
eternal sensibles, the Forms were at least eternal particulars. It is, however, a mistake to say, as Aristotle does here and in *E. N.* 1096ᵇ 3,
that the Platonists rested the whole difference between Ideas and
particulars on the eternity of the Ideas. That they are eternal was
only one way out of several of describing their nature.

16. τούτων, ' of the mathematical sciences ', referring to l. 2.

21. ἡ ἐν τοῖς μαθήμασιν ἁρμονική, the mathematical as opposed to the
experimental study of musical harmony.

25. περὶ ποῖα. Bonitz reads παρὰ ποῖα and cites ll. 28, 29, 31 in
support. But the cases are not parallel. There Aristotle is speaking
of a science apart from that of medicine, of healthy things apart from
those which are sensible. Here he is speaking of the relation between
certain sciences and certain objects, and παρά is inappropriate. Its
occurrence in ll. 28, 29, 31 has led to its intrusion here in some
manuscripts.

26. γεωδαισίας. This science, as Heath observes (Gk. *Math.* i. 16),
was not confined to land-measuring, but covered generally the practical
measurement of surfaces and volumes. Cf. Geminus *ap.* Procl. *in
Eucl.* i, p. 39. 20—40. 2.

32. The difference between geometry and mensuration, like that between arithmetic and harmonics (*An. Post.* 87ᵃ 33), is that one is not καθ' ὑποκειμένου and the other is. This does not mean that there are separately existing non-sensible planes for geometry to study, nor that mensuration studies only particular visible fields. Both sciences alike deal with certain universal attributes of certain classes of sensible things in abstraction from other attributes (ἐξ ἀφαιρέσεως). Geometry studies planes in abstraction from the underlying matter (μὴ καθ' ὑποκειμένου); mensuration studies planes not in abstraction from matter but in abstraction from any particular kind of matter.

998ᵃ 3. ἀλλ' ὥσπερ Πρωταγόρας ἔλεγεν, ' but along a line, as Protagoras used to say'. Protagoras, as we should expect, appealed simply to the visible circle. He is said (Diog. Laert. ix. 55) to have written a book περὶ τῶν μαθημάτων, in which he presumably expressed similar views; and he displays contempt for mathematics in Plato's *Protagoras* (318 D, E). Burnet suggests (*G. P.* § 91) that it was from taking the common-sense view thus opposed to the mathematical view in questions about commensurability that he was led to use the curious phrase ' man is the *measure* of all things'. The similar views about mathematics referred to in N. 1089ᵃ 21, *An. Post.* 76ᵇ 39, 87ᵇ 37 may perhaps be assigned to Protagoras, cf. Apelt, *Beiträge*, 261. Sir T. Heath suggests (*Gk. Math.* i. 179) that it was against such attacks on geometry that Democritus wrote his work, ' On the contact of a circle and of a sphere'.

5. ἕλικες. For the belief in spiral movements of the planets cf. Pl. *Tim.* 39 A, Tim. Locr. 97 c, Theo Smyrn. p. 178. 13, 179. 4, 186. 12, 200. 24, 203. 15 Hiller.

ὅμοιαι περὶ ὧν, ' like those about which'.

W. Jaeger holds (*Hermes*, lii. 488) that, as we have τοιαῦταί εἰσιν οἵας in l. 1 and τὴν αὐτὴν ἔχει φύσιν in l. 6, so here we need words expressing identity of nature, not mere similarity. Alexander has (200. 23) τοιαῦται ὁποίας ὁ ἀστρολόγος λαμβάνει, and Jaeger would accordingly read οἷαι περὶ ὧν. But Alexander is evidently paraphrasing, and may well be paraphrasing ὅμοιαι.

6. τὰ σημεῖα. Schwegler takes this to mean the constellations. The word is found in this sense as early as Euripides (*Ion* 1157, *Rhes.* 529); but this meaning is unparalleled in Aristotle, and it is better to take the word with Alexander as meaning the points which the astronomer uses as symbols of the stars. This carries out the opposition which is being stated between sensible things and the objects of mathematics; σημεῖα as ' constellations could not be opposed to the stars which compose them.

7. εἰσὶ δέ τινες κτλ. This view is mentioned again in M. 1076ᵃ 33, 38–ᵇ 11. In N. 1090ᵃ 20 it is ascribed to the Pythagoreans. But Aristotle is speaking here of people who believe in the Forms as well as in the mathematicals (ll. 7, 8, 12), so that some Platonists must be meant. Schwegler suggests Eudoxus, cf. A. 991ᵃ 14–18; but Alexander in his commentary on that passage says that Eudoxus believed in the presence of *Ideas* in sensible things (and in saying so

appears to depend on statements of Aristotle's in the dialogue *De Ideis* ;
v. Al. 98. 21), while the persons here referred to evidently do not
believe in the immanence of Ideas but only in that of mathematicals
(l. 12).

10. τὰ τοιαῦτα.   For τοιοῦτος referring forward cf. A. 987ᵇ 4 n.

Problems 6, 7 (ch. 3).

Sixth problem.

998ᵃ 20. Are the genera, or the simplest constituent parts, the first
principles of things ?

Thesis. (*a*) The elements of speech are the constituent parts.
(*b*) The elements of geometry are the propositions whose proof
is involved in the proof of other propositions.

28. (*c*) Those who said that bodies have one element, or more than
one element, meant their constituents, not the genera of them.
(*d*) Generally, if we want to know the nature of a thing, we investigate
its parts.

ᵇ **4.** *Antithesis.* (*a*) If we know things by their definition, and
genera are the starting-points of definition, they must be the first
principles of the things defined.   (*b*) If to know things is to know
their species, genera are at any rate the first principles of species.
(*c*) Some of those who named unity, being, &c., as elements of things
were thinking of them as genera.

11. We cannot say that *both* genera *and* constituents are first
principles, for then there would be two definitions of the essence of a
thing, which there cannot be.

Seventh problem.

14. If classes *are* first principles, is it *summa genera* or *infimae
species* that are so?

Thesis. (*a*) If the more universal is more of a principle, the *summa
genera* will be so, i. e. being and unity.

22. But neither of these can be one genus of existing things.   For
the differentiae of each genus must be, and be one each, but the genus,
if it is taken apart from its species, cannot be predicated of its differentiae.
But if unity and being are not genera they are not first principles.

28. (*b*) The terms in which the genus is combined with successive
differentiae will all be genera, and still more so the differentiae themselves, so that there would be an infinite number of first principles.

999ᵃ 1. (*c*) Even if unity is of the nature of a principle, still if the indivisible is one and indivisibility means primarily indivisibility in kind, the *infimae species* will be more truly one and therefore more truly a principle.

6. (*d*) Where terms are respectively prior and posterior, that which is predicable of them does not exist apart from them ; thus there is no such thing as number or figure apart from the particular numbers or figures, and if these genera do not exist apart from the species, *a fortiori* no other genus does. But individuals are not prior or posterior to each other.

16. *Antithesis.* The principle should exist apart from that of which it is a principle, but why should one suppose an *infima species* to exist apart from its members, except because it is universally predicated of them ? But at that rate the more universal classes, i. e. the *summa genera*, would be more truly principles.

998ᵃ 20–ᵇ 14.   *Sixth* ἀπορία.

This problem is nowhere answered explicitly by Aristotle, but in Z. 10 we learn that the ἐνυπάρχοντα or parts of a thing are included in its definition only when they are included in its form ; while in Z. 13 we learn that universals (among which the γένη named in this problem are included) cannot constitute the substance of individuals. The nature of an individual cannot, in fact, be exhausted by naming either the classes under which it falls or the parts which it includes.

25. τῶν διαγραμμάτων, as Asclepius says (174. 9), means geometrical propositions rather than figures, cf. Δ. 1014ᵃ 36, *Cat.* 14ᵃ 39. Θ. 1051ᵃ 22, *Soph. El.* 175ᵃ 27 are difficult cases of the use of the word.

26. στοιχεῖα. For this use cf. Δ. 1014ᵃ 35, *Cat.* 14ᵃ 39, *Top.* 158ᵇ 35, 163ᵇ 24. *Elements* of geometry were written (1) by Socrates' contemporary Hippocrates of Chios (Procl. *in Eucl.* p. 66. 7 Friedlein) ; (2) by Leon (born *c.* 410) (ib. 20) ; (3) by Theudius of Magnesia, whose work was the geometrical text-book of the Academy, and was no doubt that used by Aristotle. Theudius' *Elements* were the immediate precursor of those of Euclid, who flourished *c.* 300. The term is frequently used of elementary propositions without special reference to geometry (cf. Bonitz, *Index*, 702ᵇ 53—703ᵃ 10), and in this usage Aristotle was anticipated by Xenophon (*Mem.* ii. 1. 1).

30. τὰ μετὰ τούτων. Christ reads, with Aᵇ, τὰ μεταξὺ τούτων. Empedocles does not seem to have treated air and earth as intermediate between fire and water. Rather he opposed fire to all the other elements (A. 985ᵇ 1, *de Gen. et Corr.* 330ᵇ 20). But Aristotle, for whom fire is the hot and dry, water the cold and moist, might naturally treat air (hot and moist) and earth (cold and dry) as bridging the differences between them (though *they* bridge the difference no less between air and earth). It is preferable, however, to read τὰ μετὰ τούτων, which is the better supported reading.

998ᵇ 1. With the vulgate reading the structure of the sentence is somewhat loose. Since Aᵇ reads καὶ τότε γνωρίζει in l. 2, Christ suggests ⟨ἀθρεῖ⟩ καὶ τότε γνωρίζει, but ἀθρεῖ would be more likely to have fallen out immediately after ἀθρεῖν. The reading εἰ . . . ἀθρεῖν, ἀθρεῖ—οἶον κλίνην—ἐξ ὧν . . . συγκειμένων, καὶ τότε γνωρίζει would give a good sense. But neither emendation is very probable, and it seems preferable to accept the traditional reading, as a not unnatural blend of two constructions which can easily be supplied.

9. τινες. The Pythagoreans and Plato made unity and being elements of things (996ᵃ 6); and Plato made the great-and-small an element (987ᵇ 20).

14—999ᵃ 23.   *Seventh ἀπορία.*

Aristotle answers this question by saying in Z. 12. 1038ᵃ 19 that the last differentia (or *infima species*) is the substance of a thing, and in Z. 13 that no universal ever constitutes the substance of an individual.

Bz. takes 998ᵇ 17—999ᵃ 1 as presenting the thesis (that *summa genera* are the first principles), 999ᵃ 1–16 the antithesis, and 999ᵃ 16–23 as returning to the thesis. But a study of the arguments shows that 998ᵇ 20—999ᵃ 16 is directed to showing that *summa genera* cannot be the principles, 999ᵃ 16–23 to showing that *infimae species* cannot be so.

16. τῶν ἀτόμων, cf. 995ᵇ 29 n.

24-26. 'Neither (1) can species be predicated of their proper differentiae, nor (2) can the genus, if it be taken apart from its species, be predicated of its differentiae'. The first point is made here for the sake of completeness though irrelevant to what Aristotle is proving. The reasons why species cannot be predicated of their differentiae are given in *Top.* 144ᵇ 5-11. (*a*) The differentia extends more widely than the species. If A is defined as a B (genus) which is C (differentia), C as well as B is wider than A. (*b*) If 'man' is predicated of its differentia, the differentia will be a sub-species— a kind of man. (*c*) If the species is predicated of its differentia it is prior to it; but in reality it is posterior.

The reasons why a genus cannot be predicated of its differentiae are given ib. 144ᵃ 36-ᵇ 3. (*a*) If it were so predicated, the genus would be predicated of the species many times over, since it would be predicated of each of the successive differentiae which constitute the species. (*b*) If 'animal' is predicable of each of its differentiae, each of them will be either a species or an individual, since 'an animal' always means one or the other. The genus, then, is predicated not of the differentiae, but of the species of which the differentiae are also predicated.

28—999ᵃ 1. This argument does not seem to bear on the question whether the *summa genera* or the *infima species* are ἀρχαί. Rather, as Alexander partially sees (207. 9), it bears on the question whether the genera are ἀρχαί at all. Aristotle in fact does not treat the two questions as entirely independent. In ll. 14–16 he raises the question whether the highest or the lowest genera are ἀρχαί, as a further difficulty in the view that genera are ἀρχαί. Thus a reference to the earlier question amidst the discussion of the later is not unnatural. Lines 28–30 seem to mean 'further, the intermediate terms (species) in which the *summum genus* is combined with the successive differentiae, right down to the indivisibles, will be genera ⟨and therefore ἀρχαί⟩— though only some are in fact commonly held to be so'. The point lies in the clause which is not expressed but can easily be supplied from l. 28 εἴπερ ἀρχαὶ τὰ γένη; and it is the same point as is expressed in l. 32, viz. that those who think the genera to be ἀρχαί will find an unconscionable number of ἀρχαί on their hands. This is fatal to their view, since it is in the pursuit of unity that they make the genera ἀρχαί.

29. τῶν ἀτόμων, *sc.* εἰδῶν, says Al. (207. 28), and this usage is not uncommon (cf. 995^b 29 n.). But the individuals may equally well be meant (cf. l. 16, 999^a 12). On the first interpretation, μέχρι may be either inclusive or exclusive; on the second, it must of course be exclusive.

30. νῦν . . . οὐ δοκεῖ, if our view of the passage be right, does not state Aristotle's objection to the theory. He does not mean that in fact not all the intermediate terms are genera though the theory requires that they should be; he himself can call all the species except the *infimae species* (and sometimes even these) genera. Rather he points out incidentally that common usage does not recognize them all as genera, either because some of them have no single names (Al. 207. 14) or because a genus combined with a privative differentia is not thought to make a genuine class (Al. 207. 17, cf. *De Part. An.* i. 3). In any case the remark is parenthetical.

31. τὰ γένη, the genera just referred to, i. e. those below the *summum genus*. If A is defined as a B (genus) which is C (differentia), C is wider than A (cf. *Top.* 144^b 5–11) and therefore more of an ἀρχή. Aristotle ignores his own doctrine that the differentia should be one which is confined to the genus and therefore no wider than the species (*Top.* 143^a 31, cf. Z. 1038^a 9).

32. ἄλλως τε κἂν τις κτλ. The higher up in the scale of genera one begins in enumerating the ἀρχαί, the more ἀρχαί one will have to recognize.

999^a 1. Aristotle returns to the view, disproved in 998^b 19–28, that unity is one of the ἀρχαί. He now deduces from it a consequence fatal to it. Even if unity *is* (γε) more of the nature of an ἀρχή, it is best found not in a *summum genus* like unity itself but in an *infima species*.

2–3. ἀδιαίρετον δὲ . . . εἶδος. This antithesis, which appears also in *De An.* 430^b 14, seems to be identical with the antithesis in I. 1053^b 6 between the indivisible in quantity and the indivisible in quality. There, however, indivisibility in quantity, here indivisibility in form, is said to be the prior kind of unity. The present argument is, it must be remembered, purely dialectical. But perhaps the two statements

are not really contradictory. In I Aristotle is dealing with the meaning of the word ' one ', and finds that its original meaning is ' a
measure'. It is properly quantities that are measured ; therefore
' one ' refers primarily to quantity. But the essential nature of a
thing is found in form rather than in quantity (cf. Γ. 1010ᵃ 24), so that
indivisibility in form or species is more important than indivisibility
in quantity.

5-6. οὐ γάρ . . . ἀνθρώπων appears to be a note to the clause τὰ δὲ γένη
διαιρετὰ εἰς εἴδη. Genera are divisible into species (for man, which is
not divisible into species, is not the genus but the species of individual
men).

6-10. Aristotle states here the rule that where one of two species is
prior to the other their common predicate is nothing separable from
them. Instances of such priority are the different numbers or figures
or forms of government. If you set number, for instance, on one
side as that in which the various numbers agree, and ask what it is in
which they differ, you find that this too is number. ' Numberness
does not exist apart from the rest of the nature of the numbers, but
penetrates their whole nature, and exists only in the various numbers.
Remove the genus number, and you remove the differentiae of the
numbers as well. Zeller argues (ii. 1. 683–686) that the ideal
numbers are meant. Now according to the Platonists ideal numbers
had, and mathematical numbers had not, this relation of priority and
posteriority (M. 1080ᵇ 11), so that if Aristotle had only the Platonists
in view here, he could only mean the ideal numbers. But the principle
he here states is not a specially Platonic one. It was accepted by the
Platonists (E. N. 1096ᵃ 17), but also by Aristotle himself (Pol.
1275ᵃ 34, cf. De An. 414ᵇ 21). He has not in his mind the distinction
between ideal and mathematical numbers, but simply the plain fact
that the number 2 is prior to the number 3 because there can be two
things without there being three, but there cannot be three without
there being two. On the whole question cf. Cook Wilson in Classical
Review, xviii. 247–260, esp. §§ 1, 7.

8. πρώτη τῶν ἀριθμῶν ἡ δυάς. The Greeks did not reckon one
as a number but opposed it to number. Cf. N. 1088ᵃ 4–8, Phys.
220ᵃ 27.

11. τούτων γάρ κτλ. The Pythagoreans and Plato, of whom
Aristotle is now speaking (cf. 996ᵃ 6), attached peculiar importance to
numbers and figures, and, as he says, would find it hard to say that
there are separate genera of anything, if not of these.

12. ἐν δὲ τοῖς ἀτόμοις. Among the individuals (for the meaning of
ἀτόμοις cf. 995ᵇ 29 n.) there is no priority, and therefore there can
conceivably be a separate genus of them. Aristotle suggests dialectically, then, that while to certain species there cannot answer any genus
which is παρὰ ταῦτα, to individuals there does answer an infima
species which is παρὰ ταῦτα. But this is in contradiction with his
doctrine that the universal is always κατὰ πολλῶν, never παρὰ τὰ
πολλά.

PROBLEMS 8–11 (ch. 4).

Eighth problem.

999ᵃ 24. *Thesis.* If there is nothing apart from individual things, how can we know the infinitely many individuals? All the things we know we know by virtue of their having some common characteristic.

29. *Antithesis.* If there is something apart from the individuals, it must be either *infimae species* or *summa genera*; and we have shown that it cannot be either.

32. If there is something apart from the concrete whole, does it exist apart from all concrete wholes or only from some? *Thesis.* If there is nothing apart from the individuals, there will be (*a*) nothing knowable, (*b*) nothing eternal or unchangeable, and therefore (*c*) no generation.

ᵇ6. For (i) generation implies an ultimate ungenerated material;

8. (ii) If generation and motion exist there must be a limit to them; a thing is not coming to be unless it can actually come to be, and as soon as it has come to be it is (and is no longer coming into being).

12. (iii) If matter must exist apart from the individual, still more must form.

17. *Antithesis.* If form exists apart, in which cases does it do so? (*a*) It obviously cannot exist apart in the case of all individuals, e. g. individual houses. (*b*) The form of all the individuals cannot be one, for then the individuals would be one; nor can their forms be different. (*c*) How does the matter become each of the individuals? How are matter and form combined in them?

Ninth problem.

24. *Thesis.* If the principles are one only in kind, none of them will be one in number, not even unity or being, and knowledge will be impossible.

27. *Antithesis.* If they are one in number, not in kind like the principles of sensible things, there will be nothing apart from the elements. It is as if the letters were limited in number; all literature would be confined to the alphabet, since no letter could be repeated.

Tenth problem.

1000ᵃ 5. Are the principles of perishable and imperishable things the same? *Thesis.* If they are, why are some things perishable, others imperishable? (*a*) The theologians say that the gods who did not taste of nectar and ambrosia became mortal, but this explanation was only meant to satisfy its authors and does not satisfy *us*.

19. (*b*) Those who use more scientific methods give no explanation, and indeed the supposition is unreasonable ; the principles cannot be the same.

24. Empedocles, the most consistent of these thinkers, makes strife the cause of destruction, but it is equally true that in his system it generates everthing except the One, i. e. God ; if there were no strife, all things would be one.

(ᵇ **3.** Hence his God is less wise than all other beings, for He has no strife in Him, and knowledge is of like by like.)

11. Similarly love is not the cause of being any more than of destruction. Empedocles assigns no cause for the change from the reign of love to that of strife save that this is the nature of things.

17. He alone is consistent, however, in not making some things perishable, others imperishable, but all perishable except the elements ; but this does not answer our problem.

23. *Antithesis.* If the principles are different, (*a*) are they imperishable or perishable ? (i) If perishable, (*a*) they presuppose previous principles (for things perish by resolution into what they come from) ; but this is impossible. (*β*) How will perishable things exist if their first principles are thus shown not to be first principles ?

29. (ii) If imperishable, how can some imperishable principles produce perishable things, others imperishable things ?

32. (*b*) No one has attempted to distinguish the principles of perishable from those of imperishable things.

Eleventh problem.

1001^a **4.** The hardest and most important question : Are being and unity the substances of things, or attributes implying a substratum ?

9. Plato and the Pythagoreans take the former view ; the physicists, on the other hand, reduce the one to something which is considered more familiar—friendship, fire, or air ; those who posit more than one element make the one and being as numerous as the principles they allege.

19. *Thesis.* (*a*) If we do not make unity and being, the most universal terms, substance; no other universal will be a substance.

24. (*b*) If unity is not a substance, number will not exist apart from sensible things.

27. *Antithesis.* If there is a One itself and a Being itself, unity and being must be their substance, for there is no other term that is universally predicated of them. But if they are substance, (*a*) how

can there be anything beside them ?   What is other than being is not,
so that according to Parmenides' argument all things will be one and
this will be being.

b 1. Whether unity is or is not a substance, number cannot be
a substance.   We have seen why it cannot if unity is not a substance ;
if it is, what can produce another than *the* One ?   It must be not-one,
but everything is either one or a plurality of ones.

7. (*b*) If the One itself is indivisible, according to Zeno's principle
it will be nothing ; for that which does not make things bigger is on
his view nothing real, the real being the solid, which alone makes
things bigger in whatever way it is added to them.

13. Zeno's view is a vulgar one ; a thing may be indivisible and yet
be, for it may add to the number of things though not to their size.
But how can *magnitude* be produced out of one or many such
indivisibles ?   It is like making a line out of points.

19. (*c*) If one supposes number to be produced out of the One itself
and something else, still we must ask how the product can be now
a number, now a spatial magnitude, if the pre-existent principle other
than the One is always the same thing—inequality.   Magnitudes cannot
be produced out of this combined either with One or with a number.

999ᵃ 24–ᵇ 24.   *Eighth* ἀπορία.

This problem is not very different from that discussed in 997ᵃ
34—998ᵃ 19, but is raised from a different point of view.   There
Aristotle had in mind the Platonic doctrine of the separate existence of Forms and mathematical objects, and confined himself to
arguing against this.   Here he considers on its own merits the question whether the existence of perishable individual objects itself implies
the existence of other realities.   To this his answer will be an affirmative one, which may be summed up thus : (1) every concrete substance
includes as elements eternal matter and eternal form, which, however,
exist only as united in a concrete substance (Z. 8).   (2) Besides this
there are pure forms which exist separately, viz. God and the beings
that move the planetary spheres (Λ. 6–10).   Cf. Z. 13, 14, M. 10.

26. τὰ καθ' ἕκαστα.   In this phrase the plural ἕκαστα sometimes
retains its proper meaning, so that the phrase means ' things arranged
according to their several *groups* ' (e. g. *An. Post.* 97ᵇ 29, *H. A.* 539ᵇ
15).   But more often, as here, τὰ καθ' ἕκαστα is used simply as the
plural of τὸ καθ' ἕκαστον, in the sense of ' individuals ' (e. g. Z. 1039ᵇ
28, 30, K. 1060ᵃ 3, M. 1077ᵃ 6, *An. Post.* 71ᵃ 23, *E. N.* 1141ᵇ 16,
1143ᵃ 32).   And since τὰ καθ' ἕκαστα can mean ' the individuals ', even
ὁ καθ' ἕκαστα is used in the sense of ' the individual ' (Z. 1035ᵇ 2).

27. For δέ *in apodosi* with an adversative suggestion cf. K. 1059ᵇ
33 n., Λ. 1071ᵃ 24, 1075ᵃ 10, *Phys.* 215ᵇ 15, *Pol.* 1287ᵇ 13.

32. ἄρτι διηπορήσαμεν, 998ª 21—999ª 23.

33. Jaeger supposes λέγω δὲ σύνολον to have fallen out by ditto-graphy after σύνολον, and refers to 995ᵇ 35 in support of his reading. But the insertion of these words seems unnecessary, and is not supported by Alexander (211. 22).

ᵇ1. ἢ παρ' οὐδέν. The question, which individuals have something (a form) apart corresponding to them, suggests to Aristotle the question whether any have. Thus the end of the sentence takes a form inconsistent with the beginning.

3. εἰ μή τις κτλ. Aristotle presumably is thinking of Protagoras (cf. Pl. *Theaet.* 151 E).

4. τὰ γὰρ αἰσθητὰ πάντα φθείρεται. This requires some correction. The heavens and the heavenly bodies are sensible but not perishable (Λ. 1069ª 30). But they are ἐν κινήσει, which is Aristotle's main point.

6. ἀνάγκη γὰρ εἶναί τι κτλ. 'For there must be something that comes to be, i. e. something out of which something is produced.' Alexander takes τι τὸ γιγνόμενον to refer to that which is produced, but a reference to this would be irrelevant, and it is preferable to take it as referring to what is in l. 7 more clearly described as ἐξ οὗ γίγνεται.

8. εἴπερ . . . ἀδύνατον. That there is an upper limit to the chain of material causes has been proved in α. 2 ; that the first material cause cannot have come out of nothing is assumed as self-evident.

8-12 appears to be not, as Alexander says (213. 26), another argument for the existence of a beginning of generation, but an argument for the existence of an end of generation, which must (it is assumed) be eternal and therefore παρὰ τὰ καθ' ἕκαστα. The difficult part of the argument is that in ll. 11, 12, which seems to mean 'and that which is incapable of completing the process of coming into being cannot be coming into being, while that which has completed the process must forthwith be' ; i. e. the becoming of anything implies that sometime it will not be becoming but will be.

12. It is only now that Aristotle comes explicitly to the existence of forms, which is what he had in mind in the framing of the problem (cf. ª 33–ᵇ 1 with ᵇ 17, 18, and note the reference to the possibility of knowledge in ª 27, ᵇ 2 ; it is form and not matter that makes knowledge possible). The proof of the eternal existence of matter (ᵇ 5–8) is a preliminary to the proof of the eternal existence of form (ᵇ 12–16) ; and the 'limit of generation' whose existence is proved in ᵇ 8–12 is simply form.

ἔτι δ' εἴπερ ἡ ὕλη ἔστι, ἔστι, *sc.* παρὰ τὰ καθ' ἕκαστα. This can be supplied in thought because the subject of the whole section is the question whether ἔστι τι παρὰ τὰ καθ' ἕκαστα (ª 26, cf. ª 30, 31, 33, 34, ᵇ 1, 2). Matter has been shown to exist παρὰ τὰ καθ' ἕκαστα because it is ungenerated while they come into being (ᵇ 4–8).

14. οὐσίαν and ὃ are not related as antecedent and relative ; ὃ . . . γίγνεται is in apposition to τὴν οὐσίαν, so that a comma is required.

14-15. εἰ γὰρ ... παράπαν. This, as Colle points out, is an answer to a supposed objection. ⟨'Nor can it be said that *neither* form *nor* matter exists,⟩ for', &c.

19. οὐ γὰρ ἂν θείημεν κτλ., cf. A. 991ᵇ 6.

24—1000ᵃ 4. *Ninth* ἀπορία.

In Z. 14, M. 10 Aristotle raises this same question with regard to the Ideas. In Λ. 4, 5 he points out that a principle such as form, privation, matter, moving cause, actuality, or potency is only analogically the same in its various manifestations; all things, however, have a prime mover which is numerically identical.

25-27. The argument may be paraphrased thus : If a principle discovered by analysis of one thing can only be one in *kind* with a principle discovered by analysis of another thing, no two things will ever have a *numerically* identical principle ; but if there is not this, if there is not a ἓν ἐπὶ πάντων, how is knowledge possible ? Even unity or being (the favourite principles of Plato and the Pythagoreans, 996ᵃ 5) will not be the same in two things ; the unity or being of one will be only *like* that in the other. εἰ μὲν ... τὸ ὄν and καὶ τὸ ἐπίστασθαι ... πάντων seem to form a single argument, and should be separated only by a colon.

1000ᵃ 1. The sentence beginning with ὥσπερ οὖν has no principal clause, and Bonitz (following Fonseca) therefore proposed to read ὥσπερ ἄν with a comma before it, treating 999ᵇ 33—1000ᵃ 1 τὸ γάρ ... τούτων as parenthetical. But later, in the *Index Aristotelicus*, he recognized ὥσπερ οὖν κτλ. as an elliptical sentence (the principal clause is very easily supplied). Cf. Θ. 1049ᵃ 3, *An. Pr.* 34ᵃ 22, *Soph. El.* 178ᵇ 1, *Rhet.* 1408ᵇ 24, ὥσπερ γάρ in *Meteor.* 390ᵃ 4, ὥσπερ in M. 1087ᵃ 7, καθάπερ in *Pol.* 1275ᵃ 14, *De Caelo* 279ᵃ 30. Cf. also Z. 1031ᵃ 8, and Vahlen, *Poet.* ed. 3, p. 276.

1000ᵃ 5—1001ᵃ 3. *Tenth* ἀπορία.

Aristotle nowhere answers this question in so many words. But in Z. 7-9, Λ. 1-5 he states the principles of perishable things, and in Z. 10, Λ. 6, 7 he points out the difference between these and the principles of imperishable things.

9. θεολόγοι, cf. A. 983ᵇ 29 n.

10. Cf. Pl. *Soph.* 243 A ὅτι λίαν τῶν πολλῶν ἡμῶν ὑπεριδόντες ὠλιγώρησαν· οὐδὲν γὰρ φροντίσαντες εἴτ' ἐπακολουθοῦμεν αὐτοῖς λέγουσιν εἴτε ἀπολειπόμεθα, περαίνουσι τὸ σφέτερον αὐτῶν ἕκαστοι.

12. τὰ μὴ γευσάμενα κτλ. So Thetis pours ambrosia and nectar into the nostrils of the dead Patroclus to make his flesh imperishable (*Il.* xix. 38).

27. Cf. A. 985ᵃ 23-9.

28. By τὸ ἕν and ὁ θεός Aristotle means (cf. ᵇ 3, A. 985ᵃ 28, *De Gen. et Corr.* 315ᵃ 7, 333ᵇ 21) the Σφαῖρος of Empedocles, i. e. the

universe in the period when Love is all-pervasive and the elements
are thoroughly united with one another. Empedocles calls this θεός in
fr. 31.

29. ἐξ ὧν κτλ., fr. 21. 9–12. By ἐξ ὧν Aristotle means 'out of the
four elements + love and strife'; in the original, however, it looks as if
only the four elements were meant. Simplicius has the line in the
form ἐκ τούτων γὰρ πάνθ' ὅσα τ' ἦν ὅσα τ' ἔστι καὶ ἔσται.

b 2. ὅταν γάρ κτλ., fr. 36. Stobaeus gives the whole verse

> τῶν δὲ συνερχομένων ἐξ ἔσχατον ἵστατο Νεῖκος.

Aristotle as usual quotes from memory. The meaning is made
clear by fr. 35. When the various elements had come together by the
force of love, love occupied the centre of the vortex and controlled the
movement, while strife was banished to the lowest or outermost edge
and thus deprived of power; things then were one just because strife
was not in them but outside them.

6. γαίῃ μέν κτλ., fr. 109.

9. Cf. A. 985^a 23–9.

14. ἀλλ' ὅτε δή κτλ., fr. 30.

ἐνὶ μελέεσσιν, sc. of the Sphairos.

15. πλατέος παρ' ἐλήλαται ὅρκου. Cf. Ar. *Ach.* 1126 κατάγελως
πλατύς, broad, flat, or downright mockery. ἐλαύνειν is, as Bonitz
says, used in the same sense as in such phrases as τάφρον ἐλαύνειν.
There may, further, be a play on ὅρκος and ἔρκος, cf. Hesiod *Theog.*
726 τὸν (Τάρταρον) πέρι χάλκεον ἔρκος ἐλήλαται. The oath 'is called
"broad" because it is a barrier or fence', Cornford, *From Religion to
Philosophy*, 237. Cornford seems wrong, however, in identifying this
barrier with Strife.

The language is reminiscent of what Hesiod says about the great
oath of the Gods by which the province of each was guaranteed
(referred to in A. 983^b 31). The whole verse means' 'which has been
traced for love and strife in turn as the result of a mighty oath'. The
oath may be supposed to have been taken by Necessity or by the gods,
like the

> Ἀνάγκης χρῆμα, θεῶν ψήφισμα παλαιόν,
> ἀΐδιον, πλατέεσσι κατεσφρηγισμένον ὅρκοις,

of which we read in fr. 115.

27. τοῦτο δ' ἀδύνατον κτλ. That there should be ἀρχαί prior to
ἀρχαί is impossible whether it be supposed that there are absolutely
primary ἀρχαί or that there is an infinite regress; for ἀρχαί that have
ἀρχαί prior to them are not ἀρχαί at all. Alexander suggests (221. 34)
that perhaps τοῦτο δ' ἀδύνατον should be treated as parenthetical, but
this seems to give an inferior sense.

29. εἰ αἱ ἀρχαὶ ἀναιρεθήσονται, 'if we are going to decide that their
so-called ἀρχαί are not ἀρχαί'. The supposition that there are first
principles of their first principles logically annihilates their first principles; for that which has a principle prior to it cannot be a first

principle. But if the supposed first principles of perishable things are thus annihilated, how can these things ever exist?

1001ᵃ 1. Of the MSS., only Aᵇ reads λέγειν after ἑτέρας. Alexander has μηδὲ τὴν ἀρχὴν εἰρηκέναι, from which Bonitz conjectured εἴρηκεν or τὴν ἀρχὴν εἴρηκεν. Vahlen (*Poet.* ed. 3, p. 158) is probably right in defending ἐγκεχείρηκεν without λέγειν, which is easily understood from the following clause (cf. Γ. 1005ᵇ 2, *De Caelo* 292ᵇ 12, *Pol.* 1313ᵇ 31, *Rhet.* 1363ᵃ 27, 1372ᵇ 36, *Poet.* 1453ᵇ 18, 1454ᵃ 1).

2. τὸ πρῶτον ἀπορηθέν, the question whether perishable and imperishable things have the same principles, discussed in 1000ᵃ 5–ᵇ 22, in distinction from the question whether the principles of perishable things are perishable, discussed in 1000ᵇ 23—1001ᵃ 1.

ἀποτρώγουσιν seems to mean, as Schwegler says, 'gulp off'. The meaning 'nibble at', which Bonitz prefers, would require the genitive.

1001ᵃ 4–ᵇ 25.   Eleventh ἀπορία.

Aristotle answers this problem in Z. 16. 1040ᵇ 16–24, I. 2 by asserting that being and unity are not substances but attributes; in M. 8. 1083ᵃ 20—1085ᵃ 2 he argues against the separate existence both of unity and of number.

12. Bonitz's emendation, τοῦ ἑνί for Aᵇ's τὸ ἕν, is certainly right.

14. Cf. 996ᵃ 8 n.

15. ἕτεροι δὲ πῦρ κτλ., cf. A. 984ᵃ 7, 5.

21. ταῦτα γάρ κτλ. The argument is: 'Since the most universal terms, being and unity, are not substances, no universals can be substances'. It certainly follows that they cannot be substances merely because of their universality, and it was because of their universality that the Pythagoreans and Plato, whom Aristotle has in view, declared them to be substances, so that the argument is a sound one.

26. ὅπερ. 'The unit is precisely what a certain kind of one is'. When A is ὅπερ B, B is not merely predicable of A but has the same intension; A and B are two names implying the same set of attributes. τὰ μὲν οὐσίαν σημαίνοντα ὅπερ ἐκεῖνο ἢ ὅπερ ἐκεῖνό τι σημαίνει, 'the terms that indicate the essence of a thing are those that indicate either it or that of which it is a kind' (*An. Post.* 83ᵃ 24). If B is the essence or definition of A, Aristotle says 'A is ὅπερ B'; if B is the genus of A, he says 'A is ὅπερ B τι' (cf. Bonitz, *Index*, 534ᵃ 6–22). So here the unit is identical with one kind of one, presumably that kind which is not thought of as having parts but as perfectly simple. The distinction between ὅπερ ἐκεῖνο and ὅπερ ἐκεῖνό τι is, however, frequently dropped, and we find 'A is ὅπερ B' when B is the genus of A. In fact ὅπερ comes almost to stand for the relation of genus to species (cf. Bonitz, *Index*, 533ᵇ 44–55).

28. καθόλου. 'For there is nothing other than unity and being that is universally predicated of the particular things that are one and existent (cf. ll. 21, 22); nothing, therefore, other than unity and being, that can be the substance of the one itself and being itself'. καθόλου

is read by all the MSS., Al., Asc., and Syr., and Bonitz's καθ' οὖ does
not seem to be necessary. His explanation ignores αὐτῶν and gives
no good sense to ἀλλὰ ταῦτα αὐτά.

32. Parmenides' argument, summed up in the line

οὐ γὰρ μήποτε τοῦτο δαμῇ εἶναι μὴ ἐόντα (fr. 7),

is this : anything other than 'what is' must be something that is not;
but what is not is not; therefore nothing other than 'what is' is.
The universe, then, has only one thing in it, 'what is', i. e. the universe
itself ; there is no plurality of any sort in the universe. This is the
argument which Aristotle now uses to refute the Platonists. So long
as 'being' is treated, as Aristotle himself treats it, as a predicate, there
is room for plurality in the universe. But if 'being' be made a substance, it follows, he says, that there is nothing other than being, and
the universe is a single substance without plurality. It is to be
noticed that τὸ ὄν covers an important ambiguity. For Parmenides it
means 'what is ', i. e. the universe ; for the Platonists it means 'being',
i. e. the attribute of existence. It is this abstraction that they make a
substance, and there is nothing in this to prevent their recognizing
other substances. Plato was quite equal to pointing out the falla-
ciousness of the principle τὸ ἕτερον τοῦ ὄντος οὐκ ἔστιν.

b 1. In ᵃ 29–ᵇ 1 Aristotle has argued that if unity and being are substances, there cannot be anything else. Now he proceeds to a fresh
point ; that number, which the Pythagoreans and the Platonists treated
as the substance of the universe, cannot be a substance. If unity is
not a substance, number cannot be a substance, for the reason given
in ᵃ 24–27 ; if unity *is* a substance, the same difficulty arises as was
in ᵃ 31–ᵇ 1 pointed out with regard to being. If unity is a substance
there can be nothing else, just as if being is a substance there is
nothing else. Any one other than the one itself (unity) must be not
one ; but everything that is, either is one or includes ones ; what is
other than unity, then, would be either non-existent or composed
of non-existent units ; there is, then, only one thing in the universe,
unity.

7. εἰ ἀδιαίρετον κτλ. Bonitz supposes that this assumption is taken
from Parmenides, and it certainly is found in him—

οὐδὲ διαιρετόν ἐστιν, ἐπεὶ πᾶν ἐστιν ὁμοῖον (fr. 8. 22).

But though the subject of this statement in Parmenides is the One,
that means the universe and not the abstract principle of unity whose
substantial existence Aristotle is attacking. If Aristotle is basing an
attack on the Platonists on this dictum of Parmenides, he is guilty of
the same confusion that was pointed out in ᵃ 32 n. But we must take
this clause in connexion with the rest of the sentence. Aristotle does
not ascribe to Zeno an attack on the One in any sense of 'the One' ;
all that he ascribes to him is the principle that that which neither makes
things greater by being added to them nor less by being subtracted
from them is not real. But this principle must have had some con-

text in Zeno's thought, and if, as seems probable, its context was an attack on 'the One' in some sense (cf. frr. 1, 2, and Diels, i.³ 170. 16–38), what is likely to have been the One which he was attacking? Not the Parmenidean One which is just what he himself believed in, but the Pythagorean indivisible units which he made it his business to attack (cf. Burnet, *E. G. P.* §§ 158, 159, 161). In fact Zeno's argument is evidently directed against what is indivisibly small, which is by no means what Parmenides meant when he called his One indivisible. What Zeno is attacking is the building up of the world out of points or units (l. 13, cf. Simpl. *Phys.* 99. 10), between which the Pythagoreans did not clearly distinguish. The argument attributed to him here is part of one of his refutations of pluralism, viz. the proof that if Being were many it would have to be both infinitely small and infinitely large (cf. Zeller, i.⁶ 749).

ἀξίωμα, 'postulate', as in M. 1077ᵃ 31.

11–12. πὼς μέν, end to end; πὼς δ', lying along one another.

13–18. 'But, since Zeno's arguments are of a low order, and an indivisible thing can exist, in such a way that we can defend it even with reference to his argument (i. e. by pointing out that an indivisible unit will increase what it is added to, in number though not in size)— yet how can a *magnitude* be composed of such a unit or several such units?'. Bonitz correctly explains the construction by saying that Aristotle meant the first clause to be followed by something like τοῦτον μὲν ἐατέον, ὅτι ἐνδέχεται ἀδιαίρετόν τι εἶναι . . . ἀλλὰ πῶς δή κτλ., and that ἀλλά remains though the intended μέν clause has been absorbed in the protasis. The anacoluthon would be removed by reading, with Apelt (following Aᵇ), ἀλλ' εἰ δὴ οὕτως, θεωρεῖ φορτικῶς. But Alexander had οὗτος, and the run of the sentence as punctuated by Apelt is unnatural.

14. φορτικῶς. Aristotle's opinion of the younger Eleatics may be inferred from the fact that he uses the same epithet of Melissus in *Phys.* 185ᵃ 10.

15. καὶ οὕτως καὶ πρὸς ἐκεῖνον. It seems impossible to make anything of this, and it is best to treat καὶ οὕτως as originally a marginal gloss referring to the variant οὕτως in l. 14. Fonseca's ὄντως is ingenious, but the word is not used by Aristotle.

21. ἄλλου μὴ ἑνός τινος. Cf. A. 987ᵇ 20 n.

23. For the Platonic description of the material principle as the unequal cf M. 1087ᵇ 5, 1088ᵇ 32, 1089ᵇ 6–15, 1091ᵇ 35.

PROBLEM 14 (ch. 5).

Fourteenth problem.

1001ᵇ 26. Are numbers, bodies, planes, points substances? *Thesis.* If not, what are the substances of things? Affections, motions, relations, states, ratios do not indicate substance, for they require a substratum and are not individual. The four elements are more like substance than heat, cold, &c., which are their affections. But body is less substantial than surface, surface than line, line than unit and point, since these are what determines body, and can exist without it while it cannot exist without them.

1002ᵃ 8. Hence, while most thinkers and the earlier thinkers thought substance was body and everything else was its attributes, the later and those reputed wiser held that substance was numbers. If these things are not substance, nothing is substance or real, for their attributes can hardly be called real.

15. *Antithesis.* (*a*) If it is agreed that lines and points are more substantial than bodies, but we do not see what sort of bodies they can be substances of (for they cannot be in *sensible* bodies), there is no substance. (*b*) These are all mere divisions of body.

20. (*c*) Any one figure is as much present in a solid as any other. If the Hermes is not determinately present in the marble, neither is the surface, line, point, or unit in the solid. If body is more substantial than its affections, and these things are more substantial than body, and these are not substance, what *is* substance?

28. (*d*) If substance passes from not being to being or *vice versa*, this implies becoming and perishing; but points, lines, and surfaces do so without becoming or perishing. When bodies touch, one surface is produced; when they are parted, two surfaces are produced; the surfaces pass out of or into being with the union or separation of the bodies. If the surfaces are generated and perish, what are they generated from?

ᵇ **5.** So too the present moment cannot become or perish, and yet is always different; it cannot, then, be substance. All these entities alike are mere limits or divisions.

1001ᵇ 26—1002ᵇ 11.   *Fourteenth* ἀπορία.

The belief in the substantiality of numbers and mathematical objects is discussed and refuted in M. 1–3, 6–9, N. 1–3, 5, 6. M. 2 refers especially to geometrical objects; M. 6–8, N. 5, 6 especially to numbers.

27. τὰ σώματα, mathematical solids.

32. τόδε τι. The meaning of this phrase is discussed by Prof. J. A. Smith in *Classical Review*, xxxv (1921). 19. Three views, he points out, are possible. (1) It may be held to mean 'this, i. e. any, member of the class of somewhats', i. e. to be the generalized form of such phrases as ὅδε ὁ ἄνθρωπος. It has been suggested that the Greek for this would be τό τι τόδε; but that would be ambiguous, for it might equally be interpreted as the generalized form of such phrases as ὁ τὶς ἄνθρωπος. τόδε τό τι would be free from any such objection, and on the analogy of ὅδε ὁ ἄνθρωπος would be the correct way of expressing this meaning. (2) It may be taken to mean 'a this', i.e. to be the generalized form of such phrases as ἄνθρωπός τις. Prof. Smith objects that it is an anachronism to ascribe to Aristotle the conception of a class of this's, and that the Greek for 'a this' is simply τόδε (cf. τόδε ἐν τῷδε, τόδε τοιόνδε). He holds that τόδε τι means (3) something which is both singular, a 'this', and possessed of a universal nature, a somewhat, i.e., is a πρώτη οὐσία.

On the whole I incline to the second view. For, generally speaking, it is singularity and not the possession of a universal nature that Aristotle seems to have in mind when he uses the phrase, e. g. *Cat.* 3ᵇ 12 τόδε τι σημαίνει, ἄτομον γὰρ καὶ ἐν ἀριθμῷ τὸ δηλούμενόν ἐστιν. And in that context τόδε τι is opposed to ποιόν τι, where τι seems to mean simply 'a'; if τι referred to the possession of a general character it would reduplicate ποιόν. It is natural, then, to suppose that in τόδε τι also τι means 'a'. It is true, however, that τόδε alone also means 'a this'; τόδε and τόδε τι seem to be interchangeable.

1002ᵃ 8. οἱ μέν κτλ. is concessive; the real point comes with οἱ δ' l. 11.

11. οἱ δ' ὕστεροι. Bonitz thinks that the Pythagoreans are meant, not the Platonists, because 'Plato's philosophy could not be rightly included within these narrow limits of mathematical objects' and because in Z. 2, while this view is mentioned in 1028ᵇ 15, Plato's view is not mentioned till 1028ᵇ 19. Alexander thinks that both the Pythagoreans and Plato are meant (230. 12), and he is probably right.

20-28. Aristotle argues here that all the surfaces involved in a solid must be in the same position with regard to existence, so that if, as he assumes, the surfaces that will bound a solid not yet cut out of the original solid do not yet exist, none of the other surfaces involved in the solid exist. So too as regards the relation between surface and line, and between line and point.

27. μηδέ, which Christ wishes away, is undoubtedly difficult. The meaning probably is 'if these are not even instances of substance'— not to speak of their being the most real substances, as the Pythagoreans and the Platonists believed.

32. τὰς δὲ στιγμάς κτλ., cf. E. 1026ᵇ 23 n.

ᵇ **3-4.** 'For it will not be suggested that the point, indivisible as it is, was divided into two'. If it were, there might be a gradual process; but as it is, the two points come into being in an instant.

6. On τὸ νῦν cf. *Phys.* iv. 13.

PROBLEMS 12, 13 (ch. 6).

1002ᵇ 12. Why should one look for Forms distinct from sensible things and from the intermediates ? *Thesis.* If it is because mathematical objects, while unlike things in this world in another respect, are like them in that there are many of one kind, so that their first principles cannot be limited in number (as the letters of the alphabet are not limited in number but only in kind), and hence, if there are not entities other than sensibles and mathematical objects, there will be no substance one in number, but only in kind, and the first principles will be limited only in kind :—if, then, the principles must be limited in number, there must be Forms.

27. Even if the supporters of the theory do not express themselves well, this is what they mean when they say that each of the Forms is a substance and none is an accident.

30. *Antithesis.* If we posit the Forms, so that the principles are one in number and not merely in kind, we have seen the difficulties that follow.

Thirteenth problem.

32. Do the elements exist potentially or in some other fashion ? *Thesis.* If in some other way, there will be something prior to the first principles ; for the potentiality is prior to the actual cause, and what is possible need not become actual. *Antithesis.* If the elements exist potentially, it is possible that everything that is should not be, for even that which is not yet is capable of being, since that which is not comes to be, but nothing incapable of being comes to be.

Twelfth problem.

1003ᵃ 5. Are the principles universal or individual ? *Thesis.* If universal, they are not substances, for no common predicate is a this, but only a such, while substance is a this ; if the common predicate is to be a this and a single thing, Socrates will be several animals, himself and man and animal.

13. *Antithesis.* If the principles are individuals, they cannot be known, so that there must be universal principles prior to them if there is to be knowledge of them.

1002ᵇ 12-32. Aristotle discusses here a problem not raised in ch. 1 but akin to problems 5 and 9.

13. τὰ μεταξύ, cf. A. 987ᵇ 14 n.

14. τίθεμεν, cf. A. 990ᵇ 9 n.

14-26. For the mode of structure of the sentence, a long protasis with
εἰ (or ἐπεί) followed by a short protasis with εἰ, ἐάν, or εἴπερ, cf. *An.
Post.* 93ᵃ 3-9, 98ᵇ 16-21, *Top.* 111ᵃ 33-ᵇ 7, *Phys.* 223ᵇ 12-20, 264ᵃ
22-31, *De Caelo* 290ᵃ 7-12, 299ᵇ 7-10, *Rhet.* 1387ᵃ 27-32. Ll. 14-
22 are an instance of 'binary structure'. Cf. A. 983ᵇ 16 n.

24. Alexander's ἀλλ' εἴδει is very attractive. If καὶ εἴδει be kept,
ἀριθμῷ καὶ εἴδει must be taken to mean 'in number as well as
in kind '.

31. εἰρήκαμεν, 999ᵇ 27—1000ᵃ 4.

32—1003ᵃ 5   *Thirteenth* ἀπορία.

The second half of the problem stated in 996ᵃ 10, 11, whether the
potentiality or actuality of the first principles refers to movement or
not, is not here discussed.

The relation of potency to actuality is discussed in Θ. 1-9; the
material element is described as potential, the formal as actual. The
priority of actuality is proved in Θ. 8. In Λ. 6, 7 it is shown that the
universe must have a first mover which is through and through
actual.

32. σύνεγγυς δὲ τούτων. This problem is akin to the previous one
because while the individual exists actually, the Form has no separate
existence but may in some sense (even if not accurately) be said to
exist potentially.

1003ᵃ 5-17   *Twelfth* ἀπορία.

For the answer to this problem cf. Z. 13, 14, where Aristotle argues
that no universal can be a substance; Z. 15, where he argues that no
individual can be defined; and M. 10, where he attempts to state the
relation of universal to individual in such a way as to solve this
paradox.—The problem is closely akin to the ninth.

10. The manuscript reading would require the rendering 'if the
common predicate *is to be* a this and *it is to be possible* to set it out apart
from the particulars' (for the meaning of ἐκθέσθαι cf. A. 992ᵇ 10 n.)—an
intolerable zeugma. I had thought of ἐκθέσθαι ⟨ἐξέσται⟩, and Jaeger
proposes ⟨δεῖ⟩ ἐκθέσθαι (to which 999ᵃ 30 offers, as he remarks, a good
parallel), but Richards's ἐν θέσθαι (cf. l. 12 τόδε τι καὶ ἕν) is better.
The corruption goes back beyond Alexander (cf. 236. 8).

BOOK Γ

Our subject—being as such (ch. 1).

1003ᵃ 21. There is a science which investigates being as being,
and is different from the sciences that investigate special parts of
being.

26. The first principles which we are seeking must belong to something in virtue of its very nature. If the early thinkers, who sought the elements of the things that are, were looking for these first principles, the elements must be elements of being *qua* being ; and so we too must grasp the first causes of being *qua* being.

1003ᵃ 21. Ἔστιν ἐπιστήμη τις κτλ. ' There is a science which investigates that which is, as being, and the attributes that belong to it in virtue of its own nature '—i. e. as being. This description of metaphysics distinguishes it from other sciences not by its method but by its subject. Other sciences cut off a part of that which is and study this as possessing certain special features ; metaphysics studies all that is, and studies it simply as being. When Aristotle describes metaphysics as a science studying the attributes of that which is, as being, we are, in view of his description of science as demonstrative, tempted to suppose him to mean that it syllogistically deduces the properties of that which is, from the mere fact of its being. But it seems clear that from bare being no properties can be deduced. Again, does τὸ ὄν mean that which is, taken collectively? Is it the attributes of the universe that he proposes to investigate ? Or does he mean that which is, taken distributively? Does he propose to investigate the properties which anything that is must have because it is ? In the former case, metaphysics would have some of the characteristics of history ; its subject—the universe—is an individual, and its propositions will be singular propositions. Only in the latter case will its propositions be universal ; that they are meant to be so is strongly suggested by the fact that it is called a science. But what important attributes are really common to *all* existing things? And is not the drawing of distinctions as much a part of metaphysics as the recognition of identities ?

To these questions Aristotle nowhere gives explicit answers ; but his attitude towards them may be divined from what he says. In the first place, though he calls metaphysics a science, he does not suppose that it is demonstrative through and through. No science is that. Every science starts with ὁρισμοί and ὑποθέσεις, unproved definitions of all its terms and unproved assumptions that there exist objects corresponding to the chief of those terms. These unproved propositions are its ἀρχαί. In some cases they are so obvious that they may be simply stated without discussion, as in geometry. In other cases the learner must be directed to facts of experience which warrant the assumptions, as in physics. In others, as in ethics, he must have lived a certain kind of life if he is to be ready to accept the assumptions. In the last two cases the statement of the assumptions is preceded or accompanied by some sort of argument which is not meant to be cogent deduction (*that* works only from principles to their conclusions), but to bring home to the learner's mind propositions which in time he will see to be self-evident though at first he may doubt or deny them.

Now if metaphysics is a science, we should expect it to behave towards the κοιναὶ ἀρχαί as the special sciences do towards the ἴδιαι ἀρχαί. The definitions it assumes will be definitions of terms not confined to one department of reality but found throughout reality—terms such as matter and form, substance and accident, quality and quantity, potency and actuality, unity and plurality. And in fact we find such a collection of unargued definitions in Book Δ. It is true that we find arguments about the proper definition of these terms in other books, such as ZHΘI. But these are not meant to be strict deductions. They are ἔλεγχοι meant to remove misconceptions and to bring the learner to admit what is ultimate and self-evident truth.

So too with regard to the ὑποθέσεις, the assumptions of existence. The chief of these are the laws of contradiction and excluded middle. It may seem strange to describe these as assumptions of existence, but this is Aristotle's way of describing them (*An. Post.* 71ᵃ 13). ὅτι ἐστι is his way of referring to synthetic propositions, as τί ἐστι is his way of referring to analytic propositions. And in Book Γ these laws are treated in the way appropriate to the treatment of ἀρχαί; they are not demonstrated but they are commended to the mind of the reader by an ἔλεγχος, a pointing out of the absurd consequences of their denial.

So far metaphysics is doing only the preliminary work of a science, the formulation and in some cases the commendation of definitions and hypotheses. Does it ever proceed to the main work of science, the drawing of conclusions from these? It seems that the answer must be in the negative. The procedure throughout the *Metaphysics* never becomes deductive; it always remains aporematic. A moment's comparison of its procedure with that of geometry, for instance, will show the difference. Aristotle's frequent description of metaphysics as the science of principles itself suggests that it is not meant to get beyond principles to conclusions. It may be noted that the method is substantially the same in nearly all Aristotle's writings. The chief exception, perhaps, is the *Prior Analytics*; formal logic is naturally capable of being treated somewhat similarly to the exact sciences. In almost all his other works the method is the aporematic method which is indeed that proper to philosophy. In particular, there is no trace in him of the view apparently held, e. g. by Plato, that metaphysics can prove the principles of the special sciences. Each science starts with principles that are unprovable.

Aristotle has in the main two ways of stating the subject-matter of metaphysics. In one set of passages it is stated as τὸ ὂν ᾗ ὄν, the whole of being, as such. This view is expressed throughout Book Γ, and occasionally elsewhere (E. 1025ᵇ 3. K. 1060ᵇ 31, 1061ᵇ 4, 26, 31); it is implied also in the description of σοφία as being occupied with the first causes and principles, *sc.* of reality as a whole (A. 981ᵇ 28,

982ᵇ 9). But more frequently metaphysics is described as studying a certain part of reality, viz. that which is χωριστόν (exists independently) and ἀκίνητον, while physics studies things that are χωριστά but not ἀκίνητα, and mathematics things that are ἀκίνητα but not χωριστά. This view of the subject of metaphysics is expressed most clearly in E. 1026ᵃ 15, but is implied in such passages as K. 1064ᵇ 4, Λ. 1069ᵇ 1, *Phys.* 192ᵃ 34, 194ᵇ 14, *De An.* 403ᵇ 15. On this view metaphysics studies not being as a whole but the highest kind of being, and when viewed in this way it may be called θεολογική (E. 1026ᵃ 19, K. 1064ᵇ 3). These two views of the business of metaphysics have been made (by Natorp) a ground for splitting up the *Metaphysics* into two. In E an attempt is made to reconcile the two views. The question is raised (1026ᵃ 23) whether first philosophy is universal or deals with a particular class of things, and the answer is given that in studying one kind of being, οὐσία ἀκίνητος, it is φιλοσοφία πρώτη, καὶ καθόλου οὕτως ὅτι πρώτη. In studying the nature of pure being, form without matter, philosophy is in effect coming to know the nature of being as a whole.

Both views are genuinely Aristotelian, but the narrower view of the scope of metaphysics is that which is more commonly present in his works, and more in keeping with the distrust of a universal science expressed in the *Posterior Analytics*.

25. For τὸ συμβεβηκός in the sense of 'necessary attribute' cf. Δ. 1025ᵃ 30 and Bonitz, *Index*, 713ᵇ 43—714ᵃ 19.

26–32. The argument is peculiar:

(1) The principles we seek must belong to some φύσις in virtue of its own character.

(2) The elements τῶν ὄντων sought for by our predecessors are the principles we seek.

∴ (3) The elements τοῦ ὄντος must be τοῦ ὄντος ᾗ ὄν.

∴ (from (2) and (3)). The principles we seek are τοῦ ὄντος ᾗ ὄν.

26–27. ἐπεὶ δὲ . . . ζητοῦμεν. This has been established in A. 1, 2.

27–8. Alexander, apparently reading καθ' αὑτάς, thinks the clause means 'clearly they must be self-subsistent causes of some kind of thing'. But the self-subsistence of the causes is irrelevant to the purpose of the chapter. Bonitz therefore rightly reads, with EJ, καθ' αὑτήν. (The reading αὑτάς is due to the same confusion which produced the reading αὑτά in l. 22.) He interprets the clause, however, as meaning 'clearly they must be causes of some self-subsistent kind of thing'. But the self-subsistence of the φύσις is equally irrelevant. The meaning must be 'clearly they must be causes pertaining to some kind of thing in virtue of its own nature'; i. e., in point of fact, to being in virtue of its own nature (τοῦ ὄντος ᾗ ὄν). It is not the self-subsistence of either the causes or the φύσις that is in point, but the essential relation between the two. The causes studied by the special sciences are ἀρχαὶ τοῦ ὄντος but not ᾗ ὄν; only those studied by metaphysics are τοῦ ὄντος ᾗ ὄν.

28–32. Schwegler proposed (l. 29) τοιαύτας ἀρχὰς ἐζήτουν ὡς ἀναγκαῖον (ὂν ?) τὰ στοιχεῖα κτλ., omitting διό in l. 31. The changes would improve the logic of the passage but are not absolutely necessary and are unsupported by testimony.

We must therefore study (1) *substance—the central mode of being to which the other modes are related,* (2) *the species of being,* (3) *the species of unity,* (4) *the species of substance,* (5) *the species of plurality. Confirmations of the view that these form the subject of philosophical study* (ch. 2).

1003ᵃ 33. (1) Being has many meanings, but these are related to one thing, not merely equivocal (cf. the meanings of ‘healthy’ and ‘medical’); they are all related to *substance*, and therefore are dealt with by one science. Meanings related to some one thing are in a sense univocal, and therefore the subject of one science.

ᵇ 16. A science deals especially with that part of its subject which is primary. Therefore the philosopher must grasp the principles of substances.

19. (2) Of every class of things there is one sense and one science, e. g. the single science of grammar investigates all articulate sounds. Therefore a science that is one in genus will study all the species of being, and its species will study the several species.

22. (3) Being and one are, like principle and cause, one not in definition but in that the one is predicable wherever the other is. One man = man, and existent man = man. ‘One *existent* man’ = ‘one man’ (being inseparable from it whether in coming to be or in ceasing to be), and ‘*one* existent man’ = ‘existent man’. The one is therefore nothing apart from the existent. And, further, the substance of anything is essentially one and essentially existent.

33. Therefore the species of unity are also the species of being, and will be investigated by the same science,—viz. the same, the like, and other such terms. Nearly all contraries can be reduced to these heads (*sc.* being and not-being, or one and many)—cf. our ‘Selection of Contraries’.

1004ⁿ 2. (4) There are as many parts of philosophy as there are kinds of substance, and one part of philosophy, as of mathematics, will be primary, and others derivative.

9. (5) Unity and plurality are opposites, and opposites are dealt with by the same science, for light is thrown on a term by the study either of its negative (in which merely the absence of the term is indicated) or of its privative (in which a definite underlying nature is further implied). Therefore the science which discusses the species of unity will discuss also the species of plurality—the other, the dissimilar, the unequal—and therefore also contrariety, for this is a sort of difference and difference is a sort of otherness.

22. These, like unity, will have different meanings, but the different meanings can still be discussed by one science. In each case the derivative meanings must be viewed in their relation to the central meaning.

31. In deciding that the same science will discuss substance and these its properties, we have solved one of our problems. It is characteristic of the philosopher to be able to discuss all things. Who else would consider such questions as, Is Socrates the same as Socrates sitting?

^b **5.** As the arithmetician considers number and its proper attributes, the philosopher considers being and its proper attributes. The mistake made by some people is not that they study the attributes, but that they ignore substance, which is prior to its attributes.

17. That the attributes fall within the scope of philosophy is indicated by the fact that they are discussed by the dialectician and the sophist, who ape the philosopher in the generality of their discussions. Dialectic differs from philosophy in its method—it is critical where philosophy gives positive knowledge; sophistic differs in the life-purpose it implies—it is merely the appearance of wisdom.

27. Of every two contraries one is privative, and all contraries can be referred to being or unity and its privation not-being or plurality (e. g. rest to unity, motion to plurality). Now almost all thinkers agree that existing things are composed of contraries (odd and even, hot and cold, limit and unlimited, friendship and strife). Since, then, unity and plurality are the subject of one science, being as such will be the subject of one science.

1005ª 6. Even if unity has many meanings, it (and its contrary) still have a primary meaning to which the others are related—even if unity is not a universal and is not separate from particular things which are one, but has in its meanings only a unity of reference or a serial unity. Therefore it is the business of the metaphysician to investigate being and these its properties: the geometer assumes these properties and considers their application in his special sphere.

13. Clearly, then, it is the work of one science to discuss being as being and its essential attributes, substances and their attributes,— both those mentioned and others such as prior and posterior, genus and species, whole and part.

1003ª 33–ᵇ 5. τὸ δὲ ὂν λέγεται . . . ὥσπερ καὶ τὸ ὑγιεινὸν . . . οὕτω δὲ καὶ τὸ ὂν λέγεται, a good instance of 'binary structure' (Riddell, *Apology of Plato*, p. 198, § 209). Cf. A. 983ᵇ 16 n.

33. πρὸς ἕν. Terms which are πρὸς ἕν or ἀφ' ἑνός or κατ' ἀναλογίαν ἕν (*E. N.* 1096ᵇ 27) are intermediate between συνώνυμα, which are καθ' ἕν and have both a common name and a common definition (*Cat.* 1ª 6), and ὁμώνυμα, which have only a common name (ib. 1ª 1). ὑγιεινόν and ἰατρικόν answer to the definition of the third class recognized in the *Categories* alongside of συνώνυμα and ὁμώνυμα, viz. παρώνυμα, things called by a name derived from some other name (1ª 12), or, to put the matter in a less purely grammatical form, things called by a common name and, though not having the same definition, yet definable by their various relations to one single thing. 'Being' has not always the same meaning, but it is no mere accident that all 'beings' are so called; all stand in some relation to οὐσία, the primary ὄν. Other terms which are in this respect like 'being' are 'one' (I. 1053ᵇ 22, H. 1045ᵇ 6, K. 1059ᵇ 33) and 'good' (*E. N.* 1096ᵇ 27). Alexander (242. 5) names also figure and number. But these have not the wide range of the terms in question; number is contained in the category of quantity (*Cat.* 4ᵇ 23) and figure in that of quality (ib. 10ª 11). The Schoolmen grouped *ens, unum, bonum* with *res, aliquid, verum* as the *transcendentalia*.

If we ask what reason Aristotle offers for denying that being, unity, and good are proper 'synonymous' terms, we must turn to B. 998ᵇ 22, K. 1059ᵇ 31. Being and unity cannot be genera because no genus is predicable of its differentiae, while being and unity are predicable of all terms whatever and therefore if they were genera would be predicable of their differentiae. For the reasons why a genus cannot be predicated of its differentiae cf. B. 998ᵇ 24–26 n.

ᵇ 5. For δέ *in apodosi* after a comparison cf. Plat. *Prot.* 326 D 5, 328 A 7, *Meteor.* 355ᵇ 15, *E. N.* 1094ª 14, Λ. 1075ª 10. Cf. also B. 999ª 27 n.

12–13. οὐ . . . μιᾶς, an irregular combination of the constructions οὐ γὰρ μόνον τῶν καθ' ἕν λεγομένων ἐπιστήμη ἔστι μία and οὐ γὰρ μόνον τὰ καθ' ἕν λεγόμενα ἐπιστήμης ἐστὶ θεωρῆσαι μιᾶς.

19–1004ª 31. This section consists of three sub-sections, (1) 19–36, in which Aristotle specifies various εἴδη of τὸ ἕν which are at the same time εἴδη of τὸ ὄν, viz. the same, the like, &c. (36–1004ª 2 is probably out of place, v. n. *ad loc.*); (2) 1004ª 2–9, in which he says that there are branches of philosophy answering to the various kinds of οὐσία, by which he doubtless means 'first philosophy' or 'theology' dealing with substances which are χωριστά and ἀκίνητα, and physics dealing with those which are χωριστά but not ἀκίνητα (E. 1026ª 13–19—mathematics, which is there mentioned as a third, does not deal with οὐσίαι but with ἀχώριστα, things that have no separate existence); (3) 1004ª 9–31, in which he points out that philosophy will study the opposites of the εἴδη of τὸ ἕν mentioned in (1). It is obvious therefore that sub-section (2) breaks the continuity of the thought. Alexander wished to insert it at

1003ᵇ 22 ; Schwegler and Natorp, with more probability, to insert it at 1003ᵇ 19.

20-22 may mean either of two things. (1) Alexander and Bonitz, reading τὰ δὲ εἴδη τῶν εἰδῶν, take it to mean, ' Wherefore to study all the species of being as such is the work of a science generically one, and to study the various species is the work of its various species'. To this it may be objected (*a*) that the opposition of ὅσα εἴδη and τὰ εἴδη is not a good one, (*b*) that there is no trace elsewhere in Aristotle of a division of philosophy into species studying identity, likeness, &c., respectively, and (*c*) that such a division would cut clean across that referred to in sub-section (2). Therefore (2) Schuppe, Natorp, and Apelt, reading with the manuscripts τά τε εἴδη τῶν εἰδῶν, translate ' wherefore to study the various species of being as such, and the species of the species, is the work of the same science as studies the genus'. But the other interpretation is very much the more natural, and the objections to it can easily be met. It is not, however, necessary to read δέ for τε.

22. εἰ δή κτλ. The protasis extends to ὄν τι (33) and the apodosis begins irregularly with ὥστε, as often happens in Aristotle after a long protasis.

23. τῷ ἀκολουθεῖν ἀλλήλοις, or, as Alexander says (246. 31) κατὰ τὸ ὑποκείμενον, i.e. in the sense that whatever is existent is one and whatever is one is existent. Such terms Alexander describes as ἑτερώνυμα. a word not found in Aristotle.

24. ἀρχή and αἴτιον differ (Al. 247. 15) as τὸ ἐξ οὗ and τὸ δι᾽ ὅ.

25. οὐδ᾽ ἂν ὁμοίως (*sc*. ὡς τὰ ἐνὶ λόγῳ δηλούμενα) ὑπολάβωμεν, i. e. our case is still stronger if being and unity are πολυώνυμα (Al. 247. 27, cf. *H. A.* 489ᵃ 2), i. e. two words which would be defined in exactly the same way.

26-33. Bonitz treats ταὐτὸ ... ὄν τι as defending the statement (25, 26) that the case is still stronger if being and unity are πολυώνυμα. But (1) surely this needs no argument, (2) it is unlikely that Aristotle would devote so much space to detailing the consequences of an identification which he is himself far from making, and (3) if he did so he would almost certainly state its consequences in the future indicative or in the optative with ἄν, not in the present indicative, which we find throughout the argument in ll. 26-33. διαφέρει . . . μᾶλλον (25, 26) must therefore be taken as parenthetical, and ll. 26-33 as being aimed at showing that being and unity are one κατὰ τὸ ὑποκείμενον (cf. Al. 249. 22).

26. I have restored the true reading of Aᵇ Γ, which was evidently also that of Alexander. ταὐτὸ γὰρ εἶς ἄνθρωπος καὶ ἄνθρωπος, καὶ ὢν ἄνθρωπος καὶ ἄνθρωπος

One man = man	(τῷ ἀκολουθεῖν ἀλλήλοις)
Existent man = man	,, ,, ,,)
(∴ One man = existent man	,, ,, ,,
∴ One = existent	,, ,, ,,)

27-30. Alexander supposes Aristotle to be arguing that as ἔστι ἄνθρωπος ἄνθρωπος means no more than ἔστιν ἄνθρωπος (cf. Asc. 236. 27), so ἔστιν ὢν ἄνθρωπος and ἔστιν εἷς ἄνθρωπος convey the same meaning as ἔστιν ἄνθρωπος and therefore as one another, i. e. everything that is ὄν is ἕν and everything that is ἕν is ὄν. But ἔστιν ὢν (or εἷς) ἄνθρωπος cannot be treated as really parallel to ἔστιν ἄνθρωπος ἄνθρωπος: the latter is a mere tautology, but ὢν and εἷς differ from ἄνθρωπος in λόγος though not in ὑποκείμενον.

One point seems to be clear. ὁμοίως δὲ καὶ ἐπὶ τοῦ ἑνός implies that in what precedes Aristotle has spoken not of τὸ ἕν but of τὸ ὄν. None of the recorded readings, then, is satisfactory. We may suppose (1) that Aristotle wrote οὐχ ἕτερόν τι δηλοῖ κατὰ τὴν λέξιν ἐπαναδιπλούμενον τὸ ἔστιν ἄνθρωπος καὶ ὢν ἄνθρωπος (ὢν appears in Γ and Syr. and in the quotation in Asc.). 'Nothing is added if we repeat ourselves and say "he is a man and an existent man" (it is clear that his humanity and his existence are not separated either in their coming to be or in their ceasing to be); and what we have said of existence we may say of unity, so that clearly the addition of "existent" and of "one" has the same significance' (i. e. that of bringing out a feature already implied though not expressed in 'man'), 'and unity is nothing apart from existence'.

But ll. 27-29 are then a rather tame repetition of ll. 26-27 ταὐτὸ ... ὢν ἄνθρωπος καὶ ἄνθρωπος, and, further, ἔστιν is somewhat suspicious; there is no point in the change from the terms 'existent man' and 'man' to the propositions 'he is a man' and 'he is an existent man'. It seems better (2) to suppose that there is an ἐπαναδίπλωσις here additional to that in ὢν ἄνθρωπος καὶ ἄνθρωπος, and of this Syr.'s phrase εἷς ὢν ἄνθρωπος (61. 7) preserves a trace. I read therefore τὸ εἷς ἄνθρωπος καὶ εἷς ὢν ἄνθρωπος. 'One existent man' adds nothing to 'one man'; the two things are inseparable whether in coming to be or in ceasing to be; and similarly 'one existent man' adds nothing to 'existent man'.

33. The meaning of ὅπερ here is sufficiently indicated by its opposition to κατὰ συμβεβηκός. For an exact account of its meaning in Aristotle cf. Bonitz, *Index*, 533ᵇ 36—534ⁿ 23.

33-35. Cf. B. 995ᵇ 20-27 n.

33. τοῦ ἑνὸς εἴδη. But it must be noted that ἕν and ὄν are not really genera (B. 998ᵇ 22, H. 1045ᵇ 6, I. 1053ᵇ 22).

36. καὶ τῶν τούτοις ἀντικειμένων is read only by the inferior manuscripts S, 1ᵇ, the Aldine edition, and perhaps by Alexander (250. 9). It seems, however, to be implied by the next sentence. But that sentence (l. 36-1004ᵃ 2) seriously disturbs the argument. After 1004ᵃ 2-9, which, as we have seen, is probably out of place, there follows an argument to show that the science which studies being, unity, and their species, must study also the opposites of these. The implication in 1003ᵇ 36—1004ⁿ 2 that it must do so is thus premature. It may be suggested that σχεδὸν . . . ἐναντίων is a mere variant of πάντα . . . ἡμῖν (1004ᵇ 33—1005ⁿ 1) wrongly inserted here, and that καὶ τῶν τούτοις ἀντικειμένων was added later to lead up to these words.

1004^a 2. τῇ ἐκλογῇ τῶν ἐναντίων. Cf. ἐν τῇ διαιρέσει τῶν ἐναντίων
I. 1054^a 30, and Γ. 1004^b 34. Alexander elsewhere refers simply to
the (now lost) *De Bono* (Bk. II) for a discussion of this subject (262.
18, 23, 615. 14, 643. 2, 695. 26), but here (250. 17) he supposes that
besides the discussion in the second book of the *De Bono* there was
a separate treatise entitled Ἐκλογὴ τῶν ἐναντίων. The reference is
probably to the work Περὶ ἐναντίων mentioned in the catalogues of
Diogenes Laertius and Hesychius. For its nature see Rose, frr. 115–
121 (= 118–124 Teubner).

2-9. This section answers the third problem set in Book B (995^b
10-13, 997^a 15-25).

5. If we are right in supposing that 1004^a 2-9 should come before
1003^b 19-36, a reference to τὸ ἕν here is out of place and Natorp is
right in excising it.

8. πρώτη τις, arithmetic ; δευτέρα, plane geometry ; ἄλλαι ἐφεξῆς,
solid geometry, astronomy, harmonics, &c.

10. τῷ δὲ ἑνὶ ἀντίκειται πλῆθος. The recurrence of these words in
l. 16 is suspicious. What we should expect is a general argument
proving the major premise that one science studies opposites ; then the
minor premise 'unity and plurality are opposites' ; and then the conclusion 'one science studies unity and plurality'. These words, then,
at first sight seem appropriate in l. 11 and not in l. 10. Luthe therefore would cut them out here. But (1) the preceding and the
following clause do not run very naturally if taken continuously, and
(2) it is certain that Alexander had τῷ δὲ ἑνί κτλ. in l. 10, and not
certain that he had these words in l. 16. It seems preferable therefore to excise the words in l. 16.

12. Schwegler's emendation ἢ γὰρ ἁπλῶς λέγομεν seems to be required, though it is not clear that Alexander had not the same reading
as our manuscripts (cf. Al. 253. 1, 6).

13. ἔνθα μὲν οὖν κτλ. Alexander interprets (1) (253. 10), 'Here the
difference, i.e. the negative, is added to "one" everywhere except in the
case of the positive term which occurs in the negation'. I.e. 'not-
one' is true of everything except what is one. (2) (253. 16) 'where
the difference, i.e. the negative, is added to "one", everything is indicated except what is denied'. In other words, the negative 'not-
one' is applicable to everything except the one, to which from its very
form it is inapplicable. The privative of 'one' on the other hand,
is applicable only to those things which, though not one, belong to the
genus, and have the underlying nature, which is susceptible of the
predicate 'one'.

These are obviously forced interpretations. The use of διαφορά for
the negative particle would be unique ; in fact διαφορά expressly implies
a distinction within a genus and is not appropriate to bare negation
(cf., for example, I. 1054^b 25, 1055^a 26). The use of τὸ ἐν τῇ ἀποφάσει
for the positive term would be very strange. Further, if ἔνθα . . .
πρόσεστι is taken to be a relative clause, as in Alexander's second
interpretation, the supplying of τὰ ἄλλα πάντα δηλοῦται with παρὰ τὸ ἐν

τῇ ἀποφάσει is extremely difficult, not to say impossible. Bonitz avoids the latter difficulty by interpreting 'here, i. e. in negation, ⟨only⟩ the difference, i. e. the negation, is present over and above what is comprised in the negation, i. e. the quality denied'. Thus he retains the objectionable interpretation of διαφορά and of τὸ ἐν τῇ ἀποφάσει, inserts an illegitimate 'only', and gives no account of τῷ ἑνί. In fact, on his interpretation either τῷ ἑνί or παρὰ τὸ ἐν τῇ ἀποφάσει is superfluous. Schwegler's emendation παρὰ τὸ ἕν, ἐν τῇ ἀποφάσει does not meet the difficulties. We may suggest, with some hesitation, that τῷ ἑνί and ἢ should be omitted, and that the passage should be interpreted as follows : 'Here, i. e. in *privation*, difference is present over and above what is implied in bare negation ; for negation implies the absence of the attribute in question, but in privation there is also an underlying nature of which the privation is asserted'. διαφορά is then used in its proper sense of specific difference within a genus as opposed to the mere 'otherness' which subsists between a term and its bare negative. For ἔνθα μέν referring to the latter of two cases mentioned cf., for example, *Pol.* 1308ᵇ 7. For the absence of a clause opposed to the μέν clause cf. Waitz on *An. Pr.* 61ᵃ 19.

Bullinger interprets ἔνθα μέν as we have done, but gives an indefensible explanation of τῷ ἑνί.

21. διαφορά· κτλ. Contrariety is μεγίστη διαφορά (I. 1055ᵃ 4), διαφορὰ τέλειος (1055ᵃ 16). Difference is 'otherness which makes the genus itself other' (1058ᵃ 7, cf. 1054ᵇ 23–31, Δ. 1018ᵃ 12–15).

29. Bonitz is clearly right in taking κατηγορία to mean not 'category' but 'predicate'—'in the case of each of the predicates in question', i. e. the same, other, &c. Bullinger interprets 'we must explain the term in each category by reference to its primary sense, i. e. its sense in the category of substance'; but the order of the words is strongly against this.

30. Natorp urges that ἐκεῖνο is the subject of ἔχειν (cf. 1005ᵃ 14, Al. 256. 16), but it seems more likely to be object.

33. ἐν τῶν ἐν τοῖς ἀπορήμασιν, viz. the fifth problem (B. 995ᵇ 18–27, 997ᵃ 25–34). The discussion extends from 1003ᵇ 32 to 1005ᵃ 18.

34. πάντων. Bz. understands ὅσα τῷ ὄντι καθ' αὐτὸ ὑπάρχει, but the natural interpretation is quite general, 'all things'. Cf. ᵇ 20, A. 982ᵃ 8.

ᵇ 1–6. Cf. B. 995ᵇ 20–27 n.

3. εἰ ἐν ἑνὶ ἐναντίον is discussed in I. 1055ᵃ 19–23, τί ἐστι τὸ ἐναντίον in 1055ᵃ 3–17, 23–33, 38–ᵇ 20, ποσαχῶς λέγεται in 1055ᵃ 33–38, ᵇ 20–25.

25. πειραστική, i. e. it makes trial of the opinions of others (*Soph. El.* 171ᵇ 3–4). In *Soph. El.* c. 2 πειραστικοὶ λόγοι are one of the four kinds of οἱ ἐν τῷ διαλέγεσθαι λόγοι and are distinguished from διαλεκτικοί, the latter being οἱ ἐκ τῶν ἐνδόξων συλλογιστικοὶ ἀντιφάσεως, the former οἱ ἐκ τῶν δοκούντων τῷ ἀποκρινομένῳ καὶ ἀναγκαίων εἰδέναι τῷ προσποιουμένῳ ἔχειν τὴν ἐπιστήμην. In *Soph. El.* 169ᵇ 25, 171ᵇ 4, however, peirastic is treated as part of dialectic, while in 171ᵇ 9,

172ᵃ 21 dialectic is described as being peirastic. Thus Aristotle has no settled distinction between the terms.

27. συστοιχία, cf. A. 986ᵃ 23 n.

31-32. οἱ μέν, the Pythagoreans; οἱ δὲ θερμόν, Alexander suggests the thinkers who generated things by μάνωσις and πύκνωσις (sc. Anaximenes)or else Parmenides. Parmenides' 'way of opinion' is doubtless what Aristotle has in his mind, cf. A. 984ᵇ 4 n., 986ᵇ 33.

32-33. οἱ δὲ πέρας, the Platonists; οἱ δὲ φιλίαν, Empedocles.

34. εἰλήφθω γάρ κτλ. Cf. ᵃ 2 n.

1005ᵃ 2. εἰς γένη ταῦτα πίπτουσιν. For the phrase cf. Δ. 1013ᵇ 16, Λ. 1071ᵃ 7.

6. ἴσως, cf. A. 987ᵃ 26 n.

9. ἢ χωριστόν. For this question cf. B. 996ᵃ 4-9, 1001ᵃ4-ᵇ 25, Z. 1040ᵇ 16-24, I. 2, M. 1083ᵃ 20—1085ᵃ 2.

10. ἴσως, cf. A. 987ᵃ 26 n.

11-18. Cf. B. 995ᵇ 20-27 n.

13. ἐξ ὑποθέσεως. Alexander explains that the geometer does not speculate about the meaning of 'contrariety' and the like but merely presupposes such terms and uses them. On this view ἀλλ' ἢ ἐξ ὑποθέσεως does not mean 'except ex hypothesi' but 'but only proceeds from the assumption of them'. This is, of course, Plato's view of the relation of the sciences to philosophy. Bz. on the other hand interprets 'except in so far as pertains to the object set before itself by geometry' (τὸ ὑποτεθὲν τῇ γεωμετρίᾳ). Alexander's interpretation is amply confirmed by E. 1025ᵇ 11 αἱ δ' (some of the sciences, which are there, as here, being distinguished from philosophy) ὑπόθεσιν λαβοῦσαι τὸ τί ἐστιν. For the use of ἀλλ' ἢ cf. Z. 1038ᵃ 14 n.

ὅτι μὲν οὖν κτλ. Aristotle has now answered the fifth of the problems in Book B (995ᵇ 18-27, 997ᵃ 25-34).

16. τῶν . . . εἰρημένων, i. e, 'contrary', 'perfect', 'real', 'one', 'the same', 'other', mentioned in l. 12. Thus the things which were in 1003ᵇ 21-36 treated as εἴδη τοῦ ὄντος are now (presumably to avoid clashing with the division of τὸ ὄν into the categories) described as attributes of being or of substance.

We must study also the axioms and, primarily, the law of contradiction
(ch. 3).

1005ᵃ 19. The philosopher must also consider the things that are in mathematics called axioms, for these are true of all existing things— of being as being. They are used in the special sciences in so far as they apply to the special subjects.

29. No special science inquires into their truth; some physicists have done so, and naturally enough, because they thought they were inquiring into being in general. But since there is some one who stands higher than the physicist, it belongs to him—the student of the universal and of primary substance—to investigate the axioms. Physics is a form of philosophy, but not the primary form.

ᵇ 2. The essays of some people at determining the conditions under which statements should be accepted as truth are due to ignorance of logic, which should be learned before one approaches the study of any science.

5. It belongs tc the philosopher, then, to study the starting-points of syllogism. He who knows most about a genus must be able to state the best-established principles of the genus, and therefore the philosopher must be able to state the best established of all principles, i.e. those about which one cannot be deceived, which are best known and rest on no hypothesis, and which must be known if one is to know anything.

18. The best established of all principles is that the same attribute cannot at the same time belong and not belong to the same subject in the same respect—with any qualifications which may be necessary in order to guard against objections. This corresponds to the definition of the best-established principle. For no one can suppose the same thing to be and not to be—the alleged doctrine of Heraclitus.

25. For a man need not believe everything that he says; if contrary attributes cannot attach to the same subject, and any belief is, as an attribute of the thinker, contrary to the contradictory belief, obviously no one can at the same time believe the same thing to be and not to be. And therefore every one in argument falls back on this ultimate law, on which even the other axioms rest.

In this chapter Aristotle discusses the second of the problems in Book B (995ᵇ 6–10, 996ᵇ 26—997ᵃ 15).

1005ᵃ 20. τῶν . . . ἀξιωμάτων. The only axioms or κοιναὶ ἀρχαί discussed by Aristotle in this book are the laws of contradiction and of excluded middle; but the principle that if equals be taken from equals equals remain is included among the axioms in K. 1061ᵇ 20, *An. Post.* 76ᵃ 41, ᵇ 20, 77ᵃ 30. This principle is strictly of a sort intermediate between κοιναί and ἴδιαι ἀρχαί, for, while extending beyond the bounds of any one science, it does not extend beyond the sciences of quantity, since equality is a *proprium* of quantity (*Cat.* 6ᵃ 26, cf. Δ. 1021ᵃ 12).

31. τῶν φυσικῶν ἔνιοι, presumably thinkers who developed the sceptical elements in Heraclitus, Empedocles, Anaxagoras, and Democritus. Cf. 1006ᵃ 2.

ᵇ 2–5. Alexander would place this sentence after δῆλον, l. 8, arguing that it has more affinity with what follows (cf l. 5 with l. 17). But

as Bz. points out it connects directly with what has been said in
ᵃ 29–31 and is quite in place.

Certain persons had evidently introduced into discussions of ἡ ἀλήθεια,
i. e. of the ultimate nature of reality (cf. A. 983ᵇ 2 n.), an inquiry
into the conditions under which beliefs are to be accepted as true.
This question, Aristotle points out, should not be mixed up with
questions about the nature of reality. It belongs to logic, which you
should study before you approach such questions. And if you study
it you will learn that proof should not be always expected, that there
are ἀρχαί which neither need it nor admit of it (1006ᵃ 5–8; cf.
An. Post. I. 3).

Antisthenes is perhaps referred to here and in 1006ᵃ 5–8 (where the
word ἀπαιδευσία recurs), 1009ᵃ 20–22, 1011ᵃ 7–13, 1012ᵃ 21. Cf.
H. 1043ᵇ 24 οἱ Ἀντισθένειοι καὶ οἱ οὕτως ἀπαίδευτοι, Δ. 1024ᵇ 32
Ἀντισθένης ᾤετο εὐήθως. τῶν λεγόντων τινὲς περὶ τῆς ἀληθείας may be
an allusion to his book called Ἀλήθεια. Aristotle's refutation of these
thinkers turns on the necessity of a fixed meaning for ὀνόματα (ch. 4),
and is described as ἔλεγχος . . . τοῦ ἐν τῇ φωνῇ λόγου καὶ τοῦ ἐν τοῖς
ὀνόμασιν (1009ᵃ 21): this recalls the saying of Antisthenes ἀρχὴ παιδεύ-
σεως ἡ τῶν ὀνομάτων ἐπίσκεψις. Further, Antisthenes' theory implied
that 'there is no such thing as contradiction or (we may almost say)
as falsehood' (Δ. 1024ᵇ 34), so that he would naturally be referred to
in 1006ᵃ 5–8 among the opponents of the law of contradiction.

These arguments for supposing Antisthenes to be referred to are
stated by Maier (*Syll. d. Ar.* ii. 2. 15 n. 2). Maier seems to follow
Dümmler too readily in scenting allusions to Antisthenes in Plato.
Bz. thinks that the τινές here referred to are the τῶν φυσικῶν ἔνιοι of
ᵃ 31, and if so the reference cannot be to Antisthenes. But it is
equally possible that others besides the physicists had discussed the
ἀρχαί of knowledge.

8. Aristotle has now answered the second problem raised in Book B,
whether metaphysics should study the axioms. He now proceeds to
show what the chief of the axioms is, to refute its opponents, and
to indicate the reasons that led to their opposition. Cf. the summary
in 1011ᵇ 13–15.

14. ἀνυπόθετον is used quite in the Platonic sense of the word. With
this we may compare Aristotle's use of ὑπόθεσις as synonymous with
συνθήκη (*An. Pr.* 50ᵃ 16, 18, *E. N.* 1133ᵃ 29, ᵇ 21), and the common
use of ἐξ ὑποθέσεως where it is often implied that the premise is not
known but merely assumed. This has to be distinguished from two
other senses of ὑπόθεσις, (1) quite general = ἀρχή, cf. *Ind. Ar.* 796ᵇ 59—
797ᵃ 15, (2) technical = the assumption of the existence of one of the
primary objects of the science one is studying, *An. Post.* 72ᵃ 20.
ὑπόθεσις in the latter sense has this in common with the sort of
hypothesis Aristotle has in mind here, that it is not a necessary
preliminary to all knowledge (cf. 1005ᵇ 15 with *An. Post.* 72ᵃ 14–21);
but it is a necessary preliminary to the knowledge of the particular
science to which it belongs.

19. It is to be noticed that the law of contradiction is for Aristotle primarily a law of being, 'the same attribute cannot at the same time belong and not belong to the same subject and in the same respect'.

25. Ἡράκλειτον. For his doctrine cf. 1010ᵃ 10, 1012ᵃ 24, 34, K. 1062ᵃ 32, 1063ᵇ 24.

οὐκ ἔστι γὰρ ἀναγκαῖον κτλ. Aristotle is not accusing Heraclitus of insincerity, but suggesting that he did not express his meaning exactly, or did not understand the full meaning of the words he used. Cf. K. 1062ᵃ 34.

26-32. Aristotle here restates the law of contradiction in a new form, ' contrary attributes cannot at the same time belong to the same subject' (contrast l. 19 n.). The connexion between the two forms is established in 1011ᵇ 15-22. Meantime the new form of the law of being is made the basis of a law of thought, ' the same man cannot at the same time suppose the same thing to be and not to be ', the holding of contrary suppositions being an instance of the having of contrary attributes.

The law of contradiction established by pointing out the difficulties involved in its denial (ch. 4).

1005ᵇ 35. There are some—e. g. many physicists—who say (1) that the same thing can be and not be, and (2) that it can be judged both to be and not to be. We have (1) assumed that a thing cannot both be and not be, and (2) shown this to be the least dubitable of all principles.

1006ᵃ 5. The demand that we should prove the law argues a lack of education; the educated man knows what should be proved and what should not. The attempt to prove everything leads to an infinite regress, and nothing can be suggested which is fitter than this law to be an indemonstrable principle.

11. It is possible to prove the law by refuting our opponent, if he will but say something. If he will not, he need not be argued with and is no better than a vegetable. If one used demonstration one might be thought to be begging the question; when our opponent himself assumes the point we are arguing for, there is proof by way of refutation, not of demonstration.

18. We begin by assuming not that our opponent must affirm or deny something (which might be thought a *petitio principii*), but that he means something (if he does not he cannot have intelligent intercourse with himself, nor with any one else). If this be granted, we can go on to argue, for we have a fixed point,—and the responsibility rests with our opponent. And he who grants this grants that something is true though unproved.

First Proof.

28. (1) The words 'is' and 'is not' have a definite meaning, so that not everything is 'so and not so'. (2) 'Man' means some one thing; let this be 'two-footed animal'. In meaning one thing it is implied that if 'man' means so-and-so, then if A is a man, so-and-so is what being a man means for A.

34. It does not matter if a word has several meanings, if only they are limited in number; for a separate word might be assigned to each meaning. If the meanings are unlimited, no account can be given of the thing. Not to mean one thing is to mean nothing, and if words mean nothing rational intercourse with others is destroyed, and even with oneself, for if we do not think one thing we do not think at all.

ᵇ**11.** Let us assume, then, that words have one definite meaning.

13. (3) Being man', then, does not mean the same as 'not being man', if 'man' not only signifies something about one subject but has one meaning.

15. (If signifying something about one thing were the same as having one meaning, 'musical', 'white', and 'man' would mean the same thing, and all things would be one—the same thing called by different names.)

18. It will not be possible to be and not be the same thing, except by equivocation, just as that which I call man, others may call not-man. The question, however, is whether the same thing can be man and not man actually, not verbally.

22. If 'man' means the same as 'not-man', 'being man' is 'being not-man'. 'Being man' and 'being not-man' will be, like 'garments' and 'clothes', two expressions for the same meaning. But it has been shown that the meanings are different.

28. According to the above definition, if anything is a man it is *necessarily* a two-footed animal; and then it is impossible for it not to be a two-footed animal, for necessity means just the impossibility of the opposite. It cannot, therefore, be true to say that the same thing is and is not a man.

34. (4) As 'being man' has a fixed meaning, so has 'not being man'. If 'being white' and 'being man' are different in meaning, 'being man' and 'being not-man' are much more different. If, then, opposites are one, all things are one, and as all things are not one our point is proved, if our opponent will only answer our question.

1007ᵃ8. If he answers 'A is B and not B', he is not answering the question. The same thing may be man and white and many other things, but if I ask whether it is man, I ought not to get the answer, 'Yes—and white and tall'. The accidental attributes are innumerable—let a man name either all or none of them. And similarly even if the same thing were man and not-man, my opponent should not add 'and not-man' any more than he should add the other accidental attributes.

20. Our opponents are really making away with substance and essence. They must say that all attributes are accidental. For if there is such a thing as being essentially a man, this will not = being not-man or not being man,—yet these are its contradictories. To signify the substance of a thing means just that the essence of the thing is nothing else; but if the thing's being A = not being A, or being not A, its essence *will* be something else. Our opponents must therefore say that nothing can be defined—that all attributes are accidental. The distinction between substance and accident is just this : whiteness is accidental to man because he is not essentially white.

33. But if all things are accidental, there will be no original substratum for accidents to inhere in. This means an infinite regress, which is impossible because not more than two accidents can be combined. (*a*) An accident can be an accident of an accident, only if both are accidents of the same subject. The white can be musical, and the musical white, because man is both. But (*b*) 'musical' is an accident of Socrates, not in the sense that both are accidents of something else. These are the two sorts of accidental proposition. But we cannot go on to say that something else is an accident, in the second sense, of white Socrates,—for such a collection of attributes makes no unity. Nor, in the first sense, is 'musical' really an accident of 'white', for it is no more so than 'white' is an accident of 'musical'. Thus in either case we are brought back to substance ; but we have shown that if there is such a thing as substance, the law of contradiction is true.

Second Proof.

ᵇ **18.** If all contradictories are compatible, all things will be one. The same thing will be both ship and wall and man, if we can indifferently either assert or deny a predicate of any subject, as the Protagoreans must admit. For, according to them, if any one thinks the man is not a ship he is not, and therefore (if contradictories are both true) is, a ship. This lands us in Anaxagoras' 'all things together'; these thinkers seem to be speaking of the indeterminate— that which exists only potentially ; in fact, that which is not, instead of that which is.

29. But they *must* admit that *any* predicate may be affirmed and denied of *any* subject. For if not-A is predicable of A, not-B will *a fortiori* be predicable of A. If, then, A is B, it is also not-B; and if it is not B, it must be not-B more than it is not-A. Since, then, A *is* not-A, it is *a fortiori* not-B, and therefore B.

Third Proof.

1008ᵃ 2. Our opponents will have to deny the law of excluded middle. For if A is man and not-man, it will also be neither man nor not-man, whether we treat this as two propositions contradictory of the former two, or as one contradictory of the former one.

Fourth Proof.

7. Their denial of the law of contradiction must be either total or partial. (1) If partial, the exceptional cases are admitted to have an attribute and not its contradictory.

12. (2) If total, then (*a*) where we may affirm we may deny, but where we may deny we may not always affirm—in which case there is something which definitely is not; and if something is known not to be the opposite affirmation will be still better known.

18. Or else (*b*) where we may affirm we may deny, and where we may deny we may affirm. Then either (i) we may not say separately ' A is B ' and ' A is not B ',—but then our opponent is not saying what he professes to say, and ultimately nothing is; how then can he talk or walk ? And it follows also that all things will be one—the same thing will be man, god, ship, and the contradictories of these.

27. Or else (ii) we can say separately that ' A is B ' and ' A is not B '—in which case again all things are indistinguishable, and, further, all statements are true and all are untrue, and our opponent admits his own statement to be untrue. And clearly argument is useless with such an opponent, who will say nothing definite.

Fifth Proof.

34. If where affirmation is true negation is false, and *vice versa*, the same thing cannot at the same time be truly affirmed and denied. But this might be called a *petitio principii*.

Sixth Proof.

ᵇ 2. Are the judgements ' A is B ' and ' A is not B ' false, but the judgement ' A is B and not B ' true ? (1) If this statement is true, what is the meaning of saying that the nature of things is such ? (2) If this statement is false, but less false than the other two, then things are to this extent determinate—this judgement at least is true and not false.

(3) If all judgements are alike false and true, he who thinks so can say nothing, and is no better than a vegetable.

12. From this point of view it is easy to see that no one really is in this state of mind. Why does one walk to Megara and not remain at rest, when one thinks one ought to walk there? Clearly we judge one thing, e. g. to see a man, to be better, another to be worse. And if so, we must judge one thing to be a man, another not to be a man, and so on. The practice of our opponents refutes their theory; practical judgements at least do not obey their rule.

27. If they say that they do not know but merely think some things to be better, and others worse, they should be all the more careful about the truth, as a sickly man must be more careful than a healthy one.

Seventh Proof.

31. Even if every A is both B and not B, there is a more and a less in the nature of things; three is at least not as even as two. The statement which is less false is more true, and there must be some truth which it is nearer. Even if there is not, we have at least got rid of the extreme view which would make definite thought impossible.

1005^b 35. Maier, *Syllogistik des Aristoteles*, ii. 2. 7. n. 1, tries to show by a comparison of 1006^b 15–17, 1007^a 10–14 with Simpl. in *Phys.* 120. 12 ff., that the Megaric school among others is referred to, but the evidence is not definite enough, though the suggestion is highly probable.

αὐτοί τε. These words, which are excised by Christ, are quite in place. 'There are some who both themselves say that the same thing can be and not be, and say that it is possible to judge so.' I.e. they maintain the possibility of contradiction (1) in fact—'A may be both B and not B', and (2) in belief—'a man may judge that A is B and also that A is not B'.

1006^a 2. πολλοὶ τῶν περὶ φύσεως, e. g. Heraclitus (1012^a 24, 34) and the Heracliteans (1010^a 10), Empedocles (1009^b 15), Anaxagoras (1009^a 27, ^{b} 25), Democritus (1009^a 27, ^{b} 11, 15).

4. διὰ τούτου ἐδείξαμεν refers to 1005^b 22–32; the law of thought has been proved from the law of being.

5–8. Cf. 1005^b 2–5 n.

6. ἀπαιδευσίαν, *sc.* τῶν ἀναλυτικῶν, cf. 1005^b 3.

13. γελοῖον τὸ ζητεῖν λόγον κτλ. 'It is absurd to seek to give an account of our views to one who cannot give an account of anything.'

26–28. The whole sentence is excised by Bz., on the assumption that there is no trace of it in Alexander's commentary. But ὁ τοῦτο συγχωρῶν, τὸν ἅπαξ συγχωρήσαντα τοῦτο (Al. 275. 2, 6) refer to it. Only the last clause, of which there is no trace in Alexander, should be omitted, as an intruder from l. 30.

28. Aristotle has shown in l. 21 that all judgement must have meaning. Coming to details, he now begins by pointing out that the 'is' or 'is not' in a judgement must mean something. (Alexander takes τὸ εἶναι ἢ μὴ εἶναι to be thus explicative of τὸ ὄνομα. An equally good sense can be got by taking τὸ εἶναι ἢ μὴ εἶναι τοδί to be the object of σημαίνει.) Next (l. 31) he goes on to the predicate, e. g. 'man', and points out that it too must have meaning.

32. εἰ τοῦτ' ἔστιν κτλ. 'If "man" means X, then if anything is a man, its being man will be being X.'

ᵇ 12. κατ' ἀρχάς, ª 21, 31.

15. Having one signification is not the same thing as signifying something about one subject. If it were, 'musical', 'white', and 'man' would have one signification, so that all things would be one; for they would be συνώνυμα. In spite of Bz., Alexander must be right in saying (280. 19) that συνώνυμα is used in the sense of πολυώνυμα (for which cf. *H. A.* 489ª 2). What is συνώνυμον, strictly speaking, has a single name as well as a single definition (*Cat.* 1ª 6); but, the singleness of the definition being the important thing, which distinguishes συνώνυμα from ὁμώνυμα, Aristotle uses the word here even of things which have one definition but different names. Cf. *Top.* 162ᵇ 37, 167ª 24, *Rhet.* 1405ª 1.

18. καὶ οὐκ ἔσται κτλ., 'and it will not be possible to be and not be the same thing'.

22-28. It is hard to see the point of this section, and it comes near to reasoning in a circle. Alexander feels a difficulty, and suggests that ὥστ' ἔσται κτλ. l. 24 follows in sense either on ἀλλὰ τὸ πρᾶγμα l. 22 or on ἄλλοι μὴ ἄνθρωπον καλοῖεν l. 20, the intervening words being parenthetical. Neither of these suggestions appears to help the sense. In εἰ δὲ μὴ σημαίνει ἕτερον τὸ ἄνθρωπος καὶ τὸ μὴ ἄνθρωπος, Aristotle seems to be pursuing the suggestion in l. 19 of an equivocation in the meaning of 'man' whereby what A calls 'man', B calls 'not-man'. If there is such an equivocation, he now proceeds,—if 'man' means nothing other than 'not-man', clearly 'not being **man**' will mean nothing other than 'being man', so that 'being man' will be 'being not-man'; for they will be one. For this is what being one means—being like 'garment' and 'cloak', i. e. two names the account (or meaning) of which is one; and if 'being man' and 'being not-man' are to *be* one, they will have to *mean* one thing. But it had been shown that they mean different things' (*sc.* in ll. 11–15, where the difference in meaning between 'being man' and 'not being man' was inferred from the necessity of there being a single meaning for 'man'), so that we need not consider further the consequences of the hypothesis that 'man' and 'not-man' are two names for the same thing.

In ll. 24, 25 Aristotle says that the identity (i. e. identity in meaning) of being man and being not-man would follow from their being one. He defends this in ll. 25–28. τὸ μουσικόν, τὸ λευκόν, and ἄνθρωπος are one in a sense (i. e. they are predicable of one subject) and yet are not

identical in meaning. But this sense of being one has been rejected
(ll. 15–18). Being one is to mean having one meaning (ll. 25–27),
and therefore if being-man and being-not-man are one, they will be
identical in meaning.

26. λώπιον does not seem to be found before Aristotle; it is
a diminutive of the poetical words λώπη, λῶπος (cf. λωποδύτης).

27. σημανεῖ seems to have been read by Alexander (ἐν ἔσται σημαίνοντα 281. 25) and to be required by the sense and the idiom.

30. ἐσήμαινε, 'was assumed to mean', sc. in ᵃ 32.

34. Aristotle passes from his argument derived from the necessity
of a fixed meaning for ' being man ' to one derived from the necessity
of a fixed meaning for ' not being man ' or ' being not-man '. Christ
thinks that the notion now referred to must be definitely the latter of
these two, ' being not-man ', and accordingly reads μὴ ἄνθρωπον εἶναι
in 1007ᵃ 1. But, though Aristotle recognizes the verbal difference
between μὴ εἶναι ἀνθρώπῳ and μὴ ἀνθρώπῳ εἶναι, he evidently treats
them as logically equivalent (1007ᵃ 24, 28, and cf. 1006ᵇ 25 with
1006ᵇ 13, 21, 24, 34). When he wishes to compare the relation
of the positive to the negative notion with the relation of τὸ λευκὸν
εἶναι to τὸ ἄνθρωπον εἶναι he naturally passes (1007ᵃ 2) to the form τὸ
μὴ ἀνθρώπῳ εἶναι.

1007ᵃ 6. πρότερον ἐλέχθη, 1006ᵇ 17.

30. τοιοῦτος λόγος, i. e. οὐσιώδης λόγος (Alexander 287. 7).

34. Alexander's conjecture καθ' οὗ for καθόλου is plainly right. The
same emendation should be made in Θ. 1049ᵃ 28. If all things are
accidental, there will be no first thing which is the subject, since the
accidental always means the predication of something *about* a subject.

ᵇ 9. ἐπὶ τὸ ἄνω, in the direction of the predicate.

10. οὐ γὰρ γίγνεταί τι ἓν ἐξ ἁπάντων, i. e. 'Socrates, who is white,
is also *a* and *b* and *c*, and so *ad infinitum*' is not really a single
statement at all.

16. ἔσται ἄρα τι κτλ., ' even if we start with accidental predication,
we come to something that signifies substance'. In the vulgate reading καὶ ὡς οὐσίαν σημαῖνον, ὡς is superfluous. I have therefore read
καὶ ὧς, ' even so '. Cf. *De Caelo* 302ᵇ 24, *De Sensu* 444ᵇ 5, and *D. G. C.*
329ᵇ 3, where Prof. Joachim has made the same correction.

17. εἰ δὲ τοῦτο κτλ. ' But we have shown that if this is so, contradictories cannot be predicated at the same time.' The original proof
in 1006ᵃ 28—1007ᵃ 20 depended on the assumption that there is something which each term essentially means, that there is an ' essence of
man ', &c. Now the opponents of the law of contradiction deny the
existence of essence ; they say that ' A is B ' always means '' A happens
to be B '. Aristotle has therefore had to show (1007ᵃ 33–ᵇ 17) that
this view is incorrect, and has thus supplied the link which was
necessary in order to make the original proof complete.

23–25. εἰ γάρ κτλ. This is not meant to prove that followers of
Protagoras must admit that contradictories are compatible. That
they do so is assumed here (εἴπερ ἡ ἀντίφασις ἀληθής); that they

must do so is proved in ch. 5. The present sentence shows that *if* they do so they must make 'all things one'.

25. καὶ γίγνεται δή κτλ. The phrase is borrowed from *Phaedo* 72 c ταχὺ ἂν τὸ τοῦ Ἀναξαγόρου γεγονὸς εἴη, ὁμοῦ πάντα χρήματα. Cf. fr. 1 of Anaxagoras (Diels).

28. 'For it is that which is potentially and not actually that is indeterminate.' I. e. A cannot be actually both B and not B, but may be potentially both B and not B. It is only that in which opposite actualities are still latent that can truly be said to be (potentially) each of two opposites, or to be indeterminate.

29. ἀλλὰ μὴν λεκτέον γ' κτλ. Cf. M. 1082ᵃ 11–15 n.

33. The logic of the passage requires Aᵇ's reading ἢ τριήρης ἢ οὐ τριήρης. The vulgate reading is due to homoioteleuton.

1008ᵃ 19. We may place a comma either (with Alexander and Bonitz) after or (with Bekker and Christ) before ἀνάγκη. In ll. 13–15 the word to be understood with the infinitives is not ἀνάγκη but ἔστιν, 'it is possible', and we should expect φάναι to be in the same construction here and ἀνάγκη to go with what follows. But if it does, ἀληθὲς διαιροῦντα λέγειν must be construed differently in ll. 19, 21. In l. 19 the construction will be 'one must either be saying what is true when one divides'; in l. 21 'if it is not true to speak dividing'; i. e. asserting 'A is B' and 'A is not B' separately. This objection is less serious than the objection to taking ἀνάγκη with φάναι.

21. οὐ λέγει τε ταῦτα, 'he does not say what he professes to say'.

23. πρότερον εἴρηται, 1006ᵇ 17, 1007ᵃ 6.

31. οὔτε γὰρ οὕτως οὔτ' οὐχ οὕτως, a reminiscence of *Theaet.* 183 A.

ᵇ 2. The question is, 'Is the man who thinks either that A is B, or that A is not B, wrong, but the man who thinks both right?' According to the reading of Aᵇ and Alexander, two alternatives are suggested in ll. 3–7: (1) If the latter is not right, what is meant by saying 'such is the nature of things'? Surely this view means that things have *no* nature. (2) If he is not right, but more right than the man who thinks that A is B or that A is not B, then a determinate character is already assigned to things.

The obvious third possibility, that the man who thinks both *is* right, is omitted, and the omission is unaccountable. Alexander twice (297. 33, 298. 6) introduces this possibility, but it is not clear that he had it in his text.

If we follow the reading of EJ, the two alternatives mentioned are: (1) If the man who thinks both is right, what is meant by saying that such is the nature of things? (2) If he is not right, but the man who thinks definitely that A is B or that A is not B is more right, a determinate nature is already assigned to things.

This can hardly be the meaning. The second alternative is just that which Aristotle's opponents would not admit, so that no statement of the consequences of it has any force as against them. One may feel sure at any rate that ἤ in l. 5 is needed. On the other hand EJ are probably right in not reading μή in l. 3. Without μή the sentence may be interpreted in either of two ways. 'What is meant by saying that the nature of things is such?' I. e. (1) what intelligible account can be given of a state of things in which, whatever A and B are, the only truth is 'A is both B and not B'? Or, (2) they have no right to say that the nature of things is such as they describe it, for it will be true only to say that it both is and is not such.

15. I have restored the reading of A[b] and Alexander, βαδίζειν δεῖν. The point is, as the corresponding instance of the precipice shows, not that a man cannot think both that he is walking to Megara and that he is not, but that he cannot think both that he ought to walk to Megara and that he ought not.

ἔωθεν is bracketed by Christ as due to dittography of εὐθέως, but may be defended by reference to νύκτωρ 1010[b] 10. In both cases Aristotle seems to be thinking of people who may dream something foolish but do not act on it when they wake up.

19–27. The admission of objective truth in judgements of value, Aristotle contends, involves the admission of objective truth in judgements of fact. There is no sense in saying that 'it would be a good thing to see a man' is objectively true, if everything that is a man can with equal truth be said not to be a man. Judgements of value are meaningless apart from judgements of fact.

Further, people's actions show that they ascribe objective truth to judgements of value, and therefore also to judgements of fact.

27. ἀλλὰ περὶ τὸ ἄμεινον καὶ χεῖρον, a reminiscence of *Theaet.* 171 E— 172 B.

Refutation of the arguments for the denial of the law of contradiction, and for asserting that all appearances are true (ch. 5).

1009ᵃ 6. The denial of the law of contradiction stands or falls with the theory of Protagoras. (1) If everything that is thought is true, every statement must be both true and false, for many people make contrary judgements and each believes the other to be wrong. And (2) if everything both is and is not, all opinions must be true, for the opinions people hold are opposite to one another.

16. Those who are led to this view by real difficulties can easily be cured, because it is their way of thinking and not their arguments that we must meet; those who argue for the sake of argument can only be cured by refuting their very words.

22. (1) For the former, the view that contradictories are alike true arises from observation of the fact that in the sensible world contraries come from the same thing. If that which is not cannot come to be, the thing must have previously had both the contrary qualities—cf. the 'everything in everything' of Anaxagoras and Democritus.

30. We shall reply that (a) they are in a sense right, but also in a sense wrong because they forget that being has two senses. The same thing is potentially, but not actually, possessed of contrary qualities. (*b*) We shall ask them to admit another kind of substance, which is unchangeable.

38. (2) The belief that all appearances are true comes also, to some people, from observation of the sensible world. (*a*) Truth, they think, should not be tested by merely counting heads, and people have contrary opinions, so that if the majority were ill or mad, the healthy or sane minority would (if counting heads were decisive) be judged to be ill or mad.

^{b} **7.** (*b*) Again, the sensations of other animals conflict with ours, and a man's own sensations vary with time, and there is no reason for calling one truer than another. Cf. Democritus.

12. (*c*) They identify thought with sensation, and sensation with physical impression. This view is found in Empedocles, Democritus, Parmenides, Anaxagoras, and even (it is said) in Homer. If the great masters are so sceptical about truth, the beginner may well despair.

1010^a 1. The ground of this opinion is the identification of reality with the sensible world, in which there is much of the indeterminate. These thinkers reflected that the sensible world is always changing, and that about the changing nothing true can be said. Hence the extreme view of the Heracliteans like Cratylus, who would not commit himself to saying anything at all, and held that so far from entering the same river twice, one cannot enter it even once.

15. We answer : (*a*) It is not so certain that the changing, when it is changing, is not. That which is losing an attribute still has something of what it loses ; of that which is coming to be, something must already be. If something is perishing, there must *be* something which perishes, and if something is coming to be, there must *be* something out of which, and something by whose agency, it comes to be.

22. (*b*) Qualitative change is different from quantitative. Quantity may be always changing, but it is in respect of their quality that we know things.

25. (*c*) It is only a small part—the part that immediately surrounds us—even of the sensible world that exhibits constant change ; it would be more reasonable to deny change of the universe because the greater part is unchanging.

32. (*d*) We must try to convince these thinkers too that there is an unchanging reality. After all, those who deny the law of contradiction imply that all things are at rest rather than in motion, for if all things have already all attributes there is nothing for them to change to.

Further arguments against the Protagorean view.

^b **1.** (*a*) Even if the senses cannot be deceived about their special objects, imagination is not the same thing as sensation.

3. (*b*) Surely people cannot really feel doubtful whether things are such as they appear at a distance or near at hand, to the sick or to the healthy, the weak or the strong, the sleeping or the waking. For (i) people do not as a matter of fact put their dreaming fancies into action.

11. (ii) Regarding the future, as Plato says, the opinion of the man who knows and that of the layman are not equally valid.

14. (iii) The opinion with which a sense furnishes us about its own object is more valid than that which it suggests regarding the object of another (even a kindred) sense. No sense contradicts itself at the same moment about the same object, nor at different moments with regard to the actual sensation, but only with regard to the object. A wine may taste sweet at one time and not at another, if it or the taster has changed, but sweetness is always the same definite character, which everything that is to be sweet must *necessarily* possess. But these theories destroy necessity as they destroy substance.

30. (*c*) In general, if only the perceptible exists, there would be nothing if there were not living beings; for there would be no sensation. But there must be, independent of sensation, substrata which cause the sensation; for sensation is not its own object, and there must be something prior to sensation, for the mover is prior to the moved. The fact that sentient being and *sensum* are correlative makes no difference to the argument.

1009ª 7. εἴτε is answered by καὶ εἰ l. 12.

18. βίας. This means intellectual, not physical compulsion. Cf. 1011ª 15 and *Top.* 105ª 16 ἔστι δ᾽ ἡ μὲν ἐπαγωγὴ πιθανώτερον . . . ὁ δὲ συλλογισμὸς βιαστικώτερον καὶ πρὸς τοὺς ἀντιλογικοὺς ἐνεργέστερον.

20–22. Cf. 1005ᵇ 2–5 n.

21. The sense demands that ἴασις shall go with τούτων and ἔλεγχος with τοῦ ἐν τῇ φωνῇ λόγου, and Alexander (303. 14) takes the words so.

21–22. τοῦ ἐν τῇ φωνῇ λόγου and τοῦ ἐν τοῖς ὀνόμασιν are alternative ways of speaking of the same thing; τ᾽ therefore is to be omitted, with Aᵇ and apparently Alexander (303. 12).

34. οὐ κατὰ ταὐτὸ ὄν would have to mean 'not according to the same sense of "being"'. But it is doubtful Greek for this. Alexander seems to have read κατὰ ταὐτό· ὂν δυνάμει κτλ. (304. 20–22), but it is better to treat ὄν as an emblema.

37. ἄλλην τινὰ οὐσίαν κτλ. 'Another substance is contained among existing things.'

ᵇ 1. ἡ περὶ τὰ φαινόμενα ἀλήθεια, 'the "truth in appearances" doctrine'.

11-33. Bonitz argues that Aristotle attaches too much importance to isolated phrases of the early thinkers. Certainly neither Empedocles nor Democritus nor Parmenides nor Anaxagoras can fairly be charged with consistent sensationalism. Empedocles' denial of the reality of generation and destruction ; Democritus' denial of the reality of the secondary qualities ; Parmenides' antithesis between the way of truth and the way of opinion (it is from the latter that the passage quoted from him comes) are sufficient evidence of a rationalistic strain in them ; and as for Anaxagoras, all that Aristotle cites against him is a traditional *obiter dictum*, itself capable of a harmless enough interpretation. They did not deliberately identify thought with sensation, but in their time the two things had not been clearly distinguished, so that it was impossible for them to be definitely either rationalists or sensationalists.

18. τὴν ἕξιν, clearly 'their bodily state', and παρεόν, 'the object present to sense' (so Al. 263. 7, Phil. in *De An.* 485. 24) ; only thus can the identification of φρόνησις with ἀλλοίωσις be established. But Empedocles failed to distinguish, rather than expressly identified them. Diels's translation of πρὸς παρεόν, 'nach dem jeweiligen körperlichen Verhältnis' (Emp. fr. 106), is less likely to be right.

20-21. ὅσσον . . . παρίστατο = fr. 108.

22-25. Theophr. *De Sensu* 3 quotes this fragment(fr. 16) in the form

ὡς γὰρ ἑκάστοτ' ἔχειν κρᾶσιν μελέων πολυπλάγκτων,
τὼς νόος ἀνθρώποισι παρέστηκεν.

Aristotle is probably as usual quoting from memory, but his παρίστᾱται (for which Diels compares ἔρᾱσαι Theocr. 1. 78, ἔρᾱται ib. 2. 149, Sappho fr. 13) is more likely to be the original form than the easier παρέστηκεν. I have restored ἑκάστοτ', the best attested reading (EJ Theophr.).

25. τὸ γὰρ πλέον ἐστὶ νόημα. πλέον in the other passage of Parmenides in which we find it (fr. 9. 3 Diels) means 'full', but the first line of the present fragment suggests that Theophrastus' interpretation of τὸ πλέον as τὸ ὑπερβάλλον is right (cf. Asc.). Thought varies according as the hot or the cold in one's body predominates ; it is better and purer when the hot predominates.

25-28. Anaxagoras was not a subjectivist; he believed in the objective validity of science, and can have meant by this remark little more than that we can find good or evil in the world according to the presumptions with which we approach it.

28. Aristotle does not commit himself to this interpretation of Homer, and in A. 983ᵇ 33 he declines to rationalize Oceanus, Tethys, and Styx into a philosophy.

30. κεῖσθαι ἀλλοφρονέοντα. The phrase, quoted again in *De An.* 404ª 30, is not to be found in the text of Homer, and *Il.* xxiii. 698 κὰδ δ' ἀλλοφρονέοντα μετὰ σφίσιν εἷσαν ἄγοντες does not refer to Hector. For similar instances of loose quotation from Homer cf. *Ind. Ar.*

507. 52. In *De An.* 404ᵃ 29 Democritus is said to have quoted the phrase, and he may have had it in his text of Homer.

31-33. These lines bring out most clearly the fact that Aristotle is taking φρόνησις as meaning knowledge, not merely thought.

38. τὰ πετόμενα διώκειν is a proverbial phrase, cf. Leutsch and Schneidewin, *Paroemiographi Graeci*, ii. 677.

1010ᵃ 6. Ἐπίχαρμος, fr. 252 Kaibel. Timaeus *ap.* Clem. *Strom.* 1. 14. 64. 2 says that Xenophanes was contemporary with Epicharmus (*fl. c.* 486), but another account makes him considerably older (born *c.* 618). We cannot be sure of his date, but the most probable view is that he was born about 565 (Burnet § 55). In *Theaet.* 152 E Epicharmus appears in opposition to the Eleatics, as maintaining the eternal becoming and perishing of all things. Diogenes Laertius (iii. 12) has preserved several verses of his in the Heraclitean vein. Schwegler suggests that Epicharmus may have said of Xenophanes οὔτ᾽ εἰκότως λέγει οὔτ᾽ ἀληθῆ, while Zeller and Gomperz think he said the views of Xenophanes were true but paradoxical. Gomperz suggests the line

εἰκότως μὲν οὐκ ἔφα τόδ᾽ ἀλλ᾽ ἀλαθέως ἔφα.

12. Cratylus is especially important in view of the fact that according to Aristotle (A. 987ᵃ 32) his was the earliest philosophical influence under which Plato came.

15-35. Bz. rightly points out that in these arguments Aristotle only succeeds in showing that there are unchanging elements in the universe, not that there is no change (which he would not have wished to show) nor that change is reconcilable with the law of contradiction. But most certainly the reconciliation is not to be achieved, as Bz. suggests, by making the law of contradiction apply not to things but only to notions. Rather it is to be met by emphasizing the ἅμα in the law of contradiction; once this is done, no fact of change can impair its validity.

16. Christ's instinct was not at fault in suspecting the phrase ἔχει τινὰ ἀληθῆ λόγον, which is unexampled in Aristotle. ἀληθῆ does not occur in Aʰ and does not seem to have been read by Asclepius; it is doubtless a gloss.

22. Bekker is probably right in reading ἰέναι εἰς ἄπειρον. εἶναι ἐπ᾽ ἄπειρον occurs in most manuscripts in α. 994ᵃ 3, and εἰς ἄπειρον οὔσης in *Pol.* 1258ᵃ 1. But in the former Aʰ reads ἰέναι, and in the latter ἰούσης is an easy emendation. Λ. 1074ᵃ 29, *Pol.* 1257ᵇ 25, 26, 27 are not very good parallels to the manuscript reading in the present passage.

23. The change of quality here contrasted with change of quantity is not alteration but generation and destruction. This is change κατὰ τὸ εἶδος or κατὰ τὴν οὐσίαν, and one sense of τὸ ποιόν is ἡ τῆς οὐσίας διαφορά (Δ. 1020ᵇ 14, cf. *Cat.* 3ᵇ 20, *Soph. El.* 178ᵇ 37).

33. πάλαι, 1009ᵃ 36.

ᵇ 2-3. With the manuscript reading we must interpret ' first they say

that not even sensation is false if it be of an object peculiar to one sense;
but imagination is not the same as sensation'. ' Not even' here is
pointless, and it is difficult to supply ' they say'. Alexander (as Bz.
pointed out) and Asclepius seem to have read οὐδ' εἰ ἡ αἴσθησις μὴ
ψευδής, and this is probably right. ἀλλά *in apodosi* after a conditional
clause is common in Aristotle (cf. *Ind. Ar.* 33ᵃ 42), but is irregular
enough, especially in the double negative form οὐδ' . . . ἀλλ' οὐ, to
account for the corruption.

2. τοῦ γε ἰδίου itself contains a criticism of the sensationalist view.
' Our first point is that not even if perception is true—not perception in general, as *they* say, but perception of an object peculiar to
one sense', &c. For the most part Aristotle holds that perception of
the ἴδια αἰσθητά is infallible (*De An.* 418ᵃ 12, 427ᵇ 12, 430ᵇ 29, *De
Sensu* 442ᵇ 8), but in *De An.* 428ᵇ 18 he says ' it is true or has as little
falsity as possible'.

3. ἡ φαντασία οὐ ταὐτὸν τῇ αἰσθήσει. In *Theaet.* 152 c Plato says
φαντασία ἄρα καὶ αἴσθησις ταὐτόν, but Aristotle has assigned a special
meaning to φαντασία. He uses it often in the general sense, corresponding exactly to φαίνεσθαι, and meaning ' appearance to sense or thought'.
But it also means the action of the mind which we call imagination,
and is then defined as κίνησις ἀπὸ τῆς αἰσθήσεως τῆς κατ' ἐνέργειαν
γιγνομένη (*De An.* 429ᵃ 1) or αἴσθησίς τις ἀσθενής (*Rhet.* 1370ᵃ 28).

3-9. There is no real difficulty, Aristotle thinks, in distinguishing
the normal from the abnormal. So in the *Ethics* he defines virtue by
reference to the φρόνιμος and thinks that it is easy to recognize the
φρόνιμος. Cf. his answer to the question why men like to be in the
society of the beautiful : τυφλοῦ τὸ ἐρώτημα (Diog. Laert. v. 1. 20).

8. πότερον ἃ τοῖς καθεύδουσιν κτλ. The objection is borrowed from
Theaet. 157 E sq.

12. ὥσπερ καὶ Πλάτων λέγει, *Theaet.* 171 E, 178 c sq.

15. ἡ τοῦ ἀλλοτρίου καὶ ἰδίου, i. e. the perception κατὰ συμβεβηκός
by one sense of the object of another sense, as of the sweetness of an
orange by sight, is not equally valid with the perception of the object
proper to the sense in question. For the doctrine of perception κατὰ
συμβεβηκός (which is really not perception but inference) cf. *De An.*
418ᵃ 20.

16. τοῦ πλησίον καὶ τοῦ αὐτῆς. Alexander interprets ' nor, of the
objects of the sense itself, is the perception of the near no more valid
(than that of the distant)'. But the supplying of ἡ τοῦ πόρρω is
difficult, and, further, the reference to the distance of the object has
already been made in l. 5 and would be a mere repetition here. The
first difficulty, but not the second, is met by Bz.'s conjecture of ἄποθεν
for αὐτῆς, which is to some extent confirmed by Asc. 282. 3.
Probably Bullinger and Goebel are right in supposing Aristotle to mean
that a sense perceives its own object more accurately than it perceives
κατὰ συμβεβηκός the object of a *cognate* sense. Taste and smell are
cognate senses (*De Sensu* 440ᵇ 29 σχεδὸν γάρ ἐστι τὸ αὐτὸ πάθος, cf.
443ᵇ 7, *De An.* 421ᵃ 16, 26). This distinction is more akin to that

mentioned in the first part of the sentence than that between a near and a distant object.

19-30. Bz. thinks that Aristotle here comes round to the true form of the law of contradiction, in which it refers to the eternal identity of the notion, not to the impossibility of contradiction in a thing at a given time. The distinction, however, which Aristotle draws is not that between thing and notion but that between the combination of subject and attribute and the bare attribute. A subject which now has one attribute may later have another, but the attribute remains always self-identical and never becomes its opposite.

32. μήτε τὰ αἰσθητὰ ... αἰσθήματα, 'neither the sensible qualities nor the sensations'. Alexander's interpretation seems in one place (315. 35) to presuppose the reading μηδὲ τὰ αἰσθήματα, which Christ adopts. But elsewhere (316. 20) he implies a reference to both αἰσθητά and αἰσθήματα, though perhaps in the reverse order to that in EJ. A^b's reading μηδὲ τὰ αἰσθητὰ εἶναι is to be explained by homoioteleuton. A reference merely to αἰσθήματα would be rather pointless; the interesting thing is the statement that if the senses disappeared the sensible qualities would disappear. This is in accordance with Aristotle's usual doctrine : ἡ τοῦ αἰσθητοῦ ἐνέργεια καὶ τῆς αἰσθήσεως ἡ αὐτὴ μέν ἐστι καὶ μία, τὸ δ' εἶναι οὐ ταὐτὸν αὐταῖς, *De An.* 425^{b}25. Apart from the αἰσθητικόν, the αἰσθητόν has a merely potential existence. Cf. the whole passage 425^{b}25—426^{b}8. On the other hand in the *Categories* (7^{b}36—8^{a}12) he argues that the αἰσθητόν is prior to the αἴσθησις and not destroyed by its destruction ; but there τὸ αἰσθητόν seems to mean the sensible body, what Aristotle here calls τὸ ὑποκείμενον. It is true that he there describes θερμόν, γλυκύ, πικρόν as persisting as well as body when αἴσθησις is destroyed, but this may be reconciled with his other statements if we take it to mean that when sensation ceases something persists which is capable of being perceived, when there is sensation again, as hot, sweet, or bitter.

1011^a 1. κἂν εἰ λέγεται κτλ. In *Cat.* 7^{b}15—8^{a}12 it is argued that though most terms which are πρὸς ἄλληλα are ἅμα τῇ φύσει so that neither exists in the absence of the other, the relation of the knowable to knowledge and of the perceptible to perception is an exception. In Δ. 15 one of the three kinds of πρός τι, that of which the measurable, the knowable, the perceptible are instances, is said to be πρός τι because something else is relative to it ; i. e. it is implied that these terms are logically prior to their correlatives.

Refutation of Protagoras continued (ch. 6).

1011^a 3. Some of our opponents, whether genuinely convinced or arguing for argument's sake, ask who is to decide which is the healthy man, and generally who is to judge. This is like asking whether we are asleep or waking. All such questions imply the demand for a proof of everything; our opponents forget that the starting-point of demonstration is not demonstration. Our genuine opponents can easily be persuaded of this.

15. Those who demand to be refuted by a 'knock-down' argument ask for what is impossible, since they claim the privilege of self-contradiction—a claim, it is true, which contradicts itself. But we can argue as follows: (*a*) Unless all things are relative, it is not the case that all that seems is true; for what seems always seems to some one. Those, therefore, who are willing to subject their view to discussion must say, not that that which seems is, but that it is for him to whom it seems, when it seems, to the sense to which and under the conditions under which it seems. Otherwise they will contradict themselves, for the same thing may seem honey to the sight but not to the taste.

28. For to those who maintain the theory in its unqualified form, because the same things appear different to different people, at different times, or to different senses, we may answer that things do not appear with contradictory attributes to the same sense, in the same respect, manner, and time. With these qualifications, my sensation is true. Or perhaps our eristic opponents will answer ' only true for you '. They must, in fact, make everything relative, so that nothing has come into being or will be unless some one has first thought it. If anything has come into being, or will be, without any one's having thought so, all things are not relative to opinion.

^b **7.** (*b*) If a thing is one, it is one in relation to one thing or to a definite number of things; if the same thing is half and equal, at all events its equality is not relative to that which is double of it. (i) If, then, in relation to a thinker, man is that which is thought, the thinker cannot be a man. (ii) If everything is in relation to a thinker, the thinker will be in relation to an infinite number of specifically different things.

13. We have shown, then, that the law of contradiction is the most indubitable of all laws, what absurdities follow from its denial, and on what grounds the denial rests. Now since contradictories cannot be truly predicated of the same subject, the same thing cannot have contrary attributes. For of two contraries one is a privation of substance, i. e. the denial of a predicate to a definite subject class. If a subject has contrary attributes, then, it has them in different respects, or one in a particular respect and another without qualification.

1011^a **3.** ταῦτα. What Aristotle has been discussing immediately before is the doctrine that whatever appears is true, and it is this,

rather than the denial of the law of contradiction, that ταῦτα refers to.
It is this that he endeavours to refute in l. 17 sqq. He divides the
supporters of this view into 'those who are convinced' and 'those
who maintain it for the sake of argument'. Yet he says (l. 10) that
they are evidently *not* convinced. He must mean that, though convinced by the considerations adduced in 1009^b 2–11 that everything
that appears is true, they are not convinced, to the extent of expressing
their conviction in practice, that there is any real difficulty in distinguishing health from disease or waking from sleeping.

What Aristotle says in ll. 6–13 is said as though it applied to both
types of believers·in πᾶν τὸ φαινόμενον ἀληθές. Yet he continues
(l. 13), 'these can easily be persuaded, but those who are satisfied
only with compulsion in argument are asking what is impossible'.
The latter are clearly οἱ τοὺς λόγους τούτους μόνον λέγοντες, and οὗτοι
(l. 13) must be οἱ πεπεισμένοι (l. 3). οὗτοι then implies that in ll. 6–13
it is the honest believers that he has had in view. If you point out to
them that their actions are inconsistent with their theory (l. 11)
and that a study of logic would have shown them that demonstration
must not be expected everywhere (ll. 11–13, cf. 1005^b 3), they
will give up their view. But those who argue merely for the sake
of argument are harder to deal with. Arguments from practice will
not appeal to them, and it is no use pointing out that their views are
inconsistent, since they hold that contradictories can both be true
(ll. 15, 16). Nevertheless, in the hope of finding them accessible to
argument somewhere, Aristotle proceeds in l. 17 to point out weak-
nesses in their view.

Christ (*Studia* 65) proposed to meet the difficulty about οὗτοι by
reading οὗτοι . . . λέγοντες l. 16 before εἰσὶ δέ τινες l. 3. But the
accepted order can be interpreted as above, though no doubt the
passage is a confused one.

6. τῷ ἀπορεῖν κτλ. The question here dismissed by Aristotle is
mentioned by Plato (*Theaet.* 158 B) and plays an important part in
Descartes (*Med.* i. 1).

7–13. Cf. 1005^b 2–5 n.

13. ἀποδείξεως γὰρ ἀρχὴ οὐκ ἀπόδειξίς ἐστιν, cf. *Post An.* i. 3.

15. τὴν βίαν, cf. 1009^a 18.

16. ἐναντία γάρ κτλ. (1) Alexander interprets: 'They demand
to be made to contradict themselves, when the very substance of their
theory is self-contradiction.' But this interpretation of ἐναντία . . . εἰπεῖν ἀξιοῦσιν is difficult to accept. (2) Bullinger interprets: 'They
claim the right to make contrary statements, while their very demand
that they shall be refuted logically (l. 15) implies the contrary of this',
since logical proof implies the law of contradiction. But since the
first ἐναντία means '*mutually* contrary statements', the second ἐναντία
must also mean this, or the epigram is spoilt. (3) The most natural
meaning of the words in themselves is perhaps, 'their claim to the
privilege of self-contradiction is in itself a self-contradictory claim',—
as Aristotle points out, e. g., in 1012^b 15–17. This does not connect

so readily as Alexander's interpretation with the preceding words, οἱ δ' ἐν τῷ λόγῳ τὴν βίαν μόνον ζητοῦντες ἀδύνατον ζητοῦσιν, but the connexion intended *may* be that since the claim of these thinkers is a nakedly self-contradictory one, they are not likely to be convinced by any refutation, which could only amount to pointing out contradictions in their view. It is, however, not so much because their claim is self-contradictory, but because it is a claim to the privilege of self-contradiction, that no refutation they can meet with will satisfy them (ἀδύνατον ζητοῦσιν). It is better therefore (4) to take ἐναντία γὰρ εἰπεῖν ἀξιοῦσιν as giving the reason for the previous words, and εὐθὺς ἐναντία λέγοντες as a supplementary criticism, akin to that expressed in 1012ᵇ 15–17. 'For they claim the privilege of self-contradiction—a claim, it is true, which from the outset contradicts itself.' This seems on the whole the best interpretation. (5) It has been suggested that the words mean 'for the instant they contradict themselves, they claim that they have a right to do so'. For this construction we might compare *Meteor.* 371ᵃ 6 σβέννυσιν εὐθὺς γιγνομένην. But most readers will probably feel that Aristotle would have expressed this meaning otherwise. (6) Richards's ⟨οὐκ⟩ ἀξιοῦσιν, 'they demand that we shall not contradict ourselves, when *they* contradict themselves from the outset' gives no satisfactory connexion with the previous clause.

24. ᾗ, 'to the sense to which it appears'. This is inserted to meet the difficulty that what appears of a certain quality to one sense may *per accidens* appear of a contrary quality to another (so Al. 319. 37—320. 7, cf. 1010ᵇ 14–19 and τῇ αὐτῇ γε αἰσθήσει 1011ᵃ 34).

ὥς. Alexander (320. 7–14) explains this as meaning 'for that organ to which it appears', and supposes it is inserted to meet the fact that if one eye is healthy and the other diseased, a thing may look both white and not white. This seems to be what is conveyed by τῇ αὐτῇ γε καὶ κατὰ τὸ αὐτὸ αἰσθήσει in l. 34; ὥς answers rather to ὡσαύτως in l. 35. Bz. is therefore probably right in supposing that the reference is to differences such as those of distance (cf. 1010ᵇ 5, 6). 'What appears *x* is *x* at the distance at which, and generally under the conditions under which, it appears *x*.'

The effect of the sentence is that if the people who believe that appearances are true wish their view to bear discussion (ὑπέχειν λόγον) they must qualify the statement in such a way as to avoid asserting the absolute existence of anything. The necessary qualifications of their view will deprive it of half its meaning, since they will restrict the authority of sense to the precise circumstances in which the sensation occurs. But instead of pointing this out Aristotle goes on to say (l. 24) that if they do not qualify their statement, they will break the law of contradiction—which of course to them is no objection at all.

28–31. πρός γε τοὺς ... ἀληθῆ. Aristotle meant to continue with something like ῥᾳδία ἡ ἀπάντησις (Al. 321. 1), 'we can easily reply', but instead the actual reply is given in l. 34 ἀλλ' οὔ τι τῇ αὐτῇ, &c. Jaeger points out that Alexander (321. 3) treats καὶ διὰ τοῦτο πάνθ'

ὁμοίως εἶναι ψευδῆ καὶ ἀληθῆ not as part of the statement of the Protagorean theory (as our interpretation takes it to be) but as the beginning of Aristotle's reply, the statement of an absurd consequence
following from the theory. He therefore supposes some such words
as ἐροῦμεν ὅτι συμβαίνει αὐτοῖς τὸ πᾶσι φαινόμενον ἀληθὲς εἶναι to have
dropped out by homoioteleuton after ἀληθὲς εἶναι (l. 30), and takes
οὔτε . . . οὔτε . . . ἀλλ᾽ οὔ τι . . . (ll. 31–34) to form a continuous statement of the situation with regard to contradictions of the senses. But
the inserted words are somewhat pointless when the Protagoreans have
just been described as τὸ φαινόμενον φάσκοντας ἀληθὲς εἶναι. Further,
while οὔτε γὰρ . . . ἕν refers to the contradictions of the senses which
prima facie lend colour to Protagoras' theory, in ἀλλ᾽ οὔ τι . . . χρόνῳ
Aristotle takes his stand on the fact which enables him to refute the
theory. For these reasons I prefer Bonitz's interpretation. But
οὔτε γὰρ . . . ἕν should not be put within brackets, as it is by Bonitz,
since τἀναντία φαίνεται has to be understood with τῇ αὐτῇ . . . αἰσθήσει.

29. τὰς πάλαι εἰρημένας αἰτίας, cf. 1009ᵃ 38—1010ᵃ 15. These
reasons are briefly summarized in 1011ᵃ 31–34.

33. ἡ μὲν γὰρ ἀφή κτλ. The famous experiment of holding an
object between two crossed fingers is referred to again in *De Insomn.*
460ᵇ 20, *Probl.* 958ᵇ 14, 959ᵃ 15, 965ᵃ 36. The reason for the
illusion given in 965ᵃ 37, διότι δυσὶν αἰσθητηρίοις ἁπτόμεθα, is insufficient. If that were the whole explanation we should feel the
object as two when we hold it between two fingers in their ordinary
position. The reason rather is that we are perceiving one object with
two organs which are not used to being in contact with a single
object.

34. For ἀλλ᾽ οὔ τι . . . γε, the reading of all the best manuscripts, cf.
Phys. 258ᵇ 22, *Pol.* 1282ᵃ 11, *Cat.* 6ᵃ 2, *De Caelo* 271ᵃ 18, *De Sensu*
439ᵃ 32. Bz.'s conjecture οὔ τοι is apparently not supported, as he
thinks, by Al. 322. 2.

ᵇ1. τοῦτ᾽ ἂν εἴη ἀληθές κτλ., i. e. τὸ φαινόμενον ἂν εἴη ἀληθὲς ᾧ φαίνεται καὶ ὅτε φαίνεται καὶ ᾗ καὶ ὥς (ᵃ 23). But if this is so, these
thinkers must always state this qualification (ᵇ 1–3); they must make
everything relative to opinion and sensation (ᵇ 4, 5), which is absurd
in view of the fact that things often happen without being thought of
beforehand (ᵇ 5–7).

7. ἔτι εἰ ἕν κτλ. 'Further, if a thing is one, it is relative to one
thing or to some determinate number of things; and if the same thing
is both half and equal, still the equal as such is not relative to the
double to which the half as such is relative.' From this two conclusions follow : (1) 'If, in relation to the thinking subject, man and
the object of thought be the same, man will not be the thinking subject
but the object of thought.' This argument may be put thus : If
man is man simply because he is thought to be so, his being is
comprised in a relation to a thinking subject. In this relation he can
only be that which is relative to thinking subject, viz., object of
thought ; and since the relation is his whole being he cannot also be

a thinking subject. I. e. if the *esse* of man be *percipi*, he cannot *percipere*. Which is absurd.

(2) The second argument may be put thus : ' If everything is relative to the thinking subject, the thinking subject is relative to an infinite number of specifically different things', and therefore, since each relative term has a correlative different from that of any other relative term (ll. 7–9), the thinking subject will have to include in it an infinite number of specifically different aspects, so that definition of it will be impossible. Which is absurd.

The balance of authority is in favour of πρὸς ἄπειρα in l. 12, but evidently ἄπειρα would give a good sense.

13–15. The summary here given covers the contents of 1005ᵇ 8— 1011ᵇ 12. ὅτι ... φάσεις, cf. 3. 1005ᵇ 8–34 ; τί συμβαίνει τοῖς οὕτω λέγουσι, cf. ch. 4 ; διὰ τί οὕτω λέγουσι, cf. chs. 5, 6.

18. οὐχ ἧττον, ' no less than it is a contrary '. For the doctrine cf. I. 1055ᵇ 11–29. Contrariety is στέρησις τελεία (1055ᵃ 34) or πρώτη (Θ. 1046ᵇ 14).

19. οὐσίας δὲ στέρησις, ' and privation of the positive, substantial nature '—more commonly in this connexion called εἶδος.

Law of excluded middle proved (ch. 7).

1011ᵇ 23. (1) We start by defining truth and falsehood. Falsehood is saying of that which is that it is not, or of that which is not that it is ; truth is saying of that which is that it is, or of that which is not that it is not. Therefore he who says that a thing is or is not says what is either true or false ; but if the subject is a middle term between contradictories, neither that which is nor that which is not is being said to be or not to be.

29. (2) The middle term will be either a real intermediate (as grey is between black and white) or a neutral (as that which is neither man nor horse is intermediate between them). In the latter case it cannot change, for change is from not-A to A or from A to not-A ; but the intermediates that really exist are constantly being observed to change. In the former case there would be change to white which was not from not-white—but it is never observed.

1012ᵃ 2. (3) The law may be proved from the principle that thought must either affirm or deny whenever it is true or false, which follows from the definition of true and false judgement (the former means affirming or denying in one way, the latter affirming or denying in another).

5. (4) There must be a middle between *every* two contradictories, if the theory is genuinely maintained ; so that (on the logical side) a man can say what is neither true nor untrue, and (on the metaphysical) there will be a middle between being and not-being, and therefore a sort of change other than generation and decay.

9. (5) In classes in which the denial of one term implies the assertion of its contrary there must still be a middle (e. g. a number which is neither odd nor not odd) ; but the absurdity of this is seen from the definition of such contraries.

12. (6) The denial of the law multiplies indefinitely the number of reals. If besides A and not-A there is B which is neither, there will be also C which is neither B nor not-B, D which is neither C nor not-C, and so on.

15. (7) A negation indicates merely the absence of a positive quality, so that there is no room for a middle between negation and affirmation.

17. Some thinkers have been led to this, as to other paradoxical beliefs, by the failure to cope with eristic arguments ; others by the demand for a proof of everything. In answering all alike we take our stand on definition, which is implied in all significant speech.

24. While the saying of Heraclitus, that all things are and are not, seems to make all statements true, the view of Anaxagoras, that there is a middle between contradictories (for his ' mixture ' can be called neither good nor not good), seems to make all statements false.

1011ᵇ **28.** The reading of Al.ᶜ and Bz., καὶ ὁ λέγων τοῦτο (sc. τὸ μεταξὺ ἀντιφάσεως), gives a less good sense than that of EJΓ Asc.ᶜ, καὶ ὁ λέγων. Aristotle has laid it down (ll. 26, 27) that to say of τὸ ὄν that it is not or of τὸ μὴ ὄν that it is is false, and that to say of τὸ ὄν that it is or of τὸ μὴ ὄν that it is not is true. It does not follow from this that to say of τὸ μεταξὺ ἀντιφάσεως that it is or that it is not is either true or false, since τὸ μεταξὺ ἀντιφάσεως is just neither ὄν nor μὴ ὄν. Rather it follows that to say of *anything* (which is the sense we get if we omit τοῦτο) that it is or that it is not is either true or false. But (28, 29) our opponent, in saying that τὸ μεταξὺ ἀντιφάσεως is, is not saying either of τὸ ὄν or of τὸ μὴ ὄν that it is or that it is not, and therefore his statement is neither true nor false ; which is absurd. Therefore τὸ μεταξὺ ἀντι-φάσεως is not anything. It is to be noted (1) that Aristotle does not assume merely that to say of what is that it is not or of what is not that it is is false, and that to say of what is that it is or of what is not that it is not is true, but that these are the definitions of falsity and truth, i. e. are convertible propositions. It is only on this assumption that it follows that the opponent, who maintains the existence of what neither is nor is not, is saying what is neither true nor false. (2) That the opponent is assumed to admit (*a*) the correctness of the definition of truth and falsity, and (*b*) that every judgement must be either true or

false. Thus Aristotle is inferring the metaphysical form of the law of
excluded middle—that there is no objective intermediate between
contradictories—from the logical form. The argument thus has value
only *ad hominem*. But of this Aristotle is well aware; he knows that
first principles cannot be demonstrated.

29. ἔτι ἤτοι κτλ. The μεταξύ may be thought of either as a genuine
intermediate, coming somewhere between the contradictories, or as
between them merely in the sense of being neither of them. On the
latter supposition, it cannot change (for change is from not-good to
good or from good to not-good, but the μεταξύ is neither good nor
not-good); but wherever there is a μεταξύ, we can observe it changing
into the extremes between which it lies (for change is just from
extreme to extreme, from extreme to intermediate, or from intermediate to extreme). Therefore there is no such thing as a μεταξύ
of contradictories in the sense of a mere neutral between them. But
secondly, if the μεταξύ is a genuine intermediate, since there can
be change from intermediate to extreme there can be change from
what is not not-white to white; but this is evidently not the case.—The
argument is again necessarily circular.

35. Aᵇ reads ἢ ἡ ἀντίφασις, EJΓ (and perhaps Asc.) εἴη ἄν τις.
Bz. thinks that Alexander read ἡ ἀντίφασις, εἴη ἄν τις, and that this is
probably the true reading. But Alexander seems to have read καὶ
οὕτως ἡ ἀντίφασις, εἰς λευκὸν οὐκ ἐκ μὴ λευκοῦ ἡ γένεσις (329. 36—330.
4). καὶ οὕτως ἡ ἀντίφασις would be difficult to interpret strictly, and
probably εἴη ἄν τις is the true reading. Bz.'s argument that καὶ οὕτως
εἴη ἄν τις κτλ. would imply that the same conclusion had been shown
to follow from the previous supposition is not conclusive. On either
supposition, change from the μεταξύ would imply change from what
is not not-white to white, and this is enough identity to justify καὶ
οὕτως.

1012ᵃ 1. νῦν δ' οὐχ ὁρᾶται. There is of course transition to white
from grey, which is not *simpliciter* not-white. But the transition is
from grey *qua* not-white; it is the specks of black in the grey that
change to white.

2. διάνοια and νοῦς are sometimes used indifferently, e. g. *De An.*
433ᵃ 2, cf. 429ᵃ 23; sometimes they appear as species of one genus,
e. g. *De An.* 414ᵇ 18, *An. Post.* 89ᵇ 7; sometimes νοῦς appears as one
of the ἕξεις of διάνοια, e. g. *An. Post.* 100ᵇ 6. In the first sense either
term is used for the whole intellectual faculty, in the second διάνοια
is specialized so as to denote discursive, and νοῦς so as to denote
intuitive thought (for the distinction cf. Θ. 10). It is probably in this
sense that Aristotle here uses the words διανοητόν and νοητόν.

3. The editions print τοῦτο δ' ἐξ ὁρισμοῦ δῆλον ὅταν ἀληθεύῃ ἢ ψεύδηται.
But the construction of ὅταν κτλ. as dependent on ὁρισμοῦ is difficult
and (I think) unexampled in Aristotle. It is better to treat τοῦτο . . .
δῆλον as parenthetical. Alexander seems to have taken it so (330.
20–23). The argument then is: 'Thought always either affirms or
denies, whenever it is true or false; it is true when, and only when,

it puts subject and predicate together in one way either by affirmation or by negation; false when, and only when, it puts them together in another way, again either by affirmation or by negation. ⟨But it is always true or false. I. e. it always affirms or denies.⟩ I. e. the actual process of thought confirms the law of excluded middle, which states that one *must* always affirm or deny (1011ᵇ 24). The argument, as Bz. says, comes very near to the first, but is distinguishable from it.

ἐξ ὁρισμοῦ, i. e. from the definition of true and false as stated in 1011ᵇ 26 or in 1012ᵃ 4.

8. μεταβολή τις, i. e. another substantial change. Of course there are other, non-substantial, kinds of change—alteration of quality, change of size, motion in space.

9. ἔτι ἐν ὅσοις γένεσιν κτλ. If there is a middle between contradictories, there will be a middle also between terms which are *ex vi formae* contraries but *ex vi materiae* contradictories as applied to a particular genus, e. g. odd and even in number.

11. τοῦ ὁρισμοῦ. Alexander thinks the definition of number is meant; but number is defined simply as ποσὸν διωρισμένον or πλῆθος ἑνὶ μετρητόν or πλῆθος μέτρων, μονάδων, or ἀδιαιρέτων (*Index Ar*. 94ᵃ 8–12). The definition of number should contain no reference to odd or even; rather, odd and even are defined by reference to it (*An. Post.* 73ᵃ 39). Aristotle is probably thinking of a definition of even as 'the quality of the numbers that are not odd'. Bz.'s view that he means the definition of the ἄμεσον ἐναντίον does not appear so likely.

In any case, as Bz. remarks, the principle that there cannot be a middle between contradictories, which from their nature as contradictories exclude it, cannot well be proved by an appeal to contraries, which so far as their being contraries goes might have a middle between them. But it is sometimes more easy to see the truth of a principle in a particular type of case than in its general form, and there is an *ad hominem* value in the appeal to the very obvious fact that every number is either odd or even.

13. πάλιν γὰρ ἔσται κτλ. Bz.'s interpretation is: If besides A and not-A there is B which is neither, there will be C which is neither A nor B, and D which is neither not-A nor B, and so on. But (1) this does not translate the Greek, and (2) there is nothing in the opponent's premises which drives him to this conclusion. A and B, not-A and B, not being contradictories, he is not bound to say there is a middle between them. The true interpretation must be that given by Alexander. If besides A and not-A there is B which is neither, then besides B and not-B there will be C which is neither, and so on. 'For again it will be possible to deny B both in the direction of its affirmation and of its negation, and the term thus produced ("neither B nor not-B") will be something.' πρὸς τὴν φάσιν κτλ., is difficult, but no other interpretation seems possible.

16. EAᵇ read ἀποπέφυκεν, which gives no sense. J reads ἀποπέφηκεν, and Al.'s ἀποφάσκει (333. 22) confirms this. I can find no

other instance of the perfect of φημί, but ἀποπέφηκεν appears more
likely than Christ's conjecture ἀποπέφακεν.

19. λόγους ἐριστικούς. It is not clear what particular argument
Aristotle has in view. Alexander cites the argument (334. 22) that
since contraries are produced from the same thing, they must have
been contained in it, so that it neither was nor was not either of them,
and the further argument (334. 35) that 'neither is nor is not' is not
the same as either 'is' or 'is not.' and therefore must be intermediate
between them. As regards the first of these arguments Bz. objects
that it cannot be called eristic since in 1009ᵃ 22–25 it (or rather a
similar argument leading up to the denial of the law of *contradiction*)
was described as arising from a study of sensible facts. Alexander
may be right; an argument derived from a study of facts may be
turned to an eristic use, or an argument invented for eristic purposes
may seem to simple people to present a difficulty naturally arising out
of the facts. But the reference may be more general—to eristic
arguments aiming not at disproving the law of excluded middle but
at bamboozling the simple-minded by disproving both a proposition
and its contradictory. In face of such arguments the simple-minded
may be ready to say 'the proposition is neither true nor not true'.

21. διὰ τὸ πάντων ζητεῖν λόγον, cf. 1005ᵇ 2–5 n.

22. ἅπαντας τούτους, i. e. both the classes just mentioned.

ἐξ ὁρισμοῦ. Aristotle has in his defence of the law of contradiction
(1006ᵃ 18 sqq.) used an argument derived from the necessity of a fixed
meaning for *every* term; he has also in his defence of the law of
excluded middle (1011ᵇ 25) used an argument derived from the
definitions of truth and falsity. If we suppose him to be thinking of
the earlier argument, there is no very close connexion between 1012ᵃ
24–28 and what precedes it. On the other view 22–28 forms
a continuous argument. Heraclitus makes everything true, Anaxagoras makes everything false; but the very definitions of truth and
falsity (1011ᵇ 26, 27) show both these views to be mistaken. So
Al. 336. 10. But the text does not naturally suggest this connexion.
Lines 22–24 point clearly to the *general* argument; cf. ἐκ τοῦ σημαίνειν
τι ἀναγκαῖον εἶναι αὐτούς with 1006ᵃ 21. Lines 22–24 say briefly with
regard to the law of excluded middle what Aristotle has shown at
length with regard to the law of contradiction, that it is implied by
the necessity of a fixed meaning for every term. Aristotle then
concludes his discussion of the law of excluded middle by pointing
out that while (the clause is in sense subordinate) the doctrine of
Heraclitus makes all judgements true, that of Anaxagoras implies
a μεταξὺ τῆς ἀντιφάσεως and thus makes all judgements false. And
with this note the next chapter directly connects itself.

25. λέγων πάντα εἶναι καὶ μὴ εἶναι. Aristotle may have in mind
such sayings of Heraclitus as that it is the same thing to be good and
to be bad (*Top.* 159ᵇ 30, *Phys.* 185ᵇ 21, and frr. 58–62 Diels). But
more probably the reference is to the doctrine of πάντα ῥεῖ, cf. 1010ᵃ
10–15.

Falsity of the views that all judgements are true, or that all are false,
that all things are at rest, or all in motion (ch. 8).

1012ᵃ 29. These discussions show the error of the sweeping statements that no judgements are true, or that all are true. (1) These
statements stand or fall with the remark of Heraclitus that all judgements are true *and* false.

ᵇ 2. (2) There are evidently contradictories which are not both true,
and some which are not both false, though the latter seems more
possible in view of what has been said. Our argument must start by
defining truth and falsehood. If that which it is true to assert is just
that which it is false to deny, everything cannot be false. And if
everything must be either affirmed or denied, both statements cannot
be false.

13. (3) These theories are open to the common objection that they
refute themselves. He who says everything is true must admit that his
opponent's view is true and therefore his own false; and he who says
everything is false must include his own view in the indictment. Nor
will it do for the former to say ' only my opponent's view is false ', nor
for the latter to say ' only my view is true '. If they do this they must
admit an indefinite number of exceptions ; e. g. the latter must hold
that the view which says the true view is true is itself true.

22. Nor is it true to say that all things are at rest (for then the same
things would be always true—or false ; but there is change in this
respect—the very holder of the view at one time was not and again will
cease to be), nor that all things are in motion (for then everything
would be false—a view which has been disproved—and further that
which changes must itself *be* something). Nor are all things at one
time resting, at another moving ; there is something which always
moves the things that are moved, and the first mover must be itself
unmoved.

1012ᵃ 32. τὸ τὴν διάμετρον σύμμετρον εἶναι is Aristotle's favourite
instance of what is not only false but impossible, cf. A. 983ᵃ 19,
Θ. 1047ᵇ 6.

ᵇ 1-2. ' So that if the statements taken separately are impossible,
the combination of them is impossible too.'

2. ἀντιφάσεις εἰσίν, presumably in the realm of pure thought, where
one judgement is plainly true and its contradictory plainly false ; in
judgements of sense there may seem to be some ground for holding
that contradictories may both be true. The opponents of the law of
contradiction should oppose it in the former case as well as in the
latter.

4. καίτοι δόξειέ γ' ἂν κτλ. From Heraclitus' doctrine of flux (1010ᵃ 7–15) the natural conclusion is that every statement becomes false before we have finished making it ; and according to Anaxagoras' doctrine of mixture (1009ᵃ 27) every statement which either asserts or denies the identity of a mixture with any of its elements must be false.

6. ἐν τοῖς ἐπάνω λόγοις, 1006ᵃ 18–22.

9. The tradition is much divided as to the reading here. Neither of the manuscript readings makes sense, but with a minimum of alteration we get an excellent sense by reading εἰ δὲ μηθὲν ἄλλο τὸ ἀληθὲς φάναι ἢ (ὃ) ἀποφάναι ψεῦδός ἐστιν. Asclepius has ὅπερ, which is doubtless his interpretation of ὅ. ' If the true-to-say (i.e. what it is true to say) is nothing other than what it is false to deny.' φάναι dependent on ἀληθές, while good Aristotelian Greek (*An. Post.* 28ᵇ 29 is perhaps the clearest instance, but Bz. cites many cases in *Ind. Ar.* 32ᵃ 23–26 and in his note on A. 989ᵇ 7), is a peculiar enough idiom to have given rise to corruption.

12. θάτερον γὰρ μόριον κτλ., 'for one *and only one* side of a contradiction is false '.

14. τὸ θρυλούμενον, e. g. by Plato, *Theaet.* 171 A sqq.

22–31. Alexander tells us that this section was omitted in some manuscripts as being more appropriate to physics than to metaphysics. The suspicion is unfounded. Aristotle apparently makes little effort in his actual treatment to keep the domains of physics and metaphysics absolutely distinct.

28. ' Further, what changes must be something that is.'

30–31. ἔστι . . . κινούμενα. Alexander, no doubt rightly, takes this to refer to the πρῶτος οὐρανός or sphere of the fixed stars, which is always moving the whole physical universe, being itself an ἀεὶ κινούμενον. On the other hand God, who moves this, is an ἀεὶ ἠρεμοῦν (καὶ . . . αὐτό l. 31).

BOOK Δ

The subjects treated of in this book fall into certain groups which may be arranged thus :

1. ἀρχή.   2. αἴτιον.   3. στοιχεῖον.

4. φύσις.   5. ἀναγκαῖον.

6. ἕν.   7. ὄν.   8. οὐσία.

9. ταὐτά.   10. ἀντικείμενα.

11. πρότερα καὶ ὕστερα.

12. δύναμις.

13. ποσόν.   14. ποιόν.   15. πρός τι.

16. τέλειον.   17. πέρας.

18. καθ' ὅ.

19. διάθεσις.   20. ἕξις.   21. πάθος.   22. στέρησις.   23. ἔχειν.

24. ἔκ τινος.   25. μέρος.   26. ὅλον.   27. κολοβόν.

28. γένος.

29. ψεῦδος.

30. συμβεβηκός.

'Beginning' (ch. 1).

1012ᵇ 34. ἀρχή means (1) the starting-point of movement (e. g. the beginning of a road),

1013ᵃ 1. (2) the best starting-point (e. g. for learning a subject),

4. (3) that part of a thing from which genesis begins (e.g. the keel of a ship),

7. (4) the external starting-point of genesis or movement (efficient cause),

10. (5) that which moves something else at its will (e. g. the ἀρχαί in cities),

14. (6) that from which knowledge of a thing starts (*causa cognoscendi*).

16. 'Cause' has the same variety of meanings, for all causes are ἀρχαί. What is common to all ἀρχαί is to be the starting-point, whether internal or external, of being, becoming, or knowledge. Thus nature, the elementary constituent, thought, will, essence, final cause are all ἀρχαί.

Aristotle offers in this chapter quite a different classification from that in A. 3. There he takes ἀρχή in a slightly technical sense, for which 'principle' is perhaps the nearest equivalent, and states the four main principles of things—the material, the formal, the efficient, and the final. Here he takes the word as it is used in ordinary language, in which it means not only various kinds of beginning but also 'rule' and even 'ruler'. Only the fourth sense here recognized coincides with one of those recognized in A. 3. The material, formal, and final principles, however, find a place in the rough list he gives at the end of the chapter (1013ᵃ 20, 21).

1013ᵃ 2. οὐκ ἀπὸ τοῦ πρώτου κτλ. Aristotle is referring to the πρότερον καὶ γνωριμώτερον ἡμῖν as opposed to the πρότερον καὶ γνωριμώτερον ἁπλῶς which comes in ll. 14–16.

4–7. ἐνυπάρχοντος . . . μὴ ἐνυπάρχοντος, as if not ὅθεν but ἐξ οὗ had preceded.

5. οἱ μὲν καρδίαν, Empedocles (A. 84. 97 Diels), Democritus (B. 1. 10 Diels), Aristotle himself (*De Somno* 456ᵃ 5, *De Vita* 468ᵇ 28, 469ᵃ 4, 17, *De Resp.* 478ᵇ 33, *P. A.* 647ᵃ 31).

6. οἱ δὲ ἐγκέφαλον, Alcmaeon (A. 8 Diels), Hippo (A. 3 Diels), Plato (*Tim.* 44 D).

9. ἡ μάχη ἐκ τῆς λοιδορίας, cf. 1023ᵃ 30, *De Gen. An.* 724ᵃ 28. From the latter passage it appears that the reference is to a poem by Epicharmus of the ' House that Jack built ' type. It has been conjectured that the original verse was ἐκ διαβολᾶς λοιδορησμός, λοιδορησμοῦ δ' ἐκ μαχά (Lorenz, *Epicharm.* 271). For a similar instance of ἐποικοδόμησις by Epicharmus cf. fr. 44 Lorenz.

16. αἱ ὑποθέσεις is used as in ᵇ 20 in the general sense of 'premises'. Cf. *Index Ar.* 796ᵇ 59—797ᵃ 15.

17. πάντα γὰρ τὰ αἴτια ἀρχαί. Sometimes Aristotle distinguishes ἀρχή from αἴτιον as being the first in a series of causes (*De Gen. et Corr.* 324ᵃ 27, α. 994ᵃ 1) but much more often they are treated as synonymous. Though, however, they coincide in denotation, there is a difference between their definitions (Γ. 1003ᵇ 24 n.).

20. φύσις may mean here, as Alexander supposes, the matter of the thing (cf. 1014ᵇ 26). Or it may mean the power of initiating movement which is in living things (1014ᵇ 18). In either case it falls, like στοιχεῖον, under the heading of ὅθεν πρῶτον γίγνεται ἐνυπάρχοντος, though the instances given in l. 4 are of a different type.

20–21. διάνοια and προαίρεσις answer to οὗ κατὰ προαίρεσιν κινεῖται τὰ κινούμενα (l. 10).

21. οὐσία does not answer exactly to any of the senses of ἀρχή above, but has most affinity with ὅθεν γνωστὸν τὸ πρᾶγμα πρῶτον (l. 14).

τὸ οὗ ἕνεκα, as Aristotle proceeds to observe, refers both to the sense of ἀρχή given in ll. 7–10, and to that given in ll. 14–16. The end which a thing serves is both the efficient cause of it and what renders it intelligible.

22. τἀγαθὸν καὶ τὸ καλόν. For the difference cf. M. 1078ᵃ 31, *Rhet.* 1366ᵃ 33, *E. E.* 1248ᵇ 18, *M. M.* 1207ʰ 29.

' *Cause*' (ch. 2).

1013ᵃ 24. ' Cause ' means (1) the material cause,

26. (2) the form, pattern, or definition (formal cause),

29. (3) the principle of change or rest (efficient cause),

32. (4) the final cause (of means to a final cause some are instruments, others actions).

ᵇ 4. A thing may have causes of more than one of these kinds (and this not merely incidentally), and what is the cause of a thing in one sense may be its effect in another.

11. That which by its presence causes one thing, by its absence causes the contrary.

16. All causes fall under these four types. (1) Letters are the cause of syllables, the material is the cause of *artefacta*, the elements are the cause of bodies, and the premises the cause of the conclusion in the sense of 'that out of which'.

22. (2) But the essence, whole, synthesis, or form also falls under 'that out of which'.

23. (3) The seed, the doctor, the adviser, and in general the agent fall under the efficient cause.

25. (4) Other things are causes in the sense of final cause; this is the good or the apparent good.

29. Cutting across this classification there are various distinctions,

32. (1) that of causes commensurate with the effects, and the classes that include these (particular and universal);

34. (2) that of proper and incidental; incidental causes include

    (*a*) the subject of that attribute which is the cause proper,

    (*b*) classes including the subject,

    (*c*) other attributes of it;

1014^a **7.** (3) that of potential and actual.

10. Of effects also we may distinguish the specific and the generic.

13. The combination of the cause proper with an incidental cause may be described as the cause of a thing.

15. Thus there are six kinds of cause,

    (1) the individual cause,

    (2) the genus of the individual cause,

    (3) the incidental cause,

    (4) the genus of the incidental cause,

    (5) the combination of (1) and (3),

    (6) the combination of (2) and (4).

19. Any of these may be either actual or potential. But while the actual and particular causes exist just so long as the effects do, the potential do not.

This chapter is almost word for word identical with *Phys.* 194^b 23— 195^b 21. Asc. 305. 19 tells us that 'they' (the editors of the *Metaphysics*) 'said that some parts of Δ had been lost, and they supplied the deficiency out of Aristotle's own writings'. That the chapter belongs originally to the *Physics* is suggested by the fact that the classification of the senses of αἴτιον does not follow that of the senses of ἀρχή, though Aristotle has said in ch. 1 that ἰσαχῶς . . . λέγεται $(1013^a 16)$. Bz. thinks that the reference to αἴτια in ch. 1 makes ch. 2 superfluous, and that it is an interpolation from the *Physics*. But when the mode of composition of Aristotle's works is borne in mind, doublets need create no suspicion. Aristotle probably himself inserted the passage in both works.

The main other passage on the four causes (apart from A. $983^a 26-32$, which agrees with the present passage) is *An. Post.* ii. 11. The general account there agrees with the present account, but instead of the material cause we have one which is called τὸ τίνων ὄντων ἀνάγκη τοῦτ' εἶναι, and is in fact the *causa cognoscendi*, the premises of a syllogism. This appears in the present chapter as an *instance* of the material cause (1013ᵇ 20). The conception of the material cause in its wider sense occurs in *De Gen. et Corr.* 318ᵃ 9, 335ᵇ 5, *Meteor.* 342ᵃ 28, *P. A.* 640ᵇ 5, *G. A.* 715ᵃ 9, 762ᵇ 1, 778ᵇ 8, as well as in the *Physics* and the *Metaphysics.*

1013ᵃ 35. καὶ ὅσα δή κτλ. The principal verb must be supplied from the context. 'We assign in the same way the causes of those things which', &c.

ᵇ 16. εἰς τέτταρας τρόπους πίπτει. For this phrase cf. Γ. 1005ᵃ 2 n.

17-23. At the beginning of the chapter Aristotle distinguished that ἐξ οὗ γίγνεταί τι ἐνυπάρχοντος and the εἶδος or παράδειγμα; he now includes both under the ἐξ οὗ, which is of two kinds, the ὑποκείμενον and the τί ἦν εἶναι. Matter and form are similarly called the ἐνυπάρχοντα αἴτια in Λ. 1070ᵇ 22.

22. τὸ ὅλον, Alexander points out, here means not the unity of form and matter but the ὁλότης or τελειότης which supervenes on the parts. It is the σύνθεσις or form of combination of the elements.

30-34. The antithesis between the καθ' ἕκαστον and the περιέχον is not exactly that of specific and generic, nor that of individual and universal. It seems to include both of these as varieties. The language here points to the former, but ᵇ 35, 1014ᵃ 22 show that the latter is also intended.

34. The chapter so far has dealt with proper causes; Aristotle now passes to incidental causes. If the sculptor is the proper cause of the statue, then (1) if the sculptor is Polyclitus, Polyclitus may be called the cause; (2) since Polyclitus is a man and man is an animal, 'a man' or 'an animal' may be said to be the cause; (3) if Polyclitus is white or musical, 'a white (man)' or 'a musical (man)' may be called, more remotely, the cause. (2) and (3) answer to the distinction in the *Categories* (ch. 2) between τὸ καθ' ὑποκειμένου and τὸ ἐν ὑποκειμένῳ, while (1) answers to the ὑποκείμενον itself.

1014ᵃ 7. παρὰ πάντα κτλ. For παρά referring to two independent and intersecting lines of division cf. E. 1026ᵃ 35, ᵇ 1. It is unnecessary to excise it, with Bz.

12. καὶ χαλκοῦ τοῦδε ἢ χαλκοῦ ἢ ὅλως ὕλης. It is surprising to find ὕλη described as an effect. Bz. therefore takes the sentence to mean that this statue, a statue, or (more generally) an image may be said to be the effect, as (ὁμοίως καί) this bronze, bronze, or matter may be said to be the cause. But the genitives χαλκοῦ, &c., are on this view quite inexplicable, and the structure of the sentence does not suggest this way of taking καί. It seems better to suppose Aristotle to mean that the metal-worker may be said to produce this bronze, bronze, or (in general) material, *sc.* for the sculptor. Cf. *Phys.* 194ᵃ 33 ποιοῦσιν αἱ τέχναι τὴν ὕλην αἱ μὲν ἁπλῶς αἱ δ' εὐεργόν, ᵇ 4 ἡ δὲ ὡς ποιητικὴ τῆς ὕλης. Alexander gives both interpretations, Simpl. *in Phys.* the latter.

16. τὸ μὲν πλῆθος ἕξ. The cause of a statue may be said to be (1) a sculptor, (2) an artist, (3) Polyclitus, (4) a man, (5) a sculptor, Polyclitus, (6) an artistic man.

20. τὰ μὲν ἐνεργοῦντα καὶ τὰ καθ' ἕκαστον. Aristotle has treated the antithesis of καθ' ἕκαστον and περιέχον and that of ἐνεργοῦν and κατὰ δύναμιν as distinct. But here he suggests that the καθ' ἕκαστον is the same as the ἐνεργοῦν (καί being explicative). This is partly justifiable. For the universal is never operative save in so far as it is realized in individuals; it is not 'the artist' but a particular artist who actually produces a house (cf. Λ. 1071ᵃ 17–24). But within the individual artist there is a further distinction between potentiality and actuality; the οἰκοδόμος is different from the οἰκοδομῶν. In l. 23 strict logic would require ὅδε ὁ οἰκοδομῶν (which is the reading in the *Physics*), but owing to the confusion between the ἐνεργοῦν and the καθ' ἕκαστον Aristotle writes ὅδε ὁ οἰκοδόμος.

'Element' (ch. 3).

1014ᵃ 26. 'Element' means (1) the primary constituent which is indivisible into parts specifically different from itself, e. g. letters of the alphabet, the physical elements.

35. So too we speak of the elements of geometrical proof or of proof in general.

ᵇ 3. (2) Whatever is one, small, and capable of many uses; and so whatever is most universal, e.g. the unit, the point.

9. Hence genera are said by some to be elements, and more so than their differentiae.

On the treatment of στοιχεῖον in this chapter cf. Diels, *Elementum*, 23–32.

1014ᵃ 26. ἐνυπάρχοντος marks the difference between στοιχεῖον and ἀρχή or αἴτιον. Thus ὕλη, στέρησις, εἶδος are στοιχεῖα; the external efficient cause is ἀρχή but not στοιχεῖον (Λ. 1070ᵇ 22, *Phys.* 189ᵇ 16).

27. ἀδιαιρέτου . . . εἶδος. Diels (23 n. 3) says that the definition ought to have run ἀδιαιρέτου, ἢ εἰ ἄρα, εἰς ἕτερον εἶδος (*sc.* ἀδιαιρέτου): this would have distinguished the case of the letters, which are indivisible, from that of the physical elements, which are only divisible into μόρια ὁμοειδῆ. But Aristotle's definition applies correctly enough to both cases. A long vowel can be divided, but only into shorter vowels of the same kind.

32. λέγουσιν οἱ λέγοντες. Aristotle frequently refers to elements in this sense as τὰ καλούμενα or λεγόμενα στοιχεῖα (e. g. *Phys.* 187ᵃ 26, *Meteor.* 339ᵇ 5, *P. A.* 646ᵃ 13). It is clear that this usage of the word was not yet fully established.

35. τῶν διαγραμμάτων. For the meaning cf. B. 998ᵃ 25 n., and for this use of στοιχεῖον cf. 998ᵃ 26 n.

36. καὶ ὅλως τὰ τῶν ἀποδείξεων, cf. *Pol.* 1295ᵃ 34.

ᵇ **2.** Diels prefers the reading of Alexander, οἱ πρῶτοι τῶν τριῶν, and interprets it with Alexander as meaning syllogisms in the first of the three figures. But there is not much point in a reference to the first figure in particular, and it seems better to follow EJ. Aristotle means then 'the primary syllogisms which (as opposed to sorites) have only three terms and only one middle term'.

4. ἐπὶ πολλὰ ᾖ χρήσιμον. To this sense, as Bz. observes, may be referred the use of στοιχεῖον in the sense of τόπος, an argument applicable to a variety of subjects (*Top.* 120ᵇ 13, 121ᵇ 11, 151ᵇ 18, *Rhet.* 1358ᵃ 35, 1396ᵇ 21, 1403ᵃ 17).

6. For the omission of τό with the infinitive cf. Z. 1030ᵃ 1–2 n., 1031ᵇ 11, 1033ᵃ 32, *An. Pr.* 67ᵇ 13, Pl. *Menex.* 247 B 4, *Symp.* 194 D 3, *Rep.* 493 D 1, 523 E 5.

8–9. To account for the accusative ἀρχάς in l. 9 we must omit διό and read δοκεῖν (with EJ), and treat καὶ τὸ ἓν . . . εἶναι as going with ἐλήλυθε (like τὰ μάλιστα καθόλου στοιχεῖα εἶναι).

Aristotle is referring to Pythagorean and Platonic views (cf. A. 986ᵃ 1, B. 3, Z. 1028ᵇ 15–18, Λ. 1069ᵃ 26–28, &c.).

10. οὐ γὰρ ἔστι λόγος αὐτῶν, the reading of Aᵇ and of the lemma in Alexander, gives a better sense than εἷς γὰρ ἔστι λόγος αὐτῶν. τὰ καλούμενα γένη here must mean *summa genera*, and these are indefinable since they cannot be analysed into genus and differentia.

'*Nature*' (ch. 4).

1014ᵇ 16. φύσις means (1) the genesis of growing things,

17. (2) the part from which growth begins,

18. (3) the internal principle of movement in natural objects.

20. Growth is the drawing of increase from something without by contact and concretion or accretion.

26. (4) the unshaped and unchanging matter from which natural objects are produced;

32. in this sense one or more of the four elements is said to be the 'nature' of natural objects;

35. (5) the essence of natural objects;

1015ᵃ 3. thus we say a thing has not its nature till it has its form. A natural object is the union of (4) and (5).

7. Thus both the first (which may mean either the proximate or the ultimate) matter, and the form which is the end of the process of becoming, are nature.

11. (6) Essence in general.

13. The primary meaning is 'the essence of things that have a principle of movement in themselves *qua* themselves'; the other meanings are derivatives of this.

17. Nature in this sense is the principle of movement of natural objects, present in them potentially or actually.

The senses of φύσις are discussed also in *Phys.* ii. 1, and the two chapters correspond as follows:

1014ᵇ 16, 17 to 193ᵇ 12–18.
18–20 to 192ᵇ 8—193ᵃ 2.
26–32 to 193ᵃ 9–17.
32–35 to 193ᵃ 17–30.
35—1015ᵃ 5 to 193ᵃ 30–ᵇ 12.

There is nothing in the *Physics* answering to 1014ᵇ 17–18, 20–26, 1015ᵃ 6–19.

1014ᵇ 17. οἶον εἴ τις ἐπεκτείνας λέγοι τὸ υ, i.e. so as to bring out the derivation of φύσις from φύω, in most of the tenses of which υ is long. It seems doubtful whether φύσις ever had this meaning of 'birth' or 'growth'. In the single passage of Homer in which the word occurs, *Od.* x. 302–3 ὡς ἄρα φωνήσας πόρε φάρμακον ἀργειφόντης | ἐκ γαίης ἐρύσας, καί μοι φύσιν αὐτοῦ ἔδειξε, it may be translated 'growth' but more likely means 'nature'. Diels cites it as meaning *Entstehung* in two fragments of Empedocles, fr. 8 (quoted below 1015ᵃ 1) and fr. 63 ἀλλὰ διέσπασται μελέων φύσις· ἡ μὲν ἐν ἀνδρός . . ., but in the first of them it seems to mean 'substantial, permanent nature', and in the second 'substance'; and the general meaning in the pre-Socratics is pretty much the same, 'stuff' or 'material'. The references I have traced to φύσις in the meaning of γένεσις are Pl. *Laws* 892 c φύσιν βούλονται λέγειν γένεσιν τὴν περὶ τὰ πρῶτα, Ar. *Phys.* 193ᵇ 12 ἔτι δ' ἡ φύσις ἡ λεγομένη ὡς γένεσις ὁδός ἐστιν εἰς φύσιν, and the present passage; and these seem to be 'learned' references to a supposed etymological meaning. But, as Prof. Burnet points out (*E. G. P.*³ 363) though φύομαι means 'I grow', 'the simple root φυ is the equivalent of the Latin *fu* and the English *be*, and need not necessarily have this derivative meaning'. On the whole subject cf. Burnet 10–12, 363–364.

17. ἔνα δὲ ἐξ οὖ κτλ. This does not mean simply, as Alexander takes it to mean, the matter of which a natural object is made; that sense— the sense in which the word was used by many of the pre-Socratics who wrote περὶ φύσεως (cf. Diels, *Vorsokr.* Index 650ᵃ 41 sqq.)—comes in ll. 26–35. What is referred to here is the inherent starting-point of growth (ἐξ οὖ φύεται), and Bz. is probably right in supposing that the seed is meant.

20–26. τὸ ἅπτεσθαι, τὸ συμπεφυκέναι, τὸ προσπεφυκέναι are not three alternative modes of growth. τὸ ἅπτεσθαι, contact between the growing thing and its nutriment, is the first condition, but there must be in addition either τὸ συμπεφυκέναι or τὸ προσπεφυκέναι, either the

complete absorption of the nutriment by the living body or the looser but
still organic attachment of the embryo to the parent (the opposition
between the two cases is, however, not well thought out, for in the
latter case also there must be a complete absorptibn of the nutriment).
For the opposition between ἀφή and σύμφυσις or συνέχεια cf. K.
1069ᵃ 5–12.

26. ἀλλὰ μὴ κατὰ τὸ ποιόν. Thus there is σύμφυσις and συνέχεια
between bone and muscle, but not qualitative identity.

27. The reading τῶν φύσει ὄντων is confirmed by Al., Asc., and by
Phys. 193ᵃ 10 (and Simpl. and Phil. *ad loc.*), where also similar
instances are given, οἷον κλίνης φύσις τὸ ξύλον, ἀνδριάντος δ' ὁ χαλκός.
Otherwise Aᵇ's τῶν μὴ φύσει ὄντων would have had strong claims to
consideration, as the examples given are actually artificial, not natural
objects. It is highly unlikely that both here and in the *Physics* οἷον
should have the force assigned to it by Bz., that of introducing not an
example but a comparison. Rather, the statue is introduced as an
example of τὰ φύσει ὄντα because *qua bronze* it does exist by nature.
Later, however, forgetting that he has so described the statue, Aristotle
says (l. 32) that this usage applies *also* to τὰ φύσει ὄντα.

ἀρρυθμίστου 'unshaped' in comparison with that which is made out
of it.

28. ἀμεταβλήτου ἐκ τῆς δυνάμεως τῆς αὐτοῦ, 'not capable of being
changed from its own potency'. ἐκ = 'out of', not 'by virtue of';
this is shown by *Phys.* 193ᵃ 26 καὶ τούτων μὲν (*sc.* τῶν στοιχείων)
ὁτιοῦν εἶναι ἀίδιον (οὐ γὰρ εἶναι μεταβολὴν αὐτοῖς ἐξ αὐτῶν); cf. 1014ᵇ 31
διασωζομένης τῆς πρώτης ὕλης.

1015ᵃ 1. φύσις οὐδενὸς ἔστιν ἐόντων κτλ., fr. 8 Diels. The full form of
the fragment is

ἄλλο δέ τοι ἐρέω. φύσις οὐδενὸς ἔστιν ἁπάντων
θνητῶν, οὐδέ τις οὐλομένου θανάτοιο τελευτή,
ἀλλὰ μόνον κτλ.

Plutarch (*Adv. Col.* 1112 A) takes φύσις = γένεσις. Subsequent
scholars have followed him in this and have interpreted θανάτοιο τελευτή
as = θάνατος; Plutarch himself reads θανάτοιο γενέθλη, which also
practically = θάνατος. But Prof. Lovejoy argues (*Philosophical Review*,
xviii. 371 ff.) that Empedocles can hardly have said 'there is no death
of mortal things', and that his point must be that things other than the
four elements have no *permanent nature* and are *always* dying. It is
clear that Aristotle interprets φύσις in Empedocles as = permanent
nature; if he had interpreted it as = γένεσις he would have quoted
Empedocles in illustration of the first sense of φύσις (1014ᵇ 16, 17),
not of the fifth. So, too, in *De Gen. et Corr.* 333ᵇ 13–18 we have
τοῦτο δ' ἐστὶν ἡ οὐσία ἡ ἑκάστου, ἀλλ' οὐ μόνον "μῖξίς τε διάλλαξίς τε
μιγέντων" ... τῶν δὴ φύσει ὄντων αἴτιον τὸ οὕτως ἔχειν, καὶ ἡ ἑκάστου
φύσις αὕτη, περὶ ἧς οὐδὲν λέγει· οὐδὲν ἄρα περὶ φύσεως λέγει, where again
φύσις in Empedocles is interpreted by οὐσία, permanent nature. In
De Gen. et Corr. 314ᵇ 7, where Aristotle again quotes the passage, it

is not clear whether Aristotle interprets φύσις as = γένεσις or = οὐσία, but in the light of the other two passages of Aristotle the latter seems more probable. In *MXG.* 975ᵇ 6 φύσις is taken as = γένεσις.

It is another question what Empedocles himself meant by φύσις. Prof. Lovejoy's argument is not conclusive against the older interpretation. It would be quite possible for Empedocles to say ' (so-called) mortal things do not really come into being and pass away in death '. But though Aristotle recognizes γένεσις as a meaning of φύσις (l. 16), this is perhaps merely an acknowledgement of the derivation of the word. There seems to be no other passage in the pre-Socratics in which φύσις has this meaning; in Emp. fr. 63 ἀλλὰ διέσπασται μελέων φύσις· ἡ μὲν ἐν ἀνδρός . . ., which Diels cites in his Index under this sense, Burnet's 'substance' seems more likely to be the correct translation. On the whole therefore Prof. Lovejoy's view seems to be the more probable. Cf. 1014ᵇ 17 n.

2. διάλλαξις. *MXG.* 975ᵇ 15 paraphrases this by διάκρισις, Aetius by διάστασις, Plutarch by διάλυσις. Diels translates *Austausch* (interchange), but though διαλλάττειν usually means 'to change' or 'exchange', that meaning is rather pointless here. Aetius' and Plutarch's interpretation is confirmed by such passages as Hippoc. *de Victu* i. 6 προσίζει γὰρ τὸ σύμφορον τῷ συμφόρῳ, τὸ δὲ ἀσύμφορον πολεμεῖ καὶ μάχεται καὶ διαλλάσσει ἀπ' ἀλλήλων, Xen. *Hell.* iv. 3. 3 διαλλάττειν τὴν χώραν, Pl. *Soph.* 223 D τὸ . . . ἐξ ἄλλης εἰς ἄλλην πόλιν διαλλάττον, *E. N.* 1161ᵃ 5, 1165ᵇ 24, 1176ᵃ 10.

6. ἀμφοτέρων τούτων, i. e. the matter (ἐξ οὗ πέφυκε γίγνεσθαι ἢ εἶναι) and the form.

8. ἡ ὅλως πρώτη. This is not a reference to *materia prima* in the technical sense in which it is used by the schoolmen, but only to what is, if we may so put it, comparatively ultimate. Water is not *materia prima*, qualityless matter.

10. εἰ πάντα τὰ τηκτὰ ὕδωρ, cf. 1023ᵃ 28. This is the doctrine of the *Timaeus* (58 D). Aristotle's own doctrine (*Meteor.* 382ᵇ 31) is that things capable of being solidified and melted are composed either of water, *or* of water and earth.

17–19. καὶ ἡ ἀρχὴ . . . ἐντελεχείᾳ: i. e. φύσις in the fifth sense is also φύσις in the third.

18–19. δυνάμει, as the soul is present in the seed; ἐντελεχείᾳ, as it is in the grown animal—so Alexander.

'Necessary' (ch. 5).

1015ᵃ 20. 'Necessary' is applied to (1) (*a*) a condition without which one cannot live,

22. (*b*) that without which the good cannot be or come to be,

26. (2) the compulsory, i. e. that which hinders something and resists its impulse,

33. (3) that which cannot be otherwise;

35. to this sense the others may be referred.

ᵇ **6.** In this sense too demonstration is necessary; its necessity depends on the necessity of the premises.

9. All things that are necessary are so either by reason of something else or in their own right. What is so in the latter sense is the simple, that which can only be in one way. Therefore if there are eternal and unchangeable entities, nothing compulsory or unnatural can pertain to them.

Aristotle recognizes in this chapter three main senses of 'necessary', answering to the three which are briefly mentioned in Λ. 1072ᵇ 11. 1015ᵃ 20–26 answers to οὗ οὐκ ἄνευ τὸ εὖ, 26–33 to τὸ βίᾳ ὅτι παρὰ τὴν ὁρμήν, 33–ᵇ 9 to τὸ μὴ ἐνδεχόμενον ἄλλως ἀλλ᾽ ἁπλῶς. The first of the three is sometimes referred to as τὸ ἐξ ὑποθέσεως (*Phys.* 199ᵇ 34, *De Somno* 455ᵇ 26, *P. A.* 639ᵇ 24, 642ᵃ 9). We get the first and the third in *P. A.* 639ᵇ 24, 642ᵃ 32, the last two in E. 1026ᵇ 28, *An. Post.* 94ᵇ 37.

1015ᵃ 25. τὸ πλεῦσαι εἰς Αἴγιναν ἵνα ἀπολάβῃ τὰ χρήματα. Christ connects this ingeniously with the reference in the 13th Platonic letter (362 B) to Plato's sending for money to one Andromedes of Aegina, presumably a banker.

29. Εὔηνος, of Paros, a sophist and elegiac poet of the time of Socrates. The line quoted is fr. 8 in Hiller, and is quoted also in *Rhet.* 1370ᵃ 10, *E. E.* 1223ᵃ 31.

30. Σοφοκλῆς, *El.* 256 ἀλλ᾽ ἡ βία γὰρ ταῦτ᾽ ἀναγκάζει με δρᾶν.

36. τό τε γὰρ βίαιον ἀναγκαῖον κτλ., 'a thing is said to do or suffer what is necessary in the sense of compulsory'.

ᵇ **8.** ἁπλῶς, i. e. not with a qualification nor merely *ad hominem*.

9. The point he has made, that the necessity of demonstration depends on the necessity of the premises, leads Aristotle to divide τὰ ἀναγκαῖα in general into those which are so in their own right and those which are so derivatively. That which is necessary in the first sense is the simple (l. 12), whose nature admits of no variation; in other words the eternal and unchangeable (l. 14). What is necessary in this sense cannot be subject to necessity in the sense of compulsion (l. 15).

Evidently τὰ ἀναγκαῖα in the senses explained in ᵃ 20–33, and some of τὰ ἀναγκαῖα in the senses explained in ᵃ 33–ᵇ 9 (i.e. the conclusions of demonstration) are derivative ἀναγκαῖα. It is only τὰ πρῶτα, the ultimate premises of demonstration, that are necessary in their own right.

15. οὐδὲν ἐκείνοις κτλ. Since they can only be in one condition, they cannot be in a condition that is forced on them or contrary to their nature. Jaeger argues for the reading οὐδὲν ἐν ἐκείνοις, but cf. B. 996ᵃ 23 n.

'One', *'Many'* (ch. 6).

1015^b 16. Things that form a unity may do so (1) *accidentally*, as

    (*a*) 'Coriscus' and 'the musical' (or 'musical Coriscus'),

    (*b*) 'the musical' and 'the just',

    (*c*) 'musical Coriscus' and 'just Coriscus'.

20. The two things in (*b*) are one because they are attributes of one substance·; those in (*a*) are one because one is an attribute of the other (so too (*d*) 'musical Coriscus' is one with 'Coriscus' because one part of the complex is an attribute of the other); those in (*c*) because 'musical' and 'just' are attributes of one substance.

28. Similarly (*e*) 'man' and 'musical man' are one, either because 'musical' belongs to 'man', which is one substance, or because both 'man' and 'musical' belong to one individual, though in different ways.

36. (2) Things *essentially* one are so (*a*) by continuity; things continuous by nature are more one than those made continuous by art.

1016^a 5. The continuous is that whose movement essentially is and must be one, i.e. indivisible in time. Contact does not constitute continuity.

9. The continuous is the more one if it has no bend, because then its motion must be simultaneous.

17. (*b*) (i) Because their substratum is one in kind, i.e. indistinguishable to sensation. The substratum referred to may be either the proximate or the ultimate.

24. (ii) Because their genus is one. Horse and man are one because they are both animals ; isosceles and equilateral are one figure because they are both triangles.

32. (*c*) Because their definitions are indistinguishable.

^{b} **1.** That is most fully one which thought cannot divide in respect of time, place, or definition—especially if it be a substance. A thing is one in that respect in which it is indivisible.

6. Most things that are one are one by virtue of some relation to what is directly one ; those things are primarily one whose substance is one in continuity (cf. 1015^b 36—1016^a 17), kind (1016^a 17–32), or definition (32–^{b} 6).

11. In some things we require unity of form as well as continuity before we call them one.

17. (3) To be one is to be a starting-point of number, or the first measure of a genus. Different genera have different units.

23. In every case the unit is indivisible either in quantity or in kind. In quantity there is the absolutely indivisible and positionless (the unit), the absolutely indivisible which has position (the point), that which is divisible in one, two, or three dimensions (the line, the plane, the solid).

31. Again, there is unity in number, species, genus, or by analogy. Each of these implies those that follow it, but not vice versa.

1017ª 3. ' Many' has senses corresponding to the three kinds of essential unity.

There is a partial correspondence between this chapter and I. 1, which may be shown as follows :

1015ᵇ 36—1016ª 17 = 1052ª 19-21.
10.16ª 32–ᵇ 6 = 1052ª 29-34.
1016ᵇ 11–17 = 1052ª 22–28.
1016ᵇ 17–31 = 1052ᵇ 15—1053ᵇ 8.

In I. 1 the accidentally one is expressly excluded from consideration ; the one in matter and the one in genus do not reappear as such; and interest is concentrated chiefly on the primary meaning of ἕν, viz. measure. The senses treated of in 1015ᵇ 36—1016ª 17, 1016ᵇ 17–31, ª 32–ᵇ 6 reappear in *Phys.* 185ᵇ 7.

1015ᵇ 16–34. By an accidental unity Aristotle means one grounded on a *de facto* conjunction, not on the essential nature of that which forms the unity. The various kinds of accidental unity referred to are

(*a*) that of substance and accident (ll. 17, 22),
(*b*) that of accident and co-accident (19, 21),
(*c*) that of substance + accident and the same substance + another accident (20, 26),
(*d*) that of substance + accident and substance (23–26),
(*e*) that of genus + accident and genus (29).

Of these (*a*) is the primary kind on which the others depend.

17. Κορίσκος occurs again as an example in E. 1026ᵇ 18, Z. 1037ª 7 ; also in *An. Pr.*, *Top.*, *Phys.*, *Parv. Nat.*, *P. A.*, *G. A.*, *E. E.* Coriscus of Scepsis was a member of a school of Platonists with whom Aristotle probably had associations while at the court of Hermias at Assos, *c.* 347–344. He is one of those to whom the (genuine) Sixth Letter of Plato is addressed. Cf. Zeller ii. 1. 982 n. 1, Jaeger, *Entst. der Met.* 34, 35, and *Arist.* 112–117, 268.

20. μουσικὸς Κορίσκος καὶ δίκαιος Κορίσκος, the reading of Alexander, is what the sense requires, for this is the kind of unity referred to in l. 26 καὶ ὁ μουσικὸς Κορίσκος δικαίῳ Κορίσκῳ.

28. For the distinction between γένος and καθόλου cf. A. 992ᵇ 12, Z. 1028ᵇ 34. τὸ καθόλου includes differentiae and properties as well as genus.

33. ἴσως, cf. A. 987ª 26 n.

1016ª 1. φάκελλος, the form given by most of the manuscripts, is a corruption. In H. 1042ᵇ 17 all the manuscripts give φάκελος, the ordinary form. That this is the correct form is evident from metrical considerations (Eur. *Cycl.* 242, Ar. *Ran.* 839). The manuscripts in

Hdt. iv. 62, 67 give φάκελος, those in Thuc. ii. 77 φάκελλος. Crönert, *Mem. Graec. Herculanensis* 75, relies on φακελων in Philodemus, *Rhet.* i. 74. 21 Sudhaus (one of the most carefully written of the Philodemus papyri), and on φάκελος in Hesych. and *Etym. Magn.* as against φάκελλος in Aen. Tact. 78. 3 Hug and in Suidas. The corruption is due to the false analogy of the Latin diminutive, and survives in the modern Greek φάκελλος, 'an envelope'.

5. The continuous is better defined in *Phys.* v. 3 without reference to movement, which is not really an element in the notion.

6. 'One motion' is defined more exactly in *Phys.* v. 4 as that in which both ὅ and ἐν ᾧ and ὅτε κινεῖται are one.

ἀδιαίρετος δὲ κατὰ χρόνον, i. e. so that when one part moves all must move. Contrast l. 11 ἐνδέχεται μὴ μίαν εἶναι τὴν κίνησιν τοῦ σκέλους.

9. ἄλλο συνεχὲς οὐδέν must clearly be the predicate, not the subject of the clause depending on φήσεις. The translation therefore is: 'you will not say that these are one piece of wood, or one body, or one continuum at all'.

16. μόριον ἔχον μέγεθος, to exclude, as Bz. observes, the case of a straight line rotating round its end *point*. Strictly, of course, a point is not a μόριον at all.

17-ᵇ17. Unity of the substratum in kind (ll. 17–24) and unity of genus (24–32) are introduced as if they were different types of unity, and these with unity by continuity (1015ᵇ 36—1016ᵃ 17) and unity of definition (1016ᵃ 32–ᵇ 1) make four kinds. But in 1016ᵇ 9 and 1017ᵃ 4 Aristotle speaks of only three. εἴδει in 1016ᵇ 9 might refer to either unity of the substratum in kind, or unity of genus; τῷ διαιρετὴν ἔχειν τὴν ὕλην κατὰ τὸ εἶδος 1017ᵃ 4 refers clearly to unity of genus. But it seems that these two are not distinguished so strongly by Aristotle from one another as they are from the other two. Unity of genus is introduced not by ἔτι, the usual mode of introducing a new sense, but by λέγεται δ' ἐν καί, and this sense is said to be analogous to the second (ll. 27, 28). Both these kinds of unity are unity of substratum; but in the one case it is the material substratum, in the other the genus as substratum of the differentiae, that is in question.

It is to be noted also that the second, third, and fourth senses may be considered as forming a group opposed to the first. They are all forms of unity τῷ εἴδει as opposed to τῷ ποσῷ (ᵇ 23).

18. ἀδιάφορον . . . ὧν = ἀδιάφορόν ἐστιν ἐν τούτοις ὧν.

20. τὸ πρῶτον might mean either the prime or the proximate matter (cf. 1015ᵃ 7); but ἔσχατον in l. 23 means 'ultimate', so that πρῶτον presumably means 'proximate'. τὸ τελευταῖον πρὸς τὸ τέλος must then mean 'last, counting from the end'.

23. ὕδωρ γὰρ ἢ ἀήρ. Aristotle himself connects χυμοί rather with moisture (*De An.* 422ᵃ 10, 17), and so wine is said to be a form of water (*Meteor.* 382ᵇ 13, 389ᵃ 27). But oil he calls a product of air (384ᵃ 1) or of air and water (384ᵃ 15, 388ᵃ 31). His remark here is thrown out rather at a venture. Only ὕδωρ, not ἀήρ, is meant to apply to τὰ τηκτά, and for this cf. 1015ᵃ 10 n.

28–32. Having pointed out that different species are 'one' if they belong to the same genus, Aristotle now points out that *infimae species* of the genus *x*, if this is itself a species of the genus *y*, are said to be 'one *y*' but not 'one *x*'. The isosceles and the equilateral triangle are one (kind of) figure but not of triangle (really, this is true not only of *infimae species* but of any included in a genus that is itself included in another). 'Sometimes they are said to be the same in respect of the higher genus (if they are *infimae species* of their genus), viz. of the genus above the genera of which their proximate genus is one.' τὸ ἀνωτέρω τούτων, which it seems best to read with Alexander, is epexegetic of τὸ ἄνω γένος, and τούτων, it seems, must mean the proximate genus and its co-ordinate genera; otherwise ἀνωτέρω τούτων would have to mean not 'above these' but 'higher above these', which it cannot mean. But the words are suspiciously like a gloss.

32. From generic unity Aristotle now proceeds to specific.

33. ἀδιαίρετος πρός, 'indistinguishable from'. For this sense of ἀδιαίρετος cf. *De An.* 427ᵃ 2, 6.

34. τὸν δηλοῦντα [τί ἦν εἶναι] τὸ πρᾶγμα. The accusative appears to be found only once elsewhere in the MSS. of Aristotle with τί ἦν εἶναι (Z. 1029ᵇ 14), and is suspect there, so that τί ἦν εἶναι should in all probability be regarded as a gloss.

35. πᾶς λόγος διαιρετός. Every definition may be analysed into genus and differentia.

ᵇ **2.** χρόνῳ. The individual when growing may be distinguished from the same individual when wasting away (ᵃ 35), in time, even if not τόπῳ or λόγῳ, and so the individual at a single time is more fully one than the same individual at different times.

τόπῳ. Different members of a species may be distinguished τόπῳ even if not χρόνῳ or λόγῳ, and are thus less truly one than a single individual.

3. λόγῳ. Different aspects or attributes of the same individual may be distinguished λόγῳ even if not χρόνῳ or τόπῳ, and are thus less fully one than a single individual under a single aspect. This, then, is the most fully one of all things.

καὶ τούτων ὅσα οὐσίαι. Aristotle no doubt means that since the other categories are dependent on substance, the unity of things in them depends on the unity of substance.

5. οἷον εἰ ᾖ ἄνθρωπος κτλ. 'E. g. if two things are indistinguishable *qua* man, they are one (kind of) man', as the isosceles and the equilateral triangle were said to be one figure because they are both triangles (ᵃ 31).

6. τὰ μὲν οὖν πλεῖστα. Alexander illustrates the different cases as follows :

τῷ ἕτερόν τι ποιεῖν ἕν. Honey is one with honey because it affects things similarly.

ἢ ἔχειν. Musician is one with musician.

ἢ πάσχειν. One thing which is heated is one with another thing which is heated.

ἢ πρός τι εἶναι ἕν. Those who live to the east are all on the 'right' side of the world, and thus share in a sort of unity.

9. ἢ συνεχείᾳ, cf. 1015ᵇ 36—1016ᵃ 17.

ἢ εἴδει, cf. 1016ᵃ 17–32 (see 1016ᵃ 17–ᵇ 17 n.).

ἢ λόγῳ, cf. 1016ᵃ 32–ᵇ 6.

11. ἔτι δ' ἔστι. It seems better to read ἔτι with JTΓ γρ. E than to read ἐπεί with the other manuscripts and suppose that the apodosis is forgotten after the two parentheses in ll. 13–16, 16–17. Alexander conjectured ἔτι for ἐπεί.

17–1017ᵃ 3. Aristotle now passes from the enumeration of various kinds of things that are one to a definition of the meaning of 'one'— the meaning which καὶ μᾶλλον ἐγγὺς τῷ ὀνόματί ἐστι, τῇ δυνάμει δ' ἐκεῖνα, as he says in making the same transition in I. 1052ᵇ 6.

17–18. τὸ δὲ ἑνὶ . . . εἶναι. 'To be one is to be a starting-point of number', i.e. (as ll. 18–21 show Aristotle to mean) to be the minimum countable unit, or recognizable member of a certain class. The clause as thus interpreted seems to need no emendation.

19. Christ's emendation δέ for γάρ is not necessary. 'For the first measure is the starting-point ; for it is that by which first we recognize a class that is the first measure of that class.'

22. δίεσις, the smallest interval in music. Philolaus meant by it a minor semitone (Boethius, *Inst. Mus.* iii. 5, 8, pp. 277, 278 Friedl.). Aristoxenus, the pupil of Aristotle, recognized three varieties of δίεσις— the enharmonic (a quarter-tone), the chromatic (one-third of a tone), and the hemiolian (three-eighths of a tone) (Aristox. i. 21, iii. 61). Cf. Theo, p. 55. 11 Hiller, and I. 1053ᵃ 15 n.

23. τῷ ποσῷ answers to the unity of continuity (1015ᵇ 36—1016ᵃ 17); under τῷ εἴδει are summed up the other forms of unity discussed in 1016ᵃ 17–ᵇ 6. Cf. ᵃ 17 n.

25. τὸ δὲ πάντῃ καὶ θέσιν ἔχον στιγμή. Cf. the Pythagorean definition of the point as μονὰς θέσιν ἔχουσα (Proclus *in Eucl.* p. 95. 26).

26. τὸ δὲ μοναχῇ, *sc.* διαιρετόν.

31—1017ᵃ 3. While in ll. 24–31 Aristotle has distinguished what we may call various degrees of intensity of unity τῷ ποσῷ, he now distinguishes various degrees of intensity of unity τῷ εἴδει. This section answers to ᵃ 17–ᵇ 6 as the preceding passage answers to 1015ᵇ 36— 1016ᵃ 17.

33. γένει δ' ὦν τὸ αὐτὸ σχῆμα τῆς κατηγορίας. It is surprising to find genus treated as co-extensive with category, and Bz. therefore takes κατηγορίας 'in a more universal and primary sense', so that ὦν τὸ αὐτὸ σχῆμα τῆς κατηγορίας means 'the things to which the same predicate is attributed'. Bz. thinks that Aristotle has in mind certain main classes within each category, classes each of which has a characteristic set of predicates; e. g. number, which has the characteristic predicates 'odd', 'even', &c. There is, however, a strong presumption against taking σχῆμα τῆς κατηγορίας in a sense other than its ordinary meaning of 'category', which it bears for example in

1017ᵃ 23, E. 1026ᵃ 36. Further, in 1024ᵇ 12–16. where genus in one sense is identified with σχῆμα κατηγορίας, the examples given show that σχῆμα κατηγορίας means a category, and not one of its sub-divisions. The same identification of genus with category is implied in I. 1054ᵇ 29, 35, 1058ᵃ 13, *Phys.* 227ᵇ 4. Δ. 1024ᵇ 12–16 is fatal to Bz.'s interpretation in all these passages. The doctrine that is really implied is that the categories are the only genera proper, since they are the only genera that are not also species.

34. κατ' ἀναλογίαν. For ἀναλογία as a relation between things in different categories cf. *E. N.* 1096ᵇ 28.

ὡς ἄλλο πρὸς ἄλλο, cf. N. 1093ᵇ 18 ἐν ἑκάστῃ γὰρ τοῦ ὄντος κατη-γορίᾳ ἐστὶ τὸ ἀνάλογον, ὡς εὐθὺ ἐν μήκει οὕτως ἐν πλάτει τὸ ὁμαλόν, ἴσως ἐν ἀριθμῷ τὸ περιττόν, ἐν δὲ χροιᾷ τὸ λευκόν.

1017ᵃ 1–2. ὅσα δὲ γένει . . . ἀλλ' ἀναλογίᾳ. Alexander explains that 'as man is to man, horse is to horse ; as man is animal, horse is animal '. This, however, is hardly adequate, and it seems more likely that it is by mere inadvertence that Aristotle has extended the principle of 'the greater unity implies the less' to a case in which it is hard to attach any definite meaning to it.

3–6. In this short list of the senses of 'many', Aristotle gives senses answering to the first sense of 'one' (1015ᵇ 36—1016ᵃ 17). the second (1016ᵃ 17–24), and the fourth (1016ᵃ 32–ᵇ 6); the third (1016ᵃ 24–32) is doubtless merged in the second. Cf. 1016ᵃ 17 n.

5. ἢ τὴν πρώτην ἢ τὴν τελευταίαν, cf. 1015ᵃ 8 n., 1016ᵃ 20.

'Being' (ch. 7).

1017ᵃ 7. What 'is' may be (1) accidentally.

(*a*) The just is musical,

(*b*) the man is musical,

(*c*) the musical is a man,

13. (*a*) because both are accidents of the same subject, and this *is* ; (*b*) because the predicate is an accident of the subject. and the subject *is* ;

(*c*) because the subject is an accident of the predicate, and the predicate *is*.

22. (2) The types of essential being answer to the forms of designation (categories), substance, quality, quantity, relation, action, passivity, place, time ;

27. for any predication like 'the man is walking' can be put in the form 'the man walks'.

31. (3) 'Being' sometimes means truth, 'not-being' falsity, e. g. in the emphatic 'Socrates *is* musical', 'the diagonal *is not* commensurate with the side'.

35. (4) 'Being' means being either potentially or actually;
ᵇ **6.** this distinction applies to substances as well as to other things.

1017ᵃ 7–ᵇ 9. The same four senses of 'being', (1) τὸ κατὰ συμβεβηκός, (2) τὰ σχήματα τῆς κατηγορίας, (3) τὸ ὡς ἀληθές, (4) τὸ δυνάμει καὶ ἐντελεχείᾳ, reappear in E. 1026ᵃ 33–ᵇ 2. (2), (3), and (4) appear in Θ. 1051ᵃ 34–ᵇ 2, N. 1089ᵃ 26–28, cf. Λ. 1069ᵇ 27.

7–22. For τὸ ὄν ... τὸ ... κατὰ συμβεβηκός cf. E. 1026ᵇ 2—1027ᵇ 16. The discussion of accidental being in the present passage answers closely to that of accidental unity in 1015ᵇ 17–34.

10–13. παραπλησίως λέγοντες ὡσπερεὶ ... οὕτω δὲ καί κτλ., an instance of 'binary structure', as often with ὥσπερ in Aristotle. Cf. A. 983ᵇ 16 n.

15. τὸ μέν refers to τὸν λευκὸν μουσικὸν ἢ τοῦτον λευκόν, **16.** τὸ δ' to τὸν ἄνθρωπον ὅταν μουσικὸν λέγωμεν. The three modes of accidental being mentioned in ll. 8–10 and again in 13–18 and in 20–22 are as follows :—X is accidentally Y when (1) Y is an accident of X, (2) X is an accident of Y, or (3) X and Y are accidents of Z. (2) and (3) evidently rest on (1), and (1) itself rests on the fact that X *is* in a non-accidental sense. To these copulative uses of 'is' Aristotle adds in ll. 18, 19 an existential use of it, 'the not-white is'. This, however, can easily be turned into the copulative form 'the not-white is existent', which rests on 'something that exists is not-white' just as 'the white is man' rests on 'the man is white'; or (if we prefer to put it so) it rests on 'some substance is existent and not-white' as 'the white is musical' rests on 'the man is white and musical'.

21. ἢ ὅτι αὐτό κτλ., 'or because that to which belongs as an accident that of which it is itself predicated, itself exists'. 'The musical is a man' presupposes the existence of the man.

22–30. So far Aristotle has been examining τὸ ὂν τὸ κατὰ συμβεβηκός, i.e. the being which is implied in a proposition like 'the man is musical', the being which is nothing but an accidental and, it may be, merely temporary connexion between subject and attribute. He now proceeds to τὸ ὂν τὸ καθ' αὑτό, which must, if the opposition is to be a proper one, mean the being which is a necessary connexion. This sense of being, like 'accidental being', will be capable of being illustrated by propositions. Four kinds of proposition exhibit such a connexion—those in which there is predicated of a subject its definition, its genus, its differentia, or its property. Now 'essential being' is said to fall into kinds which are either identical with or correspond to the categories. But propositions of which the subject belongs to one category, the predicate to another, will not readily lend themselves to a classification answering to the categories; nor will the connexion of subject and predicate be in such a case of the most direct, essential kind. Now where the predicate is a property of the subject, subject and predicate may be in different categories, so that it is not propositions of this kind that Aristotle has in view. Again, where the predicate is a differentia of the subject, they may be in different

categories—the differentia of a substance, for example, is a quality
(1020ᵃ 33); so that such propositions are not intended here. And
where the predicate is the definition of the subject, the same difficulty
arises, so far as the differentia included in the definition is concerned.
The only propositions in which from the nature of the case subject
and predicate must be unambiguously in the same category are those
in which the predicate is the genus of the subject. These, then,
are the propositions which Aristotle has in view here. Being *per se* is
asserted in as many different ways as there are categories (ll. 22–24).
I. e. if we examine propositions in which the B which A is said to *be*
is the genus of A, we shall find that the being which is implied has
different meanings according to the category to which subject and
predicate belong. ' Man is an animal': ' is' takes its meaning from
the category to which the terms it connects belong. 'White is
a colour': ' is' here has a different meaning. Now if we take any
such proposition and push the question ' what is so-and-so' as far as
we can in the direction of generality, we come to one or other of ten
supreme kinds. ' Man is an animal. An animal is a living thing.
A living thing is a substance.' 'White is a colour. Colour is
a quality.' We can go no further. ' Substance is a what?' We
can only say that it is a kind of entity, and that is all we can say
of quality too. Thus essential being has ten ultimate meanings or
colourings answering to the ten ultimate kinds of things that are.

The conception of the categories as the ultimate types of answer
to the question ' what (i. e. what kind of thing) is so-and-so' is best
expressed in *Top.* 103ᵇ 27–37 δῆλον δ' ἐξ αὐτῶν ὅτι ὁ τὸ τί ἐστι σημαίνων
ὁτὲ μὲν οὐσίαν σημαίνει, ὁτὲ δὲ ποιόν, ὁτὲ δὲ τῶν ἄλλων τινὰ κατηγοριῶν.
ὅταν μὲν γὰρ ἐκκειμένου ἀνθρώπου φῇ τὸ ἐκκείμενον ἄνθρωπον εἶναι ἢ ζῷον,
τί ἐστι λέγει καὶ οὐσίαν σημαίνει· ὅταν δὲ χρώματος λευκοῦ ἐκκειμένου
φῇ τὸ ἐκκείμενον λευκὸν εἶναι ἢ χρῶμα, τί ἐστι λέγει καὶ ποιὸν σημαίνει ...
ὁμοίως δὲ καὶ ἐπὶ τῶν ἄλλων· ἕκαστον γὰρ τῶν τοιούτων, ἐάν τε αὐτὸ περὶ
αὑτοῦ λέγηται ἐάν τε τὸ γένος περὶ τούτου, τί ἐστι σημαίνει.

Aristotle makes his meaning unnecessarily obscure by citing
(1017ᵃ 27–30) propositions which do not assert essential being at all.
' The man is healthy ', ' the man is walking', ' the man is cutting ' are
purely accidental propositions just like ' the man is musical '. But
these propositions serve as well as essential propositions would to
illustrate the point he is at the moment making—that ' is ' takes its
colour from the terms it connects. ' The man is walking' means
nothing more or less than ' the man walks '; the kind of being that
is implied can be learnt only, and completely, by considering the
terms connected by it. From the occurrence of these examples
Maier infers (*Syll. des Ar.* ii. 2. 328 n. 1) that it is by inadvertence
that Aristotle associates the categories exclusively with essential being.
He holds that the classification of being according to the categories
cuts clean across the classification of it into essential and accidental.
But it is most unlikely that so important a statement (which recurs in
E. 1026ᵃ 34–36 ὧν ἕν μὲν ἦν τὸ κατὰ συμβεβηκός ... παρὰ ταῦτα

δ' ἐστὶ τὰ σχήματα τῆς κατηγορίας) should be due to carelessness. It is much more in Aristotle's manner to use an example which while illustrating his immediate point obscures his main meaning. Accidents, of course, fall within the categories (*Top.* 103ᵇ 23–25), for the categories include everything that is. But the categories are the most general answers possible to the question 'what is so-and-so *per se*', and in this sense they are the ultimate kinds of *essential* being.

It may seem surprising that Aristotle, while dwelling on the two main senses of the copulative ' is '—those in which it indicates respectively accidental and essential being—should say nothing of the existential ' is ', which nevertheless is presupposed in his account of accidental being (τῷ ὄντι συμβέβηκε l. 16, cf. ll. 19, 20, 21). The reason is that, though logically the existential 'is' may be distinguishable from the copulative, metaphysically it is not. To be is either to be a substance, or to be a quality, or to be in some other of the categories, for nothing can be without being of some kind.

Apelt goes, however, too far when he treats the doctrine of the categories as being essentially a classification of the senses of the copulative 'is' (*Beitr. zur Gesch. d. gr. Phil.* 106–131). The present passage, which is perhaps that on which he most relies, pre-supposes the doctrine of the categories and *infers* from it the existence of corresponding senses of essential being, which is a form of copulative being—ἐπεὶ οὖν τῶν κατηγορουμένων τὰ μὲν τί ἐστι σημαίνει, τὰ δὲ ποιόν, . . . ἑκάστῳ τούτων τὸ εἶναι ταὐτὸ σημαίνει (ll. 24–27).

23. τὰ σχήματα τῆς κατηγορίας. The phrase occurs also in E. 1026ᵃ 36, *Phys.* 227ᵇ 4, and in the singular in 1016ᵇ 34, I. 1054ᵇ 29. In 1024ᵇ 13 we have σχῆμα κατηγορίας τοῦ ὄντος, in Θ. 1051ᵃ 35 τὰ σχήματα τῶν κατηγοριῶν.

25–27. The full list of ten categories occurs only in *Cat.* 1ᵇ 25–27, *Top.* 103ᵇ 20–23. The present list of eight is common, cf. *An. Post.* 83ᵃ 21, *Phys.* 225ᵇ 5, and shorter lists are commoner still.

31–35. For τὸ ὂν ὡς ἀληθές cf. E. 4, Θ. 10.

The cases in which being means truth and not-being falsity are distinguished both from the accidental and from the essential sense of being. Evidently then an ordinary sentence of the type 'A is B' can hardly be used to illustrate this third sense, since it must be an instance of either the essential or the accidental sense. What we want is a proposition in which the truth or the falsity of another proposition is stated, and such propositions we find in those of the form 'A *is* B', 'A *is not* B', where the ordinary proposition 'A is B' is pronounced true or false. That this is what Aristotle has in mind is indicated by the emphatic position of ἔστι, οὐκ ἔστι in ll. 33–35.

We can have ' being as truth '

(*a*) ἐπὶ καταφάσεως, where an affirmative proposition is pronounced true, as in 'Socrates *is* musical',

(*b*) ἐπ' ἀποφάσεως, where a negative proposition is pronounced true, as in ' Socrates *is* not-pale ';

and ' not-being as falsity '

(*a*) ἐπὶ καταφάσεως, where an affirmative proposition is pronounced false, as in 'the diagonal of the square *is not* commensurate with the side'

(*b*) ἐπ' ἀποφάσεως, where a negative proposition is pronounced false, as in 'the square on the diagonal *is not* not-commensurate with the square on the side'. (Aristotle does not illustrate this case.)

35. Bz.'s reading σύμμετρος for ἀσύμμετρος is required by the sense, and amply confirmed by Alexander.

35-ᵇ 9. For τὸ ὂν δυνάμει καὶ ἐντελεχείᾳ cf. Θ. *passim.*

There is a difficulty about Aristotle's classification of the senses of being. While the first three senses seem to answer to three types of judgement,

(1) A is (accidentally) B,
(2) A is (essentially) B,
(3) A *is* B (= it is true that A is B),

the fourth answers not to a type of statement co-ordinate with these, but to two senses in which each of them may be taken (τὸ μὲν δυνάμει ῥητὸν τὸ δ' ἐντελεχείᾳ τῶν εἰρημένων τούτων).

1017ᵇ 1. ῥητόν has caused much difficulty to the editors. Elsewhere in Aristotle the word occurs only in its ordinary meaning of 'stated, fixed', which cannot be the meaning here. Yet it is not satisfactory to excise the word, for it occurs in all the manuscripts and as a variant in Alexander and Asclepius, and no plausible reason has been suggested for its intrusion if it is spurious. It seems quite possible to retain it, and it even makes the construction more natural (for τὸ εἶναι σημαίνει καὶ τὸ ὂν τὸ μὲν δυνάμει τὸ δ' ἐντελεχείᾳ τῶν εἰρημένων τούτων is not easy to construe). 'Being or "is" means, further, that some of the things we have named (i.e. of the judgements referred to under accidental being, essential being, and being as truth) *can be said* by virtue of a potentiality (resident in the subject), others by virtue of an actuality.'

ῥητῶς before ὁρῶν in l. 3 seems to be spurious; it is not found, as ῥητόν l. 1 is, in Aᵇ. Al., Asc.

6. ὁμοίως δὲ καὶ ἐπὶ τῶν οὐσιῶν. Aristotle passes now from attributes like 'seeing', 'knowing', 'resting' to substances, and among these he includes the half line which is in the whole line in the sense that it is potentially there. A line is not, on his own view, a substance; the example is a concession to Pythagorean and Platonic views (cf. l. 19). Cf. also 1020ᵃ 20 n. It is not necessary with Apelt to regard καὶ τὸ ἥμισυ τῆς γραμμῆς as interpolated from Θ. 1048ᵃ 33.

9. ἐν ἄλλοις, Θ. 7.

'*Substance*' (ch. 8).

1017ᵇ 10. 'Substance' is applied to (1) the simple bodies, or in general bodies, the animals and stars composed of them, and the parts of these; these are called substances because they are not attributes but subjects,

14. (2) the internal cause of being in such things, e. g. the soul,

17. (3) the limits which are present in bodies and define their individuality, and whose destruction involves the destruction of the bodies, e. g. planes, lines, numbers,

21. (4) the essence,

23. Thus substance means (1) the ultimate subject which is never a predicate (cf. ll. 10–14),

(2) what is individual and separable, i. e. the form (cf. 14–22).

With the senses of 'substance' recognized in this chapter cf. those recognized in Z. 2, 3. 1017ᵇ 10–14 answers to 1028ᵇ 8–13, 1017ᵇ 17–21 to 1028ᵇ 15–18. The formal cause of corporeal things (14–16) and the essence (21, 22) are not included among the generally recognized senses mentioned in Z. 2, but essence is mentioned in the less superficial list given in Z. 3. 1028ᵇ 34–36.

1017ᵇ 11. καὶ ὅσα τοιαῦτα. For the probable meaning cf. H. 1042ᵃ 8 n.

12. ζῷα. In Z. 1028ᵇ 9 Aristotle says more accurately 'animals and plants'.

δαιμόνια, i. e. the heavenly bodies, as appears from Z. 1028ᵇ 12, H. 1042ᵃ 10. They are often called θεῖα, e. g. E. 1026ᵃ 18, 20, Λ. 1074ᵃ 30.

17. μόρια. It is only loosely that planes, lines, and points can be said to be *parts* of solids, planes, and lines. According to Aristotle they are boundaries, not parts by whose summation the wholes are made up.

ὁρίζοντά τε καὶ τόδε τι σημαίνοντα, marking off individual from individual. The individual solid is bounded by planes, the plane by lines, the line by points.

19. τινες, **20** τισι, Pythagoreans and Platonists.

21. ἔτι τὸ τί ἦν εἶναι. That which is the substance of a thing in this sense is also its substance in the second sense (ll. 14–16)—cf. Z. 17. Thus soul is the substance of the animal in this sense (Z. 1035ᵇ 15) as well as in the second. But while substance in the second sense is the form of sensible bodies only, in the fourth the notion is widened so as to include the essence of anything.

22. οὗ ὁ λόγος ὁρισμός, cf. Z. 1030ᵃ 6 ff.

23. The last three of the four senses mentioned earlier are now brought under the common heading of form, 'which being a this is also separable in thought'. The first of the four is now called τὸ ὑποκεί-μενον ἔσχατον, which (it is evident from ll. 10–14) means not prime matter but the individual which comprises both matter and form.

25. The form is said to be (1) τόδε τι. It is more often the concrete unity of matter and form that is so described, but form is the element that gives individual character, and so the form is sometimes called τόδε τι (cf. H. 1042ᵃ 29, Θ. 1049ᵃ 35, Λ. 1070ᵃ 11, 13–15, *De Gen. et Corr.* 318ᵇ 32).

It is said to be (2) χωριστόν. This is difficult, for Aristotle's doctrine is that form is in general not separable from matter (cf. Λ. 1070ᵃ 13); soul, for example, is not separable from body, but only that part of it which is reason. χωριστόν must mean only 'separable in thought or definition', cf. H. 1042ᵃ 26 ἔστι δ' οὐσία . . . ὁ λόγος καὶ ἡ μορφή, ὁ τόδε τι ὂν τῷ λόγῳ χωριστόν ἐστιν, and *Phys.* 193ᵇ 4 τὸ εἶδος οὐ χωριστὸν ὂν ἀλλ' ἢ κατὰ τὸν λόγον.

'*The Same*', '*Other*', '*Different*', '*Like*', '*Unlike*' (ch. 9).

1017ᵇ 27. Things are 'the same' (1) accidentally.

(*a*) 'the white' is identical with 'the musical' because they are attributes of the same subject ;

(*b*) 'the man' with 'the musical' and *vice versa* because one is an attribute of the other ;

(*c*) 'the musical man' with 'the man' or 'the musical', and *vice versa*.

33. Because these identities are accidental, none of them can be generalized (as in 'every man is the same as the musical'), for universal propositions are essential.

1018ᵃ 5. (2) Essential identity means (*a*) unity of matter (i) in kind or (ii) in number, or (*b*) unity of essence. Identity is unity of being of two or more things, or of one thing treated as two or more.

9. Things are called 'other' if (1) their kinds, (2) their matters, or (3) their definitions are more than one (cf. (*a*) (i), (*a*) (ii), (*b*) above).

12. Things are called 'different' if they are other, being at the same time one—not in number but in species or genus or by analogy ; also things of different genus, contraries, and things that have their otherness in their essence.

15. Things are 'like' if in all respects or most they have the same attributes, or if their quality is the same, or if they agree in the greater number or the more important of the attributes in respect of which things suffer alteration. 'Unlike' has the opposite senses.

Aristotle's best classification of the types of identity is found in *Top.* I. 7. He recognizes there :

(1) identity in number, i. e. of the same thing differently designated,
  (*a*) as of ἱμάτιον and λώπιον, or of ζῷον πεζὸν δίπουν and ἄνθρωπος,
  (*b*) as of τὸ ἐπιστήμης δεκτικόν and ἄνθρωπος,
  (*c*) as of τὸ καθήμενον and Socrates.
(2) in species, as of man with man,
(3) in genus, as of horse with man.

The triple classification, identity in number, species, genus, is common in Aristotle, identity by analogy being sometimes added. In I. 1054ᵃ 32–ᵇ 3 we have

(1) identity in number, answering to (1) (*b*), (1) (*c*) in *Top*. I. 7,
(2) identity in definition and number, answering to (1) (*a*),
(3) identity in definition, answering to (2).

The reference to ὕλη in the present classification (1018ᵃ 6) indicates that this list has greater affinities with the list of types of unity in ch. 6.

(1) Accidental identity (1017ᵇ 27—1018ᵃ 4) answers to accidental unity (1015ᵇ 16–34).

(2) Essential identity (*a*) of matter (i) in εἶδος (1018ᵃ 6) answers to unity of the substratum in εἶδος (1016ᵃ 17–24),

(ii) in number (1018ᵃ 6) answers to continuity (1015ᵇ 36 - 1016ᵃ 17),
(*b*) of οὐσία (1018ᵃ 7) answers to unity of λόγος (1016ᵃ 32–ᵇ 6).

At the same time (1) answers to (1) (*c*) of the *Topics*; (2) (*a*) (i) to (2); (2) (*b*) to (1) (*a*). (2) (*a*) (ii) is a type not treated of in the *Topics*.

1017ᵇ 27—1018ᵃ 3. The accidental senses of ταὐτό answer to the accidental senses of 'one' given in ch. 6. The cases are as follows:

(1) The white = the musical, cf. 1015ᵇ 21,
(2) man = the musical and *vice versa*, cf. 1015ᵇ 22,
(3) musical man = the musical or man and *vice versa*, cf. 1015ᵇ 24.

30-31. ἑκατέρῳ . . . ἐκείνων, each of the simple terms 'man' and 'musical'. τοῦτο, the complex term 'musical man'.

33. διό, because these are *accidental* unities.

1018ᵃ 1. The text seems to be improved by the insertion of a colon after καθ' αὑτά. Aristotle establishes the fact that accidental judgements are never universal by the premises (1017ᵇ 35, 1018ᵃ 1),

Universals are essential,

Accidents are not essential.

Then he goes on 'Accidents (though, as we have seen, they cannot be predicated of universal subjects but require the subject to be qualified by a τις) are predicated of particular subjects ἁπλῶς, without any qualification'.

2. The reference to 'musical Socrates' is borrowed from Pl. *Phaedo* 60 D—61 B, where Socrates tells Cebes of the words which haunted him in dreams, Ὦ Σώκρατες, μουσικὴν ποίει καὶ ἐργάζου.

5. ὁσαχῶσπερ. Jaeger's emendation explains the origin of the otherwise mysterious reading ὅσα ὥσπερ, and gives a more forcible sense than Aᵇ's ὥσπερ. Alexander's τοσαυταχῶς . . . ὁσαχῶς (377. 17 f.) points in the same direction.

9–11. The three senses of 'other' here given do not answer exactly to the senses of 'the same' given in ll. 5–9. There is not there anything that answers obviously to τὰ εἴδη πλείω. But the two classifications really reduce themselves to the same, thus:

ἡ ὕλη μία εἴδει ✕ τὰ εἴδη πλείω,

ἡ ὕλη μία ἀριθμῷ ✕ ἡ ὕλη πλείω,

ἡ οὐσία μία ✕ ὁ λόγος τῆς οὐσίας πλείω.

Specific difference of matter is equivalent to difference of species. For another classification of senses of 'other' cf. I. 1054ᵇ 14–18.

11. ἀντικειμένως. In I. 1054ᵇ 19 Aristotle points out that the opposition is not contradictory opposition (for τὰ μὴ ὄντα are neither

the same as nor other than other things), but is that of ἕξις to
στέρησις.

12. μὴ μόνον ἀριθμῷ Alexander interprets as meaning 'only they
must not be one in number', taking μὴ μόνον as = μόνον μή. With this
Bonitz compares E. 1025^b 27 οὐσίαν τὴν κατὰ τὸν λόγον ὡς ἐπὶ τὸ πολύ,
οὐ χωριστὴν μόνον. οὐ χωριστὴν μόνον is, however, not a very close
parallel to μὴ μόνον ἀριθμῷ, and it is doubtful whether it has the
meaning corresponding to that which Alexander and Bonitz assign to
μὴ μόνον ἀριθμῷ. A different reading and punctuation seem preferable
in that passage.

But in the present passage the interpretation seems to be right. Cf.
Eur. *Cycl.* 219 ὧν ἂν θέλῃς σύ, μὴ 'μὲ καταπίῃς μόνον, 'provided only
that you don't swallow me'.

1. 1054^b 24—1055^a 2 similarly insists that διάφορα must, while
ἕτερα need not, be the same in some respect.

Both the present passage and that in Book 1 and many others
recognize that things in different genera may be διάφορα, and this
is *prima facie* inconsistent with the usual account of διαφορά as existing
only within a genus (cf. I. 1055^a 26). The same inconsistency is
found in the account of contraries, but cf. l. 25 n.

13-15. Bz. complains that we have here a cross division, since ὧν
ἕτερον τὸ γένος are simply the things which are τὸ αὐτὸ ἀναλογίᾳ, which
Aristotle has already referred to, and ὅσα ἔχει ἐν τῇ οὐσίᾳ τὴν ἑτερότητα
are simply those which are τὸ αὐτὸ γένει, while τὰ ἐναντία do not imply
a sense of 'different' co-ordinate with the others here mentioned. It
is, however, no part of Aristotle's object to avoid cross division. He
is simply giving the statements that might naturally be given of the
meaning of 'difference', and if these overlap it is his business to state
them nevertheless.

14. ὅσα ἔχει ἐν τῇ οὐσίᾳ τὴν ἑτερότητα, cf. ^b 2, 3. Alexander gives
various alternative explanations : (1) that contraries are meant, (2) that
Aristotle means things that without being contraries have some element
of contrariety, as earth *qua* dry is contrary to water *qua* wet, (3) that he
means things which have the same underlying subject but differ in
definition, as 'counterfeit' and 'drachma'.

Aristotle's language, however, is reminiscent of l. 1058^a 7 λέγω γὰρ
γένους διαφορὰν ἑτερότητα ἢ ἕτερον ποιεῖ τοῦτο αὐτό. Difference is
otherness which is not merely in the matter but enters into the very
essence of the thing and constitutes a genuine differentiation of the
genus.

15-18. Bz. again complains of overlapping in the definitions, but as
has been remarked on l. 13 the objection is beside the mark.

The senses of 'like' recognized in I. 1054^b 3-13 are
(1) 'the same in εἶδος though not identical in number', e. g. 'like'
geometrical figures,
(2) 'having the same εἶδος and not differing in degree',
(3) 'having the same πάθος in different degrees',
(4) 'having more qualities the same than different'.

Of the senses recognized in the present passage the first answers roughly to (1) and (2) in this classification, the second and fourth to (4), the third to (3).

'Opposite', 'Contrary', 'Other in species', 'The same in species' (ch. 10).

1018ª 20. The term 'opposites' is applied to contradictories, contraries, relative terms, positive terms and their privatives, the termini of generation and destruction, and incompatible attributes or their elements.

25. 'Contraries' are attributes differing in genus and incapable of belonging to the same subject; the most different attributes in the same genus or in the same subject-matter or falling under the same faculty; things whose difference is greatest absolutely or in genus or in species.

31. Other contraries are so called by virtue of some relation (e.g. that of possession, reception, action, passivity) to these.

35. The senses of 'the same', 'other', 'contrary' must vary with the senses of 'one' and those of 'being' (the categories).

38. Things 'other in species' are those which, being of the same genus, are co-ordinate; those which being in the same genus have a difference; those which have a contrariety in their essence; contraries, or contraries *per se*; things whose definitions differ in the *infima species*; attributes of the same substance which have a difference.

ᵇ 7. 'The same in species' has corresponding meanings.

The first four kinds of opposites here named constitute Aristotle's ordinary list of the kinds of opposite, cf. I. 1055ª 38, 1057ª 33, *Cat.* 11ᵇ 17, *Top.* 109ᵇ 17, ii. 8, v. 6. Waitz finds in the other two (ll. 21–25) not separate kinds of opposite but marks by which opposites may be recognized; but Bonitz points out that Aristotle's words do not suggest that these two are in a different position from the other four; and also that these marks are *not* characteristic of τὰ πρός τι. He finds therefore in the discrepancy between this list and Aristotle's ordinary list of opposites evidence of the late origin of Book Δ. Δ is much more likely to be of quite early origin. If we remember that Aristotle is jotting down the usages of 'opposite' in ordinary speech, we shall find no difficulty in a divergence from his own scientific classification.

1018ª 25–35. The first two senses of ἐναντίον answer to *Cat.* 14ª 19 ἀνάγκη δὲ πάντα τὰ ἐναντία ἢ ἐν τῷ αὐτῷ γένει εἶναι ἢ ἐν τοῖς ἐναντίοις γένεσιν ἢ αὐτὰ γένη εἶναι.

The recognition of things differing in genus as one kind of contraries is found in *Cat.* 14ª 20, *Top.* 153ª 36. Elsewhere ἐναντία are said to be necessarily in the same genus, *Cat.* 6ᵃ 17, *An. Post.* 73ᵇ 21, *De Gen. et Corr.* 324ᵃ 2, and this is implied also in I. 4. The apparent inconsistency is removed if we remember that a genus may itself be a species of a wider genus. Thus the contraries, justice and injustice, which are in the contrary genera virtue and vice (*Cat.* 14ᵃ 22), are both included in the wider genus of ἕξις, and good and bad, which are contrary genera (14ᵃ 24), are included in the genus of quality. It is evident that contraries must at all events be in the same category, even if they are not both included in any narrower genus.

In fact γένος here is used in a looser sense than in Bk. I, where difference of genus implies the absence of a common matter and the impossibility of change from the one class to the other (1054ᵇ 28, 1057ᵃ 26).

Of the senses of 'contrary' recognized here, the first (l. 26) does not appear in I. 4, the second (27) appears in I. 4. 1055ᵃ 27 f., the third (28) in 1055ᵃ 29, the fourth (29) in 1055ᵃ 31. The fifth (30) is rather a general summary of the senses than a distinct one ; the sixth (31) appears in 1055ᵃ 35.

28. καὶ τὰ πλεῖστον διαφέροντα τῶν ἐν ταὐτῷ δεκτικῷ. This may be another way of putting the previous definition ; or it may be a narrower definition, for, as Alexander says, rational and irrational, though differentiae of the same genus, are not found in the same δεκτικόν or ὕλη (δεκτικόν = ὕλη, cf. I. 1055ᵃ 29 f.). That which is ever rational is never irrational. But in *De Somno* 453ᵇ 27 Aristotle says that contraries are always in the same δεκτικόν. Maier thinks that the reference is to ἐναντιότητες ἐν τῷ συνειλημμένῳ τῇ ὕλη as opposed to those ἐν τῷ λόγῳ (I. 1058ᵇ 1), i. e. to oppositions such as that of male and female (the same seed being capable of becoming male or female, ib. 23). But it is doubtful if the meaning is so definite as this.

29. τῶν ὑπὸ τὴν αὐτὴν δύναμιν, e. g. of the objects of a single science (I. 1055ᵃ 31).

38. ὥστ' . . . κατηγορίαν. Christ brackets these words and thinks there is no trace of them in Alexander, but they are paraphrased in Al. 383. 13.

On ἕτερα . . . τῷ εἴδει cf. I. 8.

ᵇ **1–2.** καὶ ὅσα . . . διαφορὰν ἔχει. This is a wider definition than the previous one, since it will apply even to τὰ ὑπάλληλα, i. e. to species one of which includes the other.

2–3. καὶ ὅσα . . . ἔχει. Alexander illustrates by the case of water and fire, which, though not contraries, are characterized by contraries, cold and wet as opposed to hot and dry. Bonitz thinks this definition is either wider than the foregoing, by including even things that are in different genera, or narrower, by excluding differents that are not opposites. The point of ἐν τῇ οὐσίᾳ ἐναντίωσιν ἔχει seems, however, to be to exclude things which have contrary attributes that arise from their matter and do not enter into their essence. Cf. ᵃ 14 n., I. 1058ᵇ 14, 22.

4. τὰ λεγόμενα πρώτως excludes the contraries mentioned in ᵃ 31–35, which are contrary only by standing in some relation to contraries. If

A and B, for instance, possess contrary qualities C and D, it does not follow that A and B are different in species.

4–5. ὅσων ... ἕτεροι. With the manuscript reading this can only mean 'those things whose definitions differ in respect of the *infima species*'. But this use of ἐν with ἕτερος is surprising (the closest parallel I have found is *Poet.* 1448ᵃ 16 ἐν ταύτῃ δὲ τῇ διαφορᾷ καὶ ἡ τραγῳδία πρὸς τὴν κωμῳδίαν διέστηκεν); and we should expect 'differ in respect of the last *differentia*'. Alexander's words ὧν ἀτόμων εἰδῶν ἐν τῷ αὐτῷ γένει ὄντων (383. 37) suggest the reading ὅσων, ὄντων τελευταίων τοῦ γένους εἰδῶν, οἱ λόγοι ἕτεροι, which gives a good sense. If ὄντων were once corrupted into ἐν τῷ, the remaining changes would follow. But in 384. 26 Alexander presupposes the manuscript reading.

7. ὅσα ἐν τῇ αὐτῇ οὐσίᾳ ὄντα ἔχει διαφοράν. Alexander explains this as meaning (1) individuals of the same species, or (2) bodies which are different though not contrary, as earth and water. But individuals of the same species could not be called ἕτερα τῷ εἴδει, and it is difficult to see in what sense earth and water are ἐν τῇ αὐτῇ οὐσίᾳ. (Bonitz's notion that Alexander had a negative before ἔχει is a mistake; see Al. 384. 28 and the context.) The natural meaning of the words seems to be 'attributes which may belong to the same substance (at different times) and which have a difference', as hot and cold are in the same substance iron and have a difference. Cf. ᵃ 28 τὰ πλεῖστον διαφέροντα τῶν ἐν ταὐτῷ δεκτικῷ.

'Prior', 'Posterior' (ch. 11).

1018ᵇ 9. 'Prior' means (1) that which is nearer some beginning determined absolutely or relatively, e. g. in respect of

12. (*a*) place,

14. (*b*) time,

19. (*c*) movement,

21. (*d*) power,

26. (*e*) arrangement;

30. (2) the prior in knowledge

(*a*) in respect of definition, e. g. the universal as against the particular, the accident as against the complex of substance and accident,

(*b*) in respect of sensation, e. g. the particular.

37. (3) Attributes of things *per se* prior are themselves said to be prior.

1019ᵃ 2. (4) The prior in nature and substance, i. e. that which can be without another, while the other cannot be without *it* (a Platonic distinction). (If we take account of the varieties in the meaning of being,

(*a*) substratum or substance is prior to attribute,

(*b*) part as against whole, matter as against concrete substance, is prior in potentiality, posterior in actuality.)

11. All the senses of ' prior ' depend on this last sense. E. g. the whole can exist without the part in generation, the part without the whole in dissolution.

In *Cat.* 12 we have the following classification of the senses of ' prior ':

(1) in time,

(2) τῷ μὴ ἀντιστρέφειν κατὰ τὴν τοῦ εἶναι ἀκολούθησιν,

(3) κατά τινα τάξιν, e. g. ἐπὶ τῶν ἐπιστημῶν καὶ τῶν λόγων.

(4) The better is prior τῇ φύσει.

(5) Of two reciprocating terms, the cause is prior to the effect τῇ φύσει.

In the present passage, priority in time ((1) in the *Categories*) is included in a wider type, τῷ ἐγγύτερον εἶναι ἀρχῆς τινός (1018ᵇ 9–29). (2) in the *Categories* answers to the fourth main sense in the present passage (1019ᵃ 2–4). (3) in the *Categories* answers roughly to (2) in Book Δ (1018ᵇ 30–37). (4) and (5) in the *Categories* do not appear distinctly in Δ but can be brought under the very wide first sense.

More cursory distinctions of various senses of priority are found in *Phys.* 260ᵇ 18, 261ᵃ 14 (cf. *De Gen. An.* 742ᵃ 21, A. 989ᵃ 15, Θ. 1050ᵃ 4, M. 1077ᵃ 19, *Rhet.* 1392ᵃ 20), 265ᵃ 22, Z. 1028ᵃ 32. 1038ᵇ 27, Θ. 1049ᵇ 11, M. 1077ᵇ 2.

1018ᵇ 21. ἁπλῶς, without qualification, by its own nature. Cf. 1. 11 ἁπλῶς καὶ τῇ φύσει.

27. κατά τινα λόγον. It is impossible to assign any suitable meaning to κατὰ τὸν λόγον in this context, and Jaeger seems to be right in reading κατά τινα λόγον, ' in a certain ratio ' (cf. λόγῳ τινι *G. A.* 740ᵇ 32, 767ᵃ 17). Alexander's ἔν τινι λόγῳ (386. 10) points to this reading, and τόν came in owing to the copyist's running his eye on to κατὰ τὸν λόγον in l. 31 f.

38—1019ᵃ 1. τὸ μὲν . . . ἐπιφανείας. Aristotle assumes that the line is prior to the plane, which it is in the sense explained later, 1019ᵃ 8.

1019ᵃ 4. The reading ἐχρήσατο is better attested than ἐχρῆτο. There seems to be no passage in Plato in which this distinction is drawn (Apelt's attempt to find it in *Tim.* 34 c is not successful); Aristotle is thinking doubtless of an oral utterance of his master. Trendelenburg conjectures that Aristotle has in mind Plato's doctrine of the priority of one ideal number relatively to another, cf. B. 999ᵃ 8, M. 6 ; we cannot be sure whether Aristotle is thinking of this or of some more general statement about the meaning of ' prior '. Mutschmann in his edition of *Divisiones Aristotelicae*, p. xvii, holds that here and in *De Gen. et Corr.* 330ᵇ 16, *P. A.* 642ᵇ 12 there is a reference to an actual Platonic book of Divisions ; but the reference in the other two passages may be to the *Sophistes* and the *Politicus*.

ἐπεὶ δέ κτλ. Aristotle has used the word εἶναι in his statement of this final sense of ' prior ' (l. 3). He therefore now considers what bearing the different senses of ' be ' (ch. 7) have on the senses of priority. He takes first the distinction between substance and the other categories (1017ᵃ 22–30). Since substance *is* in a fuller sense than the other categories, it is prior to them.

Next, he has distinguished being potentially from being actually (1017ᵃ 35–ᵇ 8). Now ' the part is prior potentially, posterior actually'. Aristotle's meaning is hard to seize and is not very satisfactory. He seems to mean that in considering a whole we should naturally say ' the whole cannot exist without the parts, but they can exist without it, and therefore (according to l. 3) they are prior'; but that when we reflect we find that in the whole the parts do not exist actually. The half-line does not exist till the whole has been cut in two; the matter does not exist till the concrete thing has been resolved into its components. Actually, therefore, the parts will exist only when the whole has ceased to exist; 'actually they are posterior to it'. But the existence of the whole presupposes the potential existence of the parts; ' in respect of potentiality they are prior to it'.

8. ἡ ἡμίσεια τῆς ὅλης, *sc.* γραμμῆς, as 1017ᵇ 7 shows. Cf. Z. 1039ᵃ 6 n., Θ. 1048ᵃ 33 n., *De Somno* 448ᵇ 4, 10.

12. ταῦτα, not ' the distinction of potentiality and actuality', though this is what has been last mentioned. It is not true that all the meanings of ' prior' and ' posterior' can be reduced to this. Rather, as the next words show, Aristotle means that all the senses of ' prior ' can be reduced to that named in l. 3, ὅσα ἐνδέχεται εἶναι ἄνευ ἄλλων, ἐκεῖνα δὲ ἄνευ ἐκείνων μή, and in this he is saying what can easily be seen to be true. Lines 4–11 are a parenthetical comment on l. 3, and there is no difficulty in supposing Aristotle now to revert to l. 3.

What does Aristotle mean by saying that the whole can in respect of genesis exist without its parts? He means that when the whole exists the parts do not exist actually (cf. l. 4 n.). But one would naturally suppose that just as the whole is resolved into its parts so it is generated out of its parts, so that κατὰ γένεσιν as well as κατὰ φθοράν the parts would be prior. This is so where a whole is produced by the mere aggregation of parts, but probably Aristotle has in mind organic wholes in which, for instance, the branches do not exist before the whole tree, and have a separate existence only when cut off from an already existing tree, and in which, again, the tree can replace its lost branches by others. But the whole thought in ll. 4–14 is somewhat loosely expressed.

14. τἆλλα, the first three senses of ' prior'.

'*Potency*', '*Capable*', '*Incapacity*', '*Incapable*', '*Possible*', '*Impossible*' (ch. 12).

1019ᵃ **15.** ' Potency ' means (*a*) a principle of change in something other than the thing changed or in it *qua* other,

20. (*b*) a principle enabling a thing to be changed, by another or by itself *qua* other, (i) in general, or (ii) for the better,

23. (*c*) the power of producing change successfully,

26. (*d*) the power of being changed successfully,

26. (*e*) a state in virtue of which a thing cannot be changed, or cannot easily be changed, for the worse.

32. Similarly the 'potent' or 'capable' means

(1) (*a*) that which has potency (*a*),

35. (*b*) that which has potency (*b*),

ᵇ **1.** (*c*) that which has a potency of changing for the worse or for the better.

3. For even that which is destroyed must have been *capable* of being destroyed. Things are capable sometimes by virtue of having something, sometimes by virtue of being deprived of something. If privation may be called a 'having', all things that are capable are so by virtue of having something—if not by having a positive disposition, then by having its privation.

10. (*d*) That which has potency (*e*),

11. (*e*) that which has potency (*c*),

(*f*) that which has potency (*d*).

15. 'Incapacity' is the privation of such a power (α) in any subject, or (β) in one which naturally has it, or (γ) in one which naturally has it, *when* it naturally would have it. Again, it may be the opposite of potency (*a*) or (*b*) or of potency (*c*) or (*d*).

21. ἀδύνατον has a corresponding sense (1), but it means (2) that whose contrary is necessarily true.

27. So too δυνατόν means (2) (*a*) that whose contrary is not necessarily false (in l. 31 'that which is not necessarily false'), as well as (*b*) that which is true, and (*c*) that which may be true.

33. The sense of δύναμις in geometry is metaphorical.

34. Sense (2) of δυνατόν and ἀδύνατον does not imply a δύναμις ; all the varieties of sense (1) imply δύναμις in sense (*a*). (*a*) is thus the primary sense of δύναμις.

The treatment of δύναμις and its cognates in this chapter answers closely to that in Θ. First, in 1019ᵃ 15–32, Aristotle explains the varieties of δύναμις in its primary sense of 'power' rather than 'potentiality' (δυνάμεως ἧ λέγεται μάλιστα κυρίως Θ. 1045ᵇ 35)—the sense that is treated of in Θ. 1–5. Then he speaks of the corresponding senses of δυνατόν (ᵃ 32–ᵇ 15), and of ἀδυναμία (ᵇ 15–21). Then, having mentioned that ἀδύνατον has corresponding senses (21), he proceeds to say that ἀδύνατον has another meaning ('impossible' as distinct from 'incapable') which does not imply a positive power but a purely logical relation between subjects and predicates (22–27), and that δυνατόν has a corresponding meaning (27–32), as well as two others

(32, 33). This passage (22–33) presupposes that secondary meaning of δύναμις ('potentiality' as opposed to 'power') which is explained in Θ. 1048ᵃ 27–ᵇ 9. Finally he traces the first group of meanings of δυνατόν (cf. ᵃ 32–ᵇ 15) back to the primary definition of δύναμις as ἀρχὴ μεταβλητικὴ ἐν ἄλλῳ ἢ ᾗ ἄλλο (1019ᵇ 35—1020ᵃ 6).

1019ᵃ 19. What answers to ἡ μὲν οὖν ὅλως is not ἡ δ᾽ l. 20, since that also introduces a general sense. The general sense of δύναμις introduced by ἡ μὲν οὖν ὅλως is opposed to the narrower sense introduced in l. 23. Jaeger, finding a difficulty in ὅλως, would read οὕτως (cf. 1018ᵃ 4, 1019ᵃ 2, 1020ᵃ 27, 1021ᵇ 4), but this does not seem necessary.

20–26. Christ proposes to transfer καθ᾽ ἥν . . . 23 βέλτιον after πάσχειν l. 26. We thus get the following kinds of δύναμις :

(1) power of changing something else (15–20),
(2) power of being changed by something else (20),
(3) power of changing something else successfully (23–26),
(4) power of being changed successfully (26, 20–23).

This is the classification which we get in Θ. 1046ᵃ 10–13, 16, 17 (1046ᵃ 13–15 answers to 1019ᵃ 26–32). It is clear, however, that Aristotle introduces a complication which does not occur in Θ, viz. the distinction of the power of being changed for the better, from the power of being changed in general. This is not the same as the distinction between the power of acting or being acted on simply and that of acting or being acted on καλῶς ἢ κατὰ προαίρεσιν. The same two distinctions occur with regard to τὸ δυνατόν. The latter distinction is applied both to active and to passive potencies (ᵃ 23–26, cf. ταῦτα πάντα ᵇ 12), the former only to passive (ᵃ 20–23, cf. ᵇ 2). (Alexander may not have had before him καθ᾽ ἥν . . . πάσχει τι and may have read ὁτὲ μὲν οὖν ἐάν, but otherwise had our traditional text.)

23–26. The powers mentioned here as instances of the power to produce change are, as it happens, powers of producing change in oneself *qua* other.

26. ἐπὶ τοῦ πάσχειν, 'in the case of passivity'. Cf. τὰς ἐπὶ τοῦ πάσχειν Θ. 1047ᵇ 35 and the uses of ἐπί quoted in Bz. *Index* 268ᵃ 32–46.

32. Jaeger is probably right in reading τῷ . . . τῷ for τὸ . . . τό. τῷ with the infinitive is the normal mode of expression in this context (ᵃ 29 f., ᵇ 6–10, 12 f.), and τό and τῷ are very often confused in manuscripts.

32–ᵇ 15. Aristotle now gives the senses of δυνατόν answering to those of δύναμις.

ᵃ 33–35 answers to (a) above, ᵃ 35–ᵇ 1 to (b), ᵇ 10–11 to (c), 11–15 to (c) and (d).

ᵇ 1. αὐτοῦ is an objective genitive depending on δύναμιν, 'power over it'. Cf. 1020ᵃ 3.

ἕνα δ᾽ ἐάν κτλ. It is not evident at first sight how this sense differs from that mentioned in ᵃ 35–ᵇ 1. The point seems to be that in ᵃ 35–ᵇ 1 Aristotle speaks of a power in A of being changed by B, and in ᵇ 1–3 of a power in A of 'changing' simply. The difference is that between a thing's being changed by another and by itself *qua* other cf. ᵃ 20 ὑφ᾽ ἑτέρου ἢ ᾗ ἕτερον).

6. εἰ δ᾽ ἡ στέρησίς ἐστιν ἕξις πως. This, according to Aristotle, it is; a privative term differs from a merely contradictory one by implying a positive nature; ἡ στέρησις εἶδός πώς ἐστιν *Phys.* 193ᵇ 19. Only that which has a positive nature in virtue of which it might have had sight can be called blind; other things that do not see must only be called ' not-seeing'. Cf. ch. 22.

8–10. The readings both of EJΓ Asc. and of Aᵇ are unintelligible, and their common archetype was evidently corrupt. On the other hand Alexander had a text which presented no difficulty to him, and his paraphrase of which (392. 10–18) gives a clear and satisfactory sense. Reasoning from his paraphrase to what the reading before him must have been, we get one which agrees substantially with that of Aᵇ except that in Aᵇ the order is dislocated, and with that of EJΓ Asc. except that in them εἰ δὲ μή, ὁμωνύμως has disappeared and the unmeaning ὁμωνύμως δὲ λεγόμενον τὸ ὄν has been inserted. Jaeger conjectures plausibly that the latter phrase is a truncated form of the gloss ὁμωνύμως δὲ λέγομεν ὧν τὸ ὄνομα μόνον κοινόν (a reference to *Cat.* 1ᵃ 1 ὁμώνυμα λέγεται ὧν ὄνομα μόνον κοινόν).

22. οἷον δυνατόν τε καὶ ἀδύνατον, ' i. e. both δυνατόν and ἀδύνατον are used as follows'.

26. ἀσύμμετρον εἶναι is plainly a gloss. For this usage of ἀνάγκη cf. Pl. *Gorg.* 475 Β 8, 499 Β 2.

27. The impossible being that whose opposite is necessarily true, we should suppose the possible to be that whose opposite is *not* necessarily true, but Aristotle defines it as that whose opposite is not necessarily false. But in the next sentence he loosely reverts to the form we should have expected here ; he describes the possible as that which is not necessarily false, i. e. that whose opposite is not necessarily true. Both descriptions are true of the possible ; it would be not possible but impossible if its opposite were necessarily true, and not possible but necessary if its opposite were necessarily false. Similarly in *De Int.* 22ᵃ 15–17 τὸ μὴ ἀναγκαῖον εἶναι is said to follow from τὸ δυνατὸν εἶναι. The difficulty would be to some extent got over if, as Alexander seems to have done, we were to omit τό before δυνατόν in l. 28. Aristotle would then be saying ' the opposite of this (i. e. that whose opposite is not necessarily true) is possible when the opposite is not necessarily false '. But the difficulty is not entirely removed, for in ll. 29, 30, the fact that the opposite is not necessarily false is treated as if it were the sole condition of possibility, while in l. 31 the fact that the proposition itself is not necessarily false is treated as the sole condition. It seems clear that Aristotle is in some confusion.

I have rendered ἐναντίον by ' opposite'; it has not here its strict meaning of ' contrary '; Aristotle is thinking rather of the contradictory opposite.

32. τὸ ἀληθὲς εἶναι if retained must = ὃ εἶναι ἀληθές ἐστιν, εἶναι being epexegetic of ἀληθές—' that of which it is true to say that it is '. τούτεστι τὸ ἤδη ὑπάρχον, ὃ ἀληθές ἐστιν εἰπεῖν εἶναι Al. The analogy of τὸ ἀληθὲς φάναι Γ. 1012ᵇ 9, ἀληθὲς εἰπεῖν *An. Pr.* 28ᵇ 29 is not very close, and there is little doubt that εἶναι is an emblema from the next line.

It is rather surprising to find this included among the senses of 'possible' (it is so also in *De Int.* 23ᵃ 8). Alexander explains that the merely existent is reckoned under the possible because, like it, it is intermediate between the necessary and the impossible.

τὸ ἐνδεχόμενον ἀληθὲς εἶναι. It is not clear how this differs from the first sense, τὸ μὴ ἐξ ἀνάγκης ψεῦδος. ἐνδεχόμενον never implies, as δυνατόν sometimes does, the presence of a positive power to be or do the thing in question. But the first definition of δυνατόν here (30–32) has defined it without any such implication. I. e. it is τὸ δυνατόν as the possible, not as the capable, that the first definition defined, and thus the third definition seems in no way to differ from it. We must as before (1018ᵃ 13–15 n.) fall back on the reflection that Aristotle is stating the various answers that might be given to the question 'what do you mean by δυνατόν?' If two of these answers amount to the same thing, that is no reason why he should not set them both down.

The difference between δυνατόν and ἐνδεχόμενον is, as Waitz (*Organon*, i. 376) says, that the former is opposed to ἐνεργοῦν, the latter to ὑπάρχον, or again that the former expresses real, the latter logical possibility or the absence of self-contradiction. But while ἐνδεχόμενον is never used in the former sense, δυνατόν is sometimes used in the latter. Cf. Θ. 1047ᵃ 24, where δυνατόν is defined much in the same way in which ἐνδεχόμενον is defined in *An. Pr.* 32ᵃ 18. In fact τὸ ἐνδεχόμενον = τὸ δυνατὸν τὸ μὴ κατὰ δύναμιν (1019ᵇ 34). For the difference between the two terms cf. Θ. 1050ᵇ 13, *De Caelo* 274ᵇ 13.

33. ἡ ἐν γεωμετρίᾳ λέγεται δύναμις, cf. Θ. 1046ᵃ 8. A square is called a δύναμις because it is ὃ δύναται ἡ πλευρά (Al. 394. 35). Cf. Euc. *El.* X. Def. 4 αἱ δυνάμεναι αὐτά = 'the straight lines the squares on which = those areas'. In *Rep.* 587 D, *Tim.* 31 C the word means 'a square', but in *Theaet.* 148 A (cf. 147 D, *Pol.* 266 B) it is defined as a line incommensurate with another line but whose square is commensurate with that of the other ; e. g. the diagonal of the square is a δύναμις in relation to the side. Putting it arithmetically, a δύναμις is (in those passages) the square root of an integral non-square number ; but Plato does not put it arithmetically.

Plato says (*Theaet.* 167 D) that Theodorus of Cyrene wrote περὶ δυνάμεων : Theaetetus carried the theory much further. For its history cf. Heath, *The Thirteen Books of Euclid's Elements*, iii. 1–10.

34–35. ταῦτα μὲν οὖν τὰ δυνατά, those explained in ᵇ 27–33 ; τὰ δὲ λεγόμενα κατὰ δύναμιν, those explained in ᵃ 33–ᵇ 15.

οὐ κατὰ δύναμιν, i. e. they do not imply a positive power such as has been described in ᵃ 15–32.

1020ᵃ 1. τὴν πρώτην [μίαν]. Bekker and Bonitz bracket μίαν. Alexander seems not to have read it, and Asclepius treats πρώτην and μίαν as alternative readings. πρώτην μίαν probably arose from ā being expanded differently in different manuscripts (cf. *G. A.* 742ᵃ 29, *Poet.* 1450ᵇ 16). The manuscript reading is defended by Vahlen (*Poet.*³

p. 127), who refers to Θ. 1046ª 10 πρὸς πρώτην μίαν. But τήν makes the combination more difficult to accept.

2. τῷ τὰ μὲν ἔχειν κτλ., 'because in some cases something else has such a power over them'. For αὐτῶν depending on δύναμιν cf. 1019^b 1.

4. ὁμοίως δὲ καὶ τὰ ἀδύνατα, i. e. in the first sense, referred to in 1019^b 21, 22.

'Quantity' (ch. 13).

1020ª 7. 'Quantity' means that which is divided into constituents of which each is individual. (1) Numerable quantity is plurality; it is divisible into non-continuous parts. (2) Measurable quantity is magnitude; it is divisible into continuous parts, in one, two, or three dimensions. Finite plurality is a number, finite length a line, finite breadth a plane, finite depth a solid.

14. Things are quantitative (a) per se or (b) incidentally.

17. (a) Things quantitative per se are (i) entities whose definition involves quantity (e. g. the line), or (ii) attributes of such entities (e. g. much, long).

23. 'Great', 'small', 'greater', 'smaller' are of the latter type, but are applied metaphorically to non-quantitative things.

26. (b) What is incidentally quantitative is so (i) as the musical is quantitative because its subject is so, (ii) as movement is quantitative because the distance moved through is so, and as time is quantitative because movement is so.

The distinction between πλῆθος and μέγεθος answers to that in *Cat.* 4^b 20 between τὸ διωρισμένον and τὸ συνεχές, except that 'the continuous' is a wider conception than 'magnitude', including time as one of its proper kinds (contrast 4^b 24 with 1020ª 29). The distinction in the *Categories* between τὸ ἐκ θέσιν ἐχόντων τῶν ἐν αὐτοῖς μορίων and τὸ οὐκ ἐξ ἐχόντων θέσιν is not noticed here. The two kinds of ποσὸν κατὰ συμβεβηκός (1020ª 15, 26, 28) are recognized in *Cat.* 5^b 1, 3, though without distinction. The distinction between ποσὰ κατ' οὐσίαν and their πάθη (1020ª 17) is not found in the *Categories*.

1020ª 8. ἕν τι καὶ τόδε τι. This is doubtless to distinguish the division of a quantity into parts from the analysis of a subject into attributes or the division of a genus into species. So Alexander.

12. It is of course not exact to say that breadth is continuous in two and depth in three dimensions. Aristotle uses a convenient brachylogy.

13. τὸ πεπερασμένον goes with μῆκος, πλάτος, βάθος, as well as with πλῆθος. The definition of number as πλῆθος πεπερασμένον is anticipated by Eudoxus' definition of it as πλῆθος ὡρισμένον (Iambl. *in Nicom. Ar. Introd.* 10. 17). For other definitions cf. Z. 1039ª 12, I. 1053ª 30, 1057ª 3, M. 1085^b 22, N. 1088ª 5, *Phys.* 207^b 7 (ἕνα

πλείω καὶ πόσ' ἄττα). Mr. F. M. Cornford (*Class. Quart.* xvii. 8 n.)
suggests (rightly, I think) that the present definition 'goes back to the
characteristically Pythagorean conception of number as the product
of the union of πέρας and ἄπειρον'; whereas such definitions as
σύνθεσις μονάδων (Z. 1039ᵃ 12), πλῆθος μονάδων (I. 1053ᵃ 30) represent
'the crude, and so to say materialistic, view which may well have been
shared by the Egyptians and the Pythagorean mathematicians or
number-atomists' of the sixth century.

16. τὸ μουσικόν is presumably a man or an instrument, both of which
are σώματα, and therefore indirectly quantitative.

19. I read with the manuscripts τὸ ποσόν τι ὑπάρχει; Alexander's
τὸ ποσὸν ἐνυπάρχει (which Bz. adopted) is probably simply his paraphrase of this. For ὑπάρχειν in this sense cf. 1022ᵃ 28.

20. A line is not strictly a substance; it has no separate existence,
but can only be separated in thought (M. 3). But it is the subject of
which long and short are attributes; it is a step nearer to substantiality
than they are, and hence Aristotle treats it, relatively, as it were, as
a substance. Cf. 1017ᵇ 6 n.

22. βαρὺ καὶ κοῦφον. It is noticeable that βαρύτης and κουφότης are
named among *qualities* (ᵇ 10). Nor is the difficulty removed by the
transition to the nominal form. The fact is that βαρύ and κοῦφον are
out of place here among the purely mathematical attributes. They
are quantities, says Alexander, in so far as they mean excess or defect
of ῥοπή, qualities in so far as they cause the things that possess them
to move up or down. According to Aristotle's view earth naturally
moves down, fire up. Thus, if one piece of earth is heavy and another
light, the difference is one of degree and comes under quantity (though
only in the 'transferred' sense mentioned in l. 25); but the difference
between earth and fire is one of quality. Cf. *De Caelo* iv. 1.

23. In *Cat.* 5ᵇ 15 'great' and 'small' are said to be not quantities but
relative terms. According to that view there is no such thing as a great
or small *per se* (contrast 1020ᵃ 24 with 5ᵇ 16).

25. καὶ ἐπ' ἄλλα, to things which are not quantities, such as pain or
disease. 'Intensive quantity' is thus treated as a metaphor.

31. ὃ ἐκινήθη, 'that through or along which it was moved'. Aristotle's account is as follows: A spatial magnitude (μέγεθος) is a ποσὸν
καθ' αὑτό; movement, since it is through a μέγεθος, is a ποσὸν κατὰ
συμβεβηκός; and time, since movement takes place in time, is also
a ποσὸν κατὰ συμβεβηκός (cf. *Phys.* 219ʰ 1 ὁ χρόνος ἀριθμὸς κινήσεως).
It is space that is directly measurable; movement, through space;
and time, through movement. In the *Categories* (5ᵇ 3) a movement is
said to be πολλή because the time it occupies is πολύς: in the present
passage the quantity of the time is said to depend on the quantity of
the movement. The latter view is also that of the *Physics* (219ᵃ 13),
where in iv. 10, 11 the relation of time to movement is elaborately
discussed. The more elaborate view of the *Physics* and the *Metaphysics* seems clearly to be the later. The fact noted in *Phys.* 220ᵇ 23
that movement and time mutually determine one another, so that either

can be used as a measure of the other, accounts for the possibility of such a view being held as is expressed in the *Categories*.

Movement and time, though classed as only *per accidens* quantities, are distinguished from ordinary *per accidens* quantities such as ' the musical ' or ' the white '. Aristotle means doubtless that the relation of the former to the quantities *per se* is not casual as is that of the latter. All extension is a possible if not actual theatre of movement, and al movement occupies time.

Why then, it may be asked, are not movement and time classed among the quantities *per se* which are πάθη καὶ ἕξεις of the things that are quantities in the primary sense (l. 19)? The answer is that movement along a line, and the time of the movement, are not related to the line as its length is. The movement is not an attribute of the line, but an event of which the line is one element, and the time is another element in the movement, and only so related to the line.

' *Quality* ' (ch. 14).

1020ᵃ 33. ' Quality' means (1) the differentia of the essence of a thing,

ᵇ **2.** (2) that which is present, besides quantity, in the essence of unchangeable (mathematical) objects, e. g. the ' planeness ' or ' solidity ' of composite numbers,

8. (3) the affections of changeable substances, in respect of which they change, e. g. heat,

12. (4) goodness and badness.

13. These fall under two main senses, of which the first is the more proper; (2) is a variety of (1),

18. and (4) of (3).

23. Goodness and badness indicate quality primarily in the case of living things, especially those which have purpose.

In *Cat.* 8 we have the following classification of the kinds of quality :

(1) (*a*) ἕξις (e. g. the virtues) and (*b*) διάθεσις (e. g. disease),

(2) ὅσα κατὰ (*a*) δύναμιν φυσικὴν (e. g. the power of boxing) ἢ (*b*) ἀδυναμίαν (e. g. softness),

(3) παθητικαὶ ποιότητες, i. e. (*a*) powers of producing a sensuous πάθος, e. g. sweetness, (*b*) results of πάθος, e. g. paleness,

(4) Figure, straightness, &c.

The first two senses here are omitted in the *Categories*, which aims at distinguishing quality more rigidly from substance or essence ; but the first sense is recognized in *Top.* 122ᵇ 16, 128ᵃ 26, *Phys.* 226ᵃ 27. Sense (3) here answers to sense (3) of the *Categories*. Sense (4) seems to be included in sense (1) of the *Categories*.

1020ᵃ 35. Since the quality of τὰ μαθηματικά comes under the *second* sense of quality, the introduction of the circle here seems out of place. But in the end Aristotle reduces the first two senses to one (ᵇ 15), and further it seems that, in spite of the general reference to τὰ μαθηματικά, Aristotle has only numbers in mind in speaking of the second meaning (cf. ᵇ 15 ἡ ἐν τοῖς ἀριθμοῖς ποιότης). In fact the analogy between (*a*) numbers and (*b*) lines, planes, and solids is the whole basis of his recognition of the second meaning as a separate one. Besides their quantitative character, as larger or smaller sums of units, numbers have a quality according as they are prime, composed of two factors, or composed of three, and therefore analogous to lines, planes, or solids, respectively ; and further as they have equal or unequal factors and are therefore analogous to squares or to rectangles, to cubes or to parallelepipeds.

ᵇ 4. μὴ μόνον ἐφ' ἕν ὄντες κτλ., i. e. geometrically representable not merely as a line, but as a surface (because they are the products of two factors) or as a solid (because they are the products of three). Prime numbers were called εὐθυμετρικοί or εὐθυγραμμικοί (Iambl. *in Nicom.* p. 27. 3 f. Pistelli), or γραμμικοί (Theo, p. 23. 12 Hiller, *Theol. Arithm.* pp. 61, 62). This last name for them seems to go back to Philolaus (*c.* 440 B.C.).

6. ὃ παρὰ τὸ ποσὸν ὑπάρχει ἐν τῇ οὐσίᾳ. This is difficult, as Aristotle goes on to say that the οὐσία of a number is what it is once, i. e. does not include the fact that it is the product of two or more factors. It looks as though Alexander read ὑπάρχει καὶ τὴν οὐσίαν (399. 37, 400. 1), and one might be tempted to read this or ὑπάρχει τὸ ἐν τῇ οὐσίᾳ. But ὑπάρχει is thus left rather awkwardly isolated ; and Aristotle says in l. 15 that this characteristic of numbers is a differentia of them, so that it must be included in their οὐσία. It is better, then, to keep the manuscript reading and put up with the inconsistency.

7. Bz.'s ὃ ἅπαξ is not (as he thinks) supported by Alexander (399 39), but seems to be a necessary emendation.

8. We now pass to qualities which do not always attach to their subjects, separable accidents as opposed to the differentiae mentioned in ᵃ 33–ᵇ 2 and the properties mentioned in ᵇ 2–8. These are the παθητικαὶ ποιότητες of *Cat.* 9ᵃ 28, the παθητικὰ ποιά of *Phys.* 226ᵃ 29.

10. βαρύτης καὶ κουφότης, cf. ᵃ 22 n.

12. κατ' ἀρετὴν καὶ κακίαν. Finally Aristotle mentions non-physical attributes which, however, like the physical attributes in the third class, are attributes in respect of which their subjects may change, and are attributes of subjects which *qua* acting are κινούμενα.

17–18. τὰ δὲ πάθη ... διαφοραί. The clause has no expressed predicate ; the meaning seems to be : ' The differentia of substance is the first kind of quality (l. 14) ... the affections of things moved and the differentiae of movements (are the second kind).' A better grammatical construction might be got by omitting αἱ and treating everything after πάθη (or after τὰ δέ) as predicate. But αἱ is well attested, and the way

of taking the clause suggested above, though grammatically inferior, is
perhaps more natural.

23. μάλιστα κτλ. 'ἀγαθά and κακά may be found in all the categories ; it is particularly in the form in which they are found in living
things and especially in men, viz. virtue and vice, that they are qualities.' So Alexander. More probably, however, Aristotle is not
suggesting that goodness and badness are ever anything but qualities,
but that they are qualities which are most properly said to be found in
living things, above all in men.

24. τοῖς ἔχουσι προαίρεσιν, i. e. men.

'Relative' (ch. 15).

1020ᵇ 26. 'Relative' terms are so (1) as that which exceeds to that
which is exceeded, (2) as the active to the passive, (3) as the measured
to its measure.

32. (1) The first kind are related numerically, either (*a*) indefinitely
or (*b*) definitely, (i) to a number or (ii) to 1, e. g.

(*b*) (ii) 2 to 1,
(*a*) (ii) *n* to 1,
(*b*) (i) 3 to 2,
(*a*) (i) *n* + 1 to *n*.

1021ᵃ 3. The exceeding and exceeded are related quite indefinitely
as to number, since number is commensurate but the amount by
which the exceeding exceeds the exceeded is quite indefinite.

9. In another way 'equal', 'like', 'the same' are relations of this
numerical type; for sameness is oneness of substance, likeness oneness of quality, equality oneness of quantity, and 'one' is the beginning
and measure of number.

14. (2) The active and the passive imply (*a*) potency, e. g. θερμαν-
τικόν and θερμαντόν, or (*b*) activity, e. g. θερμαῖνον and θερμαινόμενον.
(Numerical relations have no activities in the sense of movement.)

21. Some relative terms implying potency also refer to particular
times, e. g. that which has made is relative to that which has been
made (father to son), that which will make to that which will be made.
Some relative terms imply privation of power, e. g. 'incapable',
'invisible'.

26. Relative terms of type (1) or (2) are relative in the sense that
what they are can only be stated by reference to something else, but
(3) the measurable, the knowable, the thinkable are called relative
because other terms are relative to them.

31. To call a thing thinkable implies that there is thought of it,
but thought is not properly described as relative to 'that of which it

is the thought ', which would be tautologous; and sight is not ' of that of which it is the sight ', but of colour.

ᵇ 3. (i) Things that are *per se* relative are

(*a*) things that are relative in mode (1), (2), or (3),

(*b*) members of classes which are relative in one of these modes, or

(*c*) attributes in virtue of which their subjects are relative in one of these modes.

8. (ii) Things that are incidentally relative are so

(*a*) as a man is relative because he is double of something, or

(*b*) as ' the white ' is relative if the same thing is double and white.

The account of relative terms in *Cat.* 7 does not classify them, but it recognizes the special nature of the relations of knowledge and perception to their correlatives (cf. 1021ᵃ 29-ᵇ 3 with 7ᵇ 22-8ᵃ 12). In I. 1056ᵇ 35 τὰ πρός τι are divided into τὰ ὡς ἐναντία, which answer loosely to the first two kinds mentioned in this chapter, and τὰ ὡς ἐπιστήμη πρὸς ἐπιστητόν, which answer to the third. The first two kinds reappear in *Phys.* 200ᵇ 28. In *Top.* 125ᵃ 33-ᵇ 4 we get a classification from a different point of view.

1020ᵇ 32—1021ᵃ 8. The passage is difficult, and the commentators do not offer any very satisfactory account of it. To begin with (l. 33) Aristotle gives a summary classification, ἢ ἁπλῶς (ἀορίστως) ἢ ὡρισμένως πρὸς αὐτούς (= ἀριθμοὺς) ἢ πρὸς ἕν. This may be supposed to be a threefold list :

(*a*) ἁπλῶς,

(*b* i) ὡρισμένως πρὸς αὐτούς,

(*b* ii) ὡρισμένως πρὸς ἕν ;

or a fourfold one,

(*a* i) ἁπλῶς πρὸς αὐτούς,

(*a* ii) ἁπλῶς πρὸς ἕν,

(*b* i) ὡρισμένως πρὸς αὐτούς,

(*b* ii) ὡρισμένως πρὸς ἕν.

But in what follows Aristotle distinguishes *five* relations, indicated by διπλάσιον, πολλαπλάσιον, ἡμιόλιον, ἐπιμόριον, ὑπερέχον, and it is hard to see how these fit into the earlier classification.

Let us start with the hypothesis that the classification is a fourfold one. It can be understood in this way. The distinction between ἁπλῶς (or κατ᾽ ἀόριστον, *sc.* ἀριθμόν) and ὡρισμένως (or κατ᾽ ἀριθμὸν ὡρισμένον) is that between a general *type* of ratio, which requires for its expression the use of a variable, and a definite ratio which can be expressed in terms of definite numbers. The distinction between πρὸς αὐτούς and πρὸς ἕν is that between a ratio which (fractions being barred) requires for its expression two numbers ·other than 1, and a ratio of which 1 is one of the terms. (Bz. objects that this would require πρὸς τὸ ἕν, but since Aristotle uses (1021ᵃ 3) πρὸς τὸ ἕν of the same relation which he had previously described as πρὸς ἕν (1020ʰ 35), the distinction does not seem very serious. For ἕν without the article = the number 1 cf. *Top.* 135ᵇ 26.)

Now the relation of the double to its half (2 : 1) is described (l. 34) as πρὸς ἕν ἀριθμὸς ὡρισμένος, i. e. as belonging to type (*b* ii). The instance evidently agrees with our description of that type.

The relation of that which is many times something else to that something (*n* : 1) is described as κατ' ἀριθμὸν πρὸς ἕν, οὐχ ὡρισμένον δέ, οἷον τόνδε ἢ τόνδε. Here the last words show that ὡρισμένον goes with ἀριθμόν, not with ἕν, Thus κατ' ἀριθμὸν πρὸς ἕν, οὐχ ὡρισμένον δέ = ἁπλῶς πρὸς ἕν. This is type (*a* ii), and it answers to our account of that type.

The relation of that which is half as big again as something else to that something (3 : 2) is described as κατ' ἀριθμὸν πρὸς ἀριθμὸν ὡρισμένον, and since this is opposed in the next line by κατὰ ἀόριστον, it is evident that ὡρισμένον goes with the first, not with the second ἀριθμόν. Thus this is related ὡρισμένως πρὸς αὐτούς (type *b* i).

The relation of the ἐπιμόριον to the ὑπεπιμόριον ($1 + \frac{1}{n}$: 1, or $n + 1$: *n*) is described as κατὰ ἀόριστον (*sc.* πρὸς ἀριθμόν, which must be understood from the previous line), ὥσπερ τὸ πολλαπλάσιον πρὸς τὸ ἕν, i. e. ἁπλῶς πρὸς αὐτούς (type *a* i). The relation between two consecutive numbers other than 1 is analogous to the relation of the πολλαπλάσιον to 1 in that it is κατ' ἀόριστον, i. e. involves a variable, *n*.

Then as an afterthought the relation of ὑπερέχον to ὑπερεχόμενον is described as being vaguer still, ὅλως ἀόριστον κατ' ἀριθμόν. The reason given for this, according to the vulgate reading, is (l. 5) ὁ γὰρ ἀριθμὸς σύμμετρος, κατὰ μὴ σύμμετρον δὲ ἀριθμὸν λέγεται. I. e. all numbers (i. e. integers) are commensurate, but that which exceeds is related to that which it exceeds 'according to an incommensurate number'. The statement is highly paradoxical, and could be explained only by supposing that Aristotle admits some wider sense of number in which it is not limited to integers; and there is no evidence that he did this.

Aᵇ reads κατὰ μὴ σύμμετρον δὲ ἀριθμὸς οὐ λέγεται. Apelt proposed κατὰ μὴ συμμέτρων δὲ ἀριθμοὶ οὐ λέγονται, and this is on the right lines; but Aᵇ's reading with the change of a single letter, συμμέτρου for σύμμετρον, gives us what is wanted. δέ must also be read with Aᵇ for γάρ in l. 6. The corruption into σύμμετρον is due to the repeated occurrence in the context of κατά with the accusative, and the other corruptions followed naturally.

1021ᵃ 8. ἢ ἴσον ἢ οὐκ ἴσον expresses Aristotle's meaning only imperfectly. The remainder may not only be either equal or unequal to the lesser amount; it may be either commensurate or incommensurate with it, and in the latter case the ratio is not expressible by whole numbers at all.

19. τῶν δὲ κατ' ἀριθμόν κτλ. Alexander offers two explanations:— (1) that numerical relations have ἐνέργειαι in the sense that they can become the object of the ἐνέργεια of thought. Cf. Θ. 1051ᵃ 29 (of geometrical propositions) τὰ δυνάμει ὄντα εἰς ἐνέργειαν ἀγόμενα εὑρίσκεται· αἴτιον δ' ὅτι ἡ νόησις ἐνέργεια. (2) That though numbers have not activities of their own, physical things act on one another in virtue of the numerical relations between them, and thus the relations may be said to act. This interpretation, however, is set aside by Aristotle's remark that αἱ κατὰ κίνησιν ἐνέργειαι (which such activities would be) do not belong to numbers. αἱ κατὰ κίνησιν ἐνέργειαι are the activities of powers as opposed to the actualizations of potentialities (Θ. 1046ᵃ 1, 1048ᵃ 25–ᵇ 9). What Aristotle means, then, is that numerical relations may be said to be actualized, though they cannot be said to have activities. All sorts of ratios are latent, for example, in the block of marble ; the sculptor actualizes certain of them and thus produces a statue in which each part bears a definite ratio to every other. Or again, elements are capable of being combined in a variety of ratios ; in the formation of any particular compound certain of these ratios are actualized. There may be, as Asclepius says, in Aristotle's words a hit at the Pythagoreans and Platonists who ascribed actual causal activity to numbers, and in this case ἐν ἑτέροις will refer to such works as the lost treatises Περὶ ἰδεῶν and Περὶ τῆς Πυθαγορικῶν δόξης.

21. The subject of the sentence must be extracted out of the partitive genitive τῶν κατὰ δύναμιν. The construction is not common, but cf. Λ. 1070ᵇ 7 οὐδὲ δὴ τῶν νοητῶν στοιχεῖόν ἐστι, *Rhet.* 1416ᵃ 21, Xen. *Anab.* iii. 5. 16 (ἔφασαν) ὁπότε πρὸς τὸν σατράπην σπείσαιντο, καὶ ἐπιμιγνύναι σφῶν τε πρὸς ἐκείνους καὶ ἐκείνων πρὸς ἑαυτούς· The construction is made easier by the subject which follows after οἷον, as in Λ. 1070ᵇ 22.

25. ἔτι ἔνια κατὰ στέρησιν δυνάμεως. I. e. as there are correlatives like ὁρατικόν and ὁρατόν, there are correlatives like μὴ ὁρατικόν and ἀόρατον, and as in general that which can do something is relative to that which it can do, so that which cannot do something is relative to that which it cannot do.

28. τῷ ὅπερ ἐστίν κτλ., 'by the fact that that which precisely they are is said to be that which it is, of (or in relation to) something else '— as the double is said to be the double of its half, or the creative of its creature—'not by the fact that something else is relative to it '.

Either ὅπερ ἐστίν or αὐτὸ ὅ ἐστιν could well be dispensed with, and there is no evidence of the latter phrase in Alexander (406. 25, 31). Jaeger is very probably right in regarding it as a gloss on ὅπερ ἐστίν.

29. τὸ δὲ μετρητὸν καὶ τὸ ἐπιστητόν. In I. 1057ᵃ 9 Aristotle points out as against this conjunction that really ἐπιστήμη is the μετρητόν, and τὸ ἐπιστητόν the μέτρον. I. e. knowledge conforms to reality, not reality to knowledge.

31. οὐκ ἔστι δ' κτλ. ' But if we are asked what thought is relative to, we must not say "to that of which it is the thought".' Aristotle's point is that that which is measured, known, thought, or seen must have a nature of its own, besides being the object of measurement, knowledge, thought, or sight. This is true enough, but does not differentiate this type of relation from the first two as he thinks it does.

It is true that if you ask what is the half half of, you can say 'its double', and if you ask what is the double double of you can say 'its half' (and so too with τὸ ποιητικόν and τὸ παθητικόν). But that which is double or half must have a nature of its own besides being double or half, just as that which is known must have a nature of its own besides being known.

There is, however, a difference. Though every particular double must have a nature of its own, there is nothing which you can say the double in general must be, except double. But you can say of the knowable in general that it must be fact, of the visible that it must be colour (or a coloured surface). It is doubtful, however, what could in general be said of the thinkable except that it must be a proposition, and here perhaps we should be involved in the tautology which Aristotle deprecates.

At the bottom of Aristotle's thought, though not very satisfactorily expressed, is the conviction that knowledge and perception are relative to reality in a way in which reality is not relative to them (ll. 29, 30). This is brought out more clearly elsewhere, where the argument takes a less logical and a more metaphysical turn, in Γ. 1010ᵇ 30, Θ. 1051ᵇ 6, I. 1053ᵃ 32, 1057ᵃ 7.

ᵇ 2. ἄλλο τι τοιοῦτον, the phosphorescent, *De An.* 419ᵃ 2.

3. Bz. conjectures that on the analogy of ᵃ 32, 33, ᵇ 1 we should read ἔστιν ἡ ὄψις οὗ ἐστιν ὄψις for the vulgate ἔστιν ὄψις οὗ ἐστιν ἡ ὄψις. But the right form is got by adopting Aᵇ's reading ὅτι ἐστὶν οὗ ἐστὶν ἡ ὄψις, 'sight is of that of which it is'. The first ὄψις is doubtless a gloss.

τὰ μὲν οὖν καθ᾽ ἑαυτά κτλ. In I. 1056ᵇ 34 the third class of relative terms (those mentioned in 1021ᵃ 29–ᵇ 3) are said to be so *not καθ᾽ αὑτά*. The two statements are, however, reconcilable. These terms are not καθ᾽ αὑτὰ τῶν πρός τι in the sense expressed in *Cat.* 8ᵃ 31, that 'their being is identical with their being related somehow to something', as 'double' is to 'half'. On the other hand they καθ᾽ αὑτὰ λέγεται πρός τι in the sense that it is they and not something of which they are mere accidents that are relative; they are not relative in the incidental way in which 'the man' is so (1021ᵇ 8).

4. τὰ δὲ ἂν τὰ γένη αὐτῶν ᾖ τοιαῦτα. In *Top.* 124ᵇ 18, *Cat.* 11ᵃ 23 Aristotle says on the other hand that if a genus is relative, it does not follow that the species are, and actually takes grammar and knowledge as the instance of this.

'*Complete*' (ch. 16).

1021ᵇ 12. 'Complete' means (1) that of which no part is outside it,
14. (2) that which is not exceeded in its kind in respect of excellence—
it may be excellence in something bad, e. g. 'a complete thief'. Ex-

cellence is a completion; a thing is complete when in respect of its proper excellence it lacks no part of its natural magnitude.

23. (3) That which possesses its end, this being good ; since the end is an extreme, we even say a thing is 'completely' spoiled when it is at the extreme of badness; hence too we call death the end, because both end and death are last things; but the final cause is also an end.

30. (i) Things *per se* complete are so (*a*) because they are not exceeded in respect of excellence (= senses (2), (3)), (*b*) because they are not exceeded by anything in their class, whatever that may be, and have nothing outside them (= sense (1)).

1022ª 1. (ii) Other things are complete through some relation to the foregoing.

1021ᵇ 12. οὗ μὴ ἔστιν ἔξω τι λαβεῖν μηδὲ ἐν μόριον. οὗ apparently depends both on ἔξω and on μόριον, 'that of which it is not possible to find any—not even one—part outside it'.

14-23. As Alexander observes, Aristotle now passes from the complete in quantity to the perfect in quality, though the quantitative expression μέγεθος is once (l. 23) used metaphorically in this connexion (cf. 1020ª 25).

16-17. From ll. 22, 23 it is evident that τῆς οἰκείας ἀρετῆς goes not with μηθὲν ἐλλείπωσιν but with κατὰ τὸ εἶδος, 'according to the form of their peculiar excellence'.

23-30. This sense of τέλειον is hardly to be distinguished from the second, and in the summary (l. 30—1022ª 1) no reference is made to it. It seems to be merely a restatement of the second sense from a slightly different point of view, viz. that of the connexion of τέλειον with τέλος.

23. The vulgate reading οἷς ὑπάρχει τὸ τέλος σπουδαῖον can only mean (and so Bz. takes it) that which has before it, or is tending towards, a good end; but such things are not naturally called perfect. The whole context (24-28) implies that it is not the having a good end before it but the having attained its end (τὸ ἔχειν τὸ τέλος) that makes a thing perfect. That the end should be good is a secondary matter; even things which have attained a bad end are called (in a secondary sense) perfect. I have therefore not hesitated to read οἷς ὑπάρχει τὸ τέλος, σπουδαῖον ὄν, 'things which have attained their end, this being good'. Alexander's interpretation requires ὄν (ὅτι τὸ οἰκεῖον τέλος ἀγαθὸν ὂν ἔχει 411. 21, cf. 412. 3). This reading gives ὑπάρχει its proper sense.

28. ἐπὶ τῷ ἐσχάτῳ seems to be the correct form. Cf. ἐπ᾽ ἐσχάτῳ Pl. *Charm.* 155 c, *Prot.* 344 A, *Rep.* 523 D, E.

29. τέλος δέ κτλ., ' but even if death is entitled to be called an end, at any rate the ultimate object of purpose is also an end'.

30—1022ª 1. The summary, as we have seen, ignores ll. 23-30 and refers first to the second sense, then to the first.

'Limit' (ch. 17).

1022ᵃ 4. 'Limit' means (1) the last point of a thing, i. e. the first point beyond which no part of it is and within which every part of it is, (2) the form of a magnitude or of a thing having magnitude, (3) the end, i. e. the *terminus ad quem* or final cause,—sometimes also the *terminus a quo*, (4) the essence; this is the limit of the knowledge of a thing, and therefore of the thing itself.

10. There are as many meanings of 'limit' as of 'beginning', and more, for the beginning is a limit but not every limit is a beginning.

1022ᵃ 5 πρώτου . . . πρώτου, to distinguish the precise boundary from the things which surround the given thing (which are *not* the first beyond which no part of the thing is to be found) and from the outermost parts of the thing (which are *not* the first within which all the parts are to be found).

6. εἶδος = σχῆμα, 'figure'.

μεγέθους ἢ ἔχοντος μέθεγος. For the absence of the article with ἔχοντος cf. Z. 1034ᵃ 24.

7. ὀτὲ δὲ ἄμφω probably has not, as Alexander and Bonitz think, any reference to the maxim τὸ ἔσχατον ἐν τῇ ἀναλύσει πρῶτόν ἐστιν ἐν τῇ γενέσει. It simply means that though 'limit' more often means the *terminus ad quem* it sometimes means the *terminus a quo*.

8. ἐφ' ὃ καὶ τὸ οὗ ἕνεκα. καί = 'i. e.'

9. τῆς γνώσεως γὰρ τοῦτο πέρας. This is what gives precise 'shape' to our knowledge of the thing, and therefore to the thing itself.

'That in virtue of which', 'In virtue of itself' (ch. 18)

1022ᵃ 14. καθ' ὅ means (1) the form or essence, (2) that in which an attribute directly resides, its matter or substratum.

19. It has meanings answering to those of 'cause'; it may be applied to (3) the final and (4) the efficient cause. It also refers (5) to position.

24. Things said to be καθ' αὐτό are (1) the essence,

27. (2) the elements in the 'what',

29. (3) attributes contained directly in the subject or in one of its parts,

32. (4) that which has no cause outside itself,

35. (5) that which belongs to one subject alone, and in virtue of its own nature.

1022ᵃ 14. There is no single English phrase that answers to the
various meanings of καθ' ὅ. 'That in virtue of which' will render
pretty well its uses in ll. 14–22, but in 22–24 it simply means 'that at,
or along, which'.

15. 'That in virtue of which a man is good is good-in-itself', the
form and essence of goodness. Christ's καθὸ ἀγαθὸς ὁ ἀγαθός is neat
but unnecessary. The statement is curiously Platonic, and Δ may well
belong to the Platonic period of Aristotle's thought.

17. Surface is that in which colour directly resides, so that surface is
that in virtue of which a thing is coloured. The καθ' ὅ in this sense,
which Aristotle describes as ὕλη (l. 18), is not πρώτη ὕλη, prime matter,
but the πρῶτον ὑποκείμενον in another sense of πρῶτος, the direct
material substratum of the given attribute.

23. τὸ κατὰ θέσιν. Alexander explains that one asks καθ' ὃ ἔστηκεν
'Αθήνησιν ὅδε ὁ ἀνδριάς, meaning, 'In what part of the city is it situated?'

25–36. Aristotle mentions five things which may be said to belong
to a subject καθ' αὑτό:

(1) Its essence (cf. Z. 1029ᵇ 13).

(2) The elements in its essence, i. e. its genus and its differentiae.
The elements in the essence of a thing are similarly described in
An. Post. 73ᵃ 34–37 as being καθ' αὑτό to it, but there the elements in
question are not the genus and differentiae but the simpler entities
involved in a complex entity (e. g. line in triangle).

(3) Attributes which reside directly in it (as whiteness resides in surface) or in a part of it (as life resides in the soul, which is a part of
man). This answers to the second sense of καθ' ὅ, as that ἐν ᾧ πρώτῳ
πέφυκε γίγνεσθαι. Surface is that 'in virtue of which' whiteness exists;
whiteness belongs to surface 'in virtue of itself'. Aristotle brings out
the onesidedness of his former identification (l. 18) of the πρῶτον
ὑποκείμενον with matter; soul, which is the *form* of man, is the ὑποκείμενον of life.

That which is καθ' αὑτό in this sense is the properties of the subject
the second type of καθ' αὑτό recognized in the *Posterior Analytics*
(73ᵃ 37–ᵇ 3).

(4) That which is predicable of the subject directly, not through the
intermediary of a cause. The instance given is a trivial one. There
are causes of man; his genus, his differentiae are formal causes of
him. But there is no cause of man's being man; man is man καθ'
αὑτό.

(5) Attributes which belong to the subject alone, and by virtue of
its own nature. This sense will include the last differentia and the
properties and thus overlaps senses (2) and (3). In general there is
a good deal of overlapping between these five senses, but that is in the
manner of Δ. Cf. 1018ᵃ 13 n.

35. The manuscripts present here a great variety of readings,
pointing to early corruption. κεχωρισμένον is, as Bz. observes,
preferable to ὡρισμένον, since it accounts better for the origin of the
reading κεχρωσμένον. There is something to be said for the variant

recognized by Alexander, διὸ τὸ κεχρωσμένον καθ᾽ αὑτό, sc. τῇ ἐπιφανείᾳ, 'wherefore being coloured is *per se* to surface' (cf. ll. 30, 31, *Top.* 131ᵇ 33, 134ᵃ 22). But the ellipse of τῇ ἐπιφανείᾳ is difficult and perhaps impossible. The reading suggested by Bz., διότι κεχωρισμένον, does not meet the difficulties.

I read, without much conviction, δι᾽ αὐτὸ κεχωρισμένον καθ᾽ αὑτό. 'Further, those attributes are *per se* to a subject which belong to it alone, and in so far as they belong to it merely by virtue of itself considered apart by itself', i. e. by virtue of its specific character, not of its generic character nor of any concomitant associated with it. The reference then is to attributes commensurate with a subject, those which are καθόλου in the strict sense defined in *An. Post.* 73ᵇ 25— 74ᵃ 3.

'Disposition' (ch. 19).

1022ᵇ 1. 'Disposition' means an arrangement of that which has parts, in respect of place, faculty, or kind; as the word shows, there must be some position.

διάθεσις occurs in *Cat.* 8ᵇ 27 as one of the kinds of quality. It is distinguished from ἕξις by its impermanence (8ᵇ 35).

1022ᵇ 2. κατὰ δύναμιν. This must mean a non-spatial arrangement of parts according to their respective functions, e.g. the hierarchy of the parts of the soul, in which reason is superior to the sensitive faculty and this to the nutritive. Cf. the distinction between πρότερον κατὰ τόπον and πρότερον κατὰ δύναμιν (1018ᵇ 12, 22).

κατ᾽ εἶδος can hardly refer as Alexander thinks to the arrangement of the parts of, e. g., a statue, which is really κατὰ τόπον. Bz. thinks with more probability that the reference is to the arrangement of the parts of a definition, and compares *An. Post.* 97ᵃ 23 τριῶν δεῖ στοχάζε- σθαι, τοῦ λαβεῖν τὰ κατηγορούμενα ἐν τῷ τί ἐστι, καὶ ταῦτα τάξαι τί πρῶτον ἢ δεύτερον, &c. Cf. Z. 1038ᵃ 30–34. But this is rather τάξις τῶν ἐν τῷ εἴδει than τάξις κατ᾽ εἶδος; it is more likely that Aristotle means the co-ordination and subordination of the species in a genus.

θέσιν. It is, of course, only metaphorically that there is position in the latter two cases.

'Having' or *'habit'* (ch. 20).

1022ᵇ 4. ἕξις means (1) the activity of that which wears and of that which is worn; this kind of ἕξις cannot itself be had, if we are to avoid an infinite regress;

10. (2) a disposition in virtue of which a thing is well or ill disposed, *per se* or with reference to another;

13. (3) a part of such a disposition; hence the excellence of part of a thing is a ἕξις of the thing.

1022ᵇ 4. ἐνέργειά τις τοῦ ἔχοντος καὶ ἐχομένου. For this sense of ἕξις cf. I. 1055ᵇ 13, *De Resp.* 474ᵃ 26, *De An. Inc.* 711ᵃ 6, Pl. *Rep.* 433 E 12, *Crat.* 414 B 9, *Theaet.* 197 B 1, *Soph.* 247 A 5, *Laws* 625 C 8. Prof. Gillespie has pointed out that *Theaet.* 197 B, *Laws* 625 C make it probable that ἕξις in this sense means originally the ἐνέργεια of wearing clothes, armour, &c. (l. 7), as opposed to the mere possession of them. ἕξις in this sense links up with the category of ἔχειν, of which the instances are ὑποδέδεται, ὥπλισται (*Cat.* 2ᵃ 3).

8. ταυτην . . . οὐκ ἐνδέχεται ἔχειν τὴν ἕξιν, while a thing *may* be said to have a ἕξις in the sense to which Aristotle proceeds in l. 10.

10. ἕξις λέγεται διάθεσίς κτλ. In *Cat.* 8ᵇ 25—9ᵃ 13 Aristotle distinguishes the two by saying that ἕξις implies relative permanence, so that while every ἕξις is a διάθεσις not every διάθεσίς is a ἕξις. This sense of ἕξις is derived from the intransitive, as the former from the transitive, use of ἔχειν.

'*Affection*' (ch. 21).

1022ᵇ 15. πάθος means (1) a quality in respect of which a thing may alter,

(2) the alterations themselves,

(3) injurious alterations, especially painful injuries,

(4) extremes of misfortune and pain.

1022ᵇ 15. ποιότης καθ' ἣν ἀλλοιοῦσθαι ἐνδέχεται, cf. 1020ᵇ 8–12. Bz. points out that ἀλλοίωσις is in turn defined by reference to ποιότης and πάθος (Λ. 1069ᵇ 12, N. 1088ᵃ 32, *Phys.* 226ᵃ 26).

The other three uses of πάθος here mentioned also imply ἀλλοίωσις, but Aristotle sometimes uses πάθος in the wider sense of 'attribute' or 'property', e. g. A. 985ᵇ 29, 986ᵃ 17, B. 997ᵃ 7, Γ. 1004ᵇ 6, 11, Δ. 1019ᵃ 1.

19. For this use of ἤδη cf. Bz. *Index* 314ᵃ 10–17.

'*Privation*' (ch. 22).

1022ᵇ 22. 'Privation' is used (1) if a thing has not some attribute that is naturally possessed, even though not by it;

24. (2) if either it or its genus would naturally have the attribute;

27. (3) if it has not the attribute, though and when it would naturally have it; other similar qualifications may be added;

31. (4) of the violent removal of anything.

32. There are as many kinds of privation as there are senses of α privative ; it may imply in general not having a thing, or having it bad, or having it small, or not easily or not well,

1023ª 4. or not at all; in which case there is a mean between the positive and the privative term, e. g. between good and bad.

1022^b 22—1023ª 7. For a briefer account of varieties of meaning of στέρησις cf. Θ. 1046ª 31.

22. ἕνα μὲν τρόπον κτλ. This sense of privation, in which all that is required is that the attribute of which a thing is said to be deprived should be such as can naturally be possessed by something, is wider than Aristotle's ordinary use of στέρησις. It distinguishes privation from negation in general only by barring absurd and self-contradictory predicates. Zeller, *Ph. d. Gr.* II. 2⁴. 216 n. 7, maintains that privation in this sense is synonymous with negation. Aristotle provides against this, however, by the words τῶν πεφυκότων ἔχεσθαι. If we take an attribute which cannot be possessed by anything, e. g. (according to Aristotle's doctrine) ' actually infinite ', ' A is not actually infinite ' is a negative judgement, but A cannot be said to suffer privation of anything. This sense recurs in I. 1055^b 4 (τὸ ἀδύνατον ὅλως ἔχειν), but is not usually included in the senses of ' privation ' by Aristotle, and does not share what is the essence of privation—that it is συνειλημμένη τῷ δεκτικῷ (I. 1055^b 8), applicable only to a particular kind of subject, that kind which might have the opposite ἕξις.

26-27. τὸ μὲν ... τὸ δέ. The mole may be said to be not merely not-seeing, but deprived of sight, or blind, because its genus, animal, naturally has sight ; a man may be so described because a man naturally has sight.

27-31. Zeller (l. c.) remarks that privation in these two senses comes under the definition of contrariety. The fact rather is that contrariety comes under the definition of privation. A subject which might have the attribute A but in any degree fails to have it can be said to be deprived of it ; but it has the contrary attribute only if it is *completely* deprived of A. Contrariety is στέρησις πρώτη (Θ. 1046^b 14) or τελεία (I. 1055ª 35).

30. The manuscript reading here cannot stand, as ἐν ᾧ ἂν ᾖ is meaningless. A tolerable sense is got by reading, as Bonitz suggests, ἐν ᾧ ἂν ᾖ καὶ καθ' ὃ καὶ πρὸς ὃ καὶ ὡς ἂν μὴ ἔχῃ πεφυκός. But ἤ καί, and the repetition of ἄν, are not entirely natural, and no parallelism is maintained with the previous sentence. The sentence should end with ἂν μὴ ἔχῃ (cf. μὴ ἔχῃ at the end of the clause in ll. 25, 28). Jaeger's transposition of πεφυκός meets all the requirements. The copyist's eye ran on from ᾧ ἂν ᾖ to ὡς, ἂν μὴ ἔχῃ and led him to add πεφυκός before its time.

' A man is also called blind if he has not sight in that medium in which, and in respect of the organ in respect of which, and with

reference to the object with reference to which, and in the circumstances
in which, he would naturally have it'. He is not called blind if he does
not see in the dark, or if he does not see with his ears, or if he does not
see sound, or if he does not see what is behind him or too far away.

'Have' or 'hold', 'In' (ch. 23).

1023ᵃ 8. ἔχειν means (1) to treat according to one's own nature or
impulse,

11. (2) to have as a receptive material has the form that is impressed
on it,

13. (3) to contain (so the whole has the parts),

17. (4) to prevent a thing from moving according to its own impulse,
e. g. to hold together.

23. 'To be in a thing' has corresponding senses.

The senses of ἔχειν are classified as follows in *Cat.* 15 :

(1) ὡς ἕξιν, (2) ὡς ποσόν, (3) ὡς τὰ περὶ τὸ σῶμα, (4) ὡς ἐν μορίῳ,
(5) ὡς μέρος, (6) ὡς ἐν ἀγγείῳ, (7) ὡς κτῆμα, (8) γυναῖκα ἔχειν καὶ ἡ γύνη
ἄνδρα.

(1) here includes (3) and (7) in the *Categories*, (2) here answers to
(1) and (2) in the *Categories*, and (3) here to (5) and (6) in the
Categories.

1023ᵃ 20. τὸν Ἄτλαντα, cf. Hes. *Theog.* 517.

21. τῶν φυσιολόγων τινές. Alexander refers to the doctrine that the
world is held in place by δίνη, i. e. to the doctrine of Empedocles
(*De Caelo* 284ᵃ 20–26, where Simplicius refers also to Anaxagoras and
Democritus).

23–25. The senses of ἐν are discussed in *Phys.* iv. 3.

24. It seems better to adopt ὁμοτρόπως (the reading of all the best
manuscripts), for which cf. *Top.* 183ᵇ 6, Pl. *Phaedo* 83 D 8. The inferior
manuscripts have altered it to the form which is much commoner in
Aristotle, ὁμοιοτρόπως.

'.From' or 'out of' (ch. 24).

1023ᵃ 26. A thing is said (1) to come from or out of its generic or
specific matter ;

29. (2) to come from its efficient cause ;

31. (3) to come from the complex of matter and form to which it
belongs, as the parts come from the whole.

35. (4) The form is said to be made out of its elements; so man
is made out of biped, syllable out of letter; this is a different relation
from that of a thing to its *perceptible* matter.

ᵇ 3. (5) A thing comes 'from' that from a part of which it proceeds
in one of the above senses; so a child comes 'from' its parents ;

5. (6) a thing comes from that which it succeeds in time. Of things so
related (*a*) some change into one another, as day and night; (*b*) in other
cases one merely succeeds the other, as one festival succeeds another.

1023ᵃ 26–ᵇ 11. For other (partial) classifications of the senses of ἐκ
cf. α. 994ᵃ 22–ᵇ 3, H. 1044ᵃ 23–25, N. 1092ᵃ 23–35. A classification
more like the present is found in *G. A.* 724ᵃ 20–30 :

(1) ὅτι τόδε μετὰ τόδε, = (6) here,
(2) ὡς ἐξ ὕλης, = (1) here,
(3) ὡς τὸ ἐναντίον ἐκ τοῦ ἐναντίου, = (6 *a*) here,
(4) ἐκ τίνος ἡ ἀρχὴ τῆς κινήσεως, = (2) here.

28. ἅπαντα τὰ τηκτὰ ἐξ ὕδατος, cf. 1015ᵃ 10 n.

30–31. ἐκ τίνος . . . μάχης; cf. 1013ᵃ 9 n.

34. τέλος . . . τέλος. These words are intended to justify ἐκ τοῦ
συνθέτου ἐκ τῆς ὕλης καὶ τῆς μορφῆς (ll. 31–32). In every such case
the whole is a union of form and matter, for a ὅλον or τέλειον is that
which has attained its τέλος, and matter has attained its τέλος only when
it has attained and (so to say) been united with the form towards which
it was moving.

36. καὶ ἡ συλλαβὴ ἐκ τοῦ στοιχείου. Aristotle is not thinking of the
letter as an element in particular syllables (this would be quite different
from the relation of biped to man and would really illustrate the *first*
sense of ἔκ τινος), but as something that has to be mentioned in defining
the syllable (Z. 1034ᵇ 25) as biped must be mentioned in defining man.

ᵇ 2. τῆς τοῦ εἴδους ὕλης does not mean the genus (though that is
called the ὕλη of the species in 1024ᵇ 8 and elsewhere), since biped is
not the genus of man, nor letter of syllable ; but rather the elements in
the definition of the form. It thus comprises both genus and differentia,
and also the components, where these have to be mentioned in the
definition of the whole, as is the case in the definition of 'syllable'.

'*Part*' (ch. 25).

1023ᵇ 12. 'Part' means (1) (*a*) that into which a quantity is divided,
(*b*) those of the 'parts' in sense (*a*) which measure the whole (2 is in
this sense not a part of 3);

17. (2) that into which the form is divided, apart from the quantity
(hence the species are parts of the genus);

19. (3) that into which the whole is divided, whole meaning either the
form or the concrete whole (e. g. both the bronze and the characteristic
angle are parts of the bronze cube) ;

22. (4) the elements in the definition (hence genus is part of species).

Senses (1 *b*), (3), (4) reappear in Z. 1034ᵇ 32—1035ᵃ 4.

1023ᵇ 20. τὸ ὅλον, ἢ τὸ εἶδος ἢ τὸ ἔχον τὸ εἶδος. For the description

of the form as a ὅλον cf. 1013ᵇ 22.   τὸ ἔχον τὸ εἶδος = the concrete unity
of matter and form, such as 'the bronze cube'.   This has two parts,
the bronze, and the angle which defines its form.   Aristotle does not
illustrate here the division of the *form* into its parts; he comes to that
in ll. 22–25, where it is carelessly treated as implying a different sense
of μέρος from that in question here.

'Whole', 'Total', 'All' (ch. 26).

1023ᵇ 26. 'A whole' means (1) that from which none of the parts of
which it is by nature the whole are lacking ;

27. (2) that which so contains its contents that they are a unity,
(*a*) in the sense that each is one with each, or (*b*) in the sense that all
together make up the unity.

29. (*a*) The phrases 'true of a whole class' and 'as a whole' imply
a whole which contains many parts by being predicated of each, and
by each being one with the rest (e. g. man, horse, god, are one by being
all of them living beings).

32. (*b*) The continuous and limited is a whole when a unity is formed
out of several constituents, (i) especially if they exist only potentially,
but (ii) failing this even if they exist actually.   Of wholes in sense (*b*)
natural wholes are more truly whole than artificial ones (cf. what we
said of unity).

1024ᵃ 1. (3) Of quantities that have a beginning, middle, and end, one
to which the position of the parts does not make a difference is a total,
one to which it does is a whole.   One to which it both may and may
not is both, i. e. one in which the nature remains after the transposition
but the shape does not (e. g. wax or a garment).

6. Water, liquids, number are totals, not wholes, except in an
extended sense.   Things which together we call a total, we speak of
singly as 'all' ('this total number', 'all these units').

1023ᵇ 26. The first definition is equivalent to the first definition of
τέλειον in ch. 16.

28–36. The various senses of 'one' given in ch. 6 are here in effect
reduced to two.   There is unity of kind, covering the senses mentioned
in 1016ᵃ 17–ᵇ 6, and unity of quantity (continuity), answering to
1015ᵇ 36—1016ᵃ 17.

28. ὡς ἕκαστον ἕν, 'in the sense that each is severally one single
thing', as man, horse, god are each of them one thing, viz. animal
(l. 32).   The unity of the universal is here opposed to the unity of the
continuous (ὡς ἐκ τούτων τὸ ἕν).

29. τὸ ὅλως λεγόμενον ὡς ὅλον τι ὄν, 'that of which we speak when we say "as a whole", implying that there is in some sense a whole.'

36. ἐπὶ τοῦ ἑνὸς ἐλέγομεν, cf. 1016^a 4.

1024^a 1-6. Aristotle gives here an account of a whole which may be a continuous whole like that described in 1023^b 32–36, or may be a discrete whole like a musical scale (1024^a 21), but is made a whole by the fact that transposition of its parts makes a difference to it. A sheet of water is a whole in the previous sense but not in this.

4. Since the nature of these things is unaffected by rearrangement of the parts, they are called alls or aggregates; since their form is affected, they are called wholes. In English we should naturally speak of 'all the wax' but of 'the whole garment', just as we speak of 'a garment' but not of 'a wax'.

8-9. πάντα δὲ λέγεται . . . ἐπὶ τούτοις τὸ πάντα. The anacolouthon is natural enough in view of the intervening clause (for a somewhat similar case cf. Θ. 1048^b 9–12). The sentence illustrates Aristotle's favourite 'binary structure', for which cf. A. 983^b 16 n., Riddell, *Apology of Plato*, p. 205, § 224.

'*Mutilated*' (ch. 27).

1024^a 11. That which is capable of 'mutilation' must be not only (1) a quantity, i. e. divisible, but (2) a whole. For not only is the number 2 not mutilated by the loss of a unit (since what is left after mutilation must be greater than what is removed), but no number can be mutilated, since after mutilation the essence must remain. The 'mutiland' must have not only unlike parts, as numbers have, but parts whose position makes a difference to it.

20. (3) It must be continuous; a musical scale is a whole in the above sense, but is discrete and therefore cannot be mutilated.

22. (4) Even wholes are not 'mutilated' by the loss of parts (*a*) requisite to their essence, (*b*) other than extremities, or (*c*) capable of growing again after being completely removed.

1024^a 11-28. τῶν ποσῶν οὐ τὸ τυχόν, ἀλλὰ μεριστόν τε δεῖ αὐτὸ εἶναι καὶ ὅλον κτλ. Every ποσόν is μεριστόν (1020^a 7), so that the stress must fall entirely on ὅλον. 'It must be a whole as well as divisible.' Aristotle goes on to say 'for two is not mutilated by the loss of one of its units . . . nor can any number be mutilated'. Now two is not 'mutilated' by the loss of a unit, for the same reason for which things that are wholes are not 'mutilated' by the loss of *certain* parts, viz. because what is removed by mutilation must be less important than what remains (cf. ll. 13, 14 with ll. 23, 24). Therefore the fact that two is not 'mutilated' by the loss of a unit does not give a reason for saying that the 'mutiland' must be a whole; the stress again falls on the second member. 'What is to be mutilated must be a whole. For not only is two not mutilated by the loss of a unit, but no number can be mutilated.' What distinguishes numbers from wholes is that, since they have no plan or structure independent of the number of units in them (for the 'quality' ascribed to them in 1020ᵇ 3-8 depends entirely on their having just so many units), every unit in them is κύριον τῆς οὐσίας, and none can be removed without altering the identity of the number. If one be removed, you get not the old number mutilated, but a new number.

Nor (ll. 16-18) is it enough to say that what is to be capable of being mutilated must have unlike parts. Every number but 2 has unlike, at least in the sense of having unequal, parts. What is to be mutilated must (ll. 18-20) be a whole in the sense defined in l. 2, that the position of its parts makes a difference to it. Five has unlike parts, two and three, but it does not matter whether it is considered as 2 + 3 or as 3 + 2. A number has not the organic structure which makes a whole on the one hand incapable of surviving certain *rearrangements* of its parts, and on the other hand capable of surviving the *loss* of certain of its parts.

Further (l. 20), what is to be mutilated must also be continuous, i.e. a whole in the sense defined in 1023ᵇ 32-34.

Finally (l. 22), even wholes are not mutilated by the loss of any part taken at random. The part that is removed must itself satisfy certain conditions.

21. The vulgate reading ἀνομοιομερῶν is clearly out of place here, and has come in from l. 16. Aᵇ preserves the true reading ἀνομοίων.

The notes of the scale are unlike, and they have position in the octave, but they are not continuous, and therefore the scale cannot be 'mutilated'.

23. οὔτε τὰ κύρια τῆς οὐσίας, since (l. 15) τὴν οὐσίαν δεῖ μένειν.

'Kind', 'Other in kind' (ch. 28).

1024ᵃ 29. 'Kind' is applied to (1) beings of the same type, of which there is continuous generation;

31. (2) beings with a common ancestor; they are more often named after the male ancestor than after the female, who only supplies the matter;

36. (3) that which underlies the differentiae;

ᵇ 4. (4) the first element in the definition.

6. Thus kind implies

    (1) continuous generation of the same type, or

    (2) a first mover of the same type as his descendants, or

    (3) a matter or substratum underlying differentiae.

9. 'Other in kind' is applied to things whose proximate substrata are different and cannot be analysed one into another or both into the same thing; e. g. form and matter, or things falling in different categories.

1024ᵃ 35. τῆς ὕλης. For the conception of the female as providing the matter, the male the form of the offspring, cf. A. 988ᵃ 5, H. 1044ᵃ 34, *G. A.* 732ᵃ 8, 736ᵇ 18, 737ᵃ 29, 738ᵇ 20, 740ᵇ 24.

ᵇ 4. ἔτι ὡς κτλ. This sense is really the same as the third, differently described. In the summary in ll. 6–9 the two are merged together.

τὸ πρῶτόν ἐνυπάρχον κτλ. According to Greek idiom this must mean not ' the first constituent which is stated in the τί ἐστι' but ' the first constituent, which is stated in the τί ἐστι'.

ὃ λέγεται ἐν τῷ τί ἐστι, 'which is stated in saying what the thing is'. Sometimes both genus and differentia are included in the τί ἐστι (*An. Post.* 97ᵃ 24, 91ᵇ 29, *Top.* 153ᵃ 17), but elsewhere, as here, the τί ἐστι is identified with the genus, and the differentia is described as answering to the question ποῖόν τι (*Top.* 102ᵃ 32–35, 122ᵇ 16, 128ᵃ 28, 142ᵇ 23–29, 144ᵃ 17, 21).

8. ὁμοειδές, 'the first mover that is of the same kind as the things it moves'. The point seems to be that if a family were descended from something non-human, it would be named not after this but after its first human ancestor

ὡς ὕλη. For the description of the genus as the matter of its species cf. Z. 1038ᵃ 6, I. 1058ᵃ 23.

10. τὸ πρῶτον ὑποκείμενον, the proximate substratum. Phlegm is not ' other in kind' than τὸ λιπαρόν, because it can be analysed into it ; nor is it other in kind than gall, because they can be analysed into the same materials (H. 1044ᵃ 18–23). But stone and bronze are other in kind because one is made of earth and the other of water, and earth and water cannot be analysed one into the other nor both into any single αἰσθητόν (Al.).

12. καὶ ὅσα καθ' ἕτερον σχῆμα κατηγορίας κτλ. Alexander thinks this is a stricter sense of ' other in genus', since form and matter, which are other in genus in the first sense, are both in the category of substance and therefore not other in genus in this sense. It is hardly true, perhaps, that ὕλη considered apart from εἶδος is placed by Aristotle in the category of substance. But better instances could be given to show that things in the same category may be incapable of being analysed into one another or into the same thing. Number and spatial extension cannot be so analysed, nor can whiteness and heat ; and the list could be indefinitely extended. In I. 1054ᵇ 28–30, however, ὧν μή ἐστι κοινὴ ἡ ὕλη μηδὲ γένεσις εἰς ἄλληλα are apparently identified with ὅσων ἄλλο σχῆμα τῆς κατηγορίας, cf. n. *ad loc.*

But ' in different categories' is not put forward as a separate sense of ' other in kind', but as falling under the already mentioned sense, viz. ' incapable of resolution one into another or both into the same thing' (cf. l. 15 with l. 11).

13. σχῆμα κατηγορίας τοῦ ὄντος. This is the only passage in which Aristotle uses this phrase. It is a compound of the more usual σχῆμα τῆς κατηγορίας and κατηγορία τοῦ ὄντος.

14. ὡς διῄρηται πρότερον, 1017ᵃ 24.

'False' (ch. 29).

1024ᵇ 17. 'False' is applied to (1) a false *thing*. This is (*a*) one which (i) is not put together, or (ii) cannot be put together, e. g. (i) that you are sitting, (ii) that the diagonal of the square is commensurate with the side ; or

21. (*b*) a thing which exists, but is such as to appear (i) not such as it is, or (ii) to be something that does not really exist. A scene-painting is a false thing in sense (i) ; a dream is so in sense (ii).

26. (2) A false *account* qua false is an account of what is not ; hence any account is untrue of anything save that of which it is true, e. g. the account of the circle is untrue of the triangle.

29. In one sense there is only one account of a thing, viz. its definition ; in another there are many, since in a way a thing is the same as itself-with-an-attribute (the false account is an account, in the first sense, of nothing).

32. Therefore Antisthenes was childish in thinking that nothing should be described.except by its proper 'account', which made contradiction, and practically falsity also, impossible. It is possible to describe a thing not only by its own 'account' but by the account of something else. This may no doubt be done falsely, but it may be done truly ; we call 8 double, using that which is the 'account' of 2.

1025ᵃ 2. (3) A false *man* is one who tends to choose such accounts for their own sake and to impress them on others, as we call things false if they make false impressions.

6. Hence the argument in the *Hippias* to show that the same man is false and true is delusive. It assumes (*a*) that he who *can* speak falsely (i. e. who knows) *is* false, and (*b*) that it is better to be willingly than unwillingly bad. This rests on a false induction, implying a confusion between willingly being, and willingly pretending to be.

1024ᵇ 17. ὡς πρᾶγμα ψεῦδος is opposed to λόγος ψευδής (1. 26). This contradicts Aristotle's real view, which is that truth and falsity are essentially characteristics of thought (E. 1027ᵇ 25, Γ. 1011ᵇ 26). Evidently there is no such thing as a false object or fact. The first

kind which he recognizes (ll. 18–21)—the objects of false opinions,
i. e. what is falsely thought, in distinction from the false thinking—are
more properly called non-existent than false. The other class (21–24),
to judge from the *description* of them, are real objects about which
people happen or may happen to entertain false opinions ; but one of
the *instances* Aristotle gives, viz., the dream, is nothing if not a state
of mind.

Throughout this book, however, Aristotle aims at classifying the
current usages of words rather than at stating a thoroughgoing meta-
physic. Some conflict between what he says here and elsewhere is
only to be expected. In particular, he seems to be adapting here the
terminology of Antisthenes (cf. l. 32), with its opposition of πρᾶγμα to
ὄνομα and λόγος.

πρᾶγμα ψεῦδος. τὸ ψεῦδος is so often opposed to τὸ ἀληθές that
ψεῦδος comes to be used as an adjective, cf. Pl. *Crat.* 385 c 16,
Polit. 281 A 13. The form ψευδές seems not to occur in Plato or
Aristotle ; ἀληθὲς καὶ ψεῦδος occurs constantly in Aristotle where we
should have expected ψευδές if he had ever used such a form. Lobeck,
Paral. 161, pronounces against this use of ψεῦδος, but does not seem
to have known all the instances.

22. ἢ μὴ οἷά ἐστιν ἢ ἃ μὴ ἔστιν κτλ. 'Scene-paintings seem to be
another sort of thing than what they are ; dreams seem to be something which in fact does not exist.' This seems to be Aristotle's
meaning ; it answers to the distinction between illusion and hallucina-
tion. A picture in two dimensions seems to be an object in three, but
at any rate it is a physical reality ; the dream, which seems a physical
reality, is not one at all.

23. σκιαγραφία is a rough sketch in light and shade, which produces
its effect best at a distance. Cf. *Rhet.* 1414ᵃ 8, Pl. *Theaet.* 208 E,
Phaedo 69 B, *Parm.* 165 c, *Rep.* 365 c, 602 D, &c.

26. The meaning of λόγος here, as is not unusual with that word in
Aristotle, is somewhat ambiguous. Two ambiguities may be detected.
(1) Aristotle begins by saying that a false λόγος, account, or statement,
is an account of that which is not. Take, e. g., the definition of the
triangle as 'a figure bounded by a line all the points on which are equi-
distant from a point called the centre'. A triangle thus characterized
is a μὴ ὄν, and this false account is an account τοῦ μὴ ὄντος. The same
may be said of any false account. But now it occurs to Aristotle that
the account which is not true of the triangle may be true of something
else ; it is not wholly false, and in so far as it is true it is τοῦ ὄντος.
He therefore qualifies the statement that it is τοῦ μὴ ὄντος by adding
ᾗ ψευδής, 'in so far as it is false'. And he continues 'hence every
account is an untrue account of anything other than that of which it is
the true account ; e. g. the account of the circle is not true of the
triangle'.

Now if for brevity we formulate a false definition in the form 'that
A is BC', A is as essential an element in this as its being BC. Now
'that A is BC' cannot be true of something else ; it is only BC, or

rather 'that it is BC', that can be true of something else.　It is
evident, then, that Aristotle passes from that notion of a λόγος which
may be formulated as 'that A is BC' to that notion of it which may
be formulated as 'that it is BC', leaving the subject indefinite.　It is
only the first that can be said to be false ; it is only the second that
can be described as being true of one thing and false of another.　It
is evident, however, that no particular statement can be formulated in
the latter way ; this is no real act of thought at all but an extract of
what may be common to several.

(2) So far λόγος has meant the essential account or definition of
a thing.　It is only in this sense that the λόγος of a circle must be untrue of a triangle ; there are many statements of another kind that are
true of both.　But Aristotle now points out that while in this sense there
is only one λόγος of a thing, viz., the account of its 'what', in another
(that in which it means 'statement' in general) there are many.
Socrates is not merely Socrates but is 'musical Socrates', and the
statement 'Socrates is musical', though it is not the definition of
Socrates, is a true account of Socrates, and there may be many such.
Of this ambiguity Aristotle is aware ; of the other, apparently, he is
not.

27. Christ's conjecture ᾗ ψευδῇ, 'a false λόγος is a λόγος of things that
are not, inasmuch as they are false '—cf. l. 21 οὕτω γὰρ οὐκ ὄντα ταῦτα
—is ingenious but unnecessary.

31. ὁ δὲ ψευδὴς λόγος οὐθενός ἐστιν ἁπλῶς λόγος.　This apparently
means that a false account is not an account in the strict sense, i. e.
a definition (ἁπλῶς = κυρίως Alexander), of anything.　There is, as we
have seen, in this sense only one λόγος of a thing, and that of course
is the true λόγος of it.

32-34. This passage must be considered in connexion with
H. 1043ᵇ 23-32 and with Pl. *Theaet.* 201 D—202 C, *Soph.* 251 B, C.
Campbell (*Theaet.*, p. xxxix) thinks that the reference in the *Theaetetus*
is not to Antisthenes but to some Pythagorean.　But if in 1043ᵇ 28-32
Aristotle is restating (as he seems to be) in his own language the
Antisthenean theory, the passage in the *Theaetetus*, which similarly
describes simple entities as indefinable, and complex entities as
definable; probably also refers to the Antistheneans.　Campbell thinks
that the passage in the *Sophistes* refers to Antisthenes.　Prof. Taylor
(*V. S.* 85) seems to cast doubt on this.　I agree with him that it is
absurd to find in 'the accidental prosodical correspondence between
ὀψιμαθής and Ἀντισθένης ' (τῶν γερόντων τοῖς ὀψιμαθέσι Soph. 251 B) an
allusion to Antisthenes.　And the εἰδῶν φίλοι of *Soph.* 248 A are
certainly not the Antistheneans.　But the persons referred to in
251 B, C are distinguished from the εἰδῶν φίλοι (v. 251 D 1, 2), and
a comparison of 251 B, C with the Aristotelian passages makes it highly
probable that Antisthenes is referred to.　The scornful tone (εὐήθως
1024ᵇ 32, οἱ οὕτως ἀπαίδευτοι 1043ᵇ 24, τῶν γερόντων τοῖς ὀψιμαθέσι
Soph. 251 B, ὑπὸ πενίας τῆς περὶ φρόνησιν κτήσεως 251 C) confirms this
(Γ. 1005ᵇ 3 ἀπαιδευσία τῶν ἀναλυτικῶν, 1006ᵃ 6 ἀπαιδευσία may also

refer to Antisthenes). *Euthyd.* 283 E—284 C, 285 E—286 D, *Crat.*
429 D, 432 D, E, 433 D seem also to refer to Antisthenes.
On the whole question cf. Procl. *in Crat.* ch. 37, Zeller ii. 1.⁴ 292–
296, Maier ii. 2. 11–16, Natorp in Pauly-Wissowa s. v. Antisthenes,
Gillespie in *Archiv f. Geschichte d. Phil.* xxvi. 479–500, xxvii. 17–38.
Prof. Gillespie illustrates the logic of Antisthenes admirably by reference to Hobbes's similar nominalistic view. The following points are
common to the two theories (xxvii. 23):

(1) The proposition is the application of names to things.

(2) The definition is a proposition in which a formula consisting of
several names is substituted for a single name (λόγος μακρός).

(3) As in the proposition of the type S is P subject and predicate
are both names of the same thing, the proposition is really assimilated
to the definition.

(4) The intensive meaning of the name is treated objectively, as
the οὐσία of the real object : this οὐσία can itself be signified by a
formula consisting of several words. For the function of the name
is to distinguish one thing from another.

(5) Thought is 'computation', involving the resolution of complexes into single elements.

(6) These simple elements are αἰσθητά.

(7) A word-formula, and hence a proposition, may be true or false
(though Antisthenes rejects the *name* ψεῦδος) or unmeaning.

A simple entity (πρᾶγμα) should have only its own name (ὄνομα)
predicated of it (*Soph.* 251 A) ; of a complex entity one may predicate
either its own name or its own λόγος, which is merely a many-worded
name (or expansion of the simple name) in which the parts of the
subject are specified (*Theaet.* 201 E ff.).

32. διὸ 'Αντισθένης ᾤετο εὐήθως. The stress is on εὐήθως. Because
in a sense there are many λόγοι of the same thing (l. 29), it was simple-
minded of Antisthenes to insist that a thing could have only its proper
λόγος or definition asserted of it.

33. ἐξ ὧν συνέβαινε μὴ εἶναι ἀντιλέγειν. This doctrine is mentioned
in Isocr. *Helena,* 10. 1, is discussed without mention of Antisthenes in
Euthyd. 285 E—286 B, and is ascribed to Antisthenes in *Top.* 104^b 21.
' A and B are supposed to be talking about the same thing . . . A
and B in their discussion make various assertions about the thing,
which they no doubt call by the same name ; but they do not necessarily attach the same or the right formula to the name. Still in
no case can they be said to contradict each other ; if both have
in mind the right formula, they agree ; if one has the right formula
and the other a wrong one, they are speaking of different things ;
if both have wrong formulae in mind, neither is speaking of the thing
at all ' (Prof. Gillespie in *A. G. P.* xxvii. 21).

34. σχεδὸν δὲ μηδὲ ψεύδεσθαι. This doctrine is mentioned in
Isoc. loc. cit., in *Euthyd.* 283 E—284 C, 286 C, D, and in *Crat.* 429 D.
Antisthenes' argument seems to have been : Any one who says any-
thing τὸ ὂν λέγει, speaks of that which is. But τὸ ὂν λέγειν is (by the

definition of ἀληθής) τἀληθῆ λέγειν. Hence no-one ψευδῆ λέγει. 'The aim of the paradox is not to deny the fact of error, but to reject the definition of ψεῦδος as saying that which is not. In other words, falsehood is ἀλλοδοξία' (*A. G. P.* xxvii. 20).

1025ᵃ 7–13. Plato, according to Aristotle, makes two mistakes : (1) He assumes that the man who can tell lies is a liar, when he should have said 'the man who chooses to tell lies'. Cf. *E. N.* 1127ᵇ 14 οὐκ ἐν τῇ δυνάμει δ' ἐστὶν ὁ ἀλαζών, ἀλλ' ἐν τῇ προαιρέσει.

(2) He assumes that the man who is willingly bad is better than the man who is unwillingly so.

The latter assumption is the result of a mistaken induction. Plato says that he who is willingly lame is better than the man who is unwillingly so. But all he has a right to say is that he who willingly *pretends* to be lame is better than the man who unwillingly *is* so; if he really were willingly lame he would presumably be worse. And so too in character, the man who willingly tells lies is worse than the man who does so unwillingly. (In its application to lameness κρείττω has of course no moral significance.)

7–8. τὸν δυνάμενον . . . φρόνιμος, cf. *Hipp. Min.* 365–369.

9. ἔτι τὸν ἑκόντα φαῦλον βελτίω, cf. ib. 371–376.

The best attested reading, ἑκόντα τὰ φαῦλα, has probably arisen by dittography :—ἑκόντα φαῦλον—ἑκόντα τὰ φαῦλον—ἑκόντα τὰ φαῦλα. Jaeger conjectures that πράττοντα has fallen out by haplography after ἑκόντα. This may be so, but we cannot be sure that Alexander *read* πράττοντα (437. 8, 11) any more than that Asclepius read λέγοντα (357. 4). Both are probably trying to make the best they can of τὰ φαῦλα.

10. τῆς ἐπαγωγῆς, cf. *Hipp. Min.* 373–375.

'*Accident*' (ch. 30).

1025ᵃ 14. 'Accident' means (1) what belongs to a thing but not of necessity nor for the most part.

21. Since there are attributes and they belong to subjects, and some of them do so only in particular places or at particular times, an attribute which belongs to a subject now or here, but not because it is this particular subject, is an accident.

24. It has therefore no determinate cause, but a chance cause. A man 'happens' to go to Aegina if he goes not by his own intention but by reason of something else, e. g. a storm.

30. (2) What belongs to a thing *per se* though not present in its essence; e. g. having its angles equal to two right angles is an accident of the triangle. Accidents of this sort may be eternal; those of the other sort cannot.

1025ᵃ 15. εἰπεῖν, epexegetic of ἀληθές, cf. A. 989ᵇ 7 n.
It is necessary to insert ὡς before ἐπὶ τὸ πολύ with Asc.ᶜ and
Eucken. ἐπὶ τὸ πολύ seems never to be found in Aristotle or Plato in
the sense of ὡς ἐπὶ τὸ πολύ.

21-24. ἐπεὶ ἔστιν ὑπάρχον τι κτλ. 'Since there are attributes and
subjects, and some of the attributes belong to the subjects only in a
particular place and at a particular time, an attribute which belongs
to a subject, but not because the subject was just this subject or the
time this time, or the place this place, will be an accident.' Even of
necessary events some are limited to certain places or times, but are
due to the nature of a particular subject and to its being in a particular place at a particular time (e. g. the rising and setting of the
heavenly bodies); events which are not due to such a determinate
cause are accidental. The cause of the husbandman's finding the
treasure is not his individual nature, nor his presence in a particular
place at a particular time, but something indefinite, i. e. something that
cannot be inferred certainly from the result. Some one must presumably have put the treasure there, but we cannot say who or when.
This would seem to be Aristotle's meaning in saying that the cause is
indeterminate. There is no lack of causation, but two causal series
meet (that of which the burying of the treasure was a member, and
that of which the husbandman's going to the field was a member),
and the result—the finding—could not be foreseen from a consideration
of the latter series only, nor can the cause be discovered from a consideration of the result. Similarly the cause of the voyager's coming
to Aegina is not his nature or his purpose, but something else—
whether winds or pirates we cannot tell by merely knowing that he has
got there.

28. ἢ ἔστι has better support in the manuscripts than καὶ ἔστι and
gives an equally good sense.

30. Aristotle now proceeds to what he elsewhere (B. 995ᵇ 20,
25, *An. Post.* 75ᵇ 1, 83ᵇ 19) calls the καθ' αὑτὸ συμβεβηκός, that
which, since it is not included in the definition of the subject, is a
συμβεβηκός, but which yet flows from the nature of the subject,—in
other words, the property.

34. ἐν ἑτέροις. That τὰ καθ' αὑτὰ συμβεβηκότα are demonstrable
(which implies that they are eternal) is stated in *An. Post.* 75ᵃ 39-41,
76ᵇ 11-15; that the others are not demonstrable is stated in E. 2,
3, K. 8, *An. Post.* 75ᵃ 18. Since Δ is apparently the earliest book of
the *Metaphysics*, the reference is no doubt to the *Posterior Analytics*.

BOOK E

Since Z init. refers, for the list of the categories, not to E. 2. 1026ᵃ 35–ᵇ 1 but to Δ, Jaeger concludes (*Arist.* 209–211) that E. 2—and with it E. 3 and 4, which arise out of the classification of the meanings of ὄν at the beginning of E. 2—are a later addition meant to bridge the gulf between the introductory part of the *Metaphysics*, ΑΒΓΕ. 1, and the substantive parts of it, Z–Θ and IM. This is not improbable, but can hardly be proved.

Division of theoretical sciences into physics, mathematics, theology (ch. 1).

1025ᵇ 3. We are seeking the causes of existing things *qua* existing. Every science is concerned with causes more or less accurately grasped.

7. The sciences (*a*) study some particular existing thing, not the existent as such ;

10. (*b*) offer no proof of essence but make it obvious to the senses or assume it, and go on to prove the properties of the genus they are studying ; whence it is clear that they make essence known not by demonstration but in some other way ;

16. (*c*) they do not discuss whether their subject genus exists—this being a matter for the same kind of thought which studies essence.

18. (1) Physics, like the more special sciences, studies a particular genus, viz. the kind of substance which has its origin of movement and rest in itself. It is not a practical nor a productive science, since the origin of things made is in the maker, that of things done in the agent. Therefore it is theoretical.

26. It studies mutable objects, and essence for the most part as inseparable from matter. It is important to observe how essences exist.

30. Some, like 'snub', already imply matter (the snub is a concave nose) ; others, like 'concave', imply no perceptible matter.

34. Since all physical objects are of the type of 'the snub' (e. g. animals and plants, and their parts), it is clear how physics should study essence, and why it studies the kind of soul that implies matter.

1026ᵃ 7. (2) Mathematics also is theoretical. Whether its objects are immutable and separately existent is not at present clear, but at all events some branches of it treat their objects as being so.

10. (3) If there is anything eternal, immutable, and existing separately, it must be studied by a theoretical science, not physics nor mathematics but prior to both. For physics deals with objects existing separately but not immutable, and some branches of mathematics deal with objects immutable but not existing separately, while the primary science deals with objects existing separately and immutable.

16. All causes must be eternal, and especially these, which act as causes on what is visible of the divine.

18. Thus there are three theoretical sciences, mathematics, physics, theology (for if the divine is present anywhere, it is in such objects), and the highest science must deal with the highest objects. The theoretical sciences are the highest of the sciences, and this is the highest of the theoretical sciences.

23. For if the question be asked whether the primary science is universal or deals with a particular genus (the distinction is found in mathematics ; geometry and astronomy deal with a particular genus, universal mathematics with all),

27. the answer is that if there is no other substance than natural substances, physics is the primary science, but if there is an immutable substance, the study of it is the primary science, and universal because primary. It studies the essence and properties of being as such.

1025^b 6. ἡ μετέχουσά τι διανοίας is designed, as Bz. says, to include bodies of so-called knowledge which rest on experience rather than on reasoning. It is these that study αἰτίας καὶ ἀρχὰς ἁπλουστέρας (l. 7), i. e. vaguely conceived causes.

7. ἡ ἀκριβεστέρας ἢ ἁπλουστέρας answers to ἢ ἀναγκαιότερον ἢ μαλακώτερον l. 13 ; for this sense of ἁπλοῦς cf. A. 987^a 21. The conditions of the ἀκρίβεια of a science are stated in A. 982^a 25–28, M. 1078^a 9–17, *An. Post.* i. 27.

7–18. Aristotle characterizes the special sciences in three ways :

(1) they deal, each of them, only with one department of being (7–10);

(2) they offer no argument to prove the essence of their subject, but make it evident to sense or assume it, and go on to prove the consequent properties (10–16);

(3) they do not discuss whether their subject exists, but simply assume that it does (16–18).

It is not very clear what light these remarks are meant to throw on the nature of metaphysics. The first point is no doubt meant to distinguish the sciences from metaphysics. They study particular ὄντα ; it studies τὸ ὂν ᾗ ὄν (cf. Γ. 1003^a 21–26). But in the end this chapter describes it as studying a particular kind of ὄντα, those which are both χωριστά and ἀκίνητα (1026^a 16). It is true that Aristotle still says it studies τὸ ὂν ᾗ ὄν (1026^a 31); it is universal in the sense that it is primary (1026ᵃ 30): i.e. its objects are those which give to all others their general character, and in studying them it is studying being as such. But Aristotle can hardly be said to have stood firm by the intention with which he evidently begins the chapter.

Again, what is the point of his reference to the other two characteristics of special sciences—that they do not offer proof of the essence nor of the existence of their subjects? Is it meant that metaphysics proves what being is, or that it is? Or that it proves the nature or the existence of the objects ôf the special sciences?

On one interpretation of 1025ᵇ 14–16, Aristotle says not merely that the special sciences do not prove the essence of their subjects, but that proof of essence is impossible. It is, then, impossible even for metaphysics. And if so, proof of existence is equally impossible for it (ll. 16–18). But probably ll. 14–16 should be interpreted otherwise, and if so, the passage throws no light on the method of metaphysics. What we may say, however, is that in practice the method of Aristotle's metaphysics is not that of 'linear inference' from a definite set of ἀρχαί, but that of aporematic discussion which discovers the ἀρχαί only as it proceeds.

11. αἱ μὲν . . . αἱ δ'. Alexander illustrates this by medicine, which, he says, simply *shows* us bodies being analysed into the four elements, and by arithmetic, which simply *assumes* that the unit is a substance without position. Assumption is the right course for a science to adopt with regard to the meaning of *all* its terms (*An. Post.* 76ᵃ 32).

15. ἐκ τῆς τοιαύτης ἐπαγωγῆς. In the parallel passage K. 1064ᵃ 8 this goes with δῆλον, which answers to φανερόν in the present passage. 'It is evident from this review of the sciences.' But if the present passage is so translated, (1) the separation of ἐκ τῆς τοιαύτης ἐπαγωγῆς from φανερόν by so many words is very curious, (2) τῆς τοιαύτης (not ταύτης τῆς) is odd, (3) it is difficult to describe the general reference to the sciences in ll. 4–13 as an ἐπαγωγή.

Alexander takes the present passage differently. ἀλλ' ἡ ἐκ τῆς αἰσθήσεως καὶ τῆς ἐπαγωγῆς πίστις οὐκ ἔστιν ἀπόδειξις (441. 38). I. e. ἡ τοιαύτη ἐπαγωγή is treated as meaning the 'leading on' of the mind to general truth by the exhibition of particular fact to sense (αἱ μὲν αἰσθήσει ποιήσασαι αὐτὸ δῆλον l. 11). If Alexander is right, the writer of K must be supposed to have misunderstood this passage.

16–17. οὐδ' εἰ ἔστιν ἢ μὴ ἔστι τὸ γένος . . . οὐδὲν λέγουσι, cf. *An. Post.* 76ᵃ 31, 35.

17. διὰ τὸ τῆς αὐτῆς κτλ. This does not, as has sometimes been thought, contradict the distinction drawn by Aristotle in *An. Post.* ii. 1, 8 between knowledge εἰ ἔστι and τί ἐστι. He says in 89ᵇ 34 that we ask what a thing is only when we already know that it is ; but this does not imply that the mode of knowledge may not be of the same type in both cases. It is in fact in both cases immediate apprehension, not demonstration, and this is what Aristotle means by τῆς αὐτῆς διανοίας.

18—1026ᵃ 7. Aristotle has already (ll. 7–10) distinguished metaphysics from the special sciences. But there is a science which makes a special claim to be the supreme science (cf. 1026ᵃ 27–29, Γ. 1005ᵃ 32), and whose relation to metaphysics it is particularly important to make clear, viz. physics. To this Aristotle accordingly devotes particular attention.

20. τὴν τοιαύτην . . . οὐσίαν κτλ. This is the strictest definition of φύσις (Δ. 1015ᵃ 13).

21. In the light of Δ. 1014ᵇ 19, 1015ᵃ 15 there is much to be said for Schwegler's conjecture ᾗ αὐτή for ἐν αὐτῇ.

22, 23. I have restored the reading of Aᵇ ποιητῶν . . . πρακτῶν in place of the vulgate ποιητικῶν . . . πρακτικῶν. E Al. read ποιητικῶν . . . πρακτῶν, which is unsatisfactory. K in the corresponding passage (1064ᵃ 11, 14) has ποιητικῆς . . . πρακτικῆς, but it is evident that ποιητῶν . . . πρακτῶν gives the better sense here, and that the vulgate reading has arisen by assimilation to πρακτική . . . ποιητική l. 21. It is the ἀρχή (or origin) of what is made or done, not the ἀρχή of the sciences that study making or doing, that Aristotle must be describing as present in the maker or doer, and identifying with νοῦς, τέχνη, δύναμίς τις, or προαίρεσις. His point is that, while the physicist studies objects that have the source of their movement in themselves, the student of an art or of morals is learning what movements he himself ought to originate—the distinction between art and conduct themselves being that artistic activity aims at an ἔργον beyond itself, while moral activity does not (E. N. vi. 4). Physics, then, is not a practical nor a productive science.

Aristotle's classification of sciences in this chapter is as follows :

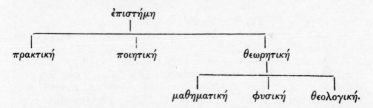

The main division into three is said by Diog. Laert. iii. 84 to be due to Plato. It reappears in Top. 145ᵃ 15, E. N. 1139ᵃ 27. The late Peripatetics and the neo-Platonists tell us that Aristotle recognized only two main divisions, θεωρητική and πρακτική (cf. a. 993ᵇ 20, E. E. 1214ᵃ 8–12), and divided the latter into ethics, economics, and politics. But their statements have no authority as against his own words. It is on the present classification that the traditional arrangement of Aristotle's works is based, the logical works being placed first as propaedeutic to the rest, and followed by the theoretical, the practical, and the productive (Poetics).

22. ἢ νοῦς ἢ τέχνη ἢ δύναμίς τις. Cf. Z. 1032ᵃ 27, where διάνοια takes the place of νοῦς. In neither passage does Alexander give a satis-

factory interpretation. The three words suggest diminishing degrees
of rationality (cf. ll. 6, 13), δύναμις being something like ἐμπειρία or rule
of thumb procedure (A. 981ᵇ 8). τέχνη and δύναμις are distinguished
(without any explanation) in Z. 1033ᵇ 8 ; they are frequently conjoined
as being practically synonymous. 27. καὶ περὶ οὐσίαν τὴν κατὰ τὸν λόγον ὡς ἐπὶ τὸ πολὺ ὡς οὐ χωριστὴν
μόνον. Bz., following Alexander, takes οὐ χωριστὴν μόνον as = μόνον
οὐ χωριστήν = ἀλλ' οὐ χωριστήν, and prints ὡς ἐπὶ τὸ πολύ, οὐ χωριστὴν
μόνον, understanding the clause to mean 'and it deals with substance
for the most part as form rather than matter, only not a form that can
exist apart from matter'. This use of μόνον is very difficult. On the
other hand, if we read τὴν . . . οὐ χωριστὴν μόνον without a comma, οὐ
for μή is a difficulty. I have therefore adopted the reading of ET
ὡς οὐ χωριστὴν μόνον (ὡς was very likely to drop out, owing to its
awkwardness after the other ὡς). I translate, 'and it deals with sub-
stance-in-the-sense-of-form for the most part only as inseparable from
matter'. μόνον thus at the end of the sentence is not uncommon
(Bz. Index 472ᵇ 44–46). This brings out the difference between
physics and metaphysics, which is Aristotle's point, better than the
other reading and interpretation ; there is no particular point here in
saying that physics studies form rather than matter, though this is of
course true (cf. Z. 1037ª 17).
29–30. ὡς . . . μηδέν ἐστι ποιεῖν. ὡς in the sense of 'since' is not
quoted in Bz.'s Index, but is of course quite good Greek. Alexander
takes it so. Possibly, however, ὡς means 'that', and the sentence
means 'the mode of existence of the essence must not escape our
notice ; we must observe that to inquire without knowing this is
fruitless'.
31. τὸ σιμόν receives fuller treatment in Z. 5.
34. ἄνευ ὕλης αἰσθητῆς. Hollowness does involve ὕλη νοητή, extension (Z. 1036ª 9).
εἰ δὴ πάντα τὰ φυσικὰ ὁμοίως τῷ σιμῷ λέγονται. All physical things,
like 'the snub', involve a union of form and matter. But there is a
difference, since 'snub' involves a union of a subject, which is itself
a unity of form and matter, with a proprium, while the other terms
here mentioned are substances, or parts of substances, involving simply
a union of form with matter.
1026ª 2. οὐθενὸς γὰρ ἄνευ κινήσεως ὁ λόγος αὐτῶν, ἀλλ' ἀεὶ ἔχει ὕλην.
ὕλη = potentiality of change, so that 'changeable' is used as synonymous with 'material' or 'sensible' (A. 989ᵇ 31 f., Z. 1036ʰ 28 f.).
5. καὶ διότι καὶ περὶ ψυχῆς ἐνίας κτλ., viz. because physics studies
form as inseparable from matter (1025ʰ 27). There seems to be
nothing in Christ's view that καὶ διότι . . . ἐστίν (l. 6) was originally meant
to go after τούτων l. 7.
περὶ ψυχῆς ἐνίας, i. e. all except the reason which comes in from
without and has no communion with the body (De An. 403ª 16–28,
429ª 24, P. A. 641ª 17–ᵇ 10, G. A. 736ᵇ 27).
For the unusual singular ἐνίας cf. Probl. 884ʰ 13, Theophr. fr. 8. 1.

8. Whether the objects of mathematics are, as the Platonists say, separately existing unchanging entities, Aristotle leaves at present uncertain ; in MN he answers that they are not. But at all events some— the pure—branches of mathematics (ἔνια μαθήματα seems to be subject, not object : cf. 14 τῆς μαθηματικῆς ἔνια περὶ ἀκίνητα, &c., *An. Post.* 79ª 7 τὰ μαθήματα περὶ εἴδη ἐστίν, *Phys.* 194ª 7 τὰ φυσικώτερα τῶν μαθημάτων, οἷον ὀπτική, *De Caelo* 302^b 29 οἱ ἐν τοῖς μαθήμασιν) study their objects *qua* unchangeable and separate. Some on the other hand, (the 'physical' or applied branches, optics, harmonics, astronomy, *Phys.* 194ª 7) study objects unchangeable indeed but not separate but 'as in matter' (l. 15). Aristotle states his position more fully in M. 2, 3.

9. Schwegler argues with much ingenuity that the correct reading must be not ᾗ χωριστά but μὴ χωριστά. This alone, he holds, would justify Aristotle in his conclusion that if there is a separately existing substance it cannot be studied by mathematics. That conclusion, however, (n.b. δέ l. 10, γάρ l. 13) is not drawn from the present sentence but from the later mentioned fact (l. 14) that τῆς μαθηματικῆς ἔνια (just *not* the ἔνια mentioned here—applied, not pure mathematics) are περὶ ἀκίνητα μὲν οὐ χωριστὰ δὲ ἴσως. It is true, as Schwegler says, that τὰ μαθηματικὰ οὐ κεχωρισμένα ὡς κεχωρισμένα νοεῖ (*De An.* 431^b 15) is not equivalent to ᾗ χωριστὰ θεωρεῖ. The latter, however, can and must mean 'studies its objects in that respect in which they are χωριστά', viz. *qua* separable in thought. Cf. *Phys.* 193^b 33 διὸ καὶ χωρίζει (ὁ μαθηματικός)· χωριστὰ γὰρ τῇ νοήσει κινήσεώς ἐστι. Regarded as concessive, the sentence is satisfactory enough with the traditional reading.

10. Natorp seeks to get rid of the difficulty about the object of metaphysics (cf. 1025^b 7–18 n.) by interpreting εἰ 'whether', and by translating καὶ περὶ χωριστὰ καὶ ἀκίνητα in l. 16 '*also* about separate and immutable objects'. He thinks it the business of first philosophy to study substantial unchangeable substance (God) *among others*, and only to determine whether and what it is, and cuts out 18 f. ὥστε . . . θεολογική and 21 f. καὶ . . . εἶναι. He points out that θεολογία and the kindred words elsewhere (except in **K**) always refer to myth, and objects to θεολογική here on that ground. There is no need, however, for such violent methods of criticism.

14. The balance of the sentence clearly requires Schwegler's emendation χωριστά. Physics studies things separate but not unchangeable, mathematics things unchangeable but not separate, metaphysics things both separate and unchangeable. ἀχώριστα μὲν ἀλλ' οὐκ ἀκίνητα would be a false antithesis, for the things that are not separate from matter are necessarily things that have movement.

The objects of physics are χωριστά in the sense that they exist separately. The reading ἀχώριστα is due to some copyist's reflection that they are not χωριστά in the sense of 'separate from matter', and in particular to a recollection of 1025^b 28. But there it is not physical things but their form that is said to be treated as οὐ χωριστήν.

15. ἴσως is as usual inserted simply out of caution, cf. A. 987ᵃ 26 n. The fact is not proved till MN.

16-18 justifies the name θεολογική which Aristotle is about to apply to the study of χωριστὰ καὶ ἀκίνητα. All causes, i. e. first causes, must be eternal, if we are to avoid an infinite regress (a. 2); and above all the unmoving first causes which act as causes on ' those among divine things which are manifest to sense ', i. e. on the heavenly bodies whose eternal revolution is itself the cause of all other events. The thought is not quite exact, for it is only *first* causes that need be eternal, and ταῦτα are not some first causes among others, but the only first causes. The heavenly bodies are only second causes. It is evident, however, that the science which studies eternal causes is properly called θεολογική, and this is Aristotle's point.

For τοῖς φανεροῖς τῶν θείων cf. *Phys.* 196ᵃ 33 τὸν δ' οὐρανὸν καὶ τὰ θειότατα τῶν φανερῶν, and also *E. N.* 1141ᵃ 34.

If we ask what exactly Aristotle means by these first causes, the answer is, God, who moves the sphere of the fixed stars, and the other immutable, eternal beings who move the spheres that account for the motion of the planets (Λ. 1072ᵃ19—1073ᵇ 3).

19. The designation of metaphysics as θεολογική is confined to this passage and the corresponding passage in K, 1064ᵇ 3. θεολογεῖν, θεολογία, θεολόγος in Aristotle always refer to the early cosmologists.

This way of naming metaphysics is connected with the view of it not as studying the general character of being as such, but as studying those beings which are χωριστὰ καὶ ἀκίνητα, in one word θεῖα.

19-21. οὐ γὰρ . . . ὑπάρχει seems to be best treated as a parenthetical clause justifying the use of the name θεολογική for the science of that which has independent and immutable existence.

22. αἱ μὲν οὖν θεωρητικαί κτλ. This has been shown in A. 982ᵇ 24 sqq.

23-32. The argument does not seem to be as obscure as Bonitz and Christ suppose it to be. Theology is more to be chosen than the other theoretical sciences; for if the question be asked whether it is universal or studies one particular kind of being, our answer is that it studies the primary kind of being, and that which gives their fundamental character to all other beings. It is thus both primary and universal, and doubly supreme among the sciences.

25. The same alternatives as have been suggested with regard to the objects of philosophy are found within mathematics. Geometry, astronomy, and (we may add) arithmetic, study special kinds of quantity, but there is a general mathematics which studies quantity in general (cf. K. 1061ᵇ 19). Bonitz thinks that this general mathematics is arithmetic. But A. 982ᵃ 28 suggests that arithmetic is a science alongside of geometry though more accurate. M. 1077ᵃ 9-12, ᵇ 17-20, *An. Post.* 74ᵃ 17-25 make it clear that Aristotle contemplates a science wider than either arithmetic or geometry; and a specimen of it is to be found in Euclid's treatment, in Bk. v of the *Elements*, of proportion as existing between *any* kind of magnitudes.

30. αὕτη, the science which studies this immutable substance.

Accidental being the subject of no science (ch. 2).

1026ª 33. 'Being' means (1) accidental being, (2) being as truth, (3) the categories, (4) the potential and the actual.

ᵇ 3. (1) Accidental being is studied by no science. For (*a*) the maker of a house does not make the infinite attributes incidental to it—its pleasantness to some people, injuriousness to others, &c.

10. (*b*) The geometer does not study the incidental attributes of figures, e. g. whether 'the triangle' is the same as 'the triangle with angles equal to two right angles'.

12. This is natural enough; the accidental is little more than a name. Plato was not far wrong in saying that sophistry deals with not-being. For it deals for the most part with the accidental—'whether the musical and the grammatical are the same', &c.—puzzles which indicate that the accidental is near to not-being.

22. This is shown also by the fact that things which exist in the proper sense are generated and destroyed by a process, while accidents are not.

24. Yet we must as far as possible state the nature and cause of the accidental; this may show why there is no science of it.

27. (*a*) The cause of it is that while some things are always alike and of necessity (in the sense that they cannot be otherwise), others are only for the most part; that which is neither always nor for the most part is the accidental.

33. E. g. cold in the dog-days is accidental, but heat is not. That a man is pale is accidental, that he is an animal is not. That a builder should cure a man, just because the builder happens to be a doctor, is accidental.

1027ª 5. Necessary or usual events are the effect of arts that tend to produce them; of accidental results there is no definite art, since the causes of accidents are themselves accidental.

8. Thus the existence of accident is due to the fact that most things are only for the most part, and therefore to the matter which admits of a departure from the usual.

15. We must start from the question whether there must not be something that is neither always nor for the most part. There are such things. We may defer the question whether there is *nothing* that is always.

19. (*b*) Evidently there is no knowledge of the accidental, since knowledge is of that which is always or for the most part; otherwise learning and teaching would be impossible. 24. We cannot state when the accidental takes place. E. g. ' honey-water is good for fever except at new moon '. If we can say this, then what happens at new moon happens then either always or usually; but the accidental happens neither always nor usually. 26. Thus we have stated the nature and cause of the accidental. and that there is no knowledge of it.

1026ᵃ 34. ἦν. The reference is to Δ. 7. Of the four senses of ' being' mentioned there, τὸ κατὰ συμβεβηκός is briefly discussed in E. 2, 3, τὸ ὡς ἀληθές in E. 4; τὸ κατὰ τὰ σχήματα τῆς κατηγορίας, or rather substance, the first category, is discussed in ZH, and τὸ κατὰ δύναμιν καὶ ἐντελέχειαν in Θ.

ᵇ 1. σημαίνει. The subject is τὸ ὄν.

6. οὔτε γὰρ ὁ ποιῶν οἰκίαν κτλ. The builder as a matter of fact makes a house which has these attributes, but he does not make it *qua* builder. His business is to make a house which is an efficient ' covering for living creatures and goods' (H. 1043ᵃ 16). Such a house may incidentally be agreeable or salubrious for some tenants and not for others, but that is not his concern ; the house is not this *qua* house. Again, it will be different from everything else in the universe ; but this it is not *qua* house, since the same could be said of anything else.

11-12. οὐδ' εἰ... ἔχον. Alexander thinks the question is whether the geometrical triangle which has its angles equal to two right angles is the same as the triangle of wood or stone. τρίγωνον alone, however, could hardly have this meaning ; it naturally means the geometrical triangle, and the question must be whether the triangle as such, i. e. thought of simply as a rectilinear figure with three sides, is the same as the triangle thought of as also having angles equal to two right angles. Nor need the fact that this is a property, i.e. a συμβε-βηκός of the type that is not in question here, a συμβεβηκὸς καθ' αὑτό (Δ. 1025ᵃ 30), disturb us. The συμβεβηκός of the triangle which Aristotle says the geometer does not discuss is not ' having angles equal to two right angles', but ' being other than, or the same as, the triangle having angles,' &c. This the geometer as such does not con-sider, just as the builder does not consider whether the house he makes is other than a man, &c. (l. 9).

These are in fact sophistical puzzles of the type referred to in ll. 15-21. If one says the two are different, the sophist asks ' how is it, then, that every triangle *has* its angles equal to two right angles ?' If one says they are the same, then for ' triangle ' one can substitute ' triangle having angles equal to two right angles', for this one can substitute

'triangle having angles, &c., having angles,' &c., and so *ad infinitum.*
Cf. *Soph. El.* 13.

13. ὥσπερ γὰρ ὄνομά τι μόνον τὸ συμβεβηκός ἐστιν. Probably no
very precise meaning is to be looked for here.   Aristotle means that the
puzzles with which the sophists occupied themselves, puzzles turning
on accidental predications such as τὸ μουσικόν ἐστι γραμματικόν, are
purely verbal and require only a clearing up of the meaning of words.
All that is necessary is to point out (1) that τὸ λευκόν here means not
white colour but a particular thing which has it, and (2) that ἐστι
means not 'is essentially' but 'happens to be'.

14. διὸ Πλάτων κτλ.   Cf. *Soph.* 254 A.

16. πότερον ἕτερον ἢ ταὐτόν κτλ.   The sophistic argument, as
Alexander says, is as follows :

Socrates is grammatical (i.e. can read and write, *Top.* 142ᵇ 30–35).
.˙. Grammatical Socrates is the same as Socrates.
Socrates is musical.
.˙. Musical Socrates is the same as Socrates.
.˙. Musical Socrates is the same as grammatical Socrates.
.˙. The musical is the same as the grammatical.
But if so, where the grammatical is the musical will be.
But Aristarchus is grammatical but not musical.
.˙. The grammatical is not the same as the musical.

17. καὶ μουσικὸς Κορίσκος καὶ Κορίσκος.   The sophistical puzzle here
would be : if Coriscus is the same as musical Coriscus, then he is the
same as musical musical Coriscus, and so *ad infinitum.*   Cf. a similar
puzzle in *Soph. El.* 173ᵃ 34.

18. καὶ εἰ πᾶν ὃ ἂν ᾖ κτλ.   The sophists seem to have opposed the
natural view that what is and has not always been must have come to
be, by the following *reductio ad absurdum* :

If a man being musical has become grammatical, then being
musical he is grammatical.
And if so, then being grammatical he is musical.
But he has not always, being grammatical, been musical.
If that which is and has not always been must have come to be,
then being grammatical he has become musical.   I.e. he must have
been grammatical before he was musical as well as musical before he
was grammatical.   Which is absurd.

Alexander gives various arguments, none of which quite suits the
text.   The argument is briefly hinted at in *Top.* 104ᵇ 25, while
a different argument for the same thesis is referred to in K. 1064ᵇ 23.

Aristotle admits the force of the reasoning, but draws not the conclusion which the sophists draw, that the belief that that which is but
has not always been must have come to be is false, but that the
supposed instance of a thing's being, by application to which they refute
the belief, viz. that the musical is grammatical, is really an instance of
not-being, and that all accidents are so too (l. 21).   Thus that Plato
was right in saying that sophistic deals with not-being is proved
thus :

Sophistic deals with the accidental.

The accidental is not-being.

Plato himself said that the sophist was concerned with not-being not in the sense of the accidental but in the sense of the false, that which seems to be what it is not (*Soph.* 235 A, 239 c).

21. φαίνεται γὰρ τὸ συμβεβηκὸς ἐγγύς τι τοῦ μὴ ὄντος. I. e. when A is κατὰ συμβεβηκός B, the connexion is so remote that A can hardly be said to *be* B in the full sense of the word 'be'.

22. τῶν τοιούτων, 'such as the following'. For τοιοῦτος referring forward cf. A. 987ᵇ 4, B. 998ᵃ 10, *De An.* 408ᵇ 1.

23. τῶν δὲ κατὰ συμβεβηκὸς οὐκ ἔστιν. Aristotle's meaning is this: If A becomes B, it is as a general rule by one part of it becoming B after another (Θ. 1049ᵇ 35, *Phys.* 237ᵇ 9, 15). But there is no gradual change in the musical by which it becomes grammatical. A gradual change takes place in the man who is musical, by which he becomes grammatical, and when this is over the musical is found to be grammatical; but it never was becoming grammatical. This conception of a thing's now not being and later being, or *vice versa*, without ever being in course of becoming or ceasing to be, is applied not only to accidental events, and to their causes (1027ᵃ 29), but also to ἐνέργειαι such as sensation (*De Sensu* 446ᵇ 4), to geometrical points, lines, and planes (B. 1002ᵃ 32, H. 1044ᵇ 21, K. 1060ᵇ 19), to moments (B. 1002ᵇ 6), to forms superinduced on matter (H. 1043ᵇ 15, 1044ᵇ 22), to contacts (*De Caelo* 280ᵇ 26). Aristotle also says that some thinkers applied it to movement (*De Caelo* 280ᵇ 6).

28. οὐ τῆς κατὰ τὸ βίαιον λεγομένης, Δ. 1015ᵃ 26.

29. ἀλλ' ἦν λέγομεν κτλ., Δ. 1015ᵃ 33–35.

30. αὕτη ἀρχή κτλ. I. e., since there are things which happen more than *n* and less than 2 *n* times out of 2 *n*, there must be things that happen *less* than *n* times out of 2 *n*.

37. καὶ τὸ ὑγιάζειν δέ κτλ. In the exposition from l. 27 to this point, the accidental has been identified with what is neither ἀεί nor ὡς ἐπὶ τὸ πολύ, i.e. with what is unusual or at best not usual. Aristotle now (35—1027ᵃ 8) calls attention to another aspect of the accidental than its lack of frequency,—the aspect to which the word συμβεβηκός 'concomitant' points. A is or does B κατὰ συμβεβηκός when it is or does it not *qua* A but *qua* C, a concomitant of A.

1027ᵃ 5. τῶν μὲν γὰρ ἄλλων [ἐνίοτε] δυνάμεις κτλ. Bonitz argues against ἐνίοτε on the ground (1) that τὰ ἄλλα, necessary or usual events, not sometimes but always have definite causes, and (2) that there is no trace of the word in Alexander or Asclepius. He conjectures αἰτίαι τε καὶ δυνάμεις from Alexander, but probably αἰτίας καὶ δυνάμεις (Al. 451. 34) is merely Alexander's expansion of δυνάμεις.

It seems better to treat ἐνίοτε as the gloss of a cautious copyist. And it should be noted that δυνάμεις ποιητικαί does not mean 'causes' in general. It is almost equivalent to τέχναι, and means something only a degree less organized than an art (cf. 1025ᵇ 22 n.).

It would also be possible to read ἄλλαι and interpret : 'for of some
of the effects thus produced by one art there are *other* faculties whose
proper business it is to produce them (as it is the business of ἰατρική,
not of οἰκοδομική, tò produce health), while of others there is *no*
definite art or faculty' (as, according to the Platonists, there is no art
of pleasure—*E. N.* 1152ᵇ 18).

8. καὶ τὸ αἴτιόν ἐστι κατὰ συμβεβηκός. This seems only to mean
that if B follows accidentally from A, A is only accidentally the
cause of B.

8–16. Bz.'s proposal to place ὥστ'... ἀνάγκης(l.13) after l. 16 ἀδύνατον
does not seem necessary nor even an improvement. It would involve
the expression of the same thought in three consecutive sentences,—
10 ἀνάγκη εἶναι τὸ κατὰ συμβεβηκὸς ὄν, 12 κατὰ συμβεβηκὸς ἔσται,
16 ἔστιν ἄρα τι παρὰ ταῦτα τὸ ὁπότερ' ἔτυχε καὶ κατὰ συμβεβηκός.
ὥστε in l. 8 is natural enough ; it introduces not a conclusion from
what Aristotle has just said, but a summary of what he has been arguing
for since 1026ᵇ 27.

15. ἀρχήν, *sc.* of the proof that accident exists.

19. ὕστερον, Λ. 6–8.

21. For the inclusion of the usual as well as the necessary among
the objects of science cf. *An. Pr.* 32ᵇ 18, *An. Post.* 87ᵇ 20.

25. ἢ γὰρ ἀεί κτλ. Bz. thinks that a better sense would be
obtained here by reading ἢ γὰρ ἀεὶ ἢ ὡς ἐπὶ τὸ πολύ, καὶ τῇ νουμηνίᾳ.
Alexander's commentary (452. 35—453. 1) does not show clearly
whether he had this or the traditional reading before him. The latter,
however, gives a good if difficult sense. ' For even that which happens
at new moon (viz. honey-water's not being beneficial) happens then
either always or for the most part '. I. e., the conditions of the
accidental as such cannot be stated. If you can state the conditions of
an event, then even if it is an exception to a wider law it has a law of
its own and is not a mere accident. This clause is very important, for
it is perhaps the only place in which Aristotle implies the view that
there is nothing which is objectively accidental. There are events
which present themselves as accidents, i. e. as unintelligible exceptions,
but if we knew more about them we should know that they obey laws
of their own. Elsewhere Aristotle speaks as if there were events which
are sheer exceptions and below the level of knowledge ; here he admits
that they are merely beyond our present knowledge.

Nature and origin of accident (ch. 3).

1027ᵃ 29. Evidently there are causes that are generable and de-
structible but are never in process of being generated or destroyed.
Otherwise all events would be necessary, if that which is generated and
destroyed by a process must have a non-accidental cause.

32. For if we ask for the conditions of a future event, and the conditions of those conditions, and so on, we finally come to conditions which are or are not in existence now, or (going further) to conditions which have or have not occurred in the past. Therefore, according to this line of thought, all future events will take place of necessity.

ᵇ 10. But in fact, though it is certain that a living man will die, it is not yet certain whether it will be by disease or by violence. This depends on something taking place. Evidently, then, the causal connexion goes back to a certain starting-point but no further. This is the cause of the chance event, and has itself no cause.

14. Whether this is a material, final, or efficient cause, is an important subject of inquiry.

1027ᵃ 29. γενητὰ καὶ φθαρτὰ ἄνευ τοῦ γίγνεσθαι καὶ φθείρεσθαι. Aristotle has already (1026ᵇ 22) pointed out that accidental events are never in process of becoming or perishing. He now says that the same is true of their causes. The passages referred to in the note on that passage (especially, for the verbal form, H. 1043ᵇ 15) are enough to vindicate the correctness of the text against such proposals as that of Apelt. Those who wish to emend the text have not sufficiently noted the fact that γίγνεσθαι and φθείρεσθαι are in the present tense. You can say of such a cause γέγονε, but you can never say of it γίγνεται. As Alexander points out, the builder gradually by a process of learning (and, we may add, of subsequent building) becomes the cause of a house; but the healthiness of the house supervenes instantaneously on this process, and he does not gradually come to be the cause of a healthy house. All we can say is that a moment ago he was not so and now he is so.

That the αἴτια of which Aristotle is speaking are the causes of accidental events is shown not only by the general drift of the chapter but by the corresponding passage in K. 1065ᵃ 6, ὅτι δὲ τοῦ κατὰ συμβεβηκὸς ὄντος οὐκ εἰσὶν αἰτίαι καὶ ἀρχαὶ τοιαῦται οἱαίπερ τοῦ καθ' αὑτὸ ὄντος, δῆλον. It cannot be maintained, however, that the chapter works out with any great clearness the thesis here put forward. In the next sentence Aristotle points out that, since that which does come into being by a process must have a non-accidental cause, i.e. one which necessarily produces it (this he assumes as in Z. 1032ᵃ 13, 1033ᵃ 24, Θ. 1049ᵇ 28), it follows that if all causes came into being by a process, they would come into being necessarily and so would all their results, immediate or remote, so that all events would be necessary. If, then, he can show that some events are not necessary, he can show that there are causes which do not come into being by a process.

He next (ᵃ 32–ᵇ 10) points out that if we start in thought from some event about which we are doubtful whether it will happen, and assume a necessary connexion at every stage, there must be conditions now in existence, and indeed there must have been conditions realized in the past (ἢ εἰς τῶν γεγονότων τι ᵇ 3, ὁμοίως δὲ κἂν ὑπερπηδήσῃ τις

κτλ. ᵇ 6), from which the event in question either necessarily will
follow or necessarily will not follow. This necessary connexion, he
admits, is up to a certain point realized. A man is eating pungent food,
therefore he will necessarily be thirsty, he will necessarily go out to get
water, he will necessarily be killed by his enemies. Again, there are
contraries present in the same living body, the harmony between them
will necessarily be dissolved, the body will necessarily die. But,
Aristotle adds (ᵇ 10), not *all* future events are thus already necessitated.
It is certain that a man will die, but it is not yet certain whether it will
be by disease or by violence. That depends on some condition not
yet in existence, and (he implies) not made necessary by anything that
is in existence—some condition which will arise, if it does arise, not by
a process but instantaneously. If the man is eating pungent food, his
fate is sealed (so we may probably interpret Aristotle), but before he eats
it there is no condition from which it necessarily follows that he will
eat it. The eating is an ἀρχή to which we can trace back the causal
nexus, but beyond it we cannot go. Therefore all events are not
necessary; therefore there are αἴτια γενητὰ ἄνευ τοῦ γίγνεσθαι.

The statement that it is not yet determined whether a man will die by
disease or by violence seems to be simply an appeal to common sense.
Aristotle does not make it clear whether these αἴτια γενητὰ ἄνευ τοῦ
γίγνεσθαι are always acts of voluntary agents. In the corresponding
passage of K (1065ᵃ 16) the matter is illustrated by an eclipse, but he
certainly did not think eclipses were accidental, and it seems that he takes
it as an instance of the cases in which he admits complete necessary connexion. In the *De Interpretatione* the instances of doubtful future events
are—whether a sea-fight will take place (18ᵇ 23), whether a garment
will be cut up or worn out (19ᵃ 12),—both clearly dependent on human
action ; and appeal is made to the fact ὅτι ἔστιν ἀρχὴ τῶν ἐσομένων καὶ
ἀπὸ τοῦ βουλεύεσθαι καὶ ἀπὸ τοῦ πρᾶξαί τι (19ᵃ 7). But he seems not
to confine contingency to human action and its results, for he goes on
to something more general, καὶ ὅτι ὅλως ἔστιν ἐν τοῖς μὴ ἀεὶ ἐνεργοῦσι
τὸ δυνατὸν εἶναι καὶ μὴ ὁμοίως. In fact he recognizes an initiative in
unconscious nature analogous to that which he allows to man ; the
former under certain conditions leads to τὸ αὐτόματον as the latter
leads to τύχη (*Phys.* ii. 4–6).

ᵇ 2. Aristotle first considers the case of death by violence, and comes
to death by disease only in ll. 6–10. νόσῳ ἤ seems to be plainly a
gloss owing its origin to νόσῳ ἢ βίᾳ l. 10.

8. ἐξ ἀνάγκης. Aristotle seems here to draw the conclusion which
follows from the supposition he is trying to prove wrong, the supposition that there are no ungenerated (i.e. accidental) causes. He gives
an example (τὸ ἀποθανεῖν τὸν ζῶντα) in which he admits that there is
certainty, but proceeds to add one (εἰ νόσῳ ἢ βίᾳ) in which he claims
that there is not. The argument is at this point very obscure.

10. σώματι, which is omitted by Aᵇ and apparently by Alexander,
is doubtless a gloss. It gives the meaning correctly enough. τὰ ἐναντία are the primary ἐναντιώσεις, the hot and the cold, the wet and the dry.

14. ἀλλ' εἰς ἀρχὴν ποίαν κτλ. Aristotle has already (ᵃ 13) said that matter is the cause of accident, but this does not mean that matter produces the accidental event; bare matter is a potentiality of opposites, without inclination to either. The meaning is that matter or the potentiality for opposite realizations is what makes accident, i. e. an unusual realization, possible. He now says it is a question for consideration, what actually brings the accidental event about, whether it is a material, final, or efficient cause. He omits the formal cause, since the accidental is just what cannot be traced to the essence of its subject. Both Alexander and Asclepius say Aristotle's view is that the ἀρχαί he has been speaking of are efficient causes. It seems clear that the positive cause of the accidental result cannot be bare matter, since that is what lends itself to opposite results. Accidental events, since they take place in time, must have an efficient cause, and Aristotle is no doubt thinking of this; e. g., a man's death at the hands of his enemies is traced to his ὄρεξις to eat tasty food, and this is an efficient cause. But wherever there is ὄρεξις there is behind it an ὀρεκτόν acting as final cause, and this also Aristotle doubtless has in mind.

Being as truth is not primary being (ch. 4).

1027ᵇ 17. (2) Being as truth and not-being as falsity depend on a putting together and a taking apart; both together are concerned with the partition of a pair of contradictory propositions

20. (for true judgement affirms when the subject and predicate are in fact combined, denies when they are separated, while the false does the opposite; how thinking things together or separately takes place is another question—I mean thinking them so that the thoughts are not a succession but a unity);

25. for falsity and truth are not in things (e. g. the good is not true, the bad false), but in thought, and with regard to simple objects, i. e. essences, there is not falsity or truth even in thought.

28. Being in the sense of truth must be discussed later, but since that which is in thought, not in things, is different from what *is* in the strict sense (the essence, quality, &c., which thought joins with or takes away from its subject), being as truth, as well as accidental being (the cause of the latter being indefinite, that of the former being some affection of thought, and both presupposing being in the strict sense and not denoting an objective existent), may be dismissed for the present.

1028ᵃ 3. We must study the causes of being itself as such.

1027ʰ 19. ἐπειδή κτλ. Bz. pointed out rightly, after Alexander, that the grammatical apodosis does not come till l. 28. But l. 29 ἐπεὶ δέ κτλ. really continues the line of thought started in l. 19 ἐπειδὴ παρὰ σύνθεσιν κτλ., and the *logical* apodosis does not come till l. 33 [τὸ μὲν ὡς συμβεβηκὸς καὶ] τὸ ὡς ἀληθὲς ὂν ἀφετέον.

It seems better to read παρά with the best manuscripts; the manuscripts of Alexander vary between παρά and περί in two places, but in 457. 20, 22, 25, 27, 38, 458. 4 give only παρά. παρά = ' dependent on ', cf. Bz. *Index* 562ᵃ 7–21.

τὸ δὲ σύνολόν κτλ., 'and the true and the false together are concerned with the sharing out of contradictories. The true affirms where the subject and the predicate are in fact united, denies where they are divided ; the false shares out the propositions in the opposite way '.

23. τὸ ἅμα . . . νοεῖν, the thinking together implied in κατάφασις, τὸ χωρὶς νοεῖν, the thinking apart implied in ἀπόφασις. This gives a better sense than taking τὸ ἅμα, τὸ χωρίς as objects of νοεῖν.

ἄλλος λόγος does not amount to an explicit reference to another book. Z. 12, to which Alexander refers, is hardly in point. *De An.* iii. 2, 6, 7 deal with the problem in question.

24. λέγω δέ κτλ. ' By thinking things together or apart I mean thinking them so that one thought does not succeed the other but they form a unity.'

25—1028ᵃ 3. Jaeger (*Stud.* pp. 21–28) argues that 1027ᵇ 29—1028ᵃ 3 ἀφείσθω cannot be a resumption of the argument in 1027ᵇ 25–29, since it overlooks the distinction there drawn between the apprehension of ἁπλᾶ and the apprehension of the truth of propositions, and since apart from this distinction the one section would be a meaningless repetition of the other. He therefore considers that ll. 25–29 are a later alternative version, just as Θ. 10, which contains the same distinction and is referred to in l. 29, is a later addition to Θ. He thinks that the recognition of the apprehension of ἁπλᾶ as distinct from judgement was due to Aristotle's coming to see that if all knowledge is a matter of judgement, of σύνθεσις and διαίρεσις, we cannot know the pure, simple forms which are the objects of metaphysics.

If Jaeger's contention be right (and it is probable enough though by no means certain), it enables us to date the older version of EΘ before *De An.* 430ᵃ 26, where the distinction is already drawn.

27. περὶ δὲ τὰ ἁπλᾶ καὶ τὰ τί ἐστιν οὐδ' ἐν διανοίᾳ. For Aristotle's doctrine of the apprehension of τὰ ἁπλᾶ καὶ τὰ τί ἐστιν cf. Θ. 1051ᵇ 17— 1052ᵃ 4 nn. τὰ τί ἐστιν is explicative of τὰ ἁπλᾶ, but a difficulty is caused by Aristotle's distinction of αἱ μὴ συνθεταὶ οὐσίαι from τὸ τί ἐστιν in 1051ᵇ 25–27 : v. n. on 1051ᵇ 17–1052ᵃ 4.

28. οὐδ' ἐν διανοίᾳ. With regard to τὰ ἁπλᾶ καὶ τὰ τί ἐστιν there is no falsity or truth even in thought. The only alternatives are apprehension of them and non-apprehension.

29. οὕτως, sc. ὡς ἀληθές.
ὕστερον ἐπισκεπτέον, Θ. 10.

31–33. Thought is always assigning or else denying to a given

subject a certain essential nature, a certain quality, quantity, &c., and
thus presupposes things which have 'being' of a more primary kind
than the being which is truth—viz. the categories.

1028ᵃ 1. τὸ λοιπὸν γένος, i. e. τὰ κυρίως (1027ᵇ 31), τὸ ἔξω ὂν καὶ
χωριστόν (K. 1065ᵃ 24), the categories, which are the various senses of
being καθ' αὐτό.

2. Natorp (*A. G. P.* i. 192) argues that ἔξω means 'outside the
categories' and that in K. 1065ᵃ 24 τὸ ἔξω ὂν καὶ χωριστόν, 'objective
being', is a later misunderstanding of Aristotle's meaning. This is
possible, but if ἔξω here were to bear the meaning Natorp assigns to it
we should expect ἔξω τούτου. For ἔξω = 'objective' cf. *De An.*
417ᵇ 20, Pl. *Theaet.* 198 c 2.

4–6. φανερὸν . . . ὄν. The remark is pointless here, as it has
already been noted (1026ᵃ 33) that 'being' has a variety of meanings
and two of them have been discussed in chs. 2–4. The sentence is
a free version of the first sentence of Z, and is evidently a later addition meant to indicate the connexion of the two books.